AMERICAN LITERATURE
A Chronological Approach

G. Robert Carlsen • Edgar H. Schuster • Anthony Tovatt • Patricia O. Tovatt

 TREASURY EDITION

WEBSTER DIVISION, McGRAW-HILL BOOK COMPANY
New York, St. Louis, San Francisco, Dallas, Atlanta

Cover Art:

RETURNING TO THE FARM
George Henry Durrie
New York Historical Society, New York City

Editorial Direction: John A. Rothermich
Editors: Steven Griffel
        Carroll Moulton
        Kenneth Pitchford
Editing and Styling: Sue McCormick
                    Ann Craig
Design Supervision: Valerie Greco
Production: Salvador Gonzales

Photo Editor: Alan Forman
Text and Cover Design: Blaise Zito Associates, Inc.
Cover Concept: Alan Forman

This book was set in Baskerville with Avant Garde Gothic by Black Dot.
The color separation was done by Black Dot.

Library of Congress Cataloging in Publication Data
Carlsen, G. Robert, 1917–
American literature, a chronological approach.

   (The McGraw-Hill literature series)
   Includes index.
   Summary: A survey of American literature from early
colonial days to the present.
   1. American literature. [1. American literature]
I. Schuster, Edgar Howard, 1930–   II. Tovatt,
Anthony. III. Title. IV. Series.
PS507.C545 1985   810′.8   83-23893
ISBN 0-07-009844-1

   4 5 6 7 8 9 10   VNHVNH   93 92 91 90 89 88 87 86

The Colonial Period Beginnings to 1750

The Revolutionary and Early National Years

1750–1830

American Romanticism 1830–1865

Regionalism and Realism 1865–1914

Modern Literature 1914–1945

Contemporary Literature 1945–

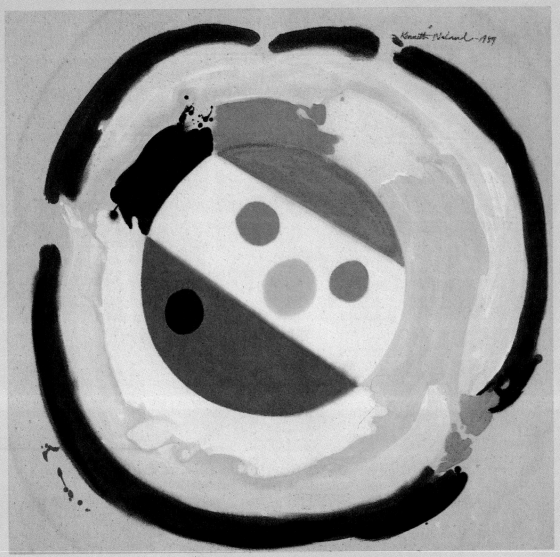

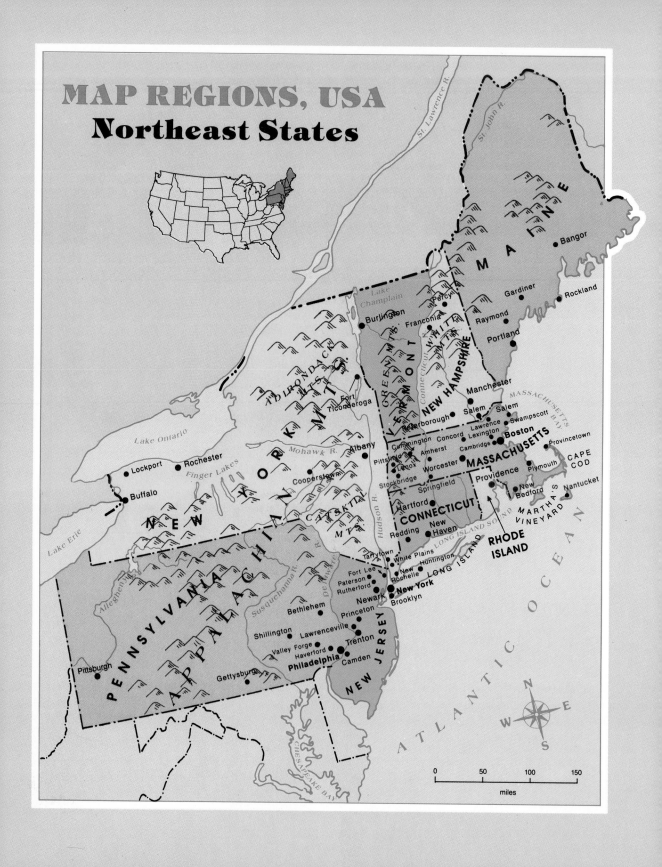

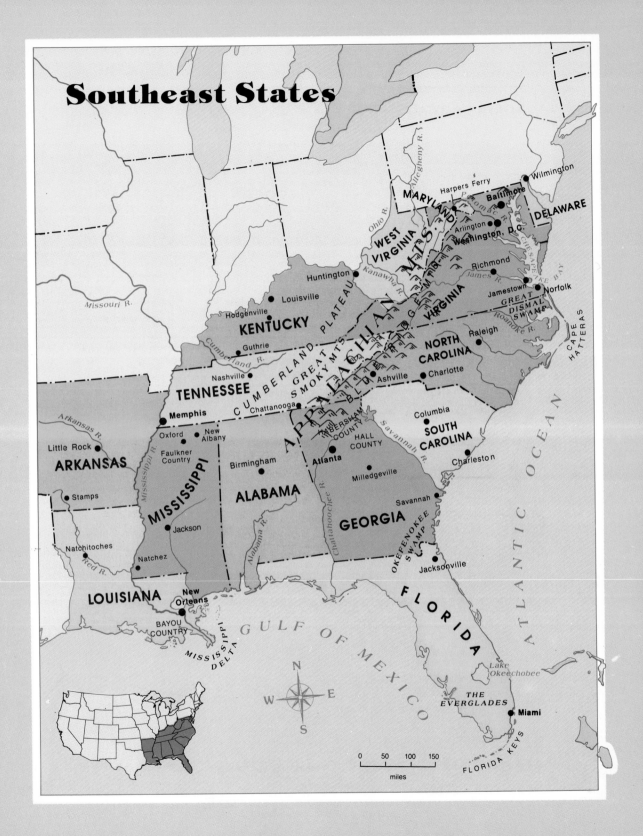

Southeast States

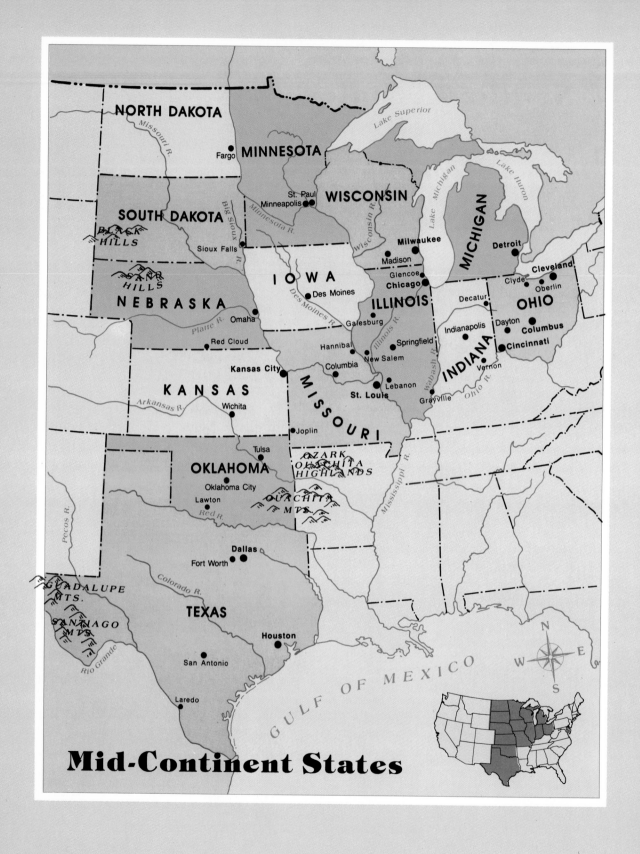

Mid-Continent States

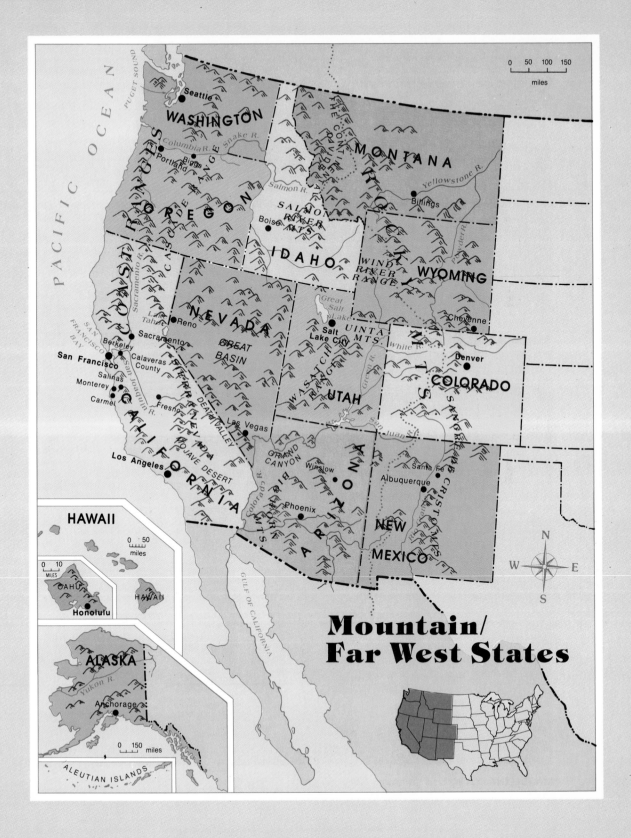

Mountain/Far West States

Scale (miles): 0 50 100 150

PACIFIC OCEAN

PUGET SOUND

WASHINGTON
Seattle
Columbia R.
Snake R.
Portland
Biggs
OREGON

COAST RANGES
CASCADE RANGE

Salmon R.
IDAHO
Boise
SALMON RIVER MTS.
THE CONTINENTAL DIVIDE

MONTANA
Yellowstone R.
Billings

WYOMING
WIND RIVER RANGE

Great Salt Lake
Salt Lake City
UINTA MTS.
White R.
Green R.
Cheyenne

NEVADA
Reno
Lake Tahoe
Sacramento R.
Berkeley
Sacramento
Calaveras County
San Francisco
SAN FRANCISCO BAY
Salinas
Monterey
Carmel
Fresno
San Joaquin R.
GREAT BASIN
SIERRA NEVADA
DEATH VALLEY
Las Vegas
WASATCH RANGE
UTAH

ROCKY MTS.
Denver
COLORADO
San Juan R.

CALIFORNIA
MOJAVE DESERT
Los Angeles
GRAND CANYON
Winslow
Colorado R.
Phoenix
ARIZONA
BIG HORN MTS.

Santa Fe
Albuquerque
SANGRE DE CRISTO MTS.
Pecos R.
Rio Grande

NEW MEXICO

GULF OF CALIFORNIA

N
W   E
S

HAWAII
Scale (miles): 0 50
OAHU
Honolulu
HAWAII

ALASKA
Scale (miles): 0 10
Yukon R.
Anchorage
Scale (miles): 0 150
ALEUTIAN ISLANDS

MAGDALENA DOUW, Artist Unknown

Courtesy, Henry Francis Du Pont Winterthur Museum, Winterthur, DE

The Colonial Period

Beginnings to 1750

THE EUROPEANS IN THE NEW WORLD

Riches, Religion, and Rejuvenation

One has only to flip the TV dial or pick up a popular magazine to realize that although nearly five hundred years have passed since "Columbus sailed the ocean blue, in fourteen hundred and ninety-two," human desires have remained much the same. How to gain wealth and power, find fulfillment, and stay forever young are aspirations of people today just as much as when explorers like Columbus sailed the high seas. At the outset, these explorers had three basic goals: to seize, in the names of their respective sovereigns, whatever new lands and precious metals they could find; to locate a water passage to the Orient that would make its coveted riches and spices more easily accessible; and to bring Christianity to native peoples. Many also sought the fabled Fountain of Youth.

Age of Exploration

Explorers such as the Genoese Columbus and the Florentine Amerigo Vespucci, who gave the new continent his name, came from a Europe in the first stages of the Renaissance—a great rebirth or reawakening of interest in the classical cultures of Greece and Rome. The Renaissance began in Italy in the 1300s and spread gradually over all of Europe in the next centuries. It is generally characterized as an age of discovery and learning, of artistic and intellectual vitality. Among other things, the printing press with movable type and the cannon are often noted as examples of Renaissance technological developments that were to have a profound influence on history.

The Renaissance

Within half a century after Columbus made his first landfall in the Caribbean, Spanish conquistadores had mercilessly plundered Mexico, Central America, and Peru. The glittering cargoes of gold and other treasure they shipped home made Spain the envy of Europe and gave her the most powerful naval force on the seas. In what is now the United States, Spanish adventurers also made extensive searches for the rumored "Seven Cities of Gold" and the magical spring that would keep one forever young.

Spain's control of the seas was finally broken in 1588, when the "Invincible Armada," the fleet of Philip II, was destroyed in the English

The
Spanish Armada

Channel by a raging storm and a tenacious British naval force. The defeat of the Armada shattered Spain's dream of expanding its empire over the North American continent. The way was now opened for France, England, and other European nations to enter the race to explore and settle the new continent.

This self-portrait, painted in Smith's old age, tells its viewers that the artist had also seen action in the navy and been a poet.

SELF-PORTRAIT, Captain Thomas Smith
Worcester Art Museum, Worcester, MA

At this time Europe was flooded with promotional booklets and verses describing the New World as a paradise veined with gold where fortunes could be had with little or no effort. It was the English who first realized the opportunities the new land offered for something other than supposed ready riches. The desperately poor from city slums and meager farms in England yearned for the chance to begin new lives. The wealthy saw possibilities for huge profits in the unbounded land that could be chartered to them by the English king and in turn parceled out by them to eager settlers. Of course, among those eager to settle were many who were persecuted in England for their religious beliefs.

Promise of a New World

Thus the steady flow of immigrants who were to found America began in the early seventeenth century. The determination of the English colonists to face hardship and peril in the new land is reflected in the following lines, taken from a popular ballad written in 1610 by a man who had been to Jamestown the previous year:

> Let England know our willingnesse, for that our work is goode,
> We hope to plant a Nation, where none before hath stood.*

EARLY LITERATURE

The New Land

The literature of a people reflects their basic concerns. Although finding fabulous riches preoccupied some of the earliest adventurers to the new continent, most early settlers were concerned primarily with establishing new homes and new lives and ensuring their right to worship in their own way. These are the things they wrote about. The literature they have handed down to us consists of descriptions, chronicles, and journals about where they lived and moralistic tracts and sermons about how to live.

The first historical writing of importance is that of Captain John Smith (see page 15). His account of the founding of Jamestown, Virginia, entitled *A True Relation* (1608), was the first book written in America. Smith's later publications about the New World include *A Description of New England* (1616) and *The General History of Virginia* (1624). For two decades he tried in his writing to popularize the idea of settlement on this seemingly boundless and fertile soil.

Captain John Smith

"The spirit of place is a great reality," wrote D. H. Lawrence in the opening chapter of his *Studies in Classic American Literature*. Works such as *Of Plymouth Plantation* (1620–1647) by William Bradford (see page 22), the *Diary* (1674–1729) of Samuel Sewall, and *The Journal of Madam Knight* (1704) by Sarah Kemble Knight (see page 43) helped establish a

"The Spirit of Place"

---

*"News from Virginia" by R. Rich.

*Harvard
Yard*

*Jamestown,
Virginia*

literary tradition in which the sense of place—the wonder and the diversity of the new land—was of primary importance. This tradition is still very much alive as can be seen in Robert Frost's poetry and John Steinbeck's *The Grapes of Wrath* and *Travels with Charley*. It is vividly exemplified in the poetry of Stephen Vincent Benét (see page 69), who, three centuries later, imagined the "childish wonderment" the Jamestown colonists experienced when they saw the Virginia landscape for the first time.

They landed and explored.
It was the first flood of Virginia Spring,
White with new dogwood, smelling of wild strawberries,
Warm and soft-voiced, cornflower-skied and kind.
And they were ravished with it, after the sea,
And half-forgot their toils, half-forgot the gold,
As they went poking and prying a little way
In childish wonderment.
A handful of men in hot, heavy, English gear,
With clumsy muskets, sweating but light at heart,
Staring about them, dubiously but ravished,
As a flying-squirrel leapt from a swaying branch
And a gray opossum squeaked and scuttled away.
Oh, the fair meadows, the goodly trees and tall,
The fresh streams running in silver through the woods!
'Twas a land, a land!*

*From "Western Star" by Stephen Vincent Benét. pub. Holt, Rinehart & Winston, Inc. Copyright 1943 by Rosemary Carr Benét. Copyright renewed © 1971 by Rachel Benét Lewis, Thomas C. Benét and Stephanie Benét Mahin.

The Puritan Influence

Some thirteen years after the English settlers landed at Jamestown, the *Mayflower* landed at Plymouth, bearing a band of people who called themselves Pilgrims, or Saints. These were Puritans who had been persecuted for their efforts to "purify" the Church of England and had fled first to Holland, where for a dozen years they worshiped as they wished. Fearing their children were losing their religious faith, however, the Pilgrims left Holland and crossed the Atlantic to what they prayed would be their Promised Land. Considering themselves truly chosen people, they resolutely set about to transform the infant settlement into a thriving community governed by their church leaders and guided, as they believed, by Divine Providence. About ten years later, their numbers were greatly swelled by a second migration of Puritans from England, where persecution continued. Under the able leadership of John Winthrop, they established a settlement in Boston. Both Puritan settlements prospered.

The Mayflower

Puritanism

The Puritans believed strongly in a Covenant of Grace between God and humanity, according to which God had promised to grant eternal life to a chosen few. These were the elect, or the saints. The early Puritans believed individuals could achieve this state of grace only through faith, and not through good works. Since grace was only achieved through the working of God on the individual soul, devout Puritans were constantly engaged in a process of spiritual self-examination. Every act, thought, word, or fantasy that could be recalled was subjected to the closest scrutiny.

The Elect

However, Puritans did impose strict ideals of moral conduct upon themselves, binding each individual not only to church doctrine but also to civil obedience. The colonial Puritan leaders also believed that in order for both church and state to flourish, the populace must be literate. Children—particularly boys—were taught from an early age to read, write, and cipher. To insure a literate ministry, Harvard College was founded in 1636.

A Literate Ministry

That their ministry was indeed literate is borne out by the enormous number of sermons, pamphlets, and books turned out by such Puritan pastors as Increase Mather, author of more than 100 tracts, and his son, Cotton (see page 38), whose output was close to 500 works. Increase Mather's father, Richard, was one of the translators of the Old Testament included in the *Bay Psalm Book* (1640), the first book printed in America. The Mathers exercised an enormous influence over writing in New England for three-quarters of a century.

The Mathers

Although the Salem witchcraft executions of 1692 caused popular reaction against the Mathers, another Puritan pastor, Jonathan Edwards (see page 53), inspired the spread of religious revivals, sometimes referred to as the Great Awakening, throughout the colonies from 1740 to 1745. The fiery, brilliant Edwards also made numerous

Salem Witchcraft

Jonathan Edwards

contributions to the field of theology. Important as it may have been in its time, most of the early Puritan writing was designed to instruct rather than to entertain; today it is read primarily by scholars. "Hoop Petticoats Arraigned and Condemned by the Light of Nature and the Law of God," for example, has little relevance now.

Bradstreet and Taylor

Of more universal appeal are the writings of our first American poets. Anne Bradstreet (see page 30) can still be read with pleasure, and the best work of Edward Taylor, physician and minister (see page 33), compares favorably with the most highly regarded poetry of seventeenth-century England.

Most Puritan poets, though, wrote verses a bit too gloomy for modern tastes; much of their work consisted of elegies, devotions, epitaphs, and maxims on morality. This is not to say that poetry was not popular in the early colonies. It was very popular, especially among

Though these early American portraits may look stiff and unnatural to us today, they represent the best skills of artists who were almost completely self-taught.

JOHN FREAKE
Artist Unknown
Worcester Art Museum, Worcester, MA
Gift of Mr. and Mrs. Albert W. Rice

those with any claim to formal schooling. It was customary not only to read and recite poems but to write them as well. The most widely read rhymes appeared in annual farmers' almanacs, which almost every family could afford or borrow. The anonymous almanac versifiers held forth endlessly, often laboriously, and often humorously, on human behavior as it related to the zodiac, the seasons, and the months of the year. The following verse comes from an almanac for 1688, published in Boston:

Puritan
Poetry

MARCH
Now if thy Body be not well
This month for Physick* doth excel;
But choose a Doctor skill'd in Art,
Not Quacks growing rich by others smart.

*Physick, medicine or medical treatment.

One of the most appealing attributes of portraits like these is that they are of ordinary people. In European lands at that time, only aristocratic families had their portraits painted.

ELIZABETH FREAKE AND BABY MARY
Artist Unknown
Worcester Art Museum, Worcester, MA
Sarah C. Garver Fund

The
Puritan
Legacy

There is little question that the Puritans had a profound influence on American life and literature. Many Americans still see this country as especially chosen by God to set an example for the world. Others believe firmly that self-esteem can only be achieved by a plain, simple, hard-working life-style. American writers from Hawthorne to Hemingway have struggled with the questions of how to live and what values to live by.

The Plantation South

A less rigorous climate and less rocky soil than New England's gave rise to a different kind of society in the southern colonies. Here the plantations, where most of the labor was performed first by indentured servants as elsewhere, but later and more importantly by black slaves, contrasted with the typical small farms, villages, and growing seaport towns of the New England and middle colonies.

William
Byrd II

Southern plantation owners (planters) were mostly Church of England gentlemen, who were apparently less self-critical and introspective than the New England Puritans. In this more relaxed atmosphere, where great attention was given to courtly manners, the literary output of the colonial Southerners was confined primarily to letters, journals, and informational pieces that were seldom published. William Byrd II (see page 48) is generally credited with making the most significant Southern contribution to American literature up to the middle of the eighteenth century.

Drama

"A Chapel
of Satan"

Banned on moral grounds by the New England Puritans and the Pennsylvania Quakers, drama was slow to develop in the colonies. Puritan ministers considered the theater "a chapel of Satan" in which truth was distorted and "profane, seditious, and bawdy stories shown forth," and where playgoers were exposed to "all things that appertain to craft, mischief, deceits, and filthiness."

Charges
of
Immorality

In the southern colonies, however, English plays were performed privately, generally in the homes of wealthy planters, lawyers, and merchants. But even in Virginia, the most cavalier colony of the plantation South, the performance of amateur theatricals sometimes prompted irate settlers to challenge drama as immoral and to drag the players before a magistrate. Court records reveal that in 1665 three actors presented an English farce, *Ye Bare and Ye Cubb*, and were immediately brought into court on a charge of immorality. After they were required to perform some scenes from the play for the judges, however, they were found "not guilty of fault."

Not surprisingly, the general public in the South did not accept play-going until the first decade of the eighteenth century, and then only grudgingly. One of the first playhouses in America open to the public was in Charleston, South Carolina, in 1716. But drama did not really begin to flourish throughout the southern and middle colonies until around 1760. Of course, it took even longer in New England.

Early Playhouses

Willing to face danger, hardship, uncertainty, and complete isolation from all they had known, the early settlers possessed rare courage and determination. They were sustained in their undertaking by the power of their faith and their commitment to the creation of a new life in a land free from persecution.

PILGRIMS GOING TO CHURCH
George H. Boughton
New York Historical Society, New York City

Below: **DEER MASK,** American Indian
Museum of the American Indian, New York City

Right: **SEAL DECOY HAT,** American Indian
Peabody Museum of Archaeology and Ethnology, Cambridge, MA

The Afro-American Literary Heritage

Sin of Slavery

The literary heritage of Afro-Americans was understandably slow in developing. A fortunate few blacks were granted freedom and literacy, but most were slaves who were denied both education and cultural advantages. Because the slaveholders feared slave uprisings, they tried to stamp out the cultural heritages of the slaves' many African homelands. In many cases, the slaves were forbidden to tell stories or

An Old Culture Survives

sing songs from their ancestral homes. Forbidden or not, songs, dances, myths, and tales were passed from one generation of slaves to another, carrying with them vestiges of their cultural heritage from Africa. These remnants of old cultures gradually evolved into the beginnings of a literature in the American tradition. Not until after the Civil War, however, were Afro-American writers in a position to be able to contribute significantly to the growing body of American literature.

American Indian Literature

American Indians had created rich literary and cultural heritages

An Oral Tradition

hundreds of years before the first Europeans cast their anchors off the coast of the New World. Many tribal groups have contributed song lyrics, stories, laws, and accounts of the creation, which have come down to us through the oral tradition. Several selections from this earliest American literature are included in this unit.

Discovery and Exploration

HENRY VII
1485–1509

HENRY VIII   1509–1547

EDWARD VI   1547–1553

MARY I   1553–1558

ELIZABETH I
1558–1603

Columbus
discovers
America, 1492

Cabot discovers
Newfoundland,
1497

The Americas
named
for Amerigo
Vespucci, 1507

Balboa sights
Pacific, 1513

Magellan, del
Cano begin
circling globe,
1519

Cortes conquers
Aztecs, 1521

Pizarro subdues
Incas, 1533

First printing
press in New
World, Mexico,
1535

DeSoto explores
Mississippi River,
1541

First college in
New World,
University of
Mexico, 1551

St. Augustine
founded, 1565

Drake maps
Pacific coast,
1577

1500

1550

Luther's
theses, 1517

Church of
England founded,
1534

Copernicus's
treatise, 1543

India's Mogul
Empire peaks in
Akbar's reign,
1556–1605

Galileo and
Shakespeare
born, Michel-
angelo dies,
1564

African Kanem
Empire at apex
under Idris III.
1571–1603

Chinese Ming
Dynasty at high
point under Wan
Li, 1573–1620

stopher Columbus

William Shakespeare

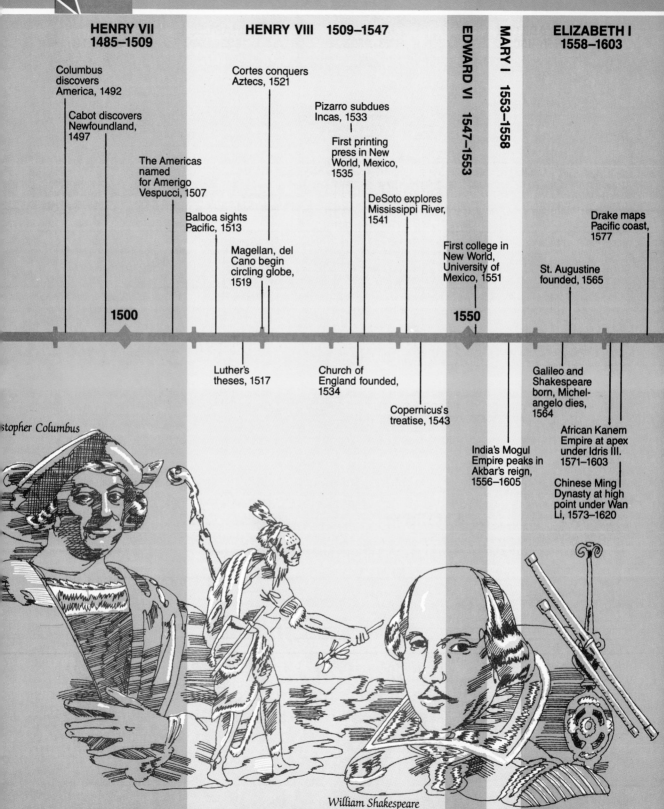

First Colonies

ELIZABETH I
1558–1603

JAMES I
1603–1625

CHARLES I
1625–1649

COMMON-WEALTH
1649–1660

Spanish Armada,
1588

Jamestown, Virginia,
founded, 1607

First African
slaves sold in
Jamestown, 1619

Pilgrims land at
Plymouth, 1620

Shah Abbas the
Great rules
Persia, 1587–
1629

Salem colony,
chartered, 1629

New Amster-
dam becomes
New York,
1664

Roanoke colony
lost , 1587

Shakespeare
dies, 1616

Harvard College
founded, 1636

King James
Bible, 1611

1600

1650

Smith's *New
England,* 1616

First book printed
in colonies, *Bay
Psalm Book,* 1640

Smith's *A True
Relation,* 1608

Smith's *History
of Virginia,* 1624

Bradford's *Of
Plymouth
Plantation,* 1647

First American
poetry, Bradstreet's
The Tenth Muse,
1650

c. 1580   **JOHN SMITH**   1631

1590   **WILLIAM BRADFORD**   1657

1612   **ANNE BRADSTREET**

c. 1642

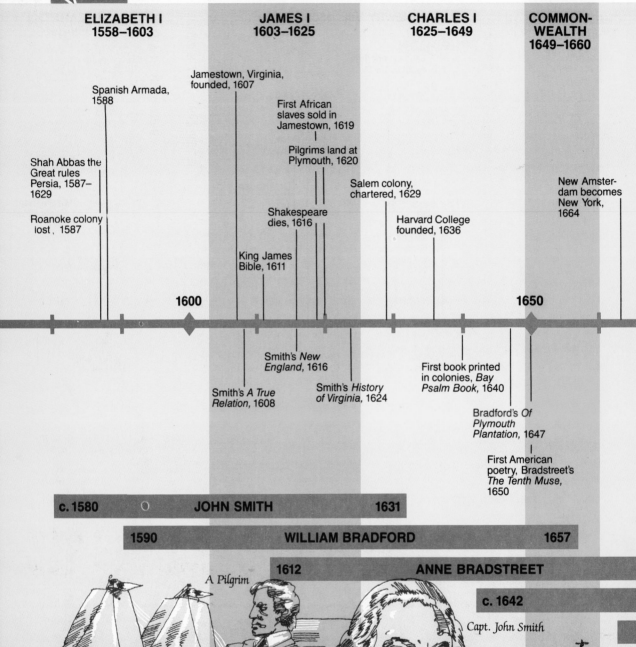

A Pilgrim

Capt. John Smith

Colonial Growth

CHARLES II 1660–1685

JAMES II 1685–1688

WILLIAM & MARY 1689–1702

ANNE 1702–1714

GEORGE I 1714–1727

GEORGE II 1727–1760

Milton's *Paradise Lost,* 1667

Philadelphia founded, 1682

Salem witch trials, 1692

William and Mary College founded, 1693

Yale College founded, 1701

First newspaper, Boston *NewsLetter,* 1704

New Orleans founded, 1718

Tuscarora join Iroquois Peace Council, 1712

Baltimore founded, 1729

Franklin founds first public library, 1731

John Peter Zenger wins fight for free press, 1735

"The Great Awakening," 1740–1745

1700

1750

Samuel Sewall's *Diary,* 1674–1729

Mather's *Wonders of the Invisible World,* 1693

Knight's *Journal,* 1704

Byrd's *History of the Dividing Line,* 1729

Franklin's first *Poor Richard's Almanack,* 1732

Edwards's "Sinners in the Hands of an Angry God," 1741

| 1674 | **WILLIAM BYRD** | 1744 |

| 1703 | **JONATHAN EDWARDS** | 1758 |

| 1672 | 1706 | **BENJAMIN FRANKLIN** | to 1790 |

| **EDWARD TAYLOR** | 1729 |

| 1663 | **COTTON MATHER** | 1728 |

| 1666 | **SARAH KEMBLE KNIGHT** | 1727 |

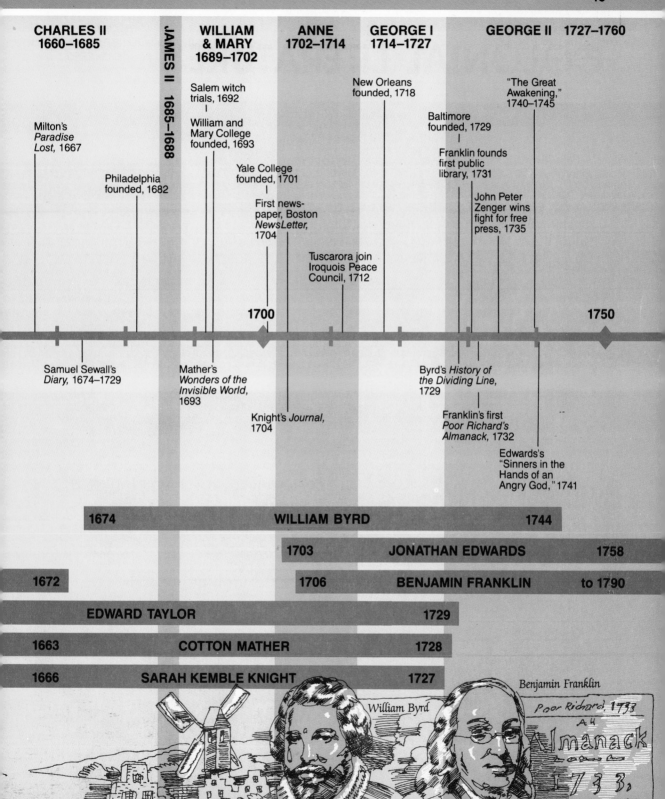

William Byrd

Benjamin Franklin

Poor Richard, 1733

A 4

Almanack

1733,

COLONIAL LITERATURE

Severe and simple as such furnishings may seem to modern eyes, they were solid, long-lasting, and extremely functional.

SEVENTEENTH-CENTURY ROOM, New England
Courtesy, Henry Francis Du Pont Winterthur Museum, Winterthur, DE

John Smith

c. 1580–1631

Soldier of fortune, explorer, promoter, and writer, Captain John Smith has come to be recognized as an important contributor to American history and literature. He remains a folk hero as well, because of his legendary rescue by the Indian princess Pocahontas. In 1607 he was instrumental in establishing Jamestown, the first permanent English settlement on American soil, and he wrote the first English book to be published about America, *A True Relation* (1608). Later, his maps of the New England coastline and his writings about the area were invaluable to the Pilgrims in founding the colony at Plymouth.

Born a commoner and faced with becoming just an ordinary apprentice when he finished grammar school at fifteen, Smith ran away from his home in Lincolnshire, England, to become a professional soldier. Only twenty-seven when he arrived in Virginia among three shiploads of settlers, he was already a survivor of shipwreck, mutiny, piracy, and bloody conflict. With various mercenary armies, he had traveled and fought throughout Europe and in the Near East, where he had been enslaved for a time by the Turks.

When the colonists landed in Virginia, John Smith was under shipboard arrest because of frequent disagreements with those in authority. Nevertheless, he proved best qualified to direct the inexperienced and quarreling settlers in building housing and defenses at Jamestown. Had it not been for his success in dealing with the Indians, the colonists would all have starved or fled back to England in panic. He was the only English leader in whom the powerful Indian chief Powhatan put any trust.

Smith was forced to return to England in 1609 because of serious gunpowder burns. He never returned to Jamestown but did make two subsequent voyages to America, during which he carefully explored and mapped much of the New England coast. He wanted desperately to found a permanent colony there but failed to get financial backing. Frustrated in his colonizing efforts and ambitions, Smith determined to find lasting fame as a historian and spent three years

PORTRAIT OF JOHN SMITH, Artist Unknown
National Portrait Gallery, Smithsonian Institution, Washington, DC

putting together his longest and most important work, *The General History of Virginia, New England, and the Summer Isles.* He died rather suddenly and in relative obscurity at fifty-one.

The first selection in the text is Smith's account of his capture by the Indians and his rescue by Pocahontas. Many historians doubt the authenticity of the rescue story, and it is often referred to as the best-known American myth. However, there is no doubt that this Indian princess did exist and aided the colonists. A vivacious young girl of about twelve when Smith first saw her, she was later to marry colonist John Rolfe and travel to England in what today we would call a publicity stunt staged by the London Company to capture public interest in settlement in Virginia.

from THE GENERAL HISTORY OF VIRGINIA

Smith's account opens after the two larger of the company's three ships have returned to London for supplies, leaving behind some 100 ragged, disease-weakened colonists out of the 144 who originally left England. It is at a time when the food supply is temporarily plentiful. Having barely survived the first summer and fall under the incompetent direction of their president and their bickering council, the settlers have given much additional responsibility to Smith, who has been exploring surrounding areas in an attempt to establish trade with the Indians.

Note that in the fashion of writers of the day, Smith uses the third person and refers to himself as "Captain Smith."

The Pocahontas Episode

December 1607–January 1608

And now the winter approaching, the rivers became so covered with swans, geese, ducks, and cranes, that we daily feasted with good bread, Virginia peas, pumpkins, persimmons, fish, fowl, and diverse sorts of wild beasts as fat as we could eat them, so that none of our tuftaffety humorists[1] desired to go for England.

But our comedies never endured long without a tragedy; some idle exceptions being muttered against Captain Smith for not discovering the head of Chickahominy River, and taxed[2] by the Council to be too slow in so worthy an attempt. The next voyage he proceeded so far that with much labor by cutting of trees asunder he made his passage; but when his barge could pass no farther, he left her in a broad bay out of danger of shot, commanding none should go ashore till his return: himself with two English[3] and two savages went up higher in a canoe, but he was not long absent but[4] his men went ashore, whose want of government gave both occasion and opportunity to the savages to surprise one George Cassen, whom they slew, and much failed not[5] to have cut off the boat and all the rest. . . .

Captain Smith Taken Prisoner. The savages having drawn from George Cassen whither Captain Smith was gone, prosecuting[6] that opportunity they followed him with three hundred bowmen, conducted by the King of Pamaunkee, who in divisions searching the turnings of the river, found Robinson and Emry by the fireside; those they shot full of arrows and slew. Then finding the Captain, . . . that used the savage that was his guide as his shield (three of them being slain and divers[7] others so galled[8]), all the rest would not come near him. Thinking thus to have returned to his boat, regarding them as he marched more than his way, slipped up to the middle in an oozy creek and his savage with him; yet durst[9] they not come to him till being

---

1. **tuftaffety humorists,** critical and pretentious colonists.
2. **taxed,** here: accused.
3. **two English,** Jehu Robinson and Thomas Emry.
4. **but,** here: until.
5. **much failed not,** did not fail by much.
6. **prosecuting,** here: seizing.
7. **divers,** here: several.
8. **galled,** wounded.
9. **durst,** dared.

"Pocahontas, the King's dearest daughter, when no entreaty could prevail, got his head in her arms, and laid her own upon his to save him from death; whereat the emperor was contented he should live. . . ."

near dead with cold, he threw away his arms. Then according to their composition[10] they drew him forth and led him to the fire, where his men were slain. Diligently they chafed his benumbed limbs.

He demanding for their captain, they showed him Opechankanough, King of Pamaunkee, to whom he gave a round ivory double compass dial. Much they marveled at the playing of the fly and needle[11], which they could see so plainly, and yet not touch it because of the glass that covered them. But when he demonstrated by that globelike jewel the roundness of the earth, the skies, the sphere of the sun, moon, and stars, and how the sun did chase the night round about the world continually; the greatness of the land

and sea, the diversity of nations, variety of complexions, and how we were to them antipodes,[12] and many other suchlike matters, they all stood as amazed with admiration. Notwithstanding, within an hour after they tied him to a tree, and as many as could stand about him prepared to shoot him, but the King holding up the compass in his hand, they all laid down their bows and arrows, and in a triumphant manner led him to Orapaks,[13]

10. **composition,** here: manner or practice.
11. **fly and needle.** The fly was a marked circle over which the needle moved.
12. **antipodes** (an tip′ ə dēz), from the other side of the world (or in the other hemisphere).
13. **Orapaks** (ôr′ ə paks), a campsite in what is now Hanover County.

where he was after their manner kindly feasted and well used. . . .

How Powhatan Entertained Him.

At last they brought him to Weronocomoco, where was Powhatan, their emperor. Here more than two hundred of these grim courtiers stood wondering at him, as he had been a monster; till Powhatan and his train had put them-selves in their greatest braveries.[14] Before a fire upon a seat like a bedstead, he sat cov-ered with a great robe, made of raccoonskins, and all the tails hanging by. On either hand did sit a young wench of sixteen or eighteen years, and along on each side the house, two rows of men, and behind them as many women, with all their heads and shoulders painted red; many of their heads bedecked with the white down of birds; but every one with something, and a great chain of white beads about their necks.

How Pocahontas Saved His Life.

At his en-trance before the King, all the people gave a great shout. The Queen of Appamatuck was appointed to bring him water to wash his hands, and another brought him a bunch of feathers, instead of a towel, to dry them. Hav-ing feasted him after their best barbarous manner they could, a long consultation was held; but the conclusion was, two great stones were brought before Powhatan: then as many as could laid hands on him, dragged him to them, and thereon laid his head, and being ready with their clubs to beat out his brains, Pocahontas, the King's dearest daughter, when no entreaty could prevail, got his head in her arms, and laid her own upon his to save him from death: whereat the emperor was contented he should live to make him hatchets, and her bells, beads, and copper; for they thought him as well of all occupa-tions as themselves. For the King himself will make his own robes, shoes, bows, arrows, pots; plant, hunt, or do anything so well as the rest.

How Powhatan Sent Him to Jamestown.

Two days after, Powhatan having disguised him-self in the most fearfullest manner he could, caused Captain Smith to be brought forth to a great house in the woods, and there upon a mat by the fire to be left alone. Not long after, from behind a mat that divided the house, was made the most dolefullest noise he ever heard; then Powhatan, more like a devil than a man, with some two hundred more as black[15] as himself, came unto him and told him now they were friends and presently he should go to Jamestown to send him two great guns and a grindstone, for which he would give him the country of Capahowosick, and forever esteem him as his son Nan-taquoud.

So to Jamestown with twelve guides Pow-hatan sent him. That night they quartered in the woods, he still expecting (as he had done all this long time of his imprisonment) every hour to be put to one death or other, for all their feasting. But almighty God (by His di-vine providence) had mollified the hearts of those stern barbarians with compassion. The next morning betimes they came to the fort, where Smith having used the savages with what kindness he could, he showed Raw-hunt, Powhatan's trusty servant, two demi-culverins[16] and a millstone to carry Powhatan: they found them somewhat too heavy, but when they did see him discharge them, being loaded with stones, among the boughs of a great tree loaded with icicles, the ice and branches came so tumbling down that the poor savages ran away half dead with fear. But at last we regained some conference with them, and gave them such toys; and sent to Powhatan, his women, and children such presents, as gave them in general full content.

---

14. **greatest braveries,** here: finest costumes.
15. **black.** They had painted themselves black.
16. **demi-culverins,** cannons weighing 3000 to 5000 pounds each.

The Third Project to Abandon the Country.
Now in Jamestown they were all in combustion,[17] the strongest preparing once more to run away with the pinnace;[18] which with the hazard of his life, with saker, falcon[19] and musket shot, Smith forced now the third time to stay or sink.

Some no better than they should be, had plotted with the President, the next day to have put him to death by the Levitical law,[20] for the lives of Robinson and Emry, pretending the fault was his that had led them to their ends: but he quickly took such order[21] with such lawyers that he laid them by the heels till he sent some of them prisoners for England.

Now every once in four or five days, Pocahontas, with her attendants, brought him so much provision that saved many of their lives that else for all this had starved with hunger. . . .

A True Proof of God's Love to the Action. His relation of the plenty he had seen, especially at Weronocomoco, and of the state and bounty of Powhatan (which till that time was unknown), so revived their dead spirits (especially the love of Pocahontas) as all men's fear was abandoned.

Thus you may see what difficulties still crossed any good endeavor; and the good success of the business being thus oft brought to the very period of destruction; yet you see by what strange means God hath still delivered it.

17. **combustion,** here: confusion.
18. **pinnace** (pin' is), the small ship left at Jamestown when the two larger ships returned to England.
19. **saker, falcon,** types of small cannons.
20. **the Levitical law,** Old Testament (Leviticus 24:17): "And he that killeth any man shall surely be put to death."
21. **took such order,** here: took control.

The following is one of the best examples of Smith's writings promoting English settlement in New England.

from A DESCRIPTION OF NEW ENGLAND

A Note for Men that Have Great Spirits and Small Means. Who can desire more content, that hath small means or but only his merit to advance his fortune, than to tread and plant that ground he hath purchased by the hazard of his life? If he have but the taste of virtue and magnanimity, what to such a mind can be more pleasant than planting and building a foundation for his posterity got from the rude earth by God's blessing and his own industry without prejudice[1] to any? If he have any grain of faith or zeal in religion, what can

he do less hurtful to any, or more agreeable to God, than to seek to convert those poor savages to know Christ and humanity, whose labors with discretion will triple requite thy charge and pains? What so truly suits with honor and honesty as the discovering things unknown: erecting towns, peopling countries, informing the ignorant, reforming things unjust, teaching virtue; and gain to

1. **prejudice,** here: harm.

our native mother country a kingdom to attend her; find employment for those that are idle because they know not what to do—so far from wronging any as to cause posterity to remember thee, and remembering thee, ever honor that remembrance with praise?

Smith goes on to explain the downfall of the Chaldean, Syrian, Greek, and Roman empires as the result of youth remaining at home in idleness rather than adventuring abroad for the good of themselves and their mother country. Then, after stating that he is "not so simple as to think that ever any other motive than wealth" would draw people from "their ease and humors at home" to erect a commonwealth in a new world, he describes the abundant agricultural, fishing, hunting, and economic opportunities New England affords. He concludes:

My purpose is not to persuade children from their parents, men from their wives, nor servants from their masters: only such as with free consent may be spared; but that each parish or village in city or country that will but apparel their fatherless children of thirteen or fourteen years of age, or young married people that have small wealth to live on, here by their labor may live exceeding well, provided always that first there be a sufficient power to command them, houses to receive them, means to defend them, and meet provisions for them. For any place may be overlain;[2] and it is most necessary to have a fortress, ere this grow to practice, and sufficient masters as carpenters, masons, fishers, fowlers, gardeners, husbandmen, sawyers, smiths, spinsters, tailors, weavers, and such like to take ten, twelve, or twenty, or as there is occasion, for apprentices. The masters by this may quickly grow rich; these may learn their trades themselves to do the like to a general and an incredible benefit for King and country, master and servant.

2. **overlain,** overrun by an enemy.

FOR UNDERSTANDING

Smith, Colonizer and Historian

1. What spurred Captain John Smith into making an expedition up the Chickahominy River? What circumstances resulted in George Cassen's death?
2. Describe Smith's two narrow escapes from death after his capture by the Indians. What effect did the friendship of Pocahontas have upon the spirits of the colonists?
3. What action was Smith forced to take when he got back to Jamestown?
4. Discuss what Captain John Smith believed to be the necessary conditions for founding a successful and profitable settlement, as revealed in the concluding paragraph from *A Description of New England.*

FOR INTERPRETATION

The purpose of the For Interpretation sections of the study notes is to encourage you to think about what you read. Reading, after all, should be both pleasurable and thought-provoking. Many times there are important ideas that are not immediately obvious. The questions and statements for discussion, like those that follow, will help you probe for insights that lie "below the surface" of the selections.

Often an author makes statements indirectly or simply suggests an important thought or idea. For example, in the first of the selections you have just read, Captain John Smith writes of the big guns he is forced to agree to give Powhatan, "They [the Indians] found them somewhat too heavy." (p. 18) Readers of Smith's time, knowing the full weight of the demi-culverins, would have chuckled at his ironic use of *somewhat.* Smith is displaying a wry sense of humor at the same time that he is showing off his skill as a negotiator.

Discuss the following:
1. John Smith's use of the word *toys* (p. 18) clearly suggests the English attitude toward the Indians.
2. The basis for much of what has come to be known as the American dream can be found in the opening paragraph of Smith's *A Note for Men that Have Great Spirits and Small Means.*

FOR APPRECIATION

Throughout this book, you will study the various techniques that writers use and that experienced readers look for in different kinds of literature. As your skill in recognizing these techniques increases, so will your capacity to appreciate and enjoy good literature.

Style

John Smith wrote in the inflated style popular at the beginning of the seventeenth century, a style generally characterized by very long, involved sentences, ornate or fancy figures of speech, and exaggeration to achieve effect.

Style can be defined as a combination of two elements: the idea to be expressed and the individuality of the writer. The idea behind most of Smith's writing is propagandistic—to popularize settlement—and thus the inflated style fits his needs admirably. However, perhaps because of his lack of a university education, Smith's style is rougher and more convoluted (turned back upon itself) than that of many of his contemporaries.

Omission of pronouns and confusion of pronoun antecedents made for a lack of clarity in much seventeenth-century writing. All writers of this time, however, expected close attention from their readers. One must read Smith's prose with great care in order to sort out confusing details and keep the thread of narration clear.

1. Discuss what you found to be the easiest passages to read and understand in the selection from *The General History . . .* What evidence is there of Smith's ability to write vivid description?

2. Discuss how Smith's early (and rough) seventeenth-century writing style contrasts with writing today.

LANGUAGE AND VOCABULARY

Just as writing style has changed since the time of Captain John Smith, so have the meanings of words and their common forms. The English language is always changing; new words are assimilated, others drop out of common usage, and still others assume new meanings. For example, the people Smith refers to as "tuftaffety humorists" would have been immediately recognized by readers of his day as individuals of gentlemanly rank, because commoners could not afford to dress in tufted taffeta, a luxurious silken fabric of high fashion.

Captain Smith uses the term "humorists" in derision, meaning people who behave capriciously, depending upon their "humors." According to medieval physiology, health and general behavior were determined by the four humors, or fluids of the body, which were designated as blood, phlegm, choler, and black bile. Smith's reference to his pettish troublemakers as "humorists" is also in keeping with the Elizabethan definition of humorist—"one that is greatly pleased, or greatly displeased, with the little things, who sets his heart upon matters of very small importance."

1. Smith uses *meet* as an adjective in the expression "meet provisions" (p. 20). In his time *meet* meant "fitting," "proper," or "adequate." What does the dictionary tell you about the adjective form of the word today?

2. The footnotes give seventeenth-century meanings for the words below. Discuss their most common twentieth-century meanings.

  a. composition

  b. braveries

  c. combustion

COMPOSITION

Imagine that you are a twentieth-century real-estate promoter and are putting out a brochure to entice homeowners to a new area or community. Write an introductory paragraph of about the same length as Smith's first paragraph from *A Description of New England*. Describe the advantages of the new development, and be sure to appeal to present-day needs.

William Bradford   1590–1657

Although he risked the penalties of going to prison or of having his nose slit or the tops of his ears cropped, as a boy of twelve, William Bradford chose to read the Bible with religious dissenters opposed to the dictates of the national Church of England. His single-minded devotion was eventually to serve him well as the leader and historian of the little troop of Pilgrims who first went to Holland and then to the colony at Plymouth in their search for religious freedom.

When Bradford was sixteen, he joined a Separatist group that met in Scrooby, a village in his native Yorkshire. Orphaned before he was a year old, Bradford was reared by relatives who warned him against his dangerous Puritan activities. Almost entirely self-educated (and principally through study of the Bible), he proved himself adept in several lines of work. After the Separatists settled in Holland, he earned his livelihood as a weaver.

At twenty-seven, Bradford was a member of the committee that arranged the pilgrimage of his people from the Netherlands to their new Zion in America. Through secret negotiations, the Pilgrims, as Bradford called them, were granted a charter by the Virginia Company for land in northern Virginia. However, as a result of a navigational error and a wintry gale off the North American shore, the *Mayflower* ended up in New England waters rather than off the coast of northern Virginia. Anarchy threatened. The mutinous "strangers" (non-Puritans) on board claimed that since the Virginia charter was now invalid, there were no legal restraints whatever to bind them, and they could do as they pleased when they went ashore. In this crisis, Bradford was instrumental in drawing up the Mayflower Compact, which established civil government by common consent of the governed. He also helped to make sure that the document was signed before the voyagers disembarked at Plymouth.

William Bradford was elected governor of Plymouth Colony some thirty times and was widely respected for his fairness. In his last

PORTRAIT OF WILLIAM BRADFORD
Fiercely devoted to the Puritan faith since his boyhood, William Bradford led the Pilgrims to Plymouth and became the colony's governor.

years, he saw the colonists losing their dedication to common goals and moral values as their prosperity increased. Understandably enough, he looked back upon the early days of hardship and struggle as days of glory.

Of Plymouth Plantation had its beginning when Bradford, like a biblical patriarch, began setting down a chronological account of the pilgrimage of his people. He wrote the first ten chapters in 1630, covering the harassment of the Separatists at Scrooby, their exile in Holland, and their settlement at Plymouth in 1620. His "Second Book," covering events at Plymouth up to 1647, was composed piecemeal, most of it before 1646. The sections you will read here begin with his account of the Atlantic crossing, after the voyagers were all "compact together" in the *Mayflower* and on their way to their Promised Land.

from OF PLYMOUTH PLANTATION

Anno 1620

Of their Voyage, and how they Passed the Sea; and of their Safe Arrival at Cape Cod

After they had enjoyed fair winds and weather for a season, they were encountered many times with cross winds and met with many fierce storms with which the ship was shroudly[1] shaken, and her upper works made very leaky; and one of the main beams in the midships was bowed and cracked, which put them in some fear that the ship could not be able to perform the voyage. So some of the chief of the company, perceiving the mariners to fear the sufficiency of the ship as appeared by their mutterings, they entered into serious consultation with the master and other officers of the ship, to consider in time of the danger, and rather to return than to cast themselves into a desperate and inevitable peril. And truly there was great distraction and difference of opinion amongst the mariners themselves; fain[2] would they do what could be done for their wages' sake (being now near half the seas over) and on the other hand they were loath[3] to hazard their lives too desperately. But in examining of all opinions, the master and others affirmed they knew the ship to be strong and firm under water; and for the buckling of the main beam, there was a great iron screw the passengers brought out of Holland, which would raise the beam into his place; the which being done, the carpenter and master affirmed that with a post put under it, set firm in the lower deck and otherways bound, he would make it sufficient. And as for the decks and upper works, they would caulk them as well as they could, and though with the working of the ship they would not long keep staunch, yet there would otherwise be no great danger, if they did not overpress her with sails. So they committed themselves to the will of God and resolved to proceed.

In sundry[4] of these storms the winds were so fierce and the seas so high, as they could not bear a knot of sail, but were forced to hull[5] for divers days together. And in one of them, as they thus lay at hull in a mighty storm, a lusty[6] young man called John Howland, coming upon some occasion above the gratings was, with a seele[7] of the ship, thrown into sea; but it pleased God that he caught hold of the topsail halyards[8] which hung overboard and ran out at length. Yet he held his hold (though he was sundry fathoms under water) till he was hauled up by the same rope to the brim of the water, and then with a boat hook and other means got into the ship again and his life saved. And though he was something ill with it, yet he lived many years after and became a profitable member both in church and commonwealth. In all this voyage there died but one of the passengers, which was William Butten, a youth, servant to

---

1. **shroudly,** dangerously.
2. **fain,** eagerly.
3. **loath** (lōth), reluctant.
4. **sundry,** several.
5. **hull,** drift with the wind under short sail.
6. **lusty,** here: strong.
7. **seele,** pitch or roll.
8. **halyards** (hal' yərdz), ropes for raising or lowering sail.

From OF PLYMOUTH PLANTATION, by William Bradford, edited by Samuel Eliot Morison. Copyright 1952 by Samuel Eliot Morison. Reprinted by permission of Alfred A. Knopf, Inc.

Samuel Fuller, when they drew near the coast.

But to omit other things (that I may be brief) after long beating at sea they fell with that land which is called Cape Cod; the which being made and certainly known to be it, they were not a little joyful. After some deliberation had amongst themselves and with the master of the ship, they tacked about and resolved to stand for the southward (the wind and weather being fair) to find some place about Hudson's River for their habitation. But after they had sailed that course about half the day, they fell amongst dangerous shoals and roaring breakers, and they were so far entangled therewith as they conceived themselves in great danger; and the wind shrinking upon them withal,[9] they resolved to bear up again for the Cape and thought themselves happy to get out of those dangers before night overtook them, as by God's good providence they did. And the next day they got into the Cape Harbor[10] where they rid in safety. . . .

Being thus arrived in a good harbor, and brought safe to land, they fell upon their knees and blessed the God of Heaven who had brought them over the vast and furious ocean, and delivered them from all the perils and miseries thereof, again to set their feet on the firm and stable earth, their proper element. . . .

But here I cannot but stay and make a pause, and stand half amazed at this poor people's present condition; and so I think will the reader, too, when he well considers the same. Being thus passed the vast ocean, and a sea of troubles before in their preparation, they had now no friends to welcome them nor inns to entertain or refresh their weatherbeaten bodies; no houses or much less towns to repair to, to seek for succour.

What could now sustain them but the Spirit of God and His grace? May not and ought not the children of these fathers rightly say: "Our fathers were Englishmen which came over this great ocean, and were ready to perish in this wilderness; but they cried unto the Lord, and He heard their voice and looked on their adversity."

[The Mayflower Compact]

I shall a little return back, and begin with a combination made by them before they came ashore; being the first foundation of their government in this place. Occasioned partly by the discontented and mutinous speeches that some of the strangers amongst them[11] had let fall from them in the ship: That when they came ashore they would use their own liberty, for none had power to command them, the patent they had being for Virginia and not for New England, which belonged to another government, with which the Virginia Company had nothing to do.[12] And partly that such an act by them done, this their condition considered, might be as firm as any patent, and in some respects more sure.

The form was as followeth:

IN THE NAME OF GOD, AMEN.
We whose names are underwritten, the loyal subjects of our dread Sovereign Lord King James, by the Grace of God of Great Britain, France, and Ireland King, Defender of the Faith, etc.

Having undertaken, for the Glory of God and advancement of the Christian Faith and Honour of our King and Country, a Voyage to plant the First Colony in the Northern Parts of Virginia, do by these presents solemnly and mutually in the presence of God

---

9. **withal** (wiTH ôl'), besides.
10. **Cape Harbor,** now Provincetown Harbor.
11. **strangers amongst them.** Among the 102 *Mayflower* passengers who reached Cape Cod, slightly over a third were members of the Pilgrim church. The rest were recruits from England, most of whom sought economic betterment in America. These the Pilgrims called strangers. The Pilgrims referred to themselves as Saints.
12. **with which . . . nothing to do.** The Pilgrims possessed a patent from the Virginia Company, but since they were now in New England, their patent was invalid.

A later artist's rendering of the Pilgrims' landing, as described by Bradford: "Being thus arrived in a good harbor, and brought safe to land, they fell upon their knees and blessed the God of Heaven who had brought them over the vast and furious ocean, and delivered them from all the perils and miseries thereof. . . ."

and one of another, Covenant and Combine ourselves together into a Civil Body Politic, for our better ordering and preservation and furtherance of the ends aforesaid; and by virtue hereof to enact, constitute and frame such just and equal Laws, Ordinances, Acts, Constitutions and Offices, from time to time, as shall be thought most meet and convenient for the general good of the Colony, unto which we promise all due submission and obedience. In witness whereof we have hereunder subscribed our names at Cape Cod, the 11th of November, in the year of the reign of our Sovereign Lord King James, of England, France and Ireland the eighteenth, and of Scotland the fifty-fourth. *Anno Domini* 1620.

After this they chose, or rather confirmed, Mr. John Carver (a man godly and well approved amongst them) their Governor for that year. And after they had provided a place for their goods, or common store (which were long in unlading for want of boats, foulness of the winter weather and sickness of divers) and begun some small cottages for their habitation; as time would admit, they met and consulted of laws and orders, both for their civil and military government as the necessity of their condition did require, still adding thereunto as urgent occasion in several times, and as cases did require.

In these hard and difficult beginnings they found some discontents and murmur-ings arise amongst some, and mutinous speeches and carriages in other; but they were soon quelled and overcome by the wisdom, patience, and just and equal carriage of things, by the Governor and better part, which clave[13] faithfully together in the main.

[The Starving Time]

But that which was most sad and lamentable was, that in two or three months' time half of their company died, especially in January and February, being the depth of winter, and wanting houses and other comforts; being infected with the scurvy[14] and other diseases which this long voyage and their inaccommodate[15] condition had brought upon them. So as there died some times two or three of a day in the foresaid time, that of 100 and odd persons, scarce fifty remained. And of these, in the time of most distress, there was but six or seven sound persons who to their great commendations, be it spoken, spared no pains night nor day, but with abundance of toil and hazard of their own health, fetched them wood, made them fires, dressed them meat, made their beds, washed their loathsome clothes, clothed and unclothed them. In a word, did all the homely and necessary offices for them which dainty and queasy stomachs cannot endure to hear named; and all this willingly and cheerfully, without any grudging in the least, showing herein their true love unto their friends and brethren; a rare example and worthy to be remembered. Two of these seven were Mr. William Brewster, their reverend Elder, and Myles Standish, their Captain and military commander, unto whom myself and many others were much beholden in our low and sick condition. And yet the Lord so upheld these persons as in this general calamity they were not at all infected either with sickness or lameness. And what I have said of these I may say of many others who died in this general visitation, and others yet living; that whilst they had health, yea, or any strength continuing, they were not wanting to any that had need of them.

And I doubt not but their recompense is with the Lord. . . .

[Indian Relations]

All this while the Indians came skulking about them, and would sometimes show themselves aloof off, but when any approached near them, they would run away; and once they stole away their tools where they had been at work and were gone to dinner. But about the 16th of March, a certain Indian came boldly amongst them and spoke to them in broken English, which they could well understand but marveled at it. At length they understood by discourse with him, that he was not of these parts, but belonged to the eastern parts where some English ships came to fish, with whom he was acquainted and could name sundry of them by their names, amongst whom he had got his language. He became profitable to them in acquainting them with many things concerning the state of the country in the east parts where he lived, which was afterwards profitable unto them; as also of the people here, of their names, number and strength, of their situation and distance from this place, and who was chief amongst them. His name was Samoset. He told them also of another Indian whose name was Squanto, a native of this place, who had been in England and could speak better English than himself.

Being, after some time of entertainment and gifts dismissed, a while after he came again, and five more with him, and they brought again all the tools that were stolen away before, and made way for the coming of their great Sachem,[16] called Massasoit. Who, about four or five days after, came with the

---

13. **clave,** clung, held fast.
14. **scurvy,** a disease caused by deficiency of vitamin C, characterized by bleeding gums, anemia, and extreme weakness.
15. **inaccommodate,** unsuitable.
16. **Sachem** (sā′ chəm), chief of a tribe or confederation.

chief of his friends and other attendance, with the aforesaid Squanto. With whom, after friendly entertainment and some gifts given him, they made a peace with him (which hath now continued this 24 years) in these terms:

1. That neither he nor any of his should injure or do hurt to any of their people.

2. That if any of his did hurt to any of theirs, he should send the offender, that they might punish him.

3. That if anything were taken away from any of theirs, he should cause it to be restored; and they should do the like to his.

4. If any did unjustly war against him, they would aid him; if any did war against them, he should aid them.

5. He should send to his neighbours confederates to certify them of this, that they might not wrong them, but might be likewise comprised in the conditions of peace.

6. That when their men came to them, they should leave their bows and arrows behind them.

After these things he returned to his place called Sowams, some 40 miles from this place, but Squanto continued with them and was their interpreter and was a special instrument sent of God for their good beyond their expectation. He directed them how to set their corn, where to take fish, and to procure other commodities, and was also their pilot to bring them to unknown places for their profit, and never left them till he died. He was a native of this place, and scarce any left alive[17] besides himself. . . .

Anno **1621**

[Mayflower *Departs and Corn Planted*]
They now began to dispatch the ship away which brought them over, which lay till about this time, or the beginning of April.[18] The reason on their part why she stayed so long, was the necessity and danger that lay upon them; for it was well towards the end of De-

cember before she could land anything here, or they able to receive anything ashore. Afterwards, the 14th of January, the house which they had made for a general rendezvous by casualty[19] fell afire, and some were fain to retire aboard for shelter; then the sickness began to fall sore amongst them, and the weather so bad as they could not make much sooner any dispatch. Again, the Governor and chief of them, seeing so many die and fall down sick daily, thought it no wisdom to send away the ship, their condition considered and the danger they stood in from the Indians, till they could procure some shelter; and therefore thought it better to draw some more charge upon themselves and friends than hazard all. The master and seamen likewise, though before they hasted the passengers ashore to be gone, now many of their men being dead, and of the ablest of them (as is before noted), and of the rest many lay sick and weak; the master durst not put to sea till he saw his men begin to recover, and the heart of winter over.

Afterwards they (as many as were able) began to plant their corn, in which service Squanto stood them in great stead, showing them both the manner how to set it, and after how to dress and tend it. Also he told them, except they got fish and set with it in these old grounds it would come to nothing. And he showed them that in the middle of April they should have store enough[20] come up the brook by which they began to build, and taught them how to take it, and where to get other provisions necessary for them. All which they found true by trial and experi-

---

17. **scarce any left alive.** Squanto, or Tisquantum, was evidently the sole survivor of the Patuxet tribe, wiped out in the pestilence of 1617.
18. **beginning of April.** The *Mayflower* sailed April 5.
19. **casualty,** unfortunate accident, usually involving loss of life.
20. **store enough.** Squanto told them enough fish for use as fertilizer could be found in the brook. He also taught them "how to take it," that is, how to build weirs to trap the fish.

The first Thanksgiving, as envisaged by a later artist. "And besides waterfowl there was great store of wild turkeys. . . . which made many afterwards write so largely of their plenty here to their friends in England. . . ."

ence. Some English seed they sowed, as wheat and pease, but it came not to good, either by the badness of the seed or lateness of the season or both, or some other defect.

[Bradford Succeeds Carver]

In this month of April, whilst they were busy about their seed, their Governor (Mr. John Carver) came out of the field very sick, it being a hot day. He complained greatly of his head and lay down, and within a few hours his senses failed, so as he never spake more till he died, which was within a few days after. Whose death was much lamented and caused great heaviness amongst them, as there was cause. He was buried in the best manner they could, with some volleys of shot by all that bore arms. And his wife, being a weak woman, died within five or six weeks after him.

Shortly after, William Bradford was chosen Governor in his stead, and being not recovered of his illness, in which he had been near the point of death, Isaac Allerton was chosen to be an assistant unto him who, by renewed election every year, continued sundry years together. Which I here note once for all.

[First Thanksgiving]

They began now to gather in the small harvest they had, and to fit up their houses and dwellings against winter, being all well recovered in health and strength and had all things in good plenty. For as some were thus employed in affairs abroad, others were exercised in fishing, about cod and bass and other fish, of which they took good store, of which every family had their portion. All the summer there was no want; and now began to come in store of fowl, as winter approached, of which this place did abound when they came first (but afterward decreased by degrees). And besides waterfowl there was great store of wild turkeys, of which they took many, besides venison, etc. Besides they had about a peck a meal a week to a person, or now since harvest, Indian corn to that proportion. Which made many afterwards write so largely of their plenty here to their friends in England, which were not feigned but true reports.

FOR UNDERSTANDING

Bradford, the Patriarch

1. Midway across the Atlantic or "halfway the seas over," as Bradford puts it, passengers on the *Mayflower* debated whether to turn back or to continue to America. How was the Pilgrims' firm faith in God reflected by the decision they made in this crisis? What other situations tested this faith as they came into harbor at Cape Cod?

2. In the Virginia Company charter that the Pilgrims carried with them, James I granted them only immunity from persecution, not religious freedom. He also placed them under the civil authority of Jamestown, which was having a difficult time governing itself. Discuss what was gained when they realized that their Virginia charter was not binding for New England and drew up the

Mayflower Compact (referred to by Bradford as "a combination made by them before coming ashore").

3. Bradford records that in "the depth of winter" two or three persons died each day, leaving scarcely fifty of their one hundred settlers. What reasons does he give for so many deaths at this time?

4. Why were the two Indians, Samoset and Squanto, of such great help to the colonists?

5. Why did the *Mayflower* stay so long before returning to England? What situation led to the selection of Bradford as governor?

FOR INTERPRETATION

In light of the information given in Bradford's history, discuss the following:

1. Togetherness and equality are strengthened in time of great hardship.

2. What is suggested by the word *feigned* in the concluding line of Bradford's description of the first Thanksgiving?

3. It is obvious the Pilgrims believed that God helps those who help themselves.

FOR APPRECIATION

The Writer's Viewpoint

Just as literary custom today demands that journalists and historians write impersonally and objectively, so in Bradford's day historians used the third-person viewpoint to keep from appearing to be braggarts. Nevertheless, as you saw in the case of John Smith, writing in the third person did not always prevent a historian from dramatizing his own exploits.

Look back over Bradford's entries to note those instances when he brings himself into his writing by using the first person *I*. Discuss in each instance what you think his purpose is. Does Bradford's writing give the reader any clue to the importance of the role he played in the successful founding of Plymouth?

Anne Bradstreet   1612–1672

Reared in aristocratic surroundings, Anne Bradstreet was given an education unusual for women at that time. "When I was about seven . . ." she wrote, "I had at one time eight tutors. . . ." In addition to schooling in music, languages, science, and mathematics, she was privileged to read in the extensive library of the Earl of Lincoln, whom her father served as steward.

In 1630 she and her husband, Simon, took part in John Winthrop's Puritan migration to Massachusetts Bay. Simon was influential in the colony's affairs and eventually became governor. Bradstreet served as a devoted mother to her eight children and as gracious hostess to friends and visitors of state. Every moment she could spare, however, she seems to have spent writing letters, verses, and journals.

In 1650, her first book of poems was published, without her knowledge or consent, by her sister's husband, who had taken the manuscript with him on an earlier trip to London. The book, *The Tenth Muse Lately Sprung Up in America, By a Gentlewoman of Those Parts,* was greeted with considerable enthusiasm in both England and the colonies, not only because readers found her subjects and their treatment agreeable, but also, one suspects, because women poets were then indeed a rarity. In 1678 a revised edition of her works was published posthumously in Boston.

Now considered one of the major poets of the colonial period, Anne Bradstreet produced learned and lengthy verses on astronomy, physics, natural history, and philosophy. Modern readers, however, generally prefer her shorter and more personal poems.

To My Dear and Loving Husband

If ever two were one, then surely we.
If ever man were lov'd by wife, then thee;
If ever wife was happy in a man,
Compare with me ye women if you can.
I prize thy love more than whole mines of gold,   5
Or all the riches that the East doth hold.
My love is such that rivers cannot quench,
Nor aught but love from thee give recompense.
Thy love is such I can no way repay,
The heavens reward thee manifold I pray.   10
Then while we live, in love let's so persever,*
That when we live no more, we may live ever.

*__persever__ (pər sev′ ər). The seventeenth-century spelling of *persevere* (at that time pronounced to rhyme with *forever*) is retained here in order to maintain the poet's end rhyme.

THE SARGENT FAMILY, Artist Unknown
National Gallery of Art, Washington, D.C.
Gift of Edgar W. and Bernice Chrysler Garbisch

Anne Bradstreet's poems deal with two important Purtian themes: domestic life and God. The poem you have just read concerns a happy marriage. The following poem concerns true wealth.

Upon the Burning of Our House

July 10th, 1666

In silent night when rest I took,
For sorrow near I did not look,
I waken'd was with thund'ring noise
And piteous shrieks of dreadful voice.
That fearful sound of fire and fire,   5
Let no man know is my desire.

I, starting up, the light did spy,
And to my God my heart did cry
To strengthen me in my distress
And not to leave me succorless.   10
Then coming out beheld a space,
The flame consume my dwelling place.

And, when I could no longer look,
I blest His name that gave and took,
That laid my goods now in the dust: 15
Yea so it was, and so 'twas just.
It was His own: it was not mine;
Far be it that I should repine.

He might of all justly bereft,
But yet sufficient for us left.   20
When by the ruins oft I past,
My sorrowing eyes aside did cast,
And here and there the places spy
Where oft I sat, and long did lie.

Here stood that trunk, and there that
    chest;   25
There lay the store I counted best:
My pleasant things in ashes lie,
And them behold no more shall I.
Under thy roof no guest shall sit,
Nor at thy table eat a bit.   30

No pleasant tale shall e'er be told,
Nor things recounted done of old.
No candle e'er shall shine in thee,
Nor bridegroom's voice ere heard shall
    be.
In silence ever shalt thou lie;   35
Adieu, adieu; all's vanity.

Then straight I gin* my heart to chide,
And did thy wealth on earth abide?
Didst fix thy hope on mould'ring dust,
The arm of flesh didst make thy trust?   40
Raise up thy thoughts above the sky
That dunghill mists away may fly.

Thou hast an house on high erect,
Fram'd by that mighty Architect,
With glory richly furnished,   45
Stands permanent tho' this be fled.
It's purchased, and paid for too
By Him who hath enough to do.

A prize so vast as is unknown,
Yet, by His gift, is made thine own.   50
There's wealth enough, I need no
    more;
Farewell my pelf, farewell my store.
The world no longer let me love,
My hope and treasure lies above.

*gin, begin.

Reprinted by permission of the publishers from THE WORKS OF ANNE BRADSTREET, ed. by Jeannine Hensley, Cambridge, Mass.: The Belknap Press of Harvard University Press, Copyright © 1967 by the President and Fellows of Harvard College.

FOR UNDERSTANDING

In "To My Dear and Loving Husband," how highly does the wife profess to value her husband's love?

FOR INTERPRETATION

1. Explain the meaning of the final two lines of "To My Dear and Loving Husband."
2. As Bradstreet views the charred ruins of her home in "Upon the Burning of Our House," what is her attitude toward the loss?

3. Explain her reference to two houses in the eighth stanza of the second poem.
4. How do the final two lines of the second poem reflect Puritan belief?

FOR APPRECIATION

1. What two words form an imperfect rhyme in "To My Dear and Loving Husband"?
2. In line 45 of "Upon the Burning of Our House," how must *furnished* be pronounced if it is to rhyme with *fled*?

Edward Taylor   c. 1642–1729

Little is known about Edward Taylor's early years. What is known is that he was born in Leicestershire, England, came to Boston in 1668, entered Harvard College, and graduated in 1671. Shortly thereafter he accepted the position of pastor and physician in the frontier village of Westfield, Massachusetts.

To reach his new post, Taylor and a companion set out after a heavy November snowfall and struggled through the 100 miles of wilderness to Westfield. In his diary, the new pastor described the ordeal in these terms: "The snow being above Mid-leg, the way unbeaten, or the track filled up again, and over the rocks and mountains, . . . Mr. Cooke of Cambridge told us it was the desperatest journey that ever Connecticut [Valley] men undertook."

For over fifty years Edward Taylor ministered to the Puritan congregation at Westfield, and during his long tenure there he wrote a considerable number of poems. For as yet undetermined reasons, however, he asked that his immediate heirs not publish any of his verses. His wish was respected. The 400-page leather-bound manuscript stayed quietly in the possession of his descendants until 1883, when a great-grandson made a gift of the manuscript to the Yale University Library.

There the handwritten volume remained until 1937, when a literary scholar discovered it and was granted permission to edit the work for publication. When the book of Taylor's poetry was published two years later, it was received with enthusiasm by most literary critics and scholars, who declared the Puritan pastor a writer of genuine power and placed him with Anne Bradstreet as a major poet of the colonial period.

An orthodox Puritan, Taylor embraced the Calvinist doctrine of predestination—the teaching that God has known and decided from the beginning of time which souls to save and which to damn. Like the early Puritans with whom he shared this belief, Taylor was deeply concerned with salvation and the state of grace and dealt frequently with these subjects in his poetry. All of his poems have religious themes.

Upon a Wasp Chilled with Cold

The Bear[1] that breathes the northern blast
Did numb, Torpedo-like,[2] a wasp
Whose stiffened limbs encramped, lay bathing
In Sol's warm breath and shine as saving,
Which with her hands she chafes and stands   5
Rubbing her legs, shanks, thighs, and hands.

1. **The Bear,** the constellation of Ursa Major, in the region of the North Celestial Pole, commonly called the Big Dipper or the Great Bear.
2. **Torpedo-like,** like the crampfish, numbfish, electric ray, or any fish of the family Torpedinidae, capable of producing a strong electrical charge.

Her petty[3] toes, and fingers' ends
Nipped with this breath, she out extends
Unto the sun, in great desire
To warm her digits at that fire.   10
Doth hold her temples in this state
Where pulse doth beat, and head doth ache.
Doth turn, and stretch her body small,
Doth comb her velvet capital,[4]
As if her little brain pan were   15
A volume of choice precepts[5] clear.
As if her satin jacket hot
Contained apothecary's shop
Of Nature's receipts,[6] that prevails
To remedy all her sad ails,[7]   20
As if her velvet helmet high
Did turret rationality.[8]
She fans her wing up to the wind
As if her pettycoat were lined
With reasons fleece,[9] and hoists sails   25
And humming flies in thankful gales[10]
Unto her dun curled palace hall
Her warm thanks offering for all.

  Lord, clear my misted sight that I
May hence view thy Divinity.   30
Some sparks whereof thou up dost hasp[11]
Within this little downy wasp
In whose small corporation[12] we
A school and a schoolmaster see
Where we may learn, and easily find   35
A nimble spirit bravely mind

---

3. **petty,** small.
4. **capital,** head.
5. **precepts,** principles that impose particular action
or conduct.
6. **apothecary's shop . . . receipts,** a pharmacist's
shop of natural medicinal formulas.
7. **ails,** ailments.
8. **Did turret rationality,** kept reason or soundness of
mind safe in the fortress of her helmeted head.
9. **As if . . . fleece,** as if the pettycoat (petticoat), or
velvety body covering, possessed rationality and directed
her when to move.
10. **flies in thankful gales,** flies in thankful cheerfulness.
11. **hasp,** fasten.
12. **corporation,** here: body.

In its freshness and simplicity, this still life on glazed velvet is a vibrant example of early American folk art.

FRUIT PLATTER, Artist Unknown
National Gallery of Art, Washington, D.C.
Gift of Edgar W. and Bernice Chrysler Garbisch

Her work in every limb: and lace
It up neat with vital grace,
Acting each part though ne'er so small
Here of this fustian[13] animal.
Till I enravished[14] up climb into
The Godhead[15] on this ladder do.
Where all my pipes[16] inspired upraise
An Heavenly music, furred[17] with praise.

40

13. **fustian,** here: covered with short pile or nap. Also, drably clothed.
14. **enravished,** transported with delight.
15. **Godhead,** here: paradise.
16. **pipes,** musical wind instrument.
17. **furred,** filled. More literally, the music is seen as a surface that is stippled with a velvety substance (praise)— a remarkably "modernistic" image.

Huswifery

Make me, O Lord, thy Spinning Wheel complete.
　　Thy Holy Word my Distaff make for me.
Make mine Affections thy Swift Flyers neat
　　And make my Soul thy holy Spool to be.
　　My Conversation make to be thy Reel　　　　　5
　　And reel the yarn thereon spun of thy Wheel.

Make me thy Loom then, knit therein this Twine:
　　And make thy Holy Spirit, Lord, wind quills:[1]
Then weave the Web thyself. The yarn is fine.[2]
　　Thine Ordinances make my Fulling Mills.[3]　　　10
　　Then dye the same in Heavenly Colors Choice,
　　All pinked[4] with Varnished[5] Flowers of Paradise.

Then clothe therewith mine Understanding, Will,
　　Affections, Judgment, Conscience, Memory,
My Words, and Actions, that their shine may fill　　15
　　My ways with glory and thee glorify.
　　Then mine apparel shall display before ye
　　That I am Clothed in Holy robes for glory.

THE POETICAL WORKS OF EDWARD TAYLOR, ed. with an Intro. and
Notes by Thomas H. Johnson. Copyright 1939 by Rockland, 1943 by
Princeton University Press.

1. **quills,** here: spindles or bobbins on which yarn is
wound in weaving.
2. **fine,** here: free from impurities.
3. **Fulling Mills,** mills in which cloth is cleaned and
thickened.
4. **pinked,** here: adorned or decorated.
5. **Varnished,** here: glossy or glistening.

FOR INTERPRETATION

"Upon a Wasp Chilled with Cold"

1. In detailing the movements of the thawing wasp, Taylor reveals himself to be a keen observer of nature. What human characteristics does the poet assign the wasp in lines 5, 6, and 7?

2. Taylor speculates that the wasp acts as if directed by precepts. Where does he suggest such precepts are located?

3. What lesson does the wasp teach the poet?

FOR APPRECIATION

Conceits in "Huswifery"

Throughout his poetry Edward Taylor uses *conceits,* elaborate and often startling comparisons between two seemingly unlike things. For example, in a poem on the creation, he likens the earth to a bowling alley and the sun to a bowling ball.

Taylor was undoubtedly influenced by the previous generation of English poets, which included John Donne and George Herbert. These poets were later called the metaphysical poets because of their extensive use of conceits. Taylor, however, differs from these earlier writers not only in his inability to match their metrical skills but also in his use of colloquial, often crude diction and of imagery derived from everyday surroundings. It is evident that Taylor believed that one's entire spiritual life could be understood through intense contemplation of the commonplace. To this end, he did not hesitate to use such homely objects as dishcloths, milk pails, and mutton roasts as images.

In "Huswifery" the conceit that forms the framework for the whole poem is the unlikely comparison of the common task of making cloth and the poet's prayer for salvation. In the first stanza, the speaker (presumably the poet) prays to be made into God's spinning wheel. The distaff, an upright spindle with a cleft end on which the unspun flax or wool is first placed, is to be Scripture ("Thy Holy Word"). Logically, one could not enjoy God's grace without knowing Scripture. Next, the poet's feelings ("Affections") are to become the flyers that adjust the spinning speed. The poet's soul is to be the spool that twists the flax or wool into thread, and his thoughts, words, and conduct ("Conversations") are to be God's reel.

In the second stanza, the poet prays that he may next become a loom on which the Lord weaves the new thread into cloth (the Web)—cloth that is cleansed through the sacraments (Ordinances) of baptism and communion (the Fulling Mills). God is then asked to dye the cloth in suitable colors and to decorate it appropriately, so as to reveal His glory.

Finally the poet petitions the Lord to clothe his spiritual, mental, and emotional being in heavenly garments made of the cloth. Then the poet, splendidly arrayed "in Holy robes" (the state of grace), can eternally glorify God.

1. What does the word "huswifery" mean? Why is this title appropriate?

2. What is the rhyme scheme of the poem?

Cotton Mather   1663–1728

Cotton Mather was fluent in Latin, Greek, and Hebrew by age eleven. At twelve he became the youngest student to enter Harvard College, where he earned two degrees. At nineteen he accepted an appointment as assistant to his famous father, Increase Mather, in the Second Congregational Church of Boston.

Young Mather came to his ministry with expectations for continuing the family influence in both church and public affairs. He was not only well-read in theology, but also broadly educated in science, medicine, history, languages, literature, and biography. Almost from the onset of his ministry, however, strict Puritan orthodoxy and church control of government crumbled rapidly. Mather, who futilely resisted the change, never realized his ambition for extensive public service and was forced to devote his energies to his ministry and to writing.

A tireless preacher and writer, he delivered well over 1000 sermons and published a staggering total of 444 bound books. Of the latter, his *Magnalia Christi Americana* (1702), a seven-volume history of early American

Puritanism, is judged his best work. Mather's *Bonifacius, or Essays to Do Good* (1710) captivated Benjamin Franklin, who wrote in his famous *Autobiography* that Mather's essays "perhaps gave me a turn of thinking that had an influence on some of the principal events in my life."

Mather's two books on witchcraft have been of considerable interest both to scholars and to the general public since the time they were written. The first book, *Memorable Providences, Relating to Witchcraft and Possessions* (1689), deals largely with a group of children supposedly "possessed" by witches. The second, *The Wonders of the Invisible World* (1693), is a report of testimony taken in one of the Salem witchcraft trials and was written in support of the judges who condemned the nineteen people to death.

The colonists' concern over witchcraft and its frenzied outcome at Salem were not, however, isolated phenomena. In Europe in the sixteenth and seventeenth centuries, thousands of men, women, children, and even animals were put to death because they were judged tainted by the devil.

from THE WONDERS OF THE INVISIBLE WORLD

The Trial of Martha Carrier at the Court of Oyer and Terminer,[1] *Held by Adjournment at Salem,*[2] *August 2, 1692*

I. Martha Carrier was indicted for the bewitching of certain persons, according to the form usual in such cases, pleading not guilty to her indictment. There were first brought in a considerable number of the bewitched persons, who not only made the court sensible of an horrid witchcraft committed upon them, but also deposed that it was Martha Carrier or her shape[3] that grievously tormented them by biting, pricking, pinching, and choking of them. It was further deposed that while this Carrier was on her examination before the magistrates, the poor people were so tortured that everyone expected their death upon the very spot, but that upon the binding[4] of Carrier they were eased. Moreover the look of Carrier then laid the afflicted people for dead, and her touch, if her eye at the same time were off them, raised them again, which things were also now seen upon her trial. And it was testified that upon the mention of some having their necks twisted almost round by the shape of this Carrier, she replied, "It's no matter though their necks had been twisted quite off."

II. Before the trial of this prisoner several of her own children had frankly and fully confessed not only that they were witches themselves, but that this, their mother, had made them so. This confession they made with great shows of repentance and with much demonstration of truth. They related place, time, occasion; they gave an account of journeys, meetings, and mischiefs by them performed, and were very credible in what they said. Nevertheless, this evidence was not produced against the prisoner at the bar, inasmuch as there was other evidence enough to proceed upon.

III. Benjamin Abbot gave in his testimony that last March was a twelve-month this Carrier was very angry with him upon laying out some land near her husband's. Her expressions in this anger were that she would stick as close to Abbot as the bark stuck to the tree, and that he should repent of it afore seven years came to an end so as Doctor Prescot should never cure him. These words were heard by others besides Abbot himself, who also heard her say she would hold his nose as close to the grindstone as ever it was held since his name was Abbot. Presently after this he was taken with a swelling in his foot, and then with a pain in his side, and exceedingly tormented. It bred unto a sore, which was lanced by Doctor Prescot, and several gallons of corruption ran out of it. For six weeks it continued very bad, and then another sore bred in his groin, which was also lanced by Doctor Prescot. Another sore then bred in his groin, which was likewise cut and put him to very great misery. He was brought unto death's door and so remained until Carrier was taken and carried away by the constable, from which very day he began to mend and

1. **Court of Oyer and Terminer** (ō′ yər, tĕr′mə nər), a higher court authorized to hear (oyer) and determine (terminer) criminal cases.
2. **Salem,** now Danvers, Massachusetts.
3. **shape,** here: a visible but disembodied shape; also, a specter.
4. **binding,** here: placing in jail.

so grew better every day and is well ever since.

Sarah Abbot also, his wife, testified that her husband was not only all this while afflicted in his body, but also that strange, extraordinary, and unaccountable calamities befell his cattle, their death being such as they could guess at no natural reason for.

IV. Allin Toothaker testified that Richard, the son of Martha Carrier, having some difference with him, pulled him down by the hair of the head. When he rose again, he was going to strike at Richard Carrier, but fell down flat on his back to the ground and had not power to stir hand or foot until he told Carrier he yielded, and then he saw the shape of Martha Carrier go off his breast.

This Toothaker had received a wound in the wars, and he now testified that Martha Carrier told him he should never be cured. Just afore the apprehending of Carrier, he could thrust a knitting needle into his wound, four inches deep; but presently after her being seized he was thoroughly healed.

He further testified that when Carrier and he sometimes were at variance she would clap her hands at him and say he should get nothing by it; whereupon he several times lost his cattle by strange deaths, whereof no natural causes could be given.

V. John Rogger also testified that upon the threatening words of this malicious Carrier his cattle would be strangely bewitched, as was more particularly then described.

VI. Samuel Preston testified that about two years ago, having some difference with Martha Carrier, he lost a cow in a strange, preternatural, unusual manner. And about a month after this, the said Carrier having again some difference with him, she told him he had lately lost a cow and it should not be long before he lost another, which accordingly came to pass; for he had a thriving and well-kept cow which without any known cause quickly fell down and died.

VII. Phebe Chandler testified that about a fortnight before the apprehension of Martha Carrier, on a Lord's day while the psalm was singing in the church, this Carrier then took her by the shoulder and shaking her asked her where she lived. She made her no answer, although as Carrier, who lived next door to her father's house, could not in reason but know who she was. Quickly after this, as she was at several times crossing the fields, she heard a voice that she took to be Martha Carrier's; and it seemed as if it was over her head. The voice told her she should within two or three days be poisoned. Accordingly, within such a little time, one half of her right hand became greatly swollen and very painful, as also part of her face, whereof she can give no account how it came. It continued very bad for some days, and several times since she has had a great pain in her breast and been so seized on her legs that she has hardly been able to go. She added that lately, going well to the house of God, Richard, the son of Martha Carrier, looked very earnestly upon her. And immediately her hand, which had formerly been poisoned, as is above said, began to pain her greatly; and she had a strange burning at her stomach, but was then struck deaf so that she could not hear any of the prayer or singing till the two or three last words of the psalm.

VIII. One Foster, who confessed her own share in the witchcraft for which the prisoner stood indicted, affirmed that she had seen the prisoner at some of their witch meetings, and that it was this Carrier who persuaded her to be a witch. She confessed that the devil carried them on a pole to a witch meeting, but the pole broke and she, hanging about Carrier's neck, they both fell down, and she then received an hurt by the fall, whereof she was not at this very time recovered.

IX. One Lacy, who likewise confessed her share in this witchcraft, now testified that she and the prisoner were once bodily present at a witch meeting in Salem village, and that she knew the prisoner to be a witch and to have been at a diabolical sacrament, and that the prisoner was the undoing of her and her chil-

In 1692, fear and ignorance combined to ignite a kind of mass hysteria in the village of Salem, Massachusetts, and nineteen people were executed for witchcraft. In this artist's rendering, one victim is arrested at her home.

dren by enticing them into the snare of the devil.

X. Another Lacy, who also confessed her share in this witchcraft, now testified that the prisoner was at the witch meeting in Salem village, where they had bread and wine administered unto them.

XI. In the time of this prisoner's trial, one Susanna Sheldon in open court had her hands unaccountably tied together with a wheel band[5] so fast that without cutting it could not be loosed. It was done by a specter, and the sufferer affirmed it was the prisoner's.

Memorandum: This rampant hag, Martha Carrier,[6] was the person of whom the confes-

sions of the witches and of her own children among the rest agreed that the devil had promised her she should be queen of hell.

5. **wheel band,** a wire or metal strip used to tie a wooden wheel firmly together.
6. **Martha Carrier.** She was hanged August 19, 1692.

FOR UNDERSTANDING

1. When her accusers testified that Martha Carrier's shape had twisted their necks almost around, what does Mather report that she said?
2. Before the trial began, what confession did Martha Carrier's children reportedly make about

their mother? According to Mather, why were the children's confessions not used during the trial?

3. Benjamin Abbot charged that Martha Carrier caused him to become so ill that he "was brought unto death's door." What event did he say caused him to regain his health?

4. According to Mather, what happened to Susanna Sheldon in the courtroom?

5. According to her children and others who testified against her, what reward was Martha Carrier supposedly promised by the devil?

FOR INTERPRETATION

1. Although Cotton Mather believed in the existence of witches, as did most of his contemporaries, he offered to use prayer, singing of psalms, patience, fasting, and maintenance of long vigils to save those accused of witchcraft rather than sending them to the gallows. He said that his offer, however, was refused by the judges and other officers of the court. Reread the final sentence of the account. Is Mather's tone forgiving? Explain.

2. Reread section VII. When Phebe Chandler testified, she said she believed Martha Carrier's voice came to her from overhead. What did this suggest about the ability of the accused to move about?

FOR APPRECIATION

Style

Were I master of the pen wherewith Palladius embalmed his Chrysostom, the Greek patriarch, or Posidonius eternized his Austin, the Latin oracle, among the ancients; or, were I owner of the quill wherewith, among the moderns, Beza celebrated his immortal Calvin, or Fabius immortalized his venerable Beza; the merits of John Cotton would oblige me to employ it, in the preserving his famous memory.

The sentence above from Cotton Mather's *Magnalia Christi Americana* is illustrative of the style of much of his writing. Often a bit vain about his intellectual accomplishments, Mather was fond of making excessive display of his learning in his prose. Thus he freighted his sentences heavily with allusions, quotations, and often involved figures of speech.

The quotation from *Magnalia Christi Americana* is the first sentence in his biographical sketch of his grandfather. His intent is plainly to eulogize John Cotton, and he sets the tone of the eulogy at once by alluding to several famous historical figures.

You will notice that Mather's style in the Martha Carrier piece, however, is very different. There is a good reason for this. In New England and the other colonies there was considerable criticism of the harsh verdicts in the Salem trials. Lieutenant Governor William Stoughton, who served as chief justice of the special court that had been created to try the witch cases, was understandably anxious to justify the verdicts of his court. As one means of doing so, he requested Cotton Mather to use court records to write a report of the trials, and to focus particularly on the large mass of evidence taken. Since he was using court records, Mather chose a plain, journalistic style rather than his usual ornate one.

Although Mather was supposedly reporting facts in his accounts of the trials, researchers have charged that he omitted testimony that might have proved embarrassing. That he was biased in his viewpoint is obvious. For example, look at the second sentence in the first paragraph of the report. Here he writes that a considerable number of "bewitched persons" were brought in. What does this indicate about his attitude toward these people? In the same sentence, note his use of the words *horrid* and *grievously*. What do these words reveal to the reader? List other words and phrases from the account that reveal Mather's subjective views on those accused of witchcraft.

Sarah Kemble Knight   1666–1727

A sharp-eyed businesswoman who competed successfully in the man's world of her era, Sarah Kemble Knight rode into American literature when she traveled from Boston to New York City on horseback in 1704. The journal she kept during her extended trip along the coastal route is the most accurate picture we have today of provincial New England.

She was born to upper-middle-class parents in Boston in April, 1666. Little is known of her education except that she became a skilled secretary and copied legal documents. In this pursuit, she learned enough law to engage in settling estates. The settlement of an estate for a relative was the business that occasioned her trip to New York City at the age of thirty-eight.

When she was left a widow with a young daughter to support, it is believed that for a time she ran a school in her home in Boston. Some historians contend that Benjamin Franklin and one of the young Mathers were among her pupils. Whether or not she had a school with such noteworthy pupils, town records verify that she did manage a shop in her home and boarded some six roomers from whom she collected rent.

Mrs. Knight was an able, cultured member of the rising merchant class in the colonies, a feminist ahead of her time, whose lively interest in her surroundings and in her fellow colonials makes her journal perennially appealing.

from THE JOURNAL OF MADAM KNIGHT

[Traveling in Connecticut]

Saturday, October 7th, we set out early in the morning, and about two o'clock afternoon we arrived at New Haven, where I was received with all possible civility. Here I discharged Mr. Wheeler[1] with a reward to his satisfaction, and took some time to rest after so long and toilsome a journey; and informed myself of the manners and customs of the place, and at the same time employed myself in the affair I went there upon.

They are governed by the same laws as we in Boston (or little differing), throughout this whole colony of Connecticut, and much the same way of Church government, and many of them good, sociable people, and I hope religious too: but a little too much independent in their principles, and, as I have

---

1. **discharged,** here: paid off (Mr. Wheeler, her guide).

Some of the first coins
made in the United States

try are on lecture days and training days[3] mostly: on the former there is riding from town to town.

And on training days the youth divert themselves by shooting at the target, as they call it (but it very much resembles a pillory[4]), where he that hits nearest the white has some yards of red ribbon presented him, which being tied to his hat-band, the two ends streaming down his back, he is led away in triumph, with great applause, as the winners of the Olympic games. They generally marry very young: the males oftener, as I am told, under twenty than above: they generally make public weddings, and have a way something singular (as they say) in some of them, viz.,[5] just before joining hands the bridegroom quits the place, who is soon followed by the bridesmen, and as it were dragged back to duty—being the reverse to the former practice among us, to steal mistress bride. . . .

They give the title of merchant to every trader; who rate their goods according to the time and specie[6] they pay in, viz., "Pay," "Money," "Pay as money," and "Trusting." "Pay" is grain, pork, beef, etc., at the prices set by the General Court that year; "Money" is pieces of eight, reals,[7] or Boston or bay shillings (as they call them), or "good hard money," as sometimes silver coin is termed by them; also "Wampum," viz., Indian beads, which serves for change. "Pay as money" is provisions, as aforesaid, one-third cheaper

been told, were formerly in their zeal very rigid in their administrations towards such as their laws made offenders, even to a harmless kiss[2] or innocent merriment among young people. Whipping being a frequent and counted an easy punishment, about which as other crimes, the Judges were absolute in their sentences. . . .

Their diversions in this part of the coun-

2. **kiss.** Colony laws forbade even the exchange of a kiss between husband and wife in public on the sabbath.
3. **lecture days** and **training days.** On lecture days citizens met to hear sermons; on training days, the young men had compulsory military instruction.
4. **pillory,** wooden frame fitted with openings to hold the head and hands of an offender.
5. **viz.,** namely.
6. **specie,** kind of currency, or articles used as money.
7. **pieces of eight, reals** (rē′ əlz). A piece of eight at that time was a Spanish dollar worth eight Spanish coins, or reals.

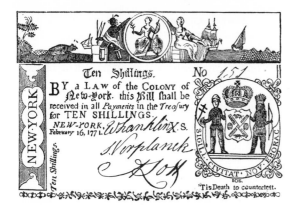

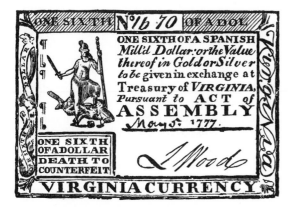

*Paper currency from the colony of
New York and the state of Virginia*

Being at a merchant's house, in comes a tall country fellow, with his alfogeos[9] full of tobacco; for they seldom loose their cud, but keep chewing and spitting as long as their eyes are open,—he advanced to the middle of the room, makes an awkward nod, and spitting a large deal of aromatic tincture,[10] he gave a scrape with his shovel-like shoe, leaving a small shovel full of dirt on the floor, made a full stop, hugging his own pretty body with his hands under his arms, stood staring round him, like a cat let out of a basket. At last, like the creature Balaam[11] rode on, he opened his mouth and said: "Have you any ribinen for hat-bands to sell, I pray?" The questions and answers about the pay being past, the ribbon is brought and opened. Bumpkin Simpers cries, "It's confounded gay, I vow;" and beckoning to the door, in comes Joan Tawdry, dropping about fifty curtsies, and stands by him: he shows her the ribbon. "Law, you," says she, "it's right gent,[12] do you take it, 'tis dreadful pretty." Then she enquires, "Have you any hood silk, I pray?" which being brought and bought, "Have you any thread silk to sew with?" says she; which being accommodated with they departed. They generally stand after they come in a great while speechless, and sometimes don't say a word till they are asked what they want, which I impute to the awe they stand in of the merchants, who they are constantly almost indebted to; and must take what they bring

than as the Assembly or General Court sets it; and "Trust" as they and the merchant agree for time.

Now, when the buyer comes to ask for a commodity, sometimes before the merchant answers that he has it, he says, "Is your pay ready?" Perhaps the chap replies, "Yes." "What do you pay in?" says the merchant. The buyer having answered, then the price is set; as suppose he wants a sixpenny knife, in pay it is twelve pence—in pay as money, eight pence, and hard money, its own price, viz., six pence. It seems a very intricate way of trade and what *lex mercatoria*[8] had not thought of.

8. **lex mercatoria** (lex mėr kə tô′ rē ə), Latin for mercantile or commercial law.
9. **alfogeos** (al fô′ jē ōs), leather or canvas saddlebags; from the Spanish. The term survives today in the western United States as alforja (al fôr′ hə), meaning a wallet or saddlebag. Here Mrs. Knight means the man's cheeks were full of tobacco.
10. **aromatic tincture,** strong-smelling mixture.
11. **Balaam** (bā′ləm), Old Testament prophet who rode on a donkey.
12. **gent,** obsolete adjective meaning elegant or fashionable.

without liberty to choose for themselves; but they serve them as well, making the merchants stay long enough for their pay.

We may observe here the great necessity and benefit both of education and conversation; for these people have as large a portion of mother wit, and sometimes a larger, than those who have been brought up in cities; but, for want of improvements, render themselves almost ridiculous, as above.

They are generally very plain in their dress, throughout all the colony, as I saw, and follow one another in their modes; that you may know where they belong, especially the women, meet them where you will.

Their chief red letter day is St. Election, which is annually observed according to charter, to choose their governor—a blessing they can never be thankful enough for, as they will find, if ever it be their hard fortune to lose it. The present governor in Connecticut is the Hon. John Winthrop, Esq., a gentleman of an ancient and honorable family, whose father was governor here sometime before, and his grandfather had been governor of the Massachusetts. This gentleman is a very courteous and affable person, much given to hospitality, and has by his good services gained the affections of the people as much as any who had been before him in that post.

FOR UNDERSTANDING

An Intriguing Journal-Keeper

1. What two kinds of diversion, or entertainment, brought the Connecticut country people together?
2. How does Mrs. Knight describe their system of trade?
3. What conclusion does she draw from her story about the young couple buying ribbon and silk?
4. According to Mrs. Knight, what was the biggest event of the year in Connecticut?

FOR INTERPRETATION

1. What do the words *harmless* and *innocent* in the second paragraph reveal about Mrs. Knight's attitude toward Connecticut's early church government?
2. What do the names the author gives the couple buying ribbon and silk suggest about her opinion of the young people in rural Connecticut?

FOR APPRECIATION

The Journal as Literature

Generally speaking, the journal was the form in which much of early American literature cast itself. Keeping a diary or a journal was the most practical way to record the day-to-day developments of life in a new frontier environment. Founding fathers set down the "simple truth" for posterity; Puritans recorded their spiritual journeys and their search for grace or vision; travelers recorded actual journeys; housewives fought off the loneliness of life in isolated areas through writing. Thus the journal proved a very flexible form and a natural literary vehicle.

This journal tradition began with William Bradford and John Winthrop; it was continued into the late seventeenth and early eighteenth centuries by such writers as Samuel Sewall, Sarah Kemble Knight, William Byrd, and the Quaker mystic John Woolman. A high point in the American tradition of journal keeping was reached in the writings of Ralph Waldo Emerson and Henry David Thoreau during the nineteenth century.

"Diary" and "journal" are more or less synonymous—both are a record of daily events, experiences, and observations—but diary usually indicates a more intimate and personal account than does journal. Thus, with the exception of some eight years, Samuel Sewall's *Diary* covers his life from 1674 to 1729 and includes not only public and family affairs but illnesses, dreams, strange coincidences, and reminiscences as well. Bradford's *Of Plymouth Plantation* can be considered a chronicle (a chronological record of historical events) in the form of a journal. Bradford's aim was to set down "in a plaine style . . . the simple truth" of the Pilgrims' history from the time of their persecution in England through their first twenty-six years as colonists in America. The actual writing he did between 1630 and 1651 from notes he kept over the years.

The Journal of Madam Knight, of course, is an example of a travel journal, another common literary form in colonial times. Mrs. Knight was meticulous in setting down her observations at the end of each day, no matter what her accommodations. Interspersed with her lively prose are lines of verse. For example, two evenings before she wrote the entry included in the text, she recorded that she could get no sleep because of "topers," or drinkers, arguing in the adjoining room. Finally she wrote:

> **I set my candle on a chest by the bedside, and sitting up, fell to my old way of composing my resentments, in the following manner:**
> > **I ask thy aid, O potent rum**
> > **To charm these wrangling topers dumb.**
> > **Thou hast their giddy brains possessed**
> > **The man confounded with the beast—**
> > **And I, poor I, can get no rest.**
> > **Intoxicate them with thy fumes:**
> > **O still their tongues till morning comes!**

How much she edited her original notes or entries is not known. Her "wonderful little journal," as it is termed by numerous scholars, was not published until 1825. Many critics agree that in its sharp portrayal of the New England backwoods folk and the intimate glance it affords into the thoughts of a cultured city-dweller of the colonial period, it exemplifies journal keeping at its most interesting and informative.

LANGUAGE AND VOCABULARY

Mrs. Knight was known as a *scrivener* and *amanuensis.* Check these words in the dictionary for meaning and origin.

COMPOSITION

Write a journal entry from your own point of view describing a contemporary event you think might be of historical interest. For example, you might write about new or unusual uses of computers or about the popularity of video games. You might describe the introduction of a new product or the implications of recent developments in astronomy, medicine, or the arts. Current magazines can provide you with ideas for a subject. Keep your journal entry brief, and be sure that your observation is a personal one. For instance, how does the event affect *your* life?

William Byrd

1674–1744

Born in Virginia to a family that achieved status through business, William Byrd was sent to England to be educated when he was only seven. By the time he returned to live in the colonies in his late twenties, he had acquired a classical education, a law degree, and a prestigious membership in The Royal Society (a group of leading scientists). He had also acquired a sophistication and urbanity that are reflected in his writings.

Byrd lived an exceedingly productive life. Over his seventy-year life span he increased the 26,000 acres of land inherited from his father to some 200,000. His renovations of Westover, the family plantation home, resulted in a library and collections of fine furniture and paintings that were unmatched by most other plantations in the South. While managing this large enterprise, he continued his studies of Latin, Greek, and Hebrew, wrote prolifically, engaged in scientific observation of plants and animals, and gave extensive political service to the Virginia colony. Yet his many accomplishments may simply reflect his dedication to a vigorous routine of morning exercises, for without fail, he "danced his dance" upon arising.

As Bradford is considered a representative of the early New England Puritans, so Byrd represents the aristocrats of the plantation South. Although he wrote poems, essays, scientific treatises, and travel books, his fame rests on a diary account, *The History of the Dividing Line betwixt Virginia and North Carolina,* considered a classic of early American literature.

Byrd was appointed head of a commission to help settle a long-standing dispute about the border between the colonies of Virginia and North Carolina. He worked with North Carolina commissioners and a surveying crew to map an acceptable division between the two colonies. The survey line began at the north end of the Currituck River or Inlet and continued through the Great Dismal Swamp beyond.

From rough notes kept daily during the survey, Byrd later transcribed two manuscripts.

PORTRAIT OF WILLIAM BYRD, Artist Unknown
Virginia Historical Society, Richmond, VA

One, entitled *The Secret History of the Dividing Line,* set down in a secret shorthand, or code, is filled with less than complimentary references and humorous names for fellow commissioners as well as satirical descriptions of other people and events. Byrd transcribed it for his own amusement and circulated it among a select audience. The other, more proper version, from which the selection in the text is taken, still displays his zesty humor, his crisp and very entertaining style, and his keen observation of nature.

from THE HISTORY OF THE DIVIDING LINE

Venturing Through Great Dismal Swamp

March 13

'Tis hardly credible how little the bordering inhabitants were acquainted with this mighty swamp, notwithstanding they had lived their whole lives within smell of it. Yet, as great strangers as they were to it, they pretended to be very exact in their account of its dimensions and were positive it could not be above seven or eight miles wide, but knew no more of the matter than stargazers know of the distance of the fixed stars. At the same time, they were simple enough to amuse our men with idle stories of the lions, panthers, and alligators they were likely to encounter in that dreadful place. In short, we saw plainly there was no intelligence of this *Terra Incognita*[1] to be got but from our own experience. For that reason it was resolved to make the requisite dispositions to enter it next morning. We allotted every one of the surveyors for this painful enterprise, with twelve men to attend them. Fewer than that could not be employed in clearing the way, carrying the chain, marking the trees, and bearing the necessary bedding and provisions. Nor would the commissioners themselves have spared their persons on this occasion but for fear of adding to the poor men's burden, while they were certain they could add nothing to their resolution.

We quartered with our friend and fellow traveler, William Wilkins, who had been our faithful pilot to Currituck[2] and lived about a mile from the place where the line ended. Everything looked so very clean and the furniture so neat that we were tempted to lodge withindoors. But the novelty of being shut up so close quite spoiled our rest, nor did we breathe so free by abundance as when we lay in the open air.

March 14

Before nine of the clock this morning the provisions, bedding, and other necessaries were made up into packs for the men to carry on their shoulders into the Dismal. They were victualed[3] for eight days at full allowance, nobody doubting but that would be abundantly sufficient to carry them through that inhospitable place; nor indeed was it possible for the poor fellows to stagger under more. As it was, their loads weighed from sixty to seventy pounds, in just proportion to the strength of those who were to bear them. 'Twould have been unconscionable to have saddled them with burdens heavier than that, when they were to lug them through a filthy bog which was hardly practicable with no burden at all. Besides this luggage at their backs, they were obliged to measure the distance, mark the trees, and clear the way for the surveyors every step they went. It was really a pleasure to see with how much cheerfulness they undertook and with how much spirit

Reprinted by permission of the publishers from THE PROSE WORKS OF WILLIAM BYRD OF WESTOVER edited by Louis B. Wright, Cambridge, Mass.: The Belknap Press of Harvard University Press, Copyright © 1966 by the President and Fellows of Harvard College.

1. **Terra Incognita** (ter′ ə in′ kog′ nə tə), Latin for unknown land.
2. **Currituck,** Currituck Inlet on the coast of North Carolina where the survey line began.
3. **victualed,** (vit′ ld), provided with food.

they went through all this drudgery. For their greater safety, the commissioners took care to furnish them with Peruvian bark,[4] rhubarb, and ipecacuanha,[5] in case they might happen, in that wet journey, to be taken with fevers or fluxes.[6]

Although there was no need of example to inflame persons already so cheerful, yet to enter the people with the better grace, the author and two more of the commissioners accompanied them half a mile into the Dismal. The skirts of it were thinly planted with dwarf reeds and gallbushes,[7] but when we got into the Dismal itself we found the reeds grew there much taller and closer and, to mend the matter, were so interlaced with bamboo briers that there was no scuffling through them without the help of pioneers.[8] At the same time we found the ground moist and trembling under our feet like a quagmire, insomuch that it was an easy matter to run a ten-foot pole up to the head in it without exerting any uncommon strength to do it. Two of the men whose burdens were the least cumbersome had orders to march before with their tomahawks and clear the way in order to make an opening for the surveyors. By their assistance we made a shift to push the line half a mile in three hours and then reached a small piece of firm land about a hundred yards wide, standing up above the rest like an island. Here the people were glad to lay down their loads and take a little refreshment, while the happy man whose lot it was to carry the jug of rum began already, like Aesop's bread carriers,[9] to find it grow a good deal lighter.

After reposing about an hour, the commissioners recommended vigor and constancy to their fellow travelers, by whom they were answered with three cheerful huzzas, in token of obedience. This ceremony was no sooner over but they took up their burdens and attended the motion of the surveyors, who, though they worked with all their might, could reach but one mile farther, the same obstacles still attending them which they had met with in the morning. However small this distance may seem to such as are used to travel at their ease, yet our poor men, who were obliged to work with an unwieldy load at their backs, had reason to think it a long way; especially in a bog where they had no firm footing but every step made a deep impression which was instantly filled with water. At the same time they were laboring with their hands to cut down the reeds, which were ten feet high, their legs were hampered with briers. Besides, the weather happened to be warm, and the tallness of the reeds kept off every friendly breeze from coming to refresh them. And indeed it was a little provoking to hear the wind whistling among the branches of the white cedars, which grew here and there amongst the reeds, and at the same time not to have the comfort to feel the least breath of it.

In the meantime the three commissioners returned out of the Dismal the same way they went in and, having joined their brethren, proceeded that night as far as Mr. Wilson's. This worthy person lives within sight of the Dismal, in the skirts whereof his stocks range and maintain themselves all the winter, and yet he knew as little of it as he did of *Terra Australis Incognita*.[10] He told us a Canterbury

4. **Peruvian bark,** the bark of cinchona trees from Peru, used in treatments for malaria and other fevers. The medicine quinine can be derived from cinchona bark.

5. **ipecacuanha** (ip′ ə kak′ yü an ə), medicine from a South American vine, used to induce vomiting.

6. **fluxes,** outpouring of body fluids as in dysentery.

7. **gallbushes,** bushes having "galls," an abnormal vegetable growth caused by certain insects or parasites.

8. **pioneers,** here: an advance party that cuts a path for the others.

9. **Aesop's bread carriers.** In Aesop's fable, the man who chose the heavy basket of bread was ridiculed. By nightfall, the bread had all been distributed, however, and this laborer had the lightest load to carry.

10. **Terra Australis** (ôs träl′ əs) **Incognita,** unknown southern lands.

An oil painting done on wood, this delightful scene is a perfect example of American folk art in its breezy directness and its almost total disregard for the laws of perspective.

THE PLANTATION, Artist Unknown
Metropolitan Museum of Art, New York City
Gift of Edgar W. and Bernice Chrysler Garbisch

tale[11] of a North Briton whose curiosity spurred him a long way into this great desert,[12] as he called it, near twenty years ago, but he, having no compass nor seeing the sun for several days together, wandered about till he was almost famished; but at last he bethought himself of a secret his countrymen make use of to pilot themselves in a dark day. He took a fat louse out of his collar and exposed it to the open day on a piece of white paper, which he brought along with him for his journal. The poor insect, having no eyelids, turned himself about till he found the darkest part of the heavens and so made the best of his way toward the North. By this direction he steered himself safe out and gave

11. **Canterbury tale,** here: a humorous comparison to the kind of ribald story that appeared in the fourteenth-century *Canterbury Tales* by Geoffrey Chaucer.
12. **desert,** here: the swamp, a place without human habitation.

such a frightful account of the monsters he saw and the distresses he underwent that no mortal since has been hardy enough to go upon the like dangerous discovery.

FOR UNDERSTANDING

Charting the Unknown

1. Byrd speaks of the cheerfulness with which the men undertook their journey through the Dismal. Why might they have felt discouraged as they began their trek?

2. What does Byrd's reference to Aesop's bread carriers show about his attitude toward life? about his sense of humor?

3. Byrd mentions Mr. Wilkins and Mr. Wilson. Who were they?

FOR INTERPRETATION

1. In an earlier diary entry, Byrd notes that an inhabitant of the environs of the Great Dismal had said of the planned venture into the swamp: "You are, to be sure, the first of the human race that ever had the boldness to attempt it, and I dare say will be the last." This individual went on to suggest that the members of the surveying party should check to see that their wills were in proper order. Byrd's entry of March 13 notes that the "bordering inhabitants" believed "lions, panthers, and alligators" lived in the swamp. What does Byrd's way of describing these people's ideas about the swamp tell you about Byrd himself?

2. Byrd implies that the surveying party might have acted differently if the people of the area had seemed knowledgeable about the swamp. What other course might he have followed?

FOR APPRECIATION

Use of Details

1. Byrd's keen observation as well as his scientific interest in nature is demonstrated by his use of details in what might otherwise be a dull account. How does he describe the vegetation and ground surface of the swamp? What kind of trees grew among the reeds? Why was the height of the reeds so irritating?

2. Whereas Puritan writers were intent on the resolution of spiritual questions, the Southern writers of the period tended to display more interest in their wilderness environment and the people around them. One thing that makes Byrd's writing so lively is his technique of taking the trouble to detail amusing anecdotes for the reader. Retell the outlandish "Canterbury" tale told Byrd by his wilderness host.

COMPOSITION

Telling an anecdote well is a skill to be developed. Write down a "tall tale" or amusing story, either original with you or one you have read or heard. What is the point of your anecdote? Be sure the point is clear. Include details to heighten listener interest and amusement. When you are sure you have the account well in mind, tell it to the class. Keep your paper at hand to refer to if necessary.

Jonathan Edwards   1703–1758

Jonathan Edwards was the last of the great voices of New England Puritanism.

Like Cotton Mather, Edwards as a boy was proficient in Latin, Greek, and Hebrew, and at eleven he wrote a perceptive essay on flying spiders. During his childhood, he began to immerse himself in religious studies and to give considerable attention to the matter of his salvation and state of grace. As a teenager at Yale, he demonstrated unusual talent in mathematics, astronomy, logic, and philosophy and began an avid study of the principles of Newton's physics and of the psychology of John Locke.

Through his considerable persuasive powers as a preacher and writer, Edwards tried to revive Puritan idealism in New England, and his sermons and tracts on sin and salvation were so enthusiastically received that they helped launch a new wave of religious fervor throughout the colonies. Called the Great Awakening, this religious revival marked the beginning of evangelism in America.

Edwards met with resistance in his own congregation, however, and was dismissed in 1750. Settling in the wilderness village of Stockbridge as minister to the Indians, he wrote two of his most highly regarded treatises: "The Freedom of the Will" (1754) and "The Great Christian Doctrine of Original Sin Defended" (1758). Edwards was a champion of the new medical treatment of inoculation against smallpox; ironically, he died soon after being inoculated.

In his "Personal Narrative" (1740–1742), Edwards carefully recorded the stages through which he passed in reaching his belief about the way God converts his chosen saints. His most widely known sermon, "Sinners in the Hands of an Angry God" (1741), was delivered not simply

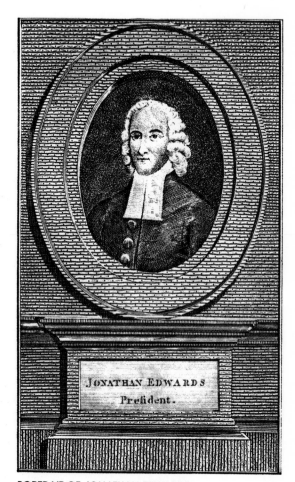

PORTRAIT OF JONATHAN EDWARDS
Amos Doolittle
National Portrait Gallery, Smithsonian Institution, Washington, DC

to terrify his listeners but to make them reexamine their beliefs about grace, salvation, and religion in their daily lives.

from PERSONAL NARRATIVE

I had a variety of concerns and exercises about my soul from my childhood; but had two more remarkable seasons of awakening, before I met with that change by which I was brought to those new dispositions, and that new sense of things, that I have since had. The first time was when I was a boy, some years before I went to college, at a time of remarkable awakening in my father's congregation. I was then very much affected for many months, and concerned about the things of religion, and my soul's salvation; and was abundant in duties. I used to pray five times a day in secret, and to spend much time in religious talk with other boys, and used to meet with them to pray together. I experienced I know not what kind of delight in religion. My mind was much engaged in it, and had much self-righteous pleasure; and it was my delight to abound in religious duties. I, with some of my schoolmates, joined together and built a booth in a swamp, in a very retired spot, for a place of prayer. And besides, I had particular secret places of my own in the woods, where I used to retire by myself, and was from time to time much affected. My affections seemed to be lively and easily moved, and I seemed to be in my element when engaged in religious duties. And I am ready to think many are deceived with such affections and such a kind of delight as I then had in religion, and mistake it for grace.

from SINNERS IN THE HANDS OF AN ANGRY GOD

The wrath of God is like great waters that are dammed for the present; they increase more and more, and rise higher and higher, till an outlet is given; and the longer the stream is stopped, the more rapid and mighty is its course, when once it is let loose. It is true, that judgment against your evil works has not been executed hitherto; the floods of God's vengeance have been withheld; but your guilt in the mean time is constantly increasing, and you are every day treasuring up more wrath; the waters are constantly rising, and waxing more and more mighty; and there is nothing but the mere pleasure of God, that holds the waters back, that are unwilling to be stopped, and press hard to go forward. If God should only withdraw his hand from the floodgate, it would immediately fly open, and the fiery floods of the fierceness and wrath of God, would rush forth with inconceivable fury, and would come upon you with omnipotent power; and if your strength were ten thousand times greater than it is, yea, ten thousand times greater than the strength of the stoutest, sturdiest devil in hell, it would be nothing to withstand or endure it.

The bow of God's wrath is bent, and the arrow made ready on the string, and justice bends the arrow at your heart, and strains the bow, and it is nothing but the mere pleasure of God, and that of an angry God, without any promise or obligation at all, that keeps the arrow one moment from being made drunk with your blood.

Thus all you that never passed under a great change of heart, by the mighty power of the Spirit of God upon your souls; all you that were never born again, and made new creatures, and raised from being dead in sin, to a state of new, and before altogether unexperienced light and life, are in the hands of an angry God. However you may have reformed your life in many things, and may have had religious affections, and may keep up a form of religion in your families and closets, and in the house of God, it is nothing but his mere pleasure that keeps you from being this moment swallowed up in everlasting destruction.

However unconvinced you may now be of the truth of what you hear, by and by you will be fully convinced of it. Those that are gone from being in the like circumstances with you, see that it was so with them; for destruction came suddenly upon most of them; when they expected nothing of it, and while they were saying, *peace and safety:* now they see, that those things on which they depended for peace and safety, were nothing but thin air and empty shadows.

The God that holds you over the pit of hell, much as one holds a spider, or some loathsome insect over the fire, abhors you, and is dreadfully provoked: his wrath towards you burns like fire; he looks upon you as worthy of nothing else, but to be cast into the fire; he is of purer eyes than to bear to have you in his sight; you are ten thousand times more abominable in his eyes, than the most hateful, venomous serpent is in ours. You have offended him infinitely more than ever a stubborn rebel did his prince; and yet it is nothing but his hand that holds you from falling into the fire every moment. It is to be ascribed to nothing else, that you did not go to hell the last night; that you were suffered to awake again in this world, after you closed your eyes to sleep. And there is no other reason to be given, why you have not dropped into hell since you arose in the morning, but that God's hand has held you up. There is no other reason to be given why you have not gone to hell, since you have sat here in the house of God, provoking his pure eyes by your sinful wicked manner of attending his solemn worship. Yea, there is nothing else that is to be given as a reason why you do not this very moment drop down into hell.

O sinner! Consider the fearful danger you are in: it is a great furnace of wrath, a wide and bottomless pit, full of the fire of wrath, that you are held over in the hand of that God, whose wrath is provoked and incensed as much against you, as against many of the damned in hell. You hang by a slender thread, with the flames of divine wrath flashing about it, and ready every moment to singe it, and burn it asunder; and you have no interest in any mediator, and nothing to lay hold of to save yourself, nothing to keep off the flames of wrath, nothing of your own, nothing that you ever have done, nothing that you can do, to induce God to spare you one moment.

FOR UNDERSTANDING

1. The paragraph from "Personal Narrative" sets forth the major concern Edwards experienced as a boy. What was this concern?

2. What did Edwards and his acquaintances build in the swamp?

3. To whom is "Sinners in the Hands of an Angry God" addressed?

4. Why, according to Edwards, is God wrathful?

5. Reread the third paragraph. According to Edwards, what people are *not* in the hands of an angry God? How is this condition achieved? What do you think Edwards would call this condition?

FOR INTERPRETATION

1. In the selection from his "Personal Narrative," note Edwards's use of the word *seemed* in the next to the last sentence. What is he suggesting in using this word?

2. What do you think is Edwards's main point in the "Personal Narrative" selection? Does the last sentence of the selection come as a surprise? What kind of sin is Edwards warning his readers against?

FOR APPRECIATION

Edwards uses metaphor effectively in the selection from "Sinners in the Hands of an Angry God." What are his primary metaphors for God's wrath? How does he elaborate on these metaphors? To what does he compare the sinners?

LANGUAGE AND VOCABULARY

The following phrases are taken from "Sinners in the Hands of an Angry God." Define each italicized word. What is the overall effect of Edwards's language?

1. would rush forth with inconceivable fury, and would come upon you with *omnipotent* power

2. as one holds a spider or some loathsome insect over the fire, he abhors you, and is dreadfully *provoked*

3. you are ten thousand times more *abominable* in his eyes than the most hateful, *venomous* serpent

4. whose wrath is provoked and *incensed*

5. to *singe* it, and burn it *asunder*

COMPOSITION

A sermon is a persuasive essay. Ideally the speaker or writer expands upon a theme and attempts to move listeners or readers—by appealing to reason, emotion, or authority—to a specific action or way of thinking. In developing a sermon, an author usually employs the other components of discourse: argumentation, description, exposition, and narration.

Edwards demonstrates skillful use of these rhetorical devices in his sermon. He appeals principally to authority and emotion and uses extended metaphor in conjunction with the four components of discourse listed above.

Think of a subject about which you hold strong convictions. Write a short essay in which you try to persuade others to think as you do about your subject or to take a specific course of action. Use at least one metaphor or whatever description, exposition, or narration techniques that fit easily into the development of your position. Before you begin this assignment, you may wish to review the definitions of these rhetorical devices in the Handbook of Literary Terms at the end of this anthology.

As you write, think about your words being spoken as in a sermon or speech. This should help you establish an effective rhythm in your essay.

EARLY AMERICAN INDIAN VOICES

American Indians had amassed a great body of oral literature hundreds of years before the arrival of the Europeans in the New World. Although the American Indian people had no written languages, they nevertheless kept alive a rich literary heritage by word of mouth, using pictographs, knotted strings, and coded wampum belts as memory aids.

Columbus, believing that he had reached India, designated all native peoples *los Indios,* the Indians. The name stuck. The hundreds of tribal groups now inhabiting North and South America, however, differ markedly both in language and culture. Some of their languages, in fact, are as different from one another as English is from Arabic. Thus, members of each tribal language group still think of themselves not as Indians but, for example, as Iroquois, Cherokee, or Apache.

In the early American Indian world, the accumulation of literary treasures was a tribal affair. Authorship of a song or story was attributed to the Great Mystery. It was the Great Mystery that gave the words to the singer, storyteller, or lawgiver. Thus through words the individual communicated with the Great Mystery. Words possessed magic and power—as did silence. Words had the power to lure game to the hunter, to cause plants to grow, to heal the sick, and to bring spiritual power to the individual. These first Americans also believed that the animate and the inanimate could converse. They believed that people could assume the shapes of animals or trees or rocks, and vice versa.

For American Indians, life was not the carefree, idyllic existence that many non-Indians have envisioned. The strong sense of tribal unity, the taboos, traditions, and rituals, the uncertainties of food supply, and the constant threat of war bound the individual to a rather restrictive pattern of living. In their daily lives and in their environment the American Indians saw and abided by divine intention— according to which, human beings were not to be masters of the world but recipients of a natural bounty that was to be protected and preserved.

Creation accounts loom large in the literature of all peoples. According to this Navaho account, the first people—that is, the insects and the birds—traveled through three underground worlds to the Fourth World. One day four gods appeared and told the people to cleanse themselves well, for in twelve days the gods would return to create new beings.

IT WAS THE WIND THAT GAVE THEM LIFE

NAVAHO

On the morning of the twelfth day the people washed themselves well. The women dried themselves with yellow cornmeal; the men with white cornmeal.[1] Soon after the ablutions were completed they heard the distant call of the approaching gods.[2] It was shouted, as before, four[3] times,—nearer and louder at each repetition,—and, after the fourth call, the gods appeared. Blue Body and Black Body each carried a sacred buckskin. White Body carried two ears of corn, one yellow, one white, each covered at the end completely with grains.[4]

The gods laid one buckskin on the ground with the head to the west; on this they placed the two ears of corn, with their tips to the east, and over the corn they spread the other buckskin with its head to the east; under the white ear they put the feather of a white eagle, under the yellow ear the feather of a yellow eagle. Then they told the people to stand at a distance and allow the wind to enter. The white wind blew from the east, and the yellow wind blew from the west, between the skins. While the wind was blowing, eight of the Mirage People[5] came and walked around the objects on the ground four times, and as they walked, the eagle feathers, whose tips protruded from between the buckskins, were seen to move. When the Mirage People had finished their walk the upper buckskin was lifted,—the ears of corn had disappeared; a man and a woman lay there in their stead.

The white ear of corn had been changed into a man, the yellow ear into a woman. It was the wind that gave them life. It is the wind that comes out of our mouths now that gives us life. When this ceases to blow we die. In the skin at the tips of our fingers we see the trail of the wind; it shows us where the wind blew when our ancestors were created.

The pair thus created were First Man and First Woman (Atsé Hastín and Atsé Estsan): The gods directed the people to build an inclosure of brushwood for the pair. When the inclosure was finished, First Man and First Woman entered it, and the gods said to them: "Live together now as husband and wife."

1. **cornmeal.** In Navaho ceremonies, yellow corn or cornmeal pertains to the female, white corn or cornmeal to the male.
2. **the approaching gods.** The four gods were White Body, Blue Body, Yellow Body, and Black Body.
3. **four,** a number sacred to the Navaho. The gods always announced their coming by calling four times.
4. **grains.** For sacred purposes an ear of corn must be completely covered with full grains.
5. **Mirage People.** Like other elements of nature, mirages were personified.

UNDERSTANDING AND INTERPRETATION

1. In what way were the eagle feathers matched with the ears of corn?
2. From what two directions did the winds blow?
3. Why is the color of the corn in this ceremony significant?
4. Why is the number of times that the Mirage People walked around the buckskins significant?
5. According to the Navaho, what on the human hand indicates that the wind gave us life?

Reproduced by permission of the American Folklore society from NAVAHO LEGENDS, pg. 69, 1897.

During the fourteenth century the Iroquoian-speaking peoples were constantly at war with their neighbors and among themselves. To end this bloody strife, Dekanawida, the great Huron lawgiver, and Hiawatha, the mighty Mohawk orator, struggled many years before persuading the Five Nations of the Iroquois (the Cayuga, Mohawk, Oneida, Onondaga, and Seneca) to establish the Council of the Great Peace (c. 1390.) A sixth nation, the Tuscarora, joined the Council in 1712.

The Law of the Great Peace is the world's oldest continuously observed constitution, and the central council fire that was kindled in the beginning has never been allowed to die. In the portion of the Constitution that follows, Dekanawida announces the formation of the confederacy and instructs the chosen lords in their obligations.

THE COUNCIL OF THE GREAT PEACE

IROQUOIS

I am Dekanawida, and with the Five Nations' confederate lords I plant the Tree of the Great Peace. . . . I name the Tree the Tree of the Great Long Leaves.[1] Under the shade of this Tree of the Great Peace we spread the soft, white, feathery down of the globe thistle[2] as seats for you, Adodarhoh,[3] and your cousin lords. . . . There shall you sit and watch the council fire of the Confederacy of the Five Nations.

Roots have spread out[4] from the Tree of the Great Peace . . . and the name of these roots is the Great White Roots of Peace. If any men of any nation outside of the Five Nations shall show a desire to obey the laws of the Great Peace . . . they may trace the roots to their source . . . and they shall be welcomed to take shelter beneath the Tree of the Long Leaves. The smoke of the confederate council fire shall pierce the sky so that all nations may discover the central council fire of the Great Peace.

I, Dekanawida, and the confederate lords now uproot the tallest pine tree and into the cavity thereby made we cast all weapons of war. Into the depths of the earth, down into the deep underearth currents of water flowing into unknown regions, we cast all weapons of strife. We bury them from sight forever and plant again the tree. . . .

Whenever the confederate lords shall assemble for the purpose of holding council, the Onondaga lords shall open it by expressing their gratitude to their cousin lords and greeting them, and they shall make an address and offer thanks to the earth where men dwell, to the streams of water, the pools, the springs and the lakes, to the maize and the fruits, to the medicinal herbs and trees, to the forest trees for their usefulness, to the animals that serve as food and give their pelts

From William N. Fenton, editor, PARKER ON THE IROQUOIS, Book III, Pages 30-31, 49, 38-39, Syracuse, N.Y.: © 1968, Syracuse University Press. By permission of Syracuse University Press.

1. **Tree . . . Leaves,** a great white pine.
2. **down . . . thistle.** The down stands for the Laws of the Great Peace.
3. **Adodarhoh.** He was the first to serve as chief lord of the Council, a position that still carries his name.
4. **spread out.** Symbolically, the roots spread in four directions—north, east, south, and west.

for clothing, to the great winds and the lesser winds, to the Thunderers, to the Sun, the mighty warrior, to the moon, to the messengers of the Great Creator who dwells in the skies above, who gives all things useful to men, and who is the source and ruler of health and life.

We now crown you with the sacred emblem of the deer's antlers, the emblem of your lordship. You shall now become a mentor of the people of the Five Nations. The thickness of your skin shall be seven spans—which is to say that you shall be proof against anger, offensive actions, and criticism. . . . With endless patience you shall carry out your duty and your firmness shall be tempered with tenderness for your people. Neither anger nor fear shall find lodgement in your mind and all your words and actions shall be marked with calm deliberation. In all your official acts, self-interest shall be cast into oblivion. Look and listen for the welfare of the whole people and have always in view not only the present but also the coming generations, even those whose faces are yet beneath the surface of the ground—the unborn of the future Nation.

FOR UNDERSTANDING

1. If people outside the council wish to join, what must they be willing to do?
2. What is used to crown the council lords?
3. Whose welfare must the council lords consider above all else?

FOR INTERPRETATION

1. Why do the lords offer thanks in opening each meeting?
2. Why do the lords need skins "seven spans" thick?

FOR APPRECIATION

Metaphor
1. Dekanawida compares his real act of organizing the council and setting forth the Laws of the Great Peace to an imaginary act of planting a huge pine tree. Through what imaginary act are all weapons of war to be destroyed?
2. Why is the metaphor of the tree appropriate to convey Dekanawida's message?

Early American Indian Songs

Generally speaking, the translations of early American Indian poems that appear in many literature anthologies were originally songs in which the words were inseparable from music and dance. There were vision and dream songs, love songs, tribal prayers, and lyrical expressions of joy and sorrow. Song, to these early peoples, was a powerful medium for communicating with the Great Mystery.

Because American Indian languages are so different from English in grammar, vocabulary, and syntax, the literal word-for-word translation of a song into English is usually incomprehensible to the non-Indian. Translators must use word sequences that are familiar to those accustomed to the accents and cadence of English verse. The arrangement of words on the page is an attempt to approximate the original rhythms and sense.

The early American Indians did not use rhyme. They did, however, use rhythmic repetition that has been likened to "rhyming thoughts." As you read the following song-poems, note the emphasis on repetition and the pairings of words, colors, animals, and expressions.

Hohokam pottery, c. 900 A.D.

PAINTED BOWL, American Indian
Arizona State Museum, Tucson, AZ

Traditionally, young American Indian men in certain tribes sought a vision to gain spiritual power for the warpath or hunt. For this ceremony a young man underwent purification rites, then withdrew to a secluded spot to petition the Great Mystery. In a long vigil, without food or shelter, the young man strove to submerge his own identity in order to identify more closely with his environment. If he was fortunate enough to be granted a vision, a tree, an animal, cloud, thunder, or a bird might be sent by the Great Mystery to act as the vision-seeker's guardian. Shaped into words and song with the aid of the Mysterious Unseen, the vision might later be sung and danced by the man for his tribe or fellow warriors.

Spring Song

As my eyes
search
the prairie
I feel the summer
in the spring.

CHIPPEWA

Song of a Man Who Received a Vision

Friends, behold!
Sacred I have been made.
Friends, behold!
In a sacred manner
I have been influenced
At the gathering of the clouds.
Sacred I have been made,
Friends, behold!
Sacred I have been made.

TETON SIOUX

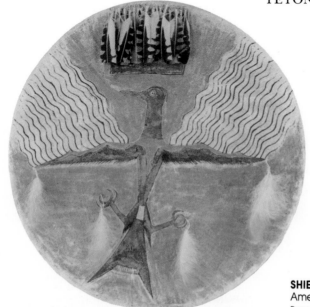

SHIELD
American Indian
Denver Art Museum, Denver, CO

Traditionally, these three songs were sung by young women. Jilted or jealous maidens would reportedly lie facedown on the prairie and sing the second song over and over. Occasionally a jealous young man might also sing this song.

I Have Found My Lover

Oh
I am thinking
Oh
I am thinking
I have found
my lover
Oh
I think it is so.

CHIPPEWA

Why Should I Be Jealous?

Why should
I, even I
Be jealous
Because of that bad boy?

CHIPPEWA

My Love Has Departed

A loon I thought it was
But it was
My love's
Splashing oar.

CHIPPEWA

HOUSE POST
Delaware Indians
Philbrook Art Center, Tulsa, OK

By permission of the Smithsonian Institution Press from the following BAE Bulletins: Bulletin 61, "Song of a Man Who Received a Vision," p. 165, 1918. Bulletin 53, "Spring Song," p. 254, and "I Have Found My Lover," p. 300, 1913. Bulletin 45, "Why Should I Be Jealous?", p. 151, and "My Love Has Departed," p. 150, 1910, Smithsonian Institution, Washington, D.C.

The Navaho hunter sits motionless and chants
his ancient hunting song over and over. The deer,
always a curious animal, comes directly to the hunter
to find out what is making the monotonous, rhythmic sound.

Hunting Song

Comes the deer to my singing,
Comes the deer to my song,
Comes the deer to my singing.

He, the blackbird, he am I,
Bird beloved of the wild deer.   5
   Comes the deer to my singing.

From the Mountain Black,
From the summit,
Down the trail, coming, coming now,
   Comes the deer to my singing.   10

Through the blossoms,
Through the flowers, coming, coming
      now,
   Comes the deer to my singing.

Through the flower dew-drops,
   Coming, coming now,   15
   Comes the deer to my singing.

Through the pollen, flower pollen,
   Coming, coming now,
   Comes the deer to my singing.

Starting with his left fore-foot,*   20
Stamping, turns the frightened deer,
   Comes the deer to my singing.

Quarry mine, blessed am I
In the luck of the chase.
   Comes the deer to my singing.   25

   Comes the deer to my singing,
   Comes the deer to my song,
   Comes the deer to my singing.

NAVAHO

"Hunting Song" from *The Indians' Book* by Natalie Curtis, 1967. By permission of Dover Publications, Inc., New York.

* **left fore-foot.** An ancient Navaho belief asserts that the male deer starts with the left fore-foot, the female with the right.

*For centuries the Tewa (tā'wə) Indians have lived in pueblos in New Mexico and
northeastern Arizona. According to the translator of this prayer, Dr. Herbert Spinden,
the sky loom refers to the desert rains so characteristic of this part of the country. Like
wandering looms the rain showers hang from the sky.*

Song of the Sky Loom

O our Mother the Earth, O our Father the Sky,
Your children are we, and with tired backs
We bring you the gifts you love.
Then weave for us a garment of brightness;
May the warp be the white light of morning,   5
May the weft be the red light of evening,
May the fringes be the falling rain,
May the border be the standing rainbow.
Thus weave for us a garment of brightness,
That we may walk fittingly where birds sing,   10
That we may walk fittingly where grass is green,
O our Mother the Earth, O our Father the Sky.

TEWA

From SONGS OF THE TEWA. Herbert J. Spinden, editor and translator,
N.Y.: Published under the auspices of the Exposition of Indian Tribal Arts,
Inc. 1933.

Songs of the Great Mystery

1. What do you think might be the warrior's
guardian in the ancient Sioux song?
2. What do you think the singer in the Chippewa
song sees as he looks out over the prairie?
3. The dream song of the Chippewa warrior is
entirely different in tone from the Sioux song.
How would you explain the difference in tone? in
the effects of the two songs?

Three Chippewa Love Songs

1. Which song might be called an example of
self-therapy? Which expresses exultation? Which
expresses sadness?
2. How are the songs like Japanese haiku?

"Hunting Song"

1. The hunter believes the magic in the song
words will help him kill the deer. As a means of
attracting the deer, what creature does he imitate?
2. Where is the deer coming from?
3. What does the deer do when it sees the hunter?

4. In line 14, the singer reveals that the deer
moves through "flower dew-drops." What time of
day does this imply?
5. What do lines 23 and 24 reveal about the
outcome of the hunt?
6. From line 7 on, what prepositions begin the
lines describing the deer's progress? What is the
effect of this use of repetition?

"Song of the Sky Loom"

1. Whom do the Tewa address as their mother and
father?
2. To what are the warp and the weft of the
material compared?
3. What is the "garment of brightness," and why
do the people pray for it?
4. What does the expression "That we may walk
fittingly" in lines 10 and 11 mean?
5. The repetition used in American Indian songs
gives the lines distinct rhythm and cadence. Which
lines of the song are exactly the same? What
purpose do these two lines serve?
6. What other repetitions are used in the song?

Ohiyesa

1858–1939

Charles A. Eastman, born with the Indian name Ohiyesa, lived the free and war-filled life of the Dakota Sioux until he was fifteen years old. Later, he attended both Dartmouth College and Boston University and became a physician, spokesman for the American Indians, and author of several books on Sioux life.

This brief selection from Eastman's

The Soul of the Indian (1911) is included with early American Indian literature because the author's early years were lived in a world not unlike that of the pre-Columbian Indians. His later life as part of mainstream America in the late nineteenth and early twentieth centuries gave Eastman a unique perspective on both worlds.

STRUTTING PIGEON, WIFE OF WHITE CLOUD, George Catlin
Haida Indians
National Museum of American Art, Smithsonian Institution

from THE SOUL OF THE INDIAN

Ohiyesa Remembers

As a child I understood how to give; I have forgotten this grace since I became civilized. I lived the natural life, whereas I now live the artificial. Any pretty pebble was valuable to me then; every growing tree an object of reverence. Now I worship with the white man before a painted landscape whose value is estimated in dollars! Thus the Indian is reconstructed, as the natural rocks are ground to powder and made into artificial blocks which may be built into the walls of modern society.

The first American mingled with his pride a singular humility. Spiritual arrogance was foreign to his nature and teaching. He never claimed that the power of articulate speech was proof of superiority over the dumb creation; on the other hand, it is to him a perilous gift. He believes profoundly in silence—the sign of a perfect equilibrium. Silence is the absolute poise or balance of body, mind, and spirit. The man who preserves his selfhood is ever calm and unshaken by the storms of existence—not a leaf, as it were, astir on the tree; not a ripple upon the surface of the shining pool—his, in the mind of the unlettered sage, is the ideal attitude and conduct of life.

If you ask him: "What is silence?" he will answer: "It is the Great Mystery!" "The holy silence is His voice!" If you ask: "What are the fruits of silence?" he will say: "They are self-control, true courage or endurance, patience, dignity, and reverence. Silence is the cornerstone of character."

"Guard your tongue in youth," said the old chief, Wabashaw, "and in age you may mature a thought that will be of service to your people!"

From THE SOUL OF THE INDIAN by Charles A. Eastman (Ohiyesa), New York: Houghton-Mifflin, 1911. By permission of Virginia Eastman Whitbeck and Eleanor Eastman Mensel.

UNDERSTANDING AND APPRECIATION

1. According to Ohiyesa, what qualities has the American Indian lost in becoming a part of modern society?
2. What comparison does Ohiyesa use to explain what happens to the American Indian?
3. What does the image imply?

COMPOSITION

The American Indian expression "Do not judge a man until you have walked a mile in his moccasins" emphasizes the great need among all peoples for mutual understanding.

In a short composition, explain the insights into American Indian life and character that you have gained through reading these selections from early Indian literature. Why might these insights be important?

A TWENTIETH-CENTURY WRITER LOOKS BACK

Our writers and artists often look back into our nation's past, where myth merges with reality. These backward glances create new perspectives through which we can rediscover the vivid landscape of dream and fact that makes up the living memory of our country.

In "Trials at Salem," Stephen Vincent Benét looks back to 1692 when terror, tragedy, and lurid drama gripped the inhabitants of the little village of Salem and threatened to engulf the whole colony of Massachusetts. Benét's view of what occurred is considerably different from that of Cotton Mather, whose contemporary report on "The Trial of Martha Carrier" can be found on page 39.

Here literature offers the reader an opportunity to see the same tragedy through the eyes of writers separated by two and a half centuries.

Stephen Vincent Benét   1898–1943

Stephen Vincent Benét was born into a military family in Bethlehem, Pennsylvania. His father, a West Point graduate, had a library overflowing with books. Colonel Benét loved poetry and often played host to literary acquaintances. Stephen's mother wrote verses. This background may have inspired the three Benét children, William Rose, Laura, and Stephen, all of whom achieved some literary fame.

After graduating from Yale, Stephen married Rosemary Carr, who was later to become his collaborator on *A Book of Americans.* By 1926, Stephen had published two collections of verse and three novels. He had sold thirty-two of the thirty-four short stories he had written. He had won national prizes, gold medals, and other recognition for both his prose and his poetry. Like many another writer, Benét was to find that literary fame does not necessarily produce financial security. Over the years he did a great deal of hack work to make ends meet—including the novelization of a Broadway thriller, *The Bat.*

Then, in 1926, Benét was granted a Guggenheim Fellowship of $2500 a year. This grant enabled him to put aside the contrived love stories of Manhattan office workers and Long Island heiresses he had been writing. He turned to the American past for his subject matter. "We have our own folk-gods and giants . . . in this country," he said. Two years later, he produced his monumental narrative poem, *John Brown's Body,* a best seller, a Pulitzer Prize winner, and a literary classic. Following this success, he did some of his best writing, combining American dialects, folklore, and history to capture the flavor, excitement, and

STEPHEN VINCENT BENÉT

color of the robust young America. His famed "The Devil and Daniel Webster" has attained a secure place in American literature. His second epic poem, the unfinished *Western Star,* posthumously won a second Pulitzer Prize.

TRIAL OF GEORGE JACOBS
T. H. Matteson
Essex Institute, Salem, MA

T. H. Matteson's depiction of one of the Salem witchcraft trials captures the mood of hysteria and accusation that gripped the village in 1692.

TRIALS AT SALEM

Salem Village had got a new minister—the Reverend Samuel Parris, ex-merchant in the West Indies. The most important thing about Samuel Parris was the fact that he brought with him to Salem Village two West Indian servants—a man known as John Indian and a woman named Tituba. And when he bought those two or their services in the West Indies, he was buying a rope that was to hang nineteen men and women of New England—so odd are the links in the circumstantial chain.

Perhaps the nine-year-old Elizabeth Parris, the daughter of the parsonage, boasted to her new friends of the odd stories Tituba told and the queer things she could do. Perhaps Tituba herself let the report of her magic powers be spread about the village. She must have been as odd and imagination-stirring a figure as a parrot or a tame monkey in the small New England town. And the winters were long and white—and any diversion a godsend.

In any case, during the winter of 1691–92 a group of girls and women began to meet nightly at the parsonage, with Tituba and her fortune telling as the chief attraction. Elizabeth Parris, at nine, was the youngest; then came Abigail Williams, eleven, and Ann Putnam, twelve. The rest were older—Mercy Lewis, Mary Wolcott, and Elizabeth Hubbard were seventeen; Elizabeth Booth and Susan Sheldon, eighteen; and Mary Warren and Sarah Churchill, twenty. Three were servants —Mercy Lewis had been employed by the

Reverend George Burroughs, a previous minister of Salem Village, and now worked for the Putnams; Mary Warren was a maid at the John Procters'; Sarah Churchill, at the George Jacobs'. All, except for Elizabeth Parris, were adolescent or just leaving adolescence.

The elder women included a pair of gossipy, superstitious busybodies—Mrs. Pope and Mrs. Bibber; and young Ann Putnam's mother, Ann Putnam, Sr., who deserves a sentence to herself.

For the Putnams were a powerful family in the neighborhood and Ann Putnam, married at seventeen and now only thirty, is described as handsome, arrogant, temperamental, and high-strung. She was also one of those people who can cherish a grudge and revenge it.

The circle met—the circle continued to meet—no doubt with the usual giggling, whispering, and gossip. From mere fortune telling it proceeded to other and more serious matters—table rapping, perhaps, and a little West Indian voodoo—weird stories told by Tituba and weird things shown, while the wind blew outside and the big shadows flickered on the wall. Adolescent girls, credulous servants, superstitious old women—and the two enigmatic figures of Tituba, the West Indian, and Ann Putnam, Sr.

But soon the members of the circle began to show hysterical symptoms. They crawled under tables and chairs; they made strange sounds; they shook and trembled with nightmare fears. The thing became a village celebrity—and more. Something strange and out of nature was happening—who had ever seen normal young girls behave like these

"Trials at Salem" from: WE AREN'T SUPERSTITIOUS by Stephen Vincent Benét. Copyright, 1937 by Esquire, Inc. Copyright © renewed 1965 by Thomas C. Benét, Rachel Benét Lewis, and Stephanie Benét Mahin. Reprinted by permission of Brandt & Brandt Literary Agents.

"Perhaps Tituba herself let the report of her magic powers be spread about the village. She must have been as odd and imagination-stirring a figure as a parrot or a tame monkey in the small New England town. And the winters were long and white—and any diversion a godsend."

young girls? And no one—certainly not the Reverend Samuel Parris—even suggested that a mixed diet of fortune telling, ghost stories, and voodoo is hardly the thing for impressionable minds during a long New England winter. Hysteria was possession by an evil spirit; pathological lying, the devil putting words into one's mouth. The Reverend Samuel became very busy. Grave ministers were called in to look at the afflicted children. A Dr. Gregg gave his opinion. It was almost too terrible to believe, and yet what else could be believed? Witchcraft!

Meanwhile, one may suppose, the "afflicted children," like most hysterical subjects, enjoyed the awed stares, the horrified looks, the respectful questions that greeted them, with girlish zest. They had been unimportant girls of a little hamlet;[1] now they were, in every sense of the word, spot news. And any reporter knows what that does to certain kinds of people. They continued to writhe and demonstrate—and be the center of attention.

1. **hamlet,** a small village.

There was only one catch about it. If they were really bewitched, somebody must be doing the bewitching.

On the twenty-ninth of February, 1692, in the midst of an appropriate storm of thunder and lightning, three women—Sarah Good, Sarah Osburn, and Tituba—were arrested on the deadly charge of bewitching the children.

The next day, March 1, two magistrates, Justice Hawthorne[2] and Justice Corwin, arrived with appropriate pomp and ceremony. The first hearing was held in the crowded meetinghouse of the village; and all Salem swarmed to it, as crowds in our time have swarmed to other sleepy little villages suddenly notorious.

The children—or the children and Tituba—had picked their first victims well. Sarah Good and Sarah Osburn were old women of no particular standing in the community.

We can imagine that meetinghouse—and the country crowd within it—on that chill March day. At one end was the majesty of the law—and the "afflicted children," where all might see them and observe. Dressed in their best, very likely, and with solicitous relatives near at hand. Do you see Mercy Lewis? Do you see Ann Putnam? And then the whole crowd turned to one vast, horrified eye. For there was the accused—the old woman—the witch!

The justices—grim Justice Hawthorne in particular—had, evidently, arrived with their minds made up. For the first question addressed to Sarah Good was, bluntly:

"What evil spirit have you familiarity with?"

"None," said the piping old voice. But everybody in the village knew worthless Sarah Good. And the eye of the audience went from her to the deadly row of "afflicted children" and back again.

"Have you made no contracts with the devil?" proceeded the Justice.

"No."

The Justice went to the root of the matter at once.

"Why do you hurt these children?"

A rustle must have gone through the meetinghouse at that. Aye, that's it; the Justice speaks shrewdly; hark to the Justice! Aye, but look too! Look at the children! Poor things, poor things!

"I do not hurt them. I scorn it," said Sarah Good defiantly. But the Justice had her now; he was not to be brushed aside.

"Who, then, do you employ to do it?"

"I employ nobody."

"What creature do you employ then?" For all witches had familiars.

"No creature, but I am falsely accused." But the sweat must have been on the old woman's palms by now.

The Justice considered. There was another point, minor but illuminating.

"Why did you go away muttering from Mr. Parris, his house?"

"I did not mutter, but I thanked him for what he gave my child."

The Justice returned to the main charge, like any prosecuting attorney.

"Have you made no contract with the devil?"

"No."

It was time for Exhibit A. The Justice turned to the children. Was Sarah Good one of the persons who tormented them? Yes, yes!—and a horrified murmur running through the crowd. And then, before the awe-stricken eyes of all, they began to be tormented. They writhed; they grew stiff; they contorted; they were stricken moaning or speechless. Yet, when they were brought to Sarah Good and allowed to touch her, they grew quiet and calm. For, as everyone knew, a witch's physical body was like an electric

2. **Justice Hawthorne,** distant relative of Nathaniel Hawthorne. The Justice actually spelled his name Hathorne; the *w* was added by Nathaniel.

EXAMINATION OF A WITCH
T. H. Matteson
Essex Institute, Salem, MA

conductor—it reabsorbed, on touch, the malefic force discharged by witchcraft into the bodies of the tormented. Everybody could see what happened—and everybody saw. When the meetinghouse was quiet, the Justice spoke again.

"Sarah Good, do you not see now what you have done? Why do you not tell us the truth? Why do you torment these poor children?"

And with these words Sarah Good was already hanged. For all that she could say was, "I do not torment them." And yet everyone had seen her, with their own eyes.

Sarah Osburn's examination followed the same course, the same prosecutor's first ques-

tion, the same useless denial, the same epileptic feats of the "afflicted children," the same end.

Then Tituba was examined and gave them their fill of marvels, prodigies, and horrors.

The West Indian woman, a slave in a strange land, was fighting for her life, and she did it shrewdly, and desperately. She admitted, repentantly, that she had tormented the children. But she had been forced to do so. By whom? By Goody Good and Goody Osburn and two other witches whom she hadn't yet been able to recognize. Her voodoo knowledge aided her—she filled the open ears of Justices and crowd with tales of hairy familiars and black dogs, red cats and black cats and yellow birds, the phantasm of a woman with legs and wings. And everybody could see that she spoke the truth. For, when she was first brought in, the children were tormented at her presence; but as soon as she had confessed and turned King's evidence, she was tormented herself, and fearfully. To Boston Jail with her—but she had saved her neck.

The hearing was over; the men and women of Salem and its outlying farms went broodingly or excitedly back to their homes to discuss the fearful workings of God's providence. Here and there a common sense voice murmured a doubt or two—Sarah Good and Sarah Osburn were no great losses to the community; but still, to convict two old women of heinous crime on the testimony of greensick girls and a West Indian slave! But, on the whole, the villagers of Salem felt relieved. The cause of the plague had been found; it would be stamped out and the afflicted children recover. The Justices, no doubt, congratulated themselves on their prompt and intelligent action. The "afflicted children" slept, after a tiring day—they were not quite so used to such performances as they were to become.

As for the accused women, they went to Boston Jail—to be chained there while waiting trial and gallows.

Meanwhile, on an outlying farm, Giles Corey, a turbulent, salty old fellow of eighty-one, began to argue the case with his wife, Martha. He believed, fanatically, in the "afflicted children." She did not, and said so—even going so far as to say that the magistrates were blinded and she could open their eyes. It was one of those marital disputes that occur between strong-willed people. And it was to bring Martha Corey to the gallows and Giles Corey to an even stranger doom.

Yet now there was a lull, through which people whispered.

As for what went on in the minds of the "afflicted children" during that lull we may

not say. But this much is evident. They had seen and felt their power. The hearing had been the greatest and most exciting event of their narrow lives. And it was so easy to do; they grew more and more ingenious with each rehearsal. You twisted your body and groaned—and grown people were afraid.

Add to this the three girl-servants, with the usual servants' grudges against present or former masters. Add to this that high-strung, dominant woman Ann Putnam, Sr., who could hold a grudge and remember it. Such a grudge as there might be against the Towne sisters, for instance—they were all married women of the highest standing, particularly Rebecca Nurse. So suppose—just suppose—that one of them were found out to be a witch? And hadn't Tituba deposed that there were other women, besides Good and Osburn, who made her torment the children?

On March 19 Martha Corey and Rebecca Nurse were arrested on the charge of witchcraft. On March 21 they were examined and committed. And with that the real reign of terror began.

Salem Village, as a community, was no longer sane.

Let us get it over quickly. The Salem witches ceased to be Salem's affair—they became a matter affecting the whole colony. Sir William Phips, the new governor, appointed a special court of oyer and terminer[3] to try the cases. And the hangings began.

On January 1, 1692, no one, except possibly the "circle children," had heard of Salem witches. On June 10 Bridget Bishop was hanged. She had not been one of the first accused, but she was the first to suffer. She had been married three times, kept a roadhouse on the road to Beverly where people drank rum and played shovelboard, and dressed, distinctively for the period, in a "black cap and black hat and red paragon bodice broi-

---

3. **court of oyer and terminer** (ō′yər tėr′mə nər), a high court which hears and determines criminal cases.

dered and looped with diverse colors." But those seem to have been her chief offenses. When questioned, she said, "I never saw the devil in my life."

All through the summer the accusations, the arrests, the trials, came thick and fast till the jails were crowded. Nor were those now accused friendless old beldames like Sarah Good. They included Captain John Alden (son of Miles Standish's friend[4]), who saved himself by breaking jail, and the wealthy and prominent Englishes, who saved themselves by flight. The most disgraceful scenes occurred at the trial of the saintly Rebecca Nurse. Thirty-nine citizens of Salem were brave enough to sign a petition for her, and the jury brought in a verdict of "not guilty." The mob in the sweating courtroom immediately began to cry out, and the presiding judge as much as told the jury to reverse the verdict. They did so, to the mob's delight. Then the governor pardoned her. And "certain gentlemen of Salem"—and perhaps the mob—persuaded him into reversing his pardon. She was hanged on Gallows Hill on July 19 with Sarah Good, Sarah Wilds, Elizabeth How, and Susanna Martin.

Susanna Martin's only witchcraft seems to have been that she was an unusually tidy woman and had once walked a muddy road without getting her dress bedraggled. No, I am quoting from testimony, not inventing. As for Elizabeth How, a neighbor testified, "I have been acquainted with Goodwife How as a naybor for nine or ten years and I never saw any harm in her but found her just in her dealings and faithful to her promises . . . I never heard her revile any person but she always pitied them and said, 'I pray God forgive them now.'" But the children cried, "I am stuck with a pin. I am pinched," when they saw her—and she hanged.

It took a little more to hang the Reverend George Burroughs. He had been Salem Village's second minister—then gone on to a parish in Maine. And the cloth had great sanctity. But Ann Putnam and Mercy Lewis managed to doom him between them, with the able assistance of the rest of the troupe. Mr. Burroughs was unfortunate enough to be a man of unusual physical strength—anyone who could lift a gun by putting four fingers in its barrel must do so by magic arts. Also, he had been married three times. So when the ghosts of his first two wives, dressed in winding sheets, appeared in a sort of magic lantern show to Ann Putnam and cried out that Mr. Burroughs had murdered them—the cloth could not save him then.

Here and there in the records gleams a flash of frantic common sense. Susanna Martin laughs when Ann Putnam and her daughter go into convulsions at her appearance. When asked why, she says, "Well I may, at such folly. I never hurt this woman or her child in my life." John Procter, the prosperous farmer who employed Mary Warren, said sensibly, before his arrest, "If these girls are left alone, we will all be devils and witches. They ought all to be sent to the whipping post." He was right enough about it—but his servant helped hang him.

Judge, jury, and colony preferred to believe the writhings of the children; the stammerings of those whose sows had died inexplicably; the testimony of such as Bernard Peach, who swore that Susanna Martin had flown in through his window, bent his body into the shape of a "Whoope," and sat upon him for an hour and a half.

One hanging on June 10, five on July 19, five on August 19, eight on September 22, including Mary Easty and Martha Corey. And of these the Reverend Noyes remarked, with unction, "What a sad thing it is to see eight firebrands of hell hanging there!" But for stubborn Giles Corey a different fate was reserved.

The old man had begun by believing in the whole hocus-pocus. He had quarreled

---

4. **Miles Standish's friend,** John Alden, Sr., who with Standish founded Duxbury.

with his wife about it. He had seen her arrested as a witch, insulted by the magistrates, condemned to die. Two of his sons-in-law had testified against her; he himself had been closely questioned as to her actions and had made the deposition of a badgered and simple man. Yes, she prayed a good deal; sometimes he couldn't hear what she said—that sort of thing. The memory must have risen to haunt him when she was condemned. Now he himself was in danger.

Well, he could die as his wife would. But there was the property—his goods, his prospering lands. By law, the goods and property of those convicted of witchcraft were confiscated by the state and the name attainted. With a curious, grim heroism, Giles Corey drew up a will leaving that property to the two sons-in-law who had not joined in the prevailing madness. And then at his trial, he said, "I will not plead. If I deny, I am condemned already in courts where ghosts appear as witnesses and swear men's lives away."

A curious, grim heroism? It was so. For those who refused to plead either guilty or not guilty in such a suit were liable to the old English punishment called *peine forte et dure*.[5] It consisted in heaping weights or stones upon the unhappy victim till he accepted a plea—or until his chest was crushed. And exactly that happened to old Giles Corey. They heaped the stones upon him until they killed him—and two days before his wife was hanged, he died. But his property went to the two loyal sons-in-law, without confiscation—and his name was not attainted. So died Giles Corey, New England to the bone.

And then, suddenly and fantastically as the madness had come, it was gone.

The "afflicted children," at long last, had gone too far. They had accused the governor's lady. They had accused Mrs. Hall, the wife of the minister at Beverly and a woman known throughout the colony for her virtues. And there comes a point when driven men and women revolt against blood and horror. It was that which ended Robespierre's[6] terror

—it was that which ended the terror of the "afflicted children." The thing had become a *reductio ad absurdum*.[7] If it went on, logically, no one but the "afflicted children" and their protégées would be left alive.

In 1706 Ann Putnam made public confession that she had been deluded by the devil in testifying as she had. She had testified in every case but one. And in 1711 the colony of Massachusetts paid fifty pounds to the heirs of George Burroughs, twenty-one pounds to the heirs of Giles Corey—five hundred and seventy-eight pounds in all to the heirs of various victims. An expensive business for the colony, on the whole.

What happened to the survivors? Well, the Reverend Samuel Parris quit Salem Village to go into business in Boston and died at Sudbury in 1720. And Ann Putnam died in 1716 and from the stock of the Putnams sprang Israel Putnam, the Revolutionary hero. And from the stock of the "Witches," the Nurses and the others, sprang excellent and distinguished people of service to state and nation. And hanging Judge Hawthorne's descendant was Nathaniel Hawthorne.

We have no reason to hold Salem up to obloquy. It was a town, like another, and a strange madness took hold of it. But it is not a stranger thing to hang a man for witchcraft than to hang him for the shape of his nose or the color of his skin. We are not superstitious, no. Well, let us be a little sure we are not. For persecution follows superstition and intolerance as fire follows the fuse. And once we light that fire we cannot foresee where it will end or what it will consume—any more than they could in Salem two hundred and sixty-seven years ago.

---

5. ***peine forte et dure*** (pen'fôr' tā dür'), French: literally, strong and hard pain or punishment; used to indicate the procedure described in the text.
6. **Robespierre** (rô'bes'pyär'), French revolutionist responsible for much of the reign of terror.
7. **reductio ad absurdum** (ri duk'shē ō ad ab sér'dəm), Latin: proof of the falsity of a conclusion by reducing it to absurdity.

FOR UNDERSTANDING

Laws in themselves never guarantee justice. Injustice was done at Salem largely because the citizens temporarily lost their collective sanity, their ability to distinguish between the real and the unreal.
1. Who were the first three people in Salem to be accused?
2. What was their crime supposed to be?
3. Which of the accused saved herself? How?
4. Why did the judge, jury, and colony prefer to believe the children rather than honest and sensible people?
5. What did the "afflicted children" finally do that stopped the madness?

FOR INTERPRETATION

Discuss how Benét suggests the following ideas in "Trials at Salem."
1. The social standing of those accused of a crime may influence justice in the courts.
2. So long as people can remain secure from what might be injustice, they are not concerned enough to do anything about it.

FOR APPRECIATION

Theme

Theme may be defined as the central idea in a work of literature. This central idea may be expressed both directly and indirectly. A theme can often be formulated by completing the sentence, The writer is trying to tell me that. . . . Of course, in many instances, it is difficult to arrive at a concise statement of theme, and opinions differ about the same piece of literature.

When Cotton Mather wrote about the trial of Martha Carrier, his intention was to justify the condemnation of the witches. When Stephen Vincent Benét looked back upon what historians now agree was an extreme miscarriage of justice, he wrote with clear intention also. A writer's intention dictates his or her choice of words. The kinds of words a writer chooses can indirectly lead the reader to the theme. Thus when Mather referred to the supposed victims of Martha Carrier's witchcraft as "poor" people, he obviously intended to convince people that it was right that she was condemned.
1. In the fourth paragraph, what does Benét call Mrs. Pope and Mrs. Bibber? In the following paragraph, what does he tell you about Ann Putnam, Sr.?
2. What journalistic term does he use to tell the reader how the importance of the children had changed?
3. What sentence from the selection do you think directly states his theme?

LANGUAGE AND VOCABULARY

Benét's writing is made vivid and interesting with fresh and seldom-used words which he weaves so skillfully into the context of his paragraphs that the reader is not troubled for meaning. The following are phrases and sentences from "Trials at Salem." Give logical definitions for the italicized words based on their contexts. Check the accuracy of your definitions in the Glossary.
1. The *phantasm* of a woman with legs and wings
2. To convict two old women of *heinous* crime on the testimony of *greensick* girls
3. Nor were those now accused friendless old *beldames* like Sarah Good.
4. By law, the goods and property of those convicted of witchcraft were *confiscated* by the state and the name *attainted.*
5. We have no reason to hold Salem up to *obloquy.*

COMPOSITION

The opening paragraph of "Trials of Salem" illustrates the writer's technique of *foreshadowing,* that is, creating suspense with a clue or clues about what is to happen later. When Benét writes of the Reverend Samuel Parris's purchase of John Indian and Tituba, he states: "And when he bought those two or their services in the West Indies, he was buying a rope that was to hang nineteen men and women of New England—so odd are the links in the circumstantial chain."

Write a brief story in which something such as a purchase, a gift, a chance remark, a joke, or a job offer has an unexpected effect or result. Foreshadow that result in your opening paragraph.

COMPOSITION WORKSHOP

RESEARCHING LITERATURE

The word "research" sometimes frightens students because it seems to suggest a lengthy paper that is difficult and time-consuming to write. There's really no need for research to appear threatening, however, if it is recognized as being nothing more than organized and systematic investigation. The word comes from a French root, meaning "to investigate thoroughly"—which is precisely what the researcher does.

The purpose of research is to develop new ideas, to revise old ones, or to increase our understanding of complex or perplexing problems. In each instance, research does its work by bringing new facts to light or by proposing new applications or arrangements for existing materials. Everyone is familiar with popularized notions of scientific research, particularly as typified by laboratory experimentation. Just think of all the white-coated scientists you have seen in movies or on television, holding up test tubes to the light. Research can, of course, be dramatic—as when a cure for a disease like polio is found. But such breakthroughs are really only the cumulative result of long, plodding years of work.

In various fields in the humanities, research may seem unglamorous or even boring. A historian, for example, using a library rather than a laboratory, may spend years studying the administration of a former president, work carried out without fanfare and far from the limelight. Yet by examining documents and published reports previously overlooked, the historian may bring to light facts previously unknown. By clarifying historical decisions or actions that were ignored or misunderstood before, such research may help us deal with present and future problems of a similar nature and thus perform a vital service.

Research goes on in the field of literature as well. In one area of literary research, the emphasis is on historical or biographical material. In another area, the approach is critical in nature. One of the major goals of critical research is to shed light on the meaning of literature.

Newly discovered facts about a particular work, for example, can make possible new interpretations of the work or relate it in new ways to the major themes of an author or the period in which it was written. Taken most broadly, critical research can deepen our understanding not only of a work, an author, or a period but also of the human imagination and, ultimately, the human condition.

For research to be available to others, of course, it must be eventually written down. The research paper is the form that has been developed for this purpose. Formal and objective in approach, it makes use of several unique mechanical features. None of these elements are insurmountable, especially if taken one by one, as we will do in these Composition Workshop assignments. Ultimately, you will see the research paper as simply another writing task that can be approached and accomplished systematically—and enjoyably.

THE ONE-PARAGRAPH SUMMARY

Of the many skills required for writing a research paper, none is more basic than the ability to summarize material too long to quote in detail. In literary research, you must be able to summarize not only works under discussion but also what other writers or critics have said about these works. You can never assume that your readers will be familiar with all the material in your discussion, nor can you quote every key interpretation in full.

The summary serves another purpose in research writing, since you will often want to restate the ground you've covered in one section of your paper before proceeding to the next. There may also be a summary at the end of your report, reiterating the important points you have made and the conclusion you have reached.

The ability to summarize can be developed easily with a little practice. If, for example, you need a plot summary of a work, state only the main thrust of the main action, and avoid being sidetracked by secondary characters or subplots. If you are summarizing a critic's or researcher's findings, cite only those elements absolutely essential to the point being made, and leave out examples or subsidiary arguments. The more succinct a summary is, the better. The ability to write a one-paragraph summary of a novel or story, in fact, is often an absolute necessity in literary research.

Since economy is so crucial, even experienced writers often rework a summary four or five times until they arrive at a version that captures the essence of a work in as few words as possible. Study the following summary of Stephen Crane's classic American novel *The Red Badge of Courage*. A 150-page novel is summarized in five sentences:

> The central character in the book is a young private, Henry Fleming, who is filled with romantic notions about the glory of war. In his first engagement, however, fear overcomes him and he flees from battle, only to stumble upon the agonizing death-scene of a wounded friend, Jim Conklin. After hiding in the depths of a forest, Fleming again meets up with friendly troops but is struck down by a frenzied soldier retreating from battle. Ironically, this wound allows him to return to his own unit without disgrace. Finally, cleansed of his grandiose notions of war and his own fearful selfishness, he carries a flag to victory in the next engagement.

ASSIGNMENT 1

For practice, write a summary of the following paragraph. Summarize the paragraph in as few sentences as possible. Compare your summary with those of your classmates.

> Even in the present day of inflated figures, the actual numbers involved in the emigration to America are astonishing. It is not known exactly how many people came to the colonies before 1776 but the so-called Puritans' migration to Massachusetts between 1628 and 1640 totaled only 20,000 people. For 30 years after independence, the arrivals didn't increase much. Then, from the close of the Napoleonic Wars until the restrictive laws were enacted in the 1920's, a total of 35 million people entered the U.S., eventually at the rate of a million a year.
>
> Terrence O'Flaherty
> *The San Francisco Chronicle*
> June 9, 1976

ASSIGNMENT 2

Write a summary of one of the prose selections in this unit. Be sure that your summary is no longer than half a page. Or, if you wish, you may prepare a summary of a novel or a short story that you have read recently.

The
and Early

LIBERTY, Artist Unknown
National Gallery of Art
Washington, DC
Gift of Edgar W. and Bernice
Chrysler Garbisch

Revolutionary National Years

Because of widespread changes in European thinking that occurred during the eighteenth century, this period is commonly known as the Age of Enlightenment. Many of those who founded our country were familiar with the ideas of such Enlightenment thinkers as Locke and Hume in Britain and Voltaire and Jean Jacques Rousseau in France.

Age of Enlightenment

These philosophers believed that human reason should be used to examine previously accepted ideas and institutions. Anything that could not stand up to rational scrutiny should then be modified or discarded. Some of these thinkers also sought to prove that nearly everything was subject to physical laws, just as nature was.

Human Reason

Two key political ideas of the age were the doctrine of natural rights and the notion of government by contract. Of all the Enlightenment ideals, however, those that most strongly influenced the founders of our nation were the beliefs in the inherent goodness of nature and in the perfectibility of humankind. This was particularly true of Benjamin Franklin (see page 92), which makes him, perhaps, the most typically American writer of the second half of the eighteenth century, as well as the best-known. (Of course, Franklin's early writing appeared in the first half of the century; he began his almanac in 1732.)

Natural Rights and Government by Contract

Benjamin Franklin

Franklin's spirit was in many ways the antithesis of the Puritan cast of mind. Whereas Jonathan Edwards, the quintessential Puritan, could be described as gloomy and introverted, Franklin was optimistic and practical. It can be argued, however, that both Franklin and Edwards considered themselves servants of a higher power, as you will see in one of the selections from Franklin's *Autobiography*, in which he examines his vices and virtues and attempts to purify his life. Unlike the sin-obsessed Edwards, Franklin thought he could best serve God by helping humankind—including himself—in *this* world.

To this end, Franklin probed the nature of the physical universe; he invented useful things; he established a school, a lending library, and the first police and fire departments. In the character of Poor Richard, he dispensed practical wisdom to a wide audience. He played leading roles in local, national, and international politics. Not least of all, he made a fortune. Franklin might be called our first self-made man, the embodiment of the American dream of success.

Franklin's Genius

THE REVOLUTION: A CAUSE FOR WORDS, WORDS FOR A CAUSE

*Political
Literature* It is fruitless to speculate how American literature might have developed had Britain treated the colonies differently. The fact is that in response to such punitive British measures as the Sugar Act (1764), the Stamp Act (1765), the Quartering Act (1765), and the Townshend Acts (1767), the more radical colonists found ample cause for words. Considering that by 1763 all the colonies had at least one printing press, it is not surprising that words poured forth profusely in support of that cause. From the early 1760s on, politics moved to center stage, not only in speeches, but also in newspapers, magazines, broadsides, and pamphlets. Many of the speeches, such as most of those by Patrick

*Considered colonial America's foremost artist, Copley
excelled at capturing his subjects' character on canvas.*

THE COPLEY FAMILY, John Singleton Copley
National Gallery of Art, Washington, DC Andrew W. Mellon Fund

Henry (see page 100), were not recorded, unfortunately. One historian asserts that from 1763 to 1783 over 9000 "little books," or pamphlets, issued from American presses. Certainly many of our first-rank writers were producing such work. To study them is to study both American literature and the history of the Revolutionary period. It is also to read some of the greatest political writing of all time.

One of the earliest little books, James Otis's *The Rights of the British Colonies Asserted and Proved* (1764), summarized the "no taxation without representation" arguments of the colonies. Then in 1765, Parliament, the law-making body of Britain, passed the Stamp Act, which required that taxes be paid on all legal and commercial paper. On February 13, 1766, Benjamin Franklin stood before the House of

The Power of "Little Books"

Monticello, the home that Thomas Jefferson designed and built on a hilltop in Albemarle County, Virginia

Pine hutch (detail) from New England, 1740–1770

Commons in London and argued against the act. A record of this session, a series of 174 questions and Franklin's answers, was published as *Examination Before the House of Commons.* Another important protest against the Stamp Act, a series of essays written by John Adams, was published in 1768 under the title *A Dissertation on the Canon and Feudal Law.*

Though the Stamp Act was repealed, other repressive acts were passed, some of which ultimately resulted in bloodshed, such as the Boston Massacre of March 5, 1770. To punish Massachusetts for the famous Boston Tea Party, Parliament passed the Coercive Acts in 1774. Called the Intolerable Acts in America, they led directly to the assembling of the First Continental Congress, September–October 1774. While the delegates had no legal authority, they issued a Declaration of Rights and Grievances, written by John Adams and others, and agreed to meet again the following May if the British failed to repeal the Coercive Acts.

In 1775 war edged nearer with Patrick Henry's "Liberty or Death" speech, the battles of Lexington and Concord, and the convening of the Second Continental Congress. But the next great political document was *Common Sense* by Thomas Paine (see page 104), a little book published on January 10, 1776. It sold over 100,000 copies in a three-month period. In July of the same year, Thomas Jefferson (see page 111), urged by the Second Continental Congress, wrote the Declaration of Independence. At the end of the year, Paine's first essay in *The American Crisis* series buoyed the spirits of General Washington and his men as they crossed the icy Delaware River to attack the British at Trenton on Christmas Day.

The war dragged on for many years. It was fought first in the northern and middle colonies, where General Washington and his troops often came perilously close to defeat. Then the action shifted to the southern colonies, where the British hoped the population might be more sympathetic to their side. But the American victory was finally achieved at Yorktown, Virginia, where the British under Cornwallis surrendered to the Americans and French under Washington on October 19, 1781. Though a peace treaty was not signed until 1783, there was no further fighting after Yorktown.

Even after the cause was officially won, words for the cause continued to pour forth. The most notable documents were, of course, the United States Constitution and the Bill of Rights, embodying the ideals for which the war had been fought. To rally support for ratification of the Constitution, Alexander Hamilton, James Madison, and John Jay wrote the famous set of essays called *The Federalist* papers in 1787 and 1788. With the inauguration of George Washington as President on April 30, 1789, the Revolutionary period officially came to an end.

Port Royal parlor, Philadelphia, 1760-1785. Fashioned after the style popular during the reign of England's Queen Anne, colonial American furniture made between 1725 and 1780 was heavy but graceful, characterized by elegant simplicity and curving lines. For a comparison with furnishings of the previous century, see page 14.

A Stately Legacy What was the legacy of such writers as Benjamin Franklin, Thomas Paine, John Adams, Thomas Jefferson, and the others? Although we cannot readily establish that they had any direct influence on the major literary figures of succeeding generations, they wrote a crisp, clear, economical, straightforward prose that has been admired ever since. You will perhaps find echoes of it in the work of American writers like Henry David Thoreau, Mark Twain, and Ernest Hemingway, among others.

NYMPH AND BITTERN
William Rush
Fairmont Park Commission, PA

EARLY IMAGINATIVE WRITING

Although imaginative writing was clearly upstaged by political writing during the Revolutionary period, some plays, verse satires, early novels, and lyric poems should be noted, if only for their historical significance.

In 1759, Thomas Godfrey, a Philadelphia poet, wrote a tragedy, *The Prince of Parthia*, which in 1767 became the first American play to be produced on an American stage—the New Theatre in Philadelphia. Twenty years later, Royall Tyler's *The Contrast*, in which a British man of manners is compared unfavorably with an American, became the first American comedy to be acted by professionals (April 16, 1787). Verse satires of note include John Trumbull's *The Progress of Dulness* (1772–1773), a satire on college education featuring such characters as Tom Brainless, Dick Harebrain, and Miss Harriet Simper; a mock epic by the same author, *M'Fingal* (1776, lengthened 1782); and Francis Hopkinson's *Battle of the Kegs* (1778), a Revolutionary War ballad satirizing the British.

The first American novel, *The Power of Sympathy*, was published in 1789. Written by William Hill Brown, it was originally attributed to a Boston writer, Sarah Wentworth Morton, since it dealt with events that occurred in her family. Other noteworthy early novels were Susanna Rowson's best-seller (*Charlotte Temple*, 1794) and Charles Brockden Brown's six melodramatic novels, all of which he published between 1798 and 1801.

America's first black poet, Phillis Wheatley (see page 119), published *Poems on Various Subjects* in 1773 but unfortunately died young. Perhaps Philip Freneau (see page 116) most deserves being called our first great imaginative writer. He began writing verse in the early 1770s while still in college and continued until the final edition of his collected poems was published in 1815. Freneau was a very good if uneven poet, who spent much of his energy on journalistic and political activities. Ironically, some of his very best poetry was largely ignored in his own time.

Pat Lyon was a wealthy manufacturer, but he wished to be remembered in his portrait as he had been in his youth: a hardworking Irish locksmith. Neagle fulfilled his wish, and in the process painted his most famous portrait.

PAT LYON AT THE FORGE
John Neagle
Museum of Fine Arts, Boston
Herman and Zoe Oliver
Sherman Fund

THE DAWNING OF A NATIONAL LITERATURE

After 1789, with the land at peace and Washington elected as America's first President, a new sense of citizenship among the people also gave rise to the notion that the country's literature should be as uniquely American as its land and government. Certainly most literature of the Revolutionary period can be described as pro-American, both in subject and theme. But the style in which writers wrote necessarily reflected English standards. Consequently, no American author was acclaimed abroad to the extent that European writers were acclaimed both here and there.

Uniquely American Literature

Irving, Cooper, and Bryant

This was changed by Washington Irving (see page 122), James Fenimore Cooper (see page 134), and William Cullen Bryant (see page 143). All wrote essays, but each achieved lasting international fame in a distinct genre of imaginative literature. Irving created the first American short stories in his *Sketch Book*, published in 1820. A year later, Cooper published his first important novel, *The Spy*, and shortly after, became America's first internationally known novelist. Also in 1821, William Cullen Bryant's first mature collection of poetry appeared.

With these three writers, a national literature had dawned. More than a hundred years before, the American Indians, the explorers, and the colonists had loved the land and drawn sustenance from its spirit. But unlike their Puritan ancestors, Irving, Cooper, and Bryant largely sidestepped such great moral dilemmas as the problem of good and evil. It remained for later writers—like Nathaniel Hawthorne, Edgar Allan Poe, and Herman Melville—to probe the depths of the American conscience and the remoter mysteries of the human heart. With their work, American literature reached a zenith that put it on a level with the best that Europe had to offer.

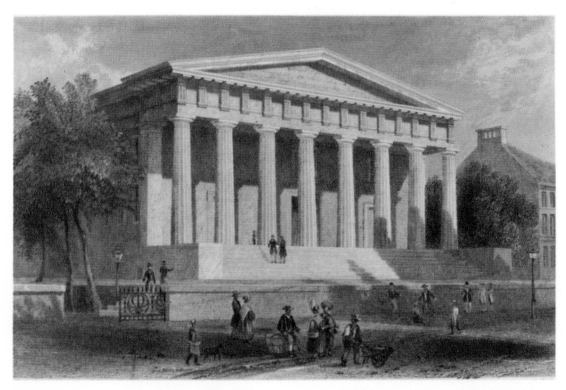

A good example of the stately, simple Greek Revival style of architecture favored throughout the colonies during the first half of the nineteenth century.

SECOND BANK OF THE UNITED STATES, PHILADELPHIA
William Strickland
Historical Society of Pennsylvania, Philadelphia, PA

Gilbert Stuart painted some of early America's best-known portraits (including George Washington's). Working directly on canvas with quick brushstrokes, he expertly captured the inner spirit of his subjects.

MRS. PEREZ MORTON
Gilbert Stuart
Worcester Art Museum, Worcester, Massachusetts
Gift of the Grandchildren of Joseph Tuckerman

The Revolutionary and

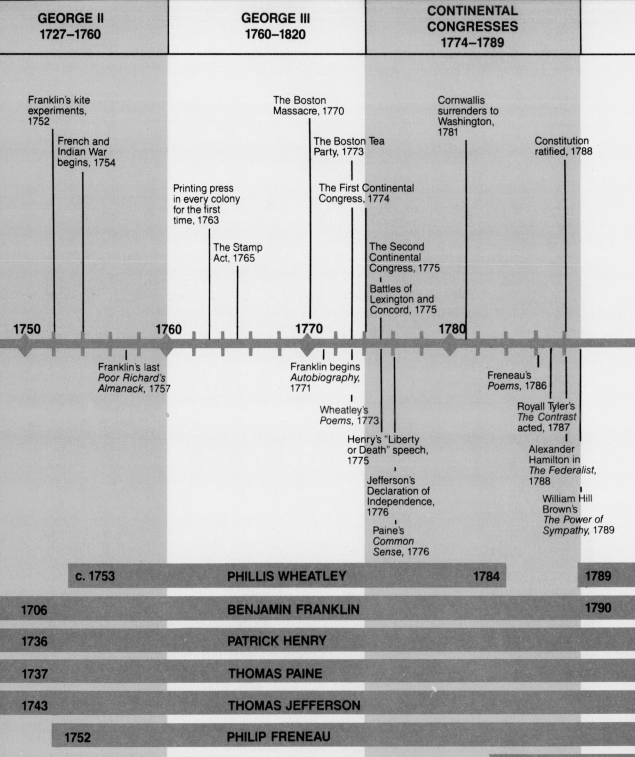

| GEORGE II 1727–1760 | GEORGE III 1760–1820 | CONTINENTAL CONGRESSES 1774–1789 | |

Franklin's kite experiments, 1752

French and Indian War begins, 1754

Printing press in every colony for the first time, 1763

The Stamp Act, 1765

The Boston Massacre, 1770

The Boston Tea Party, 1773

The First Continental Congress, 1774

The Second Continental Congress, 1775

Battles of Lexington and Concord, 1775

Cornwallis surrenders to Washington, 1781

Constitution ratified, 1788

1750　　　**1760**　　　**1770**　　　**1780**

Franklin's last *Poor Richard's Almanack*, 1757

Franklin begins *Autobiography*, 1771

Wheatley's *Poems*, 1773

Henry's "Liberty or Death" speech, 1775

Jefferson's Declaration of Independence, 1776

Paine's *Common Sense*, 1776

Freneau's *Poems*, 1786

Royall Tyler's *The Contrast* acted, 1787

Alexander Hamilton in *The Federalist*, 1788

William Hill Brown's *The Power of Sympathy*, 1789

c. 1753	PHILLIS WHEATLEY	1784	1789
1706	BENJAMIN FRANKLIN		1790
1736	PATRICK HENRY		
1737	THOMAS PAINE		
1743	THOMAS JEFFERSON		
1752	PHILIP FRENEAU		
			1783

Early National Years

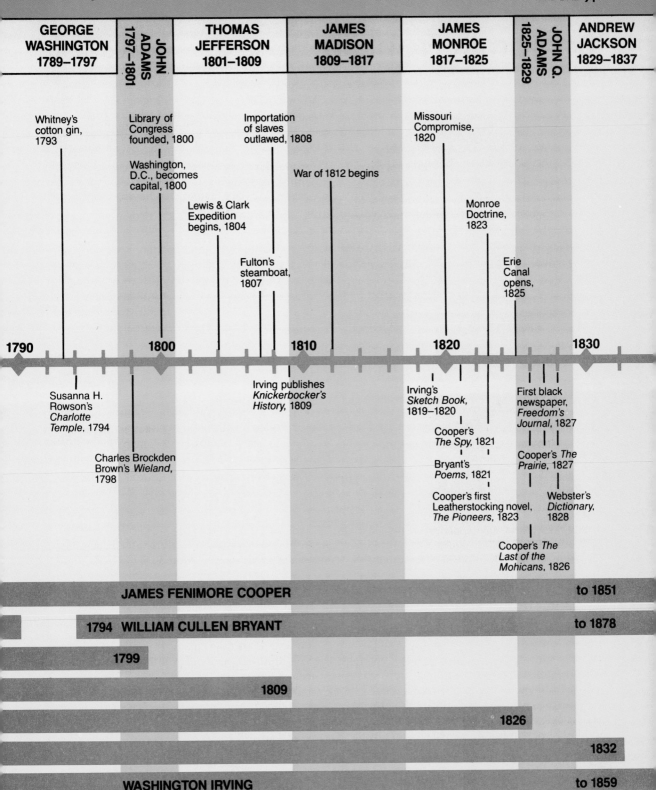

| GEORGE WASHINGTON 1789–1797 | JOHN ADAMS 1797–1801 | THOMAS JEFFERSON 1801–1809 | JAMES MADISON 1809–1817 | JAMES MONROE 1817–1825 | JOHN Q. ADAMS 1825–1829 | ANDREW JACKSON 1829–1837 |

Whitney's cotton gin, 1793

Library of Congress founded, 1800

Washington, D.C., becomes capital, 1800

Importation of slaves outlawed, 1808

Missouri Compromise, 1820

War of 1812 begins

Lewis & Clark Expedition begins, 1804

Monroe Doctrine, 1823

Fulton's steamboat, 1807

Erie Canal opens, 1825

1790   **1800**   **1810**   **1820**   **1830**

Susanna H. Rowson's *Charlotte Temple*, 1794

Irving publishes *Knickerbocker's History*, 1809

Irving's *Sketch Book*, 1819–1820

First black newspaper, *Freedom's Journal*, 1827

Charles Brockden Brown's *Wieland*, 1798

Cooper's *The Spy*, 1821

Cooper's *The Prairie*, 1827

Bryant's *Poems*, 1821

Cooper's first Leatherstocking novel, *The Pioneers*, 1823

Webster's *Dictionary*, 1828

Cooper's *The Last of the Mohicans*, 1826

JAMES FENIMORE COOPER   **to 1851**

1794 WILLIAM CULLEN BRYANT   **to 1878**

1799

1809

1826

1832

WASHINGTON IRVING   **to 1859**

Benjamin Franklin 1706–1790

PORTRAIT OF BENJAMIN FRANKLIN
Pierre Michel Alix
National Portrait Gallery, Smithsonian Institution

"Printer, postmaster, almanac maker, essayist, chemist, orator, tinker, statesman, humorist, philosopher, parlor man, political economist, professor of housewifery, ambassador, projector, maximonger, herb doctor, wit:—Jack of all trades, master of each and mastered by none—the type and genius of his land." So wrote the great American novelist Herman Melville of Benjamin Franklin in 1855, two generations after Franklin's death. Today, some four generations later, we remain fascinated and confounded by the many-sided genius of the first American man of the world.

Our admiration and awe grow all the greater when we consider Franklin's humble beginnings. He was the youngest son of a candlemaker who had seventeen children in all.

Born in Boston, Franklin went to grammar school there at the age of eight, but at ten he left school to assist his father in candlemaking and soapmaking; thereafter, he educated himself. A printer's apprentice to an older brother at twelve, Franklin first learned the trade, then ran away to seek his own fortune. He was only seventeen years old at the time.

By the age of twenty, Franklin had finally settled in Philadelphia as a printer. Within the next two dozen years he accumulated a small fortune and was able to live the remainder of his life as he pleased. As Melville's description suggests, Franklin was pleased to live his life in many ways—too many to explore here. Of course, everyone recalls his experiments with electricity, which brought him international fame as a scientist. But most important of all for our country were his many diplomatic activities.

As ambassador to Britain for most of the pre-Revolutionary American colonies from 1764 to 1775, Franklin formally protested the Stamp Act and Townshend Acts, among others. During this period Franklin also began his famous *Autobiography*, two sections of which follow. On the eve of the Revolution, he returned to America to attend the Second Continental Congress and to help draft the Declaration of Independence. During the war years, he served in Paris, negotiating French naval, military, and monetary assistance for the Revolution. Without this assistance, our victory over the British would have been impossible.

Franklin signed the Treaty of Paris, which officially ended the war on September 3, 1783, then returned home to become a member of the Constitutional Convention. He signed the Constitution as a member of the Pennsylvania delegation on September 17, 1787. The following year, just two years before his death, he finished the bulk of his *Autobiography*. His last public act was to sign a memorial to Congress urging the abolition of slavery.

from **AUTOBIOGRAPHY**

Arrival in Philadelphia

I have been the more particular in this description of my journey, and shall be so of my first entry into that city, that you may in your mind compare such unlikely beginnings with the figure I have since made there. I was in my working dress, my best cloaths being to come round by sea. I was dirty from my journey; my pockets were stuff'd out with shirts and stockings, and I knew no soul nor where to look for lodging. I was fatigued with travelling, rowing and want of rest, I was very hungry; and my whole stock of cash consisted of a Dutch dollar, and about a shilling in copper. The latter I gave the people of the boat for my passage, who at first refus'd it, on account of my rowing; but I insisted on their taking it. A man being sometimes more generous when he has but a little money than when he has plenty, perhaps thro' fear of being thought to have but little.

Then I walked up the street, gazing about till near the market-house I met a boy with bread. I had made many a meal on bread, and, inquiring where he got it, I went immediately to the baker's he directed me to, in Second-street, and ask'd for bisket, intending such as we had in Boston; but they, it seems, were not made in Philadelphia. Then I asked for a three-penny loaf, and was told they had none such. So not considering or knowing the difference of money, and the greater cheapness nor the names of his bread, I bad him give me three-penny worth of any sort. He gave me, accordingly, three great puffy rolls. I was surpriz'd at the quantity, but took it, and, having no room in my

From AUTOBIOGRAPHY. POOR RICHARD. LETTERS. Benjamin Franklin. The World's Great Books. D. Appleton and Company, 1899.

pockets, walk'd off with a roll under each arm, and eating the other. Thus I went up Market-street as far as Fourth-street, passing by the door of Mr. Read, my future wife's father; when she, standing at the door, saw me, and thought I made, as I certainly did, a most awkward, ridiculous appearance. Then I turned and went down Chesnut-street and part of Walnut-street, eating my roll all the way, and, coming round, found myself again at Market-street wharf, near the boat I came in, to which I went for a draught of the river water; and, being filled with one of my rolls, gave the other two to a woman and her child that came down the river in the boat with us, and were waiting to go farther.

Thus refreshed, I walked again up the street, which by this time had many clean-dressed people in it, who were all walking the same way. I joined them, and thereby was led into the great meeting-house of the Quakers near the market. I sat down among them, and, after looking round awhile and hearing nothing said, being very drowsy thro' labor and want of rest the preceding night, I fell fast asleep, and continu'd so till the meeting broke up, when one was kind enough to rouse me. This was, therefore, the first house I was in, or slept in, in Philadelphia. . . .

Project of Arriving at Moral Perfection

It was about this time I conceiv'd the bold and arduous project of arriving at moral perfection. I wish'd to live without committing any fault at any time; I would conquer all that either natural inclination, custom, or company might lead me into. As I knew, or thought I knew, what was right and wrong, I did not see why I might not always do the one and avoid the other. But I soon found I had undertaken a task of more difficulty than I had imagined. While my care was employ'd in guarding against one fault, I was often surprised by another; habit took the advantage of inattention; inclination was sometimes too strong for reason. I concluded, at length, that the mere speculative conviction that it was our interest to be completely virtuous was not sufficient to prevent our slipping; and that the contrary habits must be broken, and good ones acquired and established, before we can have any dependence on a steady, uniform rectitude of conduct. For this purpose I therefore contrived the following method.

In the various enumerations of the moral virtues I had met with in my reading, I found the catalogue more or less numerous, as different writers included more or fewer ideas under the same name. *Temperance*, for example, was by some confined to eating and drinking, while by others it was extended to mean the moderating of every other pleasure, appetite, inclination, or passion, bodily or mental, even to our avarice and ambition. I propos'd to myself, for the sake of clearness, to use rather more names, with fewer ideas annex'd to each, than a few names with more ideas; and I included under thirteen names of virtues all that at that time occurr'd to me as necessary or desirable, and annex'd to each a short precept, which fully express'd the extent I gave to its meaning.

These names of virtues, with their precepts, were:

1. *Temperance*
Eat not to dullness; drink not to elevation.

2. *Silence*
Speak not but what may benefit others or yourself; avoid trifling conversation.

3. *Order*
Let all your things have their places; let each part of your business have its time.

4. *Resolution*
Resolve to perform what you ought; perform without fail what you resolve.

5. *Frugality*
Make no expense but to do good to others or yourself; *i. e.,* waste nothing.

6. *Industry*
Lose no time; be always employ'd in something useful; cut off all unnecessary actions.

7. *Sincerity*
Use no hurtful deceit; think innocently and justly; and, if you speak, speak accordingly.

8. *Justice*
Wrong none by doing injuries, or omitting the benefits that are your duty.

9. *Moderation*
Avoid extremes; forbear resenting injuries so much as you think they deserve.

10. *Cleanliness*
Tolerate no uncleanliness in body, cloaths, or habitation.

11. *Tranquillity*
Be not disturbed at trifles, or at accidents common or unavoidable.

12. *Chastity*
Rarely use venery but for health or offspring, never to dullness, weakness, or the injury of your own or another's peace or reputation.

13. *Humility*
Imitate Jesus and Socrates.

My intention being to acquire the *habitude* of all these virtues, I judg'd it would be well not to distract my attention by attempting the whole at once, but to fix it on one of them at a time; and, when I should be master of that, then to proceed to another, and so on, till I should have gone thro' the thirteen; and, as the previous acquisition of some might facilitate the acquisition of certain others, I arrang'd them with that view, as they stand above. *Temperance* first, as it tends to procure that coolness and clearness of head, which is so necessary where constant vigilance was to be kept up, and guard maintained against the unremitting attraction of ancient habits, and the force of perpetual temptations. This being acquir'd and establish'd, *Silence* would be more easy; and my desire being to gain knowledge at the same time that I improv'd in virtue, and considering that in conversation it was obtain'd rather by the use of the ears than of the tongue, and therefore wishing to break a habit I was getting into of prattling, punning, and joking, which only made me acceptable to trifling company, I gave *Silence* the second place. This and the next, *Order*, I expected would allow me more time for attending to my project and my studies. *Resolution*, once become habitual, would keep me firm in my endeavors to obtain all the subsequent virtues; *Frugality* and *Industry* freeing me from my remaining debt, and producing affluence and independence, would make more easy the practice of *Sincerity* and *Justice*, etc., etc. Conceiving then that, agreeably to the advice of Pythagoras in his Golden Verses, daily examination would be necessary, I contrived the following method for conducting that examination.

I made a little book, in which I allotted a page for each of the virtues. I rul'd each page with red ink, so as to have seven columns, one for each day of the week, marking each column with a letter for the day. I cross'd these columns with thirteen red lines, marking the beginning of each line with the first letter of one of the virtues, on which line, and in its proper column, I might mark, by a little black spot, every fault I found upon examination to have been committed respecting that virtue upon that day.

I determined to give a week's strict attention to each of the virtues successively. Thus, in the first week, my great guard was to avoid every the least offence against *Temperance*, leaving the other virtues to their ordinary chance, only marking every evening the faults of the day. Thus, if in the first week I could keep my first line, marked T, clear of spots, I suppos'd the habit of that virtue so much strengthen'd, and its opposite weaken'd, that I might venture extending my attention to include the next, and for the following week keep both lines clear of spots.

Form of the pages

TEMPERANCE.							
EAT NOT TO DULLNESS; DRINK NOT TO ELEVATION.							
	S.	M.	T.	W.	T.	F.	S.
T.							
S.	*	*		*		*	
O.	**	*	*			*	*	
R.			*			*	
F.		*			*		
I.			*				
S.							
J.							
M.							
C.							
T.							
C.							
H.							

Proceeding thus to the last, I could go thro' a course compleat in thirteen weeks, and four courses in a year. And like him who, having a garden to weed, does not attempt to eradicate all the bad herbs at once, which would exceed his reach and his strength, but works on one of the beds at a time, and, having accomplish'd the first, proceeds to a second, so I should have, I hoped, the encouraging pleasure of seeing on my pages the progress I made in virtue, by clearing successively my lines of their spots, till in the end, by a number of courses, I should be happy in viewing a clean book, after a thirteen weeks' daily examination. . . .

The precept of *Order* requiring that *every part of my business should have its allotted time*, one page in my little book contain'd the following scheme of employment for the twenty-four hours of a natural day.

THE MORNING. *Question.* What good shall I do this day?	⎧ 5 ⎪ 6 ⎨ ⎪ ⎩ 7	Rise, wash, and address *Powerful Goodness!* Contrive day's business, and take the resolution of the day; prosecute the present study, and breakfast.
	8 9 10 11	} Work.
NOON.	⎰ 12 ⎱ 1	Read, or overlook my accounts, and dine.
	2 3 4 5	} Work.
EVENING. *Question.* What good have I done to-day?	⎧ 6 ⎪ 7 ⎨ 8 ⎪ ⎩ 9	Put things in their places. Supper. Music or diversion, or conversation. Examination of the day.
NIGHT.	⎧ 10 ⎪ 11 ⎪ 12 ⎨ 1 ⎪ 2 ⎪ 3 ⎩ 4	} Sleep.

I enter'd upon the execution of this plan for self-examination, and continu'd it with occasional intermissions for some time. I was surpris'd to find myself so much fuller of faults than I had imagined; but I had the satisfaction of seeing them diminish. To avoid the trouble of renewing now and then my little book, which, by scraping out the marks on the paper of old faults to make room for new ones in a new course, became full of holes, I transferr'd my tables and precepts to the ivory leaves of a memorandum book, in which the lines were drawn with red ink, that made a durable stain, and on those lines I mark'd my faults with a black-lead pencil, which marks I could easily wipe out with a wet sponge. After a while I went thro' one course only in a year, and afterward only one in several years, till at length I omitted them entirely, being employ'd in voyages and business abroad, with a multiplicity of affairs that interfered; but I always carried my little book with me. . . .

In truth, I found myself incorrigible with respect to *Order*; and now I am grown old, and my memory bad, I feel very sensibly the want of it. But, on the whole, tho' I never arrived at the perfection I had been so ambitious of obtaining, but fell far short of it, yet I was, by the endeavor, a better and a happier man than I otherwise should have been if I had not attempted it; as those who aim at perfect writing by imitating the engraved copies, tho' they never reach the wish'd-for excellence of those copies, their hand is mended by the endeavor, and is tolerable while it continues fair and legible.

It may be well my posterity should be informed that to this little artifice, with the blessing of God, their ancestor ow'd the constant felicity of his life, down to his 79th year, in which this is written. What reverses may attend the remainder is in the hand of Providence; but, if they arrive, the reflection on past happiness enjoy'd ought to help his bearing them with more resignation. To *Temperance* he ascribes his long-continued health, and what is still left to him of a good constitution; to *Industry* and *Frugality*, the early easiness of his circumstances and acquisition of his fortune, with all that knowledge that enabled him to be a useful citizen, and obtained for him some degree of reputation among the learned; to *Sincerity* and *Justice*, the confidence of his country, and the honorable employs it conferred upon him; and to the joint influence of the whole mass of the virtues, even in the imperfect state he was able to acquire them, all that evenness of temper, and that cheerfulness in conversation, which makes his company still sought for, and agreeable even to his younger acquaintance. I hope, therefore, that some of my descendants may follow the example and reap the benefit.

FOR UNDERSTANDING

1. What was the goal of the plan that Franklin describes in this selection?
2. What reason does Franklin give for putting *Temperance* first on his list of virtues?
3. How does Franklin define *Resolution*? *Frugality*? *Tranquillity*? Try to use your own words in your answer.
4. What are the three types of *Cleanliness* that Franklin considers important?
5. What was the final outcome of Franklin's plan?

FOR INTERPRETATION

1. Using the selections and what you know about Franklin from the unit introduction and the biographical note, defend the idea that Franklin's story portrays a man who rose "from rags to riches."
2. Argue the merits of Franklin's scheme for living a virtuous life.
3. Elsewhere in his *Autobiography*, Franklin says that he added *Humility* to his virtues only after a friend told him that he (Franklin) was a proud man. What evidence do you find in the selections that humility was a virtue Franklin lacked?
4. Discuss this statement: Franklin was not a religious man in the ordinary sense. He did not regularly attend church, read the Scriptures, or receive sacraments. Yet the selection from his *Autobiography* reveals him to be a very moral man.
5. Compare Franklin's list of virtues with some other list you may know, or with a made-up list of your own. What virtues on your list might make Franklin's more complete? Be sure not to duplicate a virtue he lists under another name.

FOR APPRECIATION

Style

Franklin is known for the simplicity, economy, and clarity of his style. Let us look closely at one of the paragraphs from the *Autobiography* to see how he achieves these effects.

Consider the paragraph on page 95 of the text, beginning "I made a little book. . . ." Here are the key parts of the three sentences in that paragraph:

I made a book . . . in which . . . a page. . . .
I rul'd each page . . . so as . . . columns . . . day . . . column . . . day.
I cross'd these columns . . . I found . . . virtue upon that day.

First notice that each sentence begins with *I*, the doer of the action. In each case *I* is followed by a verb telling what *I* did. Next, notice how a key word following each verb is picked up in the next sentence (*page, columns, day*).

This repetition of structure and key words links each sentence to the next and, along with the logical order in which Franklin expresses himself, makes the paragraph coherent. Coherence, in turn, helps to assure clarity.

1. Study the first sentence of the next paragraph in the text ("I determined to give. . . ."). Try to describe how it is linked to the last sentence of the previous paragraph.
2. What specific connective or linking word helps Franklin connect several other sentences in the second of the two paragraphs we have been discussing?

COMPOSITION

In a paragraph of about 100 words—the one beginning "I made a little book"—Franklin describes a simple process with great clarity. Following a method similar (though not necessarily identical) to his, write a paragraph of about the same length as Franklin's on a process with which you are familiar. (The process might be something like starting a car, making breakfast, playing an instrument, or swinging a hockey stick.) Pay special attention to *coherence*, the logical and orderly connection of your ideas.

from POOR RICHARD'S ALMANACK

He that lives upon hope will die fasting.

Fish and visitors smell in three days.

If your head is wax, don't walk in the sun.

Necessity never made a good bargain.

He that won't be counselled, can't be helped.

There are three things extremely hard: steel, a diamond, and to know one's self.

Keep thy shop, and thy shop will keep thee.

No gains without pains.

Diligence is the mother of good luck.

He that falls in love with himself will have no rivals.

Three may keep a secret if two of them are dead.

Fools make feasts, and wise men eat them.

God heals and the doctor takes the fee.

Early to bed, and early to rise, makes a man healthy, wealthy, and wise.

The rotten apple spoils his companions.

Lost time is never found again.

Now I have a sheep and cow, everybody bids me good morrow.

The cat in gloves catches no mice.

If Jack's in love, he's no judge of Jill's beauty.

Genius without education is like silver in the mine.

FOR UNDERSTANDING

The thoughts expressed in Franklin's sayings are not original with him. He drew from a variety of sources, though the wording is his own. Study the four sayings below, each written by Titan Leeds, the publisher of a rival almanac in the 1730s. In the list of Franklin sayings, can you find his paraphrase for each Leeds aphorism?

1. Bad hours and ill company have ruined many fine young people.
2. Necessity is a mighty weapon.
3. 'Tis best to make a good use of another's folly.
4. Be careful of the main chance, or it will never take care of you.

FOR INTERPRETATION

One of the main strengths of Franklin's sayings is that he usually does not state directly what he means. You must think about the quotation before the full meaning becomes clear. Thus, Franklin requires you to participate actively in the thought and *discover* it for yourself. Go back to the sayings and look again at three or four that you didn't understand. Think about them for a time; then try to write in your own words what you believe Franklin means.

FOR APPRECIATION

Style
Generally, Franklin's sayings are shorter than those of Leeds. Why might a brief saying be better than a longer one? Can you give other reasons why Franklin's sayings are better than Leeds's?

LANGUAGE AND VOCABULARY

Adage, aphorism, epigram, maxim, proverb, and *saying* all refer to briefly expressed words of wisdom or wit. Try to answer the following questions about these words. Use a dictionary if necessary. Use each word only once as an answer.

1. Which word is the most general in meaning?

2. Which word usually refers to a rule of conduct?

3. Which word generally implies that the bit of wisdom has been expressed with great wit?

4. Which word refers to wisdom that has gained credit through long use?

5. Which word refers to an old and familiar saying that states a basic truth?

6. Which word might best describe the sayings of Benjamin Franklin?

COMPOSITION

Try your own hand at saying something in as few words as possible. Below are ten wordy statements. Rewrite three of them in a manner similar to that of Franklin.

1. A person who is lazy probably will be a person who does not earn much money.

2. Nothing is more important to the successful completion of a task than a good beginning.

3. If something is working well, don't try to make it work better.

4. As long as people have jobs, their families will not go hungry, even though they may not have a lot to eat.

5. A wise person readily recognizes good advice.

6. One is more likely to get oneself into trouble from not being sufficiently careful than from not knowing enough about what one is doing.

7. If you try to do a job too quickly, you may make mistakes and may have to start all over again.

8. Empty-headed people are often the ones who do the most talking.

9. Although you may think you will never get over a particular injury or loss, you will eventually.

10. People ought to study the past so that they do not make the same mistakes as their predecessors.

Patrick Henry   1736–1799

George Washington has been called the Sword of the American Revolution, and Thomas Jefferson, the Pen. Patrick Henry was neither a great general nor a great writer, but he earned the title of the Trumpet of the Revolution for his fiery speeches, some of whose words still ring in the ears of Americans today. That we still admire Patrick Henry is not surprising; Thomas Jefferson, who took the opposite side from Henry on many political issues, nevertheless wrote that Patrick Henry throughout his life had been "the idol of his country beyond any man who ever lived."

The Trumpet of the Revolution was born on May 29, 1736, on his father's plantation in Hanover County, Virginia, then on the edge of the frontier. Henry had little formal schooling, but nonetheless passed an examination in 1760 that enabled him to practice law. A few years later, while in his twenties, he won an important case and in 1765 was selected for a seat in the House of Burgesses, Virginia's legislature. He had been there less than two weeks when he offered resolutions against the Stamp Act, claiming that England had no right to tax the colonies. One passage in his speech reminded King George III of England that Julius Caesar and Charles I had both been killed by their political opponents. According to legend, when he had completed this passage, members of his audience called out, "Treason! Treason!" To this outcry Patrick Henry replied, "If this be treason, make the most of it."

Patrick Henry was a Virginia delegate to both the First and Second Continental Congresses. Between the two congresses, at the Virginia provincial convention (1775), he delivered his famous "Liberty or Death" speech, which appears below. Although Henry was elected commander in chief of Virginia's regular military forces in 1775, it is as an orator and political figure that he is remembered. In July

PORTRAIT OF PATRICK HENRY

A lifelong champion of the republic, Patrick Henry is best remembered for his powerful, fiery speeches.

1776, Patrick Henry became the first elected governor of Virginia and was reelected to that position four more times. He was also a powerful leader in the colonial House of Burgesses and, after independence, in the General Assembly of his commonwealth. Although offered such federal posts as senator, secretary of state, and chief justice of the Supreme Court, Patrick Henry refused them all. He preferred to remain in the General Assembly of his native Virginia, to which he had been reelected just before he died in 1799.

LIBERTY OR DEATH

No man thinks more highly than I do of the patriotism, as well as abilities, of the very worthy gentlemen who have just addressed the house. But different men often see the same subject in different lights; and, therefore, I hope it will not be thought disrespectful to those gentlemen, if, entertaining as I do, opinions of a character very opposite to theirs, I should speak forth my sentiments freely, and without reserve. This is no time for ceremony. The question before this house is one of awful moment to the country. For my own part, I consider it as nothing less than a question of freedom or slavery. And in proportion to the magnitude of the subject, ought to be the freedom of the debate. It is only in this way that we can hope to arrive at truth, and fulfil the great responsibility which we hold to God and our country. Should I keep back my opinions at such a time, through fear of giving offence, I should consider myself as guilty of treason toward my country, and of an act of disloyalty toward the majesty of heaven, which I revere above all earthly kings.

Mr. President, it is natural to man to indulge in the illusions of hope. We are apt to shut our eyes against a painful truth—and listen to the song of that siren, till she transforms us into beasts. Is this the part of wise men, engaged in a great and arduous struggle for liberty? Are we disposed to be of the number of those, who having eyes, see not, and having ears, hear not, the things which so nearly concern their temporal salvation? For my part, whatever anguish of spirit it might

cost, I am willing to know the whole truth; know the worst, and to provide for it.

I have but one lamp by which my feet are guided; and that is the lamp of experience. I know of no way of judging of the future but by the past. And judging by the past, I wish to know what there has been in the conduct of the British ministry for the last ten years, to justify those hopes with which gentlemen have been pleased to solace themselves and the house? Is it that insidious smile with which our petition has been lately received? Trust it not, sir; it will prove a snare to your feet. Suffer not yourselves to be betrayed with a kiss. Ask yourselves how this gracious reception of our petition comports with those warlike preparations which cover our waters and darken our land. Are fleets and armies necessary to a work of love and reconciliation? Have we shown ourselves so unwilling to be reconciled, that force must be called in to win back our love? Let us not deceive ourselves, sir. These are the implements of war and subjugation—the last arguments to which kings resort. I ask gentlemen, sir, what means this martial array, if its purpose be not to force us to submission? Can gentlemen assign any other possible motive for it? Has Great Britain any enemy in this quarter of the world, to call for all this accumulation of navies and armies? No, sir, she has none. They are meant for us: they can be meant for no other. They are sent over to bind and rivet upon us those chains which the British ministry have been so long forging. And what have we to oppose to them? Shall we try argument? Sir, we have been trying that for the last ten years. Have we any thing new to offer upon the subject? Nothing. We have held the subject up in every light of which it is capable; but it has been all in vain. Shall we resort to

Note: There is no record of Henry's speeches. They are read as reconstructions pieced together from the notes and recollections of people who heard them. The material here is from SKETCHES OF THE LIFE AND CHARACTER OF PATRICK HENRY, William Wert.

entreaty and humble supplication? What terms shall we find, which have not been already exhausted? Let us not, I beseech you, sir, deceive ourselves longer. Sir, we have done every thing that could be done, to avert the storm which is now coming on. We have petitioned—we have remonstrated—we have supplicated—we have prostrated ourselves before the throne, and have implored its interposition to arrest the tyrannical hands of the ministry and parliament. Our petitions have been slighted; our remonstrances have produced additional violence and insult; our supplications have been disregarded; and we have been spurned, with contempt, from the foot of the throne. In vain, after these things, may we indulge the fond hope of peace and reconciliation. *There is no longer any room for hope.* If we wish to be free—if we mean to preserve inviolate those inestimable privileges for which we have been so long contending—if we mean not basely to abandon the noble struggle in which we have been so long engaged, and which we have pledged ourselves never to abandon, until the glorious object of our contest shall be obtained—we must fight! —I repeat it, sir, we must fight!! An appeal to arms and to the God of hosts, is all that is left us!

They tell us, sir, that we are weak—unable to cope with so formidable an adversary. But when shall we be stronger? Will it be the next week or the next year? Will it be when we are totally disarmed, and when a British guard shall be stationed in every house? Shall we gather strength by irresolution and inaction? Shall we acquire the means of effectual resistance by lying supinely on our backs, and hugging the delusive phantom of hope, until our enemies shall have bound us hand and foot? Sir, we are not weak, if we make a proper use of those means which the God of nature hath placed in our power. Three millions of people armed in the holy cause of liberty, and in such a country as that which we possess, are invincible by any force which our enemy can send against us. Be-sides, sir, we shall not fight our battles alone. There is a just God who presides over the destinies of nations, and who will raise up friends to fight our battles for us. The battle, sir, is not to the strong alone; it is to the vigilant, the active, the brave. Besides, sir, we have no election. If we were base enough to desire it, it is now too late to retire from the contest. There is no retreat but in submission and slavery! Our chains are forged. Their clanking may be heard on the plains of Boston! The war is inevitable—and let it come!! I repeat it, sir, let it come!!!

It is vain, sir, to extenuate the matter. Gentlemen may cry, peace, peace—but there is no peace. The war is actually begun! The next gale that sweeps from the north will bring to our ears the clash of resounding arms! Our brethren are already in the field! Why stand we here idle? What is it that gentlemen wish? What would they have? Is life so dear, or peace so sweet, as to be purchased at the price of chains and slavery? Forbid it, Almighty God!—I know not what course others may take; but as for me, give me liberty, or give me death!

FOR UNDERSTANDING

1. According to Patrick Henry's own statement, what was the basic question being debated by the Virginia convention?
2. What reasons does Henry give for suggesting that Great Britain could not be trusted at the time?
3. How does Henry argue against the notion that the colonies are too weak to fight the British?

FOR INTERPRETATION

1. In the early part of his speech, Henry says that "different men often see the same subject in different lights." To what subject is he referring here? How were some other men's "lights" different from his? Give an example of someone seeing things differently from you in light of experience different from your own.

2. What is the deeper significance of Henry's statement that he is loyal to "the majesty of heaven, . . . above all earthly kings"?

3. Try to suggest some reasons for the effectiveness and memorable quality of Henry's famous concluding words.

FOR APPRECIATION

Structure

A case could easily be made that Patrick Henry in this speech tramples upon "the rules of persuasion." It is true that he uses emotional language at times—for example, "the holy cause of liberty." His speech, however, is not a mere emotional outburst but a carefully structured oration. After a relatively calm introduction, tension rises when he points up such facts as the presence of British fleets and troops. Next, he goes on to anticipate the arguments of the other side, then arrives at a stirring conclusion. As you analyze the structure of the speech in greater detail, try answering the following questions.

1. Henry gathers momentum as he moves along. In what two places, just before the final climax, does he intensify his pitch by repetitions? Why is repetition an effective oratorical device?

2. Study the conclusion of the speech carefully. What two or three key items in the final paragraph are anticipated in the *opening* of the speech?

3. Even within a section of the speech, Patrick Henry sometimes has a distinct, well-structured rhythm. Look, for instance, at the end punctuation of the final paragraph. What interesting pattern do you find?

4. Notice the large number of questions Henry asks, especially in the middle sections of the speech. Questions such as these, whose answers are intended to be obvious, are known as *rhetorical questions*. What might be the point of a speaker's using such questions?

LANGUAGE AND VOCABULARY

Synonyms

In the third paragraph from the end of the speech, notice this string of verbs: *petitioned, remonstrated, supplicated, implored*. They are roughly in climactic order, moving from the mildest to the strongest. To petition is to make a (more or less formal) request. To remonstrate is to object by arguing. To supplicate is to beseech humbly. To implore is to beg earnestly.

Match each of the four words below with its best synonym in Patrick Henry's sequence of verbs. Why might he have preferred the longer, more formal words that he used?

object   entreat   plead   pray

Thomas Paine   1737–1809

It would be difficult to find a more vigorous and dedicated champion of human rights in his day than Thomas Paine. He not only defended the rights of farmers and laborers but also those of women, the elderly, and the poor. Along with Benjamin Franklin, he drew up the Pennsylvania constitution, which gave voting rights to a broader range of people than ever before. He also attacked the institution of slavery and wrote the preamble to the first legislative measure passed in America for the emancipation of slaves—a 1780 act of the Pennsylvania legislature. That this same man should have been one of the earliest and strongest advocates of independence from Britain is no surprise.

Yet oddly enough, this great defender of liberty and advocate of independence for the colonies was born in England and did not even come to America until 1774. Within a year and a half of his arrival, however, he had published *Common Sense* (January 1776), a pamphlet arguing for independence from Great Britain. It immediately became a best seller. In the same year, he began a series of sixteen essays called *The Crisis,* issued periodically from 1776 to 1783. Historians agree that these essays aided the American cause enormously and contributed significantly to the colonies' ultimate victory.

After a few years of relative inactivity following the Revolution, Paine went to England and France on a business matter in 1787 and was soon embroiled in the French Revolution. *The Rights of Man,* which he published in two parts (1791 and 1792), defended that revolution and urged the English to create a republic. Paine was subsequently tried in England for treason and sentenced to banishment, but by 1792 he was already a French citizen living in France. When the tide of affairs in France turned against his faction, he spent eleven months in prison. James Monroe, then American minister to France, arranged Paine's release from prison and nursed the ailing writer back to health in his own home. Before his prison stay and after his release, Paine wrote *The Age of Reason* (1794–1795), an

PORTRAIT OF THOMAS PAINE
Charles W. Peale and James Watson
National Portrait Gallery, Smithsonian Institution

An eloquent defender of liberty and human rights, Thomas Paine died penniless and persecuted.

attack on organized religion that won him many new enemies.

After several more years in France, Thomas Paine finally returned to America in 1802 at the urging of Thomas Jefferson, who had become President the previous year. The old patriot found new persecution directed at him by those who feared his radical views and hated both Jefferson and Paine. Outbursts of malevolent criticism, as well as poverty and ill health, dogged this champion of human rights until his death in 1809. The ultimate indignity came in New Rochelle, New York, in 1806, when he was denied the right to vote by a federal official on the charge that he was not an American citizen.

from **THE CRISIS**

Number I

These are the times that try men's souls. The summer soldier and the sunshine patriot will in this crisis, shrink from the service of his country; but he that stands it NOW, deserves the love and thanks of man and woman. Tyranny, like hell, is not easily conquered; yet we have this consolation with us, that the harder the conflict, the more glorious the triumph. What we obtain too cheap, we esteem too lightly; 'tis dearness only that gives everything its value. Heaven knows how to put a proper price upon its goods; and it would be strange indeed, if so celestial an article as FREEDOM should not be highly rated. Britain, with an army to enforce her tyranny, has declared that she has a right (*not only to* TAX) but *"to* BIND *us in* ALL CASES WHATSO-EVER,"[1] and if being *bound in that manner,* is not slavery, then is there not such a thing as slavery upon earth. Even the expression is impious, for so unlimited a power can belong only to God.

Whether the independence of the continent was declared too soon, or delayed too long, I will not now enter into as an argument; my own simple opinion is, that had it been eight months earlier, it would have been much better. We did not make a proper use of last winter, neither could we, while we were in a dependent state. However, the fault, if it were one, was all our own; we have none to blame but ourselves. But no great deal is lost yet; all that Howe[2] has been doing for this month past, is rather a ravage than a conquest, which the spirit of the Jerseys[3] a

year ago would have quickly repulsed, and which time and a little resolution will soon recover.

I have as little superstition in me as any man living, but my secret opinion has ever been, and still is, that God Almighty will not give up a people to military destruction, or leave them unsupportedly to perish, who have so earnestly and so repeatedly sought to avoid the calamities of war, by every decent method which wisdom could invent. Neither have I so much of the infidel in me, as to suppose that he has relinquished the government of the world, and given us up to the care of devils; and as I do not, I cannot see on what grounds the king of Britain can look up to heaven for help against us: a common murderer, a highwayman, or a house-breaker, has as good a pretence as he.

'Tis surprising to see how rapidly a panic[4] will sometimes run through a country. All nations and ages have been subject to them: Britain has trembled like an ague at the report of a French fleet of flat-bottomed boats; and in the fourteenth century the whole En-

---

1. **in all cases whatsoever.** Paine is referring to the first paragraph of the Declaratory Act, February 24, 1766, which stated: "That the King's Majesty . . . had, hath, and of right ought to have full power and authority to make laws . . . to bind the colonies and people of America . . . in all cases whatsoever."

2. **Howe,** Sir William Howe, British commander in chief in America, 1775–1778. Howe was directly in charge of the British armies during Bunker Hill, Long Island, and other early battles, as well as at Brandywine and Germantown.

3. **the Jerseys.** At the time, the state of New Jersey was divided into East and West Jersey.

4. **a panic.** Paine is probably referring to the "cowardly and disaffected inhabitants" who spread false rumors that the war was lost. (See the last paragraph of the essay.)

From THE SELECTED WORK OF TOM PAINE, Howard Fast, ed. Duell, Sloan and Pearce, New York, 1945.

glish army, after ravaging the kingdom of France, was driven back like men petrified with fear; and this brave exploit was performed by a few broken forces collected and headed by a woman, Joan of Arc. Would that heaven might inspire some Jersey maid to spirit up her countrymen, and save her fair fellow sufferers from ravage and ravishment! Yet panics, in some cases, have their uses; they produce as much good as hurt. Their duration is always short; the mind soon grows through them, and acquires a firmer habit than before. But their peculiar advantage is, that they are the touchstones of sincerity and hypocrisy, and bring things and men to light, which might otherwise have lain forever undiscovered. In fact, they have the same effect on secret traitors which an imaginary apparition would have upon a private murderer. They sift out the hidden thoughts of man, and hold them up in public to the world. Many a disguised tory[5] has lately shown his head, that shall penitentially solemnize with curses the day on which Howe arrived upon the Delaware.

As I was with the troops at Fort Lee,[6] and marched with them to the edge of Pennsylvania, I am well acquainted with many circumstances, which those who live at a distance, know but little or nothing of. Our situation there, was exceedingly cramped, the place being a narrow neck of land between the North River and the Hackensack. Our force was inconsiderable, being not one-fourth so great as Howe could bring against us. We had no army at hand to have relieved the garrison, had we shut ourselves up and stood on our defence. Our ammunition, light artillery, and the best part of our stores, had been removed, on the apprehension that Howe would endeavor to penetrate the Jerseys, in which case Fort Lee could be of no use to us; for it must occur to every thinking man, whether in the army or not, that these kind of field forts are only for temporary purposes, and last in use no longer than the enemy directs his force against the particular object,

which such forts are raised to defend. Such was our situation and condition at Fort Lee on the morning of the 20th of November, when an officer arrived with information that the enemy with 200 boats had landed about seven miles above: Major General Greene, who commanded the garrison, immediately ordered them under arms, and sent express to General Washington at the town of Hackensack, distant by the way of the ferry, six miles. Our first object was to secure the bridge over the Hackensack, which laid up the river between the enemy and us, about six miles from us, and three from them. General Washington arrived in about three-quarters of an hour, and marched at the head of the troops towards the bridge, which place I expected we should have a brush for; however, they did not choose to dispute it with us, and the greatest part of our troops went over the bridge, the rest over the ferry except some which passed at a mill on a small creek, between the bridge and the ferry, and made their way through some marshy grounds up to the town of Hackensack, and there passed the river. We brought off as much baggage as the wagons could contain, the rest was lost. The simple object was to bring off the garrison, and march them on till they could be strengthened by the Jersey or Pennsylvania militia, so as to be enabled to make a stand. We stayed four days at Newark, collected our out-posts with some of the Jersey militia, and marched out twice to meet the enemy, on being informed that they were advancing, though our numbers were greatly inferior to theirs. Howe, in my little opinion, committed a great error in generalship in not throwing a body of forces off from Staten Island through Amboy, by which means he might have seized all our stores at Brunswick, and intercepted

5. **tory** (usually capitalized), here: an American who favored reconciliation with Britain rather than independence. Also, a British political party at that time.
6. **Fort Lee.** Paine was stationed at Fort Lee, New Jersey, in September 1776, when General Greene appointed him aide-de-camp.

our march into Pennsylvania: but if we believe the power of hell to be limited, we must likewise believe that their agents are under some providential control.

I shall not now attempt to give all the particulars of our retreat to the Delaware; suffice for the present to say, that both officers and men, though greatly harassed and fatigued, without rest, covering, or provision, the inevitable consequences of a long retreat, bore it with a manly and martial spirit. All their wishes centred in one, which was, that the country would turn out and help them to drive the enemy back. Voltaire has remarked that King William never appeared to full advantage but in difficulties and in action; the same remark may be made on General Washington, for the character fits him! There is a natural firmness in some minds which cannot be unlocked by trifles, but which, when unlocked, discovers a cabinet of fortitude; and I reckon it among those kind of public blessings, which we do not immediately see, that God hath blest him with uninterrupted health, and given him a mind that can even flourish upon care.

I shall conclude this paper with some miscellaneous remarks on the state of our affairs; and shall begin with asking the following question: Why is it that the enemy have left the New-England provinces, and made these middle ones the seat of war? The answer is easy: New-England is not infested with tories, and we are. I have been tender in raising the cry against these men, and I used numberless arguments to show them their danger, but it will not do to sacrifice a world either to their folly or their baseness. The period is now arrived, in which either they or we must change our sentiments, or one or both must fall. And what is a tory? Good God! what is he? I should not be afraid to go with a hundred whigs[7] against a thousand tories, were they to attempt to get into arms. Every tory is a coward; for servile, slavish, self-interested fear is the foundation of toryism; and a man under such influence, though he may be cruel, never can be brave.

But, before the line of irrecoverable separation be drawn between us, let us reason the matter together: your conduct is an invitation to the enemy, yet not one in a thousand of you has heart enough to join him. Howe is as much deceived by you as the American cause is injured by you. He expects you will all take up arms, and flock to his standard, with muskets on your shoulders. Your opinions are of no use to him, unless you support him personally, for 'tis soldiers, and not tories that he wants.

I once felt all that kind of anger, which a man ought to feel, against the mean principles that are held by the tories: a noted one, who kept a tavern at Amboy, was standing at his door, with as pretty a child in his hand, about eight or nine years old, as I ever saw, and after speaking his mind as freely as he thought was prudent, finished with this unfatherly expression, *"Well! give me peace in my day."* Not a man lives on the continent but fully believes that a separation must some time or other finally take place, and a generous parent should have said, *"If there must be trouble let it be in my day, that my child may have peace,"* and this single reflection, well applied, is sufficient to awaken every man to duty. Not a place upon earth might be so happy as America. Her situation is remote from all the wrangling world, and she has nothing to do but to trade with them. A man can distinguish himself between temper and principle, and I am as confident, as I am that God governs the world, that America will never be happy till she gets clear of foreign dominion. Wars, without ceasing, will break out till that period arrives, and the continent must in the end be conqueror; for though the flame of liberty may sometimes cease to shine, the coal can never expire.

America did not, nor does not want

7. **whigs** (usually capitalized), the political party in England in the eighteenth and nineteenth centuries that opposed the Tories. In the American Revolution, a Whig was an American who supported the war against England.

force; but she wanted a proper application of that force. Wisdom is not the purchase of a day, and it is no wonder that we should err at the first setting off. From an excess of tenderness, we were unwilling to raise an army, and trusted our cause to the temporary defence of a well-meaning militia.[8] A summer's experience has now taught us better; yet with those troops, while they were collected, we were able to set bounds to the progress of the enemy, and, thank God! they are again assembling. I always consider militia as the best troops in the world for a sudden exertion, but they will not do for a long campaign. Howe, it is probable, will make an attempt on this city;[9] should he fail on this side the Delaware, he is ruined: if he succeeds, our cause is not ruined. He stakes all on his side against a part on ours; admitting he succeeds, the consequence will be, that armies from both ends of the continent will march to assist their suffering friends in the middle states; for he cannot go everywhere; it is impossible. I consider Howe the greatest enemy the tories have; he is bringing a war into their country, which, had it not been for him and partly for themselves, they had been clear of. Should he now be expelled, I wish with all the devotion of a *Christian,* that the names of whig and tory may never more be mentioned; but should the tories give him encouragement to come, or assistance if he come, I as sincerely wish that our next year's arms may expel them from the continent, and that congress appropriate their possessions to the relief of those who have suffered in well doing. A single successful battle next year will settle the whole. America could carry on a two years' war by the confiscation of the property of disaffected persons; and be made happy by their expulsion. Say not that this is revenge, call it rather the soft resentment of a suffering people, who, having no object in view but the *good* of *all,* have staked their *own all* upon a seemingly doubtful event. Yet it is folly to argue against determined hardness; eloquence may strike the ear, and the language of sorrow draw forth the tear of compassion, but nothing can reach the heart that is steeled with prejudice.

Quitting this class of men, I turn with the warm ardor of a friend to those who have nobly stood, and are yet determined to stand the matter out: I call not upon a few, but upon all; not on *this* state or *that* state, but on *every* state; up and help us; lay your shoulders to the wheel; better have too much force than too little, when so great an object is at stake. Let it be told to the future world, that in the depth of winter, when nothing but hope and virtue could survive, that the city and the country, alarmed at one common danger, came forth to meet and to repulse it. Say not that thousands are gone, turn out your tens of thousands; throw not the burden of the day upon Providence, but *"show your faith by your works,"* that God may bless you. It matters not where you live, or what rank of life you hold, the evil or the blessing will reach you all. The far and the near, the home counties and the back, the rich and the poor, will suffer or rejoice alike. The heart that feels not now, is dead: the blood of his children will curse his cowardice, who shrinks back at a time when a little might have saved the whole, and made *them* happy. (I love the man that can smile at trouble; that can gather strength from distress, and grow brave by reflection.) 'Tis the business of little minds to shrink; but he whose heart is firm, and whose conscience approves his conduct, will pursue his principles unto death. My own line of reasoning is to myself as straight and clear as a ray of light. Not all the treasures of the world, so far as I believe, could have induced me to support an offensive war, for I think it murder; but if a thief breaks into my house, burns and destroys my property, and kills or threatens to

8. **militia,** a citizen army, as distinct from a professional army. Paine, like Washington, wanted a permanent army raised for the duration of the war.
9. **this city,** Philadelphia, where Paine arranged for the publication of this essay. Howe in fact wintered in Philadelphia in 1777–1778, while Washington and his troops were at Valley Forge, just outside the city.

kill me, or those that are in it, and to *"bind me in all cases whatsoever,"* to his absolute will, am I to suffer it? What signifies it to me, whether he who does it is a king or a common man; my countryman, or not my countryman; whether it be done by an individual villain or an army of them? If we reason to the root of things we shall find no difference; neither can any just cause be assigned why we should punish in the one case and pardon in the other. Let them call me rebel, and welcome, I feel no concern from it; but I should suffer the misery of devils, were I to make a whore of my soul by swearing allegiance to one whose character is that of a sottish, stupid, stubborn, worthless, brutish man.[10] I conceive likewise a horrid idea in receiving mercy from a being, who at the last day shall be shrieking to the rocks and mountains to cover him, and fleeing with terror from the orphan, the widow, and the slain of America.

There are cases which cannot be over-done by language, and this is one. There are persons too who see not the full extent of the evil which threatens them; they solace them-selves with hopes that the enemy, if he suc-ceed, will be merciful. Is this the madness of folly, to expect mercy from those who have refused to do justice; and even mercy, where conquest is the object, is only a trick of war; the cunning of the fox is as murderous as the violence of the wolf; and we ought to guard equally against both. Howe's first object is partly by threats and partly by promises, to terrify or seduce the people to deliver up their arms and to receive mercy. The ministry recommended the same plan to Gage,[11] and this is what the tories call making their peace, *"a peace which passeth all understanding,"* indeed! A peace which would be the immediate fore-runner of a worse ruin than any we have yet thought of. Ye men of Pennsylvania, do rea-son upon these things! Were the back coun-ties to give up their arms, they would fall an easy prey to the Indians, who are all armed; this perhaps is what some tories would not be sorry for. Were the home counties to deliver up their arms, they would be exposed to the resentment of the back counties, who would then have it in their power to chastise their defection at pleasure. And were any one state to give up its arms, *that* state must be garri-soned by Howe's army of Britains and Hes-sians[12] to preserve it from the anger of the rest. Mutual fear is the principal link in the chain of mutual love, and woe be to that state that breaks the compact. Howe is mercifully inviting you to barbarous destruction, and men must be either rogues or fools that will not see it. I dwell not upon the powers of imagination; I bring reason to your ears; and in language as plain as A, B, C, hold up truth to your eyes.

I thank God that I fear not. I see no real cause for fear. I know our situation weil and can see the way out of it. While our army was collected, Howe dared not risk a battle, and it is no credit to him that he decamped from the White Plains,[13] and waited a mean opportuni-ty to ravage the defenceless Jerseys; but it is great credit to us, that, with a handful of men, we sustained an orderly retreat for near an hundred miles, brought off our ammuni-tion, all our field pieces, the greatest part of our stores, and had four rivers to pass. None can say that our retreat was precipitate, for we were near three weeks in performing it, that the country might have time to come in. Twice we marched back to meet the enemy, and remained out till dark. The sign of fear was not seen in our camp, and had not some of the cowardly and disaffected inhabitants spread false alarms through the country, the

---

10. **brutish man.** Paine is referring to King George III, king of England from 1760 to 1820.
11. **Gage,** General Thomas Gage (1721–1787), who preceded Howe as commander in chief of the British armed forces.
12. **Hessians,** German mercenary troops who were hired by the British to fight against American forces. Many of them came from a region in Germany called Hesse.
13. **White Plains,** an area north of New York City, where Washington and Howe fought an indecisive battle in October 1776.

Jerseys had never been ravaged. Once more we are again collected and collecting, our new army at both ends of the continent is recruiting fast, and we shall be able to open the next campaign with sixty thousand men, well armed and clothed. This is our situation, and who will may know it. By perseverance and fortitude we have the prospect of a glorious issue; by cowardice and submission, the sad choice of a variety of evils—a ravaged country—a depopulated city—habitations without safety, and slavery without hope—our homes turned into barracks and bawdy-houses for Hessians, and a future race to provide for, whose fathers we shall doubt of. Look on this picture and weep over it! and if there yet remains one thoughtless wretch who believes it not, let him suffer it unlamented.

FOR UNDERSTANDING

1. In what sense does Paine use the verb *try* in the first sentence of the essay?
2. To what three specific types of criminal does Paine indirectly compare George III?
3. What famous American does Paine praise highly? What does Paine say of him?
4. What was the great hope of Washington's army as it retreated across New Jersey?
5. What does Paine mean by an "offensive war"? What reason does he give for not supporting such a war? What kind of war does he believe the American Revolution to be?

FOR INTERPRETATION

1. Why is it ironic that Paine called General Howe the greatest enemy the American Tories had? How does he justify this observation?
2. Paine argues that the Tory hope of avoiding a war with Britain is a vain hope. What fundamental assumption underlies this view? What is your own opinion of this assumption? What arguments would you use to support your opinion?

3. How does Paine go about arguing that God Himself is on the side of those favoring independence from England?
4. Interpret the following quotation from the essay: "Is this the madness of folly, to expect mercy from those who have refused to do justice."
5. Argue for or against the proposition that Paine's views, as expressed in *The Crisis,* "Number 1," were indeed "common sense."

FOR APPRECIATION

Author's Intention
One of Paine's intentions was to stir the hearts of the troops that remained loyal to Washington. Put yourself in the place of one of these men and try to point out two or three phrases or sentences that might have raised your spirits.

Another intention of the author was to rally the support of those still aloof from the battle or predisposed toward the Tories. What are some of the details that Paine uses to help realize this intention?

LANGUAGE AND VOCABULARY

1. The word *propaganda* may be defined as the spreading of ideas, information, or rumor for the purpose of helping or injuring an institution, a cause, or a person. Using this definition, argue that Paine was or was not a *propagandist.*
2. Look up the origin of the word *propaganda,* and be prepared to share your findings with your classmates.

COMPOSITION

Thomas Paine wrote effectively because he was writing to rally support for a cause he really believed in. Think about something you believe in, some concern or issue you'd like others to view as you do. Write a paragraph or two making a convincing argument for believing as you do and building a case that will sway your reader to share your beliefs.

Thomas Jefferson

1743–1826

The Greek philosopher Plato argued in his *Republic* that the best possible ruler for a country would be a "philosopher-king." When Thomas Jefferson became the third President of the United States in 1801, our country was indeed led by a "philosopher-president" of the highest order. Jefferson acquired a lifelong passion for reading in youth and received a thorough classical education, studying two years at the College of William and Mary. Then he spent five years (1762–1767) as an apprentice law student, reading not only law books but also ancient classics, English literature, and political philosophy. Because of his zeal for learning, Jefferson achieved a scholarly knowledge of such fields as science, languages, and philosophy. He read all the great thinkers of his time and applied their ideas, notably in the Declaration of Independence. Jefferson was also a connoisseur and patron of the arts; in fact, he designed his home, Monticello, and planned the buildings and campus of the University of Virginia, which he founded in 1824.

Jefferson believed deeply that every human being was entitled to freedom and happiness. It was the function of government to secure for people such "natural rights." He would not support the new Constitution until the Bill of Rights, with its guarantees of individual freedoms, was adopted. Jefferson also believed that a good government rules by the consent of the governed and in the interests of all citizens, not by and for a privileged few.

In 1769, Thomas Jefferson became a member of Virginia's legislature, the House of Burgesses, in his mid-twenties. His first great contribution to the Revolutionary cause, however, was his pamphlet *A Summary View of the Rights of British America,* published in 1774. In this document he argued persuasively that Parliament had no authority in the colonies. After this, his political career unfolded rapidly. He was elected delegate to the Second Continental Congress, 1775–1776, where he

THOMAS JEFFERSON
Rembrandt Peale
New York Historical Society, New York City

A man of supreme intelligence and ability, Jefferson has been called "America's philosopher-president."

wrote the Declaration of Independence. He served in the Virginia House of Representatives, 1776–1779, was elected governor of Virginia, 1779–1781, and headed the Virginia delegation to Congress in 1783. He was appointed minister to France, replacing Benjamin Franklin, and serving 1785–1789. He went on to become our first secretary of state, 1789–1794, under George Washington, then served as Vice President under John Adams, 1797–1801. The peak of his political career was reached during his two terms as President, 1801–1809.

After 1809, Jefferson turned his attention mostly to the University of Virginia, an institution "based on the illimitable freedom of the human mind to explore every subject."

Thomas Jefferson died on July 4, 1826, the fiftieth anniversary of the Declaration of Independence.

DECLARATION OF INDEPENDENCE
In Congress, July 4, 1776

The Unanimous Declaration of the Thirteen United States of America

When in the course of human events, it becomes necessary for one people to dissolve the political bands which have connected them with another, and to assume among the powers of the earth the separate and equal station to which the Laws of Nature and of Nature's God entitle them, a decent respect to the opinions of mankind requires that they should declare the causes which impel them to the separation.

We hold these truths to be self-evident, that all men are created equal, that they are endowed by their Creator with certain unalienable rights, that among these are life, liberty, and the pursuit of happiness. That to secure these rights, governments are instituted among men, deriving their just powers from the consent of the governed. That whenever any form of government becomes destructive of these ends, it is the right of the people to alter or to abolish it, and to institute new government, laying its foundation on such principles and organizing its powers in such form, as to them shall seem most likely to effect their safety and happiness. Prudence, indeed, will dictate that governments long established should not be changed for light and transient causes; and accordingly all experience hath shown, that mankind are more disposed to suffer, while evils are sufferable, than to right themselves by abolishing the forms to which they are accustomed. But when a long train of abuses and usurpations,[1] pursuing invariably the same object evinces a design to reduce them under absolute despotism, it is their right, it is their duty, to throw off such government, and to provide new guards for their future security. Such has been the patient sufferance of these Colonies; and such is now the necessity which constrains them to alter their former systems of government. The history of the present King of Great Britain is a history of repeated injuries and usurpations, all having in direct object the establishment of an absolute tyranny over these States. To prove this, let facts be submitted to a candid world.

He has refused his assent to laws, the most wholesome and necessary for the public good.

He has forbidden his Governors to pass laws of immediate and pressing importance, unless suspended in their operation till his assent should be obtained; and when so suspended, he has utterly neglected to attend to them.

He has refused to pass other laws for the accommodation of large districts of people, unless those people would relinquish the right of representation in the legislature, a right inestimable to them and formidable to tyrants only.

He has called together legislative bodies at places unusual, uncomfortable, and distant from the depository of their public records, for the sole purpose of fatiguing them into compliance with his measures.

He has dissolved representative houses

---

1. **usurpations** (yü sər pā' shənz), unjust or unlawful seizures of power or position belonging to another.

SIGNING OF THE DECLARATION OF INDEPENDENCE
John Trumbull, Yale University Art Gallery

repeatedly, for opposing with manly firmness his invasions on the rights of the people.

He has refused for a long time, after such dissolutions, to cause others to be elected; whereby the legislative powers, incapable of annihilation, have returned to the people at large for their exercise; the State remaining in the meantime exposed to all the dangers of invasion from without and convulsions within.

He has endeavored to prevent the population of these States; for that purpose obstructing the laws for naturalization of foreigners; refusing to pass others to encourage their migration hither, and raising the conditions of new appropriations of lands.

He has obstructed the administration of justice, by refusing his assent to laws for establishing judiciary powers.

He has made judges dependent on his will alone, for the tenure of their offices, and the amount and payment of their salaries.

He has erected a multitude of new offices, and sent hither swarms of officers to harass our people, and eat out their substance.

He has kept among us, in times of peace, standing armies without the consent of our legislatures.

He has affected to render the military independent of and superior to the civil power.

He has combined with others to subject us to a jurisdiction foreign to our constitution, and unacknowledged by our laws; giving his assent to their acts of pretended legislation:

For quartering large bodies of armed troops among us:

For protecting them, by a mock trial,

from punishment for any murders which they should commit on the inhabitants of these States:

For cutting off our trade with all parts of the world:

For imposing taxes on us without our consent:

For depriving us in many cases of the benefits of trial by jury:

For transporting us beyond seas to be tried for pretended offences:

For abolishing the free system of English laws in a neighbouring Province,[2] establishing therein an arbitrary government, and enlarging its boundaries so as to render it at once an example and fit instrument for introducing the same absolute rule into these Colonies:

For taking away our Charters, abolishing our most valuable laws, and altering fundamentally the forms of our governments:

For suspending our own Legislatures, and declaring themselves invested with power to legislate for us in all cases whatsoever.

He has abdicated government here, by declaring us out of his protection and waging war against us.

He has plundered our seas, ravaged our coasts, burnt our towns, and destroyed the lives of our people.

He is at this time transporting large armies of foreign mercenaries to compleat the works of death, desolation, and tyranny, already begun with circumstances of cruelty and perfidy scarcely paralleled in the most barbarous ages, and totally unworthy the head of a civilized nation.

He has constrained our fellow citizens taken captive on the high seas to bear arms against their country, to become the executioners of their friends and brethren, or to fall themselves by their hands.

He has excited domestic insurrections amongst us, and has endeavoured to bring on the inhabitants of our frontiers the merciless Indian savages, whose known rule of warfare is an undistinguished destruction of all ages, sexes, and conditions.

In every stage of these oppressions we have petitioned for redress in the most humble terms: our repeated petitions have been answered only by repeated injury. A prince whose character is thus marked by every act which may define a tyrant, is unfit to be the ruler of a free people.

Nor have we been wanting in attention to our British brethren. We have warned them from time to time of attempts by their Legislature to extend an unwarrantable jurisdiction over us. We have reminded them of the circumstances of our emigration and settlement here. We have appealed to their native justice and magnanimity, and we have conjured[3] them by the ties of our common kindred to disavow these usurpations, which would inevitably interrupt our connections and correspondence. They too have been deaf to the voice of justice and of consanguinity.[4] We must, therefore, acquiesce in the necessity, which denounces[5] our separation, and hold them, as we hold the rest of mankind, enemies in war, in peace friends.

We, therefore, the Representatives of the United States of America, in General Congress assembled, appealing to the Supreme Judge of the world for the rectitude of our intentions, do, in the name, and by authority of the good people of these Colonies, solemnly publish and declare, That these United Colonies are, and of right ought to be Free and Independent States; that they are absolved from all allegiance to the British Crown, and that all political connection between them and the State of Great Britain is

---

2. **neighbouring Province.** This refers to Quebec, acquired by Britain in the French and Indian War and enlarged to include much of the land between the Ohio and Mississippi Rivers.

3. **conjured** (kon′ jŭrd), here: called upon solemnly.

4. **consanguinity** (kon′sang gwin′ ə tē), blood relationship.

5. **denounces,** here: proclaims.

and ought to be totally dissolved; and that as Free and Independent States they have full power to levy war, conclude peace, contract alliances, establish commerce, and to do all other acts and things which independent States may of right do. And for the support of this declaration, with a firm reliance on the protection of Divine Providence, we mutually pledge to each other our lives, our fortunes and our sacred honor.

FOR UNDERSTANDING

1. What reason for writing the Declaration does Jefferson give in its first paragraph?
2. According to the Declaration, where does a government get its powers?
3. What are the "unalienable rights" that Jefferson mentions?
4. What person or thing does Jefferson blame most for the ills of the colonies?
5. What pledge did the signers of the Declaration make to each other?

FOR INTERPRETATION

1. What do you suppose Jefferson meant by "the Laws of Nature and of Nature's God"? How might such laws differ from or be the same as other laws?
2. Jefferson basically mentions four "self-evident" truths. Name them. Then argue for or against the notion that they are in fact self-evident.
3. Jefferson says that it is the "right and duty" of mankind to throw off "absolute despotism." What does he mean by the latter phrase? Why would it be the "duty" of mankind to throw off such a despotism?
4. Compare the attitude expressed in the Declaration toward the British people with that toward King George III.
5. Argue for or against the notion that the Declaration of Independence was a piece of "propaganda." (See page 110 in the Paine study notes for a definition of *propaganda.*) How would you compare Paine's *The Crisis* with the Declaration of Independence in terms of purpose and style? in terms of the place each holds in our history?

FOR APPRECIATION

Style and Concreteness

1. Jefferson has often been praised for his writing style. Pick out and write on a piece of paper two or three phrases or sentences that you think are particularly well expressed.
2. Well-chosen words and phrases and a smooth and clear style help a writer to persuade someone of her or his point of view. But language alone is not likely to win an argument if one is trying to convince a mature, thoughtful audience. The bulk of Jefferson's Declaration is composed of solid, *concrete* details that help *prove* his case against the king of England.

How many reasons for declaring independence does Jefferson give? Which three or four would you have considered most persuasive if you had been an American colonist at the time? At one point in the Declaration, Jefferson shifts from "He" as a paragraph opener to "For." Why does he do this?

COMPOSITION

Write a persuasive composition addressed to a specific audience. Try to convince them of your point of view on some issue of importance to you. (For example, you might address your family, school, or government about duties or responsibilities you feel people your age should or should not exercise.) Or you might try to persuade your readers to share a personal opinion of yours (for example, that one athlete or film director is more valuable than others in the same field.)

Organize your composition like Jefferson's Declaration; that is, begin with an introduction and end with a summing up, but make the middle part—which will give your reasons—the longest part of your work.

Philip Freneau   1752–1832

Philip Freneau is commonly known as the poet of the American Revolution, a title he earned by publishing such poems as "American Liberty," "General Gage's Soliloquy," and "General Gage's Confession" on the eve of the Revolution. Later, his poems are said to have lifted the spirits of the soldiers at Valley Forge and elsewhere during the darkest days of the war. In the early 1780s Freneau worked as a writer and editor for the *Freeman's Journal,* in which he poured forth a steady stream of satirical, anti-British poetry. Far from being an ivory-tower poet, Freneau served a brief term in the militia in 1778. Captured by the British in 1780, he was treated brutally and starved while a prisoner.

It would be a mistake, however, to think of Freneau only as a poet of the Revolution. The first American poet to regard himself as a professional, he spent a lifetime writing a wide variety of poems—poems of romantic fancy (such as "The Indian Student"), poems of life at sea, philosophical poems, and excellent nature poetry. Though he both experienced and wrote about the Revolution and the War of 1812, many of his best lyrics do not mention either of these wars, or even his favorite theme, freedom.

Philip Freneau was also a farmer, a first-rate sea captain, and a noteworthy journalist and editor. In this last capacity, he edited a Jeffersonian paper from 1791 to 1793 that severely attacked Alexander Hamilton, causing the latter to accuse Freneau of being Jefferson's anti-Federalist mouthpiece.

Freneau spent his last years in New Jersey, where his family had a plantation in Mount

PORTRAIT OF PHILIP FRENEAU
Known as "the poet of the American Revolution," Freneau was also a farmer, editor, and sea captain.

Pleasant, Monmouth County. He had been educated there at the College of New Jersey—now called Princeton University—and had roomed with James Madison, who became the fourth president of the United States. The final edition of Freneau's poems that was published during his lifetime appeared in 1815.

To the Memory of the Brave Americans

Under General Greene, in South Carolina,
who fell in the action of September 8, 1781.

At Eutaw springs the valiant died:
Their limbs with dust are cover'd o'er—
Weep on, ye springs, your tearful tide;
How many heroes are no more!

If in this wreck of ruin, they   5
Can yet be thought to claim a tear,
O smite thy gentle breast, and say
The friends of freedom slumber here!

Thou, who shalt trace this bloody plain,
If goodness rules thy generous breast,   10
Sigh for the wasted rural reign;
Sigh for the shepherds, sunk to rest!

Stranger, their humble graves adorn;
You too may fall, and ask a tear:
'Tis not the beauty of the morn   15
That proves the evening shall be clear—

They saw their injur'd country's woe;
The flaming town, the wasted field;
Then rush'd to meet the insulting foe;
They took the spear—but left the shield,   20

Led by thy conquering genius, GREENE,
The Britons they compell'd to fly:
None distant view'd the fatal plain,
None griev'd, in such a cause, to die—

But, like the Parthian, fam'd of old,   25
Who, flying, still their arrows threw;
These routed Britons, full as bold,
Retreated, and retreating slew.

Now rest in peace, our patriot band;
Though far from Nature's limits thrown,   30
We trust, they find a happier land,
A brighter sun-shine of their own.

The Wild Honey Suckle

Fair flower, that dost so comely grow,
Hid in this silent, dull retreat,
Untouched thy honied blossoms blow,
Unseen thy little branches greet:
    No roving foot shall crush thee here,   5
    No busy hand provoke a tear.

By Nature's self in white arrayed,
She bade thee shun the vulgar eye,
And planted here the guardian shade,
And sent soft waters murmuring by;   10
    Thus quietly thy summer goes,
    Thy days declining to repose.

Smit with those charms, that must decay,
I grieve to see your future doom;
They died—nor were those flowers more gay,   15
The flowers that did in Eden bloom;
    Unpitying frosts, and Autumn's power
    Shall leave no vestige of this flower.

From morning suns and evening dews
At first thy little being came: 20
If nothing once, you nothing lose,
For when you die you are the same;
    The space between, is but an hour,
    The frail duration of a flower.

From POEMS OF FRENEAU. Harry Hayden Clark, ed., Hafner Publishing Co., New York.

UNDERSTANDING AND APPRECIATION

"To the Memory of the Brave Americans"

1. Personification is a figure of speech that gives animals, ideas, or inanimate objects human forms or qualities. Find an example of personification in the first stanza of this poem.

2. A defining quality of poetry is structured sound. In the third stanza of Freneau's poem, what two consonant sounds are used repeatedly throughout? How many words can you find in which both sounds are present in the same word?

3. What is the effect of having a stranger "trace" the battlefield after the battle?

4. What consolation does the poet offer the slain in the last stanza?

"The Wild Honey Suckle"

1. The poem is about a flower—the wild honey suckle. Point to some specific details that describe the flower in terms of the senses.

2. Although the poem is truly about a flower, it also manages to suggest that human life—like the life of the flower—is brief. How does it manage to do this?

3. What is the significance of the poet's bringing Eden into the poem?

4. What does the honey suckle symbolize?

5. Hyperbole is a figure of speech in which the poet consciously exaggerates in order to heighten an effect. Find an example of hyperbole in the last stanza. How does this figure of speech relate to the symbolic meaning of the flower?

Phillis Wheatley

c. 1753–1784

Phillis Wheatley, America's first black poet, was born in Senegal, Africa, about 1753. In 1761, she was brought to America on a slave ship and was purchased by a Boston merchant, John Wheatley. Growing fond of her and recognizing her talent, he and his wife gave her a good education and eventually—in 1773—her freedom. Wheatley published a poem in a newspaper when she was only thirteen. She had a book, *Poems on Various Subjects, Religious and Moral,* published in London in 1773, after a visit there.

During the Revolutionary War, Phillis Wheatley enthusiastically supported American independence and wrote several poems on behalf of the patriot cause. In April 1776, one of these, printed here, originally appeared in the *Pennsylvania Magazine,* which at the time was edited by Thomas Paine. Washington was so impressed by this poem that he invited Wheatley to the American army camp, where he received her in his headquarters.

Wheatley's poetry is derivative and typical of her century, as one might expect from someone as young as she. Nevertheless, there was sufficient genius in her early work to win praise from a wide range of people, including Benjamin Franklin and Voltaire. It seems probable that her talents would have developed as she grew older, but we shall never know. Although she completed a second volume of her

ENGRAVING OF PHILLIS WHEATLEY, Artist Unknown
National Portrait Gallery, Smithsonian Institution

verse, which was advertised in 1779, the only copy of it was stolen and lost before it reached publication. She died in poverty and obscurity about the age of thirty.

To His Excellency General Washington

Celestial choir! enthron'd in realms of light,
    Columbia's scenes[1] of glorious toils I write.
While freedom's cause her anxious breast alarms,
She flashes dreadful in refulgent arms.

1. **Columbia's scenes.** Columbia is a female figure who personifies America. The poet is telling the "celestial choirs" (angels) that she is going to write about America's scenes of glorious toils—the Revolution.

See mother earth her offspring's fate bemoan,   5
And nations gaze at scenes before unknown!
See the bright beams of heaven's revolving light
Involved in sorrows and the veil of night!
    The goddess[2] comes, she moves divinely fair,
Olive and laurel binds her golden hair: 10
Wherever shines this native of the skies,
Unnumber'd charms and recent graces rise.
    Muse![3] bow propitious while my pen relates
How pour her armies through a thousand gates,
As when Eolus[4] heaven's fair face deforms,   15
Enwrapp'd in tempest and a night of storms;
Astonish'd ocean feels the wild uproar,
The refluent surges beat the sounding shore;
Or thick as leaves in Autumn's golden reign,
Such, and so many, moves the warrior's train.   20
In bright array they seek the work of war,
Where high unfurl'd the ensign waves in air.
Shall I to Washington their praise recite?
Enough thou[5] know'st them in fields of fight.
Thee, first in peace and honours,—we demand   25
The grace and glory of thy martial band.
Fam'd for thy valour, for thy virtues more,
Hear every tongue thy guardian aid implore!
    One century scarce perform'd its destined round,
When Gallic powers Columbia's fury found;[6]   30
And so may you, whoever dares disgrace
The land of freedom's heaven-defended race!
Fix'd are the eyes of nations on the scales,[7]
For in their hopes Columbia's arm prevails.
Anon Britannia[8] droops the pensive head,   35
While round increase the rising hills of dead.
Ah! cruel blindness to Columbia's state!
Lament thy thirst of boundless power too late.

---

2. **The goddess,** that is, Columbia.
3. **Muse!** Here the poet is addressing a classical goddess who presided over poetry. It was common in Wheatley's time for a poet to ask the assistance of a muse, as she does here.
4. **Eolus,** the Greek god of the winds.
5. **thou.** The reference here and subsequently is to George Washington. The point being made here is that Washington does not need to hear praise of the armies because he knows of their bravery.
6. **Gallic . . . found,** French forces (Gallic powers) that America fought powerfully in the French and Indian War, which France lost.
7. **the scales,** the scales of justice or of fate.
8. **Britannia,** England.

WASHINGTON AT DORCHESTER HEIGHTS, Gilbert Stuart
Museum of Fine Arts, Boston

Proceed, great chief,[9] with virtue on thy side,
Thy ev'ry action let the goddess guide.   **40**
A crown, a mansion, and a throne that shine,
With gold unfading, WASHINGTON! be thine.

9. **great chief,** Washington.

From THE POEMS OF PHILLIS WHEATLEY, edited by Julian D. Mason,
Jr., Copyright © 1966 The University of North Carolina Press. Reprinted
by permission of the publisher.

UNDERSTANDING AND INTERPRETATION

1. What images does the poet use to suggest the size of the American army? Is Wheatley using hyperbole here?
2. According to the poet, for what two personal qualities was Washington famous?
3. According to the poem, what was the cause of the British decision to fight against the colonies?
4. What is the significance of the fact that "olive and laurel" bind Columbia's hair? What does the olive branch symbolize? the laurel wreath?
5. What three things does the poet wish for Washington? Are these to be taken literally or symbolically, or both? Do you think these are appropriate wishes? Why or why not?

Washington Irving   1783–1859

In 1820, Sydney Smith, an English minister, asked in the pages of the *Edinburgh Review:* "In the four quarters of the globe, who reads an American book? or goes to an American play? or looks at an American picture or statue?" He did not have to wait long for his answer. Washington Irving was our first genuine author of *belles lettres*—witty, entertaining essays that incorporate history, biography, legend, and a fertile imagination. The British who had delighted in looking down on the American colonies were happy to welcome him to the company of Byron and Coleridge and Scott. America, to be sure, had produced political writers, competent historians, and even a few poets in the years before the Revolution; but our stylists were few in number. That Irving came to a literary career through a side door, as it were, makes his life and his achievements all the more fascinating.

Born in New York City, the youngest of eleven children, he began reading for the law at the age of sixteen, but his heart was not in his studies. "I was always fond of visiting new scenes and observing strange characters and manners," he later recalled. "Even when a mere child I began my traveling, and made many tours of discovery into foreign parts and unknown regions of my native city, to the frequent alarm of my parents." Travel continued to entice him, first to the Hudson Valley and Canada, then to France, Italy, and Holland. He spent two years in Europe as a literary vagabond, reading whatever he pleased, observing European customs, and attending the theater.

When he became a lawyer at the age of twenty-three, his family expected him to settle down. Irving preferred the literary to the legal world. He and his brother William published the *Salmagundi* papers—satirical essays and poems written to ridicule local theater, politics, and fashions. The next year, 1809, he began *A History of New York,* signing it Diedrich Knickerbocker. It was one of America's first pieces of comic literature, a burlesque of serious history that dared to satirize the persons and

PORTRAIT OF WASHINGTON IRVING
Rintoul & Rockwood Studio
National Portrait Gallery, Smithsonian Institution

policies of John Adams, Madison, and Jefferson as well as the Dutch administrator and symbol of the old aristocracy, Peter Stuyvesant "the Headstrong." One of Irving's favorite character studies in this history is still a delight today: the "golden reign of Wouter Van Twiller," governor of New Amsterdam. A "model of majesty and lordly grandeur," he was "exactly five feet six inches in height, and six feet five inches in circumference," and when he stood erect "he had not a little the appearance of a beer barrel on skids."

As Diedrich Knickerbocker, Irving established an enviable reputation. New York feted the young, witty lawyer, but again he was restless and by no means convinced that he could sustain a literary career. He worked for a while

Sunnyside, Washington Irving's residence near Tarrytown, New York. He retired there in 1836, and spent the next two decades writing and being a country squire.

in the family hardware business, then served as a staff colonel during the War of 1812. He sailed again for Europe in 1815, little realizing that he would remain abroad for seventeen years. For business reasons he lived chiefly in England; but when the family business failed, he had to find other means to support himself, and literary work seemed the most attractive. Always a collector of tales, a keen observer, and an amateur artist, he naturally drifted into writing essays and sketches. Under the pseudonym Geoffrey Crayon, Gent., these writings were published serially in the United States in 1819–1820. When gathered into a volume called *The Sketch Book,* published in England in 1820, Irving was greeted with a reception such as no American author had ever received from the

British public. Lord Byron declared that "Crayon is very good"; Sir Walter Scott and Thomas Moore, personal friends by now, gave him public acclaim. American literary critics were as quick to recognize his considerable achievement.

As a visitor to England, Irving had filled his journals with anecdotes, quotations, travel notes, and details of English life. *The Sketch Book* is a graceful reworking of these notes. Most of the thirty-six pieces recount the pleasures of the English countryside, typical village life, and landmarks no visitor should miss. With much genial humor, he describes Westminster Abbey, Stratford-on-Avon, the Boar's Head Tavern, an English Christmas, and more. Six of the book's chapters, however, treat American subjects; not surprisingly, these were the ones to achieve lasting fame, especially "Rip Van Winkle" and "The Legend of Sleepy Hollow."

Irving wrote these American narratives as though he were recounting well-known legends of colonial Dutch-American life in the lower Hudson Valley. We know now that he borrowed the tales from German folklore and simply blended the two cultures, creating the first American short stories. Irving could not have foreseen how widely his *Sketch Book* would be read in the next decades, but he had certainly caught the mood of romantic melancholy so popular with both English and American readers. "The truth presses home upon us as we advance in life," wrote Irving in his notebook, "that everything around us is transient and uncertain. . . . When I look back for a few short years, what changes of all kind have taken place, what wrecks of time and fortune are strewn around me." In these tales and essays of time past, Irving had found his talent, and he knew it.

Bracebridge Hall followed in 1822. Like so many sequels, it hardly measures up to the charms of his first success. This collection of Irving sketches begins in England, then moves across the channel to France and Spain for its settings; but only "Dolph Heyliger" and "The Storm-Ship" are remembered. Irving's interest in tales of the supernatural continued to grow, however, and he crossed the Rhine to visit Dresden and Vienna, to explore "the rich mine of German literature." *Tales of a Traveller* (1824) resulted, a highly uneven collection but notable for "The Devil and Tom Walker," a short story far superior to the Gothic romances—tales filled with magic, mystery, and medieval trappings— that make up most of the volume.

During the next eight years before his return to the United States, Irving made two diplomatic journeys to Spain, living for a time in the Alhambra as attaché to the American envoy; he also served in London as secretary to the American legation. These were highly productive years in terms of his reputation abroad and of newly published volumes. A life of Christopher Columbus appeared in 1828, and *The Conquest of Granada,* a mixture of romance and history, in 1829. Both works were the result of prodigious research, but there is no doubt that *The Alhambra* (1832) struck the familiar chord and more clearly reflects Irving's genuine talents. His American public called it the "Spanish Sketch

Book." They welcomed his return to the leisurely narrative, the legends of barbaric Spain, the sights and sounds of an opulent era of history.

The United States seemed strange to Irving when he returned in 1832, and some of his American critics were quick to suggest that his long stay abroad had "Europeanized" him. Irving set out to prove the charge exaggerated. After a journey to the West, he set down his impressions in *A Tour on the Prairies* (1835). Compared with H. L. Ellsworth's account of the same trip, Irving's impressions are more quaint than accurate, more idealized than realistic. But his eastern readers were accustomed to this aspect of his art. They were willing to accept the picturesque, even the sentimental, because Irving could hold their attention with intimate, vibrant description. What is more, they had never seen a savage Indian or a buffalo hunt. Irving never again equaled the quality of his *Sketch Book* prose, but he supplied his public with what they wanted. *Astoria* (1836) is a history of John Jacob Astor's fur trade in the Northwest, written from original materials in a New York library, not from notes of personal expeditions. *The Adventures of Captain Bonneville* (1837) recounts life in the Rocky Mountains, but it too was done under Astor's patronage.

Perhaps if Irving had not achieved such acclaim as a young man, his later years would not strike us as anticlimactic. In 1836, he moved into Sunnyside, his home near Tarrytown, New York, and for the next two decades he played country squire and successful writer pursued by politicians and public alike.

American letters will always be in Irving's debt. For too long the colonies and the young nation had been fed on political tracts, harsh sermons, propaganda, and factual histories. What James Fenimore Cooper did for the early American novel and William Cullen Bryant for poetry, Irving did for *belles lettres*. These three American writers earned international reputations at a time when American letters were in their infancy, acquainting European audiences with American regional life and establishing a respect for literary artists in a young country only beginning to discover its cultural heritage. It is not surprising that Washington Irving's sketches and short stories inspired Hawthorne and Poe and many of their contemporaries. Irving set high standards.

THE DEVIL AND TOM WALKER

A few miles from Boston in Massachusetts, there is a deep inlet, winding several miles into the interior of the country from Charles Bay, and terminating in a thickly-wooded swamp or morass. On one side of this inlet is a beautiful dark grove; on the opposite side the land rises abruptly from the water's edge into a high ridge, on which grow a few scattered oaks of great age and immense size. Under one of these gigantic trees, according to old stories, there was a great amount of treasure buried by Kidd[1] the pirate. The inlet allowed a facility to bring the money in a boat secretly and at night to the very foot of the hill; the elevation of the place permitted a good look-out to be kept that no one was at hand; while the remarkable trees formed good landmarks by which the place might easily be found again. The old stories add, moreover, that the devil presided at the hiding of the money, and took it under his guardianship; but this, it is well known, he always does with buried treasure, particularly when it has been ill-gotten. Be that as it may, Kidd never returned to recover his wealth; being shortly after seized at Boston, sent out to England, and there hanged for a pirate.

About the year 1727, just at the time that earthquakes were prevalent in New England, and shook many tall sinners down upon their knees, there lived near this place a meagre, miserly fellow, of the name of Tom Walker. He had a wife as miserly as himself; they were so miserly that they even conspired to cheat each other. Whatever the woman could lay hands on, she hid away; a hen could not cackle but she was on the alert to secure the new-laid egg. Her husband was continually prying about to detect her secret hoards, and many and fierce were the conflicts that took place about what ought to have been common property. They lived in a forlorn-looking house that stood alone, and had an air of starvation. A few straggling savin-trees, emblems of sterility, grew near it; no smoke ever curled from its chimney; no traveller stopped at its door. A miserable horse, whose ribs were as articulate as the bars of a gridiron, stalked about a field, where a thin carpet of moss, scarcely covering the ragged beds of pudding-stone, tantalized and balked his hunger; and sometimes he would lean his head over the fence, look piteously at the passer-by, and seem to petition deliverance from this land of famine.

The house and its inmates had altogether a bad name. Tom's wife was a tall termagant, fierce of temper, loud of tongue, and strong of arm. Her voice was often heard in wordy warfare with her husband; and his face sometimes showed signs that their conflicts were not confined to words. No one ventured, however, to interfere between them. The lonely wayfarer shrunk within himself at the horrid clamor and clapper-clawing; eyed the den of discord askance; and hurried on his way, rejoicing, if a bachelor, in his celibacy.

One day that Tom Walker had been to a distant part of the neighborhood, he took what he considered a short cut homeward, through the swamp. Like most short cuts, it was an ill-chosen route. The swamp was thickly grown with great gloomy pines and hemlocks, some of them ninety feet high, which made it dark at noonday, and a retreat for all the owls of the neighborhood. It was full of pits and quagmires,[2] partly covered with weeds and mosses, where the green sur-

---

1. **William Kidd** (1645?–1701), known as Captain Kidd, tried and convicted for murder and piracy; hanged in London, 1701.
2. **quagmires** (kwag' mīrz), areas of soft, wet, miry land that give way underfoot.

face often betrayed the traveller into a gulf of black, smothering mud: there were also dark and stagnant pools, the abodes of the tadpole, the bullfrog, and the water-snake; where the trunks of pines and hemlocks lay half-drowned, half-rotting, looking like alligators sleeping in the mire.

Tom had long been picking his way cautiously through this treacherous forest; stepping from tuft to tuft of rushes and roots, which afforded precarious footholds among deep sloughs; or pacing carefully, like a cat, along the prostrate trunks of trees; startled now and then by the sudden screaming of the bittern, or the quacking of a wild duck rising on the wing from some solitary pool. At length he arrived at a firm piece of ground, which ran out like a peninsula into the deep bosom of the swamp. It had been one of the strongholds of the Indians during their wars with the first colonists. Here they had thrown up a kind of fort, which they had looked upon as almost impregnable, and had used as a place of refuge for their squaws and children. Nothing remained of the old Indian fort but a few embankments, gradually sinking to the level of the surrounding earth, and already overgrown in part by oaks and other forest trees, the foliage of which formed a contrast to the dark pines and hemlocks of the swamp.

It was late in the dusk of evening when Tom Walker reached the old fort, and he paused there awhile to rest himself. Any one but he would have felt unwilling to linger in this lonely, melancholy place, for the common people had a bad opinion of it, from the stories handed down from the time of the Indian wars; when it was asserted that the savages held incantations here, and made sacrifices to the evil spirit.

Tom Walker, however, was not a man to be troubled with any fears of the kind. He reposed himself for some time on the trunk of a fallen hemlock, listening to the boding cry of the tree-toad, and delving with his walking-staff into a mound of black mould at his feet.

As he turned up the soil unconsciously, his staff struck against something hard. He raked it out of the vegetable mould, and lo! a cloven skull, with an Indian tomahawk buried deep in it, lay before him. The rust on the weapon showed the time that had elasped since this deathblow had been given. It was a dreary memento of the fierce struggle that had taken place in this last foothold of the Indian warriors.

"Humph!" said Tom Walker, as he gave it a kick to shake the dirt from it.

"Let that skull alone!" said a gruff voice. Tom lifted up his eyes, and beheld a great black man seated directly opposite him, on the stump of a tree. He was exceedingly surprised, having neither heard nor seen any one approach; and he was still more perplexed on observing, as well as the gathering gloom would permit, that the stranger was neither negro nor Indian. It is true he was dressed in a rude half-Indian garb, and had a red belt or sash swathed round his body; but his face was neither black nor copper-color, but swarthy and dingy, and begrimed with soot, as if he had been accustomed to toil among fires and forges. He had a shock of coarse black hair, that stood out from his head in all directions, and bore an axe on his shoulder.

He scowled for a moment at Tom with a pair of great red eyes.

"What are you doing on my grounds?" said the black man, with a hoarse growling voice.

"Your grounds!" said Tom, with a sneer, "no more your grounds than mine; they belong to Deacon Peabody."

"Deacon Peabody be d——d," said the stranger, "as I flatter myself he will be, if he does not look more to his own sins and less to those of his neighbors. Look yonder, and see how Deacon Peabody is faring."

Tom looked in the direction that the stranger pointed, and beheld one of the great trees, fair and flourishing without, but rotten at the core, and saw that it had been nearly hewn through, so that the first high wind was likely to blow it down. On the bark of the tree was scored the name of Deacon Peabody, an eminent man, who had waxed wealthy by driving shrewd bargains with the Indians. He now looked around, and found most of the tall trees marked with the name of some great man of the colony, and all more or less scored by the axe. The one on which he had been seated, and which had evidently just been hewn down, bore the name of Crown-inshield; and he recollected a mighty rich man of that name, who made a vulgar display of wealth, which it was whispered he had acquired by buccaneering.

"He's just ready for burning!" said the black man, with a growl of triumph. "You see I am likely to have a good stock of firewood for winter."

"But what right have you," said Tom, "to cut down Deacon Peabody's timber?"

"The right of a prior claim," said the other. "This woodland belonged to me long before one of your white-faced race put foot upon the soil."

"And pray, who are you, if I may be so bold?" said Tom.

"Oh, I go by various names. I am the wild huntsman in some countries; the black miner in others. In this neighborhood I am known by the name of the black woodsman. I am he to whom the red men consecrated this spot, and in honor of whom they now and then roasted a white man, by way of sweet-smelling sacrifice. Since the red men have been exterminated by you white savages, I amuse myself by presiding at the persecutions of Quakers and Anabaptists;[3] I am the great patron and prompter of slave-dealers, and the grand-master of the Salem witches."

"The upshot of all which is, that, if I mistake not," said Tom, sturdily, "you are he commonly called Old Scratch."

"The same, at your service!" replied the black man, with a half civil nod.

Such was the opening of this interview, according to the old story; though it has al-

most too familiar an air to be credited. One would think that to meet with such a singular personage, in this wild, lonely place, would have shaken any man's nerves; but Tom was a hard-minded fellow, not easily daunted, and he had lived so long with a termagant wife, that he did not even fear the devil.

It is said that after this commencement they had a long and earnest conversation together, as Tom returned homeward. The black man told him of great sums of money buried by Kidd the pirate, under the oak trees on the high ridge, not far from the morass. All these were under his command, and protected by his power, so that none could find them but such as propitiated his favor. These he offered to place within Tom Walker's reach, having conceived an especial kindness for him; but they were to be had only on certain conditions. What these conditions were may be easily surmised, though Tom never disclosed them publicly. They must have been very hard, for he required time to think of them, and he was not a man to stick at trifles when money was in view. When they had reached the edge of the swamp, the stranger paused. "What proof have I that all you have been telling me is true?" said Tom. "There's my signature," said the black man, pressing his finger on Tom's forehead. So saying, he turned off among the thickets of the swamp, and seemed, as Tom said, to go down, down, down, into the earth, until nothing but his head and shoulders could be seen, and so on, until he totally disappeared.

When Tom reached home, he found the black print of a finger burnt, as it were, into his forehead, which nothing could obliterate.

The first news his wife had to tell him was the sudden death of Absalom Crowninshield, the rich buccaneer. It was announced in the

3. **Anabaptists,** a radical Protestant sect, originating in Zurich in 1524, that advocated return to primitive Christianity, denied necessity of infant baptism, and opposed union of church and state.

papers, with the usual flourish, that "A great man had fallen in Israel."

Tom recollected the tree which his black friend had just hewn down, and which was ready for burning. "Let the freebooter roast," said Tom, "who cares!" He now felt convinced that all he had heard and seen was no illusion.

He was not prone to let his wife into his confidence; but as this was an uneasy secret, he willingly shared it with her. All her avarice was awakened at the mention of hidden gold, and she urged her husband to comply with the black's man terms, and secure what would make them wealthy for life. However Tom might have felt disposed to sell himself to the devil, he was determined not to do so to oblige his wife; so he flatly refused, out of the mere spirit of contradiction. Many and bitter were the quarrels they had on the subject; but the more she talked, the more resolute was Tom not to be damned to please her.

At length she determined to drive the bargain on her own account, and if she succeeded, to keep all the gain to herself. Being of the same fearless temper as her husband, she set off for the old Indian fort towards the close of a summer's day. She was many hours absent. When she came back, she was reserved and sullen in her replies. She spoke something of a black man, whom she had met about twilight hewing at the root of a tall tree. He was sulky, however, and would not come to terms: she was to go again with a propitiatory offering, but what it was she forebore to say.

The next evening she set off again for the swamp, with her apron heavily laden. Tom waited and waited for her, but in vain; midnight came, but she did not make her appearance: morning, noon, night returned, but still she did not come. Tom now grew uneasy for her safety, especially as he found she had carried off in her apron the silver tea-pot and spoons, and every portable article of value. Another night elapsed, another morning

came; but no wife. In a word, she was never heard of more.

What was her real fate nobody knows, in consequence of so many pretending to know. It is one of those facts which have become confounded by a variety of historians. Some asserted that she lost her way among the tangled mazes of the swamp, and sank into some pit or slough; others, more uncharitable, hinted that she had eloped with the household booty, and made off to some other province; while others surmised that the tempter had decoyed her into a dismal quagmire, on the top of which her hat was found lying. In confirmation of this, it was said a great black man, with an axe on his shoulder, was seen late that very evening coming out of the swamp, carrying a bundle tied in a check apron, with an air of surly triumph.

The most current and probable story, however, observes, that Tom Walker grew so anxious about the fate of his wife and his property, that he set out at length to seek them both at the Indian fort. During a long summer's afternoon he searched about the gloomy place, but no wife was to be seen. He called her name repeatedly, but she was nowhere to be heard. The bittern alone responded to his voice, as he flew screaming by: or the bull-frog croaked dolefully from a neighboring pool. At length, it is said, just in the brown hour of twilight, when the owls began to hoot, and the bats to flit about, his attention was attracted by the clamor of carrion crows hovering about a cypress-tree. He looked up, and beheld a bundle tied in a check apron, and hanging in the branches of the tree, with a great vulture perched hard by, as if keeping watch upon it. He leaped with joy; for he recognized his wife's apron, and supposed it to contain the household valuables.

"Let us get hold of the property," said he, consolingly to himself, "and we will endeavor to do without the woman."

As he scrambled up the tree, the vulture

A contemporary illustrator of Irving's works, Quidor was an American Romantic whose imaginative style of painting matched the flamboyance of his life.

THE DEVIL AND TOM WALKER
John Quidor
Cleveland Museum of Art

spread its wide wings, and sailed off, screaming, into the deep shadows of the forest. Tom seized the checked apron, but, woeful sight! found nothing but a heart and liver tied up in it!

Such, according to this most authentic old story, was all that was to be found of Tom's wife. She had probably attempted to deal with the black man as she had been accustomed to deal with her husband; but though a female scold is generally considered a match for the devil, yet in this instance she appears to have had the worse of it. She must

have died game, however; for it is said Tom noticed many prints of cloven feet deeply stamped about the tree, and found handfuls of hair, that looked as if they had been plucked from the coarse black shock of the woodman. Tom knew his wife's prowess by experience. He shrugged his shoulders, as he looked at the signs of a fierce clapper-clawing. "Egad," said he to himself, "Old Scratch must have had a tough time of it!"

Tom consoled himself for the loss of his property, with the loss of his wife, for he was a man of fortitude. He even felt something like gratitude towards the black woodman, who, he considered, had done him a kindness. He sought, therefore, to cultivate a further acquaintance with him, but for some time without success; the old blacklegs played shy, for whatever people may think, he is not always to be had for calling for: he knows how to play his cards when pretty sure of his game.

At length, it is said, when delay had whetted Tom's eagerness to the quick, and prepared him to agree to anything rather than not gain the promised treasure, he met the black man one evening in his usual woodman's dress, with his axe on his shoulder, sauntering along the swamp, and humming a tune. He affected to receive Tom's advances with great indifference, made brief replies, and went on humming his tune.

By degrees, however, Tom brought him to business, and they began to haggle about the terms on which the former was to have the pirate's treasure. There was one condition which need not be mentioned, being generally understood in all cases where the devil grants favors; but there were others about which, though of less importance, he was inflexibly obstinate. He insisted that the money found through his means should be employed in his service. He proposed, therefore, that Tom should employ it in the black traffic; that is to say, that he should fit out a slave-ship. This, however, Tom resolutely refused: he was bad enough in all conscience; but the devil himself could not tempt him to turn slave-trader.

Finding Tom so squeamish on this point, he did not insist upon it, but proposed, instead, that he should turn usurer; the devil being extremely anxious for the increase of usurers, looking upon them as his peculiar people.

To this no objections were made, for it was just to Tom's taste.

"You shall open a broker's shop in Boston next month," said the black man.

"I'll do it to-morrow, if you wish," said Tom Walker.

"You shall lend money at two per cent a month."

"Egad, I'll charge four!" replied Tom Walker.

"You shall extort bonds, foreclose mortgages, drive the merchants to bankruptcy"——

"I'll drive them to the d——," cried Tom Walker.

"You are the usurer for my money!" said black-legs with delight. "When will you want the rhino?"[4]

"This very night."

"Done!" said the devil.

"Done!" said Tom Walker.—So they shook hands and struck a bargain.

A few days' time saw Tom Walker seated behind his desk in a counting-house in Boston.

His reputation for a ready-moneyed man, who would lend money out for a good consideration, soon spread abroad. Everybody remembers the time of Governor Belcher, when money was particularly scarce. It was a time of paper credit. The country had been deluged with government bills, the famous Land Bank had been established; there had been a rage for speculating; the people had run mad with schemes for new settlements; for building cities in the wilderness; land-jobbers went about with maps of grants, and townships, and Eldorados,[5] lying nobody knew where, but which everybody was ready to purchase. In a word, the great speculating fever which breaks out every now and then in the country, had raged to an alarming degree, and everybody was dreaming of making sudden fortunes from nothing. As usual the fever had subsided; the dream had gone off,

4. **rhino,** money, cash (origin of the word unknown).
5. **Eldorado,** the legendary "city of gold" in the Americas that sixteenth-century Spanish explorers searched for in vain.

and the imaginary fortunes with it; the patients were left in doleful plight, and the whole country resounded with the consequent cry of "hard times."

At this propitious time of public distress did Tom Walker set up as usurer in Boston. His door was soon thronged by customers. The needy and adventurous; the gambling speculator; the dreaming land-jobber; the thriftless tradesman; the merchant with cracked credit; in short, everyone driven to raise money by desperate means and desperate sacrifices, hurried to Tom Walker.

Thus Tom was the universal friend of the needy, and acted like a "friend in need"; that is to say, he always exacted good pay and good security. In proportion to the distress of the applicant was the highness of his terms. He accumulated bonds and mortgages; gradually squeezed his customers closer and closer: and sent them at length, dry as a sponge, from his door.

In this way he made money hand over hand; became a rich and mighty man, and exalted his cocked hat upon 'Change. He built himself, as usual, a vast house, out of ostentation; but left the greater part of it unfinished and unfurnished, out of parsimony. He even set up a carriage in the fulness of his vainglory, though he nearly starved the horses which drew it; and as the ungreased wheels groaned and screeched on the axle-trees, you would have thought you heard the souls of the poor debtors he was squeezing.

As Tom waxed old, however, he grew thoughtful. Having secured the good things of this world, he began to feel anxious about those of the next. He thought with regret on the bargain he had made with his black friend, and set his wits to work to cheat him out of the conditions. He became, therefore, all of a sudden, a violent church-goer. He prayed loudly and strenuously, as if heaven were to be taken by force of lungs. Indeed, one might always tell when he had sinned most during the week, by the clamor of his

Sunday devotion. The quiet Christians who had been modestly and steadfastly travelling Zionward,[6] were struck with self-reproach at seeing themselves so suddenly outstripped in their career by this new-made convert. Tom was as rigid in religious as in money matters; he was a stern supervisor and censurer of his neighbors, and seemed to think every sin entered up to their account became a credit on his own side of the page. He even talked of the expediency of reviving the persecution of Quakers and Anabaptists. In a word, Tom's zeal became as notorious as his riches.

Still, in spite of all this strenuous attention to forms, Tom had a lurking dread that the devil, after all, would have his due. That he might not be taken unawares, therefore, it is said he always carried a small Bible in his coat-pocket. He had also a great folio Bible on his counting-house desk, and would frequently be found reading it when people called on business; on such occasions he would lay his green spectacles in the book, to mark the place, while he turned round to drive some usurious bargain.

Some say that Tom grew a little crack-brained in his old days, and that, fancying his end approaching, he had his horse new shod, saddled and bridled, and buried with his feet uppermost; because he supposed that at the last day the world would be turned upside down; in which case he should find his horse standing ready for mounting, and he was determined at the worst to give his old friend a run for it. This, however, is probably a mere old wives' fable. If he really did take such a precaution, it was totally superfluous; at least so says the authentic old legend; which closes his story in the following manner.

One hot summer afternoon in the dogdays, just as a terrible black thunder-gust

---

6. **Zionward** (zī′ ən wərd), heavenward. Zion is identified with Jerusalem, considered the earthly home of God by the Israelites and early Christians.

was coming up, Tom sat in his counting-house, in his white linen cap and India silk morning-gown. He was on the point of foreclosing a mortgage, by which he would complete the ruin of an unlucky land-speculator for whom he had professed the greatest friendship. The poor land-jobber begged him to grant a few months' indulgence. Tom had grown testy and irritated, and refused another day.

"My family will be ruined, and brought upon the parish," said the land-jobber.

"Charity begins at home," replied Tom; "I must take care of myself in these hard times."

"You have made so much money out of me," said the speculator.

Tom lost his patience and his piety. "The devil take me," said he, "if I have made a farthing!"

Just then there were three loud knocks at the street-door. He stepped out to see who was there. A black man was holding a black horse, which neighed and stamped with impatience.

"Tom, you're come for," said the black fellow, gruffly. Tom shrank back, but too late. He had left his little Bible at the bottom of his coat-pocket, and his big Bible on the desk buried under the mortgage he was about to foreclose: never was sinner taken more unawares. The black man whisked him like a child into the saddle, gave the horse the lash, and away he galloped, with Tom on his back, in the midst of the thunder-storm. The clerks stuck their pens behind their ears, and stared after him from the windows. Away went Tom Walker, dashing down the streets; his white cap bobbing up and down; his morning-gown fluttering in the wind, and his steed striking fire out of the pavement at every bound. When the clerks turned to look for the black man, he had disappeared.

Tom Walker never returned to foreclose the mortgage. A countryman, who lived on the border of the swamp, reported that in the height of the thunder-gust he had heard a great clattering of hoofs and a howling along the road, and running to the window caught sight of a figure, such as I have described, on a horse that galloped like mad across the fields, over the hills, and down into the black hemlock swamp towards the old Indian fort; and that shortly after a thunder-bolt falling in that direction seemed to set the whole forest in a blaze.

The good people of Boston shook their heads and shrugged their shoulders, but had been so much accustomed to witches and goblins, and tricks of the devil, in all kinds of shapes, from the first settlement of the colony, that they were not so much horror-struck as might have been expected. Trustees were appointed to take charge of Tom's effects. There was nothing, however, to administer. On searching his coffers, all his bonds and mortgages were found reduced to cinders. In place of gold and silver, his iron chest was filled with chips and shavings; two skeletons lay in his stable instead of his half-starved horses, and the very next day his great house took fire and was burnt to the ground.

Such was the end of Tom Walker and his ill-gotten wealth. Let all griping money-brokers lay this story to heart. The truth of it is not to be doubted. The very hole under the oak-trees, whence he dug Kidd's money, is to be seen to this day; and the neighboring swamp and old Indian fort are often haunted in stormy nights by a figure on horseback, in morning-gown and white cap, which is doubtless the troubled spirit of the usurer. In fact, the story has resolved itself into a proverb, and is the origin of that popular saying, so prevalent throughout New England, of "The Devil and Tom Walker."

FOR UNDERSTANDING

1. What bad character trait do Tom and his wife have in common?

2. Near what city and in what year is this story set?

3. What are the first words of "Old Scratch"?

4. In his first conversation with Tom, Old Scratch refers to Tom's race as "white savages." Why does he call them "savages"?

5. What proof does Old Scratch offer as a sign that he is telling the truth to Tom?

6. What does Tom absolutely refuse to do with his money? Why?

7. When Tom and Old Scratch are haggling about the terms of their agreement (page 130), what is the "one condition which need not be mentioned"?

8. Near the end of the story, what words of Tom's seal his doom? Why is this appropriate?

FOR INTERPRETATION

1. Explain what Irving is criticizing or satirizing in the following quotations from the story.

a. The lonely wayfarer shrunk within himself at the horrid clamor and clapper-clawing; eyed the den of discord askance; and hurried on his way, rejoicing, if a bachelor, in his celibacy.

b. Tom was the universal friend of the needy, and acted like a "friend in need"; that is to say, he always exacted good pay and good security.

c. Tom was as rigid in religious as in money matters; he was a stern supervisor and censurer of his neighbors, and seemed to think every sin entered up to their account became a credit on his own side of the page.

2. Below are opposed statements about this story. Select the statement that best expresses your own opinion.

a. The theme of Irving's story is universal; it could therefore be placed in any geographical setting.

b. The idea of selling one's soul to the devil is essentially a European theme, and Irving should have used a European setting for his story.

FOR APPRECIATION

Setting

Much of the charm of this story can be attributed to Irving's careful creation of an atmosphere foreboding mystery and evil. What specific sights, colors, sounds, and feelings contribute to this atmosphere in the swamp? at the old Indian fort? when Tom finds his wife's remains?

Characterization

1. Look back to the second paragraph. How do the house, the farm, and the horse help to show the Walkers' chief character trait?

2. What new traits of each are revealed throughout the remainder of the story?

3. What details of the black woodsman's physical appearance suggest his inner nature?

COMPOSITION

Irving was a master of description. Look back at his description of the Walkers' farm on page 125 (beginning "They lived in . . .") and at his description of the swamp on page 125 (beginning "The swamp was thickly . . ."). Try to decide what makes his descriptions so good. Then think of something you would like to describe, and try to write a brief description of your own.

James Fenimore Cooper   1789–1851

One might assume that only a born writer could produce thirty-two novels and a dozen other books in no more than three decades. Yet James Fenimore Cooper did not publish his first novel until he was over thirty, and at the time he began work on it, he disliked writing so much as a letter. The story goes that he was reading an English novel to his wife, who was ill in bed, when he threw it down in disgust and said he could write a better book himself. His first novel, *Precaution* (1820), was an imitation English novel set in England and was, in fact, very bad. But Cooper had found his trade. His next novel, *The Spy*, published only a little over a year later, was an immediate popular success.

The Spy was followed by *The Pioneers* (1823), the first of five books in which the famous Natty Bumppo appears as a major character. A year later Cooper published *The Pilot*, his first novel dealing with the sea. By this time, with the sole exception of Washington Irving, he had become the best-known American writer both at home and abroad. This was quite an achievement for a man who had found writing a disagreeable task only a half-dozen years before.

In spite of the many novels he wrote, Cooper's reputation rests mainly on what are called the "Leatherstocking Tales," five novels that embody the epic figure of Natty Bumppo, one of the most memorable heroes in American fiction. The Leatherstocking Tales get their name from the fact that Bumppo is called "Leatherstocking" in *The Pioneers*. His other nicknames include Deerslayer, Hawkeye, and Pathfinder. He is known simply as "the trapper" in the selection below.

After *The Pioneers*, Natty Bumppo next appears as a major character in Cooper's best-known work, *The Last of the Mohicans*, published in 1826. The following year Cooper published another Leatherstocking novel, *The Prairie*, in which Bumppo dies. (The selection here comes from the last chapter of this novel.) Fourteen years later, Cooper brought his hero back to life in *The Pathfinder*, making him just a

ENGRAVING OF JAMES FENIMORE COOPER
Oliver Pelton
National Portrait Gallery, Smithsonian Institution

year or two older than he is in *The Last of the Mohicans*. The final Leatherstocking novel, *The Deerslayer* (1841), concerns Bumppo as a young man of twenty-three.

The following list shows Cooper's Leatherstocking novels arranged in sequence with Natty Bumppo's life. The books' publication dates are shown to the left of the titles, and Natty Bumppo's approximate age at the time of the action is shown at the right.

Chronology of Bumppo's Life
1841 *The Deerslayer* (23)
1826 *The Last of the Mohicans* (48)
1840 *The Pathfinder* (50)
1823 *The Pioneers* (60s)
1827 *The Prairie* (80s)

It is fitting in a way that Cooper's last portrait of Leatherstocking should be of one so young, for in many ways Natty Bumppo never really grew old. Moreover, he remains young and alive in our imaginations, even today.

From 1826 to 1833, Cooper traveled abroad. Upon his return he found himself dismayed by much in American society. He soon became a strong critic of American life, expressing his own aristocratic social views in such nonfiction books as *The American Democrat* (1838). America at the time was still quite young—and still too uncertain of itself to tolerate criticism from within. The press of the day attacked both Cooper's books and his personal character, criticism that was to increasingly alienate him from society. Cooper's last novel failed in America, and he was offered only 100 pounds for it in England. He thereafter told his wife that he would no longer write novels. He continued to write, however, virtually to the day of his death in 1851.

Several months after Cooper died, the orator Daniel Webster presided over a public memorial for Cooper, held in New York. Many of the great writers of the time appeared or sent letters, praising James Fenimore Cooper as an artist and as an individual. As an artist, Cooper remains appreciated today. Perhaps we should appreciate him as much as an individual of special integrity. Speaking of this at Cooper's testimonial, William Cullen Bryant pointed out that Cooper "never thought of disguising his opinions, and he abhorred all disguises in others."

As the selection opens, a band of U.S. Army troops, commanded by Captain Middleton, are entering the Indian town where Natty Bumppo lives with his Indian friends. Middleton is a friend of Natty, who is usually called "the trapper" throughout this passage. Natty's adopted Indian son, Hard-Heart, has led the army troops into a large circle of Pawnee Indians inside the town.

from THE PRAIRIE

Chapter XXXIV
The Death of Leatherstocking

When they entered the town, its inhabitants were seen collected in an open space, where they were arranged with the customary deference to age and rank. The whole formed a large circle, in the centre of which were per-

From THE PRAIRIE (Chapter XXXIV). THE NOVELS OF JAMES FENIMORE COOPER, Volume IV, D. Appleton and Company, New York, 1883.

haps a dozen of the principal chiefs. Hard-Heart waved his hand as he approached, and, as the mass of bodies opened he rode through, followed by his companions. Here they dismounted; and as the beasts were led apart, the strangers found themselves environed by a thousand grave, composed, but solicitous faces.

Middleton gazed about him in growing concern, for no cry, no song, no shout welcomed him among a people, from whom he had so lately parted with regret. His uneasiness, not to say apprehensions, was shared by all his followers. Determination and stern resolution began to assume the place of anxiety in every eye, as each man silently felt for his arms, and assured himself that his several weapons were in a state for service. But there was no answering symptom of hostility on the part of their hosts. Hard-Heart beckoned for Middleton and Paul to follow, leading the way towards the cluster of forms that occupied the centre of the circle. Here the visitors found a solution of all the movements which had given them so much reason for apprehension.

The trapper was placed on a rude seat, which had been made, with studied care, to support his frame in an upright and easy attitude. The first glance of the eye told his former friends that the old man was at length called upon to pay the last tribute of nature. His eye was glazed, and apparently as devoid of sight as of expression. His features were a little more sunken and strongly marked than formerly; but there, all change, so far as exterior was concerned, might be said to have ceased. His approaching end was not to be ascribed to any positive disease, but had been a gradual and mild decay of the physical powers. Life, it is true, still lingered in his system; but it was as if at times entirely ready to depart, and then it would appear to re-animate the sinking form, reluctant to give up the possession of a tenement that had never been corrupted by vice or undermined by disease. It would have been no violent fancy to have imagined that the spirit fluttered about the placid lips of the old woodsman, reluctant to depart from a shell that had so long given it an honest and honorable shelter.

His body was placed so as to let the light of the setting sun fall full upon the solemn features. His head was bare, the long, thin locks of grey fluttering lightly in the evening breeze. His rifle lay upon his knee, and the other accoutrements of the chase were placed at his side, within reach of his hand. Between his feet lay the figure of a hound, with its

head crouching to the earth, as if it slumbered; and so perfectly easy and natural was its position, that a second glance was necessary to tell Middleton he saw only the skin of Hector, stuffed, by Indian tenderness and ingenuity, in a manner to represent the living animal. His own dog was playing at a distance with the child of Tachechana and Mahtoree. The mother herself stood at hand, holding in her arms a second offspring, that might boast of a parentage no less honorable than that which belonged to the son of Hard-Heart. Le Balafré was seated nigh the dying trapper, with every mark about his person that the hour of his own departure was not far distant. The rest of those immediately in the centre were aged men, who had apparently drawn near in order to observe the manner in which a just and fearless warrior would depart on the greatest of his journeys.

The old man was reaping the rewards of a life remarkable for temperance and activity, in a tranquil and placid death. His vigor in a manner endured to the very last. Decay, when it did occur, was rapid, but free from pain. He had hunted with the tribe in the spring, and even throughout most of the summer; when his limbs suddenly refused to perform their customary offices. A sympathizing weakness took possession of all his faculties; and the Pawnees believed that they were going to lose, in this unexpected manner, a sage and counsellor whom they had begun both to love and respect. But, as we have already said, the immortal occupant seemed unwilling to desert its tenement. The lamp of life flickered, without becoming extinguished. On the morning of the day on which Middleton arrived, there was a general reviving of the powers of the whole man. His tongue was again heard in wholesome maxims, and his eye from time to time recognised the persons of his friends. It merely proved to be a brief and final intercourse with the world, on the part of one who had already been considered, as to mental communion, to have taken his leave of it for ever.

When he had placed his guests in front of the dying man, Hard-Heart, after a pause, that proceeded as much from sorrow as decorum, leaned a little forward, and demanded—

"Does my father hear the words of his son?"

"Speak," returned the trapper, in tones that issued from his chest, but which were rendered awfully distinct by the stillness that reigned in the place. "I am about to depart from the village of the Loups, and shortly shall be beyond the reach of your voice."

"Let the wise chief have no cares for his journey," continued Hard-Heart, with an earnest solicitude that led him to forget, for the moment, that others were waiting to address his adopted parent; "a hundred Loups shall clear his path from briers."

"Pawnee, I die, as I have lived, a Christian man!" resumed the trapper, with a force of voice that had the same startling effect on his hearers as is produced by the trumpet, when its blast rises suddenly and freely on the air, after its obstructed sounds have been heard struggling in the distance: "as I came into life so will I leave it. Horses and arms are not needed to stand in the presence of the

Great Spirit of my people. He knows my color, and according to my gifts will He judge my deeds."

"My father will tell my young men how many Mingoes* he has struck, and what acts of valor and justice he has done, that they may know how to imitate him."

"A boastful tongue is not heard in the heaven of a white man!" solemnly returned the old man. "What I have done He has seen. His eyes are always open. That which has been well done will He remember; wherein I have been wrong will He not forget to chastise, though He will do the same in mercy. No, my son; a Pale-face may not sing his own praises, and hope to have them acceptable before his God!"

A little disappointed, the young partisan stepped modestly back, making way for the recent comers to approach. Middleton took one of the meagre hands of the trapper, and struggling to command his voice, he succeeded in announcing his presence.

The old man listened like one whose thoughts were dwelling on a very different subject; but when the other had succeeded in making him understand that he was present, an expression of joyful recognition passed over his faded features.

"I hope you have not so soon forgotten those whom you so materially served!" Middleton concluded. "It would pain me to think my hold on your memory was so light."

"Little that I have ever seen is forgotten," returned the trapper: "I am at the close of many weary days, but there is not one among them all that I could wish to overlook. I remember you, with the whole of your company; ay, and your gran'ther, that went before you. I am glad that you have come back upon these plains, for I had need of one who speaks the English, since little faith can be put in the traders of these regions. Will you do a favor to an old and dying man?"

"Name it," said Middleton; "it shall be done."

"It is a far journey to send such trifles," resumed the old man, who spoke at short intervals, as strength and breath permitted; "a far and weary journey is the same; but kindnesses and friendships are things not to be forgotten. There is a settlement among the Otsego hills—"

"I know the place," interrupted Middleton, observing that he spoke with increasing difficulty; "proceed to tell me what you would have done."

"Take this rifle, and pouch, and horn, and send them to the person whose name is graven on the plates of the stock,—a trader cut the letters with his knife,—for it is long that I have intended to send him such a token of my love!"

"It shall be so. Is there more that you could wish?"

"Little else have I to bestow. My traps I give to my Indian son; for honestly and kindly has he kept his faith. Let him stand before me."

Middleton explained to the chief what the trapper had said, and relinquished his own place to the other.

"Pawnee," continued the old man, always changing his language to suit the person he addressed, and not unfrequently according to the ideas he expressed, "it is a custom of my people for the father to leave his blessing with the son before he shuts his eyes for ever. This blessing I give to you; take it; for the prayers of a Christian man will never make the path of a just warrior to the blessed prairies either longer or more tangled. May the God of a white man look on your deeds with friendly eyes, and may you never commit an act that shall cause him to darken his face. I know not whether we shall ever meet again. There are many traditions concerning the place of Good Spirits. It is not for one like

---

* **Mingoes,** Cooper's word for enemy Indians.

THE DYING TECUMSEH, Ferdinand Pettrich
National Museum of American Art, Smithsonian Institution, Washington, DC

me, old and experienced though I am, to set up my opinions against a nation's. You believe in the blessed prairies, and I have faith in the sayings of my fathers. If both are true our parting will be final; but if it should prove that the same meaning is hid under different words, we shall yet stand together, Pawnee, before the face of your Wahcondah, who will then be no other than my God. There is much to be said in favor of both religions, for each seems suited to its own people, and no doubt it was so intended. I fear I have not altogether followed the gifts of my color, inasmuch as I find it a little painful to give up for ever the use of the rifle, and the comforts of the chase. But then the fault has been my own, seeing that it could not have been His.

Ay, Hector," he continued, leaning forward a little, and feeling for the ears of the hound, "our parting has come at last, dog, and it will be a long hunt. You have been an honest, and a bold, and a faithful hound. Pawnee, you cannot slay the pup on my grave, for where a Christian dog falls there he lies for ever; but you can be kind to him after I am gone, for the love you bear his master."

"The words of my father are in my ears," returned the young partisan, making a grave and respectful gesture of assent.

"Do you hear what the chief has promised, dog?" demanded the trapper, making an effort to attract the notice of the insensible effigy of his hound. Receiving no answering look, nor hearing any friendly whine, the old man felt for the mouth, and endeavored to force his hand between the cold lips. The truth then flashed upon him, although he was far from perceiving the whole extent of the deception. Falling back in his seat, he hung his head, like one who felt a severe and unexpected shock. Profiting by this momentary forgetfulness, two young Indians removed the skin with the same delicacy of feeling that had induced them to attempt the pious fraud.

"The dog is dead!" muttered the trapper, after a pause of many minutes; "a hound has his time as well as a man; and well has he filled his days! Captain," he added, making an effort to wave his hand for Middleton, "I am glad you have come; for though kind, and well meaning according to the gifts of their color, these Indians are not the men to lay the head of a white man in his grave. I have been thinking, too, of this dog at my feet; it will not do to set forth the opinion that a Christian can expect to meet his hound again; still there can be little harm in placing what is left of so faithful a servant nigh the bones of his master."

"It shall be as you desire."

"I'm glad you think with me in this matter. In order, then, to save labor, lay the pup at my feet; or for that matter, put him side by side. A hunter need never be ashamed to be found in company with his dog!"

"I charge myself with your wish."

The old man made a long, and apparently a musing pause. At times he raised his eyes wistfully, as if he would again address Middleton, but some innate feeling appeared always to suppress his words. The other, who observed his hesitation, inquired in a way most likely to encourage him to proceed whether there was aught else that he could wish to have done.

"I am without kith or kin in the wide world!" the trapper answered: "when I am gone there will be an end of my race. We have never been chiefs; but honest, and useful in our way I hope it cannot be denied we have always proved ourselves. My father lies bur-

ied near the sea, and the bones of his son will whiten on the prairies—"

"Name the spot, and your remains shall be placed by the side of your father," interrupted Middleton.

"Not so, not so, Captain. Let me sleep where I have lived—beyond the din of the settlements! Still I see no need why the grave of an honest man should be hid, like a Redskin in his ambushment. I paid a man in the settlements to make and put a graven stone at the head of my father's resting-place. It was of the value of twelve beaver-skins, and cunningly and curiously was it carved! Then it told to all comers that the body of such a Christian lay beneath; and it spoke of his manner of life, of his years, and of his honesty. When we had done with the Frenchers in the old war I made a journey to the spot, in order to see that all was rightly performed, and glad I am to say, the workman had not forgotten his faith."

"And such a stone you would have at your grave?"

"I! no, no, I have no son but Hard-Heart, and it is little that an Indian knows of white fashions and usages. Besides, I am his debtor already, seeing it is so little I have done since I have lived in his tribe. The rifle might bring the value of such a thing—but then I know it will give the boy pleasure to hang the piece in his hall, for many is the deer and the bird that he has seen it destroy. No, no, the gun must be sent to him whose name is graven on the lock!"

"But there is one who would gladly prove his affection in the way you wish; he who owes you not only his own deliverance from so many dangers, but who inherits a heavy debt of gratitude from his ancestors. The stone shall be put at the head of your grave."

The old man extended his emaciated hand, and gave the other a squeeze of thanks.

"I thought you might be willing to do it, but I was backward in asking the favor," he said, "seeing that you are not of my kin. Put no boastful words on the same, but just the name, the age, and the time of the death, with something from the holy book; no more, no more. My name will then not be altogether lost on 'arth; I need no more."

Middleton intimated his assent, and then followed a pause that was only broken by distant and broken sentences from the dying man. He appeared now to have closed his accounts with the world, and to await merely for the final summons to quit it. Middleton and Hard-Heart placed themselves on the opposite sides of his seat, and watched with melancholy solicitude, the variations of his countenance. For two hours there was no very sensible alteration. The expression of his faded and time-worn features was that of a calm and dignified repose. From time to time he spoke, uttering some brief sentence in the way of advice, or asking some simple questions concerning those in whose fortunes he took a friendly interest. During the whole of that solemn and anxious period each individual of the tribe kept his place, in the most self-restrained patience. When the old man spoke, all bent their heads to listen; and when his words were uttered, they seemed to ponder on their wisdom and usefulness.

As the flame drew nigher to the socket his voice was hushed, and there were moments when his attendants doubted whether he still belonged to the living. Middleton, who watched each wavering expression of his weather-beaten visage, with the interest of a keen observer of human nature, softened by the tenderness of personal regard, fancied he could read the workings of the old man's soul in the strong lineaments of his countenance. Perhaps what the enlightened soldier took for the delusion of mistaken opinion did actually occur—for who has returned from that unknown world to explain by what forms, and in what manner, he was introduced into its awful precincts? Without pretending to explain what must ever be a mystery to the quick, we shall simply relate facts as they occurred.

The trapper had remained nearly mo-

tionless for an hour. His eyes alone had occasionally opened and shut. When opened, his gaze seemed fastened on the clouds which hung around the western horizon, reflecting the bright colors, and giving form and loveliness to the glorious tints of an American sunset. The hour—the calm beauty of the season—the occasion, all conspired to fill the spectators with solemn awe. Suddenly, while musing on the remarkable position in which he was placed, Middleton felt the hand which he held grasp his own with incredible power, and the old man, supported on either side by his friends, rose upright to his feet. For a moment he looked about him, as if to invite all in presence to listen (the lingering remnant of human frailty), and then, with a fine military elevation of the head, and with a voice that might be heard in every part of that numerous assembly, he pronounced the word—

"Here!"

A movement so entirely unexpected, and the air of grandeur and humility which were so remarkably united in the mien of the trapper, together with the clear and uncommon force of his utterance, produced a short period of confusion in the faculties of all present. When Middleton and Hard-Heart, each of whom had involuntarily extended a hand to support the form of the old man, turned to him again, they found that the subject of their interest was removed for ever beyond the necessity of their care. They mournfully placed the body in its seat, and Le Balafré arose to announce the termination of the scene to the tribe. The voice of the old Indian seemed a sort of echo from that invisible world to which the meek spirit of the trapper had just departed.

"A valiant, a just, and a wise warrior, has gone on the path which will lead him to the blessed grounds of his people!" he said. "When the voice of the Wahcondah called him, he was ready to answer. Go, my children; remember the just chief of the Pale-faces, and clear your own tracks from briers!"

The grave was made beneath the shade

of some noble oaks. It has been carefully watched to the present hour by the Pawnees of the Loup, and is often shown to the traveller and the trader as a spot where a just White man sleeps. In due time the stone was placed at its head, with the simple inscription which the trapper had himself requested. The only liberty taken by Middleton was to add—"*May no wanton hand ever disturb his remains!*"

FOR UNDERSTANDING

1. In this selection, Cooper frequently refers to Natty by his occupation. What is that occupation?
2. With which Indian character does Natty have an argument? What is the subject of their quarrel?
3. What three requests does Natty make of Captain Middleton?
4. What slight change in one of these requests does Middleton take the liberty of making?
5. What is Natty's last word?

FOR INTERPRETATION

1. Discuss the implications of Natty Bumppo's final word.
2. What is the significance of the fact that Natty stands between Captain Middleton and Chief Hard-Heart?
3. Interpret the following line: "He [God] knows my color, and according to my gifts will He judge my deeds." Be sure to test your interpretation in the context in which the quotation is found.
4. What does Natty's discussion of the Christian God and Wahcondah reveal about his character?
5. In Cooper's first Leatherstocking novel, *The Pioneers*, Natty Bumppo escapes from civilization. In *The Prairie*, we find the same hero living with a Pawnee tribe, far apart from the civilization of the white man. In addition, he has few possessions and personal ties. Why might such a person be a favorite type of American hero?

FOR APPRECIATION

Setting
Cooper is famous for his descriptions of nature. In this selection, however, the natural setting is sketched with just a few details. Find some of those details near the beginning and near the end. How do they relate to the overall theme of the selection?

LANGUAGE AND VOCABULARY

One way of testing to determine whether one knows the meaning of a word is to try to name its opposite. A word opposite in meaning to another word is called an *antonym*. For example, an antonym of *good* would be *bad* or *evil*.

In column A below are ten words from the opening of this selection. An antonym for each of these words appears in column B. On your own paper, write the words in column A. Then next to each one, write its antonym from column B. Be sure to match adjectives with adjectives and nouns with nouns. Use a dictionary to find the meaning of any word you do not understand.

A	B
customary	jovial
deference	unconcerned
grave	unique
composed	indecision
solicitous	disrespect
uneasiness	amity
apprehension	hopefulness
determination	calmness
stern	impatient
hostility	lax

William Cullen Bryant   1794–1878

When William Cullen Bryant, "the father of American poetry," died in his mid-eighties on June 12, 1878, the mayor of New York ordered the city's flags flown at half-mast. By this time, Bryant had long been one of the best-known writers and editors not only in New York but in the entire country. He was the first American to write a body of poems that could stand beside the work of European poets. In addition, he had written excellent critical essays and had translated Homer's *Iliad* and *Odyssey*. As editor-in-chief of the New York *Evening Post* for nearly fifty years, he exerted a strong political influence upon the whole nation.

Born in 1794, in the town of Cummington, then on the western Massachusetts frontier, Bryant knew his beloved Nature at first hand. A precocious child, he began writing poetry at the age of eight or nine, going on to win his first public acclaim at ten, when he read a poem at the annual school exercises. It was later printed in a newspaper. He published a longer work at the age of fourteen and is thought to have written a draft of "Thanatopsis" when he was only seventeen or eighteen.

Of course, writing poetry, then as now, was no way to make a living. Bryant was apprenticed to the law and practiced in western Massachusetts for about ten years, until he moved to the city of New York (1825). He became assistant editor of the New York *Evening Post* in 1826 and editor in 1829, a position he held until his death. In the pages of that influential paper, Bryant championed Jacksonian democracy and vigorously opposed slavery.

Poems, published in 1821, was his first mature book of poetry. His collected *Poems* (1832) established him beyond question as the country's foremost poet. In addition, his essays on poetry, notably the 1825 lectures, powerfully influenced mainstream American poetry for decades. Bryant defined poetry as the art of exciting the imagination and touching the heart by selecting and arranging the symbols of thought. He also believed, however, that poetry must appeal to the understanding, and he thought poetry valuable in proportion to "the

WILLIAM CULLEN BRYANT
José Maria Mora
National Portrait Gallery,
Smithsonian Institution

direct lessons of wisdom that it delivers." He further argued that the poet was a teacher of the highest moral lessons. This didactic emphasis might seem to relate Bryant to eighteenth-century English poetry, such as that of Alexander Pope. Yet in sentiment, Bryant's work more nearly resembles the poems of the great English Romantic, William Wordsworth, whom he deeply admired.

Bryant continued publishing poetry throughout his life, but perhaps the most famous of his later works are his translations of the *Iliad* (1870) and the *Odyssey* (1871–1872). His best-known collections of prose pieces are the first and second series of the *Letters of a Traveller* (1850 and 1859). But of course it is for his poems that we will remember Bryant. As a poet of reflection, he strove for a universal note in his work. His main theme is Nature, or rather the effect of Nature upon people. Though many of his poems lack that concrete unity of effect that we value most in poetry today, his best work brings to mind what Robinson Jeffers says at the end of "The Stone-Cutters":

> Yet stones have stood for a thousand years,
>   and pained thoughts found
> The honey of peace in old poems.

Thanatopsis

To him who in the love of Nature holds
Communion with her visible forms, she speaks
A various language; for his gayer hours
She has a voice of gladness, and a smile
And eloquence of beauty, and she glides   5
Into his darker musings, with a mild
And healing sympathy, that steals away
Their sharpness ere he is aware. When thoughts
Of the last bitter hour come like a blight
Over thy spirit, and sad images   10
Of the stern agony, and shroud, and pall,
And breathless darkness, and the narrow house,
Make thee to shudder, and grow sick at heart;—
Go forth, under the open sky, and list
To Nature's teachings, while from all around—   15
Earth and her waters, and the depths of air,—
Comes a still voice—Yet a few days, and thee
The all-beholding sun shall see no more
In all his course; nor yet in the cold ground,
Where thy pale form was laid, with many tears,   20
Nor in the embrace of ocean, shall exist
Thy image. Earth, that nourished thee, shall claim
Thy growth, to be resolved to earth again,
And, lost each human trace, surrendering up
Thine individual being, shalt thou go   25
To mix for ever with the elements,
To be a brother to the insensible rock
And to the sluggish clod, which the rude swain
Turns with his share, and treads upon. The oak
Shall send his roots abroad, and pierce thy mould.   30

Yet not to thine eternal resting-place
Shalt thou retire alone,—nor couldst thou wish
Couch more magnificent. Thou shalt lie down
With patriarchs of the infant world—with kings,
The powerful of the earth—the wise, the good,   35
Fair forms, and hoary seers of ages past,
All in one mighty sepulchre. The hills
Rock-ribbed and ancient as the sun; the vales
Stretching in pensive quietness between;
The venerable woods; rivers that move   40
In majesty, and the complaining brooks
That make the meadows green; and, poured round all,
Old ocean's grey and melancholy waste—

A founder of American landscape painting, Durand excelled in capturing the mood of majestic natural scenes like this one, which illustrates Bryant's poem so well.

SCENE FROM THANATOPSIS, Asher B. Durand
Metropolitan Museum of Art, New York City
Gift of J. Pierpont Morgan

Are but the solemn decorations all
Of the great tomb of man. The golden sun,   45
The planets, all the infinite host of heaven,
Are shining on the sad abodes of death,
Through the still lapse of ages. All that tread
The globe are but a handful to the tribes
That slumber in its bosom.—Take the wings   50
Of morning, traverse Barca's desert sands,[1]
Or lose thyself in the continuous woods
Where rolls the Oregon,[2] and hears no sound,
Save his own dashings—yet—the dead are there:
And millions in those solitudes, since first   55
The flight of years began, have laid them down

1. **Barca's desert sands.** Barca was once a Greek oasis-colony on the North African coast of the Mediterranean.
2. **Oregon,** now called the Columbia River, between Washington and Oregon States.

In their last sleep—the dead reign there alone.
So shalt thou rest, and what if thou withdraw
In silence from the living, and no friend
Take note of thy departure? All that breathe   60
Will share thy destiny. The gay will laugh
When thou art gone, the solemn brood of care
Plod on, and each one as before will chase
His favourite phantom; yet all these shall leave
Their mirth and their employments, and shall come,   65
And make their bed with thee. As the long train
Of ages glide away, the sons of men,
The youth in life's green spring, and he who goes
In the full strength of years, matron, and maid,
And the sweet babe, and the grey-headed man—   70
Shall one by one be gathered to thy side,
By those, who in their turn shall follow them.

　　So live, that when thy summons comes to join
The innumerable caravan, which moves
To that mysterious realm, where each shall take   75
His chamber in the silent halls of death,
Thou go not, like the quarry-slave at night,
Scourged to his dungeon, but, sustained and soothed
By an unfaltering trust, approach thy grave
Like one who wraps the drapery of his couch   80
About him, and lies down to pleasant dreams.

To a Waterfowl

　　Whither, 'midst falling dew,
While glow the heavens with the last steps of day,
Far, through their rosy depths, dost thou pursue
　　Thy solitary way?

　　Vainly the fowler's eye   5
Might mark thy distant flight to do thee wrong.
As, darkly seen against the crimson sky,
　　Thy figure floats along.

　　Seek'st thou the plashy brink
Of weedy lake, or marge of river wide,   10
Or where the rocking billows rise and sink
　　On the chafed ocean side?

*This dramatic landscape painting is considered
Durand's masterpiece. The "Kindred Spirits" of the
title are Thomas Cole and William Cullen Bryant,
who stand together in the foreground, surveying the
magnificent view.*

KINDRED SPIRITS
Asher B. Durand
New York Public Library
Astor, Lenox, and Tilden
Collection

There is a Power whose care
Teaches thy way along that pathless coast,—
The desert and illimitable air,—   15
    Lone wandering, but not lost.

All day thy wings have fanned,
At that far height, the cold thin atmosphere,
Yet stoop not, weary, to the welcome land,
    Though the dark night is near.   20

And soon that toil shall end;
Soon shalt thou find a summer home and rest,
And scream among thy fellows; reeds shall bend,
Soon, o'er thy sheltered nest.

Thou'rt gone, the abyss of heaven   25
Hath swallowed up thy form; yet, on my heart
Deeply hath sunk the lesson thou hast given,
And shall not soon depart.

He who, from zone to zone,
Guides through the boundless sky thy certain flight,   30
In the long way that I must tread alone,
Will lead my steps aright.

From POEMS OF WILLIAM CULLEN BRYANT, Oxford Edition,
London, 1914.

FOR UNDERSTANDING

"Thanatopsis"

1. Look up the word *thanatopsis* in a dictionary and explain its origin and meaning.
2. Bryant divides his poem into three parts (at line 30 and at line 72). Discuss why you think he made these particular divisions.
3. What advice does the speaker give those who shudder at the thought of death?
4. What does the speaker mean when he says that the person who dies does not retire alone? Why does Bryant choose the word *retire?*
5. Interpret the following passage: "each one as before will chase/His favourite phantom. . . ."
6. Explain how the person addressed as "thou" gains in stature and importance as the poem progresses.
7. What is the "message" of the poet?

"To a Waterfowl"

1. List some specific details that tell at what time of day the action of the poem is taking place.
2. How would you argue for or against the idea

that the time of day suggests or symbolizes death?
3. Name two or three things that the speaker and the bird have in common.
4. As specified in the poem, what is the end of the bird's journey?
5. What might be the end of the speaker's journey?
6. What is the "lesson" that the speaker learns?
7. Discuss the idea that "To a Waterfowl" is a poem about blind faith.

FOR APPRECIATION

Scanning Poetry

Poetry, like music, has rhythm. The technical term for rhythm in traditional poetry is *meter*. It is established by the regular or nearly regular occurrence of similar units, called *feet*. Generally, a foot is defined as a unit consisting of one accented syllable with one or more unaccented syllables.

Scanning poetry is simply marking the accented or stressed syllables and the unaccented or unstressed syllables (rĕ pórt). To establish the rhythmic or metrical pattern, it is best to read and listen to the beat of several lines, since any given line may be irregular. Counting the number of syllables in the line may also be helpful, but here, too, there may be irregularities.

The following is a *scansion* of the beginning of the second part of "Thanatopsis."

> Yĕt nót / tŏ thíne / ĕ tér / năl rést / ĭng pláce
> Shălt thóu / rĕ tíre / ă lóne, / nŏr coúldst / thŏu wísh
> Coúch mŏre / măg níf / ĭ cént. / Thŏu shált / lĭe dówn
> Wĭth pá / trĭ árchs / ŏf thĕ ín / fănt wórld—/ wĭth kíngs,
> Thĕ pów / ĕr fúl / ŏf thĕ eárth—/thĕ wíse, / thĕ góod.

Obviously, there are five feet to the line. (Note that the end of each foot is marked by a perpendicular line, except for the last foot of the line.) Most of the feet in this poem consist of an unaccented syllable followed by an accented syllable. This is the most common foot in English verse and is called an *iamb*. Here is a list of the most frequently used feet, with an example of each:

iamb: an unaccented syllable followed by an accented syllable: rĕ pórt

trochee: an accented syllable followed by an unaccented syllable: rhý thm̆

anapest: two unaccented syllables followed by an accented syllable: ĭn tĕr rúpt

dactyl: an accented syllable followed by two unaccented syllables: ráp ĭd lў

The following special terms are used to describe the length of the lines in poetry:

monometer: one foot per line
dimeter: two feet per line
trimeter: three feet per line
tetrameter: four feet per line
pentameter: five feet per line
hexameter: six feet per line

The lines in Bryant's "Thanatopsis" are called *iambic* (after their most characteristic foot) *pentameter* (because they typically have five feet to the line).

Note that although every line in our sample has five feet, not every line is invariably iambic.

1. Find an example of a trochee in "Thanatopsis."
2. Find two anapests.

In many respects, "To a Waterfowl" is not quite as regular as "Thanatopsis." How many accents are there in the first and fourth lines of each stanza? How many accents are in the second and third lines of each stanza? To scan this poem, use the third stanza, since it is more regular than most of the others. In what one line is even the third stanza irregular?

Another difference between "Waterfowl" and "Thanatopsis" is that the former has rhyme. Which lines rhyme with which in each stanza?

In conclusion, we scan poems primarily to get a sense of their basic rhythm and its variations. When we read poetry, however, we should not slavishly follow some predetermined rhythm. We must respond to punctuation and other indications of pauses or emphases in a line. Above all, we must respond to the sense, the meaning of a line. Consider the last line of "To a Waterfowl" as an example. The dum-ty, dum-ty, dum-ty reading would be:

Wĭll leád mў stĕps ă ríght

While this might seem to be the "correct" analysis, we achieve a more dramatic reading by putting primary stress on "my":

Wĭll leád mý stĕps ă ríght

Note also that this reading helps to call attention to the parallels between the speaker and the waterfowl. To those who would argue that "steps" must be stressed, we would suggest that it receives a *secondary* stress, while "my" gets a *primary* stress. The notion of two degrees of stress more accurately reflects our normal speech. In most dictionaries, too, you will find both a light and a heavy stress mark on some words. These are the primary (heavy) and secondary (light) stresses we have just mentioned.

A TWENTIETH-CENTURY WRITER LOOKS BACK

It is easy to appreciate why a twentieth-century writer would want to look back on the Revolutionary period, the era in which our nation was born. It is also easy to appreciate why a biographer would be interested in John Adams, one of our founding fathers, our first Vice President, and our second President. Adams is also interesting because he was married to one of the most engaging and articulate women in early American history, Abigail Smith Adams. Aside from being the wife of one President and mother of another (John Quincy Adams), she was a marvelous letter-writer whose work is being read with renewed interest today.

When he was only twenty years old, John Adams wrote in his diary: "I am resolved to rise with the sun. May I blush whenever I suffer one hour to pass unimproved. I will rouse my mind and fix my attention; I will stand collected within myself and think upon what I read and what I see."

What would a man with that much self-discipline and that fierce a determination become in later years? To answer many such questions, Catherine Drinker Bowen spent five years of her life probing the life of Adams. Originally planned as a full-length portrait of the entire life, the resulting book, *John Adams and the American Revolution,* concentrates instead on her subject's tenth to fortieth years (1745–1776).

The excerpt that follows is from the final section of the book, telling of Adams's participation in the Second Continental Congress, to which he had been elected as one of the Massachusetts delegates.

The First Continental Congress met from September 5 to October 25, 1774, in Philadelphia, to discuss the so-called Coercive or Intolerable Acts—laws passed by Britain to punish Massachusetts for the Boston Tea Party. During that congress, John Adams, along with his cousin Sam Adams and others, wrote a *Declaration of Rights and Grievances* on behalf of the colonies. The delegates agreed to meet again the following May if Britain failed to remove the Coercive Acts.

They did meet again, beginning May 10, 1775, and all the world knows the Declaration of Independence that brought this second gathering to a dramatic climax over a year later. What was it like to be there? What exactly led up to the signing of the Declaration? Bowen recreates some of these scenes from the opening months of the Second Continental Congress, largely through the eyes of one of the most radical of all the delegates, young John Adams.

Catherine Drinker Bowen   1897–1973

Catherine Drinker Bowen was one of the most prolific and popular biographers of the twentieth century. Born in Haverford, Pennsylvania, in 1897, the youngest of six children, she expressed her first love—for music—by becoming an excellent violinist. Not surprisingly, her earliest published work includes biographies of musicians, notably *Beloved Friend* (1937), about the Russian composer Tchaikowsky, and *Free Artist* (1939), about the Russian composer and pianist Anton Rubinstein and his brother Nicholas. She first achieved widespread critical and popular acclaim with *Yankee from Olympus* (1944), a biography of Justice Oliver Wendell Holmes and his family. This was followed by *John Adams and the American Revolution* (1950) and her biography of the English jurist Sir Edward Coke, *The Lion and the Throne*, which won the National Book Award for nonfiction in 1958.

Bowen developed a strong interest in the Revolutionary period and subsequently wrote two additional books dealing with events of that time. In 1966, she published *Miracle at Philadelphia: The Story of the Continental Convention, May to September 1787*. Her last book, published posthumously in 1974, was *The Most Dangerous Man in America: Scenes from the Life of Benjamin Franklin*.

Bowen wrote several other biographies, including a personal account, *Family Portrait* (1970). She also reflected on her career as a biographer in such works as *Adventures of a Biographer* (1959) and *Biography: The Craft and the Calling* (1969).

from JOHN ADAMS AND THE AMERICAN REVOLUTION

The Second Continental Congress

1

In the State House yard the Philadelphia Associators[1] drilled their new-formed battalions, the bucktails on their cockaded hats standing up bravely in the early May breeze.

Twenty blocks away in the Factory yard, the Quaker Blues went through the manual of arms as smartly as any veterans, aware they had been read out of Meeting[2] for what they did. And in John Cadwalader's garden the Silk Stocking Company drilled, determined

1. **Philadelphia Associators.** This group, together with the Quaker Blues and the Silk Stocking Company, was simply a group of American citizens training to be soldiers in the Revolution.
2. **read out of Meeting.** Since Quakers are traditionally pacifists, those training for war were expelled from the church (Meeting).

to outdo the Blues. Their light green uniforms were crossed over the breast with white leather belts; they wore green jockey caps, and on their cartouche boxes[3] the word LIBERTY stood out large.

Crowds gathered in the late afternoons to watch them. Often enough, John Adams was among the crowd. He was touched and cheered by the martial spirit that everywhere prevailed. "Uniforms and Regimentals are thick as Bees," he wrote home. "Oh, that I were a soldier! I will be. I am reading military books. Everybody must, and will, and shall be a soldier."

Coming through New York, John had seen thousands of troops at drill—a sight especially heartening because that large province last winter had rejected the First Continental Congress and refused to send delegates to the Second. They had even prepared humble petitions to King and Parliament, inscribed on paper bearing the significant watermark *Liberty and Prudence*. But Lexington[4] had changed their minds: they had elected a dozen delegates for Philadelphia. John hoped all twelve would not be as conciliatory as Duane and Jay. Tidings of Lexington had traveled amazingly fast. Kentucky should have it soon, and Savannah. Surely, the news would bring Georgia into the union!

Congress sat in the State House now, two blocks up Chestnut Street from Carpenters' Hall. The Pennsylvania Assembly had lent their room on the ground floor at the east end, a large, beautiful, white-paneled chamber, lined on two sides with windows. A handsome glass-prismed chandelier hung in the center. At the far end were twin fireplaces; the President's table faced the room. The place had an air auspicious, inspiring.

Forty-eight delegates answered to the roll call. (There would eventually be sixty-five.) Virginia had her old delegation. Thomas Jefferson was to come later, as alternate for Peyton Randolph, should the latter be called

back to Virginia. John saw few new faces. Hancock of course was with the Massachusetts delegation now, Pennsylvania had added a distinguished young Scottish-born constitutional scholar, James Wilson. But among newcomers the most celebrated by far was Dr. Franklin, just landed from England. It was wonderful to see him, his chair at the end of the row pulled out a little from the rest, tranquil and composed in his brown Quaker suit, the gray hair falling almost to his shoulders. Here was a man who knew the riddle of ministerial Britain at first hand, who had met Lord North[5] face to face, a man wise in the ways of courts and empires.

The first morning, Colonel Washington created a sensation by appearing in his uniform of the Virginia militia—blue and buff coat with rich gold epaulets, a small elegant sword at his side and a black cockade in his hat. Some, jealous of his wealth and social position, said sourly that the Virginian had found a pretty way to advertise his military ambitions. After all, Colonel Dickinson sat in Congress sans regimentals; so did Major Mifflin. But the New England men declared it a glorious idea. And how skillful, how natural to the man, this tacit yet open reminder that the business of the Congress might well be not negotiation but war!

It was a reminder, John discovered very soon, that was most burningly necessary. The New England men had come to Philadelphia with a program definite, immediate, practical: First, to put the continent in a state of strong defense. Second, to institute a people's government in every colony, entirely independent of royal governors, Parliament, and

---

3. **cartouche boxes** (kär tüsh′), containers holding ammunition or cartridges for firearms.
4. **Lexington,** the battle fought at Lexington, Massachusetts. John goes on to speculate that news of the same battle will bring both Kentucky and Georgia into the camp of those favoring independence.
5. **Lord North,** Frederick North, British prime minister from 1770 to 1782.

Britain. They had expected to put it through without delay.

Now they found they could not even mention the word *independence*, let alone the words *American Army*. In spite of Lexington, the Middle and Southern colonies were not ready to accept a state of war for the whole continent. They had every sympathy with Massachusetts and said so with tears in their eyes. They approved the drilling, the battalions, the martial spirit out-of-doors. But they approved it, John discovered, conditionally, only should negotiation fail.

Sitting in the wide, white-paneled chamber, discouragement swept over John. At the expense of three precious days, Congress prepared an elaborate memorial for London, proving that Britain, not America, had fired the first shot at Lexington. What was to be gained, John thought disgustedly, by proving who fired first? In Congress last summer a Pennsylvania member had suggested bluntly that Massachusetts be left to conduct by herself what quarrels she chose. Was it possible Congress might repeat this proposal? *"Don't let New England start a war,"* Dr. Franklin had written from London, *"without the approval of the Continental Congress. If they do, they may have to fight a war alone."*

John recalled it now with foreboding. Yet a display of anger, contempt, impatience, would persuade of nothing, and might lose much. Even in letters home, John told himself he must be careful, hint rather than say what he felt. "America," he wrote to Abigail,[6] "is a great unwieldy body. Its progress may be slow. It is like a large fleet sailing under convoy. The fastest sailors must wait for the dullest and slowest."

2

After the Lexington depositions, Congress turned its attention to the Continental Association. No more goods must be shipped to Georgia, East and West Florida, Quebec.

JOHN ADAMS
Gilbert Stuart
National Museum of American Art
Smithsonian Institution, Washington, DC
Gift of Miss Mary Louisa Adams Clement

Local merchants sent pleas and claims to the floor. All were solemnly entered in the *Minutes*—as if, John thought, shifting irritably in his seat, as if there were no redcoats at Boston.

The city of New York looked for a large detachment of British troops to land any day. Congress resolved that no resistance should be offered. The redcoats were to be received peacefully by the citizens, even given barrack room! Five men of Boston, who had seen their own town resist British troops since the year '68, sat silent, staring at their shoes.

Here and again, it was true, something happened to lift the gloom of these first days.

6. **Abigail,** Abigail Adams, John's wife.

There was a knock at the door one morning and a traveler entered, his face and clothes streaked with dust. It was a Dr. Hall, from the Parish of St. John's, Georgia. The Parish—a whole county—had sent him as delegate, he told Congress a trifle breathlessly. He had ridden nearly eight hundred miles. Of course he couldn't expect to vote, he added hastily, seeing that the rest of Georgia had not joined the union. But could he sit here, that his constituents might know they were part of the union? John all but wept as the Doctor walked to the seat assigned, limping a little from six consecutive weeks on horseback.

On the 18th of May, Congress heard that Fort Ticonderoga had been captured from the British. Ticonderoga, commanding the approach to the St. Lawrence River, was as important strategically as any point in America. Yet to Congress the affair caused more embarrassment than triumph. Badly as America needed the powder and arms taken by Ethan Allen, to advertise his victory would be to acknowledge before the world that the colonies had definitely taken the offensive against England, nullifying all the careful depositions and proofs about Lexington.

Toward the last of May, something happened to push John altogether beyond his powers of self-control. The Dickinson-Duane faction moved that "an humble and dutiful petition" be dispatched to His Majesty, including a plain statement that the colonies desired immediate negotiation and "accommodation of the unhappy disputes," and that they were ready to "enter into measures" to achieve it.

It was too much. John sprang to his feet and lashed out. His voice, rapid, loud, penetrated to every corner. This was an act of imbecility! Were they to sit composing humble addresses, with the earth still loose over fifty New England graves,[7] and Britain's ships of war coming ever nearer? Had not Congress wasted time enough with humble petitions that were never read, eloquent addresses that

were spurned and spat upon? Let this Congress give over petitioning and memorializing, and get to the business of defending the continent! Two precious weeks had already been wasted. Before they even breathed the word *negotiation*, certain matters should be tended to on this side of the water.

John raised a hand, ticked off his program on his fingers: Let Congress recommend to each colony that it institute an independent popular government. Let the troops at Cambridge be recognized as a Continental army with a commander-in-chief over all, and let Congress assume the entire burden of its subsistence and armament. England should be told of these plans, frankly and fully—and told also that if she continued this war, the colonies would seek help and foreign alliance where they could. John leaned forward, grasped the chair in front of him. "Yes," he repeated, "alliance with France, with the ancient enemy, if need be! With Spain, Holland, with any European power that cares to listen. Then and then only, Congress may enter into negotiation with Britain and her ministers. Then only we may indulge this talk of harmony, accommodation, loyalty, allegiance, love."

Spitting the last five words as if they were poison and would choke him, John sat down. Sullivan of New Hampshire rose immediately, continuing where John left off. His voice was rough, angry. John had scarcely got his breath when he was told a man wished to see him, outside the building in the State House yard. John made his way across the room. As he stepped to the pathway, the door banged behind him and a voice spoke his name, loud, peremptory. Dickinson had followed him out; he was in a violent passion.

"Give me the reason," he shouted, "why you New Englandmen oppose our every measure of reconciliation! Sullivan is in there

---

7. **fifty New England graves,** the graves of the men who died in the battles of Lexington and Concord, April 18 and 19, 1775.

now, haranguing against my petition to the King. Look ye, Adams! If you don't fall in with our plans, I and my friends will break off from New England, carry this Congress and this country in our own way."

John looked coolly back at Dickinson. His own speech had cleared his brain, and though he was still angry, he felt confident, exhilarated. Beyond the open window, Sullivan's voice could be heard, droning on. Out here the midday sun blazed. Sweat poured from Dickinson's face; his lips were white and his fingers twitched at his sides.

"You are wasting your time, Mr. Dickinson," John said. "I am not to be threatened. In the name of unity, I can make sacrifices as well as you. You and your friends have seen me make them. Let the Congress judge between us. If they vote against me, I will submit. And if they vote against you, let you do the same."

Dickinson opened his mouth to speak. John turned on his heel and left him.

3

But if John had won the encounter without doors, Dickinson won it within. Congress voted *Ay* to the humble petition. *Resolved unanimously*, Charles Thomson wrote in the *Minutes*. At the last, John submitted. He had to submit. Unity at all costs must be preserved —and even a dutiful petition need not stop America from fighting a war. But John thought much about Dickinson and his seeming change of front. This was a man who had done more than any of them,[8] back in the year '68, to wake the colonies to the reality of their position. Yet here he was, begging, bargaining, petitioning, praying, negotiating. John determined to fight him with all the strength and all the skill he possessed. Things were in the open now, the parties and factions defined. John and his supporters faced, John said, "not only the party in favor of a petition to the King, and the party who were

jealous of independence, but a third party—a Southern party which was against a Northern, with a jealousy against a New England army under the command of a New England general."

The quickest way to proceed would be to name a commander-in-chief from some colony south of Connecticut. The minute a Southern general was adopted, the army automatically ceased to be a New England organization and became a Continental one. From a military standpoint the move was urgent, vitally necessary. On the way down from Braintree, John had visited headquarters at Cambridge, had seen at first hand how dangerous was the confusion. Already since April, four thousand volunteers had got discouraged and gone home. Sixteen thousand remained, sprawled in lines thirty miles long from Cambridge to Roxbury, subsisting precariously on gifts from the surrounding farms, living in tents, cabins, sailcloth shelters, brush-thatched huts of turf or stone. To encourage enlistment, any man that brought in forty-nine volunteers got a captain's commission. John himself had seen one of these "captains"—a wizened little shoemaker from Weymouth—order a private from his company to fetch a pail of water for the mess. "Fetch it yourself, Keptin," the man had replied without rancor. "I got the last pail."

Artemas Ward of Shrewsbury commanded these motley thousands. He was a Harvard graduate, well known for his services in the French war,[9] and very popular. But he was nearing fifty, suffered from the bladder stone, and had no experience in dealing with such vast numbers of men. John Hancock was New England's candidate to succeed him.

---

8. **a man . . . them.** John Dickinson wrote *Letters from a Farmer in Pennsylvania* (published 1767–1768), anti-British articles in response to the Townshend Acts, most of which were repealed in 1770.
9. **the French war,** the French and Indian War, 1754–1763, in which George Washington also fought.

Hancock had seen no service in the field; besides which he was frequently crippled with gout. But as Colonel of the Boston Cadets he had long cut a fine figure on the parade ground, escorting governors, officiating at civic celebrations. There was little doubt he expected the position, or at least the refusal of it. Hancock moreover had come into special prominence lately by reason of having been named President of Congress pro tem, when Peyton Randolph was called home to Virginia.

John had no slightest intention of nominating Hancock. George Washington was his man. Not only did John admire Washington personally, but unless a Southerner commanded the troops, there would be few enlistments south of Connecticut. Canvassing the delegates, John found little serious support for Hancock; it was Artemas Ward who was Washington's most formidable rival. Yet John felt sure he could persuade his countrymen that local pride should give way to urgent necessity. Colonel Washington, moreover, could afford the job financially, having a large independent fortune. This would count heavily with the Middle and Southern delegates, men like Dickinson, Duane, the Rutledges, who considered an independent fortune the first step to prestige. Washington had more military experience than any other man in America—except of course, the much talked of Colonel Charles Lee, a retired half-pay British officer who lived on his estates in Virginia and advertised himself as more American than the Americans. . . .

John worked hard. By the middle of June, he decided the moment was ripe. On a dull, muggy morning, he walked alone to Congress, determined to nominate Washington before the noon bell sounded from the tower. As soon as the members were seated, John rose and spoke briefly for the establishment of a Continental army, outlining the present dangers, chief of which was that the forces at Cambridge might dissolve entirely.

What was to prevent the British from profiting by this delay, marching out of Boston and "spreading desolation as far as they could go"? For commander-in-chief of a Grand American Army he would like, John finished, to suggest "*a gentleman whose skill as an officer, whose independent fortune, great talents and universal character would command the respect of America and unite the full exertions of the Colonies better than any other person alive.*"

All the time John was speaking, Hancock wore a look of pleased, even radiant, expectancy. Facing the room in his chair behind the President's table, he was plainly visible to everyone, including John, who stood near the front. No one loved glory more than Hancock; he had the vanity of a child, open and vulnerable. John saw his face and hastened on, raising his voice a little: "A gentleman *from Virginia*, who is among us here, and well known to all."

Hancock shrank as at a blow. ("I never," John wrote later, "remarked a more sudden and striking change of countenance. Mortification and resentment were expressed as forcibly as his face could exhibit them.") Washington, who was on the south side of the room, left his seat at the word *Virginia* and slipped quietly out the door before his name was pronounced.

John finished and sat down. Sam Adams rose at once to second the motion. Hancock's face grew hard and dark with anger: he made no attempt to hide his feelings. Since the year '65, Sam Adams's open palm had received the Hancock money—thousands of pounds poured out for the use of the liberty party. Was this to be his reward? Hancock's eyes swept the room. Sherman of Connecticut, then Cushing of Boston, rose. The army around Cambridge, they argued, would not fight under a Southern commander. There had been trouble enough already over the local election of New England officers. Many a regiment had broken up entirely because of these local jealousies.

Samuel F. B. Morse, inventor of the telegraph, was also a painter. He favored historical subjects like this one—"The Old House of Representatives," with its eighty-six legislators and one Indian.

THE OLD HOUSE OF REPRESENTATIVES
Samuel F. B. Morse
Corcoran Gallery of Art, Washington, DC
Museum Purchase

Colonel Washington was indeed a splendid soldier and patriot, someone else interposed. But he could speak no French, an accomplishment that might prove indispensable should this war continue, and foreign alliances, foreign legions, be sought.

The debate went on. Most of the talk, John noted with relief, came from a very small group. Three-quarters, perhaps seven-eighths, of the room sat silent. They were the Washington men. John had worked hard enough by now to know it, and know they were merely waiting for the vote. Late in the afternoon, Congress rose without taking the count. That evening the brace of Adamses were very busy, and next morning when Johnson of Maryland put the motion a sec-ond time, Congress voted unanimously for Washington.

A week later, on Friday, June 23rd, John got on his horse and with most of Congress, escorted General Washington and his military entourage out of town on the journey northward. They had not ridden twenty miles from Philadelphia when the little cavalcade was stopped by a very dusty courier posting down from Connecticut. Gage had attacked the Provincial entrenchments. There had been a battle on the hills above Boston— Breed's Hill, Bunker's Hill;[10] . . . Charles-

10. **Breed's Hill, Bunker's Hill.** The so-called battle of Bunker Hill, June 17, 1775, was actually fought on nearby Breed's Hill.

town was burned by the enemy. Out of two thousand British, a thousand had been lost, and four hundred Americans. . . . The militia were driven from their position.

4

After Bunker Hill, Congress seemed to bestir itself, jolted into more decisive action. Articles of War were adopted for the army, a hospital service organized, with doctors, nurses, and such medicines as could be found. Congress scoured the country for gunpowder and for saltpeter to make it, niter, sulphur, for brass fieldpieces, and above all for muskets that would shoot. A General Post Office was set up to facilitate communications. Loans of money were arranged to buy army supplies; two millions of paper dollars were ordered printed and put in circulation. A department of Indian Affairs was organized; a skillful and most necessary appeal composed, praying the powerful Six Nations to remain neutral in this war.

Yet even now, in all that Congress did, it proceeded conditionally, John noted. Always conditionally, on the assumption, the hope, the prayer, that Britain would capitulate, make peace, forgive, return to the old free system of government. Early in July, Dickinson's *Petition to the King* went off to London, carried by Richard Penn and signed, of course, by every member of Congress. John wrote his name below Sam's and, thoroughly disgusted, threw down his pen. The *Address to the People of Great Britain* which went in the same ship affected him as strongly. The times were too desperate, the situation too serious, for such polite and fruitless trafficking. "Prettynesses," John wrote in disgust, "juvenilities—and much less, Puerilities, became not a great assembly like this, the Representatives of a great People."

There was one member of Congress, a new member, who occupied himself with neither prettinesses nor puerilities. Late in June,

Thomas Jefferson had arrived from Virginia. John was immediately drawn to him. ("He soon seized upon my heart," John said.) Jefferson at thirty-two was tall, thin, sandy-haired, with a fair complexion—in no way celebrated unless it was for his trick of writing fluent English. The Virginia delegates had boasted about it. Jefferson was not a speechmaker like Patrick Henry or Richard Henry Lee. His eloquence lay all on paper. He could translate into warm and even burning words the most abstract ideas concerning government, liberty, freedom. Jefferson was a natural scholar, his friends reported further, deeply read in history and natural science—"the greatest rubber-off-of-dust," Duane told John, that he had ever met, with a knowledge of French, Italian, and Spanish, and the ambition to learn German. What particularly attracted John, these first weeks, was Jefferson's quick, decisive way in committee. "He was prompt," John said; "frank, explicit as Samuel Adams himself."

Not long after Jefferson's arrival, he was put on a committee to draft a *Declaration of the Causes and Necessity for Taking up Arms*, a document designed chiefly for the troops at Cambridge. Jefferson was asked to write it. He proceeded very carefully, making several drafts, striking out phrases that seemed verbose or slipshod. But the committee disapproved. ("It was too strong for Mr. Dickinson," Jefferson said later.) Dickinson went over it, and though he strengthened rather than toned it down, Congress accepted his version. *"Our cause is just,"* a final paragraph ran, *"our union is perfect. We fight not for glory or for conquest. In our own native land, in defence of the freedom that is our birthright, we have taken up arms. We shall lay them down when hostilities shall cease on the part of the aggressors, and all danger of their being renewed shall be removed, and not before."*

Yet the *Declaration on Taking Arms*, spirited though it might be, was balanced on the other side by the humble petition. John could not forget it. "In exchange for these Petitions, Declarations and Addresses," he wrote home, "I suppose we shall receive Bills of Attainder and other such like Expressions of Esteem and Kindness."

"Does every member of Congress feel for us?" Abigail had written after Bunker Hill. "Can they realize what we suffer?"

"No!" John answered. "They don't! They can't. A ship is dearer to some of them than a city, and a few barrels of flour than a thousand men's lives—other men's lives, I mean."

5

The British burned Falmouth in October of 1775, shelling it from the sea, a pointed answer to Dickinson's humble *Petition to the King*. One hundred and fifty buildings, churches, houses were leveled to the ground. The news shocked the entire country. Here was no midnight raid by naked, painted savages. The British had done this. America's own brothers had done it. Captain Mowett, commander of the ship *Canceaux* that had led the shelling, showed papers ordering him to destroy all towns from Boston to Halifax, and announced that Portsmouth would be next.

"Death and desolation mark their footsteps," General Nathanael Greene wrote to the newspapers from Washington's headquarters outside of Boston. "Fight or be slaves is the American motto now." This was civil war with a vengeance.

Yet there were men in the patriot party who showed little sympathy for Falmouth. One of them was John's old friend, Major Hawley of Northampton. By whose fault was it, Hawley demanded, that Falmouth had been a "defenseless victim"? The town had refused to arm, had taken no measures to blockade the harbor. Would its citizens believe, at last, that Britain was an enemy not a friend, or must Boston be burned to prove it, and Philadelphia? Let Falmouth and her sister towns cease to mourn and whimper! Let

them abandon their mistaken "loyalty" and enter this contest with their whole heart and strength, taking pride in the rightness of the cause. This was not the first civil war of history. The Scriptures themselves bore witness: "And the children of Israel wept before the Lord and asked counsel, saying, Shall I go up to battle against the children of Benjamin my brother? And the Lord said, Go up against him."

Go up against thy brother. America was not yet ready for such counsel. America was still two-thirds Tory and four-fifths totally indifferent to the war. Thirteen colonies as yet had no conception of themselves as a nation, though they had begun cautiously to talk of a confederacy, and newspapers used the phrase *United American Colonies*. Even the patriots still regarded the war as an affair wholly sectional. Each colony felt justified in taking what individual stand it chose. New Jersey threatened a separate peace treaty with Britain, Massachusetts a separate declaration of independence. Congress found it necessary to pass a resolution *"that it will be very dangerous to the liberties and welfare of America, if any Colony should separately petition the King or either house of Parliament."*

The Middle colonies seemed more concerned over internal squabbles than over the war with Britain, putting their hope in the King of England, nursing the kind illusion that it was the British ministry and not George III who burned their towns and murdered their brothers. In spite of Lexington, Bunker Hill, Falmouth, in spite even of Hessian mercenaries coming to kill them, Americans still believed that kings were half divine. *George Rex* ruled by godly sanction. Every warrant bore his name, every office was conferred under the power of his royal seal and signature. To deny him, dethrone him, would be not only dangerous but impious.

Led by Dickinson, the "conciliation men" had no slightest intention of knuckling under to Britain, no intention of renouncing the fight for a free representative government in America. They still hoped, by threat or persuasion, to gain a free government not separate from the British Empire but within it. Their position had not changed since August, 1774, when Congress first met to protest the Boston Port Bill.[11] The trouble was, Britain had not reacted according to their prophecies or their plans. The commercial blockade had failed to force Britain's hand, the use of arms had failed to force it. Parliament and King were no nearer yielding than they had been when Peyton Randolph called the first meeting to order in Carpenters' Hall.

The radical party in Congress, the "violent men," the "independence men," were led now by the two Adamses, Gadsden of South Carolina, the two Lees and George Wythe of Virginia. Washington of course was with the army; Patrick Henry had stayed in Virginia as Colonel of the militia. Jefferson, called home by illness in his family, would not return until May of '76. Their party differed from the Dickinson-Duane-Wilson faction only in having abandoned all hope of reconciliation. This was not to say they did not still desire it in their hearts. Every one of them, except perhaps Sam Adams, would have rejoiced to see America remain—on her own terms—within the British Empire. But they were realistic, knew that separation was now inevitable —and recognized further that Britain would destroy the colonies altogether rather than yield.

To this last, the conciliatory party remained blind, preferring to deceive themselves and their followers with visions of an olive branch extended across the seas. Peace commissioners were coming from London in the spring or summer, said Dickinson, Rutledge, Duane. They had positive news of it, positive promises. What folly, then, and what wickedness, to scream separation from England! The independence men would be guilty of plunging their country in endless, tragic civil war, compared with which the few skirmishes already fought would be nothing. A wise delay of a few months might save the situation.

John Adams said openly and contemptuously that he did not believe a word of this commissioner talk. "A bubble," he called it. "As arrant an illusion as ever was hatched in the brain of an enthusiast, a politician or a maniac."

For the conciliation men, John Adams had become, by January of 1776, an adversary more dangerous even than his cousin Samuel. Sam at least was opposed to a large standing army; Sam recognized and valued local attachments, local sentiments. One had the feeling that the *Grand Incendiary*[12] was a Massachusetts man first, an American second. But John Adams put a Continental army and a Continental confederated government over and beyond all else.

There was about this Braintree Adams something maddeningly obdurate. He seemed not to care how many enemies he made, and he was sure of himself and his convictions! When he rose he spoke arrogantly, let his voice ring out with royal impatience, thumped his hickory walking stick against the floor to make his points tell. He had a way of drawing in his lips, sucking loudly against his teeth, raising his thick powerful chest as if to gather the force of a tremendous bellows and then letting fly, repeating himself inexorably, like a bell that clangs and clangs and will not be denied. "Nothing can save us but discipline in the army, governments in every colony and a confederation of the whole. . . . *Discipline in the army*! (thump with the hickory cane) *A written constitution in every state*! (thump again) *A union and a confederation of thirteen states, independent of Parliament, of Minister and of King*!"

11. **Boston Port Bill,** a reference to the Coercive Acts, passed March–June 1774 in response to the Boston Tea Party. One act closed the port of Boston until the ruined tea was paid for.
12. **the Grand Incendiary,** a nickname of Sam Adams.

FOR UNDERSTANDING

1. As expressed in a letter that he wrote home, what was John Adams's attitude toward those training to be soldiers?

2. What was significant about George Washington's appearance at the congress?

3. Why was the capture of Fort Ticonderoga an "embarrassment" to the congress?

4. When John Adams finally spoke at the congress for the first time, what proposals did he make?

5. Who became president of the congress when Peyton Randolph was called home? What other specially significant event occurred as a result of his being called home to Virginia?

6. Why was it particularly important in John Adams's mind for a southerner to be in command of the army?

7. What important events in the Boston area finally jolted the congress into stronger action?

8. What terrible final recognition did members of the radical party in the congress come to?

FOR INTERPRETATION

1. Why did John Adams almost weep at the sight of the delegate from Georgia?

2. Why was the conciliatory party even more strongly against John than against his cousin Sam?

3. Assuming that it is true that at the time of the Second Continental Congress two-thirds of all Americans were sympathetic to the British and 80 percent of them were indifferent to the war, does this mean that the delegates were acting against the wishes of Americans when they ultimately adopted the Declaration of Independence? Why or why not?

4. John Adams was a member of the radical party at the Continental Congress—we might even call him an extremist today. Yet his side eventually prevailed. What personal qualities helped Adams win victory for his side in spite of the great odds against him?

5. What events helped John Adams's side to win? (In trying to answer this question, you might turn back to some earlier selections in this unit.)

6. Henry David Thoreau (see page 190) in his essay "Civil Disobedience" wrote, "Any man more right than his neighbor constitutes a majority of one." Discuss the meaning of this quotation in the light of the selection you have just read.

FOR APPRECIATION

The Art of Biography

A good biographer tries to get inside her or his subject and relive events as the subject lived them. How does Catherine Drinker Bowen, writing in this century, manage to relive events John Adams experienced 200 years previously? How does she give her readers the illusion that they know John Adams? To answer these questions, respond to each of the following:

1. Look carefully at the opening paragraph of the selection. How many proper nouns do you find? Why might this be significant?

2. What other examples of good concrete details can you find in the opening paragraph?

3. Now focus on the second paragraph of the selection. How does Bowen know that John Adams was "often enough . . . among the crowd"? How does she know he was "touched and cheered by the martial spirit"?

4. At the end of the third paragraph of the selection, we find this sentence: "Surely, the news would bring Georgia into the union!" Who is speaking here? How do you know?

5. How does the author refer to Adams when she first mentions him? How does she refer to him in the next paragraph? Can you explain the slight change?

COMPOSITION WORKSHOP

THE BOOK REVIEW

Of all the different kinds of writing assignments you have been given so far by your teachers, the book report is probably one of the most familiar. It usually involves a brief, informative account of a book, summarizing its contents. This is, incidentally, one convenient way of making sure you have completed a particular reading assignment.

A book review is like a book report in giving a brief summary of the writing being discussed. It goes beyond a mere report of its contents, however, by offering a closer inspection of the work and an evaluation of it as well. In this respect, a book review resembles a third kind of writing about books—called literary criticism—in which the whole emphasis is on evaluation and analysis. As you can see, the book review itself stands midway between the book report and a piece of literary criticism. Like the first, it summarizes the work. Like the second, it gives an evaluation of it. Like neither, it tries to suggest in brief terms how good the book is—that is, how well-written it is. It must also indicate how well the book does its particular job—how effective, informative, or moving it is.

Let's look more closely at the kind of book review that most often appears in newspapers and magazines. This type of review is usually about 500 words long and is broken into five or six paragraphs. The text of the review is preceded by a heading that gives basic information about the book: title and author, publisher and city of publication, number of pages, kind of binding (hardcover or paperback), and price. For example:

The Red Badge of Courage, by Stephen Crane. Washington Square Press, New York. 156 pp. Soft cover, $4.95.

The first section of a review provides a general context for the discussion, explaining what kind of book is being examined and giving a few pertinent facts about the author. If the book is not a recent one, some historical background may help to suggest the work's place in the literature of its time as compared with its standing now.

The second section of the review typically gives a brief summary of the book, seldom longer than one paragraph. Reviewers of new fiction often avoid giving away the book's ending, but in reviewing classic works this isn't always considered necessary. In any case, the summary should give the reader some idea of what the book is about.

The final section of the book review offers a critical evaluation of the work. This is the hardest element of a review to define because there are so many different ways to judge a work. To speak only of fiction meant for the general reader, more questions arise than can be answered at such short length: How well-written is the work? How moving is it? How does the work achieve its effect? Are the characters believable? Is the situation true to life? Does the sequence of events show us, rather than tell us, the theme of the book? Is the plot well handled, or is it artificial and mechanical? Is the theme illuminating and thought-provoking or dull and obvious?

Much will depend on the nature of the book being discussed. For example, a work of realistic fiction attempts to show us recognizable characters from the "real" world and can be judged in part by its skill in creating an illusion of that reality. But realism as such may not be the most important goal of the author, as in fantasy, science fiction, myths, fables, and visionary or experimental work. Here, the goal is to get us, temporarily, to believe in the unbelievable—in characters and events that are *not* true to life as we know it. But we would still want to investigate how the author achieves these effects.

Regardless of whether a work of literature is realistic or fantastic, it is presumably written to have an emotional impact upon its reader and, ultimately, to add to our understanding of what it means to be human. Since every reader is a human being and thus an "expert" on the human condition, the personal reaction of any reader is a valid possible starting place for evaluation. One need not have been in a war to judge a war novel. One need not have gone to the moon to judge a story about space travel. Standards will vary, but the good writer will find a way to make the subject, however familiar or remote, come alive in the reader's imagination.

No matter what questions are raised for evaluation, they must be answered succinctly, since the final section of a book review should generally be only one to three paragraphs long.

Here is the text of a sample review. It follows immediately upon the heading presented earlier. Note the points it raises and the order in which they are presented.

This classic American novel, published in 1895, appeared thirty years after the Civil War, when its author was only twenty-four years old. Stephen Crane died five years later and while he wrote other important work, both fiction and poetry, it is on the strength of this novel alone that he has attained a permanent place in American literature.

The Red Badge of Courage was immediately celebrated as a powerful war novel for its realistic description of the Civil War, particularly by those who had experienced the war firsthand. There was widespread amazement when it became known that Crane hadn't been born till after the Civil War and had, in fact, never taken part in or witnessed military combat. Later, when he experienced battle as a correspondent in Greece and Cuba, he said that war was exactly as he imagined it to be in his novel.

The central character in the book is a young private, Henry Fleming, who is filled with romantic notions about the glory of war. In his first engagement, however, fear overcomes him, and he flees from battle, only to stumble upon the agonized death-scene of a wounded friend, Jim Conklin. After hiding in the depths of a forest, Fleming again meets up with friendly troops but is struck down by a frenzied soldier retreating from battle. Ironically, this wound allows him to return to his unit without disgrace. Finally, cleansed of his grandiose notions of war and his own fearful selfishness, he carries a flag to victory in the next engagement.

The most remarkable thing about this novel is the vividness and intensity with which Crane evokes his hero's harrowing growth from self-preoccupied fear toward a more mature self-confidence. A strong sense of reality is projected despite a somewhat plotless movement of blurred and disjointed scenes. Yet these rapid shifts from one feverish emotional state to another are given unity and solidity by a skein of metaphor and symbol.

Most noticeably, certain colors come to symbolize the thematic elements of the book. The red god of war, the pastelike gray of death, the purity and hope of the unclouded blue sky, the golden rays of the sun in the book's last sentence—all of these are used by Crane much as an impressionist painter uses dabs of color to catch the vibrant atmosphere of a particular landscape.

There is also a repeated use of religious symbols to suggest the profundity of the change that Fleming undergoes. This change is set in motion by the death of Jim Conklin (whose initials are those of Jesus Christ). As Conklin dies, Crane says, "The red sun was pasted in the sky like a wafer." This sacramental image is deepened in the "cathedral-forest" scene that follows; here Fleming expresses his contrition and confronts his own fear of death.

The headlong rush of the book is given emotional depth by the coherence of these strands of imagery, tying action and theme securely together. The imagery remains astonishingly fresh even today and contributes to the novel's enduring impact. Unique in its combination of realistic and impressionistic elements, the novel remains a forward-looking landmark in American fiction.

ASSIGNMENT 1

Choose an American novel to review. You may select any novel discussed in this book or one that your teacher recommends. Read the book carefully, with an awareness that you will be reviewing it.

ASSIGNMENT 2

Write a book review of the work you read for Assignment 1. Make sure that your review contains the sections found in a typical book review.

BOSTON HARBOR FROM CONSTITUTION WHARF (detail), Robert Salmon
United States Naval Academy Museum, Anapolis, MD

American Romanticism

1830–1865

Between the years 1830 and 1865 the early national literature of America matured. Our country produced a galaxy of writers whose light shines even more brilliantly today than it did 100 years ago. At the beginning of this period, Edgar Allan Poe (see page 231) published his first poems and began composing his highly original short stories. By the end, Emily Dickinson had her extraordinary "letter to the world" (as she called her poetry) well underway. The middle of the era saw the production of important works by five of America's most famous writers: Ralph Waldo Emerson (see page 180), Henry David Thoreau (see page 190), Nathaniel Hawthorne (see page 210), Herman Melville (see page 252), and Walt Whitman (see page 313). How can we account for this enormous outpouring of creative energy on the part of such disparate writers? Despite considerable differences in form and style, most of them approached their themes with an essentially Romantic outlook. We therefore sum up this era by calling it the Age of Romanticism in American letters.

A Galaxy of Writers

Romanticism refers to a set of loosely connected attitudes toward nature and mankind, rather than to the specific theme of romantic love. In Europe and in England, starting around the middle of the eighteenth century, Romanticism in the arts meant the creation of new themes: the celebration of the self, exaltation in the natural landscape, scrutiny of the artist's own personality and imagination. Romantic poetry rejected the strict styles and forms of eighteenth-century verse and sought new freedom. The greatest of the English Romantics— William Wordsworth (1770–1850), Samuel Taylor Coleridge (1772–1834), George Gordon, Lord Byron (1788–1824), Percy Bysshe Shelley (1792–1822), and John Keats (1795–1821)—focused on individual aspirations and emotions rather than on the standards and norms of society as a whole.

Age of Romanticism

Romanticism came relatively late to American literature. But it produced a splendidly diverse harvest. Emerson and Thoreau elaborated the philosophy of Transcendentalism, essentially a humanist, individualistic system of thought, celebrating the individual's power to create his or her own universe. Nathaniel Hawthorne and Herman Melville, our two greatest novelists of the mid-nineteenth century, shared the preference of the Romantics for exotic or remote settings.

American landscape painting of the nineteenth century closely paralleled the major literary movements of the period. A case in point is this luminously romantic seascape by Martin Johnson Heade.

Hawthorne's tales explored America's Puritan past, whereas Melville created universal, symbolic worlds from his experiences in the South Pacific and on board whaling vessels. Both Hawthorne and Melville presented the interior psychology of their characters with a new subtlety, and they may be said to have paved the way for realism in American literature later in the century.

Romantic Traits: the Individual and the Unique

Edgar Allan Poe shared with the novelists a Romantic preoccupation with unusual states of mind: madness, terror, and dreams. Acclaimed now as the inventor of the detective story, Poe also used exotic settings in his tales (as in "The Fall of the House of Usher") and depicted his mysterious characters with keen psychological insight. The themes of Poe, Hawthorne, and Melville are darker than the sunny optimism of Emerson or the prickly independence of Thoreau. What marks them all as Romantic writers is their focus on the individual and their determination to explore the limits of unique personalities.

The poetry of this period moved from popular traditionalism to extraordinary originality. The "fireside poets"—Henry Wadsworth Longfellow, John Greenleaf Whittier, and Oliver Wendell Holmes—

wrote of the American past and the American landscape in a fluent, accessible style. Their themes were popular: love, family, patriotism. They were Romantic in their shared recognition of life's mixture of pleasure and pain; much of their work displays an autumnal quality tinged with melancholy. Perhaps the most dynamically Romantic poet of the period—and certainly the most original—was Walt Whitman. Whitman set out in his poetry to fuse his own individual personality with the collective personality of the nation. Aspiring, exuberant, sensitive, he gloried in America's diversity of peoples and landscapes. The "I" in his poetry encompasses the merchant prince and the

Poetry:
Popular and
Original

One of the best-known of all American landscape paintings is this peaceful river scene by George Caleb Bingham. The artist grew up in Missouri, a region that inspired some of his most famous paintings.

FUR TRADERS DESCENDING THE MISSOURI
George Caleb Bingham
Metropolitan Museum of Art, New York City
Morris K. Jessup Fund

This little plaster group of checker players was one of many made by naturalist sculptor John Rogers and sold in general stores around the country for about $15 in the mid-1800s.

humble dock-worker, the teeming cities and the vast prairies. His optimism and compassion were the irresistible hallmarks of his work. Even as he rejected the restraints of strict meter and rhyme in poetry to create free verse, he became America's first truly democratic poet.

We will focus in this unit on most of these major figures of American Romanticism, but it should be mentioned that many other significant writers flourished at this time. Margaret Fuller (1810–1850), the gifted editor of the Transcendentalist magazine *The Dial,* published *Woman in the Nineteenth Century* (1845), a feminist classic. She probably would have made many other significant contributions to literature had it not been for her untimely death. And no account of the novelists of the period should omit the names of Harriet Beecher Stowe and Louisa May Alcott, who wrote *Uncle Tom's Cabin* (1852) and *Little Women* (1868) respectively—two of the most popular books ever published.

EMERSON, THOREAU, AND TRANSCENDENTALISM

Many foreign writers and thinkers as well as many Americans contributed to the philosophy that goes by the name of Transcendentalism. But it is generally agreed that the authors who contributed most heavily were the Americans Ralph Waldo Emerson and Henry David Thoreau. Emerson's essay *Nature* (1836) is usually considered the best and most systematic expression of the philosophy, although its premises are further elaborated in some of Emerson's other essays, in his poems, and in Thoreau's famous *Walden* (1854). Let us try to define Transcendentalism.

To Go Beyond

Its root, *scandere,* means "to climb." (We find the same root in such familiar words as *ascend* and *descend.*) Its prefix, *trans-,* means "over." Thus, *to transcend* is *to climb over* or, more broadly, *to go beyond.*

"To go beyond what?" is the next question we might ask. For the Transcendentalists of the middle part of the nineteenth century, the "what" was the limitations of the senses and of everyday experience. When Thoreau writes, "I have never yet met a man who was quite awake," he is commenting on these everyday limitations, saying that we do not see to the roots of things.

The Inner Light

A next question might be, "How do we go beyond everyday experience?" The Transcendentalists would answer: "By depending upon our intuition rather than on reason or logic." Reliance on intuition was nothing new in America. The Puritans had hoped for an intuitive revelation that they were among God's "chosen"; the Quakers tried to live by the "inner light."

Higher Truths and Insights

Finally we may ask, "What happens when, by use of intuition, we go beyond everyday human experience?" The broadest answer, according to the Transcendentalists, is that we discover higher truths and insights. For Emerson, one of the specific discoveries was "the all in

SEE NON TY A, AN IOWA MEDICINE MAN, George Catlin

National Gallery of Art, Washington D.C., Paul Mellon Collection

The December 29, 1860, cover of Harper's Weekly, *one of the most popular American magazines of the nineteenth century. Note the price of the magazine and its "civilizing" intent, as stated in its subtitle.*

Mount was the outstanding American genre painter of the nineteenth century. Clear, direct, simple and wholesome, genre painting celebrated the workaday life of the common man and woman, extolling the democratic virtues and activities of everyday American country life.

CIDER MAKING
William Sidney Mount
Metropolitan Museum of Art, New York City
Charles Allen Munn Bequest

each." He discovered that "the individual is the world." He placed the individual squarely at the spiritual center of the universe. This credo does not mean that the Transcendentalists did not believe in God; it does mean that they did not think of God as something apart from human beings or nature. Thoreau thought God was so much a part of himself that when he was asked on his deathbed whether he had made peace with God, he answered, "I didn't know we had ever quarreled."

Transcendentalism was, then, a radically humanistic philosophy. In this respect it was opposed to the otherworldly philosophy of the

*The Individual
Is the World*

Porcelain vase, 1884

Puritans. But it was similar to Puritanism in at least one respect: it was highly moralistic. Emerson and Thoreau were concerned with how human beings should live. Democracy, equality, individualism, self-reliance, integrity, optimism—these were among their key values. It is significant that one of the last and best of Emerson's works was a series of essays entitled *The Conduct of Life* (1860).

POE, HAWTHORNE, MELVILLE

Edgar Allan Poe, Nathaniel Hawthorne, and Herman Melville shared many values with Emerson and Thoreau. Yet none of these great writers subscribed to Transcendentalism. If they were influenced by it at all, they were negatively influenced: Transcendentalism was something for them to react against.

The main reason for their rejection of the philosophy was their denial of some of Emerson's major premises and attitudes: his insistence on optimism, his belief in progress, and, above all, his failure to recognize fully the reality of evil. Emerson, whom we still see as more characteristically American than the other three, was full of sun and light. But Melville, who was speaking about Hawthorne and who could have been speaking for Poe, wrote of the "great power of blackness [which] derives its force from its appeals to that Calvinistic sense of Innate Depravity and Original Sin, from whose visitations . . . no deeply thinking mind is always and wholly free." In their concern with blackness, with evil and sin, Poe, Hawthorne, and Melville had more in common with the Puritans than they did with Emerson and Thoreau.

Edgar Allan Poe knew blackness firsthand. From the beginning, his life was a series of catastrophes (for instance, his father deserted the family, and his mother died before he was three). For most of his forty years, he struggled against poverty, in spite of the fact that his story "The Gold Bug" and his poem "The Raven" were instant successes.

Yet, undaunted by hardship, misfortune, and acute emotional anguish, Poe achieved eminence in three fields. He was an exceptional critic (the first professional to appreciate Hawthorne), a poet, and a short-story writer of marked originality. And although some American critics and writers have disdained Poe, he had a profound effect on literature both here and abroad. Specifically, Poe strongly influenced the French Symbolist poets and thus, indirectly, such Americans as T. S. Eliot and Wallace Stevens. He also virtually invented the detective story, and some of his own works remain classics of that genre. Finally, Poe was one of the first to use fiction to explore morbid states of mind. Thus, he is an early link in a chain that includes some of the best fiction of our own time.

The Impact of Poe

Nathaniel Hawthorne

Nathaniel Hawthorne, too, was an intrepid explorer of the darker side of the human soul, and he is often given credit for founding the

*The interior of a well-to-do New Jersey home about 1820. The room is
furnished in neoclassic style, a fashion borrowed from the French,
who in turn had copied it from early Greek and Roman forms.*

psychological novel. Like Poe (and Melville), his own early life was
marked by the loss of a father and subsequent poverty. Moreover, his
mother never quite recovered from the loss of her husband, and her
periods of seclusion must have affected her son. In any event, he
himself became reclusive, spending most of his time in a third-floor
room of his uncle's house in Salem, Massachusetts, learning to become
a writer—for twelve long years.

*Dark Side
of the
Human Soul*

His first book of stories, *Twice-Told Tales* (1837), marked his reentry
into the world. Its tales, however, probed the inner and outward effects
of Puritanism and centered on such themes as guilt, pride, and

alienation. While this book was not a financial success, it was hailed by many, including Edgar Allan Poe, who said it belonged to "the highest region of Art." A second collection of stories, *Mosses from an Old Manse* (1846), was also concerned with darker themes and the mysteries of the human heart. It won Hawthorne the admiration and the friendship of Herman Melville.

It was, however, his first major novel, *The Scarlet Letter* (1850), that established Hawthorne's reputation—and his immortality. A tale of sin, perdition, and redemption, it was unlike any work of fiction that had appeared previously. Hawthorne went on to write other novels, notably *The House of the Seven Gables* (1851), but his earlier work is his deepest and best.

Melville's South Sea Successes

Herman Melville's career began brightly enough with the successful novels *Typee* and *Omoo*, which were semiromanticized adventures about his own experiences in the South Seas. But he soon determined to follow his own genius—to tell the truth as he saw it rather than to please readers. And his pursuit of truth led him into poverty and profound despair.

Unlike the Transcendentalists, who believed in a congruity between the structure of the human spirit and the structure of the universe, Melville believed that the structure of the universe was tragically flawed. He could not account for the inequities and injustices of the world and said, "NO! in thunder" to that world. He used his later novels—especially *Moby-Dick* (1851), *Pierre* (1852), and *The Confidence Man* (1857)—to communicate that message, but few cared to hear it during his lifetime.

Moby-Dick

Today, however, Melville's reputation as one of our greatest writers is firmly established. *Moby-Dick*, the story of Captain Ahab's maniacal pursuit of the white whale, is acknowledged to be one of the greatest novels of world literature. And short works such as "Bartleby the Scrivener," "Benito Cereno," and *Billy Budd* are undisputed American classics. The last of these, incidentally, was finished just five days before Melville's death and was not published until thirty years later. *Billy Budd* is a tragedy—true to Melville's vision—but it also strikes an affirmative note.

LONGFELLOW, WHITTIER, HOLMES

The Fireside Poets

Writing at the same time as Poe, Hawthorne, and Melville, but on very different themes and with equally different emphases, were the so-called fireside poets, a group whose most famous members were William Cullen Bryant (see page 143), Henry Wadsworth Longfellow (see page 281), John Greenleaf Whittier (see page 287), Oliver Wendell Holmes (see page 291), and James Russell Lowell (1819–1891). They were not a group in the sense that they communicated frequently with

A founder of the Hudson River School, Cole brought both realism and idealism to his paintings. The scenes he painted were on a heroic scale, and embued with an almost religious awe for the grandeur of the American wilderness.

THE OXBOW, Thomas Cole
Metropolitan Musuem of Art, New York City
Gift of Mrs. Russell Sage

one another, although they did know one another. They were called "fireside poets" because their poetry could be understood by the literate common man and woman, who often read it by their firesides.

It was remarkable that five major poets should have shared an appreciative audience over a long period of time—they were widely known, read, and loved over the whole second half of the nineteenth century, and even beyond. Still more remarkable was the fact that these poets appealed to highly educated readers as well as to less educated ones. In this century, we have had poets who appealed to the average reader and poets who appealed to the intellectual, but only rarely have we seen major talents who appealed to both.

What gave these poets such a broad appeal? They seem to have had

*Widely Read,
Widely Loved*

Traditional Forms,
Popular Themes

four things in common. First, they used traditional forms and metrical arrangements; they were not "experimental" poets like Walt Whitman and Emily Dickinson. Second, they wrote for the most part on "popular" themes—idealized love and nature, God and religion, home, family, children, and country. Third, they all shared the view that the function of poetry was to teach, and their "lessons," on the whole, were clearly communicated. Finally, there is a shared tone in much of their work, one we might identify as bittersweet in its recognition that life combines delight and regret, pleasure and sadness. A touch of melancholy and a yearning for youth or for the past characterizes many of their poems.

CONFLICT AND CONTINUITY

The Civil War

Toward the end of this period in which so many outstanding writers flourished, a great war between the states was fought. Provoked in large measure by the issue of slavery, it raised the critical question of whether the newfound experiment with democracy and freedom could survive in one piece.

Douglass,
Lincoln,
and Lee

There was a prevailing gloom over the land through much of this time, and literary production was definitely inhibited. In 1864, William Wells Brown published the first novel to be written by a black American. But his book—*Clotelle: A Tale of the Southern States*—had been previously published much earlier (1853) in London. In fact, no really major work of American fiction was published during the war years, though the period inspired much impassioned prose of other kinds. In the years before the war, the autobiography of Frederick Douglass (see page 299), a fugitive slave and self-educated man, was read by thousands of Americans. During the war, Abraham Lincoln (see page 303) gave memorable expression to some of our national dreams and aspirations, notably in his address at Gettsyburg. Robert E. Lee (see page 306) could have spoken eloquently for the South and did write some fine letters; but he was no speechmaker and refused to write memoirs of the war.

While the war temporarily silenced America's major novelists, it stimulated her poets. All the fireside poets were writing during this period, as was Herman Melville, who turned from prose to poetry, publishing a number of excellent poems on the war. There was also a fresh young poetic talent from the South, Henry Timrod (see page 309), who wrote a number of excellent poems on behalf of the Southern cause.

Walt Whitman

But the greatest of all poetic talents, who was also the reassuring voice of continuity, was Walt Whitman. He had already been shaping *Leaves of Grass*—the title of each of the nine editions of his poems—since 1855. But the war prompted *Drum-Taps*, a book of war poems, and its "Sequel" of poems about Abraham Lincoln, written after that

This painting dramatically captures the impressive natural setting of the burgeoning settlements along the river in the 1800s.

VIEW OF THE HUDSON, Thomas Havell
New York Historical Society, New York City

symbol of democracy had been assassinated. A poem like "When Lilacs Last in the Dooryard Bloom'd" promised that democracy would always be reborn, even out of the ashes of the deepest tragedy.

Above all, Whitman was affirmative. As determined as Melville had been to say "NO! in thunder," the author of *Leaves of Grass* was determined to say "Yes!" in a sunburst of optimism and energy that far surpassed Emerson's. Whitman loved everything, affirmed everything, took everything in.

A Sunburst of Optimism

But most important of all was Whitman's identification with the common man and woman. Other writers before him had expressed concern for the average citizen, and nearly all had believed deeply in the democratic ideal, but Whitman *was* a common man—a printer's apprentice, a reporter, a schoolteacher, a politician, a housebuilder, a volunteer nurse, a government employee. Whitman celebrated himself, to be sure, but he did so as a symbol of the "divine average," as a traveler along the open road on the long journey of the American people toward freedom and self-development.

Democracy and the Common Person

American Romanticism

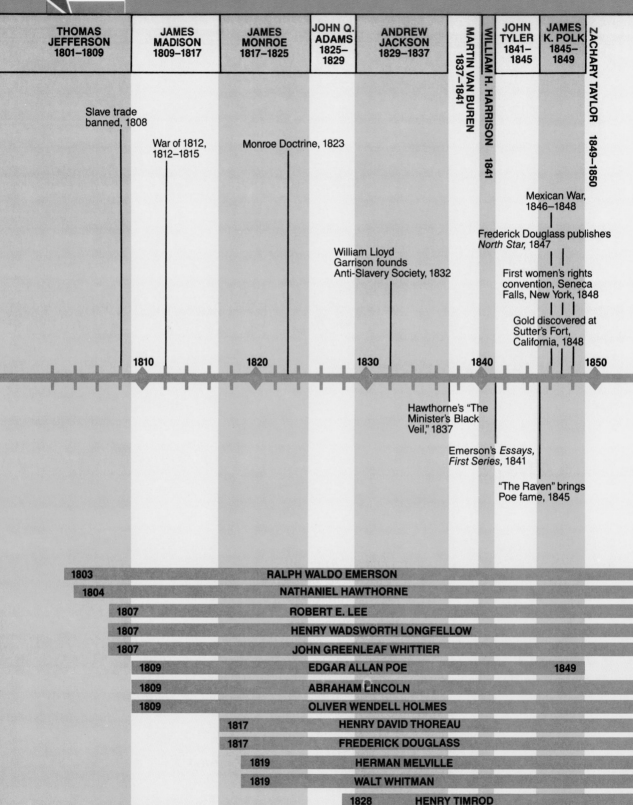

THOMAS JEFFERSON 1801–1809	JAMES MADISON 1809–1817	JAMES MONROE 1817–1825	JOHN Q. ADAMS 1825–1829	ANDREW JACKSON 1829–1837	MARTIN VAN BUREN 1837–1841	WILLIAM H. HARRISON 1841	JOHN TYLER 1841–1845	JAMES K. POLK 1845–1849	ZACHARY TAYLOR 1849–1850

Slave trade banned, 1808

War of 1812, 1812–1815

Monroe Doctrine, 1823

Mexican War, 1846–1848

Frederick Douglass publishes *North Star,* 1847

William Lloyd Garrison founds Anti-Slavery Society, 1832

First women's rights convention, Seneca Falls, New York, 1848

Gold discovered at Sutter's Fort, California, 1848

1810   1820   1830   1840   1850

Hawthorne's "The Minister's Black Veil," 1837

Emerson's *Essays, First Series,* 1841

"The Raven" brings Poe fame, 1845

1803	RALPH WALDO EMERSON	
1804	NATHANIEL HAWTHORNE	
1807	ROBERT E. LEE	
1807	HENRY WADSWORTH LONGFELLOW	
1807	JOHN GREENLEAF WHITTIER	
1809	EDGAR ALLAN POE	1849
1809	ABRAHAM LINCOLN	
1809	OLIVER WENDELL HOLMES	
1817	HENRY DAVID THOREAU	
1817	FREDERICK DOUGLASS	
1819	HERMAN MELVILLE	
1819	WALT WHITMAN	
1828	HENRY TIMROD	

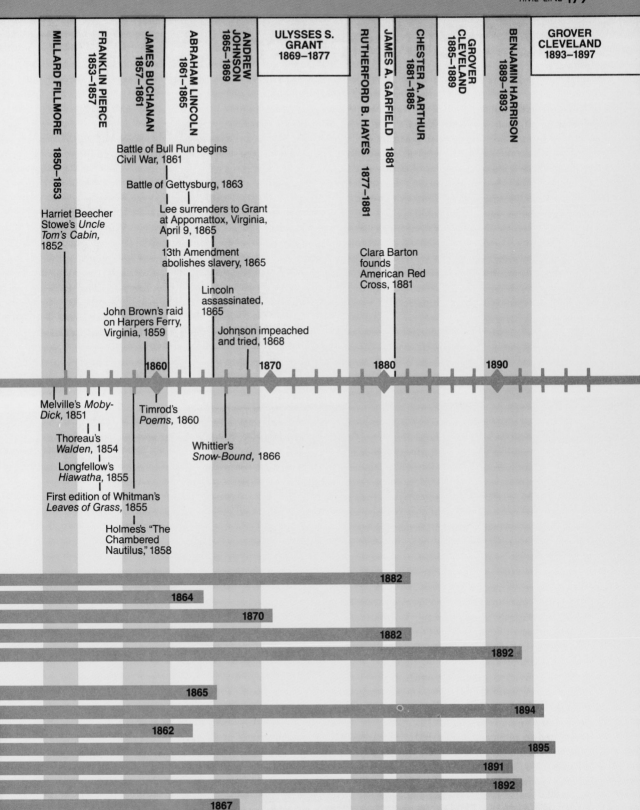

MILLARD FILLMORE   1850–1853

FRANKLIN PIERCE
1853–1857

JAMES BUCHANAN
1857–1861

ABRAHAM LINCOLN
1861–1865

ANDREW
JOHNSON
1865–1869

ULYSSES S.
GRANT
1869–1877

RUTHERFORD B. HAYES   1877–1881

JAMES A. GARFIELD   1881

CHESTER A. ARTHUR
1881–1885

GROVER
CLEVELAND
1885–1889

BENJAMIN HARRISON
1889–1893

GROVER
CLEVELAND
1893–1897

Battle of Bull Run begins
Civil War, 1861

Battle of Gettysburg, 1863

Lee surrenders to Grant
at Appomattox, Virginia,
April 9, 1865

13th Amendment
abolishes slavery, 1865

Harriet Beecher
Stowe's *Uncle
Tom's Cabin,*
1852

Clara Barton
founds
American Red
Cross, 1881

Lincoln
assassinated,
1865

John Brown's raid
on Harpers Ferry,
Virginia, 1859

Johnson impeached
and tried, 1868

1860   1870   1880   1890

Melville's *Moby-
Dick,* 1851

Timrod's
Poems, 1860

Thoreau's
Walden, 1854

Longfellow's
Hiawatha, 1855

Whittier's
Snow-Bound, 1866

First edition of Whitman's
Leaves of Grass, 1855

Holmes's "The
Chambered
Nautilus," 1858

1882

1864

1870

1882

1892

1865

1894

1862

1895

1891

1892

1867

Ralph Waldo Emerson   1803–1882

Ralph Waldo Emerson, "the Sage of Concord," is considered by many to be America's first philosopher. Admittedly, his philosophy of "Transcendentalism" (see page 168) was neither very original nor very consistently developed, yet his life's work comprises a considerable body of speculative thought. If we except thinkers like Jonathan Edwards, whose primary concern was religion; Thomas Jefferson, whose main interest was politics; and Benjamin Franklin, whose chief focus was the practical application of ideas, Emerson qualifies as America's first significant abstract thinker.

Emerson's thought has always had a special appeal for the young, a fact accounted for by his optimism, by his belief that everyone should follow his or her own path, and by the decidedly antiestablishment strain in his thinking. Emerson's strong opposition to materialism— typified by his famous remark that "things are in the saddle and ride mankind"—also strikes a responsive chord in many young people, as does his unswerving optimism and belief in the value of the individual.

Born in 1803 in Boston, Massachusetts, Ralph Waldo Emerson lost his father, a notable Unitarian minister, in 1811. For some time thereafter, he lived on the edge of poverty, but his education was not neglected. He went to the Boston Latin School, and then—at the age of fourteen—to Harvard College, from which he graduated in 1821. After teaching for a few years, Emerson decided to become a minister and entered Harvard Divinity School in 1825. Four years later, he became pastor of the Second Church in Boston, becoming the eighth consecutive clergyman in his family.

Emerson liked the life of a clergyman in many ways, and his parishioners liked him. However, he was much too independent a thinker to subscribe for long to any established church. In 1832, against the wishes of his congregation, he resigned his pastorate. He continued to preach as a substitute minister for several years, but in 1839 he left the pulpit forever.

PORTRAIT OF RALPH WALDO EMERSON
National Portrait Gallery
Smithsonian Institution

After his resignation Emerson traveled to Europe, where he met many of the most famous English writers of the time, including Thomas Carlyle and the Romantic poets William Wordsworth and Samuel Taylor Coleridge. There also, he resolved to prove that Christianity was not only a system of doctrines but a system of moral truth—"a rule of life, not a rule of faith."

Although Emerson had resigned from one pulpit, it soon became obvious that he had found another: he began his career as a public lecturer in the winter of 1833–1834. He continued to lecture for nearly forty years, speaking not only in New England but also in the middle states and in such "western" cities as Cincinnati, Cleveland, Chicago, Milwaukee, and St. Louis.

About the same time he began his career as a lecturer, Emerson also settled for good in Concord, Massachusetts, the home of his ancestors. There he was in touch with some of the greatest minds of his time, among them Henry David Thoreau, Bronson Alcott, Margaret Fuller, and Nathaniel Hawthorne. There, too, he helped to establish—and wrote articles for—the famous Transcendentalist magazine, *The Dial*, which lasted from 1840 to 1844. Initially edited by Margaret Fuller, the magazine was later edited by Emerson himself.

The group of intellectuals who met informally in Emerson's home and elsewhere to discuss philosophy, religion, and literature (and who were known by outsiders as the "Transcendental Club") caused a good deal of intellectual ferment. But no one was quite as controversial as Emerson himself. He began his career as an intellectual iconoclast with his lengthy essay *Nature*, published in 1836. The next year he gave the Phi Beta Kappa address at Harvard, an address later published as "The American Scholar," which Oliver Wendell Holmes called "our intellectual Declaration of Independence." In 1838 Emerson continued his independent thinking in his address at the Harvard Divinity School, in which he discussed some "defects of historical Christianity" and urged the graduating ministers to "Go alone, refuse the good models, even those which are sacred in the imagination of men." This was strong preaching from a commencement speaker, and it was many years before Emerson was invited to speak at Harvard again, though his alma mater did grant him an honorary degree when he was in his sixties.

Emerson's next major contributions were two collections of essays, entitled simply *Essays, First Series* and *Essays, Second Series*, published in 1841 and 1844, respectively. These essays were fashioned from material he had written in his journals or that he had used in his public lectures. (Emerson began his journals while he was still a teenager and kept them all his life.) The individual pieces in these collections probably remain Emerson's best-known works. They include such essays as "Self-Reliance," "Compensation," "Love," "Friendship," and "The

Caricature of Ralph Waldo Emerson as a scholar and lecturer. Note the titles of the books at his feet.

Over-Soul" from the *First Series*, and "Experience," "Character," "Gifts," and "Manners" from the *Second*.

Viewed collectively, the *Essays* favor a radical individualism, an insistence on self-reliance, and a refusal to measure conduct by traditional social values. On the other hand, Emerson insisted on belief in a God, a force he variously named as the "aboriginal Self," the "ever-blessed ONE," and "the Over-Soul." It is paradoxical that he should have put so much stress on the individual while at the same time acknowledging the overwhelming importance of the One.

Perhaps the resolution of the paradox—an instance of the familiar paradox of the One and the Many—lies in Emerson's *pantheism*. A pantheist (*pan* means "all") believes that God is in all things. Thus God is also in the individual self—the *same* God is in all individual selves. Possibly the phrase that best sums up Emerson's thinking is this: "I have taught one doctrine, namely, the infinitude of the private man."

Not long after the second series of essays,

Emerson published his first collection of *Poems* (1847). This was followed twenty years later by another collection, *May-Day and Other Pieces*. While one never thinks of the great essayist as a poet first, poet-critic Mark Van Doren has said of Emerson's verse, "the best of him belongs with the best American poetry." As we might expect, many of Emerson's poems are intellectual and metaphysical, but he could write simple poems, too, and he had an exceptional eye for naturalistic details.

After his first volume of poems, Emerson's next book was *Representative Men* (1850), a series of essays written on the philosopher Plato, the Swedish mystic Emanuel Swedenborg, the French essayist Michel de Montaigne, the poet Shakespeare, Napoleon, who represented "the man of the world," and the German author Johann Wolfgang von Goethe. All of these men were admired by Emerson; all influenced his own thinking. A sentence from the last paragraph of the introduction of *Representative Men* might well serve as its optimistic, idealistic motto: ". . . great men exist that there may be greater men."

Emerson made a second trip to Europe in 1847–1848, where he renewed his friendship with Thomas Carlyle and made friends with some of the greatest European thinkers and writers of the time. Using material gleaned from this trip, Emerson gave a series of lectures on England. These became the basis of his next book, *English Traits*, published in 1856. Many believe that the culmination of his career as an essayist came with his next volume, *The Conduct of Life* (1860).

In this collection of essays, speculating on such topics as "Power," "Wealth," "Culture," and "Behavior," Emerson was in his element as a moralist. Here is a sample from the last essay in the book, "Illusions":

In this kingdom of illusions we grope eagerly for stays and foundations. There is none but a strict and faithful dealing at home and a severe barring out of all duplicity or illusion there. Whatever games are played with us, we must play no games with ourselves, but deal in our privacy with the last honesty and truth. I look upon the simple and childish virtues of veracity and honesty as the root of all that is sublime in character. Speak as you think, be what you are, pay your debts of all kinds. . . . This reality is the foundation of friendship, religion, poetry and art.

Though Emerson may have given up the clerical garb before his thirtieth year, expressions like this show that he never left the ministry in a larger sense.

In *Society and Solitude* (1870), a collection of essays based on lectures delivered earlier, Emerson argued for a balance between social and solitary manners of living. It was a balance he himself admirably achieved. In the same year in which this collection appeared, Emerson gave a series of sixteen lectures at Harvard, later published as *The Natural History of the Intellect* (1893). But his powers by this time were waning, and most of the material for the lectures came from courses he had given earlier. The last work published under his own editorial supervision was *Letters and Social Aims*, in 1875. Several other volumes of work were edited and published by his friend James Elliot Cabot and his son Edward Emerson. The latter edited the famous *Journals*, published in ten volumes, 1909–1914.

One of Emerson's last poems is entitled "Terminus." It ends with the following stanza, in the serene and optimistic voice of its creator:

As the bird trims her to the gale,
I trim myself to the storm of time,
I man the rudder, reef the sail,
Obey the voice at eve obeyed at prime:
"Lowly faithful, banish fear,
Right onward drive unharmed;
The port, well worth the cruise, is near,
And every wave is charmed."

Concord Hymn

Sung at the Completion of the Battle Monument,
July 4, 1837

By the rude bridge that arched the flood,
　　Their flag to April's breeze unfurled,
Here once the embattled farmers stood
　　and fired the shot heard round the world.

The foe long since in silence slept;　　　　　　　5
　　Alike the conqueror silent sleeps;
And Time the ruined bridge has swept
　　Down the dark stream which seaward creeps.

On this green bank, by this soft stream,
　　We set to-day a votive* stone;　　　　　　　10
That memory may their deed redeem,
　　When, like our sires, our sons are gone.

Spirit, that made those heroes dare
　　To die, and leave their children free,
Bid Time and Nature gently spare　　　　　　　15
　　The shaft we raise to them and thee.

*__votive__ (vō′tiv),   dedicated in fulfillment of a vow or in
gratitude.

UNDERSTANDING AND APPRECIATION

1. What does the poet mean by "the shot heard round the world"? What kind of figurative language does this represent?
2. The tone of this poem could be described as one of quiet reverence. What two frequently repeated consonants help it achieve that tone?

3. Notice that the "flood" in line 1 becomes the "soft stream" in line 9. Why is this an appropriate shift?
4. What is the declared purpose of the "votive stone" (i.e., memorial statue)?
5. How would you describe the "Spirit" that the speaker addresses in the final stanza of Emerson's "Concord Hymn"?

from **NATURE**

To go into solitude, a man needs to retire as much from his chamber as from society. I am not solitary whilst I read and write, though nobody is with me. But if a man would be alone, let him look at the stars. The rays that come from those heavenly worlds will separate between him and what he touches. One might think the atmosphere was made transparent with this design, to give man, in the heavenly bodies, the perpetual presence of the sublime. Seen in the streets of cities, how great they are! If the stars should appear one night in a thousand years, how would men believe and adore; and preserve for many generations the remembrance of the city of God which had been shown! But every night come out these envoys of beauty, and light the universe with their admonishing smile.

The stars awaken a certain reverence, because though always present, they are inaccessible; but all natural objects make a kindred impression, when the mind is open to their influence. Nature never wears a mean appearance. Neither does the wisest man extort her secret, and lose his curiosity by finding out all her perfection. Nature never became a toy to a wise spirit. The flowers, the animals, the mountains, reflected the wisdom of his best hour, as much as they had delighted the simplicity of his childhood.

When we speak of nature in this manner, we have a distinct but most poetical sense in the mind. We mean the integrity of impression made by manifold natural objects. It is this which distinguishes the stick of timber of the wood-cutter from the tree of the poet. The charming landscape which I saw this morning is indubitably made up of some twenty or thirty farms. Miller owns this field, Locke that, and Manning the woodland beyond. But none of them owns the landscape.

There is a property in the horizon which no man has but he whose eye can integrate all the parts, that is, the poet. This is the best part of these men's farms, yet to this their warranty-deeds give no title.

To speak truly, few adult persons can see nature. Most persons do not see the sun. At least they have a very superficial seeing. The sun illuminates only the eye of the man, but shines into the eye and the heart of the child. The lover of nature is he whose inward and outward senses are still truly adjusted to each other; who has retained the spirit of infancy even into the era of manhood. His intercourse with heaven and earth becomes part of his daily food. In the presence of nature a wild delight runs through the man, in spite of real sorrows. Nature says,—he is my creature, and maugre[1] all his impertinent griefs, he shall be glad with me. Not the sun or the summer alone, but every hour and season yields its tribute of delight; for every hour and change corresponds to and authorizes a different state of the mind, from breathless noon to grimmest midnight. Nature is a setting that fits equally well a comic or a mourning piece. In good health, the air is a cordial of incredible virtue. Crossing a bare common, in snow puddles, at twilight, under a clouded sky, without having in my thoughts any occurrence of special good fortune, I have enjoyed a perfect exhilaration. I am glad to the brink of fear. In the woods, too, a man casts off his years, as the snake his slough,[2] and at what period soever of life is always a child. In the woods is perpetual youth. Within these plantations of God, a decorum and sanctity

1. **maugre** (mô′ gər), in spite of (archaic usage).
2. **slough** (sluf), here: skin.

VIEW OF THE FALLS OF MUNDA
Thomas Cole
Museum of Art, Rhode Island School of Design
Jesse Metcalf Fund

reign, a perennial festival is dressed, and the guest sees not how he should tire of them in a thousand years. In the woods, we return to reason and faith. There I feel that nothing can befall me in life,—no disgrace, no calamity (leaving me my eyes), which nature cannot repair. Standing on the bare ground,—my head bathed by the blithe air and uplifted into infinite space,—all mean egotism vanishes. I become a transparent eyeball; I am nothing; I see all; the currents of the Universal Being circulate through me; I am part or parcel of God. The name of the nearest friend sounds then foreign and accidental: to be brothers, to be acquaintances, master or servant, is then a trifle and a disturbance. I am the lover of uncontained and immortal beauty. In the wilderness, I find something more dear and connate³ than in streets or villages. In the tranquil landscape, and especially in the distant line of the horizon, man beholds somewhat as beautiful as his own nature.

The greatest delight which the fields and woods minister is the suggestion of an occult relation between man and the vegetable. I am not alone and unacknowledged. They nod to me, and I to them. The waving of the boughs in the storm is new to me and old. It takes me by surprise, and yet is not unknown. Its effect is like that of a higher thought or a better emotion coming over me, when I deemed I was thinking justly or doing right.

Yet it is certain that the power to produce this delight does not reside in nature, but in man, or in a harmony of both. It is necessary to use these pleasures with great temperance. For nature is not always tricked⁴ in holiday attire, but the same scene which yesterday breathed perfume and glittered as for the frolic of the nymphs is overspread with melancholy to-day. Nature always wears the colors of the spirit. To a man laboring under calamity, the heat of his own fire hath sadness in it. Then there is a kind of contempt of the landscape felt by him who has just lost by death a dear friend. The sky is less grand as it shuts down over less worth in the population.

3. **connate** (kon′ āt), having the same origin or nature.
4. **tricked,** here: clothed, arrayed.

FOR UNDERSTANDING

1. According to Emerson, what is one of the best ways one can really be alone?
2. What distinguishes the "stick of timber of the wood-cutter from the tree of the poet"?
3. In what part of *Nature* does Emerson describe the most profound change taking place?
4. Where does Emerson find the source of the power to produce delight?

FOR INTERPRETATION

1. Interpret the following quotation from *Nature:* "The sun illuminates only the eye of the man, but shines into the eye and heart of the child."
2. What does Emerson mean when he says (in paragraph 4), "I am nothing"?
3. Try to relate that statement ("I am nothing") to Emerson's pantheism.
4. Does nature have the potential to lift man's spirits at all times, or only occasionally? Explain in detail, looking at the whole selection.

from **SELF-RELIANCE**

There is a time in every man's education when he arrives at the conviction that envy is ignorance; that imitation is suicide; that he must take himself for better, for worse, as his portion; that though the wide universe is full of good, no kernel of nourishing corn can come to him but through his toil bestowed on that plot of ground which is given to him to till. The power which resides in him is new in nature, and none but he knows what that is which he can do, nor does he know until he has tried.

Trust thyself: every heart vibrates to that iron string. Accept the place the Divine Providence[1] has found for you; the society of your contemporaries, the connection of events. Great men have always done so and confided themselves childlike to the genius of their age, betraying their perception that the Eternal was stirring at their heart, working through their hands, predominating in all their being.

Society everywhere is in conspiracy against the manhood of every one of its members. The virtue in most request is conformity. Self-reliance is its aversion. It loves not realities and creators, but names and customs.

Whoso would be a man, must be a nonconformist. He who would gather immortal palms[2] must not be hindered by the name of goodness, but must explore if it be goodness. Nothing is at last sacred but the integrity of your own mind.

What I must do is all that concerns me, not what the people think. This rule, equally arduous in actual and in intellectual life, may serve for the whole distinction between greatness and meanness. It is harder because you will always find those who think they know

what is your duty better than you know it. It is easy in the world to live after the world's opinion; it is easy in solitude to live after your own; but the great man is he who in the midst of the crowd keeps with perfect sweetness the independence of solitude.

For noncomformity the world whips you with its displeasure.

The other terror that scares us from self-trust is our consistency; a reverence for our past act or word because the eyes of others have no other data for computing our orbit[3] than our past acts, and we are loath to disappoint them.

But why should you keep your head over your shoulder? Why drag about this corpse of your memory, lest you contradict somewhat[4] you have stated in this or that public place? Suppose you should contradict yourself; what then? It seems to be a rule of wisdom never to rely on your memory alone, scarcely even in acts of pure memory, but to bring the past for judgment into the thousand-eyed present, and live ever in a new day.

A foolish consistency is the hobgoblin[5] of little minds, adored by little statesmen and philosophers and divines. With consistency a great soul has simply nothing to do. He may as well concern himself with his shadow on the wall. Speak what you think now in hard words and tomorrow speak what tomorrow

---

1. **Divine Providence,** benevolent guidance of God for the future.
2. **immortal palms,** lasting victories.
3. **eyes of others . . . orbit,** that is, they don't have any basis for judging our merit other than what we have already done.
4. **somewhat,** here: something.
5. **hobgoblin,** frightening apparition.

The summer school at Concord, Massachusetts, where Emerson gave his lectures

thinks in hard words again, though it contradict everything you said today.—"Ah, so you shall be sure to be misunderstood."—Is it so bad then to be misunderstood? Pythagoras[6] was misunderstood, and Socrates,[7] and Jesus, and Luther,[8] and Copernicus,[9] and Galileo,[10] and Newton,[11] and every pure and wise spirit that ever took flesh. To be great is to be misunderstood.

6. **Pythagoras,** Greek philosopher and mathematician of the fifth century B.C.
7. **Socrates,** Athenian idealist philosopher and teacher of the fifth century B.C.
8. **Luther,** Martin (1483–1546), leader of the German Protestant Reformation.
9. **Copernicus,** Nicolaus (1473–1543), Polish astronomer. Founder of modern astronomy.
10. **Galileo** (1564–1642), Italian astronomer and physicist. Founder of modern experimental science.
11. **Newton,** Sir Isaac (1642–1727), English mathematician and philosopher.

FOR UNDERSTANDING

1. What virtue does Emerson say is in most demand by society?
2. What kind of treatment can the nonconformist expect from "the world," according to Emerson?
3. What adjective does Emerson use to modify "consistency"? Why might this adjective be important?

FOR INTERPRETATION

Answer one or more of the following, according to the directions of your teacher.
1. For what does "no kernel of nourishing corn" stand?
2. Why does Emerson find conformity harmful?
3. If conformity is harmful, why does society demand it?
4. Restate in your own words and discuss the following statement: "The great man is he who in the midst of the crowd keeps with perfect sweetness the independence of solitude."
5. Emerson tells us not to be concerned about being misunderstood. How does he justify or rationalize this? What do you think of his justification or rationalization?

FOR APPRECIATION

Style
It has often been observed that the unit of thought in Emerson's essays is not the paragraph but rather "the carefully wrought sentence." Sometimes there does not even seem to be a logical sequence within Emerson's paragraphs or very clear connections between paragraphs. These stylistic peculiarities make Emerson difficult to read.

Select a sentence or two from either of the two essays you have read, a sentence that you find especially meaningful or well expressed. Be prepared to discuss it in class.

LANGUAGE AND VOCABULARY

The following key words are from Emerson's "Self-Reliance": *imitation, society, independence, consistency, self-reliance.* Try to think of an *antonym* for each. When you have your five antonyms, group the total of ten words in two columns. In the left-hand column, put the words for qualities or things that Emerson seems to regard *positively.* In the right-hand column, list the qualities or things he seems to regard *negatively.* Discuss your lists in class.

Henry David Thoreau   1817–1862

Few writers in America have felt a sense of place as strongly as Henry David Thoreau. He was born in Concord, Massachusetts, lived most of his life in and around the village, died, and was buried there. Yet he was not a hermit, in spite of his resolve at the age of twenty-eight to spend more than two years alone at Walden Pond, a mile and a half south of Concord. Thoreau's neighbors knew him as a strong-minded, restless individual, a man of dry wit, frank opinions, and unquestioned integrity. Clearly he was in love with life, but less with the bustle of Concord village than with the natural world of the fields and nearby ponds. He could do without the post office and the church more easily than he could give up his walks in the woods. "If a man does not keep pace with his companions," he once wrote, "perhaps it is because he hears a different drummer. Let him step to the music which he hears, however measured or far away. It is not important that he should mature as soon as an apple tree or an oak."

The "different drummer" Thoreau stepped to set him apart from Concord even before he returned from four years' study at Harvard College. He questioned authority when it was unreasonable or untested; he resented traditions when they were hollow gestures to the past; above all he fought his neighbors' "desperate haste to succeed and in such desperate enterprises." On graduation he applied for a teaching position in Concord but kept it only a few weeks. When a member of the school committee insisted Thoreau must not "spare the rod" on unruly pupils, he chose six of his students at random, whipped them soundly, and then resigned. Some months later he and his brother John opened a private school in Concord which prospered for about three years in spite of its progressive theories of education. The rod was abandoned; students were encouraged to make their own observations and form their own opinions, not merely parrot what they read in books; classes were held outdoors whenever possible so that the natural world

PORTRAIT OF HENRY DAVID THOREAU
National Portrait Gallery
Smithsonian Institution

could mix with the academic. Had it not been for John Thoreau's failing health, Henry might have devoted much of his life to teaching, since it provided him with the leisure to transact what he called "private business"—the writing of poetry, keeping his journals, reading, nature study, conversation.

After his brother's premature death in 1842, he resolved that making a living should never interfere with life itself, and so he spent the next twenty years earning only the minimum he needed, never letting work become an end in itself. He helped his father in the family's pencil factory; he lived with Ralph Waldo Emerson, the famous essayist, lecturer, and poet, and his wife as caretaker of their property; he worked in

Concord as a gardener, surveyor, magazine editor, and curator of the lyceum; he lectured, with only fair success, from Bangor, Maine, to Philadelphia; he tutored the children of Emerson's brother William on Staten Island until homesickness drove him back to Concord. All the while, of course, he was confiding his inward life in his journals. What passed for the world's business—"desperate enterprises," that is—little interested him.

If Thoreau had written nothing else but his journals—he began them in 1837, just a few months after graduation from Harvard, and made the last entry a few months before his death—fame might have been even slower in coming than it was. For years he had mined the journals for lecture material and for the few essays he published in *The Dial*, at Emerson's suggestion. But it was not until 1845 that he made a decision that altered his life. Making his living in town was consuming more of his time than he had bargained for. "Actually," he was to write later, "the laboring man has not leisure for a true integrity day by day; he cannot afford to sustain the manliest relations to man; his labor would be depreciated in the market. He has no time to be anything but a machine." To escape the market and the machine, Thoreau conceived of building a cabin in comparative solitude and spending uninterrupted nights and days sorting out his philosophies. He considered Flint's Pond in nearby Lincoln, but he could not convince the owner of the land that his idea was sensible. Late in 1844, Emerson purchased some wood lots on the north shore of Walden Pond, and five months later Thoreau was borrowing an ax to build his own cabin there. For "rent," he would clear the fields for gardening and leave the cabin on the edge of the pine grove after he had finished his "experiment in living." On Independence Day, 1845, he moved in. He stayed slightly more than two years and two months.

Walden; or Life in the Woods is the record of that sojourn, and much more. The writing of this book and the reasons for writing it, however, are often misunderstood. Thoreau moved to Walden to simplify his life. "I wished to live deliberately," he wrote, "to front only the essential facts of life, and see if I could not learn what it had to teach, and not, when I came to die, discover that I had not lived." But there were other reasons. He thought of himself as a philosopher and "to be a philosopher," he said, "is not merely to have subtle thoughts, nor even to found a school, but so to love wisdom as to live according to its dictates. . . . It is to solve some of the problems of life, not only theoretically but practically." He also wished to write a book. Not *Walden;* that was his second book. He and his brother John had made a memorable excursion in 1839 on the Concord and Merrimack Rivers, and he had delayed too long in publishing an account of the trip from the notes he had made in his journals. Possibly Thoreau had also felt the enmity of his fellow townspeople long enough. After he had refused to pay his church taxes in 1838, he was looked upon as an extremist. Then, in 1844, when he and Edward Hoar let a cooking fire on the banks of Fairhaven Bay get out of hand and burn a hundred acres of Concord woodland, his reputation was thoroughly tarnished.

His return to civilization in 1847 was dictated by equally practical considerations. Now that he had made his experiment, he had "several more lives to live, and could not spare any more time for that one." Emerson, moreover, was leaving in September for a lecture tour in England and had persuaded Thoreau once again to live in his Concord home and take care of his family. And his book was almost finished. He was eager to see it in print. Publishers in New York and Boston, alas, were not eager to accept it. It was 1849 before *A Week on the Concord and Merrimack Rivers* appeared, and then only at Thoreau's own expense. He had agreed to pay for a thousand copies. It was soon evident that the book was a total failure. The account of the voyage was vivid enough, but he bored some readers and offended others with his long digressions on history, ancient authors, philosophy, and especially religion. By 1853, the Boston publishers had sold only 219 copies. When they shipped the rest to Thoreau in October of that year he wrote in his journal: "They are something more substantial than fame, as my back knows, which has borne them up two flights of stairs to a place similar to that to which they trace their origin. . . . I have now a library of nearly nine hundred volumes, over seven hundred of which I wrote myself."

Thoreau never lost his sense of humor, particularly about the eccentricities of his neighbors or about the foibles of life.

The publication of *Walden* is another story. Emerson persuaded Ticknor and Fields of Boston to print it. Before its appearance in August, 1854, excerpts appearing in the New York *Tribune* helped to spread the author's name. Even though the reviewers were not wholly satisfied, Thoreau was, with the general reception of the book and its sales. He knew he had written a masterpiece, and if it took several decades before America realized it, he was prepared for that. Surprisingly he never attempted a sequel to the book, nor did he ever cull his journals for a third volume of any kind. The last eight years of his life were concentrated on brief travels—New Jersey, the Maine woods, Brooklyn (to meet Walt Whitman), Minnesota (to regain his health)—and on social issues on which he felt compelled to speak.

As early as 1849 he had published a remarkable essay called "On the Duty of Civil Disobedience." (In this century it became Gandhi's textbook during his passive resistance campaign in India.) Thoreau also lectured and debated on the Abolition movement, though he never formally joined any organizations. He forever remained the staunch individualist, standing apart from, but not above, his fellows, the better to observe them and their problems. When in 1859 he rose to defend another strong-minded man, Captain John Brown, a few days after the Harper's Ferry attack, he was advised by his Concord neighbors that such a defense was ill-timed. Thoreau assured them that he was not asking for advice but calling a meeting. When the selectmen refused to toll the bell for that meeting, he pulled the rope himself. Concord should have known by that time that Henry Thoreau made most of his decisions with little thought to their popularity and much to their necessity and their rightness.

Walden is based on similar assumptions. "I do not propose to write an ode to dejection," he writes on its title page, "but to brag as lustily as chanticleer in the morning, standing on his roost, if only to wake my neighbors up." Whether they wished to be waked or not, we might add. He is not writing for the "strong and valiant natures, who will mind their own affairs whether in heaven or hell." Nor is he addressing "those who are well employed, in whatever circumstances, and [who] know whether they are well employed or not." But to "the mass of men who are discontented and idly complaining of the hardness of their lot or of the times," Thoreau offers advice, inspiration, severe criticism, encouragement, even practical remedies. Modern critics see something of *Robinson Crusoe* in Thoreau's experiment in solitary life, something also of Jonathan Swift's *Gulliver's Travels* in his severe criticism of so-called civilization. Thoreau's contemporaries on reading *Walden* looked back to Emerson's essays, particularly "Self-Reliance," and to the sermons of colonial New England preachers. But whatever comparisons are made, certain distinguishing characteristics set this book apart and give it a flavor of its own.

Thoreau first of all begins his opening sentence with the first-person pronoun and continues in that relaxed informal tone. We never lose sight of a humble citizen of Concord seeking to learn about life in observing nature and sharing his discoveries. Second, he warns us that he "would not have any one adopt *[his]* mode of living on any account." He is not advocating our leaving home to live on the edge of a pond in a timbered cabin. "I would have each one be very careful to find out and pursue *his own way*," he tells us more than once, so long as each one knows where one is going and why. Finally, Thoreau's sense of humor (often missed by the hurried reader), his keen eye for the illustrative anecdote, his respect for the forces of nature, his alertness to the way language carefully shaped can reflect those forces, and above all his quality of "being," as Emerson called it, make *Walden* a unique experience. This book is not merely about nature, it *is* nature, captured. "I have travelled a good deal in Concord," he tells us with tongue in cheek early in the first chapter. We, too, can "travel" widely in Thoreau's world. Concord and Walden Pond have been reduced, in his prose, to a capsule of the human condition. He is writing not merely about life in the 1840s, but about us.

WALDEN.

By HENRY D THOREAU,

AUTHOR OF "A WEEK ON THE CONCORD AND MERRIMACK RIVERS."

I do not propose to write an ode to dejection, but to brag as lustily as chanticleer in the morning, standing on his roost, if only to wake my neighbors up. — Page 92.

BOSTON:
JAMES R. OSGOOD AND COMPANY,
LATE TICKNOR & FIELDS, AND FIELDS, OSGOOD, & CO.

from **WALDEN**

I. Economy

When I wrote the following pages, or rather the bulk of them, I lived alone, in the woods, a mile from any neighbor, in a house which I had built myself, on the shore of Walden Pond, in Concord, Massachusetts, and earned my living by the labor of my hands only. I lived there two years and two months. At present I am a sojourner in civilized life again.

I should not obtrude my affairs so much on the notice of my readers if very particular inquiries had not been made by my townsmen concerning my mode of life, which some would call impertinent, though they do not appear to me at all impertinent, but, considering the circumstances, very natural and pertinent. Some have asked what I got to eat; if I did not feel lonesome; if I was not afraid; and the like. Others have been curious to learn what portion of my income I devoted to charitable purposes; and some, who have large families, how many poor children I maintained. I will therefore ask those of my readers who feel no particular interest in me to pardon me if I undertake to answer some of these questions in this book. In most books, the *I*, or first person, is omitted; in this it will be retained; that, in respect to egotism, is the main difference. We commonly do not remember that it is, after all, always the first person that is speaking. I should not talk so much about myself if there were anybody else whom I knew as well. Unfortunately, I am confined to this theme by the narrowness of my experience. Moreover, I, on my side, require of every writer, first or last, a simple and sincere account of his own life, and not merely what he has heard of other men's lives; some such account as he would send to

his kindred from a distant land; for if he has lived sincerely, it must have been in a distant land to me. Perhaps these pages are more particularly addressed to poor students. As for the rest of my readers, they will accept such portions as apply to them. I trust that none will stretch the seams in putting on the coat, for it may do good service to him whom it fits. . . .

I see young men, my townsmen, whose misfortune it is to have inherited farms, houses, barns, cattle, and farming tools; for these are more easily acquired than got rid of. Better if they had been born in the open pasture and suckled by a wolf, that they might have seen with clearer eyes what field they were called to labor in. Who made them serfs of the soil? Why should they eat their sixty acres, when man is condemned to eat only his peck of dirt? Why should they begin digging their graves as soon as they are born? They have got to live a man's life, pushing all these things before them, and get on as well as they can. How many a poor immortal soul have I met well nigh crushed and smothered under its load, creeping down the road of life, pushing before it a barn seventy-five feet by forty, its Augean stables[1] never cleansed, and one hundred acres of land, tillage, mowing, pasture, and woodlot! The portionless, who struggle with no such unnecessary inherited encumbrances, find it labor enough to subdue and cultivate a few cubic feet of flesh.

But men labor under a mistake. The better part of the man is soon ploughed into the soil for compost. By a seeming fate, commonly called necessity, they are employed, as it

---

1. **Augean** (ô jē′ ən) **stables,** stables in which 3,000 oxen were kept, left uncleaned for 30 years; Hercules cleaned the stables in one day.

says in an old book, laying up treasures which moth and rust will corrupt and thieves break through and steal. It is a fool's life, as they will find when they get to the end of it, if not before. . . .

When I consider my neighbors, the farmers of Concord, who are at least as well off as the other classes, I find that for the most part they have been toiling twenty, thirty, or forty years, that they may become the real owners of their farms, which commonly they have inherited with encumbrances, or else bought with hired money,—and we may regard one third of that toil as the cost of their houses,—but commonly they have not paid for them yet. It is true, the encumbrances sometimes outweigh the value of the farm, so that the farm itself becomes one great encumbrance, and still a man is found to inherit it, being well acquainted with it, as he says. On applying to the assessors, I am surprised to learn that they cannot at once name a dozen in the town who own their farms free and clear. If you would know the history of these homesteads, inquire at the bank where they are mortgaged. The man who has actually paid for his farm with labor on it is so rare that every neighbor can point to him. I doubt if there are three such men in Concord. What has been said of the merchants, that a very large majority, even ninety-seven in a hundred, are sure to fail, is equally true of the farmers. With regard to the merchants, however, one of them says pertinently that a great part of their failures are not genuine pecuniary failures, but merely failures to fulfil their engagements, because it is inconvenient; that is, it is the moral character that breaks down. But this puts an infinitely worse face on the matter, and suggests, beside, that probably not even the other three succeed in saving their souls, but are perchance bankrupt in a worse sense than they who fail honestly. Bankruptcy and repudiation are the springboards from which much of our civilization vaults and turns its somersets, but the savage stands on the unelastic plank of famine. . . .

Near the end of March, 1845, I borrowed an axe and went down to the woods by Walden Pond, nearest to where I intended to build my house, and began to cut down some tall arrowy white pines, still in their youth, for timber. It is difficult to begin without borrowing, but perhaps it is the most generous course thus to permit your fellow-men to have an interest in your enterprise. The owner of the axe, as he released his hold on it, said that it was the apple of his eye; but I returned it sharper than I received it. It was a pleasant hillside where I worked, covered with pine woods, through which I looked out on the pond, and a small open field in the woods where pines and hickories were springing up. The ice in the pond was not yet dissolved, though there were some open spaces, and it was all dark colored and saturated with water. There were some slight flurries of snow during the days that I worked there; but for the most part when I came out on to the railroad, on my way home, its yellow sand heap stretched away gleaming in the hazy atmosphere, and the rails shone in the spring sun, and I heard the lark and pewee and other birds already come to commence another year with us. They were pleasant spring days, in which the winter of man's discontent was thawing as well as the earth, and the life that had lain torpid began to stretch itself. One day, when my axe had come off and I had cut a green hickory for a wedge, driving it with a stone, and had placed the whole to soak in a pond hole in order to swell the wood, I saw a striped snake run into the water, and he lay on the bottom, apparently without inconvenience, as long as I stayed there, or more than a quarter of an hour; perhaps because he had not yet fairly come out of the torpid state. It appeared to me that for a like reason men remain in their present low and primitive condition; but if they should feel the influence of the spring of springs arousing them, they would of necessity rise to a higher and more ethereal life. I had previously seen the snakes in frosty mornings in my path with portions of their bodies still numb and inflexible, waiting for the sun to thaw them. On the 1st of April it rained and melted the ice, and in the early part of the day, which was very foggy, I heard a stray goose groping about over the pond and cackling as if lost, or like the spirit of the fog.

So I went on for some days cutting and hewing timber, and also studs and rafters, all with my narrow axe, not having many communicable or scholar-like thoughts, singing to myself,—

> Men say they know many things;
> But lo! they have taken wings,—
> The arts and sciences,
> And a thousand appliances;
> The wind that blows
> Is all that anybody knows.

I hewed the main timbers six inches square, most of the studs on two sides only, and the rafters and floor timbers on one side, leaving the rest of the bark on, so that they were just as straight and much stronger than sawed ones. Each stick was carefully mortised or tenoned by its stump, for I had borrowed other tools by this time. My days in the woods were not very long ones; yet I usually carried my dinner of bread and butter, and read the newspaper in which it was wrapped, at noon, sitting amid the green pine boughs which I had cut off, and to my bread was imparted some of their fragrance, for my hands were covered with a thick coat of pitch. Before I had done I was more the friend than the foe of the pine tree, though I had cut down some of them, having become better acquainted with it. Sometimes a rambler in the wood was attracted by the sound of my axe, and we chatted pleasantly over the chips which I had made.

By the middle of April, for I made no haste in my work, but rather made the most of it, my house was framed and ready for the raising. I had already bought the shanty of James Collins, an Irishman who worked on the Fitchburg Railroad, for boards. James Collins' shanty was considered an uncommonly fine one. When I called to see it he was not at home. I walked about the outside, at first unobserved from within, the window was so deep and high. It was of small dimensions, with a peaked cottage roof, and not much else to be seen, the dirt being raised five feet all around as if it were a compost heap. The roof was the soundest part, though a good deal warped and made brittle by the sun. Door-sill there was none, but a perennial passage for the hens under the door board. Mrs. C. came to the door and asked me to view it from the inside. The hens were driven in by my approach. It was dark, and had a dirt floor for the most part, dank, clammy, and aguish, only here a board and there a board which would not bear removal. She lighted a lamp to show me the inside of the roof and the walls, and also that the board floor extended under the bed, warning me not to step into the cellar, a sort of dust hole two feet deep. In her own words, they were "good boards overhead, good boards all around, and a good window,"—of two whole squares originally, only the cat had passed out that way lately. There was a stove, a bed, and a place to sit, an infant in the house where it was born, a silk parasol, gilt-framed looking-glass, and a patent new coffee-mill nailed to an oak sapling, all told. The bargain was soon concluded, for James had in the meanwhile returned. I to pay four dollars and twenty-five cents to-night, he to vacate at five to-morrow morning, selling to nobody else meanwhile: I to take possession at six. It were well, he said, to be there early, and anticipate certain indistinct but wholly unjust claims on the score of ground rent and fuel. This he assured me was the only encumbrance. At six I passed him and his family on the road. One large bundle held their all,—bed, coffee-mill, looking-glass, hens,—all but the cat; she took to the woods and became a wild cat, and, as I learned afterward, trod in a trap set for woodchucks, and so became a dead cat at last.

I took down this dwelling the same morning, drawing the nails, and removed it to the pond side by small car-loads, spreading the boards on the grass there to bleach and warp back again in the sun. One early thrush gave me a note or two as I drove along the woodland path. I was informed treacherously by a young Patrick that neighbor Seeley, an Irishman, in the intervals of the carting, transferred the still tolerable, straight, and drivable nails, staples, and spikes to his pocket, and then stood when I came back to pass the time of day, and look freshly up, unconcerned, with spring thoughts, at the devastation; there being a dearth of work, as he said. He was there to represent spectatordom, and help make this seemingly insignificant event one with the removal of the gods of Troy.[2]

I dug my cellar in the side of a hill sloping to the south, where a woodchuck had formerly dug his burrow, down through sumach[3] and blackberry roots, and the lowest stain of vegetation, six feet square by seven deep, to a fine sand where potatoes would not freeze in any winter. The sides were left shelving, and not stoned; but the sun having never shone on them, the sand still keeps its place. It was but two hours' work. I took particular pleasure in this breaking of ground, for in almost all latitudes men dig into the earth for an equable temperature. Under the most splendid house in the city is still to be found the cellar where they store their roots as of old, and long after the superstructure has disappeared posterity remark its dent in the earth. The house is still but a sort of porch at the entrance of a burrow.

At length, in the beginning of May, with the help of some of my acquaintances, rather to improve so good an occasion for neighborliness than from any necessity, I set up the frame of my house. No man was ever more honored in the character of his raisers than I. They are destined, I trust, to assist at the raising of loftier structures one day. I began to occupy my house on the 4th of July, as soon as it was boarded and roofed, for the boards were carefully feather-edged and lapped, so that it was perfectly impervious to rain, but before boarding I laid the foundation of a chimney at one end, bringing two cartloads of stones up the hill from the pond in my arms. I built the chimney after my hoeing in the fall, before a fire became necessary for warmth, doing my cooking in the mean while out of doors on the ground, early in the morning: which mode I still think is in some respects more convenient and agreeable than the usual one. When it stormed before my bread was baked, I fixed a few boards over the fire, and sat under them to watch my loaf, and passed some pleasant hours in that way. In those days, when my hands were much employed, I read but little, but the least scraps of paper which lay on the ground, my holder, or tablecloth, afforded me as much entertainment, in fact answered the same purpose as the Iliad.[4] . . .

Before winter I built a chimney, and shingled the sides of my house, which were already impervious to rain, with imperfect and sappy shingles made of the first slice of the log, whose edges I was obliged to straighten with a plane.

I have thus a tight shingled and plastered house, ten feet wide by fifteen long, and eight-feet posts, with a garret and a closet, a large window on each side, two trap doors, one door at the end, and a brick fireplace opposite. The exact cost of my house, paying the usual price for such materials as I used, but not counting the work, all of which was done by myself, was as follows; and I give the details because very few are able to tell exactly what their houses cost, and fewer still, if any,

---

2. **gods of Troy,** probably an allusion to Virgil's *Aeneid,* in which the destruction of Troy is told.
3. **sumach, sumac** (sü′ mak), any of a family of small trees, shrubs, and woody vines that produce small fleshy fruit and a milky juice.
4. **Iliad** (il′ ē əd), Greek epic composed by Homer, describing the siege of Troy and the terrible effects of Achilles' wrath.

the separate cost of the various materials which compose them:—

Boards	$8 03½,	mostly shanty boards
Refuse shingles for roof and sides	4 00	
Laths	1 25	
Two second-hand windows with glass	2 43	
One thousand old brick	4 00	
Two casks of lime	2 40	That was high. More than I needed.
Hair	0 31	
Mantle-tree iron	0 15	
Nails	3 90	
Hinges and screws	0 14	
Latch	0 10	
Chalk	0 01	
Transporation	1 40	I carried a good part on my back.
In all	$28 12½	

These are all the materials excepting the timber, stones, and sand, which I claimed by squatter's right. I have also a small woodshed adjoining, made chiefly of the stuff which was left after building the house.

I intend to build me a house which will surpass any on the main street in Concord in grandeur and luxury, as soon as it pleases me as much and will cost me no more than my present one. . . .

For more than five years I maintained myself solely by the labor of my hands, and I found, that by working about six weeks in a year, I could meet all the expenses of living. The whole of my winters, as well as most of my summers, I had free and clear for study. I have thoroughly tried school-keeping, and found that my expenses were in proportion, or rather out of proportion, to my income, for I was obliged to dress and train, not to say think and believe, accordingly, and I lost my time into the bargain. As I did not teach for the good of my fellow-men, but simply for a livelihood, this was a failure. I have tried trade; but I found that it would take ten years to get under way in that, and that then I should probably be on my way to the devil. I was actually afraid that I might by that time be doing what is called a good business. When formerly I was looking about to see what I could do for a living, some sad experience in conforming to the wishes of friends being fresh in my mind to tax my ingenuity, I thought often and seriously of picking huckleberries; that surely I could do, and its small profits might suffice,—for my greatest skill has been to want but little,—so little capital is required, so little distraction from my wonted moods, I foolishly thought. While my acquaintances went unhesitatingly into trade or the professions, I contemplated this occupation as most like theirs; ranging the hills all summer to pick the berries which came in my way, and thereafter carelessly dispose of them; so, to keep the flocks of Admetus.[5] I also dreamed that I might gather the wild herbs, or carry evergreens to such villagers as loved to be reminded of the woods, even to the city, by hay-cart loads. But I have since learned that trade curses everything it handles; and though you trade in messages from heaven, the whole curse of trade attaches to the business.

As I preferred some things to others, and especially valued my freedom, as I could fare hard and yet succeed well, I did not wish to spend my time in earning rich carpets or other fine furniture, or delicate cookery, or a house in the Grecian or the Gothic style just yet. If there are any to whom it is no interrup-

---

5. **Admetus** (ad mē′ təs), husband of Alcestis, who saved the life of Admetus by dying in his place; she was brought back from Hades by Hercules.

tion to acquire these things, and who know how to use them when acquired, I relinquish to them the pursuit. Some are "industrious," and appear to love labor for its own sake, or perhaps because it keeps them out of worse mischief; to such I have at present nothing to say. Those who would not know what to do with more leisure than they now enjoy, I might advise to work twice as hard as they do, —work till they pay for themselves, and get their free papers. For myself I found that the occupation of a daylaborer was the most independent of any, especially as it required only thirty or forty days in a year to support one. The laborer's day ends with the going down of the sun, and he is then free to devote himself to his chosen pursuit, independent of his labor; but his employer, who speculates from month to month, has no respite from one end of the year to the other.

In short, I am convinced, both by faith and experience, that to maintain one's self on this earth is not a hardship but a pastime, if we will live simply and wisely; as the pursuits of the simpler nations are still the sports of the more artificial. It is not necessary that a man should earn his living by the sweat of his brow, unless he sweats easier than I do. . . .

FOR UNDERSTANDING

1. Why does Thoreau say he will talk about himself in *Walden*?
2. What does Thoreau say about the "misfortune" of young men who inherit property?
3. Where did Thoreau get the boards for his house on Walden Pond? What happened to some of his nails?
4. Why does Thoreau proudly detail the cost of his house?
5. How long each year does Thoreau say he worked as a day laborer to meet his living expenses? Why did Thoreau like working as a day laborer?

FOR INTERPRETATION

Discuss what Thoreau might have said about each of the following statements. What do you say about them?
1. The more possessions one has, the more difficult it is to practice economy.
2. Most of us today are overly concerned with the future, whereas we should be primarily concerned with the present.
3. Too much of our time is spent in trying to impress others; too little is spent in trying to satisfy our own inner needs.
4. It is foolish for a person to become a doctor, say, or a teacher, for such occupations leave one with too little time for oneself.
5. Self-discipline is a necessary preliminary to spiritual growth and realization.

FOR APPRECIATION

Style

In literature, *style* refers to *how* writers say whatever they say. Naturally, how someone expresses a thought—in speech as well as in writing—can tell us a good deal about that person. To put it in the famous words of the French naturalist Georges de Buffon (1707–1788), "The style is the man himself."

Thoreau's style tells us much about him. One need not read very far in *Walden,* for example, to discover that its author was well acquainted with both Greek and Oriental literature. References to such things as "Augean stables" (see p. 194) or the *Harivamsa* (see p. 200) tell us that Thoreau was not simply an articulate vagabond but a well-read and well-educated man.

Thoreau is also very much a man of his time and place, and his references to his native environment far outweigh his references to antiquity. There is also much of the New England Yankee in two of the most salient characteristics of his style—its *economy* and its *concreteness.* Study the first paragraph of *Walden,* looking for these characteristics. On the basis of the economy and concreteness of his style as well as your knowledge of Thoreau himself, be prepared to discuss de Buffon's statement on style.

II. Where I Lived, and What I Lived For

When first I took up my abode in the woods, that is, began to spend my nights as well as days there, which, by accident, was on Independence day, or the fourth of July, 1845, my house was not finished for winter, but was merely a defence against the rain, without plastering or chimney, the walls being of rough weather-stained boards, with wide chinks, which made it cool at night. The upright white hewn studs and freshly planed door and window casings gave it a clean and airy look, especially in the morning, when its timbers were saturated with dew, so that I fancied that by noon some sweet gum would exude from them. To my imagination it retained throughout the day more or less of this auroral[1] character, reminding me of a certain house on a mountain which I had visited a year before. This was an airy and unplastered cabin, fit to entertain a travelling god, and where a goddess might trail her garments. The winds which passed over my dwelling were such as sweep over the ridges of mountains, bearing the broken strains, or celestial parts only, of terrestrial music. The morning wind forever blows, the poem of creation is uninterrupted; but few are the ears that hear it. Olympus[2] is but the outside of the earth everywhere.

The only house I had been the owner of before, if I except a boat, was a tent, which I used occasionally when making excursions in the summer, and this is still rolled up in my garret,[3] but the boat, after passing from hand to hand, has gone down the stream of time. With this more substantial shelter about me, I had made some progress toward settling in the world. This frame, so slightly clad, was a sort of crystallization around me, and reacted on the builder. It was suggestive somewhat as a picture in outlines. I did not need to go out doors to take the air, for the atmosphere within had lost none of its freshness. It was

not so much within doors as behind a door where I sat, even in the rainiest weather. The Harivamsa[4] says, "An abode without birds is like a meat without seasoning." Such was not my abode, for I found myself suddenly neighbor to the birds; not by having imprisoned one, but having caged myself near them. I was not only nearer to some of those which commonly frequent the garden and the orchard, but to those wilder and more thrilling songsters of the forest which never, or rarely, serenade a villager,—the woodthrush, the veery, the scarlet tanager, the field-sparrow, the whippoorwill, and many others.

I was seated by the shore of a small pond, about a mile and a half south of the village of Concord and somewhat higher than it, in the midst of an extensive wood between that town and Lincoln, and about two miles south of that our only field known to fame, Concord Battle Ground; but I was so low in the woods that the opposite shore, half a mile off, like the rest, covered with wood, was my most distant horizon. For the first week, whenever I looked out on the pond it impressed me like a tarn high up on the side of a mountain, its bottom far above the surface of other lakes, and, as the sun arose, I saw it throwing off its nightly clothing of mist, and here and there, by degrees, its soft ripples or its smooth reflecting surface was revealed, while the mists, like ghosts, were stealthily withdrawing in every direction into the woods, as at the breaking up of some nocturnal conventicle.[5] The very dew seemed to hang upon the trees later into the day than usual, as on the sides of mountains. . . .

Every morning was a cheerful invitation to make my life of equal simplicity, and I may

1. **auroral** (ô rôr′ əl),   pertaining to the dawn.
2. **Olympus** (ō lim′ pəs),   a mountain in Thessaly considered by the ancient Greeks to be the home of the gods.
3. **garret,**   set of rooms in an attic.
4. **Harivamsa** (ha rē′ vam sa),   a supplement to the great Hindu epic *Mahābhārata.*
5. **conventicle** (kən ven′ tə kəl),   a secret religious assembly.

THE OLD HUNTING GROUND, Worthington Whittredge
Reynolda House
Winston-Salem, North Carolina

say innocence, with Nature herself. I have been as sincere a worshipper of Aurora[6] as the Greeks. I got up early and bathed in the pond; that was a religious exercise, and one of the best things which I did. They say that characters were engraven on the bathing tub of king Tching-thang to this effect: "Renew thyself completely each day; do it again, and again, and forever again." I can understand that. Morning brings back the heroic ages. I was as much affected by the faint hum of a mosquito making its invisible and unimaginable tour through my apartment at earliest dawn, when I was sitting with door and windows open, as I could be by any trumpet that ever sang of fame. It was Homer's requiem; itself an Iliad and Odyssey in the air, singing its own wrath and wanderings. There was something cosmical about it; a standing advertisement, till forbidden, of the everlasting vigor and fertility of the world. The morning, which is the most memorable season of the day, is the awakening hour. Then there is least somnolence in us; and for an hour, at least, some part of us awakes which slumbers all the rest of the day and night. Little is to be expected of that day, if it can be called a day, to which we are not awakened by our Genius, but by the mechanical nudgings of some servitor, are not awakened by our own newly-acquired force and aspirations from within, accompanied by the undulations of celestial music, instead of factory bells, and a fragrance filling the air—to a higher life than we fell asleep from; and thus the darkness bear its fruit, and prove itself to be good, no less than the light. That man who does not believe that each day contains an earlier, more sacred, and auroral hour than he has yet profaned, has despaired of life, and is pursuing a descending and darkening way. After a partial cessation of his sensuous life, the soul of man, or its organs rather, are reinvigorated each day, and his Genius tries again what noble life it can make. All memorable events, I should say, transpire in morning time and in a morning atmosphere. The Vedas[7] say,

"All intelligences awake with the morning." Poetry and art, and the fairest and most memorable of the actions of men, date from such an hour. All poets and heroes, like Memnon,[8] are the children of Aurora, and emit their music at sunrise. To him whose elastic and vigorous thought keeps pace with the sun, the day is a perpetual morning. It matters not what the clocks say or the attitudes and labors of men. Morning is when I am awake and there is a dawn in me. Moral reform is the effort to throw off sleep. Why is it that men give so poor an account of their day if they have not been slumbering? They are not such poor calculators. If they had not been overcome with drowsiness they would have performed something. The millions are awake enough for physical labor; but only one in a million is awake enough for effective intellectual exertion, only one in a hundred millions to a poetic or divine life. To be awake is to be alive. I have never yet met a man who was quite awake. How could I have looked him in the face? . . .

I went to the woods because I wished to live deliberately, to front only the essential facts of life, and see if I could not learn what it had to teach, and not, when I came to die, discover that I had not lived. I did not wish to live what was not life, living is so dear; nor did I wish to practise resignation, unless it was quite necessary. I wanted to live deep and suck out all the marrow of life, to live so sturdily and Spartan-like as to put to rout all that was not life, to cut a broad swath and shave close, to drive life into a corner, and reduce it to its lowest terms, and, if it proved to be mean, why then to get the whole and genuine meanness of it, and publish its meanness to the world; or if it were sublime, to know it by

6. **Aurora** (ô rôr′ a),   the goddess of dawn.
7. **Vedas** (vā′ dəz),   sacred literature of Hinduism written in Sanskrit.
8. **Memnon,** a gigantic statue of an Egyptian king at Thebes, said to emit musical sound at sunrise.

experience, and be able to give a true account of it in my next excursion. For most men, it appears to me, are in a strange uncertainty about it, whether it is of the devil or of God, and have *somewhat hastily* concluded that it is the chief end of man here to "glorify God and enjoy him forever."

Still we live meanly, like ants; though the fable tells us that we were long ago changed into men; like pygmies we fight with cranes; it is error upon error, and clout upon clout, and our best virtue has for its occasion a superfluous and evitable wretchedness. Our life is frittered away by detail. An honest man has hardly need to count more than his ten fingers, or in extreme cases he may add his ten toes, and lump the rest. Simplicity, simplicity, simplicity! I say, let your affairs be as two or three, and not a hundred or a thousand; instead of a million count half a dozen, and keep your accounts on your thumb nail. In the midst of this chopping sea of civilized life, such are the clouds and storms and quicksands and thousand-and-one items to be allowed for, that a man has to live, if he would not founder and go to the bottom and not make his port at all, by dead reckoning, and he must be a great calculator indeed who succeeds. Simplify, simplify. Instead of three meals a day, if it be necessary eat but one; instead of a hundred dishes, five; and reduce other things in proportion. Our life is like a German Confederacy, made up of petty states, with its boundary forever fluctuating, so that even a German cannot tell you how it is bounded at any moment. The nation itself, with all its so-called internal improvements, which, by the way, are all external and superficial, is just such an unwieldy and overgrown establishment, cluttered with furniture and tripped up by its own traps, ruined by luxury and heedless expense, by want of calculation and a worthy aim, as the million households in the land; and the only cure for it as for them is in a rigid economy, a stern and more than Spartan simplicity of life and elevation of purpose. It lives too fast. Men think that it

is essential that the *Nation* have commerce, and export ice, and talk through a telegraph, and ride thirty miles an hour, without a doubt, whether *they* do or not; but whether we should live like baboons or like men, is a little uncertain. If we do not get out sleepers, and forge rails, and devote days and nights to the work, but go to tinkering upon our *lives* to improve *them,* who will build railroads? And if railroads are not built, how shall we get to heaven in season? But if we stay at home and mind our business, who will want railroads? We do not ride on the railroad; it rides upon us. Did you ever think what those sleepers are that underlie the railroads? Each one is a man, an Irishman, or a Yankee man. The rails are laid on them, and they are covered with sand, and the cars run smoothly over them. They are sound sleepers, I assure you. And every few years a new lot is laid down and run over; so that, if some have the pleasure of riding on a rail, others have the misfortune to be ridden upon. And when they run over a man that is walking in his sleep, a supernumerary sleeper in the wrong position, and wake him up, they suddenly stop the cars, and make a hue and cry about it, as if this were an exception. I am glad to know that it takes a gang of men for every five miles to keep the sleepers down and level in their beds as it is, for this is a sign that they may sometime get up again.

Why should we live with such hurry and waste of life? We are determined to be starved before we are hungry. Men say that a stitch in time saves nine, and so they take a thousand stitches to-day to save nine to-morrow. As for *work,* we haven't any of any consequence. We have the Saint Vitus' dance,[9] and cannot possibly keep our heads still. If I should only give a few pulls at the parish bell-rope, as for a fire, that is, without setting the bell, there is hardly a man on his

9. **Saint Vitus' dance,** a nervous disorder in which there is involuntary movement of the muscles.

farm in the outskirts of Concord, notwithstanding that press of engagements which was his excuse so many times this morning, nor a boy, nor a woman, I might almost say, but would forsake all and follow that sound, not mainly to save property from the flames, but, if we will confess the truth, much more to see it burn, since burn it must, and we, be it known, did not set it on fire,—or to see it put out, and have a hand in it, if that is done as handsomely; yes, even if it were the parish church itself. Hardly a man takes a half hour's nap after dinner, but when he wakes he holds up his head and asks, "What's the news?" as if the rest of mankind had stood his sentinels. Some give directions to be waked every half hour, doubtless for no other purpose; and then, to pay for it, they tell what they have dreamed. After a night's sleep the news is as indispensable as the breakfast. "Pray tell me anything new that has happened to a man anywhere on this globe,"—and he reads it over his coffee and rolls, that a man has had his eyes gouged out this morning on the Wachito River,[10] never dreaming the while that he lives in the dark unfathomed mammoth cave of this world, and has but the rudiment of an eye himself.

For my part, I could easily do without the post-office. I think that there are very few important communications made through it. To speak critically, I never received more than one or two letters in my life—I wrote this some years ago—that were worth the postage. The penny-post is, commonly, an institution through which you seriously offer a man that penny for his thoughts which is so often safely offered in jest. And I am sure that I never read any memorable news in a newspaper. If we read of one man robbed, or murdered, or killed by accident, or one house burned, or one vessel wrecked, or one steamboat blown up, or one cow run over on the Western Railroad, or one mad dog killed, or one lot of grasshoppers in the winter,—we never need read of another. One is enough. If you are acquainted with the principle, what do you care for a myriad instances and applications? To a philosopher all *news*, as it is called, is gossip, and they who edit and read it are old women over their tea. Yet not a few are greedy after this gossip. . . .

10. **Wachito River,** apparently a phonetic spelling of the Ouachita River, which flows southeast through southern Arkansas and northeastern Louisiana.

FOR UNDERSTANDING

1. How does Thoreau describe the atmosphere of his house when he moved into it?
2. According to Thoreau, what is the best part of the day and why?
3. What did Thoreau endeavor to learn by going to live in the woods?
4. What opinion does he express about the railroads?
5. Why does Thoreau feel that newspapers are not essential?
6. What is the one-word formula Thoreau gives us to help us arrange our lives more satisfyingly and effectively?

FOR INTERPRETATION

Discuss the following statements:
1. Thoreau's advice—to simplify—applies only to those who, like him, want to live the life of a thinker.
2. It is foolish to suppose that a modern nation like ours would prosper very long if it were to adopt the kind of "rigid economy" and "Spartan simplicity" that Thoreau recommends.
3. A civilization necessarily "pays for" every technological advance it makes; in a real sense there has been no progress since the beginning of recorded time.
4. Times have changed to such an extent that many things Thoreau considered nonessential for his time are essential for ours.

XII. Brute Neighbors

Why do precisely these objects which we behold make a world? Why has man just these species of animals for his neighbors; as if nothing but a mouse could have filled this crevice? I suspect that Pilpay & Co. have put animals to their best use, for they are all beasts of burden, in a sense, made to carry some portion of our thoughts. . . .

The mice which haunted my house were not the common ones, which are said to have been introduced into the country, but a wild native kind not found in the village. I sent one to a distinguished naturalist, and it interested him much. When I was building, one of these had its nest underneath the house, and before I had laid the second floor, and swept out the shavings, would come out regularly at lunch time and pick up the crumbs at my feet. It probably had never seen a man before; and it soon became quite familiar, and would run over my shoes and up my clothes. It could readily ascend the sides of the room by short impulses, like a squirrel, which it resembled in its motions. At length, as I leaned with my elbow on the bench one day, it ran up my clothes, and along my sleeve, and round and round the paper which held my dinner, while I kept the latter close, and dodged and played at bo-peep with it; and when at last I held still a piece of cheese between my thumb and finger, it came and nibbled it, sitting in my hand, and afterward cleaned its face and paws, like a fly, and walked away.

A phoebe[1] soon built in my shed, and a robin for protection in a pine which grew against the house. In June the partridge *(Tetrao umbellus)*, which is so shy a bird, led her brood past my windows, from the woods in the rear to the front of my house, clucking and calling to them like a hen, and in all her behavior proving herself the hen of the woods. The young suddenly disperse on your approach, at a signal from the mother, as if a whirlwind had swept them away, and they so exactly resemble the dried leaves and twigs that many a traveller has placed his foot in the midst of a brood, and heard the whir of the old bird as she flew off, and her anxious calls and mewing, or seen her trail her wings to attract his attention, without suspecting their neighborhood. The parent will sometimes roll and spin round before you in such a dishabille,[2] that you cannot, for a few moments, detect what kind of creature it is. The young squat still and flat, often running their heads under a leaf, and mind only their mother's directions given from a distance, nor will your approach make them run again and betray themselves. You may even tread on them, or have your eyes on them for a minute, without discovering them. I have held them in my open hand at such a time, and still their only care, obedient to their mother and their instinct, was to squat there without fear or trembling. So perfect is this instinct, that once, when I had laid them on the leaves again, and one accidentally fell on its side, it was found with the rest in exactly the same position ten minutes afterward. They are not callow like the young of most birds, but more perfectly developed and precocious even than chickens. The remarkably adult yet innocent expression of their open and serene eyes is very memorable. All intelligence seems reflected in them. They suggest not merely the purity of infancy, but a wisdom clarified by experience. Such an eye was not born when the bird was, but is coeval with the sky it reflects. The woods do not yield another such a gem. The traveller does not often look into such a limpid well. The ignorant or reckless sportsman often shoots the parent at such a time, and leaves these innocents to fall a prey to some prowling beast or bird, or gradually mingle with the decaying

---

1. **phoebe** (fē′ bē), an American flycatcher common in eastern United States.
2. **dishabille** (dis′ ə bēl′), state of being carelessly or partially dressed.

leaves which they so much resemble. It is said that when hatched by a hen they will directly disperse on some alarm, and so are lost, for they never hear the mother's call which gathers them again. These were my hens and chickens.

It is remarkable how many creatures live wild and free though secret in the woods, and still sustain themselves in the neighborhood of towns, suspected by hunters only. How retired the otter manages to live here! He grows to be four feet long, as big as a small boy, perhaps without any human being getting a glimpse of him. I formerly saw the raccoon in the woods behind where my house is built, and probably still heard their whinnering at night. Commonly I rested an hour or two in the shade at noon, after planting, and ate my lunch, and read a little by a spring which was the source of a swamp and of a brook, oozing from under Brister's Hill, half a mile from my field. The approach to this was through a succession of descending grassy hollows, full of young pitchpines, into a larger wood about the swamp. There, in a very secluded and shaded spot, under a spreading white-pine, there was yet a clean firm sward to sit on. I had dug out the spring and made a well of clear gray water, where I could dip up a pailful without roiling it, and thither I went for this purpose almost every day in midsummer, when the pond was warmest. Thither too the wood-cock led her brood, to probe the mud for worms, flying but a foot above them down the bank, while they ran in a troop beneath; but at last, spying me, she would leave her young and circle round and round me, nearer and nearer till within four or five feet, pretending broken wings and legs, to attract my attention, and get off her young, who would already have taken up their march, with faint wiry peep, single file through the swamp, as she directed. Or I heard the peep of the young when I could not see the parent bird. There too the turtle-doves sat over the spring, or fluttered from bough to bough of the soft white-pines over

my head; or the red squirrel, coursing down the nearest bough, was particularly familiar and inquisitive. You only need sit still long enough in some attractive spot in the woods that all its inhabitants may exhibit themselves to you by turns.

I was witness to events of a less peaceful character. One day when I went out to my wood-pile, or rather my pile of stumps, I observed two large ants, the one red, the other much larger, nearly half an inch long, and black, fiercely contending with one another. Having once got hold they never let go, but struggled and wrestled and rolled on the chips incessantly. Looking farther, I was surprised to find that the chips were covered with such combatants, that it was not a *duellum*, but a *bellum*,[3] a war between two races of ants, the red always pitted against the black, and frequently two red ones to one black. The legions of these Myrmidons[4] covered all the hills and vales in my wood-yard, and the ground was already strewn with the dead and dying, both red and black. It was the only battle which I have ever witnessed, the only battle-field I ever trod while the battle was raging; internecine war; the red republicans on the one hand, and the black imperialists on the other. On every side they were engaged in deadly combat, yet without any noise that I could hear, and human soldiers never fought so resolutely. I watched a couple that were fast locked in each other's embraces, in a little sunny valley amid the chips, now at noon-day prepared to fight till the sun went down, or life went out. The smaller red champion had fastened himself like a vise to his adversary's front, and through all the tumblings on that field never for an instant ceased to gnaw at one of his feelers near the root, having already caused the other to go by

---

3. *duellum, bellum,* Latin for "duel" and "war."
4. **Myrmidons** (mėr′ mə donz), an allusion to Homer's *Iliad;* the Greek hero Achilles led his army, the Myrmidons. They were his faithful unquestioning followers.

the board; while the stronger black one dashed him from side to side, and, as I saw on looking nearer, had already divested him of several of his members. They fought with more pertinacity than bull-dogs. Neither manifested the least disposition to retreat. It was evident that their battle-cry was Conquer or die.

In the meanwhile there came along a single red ant on the hillside of this valley, evidently full of excitement, who either had despatched his foe, or had not yet taken part in the battle; probably the latter, for he had lost none of his limbs; whose mother had charged him to return with his shield or upon it. Or perchance he was some Achilles, who had nourished his wrath apart, and had now come to avenge or rescue his Patroclus.[5] He saw this unequal combat from afar,—for the blacks were nearly twice the size of the red,—he drew near with rapid pace till he stood on his guard within half an inch of the combatants; then, watching his opportunity, he sprang upon the black warrior, and commenced his operations near the root of his right fore-leg, leaving the foe to select among his own members; and so there were three united for life, as if a new kind of attraction had been invented which put all other locks and cements to shame. I should not have wondered by this time to find that they had their respective musical bands stationed on some eminent chip, and playing their national airs the while, to excite the slow and cheer the dying combatants. I was myself excited somewhat even as if they had been men. The more you think of it, the less the difference. And certainly there is not the fight recorded in Concord history, at least, if in the history of America, that will bear a moment's comparison with this, whether for the numbers engaged in it, or for the patriotism and heroism displayed. For numbers and for carnage it was an Austerlitz[6] or Dresden. Concord Fight! Two killed on the patriots' side, and Luther Blanchard wounded! Why here every ant was a Buttrick,[7]—"Fire! for God's sake

fire!"—and thousands shared the fate of Davis and Hosmer. There was not one hireling there. I have no doubt that it was a principle they fought for, as much as our ancestors, and not to avoid a three-penny tax on their tea; and the results of this battle will be as important and memorable to those whom it concerns as those of the battle of Bunker Hill, at least.

I took up the chip on which the three I have particularly described were struggling, carried it into my house, and placed it under a tumbler on my window-sill, in order to see the issue. Holding a microscope to the first-mentioned red ant, I saw that, though he was assiduously gnawing at the near fore-leg of his enemy, having severed his remaining feeler, his own breast was all torn away, exposing what vitals he had there to the jaws of the black warrior, whose breastplate was apparently too thick for him to pierce; and the dark carbuncles of the sufferer's eyes shone with ferocity such as war only could excite. They struggled half an hour longer under the tumbler, and when I looked again the black soldier had severed the heads of his foes from their bodies, and the still living heads were hanging on either side of him like ghastly trophies at his saddle-bow, still apparently as firmly fastened as ever, and he was endeavoring with feeble struggles, being without feelers and with only the remnant of a leg, and I know not how many other wounds, to divest himself of them; which at length, after half an hour more, he accomplished. I raised the glass, and he went off over the window-sill in that crippled state. Whether he finally survived that combat, and spent the remainder

5. **Patroclus** (pə trō′ kləs), in the *Iliad*, Achilles's dear friend, killed by the Trojan hero Hector.
6. **Austerlitz** (ô′ ster lits), town in Czechoslovakia and site of Napoleon's victory over Austrian and Russian armies, 1805.
7. **Buttrick**, Maj. John, leader of the provincials who turned back the British advance at the North Bridge, Concord, Mass., in 1775. Blanchard, Davis, and Hosmer were casualties in the skirmish.

of his days in some Hotel des Invalides,[8] I do not know; but I thought that his industry would not be worth much thereafter. I never learned which party was victorious, nor the cause of the war; but I felt for the rest of that day as if I had had my feelings excited and harrowed by witnessing the struggle, the ferocity and carnage, of a human battle before my door. . . .

XVIII. Conclusion

I left the woods for as good a reason as I went there. Perhaps it seemed to me that I had several more lives to live, and could not spare any more time for that one. It is remarkable how easily and insensibly we fall into a particular route, and make a beaten track for ourselves. I had not lived there a week before my feet wore a path from my door to the pondside; and though it is five or six years since I trod it, it is still quite distinct. It is true, I fear, that others may have fallen into it, and so helped to keep it open. The surface of the earth is soft and impressible by the feet of men; and so with the paths which the mind travels. How worn and dusty, then, must be the highways of the world, how deep the ruts of tradition and conformity! I did not wish to take a cabin passage, but rather to go before the mast and on the deck of the world, for there I could best see the moonlight amid the mountains. I do not wish to go below now.

I learned this, at least, by my experiment; that if one advances confidently in the direction of his dreams, and endeavors to live the life which he has imagined, he will meet with a success unexpected in common hours. He will put some things behind, will pass an invisible boundary; new, universal, and more liberal laws will begin to establish themselves

---

8. **Hotel des Invalides** (o tel' dä zan və lēd'), in Paris, originally a hospital for veterans; now a museum containing the tomb of Napoleon.

---

around and within him; or the old laws be expanded, and interpreted in his favor in a more liberal sense, and he will live with the license of a higher order of beings. In proportion as he simplifies his life, the laws of the universe will appear less complex, and solitude will not be solitude, nor poverty poverty, nor weakness weakness. If you have built castles in the air, your work need not be lost; that is where they should be. Now put the foundations under them. . . .

FOR UNDERSTANDING

1. What is unusual about the mouse that lived under Thoreau's house?
2. How did Thoreau manage to see so much of the wildlife that lived in the woods?
3. What is the overall effect of Thoreau's comparing the battle of the ants with human battles?
4. Define in your own words what Thoreau means by "an invisible boundary."
5. How does one cross such a boundary?
6. Reread the discussion of Transcendentalism on page 168 of the text and try to relate Thoreau's "Conclusion" to it.

FOR INTERPRETATION

The following quotations are gathered from all the foregoing passages. Discuss the meaning of each and the relevance of any five to your own life and experience.
1. But men labor under a mistake. The better part of the man is soon ploughed into the soil for compost.
2. . . . I made no haste in my work, but rather made the most of it. . . .
3. . . . my greatest skill has been to want but little. . . .
4. . . . trade curses everything it handles; and though you trade in messages from Heaven, the whole curse of trade attaches to the business.
5. . . . I am convinced . . . that to maintain one's self on this earth is not a hardship but a pastime, if we will live simply and wisely. . . .
6. Morning is when I am awake and there is a

dawn in me. Moral reform is the effort to throw off sleep.

7. I have never yet met a man who was quite awake. How could I have looked him in the face?

8. Our life is frittered away by detail.

9. . . . if railroads are not built, how shall we get to heaven in season? But if we stay home and mind our business, who will want railroads? We do not ride on the railroad; it rides upon us.

10. It is remarkable how easily and insensibly we fall into a particular route, and make a beaten track for ourselves.

FOR APPRECIATION

Tone

Tone usually refers to a writer's attitude toward his or her material. Just as a speaker's *tone of voice* shows attitude, writers reveal their attitudes toward their subjects in various ways. One of the main ways is word choice. Consider, for example, the contrast in connotation of the words "fuzz," "cop," and "law-enforcement officer," all of which may be used to refer to a police officer.

Sometimes, it is important to distinguish tone in the sense of the writer's attitude toward the subject from tone in the sense of the writer's attitude toward the reader. At one point in *Walden,* when Thoreau speaks of the "dirty institutions" of society, his tone *toward his subject* may properly be called hostile or even bitter; but he does not necessarily adopt the same tone *toward his readers.* Certainly those members of his audience who admire him do not feel that he is expressing hostility toward them; on the contrary, they are far more likely to describe his tone toward his audience as friendly, honest, sincere.

Choose three or four of the quotations from the For Interpretation section—or any others from the Thoreau selections—and discuss the differences between Thoreau's attitude toward his material and his attitude toward his readers. Note especially which of the two attitudes seems to vary more and why.

COMPOSITION

Choose one of the following for a brief paper:

1. Although Thoreau is now accounted a major American writer, he received little recognition during his lifetime. In fact, many of his contemporaries dismissed him as an eccentric who rejected the benefits of civilization. Even his best friend, Ralph Waldo Emerson, on whose woodlot Thoreau built his cabin, lamented that Thoreau, instead of using "his rare powers of action," was content to be "the captain of a huckleberry party." Write your assessment of Thoreau as a thinker and critic of society.

2. Describe an imaginary sanctuary you would like to have, a place you could go to be alone and think through any troublesome problems. Locate your sanctuary; include details of furnishings or equipment you would like to have in it.

Nathaniel Hawthorne   1804–1864

New England was in Nathaniel Hawthorne's blood, but rarely has an American writer been so consciously tied to his birthplace and his ancestry and, at the same time, so aware of his aversion to both. Born in Salem, Massachusetts, on Independence Day, 1804, he was descended from wealthy and influential citizens who, despite their prominence, left a blot on the family's history for which Hawthorne spent a lifetime trying to atone. William Hathorne (Nathaniel changed the spelling) had arrived in the American colonies in 1630. Eventually he became a judge and condemned a Quaker woman to be whipped in the streets of Salem for holding to a religion the Puritans strongly opposed. "Grave, bearded, sable-cloaked and steeple-crowned," Hawthorne described him. His son, John, was also a judge; and Hawthorne could not forget that in 1692 this ancestor "made himself so conspicuous in the martyrdom of witches that their blood may be said to have left a stain upon him." Intolerance, cruelty, pride— these sins obsessed the young Hawthorne as he listened to the history of early Salem and his ancestors.

It is true that Bold Daniel Hathorne, his grandfather, belonged to that early Salem. He was a naval captain in the Revolutionary War, of such bravery that he became the hero of a popular ballad. Other ancestors fought Indians, sailed merchant ships, built up considerable fortunes in trade. But Hawthorne grew up in nineteenth-century "joyless" Salem, as he called it, in the "chilliest of social atmospheres," and he loathed it. His own father, a sea captain, died of a fever in Dutch Guiana when Hawthorne was only four, and shortly thereafter his mother was forced to move her three children first into her parents' crowded Salem home, eventually into her brother's house in Raymond, Maine. There is no reason to believe Hawthorne's childhood was abnormally disordered, but certainly the family's impoverishment, his mother's prolonged mourning and spells of seclusion, his own distaste for school, his fragile health—these

PORTRAIT OF NATHANIEL HAWTHORNE
Emanuel Gottlieb Leutze
National Portrait Gallery, Smithsonian Institution

aspects of his youth, coupled with his sense of inherited guilt, began to shape the young man's mind.

After four years at Bowdoin College at his uncle's expense, he returned to Salem not to read law or to enter business, as his relatives expected, but to seclude himself in his mother's house and, quite simply, turn himself into a writer. "I do not want to be a doctor and live by men's diseases," he had written to his mother from Bowdoin, "nor a minister to live by their sins, nor a lawyer and live by their quarrels. So, I don't see that there is anything left for me but to be an author." For the next twelve years he lived physically in "the chamber under the eaves" of his mother's house, seldom going out except at twilight or to make a brief journey to another city. Mentally he lived in a world of books.

"I had read endlessly all sorts of good and good-for-nothing books," he recalled many years later, "and, in the dearth of other employment, had early begun to scribble sketches and stories most of which I burned." His first novel, *Fanshawe,* was published anonymously at his own expense in 1828. In anger at the lack of sales or at his own immaturity as a writer, he recalled every copy he could find and destroyed them. When a local printer delayed publishing his *Seven Tales of My Native Land,* he withdrew the manuscript and burned it "in a mood half savage, half despairing." Other stories he destroyed before publication because they were "morbid."

A weaker man would have withered under such an apprenticeship. Hawthorne only grew, in self-respect, in determination to succeed on his own terms, in patience with the world "outside." He traveled occasionally to New Haven, to Swampscott, to the mountains of Vermont, always keeping a notebook in which he jotted observations of places and people, ideas for stories, phrases which pleased him. He sold tales and sketches to New England magazines; he was even persuaded to edit a Boston magazine for six months. Finally in 1837, at the age of thirty-two, he published his first collection, *Twice-Told Tales.* Longfellow, the most popular poet of the day, gave it a full, almost flattering review. New York magazine editors read it and asked for contributions to their pages. Even Salem recognized its merits. One family in particular, the Nathaniel Peabodys, so wooed the young author that within two years he was engaged to their youngest daughter, Sophia.

Supporting a wife, Hawthorne realized, is not a task a recluse can face without qualms. He could never manage it by writing stories, so with as decisive a manner as he had entered his apprenticeship, he left Salem and his mother's house for a political appointment as measurer of coal and salt in the Boston customhouse. The contrast was a shock. He had hoped to discover what "reality" was like as well as to earn a respectable salary, and he gave it a fair try; but after two years he resigned from this "very grievous thralldom." He had been able to write little more than notebook entries, and he found "nothing in the world that [he] thought preferable to [his] old solitude." He thought

marriage might be the answer, and in one way it was. He learned to share his life.

With their moving to the Old Manse in rural Concord, Massachusetts, the Hawthornes found a happiness neither had expected out of life. "Everybody that comes here," he wrote in 1843, "falls asleep; but for my own part, I feel as if, for the first time in my life, I was awake. I have found a reality, though it looks very much like some of my old dreams." Intellectually he was still content to trust his "dreams," his secret musings, his private thoughts, in spite of conversations with extraordinary neighbors who tried to draw him out of his protective shell. Henry David Thoreau struck him as "ugly as sin, long-nosed, queer mouthed," and yet "a healthy, wholesome man to know." They had long, involved talks together. Emerson was for him "the one great original thinker," but Hawthorne looked upon him as a "poet of deep beauty" rather than a philosopher. These men stimulated Hawthorne. They showed him the optimistic side of reality, but he doubted whether either of them had a theory of tragedy, whether they could ever know the dark recesses of the human heart. He produced more than twenty tales during these three years in Concord, sold them to magazines, and then collected them in *Mosses from an Old Manse.* His reputation was growing. Edgar Allan Poe, who knew what made a short story memorable, called Hawthorne *"the* example, *par excellence,* in this country, of the privately admired and publicly unappreciated man of genius."

It took a return to Salem to bring him fame. A Bowdoin classmate, Franklin Pierce, found him a lucrative post as surveyor in the Salem customhouse. After three years of coping with the dullness of the work, he was not distressed to find himself dismissed for political reasons. "Now you can write your book," Sophia told him. In seven months it was finished. In April 1850 Ticknor and Fields of Boston published *The Scarlet Letter.* Had Hawthorne not written another word than this long tale of Puritan Boston, he would still find a high place in the history of American literature. He called it "positively a hell-fired story, into which I found it almost impossible to throw any cheering light." The contemporary critics, accustomed to Hawthorne's moralizing and his fondness for somber moods, found it unforgettable, perhaps America's first tragedy. Readers of Hester Prynne's story have agreed ever since.

The last fourteen years of Hawthorne's life were such a contrast to his long struggle for recognition that it is almost as though their chronicle belongs to another man. Ambitious with the success of *The Scarlet Letter,* he enlarged his scope with plans for novels and romances. Within a year he had finished the story of the Pyncheon family of Salem and Maule's curse, *The House of the Seven Gables.* "I think it a work more characteristic of my mind," he wrote a friend, "and more proper and natural for me to write." Perhaps it was more proper, if he meant a romance with a happy ending that would charm more readers. But it was hardly characteristic of the best part of Hawthorne's mind and talent. A year later he published *The Blithedale Romance,* a satire of Brook Farm, the famous cooperative community in West Roxbury where he had lived briefly before his marriage. In spite of a memorable villain, the cold-hearted social reformer, Hollingsworth, the story is static and uninspired. After seven years in Europe (Hawthorne had written a campaign biography for Franklin Pierce, who, after his election as president, rewarded him with the consulship at Liverpool), he tried an even more ambitious novel, *The Marble Faun,* set in contemporary Rome amid the splendors of that alluring city. He took as his theme nothing less than the origin of evil, the coming of sin into the world, and tried to illustrate it through two young couples, one of them a faunlike pagan Roman, called Donatello, and a mysterious American girl, Miriam. But the scope of the novel is too large; too many guidebook details of Rome interfere with our believing the mystery that is supposed to surround these people. Clearly Hawthorne

had achieved his most powerful work in his early tales and in his masterpiece, *The Scarlet Letter.*

The moral nature of these early sketches and tales was, for Hawthorne, the reason for their being and the secret of their strength. He began these stories with an idea, then clothed that idea in reality. He was not interested, like Irving, in picturesque description, or, like Poe, in carefully controlled suspense. That is not to say Hawthorne was intent on writing narrative sermons. His poetic imagination would never allow his tales to become treatises on the Origin of Evil. But they began with the idea of guilt or pride or intolerance and moved from there into complex personal relationships, into the secret mysteries of the human heart.

From his own years of solitude, Hawthorne discovered much about the human heart, and what he discovered left him anxious about the world. His tales reflect this anxiety, particularly those in which the pride of intellect is revealed, as in "Ethan Brand," where the protagonist searches for the Unpardonable Sin only to discover it in himself, or in "Rappaccini's Daughter," where a learned scientist poisons his daughter in a mad experiment which goes beyond nature's limit. When the mind takes precedence over the heart, Hawthorne tells us, only misery, the misery of isolation from our fellows, can be the result. In his greatest novel, *The Scarlet Letter,* it is not the adulterers, Hester Prynne and the Reverend Dimmesdale, but the evil doctor, the wronged husband, Roger Chillingworth, who is most guilty. "That old man's revenge has been blacker than my sin," Dimmesdale tells Hester. "He has violated, in cold blood, the sanctity of the human heart." Once we are accustomed to the somber colors of Hawthorne's parables, we sense as clearly as he did that through them he speaks for everyone.

THE MINISTER'S BLACK VEIL
A Parable

The sexton[1] stood in the porch of Milford meeting-house, pulling busily at the bell-rope. The old people of the village came stooping along the street. Children, with bright faces, tripped merrily beside their parents, or mimicked a graver gait, in the conscious dignity of their Sunday clothes. Spruce bachelors looked sidelong at the pretty maidens, and fancied that the Sabbath[2] sunshine made them prettier than on week days. When the throng had mostly streamed into the porch, the sexton began to toll the bell, keeping his eye on the Reverend Mr. Hooper's door. The first glimpse of the clergyman's figure was the signal for the bell to cease its summons.

"But what has good Parson Hooper got upon his face?" cried the sexton in astonishment.

All within hearing immediately turned about, and beheld the semblance of Mr. Hooper, pacing slowly his meditative way towards the meeting-house. With one accord they started, expressing more wonder than if some strange minister were coming to dust the cushions of Mr. Hooper's pulpit.

"Are you sure it is our parson?" inquired Goodman Gray of the sexton.

"Of a certainty it is good Mr. Hooper," replied the sexton. "He was to have exchanged pulpits with Parson Shute, of Westbury; but Parson Shute sent to excuse himself yesterday, being to preach a funeral sermon."

The cause of so much amazement may appear sufficiently slight. Mr. Hooper, a gentlemanly person, of about thirty, though still a bachelor, was dressed with due clerical neatness, as if a careful wife had starched his band, and brushed the weekly dust from his Sunday's garb. There was but one thing remarkable in his appearance. Swathed about his forehead, and hanging down over his face, so low as to be shaken by his breath, Mr. Hooper had on a black veil. On a nearer view it seemed to consist of two folds of crape,[3] which entirely concealed his features, except the mouth and chin, but probably did not intercept his sight, further than to give a darkened aspect to all living and inanimate things. With this gloomy shade before him, good Mr. Hooper walked onward, at a slow and quiet pace, stooping somewhat, and looking on the ground, as is customary with abstracted men, yet nodding kindly to those of his parishioners who still waited on the meeting-house steps. But so wonder-struck were they that his greeting hardly met with a return.

"I can't really feel as if good Mr. Hooper's face was behind that piece of crape," said the sexton.

"I don't like it," muttered an old woman, as she hobbled into the meeting-house. "He has changed himself into something awful, only by hiding his face."

"Our parson has gone mad!" cried Goodman Gray, following him across the threshold.

A rumor of some unaccountable phenomenon had preceded Mr. Hooper into the meeting-house, and set all the congregation astir. Few could refrain from twisting their heads towards the door; many stood upright, and turned directly about; while several little

1. **sexton,** person who tends a church.
2. **Sabbath,** day of the week for rest and worship.
3. **crape** (also crepe), a thin, light material with a crinkled surface.

boys clambered upon the seats, and came down again with a terrible racket. There was a general bustle, a rustling of the women's gowns and shuffling of the men's feet, greatly at variance with that hushed repose which should attend the entrance of the minister. But Mr. Hooper appeared not to notice the perturbation of his people. He entered with an almost noiseless step, bent his head mildly to the pews on each side, and bowed as he passed his oldest parishioner, a white-haired great-grandsire, who occupied an armchair in the centre of the aisle. It was strange to observe how slowly this venerable man became conscious of something singular in the appearance of his pastor. He seemed not fully to partake of the prevailing wonder, till Mr. Hooper had ascended the stairs, and showed himself in the pulpit, face to face with his congregation, except for the black veil. That mysterious emblem was never once withdrawn. It shook with his measured breath, as he gave out the psalm;[4] it threw its obscurity between him and the holy page, as he read the Scriptures; and while he prayed, the veil lay heavily on his uplifted countenance. Did he seek to hide it from the dread Being whom he was addressing?

Such was the effect of this simple piece of crape, that more than one woman of delicate nerves was forced to leave the meeting-house. Yet perhaps the pale-faced congregation was almost as fearful a sight to the minister, as his black veil to them.

Mr. Hooper had the reputation of a good preacher, but not an energetic one: he strove to win his people heavenward by mild, persuasive influences, rather than to drive them thither by the thunders of the Word. The sermon which he now delivered was marked by the same characteristics of style and manner as the general series of his pulpit oratory. But there was something, either in the sentiment of the discourse itself, or in the imagination of the auditors,[5] which made it greatly the most powerful effort that they had ever heard from their pastor's lips. It was tinged,

rather more darkly than usual, with the gentle gloom of Mr. Hooper's temperament. The subject had reference to secret sin, and those sad mysteries which we hide from our nearest and dearest, and would fain conceal from our own consciousness, even forgetting that the Omniscient[6] can detect them. A subtle power was breathed into his words. Each member of the congregation, the most innocent girl, and the man of hardened breast, felt as if the preacher had crept upon them, behind his awful veil, and discovered their hoarded iniquity of deed or thought. Many spread their clasped hands on their bosoms. There was nothing terrible in what Mr. Hooper said, at least, no violence; and yet, with every tremor of his melancholy voice, the hearers quaked. An unsought pathos came hand in hand with awe. So sensible were the audience of some unwonted attribute in their minister that they longed for a breath of wind to blow aside the veil, almost believing that a stranger's visage would be discovered, though the form, gesture, and voice were those of Mr. Hooper.

At the close of the services, the people hurried out with indecorous confusion, eager to communicate their pent-up amazement, and conscious of lighter spirits the moment they lost sight of the black veil. Some gathered in little circles, huddled closely together, with their mouths all whispering in the centre; some went homeward alone, wrapt in silent meditation; some talked loudly, and profaned the Sabbath day with ostentatious laughter. A few shook their sagacious heads, intimating that they could penetrate the mystery; while one or two affirmed that there was no mystery at all, but only that Mr. Hooper's eyes were so weakened by the midnight lamp, as to require a shade. After a brief interval, forth came good Mr. Hooper also, in the rear of his flock. Turning his veiled face from one

4. **psalm** (säm), any of 150 sacred songs in the Old Testament.
5. **auditors,** here: hearers, listeners.
6. **Omniscient** (om nish' ənt), all-knowing; God.

group to another, he paid due reverence to the hoary heads, saluted the middle aged with kind dignity as their friend and spiritual guide, greeted the young with mingled authority and love, and laid his hands on the little children's heads to bless them. Such was always his custom on the Sabbath day. Strange and bewildered looks repaid him for his courtesy. None, as on former occasions, aspired to the honor of walking by their pastor's side. Old Squire Saunders, doubtless by an accidental lapse of memory, neglected to invite Mr. Hooper to his table, where the good clergyman had been wont to bless the food almost every Sunday since his settlement. He returned, therefore, to the parsonage, and, at the moment of closing the door, was observed to look back upon the people, all of whom had their eyes fixed upon the minister. A sad smile gleamed faintly from beneath the black veil, and flickered about his mouth, glimmering as he disappeared.

"How strange," said a lady, "that a simple black veil, such as any woman might wear on her bonnet, should become such a terrible thing on Mr. Hooper's face!"

"Something must surely be amiss with Mr. Hooper's intellects," observed her husband, the physician of the village. "But the strangest part of the affair is the effect of this vagary, even on a sober-minded man like myself. The black veil, though it covers only our pastor's face, throws its influence over his whole person, and makes him ghostlike from head to foot. Do you not feel it so?"

"Truly do I," replied the lady; "and I would not be alone with him for the world. I wonder he is not afraid to be alone with himself!"

"Men sometimes are so," said her husband.

The afternoon service was attended with similar circumstances. At its conclusion, the bell tolled for the funeral of a young lady. The relatives and friends were assembled in the house, and the more distant acquaintances stood about the door, speaking of the good qualities of the deceased, when their talk was interrupted by the appearance of Mr. Hooper, still covered with his black veil. It was now an appropriate emblem. The clergyman stepped into the room where the corpse was laid, and bent over the coffin, to take a last farewell of his deceased parishioner. As he stooped, the veil hung straight down from his forehead, so that, if her eyelids had not been closed forever, the dead maiden might have seen his face. Could Mr. Hooper be fearful of her glance, that he so hastily caught back the black veil? A person who watched the interview between the dead and living scrupled[7] not to affirm, that, at the instant when the clergyman's features were disclosed, the corpse had slightly shuddered, rustling the shroud and muslin cap, though the countenance retained the composure of death. A superstitious old woman was the only witness of this prodigy. From the coffin Mr. Hooper passed into the chamber of the mourners, and thence to the head of the staircase, to make the funeral prayer. It was a tender and heart-dissolving prayer, full of sorrow, yet so imbued with celestial[8] hopes, that the music of a heavenly harp, swept by the fingers of the dead, seemed faintly to be heard among the saddest accents of the minister. The people trembled, though they but darkly understood him when he prayed that they, and himself, and all of mortal race, might be ready, as he trusted this young maiden had been, for the dreadful hour that should snatch the veil from their faces. The bearers went heavily forth, and the mourners followed, saddening all the street, with the dead before them, and Mr. Hooper in his black veil behind.

"Why do you look back?" said one in the procession to his partner.

"I had a fancy," replied she, "that the minister and the maiden's spirit were walking hand in hand."

---

7. **scrupled** (skrü′ pəld), hesitated.
8. **celestial,** heavenly, divine.

"And so had I, at the same moment," said the other.

That night, the handsomest couple in Milford village were to be joined in wedlock. Though reckoned a melancholy man, Mr. Hooper had a placid cheerfulness for such occasions, which often excited a sympathetic smile where livelier merriment would have been thrown away. There was no quality of his disposition which made him more beloved than this. The company at the wedding awaited his arrival with impatience, trusting that the strange awe, which had gathered over him throughout the day, would now be dispelled. But such was not the result. When Mr. Hooper came, the first thing that their eyes rested on was the same horrible black veil, which had added deeper gloom to the funeral, and could portend nothing but evil to the wedding. Such was its immediate effect on the guests that a cloud seemed to have rolled duskily from beneath the black crape, and dimmed the light of the candles. The bridal pair stood up before the minister. But the bride's cold fingers quivered in the tremulous hand of the bridegroom, and her deathlike paleness caused a whisper that the maiden who had been buried a few hours before was come from her grave to be married. If ever another wedding were so dismal, it was that famous one where they tolled the wedding knell. After performing the ceremony, Mr. Hooper raised a glass of wine to his lips, wishing happiness to the new-married couple in a strain of mild pleasantry that ought to have brightened the features of the guests, like a cheerful gleam from the hearth. At that instant, catching a glimpse of his figure in the looking-glass, the black veil involved his own spirit in the horror with which it overwhelmed all others. His frame shuddered, his lips grew white, he spilt the untasted wine upon the carpet, and rushed forth into the darkness. For the Earth, too, had on her Black Veil.

The next day, the whole village of Milford talked of little else than Parson Hooper's black veil. That, and the mystery concealed behind it, supplied a topic for discussion between acquaintances meeting in the street, and good women gossiping at their open windows. It was the first item of news that the tavernkeeper told to his guests. The children babbled of it on their way to school. One imitative little imp covered his face with an old black handkerchief, thereby so affrighting his playmates that the panic seized himself, and he well-nigh lost his wits by his own waggery.[9]

It was remarkable that of all the busybodies and impertinent people in the parish, not one ventured to put the plain question to Mr. Hooper, wherefore he did this thing. Hitherto, whenever there appeared the slightest call for such interference, he had never lacked advisers, nor shown himself averse to be guided by their judgment. If he erred at all, it was by so painful a degree of self-distrust, that even the mildest censure would lead him to consider an indifferent action as a crime. Yet, though so well acquainted with this amiable weakness, no individual among his parishioners chose to make the black veil a subject of friendly remonstrance. There was a feeling of dread, neither plainly confessed nor carefully concealed, which caused each to shift the responsibility upon another, till at length it was found expedient to send a deputation of the church, in order to deal with Mr. Hooper about the mystery before it should grow into a scandal. Never did an embassy so ill discharge its duties. The minister received them with friendly courtesy, but became silent, after they were seated, leaving to his visitors the whole burden of introducing their important business. The topic, it might be supposed, was obvious enough. There was the black veil swathed round Mr. Hooper's forehead, and concealing every feature above his placid mouth, on which, at times, they could perceive the glimmering of a melancholy smile. But that piece of crape, to their

---

9. **waggery** (wag′ ər ē), joking.

imagination, seemed to hang down before his heart, the symbol of a fearful secret between him and them. Were the veil but cast aside, they might speak freely of it, but not till then. Thus they sat a considerable time, speechless, confused, and shrinking uneasily from Mr. Hooper's eye, which they felt to be fixed upon them with an invisible glance. Finally, the deputies returned abashed to their constituents,[10] pronouncing the matter too weighty to be handled, except by a council of the churches, if, indeed, it might not require a general synod.

But there was one person in the village unappalled by the awe with which the black veil had impressed all beside herself. When the deputies returned without an explanation, or even venturing to demand one, she, with the calm energy of her character, determined to chase away the strange cloud that appeared to be settling round Mr. Hooper, every moment more darkly than before. As his plighted wife, it should be her privilege to know what the black veil concealed. At the minister's first visit, therefore, she entered upon the subject with a direct simplicity, which made the task easier both for him and her. After he had seated himself, she fixed her eyes steadfastly upon the veil, but could discern nothing of the dreadful gloom that had so overawed the multitude: it was but a double fold of crape, hanging down from his forehead to his mouth, and slightly stirring with his breath.

"No," said she aloud, and smiling, "there is nothing terrible in this piece of crape, except that it hides a face which I am always glad to look upon. Come, good sir, let the sun shine from behind the cloud. First lay aside your black veil: then tell me why you put it on."

Mr. Hooper's smile glimmered faintly.

"There is an hour to come," said he, "when all of us shall cast aside our veils. Take it not amiss, beloved friend, if I wear this piece of crape till then."

"Your words are a mystery, too," re-turned the young lady. "Take away the veil from them, at least."

"Elizabeth, I will," said he, "so far as my vow may suffer me. Know, then, this veil is a type and a symbol, and I am bound to wear it ever, both in light and darkness, in solitude and before the gaze of multitudes, and as with strangers, so with my familiar friends. No mortal eye will see it withdrawn. This dismal shade must separate me from the world: even you, Elizabeth, can never come behind it!"

"What grievous affliction hath befallen you," she earnestly inquired, "that you should thus darken your eyes forever?"

"If it be a sign of mourning," replied Mr. Hooper, "I, perhaps, like most other mortals, have sorrows dark enough to be typified by a black veil."

"But what if the world will not believe that it is the type of an innocent sorrow?" urged Elizabeth. "Beloved and respected as you are, there may be whispers that you hide your face under the consciousness of secret sin. For the sake of your holy office, do away this scandal!"

The color rose into her cheeks as she intimated the nature of the rumors that were already abroad in the village. But Mr. Hooper's mildness did not forsake him. He even smiled again—that same sad smile, which always appeared like a faint glimmering of light, proceeding from the obscurity beneath the veil.

"If I hide my face for sorrow, there is cause enough," he merely replied; "and if I cover it for secret sin, what mortal might not do the same?"

And with this gentle, but unconquerable obstinacy[11] did he resist all her entreaties.[12] At length Elizabeth sat silent. For a few moments she appeared lost in thought, considering, probably, what new methods might be tried to withdraw her lover from so dark a fantasy,

---

10. **constituents,** persons who vote or appoint.
11. **obstinacy,** stubbornness.
12. **entreaties,** earnest requests; prayers.

which, if it had no other meaning, was perhaps a symptom of mental disease. Though of a firmer character than his own, the tears rolled down her cheeks. But, in an instant, as it were, a new feeling took the place of sorrow: her eyes were fixed insensibly on the black veil, when, like a sudden twilight in the air, its terors fell around her. She arose, and stood trembling before him.

"And do you feel it then, at last?" said he mournfully.

She made no reply, but covered her eyes with her hand, and turned to leave the room. He rushed forward and caught her arm.

"Have patience with me, Elizabeth!" cried he passionately. "Do not desert me, though this veil must be between us here on earth. Be mine, and hereafter there shall be no veil over my face, no darkness between our souls! It is but a mortal veil—it is not for eternity! O! you know not how lonely I am, and how frightened, to be alone behind my black veil. Do not leave me in this miserable obscurity forever!"

"Lift the veil but once, and look me in the face," said she.

"Never! It cannot be!" replied Mr. Hooper.

"Then farewell!" said Elizabeth.

She withdrew her arm from his grasp, and slowly departed, pausing at the door, to give one long, shuddering gaze, that seemed almost to penetrate the mystery of the black veil. But, even amid his grief, Mr. Hooper smiled to think that only a material emblem had separated him from happiness, though the horrors which it shadowed forth must be drawn darkly between the fondest of lovers.

From that time no attempts were made to remove Mr. Hooper's black veil, or, by a direct appeal, to discover the secret which it was supposed to hide. By persons who claimed a superiority to popular prejudice, it was reckoned merely an eccentric whim, such as often mingles with the sober actions of men otherwise rational, and tinges them all with its own semblance of insanity. But with the multi-

tude, good Mr. Hooper was irreparably a bugbear.[13] He could not walk the street with any peace of mind, so conscious was he that the gentle and timid would turn aside to avoid him, and that others would make it a point of hardihood to throw themselves in his way. The impertinence of the latter class compelled him to give up his customary walk at sunset to the burial ground; for when he leaned pensively over the gate, there would always be faces behind the gravestones, peeping at his black veil. A fable went the rounds that the stare of the dead people drove him thence. It grieved him, to the very depth of his kind heart, to observe how the children fled from his approach, breaking up their merriest sports, while his melancholy figure was yet afar off. Their instinctive dread caused him to feel more strongly than aught else, that a preternatural horror was interwoven with the threads of the black crape. In truth, his own antipathy[14] to the veil was known to be so great, that he never willingly passed before a mirror, nor stooped to drink at a still fountain, lest, in its peaceful bosom, he should be affrighted by himself. This was what gave plausibility to the whispers, that Mr. Hooper's conscience tortured him for some great crime too horrible to be entirely concealed, or otherwise than so obscurely intimated. Thus, from beneath the black veil, there rolled a cloud into the sunshine, an ambiguity of sin or sorrow, which enveloped the poor minister, so that love or sympathy could never reach him. It was said that ghost and fiend consorted with him there. With self-shudderings and outward terrors, he walked continually in its shadow, groping darkly within his own soul, or gazing through a medium that saddened the whole world. Even the lawless wind, it was believed, respected his dreadful secret, and never blew aside the veil. But still good Mr. Hooper sadly smiled at the

---

13. **bugbear,** something feared without reason.
14. **antipathy** (an tǐ′ pə thē), strong dislike.

pale visages of the worldly throng as he passed by.

Among all its bad influences, the black veil had the one desirable effect of making its wearer a very efficient clergyman. By the aid of his mysterious emblem—for there was no other apparent cause—he became a man of awful power over souls that were in agony for sin. His converts always regarded him with a dread peculiar to themselves, affirming, though but figuratively, that, before he brought them to celestial light, they had been with him behind the black veil. Its gloom, indeed, enabled him to sympathize with all dark affections. Dying sinners cried aloud for Mr. Hooper, and would not yield their breath till he appeared; though ever, as he stooped to whisper consolation, they shuddered at the veiled face so near their own. Such were the terrors of the black veil, even when Death had bared his visage! Strangers came long distances to attend service at his church, with the mere idle purpose of gazing at his figure, because it was forbidden them to behold his face. But many were made to quake ere they departed! Once, during Governor Belcher's administration, Mr. Hooper was appointed to preach the election sermon. Covered with his black veil, he stood before the chief magistrate, the council, and the representatives, and wrought so deep an impression, that the legislative measures of that year were characterized by all the gloom and piety of our earliest ancestral sway.

In this manner Mr. Hooper spent a long life, irreproachable[15] in outward act, yet shrouded[16] in dismal suspicions; kind and loving, though unloved and dimly feared; a man apart from men, shunned in their health and joy, but ever summoned to their aid in mortal anguish. As years wore on, shedding their snows above his sable[17] veil, he acquired a name throughout the New England churches, and they called him Father Hooper. Nearly all his parishioners who were of mature age when he was settled had been borne away by many a funeral: he had one congregation in

the church, and a more crowded one in the churchyard; and having wrought so late into the evening, and done his work so well, it was now good Father Hooper's turn to rest.

Several persons were visible by the shaded candle-light, in the death chamber of the old clergyman. Natural connections he had none. But there was the decorously[18] grave, though unmoved physician, seeking only to mitigate the last pangs of the patient whom he could not save. There were the deacons,[19] and other eminently pious members of his church. There, also, was the Reverend Mr. Clark, of Westbury, a young and zealous divine, who had ridden in haste to pray by the bedside of the expiring minister. There was the nurse, no hired handmaiden of death, but one whose calm affection had endured thus long in secrecy, in solitude, amid the chill of age, and would not perish, even at the dying hour. Who, but Elizabeth! And there lay the hoary head of good Father Hooper upon the death pillow, with the black veil still swathed about his brow, and reaching down over his face, so that each more difficult gasp of his faint breath caused it to stir. All through life that piece of crape had hung between him and the world: it had separated him from cheerful brotherhood and woman's love, and kept him in that saddest of all prisons, his own heart; and still it lay upon his face, as if to deepen the gloom of his darksome chamber, and shade him from the sunshine of eternity.

For some time previous, his mind had been confused, wavering doubtfully between the past and the present, and hovering forward, as it were, at intervals, into the indistinctness of the world to come. There had been feverish turns, which tossed him from

15. **irreproachable,** blameless, faultless.
16. **shrouded,** covered.
17. **sable,** black, dark.
18. **decorously** (dek′ ər əs lē), showing propriety and good taste.
19. **deacons,** laity appointed to help the minister.

side to side, and wore away what little strength he had. But in his most convulsive struggles, and in the wildest vagaries of his intellect, when no other thought retained its sober influence, he still showed an awful solicitude[20] lest the black veil should slip aside. Even if his bewildered soul could have forgotten, there was a faithful woman at his pillow, who, with averted eyes, would have covered that aged face, which she had last beheld in the comeliness of manhood. At length the death-stricken old man lay quietly in the torpor of mental and bodily exhaustion, with an imperceptible pulse, and breath that grew fainter and fainter, except when a long, deep, and irregular inspiration seemed to prelude the flight of his spirit.

The minister of Westbury approached the bedside.

"Venerable Father Hooper," said he, "the moment of your release is at hand. Are you ready for the lifting of the veil that shuts in time from eternity?"

Father Hooper at first replied merely by a feeble motion of his head; then, apprehensive, perhaps, that his meaning might be doubtful, he exerted himself to speak.

"Yea," said he, in faint accents, "my soul hath a patient weariness until that veil be lifted."

"And is it fitting," resumed the Reverend Mr. Clark, "that a man so given to prayer, of such a blameless example, holy in deed and thought, so far as mortal judgment may pronounce; is it fitting that a father in the church should leave a shadow on his memory, that may seem to blacken a life so pure? I pray you, my venerable brother, let not this thing be! Suffer us to be gladdened by your triumphant aspect as you go to your reward. Before the veil of eternity be lifted, let me cast aside this black veil from your face!"

And thus speaking, the Reverend Mr. Clark bent forward to reveal the mystery of so many years. But, exerting a sudden energy, that made all the beholders stand aghast, Father Hooper snatched both his hands from beneath the bedclothes, and pressed them strongly on the black veil, resolute to struggle, if the minister of Westbury would contend with a dying man.

"Never!" cried the veiled clergyman. "On earth, never!"

"Dark old man!" exclaimed the affrighted minister, "with what horrible crime upon your soul are you now passing to the judgment?"

Father Hooper's breath heaved; it rattled in his throat; but, with a mighty effort, grasping forward with his hands, he caught hold of life, and held it back till he should speak. He even raised himself in bed; and there he sat, shivering with the arms of death around him, while the black veil hung down, awful, at that last moment, in the gathered terrors of a lifetime. And yet the faint, sad smile, so often there, now seemed to glimmer from its obscurity, and linger on Father Hooper's lips.

"Why do you tremble at me alone?" cried he, turning his veiled face round the circle of pale spectators. "Tremble also at each other! Have men avoided me, and women shown no pity, and children screamed and fled, only for my black veil? What, but the mystery which it obscurely typifies, has made this piece of crape so awful? When the friend shows his inmost heart to his friend; the lover to his best beloved; when man does not vainly shrink from the eye of his Creator, loathsomely treasuring up the secret of his sin; then deem me a monster, for the symbol beneath which I have lived, and die! I look around me, and, lo! on every visage a Black Veil!"

While his auditors shrank from one another, in mutual affright, Father Hooper fell back upon his pillow, a veiled corpse, with a faint smile lingering on the lips. Still veiled, they laid him in his coffin, and a veiled corpse they bore him to the grave. The grass of many years has sprung up and withered on

---

20. **solicitude** (sə lis′ ə tüd), attentive concern.

that grave, the burial stone is moss-grown, and good Mr. Hooper's face is dust; but awful is still the thought that it mouldered beneath the Black Veil.

FOR UNDERSTANDING

1. As Reverend Hooper delivers his first sermon with the veil over his face, what is the effect on his listeners?

2. After the wedding ceremony, what causes Hooper to rush off into the night?

3. Who is the only person in the village with courage enough to ask Hooper to remove the veil? What is his reply? What is her response?

4. Although Hooper is shunned because he wears the veil for the rest of his life, to whom is he most comforting as a minister?

5. As Reverend Hooper is dying, who attempts to remove the veil?

FOR INTERPRETATION

Respond to one or more of the following, as directed by your teacher.

1. What does the wearing of the veil symbolize?

2. Why do you agree or disagree with the assertion that one's own heart is "the saddest of all prisons"?

3. There is no evidence that the Reverend Mr. Hooper had any sins to hide. His only "sin" was the wearing of the black veil itself. By wearing it, however, he ironically committed the very sin that he wished to warn others against. Thus, it was fitting that he should suffer the consequences of alienation. Discuss these statements as a possible interpretation of the story.

FOR APPRECIATION

Setting

Setting includes *time, place,* and *atmosphere.* The relative importance of these elements depends on the writer's purpose and the type of writing.

Hawthorne soon establishes the time as long in the past. The place is a small village. Note that the author suggests the distance in time by referring to the character Gray as *Goodman* Gray. In England and later in early colonial times, this term was used to refer to the male head of a household. It designated that the person was a farmer or laborer and not of the aristocracy. The mistress of the household was referred to as *Goodwife,* or simply as *Goody.*

The atmosphere or mood of the story is gloomy and mysterious. How does the black veil itself help to create this atmosphere? How does the line, "It was tinged, rather more darkly than usual, with the gentle gloom of Mr. Hooper's temperament," add to the somber mood? Find other references to *dark, darkly, dismal,* and *dreadful.*

The Structure of the Short Story

A short story has a *plot.* The simplest definition of "plot" is *action.* But this definition is too simple. If you were to describe what happened to you from the time you got up this morning till now, you would have written a narrative with action in it, but you would not have written a short story. One reason is that the action in a short story is centered about a *conflict,* a struggle between two opposed forces. The basis of plot is conflict.

Because the plot of a short story is based on conflict, it is best to define "plot" not simply as action, but as *structured* or *patterned* action. Another important part of the structured action of a story is a *climax,* the point in the story at which the action reaches its peak, the point when the reader's emotional response is the greatest. After the climax, the reader's emotions return to a more normal state. We may say that the structured action of the short story moves from a tension or imbalance (brought on by the conflict) to a peak (the climax) and then returns to a balance.

Conflicts in fiction may be either *internal* or *external.* An internal conflict occurs within a character. For instance, a given character's mind might be at war with his or her emotions. External conflicts may occur between a character and (a) another character, (b) society, or (c) some aspect of nature.

Conflict and climax are closely related. For instance, if you can locate the main climax of a story, you can usually discover from it the main forces in conflict. Similarly, if you know the main forces in conflict, you can usually locate the episode or moment when the action between these forces reaches its peak.

Another important moment in many short stories is called the *moment of illumination.* As the climax of a story is related to its plot, the moment of illumination is related to its meaning or theme. The moment of illumination may be defined as the point at which the full meaning of the story becomes clear. This point may occur at the climax, but it often occurs after the climax.

Try to put your knowledge of the structure of the short story to work by applying it to "The Minister's Black Veil."

1. What forces are in conflict in this story?

2. Where is the climax of this conflict?

3. Recalling that the moment of illumination is related to the theme, where is this moment in "The Minister's Black Veil"?

LANGUAGE AND VOCABULARY

Note that Hawthorne subtitles "The Minister's Black Veil" a "parable." What is a parable? If you do not know, look up the word. In connection with Hawthorne's works, the following additional terms

are sometimes used: *allegory, tale, sketch, romance, fable.* Adding *parable* to this list, which of the six words best fits each blank space in the sentences below?

1. A(n) _____ generally points out weaknesses or follies of humanity, often using beasts instead of persons.

2. A(n) _____ may deal with events in the long ago and far away and may contain imaginatively improbable events.

3. An allegorical tale, often relatively simple and homely, that illustrates or reinforces a spiritual truth is called a(n) _____.

4. In a(n) _____ the objects and persons are equated with meanings that lie outside the story itself.

5. _____ usually describes a relatively short narrative without a complicated plot, whose purpose is to entertain or amuse.

6. A(n) _____ presents a single scene, character, or incident. It lacks both a developed plot and much characterization.

DR. HEIDEGGER'S EXPERIMENT

That very singular man, old Dr. Heidegger, once invited four venerable friends to meet him in his study. There were three white-bearded gentlemen, Mr. Medbourne, Colonel Killigrew, and Mr. Gascoigne,[1] and a withered gentlewoman, whose name was the Widow Wycherly. They were all melancholy old creatures, who had been unfortunate in life, and whose greatest misfortune it was that they were not long ago in their graves. Mr. Medbourne, in the vigor of his age, had been a prosperous merchant, but had lost his all by a frantic speculation, and was now little better than a mendicant. Colonel Killigrew had

wasted his best years, and his health and substance, in the pursuit of sinful pleasures, which had given birth to a brood of pains, such as the gout, and divers other torments of soul and body. Mr. Gascoigne was a ruined politician, a man of evil fame, or at least had been so till time had buried him from the knowledge of the present generation, and made him obscure instead of infamous. As for the Widow Wycherly, tradition tells us that she was a great beauty in her day; but,

1. **Mr. Gascoigne** (gas coin′).

for a long while past, she had lived in deep seclusion, on account of certain scandalous stories which had prejudiced the gentry of the town against her. It is a circumstance worth mentioning that each of these three old gentlemen, Mr. Medbourne, Colonel Killigrew, and Mr. Gascoigne, were early lovers of the Widow Wycherly, and had once been on the point of cutting each other's throats for her sake. And, before proceeding further, I will merely hint that Dr. Heidegger and all his four guests were sometimes thought to be a little beside themselves—as is not unfrequently the case with old people, when worried either by present troubles or woeful recollections.

"My dear old friends," said Dr. Heidegger, motioning them to be seated, "I am desirous of your assistance in one of those little experiments with which I amuse myself here in my study."

If all stories were true, Dr. Heidegger's study must have been a very curious place. It was a dim, old-fashioned chamber, festooned with cobwebs, and besprinkled with antique dust. Around the walls stood several oaken bookcases, the lower shelves of which were filled with rows of gigantic folios[2] and black-letter quartos,[3] and the upper with little parchment-covered duodecimos.[4] Over the central bookcase was a bronze bust of Hippocrates,[5] with which, according to some authorities, Dr. Heidegger was accustomed to hold consultations in all difficult cases of his practice. In the obscurest corner of the room stood a tall and narrow oaken closet, with its door ajar, within which doubtfully appeared a skeleton. Between two of the bookcases hung a looking-glass, presenting its high and dusty plate within a tarnished gilt frame. Among many wonderful stories related of this mirror, it was fabled that the spirits of all the doctor's deceased patients dwelt within its verge, and would stare him in the face whenever he looked thitherward. The opposite side of the chamber was ornamented with the full-length portrait of a young lady, arrayed in the faded magnificence of silk, satin, and brocade, and with a visage as faded as her dress. Above half a century ago, Dr. Heidegger had been on the point of marriage with this young lady; but, being affected with some slight disorder, she had swallowed one of her lover's prescriptions, and died on the bridal evening. The greatest curiosity of the study remains to be mentioned; it was a ponderous folio volume, bound in black leather, with massive silver clasps. There were no letters on the back, and nobody could tell the title of the book. But it was well known to be a book of magic; and once, when a chambermaid had lifted it, merely to brush away the dust, the skeleton had rattled in its closet, the picture of the young lady had stepped one foot upon the floor, and several ghastly faces had peeped forth from the mirror; while the brazen head of Hippocrates frowned, and said,—"Forbear!"

Such was Dr. Heidegger's study. On the summer afternoon of our tale a small round table, as black as ebony, stood in the centre of the room, sustaining a cut-glass vase of beautiful form and elaborate workmanship. The sunshine came through the window, between the heavy festoons[6] of two faded damask[7] curtains, and fell directly across this vase; so that a mild splendor was reflected from it on the ashen visages of the five old people who sat around. Four champagne glasses were also on the table.

"My dear old friends," repeated Dr. Hei-

2. **folios,** books whose pages are more than 11 inches in height.
3. **quartos,** books of pages approximately 9 × 12 inches.
4. **duodecimos,** books consisting of pages approximately 5 × 7½ inches.
5. **Hippocrates** (hi pok' rə tēz), (c. 460–377 B.C.) Noted Greek physician known as "the Father of Medicine" and credited with devising the code known today as the Hippocratic oath, which is administered to people about to enter the medical profession.
6. **festoons,** ornamental carvings consisting of flowers or leaves linked together and looped between two points.
7. **damask,** a rich, reversible, elaborately patterned fabric.

degger, "may I reckon on your aid in performing an exceedingly curious experiment?"

Now Dr. Heidegger was a very strange old gentleman, whose eccentricity had become the nucleus for a thousand fantastic stories. Some of these fables, to my shame be it spoken, might possibly be traced back to my own veracious self; and if any passages of the present tale should startle the reader's faith, I must be content to bear the stigma of a fiction monger.

When the doctor's four guests heard him talk of his proposed experiment, they anticipated nothing more wonderful than the murder of a mouse in an air pump, or the examination of a cobweb by the microscope, or some similar nonsense, with which he was constantly in the habit of pestering his intimates. But without waiting for a reply, Dr. Heidegger hobbled across the chamber, and returned with the same ponderous folio, bound in black leather, which common report affirmed to be a book of magic. Undoing the silver clasps, he opened the volume, and took from among its black-letter pages a rose, or what was once a rose, though now the green leaves and crimson petals had assumed one brownish hue, and the ancient flower seemed ready to crumble to dust in the doctor's hands.

"This rose," said Dr. Heidegger, with a sigh, "this same withered and crumbling flower, blossomed five and fifty years ago. It was given me by Sylvia Ward, whose portrait hangs yonder; and I meant to wear it in my bosom at our wedding. Five and fifty years it has been treasured between the leaves of this old volume. Now, would you deem it possible that this rose of half a century could ever bloom again?"

"Nonsense!" said the Widow Wycherly, with a peevish toss of her head. "You might as well ask whether an old woman's wrinkled face could ever bloom again."

"See!" answered Dr. Heidegger.

He uncovered the vase, and threw the faded rose into the water which it contained. At first, it lay lightly on the surface of the fluid, appearing to imbibe none of its moisture. Soon, however, a singular change began to be visible. The crushed and dried petals stirred, and assumed a deeping tinge of crimson, as if the flower were reviving from a deathlike slumber; the slender stalk and twigs of foliage became green; and there was the rose of half a century, looking as fresh as when Sylvia Ward had first given it to her lover. It was scarcely full blown; for some of its delicate red leaves curled modestly around its moist bosom, within which two or three dewdrops were sparkling.

"That is certainly a very pretty deception," said the doctor's friends; carelessly, however, for they had witnessed greater miracles at a conjurer's show; "pray how was it effected?"

"Did you never hear of the 'Fountain of Youth,'" asked Dr. Heidegger, "which Ponce de Leon, the Spanish adventurer, went in search of two or three centuries ago?"

"But did Ponce de Leon ever find it?" said the Widow Wycherly.

"No," answered Dr. Heidegger, "for he never sought it in the right place. The famous Fountain of Youth, if I am rightly informed, is situated in the southern part of the Floridian peninsula, not far from Lake Macaco. Its source is overshadowed by several gigantic magnolias, which, though numberless centuries old, have been kept as fresh as violets by the virtues of this wonderful water. An acquaintance of mine, knowing my curiosity in such matters, has sent me what you see in the vase."

"Ahem!" said Colonel Killigrew, who believed not a word of the doctor's story; "and what may be the effect of this fluid on the human frame?"

"You shall judge for yourself, my dear colonel," replied Dr. Heidegger; "and all of you, my respected friends, are welcome to so much of this admirable fluid as may restore to you the bloom of youth. For my own part,

FLOWERS ON A WINDOW LEDGE
John La Farge
Corcoran Gallery of Art, Washington, D.C.

having had much trouble in growing old, I am in no hurry to grow young again. With your permission, therefore, I will merely watch the progress of the experiment."

While he spoke, Dr. Heidegger had been filling the four champagne glasses with the water of the Fountain of Youth. It was apparently impregnated with an effervescent gas, for little bubbles were continually ascending from the depths of the glasses, and bursting in silvery spray at the surface. As the liquor diffused a pleasant perfume, the old people doubted not that it possessed cordial[8] and comfortable properties; and though utter skeptics as to its rejuvenescent power, they were inclined to swallow it at once. But Dr. Heidegger besought them to stay a moment.

"Before you drink, my respectable old friends," said he, "it would be well that, with the experience of a lifetime to direct you, you should draw up a few general rules for your guidance, in passing a second time through the perils of youth. Think what a sin and shame it would be, if, with your peculiar advantages, you should not become patterns of virtue and wisdom to all the young people of the age!"

The doctor's four venerable friends made him no answer, except by a feeble and tremulous laugh; so very ridiculous was the idea that, knowing how closely repentance treads behind the steps of error, they should ever go astray again.

"Drink then," said the doctor, bowing: "I rejoice that I have so well selected the subjects of my experiment."

With palsied hands, they raised the glasses to their lips. The liquor, if it really possessed such virtues as Dr. Heidegger imputed to it, could not have been bestowed on four human beings who needed it more woefully. They looked as if they had never known what youth or pleasure was, but had been the offspring of Nature's dotage, and always the gray, decrepit, sapless, miserable creatures, who now sat stooping round the doctor's table, without life enough in their souls or

bodies to be animated even by the prospect of growing young again. They drank off the water, and replaced their glasses on the table.

Assuredly there was an almost immediate improvement in the aspect of the party, not unlike what might have been produced by a glass of generous wine, together with a sudden glow of cheerful sunshine brightening over all their visages at once. There was a healthful suffusion on their cheeks, instead of the ashen hue that had made them look so corpse-like. They gazed at one another, and fancied that some magic power had really begun to smooth away the deep and sad inscriptions which Father Time had been so long engraving on their brows. The Widow Wycherly adjusted her cap, for she felt almost like a woman again.

"Give us more of this wondrous water!" cried they, eagerly. "We are younger—but we are still too old! Quick—give us more!"

"Patience, patience!" quoth Dr. Heidegger, who sat watching the experiment with philosophic coolness. "You have been a long time growing old. Surely, you might be content to grow young in half an hour! But the water is at your service."

Again he filled their glasses with the liquor of youth, enough of which still remained in the vase to turn half the old people in the city to the age of their own grandchildren. While the bubbles were yet sparkling on the brim, the doctor's four guests snatched their glasses from the table, and swallowed the contents at a single gulp. Was it delusion? Even while the draught was passing down their throats, it seemed to have wrought a change on their whole systems. Their eyes grew clear and bright; a dark shade deepened among their silvery locks, they sat around the table, three gentlemen of middle age, and a woman, hardly beyond her buxom prime.

"My dear widow, you are charming!" cried Colonel Killigrew, whose eyes had been

---

8. **cordial** (kôr′ jəl),   here: pleasing.

fixed upon her face, while the shadows of age were flitting from it like darkness from the crimson daybreak.

The fair widow knew, of old, that Colonel Killigrew's compliments were not always measured by sober truth; so she started up and ran to the mirror, still dreading that the ugly visage of an old woman would meet her gaze. Meanwhile, the three gentlemen behaved in such a manner as proved that the water of the Fountain of Youth possessed some intoxicating qualities; unless, indeed, their exhilaration of spirits were merely a lightsome dizziness caused by the sudden removal of the weight of years. Mr. Gascoigne's mind seemed to run on political topics, but whether relating to the past, present, or future, could not easily be determined, since the same ideas and phrases had been in vogue these fifty years. Now he rattled forth full-throated sentences about patriotism, national glory, and the people's right; now he muttered some perilous stuff or other, in a sly and doubtful whisper, so cautiously that even his own conscience could scarcely catch the secret; and now, again, he spoke in measured accents, and a deeply deferential tone, as if a royal ear were listening to his well-turned periods. Colonel Killigrew all this time had been trolling forth a jolly bottle song, and ringing his glass in symphony with the chorus, while his eyes wandered toward the buxom figure of the Widow Wycherly. On the other side of the table, Mr. Medbourne was involved in a calculation of dollars and cents, with which was strangely intermingled a project for supplying the East Indies with ice, by harnessing a team of whales to the polar icebergs.

As for the Widow Wycherly, she stood before the mirror curtsying and simpering to her own image, and greeting it as the friend whom she loved better than all the world beside. She thrust her face close to the glass, to see whether some long-remembered wrinkle or crow's foot had indeed vanished. She examined whether the snow had so entirely melted from her hair that the venerable cap could be safely thrown aside. At last, turning briskly away, she came with a sort of dancing step to the table.

"My dear old doctor," cried she, "pray favor me with another glass!"

"Certainly, my dear madam, certainly!" replied the complaisant doctor; "see! I have already filled the glasses."

There, in fact, stood the four glasses, brimful of this wonderful water, the delicate spray of which, as it effervesced from the surface, resembled the tremulous glitter of diamonds. It was now so nearly sunset that the chamber had grown duskier than ever; but a mild and moonlike splendor gleamed from within the vase, and rested alike on the four guests and on the doctor's venerable figure. He sat in a high-backed, elaborately-carved, oaken arm-chair, with a gray dignity of aspect that might have well befitted that very Father Time, whose power had never been disputed, save by this fortunate company. Even while quaffing the third draught of the Fountain of Youth, they were almost awed by the expression of his mysterious visage.

But, the next moment, the exhilarating gush of young life shot through their veins. They were now in the happy prime of youth. Age, with its miserable train of cares and sorrows and diseases, was remembered only as the trouble of a dream, from which they had joyously awoke. The fresh gloss of the soul, so early lost, and without which the world's successive scenes had been but a gallery of faded pictures, again threw its enchantment over all their prospects. They felt like new-created beings in a new-created universe.

"We are young! We are young!" they cried exultingly.

Youth, like the extremity of age, had effaced the strongly-marked characteristics of middle life, and mutually assimilated them all. They were a group of merry youngsters, almost maddened with the exuberant frolicsomeness of their years. The most singular effect of their gayety was an impulse to mock the infirmity and decrepitude of which they had so lately been the victims. They laughed loudly at their old-fashioned attire, the wide-skirted coats and flapped waistcoats of the young men, and the ancient cap and gown of the blooming girl. One limped across the floor like a gouty[9] grandfather; one set a pair of spectacles astride of his nose, and pretended to pore over the black-letter pages of the book of magic; a third seated himself in an arm-chair, and strove to imitate the venerable dignity of Dr. Heidegger. Then all shouted mirthfully, and leaped about the room. The Widow Wycherly—if so fresh a damsel could be called a widow—tripped up to the doctor's chair, with a mischievous merriment in her rosy face.

"Doctor, you dear old soul," cried she, "get up and dance with me!" And then the four young people laughed louder than ever, to think what a queer figure the poor old doctor would cut.

"Pray excuse me," answered the doctor quietly. "I am old and rheumatic, and my dancing days were over long ago. But either of these gay young gentlemen will be glad of so pretty a partner."

"Dance with me, Clara!" cried Colonel Killigrew.

"No, no, I will be her partner!" shouted Mr. Gascoigne.

"She promised me her hand, fifty years ago!" exclaimed Mr. Medbourne.

They all gathered round her. One caught both her hands in his passionate grasp—another threw his arm about her waist—the third buried his hand among the glossy curls that clustered beneath the widow's cap. Blushing, panting, struggling, chiding, laughing, her warm breath fanning each of their faces by turns, she strove to disengage herself, yet still remained in their triple embrace. Never was there a livelier picture of youthful rivalship, with bewitching beauty for the prize. Yet, by a strange deception, owing to the duskiness of the chamber, and the antique dresses which they still wore, the tall mirror is said to have reflected the figures of the three old, gray, withered grandsires, ridiculously contending for the skinny ugliness of a shrivelled grandam.

But they were young: their burning passions proved them so. Inflamed to madness by the coquetry of the girl-widow, who neither granted nor quite withheld her favors, the three rivals began to interchange threatening glances. Still keeping hold of the fair prize, they grappled fiercely at one another's throats. As they struggled to and fro, the table was overturned, and the vase dashed into a thousand fragments. The precious Water of Youth flowed in a bright stream across the floor, moistening the wings of a butterfly, which, grown old in the decline of summer, had alighted there to die. The insect fluttered lightly through the chamber, and settled on the snowy head of Dr. Heidegger.

"Come, come, gentlemen!—come, Madam Wycherly," exclaimed the doctor, "I really must protest against this riot."

They stood still and shivered; for it seemed as if gray Time were calling them back from their sunny youth, far down into the chill and darksome vale of years. They looked at old Dr. Heidegger, who sat in his carved arm-chair, holding the rose of half a century, which he had rescued from among the fragments of the shattered vase. At the motion of his hand, the four rioters resumed their seats; the more readily, because their violent exertions had wearied them, youthful though they were.

"My poor Sylvia's rose!" ejaculated Dr. Heidegger, holding it in the light of the sunset clouds; "it appears to be fading again."

And so it was. Even while the party were looking at it, the flower continued to shrivel up, till it became as dry and fragile as when the doctor had first thrown it into the vase. He shook off the few drops of moisture which clung to its petals.

---

9. **gouty** (gou′ tē), having gout, a disease which causes swelling of the joints, especially of the feet and hands.

"I love it as well thus as in its dewy freshness," observed he, pressing the withered rose to his withered lips. While he spoke, the butterfly fluttered down from the doctor's snowy head, and fell upon the floor.

His guests shivered again. A strange chillness, whether of the body or spirit they could not tell, was creeping gradually over them all. They gazed at one another, and fancied that each fleeting moment snatched away a charm, and left a deepening furrow where none had been before. Was it an illusion? Had the changes of a lifetime been crowded into so brief a space, and were they now four aged people, sitting with their old friend, Dr. Heidegger?

"Are we grown old again, so soon?" cried they, dolefully.

In truth they had. The Water of Youth possessed merely a virtue more transient than that of wine. The delirium which it created had effervesced away. Yes! they were old again. With a shuddering impulse, that showed her a woman still, the widow clasped her skinny hands before her face, and wished that the coffin lid were over it, since it could be no longer beautiful.

"Yes, friends, ye are old again," said Dr. Heidegger, "and lo! the Water of Youth is all lavished on the ground. Well—I bemoan it not; for if the fountain gushed at my very doorstep, I would not stoop to bathe my lips in it—no, though its delirium were for years instead of moments. Such is the lesson ye have taught me!"

But the doctor's four friends had taught no such lesson to themselves. They resolved forthwith to make a pilgrimage to Florida, and quaff at morning, noon, and night, from the Fountain of Youth.

FOR UNDERSTANDING

1. Name each of the old friends of Dr. Heidegger, and briefly describe the kind of life each one lives.
2. How old is the rose, and how does Dr. Heidegger transform it?

3. What request does the old doctor make of his friends before they drink the water he says is from the Fountain of Youth?
4. How are the contents of the vase spilled? What is the effect upon the butterfly, the rose, and the Doctor's old friends?
5. Compare the nonphysical characteristics of Dr. Heidegger's friends before and after the experiment. Comment on the reason(s) for the change(s), or the lack of change(s).

FOR INTERPRETATION

Hawthorne implies all of the following ideas in his story. Discuss each.
1. In youth, and again in old age, people are not as different from one another as they are in middle age.
2. True love or affection does not change with the passage of time.
3. Human beings display no significant ability to benefit from the mistakes of the past.

FOR APPRECIATION

Setting

The atmosphere that pervades the story is not one that induces horror in the reader, even though Doctor Heidegger's study contains much that could be frightening. To help set the mood, Hawthorne employs a literary device popular in his time in which a writer interrupts the story to talk briefly with the reader. The first example of this occurs on page 223, with the sentence beginning, "And before proceeding further, I will merely hint that Dr. Heidegger and all his four guests were sometimes thought to be a little beside themselves, — . . ."

The good doctor's study, Hawthorne speculates with tongue in cheek, "must have been a very curious place." The word *curious* is used here in the sense of "interesting because of novelty or rarity."
1. What makes the study curious?
2. What does the expression "to be beside oneself" mean? How does this clue readers not to take the story too seriously?
3. For what reason does Hawthorne again suggest the story should not be taken too seriously when

he speaks directly to the reader on page 224 in the paragraph beginning, "Now Heidegger was a very strange old gentleman . . ."?

Characterization

Characterization is the means by which authors reveal to their readers the personality of the characters they create. Writers generally develop a character in one or more of the following ways:

1. by how the character acts
2. by what the character says and thinks
3. by how other characters react to the character, including what they say and think about the individual
4. by implicit or explicit comparisons between one character and another or others
5. by physical descriptions of the character
6. by direct statements revealing the writer's idea of the character

Let us see how Hawthorne uses some of these methods to establish Dr. Heidegger as a cool, detached, rather philosophical man.

Hawthorne directly says (6) that Heidegger, like the other characters, is a little odd; but for the most part, he shows his main character to be different from the others by having him stand apart from them (4). The author does not use much physical description of Heidegger (5), but the adjective *snowy*, describing his head, suggests the wisdom of age. For the most part, though, the character of Heidegger is created by what he does and says. Note that, unlike the other characters, Dr. Heidegger does not choose to dance with the widow (1), and of course his comments in the penultimate paragraph of the story (2) are particularly revealing of the kind of man he is.

Try to find on your own examples of the remaining method (3) used to establish the character of Dr. Heidegger.

Conflict and Climax

If we accept Dr. Heidegger as the protagonist, or hero, of this tale, which of the following best describes (describe) the central conflict?
1. the hero versus another person (or persons)
2. the hero versus society
3. the hero versus nature
4. the hero versus forces within himself
5. the hero versus fate

Identify the climax of the conflict or conflicts and discuss both of these elements in some detail.

Moment of Illumination

Is there any particular moment in this story that you would call its moment of illumination? If so, what is it? Also, how would you classify the last sentence of the story with reference to the meaning of the story?

LANGUAGE AND VOCABULARY

Find two synonyms for each of the words listed below. Explain the differences between the synonyms.

rejuvenescent	decrepit	torpid
portentous	fervid	coquetry
lurid	litigants	

COMPOSITION

Hawthorne's writing is formal and structured and abounds in words not commonly used. The story he tells here, however, is a simple one in which a scientific observer (Heidegger) sits in moral judgment upon vain and "sinful" people.

Rewrite the bare bones of the story in a few paragraphs, ending your account with a moral such as found in Aesop's fables.

Edgar Allan Poe

1809–1849

Edgar Poe was born in Boston on January 19, 1809, the son of a talented English actress, Elizabeth Arnold, and a much less talented American actor, David Poe. The latter deserted his wife shortly thereafter, and she died of consumption in December 1811, before Edgar's second birthday. The baby was then taken into the home of John Allan, a wealthy tobacco merchant, and thus assumed his middle name. There is no question that Poe owed a lot to the Allans, yet in his relations with his foster father, Edgar may have suffered more than he gained. He was sent, for instance, to the University of Virginia, yet he was given so small an allowance that he turned to gambling in an effort to get by and was forced to leave the college when Allan would not pay Poe's gambling debts. Again, Poe was admitted to West Point in 1830 in the hope of making up with his foster father, but the latter refused to send him any expense money. Gambling debts and innumerable violations of academy regulations resulted in Poe's having to leave West Point a few months later. When John Allan died, in 1843, he left Poe nothing.

The losses and uncertainties of Poe's early life only served to exaggerate the tendencies of an already unstable temperament. Insecure, troubled, and given to extremes, Poe was destined to lead a life of outward struggle and inner turmoil.

Personal instability notwithstanding, Poe had genius, and when he was healthy, he had strong ambitions and an enormous capacity for work. He published his first book of poems, *Tamerlane and Other Poems,* in 1829, while he was still in his teens and a second book only two years later. A third collection, published in 1831, showed great promise but sold not at all.

Poe's career as a writer of short stories began with the newspaper publication of five stories in 1832. The next year the story "MS Found in a Bottle" won a prize offered by the Baltimore *Saturday Visitor* and also helped him to get his first editorial position, on the *Southern Literary Messenger.*

PORTRAIT OF EDGAR ALLAN POE
National Portrait Gallery
Smithsonian Institution

It was at about the same time that Poe married his thirteen-year-old cousin, Virginia Clemm, a marriage that gave his life some affection and structure. Living with his new wife and her mother in Richmond, Virginia, and working for the *Messenger,* Poe wrote eighty-three reviews and four essays, six poems and three stories over a relatively brief period of time. The circulation of the magazine increased greatly, but Poe was nevertheless dismissed and moved his family to New York, where he published his first long work of fiction, the novelette *The Narrative of Arthur Gordon Pym,* in 1838.

Experiencing little success in New York, Poe and his family next moved to Philadelphia, where he assumed the literary editorship of *Burton's Gentleman's Magazine* and where he published his first book of short stories, *Tales of the Grotesque and Arabesque.* The collection included some of Poe's best work, such as "William Wilson," "Ligeia," and "The Fall of the House of Usher." In 1841 he became the editor of *Graham's Magazine,* and at about the same time he wrote "The Murders in the Rue Morgue," generally considered to be the first modern detective story. It features the intellectual amateur detective C. Auguste Dupin, who also solves the crimes in "The Purloined Letter" and "The Mystery of Marie Roget."

In 1843 Poe won $100 for his short story "The Gold Bug." "The Raven," published in 1845, brought him wider attention than he had achieved previously. But his wife died in 1847, and he more than ever fell into an abnormal state of mind and body. In October 1849 he mysteriously disappeared for five days and was finally found in a delirious state at a voting place in Baltimore. He died four days later, never having fully regained consciousness. To this day, no one is certain what befell him.

As a writer Poe has been held in both high and low esteem. Generally, he has been admired more in Europe than in his own country. Most critics agree that Poe was a brilliant literary critic and credit him with the invention of the detective story genre. And whatever the estimate of the worth of his prose and poetry may be, there is no question that both remain widely read and widely admired. Given the brevity of Poe's life and that his last eighteen years were, according to poet-critic Richard Wilbur, "a Sahara of dreariness, pain, and drudgery," it is remarkable that he developed his talent to the breadth and depth that he did. It is unthinkable that there will ever come a time when major works by Poe will not be read by American students and scholars alike.

A THEORY OF THE SHORT STORY

From Poe's Review of Nathaniel Hawthorne's *Twice-Told Tales*

Were we called upon . . . to designate that class of composition which . . . should best fulfill the demands of high genius . . . we should unhesitatingly speak of the prose tale as Mr. Hawthorne has here exemplified it. We allude to the short prose narrative, requiring from a half-hour to one or two hours

in its perusal. The ordinary novel is objectionable, from its length. . . . As it cannot be read at one sitting, it deprives itself, of course, of the immense force derivable from *totality.* Worldly interests intervening during the pauses of perusal, modify, annul, or counteract, in a greater or less degree, the impressions of the book. But simple cessation in reading would, of itself, be sufficient to destroy the true unity. In the brief tale, however, the author is enabled to carry out the fulness of his intention, be it what it may. During the hour of perusal the soul of the reader is at the writer's control. There are not external or

From MAJOR WRITERS OF AMERICA, Harcourt, © 1966. (First appeared in *Graham's Magazine,* May 1842.)

extrinsic influences—resulting from weariness or interruption.

A skillful literary artist has constructed a tale. If wise, he has not fashioned his thoughts to accommodate his incidents; but having conceived, with deliberate care, a certain unique or single *effect* to be wrought out, he then invents such incidents—he then combines such events as may best aid him in establishing this preconceived effect. If his very initial sentence tend not to the outbringing of this effect, then he has failed in his first step. In the whole composition there should be no word written, of which the tendency, direct or indirect, is not to the one pre-established design. And by such means, with such care and skill, a picture is at length painted which leaves in the mind of him who contemplates it with a kindred art, a sense of the fullest satisfaction. . . .

We have said that the tale has a point of superiority even over the poem. In fact, while the *rhythm* of this latter is an essential aid in the development of the poem's highest idea—the idea of the Beautiful—the artificialities of this rhythm are an inseparable bar to the development of all points of thought or expression, which have their basis in *Truth*. But Truth is often, and in very great degree, the aim of the tale. . . .

THE FALL OF THE HOUSE OF USHER

Son cœur est un luth suspendu;
Sitôt qu'on le touche il résonne.[1]

—*De Béranger*

During the whole of a dull, dark, and soundless day in the autumn of the year, when the clouds hung oppressively low in the heavens, I had been passing alone, on horseback, through a singularly dreary tract of country, and at length found myself, as the shades of the evening drew on, within view of the melancholy House of Usher. I know not how it was—but, with the first glimpse of the building, a sense of insufferable gloom pervaded my spirit. I say insufferable; for the feeling was unrelieved by any of that half-pleasurable, because poetic, sentiment with which the mind usually receives even the sternest natural images of the desolate or terrible. I looked upon the scene before me—upon the mere house, and the simple landscape features of the domain—upon the bleak walls—upon the vacant eye-like windows—upon a few rank sedges—and upon a few white trunks of decayed trees—with an utter depression of soul which I can compare to no earthly sensation more properly than to the after-dream of the reveller upon opium—the bitter lapse into every-day life—the hideous dropping off of the veil. There was an iciness, a sinking, a sickening of the heart—an unredeemed dreariness of thought which no goading of the imagination could torture into aught[2] of the sublime. What was it—I paused to think—what was it that so unnerved me in the contemplation of

1. "His heart is a hanging lute, which need only be touched to resound."
2. **aught** (ôt), anything.

the House of Usher? It was a mystery all insoluble; nor could I grapple with the shadowy fancies that crowded upon me as I pondered. I was forced to fall back upon the unsatisfactory conclusion, that while, beyond doubt, there *are* combinations of very simple natural objects which have the power of thus affecting us, still the analysis of this power lies among considerations beyond our depth. It was possible, I reflected, that a mere different arrangement of the particulars of the scene, of the details of the picture, would be sufficient to modify, or perhaps to annihilate its capacity for sorrowful impression; and, acting upon this idea, I reined my horse to the precipitous brink of a black and lurid tarn[3] that lay in unruffled lustre by the dwelling, and gazed down—but with a shudder even more thrilling than before—upon the remodeled and inverted images of the gray sedge, and the ghastly tree-stems, and the vacant and eye-like windows.

Nevertheless, in this mansion of gloom I now proposed to myself a sojourn of some weeks. Its proprietor, Roderick Usher, had been one of my boon companions in boyhood; but many years had elapsed since our last meeting. A letter, however, had lately reached me in a distant part of the country—a letter from him—which, in its wildly importunate nature, had admitted of no other than a personal reply. The MS.[4] gave evidence of nervous agitation. The writer spoke of acute bodily illness—of a mental disorder which oppressed him—and of an earnest desire to see me, as his best and indeed his only personal friend, with a view of attempting, by the cheerfulness of my society, some alleviation of his malady. It was the manner in which all this, and much more, was said—it was the apparent *heart* that went with his request—which allowed me no room for hesitation; and I accordingly obeyed forthwith what I still considered a very singular summons.

Although, as boys, we had been even intimate associates, yet I really knew little of my friend. His reserve had been always excessive and habitual. I was aware, however, that his very ancient family had been noted, time out of mind, for a peculiar sensibility of temperament, displaying itself, through long ages, in many works of exalted art, and manifested, of late, in repeated deeds of munificent yet unobtrusive charity, as well as in a passionate devotion to the intricacies, perhaps even more than to the orthodox and easily recognizable beauties, of musical science. I had learned, too, the very remarkable fact, that the stem of the Usher race, all time-honored as it was, had put forth, at no period, any enduring branch; in other words, that the entire family lay in the direct line of descent, and had always, with very trifling and very temporary variation, so lain. It was this deficiency, I considered, while running over in thought the perfect keeping of the character of the premises with the accredited character of the people, and while speculating upon the possible influence which the one, in the long lapse of centuries, might have exercised upon the other—it was this deficiency, perhaps, of collateral issue, and the consequent undeviating transmission, from sire to son, of the patrimony with the name, which had, at length, so identified the two as to merge the original title of the estate in the quaint and equivocal appellation of the "House of Usher"—an appellation which seemed to include, in the minds of the peasantry who used it, both the family and the family mansion.

I have said that the sole effect of my somewhat childish experiment—that of looking down within the tarn—had been to deepen the first singular impression. There can be no doubt that the consciousness of the rapid increase of my superstition—for why should I not so term it?—served mainly to accelerate the increase itself. Such, I have long known, is the paradoxical law of all sentiments having terror as a basis. And it might have been for

3. **tarn,** small lake.
4. **MS.,** abbreviation for manuscript.

this reason only, that, when I again uplifted my eyes to the house itself, from its image in the pool, there grew in my mind a strange fancy—a fancy so ridiculous, indeed, that I but mention it to show the vivid force of the sensations which oppressed me. I had so worked upon my imagination as really to believe that about the whole mansion and domain there hung an atmosphere peculiar to themselves and their immediate vicinity—an atmosphere which had no affinity with the air of heaven, but which had reeked up from the decayed trees, and the gray wall, and the silent tarn—a pestilent and mystic vapor, dull, sluggish, faintly discernible, and leaden-hued.

Shaking off from my spirit what *must* have been a dream, I scanned more narrowly the real aspect of the building. Its principal feature seemed to be that of an excessive antiquity. The discoloration of ages had been great. Minute fungi overspread the whole exterior, hanging in a fine tangled web-work from the eaves. Yet all this was apart from any extraordinary dilapidation. No portion of the masonry had fallen; and there appeared to be a wild inconsistency between its still perfect adaptation of parts, and the crumbling condition of the individual stones. In this there was much that reminded me of the specious totality of old wood-work which has rotted for long years in some neglected vault, with no disturbance from the breath of the external air. Beyond this indication of extensive decay, however, the fabric gave little token of instability. Perhaps the eye of a scrutinizing observer might have discovered a barely perceptible fissure, which, extending from the roof of the building in front, made its way down the wall in a zigzag direction, until it became lost in the sullen waters of the tarn.

Noticing these things, I rode over a short causeway to the house. A servant in waiting took my horse, and I entered the Gothic archway of the hall. A valet, of stealthy step, thence conducted me, in silence, through many dark and intricate passages in my progress to the *studio* of his master. Much that I encountered on the way contributed, I know not how, to heighten the vague sentiments of which I have already spoken. While the objects around me—while the carvings of the ceilings, the sombre tapestries of the walls, the ebon[5] blackness of the floors, and the phantasmagoric armorial trophies which rattled as I strode, were but matters to which, or to such as which, I had been accustomed from my infancy—while I hesitated not to acknowledge how familiar was all this—I still wondered to find how unfamiliar were the fancies which ordinary images were stirring up. On one of the staircases, I met the physician of the family. His countenance, I thought, wore a mingled expression of low cunning and perplexity. He accosted me with trepidation and passed on. The valet now threw open a door and ushered me into the presence of his master.

The room in which I found myself was very large and lofty. The windows were long, narrow, and pointed, and at so vast a distance from the black oaken floor as to be altogether inaccessible from within. Feeble gleams of encrimsoned light made their way through the trellissed[6] panes, and served to render sufficiently distinct the more prominent objects around; the eye, however, struggled in vain to reach the remoter angles of the chamber, or the recesses of the vaulted and fretted ceiling. Dark draperies hung upon the walls. The general furniture was profuse, comfortless, antique, and tattered. Many books and musical instruments lay scattered about, but failed to give any vitality to the scene. I felt that I breathed an atmosphere of sorrow. An air of stern, deep, and irredeemable gloom hung over and pervaded all.

Upon my entrance, Usher arose from a sofa on which he had been lying at full

5. **ebon** (eb′ ən), ebony, black.
6. **trellissed** (trel′ ist), framed with light strips of wood or metal.

length, and greeted me with a vivacious warmth which had much in it, I at first thought, of an overdone cordiality—of the constrained effort of the *ennuyé*[7] man of the world. A glance, however, at his countenance convinced me of his perfect sincerity. We sat down; and for some moments, while he spoke not, I gazed upon him with a feeling half of pity, half of awe. Surely, man had never before so terribly altered, in so brief a period, as had Roderick Usher! It was with difficulty that I could bring myself to admit the identity of the wan being before me with the companion of my early boyhood. Yet the character of his face had been at all times remarkable. A cadaverousness[8] of complexion; an eye large, liquid, and luminous beyond comparison; lips somewhat thin and very pallid but of a surpassingly beautiful curve; a nose of a delicate Hebrew model but with a breadth of nostril unusual in similar formations; a finely moulded chin, speaking, in its want of prominence, of a want of moral energy; hair of a more than web-like softness and tenuity,[9]—these features, with an inordinate expansion above the regions of the temple, made up altogether a countenance not easily to be forgotten. And now in the mere exaggeration of the prevailing character of these features, and of the expression they were wont to convey, lay so much of change that I doubted to whom I spoke. The now ghastly pallor of the skin, and the now miraculous lustre of the eye, above all things startled and even awed me. The silken hair, too, had been suffered to grow all unheeded, and as, in its wild gossamer texture, it floated rather than fell about the face, I could not, even with effort, connect its Arabesque[10] expression with any idea of simple humanity.

In the manner of my friend I was at once struck with an incoherence—and inconsistency; and I soon found this to arise from a series of feeble and futile struggles to overcome an habitual trepidancy—an excessive nervous agitation. For something of this nature I had indeed been prepared, no less by his letter,

than by reminiscences of certain boyish traits, and by conclusions deduced from his peculiar physical confirmation and temperament. His action was alternately vivacious and sullen. His voice varied rapidly from a tremulous indecision (when the animal spirits seemed utterly in abeyance) to that species of energetic concision—that abrupt, weighty, unhurried, and hollow-sounding enunciation—that leaden, self-balanced, and perfectly modulated guttural utterance, which may be observed in the lost drunkard, or the irreclaimable eater of opium, during the periods of his most intense excitement.

It was thus that he spoke of the object of my visit, of his earnest desire to see me, and of the solace he expected me to afford him. He entered, at some length, into what he conceived to be the nature of his malady. It was, he said, a constitutional and a family evil, and one for which he despaired to find a remedy—a mere nervous affection, he immediately added, which would undoubtedly soon pass off. It displayed itself in a host of unnatural sensations. Some of these, as he detailed them, interested and bewildered me; although, perhaps, the terms and the general manner of their narration had their weight. He suffered much from a morbid acuteness of the senses; the most insipid food was alone endurable; he could wear only garments of certain texture; the odors of all flowers were oppressive; his eyes were tortured by even a faint light; and there were but peculiar sounds, and these from stringed instruments, which did not inspire him with horror.

To an anomalous species of terror I found him a bounden slave. "I shall perish," said he, "I *must* perish in this deplorable folly. Thus, thus, and not otherwise, shall I be lost. I dread the events of the future, not in them-

---

7. ***ennuyé*** (än wē yā′), bored.
8. **cadaverousness** (kə dav′ ər əs nəs), paleness, as of a corpse or cadaver.
9. **tenuity** (te nyü′ ə tē), thinness, slightness.
10. **Arabesque** (ar a besk′), an elaborate and fanciful design.

selves, but in their results. I shudder at the thought of any, even the most trivial, incident, which may operate upon this intolerable agitation of soul. I have, indeed, no abhorrence of danger, except in its absolute effect—in terror. In this unnerved, in this pitiable, condition I feel that the period will sooner or later arrive when I must abandon life and reason together, in some struggle with the grim phantasm, FEAR.''

I learned, moreover, at intervals, and through broken and equivocal hints, another singular feature of his mental condition. He was enchained by certain superstitious impressions in regard to the dwelling which he tenanted, and whence, for many years, he had never ventured forth—in regard to an influence whose supposititious[11] force was conveyed in terms too shadowy here to be restated—an influence which some peculiarities in the mere form and substance of his family mansion had, by dint of long sufferance, he said, obtained over his spirit—an effect which the *physique* of the gray walls and turrets, and of the dim tarn into which they all looked down, had, at length, brought about upon the *morale* of his existence.

He admitted, however, although with hesitation, that much of the peculiar gloom which thus afflicted him could be traced to a more natural and far more palpable origin—to the severe and long-continued illness—indeed to the evidently approaching dissolution—of a tenderly beloved sister, his sole companion for long years, his last and only relative on earth. "Her decease," he said, with a bitterness which I can never forget, "would leave him (him, the hopeless and the frail) the last of the ancient race of the Ushers." While he spoke, the lady Madeline (for so was she called) passed through a remote portion of the apartment, and, without having noticed my presence, disappeared. I regarded her with an utter astonishment not unmingled with dread; and yet I found it impossible to account for such feelings. A sensation of stupor oppressed me as my eyes followed her retreating steps. When a door, at length, closed upon her, my glance sought instinctively and eagerly the countenance of the brother; but he had buried his face in his hands, and I could only perceive that a far more than ordinary wanness had overspread the emaciated fingers through which trickled many passionate tears.

The disease of the lady Madeline had long baffled the skill of her physicians. A settled apathy, a gradual wasting away of the person, and frequent although transient affections of a partially cataleptical[12] character were the unusual diagnosis. Hitherto she had steadily borne up against the pressure of her malady, and had not betaken herself finally to bed; but on the closing in of the evening of my arrival at the house, she succumbed (as her brother told me at night with inexpressible agitation) to the prostrating power of the destroyer; and I learned that the glimpse I had obtained of her person would thus probably be the last I should obtain—that the lady, at least while living, would be seen by me no more.

For several days ensuing, her name was unmentioned by either Usher or myself; and during this period I was busied in earnest endeavors to alleviate the melancholy of my friend. We painted and read together, or I listened, as if in a dream, to the wild improvisations of his speaking guitar. And thus, as a closer and still closer intimacy admitted me more unreservedly into the recesses of his spirit, the more bitterly did I perceive the futility of all attempt at cheering a mind from which darkness, as if an inherent positive quality, poured forth upon all objects of the moral and physical universe in one unceasing radiation of gloom.

I shall ever bear about me a memory of the many solemn hours I thus spent alone

---

11. **supposititious** (sə poz ə tish′ əs), hypothetical, supposed.
12. **cataleptical** (katl ep′ tik əl), condition associated with schizophrenia, in which the muscles become rigid.

with the master of the House of Usher. Yet I should fail in any attempt to convey an idea of the exact character of the studies, or of the occupations, in which he involved me, or led me the way. An excited and highly distempered ideality[13] threw a sulphureous[14] lustre over all. His long improvised dirges will ring forever in my ears. Among other things, I hold painfully in mind a certain singular perversion and amplification of the wild air of the last waltz of Von Weber.[15] From the paintings over which his elaborate fancy brooded, and which grew, touch by touch, into vaguenesses at which I shuddered the more thrillingly, because I shuddered knowing not why—from these paintings (vivid as their images now are before me) I would in vain endeavor to educe more than a small portion which should lie within the compass of merely written words. By the utter simplicity, by the nakedness of his designs, he arrested and overawed attention. If ever mortal painted an idea, that mortal was Roderick Usher. For me at least, in the circumstances then surrounding me, there arose out of the pure abstractions which the hypochondriac contrived to throw upon his canvas, an intensity of intolerable awe, no shadow of which felt I ever yet in the contemplation of the certainly glowing yet too concrete reveries of Fuseli.[16]

One of the phantasmagoric conceptions of my friend, partaking not so rigidly of the spirit of abstraction, may be shadowed forth, although feebly, in words. A small picture presented the interior of an immensely long and rectangular vault or tunnel, with low walls, smooth, white, and without interruption or device. Certain accessory points of the design served well to convey the idea that this excavation lay at an exceeding depth below the surface of the earth. No outlet was observed in any portion of its vast extent, and no torch or other artificial source of light was discernible; yet a flood of intense rays rolled throughout, and bathed the whole in a ghastly and inappropriate splendor.

"Oh, pity me, miserable wretch that I am!—I dared not—I dared not speak! We have put her living in the tomb!"

I have just spoken of that morbid condition of the auditory nerve which rendered all music intolerable to the sufferer, with the exception of certain effects of stringed instru-

13. **ideality** (ī dē al′ ə tē), something that is only ideal and has no reality.
14. **sulphureous** (sul fyur′ ē əs), containing sulfur; fiery, hellish.
15. **Karl Maria von Weber** (1786–1826), German Romantic composer; "The Last Waltz of von Weber" was composed by Karl Gottlieb Reissiger (1798–1859).
16. **Henry Fuseli** (1741–1825), Swiss painter who settled in England; he was noted for his interest in the supernatural and grotesque.

ments. It was, perhaps, the narrow limits to which he thus confined himself upon the guitar which gave birth, in great measure, to the fantastic character of his performances. But the fervid *facility* of his *impromptus*[17] could not be so accounted for. They must have been, and were, in the notes, as well as in the words of his wild fantasias (for he not unfrequently accompanied himself with rhymed verbal improvisations), the result of that intense mental collectedness and concentration to which I have previously alluded as observable only in particular moments of the highest artificial excitement. The words of one of these rhapsodies I have easily remembered. I was, perhaps, the more forcibly impressed with it as he gave it, because, in the under or mystic current of its meaning, I fancied that I perceived, and for the first time, a full consciousness on the part of Usher of the tottering of his lofty reason upon her throne. The verses, which were entitled, "The Haunted Palace," ran very nearly, if not accurately, thus:—

I

In the greenest of our valleys,
    By good angels tenanted,
Once a fair and stately palace—
    Radiant palace—reared its head.
In the monarch Thought's dominion—   5
    It stood there!
Never seraph[18] spread a pinion[19]
    Over fabric half so fair.

II

Banners yellow, glorious, golden,
    On its roof did float and flow   10
(This—all this—was in the olden
    Time long ago);
And every gentle air that dallied,
    In that sweet day,
Along the ramparts plumed and pallid,   15
    A winged odor went away.

III

Wanderers in that happy valley
    Through two luminous windows saw
Spirits moving musically

To a lute's well-tunèd law;   20
Round about a throne, where sitting
    (Porphyrogene!)[20]
In state his glory well befitting,
    The ruler of the realm was seen.

IV

And all with pearl and ruby glowing   25
    Was the fair palace door,
Through which came flowing, flowing, flowing
    And sparkling evermore,
A troop of Echoes whose sweet duty
    Was but to sing,   30
In voices of surpassing beauty,
    The wit and wisdom of their king.

V

But evil things, in robes of sorrow,
    Assailed the monarch's high estate;
(Ah, let us mourn, for never morrow   35
    Shall dawn upon him, desolate!)
And, round about his home, the glory
    That blushed and bloomed
Is but a dim-remembered story
    Of the old time entombed.   40

VI

And travellers now within that valley,
    Through the red-litten windows see
Vast forms that move fantastically
    To a discordant melody;
While, like a rapid ghastly river,   45
    Through the pale door;
A hideous throng rush out forever,
    And laugh—but smile no more.

I well remember that suggestions arising from this ballad led us into a train of thought wherein there became manifest an opinion of Usher's which I mention not so much on account of its novelty (for other men have

---

17. **impromptus** (im promp′ tüz), brief musical improvisations.
18. **seraph** (ser′ əf), one of the highest order of angels.
19. **pinion** (pin′ yən), wing.
20. **porphyrogene** (pôr fər ō jēn′), of royal descent.

thought thus), as on account of the pertinacity with which he maintained it. This opinion, in its general form, was that of the sentience of all vegetable things. But, in his disordered fancy, the idea had assumed a more daring character, and trespassed, under certain conditions, upon the kingdom of inorganization. I lack words to express the full extent, or the earnest *abandon* of his persuasion. The belief, however, was connected (as I previously hinted) with the gray stones of the home of his forefathers. The conditions of the sentence had been here, he imagined, fulfilled in the method of collocation of these stones—in the order of their arrangement, as well as in that of the many *fungi* which overspread them, and of the decayed trees which stood around —above all, in the long undisturbed endurance of this arrangement, and in its reduplication in the still waters of the tarn. Its evidence—the evidence of the sentience—was to be seen, he said (and I here started as he spoke), in the gradual yet certain condensation of an atmosphere of their own about the waters and the walls. The result was discoverable, he added, in that silent yet importunate and terrible influence which for centuries had moulded the destinies of his family, and which made *him* what I now saw him—what he was. Such opinions need no comment, and I will make none.

Our books—the books which, for years, had formed no small portion of the mental existence of the invalid—were, as might be supposed, in strict keeping with this character of phantasm. We pored together over such works as the "Ververt et Chartreuse" of Gresset; the "Belphegor" of Machiavelli; the "Heaven and Hell" of Swedenborg; the "Subterranean Voyage of Nicholas Klimm" of Holberg; the "Chiromancy" of Robert Flud, of Jean D'Indaginé, and of Dela Chambre; the "Journey into the Blue Distance" of Tieck; and the "City of the Sun" of Campanella. One favorite volume was a small octavo edition of the "Directorium Inquisitorium," by the Dominican Eymeric de Gironne; and there were passages in Pomponius Mela, about the old African Satyrs and Œgipans,[21] over which Usher would sit dreaming for hours. His chief delight, however, was found in the perusal of an exceedingly rare and curious book in quarto Gothic —the manual of a forgotten church—the *Vigiliæ Mortuorum secundum Chorum Ecclesiæ Maguntinæ*.[22]

I could not help thinking of the wild ritual of this work, and of its probable influence upon the hypochondriac, when, one evening, having informed me abruptly that the lady Madeline was no more, he stated his intention of preserving her corpse for a fortnight (previously to its final interment), in one of the numerous vaults within the main walls of the building. The worldly reason, however, assigned for this singular proceeding, was one which I did not feel at liberty to dispute. The brother had been led to his resolution (so he told me) by consideration of the unusual character of the malady of the deceased, of certain obtrusive and eager inquiries on the part of her medical men, and of the remote and exposed situation of the burial-ground of the family. I will not deny that when I called to mind the sinister countenance of the person whom I met upon the staircase, on the day of my arrival at the house, I had no desire to oppose what I regarded as at best but a harmless, and by no means an unnatural, precaution.

At the request of Usher, I personally aided him in the arrangements for the temporary entombment. The body having been encoffined, we two alone bore it to its rest. The vault in which we placed it (and which had been so long unopened that our torches, half smothered in its oppressive atmosphere, gave us little opportunity for investigation) was small, damp, and entirely without means

---

21. **Œgipans,** African goat-men.
22. **Vigiliae . . . Maguntinae,** *Vigils of the Dead, According to the Church-Choir of Mayence,* printed around 1500 at Basel in Switzerland.

of admission for light; lying, at great depth, immediately beneath that portion of the building in which was my own sleeping apartment. It had been used, apparently, in remote feudal times, for the worst purposes of a donjon-keep,[23] and, in later days, as a place of deposit for powder, or some other highly combustible substance, as a portion of its floor, and the whole interior of a long archway through which we reached it, were carefully sheathed with copper. The door, of massive iron, had been, also, similarly protected. Its immense weight caused an unusually sharp, grating sound, as it moved upon its hinges.

Having deposited our mournful burden upon tressels within this region of horror, we partially turned aside the yet unscrewed lid of the coffin, and looked upon the face of the tenant. A striking similitude between the brother and sister now first arrested my attention; and Usher, divining, perhaps, my thoughts, murmured out some few words from which I learned that the deceased and himself had been twins, and that sympathies of a scarcely intelligible nature had always existed between them. Our glances, however, rested not long upon the dead—for we could not regard her unawed. The disease which had thus entombed the lady in the maturity of youth, had left, as usual in all maladies of a strictly cataleptical character, the mockery of a faint blush upon the bosom and the face, and that suspiciously lingering smile upon the lip which is so terrible in death. We replaced and screwed down the lid, and, having secured the door of iron, made our way, with toil, into the scarcely less gloomy apartments of the upper portion of the house.

And now, some days of bitter grief having elapsed, an observable change came over the features of the mental disorder of my friend. His ordinary manner had vanished. His ordinary occupations were neglected or forgotten. He roamed from chamber to chamber with hurried, unequal, and objectless step. The pallor of his countenance had assumed, if possible, a more ghastly hue—but the luminousness of his eye had utterly gone ·out. The once occasional huskiness of his tone was heard no more; and a tremulous quaver, as if of extreme terror, habitually characterized his utterance. There were times, indeed, when I thought his unceasingly agitated mind was laboring with some oppressive secret, to divulge which he struggled for the necessary courage. At times, again, I was obliged to resolve all into the mere inexplicable vagaries of madness, for I beheld him gazing upon vacancy for long hours, in an attitude of the profoundest attention, as if listening to some imaginary sound. It was no wonder that his condition terrified—that it infected me. I felt creeping upon me, by slow yet certain degrees, the wild influences of his own fantastic yet impressive superstitions.

It was, especially, upon retiring to bed late in the night of the seventh or eighth day after the placing of the lady Madeline within the donjon, that I experienced the full power of such feelings. Sleep came not near my couch—while the hours waned and waned away. I struggled to reason off the nervousness which had dominion over me. I endeavored to believe that much, if not all of what I felt, was due to the bewildering influence of the gloomy furniture of the room—of the dark and tattered draperies, which, tortured into motion by the breath of a rising tempest, swayed fitfully to and fro upon the walls, and rustled uneasily about the decorations of the bed. But my efforts were fruitless. An irrepressible tremor gradually pervaded my frame; and, at length, there sat upon my very heart an incubus[24] of utterly causeless alarm. Shaking this off with a gasp and a struggle, I uplifted myself upon the pillows, and, peering earnestly within the intense darkness of the chamber, hearkened—I know not why,

---

23. **donjon-keep,** dungeon.
24. **incubus** (ing′ kyə bəs), an evil spirit supposed to descend on sleeping persons.

except that an instinctive spirit prompted me—to certain low and indefinite sounds which came, through the pauses of the storm, at long intervals. I knew not whence. Overpowered by an intense sentiment of horror, unaccountable yet unendurable, I threw on my clothes with haste (for I felt that I should sleep no more during the night), and endeavored to arouse myself from the pitiable condition into which I had fallen, by pacing rapidly to and fro through the apartment.

I had taken but few turns in this manner, when a light step on an adjoining staircase arrested my attention. I presently recognized it as that of Usher. In an instant afterward he rapped, with a gentle touch, at my door, and entered, bearing a lamp. His countenance was, as usual, cadaverously wan—but, moreover, there was a species of mad hilarity in his eyes—an evidently restrained *hysteria* in his whole demeanor. His air appalled me—but anything was preferable to the solitude which I had so long endured, and I even welcomed his presence as a relief.

"And you have not seen it?" he said abruptly, after having stared about him for some moments in silence—"you have not then seen it?—but, stay! you shall." Thus speaking, and having carefully shaded his lamp, he hurried to one of the casements, and threw it freely open to the storm.

The impetuous fury of the entering gust nearly lifted us from our feet. It was, indeed, a tempestuous yet sternly beautiful night, and one wildly singular in its terror and its beauty. A whirlwind had apparently collected its force in our vicinity; for there were frequent and violent alterations in the direction of the wind; and the exceeding density of the clouds (which hung so low as to press upon the turrets of the house) did not prevent our perceiving the life-like velocity with which they flew careering from all points against each other, without passing away into the distance. I say that even their exceeding density did not prevent our perceiving this—yet we had no glimpse of the moon or stars, nor was

there any flashing forth of the lightning. But the under surfaces of the huge masses of agitated vapor, as well as all terrestrial objects immediately around us, were glowing in the unnatural light of a faintly luminous and distinctly visible gaseous exhalation which hung about and enshrouded the mansion.

"You must not—you shall not behold this!" said I, shuddering, to Usher, as I led him, with a gentle violence, from the window to a seat. "These appearances, which bewilder you, are merely electrical phenomena not uncommon—or it may be that they have their ghastly origin in the rank miasma[25] of the tarn. Let us close this casement;—the air is chilling and dangerous to your frame. Here is one of your favorite romances. I will read, and you shall listen:—and so we will pass away this terrible night together."

The antique volume which I had taken up was the "Mad Trist" of Sir Launcelot Canning; but I had called it a favorite of Usher's more in sad jest than in earnest; for, in truth, there is little in its uncouth and unimaginative prolixity[26] which could have had interest for the lofty and spiritual ideality of my friend. It was, however, the only book immediately at hand; and I indulged a vague hope that the excitement which now agitated the hypochondriac, might find relief (for the history of mental disorder is full of similar anomalies) even in the extremeness of the folly which I should read. Could I have judged, indeed, by the wild overstrained air of vivacity with which he hearkened, or apparently hearkened, to the words of the tale, I might well have congratulated myself upon the success of my design.

I had arrived at that well-known portion of the story where Ethelred, the hero of the Trist, having sought in vain for peaceable admission into the dwelling of the hermit, pro-

---

25. **miasma** (mī az′ mə), bad-smelling vapor.
26. **prolixity** (prō lik′ sə tē), tedious length; wordiness.

ceeds to make good an entrance by force. Here, it will be remembered, the words of the narrative run thus:[27]

"And Ethelred, who was by nature of a doughty[28] heart, and who was now mighty withal, on account of the powerfulness of the wine which he had drunken, waited no longer to hold parley with the hermit, who, in sooth, was of an obstinate and maliceful turn, but, feeling the rain upon his shoulders, and fearing the rising of the tempest, uplifted his mace outright, and, with blows, made quickly room in the plankings of the door for his gauntleted hand; and now pulling therewith sturdily, he so cracked, and ripped, and tore all asunder, that the noise of the dry and hollow-sounding wood alarumed[29] and reverberated throughout the forest."

At the termination of this sentence I started and, for a moment, paused; for it appeared to me (although I at once concluded that my excited fancy had deceived me)—it appeared to me that, from some very remote portion of the mansion, there came, indistinctly to my ears, what might have been, in its exact similarity of character, the echo (but a stifled and dull one certainly) of the very cracking and ripping sound which Sir Launcelot had so particularly described. It was, beyond doubt, the coincidence alone which had arrested my attention; for, amid the rattling of the sashes of the casements, and the ordinary commingled noises of the still increasing storm, the sound, in itself, had nothing, surely, which should have interested or disturbed me. I continued the story:

"But the good champion Ethelred, now entering within the door, was sore enraged and amazed to perceive no signal of the maliceful hermit; but, in the stead thereof, a dragon of a scaly and prodigious demeanor, and of a fiery tongue, which sate in guard before a palace of gold, with a floor of silver; and upon the wall there hung a shield of shining brass with this legend enwritten—

Who entereth herein, a conqueror hath bin;
Who slayeth the dragon, the shield he shall win.

And Ethelred uplifted his mace, and struck upon the head of the dragon, which fell before him, and gave up his pesty breath, with a shriek so horrid and harsh, and withal so piercing, that Ethelred had fain to close his ears with his hands against the dreadful noise of it, the like whereof was never before heard."

Here again I paused abruptly, and now with a feeling of wild amazement—for there could be no doubt whatever that, in this instance, I did actually hear (although from what direction it proceeded I found it impossible to say) a low and apparently distant, but harsh, protracted, and most unusual screaming or grating sound—the exact counterpart of what my fancy had already conjured up for the dragon's unnatural shriek as described by the romancer.

Oppressed, as I certainly was, upon the occurrence of this second and most extraordinary coincidence, by a thousand conflicting sensations, in which wonder and extreme terror were predominant, I still retained sufficient presence of mind to avoid exciting, by any observation, the sensitive nervousness of my companion. I was by no means certain that he had noticed the sounds in question; although, assuredly, a strange alteration had, during the last few minutes, taken place in his demeanor. From a position fronting my own, he had gradually brought round his chair, so as to sit with his face to the door of the chamber; and thus I could but partially perceive his features, although I saw that his lips trem-

---

27. The paragraphs on Ethelred are an imaginative parody of the style of medieval romances.
28. **doughty** (dou′ tē), strong and bold.
29. **alarumed** (a lar′ əmd), sounded with alarm.

bled as if he were murmuring inaudibly. His head had dropped upon his breast—yet I knew that he was not asleep, from the wide and rigid opening of the eye as I caught a glance of it in profile. The motion of his body, too, was at variance with this idea—for he rocked from side to side with a gentle yet constant and uniform sway. Having rapidly taken notice of all this, I resumed the narrative of Sir Launcelot, which thus proceeded:

"And now, the champion, having escaped from the terrible fury of the dragon, bethinking himself of the brazen shield, and of the breaking up of the enchantment which was upon it, removed the carcass from out of the way before him, and approached valorously over the silver pavement of the castle to where the shield was upon the wall; which in sooth tarried not for his full coming, but fell down at his feet upon the silver floor, with a mighty great and terrible ringing sound."

No sooner had these syllables passed my lips, than—as if a shield of brass had indeed, at the moment, fallen heavily upon a floor of silver—I became aware of a distinct, hollow, metallic, and clangorous, yet apparently muffled, reverberation. Completely unnerved, I leaped to my feet; but the measured rocking movement of Usher was undisturbed. I rushed to the chair in which he sat. His eyes were bent fixedly before him, and throughout his whole countenance there reigned a stony rigidity. But, as I placed my hand upon his shoulder, there came a strong shudder over his whole person; a sickly smile quivered about his lips; and I saw that he spoke in a low, hurried, and gibbering[30] murmur, as if unconscious of my presence. Bending closely over him, I at length drank in the hideous import of his words.

"Now hear it?—yes, I hear it, and *have* heard it. Long—long—long—many minutes, many hours, many days, have I heard it—yet I dared not—oh, pity me, miserable wretch that I am!—I dared not—I *dared* not speak!

We have put her living in the tomb! Said I not that my senses were acute? I *now* tell you that I heard her first feeble movements in the hollow coffin. I heard them—many, many days ago—yet I dared not—I *dared not speak!* And now—to-night—Ethelred—ha! ha!—the breaking of the hermit's door, and the death-cry of the dragon, and the clangor of the shield—say, rather, the rending of her coffin, and the grating of the iron hinges of her prison, and her struggles within the coppered archway of the vault! Oh! whither shall I fly? Will she not be here anon? Is she not hurrying to upbraid[31] me for my haste? Have I not heard her footsteps on the stair? Do I not distinguish that heavy and horrible beating of her heart? Madman!"—here he sprang furiously to his feet, and shrieked out his syllables, as if in the effort he were giving up his soul—*"Madman! I tell you that she now stands without the door!"*

As if in the superhuman energy of his utterance there had been found the potency of a spell, the huge antique panels to which the speaker pointed threw slowly back, upon the instant, their ponderous and ebony jaws. It was the work of the rushing gust—but then without those doors there *did* stand the lofty and enshrouded figure of the lady Madeline of Usher. There was blood upon her white robes, and the evidence of some bitter struggle upon every portion of her emaciated frame. For a moment she remained trembling and reeling to and fro upon the threshold—then, with a low moaning cry, fell heavily inward upon the person of her brother, and in her violent and now final death-agonies, bore him to the floor a corpse, and a victim to the terrors he had anticipated.

From that chamber, and from that mansion, I fled aghast. The storm was still abroad

---

30. **gibbering** (jib′ ər ing), chattering senselessly.
31. **upbraid** (up brād′), blame, reprove.

in all its wrath as I found myself crossing the old causeway. Suddenly there shot along the path a wild light, and I turned to see whence a gleam so unusual could have issued; for the vast house and its shadows were alone behind me. The radiance was that of the full, setting, and blood-red moon, which now shone vividly through that once barely discernible fissure, of which I have before spoken as extending from the roof of the building, in a zigzag direction, to the base. While I gazed, this fissure rapidly widened—there came a fierce breath of the whirlwind—the entire orb of the satellite burst at once upon my sight—my brain reeled as I saw the mighty walls rushing asunder—there was a long tumultuous shouting sound like the voice of a thousand waters—and the deep and dank tarn at my feet closed sullenly and silently over the fragments of the *"House of Usher."*

FOR UNDERSTANDING

1. What relationship has existed between the narrator and Roderick Usher?
2. Why has Usher asked the narrator to visit him?
3. What minor fault in the building itself—barely noticed by the narrator initially—assumes great significance at the end?
4. What is symbolized by this fault?
5. What is the precise relationship between Lady Madeline and Roderick Usher?
6. What are the fundamental reasons given by Usher for burying Madeline temporarily in the vault?
7. When Usher hears the noises from Lady Madeline's vault, what is the horrible thought that occurs to him?

FOR INTERPRETATION

Since Poe believed that everything in a story had a purpose (see Poe's theory, p. 233), we may assume that the poem, "The Haunted Palace," is not merely a literary interlude. Try to determine what its significance is, and be prepared to back up your opinion. To begin with, ask yourself the significance of the following details:

1. Once a fair and stately palace—
     Radiant palace—reared its head. (ll. 3–4)
2. Banners yellow, glorious, golden,
     On its roof did float and flow (ll. 9–10)
3. Wanderers in that happy valley
     Through two luminous windows saw (ll. 17–18)
4. And all with pearl and ruby glowing
     Was the fair palace door, (ll. 25–26)

Notice, too, in whose "dominion" the palace stands.

FOR APPRECIATION

Setting

Poe is a master at creating a setting, particularly at creating atmosphere. In this story, the pervading atmosphere is one of gloom.
1. Find details that create a gloomy atmosphere in Poe's description of the following:
   a. the outside of the house
   b. the inside of the house
   c. the area around the house
   d. Roderick Usher's appearance
2. Normally, we distinguish characterization from setting. What comment, however, might you make about the following characterization of the mind of Roderick Usher: ". . . a mind from which darkness, as if an inherent positive quality, poured forth upon all objects of the moral and physical universe in one unceasing radiation of gloom"?

POE'S THEORY AND AN INTERPRETATION

Much has been made of Poe's insistence on a unified effect in the short story. Clearly, he emphasizes a self-conscious attempt on the part of the artist to create a unique or single effect. Nowhere, however, does he say that the creation of this effect is the *sole* aim of the brief tale. In fact, in the very next paragraph after he speaks of the unique effect, he emphasizes that the tale is superior even to the poem in its ability to express truth. He goes on to say that truth is "often, and in very great degree," *the aim* of the tale.

It is thus unnecessarily narrow to assume that Poe's main interest in writing a story like "The Fall of the House of Usher" was to create the effect of terror. Terror is there, to be sure, and no doubt all the details contribute to the creation of this effect, just as Poe said they should. But truth is assuredly another aim of this tale, perhaps even *the* aim of Poe's story.

That the truth of "Usher" is hard to come by is obvious from the many interpretations of the story that exist. The interpretation about to be offered is not necessarily *the* truth; it can be considered *a* truth.

The reader may begin by assuming that Roderick Usher is a prototype of the creative artist. There is ample reason for making this assumption, for the main character writes, composes music, and paints. The fragment of verse with which Poe begins his tale also suggests that his protagonist was intended to be an artist: "His heart is a hanging lute, which need only be touched to resound."

Now there is a peculiar paradox regarding artists. On the one hand, they need to have contact with other human beings; on the other, they need solitude in order to create. The artist not only needs to be alone during a particular period of creativity; he or she also needs time alone in order to master techniques.

Usher is an artist who has not left his house—a symbol of his own mind—for many years. He has consequently grown deep within himself. Note, for one thing, that he paints *ideas,* rather than people or things. Also, his senses—through which one normally perceives the external world—are virtu-ally useless; they cause him pain rather than pleasure.

This absence of contact with the real world causes an enormous strain, but Usher holds himself together as long as he has some connection with the world outside his own mind, as he does through his sister Madeline. (Madeline can also be interpreted as the feminine side of Usher's own nature—a natural, nurturing side, which of course is also wasting away.) When Madeline takes to her bed, Usher's last connection with the world outside of his own mind is gone, and he literally begins to go mad. So strained does he become that he actually buries his sister prematurely.

Madeline eventually breaks out of her vault and comes to get Usher in a vampire-like embrace that both unites and destroys them. Naturally, the house of Usher must go, too. It bursts asunder through the "wild light" that emanates from the blood-red moon and falls into the tarn, a symbol of nothingness.

The meaning of this final catastrophe for the Usher-as-artist theme is that when artists turn away from the external world, and even from their "other side" (the feminine side, in Usher's case) of their own natures, they destroy not only their capacity to create but ultimately themselves as well. "The Fall of the House of Usher" is a horror story, to be sure, but it is also a tale that tells an important truth about art and artists.

To Helen

Helen, thy beauty is to me
  Like those Nicean[1] barks of yore,
That gently, o'er a perfumed sea,
  The weary, way-worn wanderer bore
  To his own native shore.   5

On desperate seas long wont to roam,
  Thy hyacinth hair, thy classic face,
Thy Naiad[2] airs have brought me home
  To the glory that was Greece
And the grandeur that was Rome.   10

Lo! in yon brilliant window-niche
  How statue-like I see thee stand!
  The agate[3] lamp within thy hand,
Ah! Psyche,[4] from the regions which
  Are Holy Land!   15

1. **Nicean** (ni sē' ən), a reference to the ancient port city of Nicaea.
2. **Naiad** (nī ad), nymphlike.
3. **agate** (ag' it), quartz-like, with clouded colors.
4. **Psyche** (sī' kē), goddess of the soul.

The Bells

I

Hear the sledges with the bells—
  Silver bells!
What a world of merriment their melody foretells!
  How they tinkle, tinkle, tinkle,
    In the icy air of night!   5
  While the stars that oversprinkle
  All the heavens seem to twinkle
    With a crystalline delight;
    Keeping time, time, time,
    In a sort of Runic[1] rhyme,   10
To the tintinnabulation[2] that so musically wells

1. **Runic** (rü' nik), consisting of runes, the letters of an ancient Germanic alphabet.
2. **tintinnabulation** (tin tə nab yə lā' shən), ringing.

From the bells, bells, bells, bells,
Bells, bells, bells—
From the jingling and the tinkling of the bells.

II

Hear the mellow wedding bells,   15
Golden bells!
What a world of happiness their harmony foretells!
Through the balmy air of night
How they ring out their delight!
From the molten-golden notes,   20
And all in tune,
What a liquid ditty floats
To the turtle-dove that listens, while she gloats
On the moon!
Oh, from out the sounding cells   25
What a gush of euphony[3] voluminously wells!
How it swells!
How it dwells
On the Future! how it tells
Of the rapture that impels   30
To the swinging and the ringing
Of the bells, bells, bells,
Of the bells, bells, bells, bells,
Bells, bells, bells—
To the rhyming and the chiming of the bells!   35

III

Hear the loud alarum bells—
Brazen bells!
What a tale of terror, now, their turbulency tells!
In the startled ear of night
How they scream out their affright!   40
Too much horrified to speak,
They can only shriek, shriek,
Out of tune,
In a clamorous appealing to the mercy of the fire,
In a mad expostulation[4] with the deaf and frantic fire,   45
Leaping higher, higher, higher,
With a desperate desire,
And a resolute endeavor
Now—now to sit, or never,

3. **euphony** (yü′ fə nē), effect pleasing to the ear.
4. **expostulation** (ek spos chə lā′ shən), protest.

By the side of the pale-faced moon.   50
   Oh, the bells, bells, bells!
  What a tale their terror tells
    Of despair!
  How they clang, and clash, and roar!
  What a horror they outpour   55
On the bosom of the palpitating air!
   Yet the ear it fully knows,
    By the twanging,
    And the clanging,
   How the danger ebbs and flows;   60
  Yet the ear distinctly tells,
    In the jangling,
    And the wrangling,
  How the danger sinks and swells,
By the sinking or the swelling in the anger of the bells—   65
    Of the bells—
  Of the bells, bells, bells, bells,
    Bells, bells, bells—
In the clamor and the clangor of the bells!

IV

Hear the tolling of the bells—   70
    Iron bells!
What a world of solemn thought their monody compels!
   In the silence of the night,
   How we shiver with affright
At the melancholy menace of their tone!   75
   For every sound that floats
   From the rust within their throats
    Is a groan.
  And the people—ah, the people—
  They that dwell up in the steeple,   80
    All alone,
  And who tolling, tolling, tolling,
   In that muffled monotone,
  Feel a glory in so rolling
   On the human heart a stone—   85
They are neither man nor woman—
They are neither brute nor human—
    They are Ghouls:[5]
  And their king it is who tolls;
  And he rolls, rolls, rolls,   90
    Rolls

---

5. **ghouls** (gülz),   horrible demons that feed on corpses.

A pæan[6] from the bells!
And his merry bosom swells
  With the pæan of the bells!
And he dances, and he yells;   95
Keeping time, time, time,
In a sort of Runic rhyme,
  To the pæan of the bells—
    Of the bells:
Keeping time, time, time,   100
In a sort of Runic rhyme,
  To the throbbing of the bells—
Of the bells, bells, bells—
  To the sobbing of the bells;
Keeping time, time, time,   105
  As he knells, knells, knells,
In a happy Runic rhyme,
  To the rolling of the bells—
Of the bells, bells, bells—
  To the tolling of the bells,   110
Of the bells, bells, bells, bells—
  Bells, bells, bells—
To the moaning and the groaning of the bells.

---

6. **pæan** (pē′ ən), a song of joy or triumph.

UNDERSTANDING AND APPRECIATION

"To Helen"

1. Although this poem was inspired by a real person, whose name was Jane, Poe addressed it to "Helen." Why might he have done this?

2. In the final stanza, "Helen" is addressed as "Psyche," the Greek word for "breath" or "soul." (Psyche has come to personify the soul.) How do you reconcile this with the earlier references to Helen of Troy, whose legendary beauty led to the Trojan War?

3. Note that all three stanzas end with a reference to a place—"native shore," "Greece and . . . Rome," and "Holy-Land." How are these related to each other? to the meaning of the poem as a whole?

"The Bells"

1. This poem is mainly an exercise in technique, in the use of sound and rhythm to create mood. Name the mood or moods created by each of the four sections.

2. *Onomatopoeia* is the poetic device of using words that imitate the sounds they describe. Thus, the word "crack" is onomatopoetic because it resembles the sound made by a whip or the breaking of a branch. (The word "break" would not be onomatopoetic.) Since this poem is about a sound-producing mechanism, one might expect to find examples of onomatopoeia in it. Find at least one example in each section of the poem.

3. Where does the tone of the fourth section shift? What effect does this have with regard to the poem as a whole?

4. Compare the first five lines of each section. What basic similarities and differences do you find?

5. Compare the last three lines of each stanza. What basic similarities and differences do you find?

6. Why might Poe have chosen to open and close each of his four sections in similar ways?

Herman Melville 1819–1891

Probably few American writers before Herman Melville experienced a boyhood and young manhood at once so happy and so miserable, so idyllic and so bleak, so romantic and yet so harsh and depressing, as his. Certainly no novelist prior to his time so quickly reached the zenith of his career, only to plunge within half a dozen years or so to its nadir. It is easy to see how he could write to his friend Nathaniel Hawthorne, "Though I wrote the Gospels in this century, I should die in the gutter." While he did not quite die in the gutter, he did die in obscurity, and he remained unknown to a whole generation of readers. Yet this author composed "Bartleby the Scrivener," one of the most poignant stories ever written; the haunting novella *Billy Budd;* and *Moby-Dick,* one of the great novels of all time.

Herman Melville was born in 1819 in the thriving city of New York, where he himself thrived in his early years. His family was well off and able to send him to a private academy. He formed a particularly close relationship with his father, Allan Melville, a highly cultured importing merchant who traveled in Europe.

But the idyllic childhood came to a sudden end when the senior Melville went bankrupt. The family retreated to Albany, New York, in the autumn of 1830, where they had some help from relatives, and for a while it looked as if they would survive. In January, 1832, however, Melville's father collapsed, became deranged, and shortly thereafter died, leaving his wife Maria and eight children swamped with enormous debts and responsibilities. Herman was only twelve at the time and remained forever after shaken by the blow.

Religious faith might have offered solace to another young man, but Herman grew up on conservative Calvinist doctrine which held that all are "conceived in sin, and are by nature children of wrath, incapable of any saving good, prone to evil, dead in sin, and in bondage thereto." True, God offered salvation to a handful of His "elect," but there was nothing one could do to *earn* that saving grace. To young

PORTRAIT OF HERMAN MELVILLE
"Keep true to the dreams of thy youth."

Melville it must have seemed that the father whom he idolized was distinctly not among those given free grace, and life itself must have seemed inscrutable indeed.

Herman spent two years as a junior clerk in a bank, helped on his uncle's farm in Pittsfield, Massachusetts, for a time, and then worked in his older brother's store in Albany. But then that enterprise itself collapsed in the panic of 1837, and the family was once again set adrift. Herman tried teaching at first; then he briefly studied surveying and engineering in the hope of finding employment in the state canal system.

When that hope failed, he signed on a merchant ship, the *St. Lawrence,* as a "boy," and sailed in the summer of 1839 for Liverpool. The four-month voyage there and back must have been a grueling introduction to the hardships of life at sea. The five or six weeks his ship was docked at Liverpool, close to the city's worst slums, must have further opened the young man's eyes to the bleakness and brutality life could hold.

Melville returned home to the same depressing financial circumstances and lack of employment he had left, and before very long he signed up as a foremasthand on another sailing ship, the *Acushnet.* This time it was no mere skip across the Atlantic, but a trip to the South Pacific to hunt whales. Melville was gone from January 3, 1841, to October 14, 1844.

In the course of those years he jumped ship in the Marquesas Islands and lived among (supposedly) cannibalistic natives for several weeks. He spent still more time on Tahiti and a neighboring island. Winding up in the Hawaiian Islands after serving time on another whaler, he lived briefly in Honolulu before enlisting in the U.S. Navy and sailing on the frigate *United States,* which ultimately took him home. Life on a whaler in the nineteenth century has been called "perhaps the lowest condition to which free American labor has ever fallen," but it could hardly have been more rigorous and severe than life in the navy. There were sixty-three public floggings during the time Melville served on the *United States.*

The cost of all this experience in terms of emotional pain must have been very great indeed; yet at the same time there was an ironic reward—Melville had finally found a career. He spent the next seven years writing novels based at least in part on his seafaring experiences.

The first two of these—*Typee: A Peek at Polynesian Life* (1846) and *Omoo: A Narrative of Adventures in the South Seas* (1847)—dealt with his experiences on Pacific islands, and both were highly successful with the reading public here and in England. But his next novel, *Mardi* (1849), was far too allegorical for the readers he had already won, and he returned to more straightforward "stories" in his next two novels—*Redburn* (1849), which was based on his first voyage across the Atlantic, and *White-Jacket*

"Such a portentous and mysterious monster roused all my curiosity." Moby-Dick, *1851*

(1850), based on his experiences in the United States Navy. Although Melville said he wrote both of these books "almost entirely" for money, they show a far superior sense of style than his first two and they helped somewhat to restore his reading public.

It was at about this time in his life that Melville moved (with his wife, Elizabeth Shaw, whom he had married in the summer of 1847) to Pittsfield, Massachusetts, where he was to remain for thirteen years. It was an especially fortunate move, in that Nathaniel Hawthorne was living at the time in nearby Lenox. The two met for the first time on August 5, 1850. Melville admired Hawthorne's work and found in him a kindred spirit. As he wrote in a letter to the older author, "There is the grand truth about Nathaniel Hawthorne. He says NO! in thunder; but the Devil himself cannot make him say *yes*. For all men who say *yes*, lie." Whether in fact Hawthorne was saying "NO! in thunder" is moot; but knowing him helped Melville to do just that in his next book, *Moby-Dick,* which was dedicated to Nathaniel Hawthorne "in token of my admiration for his genius."

Moby-Dick; or, The Whale, published in 1851, is by every measure Herman Melville's greatest book, though it is not a book that everybody reads with pleasure, nor was it highly regarded by most readers at the time of its publication. The story is simple enough, but the story is only a small part of the total book. It begins with a character directly addressing the reader. "Call me Ishmael," he says, and goes on to tell us that he feels it high time to go to sea "whenever it is a damp, drizzly November in my soul." With his newfound friend, Queequeg, a Polynesian prince, he signs up for a whaling voyage on the ship *Pequod*.

The ship is full of fascinating characters, such as the mysterious Fedallah; the American Indian harpooner, Tashtego; the African, Daggoo; the black cabin boy, Pip; and the pacific and noble chief mate, Starbuck. But the main character, who does not even appear till the twenty-eighth chapter, is the demoniacal and driven Captain Ahab. He has a wooden leg, a token of his last encounter with the legendary white whale, Moby-Dick, and he is bent on revenge—cost what it may.

Other whales are sighted and taken. Eventually, Moby-Dick himself comes into view, and Ahab and his harpooners chase him over a three-day period. The great white whale is hit, but he gets the greater vengeance when he sinks the harpooners' boats and the *Pequod* as well. Only Ishmael, an orphan, survives to tell the tale.

Interspersed with the action of the novel are long passages about the whale, the science and history of whaling, and the whaling industry. Such "digressions" are uncharacteristic of modern novels, and many readers grow rather impatient with them. Yet *Moby-Dick* would not be the same book without them.

On another level, the novel is philosophical and symbolic. The ship itself may represent humanity; appropriately, there is a wide range of character types aboard. The whale has been taken as a symbol of evil, and it *is* that in part—we can tell that from its violence. But the whiteness of Moby-Dick suggests just the opposite, as does his nobility. Probably it is neither good nor evil that the white whale represents, but both. He is nature, the nature of things. He simply is.

Captain Ahab is certainly a monomaniac, but he is not an entirely unsympathetic character. For one thing, it is difficult not to admire his determination, his dedication to a cause. And what is that cause? Ahab will not accept the fact that Moby-Dick simply is. His attempt to kill the whale may be read as an attempt to redesign the very structure of the universe, which he sees as flawed, fatally cracked. Ahab says "NO! in thunder" to that structure—a structure that has such a large component of evil in it—and we admire him for doing so and for his bold plunge into the very depths of life's perplexities and contradictions. Like Shakespeare's King Lear, to whom he has been compared (Shakespeare and the Bible were the two most profound influences on Melville), he is a tragic hero of great stature, and he remains vividly alive in our imagination long, long after we have finished reading the book.

Melville must have been exhausted after composing *Moby-Dick;* nevertheless, by March of the next year he had finished still another novel, *Pierre* (1852). Its protagonist is a man of violent emotions who, after turning murderously on all those he loves, finally takes poison himself. Quite possibly Melville was on the verge of a mental breakdown similar to that suffered by his father, a state of mind certainly not helped by the hostility that had greeted his most recent work. Yet out of his profound despair Melville wrote his great short story, "Bartleby the Scrivener."

There was a three-year hiatus between the publication of *Pierre* and Melville's next novel, but then, in a flurry of activity, he published three books in three years: his only historical novel, *Israel Potter* (1855); a collection of long and short stories, *Piazza Tales* (1856); and the last novel he was to write, *The Confidence Man* (1857), which has been described as a book that utterly repudiates all that is heroic in humanity.

Potter is a curious book, containing a number

of historical characters, such as Benjamin Franklin, John Paul Jones, and Ethan Allen. The novel ends with Israel returning from England to America, impoverished and hoping to get a pension. He is refused the pension and dies in poverty. Melville might well have seen himself in this exiled figure and may have been expressing his own fears in the conclusion of the novel. It was increasingly clear that he could not earn enough to support his wife and four children by writing, and he had not been successful in finding any sort of governmental employment, though he had tried for many years. In 1863 he sold his home, Arrowhead, and moved to New York, the city of his birth, where in 1866 he finally succeeded in gaining a government job as district inspector of customs on the New York docks, a position he retained for nineteen years.

Thanks to this steady income and an inheritance received by his wife, Melville's last twenty-five years were as calm as his first twenty-five had been turbulent. As a writer, he turned from prose to poetry. After a book of poems stimulated by the Civil War—*Battle-Pieces and Aspects of the War* (1866)—he published an unusually long narrative poem, *Clarel: A Poem and Pilgrimage in the Holy Land* (1876). It was based on a trip he had taken to the Holy Land in 1856—1857 to restore his health. Finally, near the end of his life he published *John Marr and Other Sailors* (1888) and *Timoleon* (1891).

This was all he was to publish in his lifetime, but there was one more effort in prose, the masterpiece, *Billy Budd,* which was not published until 1924. It is a tale of an innocent, handsome sailor (Billy), who is persecuted by Claggart, an evil petty officer. The latter makes up a story about Billy being involved in a mutiny and tells it to Captain Vere. Billy is literally struck dumb by the accusation and acts instead of talking, striking Claggart a fatal blow. Captain Vere, who sympathizes with Billy and recognizes his deep-down innocence, nevertheless is forced to have him hanged. Billy dies, but his legend lives on among sailors. His last words are, "God bless Captain Vere."

The psychological parallels with Melville's own life are too direct to miss. In destroying Claggart, Melville was exorcising the "demons" that had plagued him all his life, and in the spiritual union of Billy and Vere one can read a final reconciliation between Melville and his own father, in which the former finally forgives the latter for "deserting" him. And lastly, in the living on of Billy Budd's legend, we can find Melville's own wish to immortalize himself. Found with the manuscript of *Billy Budd* after Melville's death was a clipping of his own motto: "Keep true to the dreams of thy youth." It is fitting that the last published book of prose by this great American writer should have been an expression of those dreams.

BARTLEBY THE SCRIVENER
A Story of Wall Street

I am a rather elderly man. The nature of my avocations for the last thirty years has brought me into more than ordinary contact with what would seem an interesting and somewhat singular set of men, of whom as yet nothing that I know of has ever been written —I mean, the law copyists, or scriveners.[1] I have known very many of them, professionally and privately, and if I pleased, could relate divers histories, at which good-natured gentlemen might smile, and sentimental souls

1. **scriveners,** copyists who duplicated legal documents.

might weep. But I waive the biographies of all other scriveners for a few passages in the life of Bartleby, who was a scrivener, the strangest I ever saw or heard of. While of other law copyists I might write the complete life, of Bartleby nothing of that sort can be done. I believe that no materials exist for a full and satisfactory biography of this man. It is an irreparable loss to literature. Bartleby was one of those beings of whom nothing is ascertainable except from the original sources, and in his case those are very small. What my own astonished eyes saw of Bartleby, *that* is all I know of him except, indeed, one vague report, which will appear in the sequel.

Ere introducing the scrivener, as he first appeared to me, it is fit I make some mention of myself, my employees, my business, my chambers, and general surroundings; because some such description is indispensable to an adequate understanding of the chief character about to be presented.

Imprimis:[2] I am a man who from his youth upwards has been filled with a profound conviction that the easiest way of life is the best. Hence, though I belong to a profession proverbially energetic and nervous, even to turbulence at times, yet nothing of that sort have I ever suffered to invade my peace. I am one of those unambitious lawyers who never addresses a jury or in any way draws down public applause; but in the cool tranquility of a snug retreat do a snug business among rich men's bonds and mortgages and title deeds. All who know me consider me an eminently *safe* man. The late John Jacob Astor, a personage little given to poetic enthusiasm, had no hesitation in pronouncing my first grand point to be prudence; my next, method. I do not speak it in vanity but simply record the fact that I was not unemployed in my profession by the late John Jacob Astor; a name which, I admit, I love to repeat; for it hath a rounded and orbicular sound to it and rings like unto bullion. I will freely add that I was not insensible to the late John Jacob Astor's good opinion.

Some time prior to the period at which this little history begins, my avocations had been largely increased. The good old office, now extinct in the State of New York, of a master in chancery,[3] had been conferred upon me. It was not a very arduous office, but very pleasantly remunerative. I seldom lose my temper; much more seldom indulge in dangerous indignation at wrongs and outrages; but I must be permitted to be rash here and declare that I consider the sudden and violent abrogation of the office of master in chancery by the new constitution as a ——— premature act; inasmuch as I had counted upon a life-lease of the profits, whereas I only received those of a few short years. But this is by the way.

My chambers were upstairs at No.—Wall Street. At one end, they looked upon the white wall of the interior of a spacious skylight shaft, penetrating the building from top to bottom.

This view might have been considered rather tame than otherwise, deficient in what landscape painters call "life." But, if so, the view from the other end of my chambers offered, at least, a contrast, if nothing more. In that direction, my windows commanded an unobstructed view of a lofty brick wall, black by age and everlasting shade; which wall required no spyglass to bring out its lurking beauties, but for the benefit of all nearsighted spectators was pushed up to within ten feet of my window panes. Owing to the great height of the surrounding buildings, and my chambers being on the second floor, the interval between this wall and mine not a little resembled a huge square cistern.

At the period just preceding the advent of Bartleby, I had two persons as copyists in my employment, and a promising lad as an office boy. First, Turkey; second, Nippers; third, Ginger Nut. These may seem names

2. **imprimis,** Latin word meaning "in the first place."
3. **master in chancery,** a judge in an equity court that handles contract adjustments, etc.

the like of which are not usually found in the Directory. In truth, they were nicknames, mutually conferred upon each other by my three clerks, and were deemed expressive of their respective persons or characters. Turkey was a short, pursy[4] Englishman of about my own age—that is, somewhere not far from sixty. In the morning, one might say, his face was of a fine, florid hue, but after twelve o'clock, meridian—his dinner hour—it blazed like a grate full of Christmas coals and continued blazing—but as it were with a gradual wane—till 6 o'clock, P.M., or thereabouts; after which, I saw no more of the proprietor of the face, which, gaining its meridian with the sun, seemed to set with it, to rise, culminate, and decline the following day, with the like regularity and undiminished glory. There are many singular coincidences I have known in the course of my life, not the least among which was the fact that exactly when Turkey displayed his fullest beams from his red and radiant countenance, just then, too, at that critical moment began the daily period when I considered his business capacities as seriously disturbed for the remainder of the twenty-four hours. Not that he was absolutely idle or averse to business then, far from it. The difficulty was, he was apt to be altogether too energetic. There was a strange, inflamed, flurried recklessness of activity about him. He would be incautious in dipping his pen into his inkstand. All his blots upon my documents were dropped there after twelve o'clock, meridian. Indeed, not only would he be reckless and sadly given to making blots in the afternoon, but some days he went further and was rather noisy. At such times, too, his face flamed with augmented blazonry, as if cannel coal had been heaped on anthracite.[5] He made an unpleasant racket with his chair; spilled his sandbox; in mending his pens impatiently split them all to pieces and threw them on the floor in a sudden passion; stood up and leaned over his table, boxing his papers about in a most indecorous manner very sad to behold in an elderly man like him.

Nevertheless, as he was in many ways a most valuable person to me, and all the time before twelve o'clock meridian, was the quickest, steadiest creature, too, accomplishing a great deal of work in a style not easily to be matched—for these reasons, I was willing to overlook his eccentricities, though, indeed, occasionally, I remonstrated with him. I did this very gently, however, because though the civilest, nay, the blandest and most reverential of men in the morning, yet in the afternoon he was disposed, upon provocation, to be slightly rash with his tongue—in fact, insolent. Now, valuing his morning services as I did, and resolved not to lose them—yet at the same time made uncomfortable by his inflamed ways after twelve o'clock—and being a man of peace, unwilling by my admonitions to call forth unseemly retorts from him, I took upon me one Saturday noon (he was always worse on Saturdays) to hint to him, very kindly, that perhaps now that he was growing old, it might be well to abridge his labors; in short, he need not come to my chambers after twelve o'clock, but dinner over, had best go home to his lodgings and rest himself till teatime. But no; he insisted upon his afternoon devotions. His countenance became intolerably fervid as he oratorically assured me—gesticulating with a long ruler at the other side of the room—that if his services in the morning were useful, how indispensable then in the afternoon?

"With submission, sir," said Turkey, on this occasion, "I consider myself your right-hand man. In the morning I but marshal and deploy my columns; but in the afternoon I put myself at their head, and gallantly charge the foe, thus"—and he made a violent thrust with the ruler.

"But the blots, Turkey," intimated I.

"True; but with submission, sir, behold these hairs! I am getting old. Surely, sir, a blot

---

4. **pursy,** short of breath due to overweight.
5. **cannel coal . . . on anthracite,** a brightly burning coal heaped on a slow, long-burning one.

or two of a warm afternoon is not to be severely urged against gray hairs. Old age—
even if it blot the page—is honorable. With
submission, sir, we *both* are getting old."

This appeal to my fellow feeling was
hardly to be resisted. At all events, I saw that
go he would not. So I made up my mind to let
him stay, resolving, nevertheless, to see to it
that during the afternoon he had to do with
my less important papers.

Nippers, the second on my list, was a
whiskered, sallow, and upon the whole,
practical-looking young man, of above five
and twenty. I always deemed him the victim
of two evil powers—ambition and indigestion. The ambition was evinced by a certain
impatience of the duties of a mere copyist, an
unwarrantable usurpation of strictly professional affairs, such as the original drawing up
of legal documents. The indigestion seemed
betokened in an occasional nervous testiness
and grinning irritability, causing the teeth to
audibly grind together over mistakes committed in copying; unnecessary maledictions,
hissed rather than spoken, in the heat of business; and especially by a continual discontent
with the height of the table where he worked.
Though of a very ingenious mechanical turn,
Nippers could never get this table to suit him.
He put chips under it, blocks of various sorts,
bits of pasteboard, and at last went so far as to
attempt an exquisite adjustment by final pieces of folded blotting paper. But no invention
would answer. If for the sake of easing his
back, he brought the table lid at a sharp angle
well up towards his chin and wrote there like
a man using the steep roof of a Dutch house
for his desk, then he declared that it stopped
the circulation in his arms. If now he lowered
the table to his waistbands and stooped over it
in writing, then there was a sore aching in his
back. In short, the truth of the matter was,
Nippers knew not what he wanted. Or if he
wanted anything, it was to be rid of a
scrivener's table altogether. Among the mani-
festations of his diseased ambition was a
fondness he had for receiving visits from certain ambiguous-looking fellows in seedy
coats, whom he called his clients. Indeed, I
was aware that not only was he, at times, considerable of a ward politician, but he occasionally did a little business at the Justices'
courts and was not unknown on the steps of
the Tombs.[6] I have good reason to believe,
however, that one individual who called upon
him at my chambers, and who, with a grand
air, he insisted was his client, was no other
than a dun,[7] and the alleged title deed, a bill.
But with all his failings, and the annoyances
he caused me, Nippers, like his compatriot
Turkey, was a very useful man to me; wrote a
neat, swift hand; and when he chose, was not
deficient in a gentlemanly sort of deport-
ment. Added to this, he always dressed in a
gentlemanly sort of way; and so, incidentally,
reflected credit upon my chambers. Whereas,
with respect to Turkey, I had much ado to
keep him from being a reproach to me. His
clothes were apt to look oily and smell of eating houses. He wore his pantaloons very loose
and baggy in summer. His coats were execra-
ble; his hat not to be handled. But while the
hat was a thing of indifference to me, inasmuch as his natural civility and deference as a
dependent Englishman always led him to
doff it the moment he entered the room, yet
his coat was another matter. Concerning his
coats, I reasoned with him; but with no effect.
The truth was, I suppose, that a man with so
small an income could not afford to sport
such a lustrous face and a lustrous coat at one
and the same time. As Nippers once observed, Turkey's money went chiefly for red
ink. One winter day, I presented Turkey with
a highly respectable-looking coat of my
own—a padded gray coat, of a most comfortable warmth, and which buttoned straight up
from the knee to the neck. I thought Turkey
would appreciate the favor and abate his
rashness and obstreperousness of afternoons.

6. **the Tombs,** a jail in New York City.
7. **dun,** bill collector.

But no; I verily believe that buttoning himself up in so downy and blanketlike a coat had a pernicious effect upon him—upon the same principle that too much oats are bad for horses. In fact, precisely as a rash, restive horse is said to feel his oats, so Turkey felt his coat. It made him insolvent. He was a man whom prosperity harmed.

Though concerning the self-indulgent habits of Turkey, I had my own private surmises, yet touching Nippers, I was well persuaded that whatever might be his faults in other respects he was, at least, a temperate young man. But, indeed, nature herself seemed to have been his vintner, and at his birth charged him so thoroughly with an irritable brandylike disposition that all subsequent potations[8] were needless. When I consider how, amid the stillness of my chambers, Nippers would sometimes impatiently rise from his seat, and stooping over his table, spread his arms wide apart, seize the whole desk, and move it, and jerk it, with a grim, grinding motion on the floor, as if the table were a perverse voluntary agent intent on thwarting and vexing him, I plainly perceive that, for Nippers, brandy and water were altogether superfluous.

It was fortunate for me that owing to its peculiar cause—indigestion—the irritability and consequent nervousness of Nippers were mainly observable in the morning, while in the afternoon he was comparatively mild. So that, Turkey's paroxysms only coming on about twelve o'clock, I never had to do with their eccentricities at one time. Their fits relieved each other like guards. When Nippers' was on, Turkey's was off; and vice versa. This was a good natural arrangement, under the circumstances.

Ginger Nut, the third on my list, was a lad, some twelve years old. His father was a carman, ambitious of seeing his son on the bench, instead of a cart, before he died. So he sent him to my office as student at law, errand

8. **potations,** alcoholic drinks or brews.

"At first Bartleby did an extraordinary quantity of writing . . . copying by sunlight and by candlelight. . . . But he wrote on, silently, palely, mechanically."

boy, cleaner and sweeper, at the rate of one dollar a week. He had a little desk to himself, but he did not use it much. Upon inspection, the drawer exhibited a great array of the shells of various sorts of nuts. Indeed, to this quick-witted youth the whole noble science of the law was contained in a nutshell. Not the least among the employments of Ginger Nut, as well as one which he discharged with the most alacrity, was his duty as cake and apple purveyor for Turkey and Nippers. Copying law papers being proverbially a dry, husky sort of business, my two scriveners were fain to moisten their mouths very often with Spitzenbergs,[9] to be had at numerous stalls nigh the customhouse and post office. Also, they sent Ginger Nut very frequently for that peculiar cake—small, flat, round, and very spicy—after which he had been named by them. Of a cold morning when business was but dull, Turkey would gobble up scores of these cakes as if they were mere wafers—indeed, they sell them at the rate of six or eight for a penny—the scrape of his .pen blending with the crunching of the crisp particles in his mouth. Of all the fiery afternoon blunders and flurried rashnesses of Turkey, was his once moistening a ginger cake between his lips and clapping it on to a mortgage for a seal. I came within an ace of dismissing him then. But he mollified me by making an oriental bow and saying—"With submission, sir, it was generous of me to find you in stationery on my own account."

Now to my original business—that of a conveyancer[10] and title hunter, and drawer-up of recondite documents of all sorts—was considerably increased by receiving the master's office. There was now great work for scriveners. Not only must I push the clerks already with me, but I must have additional help.

In answer to my advertisement, a motionless young man one morning stood upon my office threshold, the door being open, for it was summer. I can see that figure now—pallidly neat, pitiably respectable, incurably forlorn! It was Bartleby.

After a few words touching his qualifications, I engaged him, glad to have among my corps of copyists a man of so singularly sedate an aspect, which I thought might operate beneficially upon the flighty temper of Turkey and the fiery one of Nippers.

I should have stated before that ground-glass folding doors divided my premises into two parts, one of which was occupied by my scriveners, the other by myself. According to my humor I threw open these doors or closed them. I resolved to assign Bartleby a corner by the folding doors, but on my side of them, so as to have this quiet man within easy call in case any trifling thing was to be done. I placed his desk close up to a small side window in that part of the room, a window which originally had afforded a lateral view of certain grimy back yards and bricks, but which, owing to subsequent erections, commanded at present no view at all, though it gave some light. Within three feet of the panes was a wall, and the light came down from far above, between two lofty buildings, as from a very small opening in a dome. Still further to a satisfactory arrangement, I procured a high green folding screen, which might entirely isolate Bartleby from my sight, though not remove him from my voice. And thus, in a manner, privacy and society were conjoined.

At first Bartleby did an extraordinary quantity of writing. As if long famishing for something to copy, he seemed to gorge himself on my documents. There was no pause for digestion. He ran a day and night line, copying by sunlight and by candlelight. I should have been quite delighted with his application had he been cheerfully industrious. But he wrote on silently, palely, mechanically.

It is, of course, an indispensable part of a scrivener's business to verify the accuracy of his copy, word by word. Where there are two or more scriveners in an office, they assist

9. **Spitzenbergs,** a type of apple.
10. **conveyancer,** a lawyer who draws up deeds to transfer property titles.

each other in this examination, one reading from the copy, the other holding the original. It is a very dull, wearisome, and lethargic affair. I can readily imagine that to some sanguine temperaments it would be altogether intolerable. For example, I cannot credit that the mettlesome poet Byron would have contentedly sat down with Bartleby to examine a law document of, say, five hundred pages, closely written in a crimpy hand.

Now and then, in the haste of business, it had been my habit to assist in comparing some brief document myself, calling Turkey or Nippers for this purpose. One object I had in placing Bartleby so handy to me behind the screen was to avail myself of his services on such trivial occasions. It was on the third day, I think, of his being with me, and before any necessity had arisen for having his own writing examined, that being hurried to complete a small affair I had in hand, I abruptly called to Bartleby. In my haste and natural expectancy of instant compliance, I sat with my head bent over the original on my desk, and my right hand sideways, and somewhat nervously extended with the copy, so that immediately upon emerging from his retreat Bartleby might snatch it and proceed to business without the least delay.

In this very attitude did I sit when I called to him, rapidly stating what it was I wanted him to do—namely, to examine a small paper with me. Imagine my surprise, nay, my consternation, when, without moving from his privacy, Bartleby, in a singularly mild, firm voice, replied, "I would prefer not to."

I sat awhile in perfect silence, rallying my stunned facilities. Immediately it occurred to me that my ears had deceived me, or Bartleby had entirely misunderstood my meaning. I repeated my request in the clearest tone I could assume. But in quite as clear a tone came the previous reply, "I would prefer not to."

"Prefer not to," echoed I, rising in high excitement, and crossing the room with a stride. "What do you mean? Are you moonstruck? I want you to help me compare this sheet here—take it," and I thrust it towards him.

"I would prefer not to," said he.

I looked at him steadfastly. His face was leanly composed; his gray eye dimly calm. Not a wrinkle of agitation rippled him. Had there been the least uneasiness, anger, impatience, or impertinence in his manner; in other words, had there been anything ordinarily human about him, doubtless I should have violently dismissed him from the premises. But as it was, I should have as soon thought of turning my pale plaster-of-Paris bust of Cicero out of doors. I stood gazing at him awhile as he went on with his own writing, and then reseated myself at my desk. This is very strange, thought I. What had one best do? But my business hurried me. I concluded to forget the matter for the present, reserving it for my future leisure. So calling Nippers from the other room, the paper was speedily examined.

A few days after this, Bartleby concluded four lengthy documents, being quadruplicates of a week's testimony taken before me in my High Court of Chancery. It became necessary to examine them. It was an important suit, and great accuracy was imperative. Having all things arranged, I called Turkey, Nippers, and Ginger Nut from the next room, meaning to place the four copies in the hands of my four clerks, while I should read from the original. Accordingly, Turkey, Nippers, and Ginger Nut had taken their seats in a row, each with his document in his hand, when I called to Bartleby to join this interesting group.

"Bartleby! quick, I am waiting."

I heard a slow scrape of his chair legs on the uncarpeted floor, and soon he appeared standing at the entrance of his hermitage.

"What is wanted?" said he, mildly.

"The copies, the copies," said I, hurriedly. "We are going to examine them. There"—and I held toward him the fourth quadruplicate.

"I would prefer not to," he said, and gently disappeared behind the screen.

For a few moments I was turned into a pillar of salt,[11] standing at the head of my seated column of clerks. Recovering myself, I advanced towards the screen and demanded the reason for such extraordinary conduct.

"Why do you refuse?"

"I would prefer not to."

With any other man I should have flown outright into a dreadful passion, scorned all further words, and thrust him ignominiously from my presence. But there was something about Bartleby that not only strangely disarmed me, but in a wonderful manner touched and disconcerted me. I began to reason with him.

"These are your own copies we are about to examine. It is labor saving for you, because one examination will answer for your four papers. It is common usage. Every copyist is bound to help examine his copy. Is it not so? Will you not speak? Answer!"

"I prefer not to," he replied in a flutelike tone. It seemed to me that while I had been addressing him, he carefully revolved every statement that I made; fully comprehended the meaning; could not gainsay the irresistible conclusion; but at the same time some paramount consideration prevailed with him to reply as he did.

"You are decided, then, not to comply with my request—a request made according to *common* usage and common sense?"

He briefly gave me to understand that on that point my judgment was sound. Yes: his decision was irreversible.

It is not seldom the case that when a man is browbeaten in some unprecedented and violently unreasonable way, he begins to stagger in his own plainest faith. He begins, as it were, vaguely to surmise that, wonderful as it may be, all the justice and all the reason is on the other side. Accordingly, if any disinterested persons are present, he turns to them for some reinforcement for his own faltering mind.

"Turkey," said I, "what do you think of this? Am I not right?"

"With submission, sir," said Turkey, in his blandest tone, "I think you are."

"Nippers," said I, "what do *you* think of it?"

"I think I should kick him out of the office."

(The reader of nice[12] perceptions will have perceived that it being morning, Turkey's answer is couched in polite and tranquil terms, but Nippers replies in ill-tempered ones. Or to repeat a previous sentence, Nipper's ugly mood was on duty, and Turkey's off.)

"Ginger Nut," said I, willing to enlist the smallest suffrage in my behalf, "what do *you* think of it?"

"I think, sir, he's a little *luny,*" replied Ginger Nut, with a grin.

"You hear what they say," said I, turning towards the screen, "come forth and do your duty."

But he vouchsafed no reply. I pondered a moment in sore perplexity. But once more business hurried me. I determined again to postpone the consideration of this dilemma to my future leisure. With a little trouble we made out to examine the papers without Bartleby, though at every page or two, Turkey deferentially dropped his opinion that this proceeding was quite out of the common; while Nippers, twitching in his chair with a dyspeptic nervousness, ground out between his set teeth occasional hissing maledictions against the stubborn oaf behind the screen. And for his (Nippers') part, this was the first and the last time he would do another man's business without pay.

Meanwhile Bartleby sat in his hermitage, oblivious to everything but his own peculiar business there.

Some days passed, the scrivener being employed upon another lengthy work. His

11. **a pillar of salt,** an allusion to the Biblical story of Lot's wife, who disobeyed God's order and was consequently turned into a pillar of salt (Genesis 19).
12. **nice,** here: sensitive.

late remarkable conduct led me to regard his ways narrowly. I observed that he never went to dinner; indeed, that he never went anywhere. As yet I had never, of my personal knowledge, known him to be outside of my office. He was a perpetual sentry in the corner. At about eleven o'clock though, in the morning, I noticed that Ginger Nut would advance towards the opening in Bartleby's screen as if silently beckoned thither by a gesture invisible to me where I sat. The boy would then leave the office, jingling a few pence, and reappear with a handful of ginger nuts, which he delivered in the hermitage, receiving two of the cakes for his trouble.

He lives, then, on ginger nuts, thought I; never eats a dinner, properly speaking; he must be a vegetarian, then; but no, he never eats even vegetables, he eats nothing but ginger nuts. My mind then ran on in reveries concerning the probable effects upon the human constitution of living entirely on ginger nuts. Ginger nuts are so called because they contain ginger as one of their peculiar constituents and the final flavoring one. Now, what was ginger? A hot, spicy thing. Was Bartleby hot and spicy? Not at all. Ginger, then, had no effect upon Bartleby. Probably he preferred it should have none.

Nothing so aggravates an earnest person as a passive resistance. If the individual so resisted be of a not inhumane temper, and the resisting one perfectly harmless in his passivity, then in the better moods of the former, he will endeavor charitably to construe to his imagination what proves impossible to be solved by his judgment. Even so, for the most part, I regarded Bartleby and his ways. Poor fellow! thought I, he means no mischief; it is plain he intends no insolence; his aspect sufficiently evinces that his eccentricities are involuntary. He is useful to me. I can get along with him. If I turn him away, the chances are he will fall in with some less indulgent employer, and then he will be rudely treated and perhaps driven forth miserably to starve. Yes. Here I can cheaply purchase a delicious self-approval. To befriend Bartleby, to humor him in his strange willfulness, will cost me little or nothing, while I lay up in my soul what will eventually prove a sweet morsel for my conscience. But this mood was not invariable with me. The passiveness of Bartleby sometimes irritated me. I felt strangely goaded on to encounter him in new opposition—to elicit some angry spark from him answerable to my own. But, indeed, I might as well have essayed to strike fire with my knuckles against a bit of Windsor soap. But one afternoon the evil impulse in me mastered me, and the following little scene ensued:

"Bartleby," said I, "when those papers are all copied, I will compare them with you."

"I would prefer not to."

"How? Surely you do not mean to persist in that mulish vagary?"

No answer.

I threw open the folding doors near by, and turning upon Turkey and Nippers, exclaimed:

"Bartleby a second time says he won't examine his papers. What do you think of it, Turkey?"

It was afternoon, be it remembered. Turkey sat glowing like a brass boiler; his bald head steaming; his hands reeling among his blotted papers.

"Think of it?" roared Turkey; "I think I'll just step behind his screen and black his eyes for him!"

So saying, Turkey rose to his feet and threw his arms into a pugilistic[13] position. He was hurrying away to make good his promise when I detained him, alarmed at the effect of incautiously rousing Turkey's combativeness after dinner.

"Sit down, Turkey," said I, "and hear what Nippers has to say. What do you think of it, Nippers? Would I not be justified in immediately dismissing Bartleby?"

---

13. **pugilistic,** fighting, boxing.

"Excuse me, that is for you to decide, sir. I think his conduct quite unusual and, indeed, unjust, as regards Turkey and myself. But it may only be a passing whim."

"Ah," exclaimed I, "you have strangely changed your mind, then—you speak very gently of him now."

"All beer," cried Turkey; "gentleness is effects of beer—Nippers and I dined together today. You see how gentle *I* am, sir. Shall I go and black his eyes?"

"You refer to Bartleby, I suppose. No, not today, Turkey," I replied; "pray, put up your fists."

I closed the doors, and again advanced towards Bartleby. I felt additional incentives tempting me to my fate. I burned to be rebelled against again. I remembered that Bartleby never left the office.

"Bartleby," said I, "Ginger Nut is away; just step round to the post office, won't you? (it was but a three minutes' walk), and see if there is anything for me."

"I would prefer not to."

"You *will* not?"

"I *prefer* not."

I staggered to my desk and sat there in a deep study. My blind inveteracy[14] returned. Was there any other thing in which I could procure myself to be ignominiously repulsed by this lean, penniless wight?[15] my hired clerk? What added thing is there, perfectly reasonable, that he will be sure to refuse to do?

"Bartleby!"

No answer.

"Bartleby," in a louder tone.

No answer.

"Bartleby," I roared.

Like a very ghost, agreeably to the laws of magical invocation, at the third summons he appeared at the entrance of his hermitage.

"Go to the next room and tell Nippers to come to me."

"I prefer not to," he respectfully and slowly said, and mildly disappeared.

"Very good, Bartleby," said I, in a quiet sort of serenely severe self-possessed tone, intimating the unalterable purpose of some terrible retribution very close at hand. At the moment I half intended something of the kind. But upon the whole, as it was drawing towards my dinner hour, I thought it best to put on my hat and walk home for the day, suffering much from perplexity and distress of mind.

Shall I acknowledge it? The conclusion of this whole business was that it soon became a fixed fact of my chambers that a pale young scrivener by the name of Bartleby had a desk there; that he copied for me at the usual rate of four cents a folio (one hundred words); but he was permanently exempt from examining the work done by him, that duty being transferred to Turkey and Nippers, out of compliment, doubtless, to their superior acuteness; moreover, said Bartleby was never, on any account, to be despatched on the most trivial errand of any sort; and that even if entreated to take upon him such a matter, it was generally understood that he would "prefer not to"—in other words, that he would refuse pointblank.

As days passed on, I became considerably reconciled to Bartleby. His steadiness, his freedom from all dissipation, his incessant industry (except when he chose to throw himself into a standing revery behind his screen), his great stillness, his unalterableness of demeanor under all circumstances, made him a valuable acquisition. One prime thing was this—*he was always there*—first in the morning, continually through the day, and the last at night. I had a singular confidence in his honesty. I felt my most precious papers perfectly safe in his hands. Sometimes, to be sure, I could not, for the very soul of me, avoid falling into sudden spasmodic passions with him. For it was exceeding difficult to bear in mind all the time those strange peculiarities, privileges, and unheard of exemptions forming

14. **inveteracy,** deeply rooted habit.
15. **wight,** creature.

the tacit stipulations on Bartleby's part under which he remained in my office. Now and then, in the eagerness of despatching pressing business, I would inadvertently summon Bartleby, in a short, rapid tone, to put his finger, say, on the incipient tie of a bit of red tape with which I was about compressing some papers. Of course, from behind the screen the usual answer, "I prefer not to," was sure to come; and then, how could a human creature, with the common infirmities of our nature, refrain from bitterly exclaiming upon such perverseness—such unreasonableness. However, every added repulse of this sort which I received only tended to lessen the probability of my repeating the inadvertence.

Here it must be said that according to the custom of most legal gentlemen occupying chambers in densely populated law buildings, there were several keys to my door. One was kept by a woman residing in the attic, which person weekly scrubbed and daily swept and dusted my apartments. Another was kept by Turkey for convenience sake. The third I sometimes carried in my own pocket. The fourth I knew not who had.

Now one Sunday morning I happened to go to Trinity Church to hear a celebrated preacher, and finding myself rather early on the ground, I thought I would walk round to my chambers for awhile. Luckily I had my key with me; but upon applying it to the lock, I found it resisted by something inserted from the inside. Quite surprised, I called out; when to my consternation a key was turned from within; and thrusting his lean visage at me, and holding the door ajar, the apparition of Bartleby appeared, in his shirt sleeves and otherwise in a strangely tattered dishabille,[16] saying quietly that he was sorry, but he was deeply engaged just then and—preferred not admitting me at present. In a brief word or two, he moreover added that perhaps I had better walk round the block two or three times, and by that time he would probably have concluded his affairs.

Now the utterly unsurmised appearance of Bartleby tenanting my law chambers of a Sunday morning, with his cadaverously gentlemanly nonchalance, yet withal firm and self-possessed, had such a strange effect upon me that incontinently I slunk away from my own door and did as desired. But not without sundry twinges of impotent rebellion against the mild effrontery of this unaccountable scrivener. Indeed, it was his wonderful mildness chiefly, which not only disarmed me but unmanned me as it were. For I consider that one, for the time, is of a sort unmanned when he tranquilly permits his hired clerk to dictate to him and order him away from his own premises. Furthermore, I was full of uneasiness as to what Bartleby could possibly be doing in my office in his shirt sleeves and in an otherwise dismantled condition of a Sunday morning. Was anything amiss going on? Nay, that was out of the question. It was not to be thought of for a moment that Bartleby was an immoral person. But what could he be doing there?—copying? Nay again, whatever might be his eccentricities, Bartleby was an eminently decorous person. He would be the last man to sit down to his desk in any state approaching to nudity. Besides, it was Sunday; and there was something about Bartleby that forbade the supposition that he would by any secular occupation violate the proprieties of the day.

Nevertheless, my mind was not pacified; and full of a restless curiosity, at last I returned to the door. Without hindrance I inserted my key, opened it, and entered. Bartleby was not to be seen. I looked round anxiously, peeped behind his screen; but it was very plain that he was gone. Upon more closely examining the place, I surmised that for an indefinite period Bartleby must have ate, dressed, and slept in my office, and that, too, without plate, mirror, or bed. The cushioned seat of a rickety old sofa in one corner

---

16. **dishabille** (dis′ ə bēl′),   state of being carelessly or partially dressed.

bore the faint impress of a lean, reclining form. Rolled away under his desk, I found a blanket; under the empty grate, a blacking box and brush; on a chair, a tin basin with soap and a ragged towel; in a newspaper a few crumbs of ginger nuts and a morsel of cheese. Yes, thought I, it is evident enough that Bartleby has been making his home here, keeping bachelor's hall all by himself. Immediately then the thought came sweeping across me, what miserable friendlessness and loneliness are here revealed! His poverty is great; but his solitude, how horrible! Think of it. Of a Sunday, Wall Street is deserted as Petra;[17] and every night of every day it is an emptiness. This building, too, which of weekdays hums with industry and life, at nightfall echoes with sheer vacancy, and all through Sunday is forlorn. And here Bartleby makes his home; sole spectator of a solitude which he has seen all populous—a sort of innocent and transformed Marius[18] brooding among the ruins of Carthage.

For the first time in my life a feeling of overpowering stinging melancholy seized me. Before, I had never experienced aught but a not unpleasing sadness. The bond of a common humanity now drew me irresistibly to gloom. A fraternal melancholy! For both I and Bartleby were sons of Adam. I remembered the bright silks and sparkling faces I had seen that day in gala trim, swanlike sailing down the Mississippi of Broadway; and I contrasted them with the pallid copyist and thought to myself, Ah, happiness courts the light, so we deem the world is gay; but misery hides aloof, so we deem that misery there is none. These sad fancyings—chimeras, doubtless, of a sick and silly brain—led on to other and more special thoughts concerning the eccentricities of Bartleby. Presentiments of strange discoveries hovered round me. The scrivener's pale form appeared to me laid out, among uncaring strangers, in its shivering winding sheet.

Suddenly I was attracted by Bartleby's closed desk, the key in open sight left in the lock.

I mean no mischief, seek the gratification of no heartless curiosity, thought I; besides, the desk is mine, and its contents, too, so I will make bold to look within. Everything was methodically arranged, the papers smoothly placed. The pigeon holes were deep, and removing the files of documents, I groped into their recesses. Presently I felt something there and dragged it out. It was an old bandanna handkerchief, heavy and knotted. I opened it and saw it was a savings bank.

I now recalled all the quiet mysteries which I had noted in the man. I remembered that he never spoke but to answer; that though at intervals he had considerable time to himself, yet I had never seen him reading —no, not even a newspaper; that for long periods he would stand looking out, at his pale window behind the screen, upon the dead brick wall; I was quite sure he never visited any refectory or eating house; while his pale face clearly indicated that he never drank beer like Turkey, or tea and coffee even, like other men; that he never went anywhere in particular that I could learn; never went out for a walk, unless, indeed, that was the case at present; that he had declined telling who he was, or whence he came, or whether he had any relatives in the world; that though so thin and pale, he never complained of ill health. And more than all, I remembered a certain unconscious air of pallid—how shall I call it?—of pallid haughtiness, say, or rather an austere reserve about him, which had positively awed me into my tame compliance with his eccentricities, when I had feared to ask him to do the slightest incidental thing for me, even though I might know from his long-continued motionlessness that behind his

17. **Petra,** the ruins of an ancient city in Jordan.
18. **Marius** (c. 155–86 B.C.), a Roman general who triumphed over Carthage, a city in North Africa, but who was banished from Rome by political enemies.

screen he must be standing in one of those dead-wall reveries of his.

Revolving all these things, and coupling them with the recently discovered fact that he made my office his constant abiding place and home, and not forgetful of his morbid moodiness; revolving all these things, a prudential feeling began to steal over me. My first emotions had been those of pure melancholy and sincerest pity; but just in proportion as the forlornness of Bartleby grew and grew to my imagination, did that same melancholy merge into fear, that pity into repulsion. So true it is, and so terrible, too, that up to a certain point the thought or sight of misery enlists our best affections; but in certain special cases, beyond that point it does not. They err who would assert that invariably this is owing to the inherent selfishness of the human heart. It rather proceeds from a certain hopelessness of remedying excessive and organic ill. To a sensitive being, pity is not seldom pain. And when at last it is perceived that such pity cannot lead to effectual succor, common sense bids the soul be rid of it. What I saw that morning persuaded me that the scrivener was the victim of innate and incurable disorder. I might give alms to his body; but his body did not pain him; it was his soul that suffered, and his soul I could not reach.

I did not accomplish the purpose of going to Trinity Church that morning. Somehow, the things I had seen disqualified me for the time from churchgoing. I walked homeward, thinking what I would do with Bartleby. Finally, I resolved upon this—I would put certain calm questions to him the next morning touching his history, etc., and if he declined to answer them openly and unreservedly (and I supposed he would prefer not), then to give him a twenty-dollar bill over and above whatever I might owe him, and tell him his services were no longer required; but that if in any other way I could assist him, I would be happy to do so, especially if he desired to return to his native place, wherever that

might be, I would willingly help to defray the expenses. Moreover, if after reaching home, he found himself at any time in want of aid, a letter from him would be sure of a reply.

The next morning came.

"Bartleby," said I, gently calling to him behind his screen.

No reply.

"Bartleby," said I, in a still gentler tone, "Come here; I am not going to ask you to do anything you would prefer not to do—I simply wish to speak to you."

Upon this he noiselessly slid into view.

"Will you tell me, Bartleby, where you were born?"

"I would prefer not to."

"Will you tell me *anything* about yourself?"

"I would prefer not to."

"But what reasonable objection can you have to speak to me? I feel friendly towards you."

He did not look at me while I spoke, but kept his glance fixed upon my bust of Cicero, which, as I then sat, was directly behind me, some six inches above my head.

"What is your answer, Bartleby," said I, after waiting a considerable time for a reply, during which his countenance remained immovable, only there was the faintest conceivable tremor of the white attenuated mouth.

"At present I prefer to give no answer," he said, and retired into his hermitage.

It was rather weak in me I confess, but his manner on this occasion nettled me. Not only did there seem to lurk in it a certain calm disdain, but his perverseness seemed ungrateful considering the undeniable good usage and indulgence he had received from me.

Again I sat ruminating what I should do. Mortified as I was at his behavior, and resolved as I had been to dismiss him when I entered my office, nevertheless I strangely felt something superstitious knocking at my heart, and forbidding me to carry out my purpose, and denouncing me for a villain if I dared to breathe one bitter word against this forlornest of mankind. At last, familiarly drawing my chair behind his screen, I sat down and said: "Bartleby, never mind, then, about revealing your history; but let me entreat you, as a friend, to comply as far as may be with the usages of this office. Say now, you will help to examine papers tomorrow or next day: in short, say now, that in a day or two you will begin to be a little reasonable:—say so, Bartleby."

"At present I would prefer not to be a little reasonable," was his mildly cadaverous reply.

Just then the folding doors opened, and Nippers approached. He seemed suffering from an unusually bad night's rest, induced by severer indigestion than common. He overheard those final words of Bartleby.

"Prefer not, eh?" gritted Nippers—"I'd *prefer* him if I were you, sir," addressing me—"I'd *prefer* him; I'd give him preferences, the stubborn mule! What is it, sir, pray, that he *prefers* not to do now?"

"Mr. Nippers," said I, "I'd prefer that you would withdraw for the present."

Somehow of late I had got into the way of involuntarily using this word "prefer" upon all sorts of not exactly suitable occasions. And I trembled to think that my contact with the scrivener had already and seriously affected me in a mental way. And what further and deeper aberration might it not yet produce? This apprehension had not been without efficacy in determining me to summary measures.

As Nippers, looking very sour and sulky, was departing, Turkey blandly and deferentially approached.

"With submission, sir," said he, "yesterday I was thinking about Bartleby here, and I think that if he would but prefer to take a quart of good ale every day, it would do much towards mending him and enabling him to assist in examining his papers."

"So you have got the word, too," said I, slightly excited.

"With submission, what word, sir?" asked Turkey, respectfully crowding himself into the contracted space behind the screen, and by so doing, making me jostle the scrivener. "What word, sir?"

"I would prefer to be left alone here," said Bartleby, as if offended at being mobbed in his privacy.

"That's the word, Turkey," said I—*"that's* it."

"Oh, *prefer?* oh, yes—queer word. I never use it myself. But, sir, as I was saying, if he would but prefer—"

"Turkey," interrupted I, "you will please withdraw."

"Oh certainly, sir, if you prefer that I should."

As he opened the folding door to retire, Nippers at his desk caught a glimpse of me and asked whether I would prefer to have a certain paper copied on blue paper or white. He did not in the least roguishly accent the word *prefer.* It was plain that it involuntarily rolled from his tongue. I thought to myself, surely I must get rid of a demented man who already has in some degree turned the tongues, if not the heads, of myself and clerks. But I thought it prudent not to break the dismission at once.

The next day I noticed that Bartleby did nothing but stand at his window in his dead-wall revery. Upon asking him why he did not write, he said that he had decided upon doing no more writing.

"Why, how now? what next?" exclaimed I, "do no more writing?"

"No more."

"And what is the reason?"

"Do you not see the reason for yourself?" he indifferently replied.

I looked steadfastly at him and perceived that his eyes looked dull and glazed. Instantly it occurred to me that his unexampled diligence in copying by his dim window for the first few weeks of his stay with me might have temporarily impaired his vision.

I was touched. I said something in condolence with him. I hinted that of course he did wisely in abstaining from writing for a while; and urged him to embrace that opportunity of taking wholesome exercise in the open air. This, however, he did not do. A few days after this, my other clerks being absent, and being in a great hurry to despatch certain letters by the mail, I thought that having nothing else earthly to do, Bartleby would surely be less inflexible than usual and carry these letters to the post office. But he blankly declined. So much to my inconvenience, I went myself.

Still added days went by. Whether Bartleby's eyes improved or not, I could not say. To all appearance, I thought they did. But when I asked him if they did, he vouchsafed no answer. At all events, he would do no copying. At last, in reply to my urgings, he informed me that he had permanently given up copying.

"What!" exclaimed I; "suppose your eyes should get entirely well—better than ever before—would you not copy then?"

"I have given up copying," he answered, and slid aside.

He remained as ever, a fixture in my chamber. Nay—if that were possible—he became still more of a fixture than before. What was to be done? He would do nothing in the office; why should he stay there? In plain fact, he had now become a millstone to me, not only useless as a necklace, but afflictive to bear. Yet I was sorry for him. I speak less than truth when I say that on his own account he occasioned me uneasiness. If he would but have named a single relative or friend, I would instantly have written and urged their taking the poor fellow away to some convenient retreat. But he seemed alone, absolutely alone in the universe. A bit of wreck in the mid-Atlantic. At length, necessities connected with my business tyrannized over all other considerations. Decently as I could, I told Bartleby that in six days time he must unconditionally leave the office. I warned him to take measures, in the interval, for procuring

some other abode. I offered to assist him in this endeavor if he himself would but take the first step towards a removal. "And when you finally quit me, Bartleby," added I, "I shall see that you go not away entirely unprovided. Six days from this hour, remember."

At the expiration of that period, I peeped behind the screen, and lo! Bartleby was there.

I buttoned up my coat, balanced myself; advanced slowly towards him, touched his shoulder, and said, "The time has come; you must quit this place; I am sorry for you; here is money; but you must go."

"I would prefer not," he replied, with his back still towards me.

"You *must*."

He remained silent.

Now I had an unbounded confidence in this man's common honesty. He had frequently restored to me sixpences and shillings carelessly dropped upon the floor, for I am apt to be very reckless in such shirt button affairs. The proceeding, then, which followed will not be deemed extraordinary.

"Bartleby," said I, "I owe you twelve dollars on account; here are thirty-two; the odd twenty are yours—Will you take it?" and I handed the bills towards him.

But he made no motion.

"I will leave them here, then," putting them under a weight on the table. Then taking my hat and cane and going to the door, I tranquilly turned and added—"After you have removed your things from these offices, Bartleby, you will of course lock the door—since every one is now gone for the day but you—and if you please, slip your key underneath the mat, so that I may have it in the morning. I shall not see you again; so good-bye to you. If, hereafter, in your new place of abode, I can be of any service to you, do not fail to advise me by letter. Good-bye, Bartleby, and fare you well."

But he answered not a word; like the last column of some ruined temple, he remained standing mute and solitary in the middle of the otherwise deserted room.

As I walked home in a pensive mood, my vanity got the better of my pity. I could not but highly plume myself on my masterly management in getting rid of Bartleby. Masterly I call it, and such it must appear to any dispassionate thinker. The beauty of my procedure seemed to consist in its perfect quietness. There was no vulgar bullying, no bravado of any sort, no choleric hectoring, and striding to and fro across the apartment, jerking out vehement commands for Bartleby to bundle himself off with his beggarly traps. Nothing of the kind. Without loudly bidding Bartleby depart—as an inferior genius might have done—I *assumed* the ground that depart he must; and upon that assumption built all I had to say. The more I thought over my procedure, the more I was charmed with it. Nevertheless, next morning upon awakening I had my doubts—I had somehow slept off the fumes of vanity. One of the coolest and wisest hours a man has is just after he awakes in the morning. My procedure seemed as sagacious as ever—but only in theory. How it would prove in practice—there was the rub. It was truly a beautiful thought to have assumed Bartleby's departure; but after all, that assumption was simply my own, and none of Bartleby's. The great point was not whether I had assumed that he would quit me, but whether he would prefer so to do. He was more a man of preferences than assumptions.

After breakfast, I walked downtown, arguing the probabilities pro and con. One moment I thought it would prove a miserable failure, and Bartleby would be found all alive at my office as usual; the next moment it seemed certain that I should find his chair empty. And so I kept veering about. At the corner of Broadway and Canal Street, I saw quite an excited group of people standing in earnest conversation.

"I'll take odds he doesn't," said a voice as I passed.

"Doesn't go?—done!" said I, "put up your money."

I was instinctively putting my hand in my pocket to produce my own when I remembered that this was an election day. The words I had overheard bore no reference to Bartleby, but to the success or nonsuccess of some candidate for the mayoralty. In my intent frame of mind, I had, as it were, imagined that all Broadway shared in my excitement and were debating the same question with me. I passed on, very thankful that the uproar of the street screened my momentary absent-mindedness.

As I had intended, I was earlier than usual at my office door. I stood listening for a moment. All was still. He must be gone. I tried the knob. The door was locked. Yes, my procedure had worked to a charm; he indeed must be vanished. Yet a certain melancholy mixed with this: I was almost sorry for my brilliant success. I was fumbling under the door mat for the key, which Bartleby was to have left there for me, when accidentally my knee knocked against a panel, producing a summoning sound, and in response a voice came to me from within—"Not yet; I am occupied."

It was Bartleby.

I was thunderstruck. For an instant I stood like the man who, pipe in mouth, was killed one cloudless afternoon long ago in Virginia by summer lightning; at his own warm open window he was killed and remained leaning out there upon the dreamy afternoon till some one touched him, when he fell.

"Not gone!" I murmured at last. But again obeying that wondrous ascendancy which the inscrutable scrivener had over me, and from which ascendancy, for all my chafing, I could not completely escape, I slowly went downstairs and out into the street, and while walking round the block, considered what I should next do in this unheard-of perplexity. Turn the man out by an actual thrusting I could not; to drive him away by calling him hard names would not do; calling in the police was an unpleasant idea; and yet, per-

A visiting artist's view of Wall Street, New York City's busy financial and legal center, in the late nineteenth century

mit him to enjoy his cadaverous triumph over me—this, too, I could not think of. What was to be done? or if nothing could be done, was there anything further that I could *assume* in the matter? Yes, as before I had prospectively assumed that Bartleby would depart, so now I might retrospectively assume that departed he was. In the legitimate carrying out of this assumption, I might enter my office in a great hurry, and pretending not to see Bartleby at all, walk straight against him as if he were air. Such a proceeding would in a singular degree have the appearance of a home thrust. It was hardly possible that Bartleby could withstand such an application of the doctrine of assumptions. But upon second thoughts the success of the plan seemed rather dubious. I resolved to argue the matter over with him, again.

"Bartleby," said I, entering the office, with a quietly severe expression, "I am seriously displeased. I am pained, Bartleby. I had thought better of you. I had imagined you of such a gentlemanly organization that in any delicate dilemma a slight hint would suffice—in short, an assumption. But it appears I am deceived. Why," I added, unaffectedly starting, "you have not even touched that money yet," pointing to it, just where I had left it the evening previous.

He answered nothing.

"Will you, or will you not, quit me?" I now demanded in a sudden passion, advancing close to him.

"I would prefer *not* to quit you," he replied, gently emphasizing the *not*.

"What earthly right have you to stay here? Do you pay any rent? Do you pay my taxes? Or is this property yours?"

He answered nothing.

"Are you ready to go on and write now? Are your eyes recovered? Could you copy a small paper for me this morning? or help examine a few lines? or step round to the post office? In a word, will you do anything at all to give a coloring to your refusal to depart the premises?"

He silently retired into his hermitage.

I was now in such a state of nervous resentment that I thought it but prudent to check myself at present from futher demonstrations. Bartleby and I were alone. I remembered the tragedy of the unfortunate Adams and the still more unfortunate Colt in the solitary office of the latter; and how poor Colt, being dreadfully incensed by Adams, and imprudently permitting himself to get wildly excited, was at unawares hurried into his fatal act—an act which certainly no man could possibly deplore more than the actor himself. Often it had occurred to me in my ponderings upon the subject that had that altercation taken place in the public street, or at a private residence, it would not have terminated as it did. It was the circumstance of being alone in a solitary office, upstairs, of a building entirely unhallowed by humanizing domestic associations—an uncarpeted office, doubtless, of a dusty, haggard sort of appearance—this it must have been which greatly helped to enhance the irritable desperation of the hapless Colt.

But when this old Adam of resentment rose in me and tempted me concerning Bartleby, I grappled him and threw him. How? Why, simply by recalling the divine injunction: "A new commandment give I unto you, that ye love one another." Yes, this it was that saved me. Aside from higher considerations, charity often operates as a vastly wise and prudent principle—a great safeguard to its possessor. Men have committed murder for jealousy's sake, and anger's sake, and hatred's sake, and selfishness' sake, and spiritual pride's sake; but no man, that ever I heard of, ever committed a diabolical murder for sweet charity's sake. Mere self-interest, then, if no better motive can be enlisted, should, especially with high-tempered men, prompt all beings to charity and philanthropy. At any rate, upon the occasion in question, I strove to drown my exasperated feelings towards the scrivener by benevolently construing his conduct. Poor fellow, poor fellow! thought I, he don't mean anything; and besides, he has seen hard times and ought to be indulged.

I endeavored, also, immediately to occupy myself, and at the same time to comfort my despondency. I tried to fancy that in the course of the morning, at such time as might prove agreeable to him, Bartleby of his own free accord would emerge from his hermitage and take up some decided line of march in the direction of the door. But no. Half-past twelve o'clock came; Turkey began to glow in the face, overturn his inkstand, and become generally obstreperous; Nippers abated down into quietude and courtesy; Ginger Nut munched his noon apple; and Bartleby remained standing at his window in one of his profoundest dead-wall reveries. Will it be credited? Ought I to acknowledge it? That afternoon I left the office without saying one further word to him.

Some days now passed, during which at leisure intervals I looked a little into "Edwards on the Will,"[19] and "Priestley on Necessity."[20] Under the circumstances, those books induced a salutary feeling. Gradually I slid into the persuasion that these troubles of mine, touching the scrivener, had been all predestined from eternity, and Bartleby was billeted upon me for some mysterious purpose of an all-wise Providence, which it was not for a mere mortal like me to fathom. Yes, Bartleby, stay there behind your screen, thought I; I shall persecute you no more; you are harmless and noiseless as any of these old chairs; in short, I never feel so private as when I know you are here. At last I see it, I feel it; I penetrate to the predestinated purpose of my life. I am content. Others may have loftier parts to enact; but my mission in this world, Bartleby, is to furnish you with office room for such period as you may see fit to remain.

I believe that this wise and blessed frame of mind would have continued with me had it not been for the unsolicited and uncharitable remarks obtruded upon me by my profes-

sional friends who visited the rooms. But thus it often is, that the constant friction of illiberal minds wears out at last the best resolves of the more generous. Though to be sure, when I reflected upon it, it was not strange that people entering my office should be struck by the peculiar aspect of the unaccountable Bartleby, and so be tempted to throw out some sinister observations concerning him. Sometimes an attorney, having business with me and calling at my office and finding no one but the scrivener there, would undertake to obtain some sort of precise information from him touching my whereabouts; but without heeding his idle talk, Bartleby would remain standing immovable in the middle of the room. So after contemplating him in that position, for a time, the attorney would depart, no wiser than he came.

Also, when a reference[21] was going on, and the room full of lawyers and witnesses, and business driving fast, some deeply occupied legal gentleman present, seeing Bartleby wholly unemployed, would request him to run round to his (the legal gentleman's) office and fetch some papers for him. Thereupon, Bartleby would tranquilly decline and yet remain idle as before. Then the lawyer would give a great stare and turn to me. And what could I say? At last I was made aware that all through the circle of my professional acquaintance a whisper of wonder was running round, having reference to the strange creature I kept at my office. This worried me very much. And as the idea came upon me of his possibly turning out a long-lived man, and keep occupying my chambers, and denying my authority; and perplexing my visitors; and scandalizing my professional reputation; and casting a general gloom over the premis-

19. **"Edwards on the Will,"** Jonathan Edwards (1703–1758), a famous Puritan minister, wrote *Freedom of the Will.*
20. **"Priestley on Necessity,"** Joseph Priestley (1733–1804), the British chemist who discovered oxygen, wrote books on philosophy.
21. **reference,** meeting between lawyers.

es; keeping soul and body together to the last upon his savings (for doubtless he spent but half a dime a day), and in the end perhaps outlive me, and claim possession of my office by right of his perpetual occupancy: as all these dark anticipations crowded upon me more and more, and my friends continually intruded their relentless remarks upon the apparition in my room; a great change was wrought in me. I resolved to gather all my faculties together and forever rid me of this intolerable incubus.

Ere revolving any complicated project, however, adapted to this end, I first simply suggested to Bartleby the propriety of his permanent departure. In a calm and serious tone, I commended the idea to his careful and mature consideration. But having taken three days to meditate upon it, he apprised me that his original determination remained the same; in short, that he still preferred to abide with me.

What shall I do? I now said to myself, buttoning up my coat to the last button. What shall I do? what ought I to do? what does conscience say I *should* do with this man, or, rather, ghost? Rid myself of him, I must; go, he shall. But how? You will not thrust him, the poor, pale, passive mortal—you will not thrust such a helpless creature out of your door? you will not dishonor yourself by such cruelty? No, I will not, I cannot do that. Rather would I let him live and die here, and then mason up his remains in the wall. What, then, will you do? For all your coaxing, he will not budge. Bribes he leaves under your own paperweight on your table; in short, it is quite plain that he prefers to cling to you.

Then something severe, something unusual must be done. What! Surely you will not have him collared by a constable and commit his innocent pallor to the common jail? And upon what ground could you procure such a thing to be done?—a vagrant, a wanderer, who refuses to budge? It is because he will *not* be a vagrant, then, that you seek to count him *as* a vagrant. That is too absurd. No visible means of support: there I have him. Wrong again: for indubitably he *does* support himself, and that is the only unanswerable proof that any man can show of his possessing the means so to do. No more, then. Since he will not quit me, I must quit him. I will change my offices; I will move elsewhere and give him fair notice that if I find him on my new premises I will then proceed against him as a common trespasser.

Acting accordingly, next day I thus addressed him: "I find these chambers too far from the city hall; the air is unwholesome. In a word, I propose to remove my offices next week and shall no longer require your services. I tell you this now, in order that you may seek another place."

He made no reply, and nothing more was said.

On the appointed day I engaged carts and men, proceeded to my chambers, and having but little furniture, everything was removed in a few hours. Throughout, the scrivener remained standing behind the screen, which I directed to be removed the last thing. It was withdrawn; and being folded up like a huge folio,[22] left him the motionless occupant of a naked room. I stood in the entry watching him a moment, while something from within me upbraided me.

I re-entered, with my hand in my pocket —and—and my heart in my mouth.

"Good-bye, Bartleby; I am going—good-bye, and God some way bless you; and take that," slipping something in his hand. But it dropped upon the floor, and then—strange to say—I tore myself from him whom I had so longed to be rid of.

Established in my new quarters, for a day or two I kept the door locked and started at every footfall in the passages. When I returned to my rooms after any little absence, I would pause at the threshold for an instant

---

22. **folio,** book whose pages are over 11 inches in height.

and attentively listen ere applying my key. But these fears were needless. Bartleby never came nigh me.

I thought all was going well, when a perturbed-looking stranger visited me, inquiring whether I was the person who had recently occupied rooms at No.—Wall Street.

Full of forebodings, I replied that I was.

"Then, sir," said the stranger, who proved a lawyer, "you are responsible for the man you left there. He refuses to do any copying; he refuses to do anything; and he says he prefers not to; and he refuses to quit the premises."

"I am very sorry, sir," said I, with assumed tranquility, but an inward tremor, "but really, the man you allude to is nothing to me—he is no relation or apprentice of mine, that you should hold me responsible for him."

"In mercy's name, who is he?"

"I certainly cannot inform you. I know nothing about him. Formerly I employed him as a copyist; but he has done nothing for me now for some time past."

"I shall settle him, then—good morning, sir."

Several days passed, and I heard nothing more; and though I often felt a charitable prompting to call at the place and see poor Bartleby, yet a certain squeamishness of I know not what, withheld me.

All is over with him by this time, thought I at last, when through another week, no further intelligence reached me. But coming to my room the day after, I found several persons waiting at my door in a high state of nervous excitement.

"That's the man—here he comes," cried the foremost one, whom I recognized as the lawyer who had previously called upon me alone.

"You must take him away, sir, at once," cried a portly person among them, advancing upon me, and whom I knew to be the landlord of No.—Wall Street. "These gentlemen, my tenants, cannot stand it any longer; Mr. B———," pointing to the lawyer, "has turned him out of his room, and he now persists in haunting the building generally, sitting upon the banisters of the stairs by day, and sleeping in the entry by night. Everybody is concerned; clients are leaving the offices; some fears are entertained of a mob; something you must do, and that without delay."

Aghast at this torrent, I fell back before it and would fain have locked myself in my new quarters. In vain I persisted that Bartleby was nothing to me—no more than to any one else. In vain—I was the last person known to have anything to do with him, and they held me to the terrible account. Fearful, then, of being exposed in the papers (as one person present obscurely threatened), I considered the matter, and at length said that if the lawyer would give me a confidential interview with the scrivener in his (the lawyer's) own room, I would, that afternoon, strive my best to rid them of the nuisance they complained of.

Going upstairs to my old haunt, there was Bartleby silently sitting upon the banister at the landing.

"What are you doing here, Bartleby?" said I.

"Sitting upon the banister," he mildly replied.

I motioned him into the lawyer's room, who then left us.

"Bartleby," said I, "are you aware that you are the cause of great tribulation to me by persisting in occupying the entry after being dismissed from the office?"

No answer.

"Now one of two things must take place. Either you must do something, or something must be done to you. Now what sort of business would you like to engage in? Would you like to re-engage in copying for some one?"

"No; I would prefer not to make any change."

"Would you like a clerkship in a dry goods store?"

"There is too much confinement about

that. No, I would not like a clerkship; but I am not particular."

"Too much confinement," I cried, "why you keep yourself confined all the time!"

"I would prefer not to take a clerkship," he rejoined, as if to settle that little item at once.

"How would a bartender's business suit you? There is no trying of the eyesight in that."

"I would not like it at all; though as I said before, I am not particular."

His unwonted wordiness inspirited me. I returned to the charge.

"Well, then, would you like to travel through the country collecting bills for the merchants? That would improve your health."

"No, I would prefer to be doing something else."

"How, then, would going as a companion to Europe, to entertain some young gentleman with your conversation—how would that suit you?"

"Not at all. It does not strike me that there is anything definite about that. I like to be stationary. But I am not particular."

"Stationary you shall be, then," I cried, now losing all patience, and for the first time in all my exasperating connection with him, fairly flying into a passion. "If you do not go away from these premises before night I shall feel bound—indeed, I *am* bound—to—to—to quit the premises myself!" I rather absurdly concluded, knowing not with what possible threat to try to frighten his immobility into compliance. Despairing of all further efforts, I was precipitately leaving him, when a final thought occurred to me—one which had not been wholly unindulged before.

"Bartleby," said I, in the kindest tone I could assume under such exciting circumstances, "will you go home with me now—not to my office, but to my dwelling—and remain there till we can conclude upon some convenient arrangement for you at our leisure? Come, let us start now, right away."

"No: at present I would prefer not to make any change at all."

I answered nothing; but effectually dodging every one by the suddenness and rapidity of my flight, rushed from the building, ran up Wall Street toward Broadway, and jumping into the first omnibus, was soon removed from pursuit. As soon as tranquility returned, I distinctly perceived that I had now done all that I possibly could, both in respect to the demands of the landlord and his tenants and with regard to my own desire and sense of duty, to benefit Bartleby and shield him from rude persecution. I now strove to be entirely carefree and quiescent; and my conscience justified me in the attempt; though, indeed, it was not so successful as I could have wished. So fearful was I of being again hunted out by the incensed landlord and his exasperated tenants that, surrendering my business to Nippers for a few days, I drove about the upper part of the town and through the suburbs in my rockaway,[23] crossed over to Jersey City and Hoboken and paid fugitive visits to Manhattanville and Astoria. In fact, I almost lived in my rockaway for the time.

When again I entered my office, lo, a note from the landlord lay upon the desk. I opened it with trembling hands. It informed me that the writer had sent to the police and had Bartleby removed to the Tombs as a vagrant. Moreover, since I knew more about him than any one else, he wished me to appear at that place and make a suitable statement of the facts. These tidings had a conflicting effect upon me. At first I was indignant; but at last almost approved. The landlord's energetic, summary disposition had led him to adopt a procedure which I do not think I would have decided upon myself, and yet, as a last resort, under such peculiar circumstances, it seemed the only plan.

As I afterwards learned, the poor scrivener, when told that he must be conducted to the Tombs, offered not the slightest obstacle,

---

23. **rockaway,** four-wheeled carriage seating two.

but in his pale, unmoving way, silently acquiesced.

Some of the compassionate and curious bystanders joined the party; and headed by one of the constables, arm in arm with Bartleby, the silent procession filed its way through all the noise, and heat, and joy of the roaring thoroughfares at noon.

The same day I received the note I went to the Tombs, or to speak more properly, the Halls of Justice. Seeking the right officer, I stated the purpose of my call and was informed that the individual I described was, indeed, within. I then assured the functionary that Bartleby was a perfectly honest man, and greatly to be compassionated, however unaccountably eccentric. I narrated all I knew, and closed by suggesting the idea of letting him remain in as indulgent confinement as possible till something less harsh might be done—though, indeed, I hardly knew what. At all events, if nothing else could be decided upon, the almshouse must receive him. I then begged to have an interview.

Being under no disgraceful charge, and quite serene and harmless in all his ways, they had permitted him freely to wander about the prison and especially in the enclosed grass-plotted yards thereof. And so I found him there, standing all alone in the quietest of the yards, his face toward a high wall, while all around, from the narrow slits of the jail windows, I thought I saw peering out upon him the eyes of murderers and thieves.

"Bartleby!"

"I know you," he said, without looking round—"and I want nothing to say to you."

"It was not I that brought you here, Bartleby," said I, keenly pained at his implied suspicion. "And to you, this should not be so vile a place. Nothing reproachful attaches to you by being here. And see, it is not so sad a place as one might think. Look, there is the sky, and here is the grass."

"I know where I am," he replied, but would say nothing more, and so I left him.

As I entered the corridor again, a broad, meatlike man in an apron accosted me, and jerking his thumb over his shoulder said—"Is that your friend?"

"Yes."

"Does he want to starve? If he does, let him live on the prison fare, that's all."

"Who are you?" asked I, not knowing what to make of such an unofficially speaking person in such a place.

"I am the grub-man. Such gentlemen as have friends here, hire me to provide them with something good to eat."

"Is this so?" said I, turning to the turnkey.

He said it was.

"Well then," said I, slipping some silver into the grub-man's hands (for so they called him), "I want you to give particular attention to my friend there; let him have the best dinner you can get. And you must be as polite to him as possible."

"Introduce me, will you?" said the grub-man, looking at me with an expression which seemed to say he was all impatience for an opportunity to give a specimen of his breeding.

Thinking it would prove of benefit to the scrivener, I acquiesced; and asking the grub-man his name, went up with him to Bartleby.

"Bartleby, this is a friend; you will find him very useful to you."

"Your sarvant, sir, your sarvant," said the grub-man, making a low salutation behind his apron. "Hope you find it pleasant here, sir; nice grounds—cool apartments—hope you'll stay with us some time—try to make it agreeable. What will you have for dinner today?"

"I prefer not to dine today," said Bartleby, turning away. "It would disagree with me; I am unused to dinners." So saying, he slowly moved to the other side of the enclosure and took up a position fronting the dead wall.

"How's this?" said the grub-man, addressing me with a stare of astonishment. "He's odd, ain't he?"

"I think he is a little deranged," said I, sadly.

"Deranged? Deranged is it? Well, now, upon my word, I thought that friend of yourn was a gentleman forger; they are always pale and genteel-like, them forgers. I can't help pity 'em—can't help it, sir. Did you know Monroe Edwards?" he added touchingly and paused. Then, laying his hand piteously on my shoulder, sighed, "He died of consumption at Sing Sing. So you weren't acquainted with Monroe?"

"No, I was never socially acquainted with any forgers. But I cannot stop longer. Look to my friend yonder. You will not lose by it. I will see you again."

Some few days after this, I again obtained admission to the Tombs and went through the corridors in quest of Bartleby; but without finding him.

"I saw him coming from his cell not long ago," said a turnkey, "maybe he's gone to loiter in the yards."

So I went in that direction.

"Are you looking for the silent man?" said another turnkey, passing me. "Yonder he lies—sleeping in the yard there. 'Tis not twenty minutes since I saw him lie down."

The yard was entirely quiet. It was not accessible to the common prisoners. The surrounding walls, of amazing thickness, kept off all sounds behind them. The Egyptian character of the masonry weighed me with its gloom. But a soft imprisoned turf grew under foot. The heart of the eternal pyramids, it seemed, wherein by some strange magic, through the clefts, grass seed dropped by birds had sprung.

Strangely huddled at the base of the wall, his knees drawn up and lying on his side, his head touching the cold stones, I saw the wasted Bartleby. But nothing stirred. I paused; then went close up to him; stooped over and saw that his dim eyes were open; otherwise he seemed profoundly sleeping. Something prompted me to touch him. I felt his hand, when a tingling shiver ran up my arm and down my spine to my feet.

The round face of the grub-man peered upon me now. "His dinner is ready. Won't he dine today, either? Or does he live without dining?"

"Lives without dining," said I, and closed the eyes.

"Eh!—He's asleep, ain't he?"

"With kings and counselors,"[24] murmured I.

There would seem little need for proceeding further in this history. Imagination will readily supply the meager recital of poor Bartleby's interment. But ere parting with the reader, let me say that if this little narrative has sufficiently interested him to awaken curiosity as to who Bartleby was and what manner of life he led prior to the present narrator's making his acquaintance, I can only reply that in such curiosity I fully share, but am wholly unable to gratify it. Yet here I hardly know whether I should divulge one little item of rumor, which came to my ear a few months after the scrivener's decease. Upon what basis it rested, I could never ascertain; and hence, how true it is I cannot now tell. But inasmuch as this vague report has not been without a certain suggestive interest to me, however sad, it may prove the same with some others; and so I will briefly mention it. The report was this: that Bartleby had been a subordinate clerk in the Dead Letter Office at Washington, from which he had been suddenly removed by a change in the administration. When I think over this rumor, hardly can I express the emotions which seize me. Dead Letters! Does it not sound like dead men? Conceive a man by nature and misfortune prone to a pallid hopelessness, can any business seem more fitted to heighten it than that of continually handling these dead letters and assorting them for the flames? For by the cartload they are annually burned. Sometimes from out the folded paper the pale clerk takes a ring—the finger it was meant for, perhaps, molders in the grave; a bank note sent in swiftest charity—he whom it

---

24. **With kings and counselors,** a reference to Job 3:13-14 meaning that Bartleby is dead.

would relieve, nor eats nor hungers any more; pardon for those who died despairing; hope for those who died unhoping; good tidings for those who died stifled by unrelieved calamities. On errands of life, these letters speed to death.

Ah, Bartleby! Ah, humanity!

FOR UNDERSTANDING

1. What is a "scrivener"?

2. To what "vague report" in the "sequel" does the narrator refer at the end of the first paragraph?

3. What is the profession of the narrator?

4. What are the nicknames of the three other employees and how did they get them?

5. Why does the narrator need to hire additional help?

FOR INTERPRETATION

At one point in the story the narrator notes that Bartleby is "more a man of preferences than assumptions." Consider some of the implications stemming from Bartleby's preferences and the narrator's "doctrine of assumptions." It is generally *assumed* that persons will do what is expected of them. Indeed, it would seem as though society functions on the basis of such assumptions. Police officers are supposed to pursue lawbreakers; nurses are expected to care for the sick; it is assumed that business people will try to satisfy their customers and make profits; we could go on and on. Normally human beings act according to such assumptions and society runs smoothly.

But where do such assumptions leave the individual? Are we nothing more than the sum of the expectations of others? Are we bound by others' assumptions and not free to act on the basis of our preferences? Notice precisely what it is assumed that Bartleby will do (and cheerfully!): he will spend the greater part of his waking hours, six days a week, slavishly copying words and then go through them all a second time to make sure he has not miscopied any. During those hours he will "live" in a little cubicle, isolated from everyone, his only view of the outside world being a "dead" wall. In short, walled in on Wall Street, Bartleby is being dehumanized by a system of assumptions that

leaves no room for human preference. In his "I would prefer not to," he is reaffirming his independence against the very warp and woof of the social fabric.

1. Orally or in writing, answer one or more of the following questions, as your teacher directs.

  a. Why does Melville use the subtitle, "A Story of Wall Street"?

  b. Since the basic conflict of the story revolves around Bartleby and the narrator, why does Melville spend so much time in the opening discussing Turkey and Nippers?

  c. In what sense is Bartleby not "ordinarily human"?

  d. What is the "paramount consideration" (p. 262) that forms the basis of Bartleby's actions throughout the story?

  e. What do you make of the narrator's description of Bartleby as a "valuable acquisition"? Why did Melville choose those words to put in the narrator's mouth?

2. Be prepared to state and justify your opinions, pro or con, of the following statements:

  a. Melville's sympathies are basically with the narrator rather than with Bartleby.

  b. It is the narrator's fault that Bartleby is sent to the Tombs and dies there.

  c. Bartleby is actually a strong person, for it takes courage to buck the system.

  d. If everyone lived by preferences, society as we know it would collapse.

  e. The injunction "love one another" is generally ignored by people in the world of business and finance.

FOR APPRECIATION

Conflict

The initial moment of the conflict between the narrator and Bartleby is the latter's assertion, "I would prefer not to." This statement shocks the narrator at first, for he is a person of assumptions, and he assumes, as an employer, that he will be obeyed. Nevertheless, for some period of time it appears that Bartleby will gain the upper hand and prevail. For example, others, including the narrator, begin using the word *prefer;* and at one point, the narrator even decides to accept Bartleby on his own terms. What happens to turn the situation in the opposite direction?

Although Bartleby and the narrator are the

chief characters in the conflict, each seems to represent a force larger than himself. What are those two forces?

Climax

One climax occurs when the narrator leaves Bartleby in the bare room. How do you know that this is not to be the final climax? A second climax, which is the major one, is Bartleby's death. Of what significance, at that time, is the narrator's comment that his scrivener is asleep "with kings and counselors"? Can you connect this phrase with the fact that Bartleby is in the Tombs?

Moment of Illumination

The story finally ends with the words, "Ah, Bartleby! Ah, humanity!" These words in the story are not in quotation marks; thus it is almost as if they were spoken by Melville himself rather than by the narrator. How does this great sighing statement illuminate the meaning of the story?

In connection with this closing, we might observe that, at the time Melville wrote this story, he was in desperate financial and emotional straits. His readers had assumed that he would continue to write the kind of popular adventure stories— like *Typee* and *Omoo*—that had made him well-known. But Melville preferred to pour his energies into profoundly probing books like *Moby-Dick* and *Pierre*, both of which were dismal failures from a financial point of view.

Can you relate this biographical detail to the full meaning of the story? What does it tell you about those famous, final words—"Ah, Bartleby! Ah, humanity!"

LANGUAGE AND VOCABULARY

"Bartleby the Scrivener" is told from a first-person point of view. That is, the teller uses the pronouns *I, me, my, mine, myself*—the "first-person" pronouns. Whenever a writer decides to have a character tell a story in the first person, the author has to make the character sound like the kind of person she or he is. The narrator of "Bartleby" is a lawyer, and Melville succeeds in making him talk like a lawyer.

Melville accomplishes this in a variety of ways. For one thing, the narrator is a bit wordy and long-winded. (The third sentence below, for example, is fifty-nine words long.) But a major consideration is the vocabulary of the character. For the italicized words and phrases in the following excerpt from the end of the story, try to find more ordinary words or phrases to replace the "lawyerish" terms of the narrator.

There would seem little need for (1) *proceeding* further in this (2) *history*. Imagination will readily supply the meager (3) *recital* of poor Bartleby's (4) *interment*. But ere parting with the reader, let me say that if this little narrative has sufficiently interested him to awaken curiosity as to who Bartleby was and what manner of life he led (5) *prior to* (6) *the present narrator's* (7) *making his acquaintance,* I can only reply that in such curiosity I fully share, but am wholly unable to (8) *gratify* it. Yet here I hardly know whether I should (9) *divulge* one little item of rumor, which (10) *came to my ear* a few months after the scrivener's (11) *decease.* Upon what basis it rested, I could never (12) *ascertain;* and hence, how true it is I cannot now tell.

Henry Wadsworth Longfellow 1807–1882

In the latter half of the nineteenth century, the name Henry Wadsworth Longfellow was almost synonymous with the term "poet" in American minds. Not only was he read by virtually every American who read anything more than a newspaper, he was also translated into more than two dozen foreign languages. Toward the end of his career, in fact, he was probably the best known living poet in the world. Today, although Longfellow is much less widely read than he was at the beginning of our century, many of his works remain inscribed on the consciousness of Americans. Have you heard of "Paul Revere's Ride," "The Children's Hour," "The Wreck of the Hesperus," *The Song of Hiawatha,* "The Village Blacksmith," *Evangeline,* or *The Courtship of Miles Standish?* All were written by Henry Wadsworth Longfellow.

Although Longfellow is associated with Cambridge, the college town outside of Boston, he was born in Portland, Maine, and he went to college at Bowdoin in his native state. His alma mater offered him a position as a teacher of modern languages, and after spending a few years abroad, where he gained a firsthand experience of the languages he would teach, he began his teaching career in 1829, at the age of twenty-two.

After teaching at Bowdoin for five years, he took a year off to travel abroad again and returned to initiate a long teaching career at Harvard. For eighteen years he taught modern languages there, finally resigning in 1854 after he felt quite sure he could support himself and his family by writing poems.

Although Longfellow had begun writing poetry in his youth, he did not publish his first collection—*Voices of the Night*—until 1839, when he was over thirty years old. But fame came quickly once he started. His second book, *Ballads and Other Poems,* appeared in 1841, and it contained such all-time favorites as "The Village Blacksmith," "Excelsior," "The Wreck of the Hesperus," and "The Skeleton in Armor." His reputation was considerably enhanced by such

PORTRAIT OF HENRY WADSWORTH LONGFELLOW
Theodore Wust
National Portrait Gallery, Smithsonian Institution

long narrative poems as *Evangeline* (1847) and *The Song of Hiawatha* (1855). *The Courtship of Miles Standish* (1858) sold more than 15,000 copies on its day of publication in Boston and London. A highly successful later work was his collection of narratives, *Tales of a Wayside Inn* (1863), which contains the famous poem "Paul Revere's Ride."

Longfellow's personal life was marked by a number of long and strong friendships, several with well-known people, such as Charles Sumner, a famous liberal politician who served in the United States Senate; the poet James Russell Lowell; and Jean Louis Agassiz, the famed scientist and professor of natural history at Harvard. Longfellow, whose first wife, Mary Potter, had died in 1835, married again in 1843. His second wife was Frances Appleton, the daughter of one of the wealthiest men in Boston. When the couple married, Longfellow's father-in-law gave them a mansion, Craigie House, as a wedding gift. Unfortunately, Mrs. Longfellow died tragically in a fire in 1861. Her husband never quite recovered from the loss, though he wrote some of his best lyric poetry in his later years.

Longfellow wrote on common themes and used conventional metrical forms. He was not an innovator, and today he does not have the reputation of the more innovative poets of his day, like Emily Dickinson and Walt Whitman. Longfellow was also an antiquarian, and he rarely addressed contemporary issues. Nevertheless, he won such a place in the heart of Americans that not to know Longfellow is not to know our country. Whatever value we may put on his work, it has a way, once we have heard it, of staying alive in the chambers of our minds.

The Arsenal at Springfield

This is the Arsenal. From floor to ceiling,
    Like a huge organ, rise the burnished arms;
But from their silent pipes no anthem pealing
    Startles the villages with strange alarms.

Ah! what a sound will rise, how wild and dreary,   5
    When the death-angel touches those swift keys!
What loud lament and dismal Miserere[1]
    Will mingle with their awful symphonies!

I hear even now the infinite fierce chorus,
    The cries of agony, the endless groan,   10
Which, through the ages that have gone before us,
    In long reverberations reach our own.

On helm and harness rings the Saxon hammer,
    Through Cimbric[2] forest roars the Norseman's song,
And loud, amid the universal clamor,   15
    O'er distant deserts sounds the Tartar[3] gong.

1. **Miserere** (miz ə rer′ ē), the 51st Psalm in the Vulgate, the 50th in the Douay Bible: the first word of the Latin Version; "Have mercy!" This psalm is frequently recited in services for the dead.
2. **Cimbric** (sim′ brik), pertaining to Germanic people of central Europe, defeated in northern Italy, 101 B.C.
3. **Tartar,** refers to the Tartars who ruled Tartary, a region of Asia and eastern Europe, in the thirteenth and fourteenth centuries and who reached their greatest power under Genghis Khan.

From HENRY WADSWORTH LONGFELLOW, POETICAL WORKS, Houghton Mifflin and Company, The Riverside Press, Cambridge, 1904.

I hear the Florentine, who from his palace
  Wheels out his battle-bell with dreadful din,
And Aztec priests upon their toecallis[4]
  Beat the wild war-drums made of serpent's skin;   20

The tumult of each sacked and burning village;
  The shout that every prayer for mercy drowns;
The soldiers' revels in the midst of pillage;
  The wail of famine in beleaguered towns;

The bursting shell, the gateway wrenched asunder,   25
  The rattling musketry, the clashing blade;
And ever and anon, in tones of thunder,
  The diapason[5] of the cannonade.

Is it, O man, with such discordant noises,
  With such accursed instruments as these,   30
Thou drownest Nature's sweet and kindly voices,
  And jarrest the celestial harmonies?

Were half the power, that fills the world with terror,
  Were half the wealth bestowed on camps and courts,
Given to redeem the human mind from error,   35
  There were no need of arsenals or forts:

The warrior's name would be a name abhorred!
  And every nation, that should lift again
Its hand against a brother, on its forehead
  Would wear forevermore the curse of Cain!   40

Down the dark future, through long generations,
  The echoing sounds grow fainter and then cease;
And like a bell, with solemn, sweet vibrations,
  I hear once more the voice of Christ say, "Peace!"

Peace! and no longer from its brazen portals   45
  The blast of War's great organ shakes the skies!
But beautiful as songs of the immortals,
  The holy melodies of love arise.

4. **teocallis** (tē ə ka′ lis), temples erected by ancient
Mexicans and Central Americans.
5. **diapason** (dī ə pā′ zn), in general, a vast, majestic
production of sound. Specifically, on an organ a principal flue stop extending through the instrument's complete scale.

*To understand this poem fully, you need to know that Longfellow undertook the
enormously difficult task of translating Dante's* Divine Comedy *from Italian to
English as a means of dealing with his grief over his second wife's death. His grief is
the "burden" he refers to in line 10 of this sonnet, one of six he wrote on the* Divine
Comedy *during the years he spent translating that long poetic work. In the same
line, the "minster gate," which literally means a church gate, refers to the book he is
translating.*

Divina Commedia I

Oft have I seen at some cathedral door
    A laborer, pausing in the dust and heat,
    Lay down his burden, and with reverent feet
    Enter, and cross himself, and on the floor
Kneel to repeat his paternoster[1] o'er;   5
    Far off the noises of the world retreat;
    The loud vociferations[2] of the street
    Become an undistinguishable roar.
So, as I enter here from day to day,
    And leave my burden at this minster gate,   10
    Kneeling in prayer, and not ashamed to pray,
The tumult of the time disconsolate
    To inarticulate murmurs dies away,
    While the eternal ages watch and wait.

1. **paternoster** (pat' ər nos' tər),   the Lord's Prayer.
2. **vociferations** (vō sif ə rā' shənz),   noisy cries.

The Tide Rises, the Tide Falls

The tide rises, the tide falls,
The twilight darkens, the curlew[1] calls;
Along the sea-sands damp and brown
The traveller hastens toward the town,
    And the tide rises, the tide falls.   5

Darkness settles on roofs and walls,
But the sea, the sea in the darkness calls;

1. **curlew** (kėr' lü),   a wading bird with a long, thin bill.

This tranquil country scene reflects the mood of peace and plenty that characterized America in the first half of the 1800s. The painter was a contemporary of Longfellow and, like the poet, traveled widely abroad.

LANDSCAPE
George Inness
National Academy of Design
New York City

The little waves, with their soft, white hands,
Efface the footprints in the sands,
　And the tide rises, the tide falls.　　　10

The morning breaks; the steeds in their stalls
Stamp and neigh, as the hostler[2] calls;
The day returns, but nevermore
Returns the traveller to the shore,
　And the tide rises, the tide falls.　　　15

2. **hostler** (os′ lər),   person who takes care of horses at an inn or stable.

OYSTER SLOOP (detail), Childe Hassam
National Gallery of Art, Washington, D.C., Ailsa Mellon Bruce Collection

UNDERSTANDING AND APPRECIATION

"The Arsenal at Springfield"

1. What basic comparison is carried throughout the poem?
2. Why does the speaker go back in time to the Saxons, Tartars, etc.?
3. What is the speaker's suggestion for the avoidance of war?
4. What prediction does the speaker make?

"Divina Commedia I"

1. Why is it appropriate for the poet to compare himself to a laborer?
2. What basic comparison between the poet and the laborer is being made?

3. Where is "here" (line 9)?
4. What is the grammatical subject of "dies away" in line 13?
5. What are the "eternal ages" watching and waiting for?

"The Tide Rises, the Tide Falls"

1. The main pause in a line of poetry is called the *caesura.* It is dictated by meaning or by natural speech rhythm, and it may or may not be indicated by punctuation. In this poem, the caesuras are very strongly marked for the most part. Can you tell why?
2. How does the title of the poem foreshadow the fact that the traveler will not return?
3. Why do you suppose the traveler will not return?

John Greenleaf Whittier   1807–1892

John Greenleaf Whittier was born in the same year as Henry Wadsworth Longfellow and two years before Oliver Wendell Holmes, the next poet you will study. He knew both of them; in fact, the last poem he wrote was addressed to Holmes. Like them, too, he was born and raised in Massachusetts, though Whittier came from East Haverhill, a farming community north of Boston near the New Hampshire border. Also, like Longfellow and Holmes, Whittier was a so-called fireside poet.

But while Whittier is often mentioned in the same breath as Longfellow and Holmes, the differences between him and them are more profound than the similarities. For one thing, Whittier was born poor and remained so a good part of his life. And quite unlike the other fireside poets, he had virtually no formal education. He managed only about a year in the local academy and had no college education at all. Lastly, while they stood somewhat apart from most serious contemporary social causes, Whittier was elected to the state legislature twice—in 1835 and 1836—and he devoted about forty years of his life to the abolition of slavery.

Whittier's career as a poet may be divided into three parts. From his boyhood (he was first published in a local paper when he was eighteen) to 1832, he wrote imitative verse, which even he later recognized as bad. Some of these verses were influenced by his love of the works of the Scottish poet Robert Burns, whom he began to read at the age of fourteen. The second stage, from 1833 to about 1860, was his political phase. He wrote poems about political reforms during this period, including hosts of antislavery poems. In the latter part of this period (from 1847 to 1860), most of Whittier's writing— reviews, editorials, sketches, and letters, as well as poems—was published in *The National Era,* the weekly newspaper established by the American and Foreign Anti-Slavery Society. This paper published serially (1851–1852) Harriet Beecher Stowe's famous novel, *Uncle Tom's Cabin.*

PORTRAIT OF JOHN GREENLEAF WHITTIER
National Portrait Gallery
Smithsonian Institution

Finally, from 1860 to the end of his long life, Whittier was primarily a poet of nature, religion, and everyday life. It was during this time that most of his best-known poetry was published, including *Snow-Bound* (1866), which brought him great acclaim and even a modest, steady income. John Greenleaf Whittier was a Quaker and a man of deep spiritual convictions. This aspect of his character is also pronounced in the work of the last thirty-odd years of his life, enriching it considerably. His last words were said to have been, "Love to all the world."

from **Snow-Bound**

A Winter Idyl

The sun that brief December day
Rose cheerless over hills of gray,
And, darkly circled, gave at noon
A sadder light than waning moon.
Slow tracing down the thickening sky   5
Its mute and ominous prophecy,
A portent seeming less than threat,
It sank from sight before it set.
A chill no coat, however stout,
Of homespun stuff could quite shut out,   10
A hard, dull bitterness of cold,
That checked, mid-vein, the circling race
Of life-blood in the sharpened face,
The coming of the snow-storm told.
The wind blew east; we heard the roar   15
Of Ocean on his wintry shore,
And felt the strong pulse throbbing there
Beat with low rhythm our inland air.

Meanwhile we did our nightly chores,—
Brought in the wood from out of doors,   20
Littered the stalls, and from the mows[1]
Raked down the herd's-grass for the cows;
Heard the horse whinnying for his corn;
And, sharply clashing horn on horn,
Impatient down the stanchion[2] rows   25
The cattle shake their walnut bows;
While peering from his early perch
Upon the scaffold's pole of birch,
The cock his crested helmet bent
And down his querulous challenge sent.   30

Unwarmed by any sunset light
The gray day darkened into night,

1. **mows,**   places in a barn where hay or grain is piled.
2. **stanchion** (stan' shən),   framework which is fastened
loosely around the neck of a cow to keep her in place in a
stall.
3. **hoary** (hôr' ē),   white or gray.

From THE COMPLETE POETICAL WORK OF WHITTIER, Houghton
Mifflin, Boston, Cambridge Edition, The Riverside Press, 1894.

POESTENKILL, NEW YORK, WINTER
Joseph H. Hidley
Abby Aldrich Rockefeller Folk Art Center,
Williamsburg, Va.

A night made hoary[3] with the swarm
And whirl-dance of the blinding storm,
As zigzag, wavering to and fro,   35
Crossed and recrossed the wingèd snow:
And ere the early bedtime came
The white drift piled the window-frame,
And through the glass the clothes-line posts
Looked in like tall and sheeted ghosts.   40

So all night long the storm roared on:
The morning broke without a sun;
In tiny spherule[4] traced with lines
Of Nature's geometric signs,

4. **spherule** (sfir′ ül),   a small sphere.
5. **pellicle** (pel′ ə kəl),   very thin skin or membrane.

WINTER SCENE IN BROOKLYN (detail), Francis Guy
The Brooklyn Museum, Brooklyn, NY
Gift of the Brooklyn Institute of Arts and Sciences

In starry flake, and pellicle,⁵   **45**
All day the hoary meteor fell;
And, when the second morning shone,
We looked upon a world unknown,
On nothing we could call our own.
Around the glistening wonder bent   **50**
The blue walls of the firmament,
No cloud above, no earth below,—
A universe of sky and snow!

UNDERSTANDING AND INTERPRETATION

1. How many beats are there in each line? Describe the rhythm of the poem in technical terms.
2. What is the basic rhyme scheme? Find a variation from this in the first stanza. Find another in the fourth stanza.

3. Study the verb forms in the second stanza. Be prepared to discuss how most of them help to create a vivid picture.
4. Interpret these lines from stanza 4, lines 47–49:

And, when the second morning shone,
We looked upon a world unknown,
On nothing we could call our own.

Oliver Wendell Holmes   1809–1894

Oliver Wendell Holmes was born in Cambridge, Massachusetts, and remained in that relatively small college town across the river from Boston most of his life. Graduating from Harvard College at the age of nineteen, he first decided to study law. Soon, however, medicine became his chosen field, and after two-and-a-half years of studying in Paris hospitals, he returned to the United States and received an M.D. from the Harvard Medical School in 1836. Although he had gained national recognition as a poet for "Old Ironsides," a poem that he wrote when he was only twenty-one, he did not publish his first book of poems until the same year he graduated from medical school.

Holmes set up practice as a doctor, but his real first love was teaching. Between 1838 and 1840, he was professor of anatomy at Dartmouth College. Then from 1847 to 1882, he was Parkman Professor of Anatomy and Physiology at Harvard.

Part of his success as a teacher no doubt stemmed from the fact that he loved to talk and talked very well—wittily, widely, and often deeply. This penchant for talk also accounts for the great success of his best-known works: *The Autocrat of the Breakfast Table* (1857–1858), *The Professor at the Breakfast Table* (1860), *The Poet at the Breakfast Table* (1872), and *Over the Teacups* (1891). In all these books, a thinly disguised Oliver Wendell Holmes—as Autocrat, Professor, and Poet—leads a lively conversation with a group of people gathered around a boarding house table in Boston. Partly essay, partly prose fiction, partly drama, and containing some of his most famous poems, these books brought him nationwide fame.

Considered among the best writers of his time while he was alive, Holmes is little read today. Perhaps the main reason for this is that his works are what are described as "occasional" pieces; that is, essays or poems written to celebrate or comment upon some contemporary

PORTRAIT OF OLIVER WENDELL HOLMES
National Portrait Gallery
Smithsonian Institution

occasion or event. Unfortunately, once the occasion has passed, the writing is forgotten along with the event that stimulated it. This has happened to the great mass of Holmes's poetry; however, a handful of his poems are still read today, including the two printed below.

Holmes is also famous as the father of Oliver Wendell Holmes, Jr. (1841–1935), who pursued the profession his father had given up—the law—and became a famous associate justice of the United States Supreme Court (1902–1932). Like his father, he loved order and clarity and despised cruelty.

Holmes wrote the following poem in response to a newspaper report detailing the proposed demolition of the frigate Constitution. *The ship, nicknamed "Old Ironsides," played a leading part in the War of 1812. Holmes's poem saved the frigate.*

Old Ironsides

Ay, tear her tattered ensign down!
  Long has it waved on high,
And many an eye has danced to see
  That banner in the sky;
Beneath it rung the battle shout,   5
  And burst the cannon's roar;—
The meteor of the ocean air
  Shall sweep the clouds no more.

Her deck, once red with heroes' blood,
  Where knelt the vanquished foe,   10
When winds were hurrying o'er the flood,
  And waves were white below,
No more shall feel the victor's tread,
  Or know the conquered knee;—
The harpies of the shore shall pluck   15
  The eagle of the sea!

Oh, better that her shattered hulk
  Should sink beneath the wave;
Her thunders shook the mighty deep,
  And there should be her grave;   20
Nail to the mast her holy flag,
  Set every threadbare sail,
And give her to the god of storms,
  The lightning and the gale!

From THE COMPLETE POETICAL WORKS OF OLIVER WENDELL HOLMES, Houghton Mifflin and Company, Cambridge Edition, The Riverside Press, Cambridge, Mass., 1908.

The Constitution *in action during the War of 1812. Saved by the public's response to Holmes's poem, the frigate may still be seen in Boston harbor.*

THE CONSTITUTION AND THE GUERRIERE
American Antiquarian Society
Worcester, MA

The Chambered Nautilus[1]

This is the ship of pearl, which, poets feign,
   Sails the unshadowed main,—
   The venturous bark that flings
On the sweet summer wind its purpled wings
In gulfs enchanted, where the Siren sings,   5
   And coral reefs lie bare,
Where the cold sea-maids rise to sun their
    streaming hair.

1. **The Chambered Nautilus.** This mollusk, found in the Indian Ocean and the South Pacific, was thought to have a membrane which functioned as a sail.

Its webs of living gauze no more unfurl;
 Wrecked is the ship of pearl!
 And every chambered cell,   10

Where its dim dreaming life was wont to dwell,
As the frail tenant shaped his growing shell,
 Before thee lies revealed,—
Its irised ceiling rent, its sunless crypt unsealed!

Year after year beheld the silent toil   15
 That spread his lustrous coil;
 Still, as the spiral grew,
He left the past year's dwelling for the new,
Stole with soft step its shining archway through,
 Built up its idle door,   20
Stretched in his last-found home, and knew the old
  no more.

Thanks for the heavenly message brought by thee.
 Child of the wandering sea,
 Cast from her lap, forlorn!
Form thy dead lips a clearer note is born   25
Than ever Triton[2] blew from wreathed horn!
 While on mine ear it rings,
Through the deep caves of thought I hear a voice that
  sings:—

Build thee more stately mansions, O my soul,
 As the swift seasons roll!   30
 Leave thy low-vaulted past!
Let each new temple, nobler than the last,
Shut thee from heaven with a dome more vast,
 Till thou at length art free,
Leaving thine outgrown shell by life's unresting sea! 35

2. **Triton** (trīt′ n), a god of the sea in Greek mythology,
Triton was thought to control the waves with a horn
fashioned from a conch shell.

BOSTON HARBOR FROM CONSTITUTION WHARF (detail)
Robert Salmon
United States Naval Academy Museum
Anapolis, MD

UNDERSTANDING AND APPRECIATION

"Old Ironsides"

1. Find each reference to the flag, and list the words that the poet uses to refer to it.
2. Why does the poet mention the flag so often when it is the *ship* he wants to save?
3. What is the meaning of "the harpies of the shore"?
4. What stanza has a rhyme scheme different from the other two? Describe that difference.
5. What "solution" concerning the ship does the poet propose in the last stanza? Is he serious or not? Why do you think he proposes it?

"The Chambered Nautilus"

1. In what sense does the speaker use the word *bark* in line 3?

2. In what sense is "the ship of pearl" wrecked?
3. What important characteristic of the nautilus is dwelt upon in stanza 3?
4. Describe the rhyme and the rhythm pattern of each stanza of the poem.
5. State in your own words the moral of the poem.

COMPOSITION

You have just read six poems by three authors who have been and remain very popular with many readers of poetry. Write a brief composition discussing the poem *or* the poet that you liked best, telling *why* you preferred it or him.

If you prefer, write instead a poem of your own, perhaps one inspired by, or in some other way similar to, one of the poems you have just read.

Afro-American Spirituals

Afro-American (or Negro) spirituals are folk songs created by American slaves who lived in the South. Composed by people who came from a long African tradition, spirituals naturally contain many African musical elements. Their words, however, reflect the experience and feelings of generations of men and women who lived and worked as slaves in the United States.

Often drawing heavily on biblical stories, persons, and symbols, spirituals gave expression to the dreams and anguish of an oppressed people. Though called "spirituals," the songs were not narrowly religious. They were spiritual in the sense that they dealt with the most basic questions of human life. They offered consolation for pain and sorrow, fostered solidarity in the face of hardship, and encouraged the hope of eventual freedom—both in the sense of release from earthly suffering, and in the sense of escape from the bondage of slavery.

Many spirituals conveyed a double meaning. While the song might appear (to a listening overseer, for example) to be solely about heavenly salvation and the joys awaiting true believers in the afterlife, the spiritual's hidden, second meaning might be decoded as encouragement and advice about escape from slavery. The song "Follow the Drinking Gourd," for instance, has been interpreted as advice to runaway slaves to take their direction from the Big Dipper, which pointed the way northward to freedom. Similarly, "Moses" in the spiritual "Go Down, Moses" has been interpreted as a reference to Harriet Tubman, the runaway slave who returned to the South many times to lead other slaves to freedom. (The system of escape routes, hiding places, and sympathizers who helped slaves was called the Underground Railroad. Harriet Tubman was perhaps the best known of the "conductors" on that railroad.)

Though spirituals were created and sung as early as the first quarter of the 1700s, they were not widely known until the last quarter of the 1800s. They were first spread by the tours of the Fisk Jubilee Singers. This group, originally nine black singers (all but one of whom were ex-slaves), led by a music teacher, George L. White, began a tour in the fall of 1871 with the intention of publicizing and raising funds for their school—now Fisk University—which had been founded in 1865. They completed their original mission by spring of the following year. In 1873 they went on to create a sensation in the British Isles and thereafter toured Europe several times. Soon other concert groups were also spreading the music of the spiritual, and today the Afro-

NEGRO LIFE IN THE SOUTH, Eastman Johnson, New York Historical Society, New York City

American spiritual is known worldwide. Here, for example, is a Spanish version of the chorus of "Go Down, Moses":

Baja, Moisés	Go down, Moses,
a la tierra de Egipto.	Way down in Egypt's land.
Di al viejo Faraón	Tell old Pharaoh
que liberte a mi pueblo.	To let my people go!

It is not surprising that the Afro-American spiritual has been given credit for improving understanding between races and developing human brotherhood. Spirituals are certainly one of America's finest artistic achievements.

Swing Low, Sweet Chariot

Chorus:
Swing low, sweet chariot,
Coming for to carry me home;
Swing low, sweet chariot,
Coming for to carry me home.

I looked over Jordan, and what did I see,
Coming for to carry me home?
A band of angels coming after me,
Coming for to carry me home. *(Chorus)*

If you get there before I do,
Coming for to carry me home,
Tell all my friends I'm coming too,
Coming for to carry me home. *(Chorus)*

The brightest day that ever I saw,
Coming for to carry me home,
When Jesus wash'd my sins away,
Coming for to carry me home. *(Chorus)*

I'm sometimes up and sometimes down,
Coming for to carry me home,
But still my soul feels heavenly bound,
Coming for to carry me home. *(Chorus)*

Go Down, Moses

When Israel was in Egypt's land:
  Let my people go;
Oppress'd so hard they could not stand,
  Let my people go.

  (Chorus)
  Go down, Moses,
  Way down in Egypt's land,
  Tell ole Pharaoh,
  Let my people go.

"Thus saith the Lord," bold Moses said,
  Let my people go;
"If not I'll smite your first-born dead,"
  Let my people go. *(Chorus)*

No more shall they in bondage toil,
  Let my people go;
Let them come out with Egypt's spoil,
  Let my people go. *(Chorus)*

When Israel out of Egypt came,
  Let my people go;
And left the proud oppressive land,
  Let my people go. *(Chorus)*

O, 'twas a dark and dismal night,
  Let my people go;
When Moses led the Israelites,
  Let my people go. *(Chorus)*

'Twas good old Moses and Aaron, too,
  Let my people go;
'Twas they that led the armies through,
  Let my people go. *(Chorus)*

From AFRO-AMERICAN VOICES, 1770's–1970's, Ralph Kendricks and Claudette Levitt, Oxford Book Company, New York, 1970.

UNDERSTANDING AND INTERPRETATION

"Swing Low, Sweet Chariot"

1. References to various forms of transportation are often found in spirituals. Which one is used in this poem? Why?
2. In what sense is the word "home" used in this spiritual? the phrase "heavenly bound"?

"Go Down, Moses"

1. Why might the specific biblical story of Moses and his people in the Pharaoh's Egypt be selected as the basis of an Afro-American spiritual?
2. Of whom might the Pharaoh be a symbol?

Frederick Douglass 1817–1895

Frederick Douglass was born in 1817, a slave on a plantation in Maryland, where he lived until he was ten. He then spent several years as a house slave in Baltimore at the home of a brother of his owner. He learned to read during this period, though he never had any formal schooling. For several years in the mid-1830s he served as a field hand, finally returning to Baltimore in 1837 after an abortive attempt to escape to the North. Though he became a ship caulker and found work on his own, he was nevertheless expected to give his weekly wages to his "master."

On Monday, September 3, 1838, Frederick Douglass escaped to New York City and then to New Bedford, Massachusetts. He worked at various jobs in the latter city for three years. Then, in the summer of 1841, he went to an antislavery convention in Nantucket, where he was asked to speak of his experiences as a slave. He impressed the famous abolitionist William Lloyd Garrison to whose newspaper, *The Liberator,* he already subscribed, and he was asked to become an agent of the Massachusetts Anti-Slavery Society. The fugitive slave thus became a lecturer.

So good a speaker was Douglass that some members of his audience questioned whether he had ever been a slave. This prompted him to describe his experiences in a little book he called *Narrative of the Life of Frederick Douglass,* which was published in 1845. Douglass was a good writer as well as a good speaker, and his book sold 30,000 copies in five years. Ten years later Douglass wrote a much enlarged autobiography, *My Bondage and My Freedom,* from which our selection is taken.

In the same year he published his first book, Douglass began a twenty-one-month tour of England, Ireland, and Scotland on behalf of the antislavery cause. On returning to the United States, he decided to establish a newspaper of his own. The first issue of that paper, *North Star,* was

PORTRAIT OF FREDERICK DOUGLASS
National Portrait Gallery
Smithsonian Institution

published in December 1847, in Rochester, New York.

During the Civil War, Douglass organized two regiments of Negro soldiers, and he continued to work for his people after the war was over. He held several political offices in the last twenty years or so of his life, including that of minister to Haiti from 1889 to 1891.

from MY BONDAGE AND MY FREEDOM

Slaves are generally expected to sing as well as to work. A silent slave is not liked by masters or overseers. *"Make a noise," "make a noise,"* and *"bear a hand,"* are the words usually addressed to the slaves when there is silence amongst them. This may account for the almost constant singing heard in the southern states. There was, generally, more or less singing among the teamsters, as it was one means of letting the overseer know where they were, and that they were moving on with the work. But, on allowance day, those who visited the great house farm were peculiarly excited and noisy. While on their way, they would make the dense old woods, for miles around, reverberate with their wild notes. These were not always merry because they were wild. On the contrary, they were mostly of a plaintive cast, and told a tale of grief and sorrow. In the most boisterous outbursts of rapturous sentiment, there was ever a tinge of deep melancholy. I have never heard any songs like those anywhere since I left slavery, except when in Ireland. There I heard the same *wailing notes,* and was much affected by them. It was during the famine of 1845–6. In all the songs of the slaves, there was ever some expression in praise of the great house farm; something which would flatter the pride of the owner, and, possibly, draw a favorable glance from him.

> "I am going away to the great house
> farm,
> O yea! O yea! O yea!
> My old master is a good old master,
> Oh yea! O yea! O yea!

From MY BONDAGE AND MY FREEDOM by Frederick Douglass, Published in 1969 by Dover Publications, Inc. By permission of Dover Publications, Inc., New York.

This they would sing, with other words of their own improvising—jargon to others, but full of meaning to themselves. I have sometimes thought, that the mere hearing of those songs would do more to impress truly spiritual-minded men and women with the soul-crushing and death-dealing character of slavery, than the reading of whole volumes of its mere physical cruelties. They speak to the heart and to the soul of the thoughtful. I cannot better express my sense of them now, than ten years ago, when, in sketching my life, I thus spoke of this feature of my plantation experience:

I did not, when a slave, understand the deep meanings of those rude and apparently incoherent songs. I was myself within the circle, so that I neither saw nor heard as those without might see and hear. They told a tale which was then altogether beyond my feeble comprehension; they were tones, loud, long and deep, breathing the prayer and complaint of souls boiling over with the bitterest anguish. Every tone was a testimony against slavery, and a prayer to God for deliverance from chains. The hearing of those wild notes always depressed my spirits, and filled my heart with ineffable sadness. The mere recurrence, even now, afflicts my spirit, and while I am writing these lines, my tears are falling. To those songs I trace my first glimmering conceptions of the dehumanizing character of slavery. I can never get rid of that conception. Those songs still follow me, to deepen my hatred of slavery, and quicken my sympathies for my brethren in bonds. If any one wishes to be impressed with a sense of the soul-killing power of slavery, let him go to Col. Lloyd's plantation, and, on allowance day, place himself in the deep, pine woods, and there let him, in silence, thoughtfully analyze the sounds that shall pass through the chambers of his soul, and if he is not thus impressed, it will only be because "there is no flesh in his obdurate heart."

The remark is not unfrequently made, that slaves are the most contented and happy laborers in the world. They dance and sing, and make all manner of joyful noises—so they do; but it is a great mistake to suppose them happy because they sing. The songs of the slave represent the sorrows, rather than the joys, of his heart; and he is relieved by them, only as an aching heart is relieved by its tears. Such is the constitution of the human mind, that, when pressed to extremes, it often avails itself of the most opposite methods. Extremes meet in mind as in matter. When the slaves on board of the "Pearl" were overtaken, arrested, and carried to prison— their hopes for freedom blasted—as they marched in chains they sang, and found (as Emily Edmunson tells us) a melancholy relief in singing. The singing of a man cast away on a desolate island, might be as appropriately considered an evidence of his contentment and happiness, as the singing of a slave. Sorrow and desolation have their songs, as well as joy and peace. Slaves sing more to *make* themselves happy, than to express their happiness.

It is the boast of slaveholders, that their slaves enjoy more of the physical comforts of life than the peasantry of any country in the world. My experience contradicts this. The men and the women slaves on Col. Lloyd's farm, received, as their monthly allowance of food, eight pounds of pickled pork, or their equivalent in fish. The pork was often tainted, and the fish was of the poorest quality— herrings, which would bring very little if offered for sale in any northern market. With their pork or fish, they had one bushel of Indian meal—unbolted[1]—of which quite fifteen per cent was fit only to feed pigs. With this, one pint of salt was given; and this was the entire monthly allowance of a full grown slave, working constantly in the open field,

from morning until night, every day in the month except Sunday, and living on a fraction more than a quarter of a pound of meat per day, and less than a peck of corn-meal per week. There is no kind of work that a man can do which requires a better supply of food to prevent physical exhaustion, than the field-work of a slave. So much for the slave's allowance of food; now for his raiment. The yearly allowance of clothing for the slaves on this plantation, consisted of two tow-linen shirts—such linen as the coarsest crash towels are made of; one pair of trowsers of the same material, for summer, and a pair of trowsers and a jacket of woolen, most slazily[2] put together, for winter; one pair of yarn stockings, and one pair of shoes of the coarsest description. The slave's entire apparel could not have cost more than eight dollars per year. The allowance of food and clothing for the little children, was committed to their mothers, or to the older slave-women having the care of them. Children who were unable to work in the field, had neither shoes, stockings, jackets nor trowsers given them. Their clothing consisted of two coarse tow-linen shirts—already described—per year; and when these failed them, as they often did, they went naked until the next allowance day. Flocks of little children from five to ten years old, might be seen on Col. Lloyd's plantation, as destitute of clothing as any little heathen on the west coast of Africa; and this, not merely during the summer months, but during the frosty weather of March. The little girls were no better off than the boys; all were nearly in a state of nudity.

As to beds to sleep on, they were known to none of the field hands; nothing but a coarse blanket—not so good as those used in the north to cover horses—was given them, and this only to the men and women. The children stuck themselves in holes and cor-

1. **unbolted,** unsifted.
2. **slazily,** flimsily.

ners, about the quarters; often in the corner of the huge chimneys, with their feet in the ashes to keep them warm. The want of beds, however, was not considered a very great privation. Time to sleep was of far greater importance, for, when the day's work is done, most of the slaves have their washing, mending and cooking to do; and, having few or none of the ordinary facilities for doing such things, very many of their sleeping hours are consumed in necessary preparations for the duties of the coming day.

FOR UNDERSTANDING

1. Why were slaves expected to make noise?
2. With what two compound adjectives does the author first characterize slavery?
3. What effects do the songs of the slaves have on the author?

4. Approximately how many hours a day and how many days a week did field slaves work?
5. Were the children of slaves treated better or worse than their parents? Explain.

FOR INTERPRETATION

In describing the "physical comforts" of the slaves, Douglass lets the facts speak for themselves. He does not exaggerate or sentimentalize.
1. Why do you think he prefers this approach?
2. What facts about the slaves' condition disturbed you the most?
3. Slave owners would argue that they "paid" slaves by giving them food, clothing, shelter. The clothing allowance was $8 per year. After escaping to freedom, Douglass earned $9 *per week* working in New Bedford. How does this fact reflect on the owners' argument?
4. There are very poor people living in the United States today. Argue for or against the proposition that these poor people—of all colors—are in just as bad a condition as black slaves.

Abraham Lincoln 1809–1865

To win the vote of the common man, many candidates in American political history have pretended that they were common folk themselves—born in a log cabin, or at least near one. Abraham Lincoln did not have to pretend. He was indeed born in a log cabin, in Kentucky, and he came from the commonest of common stock—his parents were a virtually illiterate frontier couple. He did not get much schooling, but he learned to read, write, and cipher, and when he arrived in New Salem, Illinois—a town that "never had three hundred people living in it"—in his very early twenties, he was already determined to become a lawyer.

He studied law there as best he could while doing odd jobs, serving as a farmhand, as postmaster, as deputy surveyor. He even became a captain of volunteers in the Black Hawk War. He was elected to the State Assembly, and then in 1836 was reelected with the highest vote out of a field of seventeen candidates. One of the reasons he did so well was that he was a clear, pithy, witty speaker. On March 1, 1837, he was admitted to the State Bar of Illinois and moved to the new state capital at Springfield to practice law. He was able to carry all his earthly goods— books and all—on the back of a mule, and had but seven dollars in his pocket.

Lincoln was known as an outstanding lawyer. He did his work thoroughly, made use of his excellent common sense, and could be very shrewd before both judges and juries. Lincoln served a term in Congress in 1847–1849.

When a new, antislavery party was formed in 1854, Lincoln, who believed slavery to be morally wrong, became a member. Two years later he was his party's candidate for the United States Senate. He lost to the Democratic candidate—the far better-known Stephen Douglas—but he fared so well in the series of debates to which he had challenged Douglas that he emerged in a very good position to challenge him again in the future. In fact, his party nominated Lincoln for the presidency and he won the election of 1860 over Stephen Douglas;

PORTRAIT OF ABRAHAM LINCOLN
John Henry Brown
National Portrait Gallery, Smithsonian Institution

John Breckinridge, a candidate who carried the southern states; and John Bell, who captured three border states.

Lincoln had already noted in a speech of 1858 that "a house divided against itself cannot stand," and had predicted that the *whole* of the United States would have to permit slavery or reject it. When he was elected president, he found himself in the very center of a conflict based heavily on the slavery issue. He made it clear that his "paramount object" in the war was to save the Union, but on January 1, 1863, he issued his Emancipation Proclamation, which declared that all slaves in rebellious states were free. Though the proclamation itself freed no one, it greatly improved the image of the North in Europe, where antislavery feeling was very strong. Its great moral effect helped to preserve the Union and thus ultimately helped free the slaves as well.

Lincoln was reelected in 1864, defeating General George McClellan. Though he insisted on the reunification of North and South, and on the abolition of slavery, he was generous toward the South in other matters. His second inaugural address struck a conciliatory tone with the famous words:

> With malice toward none, with charity for all, with firmness in the right, as God gives us to see the right, let us strive on to finish the work we are in, to bind up the nation's wounds, to care for him who shall have borne the battle, and for his widow, and his orphan—to do all which may achieve and cherish a just and lasting peace among ourselves and with all nations.

Unfortunately, Lincoln did not live long enough to bind up the nation's wounds. On April 14, 1865, while attending a play at Ford's Theater in Washington, D.C., he was shot by John Wilkes Booth, a fanatic sympathizer with the Southern cause. He died on April 15, 1865. When Secretary of War Edwin Stanton was told of the tragedy, he declared, "Now he belongs to the ages."

This speech was delivered on November 19, 1863, at the dedication ceremony for the battlefield cemetery at Gettysburg, Pennsylvania. Four months before, one of the bloodiest battles of the Civil War had been fought there. Lincoln was not the principal speaker—an honor accorded to Edward Everett, a noted orator of the time. But it is Lincoln's "few appropriate remarks" that have been remembered.

GETTYSBURG ADDRESS

Four score and seven years ago our fathers brought forth on this continent a new nation, conceived in liberty, and dedicated to the proposition that all men are created equal.

Now we are engaged in a great civil war, testing whether that nation, or any nation so conceived and so dedicated, can long endure. We are met on a great battlefield of that war. We have come to dedicate a portion of that field as a final resting place for those who here gave their lives that that nation might live. It is altogether fitting and proper that we should do this.

But in a larger sense we cannot dedicate, we cannot consecrate, we cannot hallow this ground. The brave men, living and dead, who struggled here, have consecrated it far above our poor power to add or detract. The world will little note nor long remember what we say here, but it can never forget what they did here. It is for us, the living, rather, to be dedicated here to the unfinished work which they who fought here have thus far so nobly advanced. It is rather for us to be here dedicated to the great task remaining before us— that from these honored dead we take increased devotion to that cause for which they gave the last full measure of devotion; that we here highly resolve that these dead shall not have died in vain; that this nation, under God, shall have a new birth of freedom; and that government of the people, by the people, for the people, shall not perish from the earth.

FOR UNDERSTANDING

1. How long is "Four score and seven years"? Why might Lincoln have preferred to express the time period in this way rather than using the exact number of years?
2. For what basic purpose were the people assembled at Gettysburg when Lincoln gave this speech?
3. What resolve did Lincoln ask the crowd to make?

FOR INTERPRETATION

Be prepared to discuss or write on one or more of the following, according to the directions of your teacher.
1. What did Lincoln mean by "in a larger sense"?
2. What in Lincoln's view was "the cause" for which the dead gave their lives?
3. In what way did the speech show Lincoln's humility?
4. What in your opinion did Lincoln mean by "a new birth of freedom"?

FOR APPRECIATION

Style

The style of the Gettysburg Address contributes greatly to its memorable effect. Style is often a very subtle thing, but see if you can decide in the examples below why Lincoln decided in each case to use the "B" version rather than the "A," which he had originally written. In making your decision, do not look at the sentences alone but examine them in the context of the whole speech.

A. This we may, in all propriety, do.
B. It is altogether fitting and proper that we should do this.

A. We are met to dedicate a portion of it. . . .
B. We have come to dedicate a portion of it. . . .

A. . . . that this nation shall have a new birth of freedom; and that this government . . .
B. . . . that this nation, under God, shall have a new birth of freedom; and that government . . .

Robert E. Lee   1807–1870

Robert Edward Lee was born in Stratford, Virginia, on January 19, 1807, the third son of the famous "Light-Horse Harry" Lee, who was an outstanding officer in the Revolutionary War, a governor of Virginia, and a member of the United States Congress. While a congressman, Henry Lee wrote the Resolution on the death of Washington containing the memorable phrasing, "first in war, first in peace, and first in the hearts of his countrymen." He died when Robert was only eleven, leaving a formidable legacy for his son to live up to.

Robert E. Lee ultimately became even more famous than his father. He began his illustrious military career by graduating second in his class at West Point (1829). He was a captain of engineers and in 1841 was in charge of the defense of New York harbor. He fought in the Mexican War of 1846–1848, during which General Winfield Scott called him "the greatest military genius in America." From 1852 to 1855 Lee served as superintendent of the academy at West Point. In 1859 it was Robert E. Lee who commanded the troops that suppressed John Brown's raid on Harper's Ferry. He was then a colonel.

During this distinguished military career, he married Mary Randolph Custis of Arlington, Virginia, a great-granddaughter of Martha Washington. The marriage committed him even more deeply to his native state.

The events leading to the Civil War placed Lee in a difficult position. He was an officer in the United States Army and he believed in the Union. On the other hand, his loyalty to Virginia was even stronger. When he was offered the field command of the Union army, he declined and he later resigned his post in the federal army. He felt that under no circumstances could he fight against his beloved state. In April 1861 he agreed to lead the Army of Northern Virginia, and two months later he also became personal military advisor to President Jefferson Davis of the Confederacy.

PORTRAIT OF ROBERT E. LEE
John Dabour
National Portrait Gallery, Smithsonian Institution

Lee proved to be the military genius Scott had called him. In the early stages of the war he won many brilliant victories, notably the second Battle of Bull Run and Fredericksburg. He also fought bravely in many battles near the end of the war, though his troops were outnumbered by from two to four to one. He was finally named commander-in-chief of all Confederate armies in February 1865. By that time, however, the Confederate cause was hopeless.

Lee was a fine writer, as we can tell from the documents he wrote as well as from his letters. Nevertheless, he declined to write his memoirs after the war, preferring to assume the presidency of Washington College in Virginia, which was later named Washington and Lee in his honor.

Though he did not write books and did not occupy major public offices as had his father, Robert E. Lee became one of the most beloved military heroes in American history. Throughout the United States, children are still named for him, as are towns, parks, and schools. For over a century, Lee has continued to inspire admiration for his qualities of sincerity, courage, loyalty, and gallantry.

from LETTER TO HIS SON

January 23, 1861

The South, in my opinion, has been aggrieved by the acts of the North, as you say. I feel the aggression, and am willing to take every proper step for redress. It is the principle I contend for, not individual or private gain. As an American citizen, I take great pride in my country, her prosperity and institutions, and would defend any State if her rights were invaded. But I can anticipate no greater calamity for the country than a dissolution of the Union. It would be an accumulation of all the evils we complain of, and I am willing to sacrifice everything but honor for its preservation. I hope, therefore, that all constitutional means will be exhausted before there is a recourse to force. Secession is nothing but revolution. The framers of our Constitution never exhausted so much labor, wisdom and forbearance in its formation, and surrounded it with so many guards and securities, if it was intended to be broken by every member of the Confederacy at will. It was intended for "perpetual union" so expressed in the preamble, and for the estab-

lishment of a government, not a compact, which can only be dissolved by revolution, or the consent of all the people in convention assembled. It is idle to talk of secession. Anarchy would have been established, and not a government by Washington, Hamilton, Jefferson, Madison, and the other patriots of the Revolution. . . . Still, a Union that can only be maintained by swords and bayonets, and in which strife and civil war are to take the place of brotherly love and kindness, has no charm for me. I shall mourn for my country and for the welfare and progress of mankind. If the Union is dissolved, and the Government disrupted, I shall return to my native State and share the miseries of my people, and save in defence will draw my sword on none.

Robert E. Lee, "Letter to His Son, January 23, 1861" in *R.E. Lee* by Douglas Southall Freeman. Copyright 1934 Charles Scribner's Sons; copyright renewed © 1962 Inez Godden Freeman. Reprinted with permission of Charles Scribner's Sons.

FOR UNDERSTANDING

1. What does Lee think is the greatest calamity that could happen to the country?

2. What one thing would Lee *not* sacrifice to preserve the Union?

3. What two human qualities does Lee specifically mention (near the end of the selection) and evidently prize very highly?

FOR INTERPRETATION

1. What do words like "proper" and "principle" reveal about Robert E. Lee?

2. Discuss the meaning and implications of the sentence, "Secession is nothing but revolution."

3. What is the difference between a "government" and a "compact," as these terms are used by Lee in this letter?

4. At the time of the writing of this letter, what is Lee's final determination? Do you think he remained true to his decision or changed it in April 1861, when he took command of the Army of Northern Virginia?

LANGUAGE AND VOCABULARY

Douglass, Lincoln, and Lee all write in a relatively plain style, yet there are probably some words in each writer's work with which you are not familiar. Part of developing a good vocabulary is *remembering* the meaning of unfamiliar words you meet in your reading. Each of the following words comes from one of the three preceding selections. How many do you recall? Decide which word belongs in the blank space in each sentence below.

reverberate	anarchy	plaintive
consecrate	calamity	boisterous
incoherent	dissolution	detract
ineffable	prosperity	engage
dehumanizing	privation	consume
obdurate	recurrence	disrupt
destitute	jargon	

1. The writer was so _____ that she could not afford to eat.

2. The noise of the rock concert will _____ through the concert hall.

3. I hope you will not have a/an _____ of the asthma attack that kept you in bed yesterday.

4. The wounded soldier was so _____ that we could not understand what he was saying.

5. The _____ cries of the trapped animal made everyone feel sad.

6. In times of _____ taxpayers are more willing to spend money on schools.

7. That stained tie will _____ from your otherwise handsome clothes.

8. The _____ effects of slavery often made people feel like animals.

9. The Civil War helped to prevent the _____ of the Union.

10. If you _____ all that ice cream, you will get fat.

11. The crowd was so _____ that I could hardly hear the person standing next to me.

12. The two armies stood ready to _____ in battle.

13. We were moved by the _____ beauty of the flowers.

14. The _____ mule refused to take another step.

15. We _____ ourselves to the cause of freedom.

16. An atomic war is the greatest _____ I can imagine.

17. _____ would probably follow such a war, for the centers of government would be wiped out.

18. Fire having destroyed their home, the Smiths were left in a state of _____.

19. Only a specialist could understand the _____ he used in his essay.

20. Noise tends to _____ concentration.

Henry Timrod

1828–1867

It is generally agreed that, with the exception of Edgar Allan Poe, Henry Timrod was the best southern poet of his time. Born in 1829 in Charleston, South Carolina, the son of a bookbinder who also wrote poetry, Timrod went to schools in his native city. He began college at what is now the University of Georgia, but poverty and ill health forced him to leave in less than two years. Giving up the idea of studying law and failing to find a job as a college professor, he earned a meager living for some time as a private tutor.

Timrod began contributing poetry to literary magazines when he was only seventeen, and he was a highly regarded member of the literary coterie of Charleston, presided over by William Gilmore Simms. He published a book of nature poems in Boston in 1860, but his best poems were not written until after the Civil War had started.

When the war broke out, Timrod enlisted and even tried to get to the front lines. However, he was already suffering from the tuberculosis that ultimately killed him at an early age, and it was clear that he was not healthy enough for the army. A brave attempt at journalism as a war correspondent for the Charleston *Courier* was also short-lived.

In 1864 he became editor of the *South Carolinian* at Columbia, married, and fathered a child. The child died in infancy, however, and Timrod was so poor that in 1866 he told a friend that he would give every line he ever wrote for $100 cash in hand. He died in Columbia, South Carolina, in 1867, about two months before his thirty-eighth birthday.

Timrod did not live to see his best poetry published in book form, but a few years after his death his friend and fellow author, Paul

PORTRAIT OF HENRY TIMROD
"Laureate of the Confederacy"

Hamilton Hayne, edited *The Collected Poems of Henry Timrod* (1873). A memorial edition of Timrod's poems was published in 1899, and a monument was dedicated to this "Laureate of the Confederacy" in Charleston, South Carolina, on May 1, 1901.

THE CONSECRATION, George Cochran Lambdin
Indianapolis Museum of Art, Indianapolis, IN

Ode

*Sung on the Occasion of Decorating the Graves
of the Confederate Dead, at Magnolia Cemetery,
Charleston, S. C., 1866*

Sleep sweetly in your humble graves,
    Sleep, martyrs of a fallen cause!—
Though yet no marble column craves
    The pilgrim here to pause.

In seeds of laurels in the earth,   5
    The garlands of your fame are sown;
And, somewhere, waiting for its birth,
    The shaft is in the stone.

Meanwhile, your sisters for the years
    Which hold in trust your storied tombs,   10
Bring all they now can give you—tears,
    And these memorial blooms.

Small tributes, but your shades will smile
    As proudly on these wreaths to-day,
As when some cannon-moulded pile   15
    Shall overlook this Bay.

Stoop, angels, hither from the skies!
    There is no holier spot of ground,
Than where defeated valor lies
    By mourning beauty crowned.   20

From THE COLLECTED POEMS OF HENRY TIMROD, Winfield Parks
and Aileen Wells Parks, eds., University of Georgia Press, 1965. (First
published in 1866.)

FOR UNDERSTANDING

1. What is the "fallen cause" to which the speaker refers?

2. Explain the meaning of "Meanwhile" in line 11.

3. Why will the "shades" of the dead soldiers smile as proudly on the memorial wreaths as on a monument?

FOR APPRECIATION

Timrod calls his poem an *ode.* This term is usually used to describe a poem that is serious and formal and written in dignified language for a ceremonial occasion. Odes are often relatively long and possess a complex structure. The word itself comes from the Greek word *aeidein,* which means "to sing" or "to chant." Originally, odes were meant to be sung.

Which of the several characteristics of the ode does Timrod's poem possess? Which does it not possess?

COMPOSITION

Comparison and contrast is often an interesting and effective way of organizing a piece of writing. Trying to find the similarities and differences between or among items can also help you discover things you did not at first realize about the subject.

Consider the three selections you have just read:

Lincoln's address, Lee's letter, and Timrod's poem. They are alike in that all three deal in some manner with the Civil War, but they are quite different in form. They also differ in the time of composition: before, during, and after the war.

Lincoln's address and Timrod's poem were both written to commemorate a cemetery; but one author is full of hope, the other is full of sadness. Lincoln and Lee may be compared in that both were great leaders, important and courageous historical figures living at a critical time in our nation's history. What similarities and differences can you detect in their respective selections in the text? Still another comparison may be made between the two southerners—Lee and Timrod. Both were defenders of a lost cause, but in the selections, one is speaking before the cause was lost, the other afterwards.

A comparison and contrast may also be made between Timrod's "Ode" and Emerson's "Concord Hymn" (p. 183). Both are poems and commemorative pieces, but they also differ in significant ways.

Select one of the topics suggested above—or one of your own choice based on two or more selections in this unit—and write a brief comparison-and-contrast essay. Try to think of a topic sentence to begin your composition, such as "Emerson's 'Concord Hymn' and Timrod's 'Ode' are both great poems celebrating men who died in war." After this, in a new paragraph, you may first mention other similarities and then discuss differences. Or you may weave comparisons and contrasts as you go along.

Walt Whitman

By the mid-nineteenth century there was no longer a paucity of great writers in the United States. On balance, authors like Emerson, Hawthorne, Longfellow, Poe, Thoreau, and Melville were producing work quite as good as that being produced by their contemporaries in England: the Brownings, Arnold, Carlyle, Ruskin, Tennyson, Thackeray, and Dickens.

But one figure peculiarly missing in American letters was a thoroughly democratic American writer, a writer who could speak for the whole country. By 1850 the nation consisted of thirty-one states and stretched all the way from Massachusetts to California. The poetic voice destined to be loved throughout the length and breadth of this land was heard for the first time in 1855: it was the voice of Walt Whitman, who in singing himself sang for all America.

Whitman was born in 1819 on a farm near Huntington, Long Island, New York, but at the age of four he moved to Brooklyn, where his father earned a living as a carpenter-builder. He went to elementary school in Brooklyn but left at about the age of eleven. The five or six years in elementary school was all the formal schooling he was to have, but Whitman was amazingly adept at schooling himself and soaking up knowledge. Like Tennyson's Ulysses, he could assert, "I am a part of all that I have met."

After a brief employment as an office boy in a law office, Whitman, like Ben Franklin before him, became a printer's apprentice, and in May 1835, at the age of sixteen, he graduated as a journeyman printer. Like Franklin, too, he soon began writing for newspapers, and in 1838–1839 edited a newspaper of his own, the *Long Islander*. Also, from about 1836 to 1841 he worked as a handyman and taught in a variety of schools. (He taught his first class when he was seventeen, and some of his pupils were older than he.)

At the age of twenty-two, Whitman moved to New York, where for a period of about five years (1841–1846) he worked as a reporter, a

PORTRAIT OF WALT WHITMAN, Thomas Eakins
National Portrait Gallery, Smithsonian Institution

magazine writer, an editor, and a politician. His poems and stories of this period were mediocre and conventional, a far cry from what he was to produce just a decade later. Nevertheless, these were years during which he imbibed the bustle and brilliance of a great metropolis, and his attendance at operas and at a series of Emerson's lectures were but two of many experiences that were to have a profound influence on his life.

By 1846 Whitman was back in Brooklyn, where for nearly two years he had what he described as "one of the pleasantest sits [situations] of my life," the editorship of the Brooklyn *Daily Eagle.* It was his job to round up the news not only of Brooklyn but also of the United States and the world. It was also at about this time that he began writing in his notebooks material that would eventually become part of his famous *Leaves of Grass*.

In 1848, after being fired from the *Daily Eagle,* Whitman spent three months in New Orleans, a visit that gave him his first glimpse of a larger America than he had known. Returning through St. Louis, Chicago, and the Great Lakes, he became acquainted with what was then frontier territory. Back in Brooklyn, he edited his own paper, the Brooklyn *Freeman,* for a brief time. Then in 1850, he moved back with his family and adopted a loafing lifestyle for a period of about five years. Today, we might describe him as a dropout. He often slept late; he took long walks; he worked with his father and brothers only off and on; and, to quote his brother, he sometimes wrote "a few hours, if he took the notion."

Those five years were a time of gestation. Whitman himself later referred to the period as "days of preparation: the gathering of the forces." What he was doing—partly consciously, mostly unconsciously—was beginning to re-create himself in the form of a book; for Whitman said of *Leaves of Grass* that it was an attempt "to put *a Person,* a human being (myself, in the latter half of the Nineteenth Century, in America) freely, fully and truly on record." In the year 1855, having set part of the type himself, he published a little book of just twelve poems, with a preface, which he entitled *Leaves of Grass.*

Although highly praised by Ralph Waldo Emerson, whom Whitman called his "master" and by whom his thinking was strongly influenced, the book did not create a sensation at the time. But it was revolutionary. It was the first American effort to break free from the stock use of the iambic pentameter line for serious poetry and from other aspects of conventional metrics. In fact, Whitman used the phrase rather than the foot as the unit of rhythm and thus helped to create what has come to be called *free verse.*

Free verse was an appropriate form for Whitman's message: that humankind was free, free to expand and develop as an individual in body, mind, and soul. The seemingly artless verses were also appropriate, since Whitman was speaking for democracy and the average man—he used the term "divine average" in "Song of Myself." That is to say, it was the kind of poetry that an average person might be able to write—without the inversions, the rhyme schemes, and the regular meters of conventional poetry. (In reality, anyone who has studied Whitman's poetry or made an attempt to imitate it quickly discovers that it is not as simple as it seems.)

Whitman published a second edition of *Leaves of Grass* the next year, adding twenty poems, along with Emerson's letter of congratulations. A phrase from that letter—"I greet you at the beginning of a great career"—was stamped in gold on the spine. A very much enlarged third edition containing 122 new poems appeared in 1860, and the process of revising old poems (or sometimes dropping them) and adding new was well underway—the book grew like grass.

A particularly momentous event in Whitman's life was the Civil War. Learning late in 1862 that his brother George had been wounded in the battle of Fredericksburg, he set out immediately for the front lines. Whitman found his brother and lived in his tent near the front lines for more than a week. He then returned to Washington, D.C., and served as a volunteer nurse, ministering to thousands of sick and wounded troops on both sides of the conflict.

Whitman's artistic output during this period was a book of poems published independently of *Leaves of Grass,* but later incorporated into it. Entitled *Drum-Taps,* this new volume, together with a sequel of poems about Lincoln, was published in October 1865. The main book might have been published much earlier, but Whitman wanted to include the Lincoln poems, for Lincoln was to him the symbol of his own message to Americans, "the representative democratic man." The poet was deeply grieved by the president's death, as we see in one of the most moving elegies ever written, "When Lilacs Last in the Dooryard Bloom'd."

Whitman remained in Washington, D.C., for better than ten years. His work in the attorney general's office did not prevent him from issuing a fourth (1867) and a fifth (1871) edition of *Leaves of Grass.* When he suffered a stroke in 1873, however, he moved to Camden, New Jersey, where, after living with his brother for

A rollicking example of nineteenth-century genre painting—the depiction of everyday work and recreation in American life. The painter, a fiddle player himself, must have taken special pleasure in painting this picture.

DANCE OF THE HAYMAKERS
William Sidney Mount
The Musuems At Stony Brook
Stony Brook, NY

several years, he finally came to own a home of his own in the spring of 1884. In Camden, Whitman continued to write poetry and published four more editions of *Leaves of Grass* (1876, 1881, 1889, and 1891–1892). He also published a collection of his newspaper writing, *November Boughs*, in 1888. His *Complete Prose Works* appeared in 1892, the year he died.

Perhaps a final estimate of Walt Whitman is impossible, for he was a unique and multifaceted individual. But there is no doubt that his free verse profoundly affected twentieth-century poetry. In addition, his identification with the common man marks him as one of the most deeply democratic and inspirational artists we have ever had.

One's-Self I Sing

One's-self I sing, a simple separate person,
Yet utter the word Democratic, the word En-Masse.

Of physiology from top to toe I sing,
Not physiognomy[1] alone nor brain alone is worthy for the Muse.[2]
  I say the Form complete is worthier far,   5
The Female equally with the Male I sing.

Of Life immense in passion, pulse, and power,
Cheerful, for freest action form'd under the laws divine,
The Modern Man I sing.

---

1. **physiognomy** (fiz ē og' nə mē), features that reveal
character.
2. **Muse,** spirit that inspires poets.

I Hear America Singing

I hear America singing, the varied carols I hear,
Those of mechanics, each one singing his as it should
    be blithe and strong,
The carpenter singing his as he measures his plank or beam,
The mason singing his as he makes ready for work, or
    leaves off work,
The boatman singing what belongs to him in his boat,
    the deck hand singing on the steam-boat deck,   5
The shoemaker singing as he sits on his bench, the
    hatter singing as he stands,
The woodcutter's song, the plowboy's on his way in the
    morning, or at noon intermission or at sundown,
The delicious singing of the mother, or of the young
    wife at work, or of the girl sewing or washing,
Each singing what belongs to him or her and to none else,
The day what belongs to the day—at night the party
    of young fellows, robust, friendly.   10
Singing with open mouths their strong melodious songs.

Walt Whitman, LEAVES OF GRASS, Comprehensive Reader's Edition,
Harold W. Blodgett and Sculley Bradley, ed., New York University Press, 1965.

When I Heard the Learn'd Astronomer

When I heard the learn'd astronomer,
When the proofs, the figures, were ranged in columns before me,
When I was shown the charts and diagrams, to add, divide, and
    measure them,
When I sitting heard the astronomer where he lectured with much
    applause in the lecture-room,
How soon unaccountable I became tired and sick,   5
Till rising and gliding out I wander'd off by myself,
In the mystical moist night-air, and from time to time,
Look'd up in perfect silence at the stars.

A Noiseless Patient Spider

A noiseless patient spider,
I mark'd where on a little promontory[1] it stood isolated,
Mark'd how to explore the vacant vast surrounding,
It launch'd forth filament, filament, filament, out of itself,
Ever unreeling them, ever tirelessly speeding them.   5

And you O my soul where you stand,
Surrounded, detached, in measureless oceans of space,
Ceaselessly musing, venturing, throwing, seeking the
    spheres to connect them,
Till the bridge you will need be form'd, till the ductile[2]
    anchor hold,
Till the gossamer[3] thread you fling catch somewhere,
    O my soul.   10

---

1. **promontory** (prom′ ən tôr ē), high point of land
projecting outward, usually into the sea.
2. **ductile** (duk′ təl), capable of being drawn out or
molded.
3. **gossamer,** fine strands of spider's silk that float in
the air or are loosely suspended from something.

When Lilacs Last in the Dooryard Bloom'd

1

When lilacs last in the dooryard bloom'd,
And the great star early droop'd in the western sky in the night,
I mourn'd, and yet shall mourn with ever-returning spring.

Ever-returning spring, trinity sure to me you bring,
Lilac blooming perennial and drooping star in the west,   5
And thought of him I love.

2

O powerful western fallen star!
O shades of night—O moody, tearful night!
O great star disappear'd—O the black murk that hides the star!
O cruel hands that hold me powerless—O helpless soul of me!   10
O harsh surrounding cloud that will not free my soul.

3

In the dooryard fronting an old farm-house near the white-
    wash'd palings,
Stands the lilac-bush tall-growing with heart-shaped leaves of
    rich green,
With many a pointed blossom rising delicate, with the perfume
    strong I love,
With every leaf a miracle—and from this bush in the dooryard,   15
With delicate-color'd blossoms and heart-shaped leaves of rich
    green,
A sprig with its flower I break.

4

In the swamp in secluded recesses,
A shy and hidden bird is warbling a song.

Solitary the thrush,   20
The hermit withdrawn to himself, avoiding the settlements,
Sings by himself a song.

Song of the bleeding throat,
Death's outlet song of life, (for well dear brother I know,
If thou wast not granted to sing thou would'st surely die).   25

5

Over the breast of the spring, the land, amid cities,
Amid lanes and through old woods, where lately the violets
    peep'd from the ground, spotting the gray debris,

ABRAHAM LINCOLN
Augustus Saint-Gaudens
The Newark Museum, Newark, NJ
Gift of Franklin Murphy, Jr.

Amid the grass in the fields each side of the lanes, passing the
    endless grass,
Passing the yellow-spear'd wheat, every grain from its shroud
    in the dark-brown fields uprisen,
Passing the apple-tree blows[1] of white and pink in the
    orchards,   30
Carrying a corpse to where it shall rest in the grave,
Night and day journeys a coffin.

6

Coffin that passes through lanes and streets,
Through day and night with the great cloud darkening the
    land,
With the pomp of the inloop'd flags with the cities draped in
    black,   35

1. **blows,** blossoms.

With the show of the States themselves as of crape-veil'd
    women standing,
With processions long and winding and the flambeaus[2] of the
    night,
With the countless torches lit, with the silent sea of faces and
    the unbared heads,
With the waiting depot, the arriving coffin, and the sombre
    faces,
With dirges through the night, with the thousand voices rising
    strong and solemn,   **40**
With all the mournful voices of the dirges pour'd around
    the coffin,
The dim-lit churches and the shuddering organs—where
    amid these you journey,
With the tolling tolling bells' perpetual clang,
Here, coffin that slowly passes,
I give you my sprig of lilac.   **45**

7

(Nor for you, for one alone,
Blossoms and branches green to coffins all I bring,
For fresh as the morning, thus would I chant a song for you
    O sane and sacred death.

All over bouquets of roses,
O death, I cover you over with roses and early lilies,
But mostly and now the lilac that blooms the first,   **50**
Copious I break, I break the sprigs from the bushes,
With loaded arms I come, pouring for you,
For you and the coffins all of you O death).

8

O western orb sailing the heaven,   **55**
Now I know what you must have meant as a month since I
    walk'd,
As I walk'd in silence the transparent shadowy night,
As I saw you had something to tell as you bent to me night
    after night,
As you droop'd from the sky low down as if to my side, (while
    the other stars all look'd on),
As we wander'd together the solemn night, (for something I
    know not what kept me from sleep),   **60**

---

2. **flambeaus** (flam' bōz),   torches.

As the night advanced, and I saw on the rim of the west how
full you were of woe,
As I stood on the rising ground in the breeze in the cool transparent night,
As I watch'd where you pass'd and was lost in the netherward[3]
black of the night,
As my soul in its trouble dissatisfied sank, as where you sad
orb,
Concluded, dropt in the night, and was gone.   65

9

Sing on there in the swamp,
O singer bashful and tender, I hear your notes, I hear your
call,
I hear, I come presently, I understand you,
But a moment I linger, for the lustrous star has detain'd me,
The star my departing comrade holds and detains me.   70

10

O how shall I warble myself for the dead one there I loved?
And how shall I deck my song for the large sweet soul that has
gone?
And what shall my perfume be for the grave of him I love?

Sea-winds blown from east and west,
Blown from the Eastern sea and blown from the Western sea,
till there on the prairies meeting,   75
These and with these and the breath of my chant,
I'll perfume the grave of him I love.

11

O what shall I hang on the chamber walls?
And what shall the pictures be that I hang on the walls,
To adorn the burial-house of him I love?   80

Pictures of growing spring and farms and homes,
With the Fourth-month[4] eve at sundown, and the gray smoke
lucid and bright,
With floods of the yellow gold of the gorgeous, indolent,
sinking sun, burning, expanding the air,
With the fresh sweet herbage[5] under foot, and the pale green
leaves of the trees prolific,

---

3. **netherward,** toward the lower regions of the earth.
4. **Fourth-month,** April.
5. **herbage** (èr′ bij), grass.

In the distance the flowing glaze, the breast of the river, with a
    wind-dapple here and there,   85
With ranging hills on the banks, with many a line against the
    sky, and shadows,
And the city at hand with dwellings so dense, and stacks of
    chimneys,
And all the scenes of life and the workshops, and the workmen
    homeward returning.

12

Lo, body and soul—this land,
My own Manhattan with spires, and the sparkling and
    hurrying tides, and the ships,   90
The varied and ample land, the South and the North in the
    light, Ohio's shores and flashing Missouri,
And ever the far-spreading prairies cover'd with grass and
    corn.

Lo, the most excellent sun so calm and haughty,
The violet and purple morn with just-felt breezes,
The gentle soft-born measureless light,   95
The miracle spreading bathing all, the fulfill'd noon,
The coming eve delicious, the welcome night and the stars,
Over my cities shining all, enveloping man and land.

13

Sing on, sing on you gray-brown bird,
Sing from the swamps, the recesses, pour your chant from the
    bushes,   100
Limitless out of the dusk, out of the cedars and pines.

Sing on dearest brother, warble your reedy song,
Loud human song, with voice of uttermost woe.

O liquid and free and tender!
O wild and loose to my soul—O wondrous singer!   105
You only I hear—yet the star holds me, (but will soon depart),
Yet the lilac with mastering odor holds me.

14

Now while I sat in the day and look'd forth,
In the close of the day with its light and the fields of spring,
    and the farmers preparing their crops,
In the large unconscious scenery of my land with its lakes and
    forests,   110

SUNSET ON LONG ISLAND, William Hart
National Academy of Design, New York City

In the heavenly aerial beauty, (after the perturb'd winds and
    the storms),
Under the arching heavens of the afternoon swift passing, and
    the voices of children and women,
The many-moving sea-tides, and I saw the ships how they
    sail'd,
And the summer approaching with richness, and the fields all
    busy with labor,
And the infinite separate houses, how they all went on, each
    with its meals and minutia[6] of daily usages,   **115**
And the streets how their throbbings throbb'd, and the cities
    pent—lo, then and there,
Falling upon them all and among them all, enveloping me with
    the rest,
Appear'd the cloud, appear'd the long black trail,
And I knew death, its thought, and the sacred knowledge of
    death.

6. **minutia** (mi nü′ shē ə), smallness, triviality.

Then with the knowledge of death as walking one side of me,   **120**
And the thought of death close-walking the other side of me,
And I in the middle as with companions, and as holding the
    hands of companions,
I fled forth to the hiding receiving night that talks not,
Down to the shores of the water, the path by the swamp in the
    dimness,
To the solemn shadowy cedars and ghostly pines so still.   **125**

And the singer so shy to the rest receiv'd me,
The gray-brown bird I know receiv'd us comrades three,
And he sang the carol of death, and a verse for him I love.

From deep secluded recesses,
From the fragrant cedars and the ghostly pines so still,   **130**
Came the carol of the bird.

And the charm of the carol rapt me,
As I held as if by their hands my comrades in the night,
And the voice of my spirit tallied[7] the song of the bird.

Come lovely and soothing death,   **135**
Undulate[8] round the world, serenely arriving, arriving,
In the day, in the night, to all, to each,
Sooner or later delicate death.

Prais'd be the fathomless universe,
For life and joy, and for objects and knowledge curious,   **140**
And for love, sweet love—but praise! praise! praise!
For the sure-enwinding arms of cool-enfolding death.

Dark mother always gliding near with soft feet,
Have none chanted for thee a chant of fullest welcome?
Then I chant it for thee, I glorify thee above all,   **145**
I bring thee a song that when thou must indeed come, come
    unfalteringly.

Approach strong deliveress,
When it is so, when thou hast taken them I joyously sing the dead,
Lost in the loving floating ocean of thee,
Laved[9] in the flood of thy bliss O death.   **150**

---

7. **tallied,** corresponded with.
8. **undulate** (un′ jə lāt), move in waves.
9. **laved** (lāvd), washed.

From me to thee glad serenades,
Dances for thee I propose saluting thee, adornments and feast-
ings for thee,
And the sights of the open landscape and the high-spread sky are
fitting,
And life and the fields, and the huge and thoughtful night.

The night in silence under many a star,   155
The ocean shore and the husky whispering wave whose voice I
know,
And the soul turning to thee O vast and well-veil'd death,
And the body gratefully nestling close to thee.

Over the tree-tops I float thee a song,
Over the rising and sinking waves, over the myriad fields and the
prairies wide,   160
Over the dense-pack'd cities all and the teeming wharves and ways,
I float this carol with joy, with joy to thee O death.

15

To the tally of my soul,
Loud and strong kept up the gray-brown bird,
With pure deliberate notes spreading filling the night.   165

Loud in the pines and cedars dim,
Clear in the freshness moist and the swamp-perfume,
And I with my comrades there in the night.

While my sight that was bound in my eyes unclosed,
As to long panoramas of visions.   170

And I saw askant[10] the armies,
I saw as in noiseless dreams hundreds of battle-flags,
Borne through the smoke of the battles and pierc'd with
missiles I saw them,
And carried hither and yon through the smoke, and torn and
bloody,
And at last but a few shreds left on the staffs, (and all in
silence),   175
And the staffs all splinter'd and broken.

I saw battle-corpses, myriads of them,
And the white skeletons of young men, I saw them,

---

10. **askant,** sideways, aslant.

Abraham Lincoln's birthplace was a log cabin near Hodgenville, Kentucky.

I saw the debris and debris of all the slain soldiers of the war,
But I saw they were not as was thought,   180
They themselves were fully at rest, they suffer'd not,
The living remain'd and suffer'd, the mother suffer'd,
And the wife and the child and the musing comrade suffer'd,
And the armies that remain'd suffer'd.

16

Passing the visions, passing the night,   185
Passing, unloosing the hold of my comrades' hands,
Passing the song of the hermit bird and the tallying song of
    my soul,
Victorious song, death's outlet song, yet varying ever-altering
    song,
As low and wailing, yet clear the notes, rising and falling,
    flooding the night,
Sadly sinking and fainting, as warning and warning, and yet
    again bursting with joy,   190
Covering the earth and filling the spread of the heaven,
As that powerful psalm in the night I heard from recesses,
Passing, I leave thee lilac with heart-shaped leaves,
I leave thee there in the door-yard, blooming, returning with
    spring.

I cease from my song for thee,   195
From my gaze on thee in the west, fronting the west,
    communing with thee,
O comrade lustrous with silver face in the night.

Yet each to keep and all, retrievements out of the night,
The song, the wondrous chant of the gray-brown bird,
And the tallying chant, the echo arous'd in my soul,   200
With the lustrous and drooping star with the countenance full
    of woe,
With the holders holding my hand nearing the call of the bird,
Comrades mine and I in the midst, and their memory ever to
    keep, for the dead I loved so well,
For the sweetest, wisest soul of all my days and lands—and this
    for his dear sake,
Lilac and star and bird twined with the chant of my soul,   205
There in the fragrant pines and the cedars dusk and dim.

UNDERSTANDING AND INTERPRETATION

"One's-Self I Sing"

1. The poet says in the opening lines that he will sing of one self and of all selves simultaneously. Explain this apparent contradiction.

2. List and discuss the other themes about which Whitman promises to sing.

"I Hear America Singing"

1. Explain how this poem demonstrates Whitman's interest in all kinds of people.

2. Obviously Whitman's intention in the poem is to express in condensed form the spirit of America. Discuss whether you believe he is being realistic or romantic; that is, whether all people then actually lived this happily or whether the poet is simply giving an ideal picture.

"When I Heard the Learn'd Astronomer"

1. Whitman looks in two directions in this poem and chooses one as the shorter road to an understanding of God and nature. How would you identify these two outlooks?

2. What is the cumulative effect of words like "proofs," "figures," "charts," "diagrams"?

3. What connection is there between "applause" in line 4 and "accountable" in line 5?

4. Why is the night air "mystical" and what is implied in this word? How is the implication reinforced in the "perfect silence" of the last line?

"A Noiseless Patient Spider"

1. As in "When I Heard the Learn'd Astronomer," Whitman divides this brief poem between two subjects, only here it is a comparison between the spider and the poet's soul, dissimilar though they may seem at first. What are the attributes he admires in the spider?

2. Does the repetition of the word "filament" help to underscore these attributes? Note that the filament comes "out of itself," meaning out of the spider's body. Why is this important in the next stanza?

3. The soul in vast oceans of space is a familiar poetic way of speaking of the spirit "surrounded" by the body yet "living" in another element. How do the joined verbs "musing, venturing, throwing" connect the soul and the spider?

4. What sort of thread is a "gossamer" thread? Does the poet succeed in applying it to both the spider and the soul?

"When Lilacs Last in the Dooryard Bloom'd"

1. What is the "trinity" that spring brings to the speaker? In what sense are they a trinity?

2. Where is the hermit thrush first mentioned? In what section of the poem does it sing its song?

3. What does the "powerful western fallen star" symbolize?

4. How do you interpret "Death's outlet song of life"?

5. Whose coffin is referred to in section 5?

6. What gesture does the speaker make at the end of section 6, and what is the gesture's significance?

7. What attitude toward death does the poem express?

8. What happens to the three major images of the poem—the lilacs, the evening star, and the bird—in the final lines of the poem?

9. Trace the symbol of spring and the theme of rebirth through the poem, concentrating on sections 1, 5, 11, 12, and 14.

10. One critic has said of this poem that its true focus is a presentation of the poet's mind at work in the context of Lincoln's death and that "the true subject is . . . the poetic process." Support or argue against this statement, giving reasons.

FOR APPRECIATION

Free Verse

When we speak of the *rhythm* of a line of poetry or prose, we mean the natural rise and fall of language in wavelike motion. By *meter* we mean carefully arranged rhythm, with the accents spaced in patterned intervals of time. Poets such as Poe and Longfellow used meter to limit their lines. "Oft have I seen at some cathedral door" is a strictly ordered five-beat line; Longfellow follows it with thirteen other five-beat lines to form a sonnet. His *rhyme scheme* is equally patterned, thus further limiting the shape of the poem.

Whitman wished to forsake meter and rhyme. He wrote what we now call *free verse*. Some poets feel free verse is not verse at all, since its only distinction from rhythmical prose is the arrangement into lines, each one usually capitalized. Whitman, however, liked the liberation of free verse. It gave him more scope, more expansiveness, and he never worried about metrical count. That is not to say he wrote in paragraphs or rejected any controls that would give his stanzas unity.

We may define free verse as verse that does not conform to any fixed pattern. It is to be distinguished from *blank verse,* which does follow a fixed pattern—five stresses to each line with the accent falling on every other syllable in a rising meter ($\smile$ $'$). Free and blank verse have in common the fact that they are unrhymed.

You may find Whitman's verse more difficult to analyze than Longfellow's sonnet, but look closely at his poems to see if he does not use some of these devices to give his work controlling form:

1. End-stopped lines. The end of the line corresponds with the natural pause in speech. Invariably the line ends with a mark of punctuation.

2. Parallel constructions. A whole phrase or a single word is repeated at the beginning of each line. Occasionally Whitman merely repeats a grammatical form in parallel: noun-verb, or noun-verb-object.

3. Single-sentence stanzas.

4. Repetition.

5. Recurring symbols.

6. Alliteration (repetition of initial consonants) and assonance (repetition of vowel sounds).

A TWENTIETH-CENTURY WRITER LOOKS BACK

The Civil War was a tragic time in our history. Brother fought against brother—quite literally, sometimes—and losses in human life and property were staggering. Forty percent of all those who fought became casualties (either dead or wounded). With more than 600,000 dead, it was the bloodiest war in American history and the bloodiest in the world in the nineteenth century.

One might well wonder why a twentieth-century writer would want to look back on such a period. There really was no glory on either side. But history can be valuable for the lessons it teaches, and the study of it may enlighten us and possibly even help us to avoid repeating mistakes. Moreover, every war has behind-the-scenes inner dramas, and it is these that are the main focus of "The Battle of Finney's Ford," the selection you are about to read. What thoughts go through a young man's head as he considers taking arms against his brothers? What forces pull him in one direction or the other? How will he behave when faced with the realities of the battle?

While "The Battle of Finney's Ford" is fiction, it is based on a threatened raid by a real historical figure, the Confederate general John Hunt Morgan, who led a number of daring raids behind the Union lines in West Virginia, Indiana, and Ohio in 1862–1863. In July 1863 he actually led a force of about 2500 men from Kentucky to Vernon, Indiana, where the story takes place.

Jessamyn West was born near North Vernon, Indiana, and her great-grandparents were living in the area when Morgan's raiders arrived. These ancestors, like the fictional Birdwell family in the story, were Quakers, a religious group that believes that war is contrary to the letter and spirit of the Gospel. Quakers—or "Friends" as they are also called—are religiously committed to nonviolence and of course also accept the Old Testament injunction, "Thou shalt not kill." But what will the eighteen-year-old protagonist, Josh Birdwell, do when his town and the lives of his family are threatened?

Jessamyn West   1902–

In 1931, while still in her twenties, Jessamyn West suffered a lung hemorrhage. She spent the better part of the next two years in a sanatorium, after which she was sent home so that she could die in the company of those she loved. But in spite of the severity of her tuberculosis, with the help of her mother, her husband, and her own will, she did not die, though her convalescence did not end till 1945. Fourteen years is a long time to be ill, but from about 1933 on she was well enough to write stories. She published her first piece of fiction in 1939, and in the year of her final victory over tuberculosis, her first book, *The Friendly Persuasion,* appeared.

Jessamyn West was born in Indiana in 1902, but her family moved to Los Angeles County in 1909, and she spent her youth in California. She loved to read and thus was naturally drawn to English, which she studied at Whittier College—named after the Quaker poet John Greenleaf Whittier—and later at the University of California and at Oxford, England.

Her first book, which she once called "a love poem to Indiana," is set in that state, in the latter half of the nineteenth century. While it was not intended to be biographical, it is based to some extent on stories of her great-grandparents as she heard them from her mother. The book was ultimately made into a film by William Wyler, starring Gary Cooper, and was nominated for an Academy Award. West herself worked on the screenplay and acted as a technical advisor, an experience that she describes in a book, *To See the Dream.*

West's first novel, *The Witch Diggers* (1951), is also set in southern Indiana, and in 1967 she published a whole new set of stories on the same characters who peopled her first book, *Except for Thee and Me.* She has written other short story collections that deal primarily with growing up and girls' initiation experiences, such as *Cress Delehanty* (1953); *Love, Death, and the Ladies' Drill Team* (1955); and *Crimson Ramblers of the World, Farewell* (1970).

A good part of her recent work has been frankly autobiographical. In *Hide and Seek: A Continuing Journey* (1973), she wrote about the three months she spent alone in a trailer on a remote bank of the Colorado River, in imitation of one of her literary heroes, Henry David Thoreau. *The Woman Said Yes* (1976) tells how her mother nursed her through the darkest days of her bout with tuberculosis, and of her sister Carmen, who died of cancer. In 1980 she looked back on her first trip abroad in 1929 in *Double Discovery: A Journey.*

West has written about twenty books altogether, and her career is not easily summed up, but one of her clearest messages is that love means acceptance. Or, to quote a critic who was speaking about her 1979 novel, *The Life I Really Lived,* "love sanctifies."

from **THE FRIENDLY PERSUASION**

The Battle of Finney's Ford

Except for the name of Morgan the morning of the eleventh opened up like any other in July: clear, with promise of heat to come. Overhead arched the great cloudless sky of summer, tranquil above the reports, the rumors, the whisperings, the fears. And above the true evidence. The evidence brought in by the eye witnesses; by the boy who had hid himself and horse in the thicket while Morgan's outriders[1] galloped past; by the girl who had waded along the branch and was not seen; the stories of the burnings, the shootings, the looting.

The mind knew Morgan's name had altered the day, yet the untutored eye could find no difference, either in it or the horizon which framed it. Eliza, standing in the doorway of the summer kitchen, breakfast bell in hand, searched every crevice of the landscape, but in so far as she could see there was no shred of alteration in it. The cows, milked early, stood in the shade along the banks of the south branch; heat waves already rippled above the well-tasseled corn; the windmill turned round three or four times with considerable speed, then stopped, as if forever.

Eliza lifted her breakfast bell to ring, then let arm and soundless bell drop to her side. She felt a profound reluctance to disturb in any way the morning quiet. She had a conviction unreasoning, but deep, that the sound of her bell might be all that was needed to shatter tranquillity, call up from out of the wood lot, or across the river side, John Morgan himself.

Jess looked down at his wife. "Thee want me to ring it?" he asked.

"No," Eliza said. "I'll ring it. The boys need to be called up for their breakfasts." But she did not raise her arm nor sound the bell. "All's so quiet," she said. "It gives me the feeling I'd oughtn't disturb it. As if ringing the bell might be the beginning . . . as if hearing it, John Morgan might ride up and say, 'Has thee[2] any horses . . . any silver . . . any blankets?'"

"He don't ask, from what I hear," Jess said. "He takes."

"Ride up and take," Eliza said, as if digesting the fact. "Well, that's a happenchance. Flood or fire could do the same. One bolt of lightning's enough if it's the Lord's will. Talking's not my concern. It's what the boys would do."

"The boys?" Jess asked.

"Joshua," his wife answered.

Jess nodded.

"If hearing the name alone's enough . . . " Eliza began, "if the very sound of it's strong enough . . ."

"Yes," Jess said, nodding again.

Morgan's name had been heard in the southern counties before July, but it was in July that it began to be heard above everything else: above the rustle of the growing corn, the clack of mills, the plop of the big bass in the deep pools. Women churning stopped their dashers to listen, children stayed away from the wood lots, men worked quietly behind their horses, foregoing all talk lest their words muffle the approach of Morgan's scouts.

---

1. **Morgan's outriders,** John Hunt Morgan (1825–1864). Confederate cavalry commander famed for raids in Kentucky, Ohio, Indiana, and Tennessee.
2. **thee,** older objective form of personal pronoun still used by Quakers, often in subject position.

But it was the young men who listened most intently, the skin tightening across their cheek bones. Not with apprehension or fear so much as with wonder. What would they do? If the hoofbeats along the wood's trace were made by John Morgan's men? If the press-gang said, "Unhitch your horses, bub, bring out your hams and bacon, show us where the old man keeps his silver." Would they unhitch, the young men wondered . . . hand over Prince and Dolly, walk up through the fine dust of the field-path, lay the meat and silver on the outstretched hands? Would they? The young men did not know. They had no way of knowing.

Since childhood they had dreamed of resistance, but the foes they had resisted were mythical: the vanished Indian, the unseen highwayman, the long-gone river pirate, figures who fled easily, whose bullets ricocheted from resolute hearts. Morgan's men were not mythical, they did not flee, their bullets pierced even the most steadfast hearts. The young men at dusk on the river road, where the banks were shoulder high and foxgrapes, thick as curtains, hung between the shadowy trees, did not look back, nor hasten. But they listened. And wondered. And hearing nothing, were not reassured. Silence also was ominous.

Eliza once again lifted the breakfast bell. "Thee think I should ring it?" she asked.

"Ring it," Jess told her. "I got no mind to meet John Morgan on an empty stomach."

Breakfast was almost over when Joshua came in. He noted with astonishment the nearly empty gravy bowl, the meat platter with its single egg, the plates crusted with jam and biscuit crumbs. It was a wonder to him that people had been able on such a morning to sit down to the table, put gravy onto biscuits, spear slices of ham and then opening and shutting their mouths, chew such things with relish. Such eating, such self-concern, seemed, when their neighbors were dying, calloused and unspiritual.

It was not only that these men were their neighbors nor that their deaths were in a sense for them, since they had died defending beliefs Joshua and his family held dear: it was the whole matter of death to which Joshua was not yet reconciled. Nor was he reconciled to the apathy of his elders in the face of death, their indifference and mild acceptance. They said Amen and God's will be done. This he could have borne, had he been convinced that they really suffered, that God's name and the Amen had not come easy. Old people, and for Joshua all who were somewhat advanced beyond his own eighteen years were old, did suffer when they lost a member of their own households. This, Joshua was ready to admit.

But Joshua sorrowed over death as an abstract fact: he resented it for unknown men and women. He went without meals because of an item in The Banner *News* about a woman dead in a millpond in another county; because of a man dragged to death behind his team. He made himself forego all one fall—in so far as he was able—any sight of the frosty, autumnal constellations in which he delighted because of a conversation of his mother's which he had overheard. After a long sickness stretching through more than a year (his mother had told a visitor) a young woman, whose name was Lydia, had said, "I know I must die, but I wish I could live long enough to see Orion[3] outside my window once more." This girl (unknown to him) named Lydia had died, his mother said, in early August, long before Orion had come near her window. All that fall Joshua had kept his eyes off the evening sky, saying stubbornly, "I won't take anything she can't have. I won't look since she can't."

For the most part Josh kept these feelings to himself, for when they burst out, as they

---

3. **Orion** (ô rī′ ən), constellation of seven stars located east of Taurus.

RALPH WHEELOCK'S FARM, Francis Alexander
National Gallery of Art, Washington, D.C.
Gift of Edgar William and Bernice Chrylser Garbisch

occasionally did, what his mother and father had to say about them angered him.

"Thee should rejoice, son," Eliza once said when he had spoken sorrowfully of the death of a young boy who had gone through the ice and drowned. "Thee should rejoice. Young Quincy's in heaven, spared all this world's misery."

"Quincy didn't think this world was a miserable place," Joshua, who had known the boy, said.

"He'll find heaven a better place, Josh," his mother had insisted.

"He's cheated," Josh had flashed out. "He's cheated."

"Thee's not to question the Lord, Joshua," his mother said.

Ordinarily he was able to hear his father speak about death with more tolerance than his mother. His father was not so sure as his mother. Joshua saw that possibilities his

mother had never laid an eye on opened their long avenues of chance to his father's sight. But his father had a kind of calm, a tolerant pliability which sometimes set Joshua's teeth on edge. Old people, Josh thought, get so eroded by time and events that they are as slippery as a handful of wetted stones at a branch bottom. Rolling and tumbling against each other, slippery as soap, not a single rough, jagged spot left with which to hold on—or resist, or strike out.

"Thee'll find a lot of things worse than death, Josh," his father had said to him one day—more as if reading his mind than answering anything Josh had spoken.

Joshua had answered his father sharply. "Death was a curse, wasn't it? A curse put on man for his disobedience?"

"Well, yes," Jess had said. "In a way thee can . . ."

But Joshua had not waited for qualifications. "What's worse than the Lord's curse? If the Lord put a curse on thee, thee'd be wrong to find anything worse, wouldn't thee?"

This logic seemed inescapable to Joshua, but his father, with his usual suppleness, escaped it. "The Lord's curses," he said mildly, "can usually be borne. There are some few man devises for himself that bite deeper."

Joshua never spoke of these things to his brother, Laban, but Labe once asked him, incuriously, Josh thought, and in his usual sleepy way, "Is thee afraid to die, Josh?"

Josh had not known what to answer. He was opposed to dying . . . was he afraid of it? He didn't know. He remembered being frightened, years ago, by sounds at night which he couldn't account for, being so frightened that the thumping of his heart had stirred the bed covers like a hand. Then he had been able to calm himself by thinking: What's the worst that can happen to me? Nothing but this: the burglar will creep nearer and nearer, finally give me one hard clunk on the head and I'll be killed. This had always calmed him, had seemed so insignificant a thing that he would cease listening and fearing and sleep.

That was imagined death, though, and imagined danger; the sounds he heard, perhaps mice in back of the studding or nails snapping in a heavy frost. If the death were real death—the sounds of danger real sounds? The click of the breech-lock in the musket before firing, a man's sucked-in breath as he pressed the trigger? He didn't know.

"I don't know, Labe," he said. But like the other young men he wondered.

Now Josh stood with hands tightly clenched over the rounded top of the chair in which his brother, Little Jess, sat. He knew, in his self-conscious way, that his family was looking at him, and he made a strong effort to control his feelings. He was particularly aware of Labe's calm, cool gaze, and he supposed that Labe, in what he thought of as Labe's belittling way, was enumerating his own physical shortcomings (Labe who was muscular, smooth-jointed, supple): built like a beanpole, black hair like a wig, high, burning cheekbones, a lopsided mouth that trembles when he's in earnest.

"What kept thee, son?" his father asked.

"I went over to Whiteys'," Josh said.

"Sit, sit, Josh," his mother bade, bustling up from her place. "I'll cook thee fresh eggs."

"I couldn't swallow an egg," said Josh.

"What do they hear at the Whiteys'?" asked his father.

"Morgan's heading this way—he's following the railroad up from Vienna.[4] He's making for Vernon.[5] He'll be there today or tomorrow."

"Vernon," said his mother. She put the two eggs she had in her hand back in the egg crock. Vernon was home. Josh had as well've said the Maple Grove Nursery. Or the south forty.[6]

"How they know so much over at Whiteys'?" his father asked. "Morgan didn't cross the Ohio till evening of fourth day. Morgan's lost out there in the woods . . . got guerrillas trained to stay out of sight. Yet people'll sit at their breakfast tables and say just where John Morgan is. Tell you whether he's shaved yet this morning . . . and where he'll be this time tomorrow."

Josh felt, many times, like a stone beneath the cold waves of his father's detached unconcern. As if in spite of all he knew, and burningly believed, he would in time be worn down, effaced by all that ceaseless, quiet questioning.

"People at breakfast tables . . ." he began angrily, then stopped. "Ben Whitey was in Harrison County[7] when Morgan crossed over. He's been riding ahead of him for three days."

---

4. **Vienna,** a town in Scott County, southeast Indiana.
5. **Vernon,** a town in Jennings County, southeast Indiana.
6. **south forty,** forty-acre plot of land.
7. **Harrison County,** southwest corner of Ohio.

"Did thee talk to Ben?" asked his father.

"Yes."

"What did he say?"

This shift of approach, this willingness to learn, cutting from beneath his feet ground for reasonable anger, angered Josh anew.

"Nothing about whether Morgan'd shaved yet, or not, this morning."

"Son," said his father, "sit thyself down and tell us. Get up, Little Jess. Give thy brother thy chair."

Little Jess went around the table to Eliza's chair and hung over his mother's shoulder, awaiting Josh's word. Josh himself, without intending to do so, sat suddenly in the chair that was pushed out for him—and also without conscious intent, began to chew hurriedly on a cold biscuit. His mother made a gesture toward passing him butter and jam, but Jess shook his head and said, "Well, Josh?"

Josh spoke rapidly, his voice a little muffled by dry biscuit crumbs. "Ben Whitey passed a dozen of Morgan's outriders last night camped down this side of Blocher. Not more'n twenty miles from Vernon. They're following the railroad. They'll raid Vernon."

"Raid Vernon," said his mother. "What does that mean?" It was a word whose meaning on the page of any book she knew perfectly well. But, "Raid Vernon"—the town where she sold her eggs, the church town, the county fair town, with its whitewashed brick houses, its quiet, dusty streets, its snowball bushes dangling their white blossoms over the unpainted picket fences—what did that mean? "Raid Vernon," she said once again as if the words themselves might somehow suddenly focus, as a stereopticon glass[8] did when given just the proper shove, to show a landscape, lifelike in its dimensions, distances—and ruin.

Josh knew what the word meant. Ben Whitey had told him. "Raid means," he said, "burn, kill, take what you want."

"Are Morgan's men killing people?" Eliza asked.

For a second the world his mother saw flickered before Josh's eyes: a world of such loving companionableness that the word war had no other meaning for her than murder; where deliberate killing was unthinkable as though in her own household son should turn on son; but it flickered for a second only, then disappeared, leaving him angry again.

"Doesn't thee know there's a war?" Josh asked with intensity. "Doesn't thee know what a war is?"

"Thy mother knows there's a war, Josh," his father reminded him, "but she don't know what a war is. Let alone what a war in Vernon'd be like. She's more used to think of caring for people than killing them."

"John Morgan thinks of killing them," Josh said. "He shot a boy through the legs who didn't run fast enough. He shot an old man in the back. I don't know how many's dead in Harrison County. Ben Whitey said he could smell the smoke of Morgan's burnings the whole way up. He said he didn't think there was a mill left standing in Harrison County. He said the country's scoured of horses—and anything else in any house a trooper wanted and could carry across his saddle-bow."[9]

Eliza leaned across the table. "The earth," she said, "and the fullness thereof, is the Lord's. What's Morgan's men but a ruckus of boys with their pants in their boots? Trying to get something they've never had a taste of before? We've got more'n we need here. High time we're called on to share it with someone. If John Morgan's men came here," Eliza said —and Josh saw his mother's eyes turn toward the door of the summer kitchen as if she saw there a dusty, slouch-hatted trooper, "I'd offer them the best I had on hand. No man's my enemy," she said.

Josh stood up, crumbling in one hand the biscuit he had been quickly munching. "Some

---

8. **stereopticon glass,** apparatus for transparent slides, especially one using double pictures, each with a separate lens producing dissolving views and an effect of depth.
9. **saddle-bow,** the arch in front of a saddle.

men are my enemies," he said. "Any man's my enemy who kills innocent men and makes slaves. They're my mortal enemies."

Josh felt his sister Mattie's hand, long-fingered—and cold for so warm a morning—touch, then feel its way into his clenched fist, and he gave way to its insistent downward pressure and sat again. "I will share with my friends," he said. "If thee gives all thee's got to a thief, thy friends will have to go hungry—there's not enough to go around. What's good about that?" he asked.

No one answered his question, but Jess said evenly, "Tales like these are always a part of war times."

Tales were lies. Josh picked up a case-knife and tried to ease off some of his feelings in clenching it. "Ben Whitey don't lie . . . some he saw with his own eyes . . . some was told him. He saw the fires . . . he heard the people whose horses were stolen. He saw an outrider with a bird-cage and bird looped to his saddle. They said he'd been carrying that bird all the way from Maukport."[10]

Josh was interrupted by his mother. She had started up, taken two steps toward the kitchen window where Ebony, the starling, hung in his cage. There, after the two steps, she stopped, stood stock still in her tracks, as if just then aware of what she'd been doing. "This is thy chance," Josh told himself, "to keep thy mouth shut, not shove a contradiction down thy own mother's throat." But he could not do it. He wrapped his hand round the cutting edge of the case-knife, but there was not enough pain in its blunt edge to divert him.

"I thought thee said," Josh told his mother, his mouth trembling with scorn for himself, "that this was our chance to share? Thee's got a good chance now to share Ebony. Thee's had that bird a long time and every single man riding with Morgan's never had him once in his life time."

Eliza turned back facing the table and her family. Josh gazed at his mother's neat, dark head, saw her black eyes move for a moment toward the head of the table where his father sat, then turned resolutely toward himself. "I was thinking he might be mistreated," she said. "I've grown over-fond of the particular."

"Mistreated," Josh shouted, ignoring her admission. "Thee can worry about a bird's being mistreated while men are being shot. Thee'd try to save it and not turn thy hand to help the men. No man's thy enemy . . . unless he tries to take thy bird. Every man's enemy is my enemy. I'd do as much any day for a man as a bird."

Jess and Labe both started at once to speak, but Eliza held up her hand, as if she were in meeting. "I was wrong, Joshua," she said. "I'd give Ebony to any man who'd care for him."

"Care for him," Josh again shouted. "Thee was right the first time. Thee think that bird Ben Whitey saw's alive now? It's neck's been wrung long ago. If it was a big bird it's been boiled and eat. Ebony'd end up in no time on a forked stick over a fire."

Joshua leaned across the table toward his mother, gesturing with the case-knife, making Ebony the whole issue of war and peace, of life and death; talking to Eliza, but for his whole family . . . for Labe . . . to hear a contradict. "Thee has responsibilities. Thee can't just take birds and make them tame. Slit their tongues and fatten them so's they can't fly. Then let anybody grab them. And cook them. Thee don't have any right to be good and generous to such a price. A price thee don't pay. Old Ebony's got to pay that price. And that old man. And the boy shot in the legs. And the Harrison County Militia. And the Vernon Militia. I'd rather die," Josh said.

There was a long silence about the breakfast table. Eliza reseated herself. Little Jess looked from face to face with nervousness. He was embarrassed when grown-ups showed emotion. He thought it did not suit

10. **Maukport**, also **Mauckport**, a town in southern Indiana near the Kentucky border.

their faces. He saw it break the smooth surface of authority and knowledgeability with which they were accustomed to front him. And without that where were they? And where was he? Lost, not a thing to fall back on, floundering from notion to notion.

Mattie gazed at Ebony, jauntily cracking sunflower seeds in his wooden cage. She saw there both her mother's bird, who was first of all God's bird, and now was no man's bird, but belonged to all, and she saw Joshua's bird, the defenseless pet who would be plucked like a chicken and eaten unless they were willing to fight and die for him. And because she oscillated between the two ways of seeing Ebony, she suffered: when she was generous and peaceful, as was her mother, she thought herself a coward, and when she was, like Joshua, ready to fight (she supposed) she felt herself a renegade, an outcast from faith and scriptures.

Only Labe sat quietly at the table, his calm face touched neither by sorrow nor eagerness. One way only opened before him, and except that he believed this to be a matter between his mother and brother, and presently his father, he would have spoken, and said better words, he thought, for loving all men than his mother had said. And he would have gotten that bird from out the center of the conversation, where its feathers, its litter, its long periods of sulky quiet muffled and strangled the thing they should be really speaking of.

In the long silence . . . while there was no talk, sounds of great clarity filled the room. All, except Little Jess, harkened to them as if they were omens; as if each, properly apprehended, might carry some kind of a revelation: the slow grating start of the windmill easing into rhythmic clicking as the wind freshened; two distant notes as old Bess the bell-cow reached forward toward uncropped grass; the prolonged, sweet morning trill of a warbler, who, uncaged and undesired either by raiders or raided, flew, singing, near the windows, then flipped out of sight.

Jess, from his place at the head of the table, looked down toward his eldest son. He bent upon him a face of so much love and regard—and good humor, too, as if behind this talk of war there were still a few reasons to laugh—that Josh thought he might be unable to bear his father's gaze, would have to lay his arms across the table and bury his face in them, and so hidden, say, "Yes, pa," or "No, pa," to whatever his father had to say. But as his father continued to gaze, quizzically and lovingly, Josh knew that he had left behind him forever the happy time of freedom from decision and sat very straight, back teeth clamped together, lips trembling, waiting his father's word.

"Thee knows, Josh," his father said, "dying's only half of it. Any of us here, I hope"— and Jess included Little Jess and Mattie in the nod of his head—"is ready to die for what he believes. If it's asked of us and can be turned to good account. I'm not for dying, willy-nilly, thee understands," Jess said, his big nose wrinkling at the bridge. "It's an awful final thing, and more often and not nobody's much discommoded by it, except thyself, but there are times when it's the only answer a man can give to certain questions. Then I'm for it. But thee's not been asked such a question, now, Josh. Thee can go out on the pike, and if thee can find John Morgan, die there in front of him by his own hand if thee can manage it, and nothing'll be decided. He'll move right on, take Ebony, if he's a mind to, though I give John Morgan credit for being a smarter man than that and thee'll be back there on the pike just as dead and just as forgotten as if thee'd tied a stone round thy neck and jumped off Clifty Falls. No, Josh, dying won't turn the trick. What thee'll be asked to do now—is kill."

The word hung in the air. A fly circled the table, loudly and slowly, and still the sound of the word was there . . . louder than the ugly humming. It hung in the air like an open wound. Kill. In the Quaker household the word was bare and stark. Bare as in Cain and Abel's time with none of the panoply of wars and regiments and campaigns to clothe it. Kill. Kill a man. Kill thy brother. Josh regarded the word. He explored it, his hand tightening again about the knife.

"I know that," he said. "I am ready to fight." But that wouldn't do. He could not pretend that he was ready for the necessary act so long as he flinched away—from even the word. "I will kill these men if I have to."

"No, Josh," Eliza said.

Josh was glad to be relieved of the need of facing his father and regarding death abstractly. He turned to his mother. "Yes," he said. "I will. I'm going to meet Ben Whitey at eight. Soon as he's had two hours' rest. The Governor's made a proclamation. Every man's to join the Home Guard and help defend his town. We're going right down to Vernon and join. Morgan'll be there any time. I'd ought to've gone a week ago."

"Joshua, Joshua," cried his mother. "Thee knows what thee's turning thy back on? On thy church. On thy God. Thy great-grandfather came here with William Penn[11] to establish ways of peace. And he did," Eliza declared passionately. "With savage Indians. Men of blood. Now thee proves thyself to be worse than the Indians. They kept the peace."

Josh felt better. The picture of himself as bloodier than a savage Indian was so fantastic it hid for the time such savagery and blood-thirstiness as he did possess—and hid too, what Josh felt to be, perhaps even worse, his lack of these qualities. "The Indians," he said, "weren't dealing with John Morgan."

Jess spoke. First that bird, now William Penn and the Indians. The human mind could move, if it moved at all, only from symbol to symbol and these so chosen that sharp and even final issues were padded enough to make them more tolerable. "Josh," he said, "those who take the sword shall perish by it."

They were back to dying: only a nicer word. "I am ready to perish," said Josh.

But Jess wouldn't let them stay there.

"'Thou shalt not kill,'" said Jess.

There it was. "But He said, 'Render unto Caesar the things that are Caesar's,'" Josh said desperately. "I live here—in Jennings County. My town is Vernon. The Governor said to defend it. My body is my country's."

"Thy soul, son, is God's."

"God won't want it," Josh said, "if I don't do what I think's my duty." He was standing again, half crying, a horrible way for a man to be starting to war. "Thee can live with God now, maybe. I can't. I don't want to die . . . and I don't even know if I could kill anyone if I tried. But I got to try," he said, "as long as people around me have to. I'm no better'n they are. I can't be separated from them."

He left the table and ran toward the kitchen stairway. "I'm going," he said. "I'm meeting Ben Whitey at eight."

As he went up the stairs he heard his father say, "No, Eliza, no."

In his room Josh said, "Packing to go to war," but it didn't mean much. He scarcely believed it; though the pain that started at the bottom of his throat and seemed to run the whole length of his chest told him this was no ordinary departure. There wasn't much packing to do. Extra socks, Ben Whitey said. Spare handkerchiefs—good in case of a wound. Stout shoes—he had them on. A heavy coat—no telling how long they'd be in the field; they might have to chase Morgan the length of the state. Musket—his musket was always oiled, cleaned, ready; shot—he didn't know whether he had enough or not. He didn't know how many . . . He didn't know how good he'd be at . . . Knife—yes. Cup—he'd get that downstairs, and the tin plate. Two blankets to roll round all the stuff, saddle old Snorty—Morgan'd have to be a pretty slow runner if old Snorty was ever to catch up with him.

He was finished. Getting ready for war

---

11. **William Penn** (1644–1718), founder of the colony of Pennsylvania.

was a short horse[12] and soon curried, it seemed. There was nothing to do now but go. He'd keep that a short horse, too, but it'd be a horse of a different color. Josh marveled at himself. Cracking jokes, for that was what it was even though there was no one to hear. Ten minutes ago he'd been crying, his mouth full of death, duty and the scriptures and here he was, dry-eyed, a pain in his chest, to be sure, but somewhat outside the whole matter, far enough apart, anyway, to say it was like this or that. It was very peculiar—but the pain itself lay like a bar between him and what had gone before. There was the pain, wide, heavy, real, and he needn't, indeed he couldn't, cross over it to explore its causes.

He looked about the room—his and Labe's —neat, orderly, the bedcovers tossed back to air, the way his mother had taught them, clothes on pegs, chest drawers closed. He felt as if he wanted to say a prayer of some kind . . . God, take care of this room, or something like that, but he thought perhaps he'd better not. He wasn't sure God was with him in this move, in spite of what he had said downstairs, and there was no use involving Him in something He wouldn't approve. He'd picked up his bed-roll to go when Mattie came in. He would rather have seen almost anyone else.

As far as Josh could tell Mattie acted parts from morning to night: very delicate and fainty at one hour like she's too fine-haired to live on a farm, the next loud and yelling as if she had Comanche blood and a quarter section wasn't big enough to give her scope. She'd help him with a piece of work, doing more than her share, one time—the next sit half a day on a tree-stump, breathing, Josh supposed, but giving no sign of it.

"Oh, Joshua," said Mattie.

Josh held onto his bed-roll. Mattie'd been crying and Josh wasn't sure who he was seeing: sister Mattie or actress Mattie. A little of both, maybe, but when she threw her arms around his neck he thought he knew which one was clasping him most warmly.

"Oh, Joshua," said Mattie again.

YOUNG SOLDIER, Winslow Homer
Cooper-Hewitt Museum
Smithsonian Institution, New York City

"I've got to go, Matt," Josh said. "I'm late now."

Mattie took her arms down. "Josh," she said, "I want thee to take this." She had a little

12. **short horse,** quarter horse bred for short legs.

New Testament in her hand and she reached up and slipped it gently into Josh's shirt pocket. "There," she said. "Over thy heart it will guard thee from all harm." Then in her natural voice she added, "I read about two soldiers who'd've been shot through the heart except for their Bibles." Then sister Mattie was hidden away again, lost behind inclined head and folded hands.

Josh couldn't help laughing, so long and loud he was surprised.

"What's so funny?" Mattie asked. "Thee setting up to be an atheist?"

"No," Josh said, "I ain't. I'll take it, and read it, too, maybe." He put the little book in his hip pocket.

"Thee going to sit on it?" Mattie asked.

Josh shouldered his bed-roll again and went to the door. "It's the one sure foundation," he said.

"Why, Josh Birdwell," said Mattie. She had come upstairs expecting a pious and tearful farewell, and here was Josh laughing and joking, and not very reverently, either. Outside the door Josh turned back to reassure his sister. "Thee don't sit on thy hip pockets," he said. "Thee sits between them."

Mattie said feebly, "Good-bye, Josh."

The rest of the good-byes, Josh figured, had been said, in as far as they could be said, downstairs about the breakfast table. He went quietly out the front door and to the barn without seeing anyone. Not until he had saddled and tied his bed-roll to the saddle and led old Snorty out into the sunny barnyard did he see his mother and Little Jess standing at the bottom of the lane waiting for him. Seeing them, he was glad they were there.

Eliza's face was very serious but she wasn't crying. She held up a package to Josh. "Here's food, Josh. You'll have to eat. I didn't know what was best. This's mostly meat and cold biscuits."

Thinking of food Josh remembered the forgotten tin cup and plate.

"Run fetch them, Little Jess," Eliza said.

"Be lively," she called after him. "Josh mustn't be late."

Josh let old Snorty's reins hang and laid his arms about his mother's shoulders, hugging her tight.

"Good-bye, Joshua," his mother said, and then not a word about his coming home safe, only, "I hope thee doesn't have to kill anyone." Joshua shut his eyes for a minute. "If thee has to die that's thy own business and thee won't anyway unless it's the Lord's will— but, oh, son," Eliza said, "I hope thee don't have to kill."

Josh opened his eyes and smiled. That was just the right thing to say . . . the words he would've chosen for her. He patted his mother's shoulder. Sticking by her principles and not getting over-fond of the particular— even when it was her own son. Josh bent and kissed her. He could not have borne it if she had broken down, put his safety first.

"Good-bye," Josh said. "Don't thee worry. I'll be shaking too hard to hit or get hit." He kissed his mother and got into the saddle. Eliza made a gesture toward him of love and farewell and walked resolutely back up the lane.

Little Jess trotted along the pike beside Josh for a way. Before turning homewards he held onto the stirrup for a minute and whispered fiercely up to his brother, "Thee shoot one for me, Josh." Josh then, looking down into Little Jess' drawn face and lips thinned with whispering, saw that no man acted to himself.

Josh was to meet Ben Whitey at the Milford cut-off, but even now, riding alone, he supposed he was a soldier and he tried to carry himself, through the warm morning and down the dusty road, like a Home Guardsman: scanning the horizon for signs of smoke or dust, keeping an eye out for single horsemen. There was no telling; if outriders of Morgan's were only twenty miles away last night, they could easily be in this neighborhood now.

In spite of his conviction that his intentions made him a militiaman, sworn to hunt down and stop or kill John Morgan, Josh would fall into looking at the farmland with a country man's eyes: sizing up a field of wheat unaccountably left standing, or noting how the apples were shaping up in an orchard. To offset this he stopped and loaded his gun. If he were to meet or sight a raider it would be his duty to shoot. He tried to think how it would be to come upon a man, emerging from the woods, say, or around a sharp turn, not speak, not pause to pass the time of day, but instantly with raised musket fire and hope to blow the stranger's head off. The idea made Josh sweat. My God, Josh thought or prayed—he didn't know which—I hope it's no boy nor old man. I hope it's some hard, old slave-driving bugger. Thinking of this hard old slave-driving bugger Josh remembered that he might be a man handy with firearms himself, and he settled deeper into the saddle and listened more intently.

The pain he had felt in his chest after breakfast was gone: it its place he now had in his middle a curious, dry, empty, swollen feeling. As if he carried something inside him, hollow, but beyond his size and growing bigger.

Ben Whitey was waiting for him at the Milford cut-off, impatient, fuming. "You're half an hour late," he yelled.

"I know it," Josh said. "We'll make up for it now," but they were only fairly started when Ben, looking back down the pike, said, "Looks like Labe on Rome Beauty. He joining too?"

"No," Josh said, "he's got convictions the other way."

"Well, you forgot something then," Ben Whitey said, "and your ma's sending it you." He rode on while Josh turned back to meet Labe.

Labe came up at a long trot, the only kind Rome Beauty had, dismounted and said, "Get on. Father said for thee to take Rome."

Josh sat atop old Snorty, unmoving, unbelieving.

"Get down," said Labe. "If thee's going to fight Morgan, fight him. Don't set there like a bump on a log."

"Father's against my going," said Josh.

"He's against it, but that didn't stop thee. Now get on. He says as far as he knows, Rome's no Quaker. From all he can tell thee and Rome think about alike. Get on."

Josh got off Snorty, transferred his bedroll to Rome's saddle and stood in the dusty road beside his brother. He was taller than Labe but Labe's shoulders and stance made him feel small.

"Tell father," he began, but Labe interrupted him.

"Father said to tell thee most killing's caused by fear. . . . Rome's being under thee ought to help a little. He don't send thee Rome because his mind's changed about anything."

"Labe," Josh asked, "thee don't think about going?"

"No," said Labe, "I don't."

"I got to," said Josh. "Otherwise I'd always think maybe it was because . . ."

"Get on," said Labe, giving him no time to finish.

Astride the big red horse Josh rode after Ben Whitey, but before he overtook him he finished his sentence. "I am afraid," he said.

"You got a fine mount now," Ben Whitey told him and he drew alongside. "If you can just keep his nose headed the right direction you ought to make out."

"Never thee fear," Josh began . . . but he shut his mouth at that point. "Thee don't know," he told himself.

They rode into Vernon together; a roan, and a claybank, two rawboned farm boys: Ben Whitey, a born fighter, and Josh, who was trying to do his duty. They entered Vernon and saw it the way a man who thinks he has been dreaming wakes and sees the landscape of his dream lying all about him, the disaster real, hard and unmelting as sunlight —and dreaming the only means of escape. Deep in the country, on the farms they had believed—and not believed. To come here with loaded guns had been an act of faith and now their faith was justified. Morgan was true; he existed; he was killing and looting; he would be here at any hour. There were tens of mouths to tell them.

The town blazed under the July sun; it throbbed with the heat of the season—and the heat of fear and excitement and wonder and resolution. At first Josh thought it was alive as he had seen it for an August fair or Fourth of July celebration. And there was something of a holiday spirit in the plunging, headlong activity. As if fifty years of seeing the Muscatatuck[13] rise and fall, the crops ripen and be harvested, the summer rains harden and whiten into winter's snow and hail, were enough for Vernon, as if tired now of this placid punkin-butter existence, they would turn to something with sharper flavor.

That was the surface: the movement, the shouts, the numbers of horses in the street, the vehicles, the laughter even. That was what Josh saw when he saw everything at once and heard everything at once. A medley in which all the sounds, blending, were a holiday roar; all the sights, the excess movements of celebration when steps reach higher and higher into the air, bows go lower and lower toward earth and smiles strain at the limitations of a single face.

When he saw the sights, one by one, there was no holiday in them. There were spring wagons full of women, children and bedding headed for back country farms and supposedly greater safety.

"No sense in that," Ben Whitey said. "That way a couple of outriders can pick up the best any household has to offer without being put to the bother of ripping up the feather ticks and taking the insides out of clocks."

But in spite of what Ben Whitey thought, they were there: spring wagons, democrats, gigs, buckboards, all filled with women, children and valuables, and headed for back country and the hills. There were men throwing shovelfuls of earth out of deep holes, preparing to bury silver, money, keepsakes: whatever they and their wives cherished and thought a raider might fancy. There were boys barricading doors, boarding up windows, reinforcing bolts. There was a man who had turned his house into a store and was now busy ripping down his sign and trying to make his store look like a house again. There was an old fellow atop the gable of his house, peering off to the south through a long spy-glass. The voices, too, when Josh listened were not celebrating anything; they rasped; they started even, then broke; a man began yelling, looked around, ended whispering.

"Let's get out of this," Ben Whitey said. "Let's find the Home Guard."

They pulled up beside a one-legged man calmly taking his ease on a street corner.

"Where's Morgan?" yelled Ben Whitey.

"Don't know for sure. Reports are thicker'n toads after a rain, but he's near. Hear tell the old boy slept in Lexington last night."

"We're here to join the Home Guard," said Ben.

"'Bout a week late," said the one-legged man, sucking on a cold pipe.

"We know that," Ben told him, "but we come up as fast as we could. We're here now. We got prime horses and we'll give good accounts of ourselves. Where's the commander?"

"Not sittin' on his pratt recruiting."

Ben Whitey put his heel in his horse's flank. "Come on back," yelled the one-legged man. More quietly he said, "You johnnies rile me, through. Every drumstick of a boy comes in here from back country, brasher'n a parched pea, and ready to spit in old Johnnie

13. **Muscatatuck** (mus kə ta′ tək), river in southeast Indiana; flows into east fork of White River.

Morgan's eye. It'll take more spit'n you got, bub, or I miss my guess. Morgan's clear grit, ginger to the backbone and no more fear in him than a rifle."

"Which side you on?" Ben asked.

"Our side. I'm for whipping Morgan but you ain't gonna do it by . . ."

"Save thy breath to cool thy broth," Josh said. "Where's the Home Guard?"

"Well, I'll be," said the peg-legger. He took his pipe from his mouth and elevated his weather-beaten chops as if awaiting the salutation. "A Quaker sure's the Lord made Moses. What's thee planning to do, sonny? Pray for the boys?"

"Come on," said Ben and the two rode on down the street.

"How we going to get any place with men like that?" Josh asked.

"They ain't all like that," said Ben.

From across a picket fence an old man beckoned to them. "Want to mix in it?" he asked.

"That's what we're here for. Where's the Home Guard?"

"Everywhere," said the old man. He picked up the end of his long beard and used it to point with. "Spread thin, but mostly to the south. Morgan could circle us—but reports are he's hitting us solid from the south. Coming up the railroad from Vienna. They got companies posted at every ford, road and bridge south of town."

"Where you figger we could do the most good?"

"The bridge below the Forks. I been thinking about this for two days. I figger John Morgan being the man he is will come straight in, cross the bridge and bust into town from there. If you want to get in some telling licks that's the place I'd head for."

"That's the place we want," Ben said.

The Muscatatuck where it is bridged below the forks flows between banks of considerable height. Here the Home Guard Commander had massed as many men as could be spared from the other approaches to

Vernon. Of these, the majority and among them the men Colonel Williams considered most steady and level headed were stationed on the west bank of the stream ready to fall upon the raiders should the smaller force which was holding the approaches to the bridge be overpowered. The Colonel hoped to stop by show of force, if possible, if not, by force itself any thrust the raiders might make before they reached the bridge. Failing this the guard on the west bank would have a fine chance to pick off the men as they debouched[14] from the bridge and headed toward town.

That was the plan. The captain in command of the river could use as many men as he could get and when Ben and Josh showed up, well mounted, he sent them at once to join the company beyond the bridge.

"They're headed this way," the captain told them. "Some of them," he said, pointing, "are sitting right there on top of that hill. Them, we fooled. Our men marched across the cliff road and then out of sight of Morgan —if he's there—a half dozen times over. Musta looked like quite an army to him. But there's likely others and they may be here soon. If we don't stop them nothing will. Once they're past us, it will be Maukport and Salem and Lexington all over again. Keep your guns handy. Dismount and rest your horses, but stay by them and keep them quiet. I'm glad you're here. I need you."

Overhead the July sun had weight as well as heat. It lay across Josh's shoulders like a burning timber. Though Ben was on one side of him, and big Gum Anson, a beefy farmer, was on the other, still Josh felt bereft of shelter, unshielded and alone—a naked target.

For a long time he scanned the road before him with rigid and unrelaxing vigilance. There was not much to be seen: the dusty road, the lush growth of summer, dock, vol-

14. **debouched** (di büsht'), marched out into open ground.

unteer oats, some daisies, a small field of shoulder high corn, and beyond these a thicket and the road curving out of sight around it. Above earth and river and the river's rank growth were the heat waves, the massive clouds of noon skies, the burning sun. Josh, who felt as if the whole duty of seeing and apprising rested with him, inspected every leaf and shadow. When a sudden movement of air fluttered the leaves of the elders up the road and rasped through the corn he lifted his gun, then put it down shamefacedly. He would feel the sweat trickle down the sides of his chest, then drop to his middle and soak in around his belt.

"Have some cherries," said Gum. "You can't keep that up all afternoon." He held out a big bag. The cherries were cool and firm and Josh took a handful.

"When Nance brought these out this morning," Gum said, "I'd've thrown 'em down except to please her. Goin' off to fight Morgan with a bag of cherries tied to my saddle like a doggone picnicker." He munched away and spat pits. "Looks like they might be the handiest article I brought."

"Wait'll Morgan gets here, Gum," somebody yelled. "It's gonna take more'n cherry-stones to stop that old shite-poke."[15]

"I got more'n cherry-stones," Gum called back and the men around him laughed.

Josh shifted in his saddle and looked about. He was amazed at the sound of laughter, amazed that men waiting to kill or be killed should laugh and joke. He scanned the faces of those who were laughing: old fellows, middle-aged farmers, boys younger than himself. Sweating, chewing tobacco, some lolling in their saddles. Most, dismounted. Some in uniform, others not. Mounted on farm plugs. Mounted on fast animals he had seen at county fairs. Every kind of fire arm. One man with a bayonet even. The sight of that lifted Josh up in his saddle again. Did the raiders carry bayonets? His sweating which he had not noticed for a while had started up once more.

"Have some more cherries?" asked Gum.

Josh took another handful. "Thanks," he said. "I was awful dry. And hungry, too. I can't remember when I had anything to eat last."

"Go kinda slow on them cherries, then. They don't set too good on'n empty stomach."

"They're setting good on mine," Josh said, chewing and spitting, but keeping his eyes uproad.

"Take it easy," advised Gum. "You'll be petered out before Johnnie gets here. They's scouts up ahead. They'll let us know if anything's twitchin'."

Josh felt a fool not to have thought of that before rearing up till his backbone was petrified, and staring till his eyes popped, acting like he was scout, trooper, captain, everything; the other men were relaxed, guns dangling or laid across their bed-rolls; some smoking; a man behind him was having a nip of something that didn't smell like switchel.[16]

"Old Morgan'll never come this way," one bearded farmer was saying. "That boy's shiftier than a creased buck. He ain't never goin' to fight his way in the front door when the back door's open."

"Back door ain't so all-fired wide open's you might think."

"Open or shut—what's it to Morgan? With five thousand men you go in where it pleasures you and don't wait for the welcome mat to be put out."

"Five thousand," somebody yelled. "What the heck we doing here? Why ain't we making a good hickory[17] for Indianapolis?"

"Indianapolis, boy? You better stay clear of there. Morton's waitin' for you there with a writ."

"Five thousand or ten thousand," said a quiet voice, "I'm going to stay right here. I'm

15. **shite-poke,** a small heron.
16. **switchel** (swich' əl), drink made of molasses or honey, maple syrup, water, and sometimes rum.
17. **making a good hickory,** traveling at a rapid pace.

going to give Morgan the butt-end of my mind if nothing else before he busts over that bridge and into my store."

"Me too. Only I'm goin' to talk with lead. My folks live down in Harrison County."

"Did you hear about old man Yardell?"

"Ya—shot in the back."

"Not doin' a thing—just come to his door to see what the ruckus was about."

"Did you hear about 'em down at Versailles? Had the cannon loaded, ready to let go smack dab in the middle of the rebs."

"What happened?"

"Cannoneer dropped his coal and before they could get another the rebs took the gun."

"Oughta court-martial the feller who done that."

"'Fore the afternoon's over, Grogan, you'll likely change your tune as to that."

The afternoon wore on. To the funky[18] smell of the river and of lush river growth was added that of sweating men and horses. Josh eased Rome's girth and hoisted his blankets so a little air could flow under them. Back in the saddle he felt light-headed and detached. Gum had been right about the cherries; they weren't setting right. He felt kind of sick but happy. He'd got here, he was all right, he was where he belonged. By twisting about he could see a curve of the Muscatatuck where it flowed in shallow ripples across a sandbar, then darkened as the channel deepened near the bridge. It was three or four o'clock. The sun went through the water and onto the sandbar, then flashed, pulsing with the movement of the water in his temples. He could see the silvery glint of the little minnows, like bullets; a dragon-fly ran its darning needle in-and-out—in-and-out of the flowing water. It was July . . . a summer afternoon . . . the cool water . . . the hot sun . . . the darting . . . the silver bullets.

Josh's neck stiffened, his head snapped up, his hand closed round the stock of his gun. A horseman was pounding up the road.

"It's one of our scouts," said Ben Whitey.

" 'Boys,' he said, 'they're closing in. They're up the road a couple of miles . . . I expect them to charge.' "

The rider, a little fellow in uniform on a lathered black, pulled up beside the captain. Josh couldn't hear what he was saying, but after a minute the captain turned and told them, his voice quiet but with an edge to it that let them know that this was it, the time had come.

"Boys," he said, "they're closing in. They're up the road a couple of miles. Less of 'em than we figured. I expect them to charge. There's just two things to remember: first, stand steady. Second, don't fire till I give the word." He stood in his stirrups and pounded

18. **funky,** here: strong, offensive.

the words home. "Don't fire till I give the word. If you fire before you can make your shots good, it's all over. They'll ride you down. Hold it. Your guns carry just as far as theirs, and you're better shots. Those men've been in the saddle for weeks now, and it's telling on them. Shoot low so's if you miss a man you get a horse. But don't miss."

The scout went on past them at a gallop and Josh could hear the black's hooves ring on the bridge planking, then quiet as he hit the dust of the road on the west bank where the men in hiding were waiting the news. The captain himself wheeled round to await the attack with his men.

Josh reached for his gun. Waves of something, he didn't know what, were hitting his chest. It's like riding through the woods and being hit by branches that leave thee in the saddle, but so belabored thy chest aches, he thought. Other waves, or perhaps the same ones, pounded against his ears, broke in deafening crashes as if he were deep under water, buffeted by currents that could break bones, could rip a man out of his flesh and let him run, liquid away. Then, in the midst of the pain and crashing, Josh thought, it's thy heart beating. Nothing but thy heart.

Gum said, "Fix those lines, boy." And again, "Get those reins fixed. If your horse jerks his head he'll spoil your aim."

Josh saw that Gum was right. He got his hand out of the reins and rubbed it along Rome's neck. "Good boy," he said. "Good old Rome. Thee'll be all right." He knew he was encouraging himself. Rome didn't need cheering—he stood solid as a meeting house, only his big head moving up and down a little.

They were all waiting. Ben Whitey was cussing, a long line of words as if he was dreaming, or singing, in a kind of funny way. But they were mostly quiet—listening. Something came down, or perhaps it came up, out of the earth itself, something very thin and fine, like a spun web, and held them all together. Josh could feel it. Anybody could

break away from it, if he liked, but while they headed the same way, waited the same thing, it held them. You could lean against it like steel. Josh felt its support . . . the waves beat against him, but he leaned against that fabric and it held him.

It held him until he heard the first sounds: a rebel yell from up the road, beyond the elder thicket—then another. Josh never knew a man could make a sound like that. It was a screech such as an animal might make —only it was in a man's voice, a voice that could say "Farewell" or "Rain tomorrow" . . . and that made it worse. It sounded crazy . . . it sounded as if the tongue that gave it could lap blood. It broke the web that held them together, it left Josh alone.

He could hear far away the thud of hooves and the waves that had beat against his ears before began now to say words: Rome's fast, Rome's mighty fast. Run for it, run for it. The minute they turn the curve, run for it.

He looked around, he picked out the likely path. "Sure wish I had a cherry-stone to suck on," said Gum Anson. "Sure am parched."

Gum's words drowned out the others. The hoof beats came nearer. What's the worst can happen to thee? Josh asked himself. Get a bullet in thy gizzard. Get killed. Nothing else . . . It was all right. He settled down to wait.

"Hold it, hold it," the captain was calling. "Wait for the word. Hold it. Hold it."

From around the bend, very slowly, came a single man, carrying a white flag. A few paces behind him were perhaps twenty or thirty other mounted men.

"It's a trick, it's a trick," the Home Guardsmen were yelling. "Watch it, captain. It's funny business."

"Don't shoot," shouted the colonel who had ridden up. "Don't fire on a white flag. But watch 'em. Keep 'em covered."

He rode forward a couple of paces. "Are you surrendering?" he called.

The man with the white flag called back, "No. No surrender. We want to parley."

"Come on in," said the colonel. "You," he yelled. "You with the white flag. The rest of you stay back."

"Trying to get up inside our range and ride us down," said Gum.

The flag-bearer came up alongside the Home Guard colonel and saluted.

"Keep your guns on those men," the colonel called back, then lowered his own. Josh couldn't hear his words, but could see that the raider was talking fast and earnestly.

"Could be your brother," said Gum.

It was so. The rebel doing the talking was tow haired and young, a gaunt brown-faced boy, very broad shouldered and supple in the saddle. Josh's gun, which had been leveled on him, wavered, but he brought it to bear, once again.

The Guardsmen were getting restless. "Tell him to make up his mind. Surrender and talk—or shut his mouth and fight."

"What's he doin'? Preachin'?"

"Lectioneering for Jeff Davis."

"Shut him up, colonel. Shut him up."

"We'll make him talk outa the other corner of his mouth."

"You the one shot old man Yardell?"

The colonel turned his back on the raiders and rode up to his own men. "Don't take your guns off them," he told them. "He says we're surrounded. He says they've cut in back of us—that they've got five thousand men circled around Vernon and it's suicide to resist. He says every bridge and ford can be rushed. He says surrender and save bloodshed. He says if we surrender nobody'll be harmed. Provisions and fresh mounts taken only. What do you say?"

The storekeeper who had wanted to give Morgan the butt-end of his mind rose now in his stirrups and delivered a piece of it. "He's lying. Men don't start talking until they're past fighting."

"If he had five thousand men they'd be in Vernon now. Blood shed, so long's it's your blood, ain't nothin' to a reb."

"Horses and provisions, eh? Who appointed us quartermaster corps to the Confederate Army?"

Ben Whitey gave the final answer. He yelled. His yell wasn't practiced like the rebel screech; it hadn't the long falsetto[19] midnight quaver which could raise the hackles and slide between the bones like cold steel, but it was very strong and it lifted toward the end with a raw, unsheathed resonance of its own. It seemed what they had waited for—it seemed the only answer to give. It drained away the uncertainty, the distrust, the fear of the long wait. Above the quiet river it rose in great volume and flowed in a roiled and mounting current across the summer fields. Josh's musket quivered with the violence of his own shouting.

The colonel regarded his men quizzically, then shrugged his shoulders as if to say to the raiders, What can I do with such fire-eaters? and rode back to the rebel leader. There was another conference shorter than the first one, after which the raiders turned, cantered back down the road up which they had just ridden.

"They give us two hours," the colonel said, "to get our women and children out of town. After which, they attack."

At eight that evening they were still waiting, drawn up, ready. The new moon had set and the night was very dark and warm, filled with soft summer stars which seemed to escape from set star shapes and let light shimmer fluidly—and it almost seemed, moistly—across the sky. Some time later the captain with a militiaman came up to the group Josh was in.

"Count off here," he said. "I'm sending twenty of you men to Finney's Ford. The rebs could come through there as well as here if

---

19. **falsetto** (fôl set' ō), artifically produced voice that falls short of full voice.

they know the crick.[20] There's a company there now—but no use having any if you don't have enough." He turned to the militia-man. "Let some of your men sleep," he said, "but keep a heavy guard posted."

Josh rode with the twenty men slowly and quietly through the night, back across the bridge and to a bank above the river where any party attempting to use the ford could be fired on while in the water. He rode among strangers. Gum and Ben Whitey had been left behind, and he thought, as he had been thinking all day, Now it begins.

In the darkness the company at the ford seemed very large; the men dismounted, speaking in muffled voices, their horses tethered and resting behind them.

"The crick takes a turn here," the new men were told. "Twenty feet down to the bottom here, so keep your eyes peeled. I'm going to let you men have a couple of hours' sleep, then you can relieve some of us. Get out of your saddles and get some rest—but don't rest so hard you can't hear a raider crossin' that branch."

Josh dismounted and felt his way along the bank in the layered darkness. He felt rather than saw the stream below him, smelled it, really, he believed, though he could hear the occasional lap of a little eddy against a stone, and see here and there a prick of light reflected from a star. He ate cold biscuit and dried beef, gave Rome a biscuit, then stretched out on his blankets, somewhat withdrawn from the main body of the militia and near the bank of the stream. Rome stood behind him snuffing at the scent of the strange men and horses about him, mouthing the already cropped-over grass in search of a neglected tuft.

War, Josh thought, seemed a hard thing to come at. The dying and killing he had declared himself ready for at the breakfast table, and which he had imagined he would meet face to face as soon as he'd gotten out onto the road, seemed always to lurk around another corner. He had fortified himself for so many encounters with either or both that there were now almost no breastworks he could fling up, or armaments he could assemble. His supply of anticipation was about used up. War appeared to consist not of the dramatic and immediate sacrifice, either of his body in dying, or his spirit in killing, as he had foreseen it at the breakfast table, but of an infinite series of waitings and postponements.

This is it, he had said, and it was only Ben Whitey waiting at the cut-off. This is it, and it was Vernon as much like Fourth of July as war. This surely is it, he had said, and it was the wind in the elder clump. This, this: a man with a white flag. And now in the dark night to defend the vulnerable ford—and this was not it either, but simply lying at ease on his blankets, his cherry-addled stomach settled with good beef and biscuit, Rome munching by his side and the Milky Way banding the sky familiarly. Except for the gun under his hand it could be any summer night, lying outside for a time to cool off before bed time. And if John Morgan himself, lantern in hand, should bend over him, prod him with his toe and say, "This is it, bub," he didn't know whether he'd believe him or not. Maybe John Morgan was waiting and hunting, too, no more an authority on *its* arrival than he. Getting ready for war might be a short horse and soon curried, but war itself was a horse liable to stretch, so far as he could see, from July to eternity . . . head at Maple Grove and hocks[21] in Beulah Land.

Josh closed his eyes to sleep; but beneath his lids there flowed not only the remembered sights of the day, the faces, attitudes, gestures he had seen and noted, but the multitudinous sights that there had been in daylight no time to name, or space within the crowded mind to delineate. Now in darkness,

20. **crick,** here: dialect for creek.
21. **hocks,** hind limb of a horse, corresponding to the ankle of a human being.

behind shut lids, they lived again. He saw the L-shaped rip in the pants of the raider who had carried the white flag, and beneath the rip, the long, improperly healed wound which reddened the man's calf from knee to ankle. He saw now, what he had missed then, the downward motion of the raider's hand toward his gun when Ben Whitey's yell lunged unexpectedly toward him. He saw now, trying to sleep, the controlled drop of a spider, delicately spinning, from the spire of an unblooming head of goldenrod to the yellowed grass beneath it. He heard Gum Anson's answer to someone who asked him, "What you doing here, Gum?" "I'm a farmer," said Gum, "and you can't farm unless you keep the varmints down." He heard another voice—the storekeeper's, he thought—say, "I'm a man of peace—but there ain't any peace when your neighbors are being killed. And if it's a question of good blood, or bad, on my hands, by God, I choose bad."

At last he slept—and continued to see and hear . . . a raider was trying to take Ebony . . . he had ridden his horse inside the summer kitchen, and overturned the table, trampled the crockery and was snatching at Ebony, who above the sounds of confusion was screaming, "Wake up, wake up."

Josh woke up. He found himself in the center of a great, bubbling cauldron of noise: men shouting, screaming advice, cursing; horses neighing; and in the creek below the splash and clatter of men and animals crossing the ford. There was a spattering of shots. Someone was calling over and over, "Mount, mount, mount."

Josh stepped cautiously, felt for Rome in the dark, said his name, doubled his hands hoping to feel them close upon horse flesh, harkened to the billowing roll of sound. Then suddenly the sound fanned out, burst inside his head, roared against the bones of his skull and breaking through bone and tissue, trickled out by way of mouth and nose; it fluttered a few last times against his ear drums, then left him in quiet.

It was daylight before he was sure what had happened: he had gone over the cliff, through the branches of a willow which grew almost parallel with the stream, and now lay within hand's reach of the creek itself. At first he had tried to call out, but the sound of his own voice had detonated like gun fire inside his head and he was afraid that his skull, which he reckoned was broken, might fall apart with the effort. He was half-conscious, and wholly sick, but between bouts of retching he thought: This is it. I've come to it at last. This is war. It's falling over a cliff, cracking thy skull and puking.

It was just after sunup when Labe found him. He had about given up when he heard sound from beneath the willow.

"Josh," he cried, "thee's alive, thee's all right."

"No, I'm not," said Josh morosely.

"Oh, Josh," Labe said again, and knelt beside him, "thee's all right."

"I wish thee'd stop saying that," Josh told him. "It makes me feel sicker. I'm not all right. My head's split, I think."

Labe looked at it. "It does kind of look that way," he said, "but if thee's not died yet I reckon thee's not going to."

Josh moaned.

"Why didn't thee call out—get some help?" Labe asked.

"At first," Josh said, "because I didn't know anything. Then when I did, if I even opened my mouth to whisper, my whole head like to fell off. Then I got so's I could talk—but if I did, I puked. I still do," he said, and did. "I wish thee'd go away," he told Labe finally, "and leave me alone. I was beginning to get a little easy." He lay back for a while, then painfully lifted himself on one elbow. "Did we get Morgan?"

"They didn't come this way."

"Didn't come this way?" asked Josh. "I heard them. They crossed the crick last night."

"That wasn't Morgan," Labe said. "That was some cotton-headed farmers over'n the south bank who took a freak to drive their stock across so's the rebs wouldn't get 'em."

"I thought it was Morgan," Josh said. "I was fooled."

"Thee had plenty of company," Labe said. "They's all fooled."

"Where's Morgan now?"

"Dupont, they say. He gave Vernon the go-by."

Josh lay back again. "We stood them off," he said proudly. "We kept Morgan out of Vernon."

There was nothing Labe could say to that. Presently he asked, "If I get some help does thee think thee could move, Josh? They're worried about thee at home."

"How'd thee come to find me?" Josh asked.

"Rome came home without thee."

"I'd just as lief²² stay here," Josh said bitterly. "Go to war and fall off a cliff."

"Thee needn't let that fash²³ you," Labe said. "More did than didn't."

With the help of Guardsmen who were still lingering about the ford, discussing the night's events, Labe got Josh, unwilling and protesting, up the bank and into Rome's saddle. Labe rode behind and let Josh lean against him, and thus supported Josh was able to travel.

"Am I bleeding?" Josh asked weakly after they'd covered a mile or so. A thin trickle of blood was coming across his shoulder and down his shirt front.

"No," Labe said, "that's me."

"Thee?" asked Josh, for whom the events of the past twenty-four hours were still uncertain. "Thee wasn't fighting, was thee?"

"Well, I was a little," Labe admitted.

"In the Guard?" Josh asked.

"No," Labe said, "just kind of privately."

"Why?"

"Well," said Labe, "when I's hunting thee a man sung a song."

"I wouldn't fight anybody about any song," Josh said.

Labe didn't say anything.

"I purely hate fighting," Josh said. "Don't thee, Labe?"

"Not so much," Labe answered.

"I hate it," Josh said. "That's why I got to."

"And I got not to," Labe said, "because I like it."

Josh wanted to be with them, so they carried the sofa out of the sitting room into the summer kitchen, and he lay on it, a cool wet towel wrapped round his head. He felt as if his skull had been peeled away and his brain left so exposed that even the changed cadence of a voice could strike it like blow. He pushed the towel a little way off his eyes. Labe was in a chair, head back, wet cloth across his nose, and broken hand in a bucket of hot water. They were both awaiting a doctor if one could be found who was not busy. His mother was changing cloths and minding breakfast, stepping very light so's not to jar his head. His father was at the table where he'd been the morning before. There was a mingling of looks on his face.

"Well," Jess said, "I never had a First Day morning²⁴ like this before and never hope to again. Though I reckon everybody's done what had to be done. Josh anyway. I'm not so sure about Labe."

Labe lifted the cloth which covered mouth as well as nose. "Mine was kind of an accident," he admitted.

Jess turned toward his eldest son. Their eyes met and Jess nodded. "Well," he said again, "no reason why we can't eat, is there, Eliza? Have a sup of hot coffee and some biscuit and gravy?"

Josh groaned.

"I can't chew," Labe muttered.

Jess seemed to be feeling better and bet-

---

22. **lief** (lēf), gladly, willingly.
23. **fash,** trouble or bother.
24. **First Day morning,** Sunday.

"The hoofbeats came nearer. 'What's the worst that can happen to thee?'
Josh asked himself. 'Get a bullet in thy gizzard. Get killed. . . .'"

ter. "I ain't been doing any fighting," he said, "in the militia or on the side. I got a good appetite. If you boys don't mind, and thy mother'll set it forth, I'll have a bite. So far's I can remember there wasn't much eating done here yesterday. Eliza," he asked, "won't thee sit and eat?"

"Thee go ahead, Jess," Eliza said. "I'm busy with the boys just now."

"Mattie?"

"No," Mattie said delicately, ". . . all this blood and broken bones . . ."

"Little Jess?"

"Thee don't need to wait for me," said Little Jess.

"Well, then," Jess said heartily, "let us eat. But before we eat let's return thanks. This is First Day morning and we've much to be thankful for."

Josh listened to his father's words . . . they were a part of his happiness. When he had first come to, found himself lying at the edge of the crick, he had thought he would hate coming home, admit he'd been hurt, not by gun or saber, but by falling over a bank onto his head. Now it didn't matter. Yesterday morning and his talk of dying and killing seemed almost a life-time away . . . the past twenty-four hours a prolonged campaign from which he had emerged, a veteran, with mind much cleared as to what mattered and what did not.

Next time . . . he wouldn't talk so big . . . about fighting . . . and dying. But that didn't matter either, now. What mattered was that he had stood there . . . he had been afraid, but he had stood at the bridge. He had thought of running . . . but he hadn't done it . . . he had stood in the front line, not knowing but that Morgan himself might bear down upon them . . . he had stood at the crick's edge in the darkness and confusion and had been hunting gun and horse when he had fallen.

And there were the things he had learned . . . that talk beforehand is no good . . . that in darkness on a twenty-foot cliff it is best not to hurry . . . that death, when you moved toward it, seemed to retreat . . . that it was only when you turned your back on it . . . and ran . . . that it pursued.

With these thoughts the words of his father's grace mingled very well. . . . "Eternal Father . . . blessed Son . . . life everlasting. . . ."

He had thought his father was still praying, his tone was still so prayerful. But the words had changed. Josh once more cautiously pushed the towel away from his eyes. Jess was looking about the sunlit kitchen now, inspecting his family. "All here," he said, "right side up and forked end down." But then, maybe he was still praying, for he said next, "Amen, amen." Either way it was all right with Josh.

FOR UNDERSTANDING

1. Why doesn't Eliza want to ring the breakfast bell?
2. How old are Josh and Labe respectively?
3. Who is Ben Whitey?
4. How does Josh define "raid"?
5. How does Eliza say she would react if Morgan's raiders came to her home?
6. According to Josh, what does the governor want him to do?
7. Describe the final gifts or words to Josh by Mattie, Eliza, Little Jess, and big Jess.

8. What proposition does the man with the white flag make? How do the defenders of the town react to that proposition?
9. How is Labe injured?

FOR INTERPRETATION

Answer one or more of the following questions, either orally or in writing, according to the direction of your teacher.
1. West writes early in the story, "The young men didn't know. They had no way of knowing." Discuss the meaning of this quotation and give your reasons for agreeing or disagreeing with the point the author is making.
2. What is the fundamental difference between Josh and Labe?
3. What does Eliza mean when she says, "I've grown overfond of the particular"?
4. In what way or ways does the governor's proclamation make things easier for Josh?
5. Most mothers with children going off to war are primarily concerned for their safe return. What is Eliza's chief concern for Josh? Why is she different from most other mothers?
6. How does the one-legged man know that Josh is a Quaker?
7. What is the double meaning in Gum's comment (page 347): "Could be your brother"?

FOR APPRECIATION

Conflict
Even if one concentrates upon a single character in a story, one is likely to find that individual facing a number of different conflicts. In Josh's case, for example, there is a conflict between him and his parents over the issue of whether or not he should go to battle and kill. This is the most obvious conflict, but it is complicated and intensified by Josh's inner conflict, centering upon his need to prove his manhood. Finally, there is the larger issue of whether or not Morgan's raiders will succeed in taking Vernon, and Josh is involved in that conflict, too.
1. Which of these different conflicts interested you most?

2. Which did the author intend to be the main conflict, and how do you know this?

Climax

The central climax of this story occurs when Josh wakes up, finds himself in the middle of the rush of men and horses, and then falls off the cliff. Did this climax disappoint you?

If so, was it because you thought another climax was coming, or what?

Moment of Illumination

1. Where does the moment of illumination in this story occur?
2. How does it help you grasp the theme of the story?
3. Is it ever possible for a reader to criticize an author for not telling the sort of story the reader expects? Explain.

LANGUAGE AND VOCABULARY

Try to explain the italicized words or expressions in the following bits of dialogue from the story. Page references are given so that you can study the word or phrase in context, if necessary.
1. Well, that's a *happen-chance.* (p. 331)
2. Morgan didn't cross the Ohio till evening of *fourth day.* (p. 334)
3. That boy's shiftier than *a creased buck.* (p. 344)
4. Why ain't we making *a good hickory* for Indianapolis? (p. 344)
5. *Lectioneering* for Jeff Davis. (p. 347)
6. . . . farmers . . . who *took a freak* to drive their stock across . . . (p. 350)
7. I *purely* hate fighting. (p. 350)

COMPOSITION

In many essays you write for school you will be asked to support or argue against some basic idea or thesis. Such essays typically begin with the statement of the thesis. They may end with some sort of summary or a restatement of the thesis, unless the essay is very short. The best endings, however, do not merely restate the thesis in the same words. It is important to *end strong,* since the ending is the last thing in your reader's mind. (It may be the last thing in a teacher's mind as he or she assigns a grade!)

An unusual way of saying something, a fresh or arresting bit of figurative language, or an acute observation are all good ways of ending an essay. Final sentences may also be unusually brief, for emphasis. You might occasionally even try asking a question at the end.

A good answer for an essay-type question on "The Battle of Finney's Ford" might begin with a thesis statement such as: "The final words or gifts of Josh's father and mother, younger brother and sister reveal much about the character of each of them."

Use this or a similar statement on characterization for your essay. Write supporting sentences that illustrate the point. Spend a long time—unless you get a brilliant idea right away—thinking about how you can end strong, as described above.

COMPOSITION WORKSHOP

LITERARY RESEARCH: SELECTING A TOPIC

Like all other forms of practical writing, a research paper must begin with a plan. Writing is always a challenging task, and it is never desirable to make it more difficult than it has to be. Intelligent planning allows the writer to get the job done with a minimum of effort.

The purpose of a literary research paper is to clarify something about the work or works that will help deepen the reader's understanding and appreciation. In effect, the writer of a research paper is saying to the reader: "In my reading and study, I have discovered something about a work of literature that deepened my own appreciation of what I read. I want to tell you about it because I think my discovery will add to your own understanding and appreciation."

The selection of a topic is of critical importance in the writing of a research paper, just as it is in all other forms of practical writing. Of course, the best topics are those that the writer has some real interest in. If, no matter how hard you try, you have absolutely no appreciation for what Henry David Thoreau was trying to accomplish at Walden Pond, you should not deal with him or his works in a research paper. You cannot hope to interest a reader in the subject if you have no interest in it yourself.

Once you have found a general topic you would enjoy investigating, your next step is to be sure that it is narrow enough to serve as a topic for a short research paper. A short research paper—the kind that beginning researchers can comfortably tackle—will normally not exceed ten typewritten pages. A paper of this length usually has fifteen to twenty-five paragraphs. Given these limits, many possible topics are immediately ruled out. For example, so broad a topic as the American Civil War could only be covered in a full-length book. It would be far better to analyze a famous battle or some other single aspect of the war. This narrower topic could probably be managed in ten typewritten pages.

One effective way of narrowing a topic is to focus on a single element. If you have chosen to analyze a single literary work or a few literary works, you might find that answering the following groups of questions will help you pinpoint your topic more exactly.

1. How realistic or believable is the story line? Do the events that take place allow the reader to see the story as believable?

2. What is the theme of the work? What social or moral point does the author make? How is it made? Is the theme a common one? Is it typical of the period in which the work was written? Has the author examined the theme in other works?

3. How believable are the author's characters? What kind of a response do the characters get from the reader? What light do the characters shed upon the historical period?

4. How is the narrative structured? How well do its various parts fit together? How does the narrative affect the reader?

5. What are the outstanding features of the writer's style? Is language used memorably? What influence did the author's style have upon other writers?

6. How did people react to the work when it was published? How is it regarded today? What is it about the work that makes it still worthwhile to read?

If you find a particular author interesting and have decided to examine that author's life, the following groups of related questions might help you identify a topic more exactly.

1. What events in the author's life might have direct bearing on his or her work? Where is this influence seen in the author's works?

2. To what extent did the author participate in the life and times in which he or she wrote? What was the author's standing in the community and the nation?

3. What light do the author's nonfictional writings shed upon his or her literary writings? How are the writer's views about life and literature reflected in his or her literary works?

Good topics for research papers are often suggested by the content of a work rather than by its message or by the literary technique the work illustrates. Here are some examples that are suggested by works in this text:

A reader of William Bradford's *Of Plymouth Plantation* might become interested in the makeup of the Plymouth Colony. This broad topic could be narrowed to more manageable topics, such as the original government of the colony, the aspirations of the *Mayflower* passengers, the trials and the difficulties posed by the colonists' surroundings, or the colonists' relationship with the Indians of Massachusetts Bay.

A reader of Thomas Paine's *The Crisis* might become interested in the events that occurred before the Revolutionary War. This broad topic could be narrowed to such topics as the British economic policy toward the colonies, the plight of the Tories in colonial America, or the arguments against separation from Britain that were voiced in the North American colonies.

A reader of Frederick Douglass's *My Bondage and My Freedom* might become interested in slavery in pre–Civil War America. This broad topic could be narrowed to a more manageable topic, such as the daily life of a typical slave, the African slave-gathering expeditions, or the success of the escape route to Canada called the Underground Railroad.

Notice that the topics that arise from the content of a selection do not necessarily deal with literary analysis or technique. Nevertheless, they are appropriate topics for literary research papers for they investigate areas that arise naturally from the literature. The reader who becomes knowledgeable about these areas learns something valuable about the period in which the literature was written.

In finding a suitable topic for a short research paper, keep in mind that the writer of a research paper always presents the reader with the findings of others who have previously investigated the topic. Therefore, the topic you select should be one that you can gather information about from several sources. Your topic should never be one that can be exhaustively treated by simply consulting a single encyclopedia article. The Big Dipper would not be a suitable topic for a research paper, for enough can be learned about that constellation from a single standard reference. To investigate life on a whaling ship, however, you would have to go beyond the encyclopedia to various historical books and other articles.

ASSIGNMENT 1

Find a general topic for a research paper. The topic should be one that you would like to find out more about. Examine the selections that you have read so far. If this examination does not suggest a topic, turn to the table of contents and scan the selections in this book that you have not yet read. Examine more carefully those selections that seem promising. If no topic presents itself from this further examination, think of something by an American author that you have read in the past or are currently reading. Remember that your topic might be one that investigates a particular literary work or group of works, one that examines some aspect of an author's life, or one that arises from the content of a literary work.

ASSIGNMENT 2

Narrow the general topic that you identified in Assignment 1. Remember that it should be specific enough for development in a short research paper of approximately ten typewritten pages. Work carefully to find a topic that is sufficiently manageable. When you are finished, you might have three or four possible topics that seem promising. Keep these tentative topics for the next Composition Workshop.

UNVEILING THE STATUE OF LIBERTY, Edward Moran

Museum of the City of New York

Regionalism and Realism

A NEW DIRECTION

In the half century between the end of the Civil War and the outbreak of World War I, life in the United States underwent a change so far-reaching that it charted a new direction for our literature. During this period the nation set its continental boundaries, opened its doors to throngs of immigrants, developed into an industrial giant, and moved toward leadership in world affairs. Such unprecedented change gave rise to political problems, social disorders, and intellectual upheavals that forced younger American writers to assess and to reflect the realities of their times.

Post-Civil War America

The shabby and inhumane policies of Reconstruction in the post-Civil War South, the brutal scramble for wealth and power among corrupt and ruthless financiers in the North, the introduction of revolutionary inventions, and the new theories in scientific thought all cried out for literary interpretation. The plight of the hapless slum dweller, the low-paid laborer, and the debt-ridden farmer mocked the romantic idealism of a past era. Emerson's doctrine of self-reliance and his Transcendental philosophy were twisted by the unscrupulous into what some termed a Gospel of Greed.

Failure of Reconstruction

Industrialism and Lost Ideals

Walt Whitman in his *Democratic Vistas* (1871) sounded one of the clearest calls for reform:

> *Never was there, perhaps, more hollowness at heart than at present, and here in the United States. Genuine belief seems to have left us. The underlying principles of the States are not honestly believ'd in . . . nor is humanity believ'd in. . . . We live in an atmosphere of hypocrisy throughout. . . . The depravity of the business classes of our country is not less than has been supposed, but infinitely greater. The official services of America, national, state, and municipal, in all their branches and departments, except the judiciary, are saturated in corruption, bribery, falsehood, maladministration; and the judiciary is tainted. The great cities reek with respectable as much as with non-respectable robbery and scoundrelism. . . . I may say that our New World democracy, however a great success in uplifting the masses out of their sloughs, in materialistic development, products, and in certain highly deceptive superficial intellectuality, is, so far, an almost complete failure in its social aspects, and in really grand religious, moral, literary, and aesthetic results.*

Despite the turmoil, however, the majority of Americans still held to the "American Dream"—the belief that hard work, honesty, and reverence

The American Dream

357

Tiffany Vase
Silver, copper, and gold
The Brooklyn Museum
Brooklyn, New York

would insure economic success, national harmony, and individual well-being. Beginning in the 1890s and extending well into the twentieth century, a series of reforms did correct many of the abuses of the post-Civil War era.

In general, the realistic writers of the 1870s and 1880s, rather than treating broad social and economic issues, wrote about the plight of the individual facing hardship or moral dilemma. Since they concentrated on characters in specific regions of the country, these authors are known as regional or local-color writers. Stress on reform came in the decades following the 1880s, some of it in an extreme form of realism that was termed naturalism. We shall have more to say about these terms later.

Despite the increase in realistic writing, the works of deceased American romantic authors were still being read; in fact Cooper, Irving, Poe, and Hawthorne even increased in popularity in the last half of the century. In the 1880s and 1890s the sonorous voices of the aging Longfellow, Emerson, Lowell, Whittier, and Oliver Wendell Holmes still exerted considerable influence on writers, thinkers, and the general public. School children in the last decades of the nineteenth century and well into the twentieth were required to memorize and to recite selected passages from these romantic writers, as both an intellectual exercise and an attempt to recapture the idealism of the past.

ROMANTICISM VERSUS REALISM

Personal Passions

Perhaps the chief tendency of romantics is that they dwell on personal passions, on the subjective side of experience, on their own unique feelings and attitudes. Romantic writers value the creative function of the imagination, often claiming that this faculty helps one arrive at greater truths than those revealed by facts or logic. By transcending the actual, romantics sometimes hope to discover an absolute or ideal.

Nature Idealized

Also, romantics frequently desire to return to the past in some way, to escape from the day-to-day problems of the present. Romantic writers often make use of exotic settings, and Nature—frequently idealized and spelled with the capital letter—may figure prominently in their work. To varying degrees one can find these tendencies in the writings of Poe and Whitman, Emerson and Thoreau, Hawthorne and Melville, as well as in the work of Irving, Bryant, and Cooper.

Relishing the Facts

Realists, in contrast, are less concerned with their own subjective responses and more concerned with the tangible world outside their psyches. Usually they portray with relish the very facts that the romanticist ignores or pushes to the background. Realists, too, are generally not concerned with absolutes or ideals and may even deny their existence. Realistic writers generally deal with the social problems of real persons in real places in the present. Their settings are ordinary; their characters are ordinary; and their focus is on life as it is, rather than life as it might be. These traits describe on the whole the writers of this period, from Mark

The period between 1865 and 1914 saw a new sophistication in American arts and letters. One of the era's most worldly and well-traveled American artists was John Singer Sargent, who won international acclaim for his elegant portraits.

MR. AND MRS. ISAAC NEWTON PHELPS STOKES
John Singer Sargent
Metropolitan Museum of Art, New York City, Bequest of Edith Minton Phelps Stokes

At a time of rapid growth and change on many fronts, realist painters like Thomas Waterman Wood sought to capture the look and feel of ordinary people engaged in everyday activities.

THE VILLAGE POST OFFICE
Thomas Waterman Wood
New York State Historical Association, Cooperstown, New York

Twain (see page 442) and William Dean Howells to Mary E. Wilkins Freeman (see page 386), Hamlin Garland (see page 404), and Stephen Crane (see page 415).

REGIONAL WRITERS

Local Color

Because of the intense curiosity of readers to learn about other sections of the country, many writers specialized in describing places, events, manners, and even the speech of specific regions and locales. Such writing is known as regionalism, or local-color writing.

Although regionalism predates the Civil War, the local colorists who became best known began publishing about 1870. That was the year in which Bret Harte (see page 368) published *The Luck of Roaring Camp and*

Other Stories. (The title story had first appeared in 1868.) Harte's region was the Far West. Once very popular, Harte's melodramatic short stories are rarely read today.

Shortly after Harte's early success, Edward Eggleston published *The Hoosier School-Master* (1871), a local-color novel dealing with Decatur County, Indiana. It was an immediate best seller and remained a minor classic for a generation. Although not read today, Eggleston influenced many later Midwestern realists, such as Hamlin Garland, Theodore Dreiser, and Willa Cather.

In the South, the best-known regionalists were George Washington Cable, who wrote of life among the Louisiana Creoles; Joel Chandler Harris of Georgia, who created the Uncle Remus stories; and Thomas Nelson Page, whose work was set in Virginia, steeped in magnolias and moonlight.

Southern Regionalists

John Sloan was one of the most revolutionary and influential of the American realists painting at the turn of the century.

SOUTH BEACH BATHERS, John Sloan
Walker Art Center, Minneapolis, Minnesota

Opening of the Brooklyn Bridge, 1883, connecting Manhattan and Brooklyn. The bridge soon came to symbolize American engineering genius.

Jewett, Chopin, Freeman

A bas-relief by sculptor Augustus Saint-Gaudens

Sarah Orne Jewett and Mary E. Wilkins Freeman were among the best-known women regionalists of their time. Jewett celebrated Maine in many stories, and her *The Country of the Pointed Firs* (1896), is considered by many to be the best regional work of the nineteenth century. Freeman, who has also won recent critical attention, wrote short stories about rural Massachusetts like "A Church Mouse." Kate Chopin (see page 380) was another woman regionalist. She achieved only short-lived fame in her lifetime but is now considered a pioneer realist. Much of her work, like "A Gentleman of Bayou Têche," is set in the Louisiana bayou country.

Although some regional writing—especially in the 1870s—was romantic in the sense that its authors tended to idealize their subjects and settings, the movement as a whole is considered fundamentally realistic. Regional writers strove to write dialogue that sounded the way people actually spoke; they generally described places with great fidelity of detail; and they were basically interested in portraying and analyzing ordinary people and ordinary events. These goals are exactly what the dean of nineteenth-century realists, William Dean Howells, thought good writing should achieve.

THE MAJOR REALISTS

The major realistic writers whose important work was published in the nineteenth century were Mark Twain, William Dean Howells, Henry James, Hamlin Garland, Ambrose Bierce, and Stephen Crane. Since the others in this group are discussed in some detail later, we will focus briefly on Howells and James here.

The novelist, editor, and critic William Dean Howells (1837–1920) was the main exponent of American realism; indeed, he has been called "in himself almost an entire literary movement." He held influential positions on two of the major literary magazines of the time—first the *Atlantic Monthly* and then *Harper's*. He also knew and aided virtually every major American writer of his time.

William Dean Howells: Opponent of Romanticism

Howells maintained that the romanticism that saturated popular literature was immoral, not only because it corrupted the taste of American readers (and writers) but also because it falsified life. Fiction, he maintained, must "cease to lie about life . . . let it forbear to teach pride and revenge, folly and insanity, egotism and prejudice . . . let it not put on fine literary airs; let it speak the dialect, the language, that most Americans know—the language of unaffected people everywhere."

A believer in democracy and the common people could hardly quarrel with Howells's basic impulses, but his own novels (which, as an editor, he always wrote with an eye to the young girl reader) show that he had a narrow view of real life, especially when compared with the naturalists' view. Writing about "the more smiling aspects of life" because they were "the more American," he placed himself in what has been called the "genteel tradition." Thus he became the whipping boy of the naturalists and the hard-nosed realists like Ambrose Bierce, who called him "Miss Nancy Howells." Although little of his work is still read, no American did more than Howells to encourage realistic writing in the United States.

An artist who remained within the genteel tradition and yet made an enduring name for himself on two continents was Henry James (1843–1916). An early psychological novelist, James was most interested in what people thought and felt. He portrayed those thoughts and feelings with a subtlety, an insightfulness, and a scrupulous honesty that have not been surpassed. His main themes deal with the effect of Europe on Americans, or the reverse. This theme along with his high degree of sophistication and his absorption with problems of technique probably kept him from ever becoming a novelist of the popular press.

Henry James: Psychological Realism

NATURALISM

Naturalism is sometimes defined as realism carried to an extreme. Its fundamental premise is that people, like everything else in the universe, are subject to natural laws, that the "absolute" truths of science apply to all human experience. Naturalists often contend that human beings do not have free will, that they are driven by powerful and blind biological urges, and that people simply are slaves to their heredity and environment.

The first naturalists commonly used great masses of detail in depicting human experience, and they dealt with the uglier sides of life. Once naturalism entered the stream of American fiction, it influenced almost all American writers. There are strong naturalistic elements, for example, in the works of John Steinbeck and Richard Wright, though the major work of both was published long after the period now under discussion.

Norris and Crane

Frank Norris (1870–1902) was one of the important naturalists of the period. His violent novels exposed the sordid side of life and business. His writing strongly influenced other writers as well as legislators pushing for social and economic reform. It was Stephen Crane, however, who broke with earlier literary tradition to write *Maggie: A Girl of the Streets* (1893), the first American fully naturalistic novel. Following close upon Norris and Crane was Jack London, who stressed the helplessness of human beings and animals before all-powerful natural laws in such works as *The Call of the Wild* (1903) and *The Sea Wolf* (1904). Upton Sinclair's novel, *The Jungle* (1906), an account of the brutal lives of immigrant workers in the Chicago stockyards, led to a Congressional investigation and subsequent passage of the Meat Inspection Act of 1906.

London and Sinclair

Theodore Dreiser

The writer who brought naturalism into popular focus was Theodore Dreiser, with novels like *Sister Carrie* (first published in 1900 but suppressed until 1912) and *Jennie Gerhardt* (1911). These two novels set off a long controversy because readers and critics were unwilling to accept Dreiser's thesis that human beings are creatures of economic and biological necessities beyond their control. It was not until the changed moral climate of the 1920s that Dreiser achieved popular success with his novel, *An American Tragedy* (1925).

POETS OF THE PERIOD

Walt Whitman continued to publish poetry as well as prose early in this period, and the poems of Emily Dickinson (see page 431) were published posthumously in 1890. Sidney Lanier (see page 377), although he died before his fortieth year, became the most famous of the post-war Southern poets and is still remembered for his masterful musical verse, such as "Song of the Chattahoochee," "The Symphony," and "The Marshes of Glynn."

Other poets of the time are remembered for special reasons. James Whitcomb Riley (1849–1916) wrote poems in the dialect of the Indiana countryside and was a national favorite for a long period. Perhaps his most famous verse is "When the Frost Is on the Punkin." Eugene Field (1850–1895) was best known as a newspaper humorist in his time, but today he is remembered as the author of such childhood poems as "Wynken, Blynken, and Nod" and "Little Boy Blue."

DRAMA

By and large, American theater audiences during this period wanted sentimental melodramas, rollicking good humor, patriotic themes, or revivals of old masterpieces rather than fresh contemporary work. One notable exception is William Vaughn Moody's (1869–1910) popular drama, *The*

Frederic Remington devoted his life to capturing the vanishing world of the Old West as he'd seen it.

A careful student of the natural world, Abbot Thayer depicted outdoor scenes in a vivid, almost abstract style.

BLUE JAYS IN WINTER, Abbott Thayer
National Museum of American Art
Smithsonian Institution, Washington, D.C.
Gift of the heirs of Abbott Thayer

Great Divide (1906), in which the playwright dealt with the Puritan concept of original sin.

The most popular dramatist of the period was Clyde W. Fitch (1865–1909) whose best-known plays are *Beau Brummel* (1890), a comedy of dress and manners; *Barbara Frietchie* (1899), based on the legendary Civil War heroine; and *Nathan Hale* (1899), an emotional treatment of the short, tragic life of the American Revolutionary War hero. Fitch's plays, although fine examples of the conventional mode, are now rarely performed.

*Melodrama
and
Heroism*

Regionalism and Realism

President	Dates
ANDREW JACKSON	1829–1837
MARTIN VAN BUREN	1837–1841
WILLIAM H. HARRISON	1841
JOHN TYLER	1841–1845
JAMES K. POLK	1845–1849
ZACHARY TAYLOR	1849–1850
MILLARD FILLMORE	1850–1853
FRANKLIN PIERCE	1853–1857
JAMES BUCHANAN	1857–1861
ABRAHAM LINCOLN	1861–1865
ANDREW JOHNSON	1865–1869
ULYSSES S. GRANT	1869–1877
RUTHERFORD B. HAYES	1877–1881

First women's college, Mt. Holyoke Seminary, 1837

Irish Potato Famine, 1846

California Gold Rush begins, 1849

Civil War, 1861–65

Reconstruction Acts, 1867

Johnson impeached and tried, 1869

First transcontinental railroad, 1869

First U.S. graduate school, Johns Hopkins, 1876

Bell patents telephone, 1876

1830 1840 1850 1860 1870 1880

First edition of Walt Whitman's *Leaves of Grass,* 1855

Dickinson first submits poems for critical review, 1862

Harte's "The Outcasts of Poker Flat," 1869

Lanier's *Poems,* 1877

Chief Joseph tries to lead his people to Canada, 1877

Writer	Born
EMILY DICKINSON	1830
MARK TWAIN	1835
BRET HARTE	1836
CHIEF JOSEPH	c. 1840
SIDNEY LANIER	1842
AMBROSE BIERCE	1842
KATE CHOPIN	1851
MARY E. WILKINS FREEMAN	1852
HAMLIN GARLAND	1860
	1871
	1872

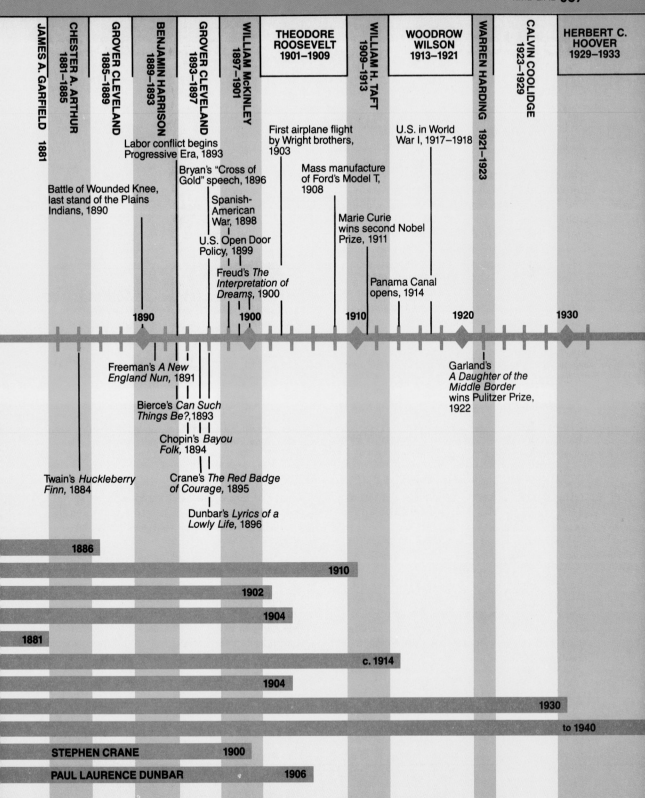

JAMES A. GARFIELD 1881

CHESTER A. ARTHUR 1881–1885

GROVER CLEVELAND 1885–1889

BENJAMIN HARRISON 1889–1893

GROVER CLEVELAND 1893–1897

WILLIAM McKINLEY 1897–1901

THEODORE ROOSEVELT 1901–1909

WILLIAM H. TAFT 1909–1913

WOODROW WILSON 1913–1921

WARREN HARDING 1921–1923

CALVIN COOLIDGE 1923–1929

HERBERT C. HOOVER 1929–1933

Labor conflict begins Progressive Era, 1893

First airplane flight by Wright brothers, 1903

U.S. in World War I, 1917–1918

Bryan's "Cross of Gold" speech, 1896

Mass manufacture of Ford's Model T, 1908

Battle of Wounded Knee, last stand of the Plains Indians, 1890

Spanish-American War, 1898

Marie Curie wins second Nobel Prize, 1911

U.S. Open Door Policy, 1899

Freud's *The Interpretation of Dreams*, 1900

Panama Canal opens, 1914

1890   **1900**   **1910**   **1920**   **1930**

Freeman's *A New England Nun*, 1891

Garland's *A Daughter of the Middle Border* wins Pulitzer Prize, 1922

Bierce's *Can Such Things Be?*, 1893

Chopin's *Bayou Folk*, 1894

Twain's *Huckleberry Finn*, 1884

Crane's *The Red Badge of Courage*, 1895

Dunbar's *Lyrics of a Lowly Life*, 1896

1886

1910

1902

1904

1881

c. 1914

1904

1930

to 1940

STEPHEN CRANE   1900

PAUL LAURENCE DUNBAR   1906

Bret Harte 1836–1902

The sentimentalized characters we have all seen in westerns—the rough miner, the noble gambler, and the coarse but warm-hearted dance-hall girl—were first introduced to the reading public by a writer who was in fact fundamentally an Easterner. Born in Albany, New York, Francis Bret Harte went West at age eighteen. His father had died when Bret was nine, leaving the family with financial problems. In California, Harte worked as a teacher, tutor, Wells Fargo messenger, drugstore clerk, and prospector. Exposed to mining-camp and frontier life, he found his richest strike in story materials that with his theatrical handling had quick appeal for a novelty-demanding public. Although his writing had insufficient depth and understanding to establish an authentic identity for the American West, it brought him almost instant fame and recognition.

In 1868, as editor of the influential *Overland Monthly,* he wrote "The Luck of Roaring Camp" to demonstrate what he saw as uniquely characteristic Western American literature. Five months later, he published "The Outcasts of Poker Flat." These stories, along with a half dozen more like them, became instantly popular in the United States and in England and gave a great boost to the beginnings of regional, or local-color, writing.

At the height of his fame, when Mark Twain was just beginning to win recognition, Harte left California in 1871 and moved to Boston. Here, the *Atlantic Monthly* contracted to pay him $10,000 (a fantastic figure in those days) for twelve western selections for the magazine. All were disappointing because Harte had lost his spark and was merely repeating his formula creations. He spent his years after 1878 abroad,

PORTRAIT OF BRET HARTE
National Portrait Gallery
Smithsonian Institution

finally dying in England of throat cancer. The author of humorous poetry and sketches as well as stories, Harte is credited with establishing the West as a literary theme that is still popular today.

Although the California gold rush was two decades in the past when the following story was written, Easterners still hungered to learn what the wild, untamed West was like. In "The Outcasts of Poker Flat" Harte recreated life in the gold camps of the Sierras, employing setting and characterization to build local color and give his tale a semblance of reality.

THE OUTCASTS OF POKER FLAT

As Mr. John Oakhurst, gambler, stepped into the main street of Poker Flat on the morning of the twenty-third of November, 1850, he was conscious of a change in its moral atmosphere since the preceding night. Two or three men, conversing earnestly together, ceased as he approached, and exchanged significant glances. There was a Sabbath lull in the air, which, in a settlement unused to Sabbath influences, looked ominous.

Mr. Oakhurst's calm, handsome face betrayed small concern in these indications. Whether he was conscious of any predisposing cause was another question. "I reckon they're after somebody," he reflected; "likely it's me." He returned to his pocket the handkerchief with which he had been whipping away the red dust of Poker Flat from his neat boots, and quietly discharged his mind of any further conjecture.

In point of fact, Poker Flat was "after somebody." It had lately suffered the loss of several thousand dollars, two valuable horses, and a prominent citizen. It was experiencing a spasm of virtuous reaction, quite as lawless and ungovernable as any of the acts that had provoked it. A secret committee had determined to rid the town of all improper persons. This was done permanently in regard to two men who were then hanging from the boughs of a sycamore in the gulch, and temporarily in the banishment of certain other objectionable characters. I regret to say that some of these were ladies. It is but due to the sex, however, to state that their impropriety was professional, and it was only in such easily established standards of evil that Poker Flat ventured to sit in judgment.

Mr. Oakhurst was right in supposing that he was included in this category. A few of the committee had urged hanging him as a possible example and a sure method of reimbursing themselves from his pockets of the sums he had won from them. "It's agin justice," said Jim Wheeler, "to let this yer young man from Roaring Camp—an entire stranger—carry away our money." But a crude sentiment of equity residing in the breasts of those who had been fortunate enough to win from Mr. Oakhurst overruled this narrower local prejudice.

Mr. Oakhurst received his sentence with philosophic calmness, none the less coolly that he was aware of the hesitation of his judges. He was too much of a gambler not to accept fate. With him life was at best an uncertain game, and he recognized the usual percentage in favor of the dealer.

A body of armed men accompanied the deported wickedness of Poker Flat to the outskirts of the settlement. Besides Mr. Oakhurst, who was known to be a coolly desperate man, and for whose intimidation the armed escort was intended, the expatriated party consisted of a young woman familiarly known as "The Duchess"; another who had won the title of "Mother Shipton,"[1] and "Uncle Billy," a suspected sluice robber and confirmed drunkard. The cavalcade pro-

---

1. **"Mother Shipton."** The original Mother Shipton is believed to have been a sixteenth-century prophetess who predicted the deaths of several notable people of the time and certain modern inventions such as the telegraph. She also predicted that the world would end in 1881.

voked no comments from the spectators, nor was any word uttered by the escort. Only when the gulch which marked the uttermost limit of Poker Flat was reached, the leader spoke briefly and to the point. The exiles were forbidden to return at the peril of their lives.

As the escort disappeared, their pent-up feelings found vent in a few hysterical tears from the Duchess, some bad language from Mother Shipton, and a Parthian[2] volley of expletives from Uncle Billy. The philosophic Oakhurst alone remained silent. He listened calmly to Mother Shipton's desire to cut somebody's heart out, to the repeated statements of the Duchess that she would die in the road, and to the alarming oaths that seemed to be bumped out of Uncle Billy as he rode forward. With the easy good humor characteristic of his class, he insisted upon exchanging his own riding horse, "Five-Spot," for the sorry mule which the Duchess rode. But even this act did not draw the party into any closer sympathy. The young woman adjusted her somewhat draggled plumes with a feeble, faded coquetry; Mother Shipton eyed the possessor of Five-Spot with malevolence, and Uncle Billy included the whole party in one sweeping anathema.[3]

The road to Sandy Bar—a camp that, not having as yet experienced the regenerating influences of Poker Flat, consequently seemed to offer some invitation to the emigrants—lay over a steep mountain range. It was distant a day's severe travel. In that advanced season the party soon passed out of the moist, temperate regions of the foothills into the dry, cold, bracing air of the Sierras. The trail was narrow and difficult. At noon the Duchess, rolling out of her saddle upon the ground, declared her intention of going no farther, and the party halted.

The spot was singularly wild and impressive. A wooden amphitheater, surrounded on three sides by precipitous cliffs of naked granite, sloped gently toward the crest of another precipice that overlooked the valley. It was, undoubtedly, the most suitable spot for a camp, had camping been advisable. But Mr. Oakhurst knew that scarcely half the journey to Sandy Bar was accomplished, and the party were not equipped or provisioned for delay. This fact he pointed out to his companions curtly, with a philosophic commentary on the folly of "throwing up their hand before the game was played out." But they were furnished with liquor, which in this emergency stood them in place of food, fuel, rest, and prescience. In spite of his remonstrances, it was not long before they were more or less under its influence. Uncle Billy passed rapidly from a bellicose state into one of stupor, the Duchess became maudlin, and Mother Shipton snored. Mr. Oakhurst alone remained erect, leaning against a rock, calmly surveying them.

Mr. Oakhurst did not drink. It interfered with a profession which required coolness, impassiveness, and presence of mind, and, in his own language, he "couldn't afford it." As he gazed at his recumbent fellow exiles, the loneliness begotten of his pariah trade, his habits of life, his very vices, for the first time seriously oppressed him. He bestirred himself in dusting his black clothes, washing his hands and face, and other acts characteristic of his studiously neat habits, and for a moment forgot his annoyance. The thought of deserting his weaker and more pitiable companions never perhaps occurred to him. Yet he could not help feeling the want of that excitement which, singularly enough, was most conducive to that calm equanimity for which he was notorious. He looked at the gloomy walls that rose a thousand feet sheer above the circling pines around him, at the sky omi-

---

2. **Parthian.** The ancient Parthians of western Asia fought on horseback with bow and arrow and after each shot turned their mounts as if in retreat. Hence, a Parthian shot came to mean any sharp parting remark.
3. **anathema** (ə nath′ ə mə), a curse.

FREIGHTING FROM FORT BENTON
Olaf C. Seltzer
Thomas Gilcrease Institute of
American History and Art, Tulsa, Oklahoma

nously clouded, at the valley below, already deepening into shadow; and, doing so, suddenly he heard his own name called.

A horseman slowly ascended the trail. In the fresh, open face of the newcomer Mr. Oakhurst recognized Tom Simson, otherwise known as "The Innocent," of Sandy Bar. He had met him sometime before over a "little game," and had, with perfect equanimity, won the entire fortune—amounting to some forty dollars—of that guileless youth. After the game was finished, Mr. Oakhurst drew the youthful speculator behind the door and thus addressed him: "Tommy, you're a good little man, but you can't gamble worth a cent. Don't try it over again." He then handed him

his money back, pushed him gently from the room, and so made a devoted slave of Tom Simson.

There was a remembrance of this in his boyish and enthusiastic greeting of Mr. Oakhurst. He had started, he said, to go to Poker Flat to seek his fortune. "Alone?" No, not exactly alone; in fact (a giggle), he had run away with Piney Woods. Didn't Mr. Oakhurst remember Piney? She that used to wait on the table at the Temperance House? They had been engaged a long time, but old Jake Woods had objected, and so they had run away, and were going to Poker Flat to be married, and here they were. And they were tired out, and how lucky it was they had found a place to camp, and company. All this the Innocent delivered rapidly, while Piney, a stout, comely damsel of fifteen, emerged from behind the pine tree, where she had been blushing unseen, and rode to the side of her lover.

Mr. Oakhurst seldom troubled himself with sentiment, still less with propriety; but he had a vague idea that the situation was not fortunate. He retained, however, his presence of mind sufficiently to kick Uncle Billy, who was about to say something, and Uncle Billy was sober enough to recognize in Mr. Oakhurst's kick a superior power that would not bear trifling. He then endeavored to dissuade Tom Simson from delaying further, but in vain. He even pointed out the fact that there was no provision, nor means of making a camp. But, unluckily, the Innocent met this objection by assuring the party that he was provided with an extra mule loaded with provisions, and by the discovery of a rude attempt at a log house near the trail. "Piney can stay with Mrs. Oakhurst," said the Innocent, pointing to the Duchess, "and I can shift for myself."

Nothing but Mr. Oakhurst's admonishing foot saved Uncle Billy from bursting into a roar of laughter. As it was, he felt compelled to retire up the canyon until he could recover his gravity. There he confided the joke to the tall pine trees, with many slaps of his leg, contortions of his face, and the usual profanity. But when he returned to the party, he found them seated by a fire—for the air had grown strangely chill and the sky overcast—in apparently amicable conversation. Piney was actually talking in an impulsive girlish fashion to the Duchess, who was listening with an interest and animation she had not shown for many days. The Innocent was holding forth, apparently with equal effect, to Mr. Oakhurst and Mother Shipton, who was actually relaxing into amiability. "Is this yer a d——d picnic?" said Uncle Billy, with inward scorn, as he surveyed the sylvan group, the glancing firelight, and the tethered animals in the foreground. Suddenly an idea mingled with

the alcoholic fumes that disturbed his brain. It was apparently of a jocular nature, for he felt impelled to slap his leg again and cram his fist into his mouth.

As the shadows crept slowly up the mountain, a slight breeze rocked the tops of the pine trees and moaned through their long and gloomy aisles. The ruined cabin, patched and covered with pine boughs, was set apart for the ladies. As the lovers parted, they unaffectedly exchanged a kiss, so honest and sincere that it might have been heard above the swaying pines. The frail Duchess and the malevolent Mother Shipton were probably too stunned to remark upon this last evidence of simplicity, and so turned without a word to the hut. The fire was replenished, the men lay down before the door, and in a few minutes were asleep.

Mr. Oakhurst was a light sleeper. Toward morning he awoke benumbed and cold. As he stirred the dying fire, the wind, which was now blowing strongly, brought to his cheek that which caused the blood to leave it— snow!

He started to his feet with the intention of awakening the sleepers, for there was no time to lose. But, turning to where Uncle Billy had been lying, he found him gone. A suspicion leaped to his brain, and a curse to his lips. He ran to the spot where the mules had been tethered—they were no longer there. The tracks were already rapidly disappearing in the snow.

The momentary excitement brought Mr. Oakhurst back to the fire with his usual calm. He did not waken the sleepers. The Innocent slumbered peacefully, with a smile on his good-humored, freckled face; the virgin Piney slept beside her frailer sisters as sweetly as though attended by celestial guardians; and Mr. Oakhurst, drawing his blanket over his shoulders, stroked his mustaches and waited for the dawn. It came slowly in a whirly mist of snowflakes that dazzled and confused the eye. What could be seen of the landscape appeared magically changed. He looked over the valley, and summed up the present and future in two words, "Snowed in!"

A careful inventory of the provisions, which, fortunately for the party, had been stored within the hut, and so escaped the felonious fingers of Uncle Billy, disclosed the fact that with care and prudence, they might last ten days longer. "That is," said Mr. Oakhurst *sotto voce*[4] to the Innocent, "if you're willing to board us. If you ain't—and perhaps you'd better not—you can wait till Uncle Billy gets back with provisions." For some occult reason, Mr. Oakhurst could not bring himself to disclose Uncle Billy's rascality, and so offered the hypothesis that he had wandered from the camp and had accidentally stampeded the animals. He dropped a warning to the Duchess and Mother Shipton, who of course knew the facts of their associate's defection. "They'll find out the truth about us *all* when they find out anything," he added significantly, "and there's no good frightening them now."

Tom Simson not only put all his worldly store at the disposal of Mr. Oakhurst, but seemed to enjoy the prospect of their enforced seclusion. "We'll have a good camp for a week, and then the snow'll melt, and we'll all go back together." The cheerful gaiety of the young man and Mr. Oakhurst's calm infected the others. The Innocent, with the aid of pine boughs, extemporized a thatch for the roofless cabin, and the Duchess directed Piney in the rearrangement of the interior with a taste and tact that opened the blue eyes of that provincial maiden to their fullest extent. "I reckon now you're used to fine things at Poker Flat," said Piney. The Duchess turned away sharply to conceal something that reddened her cheeks through their professional tint, and Mother Shipton requested Piney not to "chatter." But when Mr. Oakhurst returned from a weary search for the trail, he heard the sound of happy laughter echoed from the rocks. He stopped in some alarm, and his thoughts first naturally reverted to the whisky, which he had prudently cached.[5] "And yet it don't somehow sound like whisky," said the gambler. It was not until he caught sight of the blazing fire through the still blind storm, and the group around it, that he settled to the conviction that it was "square fun."

Whether Mr. Oakhurst had cached his cards with the whisky as something debarred the free access of the community, I cannot say. It was certain that, in Mother Shipton's words, he "didn't say 'cards' once" during that evening. Haply the time was beguiled by an accordion, produced somewhat ostentatiously by Tom Simson from his pack. Notwithstanding some difficulties attending the manipulation of this instrument, Piney Woods managed to pluck several reluctant melodies from its keys, to an accompaniment by the Innocent on a pair of bone castanets. But the crowning festivity of the evening was reached in a rude camp-meeting hymn, which the lovers, joining hands, sang with great earnestness and vociferation. I fear that a certain defiant tone and Covenanters'[6] swing to its chorus, rather than any devotional quality, caused it speedily to infect the others, who at last joined in the refrain:

"I'm proud to live in the service of the
    Lord,
And I'm bound to die in His army."

The pines rocked, the storm eddied and whirled above the miserable group, and the flames of their altar leaped heavenward, as if in token of the vow.

At midnight the storm abated, the rolling clouds parted, and the stars glittered keenly above the sleeping camp. Mr. Oakhurst, whose professional habits had enabled him to

---

4. **sotto voce** (sot′ ō vo′ chē), Italian expression, meaning in a low voice.
5. **cached** (kasht), hidden.
6. **Covenanters** (kuv′ ə nən tərz), seventeenth-century Scottish Presbyterians who agreed to defend and extend Presbyterianism against rule by the Anglican church.

live on the smallest possible amount of sleep, in dividing the watch with Tom Simson, somehow managed to take upon himself the greater part of that duty. He excused himself to the Innocent by saying that he had "often been a week without sleep." "Doing what?" asked Tom. "Poker!" replied Oakhurst sententiously. "When a man gets a streak of luck, he don't get tired. The luck gives in first. Luck," continued the gambler reflectively, "is a mighty queer thing. All you know about it for certain is that it's bound to change. And it's finding out when it's going to change that makes you. We've had a streak of bad luck since we left Poker Flat—you come along, and slap, you get into it, too. If you can hold your cards right along, you're all right. For," added the gambler, with cheerful irrelevance,

> "I'm proud to live in the service of the Lord,
> And I'm bound to die in His army."

The third day came, and the sun, looking through the white-curtained valley, saw the outcasts dividing their slowly decreasing store of provisions for the morning meal. It was one of the peculiarities of that mountain climate that its rays diffused a kindly warmth over the wintry landscape, as if in regretful commiseration of the past. But it revealed drift on drift of snow piled high around the hut—a hopeless, uncharted, trackless sea of white lying below the rocky shores to which the castaways still clung. Through the marvelously clear air the smoke of the pastoral village of Poker Flat rose miles away. Mother Shipton saw it, and from a remote pinnacle of her rocky fastness hurled in that direction a final malediction. It was her last vituperative attempt, and perhaps for that reason was invested with a certain degree of sublimity. It did her good, she privately informed the Duchess. "Just you go out there and cuss, and see." She then set herself to the task of amusing "the child," as she and the Duchess were pleased to call Piney. Piney was no chicken,

but it was a soothing and original theory of the pair thus to account for the fact that she didn't swear and wasn't improper.

When night crept up again through the gorges, the reedy notes of the accordion rose and fell in fitful spasms and long-drawn gasps by the flickering campfire. But music failed to fill entirely the aching void left by insufficient food, and a new diversion was proposed by Piney—storytelling. Neither Mr. Oakhurst nor his female companions caring to relate their personal experiences, this plan would have failed too, but for the Innocent. Some months before he had chanced upon a stray copy of Mr. Pope's[7] ingenious translation of the *Iliad*. He now proposed to narrate the principal incidents of that poem—having thoroughly mastered the argument and fairly forgotten the words—in the current vernacular of Sandy Bar. And so, for the rest of that night, the Homeric demigods again walked the earth. Trojan bully and wily Greek wrestled in the winds, and the great pines in the canyon seemed to bow to the wrath of the son of Peleus.[8] Mr. Oakhurst listened with quiet satisfaction. Most especially was he interested in the fate of "Ashheels," as the Innocent persisted in denominating the "swift-footed Achilles."

So, with small food and much of Homer and the accordion, a week passed over the heads of the outcasts. The sun again forsook them, and again from leaden skies the snowflakes were sifted over the land. Day by day closer around them drew the snowy circle, until at last they looked from their prison over drifted walls of dazzling white, that towered twenty feet above their heads. It became more and more difficult to replenish their

---

7. **Mr. Pope,** Alexander Pope, English poet (1688–1744).
8. **son of Peleus** (pē′ lē əs), **Achilles** (ə kil′ ēz), Greek warrior, killed in the Trojan War.

fires, even from the fallen trees beside them, now half-hidden in the drifts. And yet no one complained. The lovers turned from the dreary prospect and looked into each other's eyes, and were happy. Mr. Oakhurst settled himself coolly to the losing game before him. The Duchess, more cheerful than she had been, assumed the care of Piney. Only Mother Shipton—once the strongest of the party—seemed to sicken and fade. At midnight on the tenth day, she called Oakhurst to her side. "I'm going," she said, in a voice of querulous weakness, "but don't say anything about it. Don't waken the kids. Take the bundle from under my head, and open it." Mr. Oakhurst did so. It contained Mother Shipton's rations for the last week, untouched. "Give 'em to the child," she said, pointing to the sleeping Piney. "You've starved yourself," said the gambler. "That's what they call it," said the woman querulously, as she lay down again, and, turning her face to the wall, passed quietly away.

The accordion and the bones were put aside that day, and Homer was forgotten. When the body of Mother Shipton had been committed to the snow, Mr. Oakhurst took the Innocent aside, and showed him a pair of snowshoes, which he had fashioned from the old packsaddle. "There's one chance in a hundred to save her yet," he said, pointing to Piney: "but it's there," he added, pointing toward Poker Flat. "If you can reach there in two days, she's safe." "And you?" asked Tom Simson. "I'll stay here," was the curt reply.

The lovers parted with a long embrace. "You are not going, too?" said the Duchess, as she saw Mr. Oakhurst apparently waiting to accompany him. "As far as the canyon," he replied. He turned suddenly and kissed the Duchess, leaving her pallid face aflame, and her trembling limbs rigid with amazement.

Night came, but not Mr. Oakhurst. It brought the storm again and the whirling snow. Then the Duchess, feeding the fire, found someone had quietly piled beside the

hut enough fuel to last a few days longer. The tears rose to her eyes, but she hid them from Piney.

The women slept but little. In the morning, looking into each other's faces, they read their fate. Neither spoke, but Piney, accepting the position of the stronger, drew near and placed her arm around the Duchess' waist. They kept this attitude for the rest of the day. That night the storm reached its greatest fury, and, rending asunder the protecting pines, invaded the very hut.

Toward morning they found themselves unable to feed the fire, which gradually died away. As the embers slowly blackened, the Duchess crept closer to Piney, and broke the silence of many hours: "Piney, can you pray?" "No, dear," said Piney simply. The Duchess, without knowing exactly why, felt relieved, and, putting her head upon Piney's shoulder, spoke no more. And so reclining, the younger and purer pillowing the head of her soiled sister upon her virgin breast, they fell asleep.

The wind lulled as if it feared to waken them. Feathery drifts of snow, shaken from the long pine boughs, flew like white-winged birds, and settled about them as they slept. The moon through the rifted clouds looked down upon what had been the camp. But all human stain, all trace of earthly travail, was hidden beneath the spotless mantle mercifully flung from above.

They slept all that day and the next, nor did they waken when voices and footsteps broke the silence of the camp. And when pitying fingers brushed the snow from their wan faces, you could scarcely have told from the equal peace that dwelt upon them which was she that had sinned. Even the law of Poker Flat recognized this, and turned away, leaving them still locked in each other's arms.

But at the head of the gulch, on one of the largest pine trees, they found the deuce of clubs pinned to the bark with a bowie knife. It bore the following, written in pencil in a firm hand:

BENEATH THIS TREE
LIES THE BODY
OF
JOHN OAKHURST,
WHO STRUCK A STREAK OF BAD LUCK
ON THE 23D OF NOVEMBER, 1850,
AND
HANDED IN HIS CHECKS
ON THE 7TH DECEMBER, 1850.

And pulseless and cold, with a Derringer by his side and a bullet in his heart, though still calm as in life, beneath the snow lay he who was at once the strongest and yet the weakest of the outcasts of Poker Flat.

FOR UNDERSTANDING

1. Why are the outcasts forced to leave Poker Flat?
2. Why do the exiles stop midway rather than pushing on to Sandy Bar? Who joins their party?
3. Which of the outcasts is not affected by the innocence of the newcomers? How does he prove his rascality?
4. What is the fate of the party?

FOR INTERPRETATION

Verify or refute the following statements on the basis of details from the story.
1. In bad times, people commonly look for a scapegoat to blame for their troubles.
2. Justice, in the Old West, could be regarded as laughable, or absurd.
3. A crisis often brings about moral change in the persons involved.
4. The ability to remain calm and impassive in time of crisis indicates strength of character.

FOR APPRECIATION

Local-Color Writing

The main purpose of *local-color writing* is to portray the habits, dress, behavior, speech, and mannerisms of people living in a particular locality or region. Conceived to satisfy the curiosity of people living in one section of the country about those living in another, local-color writing dominated American literature around 1880. Local colorists were usually satisfied with being entertainingly informative about the surface details of a place and its people. Generally speaking, the writing of local colorists was marked by *dialect* (some of it woefully inaccurate), the use of eccentrics as characters, and an appeal to sentimentality or whimsical humor. Writers often sentimentalized or idealized their characters in order to illustrate a moral, as Harte has done in this story.

1. In choosing eccentric, or out-of-the-ordinary people, such as the outcasts, to be the main characters in his story, what kind of Westerner was Harte obviously overlooking?
2. Alexander Pope's translation of Homer's *Iliad,* telling of the adventures of the Greek hero Achilles, is very difficult reading. Discuss the believability of a young man like Tom Simson being able to read the *Iliad* and recall it in detail.
3. Do you find the circumstances of Mother Shipton's death realistic or sentimentalized? Discuss.
4. Do you think that characters like the gambler Oakhurst were common in the early West?

COMPOSITION

The sad, sentimental ending Harte chose for his story represents but one of numerous possibilities. It leaves the reader with many questions.

Write a composition explaining how you think the story might have ended more realistically.

Sidney Lanier

1842–1881

Sidney Lanier emerged for a brief period after the Civil War as the leading literary voice of the new South, exploring in both prose and poetry the injustices that beset the southern small farmer and the day laborer. Best known as a promising poet who died young, Lanier was also a talented musician who published a series of critical essays on the musical basis of poetry, a thesis he attempted to demonstrate in his own verses. Although his theories of music and poetry never won wide acceptance, his major poems—"Song of the Chattahoochee," "The Marshes of Glynn," and "The Symphony"—are still read today.

Born in Macon, Georgia, Lanier volunteered for service in the Confederate forces and served four years before he was captured. He spent five months in a Union prisoner of war camp. There he contracted the tuberculosis that finally killed him at age thirty-nine. Lanier has been classified primarily as a regionalist, but in some of his work he looked beyond his native Georgia to problems in the turbulent and growing nation in the two decades after the Civil War.

PORTRAIT OF SIDNEY LANIER
Like his predecessor, the Southern poet Henry Timrod, Lanier died young of tuberculosis.

Song of the Chattahoochee

Out of the hills of Habersham,
Down the valleys of Hall,[1]
I hurry amain[2] to reach the plain,
Run the rapid and leap the fall,
Split at the rock and together again,   **5**
Accept my bed, or narrow or wide,
And flee from folly on every side

1. **Habersham and Hall,** counties in Georgia.
2. **amain** (ə mān′), at full speed.

Sidney Lanier, "Song of the Chattahoochee," in POEMS OF SIDNEY LANIER. New York: Charles Scribner's Sons, 1884.

With a lover's pain to attain the plain
  Far from the hills of Habersham,
  Far from the valleys of Hall.   10

  All down the hills of Habersham,
  All through the valleys of Hall,
The rushes cried, *Abide, abide,*
The willful waterweeds held me thrall,[3]
The laving laurel turned my tide,   15
The ferns and the fondling grass said
    Stay,
The dewberry dipped for to work delay,
And the little reeds sighed, *Abide, abide,*
  Here in the hills of Habersham,
  Here in the valleys of Hall.   20

  High o'er the hills of Habersham,
  Veiling the valleys of Hall,
The hickory told me manifold
Fair tales of shade, the poplar tall
Wrought me her shadowy self to hold,   25
The chestnut, the oak, the walnut, the
    pine,
Overleaning, with flickering meaning
    and sign,
Said, *Pass not, so cold, these manifold*
  Deep shades of the hills of Habersham,
  These glades in the valleys of Hall.   30

  And oft in the hills of Habersham,
  And oft in the valleys of Hall,
The white quartz shone, and the smooth
    brook-stone
Did bar me of passage with friendly
    brawl,
  And many a luminous jewel lone   35
—Crystals clear or a-cloud with mist,
Ruby, garnet, and amethyst—
Made lures with the lights of streaming
    stone
  In the clefts of the hills of Haber-
    sham,
  In the beds of the valleys of Hall.   40

3. **thrall** (thrôl),   in bondage.

STUDY FROM NATURE, Asher B. Durand
New York Historical Society, New York City

But oh, not the hills of Habersham,
  And oh, not the valleys of Hall
Avail: I am fain[4] for to water the plain.
Downward the voices of Duty call—
Downward, to toil and be mixed with
    the main;[5]   45
The dry fields burn, and the mills are
    to turn,
And a myriad flowers mortally yearn,
And the lordly main from beyond the
    plain
  Calls o'er the hills of Habersham,
  Calls through the valleys of Hall.   50

4. **fain,** obliged.
5. **main,** here: the sea.

FOR UNDERSTANDING

1. Who is the speaker in the poem?
2. What things impede the river's progress?
3. Why must the river rush down to the plain?

FOR APPRECIATION

The poet uses alliteration, repetition, and internal rhyme to create a sense of the headlong rushing of the river.
1. Point out (a) the internal rhyme in lines 8 and 13; (b) the alliteration in line 7.
2. List the verbs in the first stanza that suggest the river's hurried, tumbling current.
3. What does the refrain add to the poem?

Kate Chopin

1851–1904

In 1894, when Kate Chopin published *Bayou Folk*, the first collection of her Louisiana stories, she was welcomed as a talented local colorist and for five years enjoyed considerable popularity. However, her novel *The Awakening* drew such negative criticism when it appeared in 1899 that she virtually gave up writing and published little after that time.

Chopin was born Katherine O'Flaherty in St. Louis to an Irish immigrant father and a Creole mother (Creoles are descendants of early French and Spanish colonists) and was brought up in the French Catholic tradition. A popular society belle, Kate was married at nineteen to Oscar Chopin of New Orleans. Living first in New Orleans, then in Natchitoches (Nack′ uh tush) Parish, Chopin became well acquainted with the local Creoles and 'Cadians. (The 'Cadians, or 'Cajuns, are believed to be descendants of the French settlers that the British drove from Nova Scotia in 1755.) It was these people who later provided material for many of her stories and sketches.

Reproduction of dialects is one of the characteristics of regional writing. In the following short story Chopin demonstrates her versatility in recreating the dialects of the Louisiana bayou country of a century ago.

A GENTLEMAN OF BAYOU TÊCHE

It was no wonder Mr. Sublet, who was staying at the Hallet plantation, wanted to make a picture of Evariste. The 'Cadian was rather a picturesque subject in his way, and a tempting one to an artist looking for bits of "local color" along the Têche.

Mr. Sublet had seen the man on the back gallery just as he came out of the swamp, trying to sell a wild turkey to the housekeeper. He spoke to him at once, and in the course of conversation engaged him to return to the house the following morning and have his picture drawn. He handed Evariste a couple of silver dollars to show that his intentions were fair, and that he expected the 'Cadian to keep faith with him.

"He tell' me he want' put my picture in one fine 'Mag'zine,'" said Evariste to his daughter, Martinette, when the two were talking the matter over in the afternoon. "W'at fo' you reckon he want' do dat?" They sat within the low, homely cabin of two rooms, that was not quite so comfortable as Mr. Hallet's negro quarters.

Martinette pursed her red lips that had little sensitive curves to them, and her black eyes took on a reflective expression.

"Mebbe he yeard 'bout that big fish w'at you ketch las' winta in Carancro lake. You know it was all wrote 'bout in the 'Suga

From COMPLETE WORKS OF KATE CHOPIN, Louisiana State University Press.

"He tell' me he want' put my picture in one fine 'Mag'zine . . . . W'at fo' you reckon he want' do dat?"

Bowl.'" Her father set aside the suggestion with a deprecatory[1] wave of the hand.

"Well, anyway, you got to fix yo'se'f up," declared Martinette, dismissing further speculation; "put on yo' otha pant'loon an' yo' good coat; an' you betta ax Mr. Léonce to cut yo' hair, an' yo' w'sker' a li'le bit."

"It's w'at I say," chimed in Evariste. "I tell dat gent'man I'm goin' make myse'f fine. He say', 'No, no,' like he ent please'. He want' me like I come out de swamp. So much betta if my pant'loon' an' coat is tore, he say, an' color' like de mud." They could not understand these eccentric wishes on the part of the strange gentleman, and made no effort to do so.

An hour later Martinette, who was quite puffed up over the affair, trotted across to Aunt Dicey's cabin to communicate the news to her. The negress was ironing; her irons stood in a long row before the fire of logs that burned on the hearth. Martinette seated herself in the chimney corner and held her feet up to the blaze; it was damp and a little chilly out of doors. The girl's shoes were considerably worn and her garments were a little too thin and scant for the winter season. Her father had given her the two dollars he had received from the artist, and Martinette was on her way to the store to invest them as judiciously as she knew how.

"You know, Aunt Dicey," she began a little complacently after listening awhile to Aunt Dicey's unqualified abuse of her own son, Wilkins, who was dining-room boy at Mr. Hallet's, "you know that stranger gentleman up to Mr. Hallet's? He want' to make my popa's picture; an' he say' he goin' put it in one fine *Mag'*zine yonda."

Aunt Dicey spat upon her iron to test its heat. Then she began to snicker. She kept on laughing inwardly, making her whole fat body shake, and saying nothing.

"W'at you laughin' 'bout, Aunt Dice?" inquired Martinette mistrustfully.

"I is n' laughin', chile!"

"Yas, you' laughin'."

"Oh, don't pay no 'tention to me. I jis studyin' how simple you an' yo' pa is. You is bof de simplest somebody I eva come 'crost."

"You got to say plumb out w'at you mean, Aunt Dice," insisted the girl doggedly, suspicious and alert now.

"Well, dat w'y I say you is simple," proclaimed the woman, slamming down her iron on an inverted, battered pie pan, "jis like you says, dey gwine put yo' pa's picture yonda in de picture paper. An' you know w'at readin' dey gwine sot down on'neaf dat picture?" Martinette was intensely attentive. "Dey gwine sot down on'neaf: 'Dis heah is one dem low-down 'Cajuns o' Bayeh Têche!'"

The blood flowed from Martinette's face, leaving it deathly pale; in another instant it came beating back in a quick flood, and her eyes smarted with pain as if the tears that filled them had been fiery hot.

"I knows dem kine o' folks," continued Aunt Dicey, resuming her interrupted ironing. "Dat stranger he got a li'le boy w'at ain't none too big to spank. Dat li'le imp he come a hoppin' in heah yistiddy wid a kine o' box on'neaf his arm. He say' 'Good mo'nin', madam. Will you be so kine an' stan' jis like you is dah at yo' i'onin', an' lef me take yo' picture?' I 'lowed I gwine make a picture outen him wid dis heah flati'on, ef he don' cl'ar hisse'f quick. An' he say he baig my pardon fo' his intrudement. All dat kine o' talk to a ole 'oman!"

"W'at you want 'im to say, Aunt Dice?" asked Martinette, with an effort to conceal her distress.

"I wants 'im to come in heah an' say: 'Howdy, Aunt Dicey! will you be so kine and go put on yo' noo calker dress an' yo' bonnit w'at you w'ars to meetin', an' stan' 'side f'om dat i'onin'-boa'd w'ilse I gwine take yo' photygraph.' Dat de way fo' a boy to talk w'at had good raisin'."

Martinette had arisen, and began to take

---

1. **deprecatory** (dep′ rə kə tô′ rē), serving to depreciate; making the matter seem unimportant.

slow leave of the woman. She turned at the cabin door to observe tentatively: "I reckon it's Wilkins tells you how the folks they talk, yonda up to Mr. Hallet's."

She did not go to the store as she had intended, but walked with a dragging step back to her home. The silver dollars clicked in her pocket as she walked. She felt like flinging them across the field; they seemed to her somehow the price of shame.

The sun had sunk, and twilight was settling like a silver beam upon the bayou and enveloping the fields in a gray mist. Evariste, slim and slouchy, was waiting for his daughter in the cabin door. He had lighted a fire of sticks and branches, and placed the kettle before it to boil. He met the girl with his slow, serious, questioning eyes, astonished to see her empty-handed.

"How come you did n' bring nuttin' f'om de sto', Martinette?"

She entered and flung her gingham sunbonnet upon a chair. "No, I didn' go yonda;" and with sudden exasperation: "You got to go take back that money; you mus'n' git no picture took."

"But, Martinette," her father mildly interposed, "I promise' 'im; an' he's goin' give me some mo' money w'en he finish."

"If he give you a ba'el o' money, you mus'n' git no picture took. You know w'at he want to put un'neath that picture, fo' ev'body to read?" She could not tell him the whole hideous truth as she had heard it distorted from Aunt Dicey's lips; she would not hurt him that much. "He's goin' to write: 'This is one 'Cajun' o' the Bayou Têche.'" Evariste winced.

"How you know?" he asked.

"I yeard so. I know it's true."

The water in the kettle was boiling. He went and poured a small quantity upon the coffee which he had set there to drip. Then he said to her: "I reckon you jus' as well go care dat two dolla' back, tomo' mo'nin'; me, I'll go yonda ketch a mess o' fish in Carancro lake."

Mr. Hallet and a few masculine companions were assembled at a rather late breakfast the following morning. The dining-room was a big, bare one, enlivened by a cheerful fire of logs that blazed in the wide chimney on massive andirons. There were guns, fishing tackle, and other implements of sport lying about. A couple of fine dogs strayed unceremoniously in and out behind Wilkins, the negro boy who waited upon the table. The chair beside Mr. Sublet, usually occupied by his little son, was vacant, as the child had gone for an early morning outing and had not yet returned.

When breakfast was about half over, Mr. Hallet noticed Martinette standing outside upon the gallery. The dining-room door had stood open more than half the time.

"Isn't that Martinette out there, Wilkins?" inquired the jovial-faced young planter.

"Dat 's who, suh," returned Wilkins. "She ben standin' dah sence mos' sun-up; look like she studyin' to take root to de gall'ry."

"What in the name of goodness does she want? Ask her what she wants. Tell her to come in to the fire."

Martinette walked into the room with much hesitancy. Her small, brown face could hardly be seen in the depths of the gingham sunbonnet. Her blue cottonade skirt scarcely reached the thin ankles that it should have covered.

"Bonjou',"[2] she murmured, with a little comprehensive nod that took in the entire company. Her eyes searched the table for the "stranger gentleman," and she knew him at once, because his hair was parted in the middle and he wore a pointed beard. She went and laid the two silver dollars beside his plate and motioned to retire without a word of explanation.

"Hold on, Martinette!" called out the planter, "what's all this pantomime business? Speak out, little one."

2. **Bonjou'** abbreviated form of **bonjour** (bôn zhür'), French for "Good day."

"My popa don't want any picture took," she offered, a little timorously.[3] On her way to the door she had looked back to say this. In that fleeting glance she detected a smile of intelligence pass from one to the other of the group. She turned quickly, facing them all, and spoke out, excitement making her voice bold and shrill: "My popa ent one low-down 'Cajun. He ent goin' to stan' to have that kine o' writin' put down un'neath his picture!"

She almost ran from the room, half blinded by the emotion that had helped her to make so daring a speech.

Descending the gallery steps she ran full against her father who was ascending, bearing in his arms the little boy, Archie Sublet. The child was most grotesquely attired in garments far too large for his diminutive person—the rough jeans clothing of some negro boy. Evariste himself had evidently been taking a bath without the preliminary ceremony of removing his clothes, that were now half dried upon his person by the wind and sun.

"Yere you' li'le boy," he announced, stumbling into the room. "You ought not lef dat li'le chile go by hisse'f *comme ça*[4] in de pirogue."[5] Mr. Sublet darted from his chair; the others following suit almost as hastily. In an instant, quivering with apprehension, he had his little son in his arms. The child was quite unharmed, only somewhat pale and nervous, as the consequence of a recent very serious ducking.

Evariste related in his uncertain, broken English how he had been fishing for an hour or more in Carancro lake, when he noticed the boy paddling over the deep, black water in a shell-like pirogue. Nearing a clump of cypress-trees that rose from the lake, the pirogue became entangled in the heavy moss that hung from the tree limbs and trailed upon the water. The next thing he knew, the boat had overturned, he heard the child scream, and saw him disappear beneath the still, black surface of the lake.

"W'en I done swim to de sho' wid 'im,"
continued Evariste, "I hurry yonda to Jake Baptiste's cabin, an' we rub 'im an' warm 'im up, an' dress 'im up dry like you see. He all right now, M'sieur; but you mus'n lef 'im go no mo' by hisse'f in one pirogue."

Martinette had followed into the room behind her father. She was feeling and tapping his wet garments solicitously, and begging him in French to come home. Mr. Hallet at once ordered hot coffee and a warm breakfast for the two; and they sat down at the corner of the table, making no manner of objection in their perfect simplicity. It was with visible reluctance and ill-disguised contempt that Wilkins served them.

When Mr. Sublet had arranged his son comfortably, with tender care, upon the sofa, and had satisfied himself that the child was quite uninjured, he attempted to find words with which to thank Evariste for this service which no treasure of words or gold could pay for. These warm and heartfelt expressions seemed to Evariste to exaggerate the importance of his action, and they intimidated him. He attempted shyly to hide his face as well as he could in the depths of his bowl of coffee.

"You will let me make your picture now, I hope, Evariste," begged Mr. Sublet, laying his hand upon the 'Cadian's shoulder. "I want to place it among things I hold most dear, and shall call it 'A hero of Bayou Têche.'" This assurance seemed to distress Evariste greatly.

"No, no," he protested, "it's nuttin' hero' to take a li'le boy out de water. I jus' as easy do dat like I stoop down an' pick up a li'le chile w'at fall down in de road. I ent goin' to 'low dat, me. I don't git no picture took, *va!*"

Mr. Hallet, who now discerned his friend's eagerness in the matter, came to his aid.

"I tell you, Evariste, let Mr. Sublet draw

---

3. **timorously** (tim′ ər əs lē),   fearfully.
4. **comme ça** (kum sə′),   French for "like that."
5. **pirogue** (pə rōg′),   dugout canoe.

your picture, and you yourself may call it whatever you want. I'm sure he'll let you."

"Most willingly," agreed the artist.

Evariste glanced up at him with shy and child-like pleasure. "It's a bargain?" he asked.

"A bargain," affirmed Mr. Sublet.

"Popa," whispered Martinette, "you betta come home an' put on yo' otha pant'loon' an' yo' good coat."

"And now, what shall we call the much talked-of picture?" cheerily inquired the planter, standing with his back to the blaze.

Evariste in a business-like manner began carefully to trace on the tablecloth imaginary characters with an imaginary pen; he could not have written the real characters with a real pen—he did not know how.

"You will put on'neat' de picture," he said, deliberately, "'Dis is one picture of Mista Evariste Anatole Bonamour, a gent'man of de Bayou Têche.'"

FOR UNDERSTANDING

1. Who is Mr. Sublet, and what agreement does he make with Evariste?
2. What caption does Aunt Dicey believe the artist will place under Evariste's picture?
3. Why does Aunt Dicey refuse to let Archie Sublet snap her photograph?
4. Why does Martinette go to see Mr. Sublet early the next morning?
5. Why does Evariste protest that he is no hero?
6. Under what condition does Evariste consent to have his picture drawn?

FOR INTERPRETATION

In this story does Chopin illustrate that pride and dignity exist among even the most impoverished people? Defend your answer.

FOR APPRECIATION

The opening paragraphs of the story demonstrate that interest in local color was indeed at a high level in the 1880s. Artists found it lucrative to draw "different-looking" inhabitants of particular locales for magazines and thus traveled around looking for suitable subjects.

Kate Chopin took as her literary province the bayou country along the Cane River in Louisiana. Linguists generally agree that she displayed a keen ear in reproducing the dialects and idioms of the people in that region.

1. Evariste and Martinette consider themselves 'Cadians. What is the term they do not want applied to them?
2. What information does the author give the reader of the way the 'Cadian swamp people dressed and lived?
3. Discuss whether Chopin's characters of Martinette and her father seem like real people or like stock characters such as those found in "The Outcasts of Poker Flat."

LANGUAGE AND VOCABULARY

There are interesting histories behind many of the words and expressions that we use every day. Consider, for example, the word "Gentleman" in the title of the story. *Gen* is from the Greek meaning birth. *Gentil* is an Old French word that designated one born into the nobility. Thus, a *gentleman* originally meant a male born to noble parents. Over the centuries, though, it has come to mean one who exhibits good breeding or manners.

Search for the histories of the following words taken from the story: *bayou, turkey, dollar, magazine, pantaloons.* A good unabridged dictionary should prove adequate for your needs; if your school library has the *Oxford English Dictionary,* you will find it an invaluable reference. Other good sources are *Morris Dictionary of Word and Phrase Origins,* by William and Mary Morris, and *Word Origins and Their Romantic Stories,* by Wilfred Funk.

Mary E. Wilkins Freeman 1852–1930

The New England into which Mary E. Wilkins (later Freeman) was born resembled in some ways the true democracy envisioned by Jefferson: a nation of small farmers and skilled artisans who were literate, eligible to vote, thrifty, and economically independent. In reality, especially after the Civil War and the country's massive industrialization, New England's hinterland was filled with dead or dying villages and failed or failing small farms. Families, and especially young single men, sought better prospects in the West or in the crowded cities. For the most part, young single women were left behind in their native villages to adapt to sterile and narrow lives as they guarded their meager possessions. It was these women, the frustrated and impoverished descendants of Puritans, whom Mary E. Wilkins knew so well in the fifty years she lived among them in Massachusetts and Vermont. And it is these women who are the heroines of many of her best stories.

Considered a minor writer until recently, Mary E. Wilkins Freeman is now recognized as an important American regionalist. The masterful character studies in her early work, especially of plain yet strong-willed women, make her stories engaging reading. Of her twenty volumes of fiction, perhaps the best known are two collections of her stories: *A Humble Romance* (1887) and *A New England Nun* (1891).

A CHURCH MOUSE

"I never heard of a woman's bein' saxton."[1]

"I dun' know what difference that makes; I don't see why they shouldn't have women saxtons as well as men saxtons, for my part, nor nobody else neither. They'd keep dusted 'nough sight cleaner. I've seen the dust layin' on my pew thick enough to write my name in a good many times, an' ain't said nothin' about it. An' I ain't goin' to say nothin' now again Joe Sowen, now he's dead an' gone. He did jest as well as most men do. Men git in a good many places where they don't belong, an' where they set as awkward as a cow on a hen-roost, jest because they push in ahead of women. I ain't blamin' 'em; I s'pose if I could push in I should, jest the same way. But there ain't no reason that I can see, nor nobody else neither, why a woman shouldn't be saxton."

Hetty Fifield stood in the rowen hay[2] field before Caleb Gale. He was a deacon, the chairman of the selectmen,[3] and the rich and influential man of the village. One looking at him would not have guessed it. There was nothing imposing about his lumbering figure

---

1. **saxton,** local pronunciation of *sexton*, one who is charged with caring for a church, ringing the bell, and sometimes digging graves.
2. **rowen** (rou' ən) **hay,** the second cutting of hay in a given season.
3. **selectmen,** a board of town officers chosen annually to manage certain public affairs.

From A NEW ENGLAND NUN AND OTHER STORIES by Mary Wilkins Freeman. New York: Harper & Brothers, 1891.

GOING TO CHURCH, George H. Durrie
The White House Collection, Washington, D.C.

in his calico shirt and baggy trousers. However, his large face, red and moist with perspiration, scanned the distant horizon with a stiff and reserved air; he did not look at Hetty.

"How'd you go to work to ring the bell?" said he. "It would have to be tolled, too, if anybody died."

"I'd jest as lief ring that little meetin'-house bell as to stan' out here an' jingle a cow-bell," said Hetty; "an' as for tollin', I'd jest as soon toll the bell for Methusaleh,[4] if he was livin' here! I'd laugh if I ain't got strength 'nough for that."

"It takes a kind of a knack."

"If I ain't got as much knack as old Joe Sowen ever had, I'll give up the ship."

"You couldn't tend the fires."

"Couldn't tend the fires—when I've cut an' carried in all the wood I've burned for forty year! Couldn't keep the fires a-goin' in them two little wood-stoves!"

"It's consider'ble work to sweep the meetin'-house."

"I guess I've done 'bout as much work as to sweep that little meetin'-house, I ruther guess I have."

4. **Methuselah** (mə thü' zə lə), Biblical patriarch who lived 969 years (Genesis 5:27). Since it was customary in some churches to toll the bell once for each year the deceased had lived, Hetty's reference to Methuselah implies her belief in her physical strength.

"There's one thing you ain't thought of."

"What's that?"

"Where'd you live? All old Sowen got for bein' saxton was twenty dollar a year an' we couldn't pay a woman so much as that. You couldn't have enough to pay for your livin' anywheres."

"Where am I goin' to live whether I'm saxton or not?"

Caleb Gale was silent.

There was a wind blowing, the rowen hay drifted round Hetty like a brown-green sea touched with ripples of blue and gold by the asters and goldenrod. She stood in the midst of it like a Mayweed that had gathered a slender toughness through the long summer; her brown cotton gown clung about her like a wilting leaf, outlining her harsh little form. She was as sallow as a squaw, and she had pretty black eyes; they were bright, although she was old. She kept them fixed upon Caleb. Suddenly she raised herself upon her toes; the wind caught her dress and made it blow out; her eyes flashed. "I tell you where I'm goin' to live," said she. *"I'm goin' to live in the meetin'-house."*

Caleb looked at her. *"Goin' to live in the meetin'-house!"*

"Yes, I be."

"Live in the meetin'-house!"

"I'd like to know why not."

"Why—you couldn't—live in the meetin'-house. You're crazy."

Caleb flung out the rake which he was holding, and drew it in full of rowen. Hetty moved around in front of him; he raked imperturbably; she moved again right in the path of the rake; then he stopped. "There ain't no sense in such talk."

"All I want is jest the east corner of the back gall'ry, where the chimbly goes up. I'll set up my cookin'-stove there, an' my bed, an' I'll curtain it off with my sunflower quilt, to keep off the wind."

"A cookin'-stove an' a bed in the meetin'-house!"

"Mis' Grout she give me that cookin'-stove, an' that bed I've allers slept on, before she died. She give 'em to me before Mary Anne Thomas, an' I moved 'em out. They air settin' out in the yard now, an' if it rains that stove an' that bed will be spoilt. It looks some like rain now. I guess you'd better give me the meetin'-house key right off."

"You don't think you can move that cookin'-stove an' that bed into the meetin'-house—I ain't goin' to stop to hear such talk."

"My worsted-work, all my mottoes I've done, an' my wool flowers, air out there in the yard."

Caleb raked. Hetty kept standing herself about until he was forced to stop or gather her in with the rowen hay. He looked straight at her and scowled; the perspiration trickled down his cheeks. "If I go up to the house can Mis' Gale git me the key to the meetin'-house?" said Hetty.

"No, she can't."

"Be you goin' up before long?"

"No, I ain't." Suddenly Caleb's voice changed: it had been full of stubborn vexation, now it was blandly argumentative. "Don't you see it ain't no use talkin' such nonsense, Hetty? You'd better go right along, an' make up your mind it ain't to be thought of."

"Where be I goin' tonight, then?"

"Tonight?"

"Yes; where be I a-goin'?"

"Ain't you got any place to go to?"

"Where do you s'pose I've got any place? Them folks air movin' into Mis' Grout's house, an' they as good as told me to clear out. I ain't got no folks to take me in. I dun' know where I'm goin'; mebbe I can go to your house?"

Caleb gave a start. "We've got company to home," said he, hastily. "I'm 'fraid Mis' Gale wouldn't think it was convenient."

Hetty laughed. "Most everybody in the town has got company," said she.

Caleb dug his rake into the ground as if it were a hoe; then he leaned on it and stared at the horizon. There was a fringe of yellow birches on the edge of the hay field; beyond them was a low range of misty blue hills. "You ain't got no place to go to, then?"

"I dun' know of any. There ain't no poorhouse here, an' I ain't got no folks."

Caleb stood like a statue. Some crows flew cawing over the field. Hetty waited. "I s'pose that key is where Mis' Gale can find it?" she said, finally.

Caleb turned and threw out his rake with a jerk. "She knows where 'tis; it's hangin' up behind the settin'-room door. I s'pose you can stay there tonight, as long as you ain't got no other place. We shall have to see what can be done."

Hetty scuttled off across the field. "You mustn't take no stove nor bed into the meetin'-house," Caleb called after her; "we can't have that, nohow."

Hetty went on as if she did not hear.

The goldenrod at the sides of the road was turning brown; the asters were in their prime, blue and white ones; here and there were rows of thistles with white tops. The dust was thick; Hetty, when she emerged from Caleb's house, trotted along in a cloud of it. She did not look to the right or left; she kept her small eager face fixed straight ahead, and moved forward like some little animal with the purpose to which it was born strong within it.

Presently she came to a large cottage house on the right of the road; there she stopped. The front yard was full of furniture, tables and chairs standing among the dahlias and clumps of marigolds. Hetty leaned over the fence at one corner of the yard and inspected a little knot of household goods set aside from the others. There was a small cooking-stove, a hair trunk,[5] a yellow bedstead stacked up against the fence, and a pile of bedding. Some children in the yard stood in a group and eyed Hetty. A woman appeared in the door—she was small, there was a black smutch[6] on her face, which was haggard with fatigue, and she scowled in the sun as she looked over at Hetty. "Well, got a place

to stay in?" said she, in an unexpectedly deep voice.

"Yes, I guess so," replied Hetty.

"I dun' know how in the world I can have you. All the beds will be full—I expect his mother some tonight, an' I'm dreadful stirred up anyhow."

"Everybody's havin' company; I never see anything like it." Hetty's voice was inscrutable. The other woman looked sharply at her.

"You've got a place, ain't you?" she asked, doubtfully.

"Yes, I have."

At the left of this house, quite back from the road, was a little unpainted cottage, hardly more than a hut. There was smoke coming out of the chimney, and a tall youth lounged in the door. Hetty, with the woman and children staring after her, struck out across the field in the little footpath towards the cottage. "I wonder if she's goin' to stay there?" the woman muttered, meditating.

The youth did not see Hetty until she was quite near him; then he aroused suddenly as if from sleep, and tried to slink off around the cottage. But Hetty called after him. "Sammy," she cried, "Sammy, come back here. I want you!"

"What d'ye want?"

"Come back here!"

The youth lounged back sulkily, and a tall woman came to the door. She bent out of it anxiously to hear Hetty.

"I want you to come an' help me move my stove an' things," said Hetty.

"Where to?"

"Into the meetin'-house."

"The meetin'-house."

"Yes, the meetin'-house."

The woman in the door had sodden hand.; behind her arose the steam of a washtub. She and the youth stared at Hetty, but

---

5. **hair trunk,** a trunk covered with animal hide from which the hair has not been removed.

6. **smutch,** smudge.

surprise was too strong an emotion for them to grasp firmly.

"I want Sammy to come right over an' help me," said Hetty.

"He ain't strong enough to move a stove," said the woman.

"Ain't strong enough!"

"He's apt to git lame."

"Most folks are. Guess I've got lame. Come right along, Sammy!"

"He ain't able to lift much."

"I s'pose he's able to be lifted, ain't he?"

"I dun' know what you mean."

"The stove don't weigh nothin'," said Hetty; "I could carry it myself if I could git hold of it. Come, Sammy!"

Hetty turned down the path, and the youth moved a little way after her, as if perforce. Then he stopped, and cast an appealing glance back at his mother. Her face was distressed. "Oh, Sammy, I'm afraid you'll git sick," said she.

"No, he ain't goin' to git sick," said Hetty. "Come, Sammy." And Sammy followed her down the path.

It was four o'clock then. At dusk Hetty had her gay sunflower quilt curtaining off the chimney corner of the church gallery; her stove and little bedstead were set up, and she had entered upon a life which endured successfully for three months. All that time a storm brewed; then it broke; but Hetty sailed in her own course for the three months.

It was on a Saturday that she took up her habitation in the meeting-house. The next morning, when the boy who had been supplying the dead sexton's place came and shook the door, Hetty was prompt on the other side. "Deacon Gale said for you to let me in so I could ring the bell," called the boy.

"Go away," responded Hetty. "I'm goin' to ring the bell; I'm saxton."

Hetty rang the bell with vigor, but she made a wild, irregular jangle at first; at the last it was better. The village people said to each other that a new hand was ringing. Only a few knew that Hetty was in the meeting-house. When the congregation had assem-bled and saw that gaudy tent pitched in the house of the Lord and the resolute little pilgrim at the door of it, there was a commotion. The farmers and their wives were stirred out of their Sabbath decorum. After the service was over, Hetty, sitting in a pew corner of the gallery, her little face dark and watchful against the flaming background of her quilt, saw the people below gathering in groups, whispering, and looking at her.

Presently the minister, Caleb Gale, and the other deacon came up the gallery stairs. Hetty sat stiffly erect. Caleb Gale went up to the sunflower quilt, slipped it aside, and looked in. He turned to Hetty with a frown. Today his dignity was supported by important witnesses. "Did you bring that stove an' bedstead here?"

Hetty nodded.

"What made you do such a thing?"

"What was I goin' to do if I didn't? How's a woman as old as me goin' to sleep in a pew, an' go without a cup of tea?"

The men looked at each other. They withdrew to another corner of the gallery and conferred in low tones; then they went downstairs and out of the church. Hetty smiled when she heard the door shut. When one is hard pressed, one, however simple, gets wisdom as to vantage points. Hetty comprehended hers perfectly. She was the propounder of a problem; as long as it was unguessed, she was sure of her foothold as propounder. This little village in which she had lived all her life had removed the shelter from her head; she being penniless, it was beholden to provide her another; she asked it what. When the old woman with whom she had lived died, the town promptly seized the estate for taxes—none had been paid for years. Hetty had not laid up a cent; indeed, for the most of the time she had received no wages. There had been no money in the house; all she had gotten for her labor for a sickly, impecunious[7] old woman was a frugal

---

7. **impecunious** (im pi kyü′ nē əs), poor.

board. When the old woman died, Hetty gathered in the few household articles for which she had stipulated, and made no complaint. She walked out of the house when the new tenants came in; all she asked was, "What are you going to do with me?" This little settlement of narrow-minded, prosperous farmers, however hard a task charity might be to them, could not turn an old woman out into the fields and highways to seek for food as they would a Jersey cow. They had their Puritan consciences, and her note of distress would sound louder in their ears than the Jersey's bell echoing down the valley in the stillest night. But the question as to Hetty Fifield's disposal was a hard one to answer. There was no almshouse[8] in the village, and no private family was willing to take her in. Hetty was strong and capable; although she was old, she could well have paid for her food and shelter by her labor; but this could not secure her an entrance even among this hard working and thrifty people, who would ordinarily grasp quickly enough at service without wage in dollars and cents. Hetty had somehow gotten for herself an unfortunate name in the village. She was held in the light of a long-thorned brier among the beanpoles, or a fierce little animal with claws and teeth bared. People were afraid to take her into their families; she had the reputation of always taking her own way, and never heeding the voice of authority. "I'd take her in an' have her give me a lift with the work," said one sickly farmer's wife; "but near's I can find out, I couldn't never be sure that I'd get molasses in the beans, nor saleratus[9] in my sour milk cakes, if she took a notion not to put it in. I don't dare to risk it."

Stories were about concerning Hetty's authority over the old woman with whom she had lived. "Old Mis' Grout never dared to say her soul was her own," people said. Then Hetty's sharp, sarcastic sayings were repeated; the justice of them made them sting. People did not want a tongue like that in their homes.

Hetty as a church sexton was directly opposed to all their ideas of church decorum and propriety in general; her pitching her tent in the Lord's house was almost sacrilege. But what could they do? Hetty jangled the Sabbath bells for the three months; once she tolled the bell for an old man, and it seemed by the sound of the bell as if his long, calm years had swung by in a weak delirium; but people bore it. She swept and dusted the little meeting-house, and she garnished the walls with her treasures of worsted-work. The neatness and the garniture went far to quiet the dissatisfaction of the people. They had a crude taste. Hetty's skill in fancy-work was quite celebrated. Her wool flowers were much talked of, and young girls tried to copy them. So these wreaths and clusters of red and blue and yellow wool roses and lilies hung as acceptably between the meeting-house windows as pictures of saints in a cathedral.

Hetty hung a worsted motto over the pulpit; on it she set her chiefest treasure of art, a white wax cross with an ivy vine trailing over it, all covered with silver frost-work. Hetty always surveyed this cross with a species of awe; she felt the irresponsibility and amazement of a genius at his own work.

When she set it on the pulpit, no queen casting her rich robes and her jewels upon a shrine could have surpassed her in generous enthusiasm. "I guess when they see that they won't say no more," she said.

But the people, although they shared Hetty's admiration for the cross, were doubtful. They, looking at it, had a double vision of a little wax Virgin upon an altar. They wondered if it savored of popery.[10] But the cross remained, and the minister was mindful not to jostle it in his gestures.

---

8. **almshouse,** home for very poor persons, supported by public funds.

9. **saleratus** (sal ə rā′ təs), sodium bicarbonate, used in baking.

10. **popery,** the doctrines, customs, and ceremonies of the Roman Catholic church. New England Puritans associated elaborate church decoration with Catholicism.

It was three months from the time Hetty took up her abode in the church, and a week before Christmas, when the problem was solved. Hetty herself precipitated the solution. She prepared a boiled dish in the meeting-house, upon a Saturday, and the next day the odors of turnip and cabbage were strong in the senses of the worshippers. They sniffed and looked at one another. This superseding the legitimate savor of the sanctuary, the fragrance of peppermint lozenges and wintergreen, the breath of Sunday clothes, by the homely weekday odors of kitchen vegetables, was too much for the sensibilities of the people. They looked indignantly around at Hetty, sitting before her sunflower hanging, comfortable from her good dinner of the day before, radiant with the consciousness of a great plateful of cold vegetables in her tent for her Sabbath dinner.

Poor Hetty had not many comfortable dinners. The selectmen doled out a small weekly sum to her, which she took with dignity as being her hire; then she had a mild forage in the neighbors' cellars and kitchens, of poor apples and stale bread and pie, paying for it in teaching her art of worsted-work to the daughters. Her Saturday's dinner had been a banquet to her: she had actually bought a piece of pork to boil with the vegetables; somebody had given her a nice little cabbage and some turnips, without a thought of the limitations of her housekeeping. Hetty herself had not a thought. She made the fires as usual that Sunday morning; the meeting-house was very clean; there was not a speck of dust anywhere; the wax cross on the pulpit glistened in a sunbeam slanting through the house. Hetty, sitting in the gallery, thought innocently how nice it looked.

After the meeting, Caleb Gale approached the other deacon. "Somethin's got to be done," said he. And the other deacon nodded. He had not smelt the cabbage until his wife nudged him and mentioned it; neither had Caleb Gale.

In the afternoon of the next Thursday, Caleb and the other two selectmen waited upon Hetty in her tabernacle. They stumped up the gallery stairs, and Hetty emerged from behind the quilt and stood looking at them, scared and defiant. The three men nodded stiffly; there was a pause; Caleb Gale motioned meaningly to one of the others, who shook his head; finally he himself had to speak. "I'm 'fraid you find it pretty cold here, don't you, Hetty?" said he.

"No, thank ye; it's very comfortable," replied Hetty, polite and wary.

"It ain't very convenient for you to do your cookin' here, I guess."

"It's jest as convenient as I want. I don't find no fault."

"I guess it's rayther lonesome here nights, ain't it?"

"I'd 'nough sight ruther be alone than have comp'ny, any day."

"It ain't fit for an old woman like you to be livin' alone here this way."

"Well, I dun' know of anything that's any fitter; mebbe you do."

Caleb looked appealingly at his companions; they stood stiff and irresponsive. Hetty's eyes were sharp and watchful upon them all.

"Well, Hetty," said Caleb, "we've found a nice, comfortable place for you, an' I guess you'd better pack up your things, an' I'll carry you right over there." Caleb stepped back a little closer to the other men. Hetty, small and trembling and helpless before them, looked vicious. She was like a little animal driven from its cover, for whom there is nothing left but desperate warfare and death.

"Where to?" asked Hetty. Her voice shrilled up into a squeak.

Caleb hesitated. He looked again at the other selectmen. There was a solemn, far-away expression upon their faces. "Well," said he, "Mis' Radway wants to git somebody, an'—"

"You ain't goin' to take me to that woman's!"

"You'd be real comfortable—"

"I ain't goin'."

THE CHRISTMAS TURKEY, Francis W. Edmonds
New York Historical Society, New York City

"Now, why not, I'd like to know?"

"I don't like Susan Radway, hain't never liked her, an' I ain't goin' to live with her."

"Mis' Radway's a good Christian woman. You hadn't ought to speak that way about her."

"You know what Susan Radway is, jest as well's I do; an' everybody else does too. I ain't goin' a step, an' you might jest as well make up your mind to it."

Then Hetty seated herself in the corner of the pew nearest her tent, and folded her hands in her lap. She looked over at the pulpit as if she were listening to preaching. She panted, and her eyes glittered, but she had an immovable air.

"Now, Hetty, you've got sense enough to know you can't stay here," said Caleb. "You'd better put on your bonnet, an' come right along before dark. You'll have a nice ride."

Hetty made no response.

The three men stood looking at her. "Come, Hetty," said Caleb, feebly; and another selectman spoke. "Yes, you'd better come," he said, in a mild voice.

Hetty continued to stare at the pulpit.

The three men withdrew a little and conferred. They did not know how to act. This was a new emergency in their simple, even lives. They were not constables; these three steady, sober old men did not want to drag an old woman by main force out of the meeting-house, and thrust her into Caleb Gale's buggy as if it were a police wagon.

Finally Caleb brightened. "I'll go over an' git mother," said he. He started with a brisk air, and went down the gallery stairs; the others followed. They took up their stand in the meeting-house yard, and Caleb got into his buggy and gathered up the reins. The wind blew cold over the hill. "Hadn't you better go inside and wait out of the wind?" said Caleb.

"I guess we'll wait out here," replied one; and the other nodded.

"Well, I sha'n't be gone long," said Caleb. "Mother'll know how to manage her." He drove carefully down the hill; his buggy wings rattled in the wind. The other men pulled up their coat collars and met the blast stubbornly.

"Pretty ticklish piece of business to tackle," said one, in a low grunt.

"That's so," assented the other. Then they were silent and waited for Caleb. Once in a while they stamped their feet and slapped their mittened hands. They did not hear Hetty slip the bolt and turn the key of the meeting-house door, nor see her peeping at them from a gallery window.

Caleb returned in twenty minutes; he had not far to go. His wife, stout and handsome and full of vigor, sat beside him in the buggy. Her face was red with the cold wind; her thick cashmere shawl was pinned tightly over her broad bosom. "Has she come down yet?" she called out in an imperious way.

The two selectmen shook their heads. Caleb kept the horse quiet while his wife got heavily and briskly out of the buggy. She went up the meeting-house steps and reached out confidently to open the door. Then she drew back and looked around. "Why," said she, "the door's locked; she's locked the door. I call this pretty work!"

She turned again quite fiercely and began beating on the door. "Hetty!" she called; "Hetty, Hetty Fifield! Let me in! What have you locked this door for?"

She stopped and turned to her husband.

"Don't you s'pose the barn key would unlock it?" she asked.

"I don't b'lieve 'twould."

"Well, you'd better go home and fetch it."

Caleb again drove down the hill, and the other men searched their pockets for keys. One had the key of his cornhouse, and produced it hopefully; but it would not unlock the meeting-house door.

A crowd seldom gathered in the little village for anything short of a fire; but today in a short time quite a number of people stood on the meeting-house hill, and more kept coming. When Caleb Gale returned with the barn key, his daughter, a tall, pretty young girl, sat beside him, her little face alert and smiling in her red hood. The other selectmen's wives toiled eagerly up the hill, with a young daughter of one of them speeding on ahead. Then the two young girls stood close to each other and watched the proceedings. Key after key was tried; men brought all the large keys they could find, running importantly up the hill, but none would unlock the meeting-house door. After Caleb had tried the last available key, stooping and screwing it anxiously, he turned around. "There ain't no use in it, anyway," said he; "most likely the door's bolted."

"You don't mean there's a bolt on that door?" cried his wife.

"Yes, there is."

"Then you might jest as well have tore 'round for hen's feathers as keys. Of course she's bolted it if she's got any wit, an' I guess she's got most as much as some of you men that have been bringin' keys. Try the windows."

But the windows were fast. Hetty had made her sacred castle impregnable except to violence. Either the door would have to be forced or a window broken to gain an entrance.

The people conferred with one another. Some were for retreating and leaving Hetty in peaceful possession until time drove her to capitulate. "She'll open it tomorrow," they said. Others were for extreme measures, and their impetuosity gave them the lead. The project of forcing the door was urged; one man started for a crowbar.

"They are a parcel of fools to do such a thing," said Caleb Gale's wife to another woman. "Spoil that good door! They'd better leave the poor thing alone till tomorrow. I dun' know what's goin' to be done with her when they git in. I ain't goin' to have father draggin' her over to Mis' Radway's by the hair of her head."

"That's jest what I say," returned the other woman.

Mrs. Gale went up to Caleb and nudged him. "Don't you let them break that door down, father," said she.

"Well, well, we'll see," Caleb replied. He moved away a little; his wife's voice had been drowned out lately by a masculine clamor, and he took advantage of it.

All the people talked at once; the wind was keen, and all their garments fluttered; the two young girls had their arms around each other under their shawls; the man with the crowbar came stalking up the hill.

"Don't you let them break down that door, father," said Mrs. Gale.

"Well, well," grunted Caleb.

Regardless of remonstrances, the man set the crowbar against the door; suddenly there was a cry, "There she is!" Everybody looked up. There was Hetty looking out of a gallery window.

Everybody was still. Hetty began to speak. Her dark old face, peering out of the window, looked ghastly; the wind blew her poor gray locks over it. She extended her little wrinkled hands. "Jest let me say one word," said she; "jest one word." Her voice shook. All her coolness was gone. The magnitude of her last act of defiance had caused it to react upon herself like an overloaded gun.

"Say all you want to, Hetty, an' don't be afraid," Mrs. Gale called out.

"I jest want to say a word," repeated Hetty. "Can't I stay here, nohow? It don't seem as if I could go to Mis' Radway's. I ain't nothin again' her. I s'pose she's a good woman, but she's used to havin' her own way, and I've been livin' all my life with them that was, an' I've had to fight to keep a footin' on the earth, an' now I'm gittin' too old for't. If I can jest stay here in the meetin'-house, I won't ask for nothin' any better. I sha'n't need much to keep me; I wa'n't never a hefty eater; an' I'll keep the meetin'-house jest as clean as I know how. An' I'll make some more

of them wool flowers. I'll make a wreath to go the whole length of the gallery, if I can git wool 'nough. Won't you let me stay? I ain't complainin', but I've always had a dretful hard time; seems as if now I might take a little comfort the last of it, if I could stay here. I can't go to Mis' Radway's nohow." Hetty covered her face with her hands; her words ended in a weak wail.

Mrs. Gale's voice rang out clear and strong and irrepressible. "Of course you can stay in the meetin'-house," said she; "I should laugh if you couldn't. Don't you worry another mite about it. You sha'n't go one step to Mis' Radway's; you couldn't live a day with her. You can stay jest where you are; you've kept the meetin'-house enough sight cleaner than I've ever seen it. Don't you worry another mite, Hetty."

Mrs. Gale stood majestically and looked defiantly around; tears were in her eyes. Another woman edged up to her. "Why couldn't she have that little room side of the pulpit, where the minister hangs his hat?" she whispered. "He could hang it somewhere else."

"Course she could," responded Mrs. Gale, with alacrity, "jest as well as not. She can have her stove an' her bed in there, an' be jest as comfortable as can be. I should laugh if she couldn't. Don't you worry, Hetty."

The crowd gradually dispersed, sending out stragglers down the hill until it was all gone. Mrs. Gale waited until the last, sitting in the buggy in state. When her husband gathered up the reins, she called back to Hetty: "Don't you worry one mite more about it, Hetty. I'm comin' up to see you in the mornin'!"

It was almost dusk when Caleb drove down the hill; he was the last of the besiegers, and the feeble garrison was left triumphant.

The next day but one was Christmas, the next night Christmas Eve. On Christmas Eve Hetty had reached what to her was the flood tide of peace and prosperity. Established in that small, lofty room, with her bed and her stove, with gifts of a rocking chair and table, and a goodly store of food, with no one to molest or disturb her, she had nothing to wish for on earth. All her small desires were satisfied. No happy girl could have a merrier Christmas than this old woman with her little measure full of gifts. That Christmas Eve Hetty lay down under her sunflower quilt, and all her old hardships looked dim in the distance, like faraway hills, while her new joys came out like stars.

She was a light sleeper; the next morning she was up early. She opened the meeting-house door and stood looking out. The smoke from the village chimneys had not yet begun to rise blue and rosy in the clear frosty air. There was no snow, but over all the hill there was a silver rime of frost; the bare branches of the trees glistened. Hetty stood looking. "Why, it's Christmas mornin'," she said, suddenly. Christmas had never been a gala-day to this old woman. Christmas had not been kept at all in this New England village when she was young. She was led to think of it now only in connection with the dinner Mrs. Gale had promised to bring her today.

Mrs. Gale had told her she should have some of her Christmas dinner, some turkey and plum pudding. She called it to mind now with a thrill of delight. Her face grew momentarily more radiant. There was a certain beauty in it. A finer morning light than that which lit up the wintry earth seemed to shine over the furrows of her old face. "I'm goin' to have turkey an' plum puddin' today," said she; "it's Christmas." Suddenly she started, and went into the meeting-house, straight up the gallery stairs. There in a clear space hung the bell-rope. Hetty grasped it. Never before had a Christmas bell been rung in this village; Hetty had probably never heard of Christmas bells. She was prompted by pure artless enthusiasm and grateful happiness. Her old arms pulled on the rope with a will; the bell sounded peal on peal. Down in the village, curtains rolled up, letting in the morning light; happy faces looked out of the windows.

Hetty had awakened the whole village to Christmas Day.

FOR UNDERSTANDING

1. Where does Hetty first talk with Caleb? What does she want from him?

2. How does Hetty provide food for herself after she moves into the meeting house?

3. Why do the selectmen try to remove Hetty after she has been sexton for three months?

4. To whom does Caleb turn when the selectmen fail to move Hetty out? When the three men leave the church what does Hetty do to the door?

5. Who finally says Hetty may stay in the church? What does Mrs. Gale promise to bring Hetty on Christmas day?

FOR INTERPRETATION

In this story does the author suggest that a strong bond exists among members of the same sex? Explain your answer.

FOR APPRECIATION

Characterization

1. Discuss how the title of the story fits with the description of Hetty in the following instances:

    a. Hetty hurries across the field after talking with Caleb (p. 389).

    b. We learn about Hetty's reputation in the village (p. 391).

    c. Hetty faces the selectmen who have come to remove her from the meeting-house (p. 392).

2. Mrs. Gale plays a brief but vital role in the story. From the first three paragraphs describing her arrival at the meeting house (p. 394), list at least five descriptive words or phrases the author uses to suggest Mrs. Gale's character.

COMPOSITION

In two or three paragraphs discuss how the author makes the men of the village appear in their attempts to oppose Hetty.

Ambrose Bierce 1842–1914?

Bearing his journalist's credentials, at age 70, Ambrose Bierce walked across the Texas border and disappeared into the bloody chaos of the Mexican Revolution. What finally happened to him remains a mystery. Born in Ohio, the ninth child of rigidly religious parents, at fifteen he left his family's impoverished Indiana farm to enter the printer's trade. A year at a Kentucky military academy was his only formal schooling, but from books his father owned, he became acquainted with English literary classics. During the Civil War, Bierce proved himself such a disciplined and courageous soldier that he rose in rank from drummer boy to brevet major. Later, while employed at the United States Mint in San Francisco, he began to contribute short satiric pieces to various periodicals.

Over the next decades, the scathing wit and precise craftsmanship of his journalism, short stories, and poems made him a central figure in West Coast literary circles that included such writers as Bret Harte and Mark Twain. His best collection of stories, *Tales of Soldiers and Civilians,* was published in 1891. Noteworthy also is his *Cynic's Word Book* (1906), renamed *The Devil's Dictionary,* filled with sour and stinging epigrams.

PORTRAIT OF AMBROSE BIERCE

His lasting place in American literature is due not to his vitriolic satire but to his fiction, most of which reflects the influence of his Civil War experience and a preoccupation with death. Two common characteristics of his short-story style are careful plotting and surprise endings.

A HORSEMAN IN THE SKY

I

One sunny afternoon in the autumn of the year 1861 a soldier lay in a clump of laurel by the side of a road in western Virginia. He lay at full length upon his stomach, his feet resting upon the toes, his head upon the left forearm. His extended right hand loosely grasped his rifle. But for the somewhat methodical disposition of his limbs and a slight rhythmic movement of the cartridge-box at the back of his belt he might have been thought to be dead. He was asleep at his post of duty. But if detected he would be dead shortly afterward, death being the just and legal penalty of his crime.

The clump of laurel in which the criminal lay was in the angle of a road which after ascending southward a steep acclivity to that point turned sharply to the west, running along the summit for perhaps one hundred yards. There it turned southward again and went zigzagging downward through the forest. At the salient of that second angle was a large flat rock, jutting out northward, overlooking the deep valley from which the road ascended. The rock capped a high cliff; a stone dropped from its outer edge would have fallen sheer downward one thousand feet to the tops of the pines. The angle where the soldier lay was on another spur of the same cliff. Had he been awake he would have commanded a view, not only of the short arm of the road and the jutting rock, but of the entire profile of the cliff below it. It might well have made him giddy to look.

The country was wooded everywhere except at the bottom of the valley to the northward, where there was a small natural meadow, through which flowed a stream scarcely visible from the valley's rim. This open ground looked hardly larger than an ordinary door-yard, but was really several acres in extent. Its green was more vivid than that of the inclosing forest. Away beyond it rose a line of giant cliffs similar to those upon which we are supposed to stand in our survey of the savage scene, and through which the road had somehow made its climb to the summit. The configuration of the valley, indeed, was such that from this point of observation it seemed entirely shut in, and one could but have wondered how the road which found a way out of it had found a way into it, and whence came and whither went the waters of the stream that parted the meadow more than a thousand feet below.

No country is so wild and difficult but men will make it a theatre of war; concealed in the forest at the bottom of that military rat-trap, in which half a hundred men in possession of the exits might have starved an army to submission, lay five regiments of Federal infantry. They had marched all the previous day and night and were resting. At nightfall they would take to the road again, climb to the place where their unfaithful sentinel now slept, and descending the other slope of the ridge fall upon a camp of the enemy at about midnight. Their hope was to surprise it, for the road led to the rear of it. In case of failure, their position would be perilous in the extreme; and fail they surely would should accident or vigilance apprise the enemy of the movement.

II

The sleeping sentinel in the clump of laurel was a young Virginian named Carter Druse. He was the son of wealthy parents, an only child, and had known such ease and cultivation and high living as wealth and taste were able to command in the mountain country of western Virginia. His home was but a few miles from where he now lay. One morning he had risen from the breakfast-table and said, quietly but gravely: "Father, a Union regiment has arrived at Grafton.[1] I am going to join it."

The father lifted his leonine head, looked at the son a moment in silence, and replied: "Well, go, sir, and whatever may occur do what you conceive to be your duty. Virginia, to which you are a traitor, must get on without you. Should we both live to the end of the war, we will speak further of the matter. Your mother, as the physician has informed you, is in a most critical condition; at the best she cannot be with us longer than a few weeks, but that time is precious. It would be better not to disturb her."

So Carter Druse, bowing reverently to his father, who returned the salute with a stately courtesy that masked a breaking heart, left the home of his childhood to go soldiering.

---

1. **Grafton,** county seat of Taylor County, northwest Virginia, on Tygart River.

EMBLEMS OF THE CIVIL WAR
Alexander Pope
Brooklyn Museum, Brooklyn, New York

By conscience and courage, by deeds of devotion and daring, he soon commended himself to his fellows and his officers; and it was to these qualities and to some knowledge of the country that he owed his selection for his present perilous duty at the extreme outpost. Nevertheless, fatigue had been stronger than resolution and he had fallen asleep. What good or bad angel came in a dream to rouse him from his state of crime, who shall say? Without a movement, without a sound, in the profound silence and the languor of the late afternoon, some invisible messenger of fate touched with unsealing finger the eyes of his consciousness—whispered into the ear of his spirit the mysterious awakening word which no human lips ever have spoken, no human memory ever has recalled. He quietly raised his forehead from his arm and looked between the masking stems of the laurels, instinctively closing his right hand about the stock of his rifle.

His first feeling was a keen artistic delight. On a colossal pedestal, the cliff,—motionless at the extreme edge of the capping rock and sharply outlined against the sky,—was an equestrian statue of impressive dignity. The figure of the man sat the figure of the horse, straight and soldierly, but with the repose of a Grecian god carved in the marble which limits the suggestion of activity. The gray costume harmonized with its aërial background; the metal of accoutrement[2] and caparison[3] was softened and subdued by the shadow; the animal's skin had no points of highlight. A carbine strikingly foreshortened lay across the pommel of the saddle, kept in place by the right hand grasping it at the "grip"; the left hand, holding the bridle rein, was invisible. In silhouette against the sky the profile of the horse was cut with the sharpness of a cameo; it looked across the heights of air to the confronting cliffs beyond. The face of the rider, turned slightly away, showed only an outline of temple and beard; he was looking downward to the bottom of the valley. Magnified by its lift against the sky and by the soldier's testifying sense of the formidableness of a near enemy the group appeared of heroic, almost colossal, size.

For an instant Druse had a strange, half-defined feeling that he had slept to the end of the war and was looking upon a noble work of art reared upon that eminence to commemorate the deeds of an heroic past of which he had been an inglorious part. The feeling was dispelled by a slight movement of the group: the horse, without moving its feet, had drawn its body slightly backward from the verge; the man remained immobile as before. Broad awake and keenly alive to the significance of the situation, Druse now brought the butt of his rifle against his cheek by cau-

tiously pushing the barrel forward through the bushes, cocked the piece, and glancing through the sights covered a vital spot of the horseman's breast. A touch upon the trigger and all would have been well with Carter Druse. At that instant the horseman turned his head and looked in the direction of his concealed foeman—seemed to look into his very face, into his eyes, into his brave, compassionate heart.

Is it then so terrible to kill an enemy in war—an enemy who has surprised a secret vital to the safety of one's self and comrades—an enemy more formidable for his knowledge than all his army for its numbers? Carter Druse grew pale; he shook in every limb, turned faint, and saw the statuesque group before him as black figures, rising, falling, moving unsteadily in arcs of circles in a fiery sky. His hand fell away from his weapon, his head slowly dropped until his face rested on the leaves in which he lay. This courageous gentleman and hardy soldier was near swooning from intensity of emotion.

It was not for long; in another moment his face was raised from earth, his hands resumed their places on the rifle, his forefinger sought the trigger; mind, heart, and eyes were clear, conscience and reason sound. He could not hope to capture that enemy; to alarm him would but send him dashing to his camp with his fatal news. The duty of the soldier was plain: the man must be shot dead from ambush—without warning, without a moment's spiritual preparation, with never so much as an unspoken prayer, he must be sent to his account. But no—there is a hope; he may have discovered nothing—perhaps he is but admiring the sublimity of the landscape. If permitted, he may turn and ride carelessly away in the direction whence he came. Surely it will be possible to judge at the instant of his withdrawing whether he knows. It may well

2. **accoutrement** (ə kü′ tər mənt), soldiers' equipment except clothes and weapons.
3. **caparison** (kə par′ ə sən), covering of the horse.

CIVIL WAR BATTLE, Artist Unknown
National Gallery of Art, Washington, D.C.
Gift of Edgar W. and Bernice Chrysler Garbisch

be that his fixity of attention—Druse turned his head and looked through the deeps of air downward, as from the surface to the bottom of a translucent sea. He saw creeping across the green meadow a sinuous line of figures of men and horses—some foolish commander was permitting the soldiers of his escort to water their beasts in the open, in plain view from a dozen summits!

Druse withdrew his eyes from the valley and fixed them again upon the group of man and horse in the sky, and again it was through the sights of his rifle. But this time his aim was at the horse. In his memory, as if they were a divine mandate, rang the words of his father at their parting: "Whatever may occur, do

what you conceive to be your duty." He was calm now. His teeth were firmly but not rigidly closed; his nerves were as tranquil as a sleeping babe's—not a tremor affected any muscle of his body; his breathing, until suspended in the act of taking aim, was regular and slow. Duty had conquered; the spirit had said to the body: "Peace, be still." He fired.

III

An officer of the Federal force, who in a spirit of adventure or in quest of knowledge had left the hidden bivouac in the valley, and with aimless feet had made his way to the lower edge of a small open space near the foot of the cliff, was considering what he had to gain by pushing his exploration further. At a distance of a quarter-mile before him, but apparently at a stone's throw, rose from its fringe of pines the gigantic face of rock, towering to so great a height above him that it made him giddy to look up to where its edge cut a sharp, rugged line against the sky. It presented a clean, vertical profile against a background of blue sky to a point half the way down, and of distant hills, hardly less blue, thence to the tops of the trees at its base. Lifting his eyes to the dizzy altitude of its summit the officer saw an astonishing sight—a man on horseback riding down into the valley through the air!

Straight upright sat the rider, in military fashion, with a firm seat in the saddle, a strong clutch upon the rein to hold his charger from too impetuous a plunge. From his bare head his long hair streamed upward, waving like a plume. His hands were concealed in the cloud of the horse's lifted mane. The animal's body was as level as if every hoofstroke encountered the resistant earth. Its motions were those of a wild gallop, but even as the officer looked they ceased, with all the legs thrown sharply forward as in the act of alighting from a leap. But this was a flight!

Filled with amazement and terror by this apparition of a horseman in the sky—half believing himself the chosen scribe of some new Apocalypse,[4] the officer was overcome by the intensity of his emotions; his legs failed him and he fell. Almost at the same instant he heard a crashing sound in the trees—a sound that died without an echo—and all was still.

The officer rose to his feet, trembling. The familiar sensation of an abraded[5] shin recalled his dazed faculties. Pulling himself together he ran rapidly obliquely away from the cliff to a point distant from its foot; thereabout he expected to find his man; and thereabout he naturally failed. In the fleeting instant of his vision his imagination had been so wrought upon by the apparent grace and ease and intention of the marvelous performance that it did not occur to him that the line of march of aërial cavalry is directly downward, and that he could find the objects of his search at the very foot of the cliff. A half-hour later he returned to camp.

This officer was a wise man; he knew better than to tell an incredible truth. He said nothing of what he had seen. But when the commander asked him if in his scout he had learned anything of advantage to the expedition he answered:

"Yes, sir; there is no road leading down into this valley from the southward."

The commander, knowing better, smiled.

IV

After firing his shot, Private Carter Druse reloaded his rifle and resumed his watch. Ten minutes had hardly passed when a Federal sergeant crept cautiously to him on hands and knees. Druse neither turned his head nor looked at him, but lay without motion or sign of recognition.

"Did you fire?" the sergeant whispered.

"Yes."

"At what?"

"A horse. It was standing on yonder rock —pretty far out. You see it is no longer there. It went over the cliff."

The man's face was white, but he showed no other sign of emotion. Having answered, he turned away his eyes and said no more. The sergeant did not understand.

"See here, Druse," he said, after a moment's silence, "it's no use making a mystery. I order you to report. Was there anybody on the horse?"

"Yes."

"Well?"

"My father."

The sergeant rose to his feet and walked away. "Good God!" he said.

---

4. **Apocalypse** (ə pok′ ə lips),   Book of Revelation.
5. **abraded** (ə brād′ əd),   scraped skin.

FOR UNDERSTANDING

1. Who is the soldier sleeping on duty at the beginning of the story, and what is his job?
2. How many regiments of which army lie in the valley below the cliffs?
3. What is the significance of this setting?
4. What is the "equestrian statue," the "noble work of art," that Carter sees? To which army does it belong?

FOR INTERPRETATION

Consider the following statements and discuss those that you feel best reflect the author's basic attitude and meaning in this story. Justify your choice by citing details from the story.
1. Duty to country is more important than one's feelings for family.
2. The good of the individual must be sacrificed for the good of the many.
3. War is a horrible institution.

FOR APPRECIATION

Conflict: Moment of Illumination

1. It is often argued that the best conflicts are those in which both sides are evenly balanced. This increases suspense, for the reader cannot be sure which side will prevail. In this story the young man has to weigh his safety and his regiment's against the life of his father. Would you say that this is an evenly balanced conflict? How would this story be changed if the man on the horse had not been his father?
2. Two things help young Druse make up his mind: The fact that he could shoot the horse, and his father's advice about duty. Why did Bierce bring in these details? To answer this question, consider what your reaction might have been if these factors had not been brought in.
3. In this carefully plotted story, the climax and moment of illumination do not come until the final lines. Why do you think Bierce withheld the horseman's identity until the story's end?

LANGUAGE AND VOCABULARY

A characteristic of Bierce's writing was his use of uncommon or unfamiliar words. Although he distinguished sharply between journalism and literature, he was a purist on the proper use of language. He intended his language to impress his readers so they would take very seriously the impact of experience his stories revealed.
1. Using context clues, see if you can determine the meaning of the italicized words in the following quotations from the selection. Use the dictionary to check yourself.
   a. . . . road which after ascending southward a steep *acclivity* to that point turned sharply to the west. . . .
   b. . . . and fail they surely would should accident or vigilance *apprise* the enemy of the movement.
   c. The father lifted his *leonine* head. . . .
   d. . . . in the profound silence and the *languor* of the late afternoon. . . .
   e. In his memory, as if they were a divine *mandate,* rang the words of his father. . . .
2. Using the dictionary, find a more common synonym for each of the words below.

apparition	taciturn	intrinsic
tranquil	ominous	

COMPOSITION

"A Horseman in the Sky" supports the implication that "War is a horrible institution" in that any resolution of the military situation described in the story would likely result in anguish and bloodshed. In a brief paper, narrate what you think may have happened to Carter Druse on the following morning when federal troops surprised the rebels in the adjoining valley.

Hamlin Garland 1860–1940

"Is there not something wrong in our social system when the unremitting toiler remains poor?" Hamlin Garland, who posed this question in his autobiographical *A Son of the Middle Border* (1914), was the first American writer to deal realistically with the unrewarding drudgery, toil, and poverty of farm life. Born on a pioneer homestead in Wisconsin, Garland spent his boyhood on windswept prairie farms in Iowa and South Dakota. In his writing, which he called *veritism,* he insisted upon telling the "bitter truth" and including "the mud and cold of the landscape, as well as its bloom and charm." Until the time when his collection of short stories, *Main-Travelled Roads,* was published in 1890, farm life in America had customarily been romanticized by American writers.

After four years of schooling at the Osage Seminary in Iowa, Garland left what he felt to be the hopelessness of farm existence to head east to Boston. Literally starving in a roach-infested little room while he educated himself through constant library study, Garland finally found a low-paying job at the Boston School of Oratory. After he began writing, he eventually became a protégé of William Dean Howells, although he was to go beyond Howells in the harshness of his own realism. An industrious and dedicated interpreter of the Midwest of his time, Garland won the respect of the literary world for his

PORTRAIT OF HAMLIN GARLAND

depiction of life on the prairies and his championship of the plight of the farmer. His *A Daughter of the Middle Border* won the Pulitzer Prize in 1922.

UNDER THE LION'S PAW

I

It was the last of autumn and first day of winter coming together. All day long the ploughmen on their prairie farms had moved to and fro in their wide level fields through the falling snow, which melted as it fell, wetting them to the skin—all day, notwithstanding the frequent squalls of snow, the dripping, desolate clouds, and the muck of the furrows, black and tenacious as tar.

Under their dripping harness the horses swung to and fro silently, with that marvellous uncomplaining patience which marks the horse. All day the wild geese, honking wildly, as they sprawled sidewise down the wind, seemed to be fleeing from an enemy behind, and with neck outthrust and wings extended, sailed down the wind, soon lost to sight.

Yet the ploughman behind his plough, though the snow lay on his ragged great-coat, and the cold clinging mud rose on his heavy boots, fettering[1] him like gyves,[2] whistled in the very beard of the gale. As day passed, the snow, ceasing to melt, lay along the ploughed land, and lodged in the depth of the stubble, till on each slow round the last furrow stood out black and shining as jet between the ploughed land and the gray stubble.

When night began to fall, and the geese, flying low, began to alight invisibly in the near corn-field, Stephen Council was still at work "finishing a land." He rode on his sulky plough when going with the wind, but walked when facing it. Sitting bent and cold but cheery under his slouch hat, he talked encouragingly to his four-in-hand.

"Come round there, boys!—Round agin! We got t' finish this land. Come in there, Dan! *Stiddy,* Kate,—stiddy! None o' y'r tantrums, Kittie. It's purty tuff, but got a be did. *Tchk! tchk!* Step along, Pete! Don't let Kate git y'r single-tree on the wheel. *Once* more!"

They seemed to know what he meant, and that this was the last round, for they worked with greater vigor than before.

"Once more, boys, an' then, sez I, oats an' a nice warm stall, an' sleep f'r all."

By the time the last furrow was turned on the land it was too dark to see the house, and the snow was changing to rain again. The tired and hungry man could see the light from the kitchen shining through the leafless hedge, and he lifted a great shout, "Supper f'r a half a dozen!"

It was nearly eight o'clock by the time he had finished his chores and started for supper. He was picking his way carefully through the mud, when the tall form of a man loomed up before him with a premonitory cough.

"Waddy ye want?" was the rather startled question of the farmer.

"Well, ye see," began the stranger, in a deprecating tone, "we'd like t' git in f'r the night. We've tried every house f'r the last two miles, but they hadn't any room f'r us. My wife's jest about sick, 'n' the children are cold and hungry—"

"Oh, y' want 'o stay all night, eh?"

"Yes, sir; it 'ud be a great accom—"

"Waal, I don't make it a practice t' turn

Reprinted by permission of Constance Garland Doyle and Isabel Garland Lord.

1. **fettering,** binding or shackling the feet.
2. **gyves** (jīvz), fetters or chains.

anybuddy way hungry, not on sech nights as this. Drive right in. We ain't got much, but sech as it is—"

But the stranger had disappeared. And soon his steaming, weary team, with drooping heads and swinging single-trees, moved past the well to the block beside the path. Council stood at the side of the "schooner"[3] and helped the children out—two little half-sleeping children—and then a small woman with a babe in her arms.

"There ye go!" he shouted jovially, to the children. *Now* we're all right! Run right along to the house there, an' tell Mam' Council you wants sumpthin' t' eat. Right this way, Mis'—keep right off t' the right there. I'll go an' git a lantern. Come," he said to the dazed and silent group at his side.

"Mother," he shouted, as he neared the fragrant and warmly lighted kitchen, "here are some wayfarers an' folks who need sumpthin' t' eat an' a place t' snooze." He ended by pushing them all in.

Mrs. Council, a large, jolly, rather coarse-looking woman, took the children in her arms. "Come right in, you little rabbits. 'Most asleep, hey? Now here's a drink o' milk f'r each o' ye. I'll have s'm tea in a minute. Take off y'r things and set up t' the fire."

While she set the children to drinking milk, Council got out his lantern and went out to the barn to help the stranger about his team, where his loud, hearty voice could be heard as it came and went between the haymow[4] and the stalls.

The woman came to light as a small, timid, and discouraged-looking woman, but still pretty, in a thin and sorrowful way.

"Land sakes! An' you've travelled all the way from Clear Lake t'-day in this mud! Waal! waal! No wonder you're all tired out. Don't wait f'r the men, Mis'—" She hesitated, waiting for the name.

"Haskins."

"Mis' Haskins, set right up to the table an' take a good swig o' tea whilst I make y' s'm toast. It's green tea, an' it's good. I tell Coun-

cil as I git older I don't seem to enjoy Young Hyson n'r Gunpowder.[5] I want the reel green tea, jest as it comes off'n the vines. Seems t' have more heart in it, some way. Don't s'pose it has. Council says it's all in m' eye."

Going on in this easy way, she soon had the children filled with bread and milk and the woman thoroughly at home, eating some toast and sweet-melon pickles, and sipping the tea.

"See the little rats!" she laughed at the children. "They're full as they can stick now, and they want to go to bed. Now, don't git up, Mis' Haskins; set right where you are an' let me look after 'em. I know all about young ones, though I'm all alone now. Jane went an' married last fall. But, as I tell Council, it's lucky we keep our health. Set right there, Mis' Haskins; I won't have you stir a finger."

It was an unmeasured pleasure to sit there in the warm, homely kitchen, the jovial chatter of the housewife driving out and holding at bay the growl of the impotent, cheated wind.

The little woman's eyes filled with tears which fell upon the sleeping baby in her arms. The world was not so desolate and cold and hopeless, after all.

"Now I hope Council won't stop out there and talk politics all night. He's the greatest man to talk politics an' read the *Tribune*— How old is it?"

She broke off and peered down at the face of the babe.

"Two months 'n' five days," said the mother, with a mother's exactness.

"Ye don't say! I want 'o know! The dear little pudzy-wudzy!" she went on, stirring it up in the neighborhood of the ribs with her fat forefinger.

"Pooty tough on 'oo to go gallivant'n' 'cross lots this way—"

"Yes, that's so; a man can't lift a moun-

---

3. **schooner,** covered wagon.
4. **haymow,** a part of the barn where the hay is stored.
5. **Young Hyson . . . Gunpowder,** kinds of tea.

tain," said Council, entering the door. "Mother, this is Mr. Haskins, from Kansas. He's been eat up 'n' drove out by grasshoppers."

"Glad t' see yeh!—Pa, empty that wash-basin 'n' give him a chance t' wash."

Haskins was a tall man, with a thin, gloomy face. His hair was a reddish brown, like his coat, and seemed equally faded by the wind and sun, and his sallow face, though hard and set, was pathetic somehow. You would have felt that he had suffered much by the line of his mouth showing under his thin, yellow mustache.

"Hain't Ike got home yet, Sairy?"

"Hain't seen 'im."

"W-a-a-l, set right up, Mr. Haskins; wade right into what we've got; 'tain't much, but we manage to live on it—she gits fat on it," laughed Council, pointing his thumb at his wife.

After supper, while the women put the childen to bed, Haskins and Council talked on, seated near the huge cooking-stove, the steam rising from their wet clothing. In the Western fashion Council told as much of his own life as he drew from his guest. He asked but few questions, but by and by the story of Haskins' struggles and defeat came out. The story was a terrible one, but he told it quietly, seated with his elbows on his knees, gazing most of the time at the hearth.

"I didn't like the looks of the country, anyhow," Haskins said, partly rising and glancing at his wife. "I was ust t' northern Ingyannie,[6] where we have lots o' timber 'n' lots o' rain, 'n' I didn't like the looks o' that dry prairie. What galled me the worst was goin' s' far away acrosst so much fine land layin' all through here vacant."

"And the 'hoppers eat ye four years, hand runnin', did they?"

"Eat! They wiped us out. They chawed everything that was green. They jest set around waitin' f'r us to die t' eat us, too. I swear! I ust t' dream of 'em sittin' 'round on the bedpost, six feet long, workin' their jaws. They eet the fork-handles. They got worse 'n'

worse till they jest rolled on one another, piled up like snow in winter. Well, it ain't no use. If I was t' talk all winter I couldn't tell nawthin'. But all the while I couldn't help thinkin' of all that land back here that no-buddy was usin' that I ought 'o had 'stead o' bein' out there in that cussed country."

"Waal, why didn't ye stop an' settle here?" asked Ike, who had come in and was eating his supper.

"Fer the simple reason that you fellers wantid ten 'r fifteen dollars an acre fer the bare land, and I hadn't no money fer that kind o' thing."

"Yes, I do my own work," Mrs. Council was heard to say in the pause which followed. "I'm a gettin' purty heavy t' be on m' laigs all day, but we can't afford t' hire, so I keep rackin'[7] around somehow, like a foundered horse.[8] S' lame—I tell Council he can't tell how lame I am, f'r I'm jest as lame in one laig as t'other." And the good soul laughed at the joke on herself as she took a handful of flour and dusted the biscuit-board to keep the dough from sticking.

"Well, I hain't *never* been very strong," said Mrs. Haskins. "Our folks was Canadians an' small-boned, and then since my last child I hain't got up again fairly. I don't like t' complain. Tim has about all he can bear now—but they was days this week when I jest wanted to lay right down an' die."

"Waal, now, I'll tell ye," said Council, from his side of the stove, silencing everybody with his good-natured roar, "I'd go down and *see* Butler, *anyway,* if I was you. I guess he'd let you have his place purty cheap; the farm's all run down. He's ben anxious t' let t' somebuddy next year. It 'ud be a good chance fer you. Anyhow, you go to bed and sleep like a babe. I've got some ploughin' t' do, anyhow, an' we'll see if somethin' can't be

6. **Ingyannie** (in jē an' ē), Indiana.
7. **rackin',** stretching and straining.
8. **foundered horse,** horse disabled or gone lame.

done about your case. Ike, you go out an' see if the horses is all right, an' I'll show the folks t' bed."

When the tired husband and wife were lying under the generous quilts of the spare bed, Haskins listened a moment to the wind in the eaves, and then said, with a slow and solemn tone,

"There are people in this world who are good enough t' be angels, an' only haff t' die to *be* angels."

II

Jim Butler was one of those men called in the West "land poor." Early in the history of Rock River he had come into the town and started in the grocery business in a small way, occupying a small building in a mean part of town. At this period of his life he earned all he got, and was up early and late sorting beans, working over butter, and carting his goods to and from the station. But a change came over him at the end of the second year, when he sold a lot of land for four times what he paid for it. From that time forward he believed in land speculation as the surest way of getting rich. Every cent he could save or spare from his trade he put into land at forced sale, or mortgages on land, which were "just as good as the wheat," he was accustomed to say.

Farm after farm fell into his hands, until he was recognized as one of the leading landowners of the county. His mortgages were scattered all over Cedar County, and as they slowly but surely fell in he sought usually to retain the former owner as tenant.

He was not ready to foreclose; indeed, he had the name of being one of the "easiest" men in the town. He let the debtor off again and again, extending the time whenever possible.

"I don't want y'r land," he said. "All I'm after is the int'rest on my money—that's all. Now, if y' want o' stay on the farm, why, I'll give y' a good chance. I can't have the land layin' vacant." And in many cases the owner remained as tenant.

In the meantime he had sold his store; he couldn't spend time in it; he was mainly occupied now with sitting around town on rainy days smoking and "gassin' with the boys," or in riding to and from his farms. In fishing-time he fished a good deal. Doc Grimes, Ben Ashley, and Cal Cheatham were his cronies on these fishing excursions or hunting trips in the time of chickens or partridges. In winter they went to Northern Wisconsin to shoot deer.

In spite of all these signs of easy life Butler persisted in saying he "hadn't enough money to pay taxes on his land," and was careful to convey the impression that he was poor in spite of his twenty farms. At one time he was said to be worth fifty thousand dollars, but land had been a little slow of sale of late, so that he was not worth so much.

A fine farm, known as the Higley place, had fallen into his hands in the usual way the previous year, and he had not been able to find a tenant for it. Poor Higley, after working himself nearly to death on it in the attempt to lift the mortgage, had gone off to Dakota, leaving the farm and his curse to Butler.

This was the farm which Council advised Haskins to apply for; and the next day Council hitched up his team and drove downtown to see Butler.

"You jest let *me* do the talkin'," he said. "We'll find him wearin' out his pants on some salt barrel somew'ers; and if he thought you *wanted* a place he'd sock it to you hot and heavy. You jest keep quiet; I'll fix 'im."

Butler was seated in Ben Ashley's store telling fish yarns when Council sauntered in casually.

"Hello, But; lyin' agin, hey?"

"Hello, Steve! how goes it?"

"Oh, so-so. Too dang much rain these days. I thought it was goin' t' freeze up f'r good last night. Tight squeak if I get m'

John Steuart Curry's bold paintings on Midwestern themes gave impetus to a whole school of Midwestern regionalism in the early 1900s.

HOMESTEADERS, John Steuart Curry
U.S. Department of Interior

ploughin' done. How's farmin' with *you* these days?"

"Bad. Ploughin' ain't half done."

"It 'ud be a religious idee f'r you t' go out an' take a hand y'rself."

"I don't haff to," said Butler, with a wink.

"Got anybody on the Higley place?"

"No. Know of anybody?"

"Waal, no; not eggsackly. I've got a relation back t' Michigan who's been hot an' cold on the idee o' comin West f'r some time. *Might* come if he could get a good lay-out. What do you talk on the farm?"

"Well, I d' know. I'll rent it on shares or I'll rent it money rent."

"Waal, how much money, say?"

"Well, say ten per cent, on the price—two-fifty."

"Waal, that ain't bad. Wait on 'im till 'e thrashes?"

Haskins listened eagerly to his important question, but Council was coolly eating a dried apple which he had speared out of a barrel with his knife. Butler studied him carefully.

"Well, knocks me out of twenty-five dollars interest."

"My relation'll need all he's got t' git his crops in," said Council, in the safe, indifferent way.

"Well, all right; *say* wait," concluded Butler.

"All right; this is the man. Haskins, this is Mr. Butler—no relation to Ben—the hardest-working man in Cedar County."

On the way home Haskins said: "I ain't much better off. I'd like that farm; it's a good farm, but it's all run down, an' so 'm I. I could make a good farm of it if I had half a show. But I can't stock it n'r seed it."

"Waal, now, don't you worry," roared Council in his ear. "We'll pull y' through somehow till next harvest. He's agreed t' hire it ploughed, an' you can earn a hundred dollars ploughin' an' y' c'n git the seed o' me, an' pay me back when y' can."

Haskins was silent with emotion, but at last he said, "I ain't got nothin' t' live on."

"Now, don't you worry 'bout that. You jest make your headquarters at ol' Steve Council's. Mother'll take a pile o' comfort in havin' y'r wife an' children 'round. Y' see, Jane's married off latey, an' Ike's away a good 'eal, so we'll be darn glad t' have y' stop with us this winter. Nex' spring we'll see if y' can't git a start again." And he chirruped to the team, which sprang forward with the rumbling, clattering wagon.

"Say, looky here, Council, you can't do this. I never saw—" shouted Haskins in his neighbor's ear.

Council moved about uneasily in his seat and stopped his stammering gratitude by saying: "Hold on, now; don't make such a fuss over a little thing. When I see a man down, an' things all on top of 'm, I jest like t' kick 'em off an' help 'm up. That's the kind of religion I got, an' it's about the *only* kind."

They rode the rest of the way home in silence. And when the red light of the lamp shone out into the darkness of the cold and windy night, and he thought of this refuge for his children and wife, Haskins could have put his arm around the neck of his burly companion and squeezed him like a lover. But he contented himself with saying, "Steve Council, you'll git y'r pay f'r this some day."

"Don't want any pay. My religion ain't run on such business principles."

The wind was growing colder, and the ground was covered with a white frost, as they turned into the gate of the Council farm, and the children came rushing out, shouting, "Papa's come!" They hardly looked like the same children who had sat at the table the night before. Their torpidity, under the influence of sunshine and Mother Council, had given way to a sort of spasmodic cheerfulness, as insects in winter revive when laid on the hearth.

III

Haskins worked like a fiend, and his wife, like the heroic woman that she was, bore also uncomplainingly the most terrible burdens. They rose early and toiled without intermission till the darkness fell on the plain, then tumbled into bed, every bone and muscle aching with fatigue, to rise with the sun next morning to the same round of the same ferocity of labor.

The eldest boy drove a team all through the spring, ploughing and seeding, milked the cows, and did chores innumerable, in most ways taking the place of a man.

An infinitely pathetic but common figure —this boy on the American farm, where there is no law against child labor. To see him in his coarse clothing, his huge boots, and his ragged cap, as he staggered with a pail of water from the well, or trudged in the cold and cheerless dawn out into the frosty field behind his team, gave the city-bred visitor a sharp pang of sympathetic pain. Yet Haskins loved his boy, and would have saved him from this if he could, but he could not.

By June the first year the result of such Herculean[9] toil began to show on the farm. The yard was cleaned up and sown to grass, the garden ploughed and planted, and the house mended.

Council had given them four of his cows.

"Take 'em an' run 'em on shares. I don't want 'o milk s' many. Ike's away s' much now, Sat'd'ys an' Sund'ys, I can't stand the bother anyhow."

Other men, seeing the confidence of Council in the newcomer, had sold him tools on time; and as he was really an able farmer, he soon had round him many evidences of his care and thrift. At the advice of Council he had taken the farm for three years, with

---

9. **Herculean** (her' kyü' lē an), work requiring superhuman strength, like that of Hercules.

the privilege of re-renting or buying at the end of the term.

"It's a good bargain, an' y' want 'o nail it," said Council. "If you have any kind ov a crop, you c'n pay y'r debts, an' keep seed an' bread."

The new hope which now sprang up in the heart of Haskins and his wife grew great almost as a pain by the time the wide field of wheat began to wave and rustle and swirl in the winds of July. Day after day he would snatch a few moments after supper to go and look at it.

"Have ye seen the wheat t'-day, Nettie?" he asked one night as he rose from supper.

"No, Tim, I ain't had time."

"Well, take time now. Le's go look at it."

She threw an old hat on her head—Tommy's hat—and looking almost pretty in her thin, sad way, went out with her husband to the hedge.

"Ain't it grand, Nettie? Just look at it."

It was grand. Level, russet here and there, heavy-headed, wide as a lake, and full of multitudinous whispers and gleams of wealth, it stretched away before the gazers like the fabled field of the cloth of gold.[10]

"Oh, I think—I *hope* we'll have a good crop, Tim; and oh, how good the people have been to us!"

"Yes; I don't know where we'd be t'-day if it hadn't ben f'r Council and his wife."

"They're the best people in the world," said the little woman, with a great sob of gratitude.

"We'll be in the field on Monday, sure," said Haskins, gripping the rail on the fence as if already at the work of the harvest.

The harvest came, bounteous, glorious, but the winds came and blew it into tangles, and the rain matted it here and there close to the ground, increasing the work of gathering it threefold.

Oh, how they toiled in those glorious days! Clothing dripping with sweat, arms aching, filled with briers, fingers raw and bleed-

ing, backs broken with the weight of heavy bundles, Haskins and his man toiled on. Tommy drove the harvester, while his father and a hired man bound on the machine. In this way they cut ten acres every day, and almost every night after supper, when the hand went to bed, Haskins returned to the field shocking the bound grain in the light of the moon. Many a night he worked till his anxious wife came out at ten o'clock to call him in to rest and lunch.

At the same time she cooked for the men, took care of the children, washed and ironed, milked the cows at night, made the butter, and sometimes fed the horses and watered them while her husband kept at the shocking.

No slave in the Roman galleys could have toiled so frightfully and lived, for this man thought himself a free man, and that he was working for his wife and babes.

When he sank into his bed with a deep groan of relief, too tired to change his grimy, dripping clothing, he felt that he was getting nearer and nearer to a home of his own, and pushing the wolf of want a little farther from his door.

There is no despair so deep as the despair of a homeless man or woman. To roam the roads of the country or the streets of the city, to feel there is no rood of ground on which the feet can rest, to halt weary and hungry outside lighted windows and hear laughter and song within,—these are the hungers and rebellions that drive men to crime and women to shame.

It was the memory of this homelessness, and the fear of its coming again, that spurred Timothy Haskins and Nettie, his wife, to such ferocious labor during that first year.

---

10. **field of the cloth of gold,** the field at Ardres, south of Calais, France, where King Henry VIII of England met with King Francis I of France in 1520 to discuss a possible alliance. So many of the royal tents and banners were made of gold-embroidered material that, from a distance, the field seemed to shine like gold.

IV

"'M, yes; 'm, yes; first-rate," said Butler, as his eye took in the neat garden, the pig-pen, and the well-filled barnyard. "You're gitt'n' quite a stock around yeh. Done well, eh?"

Haskins was showing Butler around the place. He had not seen it for a year, having spent the year in Washington and Boston with Ashley, his brother-in-law, who had been elected to Congress.

"Yes, I've laid out a good deal of money durin' the last three years. I've paid out three hundred dollars f'r fencin'."

"Um—h'm! I see, I see," said Butler, while Haskins went on:

"The kitchen there cost two hundred; the barn ain't cost much in money, but I've put a lot o' time on it. I've dug a new well, and I—"

"Yes, yes, I see. You've done well. Stock worth a thousand dollars," said Butler, picking his teeth with a straw.

"About that," said Haskins, modestly. "We begin to feel's if we was gitt'n' a home f'r ourselves; but we've worked hard. I tell you we begin to feel it, Mr. Butler, and we're goin' t' begin to ease up purty soon. We've been kind o' plannin' a trip back t' *her* folks after the fall ploughin's done."

"*Eggs*-actly!" said Butler, who was evidently thinking of something else. "I suppose you've kind o' calc'lated on stayin' here three years more?"

"Well, yes. Fact is, I think I c'n buy the farm this fall, if you'll give me a reasonable show."

"Um—m! What do you call a reasonable show?"

"Well, say a quarter down and three years' time."

Butler looked at the huge stacks of wheat, which filled the yard, over which the chickens were fluttering and crawling, catching grasshoppers, and out of which the crickets were singing innumerably. He smiled in a peculiar way as he said, "Oh, I won't be hard on yeh. But what did you expect to pay f'r the place?"

"Why, about what you offered it for before, two thousand five hundred, or *possibly* three thousand dollars," he added quickly, as he saw the owner shake his head.

"This farm is worth five thousand and five hundred dollars," said Butler, in a careless and decided voice.

"*What!*" almost shrieked the astounded Haskins. "What's that? Five thousand? Why, that's double what you offered it for three years ago."

"Of course, and it's worth it. It was all run down then; now it's in good shape. You've laid out fifteen hundred dollars in improvements, according to your own story."

"But *you* had nothin' t' do about that. It's my work an' my money."

"You bet it was; but it's my land."

"But what's to pay me for all my—"

"Ain't you had the use of 'em?" replied Butler, smiling calmly into his face.

Haskins was like a man struck on the head with a sandbag; he couldn't think; he stammered as he tried to say: "But—I never'd git the use—You'd rob me! More'n that: you agreed—you promised that I could buy or rent at the end of three years at—"

"That's all right. But I didn't say I'd let you carry off the improvements, nor that I'd go on renting the farm at two-fifty. The land is doubled in value, it don't matter how; it don't enter into the question; an' now you can pay me five hundred dollars a year rent, or take it on your own terms at fifty-five hundred, or—git out."

He was turning away when Haskins, the sweat pouring from his face, fronted him, saying again:

"But *you've* done nothing to make it so. You hain't added a cent. I put it all there myself, expectin' to buy. I worked an' sweat to improve it. I was workin' for myself an' babes—"

"Well, why didn't you buy when I offered to sell? What y' kickin' about?"

"I'm kickin' about payin' you twice f'r my own things,—my own fences, my own kitchen, my own garden."

Butler laughed. "You're too green t' eat, young feller. *Your* improvements! The law will sing another tune."

"But I trusted your word."

"Never trust anybody, my friend. Besides, I didn't promise not to do this thing. Why, man, don't look at me like that. Don't take me for a thief. It's the law. The reg'lar thing. Everybody does it."

"I don't care if they do. It's stealin' jest the same. You take three thousand dollars of my money—the work o' my hands and my wife's." He broke down at this point. He was not a strong man mentally. He could face hardship, ceaseless toil, but he could not face the cold and sneering face of Butler.

"But I don't take it," said Butler, coolly. "All you've got to do is to go on jest as you've been a-doin', or give me a thousand dollars down, and a mortgage at ten per cent on the rest."

Haskins sat down blindly on a bundle of oats near by, and with staring eyes and drooping head went over the situation. He was under the lion's paw. He felt a horrible numbness in his heart and limbs. He was hid in a mist, and there was no path out.

Butler walked about, looking at the huge stacks of grain, and pulling now and again a few handfuls out, shelling the heads in his hands and blowing the chaff away. He hummed a little tune as he did so. He had an accommodating air of waiting.

Haskins was in the midst of the terrible toil of the last year. He was walking again in the rain and the mud behind his plough; he felt the dust and dirt of the threshing. The ferocious husking-time, with its cutting wind and biting, clinging snows, lay hard upon him. Then he thought of his wife, how she had cheerfully cooked and baked, without holiday and without rest.

"Well, what do you think of it?" inquired the cool, mocking, insinuating voice of Butler.

"I think you're a thief and a liar!" shouted Haskins, leaping up. "A blackhearted houn'!" Butler's smile maddened him; with a sudden leap he caught a fork in his hands, and whirled it in the air. "You'll never rob another man, I swear!" he grated through his teeth, a look of pitiless ferocity in his accusing eyes.

Butler shrank and quivered, expecting the blow; stood, held hypnotized by the eyes of the man he had a moment before despised —a man transformed into an avenging demon. But in the deadly hush between the lift of the weapon and its fall there came a gush of faint, childish laughter and then across the range of his vision, far away and dim, he saw the sun-bright head of his baby girl, as, with the pretty, tottering run of a two-year-old, she moved across the grass of the dooryard. His hands relaxed; the fork fell to the ground; his head lowered.

"Make out y'd deed an' mor'gage, an git off'n my land, an' don't ye never cross my line agin; if y' do, I'll kill ye."

Butler backed away from the man in wild haste, and climbing into his buggy with trembling limbs drove off down the road, leaving Haskins seated dumbly on the sunny pile of sheaves, his head sunk into his hands.

FOR UNDERSTANDING

1. As the story opens, why is the Haskins family in such desperate circumstances?
2. How do the Councils help the Haskins?
3. How does Haskins raise the value of the Higley farm property?
4. What price does Butler want for the farm when Haskins asks to buy it? Explain which man has the protection of the law.
5. What keeps Haskins from killing Butler?

FOR INTERPRETATION

Discuss what Garland implies about justice:
1. In the metaphor indicated in the title and enlarged upon in the paragraph beginning "Haskins sat down blindly on a bundle of oats . . . " (p. 413).
2. In the paragraph about the American farm boy beginning "An infinitely pathetic but common . . . " (p. 410).

FOR APPRECIATION

Realism

As a spokesman for what he called the Middle Border—the prairie region of Wisconsin, Minnesota, Nebraska, Kansas, and the Dakotas—Garland records what happened to the farmer as the population moved west after the Civil War.

1. What does the description of Council plowing his field in the story's opening show the reader?

2. Garland makes no attempt at in-depth characterization but uses people representative of those who could be found on prairie farms and in farming communities. What was the farm wife and mother like as Garland pictures her?

3. How had Butler changed after first coming to Rock River? What kind of American does he represent?

LANGUAGE AND VOCABULARY

Garland strove to increase the realism of his writing by using the dialect commonly heard in the Border region. Supply the proper spelling for each of the following:

stiddy	purty	sez
waddy	sumpthin'	git
waal	jest	eggsackly
aint	Sat'd'ys	calc'lated

COMPOSITION

Although in his stories Garland painted a hopeless picture of prairie farm life, he was also concerned with the misery of the poor in the cities. He believed that environment, rather than natural depravity or wickedness, was at the root of human misery.

Write a brief composition in which you discuss how the characters in "Under the Lion's Paw" reflect Garland's fundamental belief in human goodness. In doing this, give particular attention to Council's statement of his "religion" (p. 410); and do not overlook the fact that Butler had changed after he sold his first farm property so profitably.

Stephen Crane

1871–1900

During his brief life span Stephen Crane demonstrated such exceptional talent that he quickly attained literary prominence in both the United States and Europe. Critics now consider him one of the major innovative writers of the nineteenth century. Through skillful use of naturalism and impressionism, he influenced such later writers as Theodore Dreiser, Sherwood Anderson, Ernest Hemingway, Willa Cather, and John Dos Passos.

Born last into the large family of a Methodist minister in Newark, New Jersey, Crane's limited schooling exceeded that of the other thirteen children. Although physically weak in early childhood, by fourteen he was an accomplished baseball player. In a day when baseball catchers spurned a glove, Crane's schoolmates boasted that no one on his team could throw a baseball so hard that he could not catch it barehanded. In fact, his brief college career—first at Lafayette College, then Syracuse University—was devoted largely to playing baseball and writing fiction and newspaper articles. He soon dropped out of school to go to New York City to pursue a writing career.

In New York he lived a hand-to-mouth existence as a free-lance reporter for various papers, and, when time allowed, as a novelist. From the brutal poverty that he observed in the slums, particularly in the Bowery, Crane shaped his first novel, *Maggie: A Girl of the Streets* (1893). The story, however, was deemed too shocking for the average reader of the time, and no editor would publish it. Undaunted, Crane borrowed money and published the novel himself, but it was a financial failure. Not until two years later, when he published *The Red Badge of Courage,* did Crane become an "immediate" success.

Although at the time that he wrote *The Red Badge of Courage,* Crane had not yet been to war—he later reported the Spanish-American and the Greco-Turkish wars—his novel was praised for its unvarnished realism, its unheroic hero, and its smell of battle smoke. Hardened combat veterans wrote to tell him how "real" his

PORTRAIT OF STEPHEN CRANE

story was, many of them refusing to believe that Crane was not also a veteran.

Before he had written the story, Crane had totally immersed himself in Matthew Brady's remarkable Civil War photographs, in books of memoirs by various ex-soldiers, and in the war reminiscences of his brother William. In this short novel that has become an American classic, Crane stripped away the glamor of combat and replaced it with a simple story of one youthful and confused soldier, Henry Fleming, a boy trying to be brave but severely frightened during his baptism of fire in the Battle of Chancellorsville.

The last four and a half years of Crane's life teemed with activity. In 1895 he published *The*

Black Riders, a volume of free verse that was followed four years later by a similar collection, *War Is Kind,* both volumes inspired by the spare lyrics of Emily Dickinson. A new novel, *George's Mother,* and a collection of tales, *The Little Regiment and Other Episodes of the American Civil War,* were published in 1896.

On his way to Cuba in 1897 to report on the revolution there, his ship sank, and he spent thirty hours at sea in a dinghy. Crane was one of the three who survived the disaster. From this experience he wrote the short story, "The Open Boat." The exposure he suffered in this ordeal and in other reporting assignments, however, weakened him physically and hastened the onset of tuberculosis which killed him three years later.

To the day of his death, Crane had not forsaken the creed he lived by: "You can never do anything good aesthetically . . . unless it has at one time meant something important to you." That is not to say that Crane believed an artist must experience every event in order to describe it realistically; if he had believed that, he would have been denying the imagination. He was, however, talking of his own formula for fiction: taking the germ of an experience and then letting that germ grow in the mind, writing from the truth of experience but always conveying that truth with acute feelings, vividly expressed.

The sights, sounds, and smells of battle and the flat and simple dialogue in the following short story seem so real that the reader is placed at once at the scene of action. The brief pictures of brutal carnage, the cruel indifference of the various characters, and the absence of moralizing or interpretive comment leave us at the story's end to fathom for ourselves the "mystery" of Fred Collins's "heroism."

A MYSTERY OF HEROISM

The dark uniforms of the men were so coated with dust from the incessant wrestling of the two armies that the regiment almost seemed a part of the clay bank which shielded them from the shells. On the top of the hill a battery was arguing in tremendous roars with some other guns, and to the eye of the infantry the artillerymen, the guns, the caissons, the horses, were distinctly outlined upon the blue sky. When a piece was fired, a red streak as round as a log flashed low in the heavens, like a monstrous bolt of lightning. The men of the battery wore white duck trousers, which somehow emphasized their legs; and when they ran and crowded in little groups at the bidding of the shouting officers, it was more impressive than usual to the infantry.

Fred Collins, of A Company, was saying: "Thunder! I wisht I had a drink. Ain't there any water round here?" Then somebody yelled: "There goes th' bugler!"

As the eyes of half the regiment swept in one machine-like movement, there was an instant's picture of a horse in a great convulsive leap of a death-wound and a rider leaning back with a crooked arm and spread fingers before his face. On the ground was the crimson terror of an exploding shell, with fibers of flame that seemed like lances. A glittering bugle swung clear of the rider's back as fell headlong the horse and the man. In the air was an odor as from a conflagration.

Sometimes they of the infantry looked down at a fair little meadow which spread at

In this painting, Eastman Johnson, an artist best known for his genre and portrait painting, depicts a scene from the conflict that disrupted American life so violently in mid-century.

CIVIL WAR SCENE, Eastman Johnson
The Brooklyn Museum
Brooklyn, New York
Dick S. Ramsay Fund

their feet. Its long green grass was rippling gently in a breeze. Beyond it was the gray form of a house half torn to pieces by shells and by the busy axes of soldiers who had pursued firewood. The line of an old fence was now dimly marked by long weeds and by an occasional post. A shell had blown the well-house to fragments. Little lines of gray smoke ribboning upward from some embers indicated the place where had stood the barn.

From beyond a curtain of green woods there came the sound of some stupendous scuffle, as if two animals of the size of islands were fighting. At a distance there were occasional appearances of swift-moving men, horses, batteries, flags, and with the crashing of infantry volleys were heard, often, wild and frenzied cheers. In the midst of it all Smith and Ferguson, two privates of A Company, were engaged in a heated discussion which involved the greatest questions of the national existence.

The battery on the hill presently engaged in a frightful duel. The white legs of the gunners scampered this way and that way, and the officers redoubled their shouts. The guns, with their demeanors of stolidity and courage, were typical of something infinitely self-possessed in this clamor of death that swirled around the hill.

One of a "swing" team[1] was suddenly smitten quivering to the ground, and his maddened brethren dragged his torn body in their struggle to escape from this turmoil and danger. A young soldier astride one of the leaders swore and fumed in his saddle and furiously jerked at the bridle. An officer screamed out an order so violently that his voice broke and ended the sentence in a falsetto shriek.

The leading company of the infantry regiment was somewhat exposed, and the colonel ordered it moved more fully under the shelter of the hill. There was the clank of steel against steel.

A lieutenant of the battery rode down and passed them, holding his right arm carefully in his left hand. And it was as if this arm was not at all a part of him, but belonged to another man. His sober and reflective charger went slowly. The officer's face was grimy and perspiring, and his uniform was tousled as if he had been in direct grapple with an enemy. He smiled grimly when the men stared at him. He turned his horse toward the meadow.

Collins, of A Company, said: "I wisht I had a drink. I bet there's water in that there ol' well yonder!"

"Yes; but how you goin' to git it?"

For the little meadow which intervened was now suffering a terrible onslaught of shells. Its green and beautiful calm had vanished utterly. Brown earth was being flung in monstrous handfuls. And there was a massacre of the young blades of grass. They were being torn, burned, obliterated. Some curious fortune of the battle had made this gentle little meadow the object of the red hate of the shells, and each one as it exploded seemed like an imprecation in the face of a maiden.

The wounded officer who was riding across this expanse said to himself: "Why, they couldn't shoot any harder if the whole army was massed here!"

A shell struck the gray ruins of the house, and as, after the roar, the shattered wall fell in fragments, there was a noise which resembled the flapping of shutters during a wild gale of winter. Indeed, the infantry paused in the shelter of the bank appeared as men standing upon a shore contemplating a madness of the sea. The angel of calamity had under its glance the battery upon the hill. Fewer white-legged men labored about the guns. A shell had smitten one of the pieces, and after the flare, the smoke, the dust, the wrath of this blow were gone, it was possible to see white legs stretched horizontally upon the ground. And at the interval to the rear where it is the business of battery horses to stand with their noses to the fight, awaiting the command to drag their guns out of the destruction, or into it, or wheresoever these incomprehensible humans demanded with whip and spur—in this line of passive and dumb spectators, whose fluttering hearts yet would not let them forget the iron laws of man's control of them—in this rank of brute-soldiers there had been relentless and hideous carnage. From the ruck[2] of bleeding and prostrate horses, the men of the infantry could see one animal raising its stricken body with its forelegs and turning its nose with mystic and profound eloquence toward the sky.

Some comrades joked Collins about his thirst. "Well, if yeh want a drink so bad, why don't yeh go git it?"

"Well, I will in a minnet, if yeh don't shut up!"

A lieutenant of artillery floundered[3] his horse straight down the hill with as little concern as if it were level ground. As he galloped past the colonel of the infantry, he threw up his hand in swift salute. "We've got to get out of that," he roared angrily. He was a black-bearded officer, and his eyes, which resem-

---

1. **"swing" team,** the center pair of horses in a team of six horses.
2. **ruck,** multitude; heap.
3. **floundered,** moved with an awkward, struggling motion.

bled beads, sparkled like those of an insane man. His jumping horse sped along the column of infantry.

The fat major, standing carelessly with his sword held horizontally behind him and with his legs far apart, looked after the receding horseman and laughed. "He wants to get back with orders pretty quick, or there'll be no batt'ry left," he observed.

The wise young captain of the second company hazarded to the lieutenant-colonel that the enemy's infantry would probably soon attack the hill, and the lieutenant-colonel snubbed him.

A private in one of the rear companies looked out over the meadow, and then turned to a companion and said, "Look there, Jim!" It was the wounded officer from the battery, who some time before had started to ride across the meadow, supporting his right arm carefully with his left hand. This man had encountered a shell, apparently, at a time when no one perceived him, and he could now be seen lying face downward with a stirruped foot stretched across the body of his dead horse. A leg of the charger extended slantingly upward, precisely as stiff as a stake. Around this motionless pair the shells still howled.

There was a quarrel in A Company. Collins was shaking his fist in the faces of some laughing comrades. "Dern yeh! I ain't afraid t' go. If yeh say much, I will go!"

"Of course, yeh will! You'll run through that there medder, won't yeh?"

Collins said, in a terrible voice: "You see now!"

At this ominous threat his comrades broke into renewed jeers.

Collins gave them a dark scowl, and went to find his captain. The latter was conversing with the colonel of the regiment.

"Captain," said Collins, saluting and standing at attention—in those days all trousers bagged at the knees—"Captain, I want t' get permission to go git some water from that there well over yonder!"

The colonel and the captain swung about simultaneously and stared across the meadow. The captain laughed. "You must be pretty thirsty, Collins?"

"Yes, sir, I am."

"Well—ah," said the captain. After a moment, he asked, "Can't you wait?"

"No, sir."

The colonel was watching Collins's face. "Look here, my lad," he said, in a pious sort of voice—"Look here, my lad"—Collins was not a lad—"don't you think that's taking pretty big risks for a little drink of water?"

"I dunno," said Collins uncomfortably. Some of the resentment toward his companions, which perhaps had forced him into this affair, was beginning to fade. "I dunno w'ether 'tis."

The colonel and the captain contemplated him for a time.

"Well," said the captain finally.

"Well," said the colonel, "if you want to go, why, go."

Collins saluted. "Much obliged t' yeh."

As he moved away the colonel called after him. "Take some of the other boys' canteens with you, an' hurry back, now."

"Yes, sir, I will."

The colonel and the captain looked at each other then, for it had suddenly occurred that they could not for the life of them tell whether Collins wanted to go or whether he did not.

They turned to regard Collins, and as they perceived him surrounded by gesticulating comrades, the colonel said: "Well, by thunder! I guess he's going."

Collins appeared as a man dreaming. In the midst of the questions, the advice, the warnings, all the excited talk of his company mates, he maintained a curious silence.

They were very busy in preparing him for his ordeal. When they inspected him carefully, it was somewhat like the examination that grooms give a horse before a race; and they were amazed, staggered, by the whole affair. Their astonishment found vent in strange repetitions.

"Are yeh sure a-goin'?" they demanded again and again.

"Certainly I am," cried Collins at last, furiously.

He strode sullenly away from them. He was swinging five or six canteens by their cords. It seemed that his cap would not remain firmly on his head, and often he reached and pulled it down over his brow.

There was a general movement in the compact column. The long animal-like thing moved slightly. Its four hundred eyes were turned upon the figure of Collins.

"Well, sir, if that ain't th' derndest thing! I never thought Fred Collins had the blood in him for that kind of business."

"What's he goin' to do, anyhow?"

"He's goin' to that well there after water."

"We ain't dyin' of thirst, are we? That's foolishness."

"Well, somebody put him up to it, an' he's doin' it."

"Say, he must be a desperate cuss."

When Collins faced the meadow and walked away from the regiment, he was vaguely conscious that a chasm, the deep valley of all prides, was suddenly between him and his comrades. It was provisional, but the provision was that he return as a victor. He had blindly been led by quaint emotions, and laid himself under an obligation to walk squarely up to the face of death.

But he was not sure that he wished to make a retraction, even if he could do so without shame. As a matter of truth, he was sure of very little. He was mainly surprised.

It seemed to him supernaturally strange that he had allowed his mind to maneuver his body into such a situation. He understood that it might be called dramatically great.

However, he had no full appreciation of anything, excepting that he was actually conscious of being dazed. He could feel his dulled mind groping after the form and color

of this incident. He wondered why he did not feel some keen agony of fear cutting his sense like a knife. He wondered at this, because human expression had said loudly for centuries that men should feel afraid of certain things, and that all men who did not feel this fear were phenomena—heroes.

He was, then, a hero. He suffered that disappointment which we would all have if we discovered that we were ourselves capable of those deeds which we most admire in history and legend. This, then, was a hero. After all, heroes were not much.

No, it could not be true. He was not a hero. Heroes had no shames in their lives, and, as for him, he remembered borrowing fifteen dollars from a friend and promising to pay it back the next day, and then avoiding that friend for ten months. When, at home, his mother had aroused him for the early labor of his life on the farm, it had often been his fashion to be irritable, childish, diabolical; and his mother had died since he had come to the war.

He saw that, in this matter of the well, the canteens, the shells, he was an intruder in the land of fine deeds.

He was now about thirty paces from his comrades. The regiment had just turned its many faces toward him.

From the forest of terrific noises there suddenly emerged a little uneven line of men. They fired fiercely and rapidly at distant foliage on which appeared little puffs of white smoke. The spatter of skirmish firing was added to the thunder of the guns on the hill. The little line of men ran forward. A color-sergeant fell flat with his flag as if he had slipped on ice. There was hoarse cheering from this distant field.

Collins suddenly felt that two demon fingers were pressed into his ears. He could see nothing but flying arrows, flaming red. He lurched from the shock of this explosion, but he made a mad rush for the house, which he viewed as a man submerged to the neck in a

Battlefield, Missionary Ridge, near Chattanooga, Tennessee

boiling surf might view the shore. In the air little pieces of shell howled, and the earthquake explosions drove him insane with the menace of their roar. As he ran the canteens knocked together with a rhythmical tinkling.

As he neared the house, each detail of the scene became vivid to him. He was aware of some bricks of the vanished chimney lying on the sod. There was a door which hung by one hinge.

Rifle bullets called forth by the insistent skirmishers came from the far-off bank of foliage. They mingled with the shells and the pieces of shells until the air was torn in all directions by hootings, yells, howls. The sky was full of fiends who directed all their wild rage at his head.

When he came to the well, he flung himself face downward and peered into its darkness. There were furtive silver glintings some feet from the surface. He grabbed one of the canteens and, unfastening its cap, swung it down by the cord. The water flowed slowly in with an indolent gurgle.

And now, as he lay with his face turned away, he was suddenly smitten with the terror. It came upon his heart like the grasp of claws. All the power faded from his muscles. For an instant he was no more than a dead man.

The canteen filled with a maddening slowness, in the manner of all bottles. Presently he recovered his strength and addressed a screaming oath to it. He leaned over until it seemed as if he intended to try to push water into it with his hands. His eyes as he gazed down into the well shone like two pieces of metal, and in their expression was a great appeal and a great curse. The stupid water derided him.

There was the blaring thunder of a shell. Crimson light shone through the swift-boiling smoke and made a pink reflection on part of the wall of the well. Collins jerked out his arm and canteen with the same motion that a man would use in withdrawing his head from a furnace.

He scrambled erect and glared and hesitated. On the ground near him lay the old well bucket, with a length of rusty chain. He lowered it swiftly into the well. The bucket struck the water and then, turning lazily over, sank. When, with hand reaching tremblingly over hand, he hauled it out, it knocked often against the walls of the well and spilled some of its contents.

In running with a filled bucket, a man can adopt but one kind of gait. So, through this terrible field over which screamed practical angels of death, Collins ran in the manner of a farmer chased out of a dairy by a bull.

His face went staring white with anticipation—anticipation of a blow that would whirl him around and down. He would fall as he had seen other men fall, the life knocked out of them so suddenly that their knees were no more quick to touch the ground than their heads. He saw the long blue line of the regiment, but his comrades were standing looking at him from the edge of an impossible star. He was aware of some deep wheel-ruts and hoofprints in the sod beneath his feet.

The artillery officer who had fallen in this meadow had been making groans in the teeth of the tempest of sound. These futile cries, wrenched from him by his agony, were heard only by shells, bullets. When wild-eyed Collins came running, this officer raised himself. His face contorted and blanched from pain, he was about to utter some great beseeching cry. But suddenly his face straightened, and he called: "Say, young man, give me a drink of water, will you?"

Collins had no room amid his emotions for surprise. He was mad from the threats of destruction.

"I can't!" he screamed, and in his reply was a full description of his quaking apprehension. His cap was gone and his hair was riotous. His clothes made it appear that he had been dragged over the ground by the heels. He ran on.

The officer's head sank down, and one elbow crooked. His foot in its brass-bound stirrup still stretched over the body of his horse, and the other leg was under the steed.

But Collins turned. He came dashing back. His face had now turned gray, and in his eyes was all terror. "Here it is! Here it is!"

The officer was as a man gone in drink. His arm bent like a twig. His head drooped as if his neck were of willow. He was sinking to the ground, to lie face downward.

Collins grabbed him by the shoulder. "Here it is. Here's your drink. Turn over. Turn over, man, for God's sake!"

With Collins hauling at his shoulder, the officer twisted his body and fell with his face turned toward that region where lived the unspeakable noises of the swirling missiles. There was the faintest shadow of a smile on his lips as he looked at Collins. He gave a sigh, a little primitive breath like that from a child.

Collins tried to hold the bucket steadily, but his shaking hands caused the water to splash all over the face of the dying man. Then he jerked it away and ran on.

The regiment gave him a welcoming roar. The grimed faces were wrinkled in laughter.

His captain waved the bucket away. "Give it to the men!"

The two genial, skylarking young lieutenants were the first to gain possession of it. They played over it in their fashion.

When one tried to drink, the other teasingly knocked his elbow. "Don't Billie! You'll make me spill it," said the one. The other laughed.

Suddenly there was an oath, the thud of wood on the ground, and a swift murmur of astonishment among the ranks. The two lieutenants glared at each other. The bucket lay on the ground, empty.

FOR UNDERSTANDING

1. Why is it difficult for Collins to get his drink of water?
2. From whom does he ask permission to go to the well? Who gives him permission?
3. At the moment he is ready to go to the well, what is Collins's main emotion?
4. When does Collins first feel fear?
5. As he returns with the bucket of water, whom does Collins find lying in the meadow? How does Collins try to help this person?
6. What happens to the water Collins brings back?

FOR INTERPRETATION

Discuss each of the following interpretations:
1. Collins's thirst concerns him more than the death of the bugler.
2. It is only as he begins to *think* about his trip to the well that Collins contemplates "heroism" but rejects it.
3. The trip back is for Collins the heroic gesture because he masters his fear, especially when he stops to give the dying man water rather than rush on to safety.

FOR APPRECIATION

Irony

In both his fiction and verse Crane often employed irony in order to point up an idea or a theme. He was particularly adept at using *irony of situation,* in which the action or the situation that is revealed is the opposite of what might be expected or seem appropriate.

Explain the irony of situation in the spilling of the water at the end of the story.

COMPOSITION

> **Too often a man's angry pride**
> **Is cap and bells for a fool.**
> **Tennyson**

Recall the way Fred Collins allowed himself to be maneuvered into making the dangerous trip to the old well simply because he wanted to save face and show his comrades he would do what he said he would. Because his angry pride forced him into his mad dash, was he any less a hero for daring to go? Was the man more fool than hero or more hero than fool?

Refresh your memory by looking up the dictionary definitions for *hero* and *fool.* Think about heroes you have read or heard about. Think back over the story and try to place yourself in Fred Collins's shoes. Then write a composition in which you support the conclusion you have reached. Your composition title is "Fred Collins: Fool or Hero?"

When first published, Crane's poetry did not please many readers because it was not like the popular poetry of the day. Yet Crane, who thought of his poems as "lines," considered them a more ambitious effort than his famous novel The Red Badge of Courage, *because the poems expressed his ideas of life as a whole. These ideas were often bitter, always antiheroic, not unlike his fiction. The form of the verses owes much to Crane's knowledge of the Bible and to his admiration for Walt Whitman and Emily Dickinson.*

As you read the following poems, think of each as an epigram, *that is, a brief and tersely worded concept.*

The Book of Wisdom

I met a seer.
He held in his hands
The book of wisdom.
"Sir," I addressed him,
"Let me read."   5
"Child—" he began.
"Sir," I said.
"Think not that I am a child,
For already I know much
Of that which you hold;   10
Aye, much."

He smiled.
Then he opened the book
And held it before me.
Strange that I should have grown so suddenly blind. 15

Think as I Think

"Think as I think," said a man,
"Or you are abominably wicked;
You are a toad."
And after I had thought of it,
I said, "I will, then, be a toad."

"The Book of Wisdom," "Think as I Think," "The Wayfarer," and "A Man Said to the Universe" from THE COLLECTED POEMS OF STEPHEN CRANE, edited by Wilson Follet. Published by Random House, Inc.

The Wayfarer

The wayfarer,
Perceiving the pathway to truth,
Was struck with astonishment.
It was thickly grown with weeds.
"Ha," he said,   5
"I see that no one has passed here
In a long time."
Later he saw that each weed
Was a singular knife.
"Well," he mumbled at last,   10
"Doubtless there are other roads."

A Man Said to the Universe

A man said to the universe:
"Sir, I exist!"
"However," replied the universe,
"The fact has not created in me
A sense of obligation."

UNDERSTANDING AND APPRECIATION

Crane's poems are in many instances structured like his fiction. In each of the four poems you have just read, for example, Crane uses the flat and direct dialogue and the ironic conclusion, or reversal, that are found in his story, "A Mystery of Heroism." Note that in "The Book of Wisdom," the narrator assures the seer quickly and confidently that he is able to read in the book of wisdom. The reversal occurs even more quickly when the seer smiles, opens the book, and the narrator is forced to the ironic conclusion that he is "so suddenly blind."

"The Book of Wisdom"
A seer is believed to possess profound knowledge and the power of foreseeing future events. Presumably persons acquire wisdom as they grow older and more experienced. The narrator addresses the seer as "Sir." What it the one word the seer utters? How does this word relate to the last line of the poem?

"Think as I Think"
What decision does the narrator make in the poem?

"The Wayfarer"
Why has no one traveled on the pathway to truth in a long time? What does the last line of the poem suggest the wayfarer will do?

"A Man Said to the Universe"
What does the universe tell the man in the poem?

Chief Joseph
1840–1904

When ordered to move his small tribe of Nez Percé from their ancestral home in the mountains of the Northwest, Chief Joseph in 1877 attempted to lead some eight hundred of his people to refuge in Canada. The United States military pursued them, however, and in the ensuing eleven weeks of fighting over 1600 miles of rugged terrain, Joseph brilliantly outmaneuvered the veteran troops. At last, with his surviving people freezing and starving, the chief surrendered to General Nelson Miles. His brief surrender statement ends with the now well-known words: "From where the sun now stands I will fight no more forever."

Until well into the present century, Indian contributions to the body of American literature were, for obvious reasons, almost exclusively oral—primarily speeches of gifted tribal orators. In addition to being a skillful military tactician, Chief Joseph was also one of the most eloquent of the Indian orators. Two years after his surrender, with his people still suffering, Joseph went to Washington to plead the cause of the Nez Percé. The following is the latter part of his

PORTRAIT OF CHIEF JOSEPH
Cyrenius Hall
National Portrait Gallery, Smithsonian Institution

rather lengthy speech to an assembly of officials as it was reported in the *North American Review,* April 1879.

CHIEF JOSEPH SPEAKS

At last I was granted permission to come to Washington and bring my friend Yellow Bull and our interpreter with me. I am glad we came. I have shaken hands with a great many friends, but there are some things I want to know which no one seems able to explain. I can not understand how the Government sends a man out to fight us, as it did General Miles, and then breaks his word. Such a government has something wrong about it. I can not understand why so many chiefs are allowed to talk so many different ways, and

promise so many different things. I have seen the Great Father Chief,* the next Great Chief, the Commissioner Chief, the Law Chief, and many other law chiefs, and they all say they are my friends, and that I shall have justice, but while their mouths all talk right I do not understand why nothing is done for my people. I have heard talk and talk, but nothing is done. Good words do not last long

---

*Great Father Chief,   Rutherford B. Hayes, U.S. President from 1877 to 1881.

unless they amount to something. Words do not pay for my dead people. They do not pay for my country, now overrun by white men. They do not protect my father's grave. They do not pay for all my horses and cattle. Good words will not give me back my children. Good words will not make good the promise of your War Chief General Miles. Good words will not give my people good health and stop them from dying. Good words will not get my people a home where they can live in peace and take care of themselves. I am tired of talk that comes to nothing. It makes my heart sick when I remember all the good words and all the broken promises. There has been too much talking by men who had no right to talk. Too many misrepresentations have been made, too many misunderstandings have come up between the white men about the Indians. If the white man wants to live in peace with the Indian he can live in peace. There need be no trouble. Treat all men alike. Give them the same law. Give them all an even chance to live and grow. All men were made by the same Great Spirit Chief. They are all brothers. The earth is the mother of all people, and all people should have equal rights upon it. You might as well expect the rivers to run backward as that any man who was born a free man should be contented when penned up and denied liberty to go where he pleases. If you tie a horse to a stake, do you expect he will grow fat? If you pen an Indian up on a small spot of earth, and compel him to stay there, he will not be contented, nor will he grow and prosper. I have asked some of the great white chiefs where they get their authority to say to the Indian that he shall stay in one place, while he sees white men going where they please. They can not tell me.

I only ask of the Government to be treated as all other men are treated. If I can not go to my own home, let me have a home in some country where my people will not die so fast. I would like to go to Bitter Root Valley. There my people would be healthy; where they are

now they are dying. Three have died since I left my camp to come to Washington.

When I think of our condition my heart is heavy. I see men of my race treated as outlaws and driven from country to country, or shot down like animals.

I know that my race must change. We can not hold our own with the white men as we are. We only ask an even chance to live as other men live. We ask to be recognized as men. We ask that the same law shall work alike on all men. If the Indian breaks the law, punish him by the law. If the white man breaks the law, punish him also.

Let me be a free man—free to travel, free to stop, free to work, free to trade where I choose, free to choose my own teachers, free to follow the religion of my fathers, free to think and talk and act for myself—and I will obey every law, or submit to the penalty.

Whenever the white man treats an Indian as they treat each other, then we will have no more wars. We shall be alike—brothers of one father and one mother, with one sky above us and one country around us, and one government for all. Then the Great Spirit Chief who rules above will smile upon this land, and send rain to wash out the bloody spots made by brothers' hands from the face of the earth. For this time the Indian race are waiting and praying. I hope that no more groans of wounded men and women will ever go to the ear of the Great Spirit Chief above, and that all people may be one people.

In-mut-too-yah-lat-lat has spoken for his people.

UNDERSTANDING AND INTERPRETATION

1. What does Chief Joseph say about General Miles?

2. What does he say about the "good words" he hears?

3. According to Chief Joseph, how would it be possible for whites and Indians to live in peace?

4. Chief Joseph says: "I know that my race must change." Explain what you think he means.

Paul Laurence Dunbar 1872–1906

Born in Dayton, Ohio, to parents who had been slaves, Paul Laurence Dunbar achieved national recognition as a poet and writer of fiction by the time he was twenty-three. The first black American poet to win a truly wide popular audience, Dunbar was considered by most of his contemporaries as essentially a writer of comic and sentimental dialect poems and stories. In the last few years of his brief life, though, he became a sharp social critic and his poems, stories, and essays on racial injustice are considered among his best work.

Dunbar was a precocious child and was reading his poetry in school assemblies and in churches long before he left elementary school. While in high school he wrote poetry and sketches for several newspapers, among them the *Westside News,* edited by flight pioneer Wilbur Wright. After graduation he used money he had earned as an elevator operator and funds borrowed from friends to publish a thousand copies of a volume of his poems, *Oak and Ivy* (1893). All copies sold quickly, but failed to attract critical attention.

His next book, *Majors and Minors* (1894), was noticed by the critics; among these was William Dean Howells, who not only wrote favorable reviews of Dunbar's work, but also assisted the young poet in publishing his next book, *Lyrics of a Lowly Life* (1896). With the appearance of this volume, Dunbar gained national prominence as a literary figure. Frederick Douglass, the black abolitionist leader, proudly pointed to Dunbar as "the poet laureate of the Negro race."

With a growing national readership, Dunbar wrote feverishly and turned out a succession of short stories, poems, and four novels, much of the work in black dialect. Although later critics were to condemn his dialect writing as marred by sentimentality and stereotypes, Dunbar was in demand not only as a writer of dialect but as a

PORTRAIT OF PAUL LAURENCE DUNBAR

platform reader as well. His appearances on the lecture circuit drew large, appreciative audiences both in the United States and England.

In 1899, when he had achieved success and some financial stability, Dunbar suffered a severe attack of pneumonia. From that time on his health deteriorated rapidly, although he continued to write at a frantic pace. At the time he died from tuberculosis four months before his thirty-fourth birthday, Paul Laurence Dunbar was one of America's most popular writers, and he is still regarded as a first-rate poet.

THE OLD MATTRESS FACTORY, William Woodward
New Orleans Museum of Art, Louisiana

Life's Tragedy

It may be misery not to sing at all
    And to go silent through the brimming day.
It may be sorrow never to be loved,
    But deeper griefs than these beset the way.

To have come near to sing the perfect song
    And only by a half-tone lost the key,   **5**

"Life's Tragedy" and "We Wear the Mask" from THE COMPLETE POEMS
OF PAUL LAURENCE DUNBAR 1913. Reprinted by permission of Dodd,
Mead & Co., Inc, New York

There is the potent sorrow, there the grief,
    The pale, sad staring of life's tragedy.

To have just missed the perfect love,
    Not the hot passion of untempered youth,   10
But that which lays aside its vanity
    And gives thee, for thy trusting worship, truth—

This, this it is to be accursed indeed;
    For if we mortals love, or if we sing,
We count our joys not by the things we have,   15
    But by what kept us from the perfect thing.

We Wear the Mask

We wear the mask that grins and lies,
It hides our cheeks and shades our eyes,
This debt we pay to human guile;
With torn and bleeding hearts we smile,
And mouth with myriad subtleties.   5

Why should the world be otherwise,
In counting all our tears and sighs?
Nay, let them only see us, while
    We wear the mask.

We smile, but, O great Christ, our cries   10
To Thee from tortured souls arise.
We sing, but oh, the clay is vile
Beneath our feet, and long the mile;
But let the world dream otherwise,
    We wear the mask.   15

UNDERSTANDING AND INTERPRETATION

"Life's Tragedy"

1. According to Dunbar, what is life's tragedy? What metaphor does the poet use to describe this tragedy?

2. What is perfect love according to the poet? What is imperfect love?

3. What do lines 15 and 16 mean? Do you agree? Explain your answer.

"We Wear the Mask"

1. Who are those identified as "we" in the poem? What does the mask symbolize?

2. To whom do the "tortured souls" reveal their true feelings? What does the poet suggest in line 14? Discuss.

AN AMERICAN ORIGINAL
Emily Dickinson

1830–1886

Emily Dickinson was no ordinary citizen of Amherst, Massachusetts. Born there December 10, 1830, she lived so private a life that piecing together her biography from the letters she left behind, the reminiscences of her friends, and especially her poems, has been a task that has led to a variety of conclusions. Surely she was "a strange and original genius," as the poet Conrad Aiken called her. Whether she was "the greatest woman poet who ever lived," as another critic claims, is difficult to say.

In the *Atlantic Monthly* for April 1862, Thomas Wentworth Higginson, a writer and former minister, published a "Letter to a Young Contributor," urging poets to forsake the old models and strive for new forms charged with life. Emily Dickinson wrote him at once, asking "Are you too deeply occupied to say if my verse is alive? The mind is so near itself it cannot see distinctly, and I have none to ask." She was thirty-one years old, the shy unmarried daughter of a prominent Amherst lawyer. She had published nothing. We think now that by this date she had written, privately, at least 300 poems. She sent Higginson four. He answered her promptly, urging her to send more and to tell him something about herself. Her answer began a long correspondence between a scholar and a teacher, as she chose to think of the relationship. Higginson was not the most perceptive of critics, and he tried too often to improve her unconventional style; but he offered her the friendship she needed. "You were not aware," she wrote years later, "that you saved my life."

Higginson not only saved her life but her poetry as well, or at least he persuaded her to go on writing. She thanked him for "the surgery," saying "it was not so painful as I supposed." Probably he had found the four poems cryptic and irregular, perhaps even jarring to his ear. If he suggested that she smooth the meters and tidy up the rhymes, he could hardly have guessed that he was dealing with a "born" poet

PORTRAIT OF EMILY DICKINSON
"If I read a book and it makes my whole body so cold no fire can warm me, I know that is poetry."

who knew how and why she broke the rules. She would continue to write as she must write.

The poet's letter of 1862 had more to say. In an almost childlike hand, she wrote to Higginson: "I have a brother and sister; my mother does not care for thought; and father; too busy with his briefs to notice what we do. He buys me many books, but begs me not to read them, because he fears they joggle the mind."

To Lavinia, her younger sister, she was always devoted, increasingly as the family diminished in size and the two unmarried sisters were left to run the big house. As the poet became more and more a recluse, Lavinia served as her only link with the outside world. It was natural that Dickinson should leave her poems in her sister's care and just as natural that Lavinia should turn to Higginson when she resolved to collect them for publication in 1890. What no one suspected was the immense number Dickinson had written: over 1700.

Though she made very few trips out of Amherst—to Boston to see a physician, to Philadelphia and Washington to pay visits to friends—she received guests in her father's house, called on new neighbors, attended local parties and church occasionally. She had eight years of schooling, first at Amherst Academy and then at Mount Holyoke Female Seminary. By 1862, however, she was seeing less of the townspeople and more of her garden where, at dusk, she could enjoy the solitude behind hemlock hedges. The poet had taken to communicating with the neighbors by means of hand-picked bouquets or freshly baked bread, accompanied by a poem as greeting or as cryptic note. By 1870, her seclusion was overtly admitted: "I do not cross my father's ground to any house or town." Her reasons are only hinted at: domestic chores (and they were many), ill health, natural shyness, poetic composition, psychic withdrawal. Whatever the causes, her seclusion was her own choosing. It was a hermit's existence as far as the town knew, but Emily Dickinson's private life was full of introspection and literary labor. "The soul selects her own society," she wrote, "then shuts the door."

Dickinson's subjects are fear, frustration, death, God, friendships, love, and the natural world around her. When she speaks in the first person—"I could not live with you," one poem begins—she does not necessarily record a personal experience, though the emotions which led to creating the poem may have begun there. Rather, she is writing of universal feelings—the agony of separation, the need for love, the fear of loneliness. Like Thoreau, Dickinson traveled widely without leaving the village where she was born; we could almost say without leaving her garden and her study. She withdrew from the world in order to know it better, to contemplate the human condition, our relation to the things of this world. "To live is so startling," she wrote Higginson, "it leaves but little room for other occupations, though friends are, if possible, an event more fair." Her poems are life distilled, not the temporal happenings of Massachusetts in 1860, not even of the Civil War, but events common to all: sorrow at the loss of a friend, joy at summer noon, despair at nightfall, the first crocus in spring, the shapes the snow takes in December, walks with her dog, small-town hypocrisy, the renunciation of hope, the nature of God. To all these subjects Dickinson brings intense personal reactions, quite oblivious of fashion or acceptability. She read deeply in Keats, Emerson, the Brownings, the Bible; but her forms are her own.

"Is my verse alive?" not "Is my poetry good poetry?" she asked of Higginson. The reader who discovers her genius will answer the question for her. Once exposed to her frankness, to the force of her lines, one does not easily forget them.

LOTUS LILIES, Charles Courtney Curran
Terra Museum of American Art, Evanston, Illinois, Daniel J. Terra Collection

GOD AND NATURE

Emily Dickinson speaks of nature as though it were a friend, or at least a confidante. Since she sees God's presence in all of nature, it is not surprising, then, to find her also thinking of God in familiar terms. Had she published these poems during her lifetime, she very likely would have drawn censure for her brashness. As it is, they remain private thoughts which we, at last, can "overhear."

This Is My Letter to the World

This is my letter to the world
That never wrote to me,—
The simple news that nature told,
With tender majesty.

Her message is committed   5
To hands I cannot see;
For love of her, sweet countrymen,
Judge tenderly of me!

POEMS, 1890.

A Little Madness in the Spring

A little madness in the Spring
Is wholesome even for the King,
But God be with the Clown,
Who ponders this tremendous scene—
This whole experiment of green,
As if it were his own!

Some Keep the Sabbath Going to Church

Some keep the Sabbath going to church;
I keep it staying at home,
With a bobolink[1] for a chorister,
And an orchard for a dome.

Some keep the Sabbath in surplice;[2]   5
I just wear my wings,
And instead of tolling the bell for church,
Our little sexton sings.

God preaches,—a noted clergyman,—
And the sermon is never long;   10
So instead of getting to heaven at last
I'm going all along!

POEMS, 1890.

1. **bobolink** (bob′ ə lingk),   a North American songbird related to the blackbird.
2. **surplice** (sẽr′ plis), a broad-sleeved white gown worn by clergymen and choir singers over their other clothes.

I Never Saw a Moor

I never saw a moor,
I never saw the sea;
Yet know I how the heather looks,
And what a wave must be.

I never spoke with God,   5
Nor visited in heaven;
Yet certain am I of the spot
As if the chart were given.

POEMS, 1890.

UNDERSTANDING AND INTERPRETATION

These four poems reflect Emily Dickinson's deep respect for creation and the Creator. With her discerning eye, she saw the evidence of God's power in the smallest creatures, the simplest gesture. In transferring these observations to poetry she set forth her personal creed.

"This Is My Letter to the World"
The poet says she writes a "letter" to the world to send nature's "message." Though we often use these two words interchangeably, they have distinct meanings here. What is nature's "message"?

"A Little Madness in the Spring"
1. What words in this poem are carefully chosen for contrast?
2. The distance from king to clown is great. Is there an equally great distance between wholesome and mad?
3. Dickinson had difficulty settling on the word "experiment" in the fifth line. She tried these lines first:
    a. This sudden legacy of green.
    b. This fair apocalypse of green.
    c. This whole apocalypse of green.
    d. This whole astonishment of green.
    e. This wild experiment of green.
    Has she made the wisest choice? What does "experiment" suggest to you?

"Some Keep the Sabbath Going to Church"
1. How does Dickinson contrast her church with the town's church?
2. Can one be "going to heaven" every Sunday? Can this be inferred from the last lines?

"I Never Saw a Moor"
We are asked to make a comparison between the two halves of this poem. Why is it vital that the poet has not seen a moor or the sea?

THE STATION ON THE MORRIS AND ESSEX RAILROAD
Edward Lamson Henry
The Chase Manhattan Bank Collection

OBSERVATIONS AND COMMENT

Society perplexed Emily Dickinson. She seldom felt comfortable in large groups of people, yet she had a keen ear and eye for society's deficiencies. In the following poems she deals tersely and perceptively with social behavior, human aspiration, and the nature of language.

Much Madness Is Divinest Sense

Much madness is divinest sense
To a discerning eye;
Much sense the starkest madness.
'Tis the majority
In this, as all, prevails.   5
Assent, and you are sane;
Demur,*—you're straightway dangerous,
And handled with a chain.

POEMS, 1890.

* **demur** (di mėr´),   hesitate or object.

Success Is Counted Sweetest

Success is counted sweetest
By those who ne'er succeed.
To comprehend a nectar
Requires sorest need.

Not one of all the purple host   5
Who took the flag today
Can tell the definition
So clear, of victory,

As he, defeated, dying,
On whose forbidden ear   10
The distant strains of triumph
Break, agonized and clear.

POEMS, 1890.

Hope Is the Thing with Feathers

Hope is the thing with feathers
That perches in the soul,
And sings the tune without the words,
And never stops at all.

And sweetest in the gale is heard;   5
And sore must be the storm
That could abash the little bird
That kept so many warm.

I've heard it in the chillest land,
And on the strangest sea;   10
Yet, never, in extremity,
It asked a crumb of me.

POEMS, 1890.

A Word Is Dead

A word is dead
When it is said,
Some say.
I say it just
Begins to live
That day.

POEMS, 1896.

UNDERSTANDING AND APPRECIATION

As a recluse, Emily Dickinson had little contact with the citizens of Amherst other than her close friends, neighbors, and family. Yet she must have been a good listener. She had strong opinions about society's decrees, what was fashionable and not fashionable, what the world expects of us, what we ask of ourselves. She would have shared with a man like Thoreau, had she known him, a strong distrust of majority opinion and mass media.

"Much Madness Is Divinest Sense"
1. What is the paradox, or apparent contradiction, on which this poem is built? To appreciate it you must be certain you understand how the poet uses the words "discerning" and "demur."
2. In line 5, the poet employs a casual parenthetical phrase: "as all." What do these two seemingly unimportant words add to the major statement of the poem?

"Success Is Counted Sweetest"
1. In the first stanza, who finds success sweetest? What is necessary to comprehend the "nectar" of success?
2. In the second stanza, who are the "purple host"? On which side are those "who took the flag"?
3. Lines 5–12 are one sentence. The strains of triumph are agony for the dying man to hear, yet he knows better than any of the victors what victory means. How do you make a connection between this image and "nectar/need" of the first stanza?

"Hope Is the Thing with Feathers"
1. In line 4 the poet states that the bird's song "never stops at all." What does this say about Hope?
2. In the second stanza, under what conditions are we told the bird sings "sweetest"?
3. What charge does Hope make for its comforting work?

"A Word Is Dead"
Rather than dying, how can a word that is uttered begin to "live"?

PORTRAITS

Emily Dickinson might not have thought of these three poems as "portraits," but read as a group they demonstrate her immense power for personifying a snake or a bird or even a train. One need not share her enthusiasm for her subject to appreciate the sharpness of her description and the intensity of the language. She makes us see common objects as clearly as she does.

A Bird Came Down the Walk

A bird came down the walk;
He did not know I saw;
He bit an angle-worm in halves
And ate the fellow, raw.

And then he drank a dew   5
From a convenient grass,
And then hopped sidewise to the wall
To let a beetle pass.

He glanced with rapid eyes
That hurried all abroad,—   10
They looked like frightened beads, I thought;
He stirred his velvet head

Like one in danger; cautious,
I offered him a crumb,
And he unrolled his feathers   15
And rowed him softer home

Than oars divide the ocean,
Too silver for a seam,
Or butterflies, off banks of noon,
Leap, plashless, as they swim.   20

POEMS, 1891.

A Narrow Fellow in the Grass

A narrow fellow in the grass
Occasionally rides;
You may have met him,—did you not,
His notice sudden is.

The grass divides as with a comb,   5
A spotted shaft is seen;
And then it closes at your feet
And opens further on.

He likes a boggy acre,
A floor too cool for corn,   10
Yet when a child, and barefoot,
I more than once, at morn,

Have passed, I thought, a whip-lash
Unbraiding in the sun,—
When, stooping to secure it,   15
It wrinkled, and was gone.

Several of nature's people
I know, and they know me;
I feel for them a transport
Of cordiality;   20

But never met this fellow,
Attended or alone,
Without a tighter breathing,
And zero at the bone.

POEMS, 1891.

I Like to See It Lap the Miles

I like to see it lap the miles,
And lick the valleys up,
And stop to feed itself at tanks;
And then, prodigious, step

Around a pile of mountains,   5
And, supercilious, peer
In shanties by the sides of roads;
And then a quarry pare

To fit its sides, and crawl between,
Complaining all the while   10
In horrid, hooting stanza;
Then chase itself down hill

And neigh like Boanerges;*
Then, punctual as a star,
Stop—docile and omnipotent—   15
At its own stable door.

POEMS, 1891.

* **Boanerges** (bō′ ə nər′ jēz),   literally, sons of thunder; name given by Jesus to sons of Zebedee; used to refer to forceful preacher.

UNDERSTANDING AND APPRECIATION

"A Bird Came Down the Walk"
1. Why is the kind of bird Emily Dickinson observes never made clear?
2. How do you know that the poet is more interested in the manner in which the bird flies away than in why he rejects the crumb?

"A Narrow Fellow in the Grass"
1. For four stanzas, this poem is chiefly description, and accurate description it is. "Spotted shaft" and "whip-lash" are not ordinarily terms to describe a snake. Why are they memorable here?
2. The last stanza sets up opposition to the earlier noncommittal description. What is Dickinson's feeling about the snake?

"I Like to See It Lap the Miles"
1. What image does Dickinson use for the train? Why is it most appropriate?
2. Considering the image used for the train, one line seems out of place: "Complaining all the while/In horrid, hooting stanza." How do you explain it?

LOSS AND DEATH

Emily Dickinson tried not to sentimentalize her life. She could become coy on occasion, but she never became maudlin, in spite of the long years she spent in solitude. These poems speak a brutal truth about loneliness, one she felt from her heart, and in their forthright language they impress on the reader the cruelty of separation and the finality of death.

Heart! We Will Forget Him!

Heart! we will forget him!
You and I—tonight!
You may forget the warmth he gave—
I will forget the light!

When you have done, pray tell me   5
That I may straight begin!
Haste! lest while you're lagging
I remember him!

POEMS, 1896.

If You Were Coming in the Fall

If you were coming in the fall,
I'd brush the summer by
With half a smile and half a spurn,
As housewives do a fly.

If I could see you in a year,   5
I'd wind the months in balls,
And put them each in separate drawers,
Until their time befalls.

If only centuries delayed,
I'd count them on my hand,   10
Subtracting till my fingers dropped
Into Van Dieman's land.*

If certain, when this life was out
That yours and mine should be,
I'd toss it yonder like a rind,   15
And taste eternity.

But now, all ignorant of the length
Of time's uncertain wing,
It goads me, like the goblin bee,
That will not state its sting.   20

POEMS, 1890.

* **Van Dieman's** (van dē′ mənz) **land,** former name for Tasmania, a state of Australia. In the poet's day it was considered extremely remote from Amherst, Mass.

Because I Could Not Stop for Death

Because I could not stop for Death,
He kindly stopped for me;
The carriage held but just ourselves
And Immortality.

We slowly drove, he knew no haste,   5
And I had put away
My labor, and my leisure too,
For his civility.

We passed the school where children played
Their lessons scarcely done;   10
We passed the fields of gazing grain,
We passed the setting sun.

We paused before a house that seemed
A swelling in the ground;
The roof was scarcely visible,   15
The cornice but a mound.

Since then 'tis centuries; but each
Feels shorter than the day
I first surmised the horses' heads
Were toward eternity.   20

POEMS, 1890.

The Bustle in a House

The bustle in a house
The morning after death
Is solemnest of industries
Enacted upon earth—

The sweeping up the heart,   5
And putting love away
We shall not want to use again
Until eternity.

POEMS, 1890.

FOR UNDERSTANDING

"Heart! We Will Forget Him!"

As the speaker in the poem urges her heart to agree to forget her lost love, why does she plead with her heart to hurry?

"If You Were Coming in the Fall"

1. How does time "build" in the poem?
2. What is the speaker's uncertainty?
3. How long will the speaker wait for the loved one to come?

"Because I Could Not Stop for Death"

1. What does the poet suggest about life in the first two lines?
2. What image has the poet chosen for death?
3. What is the house before which they pause?
4. Explain the time perspective in the final stanza.

"The Bustle in a House"

1. Why is the bustle here the "solemnest of industries"?
2. Explain the figurative language in the second stanza.

FOR APPRECIATION

Selection of Significant Details

A novelist has several hundred pages in which to build the atmosphere and setting for a narrative. A short-story writer must work faster in a relatively confined space. The poet, unless writing epics or dramas, is even more restrained and thus must make each word count. Emily Dickinson took upon herself the tightest of restrictions when she chose to write four-line stanzas, and two- or three-stanza poems. Her form is so miniature that she has little time to expand her thought and must register her impressions swiftly and with sharp immediacy.

Dickinson developed several devices to concentrate concrete details rather than generalities in the reader's mind. Note first the poem "Some Keep the Sabbath Going to Church." Here she wisely groups details to give the reader a clear view of *her* church: bobolink, orchard, wings, bird song implied in singing sexton, God preaching, a short sermon. If you inspect closely "I Like to See It Lap the Miles," you will notice how the details accumulate rapidly as the train rolls through the countryside: from valleys to tanks, from a pile of mountains (not a range but a *pile*) to shanties, then on to quarries, and down hills to the stable door. Finally, turn to "If You Were Coming in the Fall." Here Emily Dickinson chooses the homeliest details to describe the passage of time and uses them in unlikely and arresting ways: summer brushed away like a fly, months rolled into balls, centuries counted on fingers, life tossed away like the rind of fruit.

Choose the Dickinson poems that affect you most and look at them closely. Give them a second and third reading. John Crowe Ransom, a famous American poet, once said he enjoyed poetry for the logical irrelevancy of its local details. Dickinson would have understood this. Her images may, at first glance, seem strange to you. What, for example, has nectar to do with success, you may ask. But give the poem a chance to assert itself on its own terms—above all, on its own terms, not yours—and you will discover the joys of connotations, those meanings that cluster around words beyond the standard dictionary meanings.

The pleasure of discovering significant details on your own is an important part of reading poetry. Consider the specific adjectives and the important nouns in these poems:

"Hope Is the Thing with Feathers"
"A Bird Came Down the Walk"
"A Narrow Fellow in the Grass"

A mere listing is not enough. What are the connotations of these details, the suggested meanings behind the words?

AN AMERICAN ORIGINAL
Mark Twain

1835–1910

The evolution of Sam Clemens of Hannibal, Missouri, into Mark Twain, the internationally known literary artist, was a gradual, and in some respects, an accidental process. When at the age of fourteen, Clemens went to work as an apprentice to the publisher of the *Missouri Courier*, he had little thought of a career; his father had died and the sons had no choice but to support the family. Yet many years later Clemens wrote: "I became a printer and began to add one link after another to the chain which was to lead me into the literary profession." These "links" took him from Missouri to the East, then to Nevada and California, to Hawaii, to Europe, back to Buffalo, to Hartford, nine more years in Europe, and finally two lonely years in Redding, Connecticut—a crowded, busy, boisterous lifetime that brought him riches and fame. When Oxford University granted him an honorary degree in 1907, no one, looking back at his achievement, could have been more surprised than Sam Clemens himself at the distance he had come from that Mississippi River town of his birth.

Hannibal in the 1830s was a paradise for a young boy. "I can call back the solemn twilight and mystery of the deep woods, the earthy smells, the faint odors of the wild flowers, the sheen of rain-washed foliage," Twain wrote in his *Autobiography*. Nor did the hectic life on the waterfront ever quite leave his memory. It infected him with restlessness and the sweet smell of romantic journeys. At the age of seventeen, Sam left his brother's newspaper to discover for himself what the world had to offer. As a journeyman printer he wandered along the east coast and through the Midwest, never in want of work, occasionally contributing letters and humorous sketches to various papers, signing them "Grumbler" or "Rumbler" or "Thomas Jefferson Snodgrass."

After reading travel books on South America, he set out for the Amazon and the Orinoco. But once again the great Mississippi

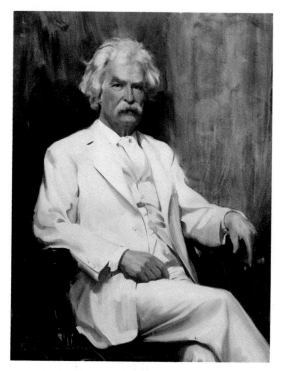

PORTRAIT OF MARK TWAIN, Frank Edwin Larson
National Portrait Gallery, Smithsonian Institution

entered his life. On the boat to New Orleans he met Horace Bixby, the river pilot, and in a short time the young Sam Clemens was apprenticed to him as a "cub," eager to "learn the river" and eventually to earn his own exalted place on a magnificent steamboat. For three years Clemens was a licensed pilot, watching more closely than perhaps he realized the motley crowds aboard—gamblers, prospectors, Southern planters, slave traders, harlots. His ear for local speech and his eye for melodramatic detail were given the best training they could have had.

But like the rest of America he was on the move. After a brief time as a hopelessly bad Confederate soldier, he trekked west when his brother, Orion, was appointed Secretary to the Territory of Nevada. When prospecting and mining proved disappointing, Clemens took employment in Virginia City as a reporter on the *Territorial Enterprise*, wiser but no richer. Now twenty-five, he realized he was happier in journalism than anywhere else, and his talent for writing humorous and satiric sketches had a chance to bloom. Sam Clemens signed his contributions with the pseudonym Mark Twain, a name he said he stole from a Captain Isaiah Sellers who used to write for the New Orleans *Picayune* and who had recently died. More likely it was a recollection from his river days, since "mark twain" was the leadsman's call telling the pilot that his ship was in two fathoms of water and therefore safe. As Mark Twain, Sam Clemens began a third and wildly successful career, but in 1862 he was still not a literary artist nor trying to be.

From Virginia City to San Francisco to Sacramento as journalist, and then to the Sandwich Islands (now called Hawaii) as travel correspondent, the talented Mark Twain was gaining a reputation as one of the wittiest writers on the west coast. He had always been a natural storyteller, a performer who genuinely enjoyed entertaining an audience with tall tales and whimsical anecdotes. It was natural for him to try the lecture platform after his travels to Hawaii. His success was instantaneous. He gave his first lecture in San Francisco at the age of thirty and continued to delight audiences all over the world well past his seventieth year, earning as much as $1,600 in one night. Before he left for the East, Mark Twain was hailed as "The Humorist of the Pacific Slope," a reputation built in part on his newspaper column but chiefly on his hilarious public lectures. One printed story, however, preceded him in the East and prepared the way for his arrival. Artemus Ward had persuaded him to write a tale about a jumping frog which Twain had heard in an Angel Camp tavern in Calaveras County. The New York *Saturday Press* published "The Celebrated Jumping Frog" in 1865. It was the beginning of literary fame, though Twain refused to call it that. He was, he said, a successful lecturer at best, a roving journalist at worst.

This roving spirit next took him eastward, to New York and Europe. He boarded the *Quaker*

Caricature of Mark Twain from the front page of The Daily Graphic, *October 26, 1874*
National Portrait Gallery, Smithsonian Institution

City in 1867 for a five-month tour of France, Italy, and the Holy Land. To meet expenses he accepted a commission to write letters periodically to the *Alta California* and the New York *Tribune*. In them Twain poured out a seemingly endless series of critical opinions based on American superiority to all things European. He knew well how to entertain the American reader. French manners, Italian guides, Greek ruins, Near Eastern monuments struck him as equally ridiculous. On his return he was besieged with offers. New York publishers insisted the *Quaker City* letters cried out for republication, and they offered Twain an irresistible contract. "I had made my mind up to *one* thing," he told his friends. "I wasn't going to touch a book unless there was *money* in it, and a good deal of it. I told them so." Money there was; too much of it. *The Innocents Abroad* appeared in 1869, an immediate best seller. Twain had been persuaded, moreover, to edit his letters, to rewrite some and destroy others. What began as journalism was soon shaped into literature. His newest career was launched.

To make money making people laugh, however, struck some of Twain's friends as an "unliterary" ambition, so he continued to call his work journalism. He bought a third interest in the Buffalo *Express* and married Olivia Langdon on the strength of *The Innocents Abroad* sales, hoping to settle down to a more sedate domestic life and to contribute nothing more than occasional satiric letters or humorous sketches to New York papers. Then he moved his family to Hartford, Connecticut. Harriet Beecher Stowe, of *Uncle Tom's Cabin* fame, was a near neighbor. William Dean Howells, editor of the *Atlantic Monthly*, became an intimate friend, and urged Twain to put some of his reminiscences about steamboating on the Mississippi into a series of papers for the magazine. The appearance of these papers in the *Atlantic Monthly* in 1875 brought such instant praise and so many demands for more of his vivid prose that Twain was ready to admit that he had become a literary figure, almost against his will. The West had nourished the ambitious Sam Clemens. Mark Twain the artist was born in New England.

Roughing It (1872) and *Life on the Mississippi* (1882) were assembled the way most of his autobiographical volumes were put together—a combination of brilliant description, humorous anecdotes, tall tales, character studies, and sharp satire held together loosely by a first-person narrator, Twain himself. He loved the western brand of humor and preserved its ribaldry as well as dialect even while he looked at life in the West realistically. As he matured, Twain let his satiric bent develop freely, and the open healthy criticism of European culture that characterized *The Innocents Abroad* turned into sharp, even bitter satire of his own society, beginning with *The Gilded Age* and ending with his extremely pessimistic novel, *The Mysterious Stranger*.

The reasons for his pessimism are numerous. He spent money carelessly, and debts from the bankruptcy of his publishing company plus the deaths of his wife and two daughters left him embittered and lonely. But before he became so cynical, he wrote the two greatest novels of his career, *The Adventures of Tom Sawyer* and *The Adventures of Huckleberry Finn*. They are children's books, seemingly melodramatic adventure stories, but beneath the surface lies more serious criticism of human foibles than some readers suspect. *Tom Sawyer* may well have been intended to entertain and do little more. It entertains supremely well, being packed with humor, midnight incantations, cruel murder, blackmail, a court trial, and the expected happy ending.

Huckleberry Finn is a much more complex book, and Twain almost abandoned the manuscript in despair several times before its completion. Huck, the son of the town drunkard, escapes his father to flee down the Mississippi on a raft with Jim, a runaway slave. Because of the friendship that grows between the two, Huck is torn between remaining loyal to the teachings of the slave-owning society in which he was reared and helping Jim become free. When he decides to help Jim, he is bringing a moral indictment against the inhumanity and injustice of the "sivilization" he knows. Huck's observation, "Human beings can be awful cruel to one another," might be considered one theme of the book.

THE CELEBRATED JUMPING FROG OF CALAVERAS COUNTY

In compliance with the request of a friend of mine who wrote me from the East, I called on good-natured, garrulous old Simon Wheeler and inquired after my friend's friend, Leonidas W. Smiley, as requested to do, and I hereunto append the result. I have a lurking suspicion that *Leonidas W.* Smiley is a myth, that my friend never knew such a personage, and that he only conjectured that if I asked old Wheeler about him, it would remind him of his infamous *Jim* Smiley and he would go to work and bore me to death with some exasperating reminiscence of him as long and as tedious as it should be useless to me. If that was the design, it succeeded.

I found Simon Wheeler dozing comfortably by the barroom stove of the dilapidated tavern in the decayed mining camp of Angel's, and I noticed that he was fat and bald-headed and had an expression of winning gentleness and simplicity upon his tranquil countenance. He roused up and gave me good day. I told him that a friend of mine had commissioned me to make some inquiries about a cherished companion of his boyhood named *Leonidas W.* Smiley—*Rev. Leonidas W.* Smiley, a young minister of the Gospel, who he had heard was at one time a resident of Angel's Camp. I added that if Mr. Wheeler could tell me anything about this Rev. Leonidas W. Smiley, I would feel under many obligations to him.

Simon Wheeler backed me into a corner and blockaded me there with his chair, and then sat down and reeled off the monotonous narrative which follows this paragraph. He never smiled, he never frowned, he never changed his voice from the gentle-flowing key to which he tuned his initial sentence, he never betrayed the slightest suspicion of enthusiasm, but all through the interminable narrative there ran a vein of impressive earnestness and sincerity which showed me plainly that, so far from his imagining that there was anything ridiculous or funny about his story, he regarded it as a really important matter and admired its two heroes as men of transcendent genius in *finesse.*[1] I let him go on in his own way and never interrupted him once.

"Rev. Leonidas W. H'm, Reverend Le—Well, there was a feller here once by the name of *Jim* Smiley, in the winter of '49—or maybe it was the spring of '50—I don't recollect exactly, somehow, though what makes me think it was one or the other is because I remember the big flume[2] warn't finished when he first come to the camp; but anyway, he was the curiousest man about always betting on anything that turned up you ever see, if he could get anybody to bet on the other side, and if he couldn't he'd change sides. Any way that suited the other man would suit *him*—any way just so's he got a bet, *he* was satisfied. But still he was lucky, uncommon lucky; he most always come out winner. He was always ready

---

1. **finesse** (fə nes′), clever maneuvering.
2. **flume** (flüm), channel for conveying water used for power, transportation, or irrigation.

"The Celebrated Jumping Frog of Calaveras County" from SKETCHES NEW AND OLD by Mark Twain. Harper & Row, Publishers, Inc.

and laying for a chance; there couldn't be no solit'ry thing mentioned but that feller'd offer to bet on it and take ary side you please, as I was just telling you. If there was a horse-race, you'd find him flush or you'd find him busted at the end of it; if there was a dog-fight, he'd bet on it; if there was a cat-fight, he'd bet on it; if there was a chicken-fight, he'd bet on it; why, if there was two birds setting on a fence, he would bet you which one would fly first; or if there was a camp-meeting, he would be there reg'lar to bet on Parson Walker, which he judged to be the best exhorter about here, and so he was too, and a good man. If he even see a straddle-bug[3] start to go anywheres, he would bet you how long it would take him to get to—to wherever he was going to, and if you took him up, he would foller that straddle-bug to Mexico but what he would find out where he was bound for and how long he was on the road. Lots of the boys here has seen that Smiley and can tell you about him. Why, it never made no difference to *him* —he'd bet on *any* thing—the dangdest feller. Parson Walker's wife laid very sick once for a good while, and it seemed as if they warn't going to save her; but one morning he come in and Smiley up and asked him how she was, and he said she was considerable better— thank the Lord for his inf'nite mercy—and coming on so smart that with the blessing of Prov'dence she'd get well yet; and Smiley, be-fore he thought, says, 'Well, I'll resk two-and-a-half she don't anyway.'

"Thish-yer Smiley had a mare—the boys called her the fifteen-minute nag but that was only in fun, you know, because of course she was faster than that—and he used to win money on that horse, for all she was so slow and always had the asthma, or the distemper, or the consumption, or something of that kind. They used to give her two or three hundred yards' start and then pass her under way, but always at the fag end of the race she'd get excited and desperate like, and come cavorting and straddling up and scat-tering her legs around limber, sometimes in the air and sometimes out to one side among the fences, and kicking up m-o-r-e dust and raising m-o-r-e racket with her coughing and sneezing and blowing her nose—and *always* fetch up at the stand just about a neck ahead, as near as you could cipher[4] it down.

"And he had a little small bull-pup, that to look at him you'd think he warn't worth a cent but to set around and look ornery and lay for a chance to steal something. But as soon as money was up on him he was a differ-ent dog; his under-jaw'd begin to stick out like the fo'castle[5] of a steamboat and his teeth would uncover and shine like the furnaces. And a dog might tackle him and bully-rag[6] him, and bite him and throw him over his shoulder two or three times, and Andrew Jackson—which was the name of the pup— Andrew Jackson would never let on but what *he* was satisfied and hadn't expected nothing else—and the bets being doubled and dou-bled on the other side all the time, till the money was all up; and then all of a sudden he would grab that other dog jest by the j'int of his hind leg and freeze to it—not chaw, you understand, but only just grip and hang on till they throwed up the sponge, if it was a year. Smiley always come out winner on that pup till he harnessed a dog once that didn't have no hind legs, because they'd been sawed off in a circular saw, and when the thing had gone along far enough and the money was all up and he come to make a snatch for his pet holt, he see in a minute how he'd been im-posed on and how the other dog had him in the door, so to speak, and he 'peared sup-rised, and then he looked sorter discouraged-like and didn't try no more to win the fight, and so he got shucked[7] out bad. He gave Smiley a look, as much as to say his heart was broke, and it was *his* fault for putting up a dog that hadn't no hind legs for him to take holt of, which was his main dependence in a fight, and then he limped off a piece and laid

---

3. **straddle-bug,** long-legged insect.
4. **cipher,** write.
5. **fo'castle** (fōk' səl), the forecastle, or upper deck of a ship.
6. **bully-rag,** to torment or harass.
7. **shucked** (shukt), stripped; cast off.

down and died. It was a good pup, was that Andrew Jackson, and would have made a name for hisself if he'd lived, for the stuff was in him and he had genius—I know it, because he hadn't no opportunities to speak of, and it don't stand to reason that a dog could make such a fight as he could under them circumstances if he hadn't no talent. It always makes me feel sorry when I think of that last fight of his'n and the way it turned out.

"Well, thish-yer Smiley had rat-tarriers, and chicken cocks, and tomcats and all them kind of things till you couldn't rest, and you couldn't fetch nothing for him to bet on but he'd match you. He ketched a frog one day and took him home, and said he cal'lated to educate him; and so he never done nothing for three months but set in his back yard and learn that frog to jump. And you bet you he *did* learn him, too. He'd give him a little punch behind, and the next minute you'd see that frog whirling in the air like a doughnut —see him turn one summerset, or maybe a couple if he got a good start, and come down flat-footed and all right, like a cat. He got him up so in the matter of ketching flies, and kep' him in practice so constant, that he'd nail a fly every time as fur as he could see him. Smiley said all a frog wanted was education and he could do 'most anything—and I believe him. Why, I've seen him set Dan'l Webster down here on this floor—Dan'l Webster was the name of the frog—and sing out, 'Flies, Dan'l, flies!' and quicker'n you could wink he'd spring straight up and snake a fly off'n the counter there, and flop down on the floor ag'in as solid as a gob of mud, and fall to scratching the side of his head with his hind foot as indifferent as if he hadn't no idea he'd been doin' any more'n any frog might do. You never see a frog so modest and straight-for'ard as he was, for all he was so gifted. And when it come to fair and square jumping on a dead level, he could get over more ground at one straddle than any animal of his breed you ever see. Jumping on a dead level was his strong suit, you understand; and when it come to that, Smiley would ante up money on

him as long as he had a red. Smiley was monstrous proud of his frog, and well he might be for fellers that had traveled and been everywheres all said he laid over any frog that ever *they* see.

"Well, Smiley kep' the beast in a little lattice box, and he used to fetch him down-town sometimes and lay for a bet. One day a feller —a stranger in the camp, he was—come acrost him with his box and says:

"'What might it be that you've got in the box?'

"And Smiley says, sorter indifferent-like, 'It might be a parrot, or it might be a canary, maybe, but it ain't—it's only just a frog.'

"And the feller took it and looked at it careful, and turned it round this way and that, and says, 'H'm—so 'tis. Well, what's *he* good for?'

"'Well,' Smiley says, easy and careless, 'he's good enough for *one* thing, I should judge—he can outjump any frog in Calaveras County.'

"The feller took the box again and took another long, particular look, and give it back to Smiley and says, very deliberate, 'Well,' he says, 'I don't see no p'ints about that frog that's any better'n any other frog.'

"'Maybe you don't,' Smiley says. 'Maybe you understand frogs and maybe you don't understand 'em; maybe you've had experience and maybe you ain't only a amature, as it were. Anyways, I've got *my* opinion, and I'll resk forty dollars that he can outjump any frog in Calaveras County.'

"And the feller studied a minute and then says, kinder sad-like, 'Well, I'm only a stranger here and I ain't got no frog; but if I had a frog, I'd bet you.'

"And then Smiley says, 'That's all right— that's all right—if you'll hold my box a minute, I'll go and get you a frog.' And so the feller took the box and put up his forty dollars along with Smiley's, and set down to wait.

"So he set there a good while thinking and thinking to himself, and then he got the frog out and prized his mouth open and took a teaspoon and filled him full of quail-shot—

filled him pretty near up to his chin—and set him on the floor. Smiley he went to the swamp and slopped around in the mud for a long time, and finally he ketched a frog and fetched him in and give him to this feller, and says:

" 'Now, if you're ready, set him alongside of Dan'l, with his forepaws just even with Dan'l's, and I'll give the word.' Then he says, 'One—two—three—*git!*' and him and the feller touched up the frogs from behind, and the new frog hopped off lively, but Dan'l give a heave and hysted up his shoulders—so—like a Frenchman, but it warn't no use—he couldn't budge; he was planted as solid as a church, and he couldn't no more stir than if he was anchored out. Smiley was a good deal surprised, and he was disgusted too, but he didn't have no idea what the matter was, of course.

"The feller took the money and started away, and when he was going out at the door, he sorter jerked his thumb over his shoulder —so—at Dan'l and says again, very deliberate, 'Well,' he says, '*I* don't see no p'ints about that frog that's any better'n any other frog.'

"Smiley he stood scratching his head and looking down at Dan'l a long time, and at last he says, 'I do wonder what in the nation that frog throw'd off for—I wonder if there ain't something the matter with him—he 'pears to look mighty baggy, somehow.' And he ketched Dan'l by the nap of the neck and hefted him, and says, 'Why, blame my cats if he don't weigh five pound!' and turned him upside down and he belched out a double handful of shot. And then he see how it was, and he was the maddest man—he set the frog down and took out after that feller, but he never ketched him. And—"

[Here Simon Wheeler heard his name called from the front yard and got up to see what was wanted.] And turning to me as he moved away, he said: "Just set where you are, stranger, and rest easy—I ain't going to be gone a second."

But, by your leave, I did not think that a continuation of the history of the enterprising vagabond *Jim* Smiley would be likely to afford me much information concerning the Rev. *Leonidas W*. Smiley and so I started away.

At the door I met the sociable Wheeler returning, and he buttonholed me and recommenced:

"Well, thish-yer Smiley had a yaller one-eyed cow that didn't have no tail, only just a short stump like a bannanner, and—"

However, lacking both time and inclination, I did not wait to hear about the afflicted cow but took my leave.

FOR UNDERSTANDING

1. How does Twain explain the fact that he asked old Simon Wheeler about Leonidas W. Smiley?
2. What evidence does Wheeler give to show that Smiley was a "betting fool"?
3. What did the mare and bull-pup have in common that made them good for finessing people?
4. How does the stranger finesse Smiley?

FOR INTERPRETATION

The West produced its legendary two-gun heroes of the "fast draw." The fact that Wheeler spoke of the two main characters of his yarn as "men of transcendent genius of finesse," implies admiration for another type of "hero" highly regarded in frontier society. Discuss the kind of character this would be.

FOR APPRECIATION

Humor
When "The Celebrated Jumping Frog" came out, even the eminent New Englander, James Russell Lowell, was ready to call it the "finest piece of humorous literature yet produced in America."
1. Twain's description of Simon Wheeler allows the reader to see the old storyteller as well as hear him. What are some of the details about his appearance and manner of speaking that make the yarn he tells especially funny?
2. Why do Twain's five short concluding paragraphs leave the reader laughing? How do they sustain Twain's humorous image of the old Western yarn-spinner?

from ROUGHING IT

My brother had just been appointed Secretary of Nevada Territory—an office of such majesty that it concentrated in itself the duties and dignities of Treasurer, Comptroller, Secretary of State, and Acting Governor in the Governor's absence. A salary of eighteen hundred dollars a year and the title of "Mr. Secretary," gave to the great position an air of wild and imposing grandeur. I was young and ignorant, and I envied my brother. I coveted his distinction and his financial splendor, but particularly and especially the long, strange journey he was going to make, and the curious new world he was going to explore. He was going to travel! I never had been away from home, and that word "travel" had a seductive charm for me. Pretty soon he would be hundreds and hundreds of miles away on the great plains and deserts, and among the mountains of the Far West, and would see buffaloes and Indians, and prairie-dogs, and antelopes, and have all kinds of adventures, and maybe get hanged or scalped, and have ever such a fine time, and write home and tell us all about it, and be a hero. And he would see the gold-mines and the silver-mines, and maybe go about of an afternoon when his work was done, and pick up two or three pailfuls of shining slugs and nuggets of gold and silver on the hillside. And by and by he would become very rich, and return home by sea, and be able to talk as calmly about San Francisco and the ocean and "the isthmus" as if it was nothing of any consequence to have seen those marvels face to face. What I suffered in contemplating his happiness, pen cannot describe. And so,

when he offered me, in cold blood, the sublime position of private secretary under him, it appeared to me that the heavens and the earth passed away, and the firmament was rolled together as a scroll! I had nothing more to desire. My contentment was complete. At the end of an hour or two I was ready for the journey. Not much packing up was necessary, because we were going in the overland stage from the Missouri frontier to Nevada, and passengers were only allowed a small quantity of baggage apiece. There was no Pacific railroad in those fine times of ten or twelve years ago—not a single rail of it.

I only proposed to stay in Nevada three months—I had no thought of staying longer than that. I meant to see all I could that was new and strange, and then hurry home to business. I little thought that I would not see the end of that three-month pleasure excursion for six or seven uncommonly long years!

I dreamed all night about Indians, deserts, and silver bars, and in due time, next day, we took shipping at the St. Louis wharf on board a steamboat bound up the Missouri River.

We were six days going from St. Louis to "St. Joe"—a trip that was so dull, and sleepy, and eventless that it has left no more impression on my memory than if its duration had been six minutes instead of that many days. . . .

The first thing we did on that glad evening that landed us at St. Joseph was to hunt up the stage-office, and pay a hundred and fifty dollars apiece for tickets per overland coach to Carson City, Nevada.

The next morning, bright and early, we took a hasty breakfast, and hurried to the starting-place. Then an inconvenience pre-

Abridged from Chapters 1, 2, 6 and 7 from ROUGHING IT, Vol. 1, by Mark Twain. Harper & Row, Publishers, Inc.

sented itself which we had not properly appreciated before, namely, that one cannot make a heavy traveling trunk stand for twenty-five pounds of baggage—because it weighs a good deal more. But that was all we could take—twenty-five pounds each. So we had to snatch our trunks open, and make a selection in a good deal of a hurry. We put our lawful twenty-five pounds apiece all in one valise, and shipped the trunks back to St. Louis again. It was a sad parting, for now we had no swallow-tail coats and white kid gloves to wear at Pawnee receptions in the Rocky Mountains, and no stove-pipe hats nor patent-leather boots, nor anything else necessary to make life calm and peaceful. We were reduced to a war-footing. Each of us put on a rough, heavy suit of clothing, woolen army shirt and "stogy"[1] boots included; and into the valise we crowded a few white shirts, some underclothing and such things. My brother, the Secretary, took along about four pounds of United States statutes and six pounds of Unabridged Dictionary; for we did not know —poor innocents—that such things could be bought in San Francisco on one day and received in Carson City the next. I was armed to the teeth with a pitiful little Smith & Wesson's seven-shooter, which carried a ball like a homeopathic[2] pill, and it took the whole seven to make a dose for an adult. But I thought it was grand. It appeared to me to be a dangerous weapon. It only had one fault—you could not hit anything with it. One of our "conductors" practiced awhile on a cow with it, and as long as she stood still and behaved herself she was safe; but as soon as she went to moving about, and he got to shooting at other things, she came to grief. The Secretary had a small-sized Colt's revolver strapped around him for protection against the Indians, and to guard against accidents he carried it uncapped. Mr. George Bemis was dismally formidable. George Bemis was our fellow-traveler. We had never seen him before. He wore in his belt an old original "Allen" revolver, such as

irreverent people called a "pepperbox." Simply drawing the trigger back, cocked and fired the pistol. As the trigger came back, the hammer would begin to rise and the barrel to turn over, and presently down would drop the hammer, and away would speed the ball. To aim along the turning barrel and hit the thing aimed at was a feat which was probably never done with an "Allen" in the world. But George's was a reliable weapon, nevertheless, because, as one of the stage-drivers afterward said, "If she didn't get what she went after, she would fetch something else." And so she did. She went after a deuce of spades nailed against a tree, once, and fetched a mule standing about thirty yards to the left of it. Bemis did not want the mule; but the owner came out with a double-barreled shotgun and persuaded him to buy it, anyhow. It was a cheerful weapon—the "Allen." Sometimes all its six barrels would go off at once, and then there was no safe place in all the region round about, but behind it.

We took two or three blankets for protection against frosty weather in the mountains. In the matter of luxuries we were modest— we took none along but some pipes and five pounds of smoking-tobacco. We had two large canteens to carry water in, between stations on the Plains, and we also took with us a little shot-bag of silver coin for daily expenses in the way of breakfasts and dinners.

By eight o'clock everything was ready, and we were on the other side of the river. We jumped into the stage, the driver cracked his whip, and we bowled away and left "the States" behind us. It was a superb summer morning, and all the landscape was brilliant with sunshine. There was a freshness and breeziness, too, and an exhilarating sense of

---

1. **stogy,** roughly made shoe or boot (after Conestoga, a town in Pennsylvania).

2. **homeopathic** (hō mē ə path′ ik), of or relating to a system of treating a disease by administering minute doses of a remedy that would produce the disease's symptoms in healthy people.

AMERICAN PASTURAGE—PRAIRIES OF THE PLATTE, George Catlin
National Gallery of Art, Washington, D.C., Paul Mellon Collection

emancipation from all sorts of cares and responsibilities, that almost made us feel that the years we had spent in the close, hot city, toiling and slaving, had been wasted and thrown away. We were spinning along through Kansas, and in the course of an hour and a half we were fairly abroad on the great Plains. Just here the land was rolling—a grand sweep of regular elevations and depressions as far as the eye could reach—like the stately heave and swell of the ocean's bosom after a storm. And everywhere were corn-fields, accenting with squares of deeper green this limitless expanse of grassy land. But presently this sea upon dry ground was to lose its "rolling" character and stretch away for seven hundred miles as level as a floor!

Our coach was a great swinging and swaying stage, of the most sumptuous description—an imposing cradle on wheels. It was drawn by six handsome horses, and by the side of the driver sat the "conductor," the legitimate captain of the craft; for it was his business to take charge and care of the mails, baggage, express matter, and passengers. We three were the only passengers, this trip. We sat on the back seat, inside. About all the rest of the coach was full of mail-bags—for we had three days' delayed mails with us. Almost touching our knees, a perpendicular wall of mail matter rose up to the roof. There was a great pile of it strapped on top of the stage, and both the fore and hind boots were full. . . .

We changed horses every ten miles, all day long, and fairly flew over the hard, level road. We jumped out and stretched our legs every time the coach stopped, and so the night found us still vivacious and unfatigued. . . .

At noon on the fifth day out, we arrived at the "Crossing of the South Platte," *alias* "Julesburg," *alias* "Overland City," four hundred and seventy miles from St. Joseph—the strangest, quaintest, funniest frontier town that our untraveled eyes had ever stared at and been astonished with.

It did seem strange enough to see a town again after what appeared to us such a long acquaintance with deep, still, almost lifeless and houseless solitude! We tumbled out into the busy street feeling like meteoric people crumbled off the corner of some other world, and wakened up suddenly in this. For an hour we took as much interest in Overland City as if we had never seen a town before. The reason we had an hour to spare was because we had to change our stage (for a less sumptuous affair, called a "mud-wagon") and transfer our freight of mails.

Presently we got under way again. We came to the shallow, yellow, muddy South Platte, with its low banks and its scattering flat sand-bars and pygmy islands—a melancholy stream straggling through the center of the enormous flat plain, and only saved from being impossible to find with the naked eye by its sentinel rank of scattering trees standing on either bank. The Platte was "up," they said—which made me wish I could see it when it was down, if it could look any sicker and sorrier. They said it was a dangerous stream to cross, now, because its quicksands were liable to swallow up horses, coach, and passengers if an attempt was made to ford it. But the mails had to go, and we made the attempt. Once or twice in midstream the wheels sunk into the yielding sands so threateningly

that we half believed we had dreaded and avoided the sea all our lives to be shipwrecked in a "mud-wagon" in the middle of a desert at last. But we dragged through and sped away toward the setting sun.

Next morning just before dawn, when about five hundred and fifty miles from St. Joseph, our mud-wagon broke down. We were to be delayed five or six hours, and therefore we took horses, by invitation, and joined a party who were just starting on a buffalo-hunt. It was noble sport galloping over the plain in the dewy freshness of the morning, but our part of the hunt ended in disaster and disgrace, for a wounded buffalo bull chased the passenger Bemis nearly two miles, and then he forsook his horse and took to a lone tree. He was very sullen about the matter for some twenty-four hours, but at last he began to soften little by little, and finally he said:

"Well, it was not funny, and there was no sense in those gawks making themselves so facetious over it. I tell you I was angry in earnest for a while. I should have shot that long gangly lubber they called Hank, if I could have done it without crippling six or seven other people—but of course I couldn't, the old 'Allen''s so confounded comprehensive. I wish those loafers had been up in the tree; they wouldn't have wanted to laugh so. If I had had a horse worth a cent—but no, the minute he saw that buffalo bull wheel on him and give a bellow, he raised straight up in the air and stood on his heels. The saddle began to slip, and I took him round the neck and laid close to him, and began to pray. Then he came down and stood up on the other end awhile, and the bull actually stopped pawing sand and bellowing to contemplate the inhuman spectacle. Then the bull made a pass at him and uttered a bellow that sounded perfectly frightful, it was so close to me, and that seemed to literally prostrate my horse's reason, and make a raving distracted maniac of him, and I wish I may die if he didn't stand on his head for a quarter of a minute and shed tears. He was absolutely out of his mind —he was, as sure as truth itself, and he really didn't know what he was doing. Then the bull came charging at us, and my horse dropped down on all fours and took a fresh start—and then for the next ten minutes he would actually throw one handspring after another so fast that the bull began to get unsettled, too, and didn't know where to start in—and so he stood there sneezing, and shoveling dust over his back, and bellowing every now and then, and thinking he had got a fifteen-hundred-dollar circus horse for breakfast, certain. Well, I was first out on his neck—the horse's, not the bull's—and then underneath, and next on his rump, and sometimes head up, and sometimes heels—but I tell you it seemed solemn and awful to be ripping and tearing and carrying on so in the presence of death, as you might say. Pretty soon the bull made a snatch for us and brought away some of my horse's tail (I suppose, but do not know, being pretty busy at the time), but *something* made him hungry for solitude and suggested to him to get up and hunt for it. And then you ought to have seen that spider-legged old skeleton go! and you ought to have seen the bull cut out after him, too—head down, tongue out, tail up, bellowing like everything, and actually mowing down the weeds, and tearing up the earth, and boosting up the sand like a whirlwind! By George, it was a hot race! I and the saddle were back on the rump, and I had the bridle in my teeth and holding on to the pommel with both hands. First we left the dogs behind; then we passed a jackass-rabbit; then we overtook a coyote, and were gaining on an antelope when the rotten girths let go and threw me about thirty yards off to the left, and as the saddle went down over the horse's rump he gave it a lift with his heels that sent it more than four hundred yards up in the air, I wish I may die in a minute if he didn't. I fell at the foot of the only solitary tree there was in nine counties adjacent (as any creature could see with the naked eye), and the next second I had hold of the

bark with four sets of nails and my teeth, and the next second after that I was astraddle of the main limb and blaspheming my luck in a way that made my breath smell of brimstone. I *had* the bull, now, if he did not think of *one* thing. But that one thing I dreaded. I dreaded it very seriously. There was a possibility that the bull might not think of it, but there were greater chances that he would. I made up my mind what I would do in case he did. It was a little over forty feet to the ground from where I sat. I cautiously unwound the lariat from the pommel of my saddle—"

"Your *saddle*? Did you take your saddle up in the tree with you?"

"Take it up in the tree with me? Why, how you talk! Of course I didn't. No man could do that. It *fell* in the tree when it came down."

"Oh—exactly."

"Certainly. I unwound the lariat, and fastened one end of it to the limb. It was the very best green rawhide, and capable of sustaining tons. I made a slip-noose in the other end, and then hung it down to see the length. It reached down twenty-two feet—half-way to the ground. I then loaded every barrel of the Allen with a double charge. I felt satisfied. I said to myself, if he never thinks of that one thing that I dread, all right—but if he does, all right anyhow—I am fixed for him. But don't you know that the very thing a man dreads is the thing that always happens? Indeed it is so. I watched the bull, now, with anxiety—anxiety which no one can conceive of who has not been in such a situation and felt that at any moment death might come. Presently a thought came into the bull's eye. I knew it! said I—if my nerve fails now, I am lost. Sure enough, it was just as I had dreaded, he started in to climb the tree—"

"What, the bull?"

"Of course—who else?"

"But a bull can't climb a tree."

"He can't, can't he? Since you know so much about it, did you ever see a bull try?"

"No! I never dreamt of such a thing."

"Well, then, what is the use of your talking that way then? Because you never saw a thing done, is that any reason why it can't be done?"

"Well, all right—go on. What did you do?"

"The bull started up, and got along well for about ten feet, then slipped and slid back. I breathed easier. He tried it again—got up a little higher—slipped again. But he came at it once more, and this time he was careful. He got gradually higher and higher, and my spirits went down more and more. Up he came—an inch at a time—with his eyes hot, and his tongue hanging out. Higher and higher—hitched his foot over the stump of a limb, and looked up, as much as to say, 'You are my meat, friend.' Up again—higher and higher, and getting more excited the closer he got. He was within ten feet of me! I took a long breath—and then said I, 'It is now or never.' I had the coil of the lariat all ready; I paid it out slowly, till it hung right over his head; all of a sudden I let go of the slack and the slip-noose fell fairly round his neck! Quicker than lightning I out with the Allen and let him have it in the face. It was an awful roar, and must have scared the bull out of his senses. When the smoke cleared away, there he was, dangling in the air, twenty foot from the ground, and going out of one convulsion into another faster than you could count! I didn't stop to count, anyhow—I shinned down the tree and shot for home."

"Bemis, is all that true, just as you have stated it?"

"I wish I may rot in my tracks and die the death of a dog if it isn't."

"Well, we can't refuse to believe it, and we don't. But if there were some proofs—"

"Proofs! Did I bring back my lariat?"

"No."

"Did I bring back my horse?"

"No."

"Did you ever see the bull again?"

"No."

"Well, then, what more do you want? I never saw anybody as particular as you are about a little thing like that."

I made up my mind that if this man was not a liar he only missed it by the skin of his teeth.

FOR UNDERSTANDING

1. What circumstances gave young Twain the opportunity to go to the Nevada Territory?
2. Describe the make and accuracy of the guns Twain and Bemis carried.
3. How did the stage passengers come to take part in a buffalo hunt, and who narrates the buffalo story?
4. What are some of the particularly ludicrous details that strain the believability of his story?
5. What evidence does he give to prove that the tall tale he has told is true?

FOR INTERPRETATION

Discuss Twain's use of irony in the following quotations:
1. He would . . . have all kinds of adventures, and maybe get hanged or scalped, and have ever such a fine time. . . . And he would see gold mines . . . and pick up two or three pailfuls of shining slugs and nuggets of gold and silver on the hillside. And . . . he would become very rich. . . .
2. Now we had no swallow-tail coats and white kid gloves to wear at Pawnee receptions in the Rocky Mountains, and no stove-pipe hats nor patent-leather boots, nor anything else necessary to make life calm and peaceful.

FOR APPRECIATION

The Tall Tale

The tall tale, boasting such famed heroes as Paul Bunyan, Davy Crockett, and Mike Fink, is recognized as an American literary genre and depends upon outlandish exaggeration for its humor. It originated in frontier conditions when men, far from any settlement, entertained themselves by "swapping lies" around their lonely campfires, with each storyteller trying to outdo those who had preceded him.

The accounts of the jumping frog and the tree-climbing buffalo bull demonstrate Twain's skill at writing the tall tale so that he holds the reader's interest throughout. After easing into a situation plausibly, he deftly supplies details that entice his audience into a properly appreciative mood before narrating the "main event."

1. Prior to Bemis's ridiculous tale about the buffalo, how does Twain characterize the luckless fellow so that the reader expects his truly ridiculous conduct?

2. Aside from the numerous exaggerated details, what factual information about the habits and capabilities of buffalo makes the whole of Bemis's yarn a preposterous "stretching" of the truth?

LANGUAGE AND VOCABULARY

Dialect: Vernacular Style

Reflecting the oral tradition of humorous storytelling so important to early Americans, Mark Twain wrote for the ear rather than the eye. Almost from the beginning of American literature, American writers made use of dialect to give their writing the *sound* of speaking. *Dialect* may be defined as the spoken language peculiar to people of a particular region, occupation, or social class. New England journalist Seba Smith (1792–1868), for example, in establishing the character of Jack Downing in his newspaper columns, had Downing's speech reveal his backwoods upbringing and lack of higher education. As a young man growing up, Twain was sharply aware of dialect differences and, in adopting a *vernacular style* of writing, he was responsible for raising the art of imitating the everyday, spoken language of people of different localities or occupations to recognized literary status. For *The Adventures of Huckleberry Finn*, in particular, Twain was accorded worldwide acclaim for his demonstrated skill in recording dialects.

The popularity of the humorous monologue, which reached its height in the middle of the nineteenth century, also influenced the development of Twain's writing style. Charles Farrar Brown, writing sketches and speaking on the lecture circuit under the pseudonym Artemus Ward, was the best-known of these professional humorists. He deliberately violated all rules for correct spelling and proper grammar to set forth his gems of shrewd common sense in an exaggeratedly uneducated dialect. It was Ward who first encouraged Twain to write down his rendition of "The Celebrated Jumping Frog" for publication.

1. In "The Celebrated Jumping Frog" Twain imitates the dialect of the Westerner to help the reader *hear* Simon Wheeler speak. Look back over the selection and make a list of usage and vocabulary items as well as colloquialisms that imitate Western dialect in the first paragraph of Wheeler's yarn.

2. Bemis, in the selection from *Roughing It*, is apparently a Midwesterner. In the four opening sentences of his yarn, what does he call persons laughing at his predicament? As he continues his tale, what is the repeated protestation he makes to convince his listeners of his truthfulness? With what two colloquialisms does he expand his last protestation?

COMPOSITION

Short, funny yarns or humorous sketches appeared regularly in many nineteenth-century newspapers and were popular with readers.

Write such a short sketch, describing a storyteller in one or two beginning paragraphs. Then have your storyteller use colloquial speech (either past or present-day) to narrate a yarn or an anecdote that may either be within the bounds of believability or be a tall tale, depending upon the extent of exaggeration you wish to employ.

from THE ADVENTURES OF HUCKLEBERRY FINN

As Huck and Jim float down the Mississippi at night on their raft, hoping to leave it at Cairo, Illinois, and take a steamboat up the Ohio into free territory, they are forced to dive overboard when the raft is overrun and damaged by a steamer in the thick fog. Unable to locate Jim, Huck swims ashore and, assuming the name George Jackson, gains shelter with the Grangerfords who are feuding with their neighbors, the Shepherdsons. In these chapters, Huck's temporary separation from Jim allows Twain to focus on what he feels to be the artificiality and sentimentality of an aristocracy maintaining itself in a raw, frontier situation. As this adventure begins, Huck, after pulling himself out of the river, has just come across a big, old-fashioned log house back from the water's edge. In his words: "I was going to rush by and get away, but a lot of dogs jumped out and went to howling and barking at me, and I knowed better than to move another peg."

Chapter XVII

In about half a minute somebody spoke out of a window, without putting his head out, and says:

"Be done, boys! Who's there?"

I says:

"It's me."

"Who's me?"

"George Jackson, sir."

"What do you want?"

"I don't want nothing, sir. I only want to go along by, but the dogs won't let me."

"What are you prowling around here this time of night for—hey?"

"I warn't prowling around, sir; I fell overboard off of the steamboat."

"Oh, you did, did you? Strike a light there, somebody. What did you say your name was?"

"George Jackson, sir. I'm only a boy."

"Look here; if you're telling the truth, you needn't be afraid—nobody'll hurt you. But don't try to budge; stand right where you are. Rouse out Bob and Tom, some of you, and fetch the guns. George Jackson, is there anybody with you?"

"No, sir, nobody."

I heard the people stirring around in the house, now, and see a light. The man sung out:

"Snatch that light away, Betsy, you old fool—ain't you got any sense? Put it on the floor behind the front door. Bob, if you and Tom are ready, take your places."

"All ready."

"Now, George Jackson, do you know the Shepherdsons?"

"No, sir—I never heard of them."

"Well, that may be so, and it mayn't. Now, all ready. Step forward, George Jackson. And mind, don't you hurry—come mighty slow. If there's anybody with you, let him keep back—if he shows himself he'll be shot. Come along, now. Come slow; push the door open, yourself—just enough to squeeze in, d' you hear?"

I didn't hurry, I couldn't if I'd a wanted to. I took one slow step at a time, and there warn't a sound, only I thought I could hear my heart. The dogs were as still as the humans, but they followed a little behind me. When I got to the three log doorsteps, I heard them unlocking and unbarring and

Chapters 17 & 18 from THE ADVENTURES OF HUCKLEBERRY FINN by Mark Twain. Harper & Row, Publishers, Inc.

Hannibal, Missouri: Twain's childhood home and the setting for many of Tom Sawyer's and Huck Finn's adventures. Years later, Twain was to write nostalgically of Hannibal in his Autobiography: *"I can call back the solemn twilight and mystery of the deep woods, the earthy smells, the faint odors of the wild flowers, the sheen of rain-washed foliage."*

unbolting. I put my hand on the door and pushed it a little and a little more, till somebody said, "There, that's enough—put your head in." I done it, but I judged they would take it off.

The candle was on the floor, and there they all was, looking at me, and me at them, for about a quarter of a minute. Three big men with guns pointed at me, which made me wince, I tell you; the oldest, gray and about sixty, the other two thirty or more—all of them fine and handsome—and the sweetest old gray-headed lady, and back of her two young women which I couldn't see right well. The old gentleman says:

"There—I reckon it's all right. Come in."

As soon as I was in, the old gentleman he locked the door and barred it and bolted it, and told the young men to come in with their guns, and they all went in a big parlor that had a new rag carpet on the floor, and got together in a corner that was out of range of the front windows—there warn't none on the side. They held the candle, and took a good look at me, and all said, "Why *he* ain't a Shepherdson—no, there ain't any Shepherdson about him." Then the old man said he hoped I wouldn't mind being searched for arms, because he didn't mean no harm by it—it was only to make sure. So he didn't pry into my pockets, but only felt outside with his hands, and said it was all right. He told me to make myself easy and at home, and tell all about myself; but the old lady says:

"Why bless you, Saul, the poor thing's as wet as he can be; and don't you reckon it may be he's hungry?"

"True for you, Rachel—I forgot."

So the old lady says to the Negro woman:

"Betsy, you fly around and get him something to eat, as quick as you can, poor thing; and one of you girls go and wake up Buck and tell him—Oh, here he is himself. Buck, take this little stranger and get the wet clothes off from him and dress him up in some of yours that's dry."

Buck looked about as old as me—thirteen or fourteen or along there, though he was a little bigger than me. He hadn't on anything but a shirt, and he was very frowsy-headed. He come in gaping and digging one fist into his eyes, and he was dragging a gun along with the other one. He says:

"Ain't they no Shepherdsons around?"

They said, no, 'twas a false alarm.

"Well," he says, "if they'd a ben some, I reckon I'd a got one."

They all laughed, and Bob says:

"Why, Buck, they might have scalped us all, you've been so slow in coming."

"Well, nobody come after me, and it ain't right. I'm always kep' down; I don't get no show."

"Never mind, Buck, my boy," says the old man, "you'll have show enough, all in good time, don't you fret about that. Go 'long with you now, and do as your mother told you."

When we got up stairs to his room, he got me a coarse shirt and a roundabout[1] and pants of his, and I put them on. While I was at it he asked me what my name was, but before I could tell him, he started to telling me about a blue jay and a young rabbit he had catched in the woods day before yesterday, and he asked me where Moses was when the candle went out. I said I didn't know; I hadn't heard about it before, no way.

"Well, guess," he says.

"How'm I going to guess," says I, "when I never heard tell about it before?"

"But you can guess, can't you? It's just as easy."

"Which candle?" I says.

"Why, any candle," he says.

"I don't know where he was," says I; "where was he?"

"Why he was in the *dark!* That's where he was!"

"Well, if you knowed where he was, what did you ask me for?"

"Why, blame it, it's a riddle, don't you see? Say, how long are you going to stay here? You got to stay always. We can just have booming times—they don't have no school now. Do you own a dog? I've got a dog—and he'll go in the river and bring out chips that you throw in. Do you like to comb up, Sundays, and all that kind of foolishness? You bet I don't, but ma she makes me. Confound these ole britches, I reckon I'd better put 'em on, but I'd rather not, it's so warm. Are you all ready? All right—come along, old hoss."

Cold corn-pone, cold corn-beef, butter and butter-milk—that is what they had for me down there, and there ain't nothing better that ever I've come across yet. Buck and his ma and all of them smoked cob pipes, except the Negro woman, which was gone, and the two young women. They all smoked and talked, and I eat and talked. The young women had quilts around them, and their hair down their backs. They all asked me questions, and I told them how pap and me and all the family was living on a little farm down at the bottom of Arkansaw, and my sister Mary Ann run off and got married and never was heard of no more, and Bill went to hunt them and he warn't heard of no more, and Tom and Mort died, and then there warn't nobody but just me and pap left, and he was just trimmed down to nothing, on ac-

---

1. **roundabout,** a short, close-fitting jacket.

count of his troubles; so when he died I took what there was left, because the farm didn't belong to us, and started up the river, deck passage, and fell overboard; and that was how I come to be here. So they said I could have a home there as long as I wanted it. Then it was most daylight, and everybody went to bed, and I went to bed with Buck, and when I waked up in the morning, drat it all, I had forgot what my name was. So I laid there about an hour trying to think, and when Buck waked up, I says:

"Can you spell, Buck?"

"Yes," he says.

"I bet you can't spell my name," says I.

"I bet you what you dare I can," says he.

"All right," says I, "go ahead."

"G-o-r-g-e J-a-x-o-n—there now," he says.

"Well," says I, "you done it, but I didn't think you could. It ain't no slouch of a name to spell—right off without studying."

I set it down, private, because somebody might want *me* to spell it, next, and so I wanted to be handy with it and rattle it off like I was used to it.

It was a mighty nice family, and a mighty nice house, too. I hadn't seen no house out in the country before that was so nice and had so much style. It didn't have an iron latch on the front door, nor a wooden one with a buckskin string, but a brass knob to turn, the same as houses in a town. There warn't no bed in the parlor, not a sign of a bed; but heaps of parlors in towns has beds in them. There was a big fireplace that was bricked on the bottom, and the bricks was kept clean and red by pouring water on them and scrubbing them with another brick; sometimes they washed them over with red water-paint that they call Spanish-brown, same as they do in town. They had big brass dog-irons that could hold up a saw log. There was a clock on the middle of the mantel-piece, with a picture of a town painted on the bottom half of the glass front, and a round place in the middle of it for the sun, and you could see the pen-

dulum swing behind it. It was beautiful to hear that clock tick; and sometimes when one of these peddlers had been along and scoured her up and got her in good shape, she would start in and strike a hundred and fifty before she got tuckered out. They wouldn't took any money for her.

Well, there was a big outlandish parrot on each side of the clock, made out of something like chalk, and painted up gaudy. By one of the parrots was a cat made of crockery, and a crockery dog by the other; and when you pressed down on them they squeaked, but didn't open their mouths nor look different nor interested. They squeaked through underneath. There was a couple of big wild-turkey-wing fans spread out behind those things. On a table in the middle of the room was a kind of a lovely crockery basket that had apples and oranges and peaches and grapes piled up in it which was much redder and yellower and prettier than real ones is, but they warn't real because you could see where pieces had got chipped off and showed the white chalk or whatever it was, underneath.

This table had a cover made out of beautiful oil-cloth, with a red and blue spread-eagle painted on it, and a painted border all around. It come all the way from Philadelphia, they said. There was some books too, piled up perfectly exact, on each corner of the table. One was a big family Bible, full of pictures. One was "Pilgrim's Progress,"[2] about a man that left his family it didn't say why. I read considerable in it now and then. The statements was interesting, but tough. Another was "Friendship's Offering,"[3] full of beautiful stuff and poetry; but I didn't read the poetry. Another was Henry Clay's Speeches, and another was Dr. Gunn's Family Medicine, which told you all about what to do

2. **Pilgrim's Progress,** a famous book by John Bunyan (1678), relating life of a Christian in allegory.
3. **Friendship's Offering,** a publication of sentimental verse and sketches.

if a body was sick or dead. There was a Hymn Book, and a lot of other books. And there was nice split-bottom chairs, and perfectly sound, too—not bagged down in the middle and busted, like an old basket.

They had pictures hung on the walls—mainly Washingtons and Lafayettes, and battles, and Highland Marys,[4] and one called "Signing the Declaration." There was some that they called crayons, which one of the daughters which was dead made her own self when she was only fifteen years old. They was different from any pictures I ever see before; blacker, mostly, than is common. One was a woman in a slim black dress, belted small under the arm-pits, with bulges like a cabbage in the middle of the sleeves, and a large black scoop-shovel bonnet with a black veil, and white slim ankles crossed about with black tape, and very wee black slippers, like a chisel, and she was leaning pensive on a tombstone on her right elbow, under a weeping willow, and her other hand hanging down her side holding a white handkerchief and a reticule,[5] and underneath the picture it said "Shall I Never See Thee More Alas." Another one was a young lady with her hair all combed up straight to the top of her head, and knotted there in front of a comb like a chair-back, and she was crying into a handkerchief and had a dead bird laying on its back in her other hand with its heels up, and underneath the picture it said "I Shall Never Hear Thy Sweet Chirrup More Alas." There was one where a young lady was at a window looking up at the moon, and tears running down her cheeks; and she had an open letter in one hand with black sealing-wax showing on one edge of it, and she was mashing a locket with a chain to it against her mouth, and underneath the picture it said "And Art Thou Gone Yes Thou Art Gone Alas." These was all nice pictures, I reckon, but I didn't somehow seem to take to them, because if ever I was down a little, they always give me the fan-tods.[6] Everybody was sorry she died, because she had laid out a lot more of these pictures to do, and a body could see by what she had done what they

had lost. But I reckoned, that with her disposition, she was having a better time in the graveyard. She was at work on what they said was her greatest picture when she took sick, and every day and every night it was her prayer to be allowed to live till she got it done, but she never got the chance. It was a picture of a young woman in a long white gown, standing on the rail of a bridge all ready to jump off, with her hair all down her back, and looking up to the moon, with the tears running down her face, and she had two arms folded across her breast, and two arms stretched out in front, and two more reaching up towards the moon—and the idea was, to see which pair would look best and then scratch out all the other arms; but, as I was saying, she died before she got her mind made up, and now they kept this picture over the head of the bed in her room, and every time her birthday come they hung flowers on it. Other times it was hid with a little curtain. The young woman in the picture had a kind of a nice sweet face, but there was so many arms it made her look too spidery, seemed to me.

This young girl kept a scrap-book when she was alive, and used to paste obituaries and accidents and cases of patient suffering in it out of the *Presbyterian Observer,* and write poetry after them out of her own head. It was very good poetry. This is what she wrote about a boy by the name of Stephen Dowling Bots that fell down a well and was drownded:

ODE TO STEPHEN DOWLING BOTS, DEC'D.

And did young Stephen sicken,
And did young Stephen die?
And did the sad hearts thicken,
And did the mourners cry?

---

4. **Highland Mary,** believed to be Mary Campbell, supposedly a sweetheart of Robert Burns (1759–1796) and the woman to whom he addressed some of his sentimental verse.
5. **reticule** (ret′ ə kyül), a woman's handbag, originally made of net.
6. **fan-tods,** an attack of fidgeting.

No; such was not the fate of
　　Young Stephen Dowling Bots;
Though sad hearts round him thickened,
　　'Twas not from sickness' shots.

No whooping-cough did rack his frame,
　　Nor measles drear, with spots;
Not these impaired the sacred name
　　Of Stephen Dowling Bots.

Despised love struck not with woe
　　That head of curly knots,
Nor stomach troubles laid him low,
　　Young Stephen Dowling Bots.

O no. Then list with tearful eye,
　　Whilst I his fate do tell.
His soul did from this cold world fly,
　　By falling down a well.

They got him out and emptied him;
　　Alas it was too late;
His spirit was gone for to sport aloft
　　In the realms of the good and great.

If Emmeline Grangerford could make poetry like that before she was fourteen, there ain't no telling what she could a done by-and-by. Buck said she could rattle off poetry like nothing. She didn't ever have to stop to think. He said she would slap down a line, and if she couldn't find anything to rhyme with it she would just scratch it out and slap down another one, and go ahead. She warn't particular, she could write about anything you choose to give her to write about, just so it was sadful. Every time a man died, or a woman died, or a child died, she would be on hand with her "tribute" before he was cold. She called them tributes. The neighbors said it was the doctor first, then Emmeline, then the undertaker—the undertaker never got in ahead of Emmeline but once, and then she hung fire on a rhyme for the dead person's name, which was Whistler. She warn't ever the same, after that; she never complained, but she kind of pined away and did not live long. Poor thing, many's the time I made my-self go up to the little room that used to be hers and get out her poor old scrap-book and read in it when her pictures had been aggravating me and I had soured on her a little. I liked all that family, dead ones and all, and warn't going to let anything come between us. Poor Emmeline made poetry about all the dead people when she was alive, and it didn't seem right that there warn't nobody to make some about her, now she was gone; so I tried to sweat out a verse or two myself, but I couldn't seem to make it go, somehow. They kept Emmeline's room trim and nice and all the things fixed in it just the way she liked to have them when she was alive, and nobody ever slept there. The old lady took care of the room herself, and she sewed there a good deal and read her Bible there, mostly.

Well, as I was saying about the parlor, there was beautiful curtains on the windows: white, with pictures painted on them, of castles with vines all down the walls, and cattle coming down to drink. There was a little old piano, too, that had tin pans in it, I reckon, and nothing was ever so lovely as to hear the young ladies sing, "The Last Link Is Broken" and play "The Battle of Prague" on it. The walls of all the rooms was plastered, and most had carpets on the floors, and the whole house was whitewashed on the outside.

It was a double house, and the big open place betwixt them was roofed and floored, and sometimes the table was set there in the middle of the day, and it was a cool, comfortable place. Nothing couldn't be better. And warn't the cooking good, and just bushels of it too!

Chapter XVIII

Col. Grangerford was a gentleman, you see. He was a gentleman all over; and so was his family. He was well born, as the saying is, and that's worth as much in a man as it is in a horse, so the Widow Douglas said, and nobody ever denied that she was of the first aristocracy in our town; and pap he always said it, too, though he warn't no more quality than a mudcat, himself. Col. Grangerford was very tall and very slim, and had a darkish-paly complexion, not a sign of red in it anywheres; he was clean-shaved every morning, all over his thin face, and he had the thinnest kind of lips, and the thinnest kind of nostrils, and a high nose, and heavy eyebrows, and the blackest kind of eyes, sunk so deep back that they seemed like they was looking out of caverns at you, as you may say. His forehead was high, and his hair was black and straight, and hung to his shoulders. His hands was long and thin, and every day of his life he put on a clean shirt and a full suit from head to foot made out of linen so white it hurt your eyes to look at it; and on Sundays he wore a blue tail-coat with brass buttons on it. He carried a mahogany cane with a silver head to it. There warn't no frivolishness about him, not a bit, and he warn't ever loud. He was as kind as he could be—you could feel that, you know, and so you had confidence. Sometimes he smiled, and it was good to see; but when he straightened himself up like a liberty-pole, and the lightning begun to flicker out from under his eyebrows you wanted to climb a tree first, and find out what the matter was afterwards. He didn't ever have to tell anybody to mind their manners—everybody was always good mannered where he was. Everybody loved to have him around, too; he was sunshine most always—I mean he made it seem like good weather. When he turned into a cloud-bank it was awful dark for a half a minute and that was enough; there wouldn't nothing go wrong again for a week.

When him and the old lady come down in the morning, all the family got up out of their chairs and give them good-day, and didn't set down again till they had set down. Then Tom and Bob went to the sideboard where the decanters was, and mixed a glass of bitters and handed it to him, and he held it in his hand and waited till Tom's and Bob's was mixed, and then they bowed and said "Our duty to you, sir, and madam;" and *they* bowed the

least bit in the world and said thank you, and so they drank, all three. . . .

Bob was the oldest, and Tom next. Tall, beautiful men with very broad shoulders and brown faces, and long black hair and black eyes. They dressed in white linen from head to foot, like the old gentleman, and wore broad Panama hats.

Then there was Miss Charlotte, she was twenty-five, and tall and proud and grand, but as good as she could be, when she warn't stirred up; but when she was, she had a look that would make you wilt in your tracks, like her father. She was beautiful.

So was her sister, Miss Sophia, but it was a different kind. She was gentle and sweet, like a dove, and she was only twenty.

Each person had their own servant to wait on them—Buck, too. My servant had a monstrous easy time, because I warn't used to having anybody do anything for me, but Buck's was on the jump most of the time.

This was all there was of the family, now; but there used to be more—three sons; they got killed; and Emmeline that died.

The old gentleman owned a lot of farms and over a hundred Negroes. Sometimes a stack of people would come there, horseback, from ten or fifteen mile around, and stay five or six days, and have such junketings round about and on the river, and dances and picnics in the woods, day-times, and balls at the house, nights. These people was mostly kinfolks of the family. The men brought their guns with them. It was a handsome lot of quality, I tell you.

There was another clan of aristocracy around there—five or six families—mostly of the name of Shepherdson. They was as high-toned, and well born, and rich and grand, as the tribe of Grangerfords. The Shepherdsons and the Grangerfords used the same steamboat landing, which was about two mile above our house; so sometimes when I went up there with a lot of our folks I used to see a lot of the Shepherdsons there, on their fine horses.

One day Buck and me was away out in the woods, hunting, and heard a horse coming. We was crossing the road. Buck says:

"Quick! Jump for the woods!"

We done it, and then peeped down the woods through the leaves. Pretty soon a splendid young man come galloping down the road, setting his horse easy and looking like a soldier. He had his gun across his pommel. I had seen him before. It was young Harney Shepherdson. I heard Buck's gun go off at my ear, and Harney's hat tumbled off from his head. He grabbed his gun and rode straight to the place where we was hid. But we didn't wait. We started through the woods on a run. The woods warn't thick, so I looked over my shoulder, to dodge the bullet, and twice I seen Harney cover Buck with his gun; and then he rode away the way he come—to get his hat, I reckon, but I couldn't see. We never stopped running till we got home. The old gentleman's eyes blazed a minute—'twas pleasure, mainly, I judged—then his face sort of smoothed down, and he says, kind of gentle:

"I don't like that shooting from behind a bush. Why didn't you step into the road, my boy?"

"The Shepherdsons don't, father. They always take advantage."

Miss Charlotte she held her head up like a queen while Buck was telling his tale, and her nostrils spread and her eyes snapped. The two young men looked dark, but never said nothing. Miss Sophia she turned pale, but the color come back when she found the man warn't hurt.

Soon as I could get Buck down by the corncribs under the trees by ourselves, I says:

"Did you want to kill him, Buck?"

"Well, I bet I did."

"What did he do to you?"

"Him? He never done nothing to me."

"Well, then, what did you want to kill him for?"

"Why nothing—only it's on account of the feud."

"What's a feud?"

"Why, where was you raised? Don't you know what a feud is?"

"Never heard of it before—tell me about it."

"Well," says Buck, "a feud is this way. A man has a quarrel with another man, and kills him; then that other man's brother kills *him;* then the other brothers, on both sides, goes for one another; then the *cousins* chip in—and by-and-by everybody's killed off, and there ain't no more feud. But it's kind of slow, and takes a long time."

"Has this one been going on long, Buck?"

"Well I should *reckon!* it started thirty year ago, or som'ers along there. There was trouble 'bout something and then a lawsuit to settle it; and the suit went agin one of the men, and so he up and shot the man that won the suit—which he would naturally do, of course. Anybody would."

"What was the trouble about, Buck?—land?"

"I reckon maybe—I don't know."

"Well, who done the shooting?—was it a Grangerford or a Shepherdson?"

"Laws, how do *I* know? it was so long ago."

"Don't anybody know?"

"Oh, yes, pa knows, I reckon, and some of the other old folks; but they don't know, now, what the row was about in the first place."

Huck learns through his servant, Jack, that Jim has salvaged the raft and is safely hidden on a little island in the nearby swamp. After the Grangerford family has returned from Sunday services, Sophia asks Huck to go back to the church to get her New Testament for her. He sees a slip of paper in it with a time written on it. The following morning he learns that Sophia has eloped with Harney Shepherdson; the two families are engaged in bloody fighting. Buck is killed along with most of the men in his family. Huck sees the sickening carnage from the fork of a cottonwood tree in which he hides.

I staid in the tree till it begun to get dark, afraid to come down. Sometimes I heard guns away off in the woods; and twice I seen little gangs of men gallop past the log store with guns; so I reckoned the trouble was still agoing on. I was mighty down-hearted; so I made up my mind I wouldn't ever go anear that house again, because I reckoned I was to blame, somehow. I judged that that piece of paper meant that Miss Sophia was to meet Harney somewheres at half-past two and run off; and I judged I ought to told her father about that paper and the curious way she acted, and then maybe he would a locked her up and this awful mess wouldn't ever happened. . . .

It was just dark, now. I never went near the house, but struck through the woods and made for the swamp. Jim warn't on his island, so I tramped off in a hurry for the crick, and crowded through the willows, red-hot to jump aboard and get out of that awful country—the raft was gone! My souls, but I was scared! I couldn't get my breath for most a minute. Then I raised a yell. A voice not twenty-five foot from me, says—

"Good lan'! is dat you, honey? Doan' make no noise."

It was Jim's voice—nothing ever sounded so good before. I run along the bank a piece and got aboard, and Jim he grabbed me and hugged me, he was so glad to see me. He says—

"Laws bless you, chile, I 'uz right down sho' you's dead agin. Jack's been heah, he say he reck'n you's ben shot, kase you didn' come home no mo'; so I's jes' dis minute a startin' de raf' down towards de mouf er de crick, so's to be all ready for to shove out en leave soon as Jack comes agin en tells me for certain you *is* dead. Lawsy, I's mighty glad to git you back agin, honey."

I says—

"All right—that's mighty good; they won't find me, and they'll think I've been killed, and floated down the river . . . so

don't you lose no time, Jim, but just shove off for the big water as fast as ever you can."

I never felt easy till the raft was two mile below there and out in the middle of the Mississippi. Then we hung up our signal lantern, and judged that we was free and safe once more. I hadn't had a bite to eat since yesterday; so Jim he got out some corn-dodgers and butter-milk, and pork and cabbage, and greens—there ain't nothing in the world so good, when it's cooked right—and whilst I eat my supper we talked, and had a good time. I was powerful glad to get away from the feuds, and so was Jim to get away from the swamp. We said there warn't no home like a raft, after all. Other places do seem so cramped up and smothery, but a raft don't. You feel mighty free and easy and comfortable on a raft.

FOR UNDERSTANDING

1. Who are the members of the Grangerford family? When Huck is first admitted to the house, how does the family's conduct show that their freedom is limited?

2. Although Huck has actually run away from a drunken and abusive father, what story does he tell the Grangerfords?

3. When Huck forgets his assumed name, how does he find out what it is?

4. Why did Emmeline Grangerford keep a scrapbook?

5. How does Huck describe the difference between the Grangerford girls, Charlotte and Sophia?

6. How do you know that Harney Shepherdson didn't want to kill Buck?

7. What does Buck tell Huck about the long-time feud between the Grangerfords and Shepherdsons that makes continuing the fighting seem so foolish?

8. What does Huck say about the raft when he and Jim are once again floating down the Mississippi River?

FOR INTERPRETATION

1. Mark Twain had a low opinion of sentimentality in art and literature. Discuss what you think his purpose was in including the titles and detailed descriptions of Emmeline's crayon drawings.

2. Huck comments that Colonel Grangerford was "well born" and "that's worth as much in a man as a horse." What does this suggest about Twain's opinion of aristocracy and class distinctions in America?

FOR APPRECIATION

Comedy: Irony of Statement

Twain's comic technique in this selection rests heavily on a device called *irony of statement*. Huck, the narrator, makes statements usually showing either approval or neutrality toward a given thing, but these attitudes are in marked contrast with those of Twain. Thus there is a contrast in the statements between what is said and what is meant. This is irony of statement.

In his description of the parlor furnishings, for example, Huck says that the clock is "beautiful" and that the fruits in the crockery basket are "prettier than real ones is." Huck, in short, approves of both. But how does Twain feel about them? The fact is that Twain thinks both the clock and the fruits are pretentious and useless, tokens of the kind of life the Grangerfords live, a life in which appearances are more important than realities.

When naïve Huck goes on to observe that the "pretty" fruits "warn't real because you could see where pieces had got chipped off and showed the white chalk or whatever it was, underneath" the reader is given insight into Twain's belief that underneath a thin veneer or paint the ugly realities of life continue to exist.

Huck said Emmeline wrote "very good poetry." How does the reader know what Twain really thought of it?

LANGUAGE AND VOCABULARY

1. The first paragraph of "The Celebrated Jumping Frog of Calaveras County" contains such literary words as *garrulous, append, personage, conjectured, infamous, reminiscence, tedious*. Find several synonyms for each word. Rewrite the paragraph using more conversational words, and then rewrite the paragraph using colloquial and slang terms. Explain how your revisions differ from and change the original.

2. Find a simple synonym for each word below:

sustenance	dogmatic	savant
remuneration	thesaurus	venerable

3. Many of our more literary words are borrowed words—words that came into the language directly from Latin or Greek or by way of French. Look up the origin of the words in number two above. Find a more learned or literary synonym for the following native words:

dark	sharp
forgive	angry
greed	deep
kind (adj.)	start (v.)

A TWENTIETH-CENTURY WRITER LOOKS BACK

When *Our Town* opened in New York in February 1938, the first-night audience was not quite prepared for the bare and dimly lit stage as it entered the theater, a stage without a curtain and without scenery. Since that time, audiences have grown accustomed to the easy informality of the Stage Manager as he introduces each scene, interrupts the action with commentary, takes the parts of several minor characters, improvises scenery, and speaks the epilogue. Playwrights of another age would have called him the Chorus. What he adds to this play is invaluable: an affectionate understanding of the simple, ordinary life that goes on day after day in Grover's Corners and an earnest desire to make us share that understanding. He wants us to see ourselves in these people, to laugh and cry with them, to enjoy life as they do. He wants us to know that ". . . this is the way we were in the provinces north of New York at the beginning of the twentieth century.—This is the way we were: in our growing up and in our marrying and in our living and in our dying." Because so many audiences willingly respond, *Our Town* is one of the most successful plays in the modern American theater.

Thornton Wilder   1897–1975

Thornton Wilder could always be counted on to try new forms, to avoid the obvious. In 1915 he first began experimenting in prose fiction and drama, but it was 1927 before he achieved critical approval and a national reputation.

Born in Madison, Wisconsin, he moved to China at the age of nine when his father was appointed consul general at Hong Kong and Shanghai. He spent six months in a German school in Hong Kong. In the following years, Wilder attended the public schools of Berkeley, California; an English mission boarding school in Cheefoo, China; and the Thacker School in Ojai, California. He was graduated from high school in Berkeley and entered Oberlin College in 1915. Later he transferred to Yale. He

interrupted his studies to serve in the Coast Artillery and, when World War I was over, completed his B.A. degree at Yale.

He spent the next year in residence at the American Academy in Rome. He returned to teach French for six years at the Lawrenceville School in New Jersey. During that time he finished his first novel, *The Cabala*, which was published in 1926. Also during that period he earned an M.A. at Princeton and wrote *The Bridge of San Luis Rey* (1927). Wilder did not, however, abandon teaching as he gained fame as a writer. He later taught at the University of Chicago and at Harvard.

It was natural that a young scholar back from Rome should want to gather his first impressions of the Eternal City into a romantic story with himself at the center. *The Cabala* is that kind of novel, but, as readers have come to expect from Wilder, it is fantasy with an ironic twist and early displayed the originality that was to become a Wilder trademark.

The Bridge of San Luis Rey not only won him a Pulitzer Prize, the first of three, but made him financially independent for several years following its publication. Like *The Cabala, The Bridge of San Luis Rey* is a philosophical novel, but it is set in eighteenth-century Peru, not Europe. Wilder was convinced that America had had enough stark realism in the novels of John Dos Passos, enough critical examination of our own society in the work of Sinclair Lewis. It was ready now for historical romance, and what he provided in *The Bridge of San Luis Rey* was made to the public's order: memorable characters, a remote and ornate setting, religious themes, a sense of mystery, and, above all, concise dialogue.

The central incident is simple: on a Friday in July 1714, a bridge collapses on the road between Lima and Cuzco, sending five people to their deaths. The plot is more complex: Brother Juniper, who was present at the accident, sets out to discover why *these* five people should have died. He tells us the story of a lonely old marquesa and her lovely daughter, then of an actor-manager and his mistress, finally of twin brothers and a secret passion. Wilder's purpose in letting Brother Juniper tell the stories is made clear in the epilogue, called "Perhaps an Intention." Here Wilder enters the book, as the omniscient narrator, in order to underscore his dominant theme: Love is a moral responsibility; the world we live in is purposeless without it. "There is a land of the living and a land of the dead," his last sentence reads, "and the bridge is love, the only survival, the only meaning."

Following his resignation from Lawrenceville, Wilder spent two years in Europe studying Continental drama. On his return he published his third novel, *The Woman of Andros,* a failure with both the public and the critics. Set in pre-Christian Greece, it tried to probe further into the hidden meanings of human life. With his next novel, however, Wilder recouped his reputation and if anything enlarged his audience. In *Heaven's My Destination* (1935) he

shifted gears, adopted the conventional realistic method for this social satire, set the story of George Brush, a traveling sales agent, in the Middle West Bible Belt about 1930, and concentrated on pitting this humanitarian hero against a materialistic society. In his travels about the country, Brush moves from comedy to pathos and back again. At one moment we laugh at his naïveté, at another we wince at the grim truths he demonstrates. The novel quite rightly has been compared to Mark Twain's *Huckleberry Finn.* Wilder commenced work on his fifth novel, *The Ides of March* (1948), after serving three years with the Intelligence Corps of the Air Force in World War II. Another best seller, it tells the familiar story of the last months of Julius Caesar's life with such originality that again Wilder turned history into perceptive character study. Using only letters and documents, all of them imaginary, to retell the events leading up to the assassination, for the first time in his fiction Wilder stood wholly outside the main action, not commenting as omniscient narrator on the moral of his story. The letters, however, are of such variety and fascination that the reader needs no guide to discover their implications.

Had Wilder published only novels, he would have had a satisfying if modest reputation among American writers. When *Our Town* opened on Broadway in 1938, the critics knew a genuine theatrical talent had blossomed. *The Skin of Our Teeth* (1942) and *The Matchmaker* (1954) are the full flowering.

"Toward the end of the twenties," Wilder said, "I began to lose pleasure in going to the theatre. I ceased to believe in the stories I saw presented there." He feared that the playwrights of his day were too timid to disturb their middle-class patrons with biting comedy or social satire and consequently soothed them with comfortable, tidy plays of little consequence. But chief among his reasons for disbelief was the box set. He was convinced that the confining three walls, the curtain, and the proscenium arch of the modern theater "shut the play up into a museum showcase." Instead of the universals he was witnessing only local happenings. "The novel," he argued, "is pre-eminently the vehicle of the unique occasion, the theatre of the generalized one. It is through the theatre's power to raise the exhibited individual action into the realm of idea and type and universal that it is able to evoke our belief."

Our Town breaks down the confinements of a box set in order to speak of universals. It was not Wilder's first attempt. As early as 1931 he had published *The Long Christmas Dinner and Other Plays*. These one-act experiments tried "to capture not versimilitude but reality," as he put it. In other words, he did not wish to hamper his audience with elaborate sets that looked like reproductions of our own dining rooms or the interior of actual Pullman cars; he avoided placing the action in a specific year or a certain town; his characters were dressed in ordinary clothes, not costumes. *The Long Christmas Dinner,* for example, spans ninety years, yet the basic set never changes. In *Pullman Car Hiawatha* plain chairs serve as berths. In *The Happy Journey to Trenton and Camden* four kitchen chairs and a low platform represent an automobile; Pa's hands hold an imaginary steering wheel; and the family travels seventy miles in twenty minutes. The Stage Manager acts as interpreter and scene changer as well as various characters in the play. In *Our Town,* Wilder experiments even further. Though set in Grover's Corners, the play was not meant, he insisted "as a picture of life in a New Hampshire village; or as a speculation about the conditions of life after death." He was attempting here "to find a value above all price for the smallest events in our daily life."

To bring belief back into the theater, in other words, Wilder strove to embody universal meaning in specific incidents, actions, and characters. Small wonder that this play has been performed in the best theaters of the world; it translates easily because the audience identification is almost immediate. Grover's Corners could be Denmark or Italy, Brazil or Japan. The need for love is a theme of much of Wilder's fiction; the need for awareness, for savoring every minute of our brief lives is at the heart of his tragic play. Failing to realize life's potential, no matter how modestly life is lived, leads only to frustration and waste. Emily Webb comes to know this truth too late. Have *we* made this discovery in time, Wilder seems to ask his audience. He does not wait for our answer, for he knows how we have trapped ourselves in our getting and spending, our overweening pride, our ignorance of the value of time. To Simon Stimson, the town drunk, Wilder gives his most biting lines, but Simon ironically speaks from the grave: "Now you know! That's what it was to be alive. To move about in a cloud of ignorance; to go up and down trampling on the feelings of those . . . of those about you. To spend and waste time as though you had a million years. To be always at the mercy of one self-centered passion, or another . . . that's the happy existence you wanted to go back to. Ignorance and blindness." *The Bridge of San Luis Rey* taught this moral to a legion of readers. *Our Town* continues to speak this truth on stages everywhere.

OUR TOWN

CHARACTERS

(in the order of their appearance)

STAGE MANAGER

DR. GIBBS

JOE CROWELL

HOWIE NEWSOME

MRS. GIBBS

MRS. WEBB

GEORGE GIBBS

REBECCA GIBBS

WALLY WEBB

EMILY WEBB

PROFESSOR WILLARD

MR. WEBB

WOMAN IN THE BALCONY

MAN IN THE AUDITORIUM

LADY IN THE BOX

SIMON STIMSON

MRS. SOAMES

CONSTABLE WARREN

SI CROWELL

THREE BASEBALL PLAYERS

SAM CRAIG

JOE STODDARD

The entire play takes place in Grover's Corners, New Hampshire.

Act I

No curtain.

No scenery.

The audience, arriving, sees an empty stage in half-light.

Presently the STAGE MANAGER, *hat on and pipe in mouth, enters and begins placing a table and three chairs downstage left, and a table and three chairs downstage right. He also places a low bench at the corner of what will be the Webb house, left.*

"Left" and "right" are from the point of view of the actor facing the audience. "Up" is toward the back wall.

As the house lights go down he has finished setting the stage and leaning against the right proscenium[1] pillar watches the late arrivals in the audience.

When the auditorium is in complete darkness he speaks:

STAGE MANAGER. This play is called "Our Town." It was written by Thornton Wilder; produced and directed by A. . . . [or: produced by A. . . . ; directed by B. . . .]. In it you will see Miss C. . . . ; Miss D. . . . ; Miss E. . . . ; and Mr. F. . . . ; Mr. G. . . . ; Mr. H. . . . ; and many others. The name of the town is Grover's Corners, New Hampshire —just across the Massachusetts line: latitude 42 degrees 40 minutes; longitude 70 degrees 37 minutes. The First Act shows a day in our town. The day is May 7, 1901. The time is just before dawn. (*A rooster crows.*)

The sky is beginning to show some streaks of light over the East there, behind our mount'in.

The morning star always gets wonderful bright the minute before it has to go,— doesn't it? (*He stares at it for a moment, then goes upstage.*)

1. **proscenium** (prō sē′ nē əm), the part of the stage in front of the curtain.

Well, I'd better show you how our town lies. Up here—(*That is: parallel with the back wall.*) is Main Street. Way back there is the railway station; tracks go that way. Polish Town's across the tracks, and some Canuck[2] families.

(*Toward the left.*) Over there is the Congregational Church; across the street's the Presbyterian.

Methodist and Unitarian are over there.

Baptist is down in the holla' by the river.

Catholic Church is over beyond the tracks.

Here's the Town Hall and Post Office combined; jail's in the basement.

Bryan[3] once made a speech from these very steps here.

Along here's a row of stores. Hitching posts and horse blocks in front of them. First automobile's going to come along in about five years—belonged to Banker Cartwright, our richest citizen . . . lives in the big white house up on the hill.

Here's the grocery store and here's Mr. Morgan's drugstore. Most everybody in town manages to look into those two stores once a day.

Public School's over yonder. High School's still farther over. Quarter of nine mornings, noontimes, and three o'clock afternoons, the hull town can hear the yelling and screaming from those schoolyards. *He approaches the table and chairs downstage right.*

This is our doctor's house,—Doc Gibbs'. This is the back door. (*Two arched trellises, covered with vines and flowers, are pushed out, one by each proscenium pillar.*) There's some scenery for those who think they have to have scenery.

This is Mrs. Gibbs' garden. Corn . . . peas . . . beans . . . hollyhocks . . . heliotrope[4] . . . and a lot of burdock.[5] (*Crosses the stage.*)

In those days our newspaper come out twice a week—the Grover's Corners *Sentinel* —and this is Editor Webb's house.

And this is Mrs. Webb's garden.

Just like Mrs. Gibbs', only it's got a lot of sunflowers, too. (*He looks upward, center stage.*)

Right here . . . 's a big butternut tree. (*He returns to his place by the right proscenium pillar and looks at the audience for a minute.*)

Nice town, y'know what I mean?

Nobody very remarkable ever come out of it, s'far as we know.

The earliest tombstones in the cemetery up there on the mountain say 1670–1680— they're Grovers and Cartwrights and Gibbses and Herseys—same names as are around here now.

Well, as I said: it's about dawn.

The only lights on in town are in a cottage over by the tracks where a Polish mother's just had twins. And in the Joe Crowell house, where Joe Junior's getting up so as to deliver the paper. And in the depot, where Shorty Hawkins is gettin' ready to flag the 5:45 for Boston. (*A train whistle is heard. The* STAGE MANAGER *takes out his watch and nods.*)

Naturally, out in the country—all around— there've been lights on for some time, what with milkin's and so on. But town people sleep late.

So—another day's begun.

---

2. **Canuck** (kə nuk'), slang for French Canadian, usually used disparagingly.
3. **Bryan,** William Jennings Bryan (1860–1925), orator and presidential candidate.
4. **heliotrope** (hē′ lē ə trōp), plant that turns toward the sun and usually bears fragrant white or purplish flowers.
5. **burdock,** coarse weed with a bur; it is also called cocklebur.

There's Doc Gibbs comin' down Main Street now, comin' back from that baby case. And here's his wife comin' downstairs to get breakfast. (MRS. GIBBS, *a plump, pleasant woman in the middle thirties, comes "downstairs" right. She pulls up an imaginary window shade in her kitchen and starts to make a fire in her stove.*)

Doc Gibbs died in 1930. The new hospital's named after him.

Mrs. Gibbs died first—long time ago, in fact. She went out to visit her daughter, Rebecca, who married an insurance man in Canton, Ohio, and died there—pneumonia —but her body was brought back here. She's up in the cemetery there now—in with a whole mess of Gibbses and Herseys —she was Julia Hersey 'fore she married Doc Gibbs in the Congregational Church over there.

In our town we like to know the facts about everybody.

There's Mrs. Webb, coming downstairs to get her breakfast, too.

—That's Doc Gibbs. Got that call at half past one this morning. And there comes Joe Crowell, Jr., delivering Mr. Webb's *Sentinel.*

[DR. GIBBS *has been coming along Main Street from the left. At the point where he would turn to approach his house, he stops, sets down his— imaginary—black bag, takes off his hat, and rubs his face with fatigue, using an enormous handkerchief.*]

[MRS. WEBB, *a thin, serious, crisp woman, has entered her kitchen, left, tying on an apron. She goes through the motions of putting wood into a stove, lighting it, and preparing breakfast.*]

[*Suddenly,* JOE CROWELL, JR., *eleven, starts down Main Street from the right, hurling imaginary newspapers into doorways.*]

JOE CROWELL, JR. Morning, Doc Gibbs.

DR. GIBBS. Morning, Joe.

JOE CROWELL, JR. Somebody been sick, Doc?

DR. GIBBS. No. Just some twins born over in Polish Town.

JOE CROWELL, JR. Do you want your paper now?

DR. GIBBS. Yes, I'll take it.—Anything serious goin' on in the world since Wednesday?

JOE CROWELL, JR. Yessir. My schoolteacher, Miss Foster, 's getting married to a fella over in Concord.

DR. GIBBS. I declare.—How do you boys feel about that?

JOE CROWELL, JR. Well, of course, it's none of my business—but I think if a person starts out to be a teacher, she ought to stay one.

DR. GIBBS. How's your knee, Joe?

JOE CROWELL, JR. Fine, Doc, I never think about it at all. Only like you said, it always tells me when it's going to rain.

DR. GIBBS. What's it telling you today? Goin' to rain?

JOE CROWELL, JR. No, sir.

DR. GIBBS. Sure?

JOE CROWELL, JR. Yessir.

DR. GIBBS. Knee ever make a mistake?

JOE CROWELL, JR. No, sir. (JOE *goes off.* DR. GIBBS *stands reading his paper.*)

STAGE MANAGER. Want to tell you something about that boy Joe Crowell there. Joe was awful bright—graduated from high school here, head of his class. So he got a scholarship to Massachusetts Tech. Graduated head of his class there, too. It was all wrote up in the Boston paper at the time. Goin' to be a great engineer, Joe was. But the war broke out and he died in France.—All that education for nothing.

HOWIE NEWSOME (*off left*). Giddap, Bessie! What's the matter with you today?

STAGE MANAGER. Here comes Howie Newsome, deliverin' the milk. (HOWIE NEWSOME, *about thirty, in overalls, comes along Main Street from the left, walking beside an invisible horse and wagon and carrying an imaginary rack with milk bottles. The sound of* *clinking milk bottles is heard. He leaves some bottles at* MRS. WEBB'S *trellis, then, crossing the stage to* MRS. GIBBS', *he stops center to talk to* DR. GIBBS.)

HOWIE NEWSOME. Morning, Doc.

DR. GIBBS. Morning, Howie.

HOWIE NEWSOME. Somebody sick?

DR. GIBBS. Pair of twins over to Mrs. Goruslawski's.

HOWIE NEWSOME. Twins, eh? This town's gettin' bigger every year.

DR. GIBBS. Goin' to rain, Howie?

HOWIE NEWSOME. No, no. Fine day—that'll burn through. Come on, Bessie.

DR. GIBBS. Hello, Bessie. (*He strokes the horse, which has remained up center.*) How old is she, Howie?

HOWIE NEWSOME. Going on seventeen. Bessie's all mixed up about the route ever since the Lockharts stopped takin' their quart of milk every day. She wants to leave 'em a quart just the same—keeps scolding me the hull trip. (*He reaches* MRS. GIBBS' *back door. She is waiting for him.*)

MRS. GIBBS. Good morning, Howie.

HOWIE NEWSOME. Morning, Mrs. Gibbs. Doc's just comin' down the street.

MRS. GIBBS. Is he? Seems like you're late today.

HOWIE NEWSOME. Yes. Somep'n went wrong with the separator. Don't know what 'twas. (*He passes* DR. GIBBS *up center.*) Doc!

DR. GIBBS. Howie!

MRS. GIBBS (*calling upstairs*). Children! Children! Time to get up.

HOWIE NEWSOME. Come on, Bessie! (*He goes off right.*)

MRS. GIBBS. George! Rebecca! (DR. GIBBS *arrives at his back door and passes through the trellis into his house.*)

MRS. GIBBS. Everything all right, Frank?

DR. GIBBS. Yes. I declare—easy as kittens.

MRS. GIBBS. Bacon'll be ready in a minute. Set down and drink your coffee. You can catch a couple hours' sleep this morning, can't you?

DR. GIBBS. Hm! . . . Mrs. Wentworth's coming at eleven. Guess I know what it's about, too. Her stummick ain't what it ought to be.

MRS. GIBBS. All told, you won't get more'n three hours' sleep. Frank Gibbs, I don't know what's goin' to become of you. I do wish I could get you to go away someplace and take a rest. I think it would do you good.

MRS. WEBB. Emileeee! Time to get up! Wally! Seven o'clock!

MRS. GIBBS. I declare, you got to speak to George. Seems like something's come over him lately. He's no help to me at all. I can't even get him to cut me some wood.

DR. GIBBS (*Washing and drying his hands at the sink.* MRS. GIBBS *is busy at the stove*). Is he sassy to you?

MRS. GIBBS. No. He just whines! All he thinks about is that baseball—George! Rebecca! You'll be late for school.

DR. GIBBS. M-m-m . . .

MRS. GIBBS. George!

DR. GIBBS. George, look sharp!

GEORGE'S VOICE. Yes, Pa!

DR. GIBBS (*as he goes off the stage*). Don't you hear your mother calling you? I guess I'll go upstairs and get forty winks.

MRS. WEBB. Wallee! Emilee! You'll be late for school! Wallee! You wash yourself good or I'll come up and do it myself.

REBECCA GIBBS' VOICE. Ma! What dress shall I wear?

MRS. GIBBS. Don't make a noise. Your father's been out all night and needs his sleep. I washed and ironed the blue gingham for you special.

REBECCA. Ma, I hate that dress.

MRS. GIBBS. Oh, hush-up-with-you.

REBECCA. Every day I go to school dressed like a sick turkey.

MRS. GIBBS. Now, Rebecca, you always look *very* nice.

REBECCA. Mama, George's throwing soap at me.

MRS. GIBBS. I'll come and slap the both of you,—that's what I'll do. (*A factory whistle sounds. The children dash in and take their* *places at the tables. Right,* GEORGE, *about six-teen, and* REBECCA, *eleven. Left,* EMILY *and* WALLY, *same ages. They carry strapped schoolbooks.*)

STAGE MANAGER. We've got a factory in our town too—hear it? Makes blankets. Cartwrights own it and it brung 'em a fortune.

MRS. WEBB. Children! Now I won't have it. Breakfast is just as good as any other meal and I won't have you gobbling like wolves. It'll stunt your growth,—that's a fact. Put away your book, Wally.

WALLY. Aw, Ma! By ten o'clock I got to know all about Canada.

MRS. WEBB. You know the rule's well as I do—no books at table. As for me, I'd rather have my children healthy than bright.

EMILY. I'm both, Mama: you know I am. I'm the brightest girl in school for my age. I have a wonderful memory.

MRS. WEBB. Eat your breakfast.

WALLY. I'm bright, too, when I'm looking at my stamp collection.

MRS. GIBBS. I'll speak to your father about it when he's rested. Seems to me twenty-five cents a week's enough for a boy your age. I declare I don't know how you spend it all.

GEORGE. Aw, Ma,—I gotta lotta things to buy.

MRS. GIBBS. Strawberry phosphates[6]—that's what you spend it on.

GEORGE. I don't see how Rebecca comes to have so much money. She has more'n a dollar.

REBECCA (*spoon in mouth, dreamily*). I've been saving it up gradual.

MRS. GIBBS. Well, dear, I think it's a good thing to spend some every now and then.

REBECCA. Mama, do you know what I love most in the world—do you?—Money.

MRS. GIBBS. Eat your breakfast.

THE CHILDREN. Mama, there's first bell.—I gotta hurry.—I don't want any more.—I gotta hurry. (*The children rise, seize their books and dash out through the trellises. They meet, down center, and chattering, walk to Main Street, then turn left. The* STAGE MANAGER *goes off, unobtrusively, right.*)

Young lovers: George Gibbs and Emily Webb

MRS. WEBB. Walk fast, but you don't have to run. Wally, pull up your pants at the knee. Stand up straight, Emily.

MRS. GIBBS. Tell Miss Foster I send her my best congratulations—can you remember that?

REBECCA. Yes, Ma.

MRS. GIBBS. You look real nice, Rebecca. Pick up your feet.

ALL. Good-by. (MRS. GIBBS *fills her apron with food for the chickens and comes down to the footlights.*)

MRS. GIBBS. Here, chick, chick, chick.

---

6. **strawberry phosphates,** beverage made of a mixture of soda water and strawberry flavoring.

No, go away, you. Go away.

Here, chick, chick, chick.

What's the matter with *you?* Fight, fight, fight,—that's all you do. Hm . . . *you* don't belong to me. Where'd you come from? *(She shakes her apron.)*

Oh, don't be so scared. Nobody's going to hurt you. (MRS. WEBB *is sitting on the bench by her trellis, stringing beans.)*

Good morning, Myrtle. How's your cold?

MRS. WEBB. Well, I still get that tickling feeling in my throat. I told Charles I didn't know as I'd go to choir practice tonight. Wouldn't be any use.

MRS. GIBBS. Have you tried singing over your voice?

MRS. WEBB. Yes, but somehow I can't do that and stay on key. While I'm resting myself I thought I'd string some of these beans.

MRS. GIBBS *(rolling up her sleeves as she crosses the stage for a chat).* Let me help you. Beans have been good this year.

MRS. WEBB. I've decided to put up forty quarts if it kills me. The children say they hate 'em, but I notice they're able to get 'em down all winter. *(Pause. Brief sound of chickens cackling.)*

MRS. GIBBS. Now, Myrtle. I've got to tell you something, because if I don't tell somebody I'll burst.

MRS. WEBB. Why, Julia Gibbs!

MRS. GIBBS. Here, give me some more of those beans. Myrtle, did one of those secondhand-furniture men from Boston come to see you last Friday?

MRS. WEBB. No-o.

MRS. GIBBS. Well, he called on me. First I thought he was a patient wantin' to see Dr. Gibbs. 'N he wormed his way into my parlor, and, Myrtle Webb, he offered me three hundred and fifty dollars for Grandmother Wentworth's highboy, as I'm sitting here!

MRS. WEBB. Why, Julia Gibbs!

MRS. GIBBS. He did! That old thing! Why, it was so big I didn't know where to put it and I almost give it to Cousin Hester Wilcox.

MRS. WEBB. Well, you're going to take it, aren't you?

MRS. GIBBS. I don't know.

MRS. WEBB. You don't know—three hundred and fifty dollars! What's come over you?

MRS. GIBBS. Well, if I could get the Doctor to take the money and go away someplace on a real trip, I'd sell it like that.—Y'know, Myrtle, it's been the dream of my life to see Paris, France.—Oh, I don't know. It sounds crazy, I suppose, but for years I've been promising myself that if we ever had the chance—

MRS. WEBB. How does the Doctor feel about it?

MRS. GIBBS. Well, I did beat about the bush a little and said that if I got a legacy—that's the way I put it—I'd make him take me somewhere.

MRS. WEBB. M-m-m . . . What did he say?

MRS. GIBBS. You know how he is. I haven't heard a serious word out of him since I've known him. No, he said, it might make him discontented with Grover's Corners to go traipsin' about Europe; better let well enough alone, he says. Every two years he makes a trip to the battlefields of the Civil War and that's enough treat for anybody, he says.

MRS. WEBB. Well, Mr. Webb just *admires* the way Dr. Gibbs knows everything about the Civil War. Mr. Webb's a good mind to give up Napoleon and move over to the Civil War, only Dr. Gibbs being one of the greatest experts in the country just makes him despair.

MRS. GIBBS. It's a fact! Dr. Gibbs is never so happy as when he's at Antietam or Gettysburg. The times I've walked over those hills, Myrtle, stopping at every bush and pacing it all out, like we were going to buy it.

MRS. WEBB. Well, if that secondhand man's really serious about buyin' it, Julia, you sell it. And then you'll get to see Paris, all right. Just keep droppin' hints from time to time—that's how I got to see the Atlantic Ocean, y'know.

MRS. GIBBS. Oh, I'm sorry I mentioned it. Only it seems to me that once in your life before you die you ought to see a country where they don't talk in English and don't even want to. (*The* STAGE MANAGER *enters briskly from the right. He tips his hat to the ladies, who nod their heads.*)

STAGE MANAGER. Thank you, ladies. Thank you very much. (MRS. GIBBS *and* MRS. WEBB *gather up their things, return into their homes and disappear.*)

Now we're going to skip a few hours.

But first we want a little more information about the town, kind of a scientific account, you might say.

So I've asked Professor Willard of our State University to sketch in a few details of our past history here.

Is Professor Willard here? (PROFESSOR WILLARD, *a rural savant,*[7] *pince-nez*[8] *on a wide satin ribbon, enters from the right with some notes in his hand.*)

May I introduce Professor Willard of our State University. A few brief notes, thank you, Professor,—unfortunately our time is limited.

PROFESSOR WILLARD. Grover's Corners . . . let me see . . . Grover's Corners lies on the old Pleistocene[9] granite of the Appalachian range. I may say it's some of the oldest land in the world. We're very proud of that. A shelf of Devonian[10] basalt crosses it with vestiges of Mesozoic[11] shale, and some sandstone outcroppings; but that's all more recent: two hundred, three hundred million years old.

Some highly interesting fossils have been found . . . I may say: unique fossils . . . two miles out of town, in Silas Peckham's cow pasture. They can be seen at the museum in our University at any time—that is, at any reasonable time. Shall I read some of Professor Gruber's notes on the meteorological situation—mean precipitation, et cetera?

STAGE MANAGER. Afraid we won't have time for that, Professor. We might have a few words on the history of man here.

PROFESSOR WILLARD. Yes . . . anthropological data: Early Amerindian stock. Cotahatchee tribes . . . no evidence before the tenth century of this era . . . hm . . . now entirely disappeared . . . possible traces in three families. Migration toward the end of the seventeenth century of English brachiocephalic[12] blue-eyed stock . . . for the most part. Since then some Slav and Mediterranean—

STAGE MANAGER. And the population, Professor Willard?

PROFESSOR WILLARD. Within the town limits: 2,640.

STAGE MANAGER. Just a moment, Professor. (*He whispers into the* PROFESSOR'S *ear.*)

PROFESSOR WILLARD. Oh, yes, indeed?—The population, *at the moment,* is 2,642. The Postal District brings in 507 more, making a total of 3,149.—Mortality and birth rates: constant.—By MacPherson's gauge: 6.032.

STAGE MANAGER. Thank you very much, Professor. We're all very much obliged to you, I'm sure.

PROFESSOR WILLARD. Not at all, sir; not at all.

STAGE MANAGER. This way, Professor, and thank you again. (*Exit* PROFESSOR WILLARD.) Now the political and social report: Editor Webb.—Oh, Mr. Webb? (MRS. WEBB *appears at her back door.*)

---

7. **savant** (sa vänt), a learned person.
8. **pince-nez** (pans' nā), eyeglasses held on the nose by a spring.
9. **Pleistocene** (plī stə sēn'), the Ice Age.
10. **Devonian** (da vō' nē ən), that period which began with the continents mainly dry. Later, large areas were flooded and sediment forming old red sandstone was laid down. The sea was full of fish. Frogs and other amphibians appeared. The land was covered with great ferns and fernlike trees.
11. **Mesozoic** (mes' ə zō' ik), the era when the Appalachians were elevated. Reptiles and dinosaurs were numerous, but became extinct when violent disturbances brought the era to an end.
12. **brachiocephalic** (brak' ē ō sə fal' ik), usually spelled brachycephalic; short-headed, with the breadth of the head at least four-fifths of its length.

MRS. WEBB. He'll be here in a minute. . . . He just cut his hand while he was eatin' an apple.

STAGE MANAGER. Thank you, Mrs. Webb.

MRS. WEBB. Charles! Everybody's waitin'. *(Exit* MRS. WEBB.*)*

STAGE MANAGER. Mr. Webb is Publisher and Editor of the Grover's Corners *Sentinel.* That's our local paper, y'know. (MR. WEBB *enters from his house, pulling on his coat. His finger is bound in a handkerchief.)*

MR. WEBB. Well . . . I don't have to tell you that we're run here by a Board of Selectmen.—All males vote at the age of twenty-one. Women vote indirect. We're lower middle class: sprinkling of professional men . . . ten percent illiterate laborers. Politically, we're eighty-six per cent Republicans; six per cent Democrats; four per cent Socialists; rest, indifferent.

Religiously, we're eighty-five per cent Protestants; twelve per cent Catholics; rest, indifferent.

STAGE MANAGER. Have you any comments, Mr. Webb?

MR. WEBB. Very ordinary town, if you ask me. Little better behaved than most. Probably a lot duller.

But our young people here seem to like it well enough. Ninety per cent of 'em graduating from high school settle down right here to live—even when they've been away to college.

STAGE MANAGER. Now, is there anyone in the audience who would like to ask Editor Webb anything about the town?

WOMAN IN THE BALCONY. Is there much drinking in Grover's Corners?

MR. WEBB. Well, ma'am, I wouldn't know what you'd call *much.* Satiddy nights the farmhands meet down in Ellery Greenough's stable and holler some. We've got one or two town drunks, but they're always having remorses every time an evangelist comes to town. No, ma'am, I'd say likker ain't a regular thing in the home here, except in the medicine chest. Right good for snake bite, y'know—always was.

BELLIGERENT MAN AT BACK OF AUDITORIUM. Is there no one in town aware of—

STAGE MANAGER. Come forward, will you, where we can all hear you—What were you saying?

BELLIGERENT MAN. Is there no one in town aware of social injustice and industrial inequality?

MR. WEBB. Oh, yes, everybody is—somethin' terrible. Seems like they spend most of their time talking about who's rich and who's poor.

BELLIGERENT MAN. Then why don't they do something about it? *(He withdraws without waiting for an answer.)*

MR. WEBB. Well, I dunno. . . . I guess we're all hunting like everybody else for a way the diligent and sensible can rise to the top and the lazy and quarrelsome can sink to the bottom. But it ain't easy to find. Meanwhile, we do all we can to help those that can't help themselves and those that can we leave alone.—Are there any other questions?

LADY IN A BOX. Oh, Mr. Webb? Mr. Webb, is there any culture or love of beauty in Grover's Corners?

MR. WEBB. Well, ma'am, there ain't much— not in the sense you mean. Come to think of it, there's some girls that play the piano at High School Commencement; but they ain't happy about it. No, ma'am, there isn't much culture; but maybe this is the place to tell you that we've got a lot of pleasures of a kind here: we like the sun comin' up over the mountain in the morning, and we all notice a good deal about the birds. We pay a lot of attention to them. And we watch the change of the seasons; yes, everybody knows about them. But those other things —you're right, ma'am,—there ain't much. —*Robinson Crusoe* and the Bible; and Handel's "Largo," we all know that; and "Whistler's Mother"—those are just about as far as we go.

LADY IN A BOX. So I thought. Thank you, Mr. Webb.

STAGE MANAGER. Thank you, Mr. Webb. (MR. WEBB *retires.*) Now, we'll go back to the town. It's early afternoon. All 2,642 have had their dinners, and all the dishes have been washed. (MR. WEBB, *having removed his coat, returns and starts pushing a lawn mower to and fro beside his house.*) There's an early-afternoon calm in our town: a buzzin' and a hummin' from the school buildings; only a few buggies on Main Street—the horses dozing at the hitching posts; you all remember what it's like. Doc Gibbs is in his office, tapping people and making them say "ah." Mr. Webb's cuttin' his lawn over there; one man in ten thinks it's a privilege to push his own lawn mower.

No, sir. It's later than I thought. There are the children coming home from school already. (*Shrill girls' voices are heard, off left.* EMILY *comes along Main Street, carrying some books. There are some signs that she is imagining herself to be a lady of startling elegance.*)

EMILY. I *can't*, Lois. I've got to go home and help my mother. I *promised*.

MR. WEBB. Emily, walk simply. Who do you think you are today?

EMILY. Papa, you're terrible. One minute you tell me to stand up straight and the next minute you call me names. I just don't listen to you. (*She gives him an abrupt kiss.*)

MR. WEBB. Golly, I never got a kiss from such a great lady before. (*He goes out of sight.* EMILY *leans over and picks some flowers by the gate of her house.* GEORGE GIBBS *comes careening down Main Street. He is throwing a ball up to dizzying heights, and waiting to catch it again. This sometimes requires his taking six steps backward. He bumps into an old lady invisible to us.*)

GEORGE. Excuse me, Mrs. Forrest.

STAGE MANAGER (*as Mrs. Forrest*). Go out and play in the fields, young man. You got no business playing baseball on Main Street.

GEORGE. Awfully sorry, Mrs. Forrest.—Hello, Emily.

Thornton Wilder, playing the Stage Manager in Our Town, *New York, 1938. He was convinced that the confining three walls, the curtain, and the proscenium arch of the modern theater "shut the play up into a museum showpiece."*

EMILY. H'lo.

GEORGE. You made a fine speech in class.

EMILY. Well . . . I was really ready to make a speech about the Monroe Doctrine, but at the last minute Miss Corcoran made me talk about the Louisiana Purchase instead. I worked an awful long time on both of them.

GEORGE. Gee, it's funny, Emily. From my window up there I can just see your head nights when you're doing your homework over in your room.

EMILY. Why, can you?

GEORGE. You certainly do stick to it, Emily. I don't see how you can sit still that long. I guess you like school.

EMILY. Well, I always feel it's something you have to go through.

GEORGE. Yeah.

EMILY. I don't mind it really. It passes the time.

GEORGE. Yeah.—Emily, what do you think? We might work out a kinda telegraph from your window to mine; and once in a while you could give me a kinda hint or two about one of those algebra problems. I don't mean the answers, Emily, of course not . . . just some little hint. . . .

EMILY. Oh, I think *hints* are allowed.—So—ah —if you get stuck, George, you whistle to me; and I'll give you some hints.

GEORGE. Emily, you're just naturally bright, I guess.

EMILY. I figure that it's just the way a person's born.

GEORGE. Yeah. But, you see, I want to be a farmer, and my Uncle Luke says whenever I'm ready I can come over and work on his farm and if I'm good I can just gradually have it.

EMILY. You mean the house and everything? (*Enter* MRS. WEBB *with a large bowl and sits on the bench by her trellis.*)

GEORGE. Yeah. Well, thanks . . . I better be getting out to the baseball field. Thanks for the talk, Emily.—Good afternoon, Mrs. Webb.

MRS. WEBB. Good afternoon, George.

GEORGE. So long, Emily.

EMILY. So long, George.

MRS. WEBB. Emily, come and help me string these beans for the winter. George Gibbs let himself have a real conversation, didn't he? Why, he's growing up. How old would George be?

EMILY. I don't know.

MRS. WEBB. Let's see. He must be almost sixteen.

EMILY. Mama, I made a speech in class today, and I was very good.

MRS. WEBB. You must recite it to your father at supper. What was it about?

EMILY. The Louisiana Purchase. It was like

silk off a spool. I'm going to make speeches all my life.—Mama, are these big enough?

MRS. WEBB. Try and get them a little bigger if you can.

EMILY. Mama, will you answer me a question, serious?

MRS. WEBB. Seriously, dear—not serious.

EMILY. Seriously,—will you?

MRS. WEBB. Of course, I will.

EMILY. Mama, am I good looking?

MRS. WEBB. Yes, of course you are. All my children have got good features; I'd be ashamed if they hadn't.

EMILY. Oh, Mama, that's not what I mean. What I mean is: am I *pretty?*

MRS. WEBB. I've already told you, yes. Now that's enough of that. You have a nice young pretty face. I never heard of such foolishness.

EMILY. Oh, Mama, you never tell us the truth about anything.

MRS. WEBB. I *am* telling you the truth.

EMILY. Mama, were *you* pretty?

MRS. WEBB. Yes, I was, if I do say it. I was the prettiest girl in town next to Mamie Cartwright.

EMILY. But, Mama, you've got to say *something* about me. Am I pretty enough . . . to get anybody . . . to get people interested in me?

MRS. WEBB. Emily, you make me tired. Now stop it. You're pretty enough for all normal purposes.—Come along now and bring that bowl with you.

EMILY. Oh, Mama, you're no help at all.

STAGE MANAGER. Thank you. Thank you! That'll do. We'll have to interrupt again here. Thank you, Mrs. Webb; thank you, Emily. (MRS. WEBB *and* EMILY *withdraw.*) There are some more things we want to explore about this town. (*He comes to the center of the stage. During the following speech the lights gradually dim to darkness, leaving only a spot on him.*) I think this is a good time to tell you that the Cartwright interests have just begun building a new bank in Grover's Corners—had to go to Vermont for the marble, sorry to say. And they've asked a friend of mine what they should put in the cornerstone for people to dig up . . . a thousand years from now. . . . Of course, they've put in a copy of the *New York Times* and a copy of Mr. Webb's *Sentinel*. . . . We're kind of interested in this because some scientific fellas have found a way of painting all that reading material with a glue—a silicate glue—that'll make it keep a thousand—two thousand years.

We're putting in a Bible . . . and the Constitution of the United States—and a copy of William Shakespeare's plays. What do you say, folks? What do you think?

Y'know—Babylon once had two million people in it, and all we know about 'em is the names of the kings and some copies of wheat contracts . . . and contracts for the sale of slaves. Yet every night all those families sat down to supper, and the father came home from his work, and the smoke went up the chimney,—same as here. And even in Greece and Rome, all we know about the *real* life of the people is what we can piece together out of the joking poems and the comedies they wrote for the theatre back then.

So I'm going to have a copy of this play put in the cornerstone and the people a thousand years from now'll know a few simple facts about us—more than the Treaty of Versailles[13] and the Lindbergh flight.[14]

See what I mean?

So—people a thousand years from now—this is the way we were in the provinces north of New York at the beginning of the twentieth century.—This is the way we were: in our growing up and in our marrying and in our living and in our dying. (*A choir partially concealed in the orchestra pit has begun singing "Blessed Be the Tie That Binds."* SIMON STIMSON *stands directing them. Two ladders have been pushed onto the stage; they serve as indication of the second story in the Gibbs and Webb houses.* GEORGE *and* EMILY *mount them, and apply themselves to their schoolwork.* DR. GIBBS *has entered and is seated in his kitchen reading.*)

Well!—good deal of time's gone by. It's evening.

You can hear choir practice going on in the Congregational Church.

The children are at home doing their schoolwork.

The day's running down like a tired clock.

SIMON STIMSON. Now look here, everybody. Music come into the world to give pleasure. —Softer! Softer! Get it out of your heads that music's only good when it's loud. You leave loudness to the Methodists. You couldn't beat 'em, even if you wanted to. Now again. Tenors!

GEORGE. Hssst! Emily!

EMILY. Hello.

GEORGE. Hello!

EMILY. I can't work at all. The moonlight's so *terrible*.

GEORGE. Emily, did you get the third problem?

EMILY. Which?

GEORGE. The *third*?

EMILY. Why, yes, George—that's the easiest of them all.

GEORGE. I don't see it. Emily, can you give me a hint?

EMILY. I'll tell you one thing: the answer's in yards.

GEORGE. !!! In yards? How do you mean?

EMILY. In *square* yards.

GEORGE. Oh . . . in square yards.

EMILY. Yes, George, don't you see?

GEORGE. Yeah.

13. **Treaty of Versailles** (ver sī′), the treaty between the Allies and Germany at the end of World War I.
14. **Lindbergh flight,** first nonstop transatlantic flight from west to east. Charles A. Lindbergh flew alone from New York to Paris in 1927, in his monoplane, *The Spirit of St. Louis.*

EMILY. In square yards of *wallpaper.*

GEORGE. Wallpaper,—oh, I see. Thanks a lot, Emily.

EMILY. You're welcome. My, isn't the moonlight *terrible?* And choir practice going on.—I think if you hold your breath you can hear the train all the way to Contoocook. Hear it?

GEORGE. M-m-m—What do you know!

EMILY. Well, I guess I better go back and try to work.

GEORGE. Good night, Emily. And thanks.

EMILY. Good night, George.

SIMON STIMSON. Before I forget it: how many of you will be able to come in Tuesday afternoon and sing at Fred Hersey's wedding?—show your hands. That'll be fine; that'll be right nice. We'll do the same music we did for Jane Trowbridge's last month.

—Now we'll do: "Art Thou Weary; Art Thou Languid?" It's a question, ladies and gentlemen, make it talk. Ready.

DR. GIBBS. Oh, George, can you come down a minute?

GEORGE. Yes, Pa. *(He descends the ladder.)*

DR. GIBBS. Make yourself comfortable, George; I'll only keep you a minute. George, how old are you?

GEORGE. I? I'm sixteen, almost seventeen.

DR. GIBBS. What do you want to do after school's over?

GEORGE. Why, you know, Pa. I want to be a farmer on Uncle Luke's farm.

DR. GIBBS. You'll be willing, will you, to get up early and milk and feed the stock . . . and you'll be able to hoe and hay all day?

GEORGE. Sure, I will. What are you . . . what do you mean, Pa?

DR. GIBBS. Well, George, while I was in my office today I heard a funny sound . . . and what do you think it was? It was your mother chopping wood. There you see your mother—getting up early; cooking meals all day long; washing and ironing;—and still she has to go out in the back yard and chop wood. I suppose she just got tired of asking you. She just gave up and decided it was easier to do it herself. And you eat her meals, and put on the clothes she keeps nice for you, and you run off and play baseball,—like she's some hired girl we keep around the house but that we don't like very much. Well, I knew all I had to do was call your attention to it. Here's a handkerchief, son. George, I've decided to raise your spending money twenty-five cents a week. Not, of course, for chopping wood for your mother, because that's a present you give her, but because you're getting older—and I imagine there are lots of things you must find to do with it.

GEORGE. Thanks, Pa.

DR. GIBBS. Let's see—tomorrow's your payday. You can count on it—Hmm. Probably Rebecca'll feel she ought to have some more too. Wonder what could have happened to your mother. Choir practice never was as late as this before.

GEORGE. It's only half past eight, Pa.

DR. GIBBS. I don't know why she's in that old choir. She hasn't any more voice than an old crow. . . . Traipsin' around the streets at this hour of the night . . . Just about time you retired, don't you think?

GEORGE. Yes, Pa. (GEORGE *mounts to his place on the ladder. Laughter and good nights can be heard on stage left and presently* MRS. GIBBS, MRS. SOAMES *and* MRS. WEBB *come down Main Street. When they arrive at the corner of the stage they stop.)*

MRS. SOAMES. Good night, Martha. Good night, Mr. Foster.

MRS. WEBB. I'll tell Mr. Webb; I *know* he'll want to put it in the paper.

MRS. GIBBS. My, it's late!

MRS. SOAMES. Good night, Irma.

MRS. GIBBS. Real nice choir practice, wa'n't it? Myrtle Webb! Look at that moon, will you? Tsk-tsk-tsk. Potato weather, for sure. *(They are silent a moment, gazing up at the moon.)*

MRS. SOAMES. Naturally, I didn't want to say a word about it in front of those others, but

MRS. SOAMES. Naturally, I didn't want to say a word about it in front of those others, but now we're alone. . . .

now we're alone—really, it's the worst scandal that ever was in this town!

MRS. GIBBS. What?

MRS. SOAMES. Simon Stimson!

MRS. GIBBS. Now, Louella!

MRS. SOAMES. But, Julia! To have the organist of the church *drink* and *drunk* year after year. You know he was drunk tonight.

MRS. GIBBS. Now, Louella! We all know about Mr. Stimson, and we all know about the troubles he's been through, and Dr. Ferguson knows too, and if Dr. Ferguson keeps him on there in his job the only thing the rest of us can do is just not to notice it.

MRS. SOAMES. *Not to notice it!* But it's getting worse.

MRS. WEBB. No, it isn't, Louella. It's getting better. I've been in that choir twice as long as you have. It doesn't happen anywhere near so often. . . . My, I hate to go to bed on a night like this.—I better hurry. Those children'll be sitting up all hours. Good night, Louella. *(They all exchange good nights. She hurries downstage, enters her house and disappears.)*

MRS. GIBBS. Can you get home safe, Louella?

MRS. SOAMES. It's as bright as day. I can see Mr. Soames scowling at the window now.

You'd think we'd been to a dance the way the menfolk carry on. *(More good nights.* MRS. GIBBS *arrives at her home and passes through the trellis into the kitchen.)*

MRS. GIBBS. Well, we had a real good time.

DR. GIBBS. You're late enough.

MRS. GIBBS. Why, Frank, it ain't any later 'n usual.

DR. GIBBS. And you stopping at the corner to gossip with a lot of hens.

MRS. GIBBS. Now, Frank, don't be grouchy. Come out and smell the heliotrope in the moonlight. *(They stroll out arm in arm along the footlights.)* Isn't that wonderful? What did you do all the time I was away?

DR. GIBBS. Oh, I read—as usual. What were the girls gossiping about tonight?

MRS. GIBBS. Well, believe me, Frank—there is something to gossip about.

DR. GIBBS. Hmm! Simon Stimson far gone, was he?

MRS. GIBBS. Worst I've ever seen him. How'll that end, Frank? Dr. Ferguson can't forgive him forever.

DR. GIBBS. I guess I know more about Simon Stimson's affairs than anybody in this town. Some people ain't made for small-town life. I don't know how that'll end; but there's nothing we can do but just leave it alone. Come, get in.

MRS. GIBBS. No, not yet . . . Frank, I'm worried about you.

DR. GIBBS. What are you worried about?

MRS. GIBBS. I think it's my duty to make plans for you to get a real rest and change. And if I get that legacy, well, I'm going to insist on it.

DR. GIBBS. Now, Julia, there's no sense in going over that again.

MRS. GIBBS. Frank, you're just *unreasonable!*

DR. GIBBS *(starting into the house).* Come on, Julia, it's getting late. First thing you know you'll catch cold. I gave George a piece of my mind tonight. I reckon you'll have your wood chopped for a while anyway. No, no, start getting upstairs.

MRS. GIBBS. Oh, dear. There's always so many things to pick up, seems like. You know, Frank, Mrs. Fairchild always locks her front door every night. All those people up that part of town do.

DR. GIBBS *(blowing out the lamp).* They're all getting citified, that's the trouble with them. They haven't got nothing fit to burgle and everybody knows it. *(They disappear.* REBECCA *climbs up the ladder beside* GEORGE.*)*

GEORGE. Get out, Rebecca. There's only room for one at this window. You're always spoiling everything.

REBECCA. Well, let me look just a minute.

GEORGE. Use your own window.

REBECCA. I did, but there's no moon there. . . . George, do you know what I think, do you? I think maybe the moon's getting nearer and nearer and there'll be a big 'splosion.

GEORGE. Rebecca, you don't know anything. If the moon were getting nearer, the guys that sit up all night with telescopes would see it first and they'd tell about it, and it'd be in all the newspapers.

REBECCA. George, is the moon shining on South America, Canada and half the whole world?

GEORGE. Well—prob'ly is. *(The* STAGE MANAGER *strolls on. Pause. The sound of crickets is heard.)*

STAGE MANAGER. Nine-thirty. Most of the lights are out. No, there's Constable Warren trying a few doors on Main Street. And here comes Editor Webb, after putting his newspaper to bed. (MR. WARREN, *an elderly policeman, comes along Main Street from the right,* MR. WEBB *from the left.)*

MR. WEBB. Good evening, Bill.

CONSTABLE WARREN. Evenin', Mr. Webb.

MR. WEBB. Quite a moon!

CONSTABLE WARREN. Yep.

MR. WEBB. All quiet tonight?

CONSTABLE WARREN. Simon Stimson is rollin' around a little. Just saw his wife movin' out to hunt for him so I looked the other way—there he is now. (SIMON STIMSON *comes down Main Street from the left, only a trace of unsteadiness in his walk.*)

MR. WEBB. Good evening, Simon . . . Town seems to have settled down for the night pretty well. . . . (SIMON STIMSON *comes up to him and pauses a moment and stares at him, swaying slightly.*) Good evening . . . Yes, most of the town's settled down for the night, Simon. . . . I guess we better do the same. Can I walk along a ways with you? (SIMON STIMSON *continues on his way without a word and disappears at the right.*) Good night.

CONSTABLE WARREN. I don't know how that's goin' to end, Mr. Webb.

MR. WEBB. Well, he's seen a peck of trouble, one thing after another. . . . Oh, Bill . . . if you see my boy smoking cigarettes, just give him a word, will you? He thinks a lot of you, Bill.

CONSTABLE WARREN. I don't think he smokes no cigarettes, Mr. Webb. Leastways, not more'n two or three a year.

MR. WEBB. Hm . . . I hope not.—Well, good night, Bill.

CONSTABLE WARREN. Good night, Mr. Webb. (*Exit.*)

MR. WEBB. Who's that up there? Is that you, Myrtle?

EMILY. No, it's me, Papa.

MR. WEBB. Why aren't you in bed?

EMILY. I don't know. I just can't sleep yet, Papa. The moonlight's so *won*-derful. And the smell of Mrs. Gibbs' heliotrope. Can you smell it?

MR. WEBB. Hm . . . Yes. Haven't any troubles on your mind, have you, Emily?

EMILY. *Troubles,* Papa? *No.*

MR. WEBB. Well, enjoy yourself, but don't let your mother catch you. Good night, Emily.

EMILY. Good night, Papa. (MR. WEBB *crosses into the house, whistling "Blessed Be the Tie That Binds" and disappears.*)

REBECCA. I never told you about that letter Jane Crofut got from her minister when she was sick. He wrote Jane a letter and on the envelope the address was like this: It said: Jane Crofut; The Crofut Farm; Grover's Corners; Sutton County; New Hampshire; United States of America.

GEORGE. What's funny about that?

REBECCA. But listen, it's not finished: the United States of America; Continent of North America; Western Hemisphere; the Earth; the Solar System; the Universe; the Mind of God—that's what it said on the envelope.

GEORGE. What do you know!

REBECCA. And the postman brought it just the same.

GEORGE. What do you know!

STAGE MANAGER. That's the end of the First Act, friends. You can go and smoke now, those that smoke.

FOR UNDERSTANDING

1. The announced purpose of the first act is to show a single day in *Our Town.* Who are the members of the two central families, and why can the audience know what is happening in both homes?

2. What dream does Mrs. Gibbs confide to Mrs. Webb? How has she suddenly been given hope that it might come true?

3. What does the Stage Manager say he is going to do with a copy of the play and why?

4. Who is Simon Stimson, and what problem does he have?

FOR INTERPRETATION

1. What conclusion about *Our Town* does one reach after hearing Mr. Webb's answers to the three questions asked by members of the audience?

2. What references in Act I could be interpreted to suggest the brevity and insignificance of human life?

FOR APPRECIATION

Structure and Staging

A play is generally designed in such a way that all the major characters and all the major tensions, or conflicts, are introduced by the end of the first act. It is, therefore, a good practice to pause at the end of the act and ask yourself what you think those tensions are and what might happen in the ensuing acts.

1. What do you think may happen to George and Emily? Discuss your reactions to Emily's emphaticly negative answer when her father questions her about any "troubles" she might have on her mind.

2. Discuss the unusual stage techniques Wilder uses to involve the audience in the action on the stage.

Act II

The tables and chairs of the two kitchens are still on the stage.

The ladders and the small bench have been withdrawn.

The STAGE MANAGER *has been at his accustomed place watching the audience return to its seats.*

STAGE MANAGER. Three years have gone by.

Yes, the sun's come up over a thousand times.

Summers and winters have cracked the mountains a little bit more and the rains have brought down some of the dirt.

Some babies that weren't even born before have begun talking regular sentences already; and a number of people who thought they were right young and spry have noticed that they can't bound up a flight of stairs like they used to, without their heart fluttering a little.

All that can happen in a thousand days.

Nature's been pushing and contriving in other ways, too; a number of young people fell in love and got married.

Yes, the mountain got bit away a few fractions of an inch; millions of gallons of water went by the mill; and here and there a new home was set up under a roof.

Almost everybody in the world gets married—you know what I mean? In our town there aren't hardly any exceptions. Most everybody in the world climbs into their graves married.

The First Act was called the Daily Life. This act is called Love and Marriage. There's another act coming after this: I reckon you can guess what that's about.

So:

It's three years later. It's 1904.

It's July 7th, just after the High School Commencement.

That's the time most of our young people jump up and get married.

Soon as they've passed their last examinations in solid geometry and Cicero's Orations, looks like they suddenly feel themselves fit to be married.

It's early morning. Only this time it's been raining. It's been pouring and thundering.

Mrs. Gibbs' garden, and Mrs. Webb's here: drenched.

All those bean poles and pea vines: drenched.

All yesterday over there on Main Street, the rain looked like curtains being blown along.

Hm . . . it may begin again any minute.

There! You can hear the 5:45 for Boston. (MRS. GIBBS *and* MRS. WEBB *enter their kitchens and start the day as in the First Act.*)

And there's Mrs. Gibbs and Mrs. Webb

come down to make breakfast, just as though it were an ordinary day. I don't have to point out to the women in my audience that those ladies they see before them, both of those ladies cooked three meals a day—one of 'em for twenty years, the other for forty—and no summer vacation. They brought up two children apiece, washed, cleaned the house,—and *never a nervous breakdown.*

It's like what one of those Middle West poets said: You've got to love life to have life, and you've got to have life to love life. . . .

It's what they call a vicious circle.

HOWIE NEWSOME (*off stage left*). Giddap, Bessie!

STAGE MANAGER. Here comes Howie Newsome delivering the milk. And there's Si Crowell delivering the papers like his brother before him. (SI CROWELL *has entered hurling imaginary newspapers into doorways;* HOWIE NEWSOME *has come along Main Street with Bessie.*)

SI CROWELL. Morning, Howie.

HOWIE NEWSOME. Morning, Si.—Anything in the papers I ought to know?

SI CROWELL. Nothing much, except we're losing about the best baseball pitcher Grover's Corners ever had—George Gibbs.

HOWIE NEWSOME. Reckon he is.

SI CROWELL. He could hit and run bases, too.

HOWIE NEWSOME. Yep. Mighty fine ballplayer. —Whoa! Bessie! I guess I can stop and talk if I've a mind to!

SI CROWELL. I don't see how he could give up a thing like that just to get married. Would you, Howie?

HOWIE NEWSOME. Can't tell, Si. Never had no talent that way. (CONSTABLE WARREN *enters. They exchange good mornings.*) You're up early, Bill.

CONSTABLE WARREN. Seein' if there's anything I can do to prevent a flood. River's been risin' all night.

HOWIE NEWSOME. Si Crowell's all worked up here about George Gibbs' retiring from baseball.

CONSTABLE WARREN. Yes, sir; that's the way it goes. Back in '84 we had a player, Si—even George Gibbs couldn't touch him. Name of Hank Todd. Went down to Maine and became a parson. Wonderful ballplayer.— Howie, how does the weather look to you?

HOWIE NEWSOME. Oh, 'tain't bad. Think maybe it'll clear up for good. (CONSTABLE WARREN *and* SI CROWELL *continue on their way.* HOWIE NEWSOME *brings the milk first to* MRS. GIBBS' *house. She meets him by the trellis.*)

MRS. GIBBS. Good morning, Howie. Do you think it's going to rain again?

HOWIE NEWSOME. Morning, Mrs. Gibbs. It rained so heavy, I think maybe it'll clear up.

MRS. GIBBS. Certainly hope it will.

HOWIE NEWSOME. How much did you want today?

MRS. GIBBS. I'm going to have a houseful of relations, Howie. Looks to me like I'll need three-a-milk and two-a-cream.

HOWIE NEWSOME. My wife says to tell you we both hope they'll be very happy, Mrs. Gibbs. Know they *will.*

MRS. GIBBS. Thanks a lot, Howie. Tell your wife I hope she gits there to the wedding.

HOWIE NEWSOME. Yes, she'll be there; she'll be there if she kin. (HOWIE NEWSOME *crosses to* MRS. WEBB'S *house.*) Morning, Mrs. Webb.

MRS. WEBB. Oh, good morning, Mr. Newsome. I told you four quarts of milk, but I hope you can spare me another.

HOWIE NEWSOME. Yes'm . . . and the two of cream.

MRS. WEBB. Will it start raining again, Mr. Newsome?

HOWIE NEWSOME. Well. Just sayin' to Mrs. Gibbs as how it may lighten up. Mrs. Newsome told me to tell you as how we hope they'll both be very happy, Mrs. Webb. Know they *will.*

MRS. WEBB. Thank you and thank Mrs. Newsome and we're counting on seeing you at the wedding.

HOWIE NEWSOME. Yes, Mrs. Webb. We hope to git there. Couldn't miss that. Come on, Bessie. (*Exit* HOWIE NEWSOME. DR. GIBBS *descends in shirt sleeves, and sits down at his breakfast table.*)

DR. GIBBS. Well, Ma, the day has come. You're losin' one of your chicks.

MRS. GIBBS. Frank Gibbs, don't you say another word. I feel like crying every minute. Sit down and drink your coffee.

DR. GIBBS. The groom's up shaving himself—only there ain't an awful lot to shave. Whistling and singing, like he's glad to leave us.—Every now and then he says "I do" to the mirror, but it don't sound convincing to me.

MRS. GIBBS. I declare, Frank, I don't know how he'll get along. I've arranged his clothes and seen to it he's put warm things on,—Frank! they're too *young*. Emily won't think of such things. He'll catch his death of cold within a week.

DR. GIBBS. I was remembering my wedding morning, Julia.

MRS. GIBBS. Now don't start that, Frank Gibbs.

DR. GIBBS. I was the scaredest young fella in the State of New Hampshire. I thought I'd make a mistake for sure. And when I saw you comin' down that aisle I thought you were the prettiest girl I'd ever seen, but the only trouble was that I'd never seen you before. There I was in the Congregational Church marryin' a total stranger.

MRS. GIBBS. And how do you think I felt!—Frank, weddings are perfectly awful things. Farces,—that's what they are! (*She puts a plate before him.*) Here, I've made something for you.

DR. GIBBS. Why, Julia Hersey—French toast!

MRS. GIBBS. 'Tain't hard to make, and I had to do something. (*Pause.* DR. GIBBS *pours on the syrup.*)

DR. GIBBS. How'd you sleep last night, Julia?

MRS. GIBBS. Well, I heard a lot of the hours struck off.

DR. GIBBS. Ye-e-s! I get a shock every time I think of George setting out to be a family man—that great gangling thing!—I tell you, Julia, there's nothing so terrifying in the world as a *son*. The relation of father and son is the darndest, awkwardest—

MRS. GIBBS. Well, mother and daughter's no picnic, let me tell you.

DR. GIBBS. They'll have a lot of troubles, I suppose, but that's none of our business. Everybody has a right to their own troubles.

MRS. GIBBS (*at the table, drinking her coffee, meditatively*). Yes . . . people are meant to go through life two by two. 'Tain't natural to be lonesome. (*Pause.* DR. GIBBS *starts laughing.*)

DR. GIBBS. Julia, do you know one of the things I was scared of when I married you?

MRS. GIBBS. Oh, go along with you!

DR. GIBBS. I was afraid we wouldn't have material for conversation more'n'd last us a few weeks. (*Both laugh.*) I was afraid we'd run out and eat our meals in silence, that's a fact.—Well, you and I been conversing for twenty years now without any noticeable barren spells.

MRS. GIBBS. Well,—good weather, bad weather—'tain't very choice, but I always find something to say. (*She goes to the foot of the stairs.*) Did you hear Rebecca stirring around upstairs?

DR. GIBBS. No. Only day of the year Rebecca hasn't been managing everybody's business up there. She's hiding in her room.—I got the impression she's crying.

MRS. GIBBS. Lord's sakes!—This has got to stop.—Rebecca! Rebecca! Come and get your breakfast. (GEORGE *comes rattling down the stairs, very brisk.*)

GEORGE. Good morning, everybody. Only five more hours to live. (*Makes the gesture of cutting his throat, and a loud "k-k-k," and starts through the trellis.*)

MRS. GIBBS. George Gibbs, where are you going?

GEORGE. Just stepping across the grass to see my girl.

MRS. GIBBS. Now, George! You put on your overshoes. It's raining torrents. You don't go out of this house without you're prepared for it.

GEORGE. Aw, Ma. It's just a *step!*

MRS. GIBBS. George! You'll catch your death of cold and cough all through the service.

DR. GIBBS. George, do as your mother tells you! (DR. GIBBS *goes upstairs.* GEORGE *returns reluctantly to the kitchen and pantomines putting on overshoes.*)

MRS. GIBBS. From tomorrow on you can kill yourself in all weathers, but while you're in my house you'll live wisely, thank you.—Maybe Mrs. Webb isn't used to callers at seven in the morning.—Here, take a cup of coffee first.

GEORGE. Be back in a minute. (*He crosses the stage, leaping over the puddles.*) Good morning, Mother Webb.

MRS. WEBB. Goodness! You frightened me! —Now, George, you can come in a minute out of the wet, but you know I can't ask you in.

GEORGE. Why not—?

MRS. WEBB. George, you know's well as I do: the groom can't see his bride on his wedding day, not until he sees her in church.

GEORGE. Aw!—that's just a superstition.— Good morning, Mr. Webb. (*Enter* MR. WEBB.)

MR. WEBB. Good morning, George.

GEORGE. Mr. Webb, you don't believe in that superstition, do you?

MR. WEBB. There's a lot of common sense in some superstitions, George. (*He sits at the table, facing right.*)

MRS. WEBB. Millions have folla'd it, George, and you don't want to be the first to fly in the face of custom.

GEORGE. How is Emily?

MRS. WEBB. She hasn't waked up yet. I haven't heard a sound out of her.

GEORGE. Emily's *asleep!!!*

MRS. WEBB. No wonder! We were up 'til all hours, sewing and packing. Now I'll tell you what I'll do; you set down here a minute with Mr. Webb and drink this cup of coffee; and I'll go upstairs and see she doesn't come down and surprise you. There's some bacon, too; but don't be long about it. (*Exit* MRS. WEBB. *Embarrassed silence.* MR. WEBB *dunks doughnuts in his coffee. More silence.*)

MR. WEBB (*suddenly and loudly*). Well, George, how are you?

GEORGE (*startled, choking over his coffee*). Oh, fine, I'm fine. (*Pause.*) Mr. Webb, what sense could there be in a superstition like that?

MR. WEBB. Well, you see,—on her wedding morning a girl's head's apt to be full of . . . clothes and one thing and another. Don't you think that's probably it?

GEORGE. Ye-e-s. I never thought of that.

MR. WEBB. A girl's apt to be a mite nervous on her wedding day. (*Pause.*)

GEORGE. I wish a fellow could get married without all that marching up and down.

MR. WEBB. Every man that's ever lived has felt that way about it, George; but it hasn't been any use. It's the womenfolk who've built up weddings, my boy. For a while now the women have it all their own. A man looks pretty small at a wedding, George. All those good women standing shoulder to shoulder making sure that the knot's tied in a mighty public way.

GEORGE. But . . . you *believe* in it, don't you, Mr. Webb?

MR. WEBB (*with alacrity*). Oh, yes; *oh, yes.* Don't you misunderstand me, my boy. Marriage is a wonderful thing,—wonderful thing. And don't you forget that, George.

GEORGE. No, sir—Mr. Webb, how old were you when you got married?

MR. WEBB. Well, you see: I'd been to college, and I'd taken a little time to get settled. But Mrs. Webb—she wasn't much older than what Emily is. Oh, age hasn't much to do with it, George,—not compared with . . . uh . . . other things.

GEORGE. What were you going to say, Mr. Webb?

MR. WEBB. Oh, I don't know.—Was I going to say something? *(Pause.)* George, I was thinking the other night of some advice my father gave me when I got married. Charles, he said, Charles, start out early showing who's boss, he said. Best thing to do is to give an order, even if it don't make sense; just so she'll learn to obey. And he said: if anything about your wife irritates you—her conversation, or anything—just get up and leave the house. That'll make it clear to her, he said. And, oh, yes! he said never, *never* let your wife know how much money you have, never.

GEORGE. Well, Mr. Webb . . . I don't think I could. . . .

MR. WEBB. So I took the opposite of my father's advice, and I've been happy ever since. And let that be a lesson to you, George, never to ask advice on personal matters.—George, are you going to raise chickens on your farm?

GEORGE. What?

MR. WEBB. Are you going to raise chickens on your farm?

GEORGE. Uncle Luke's never been much interested, but I thought—

MR. WEBB. A book came into my office the other day, George, on the Philo System of raising chickens. I want you to read it. I'm thinking of beginning in a small way in the back yard, and I'm going to put an incubator in the cellar—*(Enter MRS. WEBB.)*

MRS. WEBB. Charles, are you talking about that old incubator again? I thought you two'd be talking about things worth while.

MR. WEBB *(bitingly)*. Well, Myrtle, if you want to give the boy some good advice, I'll go upstairs and leave you alone with him.

MRS. WEBB *(pulling GEORGE up)*. George, Emily's got to come downstairs and eat her breakfast. She sends you her love but she doesn't want to lay eyes on you. Good-by.

GEORGE. Good-by. (GEORGE *crosses the stage to*

his own home, bewildered and crestfallen. He slowly dodges a puddle and disappears into his house.)

MR. WEBB. Myrtle, I guess you don't know about that older superstition.

MRS. WEBB. What do you mean, Charles?

MR. WEBB. Since the cave men: no bridegroom should see his father-in-law on the day of the wedding, or near it. Now remember that. *(Both leave the stage.)*

STAGE MANAGER. Thank you very much, Mr. and Mrs. Webb.—Now I have to interrupt again here. You see, we want to know how all this began—this wedding, this plan to spend a lifetime together. I'm awfully interested in how big things like that begin.

You know how it is: you're twenty-one or twenty-two and you make some decisions; then whisssh! you're seventy: you've been a lawyer for fifty years, and that white-haired lady at your side has eaten over fifty thousand meals with you.

How do such things begin?

George and Emily are going to show you now the conversation they had when they first knew that . . . that . . . as the saying goes . . . they were meant for one another.

But before they do it I want you to try and remember what it was like to have been very young.

And particularly the days when you were first in love; when you were like a person sleepwalking, and you didn't quite see the street you were in, and didn't quite hear everything that was said to you.

You're just a little bit crazy. Will you remember that, please?

Now they'll be coming out of high school at three o'clock. George has just been elected President of the Junior Class, and as it's June, that means he'll be President of the Senior Class all next year. And Emily's just been elected Secretary and Treasurer. I

The bare and dimly lit stage, a stage without curtain and without scenery, is a hallmark of Our Town.

don't have to tell you how important that is. *(He places a board across the backs of two chairs, which he takes from those at the Gibbs family table. He brings two high stools from the wings and places them behind the board. Persons sitting on the stools will be facing the audience. This is the counter of Mr. Morgan's drugstore. The sounds of young people's voices are heard off left.)* Yepp,—there they are coming down Main Street now. (EMILY, *carrying an armful of—imaginary—schoolbooks, comes along Main Street from the left.)*

EMILY. I can't, Louise. I've got to go home. Good-by. Oh, Ernestine! Ernestine! Can you come over tonight and do Latin? Isn't

that Cicero the worst thing—! Tell your mother you *have* to. G'by. G'by, Helen. G'by, Fred. (GEORGE, *also carrying books, catches up with her.)*

GEORGE. Can I carry your books home for you, Emily?

EMILY *(coolly).* Why . . . uh . . . Thank you. It isn't far. *(She gives them to him.)*

GEORGE. Excuse me a minute, Emily.—Say, Bob, if I'm a little late, start practice anyway. And give Herb some long high ones.

EMILY. Good-by, Lizzy.

GEORGE. Good-by, Lizzy.—I'm awfully glad you were elected, too, Emily.

EMILY. Thank you. *(They have been standing on

Main Street, almost against the back wall. They take the first steps toward the audience when GEORGE *stops and says:)*

GEORGE. Emily, why are you mad at me?

EMILY. I'm not mad at you.

GEORGE. You've been treating me so funny lately.

EMILY. Well, since you ask me, I might as well say it right out, George—*(She catches sight of a teacher passing.)* Good-by, Miss Corcoran.

GEORGE. Good-by, Miss Corcoran.—Wha— What is it?

EMILY *(not scoldingly; finding it difficult to say).* I don't like the whole change that's come over you in the last year. I'm sorry if that hurts your feelings, but I've got to—tell the truth and shame the devil.

GEORGE. A *change?*—Wha—what do you mean?

EMILY. Well, up to a year ago I used to like you a lot. And I used to watch you as you did everything . . . because we'd been friends so long . . . and then you began spending all your time at baseball . . . and you never stopped to speak to anybody any more. Not even to your own family you didn't . . . and, George, it's a fact, you've got awfully conceited and stuck-up, and all the girls say so. They may not say so to your face, but that's what they say about you behind your back, and it hurts me to hear them say it, but I've got to agree with them a little. I'm sorry if it hurts your feelings . . . but I can't be sorry I said it.

GEORGE. I . . . I'm glad you said it, Emily. I never thought that such a thing was happening to me. I guess it's hard for a fella not to have faults creep into his character. *(They take a step or two in silence, then stand still in misery.)*

EMILY. I always expect a man to be perfect, and I think he should be.

GEORGE. Oh . . . I don't think it's possible to be perfect, Emily.

EMILY. Well, my *father* is, and as far as I can see *your* father is. There's no reason on earth why you shouldn't be, too.

GEORGE. Well, I feel it's the other way round. That men aren't naturally good; but girls are.

EMILY. Well, you might as well know right now that I'm not perfect. It's not as easy for a girl to be perfect as a man, because we girls are more—more—nervous.—Now I'm sorry I said all that about you. I don't know what made me say it.

GEORGE. Emily,—

EMILY. Now I can see it's not the truth at all. And suddenly I feel that it isn't important, anyway.

GEORGE. Emily . . . would you like an ice-cream soda, or something, before you go home?

EMILY. Well, thank you . . . I would. *(They advance toward the audience and make an abrupt right turn, opening the door of Morgan's drugstore. Under strong emotion,* EMILY *keeps her face down.* GEORGE *speaks to some passers-by.)*

GEORGE. Hello, Stew,—how are you?—Good afternoon, Mrs. Slocum. *(The* STAGE MANAGER, *wearing spectacles and assuming the role of Mr. Morgan, enters abruptly from the right and stands between the audience and the counter of his soda fountain.)*

STAGE MANAGER. Hello, George. Hello, Emily. What'll you have?—Why, Emily Webb, what have you been crying about?

GEORGE *(he gropes for an explanation).* She . . . she just got an awful scare, Mr. Morgan. She almost got run over by that hardware-store wagon. Everybody says that Tom Huckins drives like a crazy man.

STAGE MANAGER *(drawing a drink of water).* Well, now! You take a drink of water, Emily. You look all shook up. I tell you, you've got to look both ways before you cross Main Street these days. Gets worse every year.—What'll you have?

EMILY. I'll have a strawberry phosphate, thank you, Mr. Morgan.

GEORGE. No, no, Emily. Have an ice-cream soda with me. Two strawberry ice-cream sodas, Mr. Morgan.

STAGE MANAGER *(working the faucets).* Two strawberry ice-cream sodas, yes sir. Yes, sir. There are a hundred and twenty-five horses in Grover's Corners this minute I'm talking to you. State Inspector was in here yesterday. And now they're bringing in those auto-mobiles, the best thing to do is to just stay home. Why, I can remember when a dog could go to sleep all day in the middle of Main Street, and nothing come along to disturb him. *(He sets the imaginary glasses before them.)* There they are. Enjoy 'em. *(He sees a customer, right.)* Yes, Mrs. Ellis. What can I do for you? *(He goes out right.)*

EMILY. They're so expensive.

GEORGE. No, no,—don't you think of that. We're celebrating our election. And then do you know what else I'm celebrating?

EMILY. N-no.

GEORGE. I'm celebrating because I've got a friend who tells me all the things that ought to be told me.

EMILY. George, *please* don't think of that. I don't know why I said it. It's not true. You're—

GEORGE. No, Emily, you stick to it. I'm glad you spoke to me like you did. But you'll *see:* I'm going to change so quick—you bet I'm going to change. And, Emily, I want to ask you a favor.

EMILY. What?

GEORGE. Emily, if I go away to State Agriculture College next year, will you write me a letter once in a while?

EMILY. I certainly will. I certainly will, George . . . *(Pause. They start sipping the sodas through the straws.)* It certainly seems like being away three years you'd get out of touch with things. Maybe letters from Grover's Corners wouldn't be so interesting after a while. Grover's Corners isn't a very important place when you think of all—New Hampshire; but I think it's a very nice town.

GEORGE. The day wouldn't come when I wouldn't want to know everything that's happening here. I know *that's* true, Emily.

EMILY. Well, I'll try to make my letters interesting. *(Pause.)*

GEORGE. Y'know, Emily, whenever I meet a farmer I ask him if he thinks it's important to go to Agriculture School to be a good farmer.

EMILY. Why, George—

GEORGE. Yeah, and some of them say that it's even a waste of time. You can get all those things, anyway, out of the pamphlets the government sends out. And Uncle Luke's getting old,—he's about ready for me to start taking over his farm tomorrow, if I could.

EMILY. My!

GEORGE. And, like you say, being gone all that time . . . in other places and meeting other people . . . Gosh, if anything like that can happen I don't want to go away. I guess new people aren't any better than old ones. I'll bet they almost never are. Emily . . . I feel that you're as good a friend as I've got. I don't need to go and meet the people in other towns.

EMILY. But, George, maybe it's very important for you to go and learn all that about— cattle judging and soils and those things. . . . Of course, I don't know.

GEORGE *(after a pause, very seriously).* Emily, I'm going to make up my mind right now. I won't go. I'll tell Pa about it tonight.

EMILY. Why, George, I don't see why you have to decide right now. It's a whole year away.

GEORGE. Emily, I'm glad you spoke to me about that . . . that fault in my character. What you said was right; but there was *one* thing wrong in it, and that was when you said that for a year I wasn't noticing people, and . . . you, for instance. Why, you say you were watching me when I did everything . . . I was doing the same about you all the time. Why, sure,—I always thought about you as one of the chief people I thought about. I always made sure where you were sitting on the bleachers, and who you were with, and for three days now I've been trying to walk home with you; but something's always got in the way. Yesterday I was standing over against the wall waiting for you, and you walked home with *Miss Corcoran*.

EMILY. George! . . . Life's awful funny! How could I have known that? Why, I thought—

GEORGE. Listen, Emily, I'm going to tell you why I'm not going to Agriculture School. I think that once you've found a person that you're very fond of . . . I mean a person who's fond of you, too, and likes you enough to be interested in your character . . . Well, I think that's just as important as college is, and even more so. That's what I think.

EMILY. I think it's awfully important, too.

GEORGE. Emily.

EMILY. Y-yes, George.

GEORGE. Emily, if I do improve and make a big change . . . would you be . . . I mean: *could* . . . you be . . .

EMILY. I . . . I am now; I always have been.

GEORGE *(pause)*. So I guess this is an important talk we've been having.

EMILY. Yes . . . yes.

GEORGE *(takes a deep breath and straightens his back)*. Wait just a minute and I'll walk you home. *(With mounting alarm he digs into his pockets for the money. The* STAGE MANAGER *enters, right.* GEORGE, *deeply embarrassed, but direct, says to him:)* Mr. Morgan, I'll have to go home and get the money to pay you for this. It'll only take me a minute.

STAGE MANAGER *(pretending to be affronted)*. What's that? George Gibbs, do you mean to tell me—!

GEORGE. Yes, but I had reasons, Mr. Morgan. —Look, here's my gold watch to keep until I come back with the money.

STAGE MANAGER. That's all right. Keep your watch. I'll trust you.

GEORGE. I'll be back in five minutes.

STAGE MANAGER. I'll trust you ten years, George,—not a day over.—Get all over your shock, Emily?

EMILY. Yes, thank you, Mr. Morgan. It was nothing.

GEORGE *(taking up the books from the counter)*. I'm ready. *(They walk in grave silence across the stage and pass through the trellis at the Webb's back door and disappear. The* STAGE MANAGER *watches them go out, then turns to the audience, removing his spectacles.)*

STAGE MANAGER. Well,—*(He claps his hand as a signal.)* Now we're ready to go on with the wedding. *(He stands waiting while the set is prepared for the next scene. Stagehands remove the chairs, tables and trellises from the Gibbs and Webb houses. They arrange the pews for the church in the center of the stage. The congregation will sit facing the back wall. The aisle of the church starts at the center of the back wall and comes toward the audience. A small platform is placed against the back wall on which the* STAGE MANAGER *will stand later, playing the minister. The image of a stained-glass window is cast from a lantern slide upon the back wall. When all is ready the* STAGE MANAGER *strolls to the center of the stage, down front, and, musingly, addresses the audience.)* There are a lot of things to be said about a wedding; there are a lot of thoughts that go on during a wedding.

We can't get them all into one wedding, naturally, and especially not into a wedding at Grover's Corners, where they're awfully plain and short.

In this wedding I play the minister. That gives me the right to say a few things more about it.

For a while now, the play gets pretty serious. Y'see, some churches say that marriage is a sacrament. I don't quite know what that means, but I can guess. Like Mrs. Gibbs said a few minutes ago: People were made to live two-by-two.

This is a good wedding, but people are so put together that even at a good wedding there's a lot of confusion way down deep in people's minds and we thought that that ought to be in our play, too.

The real hero of this scene isn't on the stage at all, and you know who that is. It's like what one of those European fellas said: Every child born into the world is nature's attempt to make a perfect human being. Well, we've seen nature pushing and contriving for some time now. We all know that nature's interested in quantity; but I think she's interested in quality, too—that's why I'm in the ministry.

And don't forget all the other witnesses at this wedding,—the ancestors. Millions of them. Most of them set out to live two-by-two, also. Millions of them.

Well, that's all my sermon. 'Twan't very long, anyway. (*The organ starts playing Handel's "Largo." The congregation streams into the church and sits in silence. Church bells are heard.* MRS. GIBBS *sits in the front row, the first seat on the aisle, the right section; next to her are* REBECCA *and* DR. GIBBS. *Across the aisle are* MRS. WEBB, WALLY *and* MR. WEBB. *A small choir takes its place, facing the audience under the stained-glass window.* MRS. WEBB, *on the way to her place, turns back and speaks to the audience.*)

MRS. WEBB. I don't know why on earth I should be crying. I suppose there's nothing to cry about. It came over me at breakfast this morning; there was Emily eating her breakfast as she's done for seventeen years and now she's going off to eat it in someone else's house, I suppose that's it.

And Emily! She suddenly said: I can't eat another mouthful, and she put her head down on the table, and *she* cried. (*She starts toward her seat in the church, but turns back and adds:*) Oh, I've got to say it: you know, there's something downright cruel about sending our girls out into marriage this way. I hope some of her girl friends have told her a thing or two. It's cruel, I know, but I couldn't bring myself to say anything. I went into it blind as a bat myself. (*In half-amused exasperation.*) The whole world's wrong, that's what's the matter.

There they come. (*She hurries to her place in*

STAGE MANAGER. *Almost everybody in the world gets married . . . . Most everybody in the world climbs into their graves married.*

the pew. GEORGE *starts to come down the right aisle of the theatre, through the audience. Suddenly three members of his baseball team appear by the right proscenium pillar and start whistling and catcalling to him. They are dressed for the ball field.*)

THE BASEBALL PLAYERS. Eh, George, George! Hast—yaow! Look at him, fellas—he looks scared to death. Yaow! George, don't look so innocent, you old geezer. We know what you're thinking. Don't disgrace the team, big boy. Whoo-oo-oo.

STAGE MANAGER. All right! All right! That'll do. That's enough of that. (*Smiling, he pushes them off the stage. They lean back to shout a few more catcalls.*) There used to be an awful lot of that kind of thing at weddings in the old days,—Rome, and later. We're more civilized now,—so they say. (*The choir*

starts singing *"Love Divine, All Love Excelling
—."* GEORGE *has reached the stage. He stares at
the congregation a moment, then takes a few steps
of withdrawal, toward the right proscenium pillar. His mother, from the front row, seems to have
felt his confusion. She leaves her seat and comes
down the aisle quickly to him.)*

MRS. GIBBS. George! George! What's the matter?

GEORGE. Ma, I don't want to grow old. Why's
everybody pushing me so?

MRS. GIBBS. Why, George . . . you wanted it.

GEORGE. No, Ma, listen to me—

MRS. GIBBS. No, no, George,—you're a man
now.

GEORGE. Listen, Ma,—for the last time I ask
you . . . All I want to do is be a fella—

MRS. GIBBS. George! If anyone should hear
you! Now stop. Why, I'm ashamed of you!

GEORGE *(He comes to himself and looks over the
scene).* What's the matter? I've been dreaming. Where's Emily?

MRS. GIBBS *(relieved).* George! You gave me
such a turn.

GEORGE. Cheer up, Ma. I'm getting married.

MRS. GIBBS. Let me catch my breath a minute.

GEORGE *(comforting her).* Now, Ma, you save
Thursday nights. Emily and I are coming
over to dinner every Thursday night . . .
you'll see. Ma, what are you crying for?
Come on; we've got to get ready for this.
(MRS. GIBBS, *mastering her emotion, fixes his tie
and whispers to him. In the meantime,* EMILY, *in
white and wearing her wedding veil, has come
through the audience and mounted onto the
stage. She too draws back, frightened, when she
sees the congregation in the church. The choir
begins: "Blessed Be the Tie That Binds.")*

EMILY. I never felt so alone in my whole life.
And George over there, looking so . . . ! I
hate him. I wish I were dead. Papa! Papa!

MR. WEBB *(leaves his seat in the pews and comes
toward her anxiously).* Emily! Emily! Now
don't get upset. . . .

EMILY. But, Papa,—I don't want to get
married . . .

MR. WEBB. Sh—sh—Emily. Everything's all
right.

EMILY. Why can't I stay for a while just as I
am? Let's go away,—

MR. WEBB. No, no, Emily. Now stop and think
a minute.

EMILY. Don't you remember that you used to
say,—all the time you used to say—all the
time: that I was *your* girl! There must be
lots of places we can go to. I'll work for you.
I could keep house.

MR. WEBB. Sh . . . you mustn't think of such
things. You're just nervous, Emily. *(He turns
and calls:)* George! George! Will you come
here a minute? *(He leads her toward* GEORGE.*)*
Why, you're marrying the best young fellow in the world. George is a fine fellow.

EMILY. But Papa,—(MRS. GIBBS *returns unobtrusively to her seat.* MR. WEBB *has one arm
around his daughter. He places his hand on*
GEORGE'S *shoulder).*

MR. WEBB. I'm giving away my daughter,
George. Do you think you can take care of
her?

GEORGE. Mr. Webb, I want to . . . I want to
try. Emily, I'm going to do my best. I love
you, Emily. I need you.

EMILY. Well, if you love me, help me. All I
want is someone to love me.

GEORGE. I will, Emily. Emily, I'll try.

EMILY. And I mean for *ever.* Do you hear? For
ever and ever. *(The fall into each other's arms.
The March from* Lohengrin* *is heard. The*
STAGE MANAGER, *as clergyman, stands on the
box, up center.)*

MR. WEBB. Come, they're waiting for us. Now
you know it'll be all right. Come, quick.
(GEORGE *slips away and takes his place beside
the* STAGE MANAGER-*clergyman.* EMILY *proceeds up the aisle on her father's arm.)*

STAGE MANAGER. Do you, George, take this
woman, Emily, to be your wedded wife, to
have . . . (MRS. SOAMES *has been sitting in the*

---

* **Lohengrin** (lō′ ən grin), opera by Richard Wagner.

last row of the congregation. She now turns to her neighbors and speaks in a shrill voice. Her chatter drowns out the rest of the clergyman's words.)

MRS. SOAMES. Perfectly lovely wedding! Loveliest wedding I ever saw. Oh, I do love a good wedding, don't you? Doesn't she make a lovely bride?

GEORGE. I do.

STAGE MANAGER. Do you, Emily, take this man, George, to be your wedded husband,—*(Again his further words are covered by those of* MRS. SOAMES.*)*

MRS. SOAMES. Don't know *when* I've seen such a lovely wedding. But I always cry. Don't know why it is, but I always cry. I just like to see young people happy, don't you? Oh, I think it's lovely. *(The ring. The kiss. The stage is suddenly arrested into silent tableau. The* STAGE MANAGER, *his eyes on the distance, as though to himself:)*

STAGE MANAGER. I've married over two hundred couples in my day.

Do I believe in it?

I don't know.

M. . . . marries N. . . . millions of them.

The cottage, the go-cart, the Sunday-afternoon drives in the Ford, the first rheumatism, the grandchildren, the second rheumatism, the deathbed, the reading of the will,—*(He now looks at the audience for the first time, with a warm smile that removes any sense of cynicism from the next line.)* Once in a thousand times it's interesting.

—Well, let's have Mendelssohn's "Wedding March"! *(The organ picks up the March. The bride and groom come down the aisle, radiant, but trying to be very dignified.)*

MRS. SOAMES. Aren't they a lovely couple? Oh, I've never been to such a nice wedding. I'm sure they'll be happy. I always say: *happiness,* that's the great thing! The important thing is to be happy. *(The bride and groom reach the steps leading into the audience. A bright light is thrown upon them. They descend into the auditorium and run up the aisle joyously.)*

STAGE MANAGER. That's all the Second Act, folks. Ten minutes' intermission.

FOR UNDERSTANDING

1. According to the Stage Manager, what were Act I and Act II called?

2. Why is the newsboy Si Crowell disappointed that George Gibbs is getting married? How does Constable Warren feel about it?

3. What makes George feel bewildered and crestfallen on his wedding morning?

4. What kind of change did Emily see take place in him over the previous year? Why did this change displease her?

5. Who takes the part of the minister at the wedding? Why do both George and Emily feel like backing out of marriage at the last moment?

FOR INTERPRETATION

1. What details of the wedding service make the service seem more symbolic than real? What do you think the wedding symbolizes?

2. In Mrs. Soames's last speech she says, "*happiness,* that's the great thing! The important thing is to be happy." By placing her speech directly following the Stage Manager's summary speech about marriage, Wilder forces the reader to question the relationship between marriage and happiness. Discuss whether you think Wilder suggests that marriage is a guarantee of happiness.

FOR APPRECIATION

Structure and Staging

1. What use does Wilder make of flashback technique in Act II? Why do you think he used flashback rather than ordinary chronological narrative?

2. Act II takes place three years after Act I, yet the two are tied together quite intimately. Note, for example, that Mrs. Soames appears very close to the end of both acts. Compare the first scene (after the Stage Manager's introductory speech) of Act I with the first scene of Act II and note the similarities. These scenes help to tie the two acts together. What other reason or reasons might Wilder have had for using such similar openings?

Act III

During the intermission the audience has seen the stagehands arranging the stage. On the right-hand side, a little right of the center, ten or twelve ordinary chairs have been placed in three openly spaced rows facing the audience.

These are graves in the cemetery.

Toward the end of the intermission the actors enter and take their places. The front row contains: toward the center of the stage, an empty chair; then MRS. GIBBS; SIMON STIMSON.

The second row contains, among others, MRS. SOAMES.

The third row has WALLY WEBB.

The dead do not turn their heads or their eyes to right or left, but they sit in a quiet without stiffness. When they speak their tone is matter-of-fact, without sentimentality and, above all, without lugubriousness.

The STAGE MANAGER *takes his accustomed place and waits for the house lights to go down.*

STAGE MANAGER. This time nine years have gone by, friends—summer, 1913.

Gradual changes in Grover's Corners. Horses are getting rarer.

Farmers coming into town in Fords.

Everybody locks their house doors now at night. Ain't been any burglars in town yet, but everybody's heard about 'em.

You'd be surprised, though—on the whole, things don't change much around here.

This is certainly an important part of Grover's Corners. It's on a hilltop—a windy hilltop—lots of sky, lots of clouds,—often lots of sun and moon and stars.

You come up here, on a fine afternoon and you can see range on range of hills—awful blue they are—up there by Lake Sunapee[1] and Lake Winnipesaukee[2] . . . and way up, if you've got a glass, you can see the White Mountains and Mt. Washington—where North Conway and Conway is. And, of course, our favorite mountain, Mt. Monadnock, 's right here—and all these towns that lie around it: Jaffrey, 'n East Jaffrey, 'n Peterborough, 'n Dublin; and *(then pointing down in the audience)* there, quite a ways down, is Grover's Corners.

Yes, beautiful spot up here. Mountain laurel and li-lacks. I often wonder why people like to be buried in Woodlawn and Brooklyn when they might pass the same time up here in New Hampshire. Over there— *(pointing to stage left)* are the old stones,— 1670, 1680. Strong-minded people that come a long way to be independent. Summer people walk around there laughing at the funny words on the tombstones . . . it don't do any harm. And genealogists come up from Boston—get paid by city people for looking up their ancestors. They want to make sure they're Daughters of the American Revolution and of the *Mayflower.* . . . Well, I guess that don't do any harm, either. Wherever you come near the human race, there's layers and layers of nonsense. . . .

Over there are some Civil War veterans. Iron flags on their graves . . . New Hampshire boys . . . had a notion that the Union ought to be kept together, though they'd

---

1. **Lake Sunapee,** boundary between Sullivan and Merrimack counties in New Hampshire; summer resort.
2. **Lake Winnipesaukee** (win' ə pə sô' kē), largest lake in New Hampshire.

never seen more than fifty miles of it themselves. All they knew was the name, friends—the United States of America. The United States of America. And they went and died about it.

This here is the new part of the cemetery. Here's your friend Mrs. Gibbs. 'N let me see—Here's Mr. Stimson, organist at the Congregational Church. And Mrs. Soames who enjoyed the wedding so—you remember? Oh, and a lot of others. And Editor Webb's boy, Wallace, whose appendix burst while he was on a Boy Scout trip to Crawford Notch.

Yes, an awful lot of sorrow has sort of quieted down up here.

People just wild with grief have brought their relatives up to this hill. We all know how it is . . . and then time . . . and sunny days . . . and rainy days . . . 'n snow . . . We're all glad they're in a beautiful place, and we're coming up here ourselves when our fit's over.

Now there are some things we all know, but we don't take'm out and look at'm very often. We all know that *something* is eternal. And it ain't houses and it ain't names, and it ain't earth, and it ain't even the stars . . . everybody knows in their bones that *something* is eternal, and that something has to do with human beings. All the greatest people ever lived have been telling us that for five thousand years and yet you'd be surprised how people are always losing hold of it. There's something way down deep that's eternal about every human being. *(Pause.)*

You know as well as I do that the dead don't stay interested in us living people for very long. Gradually, gradually, they lose hold of the earth . . . and the ambitions they had . . . and the pleasures they had . . . and the things they suffered . . . and the people they loved.

They get weaned away from earth—that's the way I put it,—weaned away.

And they stay here while the earth part of 'em burns away, burns out; and all that time they slowly get indifferent to what's goin' on in Grover's Corners.

They're waitin'. They're waitin' for something that they feel is comin'. Something important, and great. Aren't they waitin' for the eternal part in them to come out clear?

Some of the things they're going to say maybe'll hurt your feelings—but that's the way it is: mother' n daughter . . . husband 'n wife . . . enemy 'n enemy . . . money 'n miser . . . all those terribly important things kind of grow pale around here. And what's left when memory's gone, and your identity, Mrs. Smith? *(He looks at the audience a minute, then turns to the stage.)*

Well! There are some *living* people. There's Joe Stoddard, our undertaker, supervising a new-made grave. And here comes a Grover's Corners boy, that left town to go out West. (JOE STODDARD *has hovered about in the background.* SAM CRAIG *enters left, wiping his forehead from the exertion. He carries an umbrella and strolls front.)*

SAM CRAIG. Good afternoon, Joe Stoddard.

JOE STODDARD. Good afternoon, good afternoon. Let me see now: do I know you?

SAM CRAIG. I'm Sam Craig.

JOE STODDARD. Gracious sakes' alive! Of all people! I should'a knowed you'd be back for the funeral. You've been away a long time, Sam.

SAM CRAIG. Yes, I've been away over twelve years. I'm in business out in Buffalo now, Joe. But I was in the East when I got news of my cousin's death, so I thought I'd combine things a little and come and see the old home. You look well.

JOE STODDARD. Yes, yes, can't complain. Very sad, our journey today, Samuel.

SAM CRAIG. Yes.

JOE STODDARD. Yes, yes. I always say I hate to supervise when a young person is taken. They'll be here in a few minutes now. I had to come here early today—my son's supervisin' at the home.

SAM CRAIG (*reading stones*). Old Farmer McCarty, I used to do chores for him—after school. He had the lumbago.

JOE STODDARD. Yes, we brought Farmer McCarty here a number of years ago now.

SAM CRAIG (*staring at* MRS. GIBBS' *knees*). Why, this is my Aunt Julia . . . I'd forgotten that she'd . . . of course, of course.

JOE STODDARD. Yes, Doc Gibbs lost his wife two-three years ago . . . about this time. And today's another pretty bad blow for him, too.

MRS. GIBBS (*to* SIMON STIMSON: *in an even voice*). That's my sister Carey's boy, Sam . . . Sam Craig.

SIMON STIMSON. I'm always uncomfortable when *they're* around.

MRS. GIBBS. Simon.

SAM CRAIG. Do they choose their own verses much, Joe?

JOE STODDARD. No . . . not usual. Mostly the bereaved pick a verse.

SAM CRAIG. Doesn't sound like Aunt Julia. There aren't many of those Hersey sisters left now. Let me see: where are . . . I wanted to look at my father's and mother's . . .

JOE STODDARD. Over there with the Craigs . . . Avenue F.

SAM CRAIG (*reading* SIMON STIMSON'S *epitaph*). He was organist at church, wasn't he?—Hm, drank a lot, we used to say.

JOE STODDARD. Nobody was supposed to know about it. He'd seen a peck of trouble. (*Behind his hand.*) Took his own life, y' know?

SAM CRAIG. Oh, did he?

JOE STODDARD. Hung himself in the attic. They tried to hush it up, but of course it got around. He chose his own epy-taph. You can see it there. It ain't a verse exactly.

SAM CRAIG. Why it's just some notes of music —what is it?

JOE STODDARD. Oh, I wouldn't know. It was wrote up in the Boston papers at the time.

SAM CRAIG. Joe, what did she die of?

JOE STODDARD. Who?

SAM CRAIG. My cousin.

JOE STODDARD. Oh, didn't you know? Had some trouble bringing a baby into the world. 'Twas her second, though. There's a little boy 'bout four years old.

SAM CRAIG (*opening the umbrella*). The grave's going to be over there?

JOE STODDARD. Yes, there ain't much more room over here among the Gibbses, so they're opening up a whole new Gibbs section over by Avenue B. You'll excuse me now. I see they're comin'. (*From left to center, at the back of the stage, comes a procession. Four men carry a casket, invisible to us. All the rest are under umbrellas. One can vaguely see:* DR. GIBBS, GEORGE, *the* WEBBS, *etc. They gather about a grave in the back center of the stage, a little to the left of center.*)

MRS. SOAMES. Who is it, Julia?

MRS. GIBBS (*without raising her eyes*). My daughter-in-law, Emily Webb.

MRS. SOAMES (*a little surprised, but no emotion*). Well, I declare! The road up here must have been awful muddy. What did she die of, Julia?

MRS. GIBBS. In childbirth.

MRS. SOAMES. Childbirth. (*Almost with a laugh.*) I'd forgotten all about that. My, wasn't life awful—(*with a sigh*) and wonderful.

SIMON STIMSON (*with a sideways glance*). Wonderful, was it?

MRS. GIBBS. Simon! Now, remember!

MRS. SOAMES. I remember Emily's wedding. Wasn't it a lovely wedding! And I remember her reading the class poem at Graduation Exercises. Emily was one of the brightest girls ever graduated from High School. I've heard Principal Wilkins say so time after time. I called on them at their new farm, just before I died. Perfectly beautiful farm.

A WOMAN FROM AMONG THE DEAD. It's on the same road we lived on.

STAGE MANAGER. . . . *The dead don't stay interested in us living people for very long. Gradually, gradually, they lose hold of the earth . . . and the people they loved.*

A MAN AMONG THE DEAD. Yepp, right smart farm. *(They subside. The group by the grave starts singing "Blessed Be the Tie That Binds.")*

A WOMAN AMONG THE DEAD. I always liked that hymn. I was hopin' they'd sing a hymn. *(Pause. Suddenly* EMILY *appears from among the umbrellas. She is wearing a white dress. Her hair is down her back and tied by a white ribbon like a little girl. She comes slowly, gazing wonderingly at the dead, a little dazed. She stops halfway and smiles faintly. After looking at the mourners for a moment, she walks slowly to the vacant chair beside* MRS. GIBBS *and sits down.)*

EMILY *(to them all, quietly, smiling).* Hello.

MRS. SOAMES. Hello, Emily.

A MAN AMONG THE DEAD. Hello, M's Gibbs.

EMILY *(warmly).* Hello, Mother Gibbs.

MRS. GIBBS. Emily.

EMILY. Hello. *(With surprise.)* It's raining. *(Her eyes drift back to the funeral company.)*

MRS. GIBBS. Yes . . . They'll be gone soon, dear. Just rest yourself.

EMILY. It seems thousands and thousands of years since I . . . Papa remembered that that was my favorite hymn.

Oh, I wish I'd been here a long time. I don't like being new here.—How do you do, Mr. Stimson?

SIMON STIMSON. How do you do, Emily. *(*EMILY *continues to look about her with a wondering smile; as though to shut out from her mind the thought of the funeral company she starts speaking to* MRS. GIBBS *with a touch of nervousness.)*

EMILY. Mother Gibbs, George and I have

made that farm into just the best place you ever saw. We thought of you all the time. We wanted to show you the new barn and a great long ce-ment drinking fountain for the stock. We bought that out of the money you left us.

MRS. GIBBS. I did?

EMILY. Don't you remember, Mother Gibbs—the legacy you left us? Why, it was over three hundred and fifty dollars.

MRS. GIBBS. Yes, yes, Emily.

EMILY. Well, there's a patent device on the drinking fountain so that it never over-flows, Mother Gibbs, and it never sinks below a certain mark they have there. It's fine. (*Her voice trails off and her eyes return to the funeral group.*) It won't be the same to George without me, but it's a lovely farm. (*Suddenly she looks directly at* MRS. GIBBS.) Live people don't understand, do they?

MRS. GIBBS. No, dear—not very much.

EMILY. They're sort of shut up in little boxes, aren't they? I feel as though I knew them last a thousand years ago . . . My boy is spending the day at Mrs. Carter's. (*She sees* MR. CARTER *among the dead.*) Oh, Mr. Carter, my little boy is spending the day at your house.

MR. CARTER. Is he?

EMILY. Yes, he loves it there.—Mother Gibbs, we have a Ford, too. Never gives any trouble. I don't drive, though. Mother Gibbs, when does this feeling go away?—Of being . . . one of *them*? How long does it . . . ?

MRS. GIBBS. Sh! dear. Just wait and be patient.

EMILY (*with a sigh*). I know.—Look, they're finished. They're going.

MRS. GIBBS. Sh—. (*The umbrellas leave the stage.* DR. GIBBS *has come over to his wife's grave and stands before it a moment.* EMILY *looks up at his face.* MRS. GIBBS *does not raise her eyes.*)

EMILY. Look! Father Gibbs is bringing some of my flowers to you. He looks just like George, doesn't he? Oh, Mother Gibbs, I never realized before how troubled and how . . . how in the dark live persons are. Look at him. I loved him so. From morning till night, that's all they are—troubled. (DR. GIBBS *goes off.*)

THE DEAD. Little cooler than it was.—Yes, that rain's cooled it off a little. Those northeast winds always do the same thing, don't they? If it isn't a rain, it's a three-day blow.—(*A patient calm falls on the stage. The* STAGE MANAGER *appears at his proscenium pillar, smoking.* EMILY *sits up abruptly with an idea.*)

EMILY. But, Mother Gibbs, one can go back; one can go back there again . . . into the living. I feel it. I know it. Why just then for a moment I was thinking about . . . about the farm . . . and for a minute I *was* there, and my baby was on my lap as plain as day.

MRS. GIBBS. Yes, of course you can.

EMILY. I can go back there and live all those days over again . . . why not?

MRS. GIBBS. All I can say is, Emily, don't.

EMILY (*she appeals urgently to the* STAGE MANAGER). But it's true, isn't it? I can go and live . . . back there . . . again.

STAGE MANAGER. Yes, some have tried—but they soon come back here.

MRS. GIBBS. Don't do it, Emily.

MRS. SOAMES. Emily, don't. It's not what you think it'd be.

EMILY. But I won't live over a sad day. I'll choose a happy one—I'll choose the day I first knew that I loved George. Why should that be painful? (*They are silent. Her question turns to the* STAGE MANAGER.)

STAGE MANAGER. You not only live it; but you watch yourself living it.

EMILY. Yes?

STAGE MANAGER. And as you watch it, you see the thing that they—down there—never know. You see the future. You know what's going to happen afterwards.

EMILY. But is that—painful? Why?

MRS. GIBBS. That's not the only reason why you shouldn't do it, Emily. When you've been here longer you'll see that our life here is to forget all that, and think only of what's ahead, and be ready for what's ahead. When you've been here longer you'll understand.

EMILY (*softly*). But Mother Gibbs, how can I *ever* forget that life? It's all I know. It's all I had.

MRS. SOAMES. Oh, Emily. It isn't wise. Really, it isn't.

EMILY. But it's a thing I must know for myself. I'll choose a happy day, anyway.

MRS. GIBBS. *No!*—At least, choose an unimportant day. Choose the least important day in your life. It will be important enough.

EMILY (*to herself*). Then it can't be since I was married; or since the baby was born. (*To the* STAGE MANAGER, *eagerly.*) I can choose a birthday at least, can't I?—I choose my twelfth birthday.

STAGE MANAGER. All right. February 11th, 1899. A Tuesday.—Do you want any special time of day?

EMILY. Oh, I want the whole day.

STAGE MANAGER. We'll begin at dawn. You remember it had been snowing for several days; but it had stopped the night before, and they had begun clearing the roads. The sun's coming up.

EMILY (*with a cry; rising*). There's Main Street . . . why, that's Mr. Morgan's drugstore before he changed it! . . . And there's the livery stable. (*The stage at no time in this act has been very dark; but now the left half of the stage gradually becomes very bright—the brightness of a crisp winter morning.* EMILY *walks toward Main Street.*)

STAGE MANAGER. Yes, it's 1899. This is fourteen years ago.

EMILY. Oh, that's the town I knew as a little girl. And, *look,* there's the old white fence that used to be around our house. Oh, I'd forgotten that! Oh, I love it so! Are they inside?

STAGE MANAGER. Yes, your mother'll be coming downstairs in a minute to make breakfast.

EMILY (*softly*). Will she?

STAGE MANAGER. And you remember: your father had been away for several days; he came back on the early-morning train.

EMILY. No . . . ?

STAGE MANAGER. He'd been back to his college to make a speech—in western New York, at Clinton.

EMILY. Look! There's Howie Newsome. There's our policeman. But he's *dead;* he *died.* (*The voices of* HOWIE NEWSOME, CONSTABLE WARREN *and* JOE CROWELL, JR., *are heard at the left of the stage.* EMILY *listens in delight.*)

HOWIE NEWSOME. Whoa, Bessie!—Bessie! 'Morning, Bill.

CONSTABLE WARREN. 'Morning, Howie.

HOWIE NEWSOME. You're up early.

CONSTABLE WARREN. Been rescuin' a party; darn near froze to death, down by Polish Town thar. Got drunk and lay out in the snowdrifts. Thought he was in bed when I shook'm.

EMILY. Why, there's Joe Crowell. . . .

JOE CROWELL. Good morning, Mr. Warren. 'Morning, Howie. (MRS. WEBB *has appeared in her kitchen, but* EMILY *does not see her until she calls.*)

MRS. WEBB. Chil-*dren!* Wally! Emily! . . . Time to get up.

EMILY. Mama, I'm here! Oh! how young Mama looks! I didn't know Mama was ever that young.

MRS. WEBB. You can come and dress by the kitchen fire, if you like; but hurry. (HOWIE NEWSOME *has entered along Main Street and brings the milk to* MRS. WEBB'S *door.*) Good morning, Mr. Newsome. Whhhh—it's cold.

HOWIE NEWSOME. Ten below by my barn, Mrs. Webb.

MRS. WEBB. Think of it! Keep yourself wrapped up. (*She takes her bottles in, shuddering.*)

EMILY (*with an effort*). Mama, I can't find my blue hair ribbon anywhere.

MRS. WEBB. Just open your eyes, dear, that's all. I laid it out for you special—on the dresser, there. If it were a snake it would bite you.

EMILY. Yes, yes . . . (*She puts her hand on her heart.* MR. WEBB *comes along Main Street, where he meets* CONSTABLE WARREN. *Their movements and voices are increasingly lively in the sharp air.)*

MR. WEBB. Good morning, Bill.

CONSTABLE WARREN. Good morning, Mr. Webb. You're up early.

MR. WEBB. Yes, just been back to my old college in New York State. Been any trouble here?

CONSTABLE WARREN. Well, I was called up this mornin' to rescue a Polish fella—darn near froze to death he was.

MR. WEBB. We must get it in the paper.

CONSTABLE WARREN. 'Twan't much.

EMILY *(whispers).* Papa. (MR. WEBB *shakes the snow off his feet and enters his house.* CONSTABLE WARREN *goes off, right.)*

MR. WEBB. Good morning, Mother.

MRS. WEBB. How did it go, Charles?

MR. WEBB. Oh, fine, I guess. I told'm a few things.—Everything all right here?

MRS. WEBB. Yes—can't think of anything that's happened, special. Been right cold. Howie Newsome says it's ten below over to his barn.

MR. WEBB. Yes, well, it's colder than that at Hamilton College.[3] Students' ears are falling off. It ain't Christian.—Paper have any mistakes in it?

MRS. WEBB. None that I noticed. Coffee's ready when you want it. *(He starts upstairs.)* Charles! Don't forget; it's Emily's birthday. Did you remember to get her something?

MR. WEBB *(patting his pocket).* Yes, I've got something here. *(Calling up the stairs.)* Where's my girl? Where's my birthday girl? *(He goes off left.)*

MRS. WEBB. Don't interrupt her now, Charles. You can see her at breakfast. She's slow enough as it is. Hurry up, children! It's seven o'clock. Now, I don't want to call you again.

EMILY *(softly, more in wonder than in grief).* I can't bear it. They're so young and beautiful. Why did they ever have to get old? Mama, I'm here. I'm grown up. I love you all, everything.—I can't look at everything hard enough. *(She looks questioningly at the*

STAGE MANAGER, *saying or suggesting: "Can I go in?" He nods briefly. She crosses to the inner door to the kitchen, left of her mother, and as though entering the room, says, suggesting the voice of a girl of twelve:)* Good morning, Mama.

MRS. WEBB *(crossing to embrace and kiss her; in her characteristic matter-of-fact manner).* Well, now, dear, a very happy birthday to my girl and many happy returns. There are some surprises waiting for you on the kitchen table.

EMILY. Oh, Mama, you *shouldn't* have. *(She throws an anguished glance at the* STAGE MANAGER.) I can't—I can't.

MRS. WEBB *(facing the audience, over her stove).* But birthday or no birthday, I want you to eat your breakfast good and slow. I want you to grow up and be a good strong girl.

That in the blue paper is from your Aunt Carrie; and I reckon you can guess who brought the post-card album. I found it on the doorstep when I brought in the milk— George Gibbs . . . must have come over in the cold pretty early . . . right nice of him.

EMILY *(to herself).* Oh, George! I'd forgotten that. . . .

MRS. WEBB. Chew that bacon good and slow. It'll keep you warm on a cold day.

EMILY *(with mounting urgency).* Oh, Mama, just look at me one minute as though you really saw me. Mama, fourteen years have gone by. I'm dead. You're a grandmother, Mama. I married George Gibbs, Mama. Wally's dead, too. Mama, his appendix burst on a camping trip to North Conway. We felt just terrible about it—don't you remember? But, just for a moment now we're all together. Mama, just for a moment we're happy. *Let's look at one another.*

MRS. WEBB. That in the yellow paper is something I found in the attic among your grandmother's things. You're old enough to wear it now, and I thought you'd like it.

---

3. **Hamilton College,** private college in Clinton, New York.

EMILY. And this is from you. Why, Mama, it's just lovely and it's just what I wanted. It's beautiful! (*She flings her arms around her mother's neck. Her mother goes on with her cooking, but is pleased.*)

MRS. WEBB. Well, I hoped you'd like it. Hunted all over. Your Aunt Norah couldn't find one in Concord, so I had to send all the way to Boston. (*Laughing.*)

Wally has something for you, too. He made it at manual-training class and he's very proud of it. Be sure you make a big fuss about it.—Your father has a surprise for you, too; don't know what it is myself. Sh—here he comes.

MR. WEBB (*off stage*). Where's my girl? Where's my birthday girl?

EMILY (*in a loud voice to the* STAGE MANAGER). I can't. I can't go on. It goes so fast. We don't have time to look at one another. (*She breaks down sobbing. The lights dim on the left half of the stage.* MRS. WEBB *disappears.*)

I didn't realize. So all that was going on and we never noticed. Take me back—up the hill—to my grave. But first: Wait! One more look.

Good-by, Good-by, world. Good-by, Grover's Corners . . . Mama and Papa. Good-by to clocks ticking . . . and Mama's sunflowers. And food and coffee. And new-ironed dresses and hot baths . . . and sleeping and waking up. Oh, earth, you're too wonderful for anybody to realize you. (*She looks toward the* STAGE MANAGER *and asks abruptly, through her tears:*)

Do any human beings ever realize life while they live it?—every, every minute?

STAGE MANAGER. No. (*Pause.*) The saints and poets, maybe—they do some.

EMILY. I'm ready to go back. (*She returns to her chair beside* MRS. GIBBS. *Pause.*)

MRS. GIBBS. Were you happy?

EMILY. No . . . I should have listened to you. That's all human beings are! Just blind people.

MRS. GIBBS. Look, it's clearing up. The stars are coming out.

EMILY. Oh, Mr. Stimson, I should have listened to them.

SIMON STIMSON (*with mounting violence; bitingly*). Yes, now you know. Now you know! That's what it was to be alive. To move about in a cloud of ignorance; to go up and down trampling on the feelings of those . . . of those about you. To spend and waste time as though you had a million years. To be always at the mercy of one self-centered passion, or another. Now you know—that's the happy existence you wanted to go back to. Ignorance and blindness.

MRS. GIBBS (*spiritedly*). Simon Stimson, that ain't the whole truth and you know it. Emily, look at that star. I forget its name.

A MAN AMONG THE DEAD. My boy Joel was a sailor,—knew 'em all. He'd set on the porch evenings and tell 'em all by name. Yes, sir, wonderful!

ANOTHER MAN AMONG THE DEAD. A star's mighty good company.

A WOMAN AMONG THE DEAD. Yes. Yes, 'tis.

SIMON STIMSON. Here's one of them coming.

THE DEAD. That's funny. 'Tain't no time for one of them to be here.—Goodness sakes.

EMILY. Mother Gibbs, it's George.

MRS. GIBBS. Sh, dear. Just rest yourself.

EMILY. It's George. (GEORGE *enters from the left, and slowly comes toward them.*)

A MAN FROM AMONG THE DEAD. And my boy, Joel, who knew the stars—he used to say it took millions of years for that speck of light to git to the earth. Don't seem like a body could believe it, but that's what he used to say—millions of years. (GEORGE *sinks to his knees then falls full length at* EMILY'S *feet.*)

A WOMAN AMONG THE DEAD. Goodness! That ain't no way to behave!

MRS. SOAMES. He ought to be home.

EMILY. Mother Gibbs?

MRS. GIBBS. Yes, Emily?

EMILY. They don't understand, do they?

MRS. GIBBS. No, dear. They don't understand. (*The* STAGE MANAGER *appears at the right, one hand on a dark curtain which he* *slowly draws across the scene. In the distance a clock is heard striking the hour very faintly.)*

STAGE MANAGER. Most everybody's asleep in Grover's Corners. There are a few lights on: Shorty Hawkins, down at the depot, has just watched the Albany train go by. And at the livery stable somebody's setting up late and talking.—Yes, it's clearing up. There are the stars—doing their old, old crisscross journeys in the sky. Scholars haven't settled the matter yet, but they seem to think there are no living beings up there. Just chalk . . . or fire. Only this one is straining away, straining away all the time to make something of itself. The strain's so bad that every sixteen hours everybody lies down and gets a rest. *(He winds his watch.)* Hm. . . . Eleven o'clock in Grover's Corners.—You get a good rest, too. Good night.

The End

FOR UNDERSTANDING

1. How many years have elapsed since the happenings of Act II? What characters are in the cemetery when Act III opens?
2. Why does the Stage Manager say the dead remain on earth?
3. Other than the Stage Manager, who is the first *living* person on the stage in Act III? What does he tell Sam Craig about Simon Stimson's death?
4. Why does the Stage Manager tell Emily that going back among the living to relive a part of life is so painful?
5. When Emily asks to be taken back to the cemetery, what does she say about earthly life and human beings? What does Simon Stimson say?

FOR INTERPRETATION

1. Act III of *Our Town*, which deals largely with death, is filled with *irony*. Discuss the irony in Emily's speech about living people being "sort of shut up in little boxes." Why is her mother's statement that Emily could find her hair ribbon if she would just open her eyes also ironic?

2. Discuss the following statements in light of what you think Wilder's play suggests:
  a. Life in Grover's Corners is very much like life in any community, large or small.
  b. All change is superficial; there is really no significant difference between life in the past and in the present.
  c. "Wherever you come near the human race, there's layers and layers of nonsense."
  d. *Our Town* both celebrates the simple joys of small-town life and condemns the lack of awareness of that life.

FOR APPRECIATION

Structure and Staging

Using essentially a bare stage in all three acts, Wilder's original staging techniques succeed in placing an American community in significant detail before an audience. The Stage Manager figure, welding the whole together, is the most important character on the stage. Light is used to focus attention on particular actions or characters throughout the production.
1. In the funeral scene, how does Wilder very simply separate the living from the dead? Over what scene does the Stage Manager himself draw a dark curtain as Act III closes?
2. Structurally speaking, in a three-act play, we expect the first act to be the conflict or tension-raising act and the third act to resolve those tensions. One of the basic tensions in this play concerns the attitude toward life of the people in the town. Discuss whether you think *Our Town* follows the usual course of resolving tension in the final act.

COMPOSITION

Imagine you are the Stage Manager introducing an audience to the place where you were born or lived for a number of years. Choose the time of day and the landmarks with which you wish to identify your locale.

  Write a series of brief paragraphs telling about your place, introducing the people you wish and giving any historical information you feel to be significant about the place or its people.

THE AMERICAN NOVEL TO 1914

Although human beings have been telling each other stories since time beyond reckoning, the novel as we know it is a relatively new literary form, dating back only some 250 years. There seems to be no universally accepted definition for the novel. It may, however, be described as a complete prose narrative, involving real or fictional characters, and usually running to no fewer than 50,000 words. Novels are written primarily to entertain, but also, sometimes, to teach—to give readers what the authors perceive to be greater insights into the human condition.

Pamela, or Virtue Rewarded, published in 1740 by Samuel Richardson (1689–1761), is among the earliest English novels. The highly romantic and lengthy tale is told through a series of letters from the young maid servant, Pamela Andrews, to her aged parents. As the title suggests, the story recounts the valiant struggles of this unsophisticated heroine to maintain her virtue under the most trying circumstances. Although most American writers at this time imitated their English counterparts (principally because the greater number of their readers lived in Britain), it was not until nearly a half century after *Pamela* that the American writer William Hill Brown (1765–1793) published *The Power of Sympathy* (1789). *The Massachusetts Magazine* advertised this work as the first American novel published in the United States. The ponderous and preachy tale has much the same theme as Richardson's *Pamela,* uses letters to tell the story, and was ostensibly written to warn its readers, especially young women, of the dangerous consequences of falling from virtue. Today the book rates little more than a note in literary histories.

When the first installments of the satirical novel *Modern Chivalry* by Hugh Henry Brackenridge (1748–1816) appeared in 1792, they were immediately popular. This sprawling narrative, almost completely devoid of plot, was published in parts until 1815, and was loosely modeled on Cervantes's *Don Quixote* (1605, 1615). The hero of *Modern Chivalry* is Captain John Farrago, a western Pennsylvania farmer, who sallies forth to see how the people on the Western frontier cope with their newly won independence and the American experiment in democracy. Accompanying him on this lengthy tour is his scalawag Irish servant, Teague Oregan, who is represented as having more brawn than brains.

Unlike the simple-minded Don Quixote of Cervantes's tale, who confused a windmill with a giant and a flock of sheep with an enemy army, the astute Captain Farrago observes that the backwoods populace is ill-prepared to accept democracy. To rectify the situation, the good Captain offers arguments in favor of the rights and ideals in the new national constitution and advocates the canons of civilized behavior. For his efforts, however, the hero is often roughly used by the ignorant and impulsive farmers and woodsmen whom he and Oregan encounter in their wanderings. Modern scholars have speculated that, in view of the overabundance of romantic writings in this period, it was satirists like Brackenridge who helped to keep American writers in touch with the harsher realities of life.

In 1797, Royall Tyler (1757–1826), better known as a dramatist, published *The Algerine Captive,* a popular novel of the adventures of a surgeon hero who is captured by Barbary pirates.

A year later Charles Brockden Brown (1771–1810) modeled *Wieland, or the Transformation* on the English gothic novel, a form characterized by terror, violence, psychic phenomena, and mystery. The term "gothic" was applied to such novels because they were usually set against a backdrop of gothic architecture, preferably an ancient and drafty castle. Lacking such a setting in America, Brown wrote of a fiendish ventriloquist who victimizes a Pennsylvania family, some of whose members are predisposed to insanity. The novel was a success and Brown went on to turn out more of what became known as American gothic novels. His skill in this medium, however, was considerably less than that of Edgar Allan Poe and Nathaniel Hawthorne.

Brown, like other novelists of the day, was aware of the principal reason for the popularity of this new literary form. In an essay, "On the Cause of the Popularity of Novels," he wrote: "We fly for relief from the sameness of real life to compositions called *novels*. In them we find common things related in an uncommon way, which is precisely the remedy we have been seeking to vary our amusements. . . . Notwithstanding the great pains that have been taken in many hundred late novels to give a turn and variety to love affairs, by every mode of cross-purposes, and hairbreadth escapes, there must be a termination of even these, and the common adventures of novels were actually becoming as insipid as the progress of real life, when a bold and successful attempt was lately made to enliven these narratives by a certain proportion of murders, ghosts, clanking chains, dead bodies, skeletons, old castles, and damp dungeons." Although much of his essay is written tongue-in-cheek, Brown ends by cautioning that if the readers of novels seek anything beyond amusement, then they "shall often be deluded by estimates of human life and happiness that are calculated upon false foundations."

In the immediate post-Revolutionary period many patriotic American intellectuals earnestly tried to develop a "national" literature along with a "national" character. These reformers attempted to wean American writers away from slavish imitation of English writers. British commentator Sydney Smith could ask in 1820: "In the four quarters of the world, who reads an American book? or goes to an American play?" Certainly the question was valid, and it indicated the major problem of originality facing most American writers. Although there were printing presses in each new state, most publishers and the lucrative reading markets were in England.

The early 1820s marked the beginning of the national literature that had been so long sought. The years 1819–1821 saw the appearance of *The Sketch Book,* by Washington Irving (see page 122), the first collection of William Cullen Bryant's *Poems,* and *The Spy,* a Revolutionary War novel by James Fenimore Cooper (see page 134). Two years later, in 1823, Cooper published *the Pioneers,* the first in his series of historical novels of romance and adventure—the *Leatherstocking Tales.* The other novels in the series that brought the author worldwide acclaim and the title "the American Sir Walter Scott" include *The Last of the Mohicans* (1826), *The Prairie* (1827), *The Pathfinder* (1840), and *The Deerslayer* (1841). Originally Cooper had not thought of his novels as a chronicle of the events in the life of his hero, Natty Bumppo. In the year before his death, however, Cooper published a new edition of the novels in which the events in the hero's career are arranged sequentially. In creating the tall and gaunt hunter Natty Bumppo, who appears in the five stories variously as Deerslayer, Hawk-eye, Pathfinder, and Leatherstocking, Cooper established a romantic model of the American frontier hero that has appeared in countless short stories, dime novels, plays, movies, and television productions since then. Cooper's frontier hero is typically American, for nowhere else could Bumppo, his friends, and his ad-

As described by Frank Norris in The Octopus, *the tentacles of the railroad changed the landscape of America forever.*

THE LACKAWANNA VALLEY, George Inness
National Galley of Art, Washington, D.C.
Gift of Mrs. Huttleston Rogers

versaries live out a mythical history amid such pristine and primitive settings.

In addition to his Leatherstocking novels, Cooper wrote five American romances of the sea and naval combat. His first, *The Pilot* (1823), relates the adventures of Revolutionary hero John Paul Jones, as well as those of one of Cooper's most famous characters, the seaman Long Tom Coffin. Cooper also wrote three novels based on European history and three that chronicled the lives of a family of landed gentry in upstate New York.

Most of Cooper's readers today are well aware before they open his books that they will find a stilted style and dialogue, bigger-than-life heroes, genteel heroines, and impossible situations in which there is formula pursuit-and-escape action. Cooper, however,

still provides the reader with good escape reading.

Nathaniel Hawthorne (see page 210), whose first novel *Fanshawe* (1828) was considered a failure, concerned himself primarily with writing short tales until he published *The Scarlet Letter* in 1850. With its appearance American literature had its first significant symbolic novel—just one year before Hawthorne's friend Herman Melville published the second such novel, *Moby-Dick.* Hawthorne, who had steeped himself in the history of colonial New England, wrote best about the distant past and called his fiction "psychological romance," declaring his aim was to "burrow into the depths of our common nature." To do so, he fastened on the moral and psychological effects of sin.

In *The Scarlet Letter* he explores sin's tragic consequences for three individuals in early colonial New England. Following the critical and financial success of that novel, Hawthorne published in the next year *The House of the Seven Gables,* in which the Pyncheon family, who have lived in the old seven-gabled house for generations, suffer under the curse of a man hanged for witchcraft. Other Hawthorne novels include *The Blithedale Romance* (1852) and *The Marble Faun* (1860). Readers still find *The Scarlet Letter* and *The House of the Seven Gables* engaging fare.

At the turn of the century it was fashionable to dismiss *Uncle Tom's Cabin* (1851) by Harriet Beecher Stowe (1811–1896) as a novel of raw propaganda, unworthy of critical evaluation. In the 1960s, however, the critic Edmund Wilson defended it as a novel of "eruptive force" in which "a critical mind is at work." Sold in the millions of copies here and abroad for years after its publication, the highly moralistic and melodramatic novel is still read.

When Herman Melville (see page 252) published *Typee* in 1846, he based the story loosely on his own adventures during a whaling voyage in the South Pacific. Accused by one critic of consorting with man-eating natives, the author was soon identified by some of his readers as "a man who had lived among cannibals." The book was an immediate success and has become a classic model for hosts of romantic tales depicting "civilized" men adapting to the exotic and dreamlike life-style of a tropical Eden. Melville's second novel of Polynesian romance, *Omoo* (1847), was also a success. With the publication of *Mardi* (1849), though, he lost many of his readers; they were puzzled and put off by the symbolism of this tale of a mysterious voyage through the world. His exciting seafaring novels *Redburn* (1849) and *White-Jacket* (1850) did much to restore his popularity.

In 1851, Melville published his lengthy masterpiece, *Moby-Dick, or The White Whale,* which he dedicated to his friend Hawthorne.

This work, usually called a novel, in many ways defies classification. On the surface the tale is a straightforward one: the half-mad Captain Ahab, who has lost a leg to Moby Dick on a previous encounter, gathers a whaling crew to pursue the Great White Whale. Many readers of the day who missed Melville's complex symbolism simply read the story as one of vengeance. Those who dropped down to another sounding, however, read the story on a level that was almost inscrutably symbolic. The critics and pundits puzzled out many meanings, one of which is that when a man tries to destroy a force (be it a force for good or for evil) that God has set loose in the world, the result can only be total disaster.

Many early critics dismissed *Moby-Dick* as either unfathomably symbolic or poorly written and unmanageable. In the latter years of his life, Melville's readers dwindled, and the author sank into obscurity. Not until the 1920s was *Moby-Dick* re-evaluated by a new generation of critics; it soon came to be regarded as one of the great novels in American literature.

Friend and promoter of both the struggling neophyte and the literary lion, William Dean Howells (1837–1920) was for many years the undisputed leader in the late-nineteenth-century school of realism in fiction. Of his many novels, however, the one most often read today is *The Rise of Silas Lapham* (1885), the story of a crude and self-made man who amasses a vast fortune, loses it through speculation, yet in adversity reveals great strength of character.

Howells's close friend, Henry James (1843–1916), is considered by many critics to be one of America's finest novelists and short-story writers. James spent much of his life in Europe. He wrote insightfully of expatriate upper-class American characters, placed in what he described as "morally interesting situations," who worked out their destinies as they were manipulated by sophisticated Europeans. His two best novels on this theme are *The Portrait of a Lady* (1881) and *The Am-*

bassadors (1903). James has also been praised for his use of the supernatural to explore the psychological; his most famous tale in this vein is *The Turn of the Screw* (1898).

The Southern writer, George Washington Cable (1844–1925), was one of many who were encouraged by Howells. Cable's most widely read novels, *The Grandissimes* (1880) and *Madame Delphine* (1881), explore the intricacies of upper-class Creole family life in New Orleans during the early part of the last century.

The Adventures of Huckleberry Finn by Mark Twain (see page 442) was a best seller when it was published in 1885 and has since attained the stature of a classic in both American and world literature. The novel moves forward on two levels. On the first level is the heady adventure of Huck and his slave friend Jim as they float down the Mississippi; on the second level is the awakening of a boy to the hypocrisy and injustice he discovers in a wider world.

Ironically, a short novel that has been acclaimed as one of the most realistic studies of a young soldier in battle was published by a twenty-three-year-old writer who had not yet been to war. The novel is *The Red Badge of Courage* published in 1895 by Stephen Crane (see page 415). The impressionistic realism of the book helped to set a new pattern for the treatment of war in modern fiction.

In the first dozen years of the twentieth century, Edith Wharton (1862–1937) produced two significant novels in addition to her compelling short stories. *The House of Mirth* (1905) is a highly critical portrayal of end-of-the-century New York formal society. *Ethan Frome* (1911) is a small masterpiece dealing with the other end of the socio-economic spectrum. The novel chronicles the bleak, poverty-ridden lives of three rural New Englanders caught up in a tragic domestic triangle.

Although not considered a great novelist, Frank Norris (1870–1902) influenced modern American fiction through naturalistic

PORTRAIT OF EDITH WHARTON
Wharton's novels and stories often depict an orderly, mannered world, where commonplace tragedy frustrates or destroys well-meaning people.

novels that were structured much like those of the French writer, Emile Zola. Marked by sordidness, brutality, and determinism, *The Octopus* (1901) and *The Pit* (1903), considered his best work, depict the struggles of California wheat growers to survive the opportunistic pressures of the railroads and speculators.

Another novelist who wrote in the naturalistic tradition but was better known than Norris was Theodore Dreiser (1871–1945). Both Norris and Dreiser dismissed the realism espoused by Howells as too tame, even as

PORTRAIT OF THEODORE DREISER

youth, was acutely conscious of the gap between rich and poor and of the disparity between the ethics people professed and those by which they lived. He used this theme of moral ambiguity again and again in his long writing career. In the trilogy *The Financier* (1912), *The Titan* (1914), and *The Stoic* (1947), he relentlessly studied the ruthless businessman, Frank Cowperwood, whose guiding philosophy was expressed in the brief motto: "I satisfy myself." In novels like *Sister Carrie* (first published in 1900 but suppressed until 1912), *Jennie Gerhardt* (1911), and *An American Tragedy* (1925), Dreiser emphasized the idea that we are creatures of economic and biological necessities. Dreiser's most popular work, and his most controversial, is *An American Tragedy* (1925). The book created a furor because Dreiser attributed the downfall of his young central character to the American economic system. Today Theodore Dreiser's works are still widely read.

The two novels by Jack London (1876–1916) that are still popular are *The Call of the Wild* (1903) and *The Sea Wolf* (1904). His best work, however, is *Martin Eden* (1909), the semi-autobiographical novel of the struggles of a poorly educated young man to win success as a writer. Although not a first-rate novelist, London is considered in some countries to be on a plane with Whitman and Twain, a judgment not shared by American critics.

Thus by 1914, when World War I began in Europe, the American novel had definitely come into its own. However, though works by American novelists were widely read and respected, both in America and abroad, no one could have foreseen that the next thirty years would witness an even more dramatic flowering of the American novel.

dishonest. They preached the philosophy of the European naturalists: that the individual's fate is determined by heredity, environment, and inward drives and external circumstances that are uncontrollable. Literary scholars often point to naturalism as the inspiration for the flood of great fiction produced by American writers in the first half of the twentieth century. But however influential the approach of the early naturalists, style was not their strong point. One critic characterized Dreiser's prose as clumsy and elephantine, his diction as flat and lifeless.

Early in life Dreiser, who had suffered extreme poverty and family instability in his

COMPOSITION WORKSHOP

THE RESEARCH PLAN: THE LIBRARY

Experienced writers know that every moment spent in carefully preparing to write pays off once the writing begins. Even if the piece of writing is as simple as a single-paragraph biographical sketch, the experienced author doesn't just begin to write. He or she first decides where to go to locate the information on the topic. The writer then collects the needed information and makes sure that all of it relates to the topic. He or she next arranges the sorted information into some kind of sensible order. The actual writing does not begin until the author writes a topic sentence that is based on all of the gathered information. In writing a research paper you will be following the same basic process.

Once you have decided upon a topic for a research paper and narrowed it down to a manageable size, your next step is to sketch out a research plan. The research plan is a quickly drawn blueprint of the sources you will follow in collecting information for the paper. Obviously the library is of central importance in your research and you should allow sufficient time to use its resources.

Almost every plan will indicate an initial stop in the library's reference section, followed by later stops at the library's card catalog. If you know at the outset what books you should consult in the reference section and the library's main collection, you should name them in the research plan. If your personal observation or interviewing can shed some light upon the topic, name these methods of collecting information in the plan also. The purpose of the plan is to identify all the various sources of information you should investigate in your research.

GENERAL REFERENCE

Once you actually begin the research, your first stop is most likely to be the reference section of a library, where you will find several useful books that will provide basic information. Some of these sources will also lead you to other sources. Depending upon the topic, a general encyclopedia is often the first reference to consult. Although all worthwhile research must go beyond the encyclo-

pedia, articles within it usually offer a useful summary of what is known about a general topic. In a well-researched encyclopedia such as the *Encyclopaedia Britannica*, there is an additional bonus. A bibliography, or list of books, accompanies most articles. This bibliography usually includes the most important books written about the subject of the article.

The general reference section of a library also includes a number of more specialized works that provide a wealth of information in the major areas of human knowledge. Biographical and historical references are most useful for background information on writers and the historical periods that their writings reflect. Especially useful, if you are collecting information on a literary topic, are such standard references as the *Literary History of the United States*.

Another important research tool in the library's general reference section is the *Readers' Guide to Periodical Literature*. This easy-to-use guide allows a researcher to obtain a listing of articles that have appeared in the nation's 100 largest-circulation magazines. Since many of these magazines often feature literary works and people in their articles, it is always worthwhile to check the *Readers' Guide*, which lists articles by topic as well as by title and author. Depending upon the size of a library, an index called the *Social Sciences and Humanities Index* might also be available. This index lists articles in more scholarly and more specialized magazines. If your topic includes an analysis or an interpretation of a work of literature, you might find scholarly articles about that work particularly useful.

THE CARD CATALOG

While your research usually begins in the general reference section of a library, you must soon move to the card catalog, the alphabetical listing of all of the printed resources in the library's collection. Three cards are usually assigned to each of the library's nonfiction books. One card lists the book by the author's last name. A second card lists the book by its title. A third card lists the book by its subject. The subject cards are often the most useful to the writer at the beginning of the research, for the subject headings on the cards

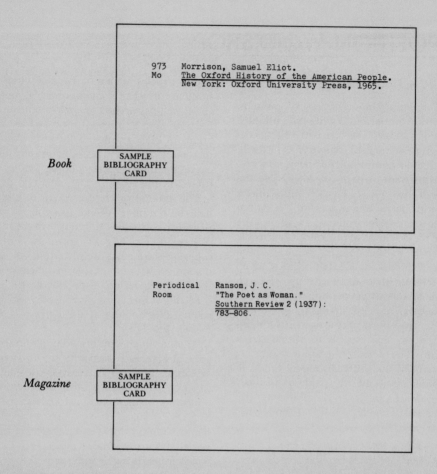

Book

SAMPLE
BIBLIOGRAPHY
CARD

```
973    Morrison, Samuel Eliot.
Mo     The Oxford History of the American People.
       New York: Oxford University Press, 1965.
```

Magazine

SAMPLE
BIBLIOGRAPHY
CARD

```
Periodical    Ransom, J. C.
Room          "The Poet as Woman."
              Southern Review 2 (1937):
              783–806.
```

permit quick identification of books that are worth examining. Be sure to check all possible headings when using the subject cards to locate books. A writer conducting research for a paper that examines features of American folklore, for example, might search for headings such as "Legends—America," "Legends—Southwest," and "Traditional Tales" as well as "Folklore." All of the cards in the card catalog, of course, include a call number that allows you quickly and easily to locate the section of the library where the book is kept.

INDEX CARDS

As you begin to identify books and articles that seem likely to supply information you can use, it is a good idea to jot down your findings on 3 x 5 inch bibliography cards. At the top of each card, write the full title of the book or article you plan to check. Be sure to include any subtitle that might be a part of the title. Then, on separate lines, write the various publication facts that will enable you to locate the item easily. These facts should include the place of publication, followed by the name of the publisher and the year of publication. All of this information is available directly from the card catalog. If the card is being made for a magazine article, the name of the magazine should be written on a separate line after the title. The name should be followed by the volume number of the magazine, the date of publication, and the page numbers on which the article can be found. For your own convenience, each bibliography card should include the book's call number or the magazine's location in the library. This information will allow you to locate each item quickly, as you do the actual research. Note the two sample bibliography cards above.

It is good practice to make out a bibliography card for any source that seems promising. If you later discover that a source provides no information you need, the card can be eliminated. The cards that remain will then be made up of all of the items that you consulted in writing the paper. Once these remaining cards are alphabetized, they can serve as the text for the bibliography that is presented at the end of every research paper.

The purpose of a bibliography is to let the reader know what resource materials the writer of a research paper consulted. If a book or an article was read or referred to, it ought to be included in the bibliography even if it was neither quoted from nor specifically referred to in the body of the paper. Works of fiction that were read are also included in the bibliography, along with the other resources. The form each bibliographical entry follows is identical to the form illustrated on the sample bibliography cards. Call numbers are not included in a bibliography.

ASSIGNMENT 1

Draw up a research plan for the topic you have chosen and narrowed down—preferably selecting a topic suggested by this unit on regionalism, realism, and naturalism. List in your plan all of the types of information that will probably be useful to you as you research your topic.

ASSIGNMENT 2

Accumulate some possible sources for a research paper that explores the topic you have chosen. Begin by consulting some general and more specialized references in the reference section of a library. Examine the bibliographies that are often provided in these references for possible books and articles that might make promising sources. Move on to the card catalog, paying special attention to the subject cards with headings that pertain to your topic. Identify as many sources as you can for further examination and study. Make a bibliographical card for each source you identify.

THE UNION JACK, NEW YORK, APRIL MORN
Childe Hassam

Hirshhorn Museum and Sculpture Garden
Smithsonian Institution, Washington, D.C.

Modern Literature

OUT OF WARS AND DEPRESSION

In the three decades between the outbreak of World War I and the end of World War II, American writers labored to interpret the new realms of thought being advanced around the world. They struggled to comprehend the theories and teachings of Darwin, Marx, Freud, and Einstein. They were also challenged to reflect issues of more immediate consequence: the impact of the great depression and two world wars on American social, political, and economic realities.

New Theories, New Realities

During these three decades, writers with an eye on the social scene were provided with many sources of inspiration and anxiety. With the twenties came the Jazz Age, new freedoms, the failure of the League of Nations, the fiasco of Prohibition, and the increase in organized crime. Widespread unemployment and poverty were wrenching social convulsions of the Great Depression of the thirties. The decade's atmosphere of militant despair provided a fertile, and sometimes explosive, field for writers who championed social and economic justice. In 1939, for example, the appearance of *The Grapes of Wrath* by John Steinbeck (see page 604) provoked such widespread shock waves that its influence has been likened to that of Harriet Beecher Stowe's 1852 antislavery novel, *Uncle Tom's Cabin.* And, of course, the forties brought the world the most terrible of anxieties: another world war and atomic age.

The Jazz Age, Depression, World Wars

Initially influenced by European writers, particularly the early symbolists, naturalists, and imagists, the writers of this period also sought inspiration in the works of such earlier American literary rebels as Walt Whitman, Emily Dickinson, Stephen Crane, and Theodore Dreiser. As a result, poets experimented with new forms of poetry, notably free verse—a form scorned by traditional poets and slow to win acceptance by the reading public.

Free Verse

Writers of fiction and drama cast aside many of the old conventions they considered limiting and tried to plumb new psychological depths in their works. Sherwood Anderson (see page 540), for example, broke new ground with his experimental novel, *Winesburg, Ohio* (1919). While

New Psychological Depths

BALLARDVALE, Charles Sheeler
Addison Gallery of American Art, Andover, Massachusetts

depicting his characters as moving through seemingly banal lives, he offered the reader occasional glimpses into their minds to reveal personalities that were frustrated and sometimes grotesque. This technique had a far-reaching influence on the work of such writers as Thomas Wolfe (see page 600), John Dos Passos (1896–1970), William Faulkner (see page 583), and Jean Toomer (1894–1967).

Stream of Consciousness Another technique inspired by the new theories of psychoanalysis was that of stream of consciousness: the revelation of a character's random thoughts. A good example of this technique is "The Jilting of

Born in Neosho, Missouri, Thomas Hart Benton became a leader of the regionalist school of painting, seeking to forge a national art based on the folklore and daily life of rural America.

HOMESTEAD, Thomas Hart Benton
The Museum of Modern Art, New York City
Gift of Marshall Field

Granny Weatherall" by Katherine Anne Porter (see page 548). It is interesting to note, however, that Ambrose Bierce, in the late nineteenth century, had already made effective use of this "new" device in his starkly grim and haunting short stories.

Nobel Prize Winners

In this period our first Nobel Prize winners—Sinclair Lewis (1885–1951), Eugene O'Neill (see page 700), Pearl Buck (1892–1973), William Faulkner, Ernest Hemingway (see page 597), and John Steinbeck were all at work. From the early twenties to the mid-forties, one can count almost a dozen great novels by almost as many novelists, including *The Great Gatsby* by F. Scott Fitzgerald (see page 566), *Main Street* and *Arrowsmith* by Sinclair Lewis, *My Ántonia* and *Death Comes for the Archbishop* by Willa Cather (see page 528), *The Sun Also Rises* and *A Farewell to Arms* by Ernest Hemingway, *Look Homeward, Angel* by Thomas Wolfe, *The Good Earth* by Pearl Buck, *Light in August* by William Faulkner, and *The Grapes of Wrath* by John Steinbeck.

*A living room decorated in the art deco style. Sleek and practical,
art deco represented all that was fashionably modern in the
fields of interior and industrial design in the 1920s and 1930s.*

"Falling Water," Bear Run, Pennsylvania, a house designed by the architect
Frank Lloyd Wright in 1936. Wright's designs were daring and original,
a radical departure from all that had gone before in American architecture.

THE FLOWERING OF AMERICAN DRAMA

With the coming of the twentieth century, American theater began to
be transformed from what had been a shallow level of sentimental
posturing to an increasingly serious and respected art form. Central to
this development was the towering genius of Eugene O'Neill, who did
much to bring serious American drama into being with such plays as
The Emperor Jones (1920), *Anna Christie* (1922), *Desire Under the Elms*
(1924), and *Mourning Becomes Electra* (1929–1931). Another playwright
whose contributions loom large during this period is Thornton Wilder,
whose drama *Our Town* plumbs the depths of ordinary life for
universal meanings and utilizes innovative staging.

O'Neill,
Wilder

    Among the other significant dramatists who helped American
theater begin reaching its potential are Robert Sherwood (1896–1955),
Maxwell Anderson (1888–1959), Clifford Odets (1906–1963), S. N.
Behrman (1893–1973), Sidney Kingsley (1906–   ), Philip Barry

THE QUEEN
Isamu Noguchi
Whitney Museum of
American Art,
New York City

Sinclair Lewis

(1896–1949), and Lillian Hellman (1905–   ). The World War II period brought to the limelight two other playwrights who were to dominate American theater for more than two decades—Tennessee Williams (1911–1983) and Arthur Miller (1915–   ). Williams's *The Glass Menagerie* (1945) and *A Streetcar Named Desire* (1947), as well as Miller's *Death of a Salesman* (1949), are plays timeless and unquestioned in their classic status in American theater.

THE AMERICAN NOVEL COMES OF AGE

The Scarlet Letter, Moby-Dick, The Adventures of Huckleberry Finn, Portrait of a Lady, The Red Badge of Courage—a number of great American novels had been written before the twentieth century. But nothing in America's earlier literary history matched the outpouring of major works by important novelists during the first five decades of this century.

In the early decades, some of America's best fiction was written by three women—Willa Cather, Ellen Glasgow (1874–1945), and Edith Wharton (1862–1937). Glasgow was the finest Southern novelist of her day—a social critic, a realist, and a defender of what her fellow-Southerner William Faulkner was later to call the "old verities and truths of the heart." Edith Wharton was more of a pessimist than either Glasgow or Cather, and she could be an abrasive satirist. Her most famous novel, *The Age of Innocence* (1920), focuses on New York society in the 1870s, a society for which she had a nostalgic attraction while retaining a sharp eye for its foibles.

A satirist with a much broader range (and a far heavier hand) was Sinclair Lewis, who was awarded America's first Nobel Prize in Literature (1930) for his uncompromising satire of American narrow-mindedness, materialism, and hypocrisy. Among the objects of his criticism were a typical midwestern town (*Main Street*, 1920), American business (*Babbitt*, 1922), science and medicine (*Arrowsmith*, 1925), and the hypocritical clergy (*Elmer Gantry*, 1927).

As America's foremost literary social critic, Lewis not surprisingly took most of his writing contemporaries to task in his Nobel acceptance speech:

> To be not only a best-seller in America but to be really beloved, a novelist must assert that all American men are tall, handsome, rich, honest, and powerful at golf; that all country towns are filled with neighbors who do nothing from day to day save go about being kind to one another; that although American girls may be wild, they change always into perfect wives and mothers; and that geographically, America is composed solely of New York, which is inhabited entirely by millionaires; of the West, which keeps unchanged all the boisterous heroism of

Strongly influenced by the European cubist movement, Max Weber's paintings distorted and reorganized their subject matter in a bold and dynamic way.

CHINESE RESTAURANT
Max Weber
Whitney Museum of American Art, New York City

1870; and of the South, where everyone lives on a plantation perpetually glossy with moonlight and scented with magnolias.

Although his assertions were not true of the pioneering realists who had been at work decades before Lewis rose to prominence nor of the realists writing in his own time, his barbs did find their mark in

An artist's rendering of Rockefeller Plaza, built in 1935. Towering seventy stories over midtown Manhattan, the RCA Building was designed as the flagship structure of the nineteen-building Rockefeller Center complex, a project that captured public imagination during the thirties.

those of his contemporaries who regularly published tidily plotted romances in the popular presses.

F. Scott Fitzgerald

The writer we associate most directly with the roaring twenties is F. Scott Fitzgerald. Of his several novels, the best is *The Great Gatsby* (1925), in which the central character, Jay Gatsby, a successful American racketeer, is now considered as significant a representative of his time as Hester Prynne, Captain Ahab, and Huck Finn are of theirs.

From the late twenties to the early fifties, the foremost novelists in the field were clearly Hemingway, Faulkner, and Steinbeck. We may speak first of Hemingway, whose two popular novels, *The Sun Also Rises* (1926) and *A Farewell to Arms* (1929), deal either with war itself or with a society shattered by war. His last novel, *The Old Man and the Sea* (1952), deals with a kind of private war. Violence, in short, is a principal part of Hemingway's world, as it was of the world of his time. The heroes of that world illustrate that life is a solitary struggle more likely to end in failure or defeat than in victory. But we may be reminded here of Melville's words in *Moby-Dick:* "The truest of all men was the Man of Sorrow." And though many of Hemingway's characters face sorrow, they face it courageously, remaining true to the code of stoic bravery by which they have lived—like the old fisherman Santiago in *The Old Man and the Sea,* who is clearly intended by his creator as a Christlike figure.

Ernest Hemingway

If Hemingway made use of his naturalistic license to write about violence on battlefields, on trout streams, on oceans, and in bullrings, William Faulkner made even more extensive use of the same license to write about a 2400 square-mile piece of land, which he called Yoknapatawpha County, Mississippi. In the novels for which he is best remembered—*The Sound and the Fury* (1929), *As I Lay Dying* (1930), *Light in August* (1932), and *Absalom, Absalom!* (1936)—there is so much sin, so much guilt, so much violence, crime, and perversion that it is as if the unconscious mind had gone on a rampage. Yet when Faulkner went to Stockholm in 1950 to receive the Nobel Prize in Literature, he delivered an optimistic and idealistic speech defending traditional values.

William Faulkner

John Steinbeck, best known for his realistic portrayal of life among the economically depressed in the United States, infused both symbolism and romantic mysticism into his carefully constructed prose. Critics have also been quick to point out the strong strain of sentimentalism running through his most starkly realistic writings. In addition to *The Grapes of Wrath* (1939), his best-known works are *Of Mice and Men* (1937), *The Pearl* (1945), and *Travels with Charley* (1962).

John Steinbeck

In addition to Faulkner, other distinguished Southern writers of the period were Thomas Wolfe and Carson McCullers (1917–1967). Wolfe, whom Faulkner once identified as the best writer of the mid-twentieth century, was more of a romantic than a naturalist, although attention has been called to many naturalistic elements in his first novel, *Look Homeward, Angel* (1929). In her later period, McCullers also moved away from naturalism toward a romantic fiction that is preoccupied with the grotesque. There is a kind of brooding terror in her novels and stories that places her in the tradition of her fellow-Southerner, Edgar Allan Poe. She is best known for her novel, *The Heart Is a Lonely Hunter* (1940); her novella, *The Ballad of the Sad Café*

Thomas Wolfe

Carson McCullers

(1951); and the novel, *The Member of the Wedding* (1946), which she rewrote as a play in 1950. Three of her longer works have been made into movies.

Richard Wright   Yet another writer from the South was Richard Wright (see page 623). His searing novel *Native Son* (1940) and his autobiography, *Black Boy* (1945), not only brought the plight of black Americans to national attention, but they also served as sources of inspiration and encouragement to a generation of black writers.

During these decades, whatever the literary emphasis of our major novelists—realism, naturalism, romanticism, or psychological analysis—each writer, according to his or her vision, attempted to delineate the enduring concerns, dreams, and rituals that inform our national character.

THE MODERN SHORT STORY

Many of the major novelists of the first half of the twentieth century also wrote excellent short stories. In the decade following World War I, however, one of the most widely read short-story writers was Ring
Ring Lardner   Lardner (1885–1933). His bitingly humorous stories and sketches of the seamier side of twentieth-century life were generally told in first

Working in wood, bronze, and plaster, sculptor Elie Nadelman brought wit and elegance to his depictions of the human figure.

WOMAN AT THE PIANO
Elie Nadelman
The Museum of Modern Art,
New York City
Philip L. Goodwin Collection

person and couched in the slang and malapropisms of baseball players, chorus girls, stockbrokers, songwriters, and gamblers. His aim was to reveal the ignorance, egotism, and depravity of the characters he loosely modeled on real people. When one of his characters refers to the World Series as the "World Serious," Lardner is simply holding up to ridicule the hero status given sports figures by a gullible public. Lardner's story "Haircut," an ironic tale of life in a small midwestern town, is perhaps his best work.

In the late twenties Lardner's lesser-known contemporary, Damon Runyon (1884–1946), began peopling his stories with characters based on people he found on New York's Broadway between Fortieth and Fiftieth Streets. These were mostly "night people," men and women who rarely saw the light of day, speaking what Runyon declared was "slanguage," but which critics referred to as "Runyonese." A major difference between Lardner's view of his characters and Runyon's view of his is that the latter was the more sympathetic and understanding. His first collection of stories, *Guys and Dolls* (1930), made him immensely popular for a time, but his popularity waned during the latter part of the great depression. When the colorful characters of *Guys and Dolls* appeared in the hit Broadway musical in 1950, Runyon's stature as one of our better humorists was reestablished.

Damon Runyon

In the early twenties, Sherwood Anderson pioneered new directions for later writers with his collections of interrelated stories and sketches: *Winesburg, Ohio* (1919), *Poor White* (1920), and *The Triumph of the Egg* (1921). One of the earliest writers to reflect Freudian psychology, he accepted the thesis that most human behavior is controlled by the subconscious, which is powerfully influenced by experiences buried in the individual's past. Anderson gave much credit for his success to Theodore Dreiser, who advised and encouraged him.

Sherwood Anderson

One of America's most durable regionalists is Jesse Stuart (see page 616). Immersed in the lives of people living in the Kentucky hills, his stories have long delighted readers around the world. Another durable short-story writer was Katherine Anne Porter, who, though she won the admiration of the most discriminating readers, never has had a popular following. During her long writing career, however, she exerted a weighty influence on both her contemporaries and successors in the realm of short fiction. Still another notable writer of this period was humorist James Thurber (see page 557), whose whimsical stories, essays, and cartoons poignantly captured and caricatured the fantasies and foibles of a generation.

The Stories of Stuart, Porter, and Thurber

The short stories in this unit reflect in varying ways the changes in life and thought in the United States during the period under study. They reflect also the subtleties, refinements, and experimental techniques that had been pioneered by such nineteenth-century naturalists as Stephen Crane and Frank Norris.

Naturalism Refined

Modern Literature

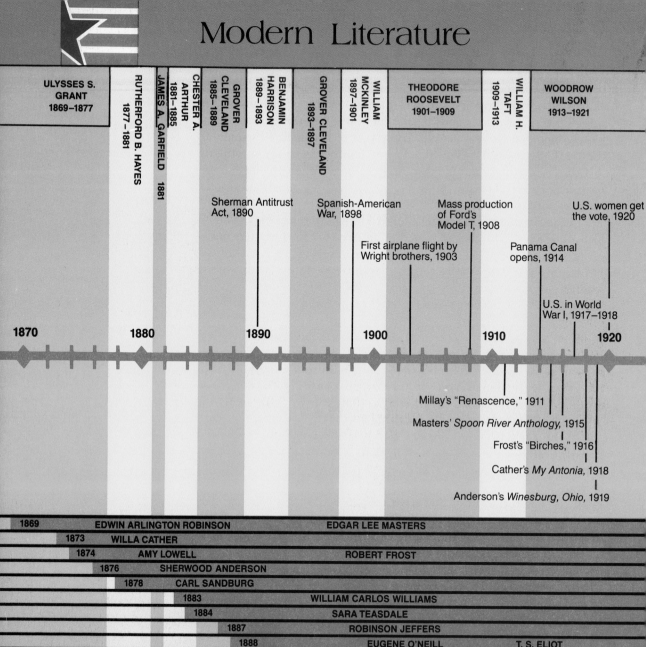

President	Dates
ULYSSES S. GRANT	1869–1877
RUTHERFORD B. HAYES	1877–1881
JAMES A. GARFIELD	1881
CHESTER A. ARTHUR	1881–1885
GROVER CLEVELAND	1885–1889
BENJAMIN HARRISON	1889–1893
GROVER CLEVELAND	1893–1897
WILLIAM MCKINLEY	1897–1901
THEODORE ROOSEVELT	1901–1909
WILLIAM H. TAFT	1909–1913
WOODROW WILSON	1913–1921

Sherman Antitrust Act, 1890

Spanish-American War, 1898

Mass production of Ford's Model T, 1908

U.S. women get the vote, 1920

First airplane flight by Wright brothers, 1903

Panama Canal opens, 1914

U.S. in World War I, 1917–1918

1870   1880   1890   1900   1910   1920

Millay's "Renascence," 1911

Masters' *Spoon River Anthology*, 1915

Frost's "Birches," 1916

Cather's *My Antonia*, 1918

Anderson's *Winesburg, Ohio*, 1919

1869	EDWIN ARLINGTON ROBINSON	EDGAR LEE MASTERS
1873	WILLA CATHER	
1874	AMY LOWELL	ROBERT FROST
1876	SHERWOOD ANDERSON	
1878	CARL SANDBURG	
1883	WILLIAM CARLOS WILLIAMS	
1884	SARA TEASDALE	
1887	ROBINSON JEFFERS	
1888	EUGENE O'NEILL	T. S. ELIOT
1890	CLAUDE MCKAY	
1892	EDNA ST. VINCENT MILLAY	
1894	e. e. cummings	
1896	F. SCOTT FITZGERALD	
1897	WILLIAM FAULKNER	
1898	STEPHEN VINCENT BENET	
1899	ERNEST HEMINGWAY	
1900	THOMAS WOLFE	
1902	LANGSTON HUGHES	
1903		
1907		
1908		
1913		
1915		

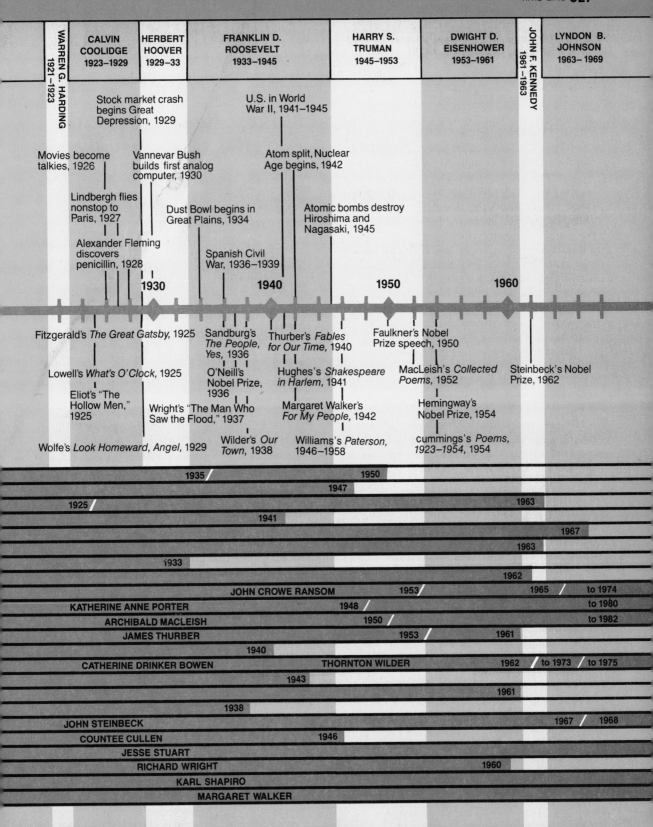

| WARREN G. HARDING 1921–1923 | CALVIN COOLIDGE 1923–1929 | HERBERT HOOVER 1929–33 | FRANKLIN D. ROOSEVELT 1933–1945 | HARRY S. TRUMAN 1945–1953 | DWIGHT D. EISENHOWER 1953–1961 | JOHN F. KENNEDY 1961–1963 | LYNDON B. JOHNSON 1963–1969 |

Stock market crash begins Great Depression, 1929

U.S. in World War II, 1941–1945

Movies become talkies, 1926

Vannevar Bush builds first analog computer, 1930

Atom split, Nuclear Age begins, 1942

Lindbergh flies nonstop to Paris, 1927

Dust Bowl begins in Great Plains, 1934

Atomic bombs destroy Hiroshima and Nagasaki, 1945

Alexander Fleming discovers penicillin, 1928

Spanish Civil War, 1936–1939

1930   **1940**   **1950**   **1960**

Fitzgerald's *The Great Gatsby*, 1925

Sandburg's *The People, Yes*, 1936

Thurber's *Fables for Our Time*, 1940

Faulkner's Nobel Prize speech, 1950

Lowell's *What's O'Clock*, 1925

O'Neill's Nobel Prize, 1936

Hughes's *Shakespeare in Harlem*, 1941

MacLeish's *Collected Poems*, 1952

Steinbeck's Nobel Prize, 1962

Eliot's "The Hollow Men," 1925

Wright's "The Man Who Saw the Flood," 1937

Margaret Walker's *For My People*, 1942

Hemingway's Nobel Prize, 1954

Wilder's *Our Town*, 1938

Williams's *Paterson*, 1946–1958

cummings's *Poems, 1923–1954*, 1954

Wolfe's *Look Homeward, Angel*, 1929

1935 / 1950
1947
1925 / 1963
1941
1967
1963
1933
1962

JOHN CROWE RANSOM   1953 / 1965 / to 1974
KATHERINE ANNE PORTER   1948 / to 1980
ARCHIBALD MACLEISH   1950 / to 1982
JAMES THURBER   1953 / 1961
1940
CATHERINE DRINKER BOWEN   THORNTON WILDER   1962 / to 1973 / to 1975
1943
1961
1938
JOHN STEINBECK   1967 / 1968
COUNTEE CULLEN   1946
JESSE STUART
RICHARD WRIGHT   1960
KARL SHAPIRO
MARGARET WALKER

Willa Cather   1873–1947

Astride a pony, Willa Cather spent many girlhood hours riding the Nebraska prairie to visit the remote sod-roofed dugouts and drab farmhouses of the Scandinavian, German, and Bohemian settlers of the region. Later, in her writing, she was to pour out her feelings about these immigrant peoples, their codes of behavior, and their love for the earth. Although she was born in the hill country near Winchester, Virginia, she moved to the midwest plains at age nine when her father established the Cather family first on a ranch outside Red Cloud, Nebraska, and later in Red Cloud itself. Here she began her schooling, having been tutored previously by her parents and her well-read grandmother.

In addition to having a good home library, Willa was able to borrow European books from French and German neighbors with whom she loved to converse in their own language. A local storekeeper, "Uncle Billy" Ducker, taught her to read Greek and Latin. A German music master taught her music history and appreciation, including opera. Willa Cather emerged from her raw frontier environment with an exceptional education.

When she entered the University of Nebraska, she thought she wanted to study medicine and classics. However, after helping found a college paper, she spent more and more of her time on English compositions and journalism, particularly dramatic criticism for the *Nebraska State Journal.* This paid off in getting her newspaper work after graduation. But in order to have more time to write the poetry and stories that she was selling occasionally to New York magazines, she spent five years, between 1901 and 1906, teaching Latin and English in Pittsburgh high schools.

A volume of verse, *April Twilights,* appeared in 1903, and in 1905 the critics praised *The Troll Garden,* her first collection of short stories. It contained two stories that attracted wide attention, "The Sculptor's Funeral" and "Paul's Case," a psychological study of a high-school boy

PORTRAIT OF WILLA CATHER

who could not face reality. In 1908 she became managing editor of *McClure's Magazine* in New York City, where her frantic schedule of duties included special assignments in Boston and in London. It was in Boston that she first met Sarah Orne Jewett, author of the highly regarded Maine sketches, *The Country of the Pointed Firs.* Jewett urged her to give over her whole life to fiction, no matter what the cost. "It is impossible for you to work so hard," she wrote, "and yet have your gifts mature as they should." After six years as an editor, Willa Cather took Jewett's advice and left *McClure's,* ready to risk her future on her pen.

While visiting with her brother in Winslow, Arizona, early in 1912, she was introduced to the ancient cliff-dwellings of nearby canyons. On the way back to New York, she spent two months contemplating the starkly beautiful environs of Winslow and the sights and sounds of Red Cloud. Though she continued to live in Greenwich Village, she was fully aware that nothing inspired her as much as the windy plains of Nebraska and the deserts of the Southwest. She remembered Sarah Orne Jewett's recommendation that she should try "to recapture in memory, people and places that might otherwise be forgotten." Except for *Shadows on the Rock* (1931), set in colonial Quebec, and *Sapphira and the Slave Girl* (1940), set in Virginia, all of Willa Cather's major works came out of her feelings for the West.

Her three great novels set on the Nebraska plains are *O Pioneers!* (1913), *The Song of the Lark* (1915), and *My Ántonia* (1918). *My Ántonia*, considered the best of the three books, records the struggle of a Bohemian immigrant girl, Ántonia Shimerda, to find selfhood on the land. Cather's well-known short novel, *Neighbor Rosicky* (1930), has as its protagonist a Bohemian-American grandfather whose natural goodness and love find fulfillment in the free and open prairie country.

After World War I, Willa Cather's short stories and eight novels evidenced general disillusionment with what she felt was the moral decline and growing materialism of the nation. In *Death Comes for the Archbishop* (1927) she wrote an enduring American masterpiece. It is a novel reaffirming the greatness of the American past as it sets forth the difficulties faced by a French bishop and his vicar in establishing a diocese in pioneer New Mexico.

In "The Sculptor's Funeral," which follows, Cather tells the story of Harvey Merrick, a sculptor of rare ability, and his return to Sand City, Kansas, where he was neither understood nor appreciated. Sand City resembles Red Cloud, and the hostility of its inhabitants is not unlike the hostility Cather met in her own career.

The values in American culture that Willa Cather admired most were drawn from the immigrants who settled the American Midwest. She showed little sympathy with the materialistic spirit of her own time, concerned with industrialism, business, and politics. Her ideal protagonists were Europeans, rich in the traditions of their heritage, who were given new life through contact with the American frontier. She was a romantic in that she was greatly interested in the past; much of her writing deals with reminiscence. Her primary interest, however, was psychological—exploring the effect of environment upon the personality.

THE SCULPTOR'S FUNERAL

A group of the townspeople stood on the station siding of a little Kansas town, awaiting the coming of the night train, which was already twenty minutes overdue. The snow had fallen thick over everything; in the pale starlight the line of bluffs across the wide, white meadows south of the town made soft, smokecoloured curves against the clear sky.

The men on the siding stood first on one foot and then on the other, their hands thrust deep into their trousers pockets, their overcoats open, their shoulders screwed up with the cold; and they glanced from time to time toward the southeast, where the railroad track wound along the river shore. They conversed in low tones and moved about restlessly, seeming uncertain as to what was expected of them. There was but one of the company who looked as if he knew exactly why he was there, and he kept conspicuously apart; walking to the far end of the platform, returning to the station door, then pacing up the track again, his chin sunk in the high collar of his overcoat, his burly shoulders drooping forward, his gait heavy and dogged. Presently he was approached by a tall, spare, grizzled man clad in a faded Grand Army suit, who shuffled out from the group and advanced with a certain deference, craning his neck forward until his back made the angle of a jack-knife three-quarters open.

"I reckon she's a-goin' to be pretty late agin tonight, Jim," he remarked in a squeaky falsetto. "S'pose it's the snow?"

"I don't know," responded the other man with a shade of annoyance, speaking from out an astonishing cataract of red beard that grew fiercely and thickly in all directions.

The spare man shifted the quill toothpick he was chewing to the other side of his mouth. "It ain't likely that anybody from the East will come with the corpse, I s'pose," he went on reflectively.

"I don't know," responded the other, more curtly than before.

"It's too bad he didn't belong to some lodge or other. I like an order funeral myself. They seem more appropriate for people of some repytation," the spare man continued, with an ingratiating concession in his shrill voice, as he carefully placed his toothpick in his vest pocket. He always carried the flag at the G. A. R.[1] funerals in the town.

The heavy man turned on his heel, without replying, and walked up the siding. The spare man rejoined the uneasy group. "Jim's ez full ez a tick, ez ushel," he commented commiseratingly.

Just then a distant whistle sounded, and there was a shuffling of feet on the platform. A number of lanky boys, of all ages, appeared as suddenly and slimily as eels wakened by the crack of thunder; some came from the waitingroom, where they had been warming themselves by the red stove, or half asleep on the slat benches; others uncoiled themselves from baggage trucks or slid out of express wagons. Two clambered down from the driver's seat of a hearse that stood backed up against the siding. They straightened their stooping shoulders and lifted their heads, and a flash of momentary animation kindled their dull eyes at that cold, vibrant scream, the worldwide call for men. It stirred them like the note of a trumpet; just as it had often stirred the man who was coming home tonight, in his boyhood.

The night express shot, red as a rocket, from out the eastward marsh lands and wound along the river shore under the long lines of shivering poplars that sentinelled the meadows, the escaping steam hanging in grey masses against the pale sky and blotting out the Milky Way. In a moment the red glare from the headlight streamed up the snow-covered track before the siding and glittered on the wet, black rails. The burly man with the dishevelled red beard walked swiftly up the platform toward the approaching train, uncovering his head as he went. The group of men behind him hesitated, glanced questioningly at one another, and awkwardly followed his example. The train stopped, and the crowd shuffled up to the express car just as the door was thrown open, the man in the G. A. R. suit thrusting his head forward with curiosity. The express messenger appeared in the doorway, accompanied by a young man in a long ulster[2] and travelling cap.

"Are Mr. Merrick's friends here?" inquired the young man.

The group on the platform swayed uneasily. Philip Phelps, the banker, responded with dignity: "We have come to take charge of the body. Mr. Merrick's father is very feeble and can't be about."

---

1. **G.A.R. (Grand Army of the Republic),** soldiers who served with the Union Army during the Civil War.
2. **ulster** (ul' stər), a long, loose overcoat, of Irish origin.

"Send the agent out here," growled the express messenger, "and tell the operator to lend a hand."

The coffin was got out of its rough-box and down on the snowy platform. The townspeople drew back enough to make room for it and then formed a close semicircle about it, looking curiously at the palm leaf which lay across the black cover. No one said anything. The baggage man stood by his truck, waiting to get at the trunks. The engine panted heavily, and the fireman dodged in and out among the wheels with his yellow torch and long oil-can, snapping the spindle boxes. The young Bostonian, one of the dead sculptor's pupils who had come with the body, looked about him helplessly. He turned to the banker, the only one of that black, uneasy, stoop-shouldered group who seemed enough of an individual to be addressed.

"None of Mr. Merrick's brothers are here?" he asked uncertainly.

The man with the red beard for the first time stepped up and joined the others. "No, they have not come yet; the family is scattered. The body will be taken directly to the house." He stooped and took hold of one of the handles of the coffin.

"Take the long hill road up, Thompson, it will be easier on the horses," called the liveryman as the undertaker snapped the door of the hearse and prepared to mount to the driver's seat.

Laird, the red-bearded lawyer, turned again to the stranger: "We didn't know whether there would be any one with him or not," he explained. "It's a long walk, so you'd better go up in the hack."[3] He pointed to a single battered conveyance, but the young man replied stiffly: "Thank you, but I think I will go up with the hearse. If you don't object," turning to the undertaker, "I'll ride with you."

They clambered up over the wheels and drove off in the starlight up the long, white hill toward the town. The lamps in the still village were shining from under the low,

snow-burdened roofs; and beyond, on every side, the plains reached out into emptiness, peaceful and wide as the soft sky itself, and wrapped in a tangible, white silence.

When the hearse backed up to a wooden sidewalk before a naked, weather-beaten frame house, the same composite, ill-defined group that had stood upon the station siding was huddled about the gate. The front yard was an icy swamp, and a couple of warped planks, extending from the sidewalk to the door, made a sort of rickety footbridge. The gate hung on one hinge, and was opened wide with difficulty. Steavens, the young stranger, noticed that something black was tied to the knob of the front door.

The grating sound made by the casket, as it was drawn from the hearse, was answered by a scream from the house; the front door was wrenched open, and a tall, corpulent woman rushed out bareheaded into the snow and flung herself upon the coffin, shrieking: "My boy, my boy! And this is how you've come home to me!"

As Steavens turned away and closed his eyes with a shudder of unutterable repulsion, another woman, also tall, but flat and angular, dressed entirely in black, darted out of the house and caught Mrs. Merrick by the shoulders, crying sharply: "Come, come, mother; you mustn't go on like this!" Her tone changed to one of obsequious solemnity as she turned to the banker: "The parlour is ready, Mr. Phelps."

The bearers carried the coffin along the narrow boards, while the undertaker ran ahead with the coffin-rests. They bore it into a large, unheated room that smelled of dampness and disuse and furniture polish, and set it down under a hanging lamp ornamented with jingling glass prisms and before a "Rogers group" of John Alden and Priscilla, wreathed with smilax.[4] Henry Steavens stared

---

3. **hack,** here: vernacular for taxicab.
4. **smilax** (smī′ laks), woody vine, usually prickly, with bright-green leaves.

about him with the sickening conviction that there had been a mistake, and that he had somehow arrived at the wrong destination. He looked at the clover-green Brussels, the fat plush upholstery, among the hand-painted china placques and panels and vases, for some mark of identification,—for something that might once conceivably have belonged to Harvey Merrick. It was not until he recognized his friend in the crayon portrait of a little boy in kilts and curls, hanging above the piano, that he felt willing to let any of these people approach the coffin.

"Take the lid off, Mr. Thompson; let me see my boy's face," wailed the elder woman between her sobs. This time Steavens looked fearfully, almost beseechingly into her face, red and swollen under its masses of strong, black, shiny hair. He flushed, dropped his eyes, and then, almost incredulously, looked again. There was a kind of power about her face—a kind of brutal handsomeness, even; but it was scarred and furrowed by violence, and so coloured and coarsened by fiercer passions that grief seemed never to have laid a gentle finger there. The long nose was distended and knobbed at the end, and there were deep lines on either side of it; her heavy, black brows almost met across her forehead, her teeth were large and square, and set far apart—teeth that could tear. She filled the room; the men were obliterated, seemed tossed about like twigs in an angry water, and even Steavens felt himself being drawn into the whirlpool.

The daughter—the tall, raw-boned woman in crêpe, with a mourning comb in her hair which curiously lengthened her long face—sat stiffly upon the sofa, her hands, conspicuous for their large knuckles, folded in her lap, her mouth and eyes drawn down, solemnly awaiting the opening of the coffin. Near the door stood a mulatto woman, evidently a servant in the house, with a timid bearing and an emaciated face pitifully sad and gentle. She was weeping silently, the corner of her calico apron lifted to her eyes, oc-

casionally suppressing a long, quivering sob. Steavens walked over and stood beside her.

Feeble steps were heard on the stairs, and an old man, tall and frail, odorous of pipe smoke, with shaggy, unkept grey hair and a dingy beard, tobacco stained about the mouth, entered uncertainly. He went slowly up to the coffin and stood rolling a blue cotton handkerchief between his hands, seeming so pained and embarrassed by his wife's orgy of grief that he had no consciousness of anything else.

"There, there, Annie, dear, don't take on so," he quavered timidly, putting out a shaking hand and awkwardly patting her elbow. She turned and sank upon his shoulder with such violence that he tottered a little. He did not even glance toward the coffin, but continued to look at her with a dull, frightened, appealing expression, as a spaniel looks at the whip. His sunken cheeks slowly reddened and burned with miserable shame. When his wife rushed from the room, her daughter strode after her with set lips. The servant stole up to the coffin, bent over it for a moment, and then slipped away to the kitchen, leaving Steavens, the lawyer, and the father to themselves. The old man stood looking down at his dead son's face. The sculptor's splendid head seemed even more noble in its rigid stillness than in life. The dark hair had crept down upon the wide forehead; the face seemed strangely long, but in it there was not that repose we expect to find in the faces of the dead. The brows were so drawn that there were two deep lines above the beaked nose, and the chin was thrust forward defiantly. It was as though the strain of life had been so sharp and bitter that death could not at once relax the tension and smooth the countenance into perfect peace—as though he were still guarding something precious, which might even yet be wrested from him.

The old man's lips were working under his stained beard. He turned to the lawyer with timid deference: "Phelps and the rest are comin' back to set up with Harve, ain't they?" he asked. "Thank 'ee, Jim, thank 'ee." He brushed the hair back gently from his son's forehead. "He was a good boy, Jim; always a good boy. He was ez gentle ez a child and the kindest of 'em all—only we didn't none of us ever onderstand him." The tears trickled slowly down his beard and dropped upon the sculptor's coat.

"Martin, Martin! Oh, Martin! come here," his wife wailed from the top of the stairs. The old man started timorously: "Yes, Annie, I'm coming." He turned away, hesitated, stood for a moment in miserable indecision; then reached back and patted the dead man's hair softly, and stumbled from the room.

"Poor old man, I didn't think he had any tears left. Seems as if his eyes would have gone dry long ago. At his age nothing cuts very deep," remarked the lawyer.

Something in his tone made Steavens glance up. While the mother had been in the room, the young man had scarcely seen any one else; but now, from the moment he first glanced into Jim Laird's florid face and blood-shot eyes, he knew that he had found what he had been heartsick at not finding before—the feeling, the understanding, that must exist in some one, even here.

The man was red as his beard, with features swollen and blurred by dissipation, and a hot, blazing blue eye. His face was strained—that of a man who is controlling himself with difficulty—and he kept plucking at his beard with a sort of fierce resentment. Steavens, sitting by the window, watched him turn down the glaring lamp, still its jangling pendants with an angry gesture, and then stand with his hands locked behind him, staring down into the master's face. He could not help wondering what link there had been between the porcelain vessel and so sooty a lump of potter's clay.

From the kitchen an uproar was sounding; when the dining-room door opened, the import of it was clear. The mother was abusing the maid for having forgotten to make the dressing for the chicken salad which had been prepared for the watchers. Steavens had never heard anything in the least like it; it was injured, emotional, dramatic abuse, unique and masterly in its excruciating cruelty, as violent and unrestrained as had been her grief of twenty minutes before. With a shudder of disgust the lawyer went into the dining-room and closed the door into the kitchen.

"Poor Roxy's getting it now," he remarked when he came back. "The Merricks took her out of the poor-house years ago; and if her loyalty would let her, I guess the poor old thing could tell tales that would curdle your blood. She's the mulatto woman who was standing in here a while ago, with her apron to her eyes. The old woman is a fury; there never was anybody like her. She made Harvey's life a hell for him when he lived at home; he was so sick ashamed of it. I never could see how he kept himself sweet."

"He was wonderful," said Steavens slowly, "wonderful; but until tonight I have never known how wonderful."

"That is the eternal wonder of it, anyway; that it can come even from such a dung heap as this," the lawyer cried, with a sweeping gesture which seemed to indicate much more than the four walls within which they stood.

"I think I'll see whether I can get a little air. The room is so close I am beginning to feel rather faint," murmured Steavens, struggling with one of the windows. The sash was stuck, however, and would not yield, so he sat down dejectedly and began pulling at his collar. The lawyer came over, loosened the sash with one blow of his red fist and sent the window up a few inches. Steavens thanked him, but the nausea which had been gradually climbing into his throat for the last half hour left him with but one desire—a desperate feeling that he must get away from this place with what was left of Harvey Merrick. Oh, he comprehended well enough now the quiet bitterness of the smile that he had seen so often on his master's lips!

Once when Merrick returned from a visit home, he brought with him a singularly feeling and suggestive bas-relief[5] of a thin, faded old woman, sitting and sewing something pinned to her knee; while a full-lipped, full-blooded little urchin, his trousers held up by a single gallows, stood beside her, impatiently twitching her gown to call her attention to a butterfly he had caught. Steavens, impressed by the tender and delicate modelling of the thin, tired face, had asked him if it were his mother. He remembered the dull flush that had burned up in the sculptor's face.

The lawyer was sitting in a rocking-chair beside the coffin, his head thrown back and his eyes closed. Steavens looked at him earnestly, puzzled at the line of the chin, and wondering why a man should conceal a feature of such distinction under that disfiguring shock of beard. Suddenly, as though he felt the young sculptor's keen glance, Jim Laird opened his eyes.

"Was he always a good deal of an oyster?" he asked abruptly. "He was terribly shy as a boy."

"Yes, he was an oyster, since you put it so," rejoined Steavens. "Although he could be very fond of people, he always gave one the impression of being detached. He disliked violent emotion; he was reflective, and rather distrustful of himself—except, of course, as regarded his work. He was sure enough there. He distrusted men pretty thoroughly and women even more, yet somehow without believing ill of them. He was determined, indeed, to believe the best; but he seemed afraid to investigate."

"A burnt dog dreads the fire," said the lawyer grimly, and closed his eyes.

Steavens went on and on, reconstructing that whole miserable boyhood. All this raw, biting ugliness had been the portion of the man whose mind was to become an exhaustless gallery of beautiful impressions—so sensitive that the mere shadow of a poplar leaf flickering against a sunny wall would be etched and held there for ever. Surely, if ever a man had the magic word in his finger tips, it was Merrick. Whatever he touched, he re-

vealed its holiest secret; liberated it from enchantment and restored it to its pristine loveliness. Upon whatever he had come in contact with, he had left a beautiful record of the experience—a sort of ethereal signature; a scent, a sound, a colour that was his own.

Steavens understood now the real tragedy of his master's life; neither love nor wine, as many had conjectured; but a blow which had fallen earlier and cut deeper than anything else could have done—a shame not his, and yet so unescapably his, to hide in his heart from his very boyhood. And without— the frontier warfare; the yearning of a boy, cast ashore upon a desert of newness and ugliness and sordidness, for all that is chastened and old, and noble with traditions.

At eleven o'clock the tall, flat woman in black announced that the watchers were arriving, and asked them to "step into the dining-room." As Steavens rose, the lawyer said dryly: "You go on—it'll be a good experience for you. I'm not equal to that crowd tonight; I've had twenty years of them."

As Steavens closed the door after him he glanced back at the lawyer, sitting by the coffin in the dim light, with his chin resting on his hand.

The same misty group that had stood before the door of the express car shuffled into the dining-room. In the light of the kerosene lamp they separated and became individuals. The minister, a pale, feeble-looking man with white hair and blond chin-whiskers, took his seat beside a small side table and placed his Bible upon it. The Grand Army man sat down behind the stove and tilted his chair back comfortably against the wall, fishing his quill toothpick from his waistcoat pocket. The two bankers, Phelps and Elder, sat off in a corner behind the dinner-table, where they could finish their discussion of the new usury law and its effect on chattel security loans.

5. **bas-relief** (bä′ ri lēf′), piece of sculpture in which the figure stands out only slightly from the background.

Despite the serenity of the scenes he painted, an eerie and disquieting aura often haunts Charles Burchfield's paintings.

THE OPEN DOOR
Charles Burchfield
Sotheby's Inc./Art Resource Inc.

The real estate agent, an old man with a smiling, hypocritical face, soon joined them. The coal and lumber dealer and the cattle shipper sat on opposite sides of the hard coal-burner, their feet on the nickelwork. Steavens took a book from his pocket and began to read. The talk around him ranged through various topics of local interest while the house was quieting down. When it was clear that the members of the family were in bed, the Grand Army man hitched his shoulders and, untangling his long legs, caught his heels on the rounds of his chair.

"S'pose there'll be a will, Phelps?" he queried in his weak falsetto.

The banker laughed disagreeably, and began trimming his nails with a pearl-handled pocket-knife.

"There'll scarcely be any need for one, will there?" he queried in his turn.

The restless Grand Army man shifted his position again, getting his knees still nearer his chin. "Why, the old man says Harve's done right well lately," he chirped.

The other banker spoke up. "I reckon he means by that Harve ain't asked him to mortgage any more farms lately, so as he could go on with his education."

"Seems like my mind don't reach back to a time when Harve wasn't bein' edycated," tittered the Grand Army man.

There was a general chuckle. The minister took out his handkerchief and blew his nose sonorously. Banker Phelps closed his knife with a snap. "It's too bad the old man's sons didn't turn out better," he remarked with reflective authority. "They never hung together. He spent money enough on Harve to stock a dozen cattle-farms, and he might as well have poured it into Sand Creek. If Harve had stayed at home and helped nurse what little they had, and gone into stock on the old man's bottom farm, they might all have been well fixed. But the old man had to trust everything to tenants and was cheated right and left."

"Harve never could have handled stock none," interposed the cattleman. "He hadn't it in him to be sharp. Do you remember when he bought Sander's mules for eight-year-olds, when everybody in town knew that Sander's father-in-law give 'em to his wife for a wedding present eighteen years before, an' they was full-grown mules then?"

The company laughed discreetly, and the Grand Army man rubbed his knees with a spasm of childish delight.

"Harve never was much account for anything practical, and he shore was never fond of work," began the coal and lumber dealer. "I mind the last time he was home; the day he left, when the old man was out to the barn helpin' his hand hitch up to take Harve to the train, and Cal Moots was patchin' up the fence; Harve, he come out on the step and sings out, in his lady-like voice: 'Cal Moots, Cal Moots! please come cord my trunk.'"

"That's Harve for you," approved the Grand Army man. "I kin hear him howlin' yet, when he was a big feller in long pants and his mother used to whale him with a rawhide in the barn for lettin' the cows git foundered in the cornfield when he was drivin' 'em home from pasture. He killed a cow of mine that-a-way onct—a pure Jersey and the best milker I had, an' the ole man had to put up for her. Harve, he was watchin' the sun set acrost the marshes when the anamile got away."

"Where the old man made his mistake was in sending the boy East to school," said Phelps, stroking his goatee and speaking in a deliberate, judicial tone. "There was where he got his head full of nonsense. What Harve needed, of all people, was a course in some first-class Kansas City business college."

The letters were swimming before Steaven's eyes. Was it possible that these men did not understand, that the palm on the coffin meant nothing to them? The very name of their town would have remained forever buried in the postal guide had it not been now and again mentioned in the world in connection with Harvey Merrick's. He remembered what his master had said to him on the day of his death, after the congestion of both lungs had shut off any probability of recovery, and the sculptor had asked his pupil to send his body home. "It's not a pleasant place to be lying while the world is moving and doing and bettering," he had said with a feeble smile, "but it rather seems as though we ought to go back to the place we came from, in the end. The townspeople will come in for a look at me; and after they have had their say, I shan't have much to fear from the judgment of God!"

The cattleman took up the comment. "Forty's young for a Merrick to cash in; they usually hang on pretty well. Probably he helped it along with whisky."

"His mother's people were not long lived, and Harvey never had a robust constitution," said the minister mildly. He would have liked to say more. He had been the boy's Sunday-school teacher, and had been fond of him; but he felt that he was not in a position to speak. His own sons had turned out badly, and it was not a year since one of them had made his last trip home in the express car, shot in a gambling-house in the Black Hills.

"Nevertheless, there is no disputin' that Harve frequently looked upon the wine when it was red, also variegated, and it shore made an oncommon fool of him," moralized the cattleman.

Just then the door leading into the parlour rattled loudly and every one started involuntarily, looking relieved when only Jim Laird came out. The Grand Army man ducked his head when he saw the spark in his blue, blood-shot eye. They were all afraid of Jim; he was a drunkard, but he could twist the law to suit his client's needs as no other man in all western Kansas could do, and there were many who tried. The lawyer closed the door behind him, leaned back against it and folded his arms, cocking his head a little to one side. When he assumed this attitude in the court-room, ears were always pricked up, as it usually foretold a flood of withering sarcasm.

"I've been with you gentlemen before," he began in a dry, even tone, "when you've sat by the coffins of boys born and raised in this town; and, if I remember rightly, you were never any too well satisfied when you checked them up. What's the matter, anyhow? Why is it that reputable young men are as scarce as millionaires in Sand City? It might almost seem to a stranger that there was some way something the matter with your progressive town. Why did Ruben Sayer, the brightest young lawyer you ever turned out, after he had come home from the university as straight as a die, take to drinking and forge a check and shoot himself? Why did Bill Merrit's son die of the shakes in a saloon in Omaha? Why was Mr. Thomas's son, here, shot in a gambling-house? Why did young Adams burn his mill to beat the insurance companies and go to the pen?"

The lawyer paused and unfolded his arms, laying one clenched fist quietly on the table. "I'll tell you why. Because you drummed nothing but money and knavery into their ears from the time they wore knickerbockers; because you carped away at them as you've been carping here tonight, holding our friends Phelps and Elder up to them for their models, as our grandfathers held up George Washington and John Adams. But the boys were young, and raw at the business you put them to, and how could they match coppers with such artists as Phelps and Elder? You wanted them to be successful rascals; they were only unsuccessful ones—that's all the difference. There was only one boy ever raised in this borderland between ruffianism and civilization who didn't come to grief, and you hated Harvey Merrick more for winning out than you hated all the other boys who got under the wheels. Yes indeed, how you did hate him! Phelps, here, is fond of saying that he could buy and sell us all out any time he's a mind to; but he knew Harve wouldn't have given a farthing for his bank and all his cattle-farms put together; and a lack of appreciation, that way, goes hard with Phelps.

"Old Nimrod thinks Harve drank too much; and this from such as Nimrod and me!"

"Brother Elder says Harve was too free with the old man's money—fell short in filial consideration, maybe. Well, we can all remember the very tone in which brother Elder swore his own father was a liar, in the county court; and we all know that the old man came out of that partnership with his son as bare as a sheared lamb. But maybe I'm getting personal, and I'd better be driving ahead at what I want to say."

The lawyer paused a moment, squared his heavy shoulders, and went on: "Harvey Merrick and I went to school together, back East. We were dead in earnest, and we wanted you all to be proud of us some day. We meant to be great men. Even I, and I haven't lost my sense of humor, gentlemen, I meant to be a great man. I came back here to practise, and I found you didn't in the least want me to be a great man. You wanted me to be a shrewd lawyer—oh, yes! Our veteran here wanted me to get him an increase of pension, because he had dyspepsia;[6] Phelps wanted a new county survey that would put the widow Wilson's little bottom farm inside his south

6. **dyspepsia** (dis pep′ sē ə), indigestion.

line; Elder wanted to lend money at five per cent a month, and get it collected; and Stark here wanted to wheedle old women up in Vermont into investing their annuities in real-estate mortgages that are not worth the paper they are written on. Oh, you needed me hard enough, and you'll go on needing me!

"Well, I came back here and became the crooked shyster you wanted me to be. You pretend to have some sort of respect for me; and yet you'll stand up and throw mud at Harvey Merrick, whose soul you couldn't dirty and whose hands you couldn't tie. Oh, you're a discriminating lot of Christians! There have been times when the sight of Harvey's name in some Eastern paper has made me hang my head like a whipped dog; and, again, times when I liked to think of him off there in the world, away from all this hog-wallow, climbing the big, clean up-grade he'd set for himself.

"And we? Now that we've fought and lied and sweated and stolen, and hated as only the disappointed strugglers in a bitter, dead little Western town know how to do, what have we got to show for it? Harvey Merrick wouldn't have given one sunset over your marshes for all you've got put together, and you know it. It's not for me to say why, in the inscrutable wisdom of God, a genius should ever have been called from this place of hatred and bitter waters; but I want this Boston man to know that the drivel he's been hearing here tonight is the only tribute any truly great man could have from such a lot of sick, side-tracked, burnt-dog, land-poor sharks as the here-present financiers of Sand City—upon which town may God have mercy!"

The lawyer thrust out his hand to Steavens as he passed him, caught up his overcoat in the hall, and had left the house before the Grand Army man had had time to lift his ducked head and crane his long neck about at his fellows.

Next day Jim Laird was drunk and unable to attend the funeral services. Steavens

called twice at his office, but was compelled to start East without seeing him. He had a presentiment that he would hear from him again, and left his address on the lawyer's table; but if Laird found it, he never acknowledged it. The thing in him that Harvey Merrick had loved must have gone under ground with Harvey Merrick's coffin; for it never spoke again, and Jim got the cold he died of driving across the Colorado mountains to defend one of Phelps's sons who had got into trouble out there by cutting government timber.

FOR UNDERSTANDING

1. Why does Henry Steavens go to Sand City? What is the only thing in the Merrick parlor that he can associate with Harvey Merrick?

2. Through whose eyes does the reader see the Merrick family? What is this person's reaction to the mother, father, sister, and maid?

3. In the parlor, next to which person does Steavens stand? With what person does he establish a feeling of mutual understanding?

4. When the townspeople are sitting in the dining room after the family has gone to bed, what is the first question asked? What does their whole conversation revolve around?

FOR INTERPRETATION

1. What does each of the following quotations reveal about the speaker, the person spoken about, or both?

a. Steavens: "He was wonderful . . . ; but until tonight I have never known how wonderful."

b. Banker Phelps: "It's too bad the old man's sons didn't turn out better. . . . He spent money enough on Harve to stock a dozen cattle-farms, and he might as well have poured it into Sand Creek."

c. The coal and lumber dealer: "Harve never was much account for anything practical, and he shore was never fond of work."

d. Jim Laird: "Harvey Merrick wouldn't have given one sunset over your marshes for all you've got put together, and you know it."

2. On the basis of this story and your own experience, discuss the following propositions:

   a. Beauty and art have no place in the business world.

   b. Great persons have overcome great obstacles.

   c. People usually find fault with those ideas and individuals they don't understand.

   d. Prophets are never honored in their own town.

FOR APPRECIATION

Conflict

In the popular imagination, conflict in a Western town means two tall Texans squared off in a dusty street in front of the local saloon. In this story, however, Willa Cather portrays a conflict, perhaps less violent, but far more serious in its implications for society. In this borderland "between ruffianism and civilization," where the rawness and bitterness of primitive struggle for physical survival sometimes fosters soul-crushing materialism, how, she asks, can the sensitive, refined, civilizing spirit find root, grow, and flourish? It is the latter, the creative mind filled with "an exhaustless gallery of beautiful impressions," that lifts life above the savage. Yet the conflict between the civilizing and the savage spirits is a warfare never wholly resolved; each age—indeed, each individual—must make the choice anew.

1. Reread the beginning of the story and discuss how Cather quickly establishes the conflict between the lawyer, Jim Laird, and his fellow townspeople.

2. Describe the dramatic scene with which this conflict reaches a climax.

3. What does the information about Laird's death tell the reader about his conflict with the town?

COMPOSITION

Willa Cather wanted the reader to be sympathetic to her belief that creative, artistic individuals such as Harvey Merrick were treated unfairly in the harsh, frontier environment. To tell her story, Cather wrote from the *omniscient,* or all-knowing, point of view that permitted her to present Merrick through the eyes of Steavens, who had loved and revered the sculptor.

However, there are two or more sides to any story. Did you wonder how Harvey's sister may have felt about her brother, upon whom her indulgent father had spent enough "to stock a dozen cattle-farms"? Imagine that you are Merrick's sister and write a two- or three-paragraph diary entry dated February 8, 1904. This is the evening the train brings home Harvey Merrick's body. Imagine what your feelings as his sister might be, and write about Harvey from *her* viewpoint.

Sherwood Anderson 1876–1941

As a boy growing up in Clyde, Ohio (the "Winesburg" of his short stories), Sherwood Anderson was nicknamed "Jobby" because of his ambitiousness in working at odd jobs to help his mother feed her brood of seven children. His father, a harness maker who made less and less money as farmers switched from using horses to using machines, was a better amateur actor and storyteller than provider. But it was from his father and from reading Mark Twain that Anderson absorbed the rhythms of the oral story that gave such naturalness to his later writing.

Though his formal schooling was sporadic, Anderson read a wide variety of books—from the Bible to Dickens, from Cooper to Twain. After a stint in the service during the Spanish-American War, he graduated from Wittenburg Academy in Springfield, Ohio, before becoming a successful advertising writer. In his early career he was a model businessman, a Horatio Alger figure bound to rise "from rags to riches." Within a few years, Anderson was the head of a paint manufacturing company in Elyria, Ohio. As he pushed to become a business success, however, he found no place for human values in a life keyed to materialistic competition. He sought answers to what had gone wrong with American ideals, and he began to write poetry and prose. Finally, mental anguish drove him to a painful break with his business career and he moved to Chicago where, along with Carl Sandburg, Vachel Lindsay, Floyd Dell, and Edgar Lee Masters, he was soon recognized as one of the "New Voices" in American literature. One member of this "Chicago Renaissance" group who influenced him greatly was the novelist Theodore Dreiser.

Neither of Anderson's first novels, *Windy McPherson's Son* (1916) nor *Marching Men* (1917), had great literary impact, but the publication of *Winesburg, Ohio* (1919), an innovative collection of short stories, brought him international acclaim and remains his masterwork. Anderson continued to write novels and his *Dark Laughter* (1925) was his most lucrative work, but his volumes of short fiction were his most successful.

PORTRAIT OF SHERWOOD ANDERSON
Soss Melik
National Portrait Gallery, Smithsonian Institution

The Triumph of the Egg (1921), *Horses and Men* (1923), and *Death in the Woods* (1933) contain many stories that show his power with simple, fluid narrative. Married four times and the father of three children, Anderson settled in Marion, Virginia, in 1924 as editor of two county newspapers. At a farewell party before leaving on a tour of Latin America, Anderson accidently swallowed a piece of toothpick which brought about his death of peritonitis soon afterward.

"Sophistication" comes from *Winesburg, Ohio* (1919), his collection of short stories and sketches about people living in a small, pre-industrial Ohio town. The stories are held together through the use of a central figure, young George Willard, who appears and reappears throughout the series as an observer, commentator, or audience, and in "Sophistication" as a leading character. George is widely thought to be the author himself, Anderson's alter ego. As you read, note the ease with which the author takes you back to Winesburg—at county fair time.

from **WINESBURG, OHIO**

Sophistication

It was early evening of a day in the late fall and the Winesburg County Fair had brought crowds of country people into town. The day had been clear and the night came on warm and pleasant. On the Trunion Pike, where the road after it left town stretched away between berry fields now covered with dry brown leaves, the dust from passing wagons arose in clouds. Children, curled into little balls, slept on the straw scattered on wagon beds. Their hair was full of dust and their fingers black and sticky. The dust rolled away over the fields and the departing sun set it ablaze with colors.

In the main street of Winesburg crowds filled the stores and the sidewalks. Night came on, horses whinnied, the clerks in the stores ran madly about, children became lost and cried lustily, an American town worked terribly at the task of amusing itself.

Pushing his way through the crowds in Main Street, young George Willard concealed himself in the stairway leading to Doctor Reefy's office and looked at the people. With feverish eyes he watched the faces drifting past under the store lights. Thoughts kept coming into his head and he did not want to think. He stamped impatiently on the wooden steps and looked sharply about. "Well, is she going to stay with him all day? Have I done all this waiting for nothing?" he muttered.

George Willard, the Ohio village boy, was fast growing into manhood and new thoughts had been coming into his mind. All that day,

amid the jam of people at the Fair, he had gone about feeling lonely. He was about to leave Winesburg to go away to some city where he hoped to get work on a city newspaper and he felt grown-up. The mood that had taken possession of him was a thing known to men and unknown to boys. He felt old and a little tired. Memories awoke in him. To his mind his new sense of maturity set him apart, made of him a half-tragic figure. He wanted someone to understand the feeling that had taken possession of him after his mother's death.

There is a time in the life of every boy when he for the first time takes the backward view of life. Perhaps that is the moment when he crosses the line into manhood. The boy is walking through the street of his town. He is thinking of the future and of the figure he will cut in the world. Ambitions and regrets awake within him. Suddenly something happens; he stops under a tree and waits as for a voice calling his name. Ghosts of old things creep into his consciousness; the voices outside of himself whisper a message concerning the limitations of life. From being quite sure of himself and his future he becomes not at all sure. If he be an imaginative boy a door is torn open and for the first time he looks out upon the world, seeing, as though they marched in procession before him, the countless figures of men who before his time have come out of nothingness into the world, lived their lives and again disappeared into nothingness. The sadness of sophistication has come to the boy. With a little gasp he sees himself as merely a leaf blown by the wind through the streets of his village. He knows that in spite of all the stout talk of his fellows he must live and die in uncertainty, a thing blown by the winds, a thing destined like corn to wilt in the sun. He shivers and looks eagerly about. The eighteen years he has lived seem but a moment, a breathing space in the long march of humanity. Already he hears death calling. With all his heart he wants to come close to some other human, touch someone with his hands, be touched by the hand of another. If he prefers that the other be a woman, that is because he believes that a woman will be gentle, that she will understand. He wants, most of all, understanding.

When the moment of sophistication came to George Willard his mind turned to Helen White, the Winesburg banker's daughter. Always he had been conscious of the girl growing into womanhood as he grew into manhood. Once on a summer night when he was eighteen, he had walked with her on a country road and in her presence had given way to an impulse to boast, to make himself appear big and significant in her eyes. Now he wanted to see her for another purpose. He wanted to tell her of the new impulses that had come to him. He had tried to make her think of him as a man when he knew nothing of manhood and now he wanted to be with her and to try to make her feel the change he believed had taken place in his nature.

As for Helen White, she also had come to a period of change. What George felt, she in her young woman's way felt also. She was no longer a girl and hungered to reach into the grace and beauty of womanhood. She had come home from Cleveland, where she was attending college, to spend a day at the Fair. She also had begun to have memories. During the day she sat in the grandstand with a young man, one of the instructors from the college, who was a guest of her mother's. The young man was of a pedantic turn of mind and she felt at once he would not do for her purpose. At the Fair she was glad to be seen in his company as he was well dressed and a stranger. She knew that the fact of his presence would create an impression. During the day she was happy, but when night came on she began to grow restless. She wanted to

drive the instructor away, to get out of his presence. While they sat together in the grandstand and while the eyes of former schoolmates were upon them, she paid so much attention to her escort that he grew interested. "A scholar needs money. I should marry a woman with money," he mused.

Helen White was thinking of George Willard even as he wandered gloomily through the crowds thinking of her. She remembered the summer evening when they had walked together and wanted to walk with him again. She thought that the months she had spent in the city, the going to theaters and the seeing of great crowds wandering in lighted thoroughfares, had changed her profoundly. She wanted him to feel and be conscious of the change in her nature.

The summer evening together that had left its mark on the memory of both the young man and the woman had, when looked at quite sensibly, been rather stupidly spent. They had walked out of town along a country road. Then they had stopped by a fence near a field of young corn and George had taken off his coat and let it hang on his arm. "Well, I've stayed here in Winesburg—yes—I've not yet gone away but I'm growing up," he had said. "I've been reading books and I've been thinking. I'm going to try to amount to something in life.

"Well," he explained, "that isn't the point. Perhaps I'd better quit talking."

The confused boy put his hand on the girl's arm. His voice trembled. The two started to walk back along the road toward town. In his desperation George boasted, "I'm going to be a big man, the biggest that ever lived here in Winesburg," he declared. "I want you to do something, I don't know what. Perhaps it is none of my business. I want you to try to be different from other women. You see the point. It's none of my business, I tell you. I want you to be a beautiful woman. You see what I want."

The boy's voice failed and in silence the

Though he began his career as a cartoonist, Walt Kuhn became known for his brooding portraits of clowns and acrobats— boldly painted figures who seem immobilized by pent-up feelings.

THE WHITE CLOWN
Walt Kuhn
National Gallery of Art, Washington, D.C.

two came back into town and went along the street to Helen White's house. At the gate he tried to say something impressive. Speeches he had thought out came into his head, but they seemed utterly pointless. "I thought—I used to think—I had it in my mind you would marry Seth Richmond. Now I know you won't," was all he could find to say as she went through the gate and toward the door of her house.

On the warm fall evening as he stood in the stairway and looked at the crowd drifting through Main Street, George thought of the talk beside the field of young corn and was ashamed of the figure he had made of himself. In the street the people surged up and down like cattle confined in a pen. Buggies and wagons almost filled the narrow thoroughfare. A band played and small boys raced along the sidewalk, diving between the legs of men. Young men with shining red faces walked awkwardly about with girls on their arms. In a room above one of the stores, where a dance was to be held, the fiddlers tuned their instruments. The broken sounds floated down through an open window and out across the murmur of voices and the loud blare of the horns of the band. The medley of sounds got on young Willard's nerves. Everywhere, on all sides, the sense of crowding, moving life closed in about him. He wanted to run away by himself and think. "If she wants to stay with that fellow she may. Why should I care? What difference does it make to me?" he growled and went along Main Street and through Hern's Grocery into a side street.

George felt so utterly lonely and dejected that he wanted to weep but pride made him walk rapidly along, swinging his arms. He came to Wesley Moyer's livery barn and stopped in the shadows to listen to a group of men who talked of a race Wesley's stallion, Tony Tip, had won at the Fair during the afternoon. A crowd had gathered in front of the barn and before the crowd walked Wesley, prancing up and down and boasting. He held a whip in his hand and kept tapping the ground. Little puffs of dust arose in the lamplight. "Quit your talking," Wesley exclaimed. "I wasn't afraid, I knew I had 'em beat all the time. I wasn't afraid."

Ordinarily George Willard would have been intensely interested in the boasting of Moyer, the horseman. Now it made him angry. He turned and hurried away along the street. "Old windbag," he sputtered. "Why does he want to be bragging? Why don't he shut up?"

George went into a vacant lot, and as he hurried along, fell over a pile of rubbish. A nail protruding from an empty barrel tore his trousers. He sat down on the ground and swore. With a pin he mended the torn place and then arose and went on. "I'll go to Helen White's house, that's what I'll do. I'll walk right in. I'll say that I want to see her. I'll walk right in and sit down, that's what I'll do," he declared, climbing over a fence and beginning to run.

On the veranda of Banker White's house Helen was restless and distraught. The instructor sat between the mother and daughter. His talk wearied the girl. Although he had also been raised in an Ohio town, the instructor began to put on the airs of the city. He wanted to appear cosmopolitan. "I like the chance you have given me to study the background out of which most of our girls come," he declared. "It was good of you, Mrs. White, to have me down for the day." He turned to Helen and laughed. "Your life is still bound up with the life of this town?" he asked. "There are people here in whom you are interested?" To the girl his voice sounded pompous and heavy.

Helen arose and went into the house. At the door leading to a garden at the back she stopped and stood listening. Her mother began to talk. "There is no one here fit to associate with a girl of Helen's breeding," she said.

Helen ran down a flight of stairs at the back of the house and into the garden. In the darkness she stopped and stood trembling. It seemed to her that the world was full of meaningless people saying words. Afire with eagerness she ran through a garden gate and, turning a corner by the banker's barn, went into a little side street. "George! Where are you, George?" she cried, filled with nervous excitement. She stopped running, and leaned against a tree to laugh hysterically. Along the dark little street came George Willard, still saying words. "I'm going to walk right into her house. I'll go right in and sit down," he declared as he came up to her. He stopped and stared stupidly. "Come on," he said, and took hold of her hand. With hanging heads they walked away along the street under the trees. Dry leaves rustled underfoot. Now that he had found her George wondered what he had better do and say.

At the upper end of the Fair Ground, in Winesburg, there is a half-decayed old grandstand. It has never been painted and the boards are all warped out of shape. The Fair Ground stands on top of a low hill rising out of the valley of Wine Creek and from the grandstand one can see at night, over a cornfield, the lights of the town reflected against the sky.

George and Helen climbed the hill to the Fair Ground, coming by the path past Waterworks Pond. The feeling of loneliness and isolation that had come to the young man in the crowded streets of his town was both broken and intensified by the presence of Helen. What he felt was reflected in her.

In youth there are always two forces fighting in people. The warm unthinking little animal struggles against the thing that reflects and remembers, and the older, the more sophisticated thing had possession of George Willard. Sensing his mood, Helen walked beside him filled with respect. When they got to the grandstand they climbed up under the roof and sat down on one of the long benchlike seats.

There is something memorable in the experience to be had by going into a fairground that stands at the edge of a Middle Western town on a night after the annual fair has been held. The sensation is one never to be forgotten. On all sides are ghosts, not of the dead, but of living people. Here, during the day just passed, have come the people pouring in from the town and the country around. Farmers with their wives and children and all the people from the hundreds of little frame houses have gathered within these board walls. Young girls have laughed and men with beards have talked of the affairs of their lives. The place has been filled to overflowing with life. It has itched and squirmed with life and now it is night and the life has all gone away. The silence is almost terrifying. One conceals oneself standing silently beside the trunk of a tree and what there is of a reflective tendency in his nature is intensified. One shudders at the thought of the meaninglessness of life while at the same instant, and if the people of the town are his people, one loves life so intensely that tears come into the eyes.

In the darkness under the roof of the grandstand, George Willard sat beside Helen White and felt very keenly his own insignificance in the scheme of existence. Now that he had come out of town where the presence of the people stirring about, busy with a multitude of affairs, had been so irritating, the irritation was all gone. The presence of Helen renewed and refreshed him. It was as though her woman's hand was assisting him to make some minute readjustment of the machinery of his life. He began to think of the people in the town where he had always lived with something like reverence. He had reverence for Helen. He wanted to love and to be loved by her, but he did not want at the moment to be confused by her womanhood. In the darkness he took hold of her hand and when she crept close put a hand on her shoulder. A wind began to blow and he shivered. With all his strength he tried to hold and to understand the mood that had come upon him. In that high place in the darkness the two oddly sensitive human atoms held each other tightly and waited. In the mind of each was the same thought. "I have come to this lonely place and here is this other," was the substance of the thing felt.

In Winesburg the crowded day had run itself out into the long night of the late fall. Farm horses jogged away along lonely country roads pulling their portion of weary people. Clerks began to bring samples of goods in off the sidewalks and lock the doors of stores. In the Opera House a crowd had gathered to see a show and further down Main Street the fiddlers, their instruments tuned, sweated and worked to keep the feet of youth flying over a dance floor.

In the darkness in the grandstand Helen White and George Willard remained silent. Now and then the spell that held them was broken and they turned and tried in the dim light to see into each other's eyes. They kissed but that impulse did not last. At the upper end of the Fair Ground a half-dozen men worked over horses that had raced during the afternoon. The men had built a fire and were heating kettles of water. Only their legs could be seen as they passed back and forth in the light. When the wind blew, the little flames of the fire danced crazily about.

George and Helen arose and walked away into the darkness. They went along a path past a field of corn that had not yet been cut. The wind whispered among the dry corn blades. For a moment during the walk back into town the spell that held them was broken. When they had come to the crest of Waterworks Hill they stopped by a tree and George again put his hands on the girl's shoulders. She embraced him eagerly and then again they drew quickly back from that impulse. They stopped kissing and stood a little apart. Mutual respect grew big in them. They were both embarrassed and to relieve their embarrassment dropped into the animalism of youth. They laughed and began to pull and haul at each other. In some way chastened and purified by the mood they had

been in, they became, not man and woman, not boy and girl, but excited little animals.

It was so they went down the hill. In the darkness they played like two splendid young things in a young world. Once, running swiftly forward, Helen tripped George and he fell. He squirmed and shouted. Shaking with laughter, he rolled down the hill. Helen ran after him. For just a moment she stopped in the darkness. There is no way of knowing what woman's thoughts went through her mind but, when the bottom of the hill was reached and she came up to the boy, she took his arm and walked beside him in dignified silence. For some reason they could not have explained they had both got from their silent evening together the thing needed. Man or boy, woman or girl, they had for a moment taken hold of the thing that makes the mature life of men and women in the modern world possible.

FOR UNDERSTANDING

1. Throughout the stories in *Winesburg, Ohio,* Anderson explores the problem of human isolation and loneliness. The period of adolescence is particularly one in which individuals feel an intensified lack of "belongingness." How old was George Willard? On the day the story opens, why was he feeling lonely among the crowds at the fair?
2. Briefly discuss the "sadness of sophistication" that comes to George as Anderson thinks it comes to every boy.
3. Why was George eager to share his feeling of sophistication with Helen White?
4. Why did Helen wish to see George? Why wasn't she really interested in the visiting college professor?
5. After they met, where did George and Helen go to sit? After a while, what thought came into the mind of each?

FOR INTERPRETATION

1. The following statement of Anderson's is of much significance to this story and particularly important to its ending: "In youth there are always two forces fighting in people. The warm unthinking little animal struggles against the thing that reflects and remembers, . . ." In light of the author's statement, what do you think is symbolic about George and Helen's exuberant play as they go down the hill?

2. Critics have commented that, in his lack of pretense and use of simple language, Anderson quite often used the word *thing* to stand for an involved, abstract idea. Discuss what you think the word means as Anderson uses it in the concluding line of "Sophistication": "Man or boy, woman or girl, they had for a moment taken hold of the thing that makes the mature life of men and women in the modern world possible."

FOR APPRECIATION

Form, Theme, Style

Sherwood Anderson thought of the book *Winesburg, Ohio* as a novel written in a form that he had invented. The book was inspired by *Spoon River Anthology* by Edgar Lee Masters (see page 639), whose free-verse poems dealt with the lives of people in southern Illinois towns. Anderson felt that in putting together a series of individual tales about lives in some way connected, he was giving the American novelist a "new looseness," a form that would better accommodate life, which itself "is a loose flowing thing." Certainly, in its overall pattern—as well as within its individual stories which have no traditional plot structure—*Winesburg, Ohio* set a literary precedent. Following its publication, Anderson became a definite influence on such writers as Hemingway and Faulkner.

In *Winesburg, Ohio,* in which he labored to point out that all people share the common bond of humanity and must recognize this kinship to avoid becoming distorted, Anderson's purpose was not to attack the small town or its people. His characters are actually composites drawn from all his experience, and his purpose was to provide insight into the anguish of people warped through their failure to reach their full potential as human beings. His interest is in understanding and loving these twisted people, introduced as "grotesques" at the beginning of the book. His stories reveal that the major problem of human beings who suffer isolation and loneliness is their inability to communicate feeling, thought, and love, and that these shortcomings create the "grotesques" in human society.

In writing style, Anderson refused to be cataloged as either a realist or a naturalist, although both influences are reflected in his writing along with much poetic lyricism. His simple language and his ability to accurately portray the inhabitants of a small, late-nineteenth-century town are clearly demonstrated in "Sophistication." What are some specific details describing life on Main Street that make his writing so vivid?

COMPOSITION

Anderson's description of the empty grandstand that remains filled with the living ghosts of those who had recently occupied it strikes a responsive chord in the reader.

Reread that vivid paragraph (p. 545) beginning, "There is something memorable in the experience to be had by going into. . . ." Using these words as a springboard, recapture a scene from your memory in which you describe *seeing* and *feeling* the presence of people after they have left a room, a stage, an auditorium, or other location.

Katherine Anne Porter   1890–1980

Katherine Anne Marie Callista Russell Porter, a lineal descendant of both Daniel Boone and Colonel Andrew Porter (a pre-Revolutionary War aide to George Washington), was born in Indian Creek, Texas, one of five children. O. Henry, the famed short-story writer whose real name was William Sidney Porter, was her father's second cousin. O. Henry, who is best remembered for having contributed the surprise ending to the American short-story form, quickly produced contrived stories in which he, as author, occasionally made an appearance to comment on the action.* By contrast, his descendant, Katherine Anne, wrote very slowly and with great patience as she struggled to perfect a completely objective style in which the author's presence could not be detected. She worked so carefully to develop this style without sacrificing sensitivity, that her total fiction amounts to one novel, five novelettes, and three collections of short stories. Although she began writing as a small child, she did not satisfy her own standards and did not begin publishing until she was thirty. But the high quality of her work was immediately recognized and she became an influence on young writers from the time her stories first appeared.

Educated at convent schools in Texas and Louisiana, Porter lived in New York for seventeen years before moving to Washington, D.C. in 1960. To supplement the income from her fiction, she worked as a newspaper reporter and editor, as well as doing an extensive study of Mexico's arts and crafts and a number of translations of Spanish, Latin-American, and French fiction. In 1930 her reputation in the literary world was confirmed when six of her short stories were published under the title of *Flowering Judas.* Her first short novel, *Hacienda* (1934), an enlarged edition of *Flowering Judas* (1935), and two other novelettes, *Noon Wine* (1937) and *Pale Horse, Pale Rider* (1939), preceded *The Leaning Tower,* a collection of seven short stories and a novella, which appeared in 1944. *The Days Before,* a masterly collection of essays, appeared in 1952. Her long-anticipated

PORTRAIT OF KATHERINE ANN PORTER

novel, *Ship of Fools* (1962), an allegory reflecting the social and political upheaval of modern times, has served to cement her position in American literature as a prose stylist of the first rank.

Family life—with all the tradition and ceremony attached to birth, marriage, and death—meant a great deal to Katherine Anne Porter. As you read "The Jilting of Granny Weatherall," you will need to stay alert to sort the past from the present. It may help you to know that John was Granny's husband, George was the man who jilted her, and her children were Cornelia, Lydia, Jimmy, and Hapsy.

---

*O. Henry allowed himself to be present on the scene as an observer who communicated directly with the reader. This was a literary device (known as "Dear Reader") commonly used by writers of a century ago, but rarely used now.

THE JILTING OF GRANNY WEATHERALL

She flicked her wrist neatly out of Doctor Harry's pudgy careful fingers and pulled the sheet up to her chin. The brat ought to be in knee breeches. Doctoring around the country with spectacles on his nose! "Get along now, take your schoolbooks and go. There's nothing wrong with me."

Doctor Harry spread a warm paw like a cushion on her forehead where the forked green vein danced and made her eyelids twitch. "Now, now, be a good girl, and we'll have you up in no time."

"That's no way to speak to a woman nearly eighty years old just because she's down. I'd have you respect your elders, young man."

"Well, Missy, excuse me." Doctor Harry patted her cheek. "But I've got to warn you, haven't I? You're a marvel, but you must be careful or you're going to be good and sorry."

"Don't tell me what I'm going to be. I'm on my feet now, morally speaking. It's Cornelia. I had to go to bed to get rid of her."

Her bones felt loose, and floated around in her skin, and Doctor Harry floated like a balloon around the foot of the bed. He floated and pulled down his waistcoat and swung his glasses on a cord. "Well, stay where you are, it certainly can't hurt you."

"Get along and doctor your sick," said Granny Weatherall. "Leave a well woman alone. I'll call for you when I want you. . . . Where were you forty years ago when I pulled through milk-leg[1] and double pneumonia? You weren't even born. Don't let Cornelia lead you on," she shouted, because Doctor Harry appeared to float up to the ceiling and out. "I pay my own bills, and I don't throw my money away on nonsense!"

She meant to wave good-by, but it was too much trouble. Her eyes closed of themselves, it was like a dark curtain drawn around the bed. The pillow rose and floated under her, pleasant as a hammock in a light wind. She listened to the leaves rustling outside the window. No, somebody was swishing newspapers: no, Cornelia and Doctor Harry were whispering together. She leaped broad awake, thinking they whispered in her ear.

"She was never like this, *never* like this!" "Well, what can we expect?" "Yes, eighty years old. . . ."

Well, and what if she was? She still had ears. It was like Cornelia to whisper around doors. She always kept things secret in such a public way. She was always being tactful and kind. Cornelia was dutiful; that was the trouble with her. Dutiful and good: "So good and dutiful," said Granny, "that I'd like to spank her." She saw herself spanking Cornelia and making a fine job of it.

"What'd you say, Mother?"

Granny felt her face tying up in hard knots.

"Can't a body think, I'd like to know?"

"I thought you might want something."

"I do. I want a lot of things. First off, go away and don't whisper."

She lay and drowsed, hoping in her sleep that the children would keep out and let her rest a minute. It had been a long day. Not that she was tired. It was always pleasant to snatch a minute now and then. There was al-

1. **milk-leg,** inflammation of femoral veins, causing a painful swelling of the leg following childbirth.

ways so much to be done, let me see: tomorrow.

Tomorrow was far away and there was nothing to trouble about. Things were finished somehow when the time came; thank God there was always a little margin over for peace: then a person could spread out the plan of life and tuck in the edges orderly. It was good to have everything clean and folded away, with the hair brushes and tonic bottles sitting straight on the white embroidered linen: the day started without fuss and the pantry shelves laid out with rows of jelly glasses and brown jugs and white stone-china jars with blue whirligigs and words painted on them: coffee, tea, sugar, ginger, cinnamon, allspice: and the bronze clock with the lion on top nicely dusted off. The dust that lion could collect in twenty-four hours! The box in the attic with all those letters tied up, well, she'd have to go through that tomorrow. All those letters—George's letters and John's letters and her letters to them both—lying around for the children to find afterward made her uneasy. Yes, that would be tomorrow's business. No use to let them know how silly she had been once.

While she was rummaging around she found death in her mind and it felt clammy and unfamiliar. She had spent so much time preparing for death there was no need for bringing it up again. Let it take care of itself now. When she was sixty she had felt very old, finished, and went around making farewell trips to see her children and grandchildren, with a secret in her mind: This is the very last of your mother, children! Then she made her will and came down with a long fever. That was all just a notion like a lot of other things, but it was lucky too, for she had once for all got over the idea of dying for a long time. Now she couldn't be worried. She hoped she had better sense now. Her father had lived to be one hundred and two years old and had drunk a noggin of strong hot toddy on his last birthday. He told the reporters it was his daily habit, and he owed his long life to that. He had made quite a scandal and was very pleased about it. She believed she'd just plague Cornelia a little.

"Cornelia! Cornelia!" No footsteps, but a sudden hand on her cheek. "Bless you, where have you been?"

"Here, Mother."

"Well, Cornelia, I want a noggin of hot toddy."

"Are you cold, darling?"

"I'm chilly, Cornelia. Lying in bed stops the circulation. I must have told you that a thousand times."

Well, she could just hear Cornelia telling her husband that Mother was getting a little childish and they'd have to humor her. The thing that most annoyed her was that Cornelia thought she was deaf, dumb, and blind. Little hasty glances and tiny gestures tossed around her and over her head saying, "Don't cross her, let her have her way, she's eighty years old," and she sitting there as if she lived in a thin glass cage. Sometimes Granny almost made up her mind to pack up and move back to her own house where nobody could remind her every minute that she was old. Wait, wait, Cornelia, till your own children whisper behind your back!

In her day she had kept a better house and had got more work done. She wasn't too old yet for Lydia to be driving eighty miles for advice when one of the children jumped the track, and Jimmy still dropped in and talked things over: "Now, Mammy, you've a good business head, I want to know what you think of this? . . ." Old. Cornelia couldn't change the furniture around without asking. Little things, little things! They had been so sweet when they were little. Granny wished the old days were back again with the children young and everything to be done over. It had been a hard pull, but not too much for her. When she thought of all the food she had cooked, and all the clothes she had cut and sewed, and all the gardens she had made —well, the children showed it. There they were, made out of her, and they couldn't get away from that. Sometimes she wanted to see John again and point to them and say, Well, I didn't do so badly, did I? But that would have to wait. That was for tomorrow. She used to think of him as a man, but now all the children were older than their father, and he would be a child beside her if she saw him now. It seemed strange and there was something wrong in the idea. Why, he couldn't possibly recognize her. She had fenced in a hundred acres once, digging the post holes herself and clamping the wires with just a boy to help. That changed a woman. John would be looking for a young woman with the peaked Spanish comb in her hair and the painted fan. Digging post holes changed a woman. Riding country roads in the winter when women had their babies was another thing: sitting up nights with sick horses and sick children and hardly ever losing one. John, I hardly ever lost one of them! John would see that in a minute, that would be something he could understand, she wouldn't have to explain anything!

It made her feel like rolling up her sleeves and putting the whole place to rights again. No matter if Cornelia was determined to be everywhere at once, there were a great many things left undone on this place. She would start tomorrow and do them. It was good to be strong enough for everything, even if all you made melted and changed and slipped under your hands, so that by the time you finished you almost forgot what you were working for. What was it I set out to do? she asked herself intently, but she could not remember. A fog rose over the valley, she saw it marching across the creek swallowing the trees and moving up the hill like an army of ghosts. Soon it would be at the near edge of the orchard, and then it was time to go in and light the lamps. Come in, children, don't stay out in the night air.

Lighting the lamps had been beautiful. The children huddled up to her and breathed like little calves waiting at the bars in the twilight. Their eyes followed the match and watched the flame rise and settle in a blue curve, then they moved away from her. The lamp was lit, they didn't have to be scared and hang on to Mother any more. Never, never, never more. God, for all my life I thank Thee. Without Thee, my God, I could never have done it. Hail, Mary, full of grace.

I want you to pick all the fruit this year and see that nothing is wasted. There's always someone who can use it. Don't let good things rot for want of using. You waste life when you waste good food. Don't let things get lost. It's bitter to lose things. Now, don't let me get to thinking, not when I am tired and taking a little nap before supper. . . .

The pillow rose about her shoulders and pressed against her heart and the memory was being squeezed out of it: oh, push down the pillow, somebody: it would smother her if she tried to hold it. Such a fresh breeze blowing and such a green day with no threats in it. But he had not come, just the same. What does a woman do when she has put on the white veil and set out the white cake for a man and he doesn't come? She tried to remember. No, I swear he never harmed me but in that. He never harmed me but in that . . . and what if he did? There was the day, the day, but a whirl of dark smoke rose and covered it, crept up and over into the bright field where everything was planted so carefully in orderly rows. That was hell, she knew hell when she saw it. For sixty years she had prayed against remembering him and against losing her soul in the deep pit of hell, and now the two things were mingled in one and the thought of him was a smoky cloud from hell that moved and crept in her head when she had just got rid of Doctor Harry and was trying to rest a minute. Wounded vanity, Ellen, said a sharp voice in the top of her mind. Don't let your wounded vanity get the upper hand of you. Plenty of girls get jilted. You were jilted, weren't you? Then stand up to it. Her eyelids wavered and let in streamers of blue-gray light like tissue paper over her eyes. She must get up and pull the shades down or she'd never sleep. She was in bed again and the shades were not down. How could that happen? Better turn over, hide from the light, sleeping in the light gave you nightmares. "Mother, how do you feel now?" and a stinging wetness on her forehead. But I don't like having my face washed in cold water!

Hapsy? George? Lydia? Jimmy? No, Cornelia, and her features were swollen and full of little puddles. "They're coming, darling, they'll all be here soon." Go wash your face, child, you look funny.

Instead of obeying, Cornelia knelt down and put her head on the pillow. She seemed to be talking but there was no sound. "Well, are you tongue-tied? Whose birthday is it? Are you going to give a party?"

Cornelia's mouth moved urgently in strange shapes. "Don't do that, you bother me, daughter."

"Oh, no, Mother. Oh, no. . . ."

Nonsense. It was strange about children. They disputed your every word. "No what, Cornelia?"

"Here's Doctor Harry."

"I won't see that boy again. He just left five minutes ago."

"That was this morning, Mother. It's night now. Here's the nurse."

"This is Doctor Harry, Mrs. Weatherall. I never saw you look so young and happy!"

"Ah, I'll never be young again—but I'd be happy if they'd let me lie in peace and get rested."

She thought she spoke up loudly, but no one answered. A warm weight on her forehead, a warm bracelet on her wrist, and a breeze went on whispering, trying to tell her something. A shuffle of leaves in the everlasting hand of God, He blew on them and they danced and rattled. "Mother, don't mind, we're going to give you a little hypodermic." "Look here, daughter, how do ants get in this bed? I saw sugar ants yesterday." Did you send for Hapsy too?

It was Hapsy she really wanted. She had to go a long way back through a great many rooms to find Hapsy standing with a baby on her arm. She seemed to herself to be Hapsy also, and the baby on Hapsy's arm was Hapsy and himself and herself, all at once, and there was no surprise in the meeting. Then Hapsy melted from within and turned flimsy as gray gauze and the baby was a gauzy shadow, and Hapsy came up close and said, "I thought you'd never come," and looked at her very searchingly and said, "You haven't changed a bit!" They leaned forward to kiss, when Cornelia began whispering from a long way off, "Oh, is there anything you want to tell me? Is there anything I can do for you?"

Yes, she had changed her mind after sixty years and she would like to see George. I want you to find George. Find him and be sure to tell him I forgot him. I want him to know I had my husband just the same and my children and my house like any other woman. A good house too and a good husband that I loved and fine children out of him. Better than I hoped for even. Tell him I was given back everything he took away and more. Oh, no, oh, no, there was something else besides the house and the man and the children. Oh, surely they were not all? What was it? Something not given back. . . . Her breath crowded down under her ribs and grew into a monstrous frightening shape with cutting edges; it bored up into her head, and the agony was unbelievable: Yes, John, get the Doctor now, no more talk, my time has come.

When this one was born it should be the last. The last. It should have been born first, for it was the one she had truly wanted. Everything came in good time. Nothing left out, left over. She was strong, in three days she would be as well as ever. Better. A woman needed milk in her to have her full health.

"Mother, do you hear me?"

"I've been telling you——"

"Mother, Father Connolly's here."

"I went to Holy Communion only last week. Tell him I'm not so sinful as all that."

"Father just wants to speak to you."

Born on an Iowa farm, Grant Wood never forgot his rural past.
His painstaking attention to detail and meticulous realism
made him one of America's best-known regionalist painters
in the years between the two world wars.

WOMAN WITH PLANTS
Grant Wood
Cedar Rapids Museum of Art, Iowa

He could speak as much as he pleased. It was like him to drop in and inquire about her soul as if it were a teething baby, and then stay on for a cup of tea and a round of cards and gossip. He always had a funny story of some sort, usually about an Irishman who made his little mistakes and confessed them, and the point lay in some absurd thing he would blurt out in the confessional showing his struggles between native piety and original sin. Granny felt easy about her soul. Cornelia, where are your manners? Give Father Connolly a chair. She had her secret comfortable understanding with a few favorite saints who cleared a straight road to God for her. All as surely signed and sealed as the papers for the new Forty Acres. Forever . . . heirs and assigns forever. Since the day the wedding cake was not cut, but thrown out and wasted. The whole bottom dropped out of the world, and there she was blind and sweating with nothing under her feet and the walls falling away. His hand had caught her under the breast, she had not fallen, there was the freshly polished floor with the green rug on it, just as before. He had cursed like a sailor's parrot and said, "I'll kill him for you." Don't lay a hand on him, for my sake leave something to God. "Now, Ellen, you must believe what I tell you. . . ."

So there was nothing, nothing to worry about any more, except sometimes in the night one of the children screamed in a nightmare, and they both hustled out shaking and hunting for the matches and calling, "There, wait a minute, here we are!" John, get the doctor now, Hapsy's time has come. But there was Hapsy standing by the bed in a white cap. "Cornelia, tell Hapsy to take off her cap. I can't see her plain."

Her eyes opened very wide and the room stood out like a picture she had seen somewhere. Dark colors with the shadows rising toward the ceiling in long angles. The tall black dresser gleamed with nothing on it but John's picture, enlarged from a little one, with John's eyes very black when they should

have been blue. You never saw him, so how do you know how he looked? But the man insisted the copy was perfect, it was very rich and handsome. For a picture, yes, but it's not my husband. The table by the bed had a linen cover and a candle and a crucifix. The light was blue from Cornelia's silk lampshades. No sort of light at all, just frippery. You had to live forty years with kerosene lamps to appreciate honest electricity. She felt very strong and she saw Doctor Harry with a rosy nimbus around him.

"You look like a saint, Doctor Harry, and I vow that's as near as you'll ever come to it."

"She's saying something."

"I heard you, Cornelia. What's all this carrying-on?"

"Father Connolly's saying——"

Cornelia's voice staggered and bumped like a cart in a bad road. It rounded corners and turned back again and arrived nowhere. Granny stepped up in the cart very lightly and reached for the reins, but a man sat beside her and she knew him by his hands, driving the cart. She did not look in his face, for she knew without seeing, but looked instead down the road where the trees leaned over and bowed to each other and a thousand birds were singing a Mass. She felt like singing too, but she put her hand in the bosom of her dress and pulled out a rosary, and Father Connolly murmured Latin in a very solemn voice and tickled her feet.[2] Will you stop that nonsense? I'm a married woman. What if he did run away and leave me to face the priest by myself? I found another a whole world better. I wouldn't have exchanged my husband for anybody except St. Michael himself, and you may tell him that for me with a thank you in the bargain.

Light flashed on her closed eyelids, and a deep roaring shook her. Cornelia, is that lightning? I hear thunder. There's going to be a storm. Close all the windows. Call the

---

2. **tickled her feet.** Father Connolly is administering the sacrament of the last rites.

children in. . . . "Mother, here we are, all of us." "Is that you, Hapsy?" "Oh, no, I'm Lydia. We drove as fast as we could." Their faces drifted above her, drifted away. The rosary fell out of her hands and Lydia put it back. Jimmy tried to help, their hands fumbled together, and Granny closed two fingers around Jimmy's thumb. Beads wouldn't do, it must be something alive. She was so amazed her thoughts ran round and round. So, my dear Lord, this is my death and I wasn't even thinking about it. My children have come to see me die. But I can't, it's not time. Oh, I always hated surprises. I wanted to give Cornelia the amethyst set—Cornelia, you're to have the amethyst set, but Hapsy's to wear it when she wants, and, Doctor Harry, do shut up. Nobody sent for you. Oh, my dear Lord, do wait a minute. I meant to do something about the Forty Acres, Jimmy doesn't need it and Lydia will later on, with that worthless husband of hers. I meant to finish the altar cloth and send six bottles of wine to Sister Borgia for her dyspepsia. I want to send six bottles of wine to Sister Borgia, Father Connolly, now don't let me forget.

Cornelia's voice made short turns and tilted over and crashed. "Oh, Mother, oh, Mother, oh, Mother. . . ."

"I'm not going, Cornelia. I'm taken by surprise. I can't go."

You'll see Hapsy again. What about her? "I thought you'd never come." Granny made a long journey outward, looking for Hapsy. What if I don't find her? What then? Her heart sank down and down, there was no bottom to death, she couldn't come to the end of it. The blue light from Cornelia's lampshade drew into a tiny point in the center of her brain, it flickered and winked like an eye, quietly it fluttered and dwindled. Granny lay curled down within herself, amazed and watchful, staring at the point of light that was herself; her body was now only a deeper mass of shadow in an endless darkness and this darkness would curl around the light and swallow it up. God, give a sign!

For the second time there was no sign. Again no bridegroom and the priest in the house. She could not remember any other sorrow because this grief wiped them all away. Oh, no, there's nothing more cruel than this—I'll never forgive it. She stretched herself with a deep breath and blew out the light.

FOR UNDERSTANDING

1. Discuss the opening situation and the significance of Granny Weatherall's name.
2. Why does she get impatient with Cornelia? How do Lydia and Jimmy still depend upon her?
3. What had happened to her sixty years before that she has prayed to forget? When she changes her mind, what does she want to tell George?
4. Why doesn't Granny feel she needs the ministrations of Father Connolly?
5. Who is at her bedside when death comes? What had she failed to do before death overtook her?

FOR INTERPRETATION

Because present and past, reality and dreams fuse throughout the story, the reader is unsure about certain details. Discuss the following:
1. what you understand about Hapsy
2. about how old Granny's husband would have been when he died
3. the importance of the jilting in Granny's life

FOR APPRECIATION

Point of View: Stream of Consciousness
Katherine Anne Porter liked to leave the reader "alone" with the characters in her stories and, as the author, to intrude as little as possible. For this reason, she spent a great deal of time and effort developing an expertise in handling *point of view*. Point of view, as you recall, determines through whose eyes an author tells a story. Common options open to the writer are using either first- or third-person narrators (or storytellers) to move a story ahead. With first-person narration, "I" be-

comes a character in the story and tells the reader what is going on. With third-person narration, the author remains invisible and manipulates the characters' speech, action, and thoughts from an unseen vantage point, referring to the characters by name and by third-person pronoun *(he, she, his, her, they)*. If the storyteller seems to know everything that is happening from *every* point of view—what *all* the characters say, do, and think—then this kind of third-person narration is called *omniscient.*

1. The beginning paragraphs of "The Jilting of Granny Weatherall" are third-person omniscient because the invisible narrator tells us not only what Doctor Harry does but what Granny says and thinks. Why must the reader be particularly alert to the use of quotation marks in the opening paragraph and throughout the story?

2. Before long, the reader is aware that Porter has shifted from third-person omniscient to third-person *limited* point of view in that the narration is limited almost entirely to Granny. Nearly all happenings are described as Granny sees them. In paragraph two, for example, the omniscient narrator recounted, "Doctor Harry spread a warm paw like a cushion on her forehead . . ." (p. 549). However in the paragraph beginning "She meant to wave good-by . . ." (p. 549), the point of view has shifted to Granny. What are Cornelia and Doctor Harry doing that annoys her?

Because *limited third-person narration* confines all that is told to the viewpoint of one character, its use demands both skill and training. It does offer advantages for in-depth characterization. To achieve this, one technique used by writers is that of allowing the reader to witness the random flow of a character's thoughts, however chaotic, jumpy, rambling, or illogical they become. This is known as *stream of consciousness.* In the flow of a character's thoughts, feelings, images, and reflections, personality traits are revealed that could never be presented as directly in any other way.

3. Development of the use of the stream-of-consciousness technique became an integral part of Katherine Anne Porter's writing style. As revealed in Granny's stream of consciousness:

   a. How does Granny feel about the "old days" and her accomplishments?

   b. What are her thoughts about the lighting of the lamps?

   c. Who do you think is driving the cart when Granny reaches for the reins?

   d. Why would Lydia need the "Forty Acres"?

COMPOSITION

Through being able to see into Granny's mind and follow the pattern of her thoughts, as well as watching her respond to those around her, the reader comes to know a great deal about Granny Weatherall. Take a few minutes to look back over the story, rereading any passages or sections that hold particular interest for you. Close your eyes and visualize Granny as she is first introduced, fussing at Doctor Harry and Cornelia, and as she reviews her life for you in her churning flow of memories, associations, and feelings.

Write a descriptive essay on Granny's character. Before you begin writing, decide what her outstanding personality traits are. Support your opinions with incidents or evidence from the story.

James Thurber

1894–1961

For over a half-century James Thurber has been recognized as one of America's leading humorists.

Born in Columbus, Ohio, and educated in the public schools there, he attended Ohio State University for a time, but left to enlist in the service during World War I. Rejected because a childhood accident had left him blind in one eye, Thurber went to France and was accepted as a code clerk in the U.S. State Department. After the war he married and returned to France as a reporter on the overseas edition of the *Chicago Tribune.* Unable to live on the meager pay in Paris, the Thurbers came back to the United States, and Thurber began writing for various newspapers until he joined the staff of the *New Yorker* magazine. There, his whimsical stories, sketches, and drawings attracted wide attention, and in the early 1930s he left the magazine to devote full time to writing.

Among his best-known works are *My Life and Hard Times* (1933), *Let Your Mind Alone* (1937), *Fables for Our Time* (1940), and *The Thurber Carnival* (1945), which was made into a popular Broadway musical. The male character in his most famous short story, "The Secret Life of Walter Mitty," has become a prototype for the daydreaming, humble man who loses himself in a variety of imaginary macho adventures.

Thurber's home town of Columbus provided him with much material for his often zany stories. *My Life and Hard Times,* from which the following selection is taken, describes domestic

PORTRAIT OF JAMES THURBER

disasters, local eccentrics, draft boards, family pets, and crises peculiar only to the Thurber family. This is autobiography as it should be written: frank, honest, slightly terrifying, and never more hilarious than in the following episode.

A tall, lanky man with bushy hair, Thurber one day said, "Everyone thinks I look like the man I draw—bald and five feet one. Actually I draw the spirit of the man I am—and I'm a pussycat." His readers knew what he meant: independent, self-assured, curious, intelligent, not above purring when something pleased him, but quick to strike at irritants and intrusions. It is difficult to be neutral to his work. He engages our minds and imaginations, but above all he helps us to laugh at human behavior. And without laughter our lives would be harder to endure.

THE NIGHT THE GHOST GOT IN

The ghost that got into our house on the night of November 17, 1915, raised such a hullabaloo of misunderstandings that I am sorry I didn't just let it keep on walking, and go to bed. Its advent caused my mother to throw a shoe through a window of the house next door and ended up with my grandfather shooting a patrolman. I am sorry, therefore, as I have said, that I ever paid any attention to the footsteps.

They began about a quarter past one o'clock in the morning, a rhythmic, quick-cadenced walking around the dining-room table. My mother was asleep in one room upstairs, my brother Herman in another; grandfather was in the attic, in the old walnut bed which, as you will remember, once fell on my father. I had just stepped out of the bathtub and was busily rubbing myself with a towel when I heard the steps. They were the steps of a man walking rapidly around the dining-room table downstairs. The light from the bathroom shone down the back steps, which dropped directly into the dining-room; I could see the faint shine of plates on the plate-rail; I couldn't see the table. The steps kept going round and round the table; at regular intervals a board creaked, when it was trod upon. I supposed at first that it was my father or my brother Roy, who had gone to Indianapolis but were expected home at any time. I suspected next that it was a burglar. It did not enter my mind until later that it was a ghost.

After the walking had gone on for perhaps three minutes, I tiptoed to Herman's room. "Psst!" I hissed, in the dark, shaking him. "Awp," he said, in the low, hopeless tone of a despondent beagle—he always half suspected that something would "get him" in the night. I told him who I was. "There's something downstairs!" I said. He got up and followed me to the head of the back staircase. We listened together. There was no sound. The steps had ceased. Herman looked at me in some alarm: I had only the bath towel around my waist. He wanted to go back to bed, but I gripped his arm. "There's something down there!" I said. Instantly the steps began again, circled the dining-room table like a man running, and started up the stairs toward us, heavily, two at a time. The light still shone palely down the stairs; we saw nothing coming; we only heard the steps. Herman rushed to his room and slammed the door. I slammed shut the door at the stairs top and held my knee against it. After a long minute, I slowly opened it again. There was nothing there. There was no sound. None of us ever heard the ghost again.

"The ghost got into our house on the night of November 17, 1915 and raised such a hullabaloo of misunderstandings. . . ."

The slamming of the doors had aroused mother: she peered out of her room. "What on earth are you boys doing?" she demanded. Herman ventured out of his room. "Nothing," he said, gruffly, but he was, in color, a light green. "What was all that running around downstairs?" said mother. So she had heard the steps, too! We just looked at her. "Burglars!" she shouted intuitively. I tried to quiet her by starting lightly downstairs.

"Come on, Herman," I said.

"I'll stay with Mother," he said. "She's all excited."

I stepped back onto the landing.

"Don't either of you go a step," said mother. "We'll call the police." Since the phone was downstairs, I didn't see how we were going to call the police—nor did I want the police—but mother made one of her quick, incomparable decisions. She flung up a window of her bedroom which faced the bed-

room windows of the house of a neighbor, picked up a shoe, and whammed it through a pane of glass across the narrow space that separated the two houses. Glass tinkled into the bedroom occupied by a retired engraver named Bodwell and his wife. Bodwell had been for some years in rather a bad way and was subject to mild "attacks." Most everybody we knew or lived near had *some* kind of attacks.

It was now about two o'clock of a moonless night; clouds hung black and low. Bodwell was at the window in a minute, shouting, frothing a little, shaking his fist. "We'll sell the house and go back to Peoria," we could hear Mrs. Bodwell saying. It was some time before mother "got through" to Bodwell. "Burglars!" she shouted. "Burglars in the house!" Herman and I hadn't dared to tell her that it was not burglars but ghosts, for she was even more afraid of ghosts than of burglars. Bodwell at first thought that she meant there were burglars in his house, but finally he quieted down and called the police for us over an extension phone by his bed. After he had disappeared from the window, mother suddenly made as if to throw another shoe, not because there was further need of it, but, as she later explained, because the thrill of heaving a shoe through a window glass had enormously taken her fancy. I prevented her.

The police were on hand in a commendably short time: a Ford sedan full of them, two on motorcycles, and a patrol wagon with about eight in it and a few reporters. They began banging at our front door. Flashlights shot streaks of gleam up and down the walls, across the yard, down the walk between our house and Bodwell's. "Open up!" cried a hoarse voice. "We're men from Headquarters!" I wanted to go down and let them in, since there they were, but mother wouldn't hear of it. "You haven't a stitch on," she pointed out. "You'd catch your death." I wound the towel around me again. Finally the cops put their shoulders to our big heavy front door with its thick beveled glass and broke it in: I could hear a rending of wood and a splash of glass on the floor of the hall. Their lights played all over the living-room and crisscrossed nervously in the dining-room, stabbed into hallways, shot up the front stairs and finally up the back. They caught me standing in my towel at the top. A heavy policeman bounded up the steps. "Who are you?" he demanded. "I live here," I said. "Well, whattsa matta, ya hot?" he asked. I was, as a matter of fact, cold; I went to my room and pulled on some trousers. On my way out, a cop stuck a gun into my ribs. "Whatta you doin' here?" he demanded. "I live here," I said.

The officer in charge reported to mother. "No sign of nobody, lady," he said. "Musta got away—whatt'd he look like?" "There were two or three of them," mother said, "whooping and carrying on and slamming doors."

"Funny," said the cop. "All ya windows and doors was locked on the inside tight as a tick."

Downstairs, we could hear the tromping of the other police. Police were all over the place; doors were yanked open, drawers were yanked open, windows were shot up and pulled down, furniture fell with dull thumps. A half-dozen policemen emerged out of the darkness of the front hallway upstairs. They began to ransack the floor: pulled beds away from walls, tore clothes off hooks in the closets, pulled suitcases and boxes off shelves. One of them found an old zither* that Roy had won in a pool tournament. "Looky here, Joe," he said, strumming it with a big paw. The cop named Joe took it and turned it over. "What is it?" he asked me. "It's an old zither our guinea pig used to sleep on," I said. It was true that a pet guinea pig we once had would never sleep anywhere except on the

---

* **zither,** musical instrument with 30 to 40 strings stretched over a shallow box and played with the fingers.

zither, but I should never have said so. Joe and the other cop looked at me a long time. They put the zither back on a shelf.

"No sign o' nuthin'," said the cop who had first spoken to mother. "This guy," he explained to the others, jerking a thumb at me, "was nekked. The lady seems historical." They all nodded, but said nothing; just looked at me. In the small silence we all heard a creaking in the attic. Grandfather was turning over in bed. "What's 'at?" snapped Joe. Five or six cops sprang for the attic door before I could intervene or explain. I realized that it would be bad if they burst in on grandfather unannounced, or even announced. He was going through a phase in which he believed that General Meade's men, under steady hammering by Stonewall Jackson, were beginning to retreat and even desert.

When I got to the attic, things were pretty confused. Grandfather had evidently jumped to the conclusion that the police were deserters from Meade's army, trying to hide away in his attic. He bounded out of bed wearing a long flannel nightgown over long woolen underwear, a nightcap, and a leather jacket around his chest. The cops must have realized at once that the indignant white-haired old man belonged in the house, but they had no chance to say so. "Back, ye cowardly dogs!" roared grandfather. "Back t' the lines, ye yellow, lily-livered cattle!" With that, he fetched the officer who found the zither a flat-handed smack alongside his head that sent him sprawling. The others beat a retreat, but not fast enough; grandfather grabbed Zither's gun from its holster and let fly. The report seemed to crack the rafters; smoke filled the attic. A cop cursed and shot his hand to his shoulder. Somehow, we all finally got downstairs again and locked the door against the old gentleman. He fired once or twice more in the darkness and then went back to bed. "That was grandfather," I explained to Joe, out of breath. "He thinks you're deserters." "I'll say he does," said Joe.

The cops were reluctant to leave without getting their hands on somebody besides

grandfather; the night had been distinctly a defeat for them. Furthermore, they obviously didn't like the "layout"; something looked—and I can see their viewpoint—phony. They began to poke into things again. A reporter, a thin-faced, wispy man, came up to me. I had put on one of mother's blouses, not being able to find anything else. The reporter looked at me with mingled suspicion and interest. "Just what the heck is the real low-down here, Bud?" he asked. I decided to be frank with him. "We had ghosts," I said. He gazed at me a long time as if I were a slot machine into which he had, without results, dropped a nickel. Then he walked away. The cops followed him, the one grandfather shot holding his now-bandaged arm, cursing and blaspheming. "I'm gonna get my gun back from that old bird," said the zither-cop. "Yeh," said Joe. "You—and who else?" I told them I would bring it to the station house the next day.

"What was the matter with that one policeman?" mother asked, after they had gone. "Grandfather shot him," I said. "What for?" she demanded. I told her he was a deserter. "Of all things!" said mother. "He was such a nice-looking young man."

Grandfather was fresh as a daisy and full of jokes at breakfast next morning. We thought at first he had forgotten all about what had happened, but he hadn't. Over his third cup of coffee, he glared at Herman and me. "What was the idee of all them cops tarry-hootin' round the house last night?" he demanded. He had us there.

FOR UNDERSTANDING

1. What noise supposedly announces the arrival of the ghost? Who discovers this noise?

2. Why do the narrator and his brother rush to get behind closed doors?
3. What does the mother assume the problem to be? How does she alert the neighbors?
4. Describe what happens when the police rush into Grandfather's attic bedroom.
5. What is the reporter's response when the narrator tells him: "We had ghosts"?

FOR INTERPRETATION AND APPRECIATION

Humor

Thurber reveals to the reader certain idiosyncrasies of his characters, thus letting the reader "in" on the humor of their behavior. He once defined humor as "a kind of emotional chaos told about calmly and quietly in retrospect."
1. How well does the above definition fit the selection you have just read?
2. We tend to feel superior to members of the Thurber family because we know more than they do. Discuss.
3. Humorists and comedians often use *malapropism*, that is, the humorous misuse of words. On page 561, what malapropism does the policeman utter when he attempts to describe the mother's emotional state? What is the author suggesting about the policeman?

Conflict

The main conflict in "The Night the Ghost Got In" is between groups rather than individuals, between the Thurber family on the one hand and the neighbors, police, and the reporter on the other. The latter represent the commonsense, "real" world; the former represents a zany, "unreal" world, a world in which—for one thing—ghosts really exist. One of the main sources of fun is the fact that when the two worlds clash, the zany world comes out victorious. The frustration and defeat of the commonsense world is well expressed by the "thin-faced, wispy" reporter who at the end of the episode asks, "Just what the heck is the real lowdown here, Bud?" Why is Bud's answer, "We had ghosts," a fitting and proper climax?

TWO FABLES

In 1940, Thurber published Fables for Our Time, *drawings and texts so wisely
critical of human behavior that they are likely to become classics of their kind.
These two, only a sample of the collection, need no commentary.*

The Very Proper Gander

Not so very long ago there was a very fine
gander. He was strong and smooth and beautiful and he spent most of his time singing to
his wife and children. One day somebody
who saw him strutting up and down in his
yard and singing remarked, "There is a very
proper gander." An old hen overheard this
and told her husband about it that night in
the roost. "They said something about propaganda," she said. "I have always suspected
that," said the rooster, and he went around
the barnyard next day telling everybody that
the very fine gander was a dangerous bird,
more than likely a hawk in gander's clothing.
A small brown hen remembered a time when
at a great distance she had seen the gander
talking with some hawks in the forest. "They
were up to no good," she said. A duck remembered that the gander had once told him
he did not believe in anything. "He said to
heck with the flag, too," said the duck. A
guinea hen recalled that she had once seen
somebody who looked very much like the
gander throw something that looked a great
deal like a bomb. Finally everybody snatched
up sticks and stones and descended on the
gander's house. He was strutting in his front

*"He was strutting in his front yard, singing to
his wife and children."*

yard, singing to his children and his wife.
"There he is!" everybody cried. "Hawk-lover!
Unbeliever! Flag-hater! Bomb-thrower!" So
they set upon him and drove him out of the
country.

*Moral: Anyone who you or your wife thinks is
going to overthrow the government by violence must
be driven out of the country.*

The Owl Who Was God

Once upon a starless midnight there was an owl who sat on the branch of an oak tree. Two ground moles tried to slip quietly by, unnoticed. "You!" said the owl. "Who?" they quavered, in fear and astonishment, for they could not believe it was possible for anyone to see them in that thick darkness. "You two!" said the owl. The moles hurried away and told the other creatures of the field and forest that the owl was the greatest and wisest of all animals because he could see in the dark and because he could answer any question. "I'll see about that," said a secretary bird, and he called on the owl one night when it was again very dark. "How many claws am I holding up?" said the secretary bird. "Two," said the owl, and that was right. "Can you give me another expression for 'that is to say' or 'namely'?" asked the secretary bird. "To wit," said the owl. "Why does a lover call on his love?" asked the secretary bird. "To woo," said the owl.

The secretary bird hastened back to the other creatures and reported that the owl was indeed the greatest and wisest animal in the world because he could see in the dark and because he could answer any question. "Can he see in the daytime, too?" asked a red fox. "Yes," echoed a dormouse and a French poodle. "Can he see in the daytime, too?" All the other creatures laughed loudly at this silly question, and they set upon the red fox and his friends and drove them out of the region. Then they sent a messenger to the owl and asked him to be their leader.

When the owl appeared among the animals it was high noon and the sun was shining brightly. He walked very slowly, which gave him an appearance of great dignity, and he peered about him with large, staring eyes, which gave him an air of tremendous importance. "He's God!" screamed a Plymouth Rock hen. And the others took up the cry "He's God!" So they followed him wherever

"He peered about him with large, staring eyes, which gave him an air of tremendous importance."

he went and when he began to bump into things they began to bump into things, too. Finally he came to a concrete highway and he started up the middle of it and all the other creatures followed him. Presently a hawk, who was acting as outrider, observed a truck coming toward them at fifty miles an hour, and he reported to the secretary bird and the secretary bird reported to the owl. "There's danger ahead," said the secretary bird. "To wit?" said the owl. The secretary bird told him. "Aren't you afraid?" he asked. "Who?" said the owl calmly, for he could not see the truck. "He's God!" cried all the creatures again, and they were still crying "He's God!" when the truck hit them and ran them down. Some of the animals were merely injured, but most of them, including the owl, were killed.

Moral: You can fool too many of the people too much of the time.

FOR UNDERSTANDING

Those who know Thurber primarily through such humorous works as "The Night the Ghost Got In" are often startled by the acid, almost cynical, comments of some of the satires in *Fables for Our Time* and especially by the dark pessimism of his later *Further Fables for Our Time* (1956). The characters in most of his fables are, of course, animals, but there can be no question that Thurber's target is human nature.

1. In "The Very Proper Gander," what remarks does the duck "remember" that the gander had once made?

2. In "The Owl Who Was God," why are the fox, the dormouse, and the French poodle set upon and driven away?

FOR INTERPRETATION

1. In the first fable why are the words "proper gander" significant?

2. Faith should never be so blind as to be completely out of touch with Reason. Discuss this statement as it relates to the second fable.

FOR APPRECIATION

Sympathy and Detachment

Characters in fables are most frequently animals. What does this fact have to do with the sympathy or detachment of the reader and with the fabulist's attempt to get a message across?

COMPOSITION

Try your hand at writing an original fable. It is usually best to begin with a moral in mind; perhaps, like Thurber, you might use a twisted maxim as the point of your fable. For inspiration, turn back to the aphorisms of Benjamin Franklin from his *Poor Richard's Almanack* (see p. 98).

You may also want to give your work an added touch by illustrating it with a simple line drawing, perhaps like the ones Thurber made.

F. Scott Fitzgerald 1896–1940

Born into a family of comfortable means in St. Paul, Minnesota, Francis Scott Key Fitzgerald was obsessed from an early age with a desire for wealth and success. Some of his education was at private schools, where he associated with sons of the well-to-do and vowed that he, too, would someday become a member of the leisure class. Ironically, it was this fascination with wealth and success that not only was his undoing but also provided him the most fruitful themes for his fiction.

At Princeton University Fitzgerald proved an indifferent student, spending much of his time in campus social life, contributing stories to literary magazines, writing plays for a drama group, and dreaming always of ways to join the ranks of the rich. Before taking a degree, however, he left college and enlisted in the army, spending two years in an Alabama training center. A year after his discharge, he published his first novel, *This Side of Paradise* (1920), and followed it a few months later with a collection of short stories, *Flappers and Philosophers*. Both were immediately successful. He repeated his successes in 1922 with the publication of *Tales of the Jazz Age* and the novel *The Beautiful and the Damned*.

On the strength of his meteoric rise to literary prominence, Fitzgerald married Zelda Sayre, also a writer. The young couple began at once the dizzying round of mad parties and alcoholic misadventures that were to mark the Fitzgeralds in the public view as the foremost representatives of the jazz age, living the flamboyant life of dissipation and wild extravagance of the characters in his fiction. Mesmerized by success, and with no sense of financial management, Fitzgerald spent money faster than he could make it. Continually in debt, he was forced to write furiously in the vain attempt to pay his creditors.

His short novel, *The Great Gatsby* (1925), the ironic tale of a high-living racketeer, is now generally judged his best work. Although the novel won critical acclaim, it was only moderately successful in bookstores when it first came out.

PORTRAIT OF F. SCOTT FITZGERALD
David Silvette
National Portrait Gallery, Smithsonian Institution

In 1930 the mad pace of the Fitzgeralds' lives resulted in the first of a series of nervous breakdowns for Zelda, requiring almost continuous hospitalization from that time on. Fitzgerald's breakdown came in 1936, two years after the publication of his novel *Tender Is the Night*. The following year, in debt and in ill health, "out of date" with the reading public, he went to Hollywood to do film scripts and to work on a novel, *The Last Tycoon*. Unfinished at the time of his death, the novel was edited and published in 1941 by Fitzgerald's friend, Edmund Wilson.

In the following short story, "Bernice Bobs Her Hair," Fitzgerald recreates a small piece of the world of the Roaring Twenties in which affluent youth busied itself with such pleasurable pastimes as house parties, all-night dances, and country club bashes. The young men were expected to exist in fashionable indolence, careening about in fast roadsters, learning the latest dance step—like the Charleston—and being ever attentive to the most popular young women in their social set. The young women—heavily lipsticked and rouged, clad in long-waisted gowns, flesh-colored silk stockings, beads, and slave bracelets—agonized over their popularity rating, the most eligible young men, and the making of such daring decisions as having their hair bobbed or shingled. When the epidemic of feminine haircutting swept the country, there were outraged cries from the press, the pulpit, prominent dowagers, and even film stars. For example, Mary Pickford, "America's Sweetheart" of the silent films, described how she had resisted having her lovely locks shorn and thus was spared watching " . . . my curls fall one by one at my feet, useless, lifeless things to be packed away in tissue paper with other outworn treasures."

BERNICE BOBS HER HAIR

I

After dark on Saturday night one could stand on the first tee of the golf-course and see the country-club windows as a yellow expanse over a very black and wavy ocean. The waves of this ocean, so to speak, were the heads of many curious caddies, a few of the more ingenious chauffeurs, the golf professional's deaf sister—and there were usually several stray, diffident waves who might have rolled inside had they so desired. This was the gallery.

The balcony was inside. It consisted of the circle of wicker chairs that lined the wall of the combination clubroom and ballroom. At these Saturday-night dances it was largely feminine; a great babble of middle-aged ladies with sharp eyes and icy hearts behind lorgnettes and large bosoms. The main function of the balcony was critical. It occasionally showed grudging admiration, but never approval, for it is well known among ladies over thirty-five that when the younger set dance in the summer-time it is with the very worst intentions in the world, and if they are not bombarded with stony eyes, stray couples will dance weird barbaric interludes in the corners, and the more popular, more dangerous girls will sometimes be kissed in the parked limousines of unsuspecting dowagers.

But, after all, this critical circle is not close enough to the stage to see the actors' faces and catch the subtler byplay. It can only frown and lean, ask questions and make satisfactory deductions from its set of postulates, such as the one which states that every young man with a large income leads the life of a hunted partridge. It never really appreciates the drama of the shifting, semicruel world of adolescence. No; boxes, orchestra-circle, principals, and chorus are represented by the medley of faces and voices that sway to the plaintive African rhythm of Dyer's dance orchestra.

From sixteen-year-old Otis Ormonde, who has two more years at Hill School, to G. Reese Stoddard, over whose bureau at home hangs a Harvard law diploma; from little Madeleine Hogue, whose hair still feels strange and uncomfortable on top of her head, to Bessie MacRae, who has been the life of the party a little too long—more than ten years—the medley is not only the centre of the stage but contains the only people capable of getting an unobstructed view of it.

With a flourish and a bang the music stops. The couples exchange artificial, effortless smiles, facetiously repeat *"la-de-da-da dum-dum,"* and then the clatter of young feminine voices soars over the burst of clapping.

A few disappointed stags caught in mid-floor as they had been about to cut in subsided listlessly back to the walls, because this was not like the riotous Christmas dances—these summer hops were considered just pleasantly warm and exciting, where even the younger marrieds rose and performed ancient waltzes and terrifying fox trots to the tolerant amusement of their younger brothers and sisters.

Warren McIntyre, who casually attended Yale, being one of the unfortunate stags, felt in his dinner-coat pocket for a cigarette and strolled out onto the wide, semidark veranda, where couples were scattered at tables, filling the lantern-hung night with vague words and hazy laughter. He nodded here and there at the less absorbed and as he passed each couple some half-forgotten fragment of a story played in his mind, for it was not a large city and every one was Who's Who to every one else's past. There, for example, were Jim Strain and Ethel Demorest, who had been privately engaged for three years. Every one knew that as soon as Jim managed to hold a job for more than two months she would marry him. Yet how bored they both looked, and how wearily Ethel regarded Jim sometimes, as if she wondered why she had trained the vines of her affection on such a wind-shaken poplar.

Warren was nineteen and rather pitying with those of his friends who had gone East to college. But, like most boys, he bragged tremendously about the girls of his city when he was away from it. There was Genevieve Ormonde, who regularly made the rounds of dances, house-parties, and football games at Princeton, Yale, Williams, and Cornell; there

was black-eyed Roberta Dillon, who was quite as famous to her own generation as Hiram Johnson[1] or Ty Cobb;[2] and, of course, there was Marjorie Harvey, who besides having a fairylike face and a dazzling, bewildering tongue was already justly celebrated for having turned five cart-wheels in succession during the last pump-and-slipper dance at New Haven.

Warren, who had grown up across the street from Marjorie, had long been "crazy about her." Sometimes she seemed to reciprocate his feeling with a faint gratitude, but she had tried him by her infallible test and informed him gravely that she did not love him. Her test was that when she was away from him she forgot him and had affairs with other boys. Warren found this discouraging, especially as Marjorie had been making little trips all summer, and for the first two or three days after each arrival home he saw great heaps of mail on the Harveys' hall table addressed to her in various masculine hand-writings. To make matters worse, all during the month of August she had been visited by her cousin Bernice from Eau Claire, and it seemed impossible to see her alone. It was always necessary to hunt round and find some one to take care of Bernice. As August waned this was becoming more and more difficult.

Much as Warren worshipped Marjorie, he had to admit that Cousin Bernice was sorta hopeless. She was pretty, with dark hair and high color, but she was no fun on a party. Every Saturday night he danced a long arduous duty dance with her to please Marjorie, but he had never been anything but bored in her company.

"Warren"—a soft voice at his elbow broke in upon his thoughts, and he turned to see Marjorie, flushed and radiant as usual. She

1. **Hiram Johnson** (1866–1945), a U.S. Senator opposed to American entry into World War I and the League of Nations.
2. **Ty Cobb** (1886–1961), a famous Detroit Tiger outfielder and batter, one of baseball's most aggressive players.

laid a hand on his shoulder and a glow settled almost imperceptibly over him.

"Warren," she whispered, "do something for me—dance with Bernice. She's been stuck with little Otis Ormonde for almost an hour."

Warren's glow faded.

"Why—sure," he answered half-heartedly.

"You don't mind, do you? I'll see that you don't get stuck."

"'Sall right."

Marjorie smiled—that smile that was thanks enough.

"You're an angel, and I'm obliged loads."

With a sigh the angel glanced round the veranda, but Bernice and Otis were not in sight. He wandered back inside, and there in front of the women's dressing-room he found Otis in the center of a group of young men who were convulsed with laughter. Otis was brandishing a piece of timber he had picked up, and discoursing volubly.

"She's gone in to fix her hair," he announced wildly. "I'm waiting to dance another hour with her."

Their laughter was renewed.

"Why don't some of you cut in?" cried Otis resentfully. "She likes more variety."

"Why, Otis," suggested a friend, "you've just barely got used to her."

"Why the two-by-four, Otis?" inquired Warren, smiling.

"The two-by-four? Oh, this? This is a club. When she comes out I'll hit her on the head and knock her in again."

Warren collapsed on a settee and howled with glee.

"Never mind, Otis," he articulated finally. "I'm relieving you this time."

Otis simulated a sudden fainting attack and handed the stick to Warren.

"If you need it, old man," he said hoarsely.

No matter how beautiful or brilliant a girl may be, the reputation of not being frequently cut in on makes her position at a dance un-fortunate. Perhaps boys prefer her company to that of the butterflies with whom they dance a dozen times an evening, but youth in this jazz-nourished generation is temperamentally restless, and the idea of fox-trotting more than one full fox trot with the same girl is distasteful, not to say odious. When it comes to several dances and the intermissions between she can be quite sure that a young man, once relieved, will never tread on her wayward toes again.

Warren danced the next full dance with Bernice, and finally, thankful for the intermission, he led her to a table on the veranda. There was a moment's silence while she did unimpressive things with her fan.

"It's hotter here than in Eau Claire," she said.

Warren stifled a sigh and nodded. It might be for all he knew or cared. He wondered idly whether she was a poor conversationalist because she got no attention or got no attention because she was a poor conversationalist.

"You going to be here much longer?" he asked, and then turned rather red. She might suspect his reasons for asking.

"Another week," she answered, and stared at him as if to lunge at his next remark when it left his lips.

Warren fidgeted. Then with a sudden charitable impulse he decided to try part of his line on her. He turned and looked at her eyes.

"You've got an awfully kissable mouth," he began quietly.

This was a remark that he sometimes made to girls at college proms when they were talking in just such half-dark as this. Bernice distinctly jumped. She turned an ungraceful red and became clumsy with her fan. No one had ever made such a remark to her before.

"Fresh!"—the word had slipped out before she realized it, and she bit her lip. Too late she decided to be amused, and offered him a flustered smile.

Warren was annoyed. Though not accustomed to have that remark taken seriously, still it usually provoked a laugh or a paragraph of sentimental banter. And he hated to be called fresh, except in a joking way. His charitable impulse died and he switched the topic.

"Jim Strain and Ethel Demorest sitting out as usual," he commented.

This was more in Bernice's line, but a faint regret mingled with her relief as the subject changed. Men did not talk to her about kissable mouths, but she knew that they talked in some such way to other girls.

"Oh, yes," she said, and laughed. "I hear they've been mooning round for years without a red penny. Isn't it silly?"

Warren's disgust increased. Jim Strain was a close friend of his brother's, and anyway he considered it bad form to sneer at people for not having money. But Bernice had had no intention of sneering. She was merely nervous.

II

When Marjorie and Bernice reached home at half after midnight they said good night at the top of the stairs. Though cousins, they were not intimates. As a matter of fact Marjorie had no female intimates—she considered girls stupid. Bernice on the contrary all through this parent-arranged visit had rather longed to exchange those confidences flavored with giggles and tears that she considered an indispensable factor in all feminine intercourse. But in this respect she found Marjorie rather cold; felt somehow the same difficulty in talking to her that she had in talking to men. Marjorie never giggled, was never frightened, seldom embarrassed, and in fact had very few of the qualities which Bernice considered appropriately and blessedly feminine.

As Bernice busied herself with toothbrush and paste this night she wondered for the hundredth time why she never had any attention when she was away from home. That her family were the wealthiest in Eau Claire, that her mother entertained tremendously, gave little dinners for her daughter before all dances and bought her a car of her own to drive round in, never occurred to her as factors in her home-town social success. Like most girls she had been brought up on the warm milk prepared by Annie Fellows Johnston[3] and on novels in which the female was beloved because of certain mysterious womanly qualities, always mentioned but never displayed.

Bernice felt a vague pain that she was not at present engaged in being popular. She did not know that had it not been for Marjorie's campaigning she would have danced the entire evening with one man; but she knew that even in Eau Claire other girls with less position and less pulchritude were given a much bigger rush. She attributed this to something subtly unscrupulous in those girls. It had never worried her, and if it had her mother would have assured her that the other girls cheapened themselves and that men really respected girls like Bernice.

She turned out the light in her bathroom, and on an impulse decided to go in and chat for a moment with her aunt Josephine, whose light was still on. Her soft slippers bore her noiselessly down the carpeted hall, but hearing voices inside she stopped near the partly opened door. Then she caught her own name, and without any definite intention of eavesdropping lingered—and the thread of the conversation going on inside pierced her consciousness sharply as if it had been drawn through with a needle.

"She's absolutely hopeless!" It was Marjorie's voice. "Oh, I know what you're going

---

3. **Annie Fellows Johnston** (1863–1931), author of children's books in which good intentions prevailed and simple virtues were glorified.

to say! So many people have told you how pretty and sweet she is, and how she can cook! What of it! She has a bum time. Men don't like her."

"What's a little cheap popularity?" Mrs. Harvey sounded annoyed.

"It's everything when you're eighteen," said Marjorie emphatically. "I've done my best. I've been polite and I've made men dance with her, but they just won't stand being bored. When I think of that gorgeous coloring wasted on such a ninny, and think what Martha Carey could do with it—oh!"

"There's no courtesy these days."

Mrs. Harvey's voice implied that modern situations were too much for her. When she was a girl all young ladies who belonged to nice families had glorious times.

"Well," said Marjorie, "no girl can permanently bolster up a lame-duck visitor, because these days it's every girl for herself. I've even tried to drop her hints about clothes and things, and she's been furious—given me the funniest looks. She's sensitive enough to know she's not getting away with much, but I'll bet she consoles herself by thinking that she's very virtuous and that I'm too fickle and will come to a bad end. All unpopular girls think that way. Sour grapes! Sarah Hopkins refers to Genevieve and Roberta and me as gardenia girls! I'll bet she'd give ten years of her life and her European education to be a gardenia girl and have three or four men in love with her and be cut in on every few feet at dances."

"It seems to me," interrupted Mrs. Harvey rather wearily, "that you ought to be able to do something for Bernice. I know she's not very vivacious."

Marjorie groaned.

"Vivacious! Good grief! I've never heard her say anything to a boy except that it's hot or the floor's crowded or that she's going to school in New York next year. Sometimes she asks them what kind of car they have and tells them the kind she has. Thrilling!"

There was a short silence, and then Mrs.

Harvey took up her refrain: "All I know is that other girls not half so sweet and attractive get partners. Martha Carey, for instance, is stout and loud, and her mother is distinctly common. Roberta Dillon is so thin this year that she looks as though Arizona were the place for her. She's dancing herself to death."

"But, mother," objected Marjorie impatiently, "Martha is cheerful and awfully witty and an awfully slick girl, and Roberta's a marvellous dancer. She's been popular for ages!"

Mrs. Harvey yawned.

"I think it's that crazy Indian blood in Bernice," continued Marjorie. "Maybe she's a reversion to type. Indian women all just sat round and never said anything."

"Go to bed, you silly child," laughed Mrs. Harvey. "I wouldn't have told you that if I'd thought you were going to remember it. And I think most of your ideas are perfectly idiotic," she finished sleepily.

There was another silence, while Marjorie considered whether or not convincing her mother was worth the trouble. People over forty can seldom be permanently convinced of anything. At eighteen our convictions are hills from which we look; at forty-five they are caves in which we hide.

Having decided this, Marjorie said good night. When she came out into the hall it was quite empty.

III

While Marjorie was breakfasting late next day Bernice came into the room with a rather formal good morning, sat down opposite, stared intently over and slightly moistened her lips.

"What's on your mind?" inquired Marjorie, rather puzzled.

Bernice paused before she threw her hand-grenade.

"I heard what you said about me to your mother last night."

Marjorie was startled, but she showed

only a faintly heightened color and her voice was quiet even when she spoke.

"Where were you?"

"In the hall. I didn't mean to listen—at first."

After an involuntary look of contempt Marjorie dropped her eyes and became very interested in balancing a stray corn-flake on her finger.

"I guess I'd better go back to Eau Claire —if I'm such a nuisance." Bernice's lower lip was trembling violently and she continued on a wavering note: "I've tried to be nice, and— and I've been first neglected and then insult-ed. No one ever visited me and got such treat-ment."

Marjorie was silent.

"But I'm in the way, I see. I'm a drag on you. Your friends don't like me." She paused, and then remembered another one of her grievances. "Of course I was furious last week when you tried to hint to me that that dress was unbecoming. Don't you think I know how to dress myself?"

"No," murmured Marjorie less than half-aloud.

"What?"

"I didn't hint anything," said Marjorie succinctly. "I said, as I remember, that it was better to wear a becoming dress three times straight than to alternate it with two frights."

"Do you think that was a very nice thing to say?"

"I wasn't trying to be nice." Then after a pause: "When do you want to go?"

Bernice drew in her breath sharply.

"Oh!" It was a little half-cry.

Marjorie looked up in surprise.

"Didn't you say you were going?"

"Yes, but——"

"Oh, you were only bluffing!"

They stared at each other across the breakfast-table for a moment. Misty waves were passing before Bernice's eyes, while Marjorie's face wore that rather hard expres-sion that she used with slightly intoxicated undergraduates.

"So you were bluffing," she repeated as if it were what she might have expected.

Bernice admitted it by bursting into tears. Marjorie's eyes showed boredom.

"You're my cousin," sobbed Bernice. "I'm v-v-visiting you. I was to stay a month, and if I go home my mother will know and she'll wah-wonder——"

Marjorie waited until the shower of bro-ken words collapsed into little sniffles.

"I'll give you my month's allowance," she said coldly, "and you can spend this last week anywhere you want. There's a very nice hotel——"

Bernice's sobs rose to a flute note, and ris-ing of a sudden she fled from the room.

An hour later, while Marjorie was in the library absorbed in composing one of those non-committal, marvellously elusive letters that only a young girl can write, Bernice reap-peared, very red-eyed and consciously calm. She cast no glance at Marjorie but took a book at random from the shelf and sat down as if to read. Marjorie seemed absorbed in her let-ter and continued writing. When the clock showed noon Bernice closed her book with a snap.

"I suppose I'd better get my railroad tick-et."

This was not the beginning of the speech she had rehearsed up-stairs, but as Marjorie was not getting her cues—wasn't urging her to be reasonable; it's all a mistake—it was the best opening she could muster.

"Just wait till I finish this letter," said Marjorie without looking round. "I want to get it off in the next mail."

After another minute, during which her pen scratched busily, she turned round and relaxed with an air of "at your service." Again Bernice had to speak.

"Do you want me to go home?"

"Well," said Marjorie, considering, "I

suppose if you're not having a good time you'd better go. No use being miserable."

"Don't you think common kindness——"

"Oh, please don't quote 'Little Women'!"[4] cried Marjorie impatiently. "That's out of style."

"You think so?"

"Heavens, yes! What modern girl could live like those inane females?"

"They were the models for our mothers."

Marjorie laughed.

"Yes, they were—not! Besides, our mothers were all very well in their way, but they know very little about their daughters' problems."

Bernice drew herself up.

"Please don't talk about my mother."

Marjorie laughed.

"I don't think I mentioned her."

Bernice felt that she was being led away from her subject.

"Do you think you've treated me very well?"

"I've done my best. You're rather hard material to work with."

The lids of Bernice's eyes reddened.

"I think you're hard and selfish, and you haven't a feminine quality in you."

"Oh, my Lord!" cried Marjorie in desperation. "You little nut! Girls like you are responsible for all the tiresome colorless marriages; all those ghastly inefficiencies that pass as feminine qualities. What a blow it must be when a man with imagination marries the beautiful bundle of clothes that he's been building ideals around, and finds that she's just a weak, whining, cowardly mass of affectations!"

Bernice's mouth had slipped half open.

"The womanly woman!" continued Marjorie. "Her whole early life is occupied in whining criticisms of girls like me who really do have a good time."

Bernice's jaw descended farther as Marjorie's voice rose.

"There's some excuse for an ugly girl whining. If I'd been irretrievably ugly I'd never have forgiven my parents for bringing me into the world. But you're starting life without any handicap—" Marjorie's little fist clenched. "If you expect me to weep with you you'll be disappointed. Go or stay, just as you like." And picking up her letters she left the room.

Bernice claimed a headache and failed to appear at luncheon. They had a matinée date for the afternoon, but the headache persisting, Marjorie made explanation to a not very downcast boy. But when she returned late in the afternoon she found Bernice with a strangely set face waiting for her in her bedroom.

"I've decided," began Bernice without preliminaries, "that maybe you're right about things—possibly not. But if you'll tell me why your friends aren't—aren't interested in me I'll see if I can do what you want me to."

Marjorie was at the mirror shaking down her hair.

"Do you mean it?"

"Yes."

"Without reservations? Will you do exactly what I say?"

"Well, I——"

"Well nothing! Will you do exactly as I say?"

"If they're sensible things."

"They're not! You're no case for sensible things."

"Are you going to make—to recommend——"

"Yes, everything. If I tell you to take boxing-lessons you'll have to do it. Write home and tell your mother you're going to stay another two weeks."

4. *Little Women,* widely read novel by Louisa May Alcott (1832–1888) about a family of properly behaved girls.

"If you'll tell me——"

"All right—I'll just give you a few examples now. First, you have no ease of manner. Why? Because you're never sure about your personal appearance. When a girl feels that she's perfectly groomed and dressed she can forget that part of her. That's charm. The more parts of yourself you can afford to forget the more charm you have."

"Don't I look all right?"

"No; for instance, you never take care of your eyebrows. They're black and lustrous, but by leaving them straggly they're a blemish. They'd be beautiful if you'd take care of them in one-tenth the time you take doing nothing. You're going to brush them so that they'll grow straight."

Bernice raised the brows in question.

"Do you mean to say that men notice eyebrows?"

"Yes—subconsciously. And when you go home you ought to have your teeth straightened a little. It's almost imperceptible, still——"

"But I thought," interrupted Bernice in bewilderment, "that you despised little dainty feminine things like that."

"I hate dainty minds," answered Marjorie. "But a girl has to be dainty in person. If she looks like a million dollars she can talk about Russia, ping-pong, or the League of Nations and get away with it."

"What else?"

"Oh, I'm just beginning! There's your dancing."

"Don't I dance all right?"

"No, you don't—you lean on a man; yes, you do—ever so slightly. I noticed it when we were dancing together yesterday. And you dance standing up straight instead of bending over a little. Probably some old lady on the side-line once told you that you looked so dignified that way. But except with a very small girl it's much harder on the man, and he's the one that counts."

"Go on." Bernice's brain was reeling.

"Well, you've got to learn to be nice to men who are sad birds. You look as if you'd been insulted whenever you're thrown with any except the most popular boys. Why, Bernice, I'm cut in on every few feet—and who does most of it? Why, those very sad birds. No girl can afford to neglect them. They're the big part of any crowd. Young boys too shy to talk are the very best conversational practice. Clumsy boys are the best dancing practice. If you can follow them and yet look graceful you can follow a baby tank across a barb-wire sky-scraper."

Bernice sighed profoundly, but Marjorie was not through.

"If you go to a dance and really amuse, say, three sad birds that dance with you; if you talk so well to them that they forget they're stuck with you, you've done something. They'll come back next time, and gradually so many sad birds will dance with you that the attractive boys will see there's no danger of being stuck—then they'll dance with you."

"Yes," agreed Bernice faintly. "I think I begin to see."

"And finally," concluded Marjorie, "poise and charm will just come. You'll wake up some morning knowing you've attained it, and men will know it too."

Bernice rose.

"It's been awfully kind of you—but nobody's ever talked to me like this before, and I feel sort of startled."

Marjorie made no answer but gazed pensively at her own image in the mirror.

"You're a peach to help me," continued Bernice.

Still Marjorie did not answer, and Bernice thought she had seemed too grateful.

"I know you don't like sentiment," she said timidly.

Marjorie turned to her quickly.

"Oh, I wasn't thinking about that. I was considering whether we hadn't better bob your hair."

Bernice collapsed backward upon the bed.

IV

On the following Wednesday evening there was a dinner-dance at the country club. When the guests strolled in Bernice found her place-card with a slight feeling of irritation. Though at her right sat G. Reece Stoddard, a most desirable and distinguished young bachelor, the all-important left held only Charley Paulson. Charley lacked height, beauty, and social shrewdness, and in her new enlightenment Bernice decided that his only qualification to be her partner was that he had never been stuck with her. But this feeling of irritation left with the last of the soup-plates, and Marjorie's specific instruction came to her. Swallowing her pride she turned to Charley Paulson and plunged.

"Do you think I ought to bob my hair, Mr. Charley Paulson?"

Charley looked up in surprise.

"Why?"

"Because I'm considering it. It's such a sure and easy way of attracting attention."

Charley smiled pleasantly. He could not know this had been rehearsed. He replied that he didn't know much about bobbed hair. But Bernice was there to tell him.

"I want to be a society vampire,[5] you see," she announced coolly, and went on to inform him that bobbed hair was the necessary prelude. She added that she wanted to ask his advice, because she had heard he was so critical about girls.

Charley, who knew as much about the psychology of women as he did of the mental states of Buddhist contemplatives, felt vaguely flattered.

"So I've decided," she continued, her voice rising slightly, "that early next week I'm going down to the Sevier Hotel barber-shop, sit in the first chair, and get my hair bobbed." She faltered, noticing that the people near her had paused in their conversation and were listening; but after a confused second Marjorie's coaching told, and she finished her paragraph to the vicinity at large. "Of course I'm charging admission, but if you'll all come down and encourage me I'll issue passes for the inside seats."

There was a ripple of appreciative laughter, and under cover of it G. Reece Stoddard leaned over quickly and said close to her ear: "I'll take a box right now."

She met his eyes and smiled as if he had said something surpassingly brilliant.

"Do you believe in bobbed hair?" asked G. Reece in the same undertone.

"I think it's unmoral," affirmed Bernice gravely. "But, of course, you've either got to amuse people or feed 'em or shock 'em." Marjorie had culled this from Oscar Wilde.[6] It was greeted with a ripple of laughter from the men and a series of quick, intent looks from the girls. And then as though she had said nothing of wit or moment Bernice turned again to Charley and spoke confidentially in his ear.

"I want to ask you your opinion of several people. I imagine you're a wonderful judge of character."

Charley thrilled faintly—paid her a subtle compliment by overturning her water.

Two hours later, while Warren McIntyre was standing passively in the stag line abstractedly watching the dancers and wondering whither and with whom Marjorie had disappeared, an unrelated perception began to creep slowly upon him—a perception that Bernice, cousin to Marjorie, had been cut in on several times in the past five minutes. He closed his eyes, opened them and looked again. Several minutes back she had been dancing with a visiting boy, a matter easily accounted for; a visiting boy would know no better. But now she was dancing with some one else, and there was Charley Paulson

5. **vampire.** In the early twentieth century the word was applied to a beautiful but heartless woman who lured men to moral destruction; the word was often shortened to "vamp."
6. **Oscar Wilde** (1854–1900), Irish-born English playwright, poet, and prose writer known for his wit.

headed for her with enthusiastic determination in his eye. Funny—Charley seldom danced with more than three girls an evening.

Warren was distinctly surprised when—the exchange having been effected—the man relieved proved to be none other than G. Reece Stoddard himself. And G. Reece seemed not at all jubilant at being relieved. Next time Bernice danced near, Warren regarded her intently. Yes, she was pretty, distinctly pretty; and to-night her face seemed really vivacious. She had that look that no woman, however histrionically proficient, can successfully counterfeit—she looked as if she were having a good time. He liked the way she had her hair arranged, wondered if it was brilliantine that made it glisten so. And that dress was becoming—a dark red that set off her shadowy eyes and high coloring. He remembered that he had thought her pretty when she first came to town, before he had realized that she was dull. Too bad she was dull—dull girls unbearable—certainly pretty though.

His thoughts zigzagged back to Marjorie. This disappearance would be like other disappearances. When she reappeared he would demand where she had been—would be told emphatically that it was none of his business. What a pity she was so sure of him! She basked in the knowledge that no other girl in town interested him; she defied him to fall in love with Genevieve or Roberta.

Warren sighed. The way to Marjorie's affections was a labyrinth indeed. He looked up. Bernice was again dancing with the visiting boy. Half unconsciously he took a step out from the stag line in her direction, and hesitated. Then he said to himself that it was charity. He walked toward her—collided suddenly with G. Reece Stoddard.

"Pardon me," said Warren.

But G. Reece had not stopped to apologize. He had again cut in on Bernice.

That night at one o'clock Marjorie, with one hand on the electric-light switch in the hall, turned to take a last look at Bernice's sparkling eyes.

"So it worked?"

"Oh, Marjorie, yes!" cried Bernice.

"I saw you were having a gay time."

"I did! The only trouble was that about midnight I ran short of talk. I had to repeat myself—with different men of course. I hope they won't compare notes."

"Men don't," said Marjorie, yawning, "and it wouldn't matter if they did—they'd think you were even trickier."

She snapped out the light, and as they started up the stairs Bernice grasped the banister thankfully. For the first time in her life she had been danced tired.

"You see," said Marjorie at the top of the stairs, "one man sees another man cut in and he thinks there must be something there. Well, we'll fix up some new stuff to-morrow. Good night."

"Good night."

As Bernice took down her hair she passed the evening before her in review. She had followed instructions exactly. Even when Charley Paulson cut in for the eighth time she had simulated delight and had apparently been both interested and flattered. She had not talked about the weather or Eau Claire or automobiles or her school, but had confined her conversation to me, you, and us.

But a few minutes before she fell asleep a rebellious thought was churning drowsily in her brain—after all, it was she who had done it. Marjorie, to be sure, had given her her conversation, but then Marjorie got much of her conversation out of things she read. Bernice had bought the red dress, though she had never valued it highly before Marjorie dug it out of her trunk—and her own voice had said the words, her own lips had smiled, her own feet had danced. Marjorie, nice girl—vain, though—nice evening—nice boys—like Warren—Warren—Warren—what's-his-name—Warren—

She fell asleep.

V

To Bernice the next week was a revelation. With the feeling that people really enjoyed looking at her and listening to her came the foundation of self-confidence. Of course there were numerous mistakes at first. She did not know, for instance, that Draycott Deyo was studying for the ministry; she was unaware that he had cut in on her because he thought she was a quiet, reserved girl. Had she known these things she would not have treated him to the line which began "Hello, Shell Shock!" and continued with the bathtub story—"It takes a frightful lot of energy to fix my hair in the summer—there's so much of it—so I always fix it first and powder my face and put on my hat; then I get into the bathtub, and dress afterward. Don't you think that's the best plan?"

Though Draycott Deyo was in the throes of difficulties concerning baptism by immersion and might possibly have seen a connection, it must be admitted that he did not. He considered feminine bathing an immoral subject, and gave her some of his ideas on the depravity of modern society.

But to offset that unfortunate occurrence Bernice had several signal successes to her credit. Little Otis Ormonde pleaded off from a trip East and elected instead to follow her with a puppylike devotion, to the amusement of his crowd and to the irritation of G. Reece Stoddard, several of whose afternoon calls Otis completely ruined by the disgusting tenderness of the glances he bent on Bernice. He even told her the story of the two-by-four and the dressing-room to show her how frightfully mistaken he and every one else had been in their first judgment of her. Bernice laughed off that incident with a slight sinking sensation.

Of all Bernice's conversation perhaps the best known and most universally approved was the line about the bobbing of her hair.

"Oh, Bernice, when you goin' to get the hair bobbed?"

"Day after to-morrow maybe," she would reply, laughing. "Will you come and see me? Because I'm counting on you, you know."

"Will we? You know! But you better hurry up."

Bernice, whose tonsorial intentions were strictly dishonorable, would laugh again.

"Pretty soon now. You'd be surprised."

But perhaps the most significant symbol of her success was the gray car of the hypercritical Warren McIntyre, parked daily in front of the Harvey house. At first the parlormaid was distinctly startled when he asked for Bernice instead of Marjorie; after a week of it she told the cook that Miss Bernice had gotta holda Miss Marjorie's best fella.

And Miss Bernice had. Perhaps it began with Warren's desire to rouse jealousy in Marjorie; perhaps it was the familiar though unrecognized strain of Marjorie in Bernice's conversation; perhaps it was both of these and something of sincere attraction besides. But somehow the collective mind of the younger set knew within a week that Marjorie's most reliable beau had made an amazing face-about and was giving an indisputable rush to Marjorie's guest. The question of the moment was how Marjorie would take it. Warren called Bernice on the 'phone twice a day, sent her notes, and they were frequently seen together in his roadster, obviously engrossed in one of those tense, significant conversations as to whether or not he was sincere.

Marjorie on being twitted only laughed. She said she was mighty glad that Warren had at last found some one who appreciated him. So the younger set laughed, too, and guessed that Marjorie didn't care and let it go at that.

One afternoon, when there were only three days left of her visit, Bernice was waiting in the hall for Warren, with whom she was going to a bridge party. She was in rather a blissful mood, and when Marjorie—also bound for the party—appeared beside her and began casually to adjust her hat in the mirror, Bernice was utterly unprepared for anything in the nature of a clash. Marjorie did her work very coldly and succinctly in three sentences.

"You may as well get Warren out of your head," she said coldly.

"What?" Bernice was utterly astounded.

"You may as well stop making a fool of yourself over Warren McIntyre. He doesn't care a snap of his fingers about you."

For a tense moment they regarded each other—Marjorie scornful, aloof; Bernice astounded, half-angry, half-afraid. Then two cars drove up in front of the house and there was a riotous honking. Both of them gasped faintly, turned, and side by side hurried out.

All through the bridge party Bernice strove in vain to master a rising uneasiness. She had offended Marjorie, the sphinx of sphinxes. With the most wholesome and innocent intentions in the world she had stolen Marjorie's property. She felt suddenly and horribly guilty. After the bridge game, when they sat in an informal circle and the conversation became general, the storm gradually broke. Little Otis Ormonde inadvertently precipitated it.

"When you going back to kindergarten, Otis?" some one had asked.

"Me? Day Bernice gets her hair bobbed."

"Then your education's over," said Marjorie quickly. "That's only a bluff of hers. I should think you'd have realized."

"That a fact?" demanded Otis, giving Bernice a reproachful glance.

Bernice's ears burned as she tried to think up an effectual comeback. In the face of this direct attack her imagination was paralyzed.

"There's a lot of bluffs in the world," continued Marjorie quite pleasantly. "I should think you'd be young enough to know that, Otis."

"Well," said Otis, "maybe so. But gee! With a line like Bernice's——"

"Really?" yawned Marjorie. "What's her latest bon mot?"

No one seemed to know. In fact, Bernice, having trifled with her muse's beau, had said nothing memorable of late.

"Was that really all a line?" asked Roberta curiously.

Bernice hesitated. She felt that wit in some form was demanded of her, but under her cousin's suddenly frigid eyes she was completely incapacitated.

"I don't know," she stalled.

"Splush!" said Marjorie. "Admit it!"

Bernice saw that Warren's eyes had left a ukulele he had been tinkering with and were fixed on her questioningly.

"Oh, I don't know!" she repeated steadily. Her cheeks were glowing.

"Splush!" remarked Marjorie again.

"Come through, Bernice," urged Otis. "Tell her where to get off."

Bernice looked round again—she seemed unable to get away from Warren's eyes.

"I like bobbed hair," she said hurriedly, as if he had asked her a question, "and I intend to bob mine."

"When?" demanded Marjorie.

"Any time."

"No time like the present," suggested Roberta.

Otis jumped to his feet.

"Good stuff!" he cried. "We'll have a summer bobbing party. Sevier Hotel barber-shop, I think you said."

In an instant all were on their feet. Bernice's heart throbbed violently.

"What?" she gasped.

Out of the group came Marjorie's voice, very clear and contemptuous.

"Don't worry—she'll back out!"

"Come on, Bernice!" cried Otis, starting toward the door.

Four eyes—Warren's and Marjorie's—stared at her, challenged her, defied her. For another second she wavered wildly.

"All right," she said swiftly, "I don't care if I do."

An eternity of minutes later, riding

down-town through the late afternoon beside Warren, the others following in Roberta's car close behind, Bernice had all the sensations of Marie Antoinette bound for the guillotine in a tumbrel. Vaguely she wondered why she did not cry out that it was all a mistake. It was all she could do to keep from clutching her hair with both hands to protect it from the suddenly hostile world. Yet she did neither. Even the thought of her mother was no deterrent now. This was the test supreme of her sportsmanship, her right to walk unchallenged in the starry heaven of popular girls.

Warren was moodily silent, and when they came to the hotel he drew up at the curb and nodded to Bernice to precede him out. Roberta's car emptied a laughing crowd into the shop, which presented two bold plate-glass windows to the street.

Bernice stood on the curb and looked at the sign, Sevier Barber-Shop. It was a guillotine indeed, and the hangman was the first barber, who, attired in a white coat and smoking a cigarette, leaned nonchalantly against the first chair. He must have heard of her; he must have been waiting all week, smoking eternal cigarettes beside that portentous, too-often-mentioned first chair. Would they blindfold her? No, but they would tie a white cloth round her neck lest any of her blood—nonsense—hair—should get on her clothes.

"All right, Bernice," said Warren quickly.

With her chin in the air she crossed the sidewalk, pushed open the swinging screen-door, and giving not a glance to the uproarious, riotous row that occupied the waiting bench, went up to the first barber.

"I want you to bob my hair."

The first barber's mouth slid somewhat open. His cigarette dropped to the floor.

"Huh?"

"My hair—bob it!"

Refusing further preliminaries, Bernice took her seat on high. A man in the chair next to her turned on his side and gave her a glance, half lather, half amazement. One barber started and spoiled little Willy Schune-

man's monthly haircut. Mr. O'Reilly in the last chair grunted and swore musically in ancient Gaelic as a razor bit into his cheek. Two bootblacks became wide-eyed and rushed for her feet. No, Bernice didn't care for a shine.

Outside a passer-by stopped and stared; a couple joined him; half a dozen small boys' noses sprang into life, flattened against the glass; and snatches of conversation borne on the summer breeze drifted in through the screen-door.

"Lookada long hair on a kid!"

"Where'd yuh get 'at stuff? 'At's a bearded lady he just finished shavin'."

But Bernice saw nothing, heard nothing. Her only living sense told her that this man in the white coat had removed one tortoise-shell comb and then another; that his fingers were fumbling clumsily with unfamiliar hairpins; that this hair, this wonderful hair of hers, was going—she would never again feel its long voluptuous pull as it hung in a dark-brown glory down her back. For a second she was near breaking down, and then the picture before her swam mechanically into her vision— Marjorie's mouth curling in a faint ironic smile as if to say: "Give up and get down! You tried to buck me and I called your bluff. You see you haven't got a prayer."

And some last energy rose up in Bernice, for she clenched her hands under the white cloth, and there was a curious narrowing of her eyes that Marjorie remarked on to some one long afterward.

Twenty minutes later the barber swung her round to face the mirror, and she flinched at the full extent of the damage that had been wrought. Her hair was not curly, and now it lay in lank lifeless blocks on both sides of her suddenly pale face. It was ugly as sin—she had known it would be ugly as sin. Her face's chief charm had been a Madonna-like simplicity. Now that was gone and she was—well, frightfully mediocre—not stagy; only ridiculous, like a Greenwich Villager who had left her spectacles at home.

As she climbed down from the chair she tried to smile—failed miserably. She saw two of the girls exchange glances; noticed Marjorie's mouth curved in attenuated mockery —and that Warren's eyes were suddenly very cold.

"You see"—her words fell into an awkward pause—"I've done it."

"Yes, you've—done it," admitted Warren. "Do you like it?"

There was a half-hearted "Sure" from two or three voices, another awkward pause, and then Marjorie turned swiftly and with serpentlike intensity to Warren.

"Would you mind running me down to the cleaners?" she asked. "I've simply got to get a dress there before supper. Roberta's driving right home and she can take the others."

Warren stared abstractedly at some infinite speck out the window. Then for an instant his eyes rested coldly on Bernice before they turned to Marjorie.

"Be glad to," he said slowly.

VI

Bernice did not fully realize the outrageous trap that had been set for her until she met her aunt's amazed glance just before dinner.

"Why, Bernice!"

"I've bobbed it, Aunt Josephine."

"Why, child!"

"Do you like it?"

"Why, Ber-nice!"

"I suppose I've shocked you."

"No, but what'll Mrs. Deyo think tomorrow night? Bernice, you should have waited until after the Deyos' dance—you should have waited if you wanted to do that."

"It was sudden, Aunt Josephine. Anyway, why does it matter to Mrs. Deyo particularly?"

"Why, child," cried Mrs. Harvey, "in her paper on 'The Foibles of the Younger Generation' that she read at the last meeting of the Thursday Club she devoted fifteen minutes to bobbed hair. It's her pet abomination. And the dance is for you and Marjorie!"

"I'm sorry."

"Oh, Bernice, what'll your mother say? She'll think I let you do it."

"I'm sorry."

Dinner was an agony. She had made a hasty attempt with a curling-iron, and burned her finger and much hair. She could see that her aunt was both worried and grieved, and her uncle kept saying, "Well, I'll be darned!" over and over in a hurt and faintly hostile tone. And Marjorie sat very quietly, intrenched behind a faint smile, a faintly mocking smile.

Somehow she got through the evening. Three boys called; Marjorie disappeared with one of them, and Bernice made a listless unsuccessful attempt to entertain the two others —sighed thankfully as she climbed the stairs to her room at half past ten. What a day!

When she had undressed for the night the door opened and Marjorie came in.

"Bernice," she said, "I'm awfully sorry about the Deyo dance. I'll give you my word of honor I'd forgotten all about it."

"'Sall right," said Bernice shortly. Standing before the mirror she passed her comb slowly through her short hair.

"I'll take you down-town to-morrow," continued Marjorie, "and the hairdresser'll fix it so you'll look slick. I didn't imagine you'd go through with it. I'm really mighty sorry."

"Oh, 'sall right!"

"Still it's your last night, so I suppose it won't matter much."

Then Bernice winced as Marjorie tossed her own hair over her shoulders and began to twist it slowly into two long blond braids until in her cream-colored negligée she looked like a delicate painting of some Saxon princess. Fascinated, Bernice watched the braids grow. Heavy and luxurious they were, moving under the supple fingers like restive snakes—

and to Bernice remained this relic and the curling-iron and a to-morrow full of eyes. She could see G. Reece Stoddard, who liked her, assuming his Harvard manner and telling his dinner partner that Bernice shouldn't have been allowed to go to the movies so much; she could see Draycott Deyo exchanging glances with his mother and then being conscientiously charitable to her. But then perhaps by to-morrow Mrs. Deyo would have heard the news; would send round an icy little note requesting that she fail to appear—and behind her back they would all laugh and know that Marjorie had made a fool of her; that her chance at beauty had been sacrificed to the jealous whim of a selfish girl. She sat down suddenly before the mirror, biting the inside of her cheek.

"I like it," she said with an effort. "I think it'll be becoming."

Marjorie smiled.

"It looks all right. For heaven's sake, don't let it worry you!"

"I won't."

"Good night, Bernice."

But as the door closed something snapped within Bernice. She sprang dynamically to her feet, clenching her hands, then swiftly and noiselessly crossed over to her bed and from underneath it dragged out her suitcase. Into it she tossed toilet articles and a change of clothing. Then she turned to her trunk and quickly dumped in two drawerfuls of lingerie and summer dresses. She moved quietly, but with deadly efficiency, and in three-quarters of an hour her trunk was locked and strapped and she was fully dressed in a becoming new travelling suit that Marjorie had helped her pick out.

Sitting down at her desk she wrote a short note to Mrs. Harvey, in which she briefly outlined her reasons for going. She sealed it, addressed it, and laid it on her pillow. She glanced at her watch. The train left at one, and she knew that if she walked down to the Marborough Hotel two blocks away she could easily get a taxicab.

Suddenly she drew in her breath sharply and an expression flashed into her eyes that a practised character reader might have connected vaguely with the set look she had worn in the barber's chair—somehow a development of it. It was quite a new look for Bernice—and it carried consequences.

She went stealthily to the bureau, picked up an article that lay there, and turning out all the lights stood quietly until her eyes became accustomed to the darkness. Softly she pushed open the door to Marjorie's room. She heard the quiet, even breathing of an untroubled conscience asleep.

She was by the bedside now, very deliberate and calm. She acted swiftly. Bending over she found one of the braids of Marjorie's hair, followed it up with her hand to the point nearest the head, and then holding it a little slack so that the sleeper would feel no pull, she reached down with the shears and severed it. With the pigtail in her hand she held her breath. Marjorie had muttered something in her sleep. Bernice deftly amputated the other braid, paused for an instant, and then flitted swiftly and silently back to her own room.

Down-stairs she opened the big front door, closed it carefully behind her, and feeling oddly happy and exuberant stepped off the porch into the moonlight, swinging her heavy grip like a shopping-bag. After a minute's brisk walk she discovered that her left hand still held the two blond braids. She laughed unexpectedly—had to shut her mouth hard to keep from emitting an absolute peal. She was passing Warren's house now, and on the impulse she set down her baggage, and swinging the braids like pieces of rope flung them at the wooden porch, where they landed with a slight thud. She laughed again, no longer restraining herself.

"Huh!" she giggled wildly. "Scalp the selfish thing!"

Then picking up her suitcase she set off at a half-run down the moonlit street.

FOR UNDERSTANDING

1. When the story opens, why does Warren dance with Bernice?

2. When does Bernice learn what Marjorie and her friends think of her?

3. What agreement do Marjorie and Bernice make?

4. Who first suggests that Bernice might bob her hair?

5. When Bernice asks Charley Paulson for advice about bobbing her hair, what reason does she give him for considering it?

6. Although Marjorie pretends to her crowd that she is indifferent to Warren's sudden interest in Bernice, what does she tell Bernice?

7. After snipping Marjorie's braids, what does Bernice do with them?

FOR INTERPRETATION

1. Bernice really had no intention of bobbing her hair. Fitzgerald says that after it was bobbed "it was ugly as sin," and that Bernice had known that it would be ugly. Why, then, did she go to get it cut?

2. What does bobbing one's hair symbolize to Bernice's aunt and uncle, and to Mrs. Deyo?

FOR APPRECIATION

1. On page 579, find the short paragraph beginning "And some energy rose up in Bernice. . . ." Discuss how this paragraph is related to her action at the story's end.

2. This story is typical of the way Fitzgerald's fiction seems to mirror the twenties. Note in the opening paragraphs how carefully he develops the setting and establishes the tone of the story. Do you think the tone is ironic, playful, or somber? Support your answer with specifics from the story that reveal how the author creates this tone.

LANGUAGE AND VOCABULARY

A. Each generation contributes new words or word "borrowings" to our language. Some are assimilated; others quickly become obsolete. Below are words from the period under study (1914–1945). Using a good modern dictionary or book of word origins, define each word and then use the word meaningfully in a sentence.

1. Babbitry	**6.** fifth column
2. bangtail	**7.** malarky
3. boondoggle	**8.** roadster
4. brownout	**9.** scofflaw
5. brunch	**10.** speakeasy

B. On page 578, Marjorie, in humiliating Bernice, uses the French expression *bon mot* (bôn mō′), literally "good word," but in English meaning "clever saying" or "witty expression." The English language has been borrowing words from the French since the Norman Conquest in 1066, and we now use hundreds of French words and expressions. Using a good modern dictionary, give the pronunciation and meaning for each of the following French words and expressions in common use in the United States. Then use each meaningfully in a sentence.

1. à la carte	**6.** faux pas
2. au revoir	**7.** hors d'oeuvre
3. cliché	**8.** ingénue
4. denouement	**9.** résumé
5. devotee	**10.** tête-à-tête

COMPOSITION

On page 569, Fitzgerald comments directly to the reader that "this jazz-nourished generation is temperamentally restless." Write several paragraphs in which you compare the "jazz-nourished" generation Fitzgerald describes with the present "rock-nourished" generation.

William Faulkner

1897–1962

"The aim of every artist is to arrest motion, which is life, by artificial means and hold it fixed so that a hundred years later, when a stranger looks at it, it moves again since it is life. Since man is mortal, the only immortality possible for him is to leave something behind him that is immortal since it will always move. This is the artist's way of scribbling 'Kilroy was here'* on the wall of the final and irrevocable oblivion through which he must someday pass." By the time William Faulkner expressed these thoughts in an interview, he had already been awarded the Nobel Prize in Literature and left his signature for immortality as the foremost American writer of his time.

When Faulkner was five, his family moved to Oxford, Mississippi, where his father, after running a livery stable and a hardware store, became business manager of the state university. A high school dropout after two years, Faulkner worked at various jobs. He served some time in the British Royal Flying Corps in Canada, studied intermittently at Mississippi University, and worked in a bookstore in New York City before returning to live in Oxford. There he acquired the "u" in the spelling of his surname (which had been *Falkner)* when a printer, setting type for his first book of poems, *The Marble Faun* (1924), spelled it *Faulkner.*

In 1924, Faulkner set off for Europe, but got only as far as New Orleans, where he did newspaper work and came to know Sherwood Anderson, who influenced him greatly and saw to it that his first novel, *Soldier's Pay* (1926), was published. However, it wasn't until the publication in 1929 of *Sartoris,* based on family history, that Faulkner found his true subject. In his imaginary Yoknapatawpha County, Mississippi—what Faulkner called "my own little postage stamp of native soil"—he created a universe of his own that he could people with characters as he willed. As he continued to write such novels as *The Sound and the Fury* (revised, 1929), *As I Lay Dying* (1930), *Sanctuary* (1931), *Light in August* (1932), *Absalom, Absalom!* (1936),

PORTRAIT OF WILLIAM FAULKNER, Soss Melik
National Portrait Gallery, Smithsonian Institution

and his short-story volume, *Go Down, Moses* (1942), he built a whole mythohistorical legend through whose characters he explored the moral and economic decline of the South. Many of the protagonists in these novels and stories are economically and morally troubled Southern aristocrats who still remain superior to the materialistic entrepreneurs from the North, the conniving Snopeses.

Much of William Faulkner's writing is structurally complex in terms of space-time relationships. He also makes extensive use of stream of consciousness and symbolism, and frequently abandons conventional grammar and

---

*"**Kilroy was here,**" a popular piece of American graffiti, probably originated by a U.S. serviceman in the late 1930s.

syntax. For these reasons, his work demands very careful reading.

Collections of his short stories which ably demonstrate his mastery of short-story form are *These Thirteen* (1931), *Dr. Martino and Other Stories* (1934), *Go Down, Moses* (1942), *Collected Stories* (1950), and *Big Woods* (1955).

Ironically, although he exposes human degradation and depravity in many of his stories, his writing affirms a faith in the fundamental nobility of humankind and the purposefulness of the universe. The following two selections of Faulkner's reflect this affirmation. After you have read "Race at Morning," an unusual hunting story told by a twelve-year-old boy, decide how it illustrates Faulkner's belief that "man will prevail," as he wrote in his Nobel Prize acceptance speech.

RACE AT MORNING

I was in the boat when I seen him. It was jest dusk-dark; I had jest fed the horses and clumb back down the bank to the boat and shoved off to cross back to camp when I seen him, about half a quarter up the river, swimming; jest his head above the water, and it no more than a dot in that light. But I could see that rocking chair[1] he toted on it and I knowed it was him, going right back to that canebrake in the fork of the bayou[2] where he lived all year until the day before the season opened, like the game wardens had give him a calendar, when he would clear out and disappear, nobody knowed where, until the day after the season closed. But here he was, coming back a day ahead of time, like maybe he had got mixed up and was using last year's calendar by mistake. Which was jest too bad for him, because me and Mister Ernest would be setting on the horse right over him when the sun rose tomorrow morning.

So I told Mister Ernest and we et supper and fed the dogs, and then I help Mister Ernest in the poker game, standing behind his chair until about ten o'clock, when Roth Edmonds said, "Why don't you go to bed, boy?"

"Or if you're going to set up," Willy Legate said, "why don't you take a spelling book to set up over? . . . He knows every cuss word in the dictionary, every poker hand in the deck and every whisky label in the distillery, but he can't even write his name . . . Can you?" he says to me.

"I don't need to write my name down," I said. "I can remember in my mind who I am."

"You're twelve years old," Walter Ewell said. "Man to man, now, how many days in your life did you ever spend in school?"

"He ain't got time to go to school," Willy Legate said. "What's the use in going to school from September to middle of November, when he'll have to quit then to come in here and do Ernest's hearing for him? And what's the use in going back to school in January, when in jest eleven months it will be November fifteenth again and he'll have to start all over telling Ernest which way the dogs went?"

"Well, stop looking into my hand, anyway," Roth Edmonds said.

1. **rocking chair,** the twelve-pointed antlers or horns of a great stag.
2. **canebrake in the fork of the bayou** (bī′ ü), a thicket of reeds and woody grasses on an island at the fork of the marshy, sluggish little river.

"What's that? What's that?" Mister Ernest said. He wore his listening button in his ear all the time, but he never brought the battery to camp with him because the cord would bound to get snagged ever time we run through a thicket.

"Willy says for me to go to bed!" I hollered.

"Don't you never call nobody 'mister'?" Willy said.

"I call Mister Ernest 'mister,'" I said.

"All right," Mister Ernest said. "Go to bed then. I don't need you."

"That ain't no lie," Willy said. "Deaf or no deaf, he can hear a fifty-dollar raise if you don't even move your lips."

So I went to bed, and after a while Mister Ernest come in and I wanted to tell him again how big them horns looked even half a quarter away in the river. Only I would 'a' had to holler, and the only time Mister Ernest agreed he couldn't hear was when we would be setting on Dan, waiting for me to point which way the dogs was going. So we jest laid down, and it wasn't no time Simon was beating the bottom of the dishpan with the spoon, hollering, "Raise up and get your four-o'clock coffee!" and I crossed the river in the dark this time, with the lantern, and fed Dan and Roth Edmondziz horse. It was going to be a fine day, cold and bright; even in the dark I could see the white frost on the leaves and bushes—jest exactly the kind of day that big old son of a gun laying up there in that brake would like to run.

Then we et, and set the stand-holder[3] across for Uncle Ike McCaslin to put them on the stands where he thought they ought to be, because he was the oldest one in camp. He had been hunting deer in these woods for about a hundred years, I reckon, and if anybody would know where a buck would pass, it would be him. Maybe with a big old buck like this one, that had been running the woods for what would amount to a hundred years in a deer's life, too, him and Uncle Ike would sholy manage to be at the same place at the same time this morning—provided, of course, he managed to git away from me and Mister Ernest on the jump. Because me and Mister Ernest was going to git him.

Then me and Mister Ernest and Roth Edmonds set the dogs over, with Simon holding Eagle and the other old dogs on leash because the young ones, the puppies, wasn't going nowhere until Eagle let them, nohow. Then me and Mister Ernest and Roth saddled up, and Mister Ernest got up and I handed him up his pump gun and let Dan's bridle go for him to git rid of the spell of bucking he had to git shut of ever morning until Mister Ernest hit him between the ears with the gun barrel. Then Mister Ernest loaded the gun and give me the stirrup, and I got up behind him and we taken the fire road[4] up toward the bayou, the five big dogs dragging Simon along in front with his single-barrel britchloader slung on a piece of plow line across his back, and the puppies moiling along in ever'body's way. It was light now and it was going to be jest fine; the east already yellow for the sun and our breaths smoking in the cold still bright air until the sun would come up and warm it, and a little skim of ice in the ruts, and ever leaf and twig and switch and even the frozen clods frosted over, waiting to sparkle like a rainbow when the sun finally come up and hit them. Until all my insides felt light and strong as a balloon, full of that light cold strong air, so that it seemed to me like I couldn't even feel the horse's back I was straddle of—jest the hot strong skin, setting up there without no weight atall, so that when old Eagle struck and jumped, me and Dan and Mister Ernest would go jest like a bird, not even touching the ground. It was jest fine. When that big old

3. **stand-holder,** a wooden platform with four legs which can be driven into soft earth or into the bottom of a bayou or marsh. On it hunters wait for the game to be driven toward them so that they may have a chance to shoot. Here, the stand-holder is floated across the bayou and set up on the far side.
4. **fire road,** a firebreak, a barrier of cleared land intended to stop a forest fire.

buck got killed today, I knowed that even if he had put it off another ten years, he couldn't 'a' picked a better one.

And sho enough, as soon as we come to the bayou we seen his foot in the mud where he had come up out of the river last night, spread in the soft mud like a cow's foot, big as a cow's, big as a mule's, with Eagle and the other dogs laying into the leash rope now until Mister Ernest told me to jump down and help Simon hold them. Because me and Mister Ernest knowed exactly where he would be—a little canebrake island in the middle of the bayou, where he could lay up until whatever doe or little deer the dogs had happened to jump could go up or down the bayou in either direction and take the dogs on away, so he could steal out and creep back down the bayou to the river and swim it, and leave the country like he always done the day the season opened.

Which is jest what we never aimed for him to do this time. So we left Roth on his horse to cut him off and turn him over Uncle Ike's standers if he tried to slip back down the bayou, and me and Simon, with the leashed dogs, walked on up the bayou until Mister Ernest on the horse said it was fur enough; then turned up into the woods about half a quarter above the brake because the wind was going to be south this morning when it riz, and turned down toward the brake, and Mister Ernest give the word to cast them,[5] and we slipped the leash and Mister Ernest give me the stirrup again and I got up.

Old Eagle had done already took off because he knowed where that old son of a gun would be laying as good as we did, not making no racket atall yet, but jest boring on through the buck vines with the other dogs trailing along behind him, and even Dan seemed to know about that buck, too, beginning to souple up and jump a little through the vines, so that I taken my holt on Mister Ernest's belt already before the time had come for Mister Ernest to touch him. Because when we got strung out, going fast behind a deer, I wasn't on Dan's back much of the time nohow, but mostly jest strung out from my holt on Mister Ernest's belt, so that Willy Legate said that when we was going through the wood fast, it looked like Mister Ernest had a boy-size pair of empty overhalls blowing out of his hind pocket.

So it wasn't even a strike, it was a jump. Eagle must 'a' walked right up behind him or maybe even stepped on him while he was laying there still thinking it was day after tomorrow. Eagle jest throwed his head back and up and said, "There he goes," and we even heard the buck crashing through the first of the cane. Then all the other dogs was hollering behind him, and Dan give a squat to jump, but it was against the curb[6] this time, not jest the snaffle,[7] and Mister Ernest let him down into the bayou and swung him around the brake and up the other bank. Only he never had to say, "Which way?" because I was already pointing past his shoulder, freshening my holt on the belt jest as Mister Ernest touched Dan with that big old rusty spur on his nigh heel, because when Dan felt it he would go off jest like a stick of dynamite, straight through whatever he could bust and over or under what he couldn't.

The dogs was already almost out of hearing. Eagle must 'a' been looking right up that big son of a gun's tail until he finally decided he better git on out of there. And now they must 'a' been getting pretty close to Uncle Ike's standers, and Mister Ernest reined Dan back and held him, squatting and bouncing and trembling like a mule having his tail roached,[8] while we listened for the shots. But never none come, and I hollered to Mister Ernest we better go on while I could still hear the dogs, and he let Dan off, but still there

---

5. **to cast them,** to let the dogs run.
6. **curb,** here: a chain or strap on the upper part of the branches of a bit used to restrain a horse.
7. **snaffle,** a simple jointed bit.
8. **tail roached,** the removal of hair from the upper part of a mule's tail.

wasn't no shots, and now we knowed the race had done already passed the standers; and we busted out of a thicket, and sho enough there was Uncle Ike and Willy standing beside his foot in a soft patch.

"He got through us all," Uncle Ike said. "I don't know how he done it. I just had a glimpse of him. He looked big as a elephant, with a rack[9] on his head you could cradle a yellin' calf in. He went right on down the ridge. You better get on, too; that Hog Bayou camp might not miss him."

So I freshened my holt and Mister Ernest touched Dan again. The ridge run due south; it was clear of vines and bushes so we could go fast, into the wind, too, because it had riz now, and now the sun was up too. So we would hear the dogs again any time now as the wind get up; we could make time now, but still holding Dan to a canter,[10] because it was either going to be quick, when he got down to the standers from that Hog Bayou camp eight miles below ourn, or a long time, in case he got by them too. And sho enough, after a while we heard the dogs; we was walking Dan now to let him blow a while, and we heard them, the sound coming faint up the wind, not running now, but trailing because the big son of a gun had decided a good piece back, probably, to put an end to this foolishness, and picked hisself up and soupled out and put about a mile between hisself and the dogs—until he run up on them other standers from that camp below. I could almost see him stopped behind a bush, peeping out and saying, "What's this? What's this? Is this whole durn country full of folks this morning?" Then looking back over his shoulder at where old Eagle and the others was hollering along after him while he decided how much time he had to decide what to do next.

Except he almost shaved it too fine. We heard the shots; it sounded like a war. Old Eagle must 'a' been looking right up his tail again and he had to bust on through the best way he could. "Pow, pow, pow, pow" and then "Pow, pow, pow, pow," like it must 'a'

been three or four ganged right up on him before he had time even to swerve, and me hollering, "No! No! No! No!" because he was ourn. It was our beans and oats he et and our brake he laid in; we had been watching him ever year, and it was like we had raised him, to be killed at last on our jump, in front of our dogs, by some strangers that would probably try to beat the dogs off and drag him away before we could even git a piece of the meat.

"Shut up and listen," Mister Ernest said. So I done it and we could hear the dogs; not just the others, but Eagle, too, not trailing no scent now and not baying no downed meat, neither, but running hot on sight long after the shooting was over. I jest had time to freshen my holt. Yes, sir, they was running on sight. Like Willy Legate would say, if Eagle jest had a drink of whisky he would ketch that deer; going on, done already gone when we broke out of the thicket and seen the fellers that had done the shooting, five or six of them, squatting and crawling around, looking at the ground and the bushes, like maybe if they looked hard enough, spots of blood would bloom out on the stalks and leaves like frogstools or hawberries.

"Have any luck, boys?" Mister Ernest said.

"I think I hit him," one of them said. "I know I did. We're hunting blood, now."

"Well, when you have found him, blow your horn and I'll come back and tote him in to camp for you," Mister Ernest said.

So we went on, going fast now because the race was almost out of hearing again, going fast, too, like not jest the buck, but the dogs, too, had took a new leash on life[11] from all the excitement and shooting.

We was in strange country now because

9. **rack,** antlers, horns.
10. **canter,** a three-beat trot, resembling a gallop, but smoother and slower.
11. **a new leash on life.** The boy means a new lease or hold on life.

we never had to run this fur before, we had always killed before now; now we had come to Hog Bayou that runs into the river a good fifteen miles below our camp. It had water in it, not to mention a mess of down trees and logs and such, and Mister Ernest checked Dan again, saying, "Which way?" I could just barely hear them, off to the east a little, like the old son of a gun had give up the idea Vicksburg or New Orleans, like he first seemed to have, and had decided to have a look at Alabama; so I pointed and we turned up the bayou hunting for a crossing, and maybe we could 'a' found one, except that I reckon Mister Ernest decided we never had time to wait.

We come to a place where the bayou had narrowed down to about twelve or fifteen feet, and Mister Ernest said, "Look out, I'm going to touch him," and done it.

I didn't even have time to freshen my holt when we was already in the air, and then I seen the vine—it was a loop of grapevine nigh as big as my wrist, looping down right across the middle of the bayou—and I thought he seen it, too, and was jest waiting to grab it and fling it up over our heads to go under it, and I know Dan seen it because he even ducked his head to jump under it. But Mister Ernest never seen it atall until it skun back along Dan's neck and hooked under the head of the saddle horn, us flying on through the air, the loop of the vine gitting tighter and tighter until something somewhere was going to have to give. It was the saddle girth.[12] It broke, and Dan going on and scrabbling up the other bank bare nekkid except for the bridle, and me and Mister Ernest and the saddle, Mister Ernest still setting in the saddle holding the gun, and me still holding onto Mister Ernest's belt, hanging in the air over the bayou in the tightened loop of that vine like in the drawed-back loop of a big rubber-banded slingshot, until it snapped back and shot us back across the bayou and flang us clear, me still holding onto Mister Ernest's belt and on the bottom now, so that when we

lit I would 'a' had Mister Ernest and the saddle both on top of me if I hadn't clumb fast around the saddle and up Mister Ernest's side, so that when we landed, it was the saddle first, then Mister Ernest, and me on top, until I jumped up, and Mister Ernest still laying there with jest the white rim of his eyes showing.

"Mister Ernest!" I hollered, and then clumb down to the bayou and scopped my cap full of water and clumb back and throwed it in his face, and he opened his eyes and laid there on the saddle cussing me.

"Why didn't you stay behind where you started out?" he said.

"You was the biggest!" I said. "You would 'a' mashed me flat!"

"What do you think you done to me?" Mister Ernest said. "Next time, if you can't stay where you start out, jump clear. Don't climb up on top of me no more. You hear?"

"Yes, sir," I said.

So he got up then, still cussing and holding his back, and clumb down to the water and dipped some in his hand onto his face and neck and dipped some more up and drunk it, and I drunk some, too, and clumb back and got the saddle and the gun, and we crossed the bayou on the down logs. If we could jest ketch Dan; not that he would have went them fifteen miles back to camp, because, if anything, he would have went on by hisself to try to help Eagle ketch that buck. But he was about fifty yards away, eating buck vines, so I brought him back, and we taken Mister Ernest's galluses[13] and my belt and the whang leather[14] loop off Mister Ernest's horn and tied the saddle back on Dan. It didn't look like much, but maybe it would hold.

"Provided you don't let me jump him

---

12. **saddle girth,** the band or strap that encircles a horse's body to hold the saddle on its back.
13. **galluses** (gal′ əs əz), suspenders.
14. **whang leather,** rawhide leather.

Fascinated all his life by the beauty and multiplicity of nature, Charles Burchfield nonetheless invested much of his work with an obsessive, almost sinister quality.

FIRST HEPATICUS, Charles Burchfield
The Museum of Modern Art, New York City
Gift of Abby Aldrich Rockefeller

through no more grapevines without hollering first," Mister Ernest said.

"Yes, sir," I said. "I'll holler first next time —provided you'll holler a little quicker when you touch him next time too." But it was all right; we jest had to be a little easy getting up. "Now which-a-way?" I said. Because we couldn't hear nothing now, after wasting all this time. And this was new country, sho enough. It had been cut over and growed up in thickets we couldn't 'a' seen over even standing up on Dan.

But Mister Ernest never even answered. He jest turned Dan along the bank of the bayou where it was a little more open, and we could move faster again, soon as Dan and us got used to that homemade cinch strop and got a little confidence in it. Which jest happened to be east, or so I thought then, because I never paid no particular attention to east then because the sun—I don't know where the morning had went, but it was gone, the morning and the frost, too—was up high now.

And then we heard him. No, that's wrong; what we heard was shots. And that was when we realized how fur we had come, because the only camp we knowed about in that direction was the Hollyknowe camp, and Hollyknowe was exactly twenty-eight miles from Van Dorn, where me and Mister Ernest lived—just the shots, no dogs nor nothing. If old Eagle was still behind him and the buck was still alive, he was too wore out now to even say, "Here he comes."

"Don't touch him!" I hollered. But Mister Ernest remembered that cinch strop, too, and he jest let Dan off the snaffle. And Dan heard them shots, too, picking his way through the thickets, hopping the vines and logs when he could and going under them when he couldn't. And sho enough, it was jest like before—two or three men squatting and creeping among the bushes, looking for blood that Eagle had done already told them wasn't there. But we never stopped this time, jest trotting on by. Then Mister Ernest swung Dan until we was going due north.

"Wait!" I hollered. "Not this way."

But Mister Ernest jest turned his face back over his shoulder. It looked tired, too, and there was a smear of mud on it where that 'ere grapevine had snatched him off the horse.

"Don't you know where he's heading?" he said. "He's done done his part, give everybody a fair open shot at him, and now he's going home, back to that brake in our bayou. He ought to make it exactly at dark."

And that's what he was doing. We went on. It didn't matter to hurry now. There wasn't no sound nowhere; it was that time in the early afternoon in November when don't nothing move or cry, not even birds, the peckerwoods and yellowhammers and jays, and it seemed to me like I could see all three of us—me and Mister Ernest and Dan—and Eagle, and the other dogs, and that big old buck, moving through the quiet woods in the same direction, headed for the same place, not running now but walking, that had all run the fine race the best we knowed how, and all three of us now turned like on a agreement to walk back home, not together in a bunch because we didn't want to worry or tempt one another, because what we had all three spent this morning doing was no play-acting jest for fun, but was serious, and all three of us was still what we was—that old buck that had to run, not because he was skeered, but because running was what he done the best and was proudest at; and Eagle and the dogs that chased him, not because they hated or feared him, but because that was the thing they done the best and was proudest at; and me and Mister Ernest and Dan, that run him not because we wanted his meat, which would be too tough to eat anyhow, or his head to hang on a wall, but because now we could go back and work hard for eleven months making a crop, so we would have the right to come back here next November—all three of us going back home now, peaceful and separate, until next year, next time.

Then we seen him for the first time. We was out of the cutover now; we could even 'a' cantered, except that all three of us was long past that. So we was walking, too, when we come on the dogs—the puppies and one of the old ones—played out, laying in a little wet swag,[15] panting, jest looking up at us when we passed. Then we come to a long open glade, and we seen the three other old dogs and about a hundred yards ahead of them Eagle, all walking, not making no sound; and then suddenly, at the fur end of the glade, the buck hisself getting up from where he had been resting for the dogs to come up, getting up without no hurry, big, big as a mule, tall as a mule, and turned, and the white underside of his tail for a second or two more before the thicket taken him.

It might 'a' been a signal, a good-by, a farewell. Still walking, we passed the other three old dogs in the middle of the glade, laying down, too; and still that hundred yards ahead of them, Eagle, too, not laying down, because he was still on his feet, but his legs was spraddled and his head was down; maybe

---

15. **wet swag,** a little wet depression.

jest waiting until we was out of sight of his shame, his eyes saying plain as talk when we passed, "I'm sorry, boys, but this here is all."

Mister Ernest stopped Dan. "Jump down and look at his feet," he said.

"Nothing wrong with his feet," I said. "It's his wind has done give out."

"Jump down and look at his feet," Mister Ernest said.

So I done it, and while I was stooping over Eagle I could hear the pump gun go "Snick-cluck. Snick-cluck. Snick-cluck" three times, except that I never thought nothing then. Maybe he was jest running the shells through to be sho it would work when we seen him again or maybe to make sho they was all buckshot. Then I got up again, and we went on, still walking; a little west of north now, because when we seen his white flag that second or two before the thicket hid it, it was on a beeline for that notch in the bayou. And it was evening, too, now. The wind had done dropped and there was a edge to the air and the sun jest touched the tops of the trees. And he was taking the easiest way, too, now, going straight as he could. When we seen his foot in the soft places he was running for a while at first after his rest. But soon he was walking, too, like he knowed, too, where Eagle and the dogs was.

And then we seen him again. It was the last time—a thicket, with the sun coming through a hole onto it like a searchlight. He crashed jest once; then he was standing there broadside to us, not twenty yards away, big as a statue and red as gold in the sun, and the sun sparking on the tips of his horns—they was twelve of them—so that he looked like he had twelve lighted candles branched around his head, standing there looking at us while Mister Ernest raised the gun and aimed at his neck, and the gun went, "Click. Snick-cluck. Click. Snick-cluck. Click. Snick-cluck" three times, and Mister Ernest still holding the gun aimed while the buck turned and give one long bound, the white underside of his tail like a blaze of fire, too, until the thicket and

the shadows put it out; and Mister Ernest laid the gun slow and gentle back across the saddle in front of him, saying quiet and peaceful, and not much louder than jest breathing, "Dawg."

Then he jogged me with his elbow and we got down, easy and careful because of that ere cinch strop, and he reached into his vest and taken out one of the cigars. It was busted where I had fell on it, I reckon, when we hit the ground. He throwed it away and taken out the other one. It was busted, too, so he bit off a hunk of it to chew and throwed the rest away. And now the sun was gone even from the tops of the trees and there wasn't nothing left but a big red glare in the west.

"Don't worry," I said. "I ain't going to tell them you forgot to load your gun. For that matter, they don't need to know we ever seed him."

"Much oblige," Mister Ernest said. There wasn't going to be no moon tonight neither, so he taken the compass off the whang leather loop in his buttonhole and handed me the gun and set the compass on a stump and stepped back and looked at it. "Jest about the way we're headed now," he said, and taken the gun from me and opened it and put one shell in the britch[16] and taken up the compass, and I taken Dan's reins and we started, with him in front with the compass in his hand.

And after a while it was full dark; Mister Ernest would have to strike a match ever now and then to read the compass, until the stars come out good and we could pick out one to follow, because I said, "How fur do you reckon it is?" and he said, "A little more than one box of matches." So we used a star when we could, only we couldn't see it all the time because the woods was too dense and we would git a little off until he would have to spend another match. And now it was good and late, and he stopped and said, "Get on the horse."

---

16. **britch,** breech, the part of the gun behind the barrel.

"I ain't tired," I said.

"Get on the horse," he said. "We don't want to spoil him."

Because he had been a good feller ever since I had knowed him, which was even before that day two years ago when maw went off with the Vicksburg roadhouse feller and the next day pap didn't come home neither, and on the third one Mister Ernest rid Dan up to the door of the cabin on the river he let us live in, so pap could work his piece of land and run his fish line, too, and said, "Put that gun down and come on here and climb up behind."

So I got in the saddle even if I couldn't reach the stirrups, and Mister Ernest taken the reins and I must 'a' went to sleep, because the next thing I knowed a buttonhole of my lumberjack was tied to the saddle horn with that ere whang cord off the compass, and it was good and late now and we wasn't fur, because Dan was already smelling water, the river. Or maybe it was the feed lot itself he smelled, because we struck the fire road not a quarter below it, and soon I could see the river, too, with the white mist laying on it soft and still as cotton. Then the lot, home; and up yonder in the dark, not no piece akchully, close enough to hear us unsaddling and shucking corn prob'ly, and sholy close enough to hear Mister Ernest blowing his horn at the dark camp for Simon to come in the boat and git us, that old buck in his brake in the bayou; home, too, resting, too, after the hard run, waking hisself now and then, dreaming of dogs behind him or maybe it was the racket we was making would wake him.

Then Mister Ernest stood on the bank blowing until Simon's lantern went bobbing down into the mist; then we clumb down to the landing and Mister Ernest blowed again now and then to guide Simon, until we seen the lantern in the mist, and then Simon and the boat; only it looked like ever time I set down and got still, I went back to sleep, because Mister Ernest was shaking me again to git out and climb the bank into the dark camp, until I felt a bed against my knees and tumbled into it.

Then it was morning, tomorrow; it was all over now until next November, next year, and we could come back. Uncle Ike and Willy and Walter and Roth and the rest of them had come in yestiddy, soon as Eagle taken the buck out of hearing, and they knowed that deer was gone, to pack up and be ready to leave this morning for Yoknapatawpha,[17] where they lived, until it would be November again and they could come back again.

So, as soon as we et breakfast, Simon run them back up the river in the big boat to where they left their cars and pickups, and now it wasn't nobody but jest me and Mister Ernest setting on the bench against the kitchen wall in the sun; Mister Ernest smoking a cigar—a whole one this time that Dan hadn't had no chance to jump him through a grapevine and bust. He hadn't washed his face neither where that vine had throwed him into the mud. But that was all right, too; his face usually did have a smudge of mud or tractor grease or beard stubble on it, because he wasn't jest a planter; he was a farmer, he worked as hard as ara one of his hands and tenants—which is why I knowed from the very first that we would git along, that I wouldn't have no trouble with him and he wouldn't have no trouble with me, from that very first day when I woke up and maw had done gone off with that Vicksburg roadhouse feller without even waiting to cook breakfast, and the next morning pap was gone, too, and it was almost night the next day when I heard a horse coming up and I taken the gun that I had already throwed a shell into the britch when pap never come home last night, and stood in the door while Mister Ernest rid up and said, "Come on. Your paw ain't coming back neither."

"You mean he give me to you?" I said.

17. **Yoknapatawpha** (yôk′ nə pə tô′ fə), the fictitious county in northern Mississippi invented by William Faulkner as the scene of many of his stories.

"Who cares?" he said. "Come on. I brought a lock for the door. We'll send the pickup truck tomorrow for whatever you want."

So I come home with him and it was all right, it was jest fine—his wife had died about three years ago—without no women to worry us or take off in the middle of the night with a durn Vicksburg roadhouse jake without even waiting to cook breakfast. And we would go home this afternoon, too, but not jest yet; we always stayed one more day after the others left because Uncle Ike always left what grub they hadn't et, and the rest of the home-made corn whisky he drunk and that town whisky of Roth Edmondziz he called Scotch that smelled like it come out of a old bucket of roof paint; setting in the sun for one more day before we went back home to git ready to put in next year's crop of cotton and oats and beans and hay; and across the river yonder, behind the wall of trees where the big woods started, that old buck laying up today in the sun, too—resting today, too, without nobody to bother him until next November.

So at least one of us was glad it would be eleven months and two weeks before he would have to run that fur that fast again. So he was glad of the very same thing we was sorry of, and so all of a sudden I thought about how maybe planting and working and then harvesting oats and cotton and beans and hay wasn't jest something me and Mister Ernest done three hundred and fifty-one days to fill in the time until we could come back hunting again, but it was something we had to do, and do honest and good during the three hundred and fifty-one days, to have the right to come back into the big woods and hunt for the other fourteen; and the fourteen days that the old buck run in front of dogs wasn't jest something to fill his time until the three hundred and fifty-one when he didn't have to, but the running and the risking in front of guns and dogs was something he had to do for fourteen days to have the right not to be bothered for the other three hundred

and fifty-one. And so the hunting and the farming wasn't two different things atall—they was jest the other side of each other.

"Yes," I said. "All we got to do now is put in that next year's crop. Then November won't be no time away."

"You ain't going to put in the crop next year," Mister Ernest said. "You're going to school."

So at first I didn't even believe I had heard him. "What?" I said. "Me? Go to school?"

"Yes," Mister Ernest said. "You must make something out of yourself."

"I am," I said. "I'm doing it now. I'm going to be a hunter and a farmer like you."

"No," Mister Ernest said. "That ain't enough any more. Time was when all a man had to do was just farm eleven and a half months, and hunt the other half. But not now. Now just to belong to the farming business and the hunting business ain't enough. You got to belong to the business of mankind."

"Mankind?" I said.

"Yes," Mister Ernest said. "So you're going to school. Because you got to know why. You can belong to the farming and hunting business and you can learn the difference between what's right and what's wrong, and do right. And that used to be enough—just to do right. But not now. You got to know why it's right and why it's wrong, and be able to tell the folks that never had no chance to learn it; teach them how to do what's right, not just because they know it's right, but because they know now why it's right because you just showed them, told them, taught them why. So you're going to school."

"It's because you been listening to that durn Will Legate and Walter Ewell!" I said.

"No," Mister Ernest said.

"Yes!" I said. "No wonder you missed that buck yestiddy, taking ideas from the very fellers that let him git away, after me and you had run Dan and the dogs durn nigh clean to death! Because you never even missed him! You never forgot to load that gun! You had done already unloaded it a purpose! I heard you!"

"All right, all right," Mister Ernest said. "Which would you rather have? His bloody head and hide on the kitchen floor yonder and half his meat in a pickup truck on the way to Yoknapatawpha County, or him with his head and hide and meat still together over yonder in that brake, waiting for next November for us to run him again?"

"And git him, too," I said. "We won't even fool with no Willy Legate and Walter Ewell next time."

"Maybe," Mister Ernest said.

"Yes," I said.

"Maybe," Mister Ernest said. "The best word in our language, the best of all. That's what mankind keeps going on: Maybe. The best days of his life ain't the ones when he said 'Yes' beforehand: they're the ones when all he knew to say was 'Maybe.' He can't say 'Yes' until afterward because he not only don't know it until then, he don't want to know 'Yes' until then . . . Step in the kitchen and make me a toddy. Then we'll see about dinner."

"All right," I said. I got up. "You want some of Uncle Ike's corn or that town whisky of Roth Edmondziz?"

"Can't you say Mister Roth or Mister Edmonds?" Mister Ernest said.

"Yes, sir," I said. "Well, which do you want? Uncle Ike's corn or that ere stuff of Roth Edmondziz?"

MAN WILL PREVAIL

Nobel Prize Acceptance Speech

Stockholm, December 10, 1950

I feel that this award was not made to me as a man, but to my work—a life's work in the agony and sweat of the human spirit, not for glory and least of all for profit, but to create out of the materials of the human spirit something which did not exist before. So this award is only mine in trust. It will not be difficult to find a dedication for the money part of it commensurate[1] with the purpose and significance of its origin. But I would like to do the same with the acclaim too, by using this moment as a pinnacle from which I might be listened to by the young men and women already dedicated to the same anguish and travail, among whom is already that one who will some day stand here where I am standing.

Our tragedy today is a general and universal physical fear so long sustained by now that we can even bear it. There are no longer problems of the spirit. There is only the question: When will I be blown up? Because of this, the young man or woman writing today has forgotten the problems of the human heart in conflict with itself which alone can make good writing because only that is worth writing about, worth the agony and the sweat.

He must learn them again. He must teach himself that the basest of all things is to be afraid; and, teaching himself that, forget it forever, leaving no room in his workshop for anything but the old verities and truths of the heart, the old universal truths lacking which

---

1. **commensurate** (kə men′ sər it), suitable in measure and importance.

any story is ephemeral[2] and doomed—love and honor and pity and pride and compassion and sacrifice. Until he does so, he labors under a curse. He writes not of love but of lust, of defeats in which nobody loses anything of value, of victories without hope and, worst of all, without pity or compassion. His griefs grieve on no universal bones, leaving no scars. He writes not of the heart but of the glands.

Until he relearns these things, he will write as though he stood among and watched the end of man. I decline to accept the end of man. It is easy enough to say that man is immortal simply because he will endure: that when the last ding-dong of doom has clanged and faded from the last worthless rock hanging tideless in the last red and dying evening, that even then there will still be one more sound: that of his puny inexhaustible voice, still talking. I refuse to accept this. I believe that man will not merely endure: he will prevail. He is immortal, not because he alone among creatures has an inexhaustible voice, but because he has a soul, a spirit capable of compassion and sacrifice and endurance. The poet's, the writer's, duty is to write about these things. It is his privilege to help man endure by lifting his heart, by reminding him of the courage and honor and hope and pride and compassion and pity and sacrifice which have been the glory of his past. The poet's voice need not merely be the record of

William Faulkner

man, it can be one of the props, the pillars to help him endure and prevail.

2. **ephemeral** (i fem′ ər əl), lasting for only a day, or for only a short time.

FOR UNDERSTANDING

1. Why does the story's twelve-year-old narrator live with Mister Ernest? What is the most important time of the year for the two?
2. What is the boy's job when hunting with Mister Ernest?
3. What is the quarry they are hunting? What happens when Mister Ernest finally gets a perfect bead on him?
4. Why won't the boy be helping to put in the

crops the following year? How does Mister Ernest answer when the boy accuses him of having unloaded his gun deliberately?

FOR INTERPRETATION

1. In his Nobel Prize acceptance speech, Faulkner says man will not merely endure but prevail, "because he has a soul, a spirit capable of compassion and sacrifice and endurance." How does

"Race at Morning" illustrate Faulkner's expressed belief?

2. Faulkner speaks of the fearful question, "When will I be blown up?" as having changed the world. Discuss any relationship you might see between this thought and Mister Ernest's saying that things are different now and the boy must "belong to the business of mankind" and help teach what is right.

3. Robert Louis Stevenson concludes his essay "El Dorado" with the words: ". . . to travel hopefully is a better thing than to arrive, and the true success is to labor." Discuss how "Race at Morning" illustrates Stevenson's idea.

FOR APPRECIATION

Style

Faulkner believed that the aim of every artist should be to arrest motion or life so that it would come alive again for a stranger a hundred years later. His descriptive passages capture life and hold it for the reader. In some instances, it is Faulkner's down-to-earth humor that makes a word picture memorable. Discuss Faulkner's humor in the following:

1. the poker game
2. settling Dan for riding
3. Willy Legate's description of Mister Ernest and the boy when they "got strung out"
4. the grapevine incident

Symbolism

Faulkner made much use of symbolism. In "Race at Morning" what, if anything, might the buck symbolize? If you decide that the animal is a symbol, try to relate its symbolic meaning to specific facts in the story, especially to the fact that Mister Ernest purposely shoots at the buck with an empty shotgun.

LANGUAGE AND VOCABULARY

A. Skilled in the use of the limited point of view, Faulkner tells "Race at Morning" in the first person. He uses words that a twelve-year-old illiterate living in Mississippi would be likely to use. Write

the word or words you would likely use in place of the italicized words in the following sentences:

1. I had *jest* fed the horses and *clumb* back down the bank.

2. I could see that rocking chair he *toted* on his head.

3. He knows every *cuss* word in the dictionary.

4. Simon was beating the bottom of the dish-pan and *hollering*.

5. The puppies were *moiling* along in ever'body's way.

6. Mister Ernest on the horse said it was *fur* enough.

7. The wind was going to be south this morning when it *riz*.

8. Dan began to *souple* up and jump a little through the vines.

9. I *clumb* down to the bayou and *scopped* my cap full of water and *clumb* back and *throwed* it in his face.

10. Home was not no *piece akchully*, it was close enough to hear things clear.

B. In "Man Will Prevail" Faulkner is not constrained by a limited point of view, and he uses words that give some indication of the richness of his vocabulary. After making sure you know the meaning of the following words from the selection, write a sentence of your own for each.

1. acclaim	**5.** verities
2. pinnacle	**6.** prevail
3. anguish	**7.** compassion
4. travail	**8.** pillar

COMPOSITION

Much of literature is concerned with the search for truths. Perhaps no other modern American writer sought answers to such questions as "Why was I born? Why am I living?" more honestly and profoundly than William Faulkner. He believed it was the writer's duty to help humankind retain a firm grasp on fundamental values.

Write a brief paper giving your opinion as to whether writers can and do influence the personal ideals of their readers. In your final paragraph, evaluate Faulkner's impact on *you*.

Ernest Hemingway   1899–1961

Ernest Hemingway is one of the best known and most widely read American writers of the twentieth century. During his lifetime, he became for many people the prototype of the outdoorsman and adventurer—hearty, tough, and courageous. His novels and stories reflect this strong, "masculine" approach to life.

While still a teenager, Hemingway served in World War I on the Italian front, first as a volunteer ambulance driver and then as an infantryman in the Italian army. Seriously wounded in a battle against Austrian forces, he was decorated and sent to Milan to recover. Like Stephen Crane, Hemingway was fascinated by war, and after the Armistice he stayed on in Europe as a war correspondent. He covered the Greco-Turkish War in 1920, and later the Spanish Civil War (1936–1939). During World War II he served in the Caribbean and in Europe.

During the twenties, Hemingway joined the group of American writers living in Paris, coming under the influence of Gertrude Stein, Ezra Pound, and Sherwood Anderson. With the assistance of F. Scott Fitzgerald he published his first novel, *The Sun Also Rises* (1926), a story about American expatriates. His other major works include *A Farewell to Arms* (1929), *Death in the Afternoon* (1932), *For Whom the Bell Tolls* (1940), and *The Old Man and the Sea* (1952). Included in several collections are such significant short stories as "The Killers," "The Snows of Kilimanjaro," "The Big Two-Hearted River," and "The Short Happy Life of Francis Macomber." Several of his works have been made into motion pictures. In successive years he was awarded the Pulitzer Prize (1953) and the Nobel Prize in Literature (1954).

Hemingway's distinctive journalistic style, with its terse rhythms, simple dialogue, and emotional detachment, had a powerful impact on a generation of American readers. The writer's reportorial approach and the "plotless" structure of his stories also had considerable impact on

PORTRAIT OF ERNEST HEMINGWAY
Waldo Peirce
National Portrait Gallery, Smithsonian Institution

later writers, who attempted to emulate his simplicity.

The younger American writers of the post-World War I period came to be called "the lost generation." The term, supposedly coined by Gertrude Stein, referred to the fact that, after the war, these men and women felt disillusioned and no longer able to uphold the traditional values of the past. Hemingway, as one of the chief speakers for this generation, often wrote about individuals caught up in forces beyond their control. In the following brief story, he gives us a glimpse of one innocent victim of the fighting between the Loyalist and Fascist sides in the Spanish Civil War.

OLD MAN AT THE BRIDGE

An old man with steel rimmed spectacles and very dusty clothes sat by the side of the road. There was a pontoon bridge across the river and carts, trucks, and men, women and children were crossing it. The mule-drawn carts staggered up the steep bank from the bridge with soldiers helping push against the spokes of the wheels. The trucks ground up and away heading out of it all and the peasants plodded along in the ankle deep dust. But the old man sat there without moving. He was too tired to go any farther.

It was my business to cross the bridge, explore the bridgehead beyond and find out to what point the enemy had advanced. I did this and returned over the bridge. There were not so many carts now and very few people on foot, but the old man was still there.

"Where do you come from?" I asked him.

"From San Carlos," he said, and smiled.

That was his native town and so it gave him pleasure to mention it and he smiled.

"I was taking care of animals," he explained.

"Oh," I said, not quite understanding.

"Yes," he said, "I stayed, you see, taking care of animals. I was the last one to leave the town of San Carlos."

He did not look like a shepherd nor a herdsman and I looked at his black dusty clothes and his gray dusty face and his steel rimmed spectacles and said, "What animals were they?"

"Various animals," he said, and shook his head. "I had to leave them."

I was watching the bridge and the African looking country of the Ebro Delta and wondering how long now it would be before we would see the enemy, and listening all the while for the first noises that would signal that ever mysterious event called contact, and the old man still sat there.

"What animals were they?" I asked.

"There were three animals altogether," he explained. "There were two goats and a cat and then there were four pairs of pigeons."

"And you had to leave them?" I asked.

"Yes. Because of the artillery. The captain told me to go because of the artillery."

"And you have no family?" I asked, watching the far end of the bridge where a few last carts were hurrying down the slope of the bank.

"No," he said, "only the animals I stated. The cat, of course, will be all right. A cat can look out for itself, but I cannot think what will become of the others."

"What politics have you?" I asked.

"I am without politics," he said. "I am seventy-six years old. I have come twelve kilometers now and I think now I can go no further."

"This is not a good place to stop," I said. "If you can make it, there are trucks up the road where it forks for Tortosa."

"I will wait a while," he said, "and then I will go. Where do the trucks go?"

"Towards Barcelona," I told him.

"I know no one in that direction," he said, "but thank you very much. Thank you again very much."

He looked at me very blankly and tiredly, then said, having to share his worry with some one, "The cat will be all right, I am sure. There is no need to be unquiet about the cat. But the others. Now what do you think about the others?"

"Why they'll probably come through it all right."

"You think so?"

"Why not," I said, watching the far bank where now there were no carts.

"But what will they do under the artillery when I was told to leave because of the artillery?"

"Did you leave the dove cage unlocked?" I asked.

"Yes."

"Then they'll fly."

"Yes, certainly they'll fly. But the others. It's better not to think about the others," he said.

"If you are rested I would go," I urged. "Get up and try to walk now."

"Thank you," he said and got to his feet, swayed from side to side and then sat down backwards in the dust.

"I was taking care of animals," he said dully, but no longer to me. "I was only taking care of animals."

There was nothing to do about him. It was Easter Sunday and the Fascists were advancing toward the Ebro. It was a gray overcast day with a low ceiling so their planes were not up. That and the fact that cats know how to look after themselves was all the good luck that old man would ever have.

FOR UNDERSTANDING

1. Why is the narrator of the story at the bridge?
2. What does the old man say he has been doing in his village? What is his major concern?

3. Why does the old man say he does not wish to go toward Barcelona?
4. What happens to the old man when he tries to stand?

FOR INTERPRETATION

1. When the narrator concludes "There was nothing to do about him," what fate does he suggest for the old man?
2. Is the narrator indifferent to the old man's predicament? Explain.

FOR APPRECIATION

The Spare Style

In April, 1938, as Fascist troops under General Franco pushed toward the Loyalist capital of Barcelona, Hemingway cabled this brief story to his American publisher. Although quite short, the story is an excellent example of Hemingway's style. The spare diction, clipped sentences, and the apparent detachment of the characters from the reality of what is happening are hallmarks of Hemingway's work.

1. What minimal descriptive details of the old man does Hemingway give the reader in the opening paragraph?
2. How does the subsequent paragraph beginning "He did not look like a shepherd nor a herdsman . . ." demonstrate Hemingway's discipline of confining description to the barest minimum?
3. Hemingway believed that the individual is helpless and exploited in a mass culture. How does he express this belief in the final paragraph?

Thomas Wolfe

Thomas Wolfe was born and reared in Asheville, North Carolina. A precocious youth, he was educated privately and entered the University of North Carolina at fifteen. During his years there, and later at Harvard, Wolfe aspired to become a playwright. Producers, however, were not interested in his work and he concentrated on writing short stories and novels. To support himself, he taught at New York University while he worked on his first novel, *Look Homeward, Angel* (1929). When the book proved a success, Wolfe devoted himself full time to writing. His second novel, *Of Time and the River* (1935), was also a success. In both books Wolfe, the most autobiographical of our major writers, tells the story of himself (as Eugene Gant) and his attempts to escape his family and what he feels is the narrowness of their environment. Most of his stories, in fact, are thinly disguised episodes in his life.

A tireless and sometimes even frantic worker with a remarkable memory for sights, sounds, and sensations, Wolfe turned out a prodigious mass of loosely organized material that talented editors helped him shape into the lyrical and moving short stories and novels that appeared before and after his untimely death. Although Wolfe has been criticized for the shapelessness and sometimes awkward style of his work, he wrote with an energy and a passion that few have matched. His death from a brain infection ended a most promising literary career.

Among Wolfe's other works are *From Death to Morning* (1935), *The Story of a Novel* (1936), *The Web and the Rock* (1939), *You Can't Go Home Again*

PORTRAIT OF THOMAS WOLFE
Soss Melik
National Portrait Gallery, Smithsonian Institution

(1940), and *The Hills Beyond* (1941). The following short story from the collection, *From Death to Morning,* is a straightforward account of one person's cherished illusions and what happens to alter them.

THE FAR AND THE NEAR

On the outskirts of a little town upon a rise of land that swept back from the railway there was a tidy little cottage of white boards, trimmed vividly with green blinds. To one side of the house there was a garden neatly patterned with plots of growing vegetables, and an arbor for the grapes which ripened late in August. Before the house there were three mighty oaks which sheltered it in their clean and massive shade in summer, and to the other side there was a border of gay flowers. The whole place had an air of tidiness, thrift, and modest comfort.

Every day, a few minutes after two o'clock in the afternoon, the limited express between two cities passed this spot. At that moment the great train, having halted for a breathing-space at the town near by, was beginning to lengthen evenly into its stroke, but it had not yet reached the full drive of its terrific speed. It swung into view deliberately, swept past with a powerful swaying motion of the engine, a low smooth rumble of its heavy cars upon pressed steel, and then it vanished in the cut. For a moment the progress of the engine could be marked by heavy billowing puffs of smoke that burst at spaced intervals above the edges of the meadow grass, and finally nothing could be heard but the solid clacking tempo of the wheels receding into the drowsy stillness of the afternoon.

Every day for more than twenty years, as the train had approached this house, the engineer had blown on the whistle, and every day, as soon as she heard this signal, a woman had appeared on the back porch of the little house and waved to him. At first she had a small child clinging to her skirts, and now this child had grown to full womanhood, and every day she, too, came with her mother to the porch and waved.

The engineer had grown old and gray in service. He had driven his great train, loaded with its weight of lives, across the land ten thousand times. His own children had grown up and married, and four times he had seen before him on the tracks the ghastly dot of tragedy converging like a cannon ball to its eclipse of horror at the boiler head—a light spring wagon filled with children, with its clustered row of small stunned faces; a cheap automobile stalled upon the tracks, set with the wooden figures of people paralyzed with fear; a battered hobo walking by the rail, too deaf and old to hear the whistle's warning; and a form flung past his window with a scream—all this the man had seen and known. He had known all the grief, the joy, the peril and the labor such a man could know; he had grown seamed and weathered in his loyal service, and now, schooled by the qualities of faith and courage and humbleness that attended his labor, he had grown old, and had the grandeur and the wisdom these men have.

But no matter what peril or tragedy he had known, the vision of the little house and the women waving to him with a brave free motion of the arm had become fixed in the mind of the engineer as something beautiful and enduring, something beyond all change and ruin, and something that would always be the same, no matter what mishap, grief or error might break the iron schedule of his days.

The heightened realism and perfect order of this scene typify the means by which Grant Wood imposed his own special vision on his rural landscapes.

STONE CITY, IOWA, Grant Wood
Joslyn Art Museum, Omaha, Nebraska

The sight of the little house and of these two women gave him the most extraordinary happiness he had ever known. He had seen them in a thousand lights, a hundred weathers. He had seen them through the harsh bare light of wintry gray across the brown and frosted stubble of the earth, and he had seen them again in the green luring sorcery of April.

He felt for them and for the little house in which they lived such tenderness as a man might feel for his own children, and at length the picture of their lives was carved so sharply in his heart that he felt that he knew their lives completely, to every hour and moment of the day, and he resolved that one day, when his years of service should be ended, he would go and find these people and speak at last with them whose lives had been so wrought into his own.

That day came. At last the engineer stepped from a train onto the station platform of the town where these two women lived. His years upon the rail had ended. He was a pensioned servant of his company, with no more work to do. The engineer walked slowly through the station and out into the streets of the town. Everything was as strange to him as if he had never seen this town before. As he walked on, his sense of bewilder-

ment and confusion grew. Could this be the town he had passed ten thousand times? Were these the same houses he had seen so often from the high windows of his cab? It was all as unfamiliar, as disquieting as a city in a dream, and the perplexity of his spirit increased as he went on.

Presently the houses thinned into the straggling outposts of the town, and the street faded into a country road—the one on which the women lived. And the man plodded on slowly in the heat and dust. At length he stood before the house he sought. He knew at once that he had found the proper place. He saw the lordly oaks before the house, the flower beds, the garden and the arbor, and farther off, the glint of rails.

Yes, this was the house he sought, the place he had passed so many times, the destination he had longed for with such happiness. But now that he had found it, now that he was here, why did his hand falter on the gate; why had the town, the road, the earth, the very entrance to this place he loved turned unfamiliar as the landscape of some ugly dream? Why did he now feel this sense of confusion, doubt and hopelessness?

At length he entered by the gate, walked slowly up the path and in a moment more had mounted three short steps that led up to the porch, and was knocking at the door. Presently he heard steps in the hall, the door was opened, and a woman stood facing him.

And instantly, with a sense of bitter loss and grief, he was sorry he had come. He knew at once that the woman who stood there looking at him with a mistrustful eye was the same woman who had waved to him so many thousand times. But her face was harsh and pinched and meager; the flesh sagged wearily in sallow folds, and the small eyes peered at him with timid suspicion and uneasy doubt. All the brave freedom, the warmth and the affection that he had read into her gesture, vanished in the moment that he saw her and heard her unfriendly tongue.

And now his own voice sounded unreal and ghastly to him as he tried to explain his presence, to tell her who he was and the reason he had come. But he faltered on, fighting stubbornly against the horror of regret, confusion, disbelief that surged up in his spirit, drowning all his former joy and making his act of hope and tenderness seem shameful to him.

At length the woman invited him almost unwillingly into the house, and called her daughter in a harsh shrill voice. Then, for a brief agony of time, the man sat in an ugly little parlor, and he tried to talk while the two women stared at him with a dull, bewildered hostility, a sullen, timorous restraint.

And finally, stammering a crude farewell, he departed. He walked away down the path and then along the road toward town, and suddenly he knew that he was an old man. His heart, which had been brave and confident when it looked along the familiar vista of the rails, was now sick with doubt and horror as it saw the strange and unsuspected visage of an earth which had always been within a stone's throw of him, and which he had never seen or known. And he knew that all the magic of that bright lost way, the vista of that shining line, the imagined corner of that small good universe of hope's desire, was gone forever, could never be got back again.

FOR UNDERSTANDING

1. How do the women respond to the engineer's greeting and how long have they done so?
2. At what point in his life does the engineer come to talk to the women?

FOR INTERPRETATION

1. Over the years, what have the women come to symbolize to the engineer?
2. Why is the engineer disillusioned after he meets and talks with the women?

FOR APPRECIATION

Theme
State the theme of the story in your own words. Completing the following statement is often helpful in setting forth the theme: In this selection the author is trying to show us that . . .

LANGUAGE AND VOCABULARY

The following five words from this story have interesting etymologies: *tidy, arbor, terrific, schedule, agony.* In a modern dictionary, preferably unabridged, or in a book of word origins, find and write the *original* meaning of each, then explain its *present* meaning.

COMPOSITION

This story graphically illustrates limited point of view. We are given the engineer's confusion and disillusionment when he sees and talks with the women. To him they are a bitter disappointment. We are not told, however, how the women feel on meeting him. Over the years have they, too, formed a romantic notion about the man? To them, was he a knight of the shining rails? Was their "dull, bewildered hostility, a sullen, timorous restraint" their normal behavior, or the result of *their* shattered illusions? Write a composition in which you visualize how the women react to the engineer. What is their point of view?

John Steinbeck

1902–1968

Banned, burned, and criticized on the floor of Congress when it was published in 1939, John Steinbeck's novel *The Grapes of Wrath* was number one on that year's best-seller list and has since been described as nothing less than a national event. As social-protest literature, it dramatically focused public attention on the callous exploitation of migrant workers. It also demonstrated the tragic loss of identity that was suffered by subsistence farm families forced from their land by a combination of natural calamity and unscrupulous speculators.

From the age of four, when the rhyme of the words *fly* and *high* first delighted him, John Steinbeck was fascinated by words and the way they could be put together. His boyhood in and around the farming community of Salinas, California, deeply influenced his writing. In addition to providing him with a setting for much of his work, it gave him a deep respect for nature, simple living, and common people. In high school Steinbeck was senior class president and a member of the track and basketball teams. However, his attendance at Stanford University was intermittent because he had to work—as a farm laborer, on a cattle boat, as a cement hauler, newspaper reporter, fruit picker, and estate caretaker—in order to earn the money to allow him to write. Although his first three novels were commercial failures, his entertaining *Tortilla Flat* (1935), about the colorful life of the raffish Spanish-speaking "paisanos" in Monterey, California, had sufficient popular appeal to make him a little money. But to nullify any idea that he might be a humorous writer, he next published *In Dubious Battle* (1936), a chilling and violent tale of strikers and strikebreakers among California's migrant fruit pickers. The next year he wrote *Of Mice and Men* (1937), an appealing and tragic story of the friendship between two unskilled workers drifting from job to job.

Of Mice and Men (the play version of which was to defeat Thornton Wilder's *Our Town* for the Drama Critics' Circle Award) and *The Grapes of Wrath,* which received the Pulitzer Prize,

PORTRAIT OF JOHN STEINBECK
James Fitzgerald
National Portrait Gallery, Smithsonian Institution

represent Steinbeck at the height of his power and popularity. In *The Grapes of Wrath,* the tragic Joad family and the other "Okies" who fled the Oklahoma dust bowl for the promise of paradise in California continue to arouse sympathy in the reader today. Like many of Steinbeck's other stories, this novel invites interpretation on more than one level. Its structure parallels the biblical migration of the Israelites from Egypt, and it has been convincingly analyzed as Christian allegory.

Steinbeck's sympathy for the wronged and his support for democracy and justice are strongly evidenced in his war novel *The Moon Is Down* (1942), said to have been very popular among those who were involved in resistance in Nazi-occupied countries. Of Steinbeck's other significant stories, his beautiful short novel *The Pearl* (1945), an allegorical story in which the Mexican hero, Kino, and his wife must throw away a fabulously valuable pearl in order to survive, is considered a masterpiece.

In 1962 John Steinbeck became the sixth American to receive the Nobel Prize in Literature. The award was given, not for any particular book, but for a career of "realistic and imaginative writings" spanning more than a generation. At the time, Steinbeck had published no fewer than sixteen novels, beginning with *Cup of Gold* in 1929 and ending with the last novel he was to publish, *The Winter of Our Discontent* in 1961. But there was much more than the novels. He was also a writer of excellent short stories,

especially those in *The Long Valley* (1938). He was a master at nonfiction, as *Travels with Charlie* (1962) attests. And he was the author of successful plays and numerous articles.

The following story comes from Steinbeck's second book, *The Pastures of Heaven* (1932), made up of ten independent episodes united by their common setting and by the recurring appearance of the Munroes, a family that seems to carry an "evil cloud" or jinx. The setting is a California valley, Corral de Tierra, near Monterey, which Steinbeck renamed "the Pastures of Heaven." After you have read "Molly Morgan" you will have to decide how much of her trouble she carries within herself and how much the Munroe curse is to blame.

---

from THE PASTURES OF HEAVEN

Molly Morgan

Molly Morgan got off the train in Salinas and waited three quarters of an hour for the bus. The big automobile was empty except for the driver and Molly.

"I've never been to the Pastures of Heaven, you know," she said. "Is it far from the main road?"

"About three miles," said the driver.

"Will there be a car to take me into the valley?"

"No, not unless you're met."

"But how do people get in there?"

The driver ran over the flattened body of a jack rabbit with apparent satisfaction. "I only hit 'em when they're dead," he apologized. "In the dark, when they get caught in the lights, I try to miss 'em."

"Yes, but how am I going to get into the Pastures of Heaven?"

"I dunno. Walk, I guess. Most people walk if they ain't met."

When he set her down at the entrance to the dirt side-road, Molly Morgan grimly picked up her suitcase and marched toward the draw in the hills. An old Ford truck squeaked up beside her.

"Goin' into the valley, ma'am?"

"Oh—yes, yes, I am."

"Well, get in, then. Needn't be scared. I'm Pat Humbert. I got a place in the Pastures."

Molly surveyed the grimy man and acknowledged his introduction. "I'm the new schoolteacher, I mean, I think I am. Do you know where Mr. Whiteside lives?"

"Sure, I go right by there. He's clerk of the board. I'm on the school board myself, you know. We wondered what you'd look like." Then he grew embarrassed at what he had said, and flushed under his coating of dirt.

"Course I mean what you'd *be* like. Last teacher we had gave a good deal of trouble. She was all right, but she was sick—I mean, sick and nervous. Finally quit because she was sick."

Molly picked at the fingertips of her gloves. "My letter says I'm to call on Mr. Whiteside. Is he all right? I don't mean that. I mean—is he—what kind of a man is he?"

"Oh, you'll get along with him all right. He's a fine old man. Born in that house he lives in. Been to college, too. He's a good man. Been clerk of the board for over twenty years."

When he put her down in front of the big old house of John Whiteside, she was really frightened. "Now it's coming," she said to herself. "But there's nothing to be afraid of. He can't do anything to me." Molly was only nineteen. She felt that this moment of interview for her first job was a tremendous inch in her whole existence.

The walk up to the door did not reassure her, for the path lay between tight little flower beds hedged in with clipped box, seemingly planted with the admonition, "Now grow and multiply, but don't grow too high, nor multiply too greatly, and above all things, keep out of this path!" There was a hand on those flowers, a guiding and a correcting hand. The large white house was very dignified. Venetian blinds of yellow wood were tilted down to keep out the noon sun. Halfway up the path she came in sight of the entrance. There was a veranda as broad and warm and welcoming as an embrace. Through her mind flew the thought, "Surely you can tell the hospitality of a house by its entrance. Suppose it had a little door and no porch." But in spite of the welcoming of the wide steps and the big doorway, her timidities clung to her when she rang the bell. The big door opened, and a large, comfortable woman stood smiling at Molly.

"I hope you're not selling something," said Mrs. Whiteside. "I never want to buy anything and I always do, and then I'm mad."

Molly laughed. She felt suddenly very happy. Until that moment she hadn't known how frightened she really was. "Oh, no," she cried. "I'm the new schoolteacher. My letter says I'm to interview Mr. Whiteside. Can I see him?"

"Well, it's noon, and he's just finishing his dinner. Did you have dinner?"

"Oh, of course. I mean, no."

Mrs. Whiteside chuckled and stood aside for her to enter. "Well, I'm glad you're sure." She led Molly into a large dining room, lined with mahogany, glass-fronted dish closets. The square table was littered with the dishes of a meal. "Why, John must have finished and gone. Sit down, young woman. I'll bring back the roast."

"Oh, no. Really, thank you, no, I'll just talk to Mr. Whiteside and then go along."

"Sit down. You'll need nourishment to face John."

"Is—is he very stern, with new teachers, I mean?"

"Well," said Mrs. Whiteside. "That depends. If they haven't had their dinner, he's a regular bear. He shouts at them. But when they've just got up from the table, he's only just fierce."

Molly laughed happily. "You have children," she said. "Oh, you've raised lots of children—and you like them."

Mrs. Whiteside scowled. "One child raised me. Raised me right through the roof. It was too hard on me. He's out raising cows now, poor devils. I don't think I raised him very high."

When Molly had finished eating, Mrs. Whiteside threw open a side door and called, "John, here's someone to see you." She pushed Molly through the doorway into a room that was a kind of a library, for big bookcases were loaded with thick, old, comfortable books, all filigreed in gold. And it was a kind of a sitting room. There was a fireplace of brick with a mantel of little red tile bricks and the most extraordinary vases on the mantel. Hung on a nail over the mantel, slung really, like a rifle on a shoulder strap, was a huge meerschaum pipe in the Jaeger fashion. Big leather chairs with leather tassels hanging to them, stood about the fireplace, all of them patent rocking chairs with the kind of springs that chant when you rock them. And lastly, the room was a kind of an office, for there was an old-fashioned rolltop desk, and behind it sat John Whiteside. When he looked up, Molly saw that he had at once the kindest and the sternest eyes she had ever seen, and the whitest hair, too. Real blue-white, silky hair, a great duster of it.

"I am Mary Morgan," she began formally.

"Oh, yes, Miss Morgan, I've been expecting you. Won't you sit down?"

She sat in one of the big rockers, and the springs cried with sweet pain. "I love these chairs," she said. "We used to have one when I was a little girl." Then she felt silly. "I've come to interview you about this position. My letter said to do that."

"Don't be so tense, Miss Morgan. I've interviewed every teacher we've had for years. And," he said, smiling, "I still don't know how to go about it."

"Oh—I'm glad, Mr. Whiteside. I never asked for a job before. I was really afraid of it."

"Well, Miss Mary Morgan, as near as I can figure, the purpose of this interview is to give me a little knowledge of your past and of the kind of person you are. I'm supposed to know something about you when you've finished. And now that you know my purpose, I suppose you'll be self-conscious and anxious to give a good impression. Maybe if you just tell me a little about yourself, everything'll be all right. Just a few words about the kind of girl you are, and where you came from."

Molly nodded quickly. "Yes, I'll try to do that, Mr. Whiteside," and she dropped her mind back into the past.

There was the old, squalid, unpainted house with its wide back porch and the round washtubs leaning against the rail. High in the great willow

tree her two brothers, Joe and Tom, crashed about crying, "Now I'm an eagle." "I'm a parrot." "Now I'm an old chicken." "Watch me!"

The screen door on the back porch opened, and their mother leaned tiredly out. Her hair would not lie smoothly no matter how much she combed it. Thick strings of it hung down beside her face. Her eyes were always a little red, and her hands and wrists painfully cracked. "Tom, Joe," she called. "You'll get hurt up there. Don't worry me so, boys! Don't you love your mother at all?" The voices in the tree were hushed. The shrieking spirits of the eagle and the old chicken were drenched in self-reproach. Molly sat in the dust, wrapping a rag around a stick and doing her best to imagine it a tall lady in a dress. "Molly, come in and stay with your mother. I'm so tired today."

Molly stood up the stick in the deep dust. "You, miss," she whispered fiercely. "You'll get whipped on your bare bottom when I come back." Then she obediently went into the house.

Her mother sat in a straight chair in the kitchen. "Draw up, Molly. Just sit with me a little while. Love me, Molly! Love your mother a little bit. You are mother's good little girl, aren't you?" Molly squirmed on her chair. "Don't you love your mother, Molly?"

The little girl was very miserable. She knew her mother would cry in a moment, and then she would be compelled to stroke the stringy hair. Both she and her brothers knew they should love their mother. She did everything for them. They were ashamed that they hated to be near her, but they couldn't help it. When she called to them and they were not in sight, they pretended not to hear, and crept away, talking in whispers.

"Well, to begin with, we were very poor," Molly said to John Whiteside. "I guess we were really poverty-stricken. I had two brothers a little older than I. My father was a traveling salesman, but even so, my mother had to work. She worked terribly hard for us."

About once in every six months a great event occurred. In the morning the mother crept silently out of the bedroom. Her hair was brushed as smoothly as it could be; her eyes sparkled, and she looked happy and almost pretty. She whispered, "Quiet, children! Your father's home." Molly and her brothers sneaked out of the house, but even in the yard they talked in excited whispers. The news traveled quickly about the neighborhood. Soon the yard was filled with whispering children. "They say their father's home." "Is your father really home?" "Where's he been this time?" By noon there were a dozen children in the yard, standing in expectant little groups, cautioning one another to be quiet.

About noon the screen door on the porch sprang open and whacked against the wall. Their father leaped out. "Hi," he yelled. "Hi, kids!" Molly and her brothers flung themselves upon him and hugged his legs, while he plucked them off and hurled them into the air like kittens.

Mrs. Morgan fluttered about, clucking with excitement, "Children, children. Don't muss your father's clothes."

The neighbor children threw handsprings and wrestled and shrieked with joy. It was better than any holiday.

"Wait till you see," their father cried. "Wait till you see what I brought you. It's a secret now." And when the hysteria had quieted a little he carried his suitcase out on the porch and opened it. There were presents such as no one had ever seen, mechanical toys unknown before—tin bugs that crawled, dancing wooden figures and astounding steam shovels that worked in sand. There were superb glass marbles with bears and dogs right in their centres. He had something for everyone, several things for everyone. It was all the great holidays packed into one.

Usually it was midafternoon before the children became calm enough not to shriek occasionally. But eventually George Morgan sat on the steps, and they all gathered about while he told his adventures. This time he had been to Mexico while there was a revolution. Again he had gone to Honolulu, had seen the volcano and had himself ridden on a surfboard. Always there were cities and people, strange people; always adventures and a hundred funny incidents, funnier than anything they had ever heard. It couldn't all be told at one time. After school they had to gather to hear more and more. Throughout the world George Morgan tramped, collecting glorious adventures.

"As far as my home life went," Miss Morgan said, "I guess I almost didn't have any father. He was able to get home very seldom from his business trips."

John Whiteside nodded gravely.

Molly's hands rustled in her lap and her eyes were dim.

One time he brought a dumpy, woolly puppy in a box, and it wet on the floor immediately.

"What kind of a dog is it?" Tom asked in his most sophisticated manner.

Their father laughed loudly. He was so young! He looked twenty years younger than their mother. "It's a dollar and a half dog," he explained. "You get an awful lot of kinds of dog for a dollar and a half. It's like this. . . . Suppose you go into a candy store and say, 'I want a nickel's worth of peppermints and gumdrops and licorice and raspberry chews.' Well, I went in and said, 'Give me a dollar and a half's worth of mixed dog.' That's the kind it is. It's Molly's dog, and she has to name it."

"I'm going to name it George," said Molly.

Her father bowed strangely to her, and said, "Thank you, Molly." They all noticed that he wasn't laughing at her, either.

Molly got up very early the next morning and took George about the yard to show him the secrets. She opened the hoard where two pennies and a gold policeman's button were buried. She hooked his little front paws over the back fence so he could look down the street at the schoolhouse. Lastly she climbed into the willow tree, carrying George under one arm. Tom came out of the house and sauntered under the tree. "Look out you don't drop him," Tom called, and just at that moment the puppy squirmed out of her arms and fell. He landed on the hard ground with a disgusting little thump. One leg bent out at a crazy angle, and the puppy screamed long, horrible screams, with sobs between breaths. Molly scrambled out of the tree, dull and stunned by the accident. Tom was standing over the puppy, his face white and twisted with pain, and George, the puppy, screamed on and on.

"We can't let him," Tom cried. "We can't let him." He ran to the woodpile and brought back a hatchet. Molly was too stupefied to look away, but Tom closed his eyes and struck. The screams stopped suddenly. Tom threw the hatchet from him and leaped over the back fence. Molly saw him running away as though he were being chased.

At that moment Joe and her father came out of the back door. Molly remembered how haggard and thin and gray her father's face was when he

*In his panoramic landscape paintings and in the etchings he did
as book illustrations, Rockwell Kent displayed a dramatic style
distinguished by bold patterns and powerful characterizations.*

AMERICA, Rockwell Kent
Courtesy, Warner Library

looked at the puppy. It was something in her
father's face that started Molly to crying. "I
dropped him out of the tree, and he hurt himself,
and Tom hit him, and then Tom ran away." Her
voice sounded sulky. Her father hugged Molly's
head against his hip.

"Poor Tom!" he said. "Molly, you must remember never to say anything to Tom about it,
and never to look at him as though you remembered." He threw a gunny sack over the puppy.
"We must have a funeral," he said. "Did I ever tell
you about the Chinese funeral I went to, about the
colored paper they throw in the air, and the little
fat roast pigs on the grave?" Joe edged in closer,
and even Molly's eyes took on a gleam of interest.
"Well, it was this way. . . ."

Molly looked up at John Whiteside and
saw that he seemed to be studying a piece of
paper on his desk. "When I was twelve years
old, my father was killed in an accident," she
said.

The great visits usually lasted about two
weeks. Always there came an afternoon when
George Morgan walked out into the town and did
not come back until late at night. The mother
made the children go to bed early, but they could
hear him come home, stumbling a little against the
furniture, and they could hear his voice through
the wall. These were the only times when his voice
was sad and discouraged. Lying with held breaths,
in their beds, the children knew what that meant.
In the morning he would be gone, and their hearts
would be gone with him.

They had endless discussions about what he
was doing. Their father was a glad argonaut, a
silver knight. Virtue and Courage and Beauty—he
wore a coat of them. "Sometime," the boys said,
"sometime when we're big, we'll go with him and
see all those things."

"I'll go, too," Molly insisted.

"Oh, you're a girl. You couldn't go, you
know."

"But he'd let me go, you know he would.

Sometime he'll take me with him. You see if he doesn't."

When he was gone their mother grew plaintive again, and her eyes reddened. Querulously she demanded their love, as though it were a package they could put in her hand.

One time their father went away, and he never came back. He had never sent any money, nor had he ever written to them, but this time he just disappeared for good. For two years they waited, and then their mother said he must be dead. The children shuddered at the thought, but they refused to believe it, because no one so beautiful and fine as their father could be dead. Some place in the world he was having adventures. There was some good reason why he couldn't come back to them. Some day when the reason was gone, he would come. Some morning he would be there with finer presents and better stories than ever before. But their mother said he must have had an accident. He must be dead. Their mother was distracted. She read those advertisements which offered to help her make money at home. The children made paper flowers and shamefacedly tried to sell them. The boys tried to develop magazine routes, and the whole family nearly starved. Finally, when they couldn't stand it any longer, the boys ran away and joined the navy. After that Molly saw them as seldom as she had seen her father, and they were so changed, so hard and boisterous, that she didn't even care, for her brothers were strangers to her.

"I went through high school, and then I went to San Jose and entered Teachers' College. I worked for my board and room at the home of Mrs. Allen Morit. Before I finished school my mother died, so I guess I'm a kind of an orphan, you see."

"I'm sorry," John Whiteside murmured gently.

Molly flushed. "That wasn't a bid for sympathy, Mr. Whiteside. You said you wanted to know about me. Everyone has to be an orphan some time."

Molly worked for her board and room. She did the work of a full time servant, only she received no pay. Money for clothes had to be accumulated by working in a store during summer vacation. Mrs. Morit trained her girls. "I can take a green girl, not worth a cent," she often said, "and when that girl's worked for me six months, she can get fifty dollars a month. Lots of women know it, and they just snap up my girls. This is the first schoolgirl I've tried, but even she shows a lot of improvement. She reads too much though. I always say a servant should be asleep by ten o'clock, or else she can't do her work right."

Mrs. Morit's method was one of constant criticism and nagging, carried on in a just, firm tone. "Now, Molly, I don't want to find fault, but if you don't wipe the silver drier than that, it'll have streaks"—"The butter knife goes this way, Molly. Then you can put the tumbler here."

"I always give a reason for everything," she told her friends.

In the evening, after the dishes were washed, Molly sat on her bed and studied, and when the light was off, she lay on her bed and thought of her father. It was ridiculous to do it, she knew. It was a waste of time. Her father came up to the door, wearing a cutaway coat, and striped trousers and a top hat. He carried a huge bouquet of red roses in his hand. "I couldn't come before, Molly. Get on your coat quickly. First we're going down to get that evening dress in the window of Prussia's, but we'll have to hurry. I have tickets for the train to New York tonight. Hurry up, Molly! Don't stand there gawping." It was silly. Her father was dead. No, she didn't really believe he was dead. Somewhere in the world he lived beautifully, and sometime he would come back.

Molly told one of her friends at school, "I don't really believe it, you see, but I don't disbelieve it. If I ever knew he was dead, why it would be awful. I don't know what I'd do then. I don't want to think about *knowing* he's dead."

When her mother died, she felt little besides shame. Her mother had wanted so much to be loved, and she hadn't known how to draw love. Her importunities had bothered the children and driven them away.

"Well, that's about all," Molly finished. "I got my diploma, and then I was sent down here."

"It was about the easiest interview I ever had," John Whiteside said.

"Do you think I'll get the position, then?"

The old man gave a quick, twinkly glance at the big meerschaum hanging over the mantel.

"That's his friend," Molly thought. "He has secrets with that pipe."

"Yes, I think you'll get the job. I think you have it already. Now, Miss Morgan, where are you going to live? You must find board and room some place."

Before she knew she was going to say it, she had blurted, "I want to live here."

John Whiteside opened his eyes in astonishment. "But we never take boarders, Miss Morgan."

"Oh, I'm sorry I said that. I just like it so much here, you see."

He called, "Willa," and when his wife stood in the half-open door, "This young lady wants to board with us. She's the new teacher."

Mrs. Whiteside frowned. "Couldn't think of it. We never take boarders. She's too pretty to be around that fool of a Bill. What would happen to those cows of his? It'd be a lot of trouble. You can sleep in the third bedroom upstairs," she said to Molly. "It doesn't catch much sun anyway."

Life changed its face. All of a sudden Molly found she was a queen. From the first day the children of the school adored her, for she understood them, and what was more, she let them understand her. It took her some time to realize that she had become an important person. If two men got to arguing at the store about a point of history or literature or mathematics, and the argument deadlocked, it ended up, "Take it to the teacher! If she doesn't know, she'll find it." Molly was very proud to be able to decide such questions. At parties she had to help with the decorations and to plan refreshments.

"I think we'll put pine boughs around everywhere. They're pretty, and they smelll so good. They smell like a party." She was supposed to know everything and to help with everything, and she loved it.

At the Whiteside home she slaved in the kitchen under the mutterings of Willa. At the end of six months, Mrs. Whiteside grumbled to her husband, "Now if Bill only had any sense. But then," she continued, "if *she* has any sense—" and there she left it.

At night Molly wrote letters to the few friends she had made in Teachers' College, letters full of little stories about her neighbors, and full of joy. She must attend every party because of the social prestige of her position. On Saturdays she ran about the hills and brought back ferns and wild flowers to plant about the house.

Bill Whiteside took one look at Molly and scuttled back to his cows. It was a long time before he found the courage to talk to her very much. He was a big, simple young man who had neither his father's balance nor his mother's humor. Eventually, however, he trailed after Molly and looked after her from distances.

One evening, with a kind of feeling of thanksgiving for her happiness, Molly told Bill about her father. They were sitting in canvas chairs on the wide veranda, waiting for the moon. She told him about the visits, and then about the disappearance. "Do you see what I have, Bill?" she cried. "My lovely father is some place. He's mine. You think he's living, don't you, Bill?"

"Might be," said Bill. "From what you say, he was a kind of an irresponsible cuss, though. Excuse me, Molly. Still, if he's alive, it's funny he never wrote."

Molly felt cold. It was just the kind of reasoning she had successfully avoided for so long. "Of course," she said stiffly, "I know that. I have to do some work now, Bill."

High up on a hill that edged the valley of the Pastures of Heaven, there was an old cabin which commanded a view of the whole country and of all the roads in the vicinity. It was said that the bandit Vasquez had built the cabin and lived in it for a year while the posses went crashing through the country looking for him. It was a landmark. All the people of the valley had been to see it at one time or another. Nearly everyone asked Molly whether she had been there yet. "No," she said, "but I will go up some day. I'll go some Saturday. I know where the trail to it is." One morning she dressed in her new hiking boots and corduroy skirt. Bill sidled up and offered to accompany her. "No," she said. "You have work to do. I can't take you away from it."

"Work be hanged!" said Bill.

"Well, I'd rather go alone. I don't want to hurt your feelings, but I just want to go alone, Bill." She was sorry not to let him accompany her, but his remark about her father had frightened her. "I want to have an adventure," she said to herself. "If Bill comes along, it won't be an adventure at all. It'll just be a trip." It took her an hour and a half to climb up the steep trail under the oaks. The leaves on the ground were as slippery as glass, and the sun was hot. The good smell of ferns and dank moss and yerba buena filled the air. When Molly came at last to the ridge crest, she was damp and winded. The cabin stood in a small clearing in the brush, a little square wooden room with no windows. Its doorless entrance was a black shadow. The place was quiet, the kind of humming quiet that flies and bees and crickets make. The whole hillside sang softly in the sun. Molly approached on tiptoe. Her heart was beating violently.

"Now I'm having an adventure," she whispered. "Now I'm right in the middle of an adventure at Vasquez' cabin." She peered in at the doorway and saw a lizard scuttle out of sight. A cobweb fell across her forehead and seemed to try to restrain her. There was nothing at all in the cabin, nothing but the dirt floor and the rotting wooden walls, and the dry, deserted smell of the earth that has long been covered from the sun. Molly was filled with excitement. "At night he sat in there. Sometimes when he heard noises like men creeping up on him, he went out of the door like the ghost of a shadow, and just melted into the darkness." She looked down

on the valley of the Pastures of Heaven. The orchards lay in dark green squares; the grain was yellow, and the hills behind, a light brown washed with lavender. Among the farms the roads twisted and curled, avoiding a field, looping around a huge tree, half circling a hill flank. Over the whole valley was stretched a veil of heat shimmer. "Unreal," Molly whispered, "fantastic. It's a story, a real story, and I'm having an adventure." A breeze rose out of the valley like the sigh of a sleeper, and then subsided.

"In the daytime that young Vasquez looked down on the valley just as I'm looking. He stood right here, and looked at the roads down there. He wore a purple vest braided with gold, and the trousers on his slim legs widened at the bottom like the mouths of trumpets. His spur rowels were wrapped with silk ribbons to keep them from clinking. Sometimes he saw the posses riding by on the road below. Lucky for him the men bent over their horses' necks, and didn't look up at the hilltops. Vasquez laughed, but he was afraid, too. Sometimes he sang. His songs were soft and sad because he knew he couldn't live very long."

Molly sat down on the slope and rested her chin in her cupped hands. Young Vasquez was standing beside her, and Vasquez had her father's gay face, his shining eyes as he came on the porch shouting, "Hi, kids!" This was the kind of adventure her father had. Molly shook herself and stood up. "Now I want to go back to the first and think it all over again."

In the late afternoon Mrs. Whiteside sent Bill out to look for Molly. "She might have turned an ankle, you know." But Molly emerged from the trail just as Bill approached it from the road.

"We were beginning to wonder if you'd got lost," he said. "Did you go up to the cabin?"

"Yes."

"Funny old box, isn't it? Just an old woodshed. There are a dozen just like it down here. You'd be surprised, though, how many people go up there to look at it. The funny part is, nobody's sure Vasquez was ever there."

"Oh, I think he must have been there."

"What makes you think that?"

"I don't know."

Bill became serious. "Everybody thinks Vasquez was a kind of hero, when really he was just a thief. He started in stealing sheep and horses and ended up robbing stages. He had to kill a few people to do it. It seems to me, Molly, we ought to teach people to hate robbers, not worship them."

"Of course, Bill," she said wearily. "You're perfectly right. Would you mind not talking for a little while, Bill? I guess I'm a little tired, and nervous, too."

The year wheeled around. Pussywillows had their kittens, and wild flowers covered the hills. Molly found herself wanted and needed in the valley. She even attended school board meetings. There had been a time when those secret and august conferences were held behind closed doors, a mystery and a terror to everyone. Now that Molly was asked to step into John Whiteside's sitting room, she found that the board discussed crops, old stories, and circulated mild gossip.

Bert Munroe had been elected early in the fall, and by the springtime he was the most energetic member. He it was who planned dances at the schoolhouse, who insisted upon having plays and picnics. He even offered prizes for the best report cards in the school. The board was coming to rely pretty much on Bert Munroe.

One evening Molly came down late from her room. As always, when the board was meeting, Mrs. Whiteside sat in the dining room. "I don't think I'll go in to the meeting," Molly said. "Let them have one time to themselves. Sometimes I feel that they would tell other kinds of stories if I weren't there."

"You go on in, Molly! They can't hold a board meeting without you. They're so used to you, they'd be lost. Besides, I'm not at all sure I want them to tell those other stories."

Obediently Molly knocked on the door and went into the sitting room. Bert Munroe paused politely in the story he was narrating. "I was just telling about my new farm hand, Miss Morgan. I'll start over again, 'cause it's kind of funny. You see, I needed a hay hand, and I picked this fellow up under the Salinas River bridge. He was pretty drunk, but he wanted a job. Now I've got him, I find he isn't worth a cent as a hand, but I can't get rid of him. That son of a gun has been every place. You ought to hear him tell about the places he's been. My kids wouldn't let me get rid of him if I wanted to. Why he can take the littlest thing he's seen and make a fine story out of it. My kids just sit around with their ears spread, listening to him. Well, about twice a month he walks into Salinas and goes on a bust. He's one of those dirty, periodic drunks. The Salinas cops always call me up when they find him in a gutter, and I have to drive in to get him. And you know, when he comes out of it, he's always got some kind of present in his pocket for my kid Manny. There's nothing you can do with a man like that. He disarms you. I don't get a dollar's worth of work a month out of him."

Molly felt a sick dread rising in her. The men were laughing at the story. "You're too soft, Bert. You can't afford to keep an entertainer on the place. I'd sure get rid of him quick."

Molly stood up. She was dreadfully afraid someone would ask the man's name. "I'm not feeling very well tonight," she said. "If you gentlemen will excuse me, I think I'll go to bed." The men stood up while she left the room. In her bed she buried her head in the pillow. "It's crazy," she said to herself. "There isn't a chance in the world. I'm forgetting all about it right now." But she found to her dismay that she was crying.

The next few weeks were agonizing to Molly. She was reluctant to leave the house. Walking to and from school she watched the road ahead of her. "If I see any kind of a stranger I'll run away. But that's foolish. I'm being a fool." Only in her own room did she feel safe. Her terror was making her lose color, was taking the glint out of her eyes.

"Molly, you ought to go to bed," Mrs. Whiteside insisted. "Don't be a little idiot. Do I have to smack you the way I do Bill to make you go to bed?" But Molly would not go to bed. She thought too many things when she was in bed.

The next time the board met, Bert Munroe did not appear. Molly felt reassured and almost happy at his absence.

"You're feeling better, aren't you, Miss Morgan?"

"Oh, yes. It was only a little thing, a kind of a cold. If I'd gone to bed I might have been really sick."

The meeting was an hour gone before Bert Munroe came in. "Sorry to be late," he apologized. "The same old thing happened. My so-called hay hand was asleep in the street in Salinas. What a mess! He's out in the car sleeping it off now. I'll have to hose the car out tomorrow."

Molly's throat closed with terror. For a second she thought she was going to faint. "Excuse me, I must go," she cried, and ran out of the room. She walked into the dark hallway and steadied herself against the wall. Then slowly and automatically she marched out of the front door and down the steps. The night was filled with whispers. Out in the road she could see the black mass that was Bert Munroe's car. She was surprised at the way her footsteps plodded down the path of their own volition. "Now I'm killing myself," she said. "Now I'm throwing everything away. I wonder why." The gate was under her hand, and her hand flexed to open it. Then a tiny breeze sprang up and brought to her nose the sharp foulness of vomit. She heard a blubbering, drunken snore. Instantly

something whirled in her head. Molly spun around and ran frantically back to the house. In her room she locked the door and sat stiffly down, panting with the effort of her run. It seemed hours before she heard the men go out of the house, calling their good-nights. Then Bert's motor started, and the sound of it died away down the road. Now that she was ready to go she felt paralyzed.

John Whiteside was writing at his desk when Molly entered the sitting room. He looked up questioningly at her. "You aren't well, Miss Morgan. You need a doctor."

She planted herself woodenly beside the desk. "Could you get a substitute teacher for me?" she asked.

"Of course I could. You pile right into bed and I'll call a doctor."

"It isn't that, Mr. Whiteside. I want to go away tonight."

"What are you talking about? You aren't well."

"I told you my father was dead. I don't know whether he's dead or not. I'm afraid—I want to go away tonight."

He stared intently at her. "Tell me what you mean," he said softly.

"If I should see that drunken man of Mr. Munroe's—" she paused, suddenly terrified at what she was about to say.

John Whiteside nodded very slowly.

"No," she cried. "I don't think that. I'm sure I don't."

"I'd like to do something, Molly."

"I don't want to go, I love it here—But I'm afraid. It's so important to me."

John Whiteside stood up and came close to her and put his arm about her shoulders. "I don't think I understand, quite," he said. "I don't think I want to understand. That isn't necessary." He seemed to be talking to himself. "It wouldn't be quite courteous—to understand."

"Once I'm away I'll be able not to believe it," Molly whimpered.

He gave her shoulders one quick squeeze with his encircling arm. "You run upstairs and pack your things, Molly," he said. "I'll get out the car and drive you right in to Salinas now."

FOR UNDERSTANDING

1. Why is Molly Morgan being interviewed by John Whiteside? What does she tell him about her father? About her schooling?
2. In the evenings at Mrs. Morit's, what dream did Molly have about her father?
3. What remark does Bill make about her father that bothers her? What does he tell her about Vasquez that she doesn't want to hear?
4. In what ways is Bert Munroe's farmhand like her father?
5. How does Molly change after hearing about Bert Munroe's farmhand? Why does she ask Mr. Whiteside to get a substitute for her?

FOR INTERPRETATION

The romantic picture Molly has of her father contrasts sharply with her picture of her mother. Steinbeck, however, gives the reader insight into what her father's life really might have been like. Discuss what the reader might understand from the following lines:
1. Throughout the world George Morgan tramped . . . (p. 608)
2. Molly remembered how haggard and thin and gray her father's face was when he looked at the puppy. (p. 608)
3. These were the only times when his voice was sad and discouraged. (p. 609)

FOR APPRECIATION

Flashback

In order to acquaint the reader with the knowledge of Molly's childhood, so essential to understanding the way she feels about her father, Steinbeck makes use of the *flashback* technique. The flashback may be thought of as a scene inserted into a story, film, play, or narrative poem that shows events that happened at an earlier time. It is a method of presenting exposition more dramatically than straight chronological narration. The flashback is a device particularly useful in films and may utilize various approaches such as dream sequences, reverie, recollections of the characters, or narration by a character or characters.
1. What is the clause with which Steinbeck introduces the first flashback in the story?
2. What reasons are given for Molly's lack of love for her mother? Why doesn't she feel a closeness to her brothers? What did she tell a school friend about believing her father was dead?

Theme

According to what Steinbeck wrote his publishers in 1931, his theme in *The Pastures of Heaven* was to show the peculiar, evil cloud that followed a certain family—he called them the Munroes—as their lives touched the lives of other families living in what once had been called "happy valley" because of the unique harmony among its people.
1. Although our knowledge of what the Munroes are like is limited to the one Munroe in this story, what kind of man does Bert Munroe show himself to be: self-righteous and insensitive, or kindhearted and tolerant? Discuss.
2. Along with the curse theme that unites the ten stories in *The Pastures of Heaven,* an individual theme for "Molly Morgan" could be the contrast between dreams and reality. Does Steinbeck suggest by the story's ending that life without some romantic idealization is not worth living? Discuss.

COMPOSITION

Write three paragraphs, using a brief flashback. Devote your opening paragraph to a situation in the present, introducing the character who is to do the "remembering," and giving sufficient detail so that the reader understands what is taking place. You may write about yourself, using the first person, or use the third person and write about someone else.

In your second paragraph write the brief flashback. In your final paragraph bring your character back to the present, telling what effect the flashback has had on him or her.

Jesse Stuart

1907–1984

For nearly a half century Jesse Stuart has been one of America's most enduring local colorists. His stories and poems of the people of the eastern Kentucky mountains have won the admiration of many critics and readers. Although the life-styles of Stuart's characters may seem a bit strange to many readers, these fiercely independent, loyal, and family-centered people are basically like people everywhere. They either yield to life's difficulties or they fight to master them; and in the telling of their trials and triumphs, their joys and their sorrows, Jesse Stuart writes with a sure knowledge of the speech and folklore of his native hills.

Born near Riverton, Kentucky, Stuart attended local schools, worked his way through college, then taught in schools near his home. Although he has traveled extensively and spent time abroad, he has chosen to make his home near Greenup, just over the hills from where he was born. There he lives an active life writing, and supervising his farm. In addition to writing hundreds of poems and short stories, he has written such popular novels as *Trees of Heaven, Taps for Private Tussie,* and *Hie to the Hunters.* Both his prose and poetry have received many awards. Land—especially the possession of it—looms large in the lives of the people of the Kentucky hills, and it is the land and its people that are the raw material of Stuart's stories. Before reading the following autobiographical account, it is important to understand that the method of surveying land in frontier Kentucky was done by "metes and bounds," rather than by the rectangular, or rectilinear, method in which the land is marked off into townships. In the metes-and-bounds method the surveyor chose as

JESSE STUART IN HIS STUDY

a starting point a prominent tree, rock, or ridge outcropping and went on from there, using other similar landmarks to set the bounds of a property. This method, especially in forested or hilly terrain, left much to interpretation and error. Thus, a deed of land surveyed by metes and bounds would carry the stipulation that the property had a certain number of acres, "more or less."

TESTIMONY OF TREES

We had just moved onto the first farm we had ever owned when Jake Timmins walked down the path to the barn where Pa and I were nailing planks on a barn stall. Pa stood with a nail in one hand and his hatchet in the other while I stood holding the plank. We watched this small man with a beardy face walk toward us. He took short steps and jabbed his sharpened sourwood cane into the ground as he hurried down the path.

"Wonder what he's after?" Pa asked as Jake Timmins came near the barn.

"Don't know," I said.

"Howdy, Mick," Jake said as he leaned on his cane and looked over the new barn that we had built.

"Howdy, Jake," Pa grunted. We had heard how Jake Timmins had taken men's farms. Pa was nervous when he spoke, for I watched the hatchet shake in his hand.

"I see ye're a-putting improvements on yer barn," Jake said.

"A-tryin' to get it fixed for winter," Pa told him.

"I'd advise ye to stop now, Mick," he said. "Jist want to be fair with ye so ye won't go ahead and do a lot of work fer me fer nothing."

"How's that, Jake?" Pa asked.

"Ye've built yer barn on my land, Mick," he said with a little laugh.

"Ain't you a-joking, Jake?" Pa asked him.

"Nope, this is my land by rights," he told Pa as he looked our new barn over. "I hate to take this land with this fine barn on it, but it's mine and I'll haf to take it."

"I'm afraid not, Jake," Pa said. "I've been around here since I was a boy. I know where the lines run. I know that ledge of rocks with that row of oak trees a-growing on it is the line!"

"No it hain't, Mick," Jake said. "If it goes to court, ye'll find out. The line runs from that big dead chestnut up there on the knoll, straight across this holler to the top of the knoll up there where the twin hickories grow."

"But that takes my barn, my meadow, my garden," Pa said. "That takes ten acres of the best land I have. It almost gets my house!"

The hatchet quivered in Pa's hand and his lips trembled when he spoke.

"Tim Mennix sold ye land that belonged to me," Jake said.

"But you ought to a-said something about it before I built my house and barn on it," Pa told Jake fast as the words would leave his mouth.

"Sorry, Mick," Jake said, "but I must be a-going. I've given ye fair warning that ye air a-building on my land!"

"But I bought this land," Pa told him. "I'm a-goin' to keep it."

"I can't hep that," Jake told Pa as he turned to walk away. "Don't tear this barn down fer it's on my property!"

"Don't worry, Jake," Pa said. "I'm not a-tearing this barn down. I'll be a-feeding my cattle in it this winter!"

Jake Timmins walked slowly up the path the way he had come. Pa and I stood watching him as he stopped and looked our barn over; then he looked at our garden that we had fenced and he looked at the new house that we had built.

"I guess he'll be a-claiming the house too," Pa said.

And just as soon as Jake Timmins crossed

the ledge of rocks that separated our farms Pa threw his hatchet to the ground and hurried from the barn.

"Where are you a-going, Pa?" I asked.

"To see Tim Mennix."

"Can I go too?"

"Come along," he said.

We hurried over the mountain path toward Tim Mennix's shack. He lived two miles from us. Pa's brogan shoes* rustled the fallen leaves that covered the path. October wind moaned among the leafless treetops. Soon as we reached the shack we found Tim cutting wood near his woodshed.

"What's the hurry, Mick?" Tim asked Pa who stood wiping sweat from his October-leaf-colored face with his blue bandanna.

"Jake Timmins is a-tryin' to take my land," Pa told Tim.

"Ye don't mean it?"

"I do mean it," Pa said. "He's just been to see me and he said the land where my barn, garden, and meadow were belonged to him. Claims about ten acres of the best land I got. I told him I bought it from you and he said it didn't belong to you to sell."

"That ledge of rocks and the big oak trees that grow along the backbone of the ledge has been the line fer seventy years," Tim said. "But lissen, Mick, when Jake Timmins wants a piece of land, he takes it."

"People told me he's like that," Pa said. "I was warned against buying my farm because he's like that. People said he'd steal all my land if I lived beside him ten years."

"He'll have it before then, Mick," Tim Mennix told Pa in a trembling voice. "He didn't have but an acre to start from. That acre was a bluff where three farms jined and no one fenced it in because it was worthless and they didn't want it. He had a deed made fer this acre and he's had forty lawsuits when he set his fence over on other people's farms and took their land, but he goes to court and wins every time."

"I'll have the County Surveyor, Finn Madden, to survey my lines," Pa said.

"That won't hep any," Tim told Pa. "There's been more people kilt over the line fences that he's surveyed than has been kilt over any other one thing in this county. Surveyor Finn Madden's a good friend to Jake."

"But he's the County Surveyor," Pa said. "I'll haf to have him."

"Jake Timmins is a dangerous man," Tim Mennix warned Pa. "He's dangerous as a loaded double-barrel shotgun with both hammers cocked."

"I've heard that," Pa said. "I don't want any trouble. I'm a married man with a family."

When we reached home, we saw Jake upon the knoll at the big chestnut tree sighting across the hollow to the twin hickories on the knoll above our house. And as he sighted across the hollow, he walked along and drove stakes into the ground. He set one stake in our front yard, about five feet from the corner of our house. Pa started out on him once but Mom wouldn't let him go. Mom said let the law settle the dispute over the land.

And that night Pa couldn't go to sleep. I was awake and heard him a-walking the floor when the clock struck twelve. I knew that Pa was worried, for Jake was the most feared man among our hills. He had started with one acre and now had over four hundred.

Next day Surveyor Finn Madden and Jake ran a line across the hollow just about on the same line that Jake had surveyed with his own eyes. And while Surveyor Finn Madden looked through the instrument, he had Jake set the stakes and drive them into the ground with a poleax. They worked at the line all day. And when they had finished surveying the line, Pa went up on the knoll at the twin hick-

*brogan shoes, coarse leather work shoes.

ories behind our house and asked Surveyor Finn Madden if his line was right.

"Surveyed it right with the deed," he told Pa. "Tim Mennix sold you land that didn't belong to him."

"Looks like this line would've been surveyed before I built my barn," Pa said.

"Can't see why it wasn't," he told Pa. "Looks like you're a-losing the best part of your farm, Mick."

Then Surveyor Finn Madden, a tall man with a white beard, and Jake Timmins went down the hill together.

"I'm not so sure that I'm a-losing the best part of my farm," Pa said. "I'm not a-goin' to sit down and take it! I know Jake's a land thief and it's time his stealing land is stopped."

"What are you a-goin' to do, Pa?" I asked.

"Don't know," he said.

"You're not a-goin' to hurt Jake over the land, are you?"

He didn't say anything but he looked at the two men as they turned over the ledge of rocks and out of sight.

"You know Mom said the land wasn't worth hurting anybody over," I said.

"But it's my land," Pa said.

And that night Pa walked the floor. And Mom got out of bed and talked to him and made him go to bed. And that day Sheriff Eif Whiteapple served a notice on Pa to keep his cattle out of the barn that we had built. The notice said that the barn belonged to Jake Timmins. Jake ordered us to put our chickens up, to keep them off his garden when it was our garden. He told us not to let anything trespass on his land and his land was on the other side of the stakes. We couldn't even walk in part of our yard.

"He'll have the house next if we don't do something about it," Pa said.

Pa walked around our house in a deep study. He was trying to think of something to do about it. Mom talked to him. She told him to get a lawyer and fight the case in court. But

Pa said something had to be done to prove that the land belonged to us, though we had a deed for our land in our trunk. And before Sunday came, Pa dressed in his best clothes.

"Where're you a-going, Mick?" Mom asked.

"A-goin' to see Uncle Mel," he said. "He's been in a lot of line-fence fights and he could give me some good advice!"

"We hate to stay here and you gone, Mick," Mom said.

"Just don't step on property Jake laid claim to until I get back," Pa said. "I'll be back soon as I can. Some time next week you can look for me."

Pa went to West Virginia to get Uncle Mel. And while he was gone, Jake Timmins hauled wagonloads of hay and corn to the barn that we had built. He had taken over as if it were his own and as if he would always have it. We didn't step beyond the stakes where Surveyor Finn Madden had surveyed. We waited for Pa to come. And when Pa came, Uncle Mel came with him carrying a long-handled double-bitted ax and a turkey of clothes across his shoulder. Before they reached the house, Pa showed Uncle Mel the land Jake Timmins had taken.

"Land hogs air pizen as copperhead snakes," Uncle Mel said, then he fondled his long white beard in his hand. Uncle Mel was eighty-two years old, but his eyes were keen as sharp-pointed briers and his shoulders were broad and his hands were big and rough. He had been a timber cutter all his days and he was still a-cuttin' timber in West Virginia at the age of eighty-two. "He can't do this to ye, Mick!"

Uncle Mel was madder than Pa when he looked over the new line that they had surveyed from the dead chestnut on one knoll to the twin hickories on the other knoll.

"Anybody would know the line wouldn't go like that," Uncle Mel said. "The line would follow the ridge."

"Looks that way to me too," Pa said.

"He's a-stealin' yer land, Mick," Uncle Mel said. "I'll hep ye get yer land back. He'll never beat me. I've had to fight too many squatters a-tryin' to take my land. I know how to fight 'em with the law."

That night Pa and Uncle Mel sat before the fire and Uncle Mel looked over Pa's deed. Uncle Mel couldn't read very well and when he came to a word he couldn't read, I told him what it was.

"We'll haf to have a court order first, Mick," Uncle Mel said. "When we get the court order, I'll find the line."

I didn't know what Uncle Mel wanted with a court order, but I found out after he got it. He couldn't chop on a line tree until he got an order from the court. And soon as Pa got the court order and gathered a group of men for witnesses, Uncle Mel started work on the line fence.

"Sixteen rods from the dead chestnut due north," Uncle Mel said, and we started measuring sixteen rods due north.

"That's the oak tree, there," Uncle Mel said. It measured exactly sixteen rods from the dead chestnut to the black oak tree.

"Deed said the oak was blazed," Uncle Mel said, for he'd gone over the deed until he'd memorized it.

"See the scar, men," Uncle Mel said.

"But that was done seventy years ago," Pa said.

"Funny about the testimony of trees," Uncle Mel told Pa, Tim Mennix, Orbie Dorton, and Dave Sperry. "The scar will allus stay on the outside of a tree well as on the inside. The silent trees will keep their secrets."

Uncle Mel started chopping into the tree. He swung his ax over his shoulder and bit out a slice of wood every time he struck. He cut a neat block into the tree until he found a dark place deep inside the tree.

"Come, men, and look," Uncle Mel said. "Look at that scar. It's as pretty a scar as I ever seen in the heart of a tree!"

And while Uncle Mel wiped sweat with his blue bandanna from his white beard, we looked at the scar.

"It's a scar, all right," Tim Mennix said, since he had been a timber cutter most of his life and knew a scar on a tree.

"Think that was cut seventy years ago," Orbie Dorton said. "That's when the deed was made and the old survey was run."

"We'll see if it's been seventy years ago," Uncle Mel said as he started counting the rings in the tree. "Each ring is a year's growth."

We watched Uncle Mel pull his knife from his pocket, open the blade, and touch each ring with his knife-blade point as he counted the rings across the square he had chopped into the tree. Uncle Mel counted exactly seventy rings from the bark to the scar.

"Ain't it the line tree, boys?" Uncle Mel asked.

"Can't be anything else," Dave Sperry said.

And then Uncle Mel read the deed, which called for a mulberry thirteen rods due north from the black oak. We measured to the mulberry and Uncle Mel cut his notch to the scar and counted the rings. It was seventy rings from the bark to the scar. Ten more rods we came to the poplar the deed called for, and he found the scar on the outer bark and inside the tree. We found every tree the deed called for but one, and we found its stump. We surveyed the land from the dead chestnut to the twin hickories. We followed it around the ledge.

"We have the evidence to take to court," Uncle Mel said. "I'd like to bring the jurymen right here to this line fence to show 'em."

"I'll go right to town and put this thing in court," Pa said.

"I'll go around and see the men that have lost land to Jake Timmins," Uncle Mel said. "I want 'em to be at the trial."

Before our case got to court, Uncle Mel had shown seven of our neighbors how to trace their lines and get their land back from Jake Timmins. And when our trial was called, the courthouse was filled with people who had lost land and who had disputes with their neighbors over line fences, attending the trial to see if we won. Jake Timmins, Surveyor Finn Madden, and their lawyer, Henson Stapleton, had produced their side of the question before the jurors and we had lawyer Sherman Stone and our witnesses to present our side, while all the landowners Jake Tim-

mins had stolen land from listened to the trial. The foreman of the jury asked that the members of the jury be taken to the line fence.

"Now here's the way to tell where a line was blazed on saplings seventy years ago," Uncle Mel said, as he showed them the inner mark on the line oak; then he showed them the outward scar. Uncle Mel took them along the line fence and showed them each tree that the deed called for, all but the one that had fallen.

"It's plain as the nose on your face," Uncle Mel would say every time he explained each line tree. "Too many land thieves in this county and a county surveyor the devil won't have in hell."

After Uncle Mel had explained the line fence to the jurors, they followed Sheriff Whiteapple and his deputies back to the courtroom. Pa went with them to get the decision. Uncle Mel waited at our house for Pa to return.

"That land will belong to Mick," Uncle Mel told us. "And the hay and corn in that barn will belong to him."

When Pa came home, there was a smile on his face.

"It's yer land, ain't it, Mick?" Uncle Mel asked.

"It's still my land," Pa said, "and sixteen men are now filing suits to recover their land. Jake Timmins won't have but an acre left."

"Remember the hay and corn he put in yer barn is yourn," Uncle Mel said.

Uncle Mel got up from his chair, stretched his arms. Then he said, "I must be back on my way to West Virginia."

"Can't you stay longer with us, Uncle Mel?" Pa said.

"I must be a-gettin' back to cut timber," he said. "If ye have any more land troubles, write me."

We tried to get Uncle Mel to stay longer. But he wouldn't stay. He left with his turkey of clothes and his long-handled, double-bitted ax across his shoulder. We waved good-by to him as he walked slowly down the path and out of sight on his way to West Virginia.

FOR UNDERSTANDING

1. What new building does Timmins claim belongs to him because it is on "his" land?
2. Who restrains Mick Stuart when he wants to do violence to Timmins? How much land did Timmins originally have?
3. What county official is aiding Timmins in his land grabs?
4. What method does Uncle Mel use to get the evidence that defeats Timmins in court?
5. What happens to Timmins after he loses the court case?

FOR INTERPRETATION

1. Why would the hay and corn Timmins had stored in the barn now belong to Mick Stuart?
2. Why is this ironic?

FOR APPRECIATION

Creating Tension

Like other good writers, Stuart builds tension and suggests conflict to come through the use of seemingly unimportant details. For example, if Jake Timmins were a friendly neighbor, would Mick Stuart stand with a hatchet poised in one hand and a nail in the other while he and his son both watch the approach of Timmins? Probably not. They would very likely go ahead with their work. But in this instance their close watchfulness suggests rising tension.

1. The reader is also alerted to the coming conflict through the unanswerable question Mick asks Jesse: "Wonder what he's after?" How does the phrasing of this question signal to the reader that Jake's presence means trouble?
2. According to Jesse, what visible signs of nervousness does his father exhibit as he holds the hatchet and answers Jake's claims?

LANGUAGE AND VOCABULARY

Usage levels fall into two broad classifications: standard and nonstandard. Standard usage includes *formal* or *literary* (spoken and written communication for a select educated group) and *informal* (speech and writing used in personal, casual situations, including regionalisms and slang words, as well as more liberal grammar). Generally we classify written work according to the appropriateness of usage, diction, and types of sentences. But when we come to informal speech, we are confronted with numerous dialects.

Study carefully "Testimony of Trees," listing variants in pronunciation, vocabulary, and grammar. Again, be careful about judging a pronunciation such as "git" for the word *get,* or "jist" for the word *just* as nonstandard. Both occur in the speech of educated people. Many Britons, for example, pronounce *ate* "et." Review your lists for examples of nonstandard usages and then for standard but regional variants.

Richard Wright

1908–1960

When Richard Wright was five years old his sharecropper father abandoned his family in Natchez, Mississippi. His mother, who soon became paralyzed and was unable to care for Richard and his younger brother, was forced to place the boys in an orphanage. Later they were shunted from one relative to another. During this period and for several years thereafter, Richard Wright knew a life of extreme poverty, hunger, fear, and violence. At nineteen, by working a series of odd jobs, he was finally able to make his way from Memphis to Chicago, then to New York. Already he was writing essays, stories, and autobiographical sketches that depicted the life at that time of black people in both the South and the North. It is small wonder that much of his writing, starkly naturalistic in method and based on his own experiences, expresses a psychology of alienation.

In 1940 Wright published his first novel, *Native Son,* a brutally powerful story of a young man raised in the so-called Black Belt slums of Chicago. The book was an immediate best seller and Wright was quickly recognized not only as a talented new voice in American letters, but also as the foremost interpreter of black life in the United States. He also emerged as a hero to younger black writers. Other stories, novels,

PORTRAIT OF RICHARD WRIGHT

essays, film scripts, and his autobiography, *Black Boy* (1945), soon followed. Invited by the French government to visit France, Wright spent the last thirteen years of his life there.

A sharecropper was a farmer who shared a crop with a plantation owner, the owner being paid a percentage of the crop (Wright's father paid fifty percent) as a return for things furnished the sharecropper, such as a cabin, seeds, tools, and so on. The money from the rest of the crop belonged to the farmer.

What often happened, however, was that sharecroppers already owed the owner more than their share was worth because they had bought food and other supplies on credit while their crops were growing. The fact that the records of such dealings were kept by the plantation owner, plus the fact that the sharecroppers were often illiterate, made cheating a fairly common practice. Even when they had a good crop, then, the sharecroppers often owed more than they earned. When the crop was poor or wiped out by a natural disaster, the poor really got poorer.

Until he was five, Richard Wright and his family lived in a sharecropper's shack that was much like the one he describes in the following story. Originally entitled "Silt" and published in 1937, the story (which begins on the next page) was given its present title and republished posthumously in the collection, Eight Men *(1961).*

THE MAN WHO SAW THE FLOOD

*When the flood waters recede,
the poor folk along the river
start from scratch.*

At last the flood waters had receded. A black father, a black mother, and a black child tramped through muddy fields, leading a tired cow by a thin bit of rope. They stopped on a hilltop and shifted the bundles on their shoulders. As far as they could see the ground was covered with flood silt. The little girl lifted a skinny finger and pointed to a mud-caked cabin.

"Look, Pa! Ain tha our home?"

The man, round-shouldered, clad in blue, ragged overalls, looked with bewildered eyes. Without moving a muscle, scarcely moving his lips, he said: "Yeah."

For five minutes they did not speak or move. The flood waters had been more than eight feet high here. Every tree, blade of grass, and stray stick had its flood mark: caky, yellow mud. It clung to the ground, cracking thinly here and there in spider web fashion. Over the stark fields came a gusty spring wind. The sky was high, blue, full of white clouds and sunshine. Over all hung a first-day strangeness.

"The henhouse is gone," sighed the woman.

"N the pigpen," sighed the man.

They spoke without bitterness.

"Ah reckon them chickens is all done drowned."

"Yeah."

"Miz Flora's house is gone, too," said the little girl.

They looked at a clump of trees where their neighbor's house had stood.

"Lawd!"

"Yuh reckon anybody knows where they is?"

"Hard t tell."

The man walked down the slope and stood uncertainly.

"There wuz a road erlong here somewheres," he said.

But there was no road now. Just a wide sweep of yellow, scalloped silt.

"Look, Tom!" called the woman. "Here's a piece of our gate!"

The gatepost was half buried in the ground. A rusty hinge stood stiff, like a lonely finger. Tom pried it loose and caught it firmly in his hand. There was nothing particular he wanted to do with it; he just stood holding it firmly. Finally he dropped it, looked up, and said:

"C mon. Les go down n see whut we kin do."

Because it sat in a slight depression, the ground about the cabin was soft and slimy.

"Gimme tha bag o lime, May," he said.

With his shoes sucking in mud, he went slowly around the cabin, spreading the white lime with thick fingers. When he reached the front again he had a little left; he shook the bag out on the porch. The fine grains of floating lime flickered in the sunlight.

"Tha oughta hep some," he said.

"Now, yuh be careful, Sal!" said May. "Don yuh go n fall down in all this mud, yuh hear?"

"Yessum."

The steps were gone. Tom lifted May and Sally to the porch. They stood a moment looking at the half-opened door. He had shut it when he left, but somehow it seemed natural that he should find it open. The planks in the porch floor were swollen and warped. The cabin had two colors; near the bottom it was a solid yellow; at the top it was the familiar gray. It looked weird, as though its ghost were standing beside it.

The cow lowed.

"Tie Pat t the pos on the en of the porch, May."

May tied the rope slowly, listlessly. When they attempted to open the front door, it would not budge. It was not until Tom placed his shoulder against it and gave it a stout shove that it scraped back jerkily. The front room was dark and silent. The damp smell of flood silt came fresh and sharp to their nostrils. Only one-half of the upper window was clear, and through it fell a rectangle of dingy light. The floors swam in ooze. Like a mute warning, a wavering flood mark went high around the walls of the room. A dresser sat cater-cornered, its drawers and sides bulging like a bloated corpse. The bed, with the mattress still on it, was like a giant casket forged of mud. Two smashed chairs lay in a corner, as though huddled together for protection.

"Les see the kitchen," said Tom.

The stovepipe was gone. But the stove stood in the same place.

"The stove's still good. We kin clean it."

"Yeah."

"But where's the table?"

"Lawd knows."

"It must've washed erway wid the rest of the stuff, Ah reckon."

They opened the back door and looked out. They missed the barn, the henhouse, and the pigpen.

"Tom, yuh bettah try tha ol pump n see ef eny watah's there."

The pump was stiff. Tom threw his weight on the handle and carried it up and down. No water came. He pumped on. There was a dry, hollow cough. The yellow water trickled. He caught his breath and kept pumping. The water flowed white.

"Thank Gawd! We's got some watah."

"Yuh bettah boil it fo yuh use it," he said.

"Yeah. Ah know."

"Look, Pa! Here's yo ax," called Sally.

Tom took the ax from her. "Yeah. Ah'll need this."

"N here's somethin else," called Sally, digging spoons out of the mud.

"Waal, Ahma git a bucket n start cleanin," said May. "Ain no use in waitin, cause we's gotta sleep on them floors tonight."

When she was filling the bucket from the pump, Tom called from around the cabin. "May, look! Ah done foun mah plow!" Proudly he dragged the silt-caked plow to the pump. "Ah'll wash it n it'll be awright."

"Ahm hongry," said Sally.

"Now, yuh jus wait! Yuh et this mawnin," said May. She turned to Tom. "Now, whutcha gonna do, Tom?"

He stood looking at the mud-filled fields.

"Yuh goin back t Burgess?"

"Ah reckon Ah have to."

"Whut else kin yuh do?"

"Nothin," he said. "Lawd, but Ah sho hate t start all over wid tha white man. Ah'd leave here ef Ah could. Ah owes im nigh eight hundred dollahs. N we need a hoss, grub, seed, n a lot mo other things. Ef we keeps on like this tha white man'll own us body n soul."

"But, Tom, there ain nothin else t do," she said.

"Ef we try t run erway they'll put us in jail."

"It coulda been worse," she said.

Sally came running from the kitchen. "Pa!"

"Hunh?"

"There's a shelf in the kitchen the flood didn git!"

"Where?"

"Right up over the stove."

"But, chile, ain nothin up there," said May.

"But there's somethin on it," said Sally.

"C mon. Les see."

High and dry, untouched by the flood-water, was a box of matches. And beside it a half-full sack of Bull Durham tobacco. He took a match from the box and scratched it on his overalls. It burned to his fingers before he dropped it.

"May!"

"Hunh?"

"Look! Here's ma bacco n some match-es!"

She stared unbelievingly. "Lawd!" she breathed.

Tom rolled a cigarette clumsily.

May washed the stove, gathered some sticks, and after some difficulty, made a fire. The kitchen stove smoked, and their eyes smarted. May put water on to heat and went into the front room. It was getting dark. From the bundles they took a kerosene lamp and lit it. Outside Pat lowed longingly into the thickening gloam and tinkled her cowbell.

"That old cow's hongry," said May.

"Ah reckon Ah'll have t be gittin erlong t Burgess."

They stood on the front porch.

"Yuh bettah git on, Tom, fo it gits too dark."

"Yeah."

The wind had stopped blowing. In the east a cluster of stars hung.

"Yuh goin, Tom?"

"Ah reckon Ah have t."

"Ma, Ah'm hongry," said Sally.

"Wait erwhile, honey. Ma knows yuh's hongry."

Tom threw his cigarette away and sighed.

"Look! Here comes somebody!"

"Thas Mistah Burgess now!"

A mud-caked buggy rolled up. The shaggy horse was splattered all over. Burgess leaned his white face out of the buggy and spat.

"Well, I see you're back."

"Yessuh."

"How things look?"

"They don look so good, Mistah."

"What seems to be the trouble?"

"Waal. Ah ain got no hoss, no grub, noth-in. The only thing Ah got is that ol cow there . . ."

"You owe eight hundred dollahs down at the store, Tom."

"Yessuh, Ah know. But, Mistah Burgess, can't yuh knock somethin off of tha, seein as how Ahm down n out now?"

"You ate that grub, and I got to pay for it, Tom."

"Yessuh, Ah know."

"It's going to be a little tough, Tom. But you got to go through with it. Two of the boys tried to run away this morning and dodge their debts, and I had to have the sheriff pick em up. I wasn't looking for no trouble out of you, Tom . . . The rest of the families are going back."

Leaning out of the buggy, Burgess wait-ed. In the surrounding stillness the cowbell tinkled again. Tom stood with his back against a post.

"Yuh got t go on, Tom. We ain't got noth-in here," said May.

Tom looked at Burgess.

"Mistah Burgess, Ah don wanna make no trouble. But this is jus *too* hard. Ahm worse off now than befo. Ah got to start from scratch."

"Get in the buggy and come with me. I'll stake you with grub. We can talk over how you can pay it back." Tom said nothing. He rested his back against the post and looked at the mud-filled fields.

"Well," asked Burgess. "You coming?" Tom said nothing. He got slowly to the ground and pulled himself into the buggy. May watched them drive off.

"Hurry back, Tom!"

"Awright."

"Ma, tell Pa t bring me some 'lasses," begged Sally.

"Oh, Tom!"

Known for many years as the dean of black American painters,
Scott was also a distinguished illustrator and muralist.

CABINS, William E. Scott
Barnett-Aden Collection
Anacostia Neighborhood Museum, Washington, D.C.

Tom's head came out of the side of the buggy.

"Hunh?"

"Bring some 'lasses!"

"Hunh?"

"Bring some 'lasses for Sal!"

"Awright!"

She watched the buggy disappear over the crest of the muddy hill. Then she sighed, caught Sally's hand, and turned back into the cabin.

FOR UNDERSTANDING

1. What does Tom spread around the outside of their cabin when they first arrive?

2. Why does the cabin now appear in two colors?

3. How does Tom get water? What will they do to the water before using it?

4. Why is Tom so depressed when his wife asks if he is going to see Burgess?

5. What does Burgess tell Tom he has done about the two men who tried to run away and "dodge their debts"?

FOR INTERPRETATION

1. In calling the main character of the story "Tom," Richard Wright is suggesting that the father is a submissive black person, an "Uncle Tom." Discuss.

2. Although the specific situation portrayed here may be rarer today than it was in Wright's time, it is still common for unscrupulous people to cheat the poor. The slum landlord is a case in point. Discuss.

FOR APPRECIATION

Intention and Theme

In judging the writer's intended theme for a story, it is often a good idea to look very closely at the end of the work. Something very curious happens at the end of this story, as you can see from the following quoted portion:

> "Ma, tell Pa t bring me some 'lasses,"
> begged Sally.
> "Oh, Tom!"
> Tom's head came out of the side of the buggy.
> "Hunh?"
> "Bring some 'lasses!"
> "Hunh?"
> "Bring some 'lasses for Sal!"

What reason or reasons might the author have had for repeating the word " 'lasses" (molasses) three times in seven lines in this important position in the story?

Another interesting fact is that the story ends with reference to the mother and daughter, thus giving a certain emphasis to them rather than to the sharecropper or the plantation owner. What effect does this have on your understanding of the theme of the story?

LANGUAGE AND VOCABULARY

A. A writer chooses words carefully. Choose from the given synonyms the one which you feel is most effective.

1. The bed, with the mattress still on it, was like a giant casket _____ of mud. (a) made (b) forged (c) constructed (d) fabricated

2. The fine grains of floating lime _____ in the sunlight. (a) flickered (b) flared (c) gleamed d) sparkled

3. The planks in the porch floor were _____ and warped. (a) swollen (b) distended (c) bloated (d) bulgy

4. Like a mute warning, a(n) _____ flood mark went high around the walls of the room. (a) uneven (b) oscillating (c) wavering (d) fluctuating

5. Two smashed chairs lay in a corner, as though _____ together for protection. (a) bunched b) grouped (c) arranged (d) huddled

B. The sounds of words, besides pleasing the ear, can also help to convey meaning. The clearest instance of this is the figure of speech known as *onomatopoeia*, which refers to a word whose sound resembles the thing or action denoted by words: *buzz, clang, jangle, rustling, bubbling,* and so on. For each of the following sentences, identify the onomatopoetic words; suggest other onomatopoetic words that could be substituted for them.

1. He took a match from the box and scratched it on his overalls.

2. The yellow water trickled.

3. In the surrounding stillness the cowbell tinkled again.

4. With his shoes sucking in mud, he went slowly around the cabin, spreading the white lime with thick fingers.

5. It was not until Tom placed his shoulder against the door and gave it a stout shove that it scraped back jerkily.

MODERN POETRY

One cannot say precisely when modern poetry began. It is difficult to isolate trends and schools that include more than a handful of poets as our early modern poets were extremely individualistic. However, most of the major poets wrote what both they and their critics referred to as the "New Poetry."

THE NEW POETRY

What has been called the New Poetry movement was well established by 1914. Essentially, the movement was an attempt by certain younger poets to say what they felt, not what they were expected to feel; to report what they saw and heard, not what they were expected to see and hear. To make their poetry new, they sought fresh and free-wheeling modes of expression and in the process proclaimed a revolution in poetic rhetoric—weary and trite verse was rejected in favor of precision and definition.

In 1912 Harriet Monroe, an editor and poet committed to publishing only innovative verse, provided considerable impetus to the movement when she established *Poetry: A Magazine of Verse.* The Chicago publication soon became the most influential poetry journal in the English-speaking world, and remained so for nearly a quarter century. Among the fledgling writers Miss Monroe published who were to become major modern poets were Carl Sandburg (see page 657), Vachel Lindsay (1879–1931), Edgar Lee Masters (see page 639), Robert Frost (see page 644), and T. S. Eliot (see page 670). Ezra Pound (1885–1972), an expatriate American poet living in London, was both a contributor to the magazine and the editor of its London edition.

One of the more individualistic of the modern poets was Wallace Stevens (1879–1955). A lawyer and vice president of an insurance firm, he did not fit the typical image of a poet. Stevens wrote in the symbolist tradition. (Symbolists use clustered images and metaphors that suggest or symbolize the basic idea or emotion the poet tries to convey.) His work, though difficult to interpret, has been judged by some critics to be among the best written by a modern American poet.

One of America's finest early modern poets was Edwin Arlington Robinson (see page 633). Not a member of any movement, he was modern in outlook, though he always used the poetic forms of the past.

Most writers of verse in the early modern period still hewed rather closely to traditional poetic forms and the treatment of "acceptable" subject matter, principally because both they and the majority of their American readers had been conditioned to accept as poetry only rhymed verse. Thus the "free verse" advocated by the new poets, together with their treatment of subjects that had once been considered unfit for poetic expression, were for several years rejected by critics, poets, and a large segment of the reading public. The poetic rebels, however, led by such formidable champions as Amy Lowell (see page 642), looked back for inspiration to nineteenth-century innovators like Walt Whitman and Stephen Crane or to contemporaries, like the Imagists in England. Eventually they made the writing and the reading of modern poetry, particularly free verse, "respectable."

THE CHICAGO GROUP

Carl Sandburg and Vachel Lindsay were members of the so-called Chicago Group—writers living in and around that city and largely devoted to writing about the Midwest. Others in the group were Theodore Dreiser and Sherwood Anderson. Initially encouraged and published by Harriet Monroe, Sandburg and Lindsay soon acquired national reputations. They had, however, little in common. Stylistically, Sandburg was a descendant of Whitman and shared Whitman's and Lincoln's faith in the people. Lindsay is best known for rhythmic poems like "General William Booth Enters into Heaven." Both became known as popular "yea-sayers" because they sought to communicate the vim, vigor, and vitality of American life.

THE IMAGISTS

Originally, the Imagists were expatriate Americans living either in London or Paris. At one time or another the group included Hilda Doolittle, who signed her work H. D. (1886–1961); Ezra Pound; Amy Lowell; and William Carlos Williams (see page 663), among others. (Williams later charged that imagistic poetry lacked structure, while Pound, the eccentric and irascible early leader of the group, left his disciples after Amy Lowell arrived and asserted her leadership. Pound later joked that the movement had been reduced to "Amygism.") The group name, *les Imagistes,* comes from their belief that poets must present firm, concrete images, not vague generalities. They rejected conventionalized romanticism, insisted on freedom of choice of subject matter, advocated the use of free verse, and stressed simple sincerity, intensity, and the language of contemporary speech when it was called for. One of the most concise and striking examples of imagistic poetry is Pound's famous two-line verse:

IN A STATION OF THE METRO*

The apparition of these faces in the crowd;
Petals on a wet, black bough.

*From *Personae* by Ezra Pound. ©1926 by Ezra Pound. Reprint permission of New Directions Publishing Corp.

The "rightness" of the images both surprises and delights the reader. The pale faces of persons emerging from a darkened subway *do* look like petals on a dark bough.

The Imagists rose to prominence for a short period in the second decade of the century and have left their mark on a good deal of both modern and contemporary verse.

IMPORTANT MODERNS

Undoubtedly the central poetic figures of the modern period were Robert Frost and T. S. Eliot. Through his long career Frost published many of the best and most popular poems written by an American. Eliot, in contrast, has never been a broadly popular poet, essentially because his work is admittedly difficult. There is, however, no question of his deep influence on American poets and critics.

Two other important modern poets were Edna St. Vincent Millay (see page 678) and Robinson Jeffers (see page 668). Millay's "Renascence" is perhaps her best-known verse. Although she has been criticized by some who prefer a more intellectual style of poetry, at her best she had a fine feel for nature and wrote some excellent lyrics. Jeffers considered himself a recorder of social decay and commented on the decadence of American society from his hilltop retreat near Carmel, California.

In this period, three of our best-known experimental poets who belonged to no particular school or movement were Edgar Lee Masters, Archibald MacLeish (see page 683), and e. e. cummings (see page 687). Masters successfully shaped the epitaph form of verse into his masterpiece, *Spoon River Anthology*. MacLeish, in his long and honored literary career, experimented successfully with both short and long verse forms as well as verse drama. It was MacLeish who concluded his instructive poem, "Ars Poetica" (1926), by asserting "A poem should not mean / But be." For years this poem was considered the most concise statement of what the Imagists believed. The innovative e. e. cummings worked at creating a new poetic convention of writing in lower case as well as using a new ordering of language that has both puzzled and delighted his readers. An example is his quiet affirmation that spring is a time "when the world is mud-luscious" and "puddle-wonderful."

THE FUGITIVES

Another group of poets whose poetic and critical contributions were to have a major impact during the first half of this century were the so-called Fugitives. Centered at Vanderbilt University, the group was led by three Southerners: John Crowe Ransom (see page 674), Robert Penn Warren (1905–   ), and Allen Tate (1899–1979). Although the three responded differently to the influence of T. S. Eliot and Ezra

Pound, and developed highly individual styles of their own, they were united in their determination to break from traditional poetic stances and methods. *The Fugitive,* the influential literary magazine they founded at Vanderbilt, was followed by the equally well-known *Sewanee Review* (founded by Allen Tate) and *Kenyon Review* (founded by John Crowe Ransom).

THE HARLEM RENAISSANCE

Among the fine black poets who figured prominently in what has been called New York's Harlem Renaissance, or Harlem Awakening, were Langston Hughes (see page 690), Claude McKay (see page 676), Countee Cullen (see page 693), Jean Toomer (1894–1967), and Arna Bontemps (1902–1973). Not only was there an "awakening" among black poets, but also among black novelists, painters, dancers, musicians, dramatists, and scholars. Basically, the aim of these men and women was two-fold: first, to remind the nation of the talents of its black artists; and second, to reveal what it meant to be black in America.

Arna Bontemps, in the introduction to his popular *American Negro Poetry*, writes of the group's concerns as follows:

> In those days a good many of the New York group went to "The Dark Tower" on 136th Street, a sort of club room maintained for them by one of their fans, to weep because they felt an injustice in the critics' insistence upon calling them *Negro* poets instead of poets. This attitude was particularly displeasing to Countee Cullen. But a few of his associates were not sure this was bad. Three decades later, considering the isolation of so many contemporary poets (including some Negroes) and their private language—well, they were still wondering. But it can be fairly said that most Negro poets in the United States remain near enough to their folk origins to prefer a certain simplicity of expression.*

The poetry of Margaret Walker (see page 697) eloquently illustrates Bontemps's assertion. One of the many fine black poets to emerge after the Harlem Renaissance, she makes skillful use of both traditional and free-verse forms to explore and celebrate the black experience in America.

*American Negro Poetry, edited by Arna Bontemps. New York: Hill and Wang. ©1963 by Arna Bontemps.

Edwin Arlington Robinson   1869–1935

At the age of eleven, Edwin Arlington Robinson decided to devote his life to writing poetry. He grew up in Gardiner, Maine (the "Tilbury Town" of his poems), studied at Harvard until straitened family circumstances forced his withdrawal, then barely supported himself at odd jobs as he wrote his first volume of poems, *The Torrent and the Night Before* (1896). Although the book attracted little attention, his second, *The Children of the Night* (1897), so impressed Theodore Roosevelt that he secured the poet a minor post in the New York customs house where he worked for four years.

In 1910 Robinson was invited to live at the MacDowell Colony in Peterborough, New Hampshire, and he spent most of the rest of his life under the patronage of this endowed colony for artists. Thus enabled to devote full time to writing, he produced his first critically admired volume of short poems, *The Man Against the Sky* (1916). More volumes followed and in the 1920s Robinson was considered our most accomplished living poet. In that decade he was awarded three Pulitzer Prizes for his poetry.

The following three poems exemplify the poet's sometimes wryly humorous but more often dark and sardonic view of life. The characters in these poems have no one with whom to share their burdens. They are alone, tragically alienated from the community. As you read, try to decide who is responsible for this alienation—the individuals, society, or both?

PORTRAIT OF EDWIN ARLINGTON ROBINSON
Richard Hood
National Portrait Gallery, Smithsonian Institution

Miniver Cheevy

Miniver Cheevy, child of scorn,
    Grew lean while he assailed the seasons;
He wept that he was ever born,
    And he had reasons.

Miniver loved the days of old   5
  When swords were bright and steeds were prancing;
The vision of a warrior bold
  Would set him dancing.

Miniver sighed for what was not,
  And dreamed, and rested from his labors;   10
He dreamed of Thebes[1] and Camelot,[2]
  And Priam's neighbors.[3]

Miniver mourned the ripe renown
  That made so many a name so fragrant;
He mourned Romance, now on the town,   15
  And Art, a vagrant.

Miniver loved the Medici,[4]
  Albeit he had never seen one;
He would have sinned incessantly
  Could he have been one.   20

Miniver cursed the commonplace
  And eyed a khaki suit with loathing;
He missed the mediaeval grace
  Of iron clothing.

Miniver scorned the gold he sought,   25
  But sore annoyed was he without it;
Miniver thought, and thought, and thought,
  and thought about it.

Miniver Cheevy, born too late,
  Scratched his head and kept on thinking;   30
Miniver coughed, and called it fate,
  And kept on drinking.

1. **Thebes** (thēbz). The poet may have had in mind either of two ancient cities named Thebes. The more ancient was in Egypt. The other was in Greece and is frequently mentioned in Greek legends.
2. **Camelot** (kam′ ə lot) was the beautiful city built for King Arthur by the magician Merlin.
3. **Priam's neighbors,** the kings of those neighboring cities in Asia Minor who helped Priam, king of Troy, resist the invading Greeks in the Trojan War.
4. **Medici** (med′ ə chē′), a family of bankers and leaders under whose tolerant rule Florence, Italy, became one of the most beautiful cities in the world. In power from the fifteenth to the eighteenth century, they were patrons and protectors of the scholars and artists who made Florence the very center of the Italian Renaissance.

Richard Cory

Whenever Richard Cory went down town,
    We people on the pavement looked at him:
He was a gentleman from sole to crown,
    Clean favored, and imperially slim.

And he was always quietly arrayed,   5
    And he was always human when he talked;
But still he fluttered pulses when he said,
    "Good-morning," and he glittered when he walked.

And he was rich—yes, richer than a king,
    And admirably schooled in every grace: 10
In fine, we thought that he was everything
    To make us wish that we were in his place.

So on we worked, and waited for the light,
    And went without the meat, and cursed the bread;
And Richard Cory, one calm summer night,   15
    Went home and put a bullet through his head.

Edwin Arlington Robinson, "Richard Cory," in THE CHILDREN OF THE NIGHT. (New York: Charles Scribner's Sons, 1897.)

Mr. Flood's Party

Old Eben Flood, climbing alone one night
Over the hill between the town below
And the forsaken upland hermitage
That held as much as he should ever know
On earth again of home, paused warily.   5
The road was his with not a native near;
And Eben, having leisure, said aloud,
For no man else in Tilbury Town to hear:

"Well, Mr. Flood, we have the harvest moon
Again, and we may not have many more;   10

Reprinted with permission of Macmillan Publishing Company from COL- LECTED POEMS by Edwin Arlington Robinson. Copyright 1921 by Edwin Arlington Robinson, renewed 1949 by Ruth Nivison.

The bird is on the wing, the poet[1] says,
And you and I have said it here before.
Drink to the bird." He raised up to the light
The jug that he had gone so far to fill,
And answered huskily: "Well, Mr. Flood,   15
Since you propose it, I believe I will."

Alone, as if enduring to the end
A valiant armor of scarred hopes outworn,
He stood there in the middle of the road
Like Roland's ghost[2] winding a silent horn.   20
Below him, in the town among the trees,
Where friends of other days had honored him,
A phantom salutation of the dead
Rang thinly till old Eben's eyes were dim.

Then, as a mother lays her sleeping child   25
Down tenderly, fearing it may awake,
He set the jug down slowly at his feet
With trembling care, knowing that most things break;
And only when assured that on firm earth
It stood, as the uncertain lives of men   30
Assuredly did not, he paced away,
And with his hand extended paused again:

"Well, Mr. Flood, we have not met like this
In a long time; and many a change has come
To both of us, I fear, since last it was   35
We had a drop together. Welcome home!"
Convivially returning with himself,
Again he raised the jug up to the light;
And with an acquiescent quaver said:
"Well, Mr. Flood, if you insist, I might.   40

"Only a very little, Mr. Flood—
For auld lang syne.[3] No more, sir; that will do."
So, for the time, apparently it did,

1. **poet,** reference to Edward Fitzgerald who made a popular translation of *The Rubaiyat of Omar Khayyam.* The "bird" here is a metaphor for time.
2. **Roland's ghost.** Roland is the legendary French hero of the medieval poem, *Chanson de Roland* (Song of Roland). While fighting under Charlemagne, the mighty Roland is betrayed and surrounded by the enemy. Too proud to sound the great horn that would summon help at once, he delays until it is too late, fights against overwhelming odds, and perishes with all his soldiers.
3. **auld lang syne** (ôld′ lang zīn′), the olden time, days gone by.

And Eben evidently thought so too;
For soon amid the silver loneliness
Of night he lifted up his voice and sang, 45
Secure, with only two moons listening,
Until the whole harmonious landscape rang—

"For auld lang syne." The weary throat gave out,
The last word wavered, and the song was done. 50
He raised again the jug regretfully
And shook his head, and was again alone.
There was not much that was ahead of him,
And there was nothing in the town below—
Where strangers would have shut the many doors 55
That many friends had opened long ago.

FOR UNDERSTANDING

"Miniver Cheevy"

1. Look up the word *miniver* in a dictionary, then explain why it seems appropriate as Cheevy's name.

2. In line 15, Cheevy mourns because Romance is "on the town." Explain this expression. Explain "vagrant" as it relates to "Art" in line 16.

3. In line 22, a khaki suit refers to a soldier's uniform. Explain the irony in lines 23–24.

4. Cheevy is a petulant dreamer as well as an alcoholic. With his absurd dreams and his constant drinking, what is he trying to avoid?

"Richard Cory"

1. In line 2, who are "we people on the pavement"? What does "clean favored" in line 4 mean?

2. Why did others wish to be in Cory's place?

3. Explain the meaning of lines 13–14.

4. What truth is the poet expressing in the last two lines of his poem?

"Mr. Flood's Party"

1. Where is Mr. Flood having his party? Why does the poet say that the old man "paused warily" in line 5?

2. In line 10, Mr. Flood says about the harvest moon: "we may not have many more." Explain.

3. We have no indication that Mr. Flood has performed any heroic feat of arms, yet in the third stanza the poet compares the old man to Roland's ghost. Explain.

4. What evidence is there in the fifth stanza to indicate that Mr. Flood, unlike Miniver Cheevy, only infrequently drinks or has a "party"?

5. Explain the wry humor in "only two moons listening" in line 47.

FOR INTERPRETATION

1. Discuss the following two statements in light of the three poems:

a. A person must be able to live with other human beings in order to be happy.

b. Great pain and personal tragedy cannot be shared; where such things are concerned we are all, always, alone.

2. You were asked to decide as you read the poems who is responsible for the alienation of the characters in each—the individual, society, or both. What is your decision?

FOR APPRECIATION

Structure

A literary work is in certain ways like a building. Both have a planned framework or structure, and the materials used—the wood or the words—are arranged according to this planned framework.

Robinson's poems tend to be highly structured. Scan at least two stanzas in "Miniver Cheevy" and "Richard Cory" and describe the rhyme scheme and rhythm in each. What regularities do you find? Are there any irregularities?

Symbolism

Not only words and phrases but also actions may have symbolic significance. Cory's suicide, for example, might be regarded as a symbolic act, for it suggests a meaning beyond the act itself. Discuss the meaning of this suicide and other symbolic acts in the Robinson poems.

LANGUAGE AND VOCABULARY

1. Having discussed synonyms and antonyms previously, we should also consider *homonyms,* words that are identical in spelling and sound, but different in meaning. For example, *base* in the "base of the column" and *base* in "base remark" are alike in sound and spelling but different in origins and meanings. *Bay* in "a bay mare" and *bay* in "bay window" are also homonyms. Find examples.

2. Words that are alike in spelling but different in origin, meaning, and pronunciation are *homographs.* The word *tear* in "a tear fell from his eye" and *tear* in "a tear in his shirt" are homographs, as are *wind* in "wind the clock" and *wind* in "the wind from the east." List other examples.

3. *Homophones* are words which sound alike but differ in origin, meaning, and spelling. For each word, find another word that sounds like it: *fair, break, minor, male, tale, right, bare, wait, plain, site.*

4. Now, if possible, find an antonym for each of the italicized words listed in the previous question. You will find that some of the words do not have antonyms.

5. Each of the following words has a homonym. Look up the origins and meanings of *bear, list, guy, mean, halter, hide, last, launch, mole, nob, palatine, palm, pan, scale.*

Varieties of Standard English

Every person has not one vocabulary but three vocabularies: a speaking vocabulary, words used when speaking with friends and with the public; a reading vocabulary, words we recognize in print; and a writing vocabulary, words we use in writing. The vocabularies are not identical; but certain words, what we might call general vocabulary, are common to all three. The guiding principle in one's choice of words is appropriateness. Is the word or phrase appropriate to the audience and to the situation? In previous exercises, we divided usage into two broad, general classes: *standard* and *nonstandard.* The term *nonstandard* generally refers to grammatical constructions, expressions, and pronunciations rejected by most educated speakers. Unfortunately there is no universally recognized system of identifying the varieties of standard English. The different varieties indicate different styles for different occasions and different audiences. One variety is no better than another if each is appropriate to the subject and to the situation.

The varieties of standard English refer more to word choice than to pronunciation, spelling, or grammar. The guiding principle of word choice is appropriateness to the subject and to the situation. For example, synonyms or near synonyms sometimes indicate degrees of refinement. Classify these words as formal, general and/or informal: *fear, terror, trepidation, goodness, virtue, probity.*

Study your own vocabulary. Make a list of the words you have learned from your readings in this book. Take an essay you have written recently and classify the nouns you have used. Try substituting nouns from your "other" vocabularies.

Edgar Lee Masters   1869–1950

Young Edgar Lee Masters, like the young Edwin Arlington Robinson, wrote poetry at an early age, and, like him, later created a fictitious town in which to center his poems. Robinson called his town Tilbury Town, while Masters called his Spoon River. Born in Kansas, but reared in southern Illinois, Masters attended Knox College briefly, studied law in his father's office, was admitted to the bar, and went to Chicago, where he became a highly respected attorney. During his youth, he wrote much poetry in traditional forms, often imitating Edgar Allan Poe and the English poets Keats and Shelley, but his work failed to attract attention.

In 1914, however, Masters wrote several free-verse monologues in imitation of those in *Epigrams from the Greek Anthology* (a collection of early Greek poems). Masters's brief verse epitaphs were poignant summaries of the lives of persons supposedly buried in the country cemetery of the imaginary town of Spoon River. The series of loosely connected monologues included nearly 250 characters and was published as the *Spoon River Anthology* (1915). The book was such a literary sensation that Masters soon gave up his law practice to write full time. Although for many years he produced an average of a book a year, he failed to achieve again the sharp and simple beauty of the first Spoon River poems. His attempt to add to the Spoon River story with *The New Spoon River* (1924) was a critical disappointment.

In his Spoon River monologues Masters deftly revealed in verse the spirit, the meanness, and the special beauty of American small town

PORTRAIT OF EDGAR LEE MASTERS
Francis J. Quirk
National Portrait Gallery, Smithsonian Institution

life—essentially what Sherwood Anderson and Sinclair Lewis revealed in prose. Most of the speakers in the *Spoon River Anthology* recite brief and bitter tales of twisted and wasted lives. But some, like Lucinda Matlock in the first of the following two epitaphs, speak with courage, conviction, and optimism.

Lucinda Matlock

I went to dances at Chandlerville,
And played snap-out at Winchester.
One time we changed partners,
Driving home in the moonlight of middle June,
And then I found Davis.   5
We were married and lived together for seventy years,
Enjoying, working, raising the twelve children,
Eight of whom we lost
Ere I had reached the age of sixty.
I spun, I wove, I kept the house, I nursed the sick,   10
I made the garden, and for holiday
Rambled over the fields where sang the larks,
And by Spoon River gathering many a shell,
And many a flower and medicinal weed—
Shouting to the wooded hills, singing to the green valleys. 15
At ninety-six I had lived enough, that is all,
And passed to a sweet repose.
What is this I hear of sorrow and weariness,
Anger, discontent, and drooping hopes?
Degenerate sons and daughters,   20
Life is too strong for you—
It takes life to love Life.

"Lucinda Matlock" and "Fiddler Jones": From the SPOON RIVER AN-
THOLOGY by Edgar Lee Masters, published by Macmillan Publishing Co.,
© 1962. Reprinted by permission of Ellen C. Masters.

**MR. AND MRS. WAYNE
MACVEAGH**
Augustus Saint-Gaudens
Corcoran Gallery of Art,
Washington, D.C.

Fiddler Jones

The earth keeps some vibration going
There in your heart, and that is you.
And if the people find you can fiddle,
Why, fiddle you must, for all your life.
What do you see, a harvest of clover?   5
Or a meadow to walk through to the river?
The wind's in the corn; you rub your hands
For beeves hereafter ready for market;
Or else you hear the rustle of skirts
Like the girls when dancing at Little Grove.   10
To Cooney Potter a pillar of dust
Or whirling leaves meant ruinous drouth;
They looked to me like Red-Head Sammy
Stepping it off, to "Toor-a-Loor."*
How could I till my forty acres   15
Not to speak of getting more,
With a medley of horns, bassoons, and piccolos
Stirred in my brain by crows and robins
And the creak of a windmill—only these?
And I never started to plow in my life   20
That some one did not stop in the road
And take me away to a dance or picnic.
I ended up with forty acres;
I ended up with a broken fiddle—
And a broken laugh, and a thousand memories,   25
And not a single regret.

*Toor-a-Loor,   a folk tune.

UNDERSTANDING AND APPRECIATION

"Lucinda Matlock"

1. How long had Lucinda's marriage lasted? How many children did she have? What had happened to them?
2. What did Lucinda do for "holiday," that is, for relaxation?
3. What of Lucinda's beliefs are suggested in the last five lines?

"Fiddler Jones"

1. The speaker compares different ways of looking at the same thing. In what two ways do two people see the same clover field? Compare the way Cooney Potter and the speaker view "a pillar of dust / Or whirling leaves."
2. What reasons does the speaker give for not tilling his forty acres?
3. What philosophy of life does Fiddler Jones express in the last four lines?

Amy Lowell 1874–1925

Born into one of the wealthiest and most distinguished families in Massachusetts, Amy Lowell was educated privately at home and abroad. In her early years she considered a stage career because she so admired actresses Sarah Bernhardt and Eleonora Duncan. But when an incurable glandular problem caused her to become abnormally obese, she gave up her dreams of the theater and eventually decided to become a poet. She did not, however, try at once to publish. Rather, since she was always thorough-going and determined, she studied poetry seriously for eight years before she published a line of verse.

In 1912 as her first book, *A Dome of Many-Colored Glass,* was being published, she heard of the few poets in London who were writing experimental, image-filled poetry under the leadership of the American expatriate, Ezra Pound. With characteristic directness, Lowell charged into the group (who called themselves Imagists) and soon convinced them that she was a better, and certainly wealthier, advisor than Pound. With considerable bitterness and acrimony Pound retreated, and she returned triumphantly to America to publish three annual volumes (1915, 1916, 1917) entitled *Some Imagist Poets.* Amy Lowell included therein not only her own verses but also those of John Gould Fletcher (1886–1950) and H. D. (Hilda Doolittle).

Although most critics ruthlessly attacked the Imagist poetry, the indomitable poet traveled up and down the country giving readings, encouraging younger poets, and writing furiously in defense of the new poetry. After a

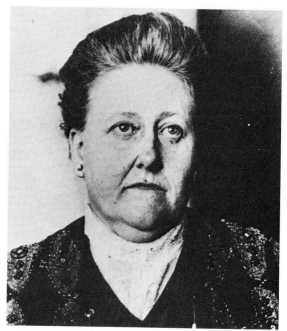

PORTRAIT OF AMY LOWELL

decade, the new forms began to win a grudging acceptance. Although Lowell expounded the Imagist standards of spareness, intensity, and firm, concrete images, much of her own poetry became simply impressionistic and sentimental. Although she turned out several volumes of verse, some of her later verse was, ironically, in the traditional mode. In 1926 she was posthumously awarded the Pulitzer Prize for her collection of poems, *What's O'Clock.*

Much of the Imagist poetry imitates the classic poetry of Greece, Rome, and the Orient. In fact, with its symbols and startling images, much of it sounds as if it were simply paraphrased from the ancient Chinese and Japanese masters. Note the rich imagery and symbols in the following two poems.

Night Clouds

The white mares of the moon rush along
    the sky
Beating their golden hoofs upon the glass
      Heavens;
The white mares of the moon are all
    standing on their hind legs
Pawing at the green porcelain doors of
    the remote Heavens.
Fly, Mares!   5
Strain your utmost,
Scatter the milky dust of stars,
Or the tiger sun will leap upon you and
    destroy you
With one lick of his vermilion tongue.

Peace

Perched upon the muzzle of a cannon
A yellow butterfly is slowly opening and
    shutting its wings.

UNDERSTANDING AND APPRECIATION

"Night Clouds"

1. Explain the metaphor in the first line: "The white mares of the moon." What is suggested by the expression "rush along the sky"?
2. The poet urges the mares to do their utmost to "Scatter the milky dust of stars." What galaxy might she be suggesting here?
3. What metaphor is used for the sun? What does the poet warn that the sun will do to the clouds?

"Peace"

This short verse is from Lowell's *Pictures of the Floating World* (1919), a collection of short verses adapted from ancient Japanese poets. How important is the title in understanding the poem? In what ways are the cannon and butterfly symbolic?

Robert Frost

1874–1963

When President Kennedy in 1961 decided to include a poet in his Inaugural Day ceremonies, it was natural for him to choose Robert Frost, a fellow New Englander and the dean of American poets. Frost published his first volume, *A Boy's Will,* in 1913; his last, *In the Clearing,* in 1962. Four times he won the Pulitzer Prize. His verse was known wherever English poetry was read. Yet Robert Frost was never one to forget that he was forty years old before his genius was recognized, that his early life was filled with hardship and disappointment.

Although Frost will always be celebrated as a New England poet, he was actually born in San Francisco, in 1874. His father had left Maine and hastened to the West Coast because he hated New England. The poet and his younger sister, Jeanie, might have spent their whole lives on the Pacific Coast had their father not died early of tuberculosis, leaving the strange request that he be buried in the New England he had loathed. After the trip East, the widow and her children settled in Salem, New Hampshire, and later in Lawrence, Massachusetts. Following graduation from Lawrence High School, Frost enrolled in Dartmouth College, but he stayed less than a year.

Until his marriage to Elinor White in 1895, Frost drifted from one job to another: mill work in Lawrence, school teaching, newspaper reporting. After his marriage he spent two years teaching in his mother's small private school, then two years at Harvard College, hoping to prepare for a career as a college instructor. Although he enjoyed the classics and philosophy, he revolted against academic discipline. Because of his poor health, he had to live in the country; so he and his growing family tried farming and chicken raising in Derry, New Hampshire. Five years of near failure as a farmer sent him back to school teaching in Derry, and then in Plymouth; but he disliked teaching as much as tilling the stubborn New Hampshire soil. From the day he sold his first poem, in 1894, he knew poetry should be his profession, indeed his whole life. In 1912 he took the gamble. Unable

PORTRAIT OF ROBERT FROST

to find a publisher for his poetry, he sold his farm and packed himself and his family off to Buckinghamshire, England, where living was cheaper and poetry had a larger audience. The decision was one of the wisest he ever made. *A Boy's Will* was issued by an English publisher in 1913 and was followed the next year by *North of Boston.* When Frost returned to the United States in 1915, his reputation was made; both books had been republished here. He bought a farm in Franconia, New Hampshire, with the hope of settling down to write the best poetry he could and to avoid the literary marketplace.

He succeeded in doing both. The National Institute of Arts and Letters elected him to membership in 1916. Amherst College offered him a professorship in English. Invitations to lecture and to give public readings came from all parts of the country. For the next forty-five years he was to become, almost against his will, a teacher-at-large. Though he was a splendid teacher and held audiences entranced by reading his own poetry, he also wished to remain close to the land. After his wife's death in 1938, he moved to the hills of Ripton, Vermont. To see Frost at home in Ripton was to see the poet next to his source, finally free from the enervating labor of cultivating the land for a living but still lovingly tied to the woodlands of Vermont where he could know "the line where man leaves off and nature starts."

There is a risk, of course, in thinking of Frost as only a New England poet and periodic visitor to college campuses. His friend and fellow-poet John Ciardi has warned us not to think of Frost as "a kindly, vague, white-haired great-grandfather" who just tells pleasant little stories in verse. Frost was a New Englander but not a mere recorder of regional folkways. He wrote of Vermont because he knew it best, but his subject was always the perils of the human condition. "It is the man we lose," Ciardi wrote after Frost's death, "a man salty and rough with the earth trace, and though towering above it, never removed from it, a man above all who could tower precisely because he was rooted in real earth." Naturally he put his characters in rural settings: small boys in deep woods, young married couples, transient farm workers, lumberjacks, gum-gatherers, just as John Steinbeck chose to write of his native California and William Faulkner of Oxford, Mississippi. But like the good teacher he was, Frost was always intent on expanding his subject or, rather, on urging his reader to expand his subject along with him, to discover that essentially New England mirrored the world.

If on occasion Frost's poems seem to be about little things in simple words—a burned house, apple-picking, birch trees, ax handles, a west-running brook, stone walls, a drumlin woodchuck—it takes only a second reading to catch the hints Frost drops along the way that there is a deceptively simple surface poem here and a vital below-the-surface meaning. Frost quite clearly used the objects of the farm world as symbols of a deeper meaning, as a way of moving from the concrete world to abstract ideas. For him a poem "begins in delight and ends in wisdom."

The delights of "Nothing Gold Can Stay" are obvious at first reading. Seven of its eight lines are direct observations of nature:

> Nature's first green is gold.
> Her hardest hue to hold.
> Her earthly leaf's a flower;
> But only so an hour.
> Then leaf subsides to leaf.   5
> So Eden sank to grief.
> So dawn goes down to day.
> Nothing gold can stay.

The opening line may sound like a paradox, a self-contradictory statement, but our own memory of spring reinforces the poet's image: the yellow weeping willows, the first trees to bud. And he reminds us that as yellow turns to green, so flower turns to leaf, and leaves will fall. Growth and decay are natural. No one can hold that "ecstasy should be static and stand still in one place," as Frost says on another occasion. Even the golden sunrise must turn to the harsher light of day.

But the chief pleasure of poetry, as the careful reader will discover, is moving from the surface delight of local details to the wisdom of suggested meanings. Frost need plant only two words in this poem to suggest ulterior, or hidden, latent meanings: *Eden* and *grief*. With line 6, the poem expands to include human nature. *Our* hardest hue to hold is innocence; *our* paradise, once golden, turned to grief. And as we reread the last line of the poem, our imagination seizes the word *gold*. In terms of the visual images—dawn's light and earth's first green—Frost is suggesting the abstract idea of loss. The verbs—*subsides, sank, goes down*—lead toward a double or triple meaning of *gold*, but the poet stops short of equating. The art is the implication. He is not telling us; he is only suggesting. "Poems can be pressed too hard for meaning," he warns us, yet at the same time our imagination plays with the hints he has given. In human terms, does gold mean innocence, or love, or perhaps life? Or all three? Delight will lead to wisdom if we allow it.

One of the reasons for Frost's popularity as a poet was that he stayed close to traditional forms: the sonnet, blank verse, the dramatic monologue, the simple lyric. He was not afraid of rhyme; he found the couplet and the quatrain a challenge, not a confinement. And like Shakespeare, he knew how to contain natural speech rhythms in blank verse. Writing free verse—poetry with rhythm but without meter and regular rhyme scheme—he likened to playing tennis with the net down. "To the right person," he wrote, "it must seem naive to distort form as such. The very words of the dictionary are a restriction to make the best of or stay out of and be silent. Coining new words isn't encouraged. We play the words as we find them. We make them do."

For Frost, poetry was very much a game he played both with the world and with his readers. The seriousness of the game did not detract from its fun nor from his joy in performance. He had, as he said, "a lover's quarrel with the world," and it was the peculiar nature of his genius that he could combine traditional forms, homely subjects, and serious insights with a perceptive sense of humor and wit. He once offered this sly warning to those about to read his verse:

It takes all kinds of in and outdoor
    schooling
To get adapted to my kind of fooling.

Though Frost's poetry is made up of observations on his New England countryside—snow, birches, rain—his real subject is human nature. His poems talk of simple things in simple words, but these simple objects become symbols leading to deeper meanings. Neither a nature poet nor a lyricist, he sees in the birch trees and hemlocks of New England something that belongs to each person everywhere: joy, doubts, horror. Frost uses New England as a means of revealing what is universal, not merely local. He accomplishes this so well because he accepts the premise that human nature is purest and most understandable when closest to nature. Here, above all, he realizes how narrowly limited is his capacity for changing the world.

Birches

When I see birches bend to left and right
Across the lines of straighter darker trees,
I like to think some boy's been swinging them.
But swinging doesn't bend them down to stay
As ice storms do. Often you must have seen them   5
Loaded with ice a sunny winter morning
After a rain. They click upon themselves
As the breeze rises, and turn many-colored
As the stir cracks and crazes their enamel.
Soon the sun's warmth makes them shed crystal shells   10
Shattering and avalanching on the snow crust—
Such heaps of broken glass to sweep away

You'd think the inner dome of heaven had fallen.
They are dragged to the withered bracken by the load,
And they seem not to break; though once they are bowed   15
So low for long, they never right themselves:
You may see their trunks arching in the woods
Years afterwards, trailing their leaves on the ground
Like girls on hands and knees that throw their hair
Before them over their heads to dry in the sun.   20
But I was going to say when Truth broke in
With all her matter of fact about the ice storm,
I should prefer to have some boy bend them
As he went out and in to fetch the cows—
Some boy too far from town to learn baseball,   25
Whose only play was what he found himself,
Summer or winter, and could play alone.
One by one he subdued his father's trees
By riding them down over and over again
Until he took the stiffness out of them,   30
And not one but hung limp, not one was left
For him to conquer. He learned all there was
To learn about not launching out too soon
And so not carrying the tree away
Clear to the ground. He always kept his poise   35
To the top branches, climbing carefully
With the same pains you use to fill a cup
Up to the brim, and even above the brim.
Then he flung outward, feet first, with a swish,
Kicking his way down through the air to the ground.   40
So was I once myself a swinger of birches.
And so I dream of going back to be.
It's when I'm weary of considerations,
And life is too much like a pathless wood
Where your face burns and tickles with the cobwebs   45
Broken across it, and one eye is weeping
From a twig's having lashed across it open.
I'd like to get away from earth awhile
And then come back to it and begin over.
May no fate willfully misunderstand me   50
And half grant what I wish and snatch me away
Not to return. Earth's the right place for love:
I don't know where it's likely to go better.
I'd like to go by climbing a birch tree,
And climb black branches up a snow-white trunk   55
Toward heaven, till the tree could bear no more,
But dipped its top and set me down again.
That would be good both going and coming back.
One could do worse than be a swinger of birches.

Mending Wall

Something there is that doesn't love a wall,
That sends the frozen-ground-swell under it
And spills the upper boulders in the sun,
And makes gaps even two can pass abreast.
The work of hunters is another thing: 5
I have come after them and made repair
Where they have left not one stone on a stone,
But they would have the rabbit out of hiding,
To please the yelping dogs. The gaps I mean,
No one has seen them made or heard them made,   10
But at spring mending-time we find them there.
I let my neighbor know beyond the hill;
And on a day we meet to walk the line
And set the wall between us once again.
We keep the wall between us as we go.   15
To each the boulders that have fallen to each.
And some are loaves and some so nearly balls
We have to use a spell to make them balance:
"Stay where you are until our backs are turned!"
We wear our fingers rough with handling them.   20
Oh, just another kind of outdoor game,
One on a side. It comes to little more:
There where it is we do not need the wall:
He is all pine and I am apple orchard.
My apple trees will never get across   25
And eat the cones under his pines, I tell him.
He only says, "Good fences make good neighbors."
Spring is the mischief in me, and I wonder
If I could put a notion in his head:
"*Why* do they make good neighbors? Isn't it   30
Where there are cows? But here there are no cows.
Before I built a wall I'd ask to know
What I was walling in or walling out,
And to whom I was like to give offense.
Something there is that doesn't love a wall,   35
That wants it down." I could say "Elves" to him,
But it's not elves exactly, and I'd rather
He said it for himself. I see him there
Bringing a stone grasped firmly by the top
In each hand, like an old-stone savage armed.   40
He moves in darkness as it seems to me,
Not of woods only and the shade of trees.
He will not go behind his father's saying,
And he likes having thought of it so well
He says again, "Good fences make good neighbors." 45

WINTER HARMONY, John H. Twachtman, National Gallery of Art, Washington, D.C., Gift of the Avelon Foundation

UNDERSTANDING AND APPRECIATION

"Birches"

1. According to Frost, what bends birches down to stay?

2. Why does Frost describe his digression (in lines 5–16) by saying "when Truth broke in / With all her matter of fact"? What is Truth opposed to here?

3. Explain the simile in lines 19–20.

4. Why does Frost say that he would like to get away from earth awhile? What simile does he use for life in line 44?

"Mending Wall"

1. What is the "something" that doesn't love a wall?

2. What damage do hunters do to a wall?

3. Why does the poet's neighbor insist on mending the wall each spring despite the fact there are no cows to keep in or out?

4. What does Frost mean when he says that his neighbor "moves in darkness"?

FOR INTERPRETATION

"Birches"

1. How is life a "pathless wood" as Frost suggests? What further meaning can you read into "cobwebs" and "twigs that lash the eye"?

2. In the last six lines, how does Frost make the birch tree an appropriate symbol for a human's dilemma: the desire both to escape the earth and to return to it?

"Mending Wall"

1. The meaning of this poem can be summed up in the problem it raises: Should we tear down the barriers that isolate us from one another, or are these boundaries and limits necessary to human life? What is the view of the speaker in the poem? What is your opinion?

2. We change people's attitudes only by putting notions in their heads, by having them see things for themselves. Discuss.

All poets, in time, face the major question: What is death? Frost saw death not as an absolute, but as perpetually involved with life and the living. These three poems will need several readings. The first is apparently simple, but proves baffling, like a riddle, and its meanings are multiple. The second suggests the many responsibilities that must be attended to in life before one can enjoy the sleep of death. The last poem is a narrative, unforgettable in its local details but also universal in its contemplation of death.

Fire and Ice

Some say the world will end in fire,
Some say in ice.
From what I've tasted of desire
I hold with those who favor fire.
But if it had to perish twice,   5
I think I know enough of hate
To say that for destruction ice
Is also great
And would suffice.

Stopping by Woods on a Snowy Evening

Whose woods these are I think I know.
His house is in the village though;
He will not see me stopping here
To watch his woods fill up with snow.

My little horse must think it queer   5
To stop without a farmhouse near
Between the woods and frozen lake
The darkest evening of the year.

He gives his harness bells a shake
To ask if there is some mistake.   10
The only other sound's the sweep
Of easy wind and downy flake.

The woods are lovely, dark and deep,
But I have promises to keep,
And miles to go before I sleep,   15
And miles to go before I sleep.

The Death of the Hired Man

Mary sat musing on the lamp-flame at the table,
Waiting for Warren. When she heard his step,
She ran on tip-toe down the darkened passage
To meet him in the doorway with the news
And put him on his guard. "Silas is back."   5
She pushed him outward with her through the door
And shut it after her. "Be kind," she said,
She took the market things from Warren's arms
And set them on the porch, then drew him down
To sit beside her on the wooden steps.   10

"When was I ever anything but kind to him?
But I'll not have the fellow back," he said.
"I told him so last haying, didn't I?
If he left then, I said, that ended it.
What good is he? Who else will harbor him   15
At his age for the little he can do?
What help he is there's no depending on.
Off he goes always when I need him most.
He thinks he ought to earn a little pay,
Enough at least to buy tobacco with,   20
So he won't have to beg and be beholden.[1]
'All right,' I say, 'I can't afford to pay
Any fixed wages, though I wish I could.'
'Someone else can.' 'Then someone else will have to.'
I shouldn't mind his bettering himself   25
If that was what it was. You can be certain,
When he begins like that, there's someone at him
Trying to coax him off with pocket money,—
In haying time, when any help is scarce.
In winter he comes back to us. I'm done."   30

"Sh! not so loud: he'll hear you," Mary said.

---

1. **be beholden,**   to be under obligation for a favor or a
gift.

"I want him to: he'll have to soon or late."

"He's worn out. He's asleep beside the stove.
When I came up from Rowe's I found him here,
Huddled against the barn door fast asleep,   35
A miserable sight, and frightening, too—
You needn't smile—I didn't recognize him—
I wasn't looking for him—and he's changed.
Wait till you see."

                    "Where did you say he'd been?"   40

"He didn't say. I dragged him to the house,
And gave him tea and tried to make him smoke.
I tried to make him talk about his travels.
Nothing would do: he just kept nodding off."

"What did he say? Did he say anything?"   45

"But little."

          "Anything? Mary, confess
He said he'd come to ditch² the meadow for me."

"Warren!"

               "But did he? I just want to know."   50

"Of course he did. What would you have him say?
Surely you wouldn't grudge the poor old man
Some humble way to save his self-respect.
He added, if you really care to know,
He meant to clear the upper pasture, too.   55
That sounds like something you have heard before?
Warren, I wish you could have heard the way
He jumbled everything. I stopped to look
Two or three times—he made me feel so queer—
To see if he was talking in his sleep.   60
He ran on³ Harold Wilson—you remember—
The boy you had in haying four years since.
He's finished school, and teaching in his college.
Silas declares you'll have to get him back.
He says they two will make a team for work: 65

---

2. **to ditch,** to dig draining ditches.
3. **He ran on,** he talked of.

Between them they will lay this farm as smooth!
The way he mixed that in with other things.
He thinks young Wilson a likely lad, though daft
On education—you know how they fought
All through July under the blazing sun,   70
Silas up on the cart to build the load,
Harold along beside to pitch it on."

"Yes, I took care to keep well out of earshot."

"Well, those days trouble Silas like a dream.
You wouldn't think they would. How some things linger!   75
Harold's young college-boy's assurance piqued[4] him.
After so many years he still keeps finding
Good arguments he sees he might have used.
I sympathize. I know just how it feels
To think of the right thing to say too late.   80
Harold's associated in his mind with Latin.
He asked me what I thought of Harold's saying
He studied Latin like the violin
Because he liked it—that an argument!
He said he couldn't make the boy believe   85
He could find water with a hazel prong—
Which showed how much good school had ever done him.
He wanted to go over that. But most of all
He thinks if he could have another chance
To teach him how to build a load of hay—"   90

"I know, that's Silas' one accomplishment.
He bundles every forkful in its place,
And tags and numbers it for future reference,
So he can find and easily dislodge it
In the unloading. Silas does that well.   95
He takes it out in bunches like big birds' nests.
You never see him standing on the hay
He's trying to lift, straining to lift himself."

"He thinks if he could teach him that, he'd be
Some good perhaps to someone in the world.   100
He hates to see a boy the fool of books.
Poor Silas, so concerned for other folk,
And nothing to look backward to with pride,
And nothing to look forward to with hope,

---

4. **piqued** (pēkt), irritated, provoked.

So now and never any different."   105
Part of a moon was falling down the west,
Dragging the whole sky with it to the hills.
Its light poured softly in her lap. She saw it
And spread her apron to it. She put out her hand
Among the harp like morning-glory strings,   110
Taut with the dew from garden bed to eaves,
As if she played unheard some tenderness
That wrought on him beside her in the night.
"Warren," she said, "he has come home to die:
You needn't be afraid he'll leave you this time."   115

"Home," he mocked gently.

                    "Yes, what else but home?
It all depends on what you mean by home.
Of course he's nothing to us, any more
Than was the hound that came a stranger to us   120
Out of the woods, worn out upon the trail."

"Home is the place where, when you have to go there,
They have to take you in."

                  "I should have called it
Something you somehow haven't to deserve."   125

Warren leaned out and took a step or two,
Picked up a little stick, and brought it back
And broke it in his hand and tossed it by.
"Silas has better claim on us you think
Than on his brother? Thirteen little miles   130
As the road winds would bring him to his door.
Silas has walked that far no doubt today.
Why doesn't he go there? His brother's rich,
A somebody—director in the bank."

"He never told us that."   135

                "We know it though."

"I think his brother ought to help, of course.
I'll see to that if there is need. He ought of right
To take him in, and might be willing to—
He may be better than appearances.   140
But have some pity on Silas. Do you think

If he had any pride in claiming kin
Or anything he looked for from his brother,
He'd keep so still about him all this time?"

"I wonder what's between them."   145

                              "I can tell you.
Silas is what he is—we wouldn't mind him—
But just the kind that kinsfolk can't abide.
He never did a thing so very bad.
He don't know why he isn't quite as good   150
As anybody. Worthless though he is,
He won't be made ashamed to please his brother."

"I can't think Si ever hurt anyone."

"No, but he hurt my heart the way he lay
And rolled his old head on that sharp-edged
          chair-back.   155
He wouldn't let me put him on the lounge.
You must go in and see what you can do.
I made the bed up for him there tonight.
You'll be surprised at him—how much he's broken.
His working days are done; I'm sure of it."   160

"I'd not be in a hurry to say that."

"I haven't been. Go, look, see for yourself.
But Warren, please remember how it is:
He's come to help you ditch the meadow.
He has a plan. You mustn't laugh at him.   165
He may not speak of it, and then he may.
I'll sit and see if that small sailing cloud
Will hit or miss the moon."

                              It hit the moon.
Then there were three there, making a dim row,   170
The moon, the little silver cloud, and she.

Warren returned—too soon, it seemed to her,
Slipped to her side, caught up her hand and waited.

"Warren?" she questioned.

                              "Dead," was all he answered.   175

UNDERSTANDING AND INTERPRETATION

It is one of the jobs of the poet to ask the ultimate questions and to suggest some penetrating, if only partial, answers. They may not be the only answers, but they are comments that reveal something about human nature. The poet extends our horizons by allowing us to see and to judge human emotions and experiences through new eyes. Through the honesty of this vision, the poet creates an empathy for all that is human. By identifying values that make us human, the poet serves as a teacher to the world.

"Fire and Ice"

1. Frost's Yankee manner is not just a way of speaking, but a mode of thought, a way of facing the world. Find in this poem evidence of these characteristics of the Yankee manner:
    a. a harsh, tight-lipped, yet humorous manner
    b. a recurrent understatement
    c. a homey, informal, and dryly factual speech
    d. a restraint of one's strongest feelings
2. Why are fire and ice such appropriate symbols for desire and hatred?

"Stopping by Woods on a Snowy Evening"

1. Why does the traveler stop at the woods? Why should his horse think this queer?
2. What similarity does the rural traveler's journey have with that of anyone journeying through life? How does the poet make a personal experience into the image of experiences common to us all?
3. Why does the traveler leave with reluctance?
4. Why does the poet repeat the last line?

"The Death of the Hired Man"

1. This poem is a dramatic narrative. Like all good drama, it is essentially psychological. What is the psychological conflict in the poem?
2. We never see or hear Silas. What does the poet gain by keeping Silas offstage?
3. Warren's gradual conversion to pity and mercy through his wife's deliberate and gentle persuasiveness is the real subject of this poem. Trace the stages in Warren's transformation and the strategies by which Mary achieves this.
4. Why is Warren's discovery of Silas's death an ironic but not surprising fulfillment and end of the dramatic conflict?
5. It is not the death of Silas, but Mary's intuitive sympathy for Silas and Warren's slow searching for justice that are the subject of "The Death of the Hired Man." Discuss.

FOR APPRECIATION

Blank Verse

Marlowe and Shakespeare first popularized *blank verse*. It is based on five stresses or beats to each line and it is unrhymed. "Mending Wall," "Birches," and "The Death of the Hired Man" are particularly fine examples of the ease with which Frost handles this traditional form. The first lines of "Birches" are built around a wholly regular beat: ten syllables, alternately unaccented and accented. We call this regular line *iambic pentameter*. But note that by line 5 Frost is ready to vary this beat, in order to avoid monotony. He still keeps five accents to each line, but their order varies. To suggest even greater naturalness, even closer approximation to ordinary speech, in "The Death of the Hired Man," Frost breaks the sentences in the middle of the line, lets sentences run on for three or four lines, splits a line between two speakers; yet the beat is always five to the line.

Frost on Poetry

Frost often discussed the art of poetry. The following quotations from Robert Frost should be studied and discussed in terms of the poems you have just read.
1. And were an epitaph to be my story
    I'd have a short one ready for my own.
    I would have written of me on my stone
    I had a lover's quarrel with the world.
2. A poem is a reaching-out toward expression: an effort to find fulfillment. A complete poem is one where an emotion has found its thought, and the thought has found the words.

Carl Sandburg 1878–1967

Carl Sandburg spoke for the common man and woman. Poet, folksinger, and journalist, this rugged son of poor Swedish immigrants had to quit school at thirteen to begin working. Leaving Galesburg, Illinois, where he was born, Sandburg roamed over Kansas, Nebraska, and Colorado working as a truck handler, harvest hand, dishwasher, brickmaker, porter, janitor, sceneshifter, and milkman, among other jobs. It wasn't until he served as a war correspondent for a Galesburg newspaper while in Puerto Rico during the Spanish-American War that he became interested in higher education. He completed four years at Lombard College in Galesburg with a good scholastic record, but did not bother to graduate. Instead he took to the road again, earning his living by reporting and writing for various newspapers.

In 1908 he became a political organizer for the Social Democrats, a reform party, and that same year married Lillian Steichen, sister of Edward Steichen, the artist-photographer. Now thirty and seeking stability, he served the next two years as the secretary to the mayor of Milwaukee. This convinced him he did not want a political career. He went back into newspaper work, at which he excelled, and in 1913 was sent to Chicago on an editorial assignment. By this time he was a serious poet, and publication of *The Chicago Poems* in 1916, followed by *Cornhuskers* in 1918, raised him to a position of leadership among the Chicago Renaissance group of innovative young American writers.

By 1920 Sandburg had reached the height of his powers and was recognized as the foremost poet of the common people. Sandburg not only extolled the American laborer in verse as free and individual as he was himself, but he also became the foremost American minstrel of his time with his collection and performance of American folk songs. Long an admirer of

PORTRAIT OF CARL SANDBURG, William A. Smith
National Portrait Gallery, Smithsonian Institution

Abraham Lincoln, he published a monumental biography of his hero, *The Prairie Years* (two volumes) and *The War Years* (four volumes), which was awarded the Pulitzer Prize in 1939. His *Complete Poems* merited another Pulitzer Prize in 1951. In addition to his volumes of verse and published collections of folk songs, he also wrote stories for children, such as *Rootabaga Stories* (1922) and *Potato Face* (1930).

As you read "Chicago," his best-known poem, first published in *Poetry* magazine in 1914, note the vigorous imagery with which he bombards the senses of the reader. Then compare this poem with "The People Will Live On" written in 1936. Decide which poem you think you will remember longer.

Chicago

Hog Butcher for the World,
Tool Maker, Stacker of Wheat,
Player with Railroads and the Nation's Freight Handler;
Stormy, husky, brawling,
City of the Big Shoulders: 5

They tell me you are wicked and I believe them, for I have seen your
    painted women under the gas lamps luring the farm boys.
And they tell me you are crooked and I answer: Yes, it is true I
    have seen the gunman kill and go free to kill again.
And they tell me you are brutal and my reply is: On the faces of
    women and children I have seen the marks of wanton hunger.
And having answered so I turn once more to those who sneer at this
    my city, and I give them back the sneer and say to them:
Come and show me another city with lifted head singing so proud
    to be alive and coarse and strong and cunning.   10
Flinging magnetic curses amid the toil of piling job on job, here is a
    tall bold slugger set vivid against the little soft cities;
Fierce as a dog with tongue lapping for action, cunning as a savage
    pitted against the wilderness,
        Bareheaded,
        Shoveling,
        Wrecking,   15
        Planning,
        Building, breaking, rebuilding,
Under the smoke, dust all over his mouth, laughing with white teeth,
Under the terrible burden of destiny laughing as a young man laughs,
Laughing even as an ignorant fighter laughs who has never lost a battle,   20
Bragging and laughing that under his wrist is the pulse, and under
    his ribs the heart of the people,
        Laughing!
Laughing the stormy, husky, brawling laughter of Youth, half-naked,
    sweating, proud to be Hog Butcher, Tool Maker,
    Stacker of Wheat, Player with Railroads and
    Freight Handler to the Nation.

Vigorous, assertive, and uninhibited, the paintings of George Bellows capture the raw look and feel of American city life in the early decades of the twentieth century.

BLUE MORNING, George Bellows
National Gallery of Art, Washington, D. C.
Gift of Chester Dale

The People Will Live On

The people will live on.
The learning and blundering people will live on.
        They will be tricked and sold and again sold
And go back to the nourishing earth for rootholds,
        The people so peculiar in renewal and comeback,   5
        You can't laugh off their capacity to take it.
The mammoth rests between his cyclonic[1] dramas.

1. **cyclonic,** having the nature of a cyclone.

The people so often sleepy, weary, enigmatic,
is a vast huddle with many units saying:
    "I earn my living.   10
    I make enough to get by
    and it takes all my time.
    If I had more time
    I could do more for myself
    and maybe for others.   15
    I could read and study
    and talk things over
    and find out about things.
    It takes time.
    I wish I had the time."   20

The people is a tragic and comic two-face:
hero and hoodlum: phantom and gorilla twisting to moan with a gargoyle² mouth: "They
buy me and sell me . . . it's a game . . .
sometime I'll break loose . . ."   25

    Once having marched
  Over the margins of animal necessity,
  Over the grim line of sheer subsistence
    Then man came
  To the deeper rituals of his bones,   30
  To the lights lighter than any bones,
  To the time for thinking things over,
  To the dance, the song, the story,
  Or the hours given over to dreaming,
    Once having so marched.   35

Between the finite limitations of the five senses
and the endless yearnings of man for the beyond
the people hold to the humdrum bidding of work and food
while reaching out when it comes their way
for lights beyond the prison of the five senses,   40
for keepsakes lasting beyond any hunger or death.
    This reaching is alive.
The panderers and liars have violated and smutted it.
    Yet this reaching is alive yet
    for lights and keepsakes.   45
    The people know the salt of the sea
    and the strength of the winds
    lashing the corners of the earth.

---

2. **gargoyle** (gär′ goil), a grotesquely carved figure.

**THE WAKE OF THE
FERRY, II**
John Sloan
The Phillips Collection,
Washington, D.C.
Acquired from the C.W.
Kraushaar Galleries

The people take the earth.
as a tomb of rest and a cradle of hope.   50
Who else speaks for the Family of Man?
They are in tune and step
with constellations of universal law.

The people is a polychrome,[3]
a spectrum and a prism   55
held in a moving monolith,[4]
a console organ of changing themes,
a clavilux[5] of color poems
wherein the sea offers fog
and the fog moves off in rain   60
and the labrador sunset shortens
to a nocturne of clear stars
serene over the shot spray
of northern lights.

3. **polychrome,**   many colored.
4. **monolith,**   a great stone in the form of a column.
5. **clavilux** (klav′ ə ləks),   an instrument that throws
patterns of light and color upon a screen.

The steel mill sky is alive.   65
The fire breaks white and zigzag
shot on a gun-metal gloaming.
Man is a long time coming.
Man will yet win.
Brother may yet line up with brother: 70

This old anvil laughs at many broken hammers.
There are men who can't be bought.
The fireborn are at home in fire.
The stars make no noise.
You can't hinder the wind from blowing.   75
Time is a great teacher.
Who can live without hope?

In the darkness with a great bundle of grief
    the people march.
In the night, and overhead a shovel of stars for   80
    keeps, the people march:
           "Where to? what next?"

UNDERSTANDING AND INTERPRETATION

"Chicago"

No doubt for added dramatic effect and impact, Sandburg *personifies* Chicago in this poem, speaking to the city as though it possessed human attributes. When words are addressed to an absent person as if he or she were present or to a thing or an idea as if it could hear or reply, this is called the use of *apostrophe*. Such a device is frequently used in oratory when the speaker wishes to arouse emotional response. Sandburg is making use of this emotional oratory technique when he addresses the city as "you."

1. What were Chicago's leading industries as revealed in the opening three lines of the poem?

2. In lines 6–8 what repetition, or *parallel structure*, does the poet use in setting forth the charges brought against Chicago? What are the charges?

3. In line 11, what metaphor does Sandburg use to describe the city? How is that image carried to the end of the poem?

"The People Will Live On"

1. What are some of the many adjectives and descriptive terms that Sandburg applies to the people in this poem?

2. According to Greek mythology, Antaeus regained his strength by touching the earth. What line in the first stanza likens the people to Antaeus in this respect?

3. What do you think Sandburg means by the "lights and keepsakes" that people reach for?

4. How are the poem's ending words, "Where to? what next?" consistent with the thought expressed in line 6?

FOR APPRECIATION

Free Verse

In conventional verse, the unit measure is the foot or perhaps the line; in *free verse,* the unit is the *stanza.* In its irregular metrical pattern, free verse has great possibilities for rhythmical effects. It is interesting to realize that historical Hebrew and much Oriental poetry is written in large rhythmical units. For example, *Psalms* and *Song of Solomon* are as much free verse as anything written by Carl Sandburg or Walt Whitman. However, a great deal of Sandburg's poetry, such as "Chicago," could be classified as having *verse paragraphs* rather than stanzas because the length of the lines is more like prose than poetry. Why is this form especially well suited to Sandburg's poetry?

William Carlos Williams   1883–1963

Although he was for a time associated with the early Imagists who gathered around Ezra Pound and Amy Lowell, William Carlos Williams soon pulled away from that group and set out to "liberate" American poetry from its conventional modes through what he called objectivism. His poetic dictum, in brief, is that the poet must celebrate what he or she *perceives* and must concentrate not on ideas but on *things*. Ideas are then conveyed through the reader's experience of the concrete realities in poetry. "Verse," he said, "to be alive must have infused into it . . . some tincture of disestablishment, something in the nature of an impalpable revolution, an ethereal reversal." To achieve his purpose Williams wrote in the vernacular about "those things which lie under the direct scrutiny of the senses, close to the nose."

Born in Rutherford, New Jersey, Williams was educated both in the United States and abroad and studied medicine at the University of Pennsylvania. As a general practitioner in Rutherford, the doctor-poet wrote and published not only verse but also fiction, essays, and autobiography. Many of his poems were written between seeing patients or during his drives to and from his office. Williams considered his major work to be *Paterson* (1946–1958), five volumes of which he completed before his death. Fragments of the sixth volume were published soon after his death. This "epic" is an objective work incorporating history, characters, and myths of Paterson, New Jersey, from its American Indian beginnings.

PORTRAIT OF WILLIAM CARLOS WILLIAMS

In the following four poems—perhaps some of his most widely read verses—note the vivid sensory impressions Williams creates, and his precise recording of details that are overlooked in our everyday living.

FOUR POEMS

The Red Wheelbarrow

so much depends
upon

a red wheel
barrow

glazed with rain
water

beside the white
chickens.

Poem

As the cat
climbed over
the top of

the jamcloset
first the right
forefoot

carefully
then the hind
stepped down

into the pit of
the empty
flowerpot

*John Sloan was a member of the "Ash Can"
school of American painting—an attempt
to record daily life as it actually happened.*

BACKYARDS, GREENWICH VILLAGE
John Sloan
Whitney Museum of American Art, New York City

This Is Just to Say

I have eaten
the plums
that were in
the icebox

and which
you were probably
saving
for breakfast

Forgive me
they were delicious
so sweet
and so cold

The Great Figure

Among the rain
and lights
I saw the figure 5
in gold
on a red
firetruck
moving
tense
unheeded
to gong clangs
siren howls
and wheels rumbling
through the dark city.

UNDERSTANDING AND APPRECIATION

1. In "The Red Wheelbarrow," what does the word *depends* suggest to the reader?
2. Williams infuses movement into "Poem" by arranging the words into tiny stanzas. Read the poem aloud to "hear" this movement, then explain how the poet achieves it.
3. What does "This Is Just to Say" suggest about the appeal to the senses of seemingly unimportant, ordinary objects? What is the humor in the poem?
4. Williams wrote "The Great Figure" in a single sentence so the reader understands that the poet is offering a single image. What senses does he use in presenting the image? What onomatopoetic words are used?

COMPOSITION

Study again the slightly varying format of Williams's four poems. Note how he handles images and movement. Then choose some ordinary thing and write an image-filled verse. You may use a sentence as Williams does in "The Red Wheelbarrow" and "The Great Figure," or you may simply break the images and movement into clusters as he does in the other two poems.

Sara Teasdale

Sara Teasdale, born in St. Louis, Missouri, came of distinguished pre-Revolutionary ancestry and graduated from a private school near her home. Having made up her mind as a young girl that she wanted to write poetry, she toured Europe and the Middle East from 1905 to 1907 to enlarge her experience. Her first volume of poetry, *Sonnets to Duse and Other Poems* (1907), established her literary reputation. As she became more involved with writing and more cynical about post-World War I conditions, she became more solitary and withdrawn. In 1918 she won the Pulitzer Prize for her *Love Poems*. Her poetry was consistently straightforward and marked by technical excellence. It was classical in style and usually expressed in simple verse forms, such as quatrains or sonnets. Nevertheless, her later work, such as *Dark of the Moon* (1926) and *Collected Poems* (1926), shows increased maturity and subtlety of expression.

Her personal life was unhappy. Her marriage failed and she spent most of her life in frail health, the last years as a semi-invalid. In 1932, while in London doing some research, she contracted pneumonia which left her in a depressed psychological state. A short time after returning to New York City, she died from taking an overdose of sleeping pills.

The Solitary

My heart has grown rich with the passing of years,
　　I have less need now than when I was young
To share myself with every comer
　　Or shape my thoughts into words with my tongue.

It is one to me that they come or go　　　　　　　　5
　　If I have myself and the drive of my will,
And strength to climb on a summer night
　　And watch the stars swarm over the hill.

Let them think I love them more than I do,
　　Let them think I care, though I go alone;　　　　10
If it lifts their pride, what is it to me
　　Who am self-complete as a flower or a stone.

In this haunting portrait, Paxton demonstrates his concern for realistic detail and his skill at capturing a subject's special individuality.

TASHKO
William McGregor Paxton,
Maryhill Museum of Art,
Goldendale, Washington

The Look

Strephon kissed me in the spring,
  Robin in the fall,
But Colin only looked at me
  And never kissed at all.

Strephon's kiss was lost in jest,
  Robin's lost in play,
But the kiss in Colin's eyes
  Haunts me night and day.

UNDERSTANDING AND APPRECIATION

Teasdale's poems exemplify lyric poetry in its most commonly expressed form—short, musical verse relating the poet's thoughts or feelings. These two poems, "The Solitary" and "The Look," demonstrate the simplicity and regularity of the kind of verse patterns she most often used.

"The Solitary"

1. How has the speaker's attitude changed over the years?
2. On what does the speaker depend for her individuality?

3. Is it possible for a person to be "self-complete as a flower or a stone"? Do you think the speaker is happy in being solitary? Is there anything selfish about such an attitude?

"The Look"

1. How does the verse pattern in "The Look" differ from that in "The Solitary"?
2. What two boys had kissed the writer? What did Colin do?
3. What happened to the kisses? What continued to haunt her?
4. Why do you think she remembered "The Look" over the passage of years?

Robinson Jeffers 1887–1962

Able to read Greek at age five and master of several languages by age fifteen, Robinson Jeffers was educated in the United States and abroad and earned a bachelor's degree at eighteen. Later Jeffers studied English, medicine, law, forestry, and zoology as he searched for a suitable profession. In 1914 he inherited his uncle's fortune and was then able to settle down to a life of writing. On Point Sur, near Carmel, California, he built a home and found a solitary existence that he prized for the rest of his life. From this solitude he wrote volumes of verse in which, like a biblical prophet, he expressed his bleak view of the self-destructive stupidities of humankind. A lasting theme in his verse is the contrast between the childishness and insignificance of human beings and the enduring grandeur of natural phenomena. Jeffers's best-known longer work is his adaptation of Euripides' drama, *Medea,* which enjoyed a successful run on Broadway.

Somewhere between free verse and blank verse, Jeffers's poetry demonstrates his firm control over both the diction and rhythms of colloquial speech. "Shine, Perishing Republic" is perhaps the most widely known of his shorter works.

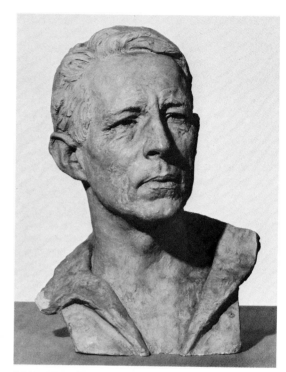

ROBINSON JEFFERS, Jo Davidson
National Portrait Gallery, Smithsonian Institution

Shine, Perishing Republic

While this America settles in the mold of its vulgarity,
    heavily thickening to empire,
And protest, only a bubble in the molten mass, pops
    and sighs out, and the mass hardens,

I sadly smiling remember that the flower fades to
    make fruit, the fruit rots to make earth.
Out of the mother; and through the spring exultances,
    ripeness and decadence; and home to the
    mother.

You making haste haste on decay: not blameworthy;
    life is good, be it stubbornly long or suddenly   **5**
A mortal splendor: meteors are not needed less than
    mountains: shine, perishing republic.

But for my children, I would have them keep their
    distance from the thickening center;
    corruption
Never has been compulsory, when the cities lie at
    the monster's feet there are left the moun-
    tains.

And boys, be in nothing so moderate as in love of
    man, a clever servant, insufferable master.
There is the trap that catches noblest spirits, that
    caught—they say—God, when he walked on
    earth.   **10**

UNDERSTANDING AND APPRECIATION

1. What did Jeffers see as the basic problem in America at that time?
2. Explain the metaphor in the second stanza.
3. What is the meaning of the following from lines 7–8: "corruption / Never has been compulsory"? What alternative to going to the center of the mass does he suggest?
4. Explain his warning in the final stanza: "be in nothing so moderate as in love of man." How is love "the trap"?

COMPOSITION

In view of the overall condition of our nation as you see it at present, write a short essay in which you tell whether you think Jeffers was a doomsayer or a prophet when he wrote "Shine, Perishing Republic."

T. S. Eliot

1888–1965

T. S. Eliot had both American and English ties. Although he was born in St. Louis, Missouri, and was educated at Harvard, he settled in London in 1915 and lived in Britain for the rest of his life.

Eliot's work as a poet, critic, and playwright represents a revolt from the cheerfulness, optimism, and hopefulness of the Victorians. Both through his verse and through his literary criticism he exerted an enormous influence on modern poetry.

Eliot's creative life falls roughly into three phases. In his first phase, which lasted into the mid-1920s, Eliot was mainly concerned with the apparently hopeless decay of Western civilization. In his second phase, after he joined the Church of England in 1927, he became more optimistic, finding a measure of hope through religious faith. In his third phase, beginning in the mid-1930s, he turned more to critical essays and to verse drama.

Eliot is difficult to comprehend at first reading. His poetry shows the influence of the French Symbolists, of some aspects of the Imagist movement, and of the metaphysical poets of the seventeenth century, especially John Donne. The Symbolists used symbols to stimulate multiple associations of ideas in the reader's mind. The Imagists emphasized the creation of sharp, concrete images. The metaphysical poets impressed Eliot with their paradoxical conceits and their intellectual toughness. All of these elements Eliot combined to communicate his own vision as a "classicist in literature, royalist in politics, and Anglo-Catholic in religion," as he said of himself. To many people, he is the poet who most clearly expresses the sense of loss and fragmentation of the modern world—a view that is apparent from the titles of poetic works such as "The Hollow Men" and *The Waste Land* (1922). Within his poems we find quotations from other authors. There are frequent allusions

PORTRAIT OF T. S. ELIOT, Wyndham Lewis
Harvard University Portrait Collection

to Dante, Shakespeare, Goethe, and other Western writers, as well as to Oriental culture and Eastern writers. Eliot alludes to so many great works of the past, both to search for help and to remind us of the spiritual, intellectual, and emotional poverty of our own time.

In 1948 Eliot was awarded the Nobel Prize in Literature. Much of his popularity in later life, both in England and the United States, came from his plays *Murder in the Cathedral* (1935) and *The Cocktail Party* (1950). In 1927 he became a British subject in deed as he had been in spirit most of his life. However, he returned periodically to the United States to lecture.

In the following poem Eliot pictures people of the mid-1920s as bereft of animal, intellectual, and spiritual values; he sees them as essentially hollow, living in "death's dream kingdom." Note, too, how his poetic method—sudden shifts, violent contrasts, apparent disunity—tends to underscore the chaos of modern life.

The Hollow Men

Mistah Kurtz—he dead.[1]

A penny for the Old Guy[2]

I

We are the hollow men
We are the stuffed men
Leaning together
Headpiece filled with straw. Alas!
Our dried voices, when   5
We whisper together
Are quiet and meaningless
As wind in dry grass
Or rats' feet over broken glass
In our dry cellar   10

Shape without form, shade without color,
Paralyzed force, gesture without motion

Those who have crossed
With direct eyes, to death's other Kingdom
Remember us—if at all—not as lost   15
Violent souls, but only
As the hollow men
The stuffed men.

II

Eyes I dare not meet in dreams
In death's dream kingdom   20
These do not appear;
There, the eyes are
Sunlight on a broken column
There, is a tree swinging
And voices are   25
In the wind's singing
More distant and more solemn
Than a fading star.

Let me be no nearer
In death's dream kingdom   30

Let me also wear
Such deliberate disguises
Rat's coat, crowskin, crossed staves
In a field
Behaving as the wind behaves   35
No nearer—

Not that final meeting
In the twilight kingdom

III

This is the dead land
This is cactus land   40
Here the stone images[3]
Are raised, here they receive
The supplication of a dead man's hand
Under the twinkle of a fading star.

Is it like this   45
In death's other kingdom
Waking alone
At the hour when we are
Trembling with tenderness
Lips that would kiss   50
Form prayers to broken stone.

1. **Mistah Kurtz,** a character in Joseph Conrad's *Heart of Darkness* who is destroyed by his own base instincts.
2. **A . . . Guy.** English children say this on Guy Fawkes Day—the anniversary of his abortive plot to blow up Parliament.
3. **stone images,** the idols, Wealth and Power, before which the poet felt America, after World War I, was bowing down.

IV

The eyes are not here
There are no eyes here
In this valley of dying stars
In this hollow valley   55
This broken jaw of our lost kingdoms

In this last of meeting places
We grope together
And avoid speech
Gathered on this beach of the tumid
    river   60

Sightless, unless
The eyes reappear
As the perpetual star
Multifoliate rose[4]
Of death's twilight kingdom   65
The hope only
Of empty men.

V

Here we go round the prickly pear
Prickly pear prickly pear
Here we go round the prickly pear   70
At five o'clock in the morning.

Between the idea
And the reality
Between the motion

And the act   75
Falls the Shadow

          For Thine is the Kingdom

Between the conception
And the creation
Between the emotion   80
And the response
Falls the Shadow

          Life is very long

Between the desire
And the spasm   85
Between the potency
And the existence
Between the essence
And the descent
Falls the Shadow   90

          For Thine is the Kingdom

For Thine is[5]
Life is
For Thine is the

This is the way the world ends   95
This is the way the world ends
This is the way the world ends
Not with a bang but a whimper.

4. **Multifoliate** (mul′ tə fō′ lē ət) **rose,** literally, the many leafed rose, perhaps many petaled. In religious symbolism a rose with many petals is the symbol of a soul unfolding spiritually.
5. **For Thine is,** note that the poem falters as from weariness. The hollow men cannot pray.

UNDERSTANDING AND INTERPRETATION

Perhaps the two most significant characteristics of "the hollow men" are fear and impotence; and note that they are fearful and powerless with respect to *all* aspects of life. They are afraid to love, afraid to think, afraid to worship or face the afterlife. These fears are symbolized in Part V by the "Shadow" that falls between ideas and realities, emotions and responses, and so on. The shadow breaks the chain before fulfillment in much the same way as the Lord's Prayer is broken off just before the words, "the Power and the Glory."

1. "A penny for the Old Guy" is what English children say when they go from door to door soliciting money for fireworks on Guy Fawkes Day (November 5). Look up Guy Fawkes or the Gunpowder Plot in a reference book and report your findings. How does knowledge of Fawkes help you to better understand the poem?
2. What is meant by a "lost violent soul"? Why are the hollow men not in this category?
3. Note as many instances as you can of the hollow men's inability to communicate effectively. How is this inability related to their fate?

4. Could a person with sincere religious convictions be a hollow man in Eliot's sense?

FOR APPRECIATION

Symbolism

A symbol is an object or condition used to suggest something else. The moon, for example, may suggest romance, mystery, purity, imagination, and other things. The particular meaning or group of meanings that the symbol calls forth will depend upon how the writer handles the symbol, upon the contexts in which it occurs.

In the last stanza of Part IV, Eliot says that the hollow men are "Sightless, unless / The eyes reappear / As the perpetual star / Multifoliate rose / Of death's twilight kingdom. . . ." The condition of sightlessness is a symbol of the lack of vision of the hollow men—they do not "see" with imagination or spirit as a poet or a saint or a prophet does. The lines say, however, that they might have such a vision if the eyes should reappear as "the perpetual star."

In trying to determine the symbolic meaning of this star, readers must call up those characteristics of stars that fit the present context. They might note that stars give light; they are in the heavens; and this star at least is "perpetual." Now especially in the context of this poem a perpetual light in the heavens can hardly fail to suggest God, or at least some aspect of divinity.

Since "Multifoliate rose" is an appositive to the perpetual star, it must suggest much the same meanings. Roses, of course, suggest brightness and beauty. Further support for thinking of the multifoliate rose as a symbol of divinity comes from the fact that this is what it symbolizes in the final portion of Dante's *Divine Comedy,* a famous poem of which Eliot was deeply fond.

1. Briefly, then, the lines suggest that the hollow men would cease to be hollow if they had spiritual vision. What are some of the advantages and disadvantages of the fact that the poet has chosen to communicate this idea symbolically rather than literally?

2. Discuss the symbolism of the earlier lines in Part IV, paying special attention to the meaning of "eyes" and to the physical setting.

John Crowe Ransom   1888–1974

As poet, literary critic, college teacher, and editor, John Crowe Ransom produced poetry that is largely devoid of sentimentality, is infused with dry wit and irony, and moves in lines that adhere strictly to conventional form. Although Ransom's poetic output is small in comparison to most American poets, his verses are polished gems of the poetic art and are highly regarded by both critics and serious readers of poetry.

After his graduation from Vanderbilt University, he went to Oxford University as a Rhodes scholar. In 1914 he returned to teach at Vanderbilt, where he founded *The Fugitive,* a "little magazine" devoted to poetry and criticism. He was also one of the leaders in the Fugitive Group of Southern writers who advocated a country, or agrarian, life because they believed such an existence represented a more stable culture than an industrial life.

In 1937 he was made Carnegie Professor of Poetry at Kenyon College where he established and became editor of the *Kenyon Review,* a quarterly literary journal. Ransom was also a widely read critic, one of the leaders of the so-called New Critics.

In the following poem, Ransom renders a moving portrait of a woman who has formally

PORTRAIT OF JOHN CROWE RANSOM

and "officially" broken with her sweetheart by letter. As you read the poem, note the contrast between the woman's emotional state at the end of the poem and her sureness in the first stanza.

Parting, Without a Sequel

She has finished and sealed the letter
At last, which he so richly has deserved,
With characters venomous and hatefully curved,
And nothing could be better.

But even as she gave it   5
Saying to the blue-capped functioner of doom,
"Into his hands," she hoped the leering groom
Might somewhere lose and leave it.

Then all the blood
Forsook the face. She was too pale for tears,   10
Observing the ruin of her younger years.
She went and stood

Under her father's vaunting oak
Who kept his peace in wind and sun, and glistened
Stoical in the rain; to whom she listened   15
If he spoke.

And now the agitation of the rain
Rasped his sere[1] leaves, and he talked low and gentle
Reproaching the wan[2] daughter by the lintel,[3]
Ceasing and beginning again.   20

Away went the messenger's bicycle,
His serpent's track went up the hill forever,
And all the time she stood there hot as fever
And cold as any icicle.

1. **sere,**   parched, withered.
2. **wan,**   pale, sickly.
3. **lintel** (lin' tl),   crosspiece over a door supporting the
weight of the structure.

UNDERSTANDING AND INTERPRETATION

1. In the first stanza, how does the woman evidently feel as she writes the letter? In the second stanza, as she hands the letter to the messenger—"the leering groom"—what does she hope he might do with it?
2. Why does she go to stand under "her father's vaunting oak"?
3. What does the title suggest about a reconciliation between the lovers?

FOR APPRECIATION

The Lyric Poet
Though some poems are written largely to communicate ideas and others are written largely to tell stories, the lyric poem is one whose primary concern is the communication of emotions.

Although there may be few story elements in lyric poetry, there is usually no lack of concrete detail. Such concrete details are used to make the reader feel the emotions the poet wishes to communicate. The poet knows that the mature reader is not going to feel an emotion merely because the poet insists on it.

Emotions in life come in response to specific situations—a strange noise heard in the middle of the night causes the heart to pound with fear; the particular person one loves enters a room and one's pulse beats faster. Through concrete details —for example, the oak "Rasped his sere leaves"— the poet tries to create a context parallel to, yet somehow more intense than, real life that will give rise to the desired emotions in readers. Concrete details meant to appeal to the reader's senses of sight, smell, touch, taste, and hearing are commonly referred to as *images*.

In the following two quotations from the poem, what is being described, and what feeling does each give you? To which of your senses does each image appeal primarily?
1. vaunting oak . . . / glistened / Stoical in the rain.
2. His serpent's track went up the hill forever.

Claude McKay   1890–1948

Born in Jamaica to poor farm workers, Claude McKay began early to write poetry in the Jamaican dialect and for his work won a prize that enabled him to emigrate to the United States when he was twenty-two. He studied briefly at Tuskegee Institute, Alabama, and at Kansas State College, but gave up formal education in 1914 and moved to Harlem. There he supported himself with odd jobs and wrote both prose and poetry.

During the 1920s McKay became one of the most vocal members of the Harlem Renaissance, writing and publishing some of his most famous social protest poems. His collection of poems, *Harlem Shadows* (1922), is his most important book and many verses from this work are often reprinted. His novel, *Home to Harlem* (1928), was a best seller and award winner.

Perhaps more than any other group, the black Americans have a right to protest. That protest is strong at times, as we see in McKay's sonnet "America," a powerful fusion of pride and outrage, love and hate.

America

Although she feeds me bread of bitterness,
And sinks into my throat her tiger's tooth,
Stealing my breath of life, I will confess
I love this cultured hell that tests my youth
Her vigor flows like tides into my blood   5
Giving me strength erect against her hate.
Her bigness sweeps my being like a flood.
Yet as a rebel fronts a king in state,
I stand within her walls with not a shred
Of terror, malice, not a word of jeer.   10
Darkly I gaze into the days ahead,
And see her might and granite wonders there,
Beneath the touch of Time's unerring hand,
Like priceless treasures sinking in the sand.

RESTING, Claude Clark
National Museum of American Art, Smithsonian Institution Washington, D.C.

UNDERSTANDING AND INTERPRETATION

Over eight hundred years ago the Persian poet
Omar Khayyám wrote the following lines:

> Ah Love! could Thou and I with Fate conspire
> To grasp this sorry Scheme of Things entire,
> Would we not shatter it to bits—and then
> Remold it nearer to the Heart's Desire!

The feeling expressed here is a familiar one in
poetry. The poet has often protested against life as
it is ("this sorry Scheme of Things") and expressed the hope that he could make it better
("Remold it nearer to the Heart's Desire").
Khayyám would begin by conspiring with Love
and Fate to shatter to bits the world as it is.

McKay is protesting against racial hatred. Underlying all the protest, however, you can detect
that the poet's outlook is basically strong and
positive.

Discuss the meaning and implications of the
following lines from the poem:

>   . . . I will confess
> I love this cultured hell that tests my youth!

Edna St. Vincent Millay   1892–1950

My candle burns at both ends;
It will not last the night;
But ah, my foes, and oh, my friends—
It gives a lovely light!*

Edna St. Vincent Millay was in her late twenties
when she expressed her philosophy of "burning
the candle at both ends" and living with reckless
abandon. Dashing, unconventional, hungry for
experience, and outspoken in her social and
political independence, she was a symbol for the
youth of her time.

Born in Rockland, Maine, she was raised
along with two younger sisters by her widowed
mother, who recognized her daughter's talent
for writing poetry. At nineteen the girl entered
her poem "Renascence" in an anthology contest
and won critical acclaim as well as a patroness
willing to pay her college expenses. When she
graduated from Vassar College in 1917, she
moved to Greenwich Village in New York City
where she began a bohemian existence; in that
same year she published *Renascence and Other
Poems.* Millay wrote continuously, publishing
several volumes of verse, including *A Few
Figs from Thistles* (1920) and *The Harp
Weaver and Other Poems*, which won the
Pulitzer Prize in 1923.

As you read "Renascence," ask yourself: Can

PORTRAIT OF EDNA ST. VINCENT MILLAY
National Portrait Gallery, Smithsonian Institution

a human soul—anguished by its own and the
world's crimes—be reborn to a fresh awareness
of faith in the world's beauty and goodness? Be
alert for the poet's shifting moods as she
searches successfully for purpose and meaning.

*From *Collected Poems,* published by Harper and Row,
reprinted by permission Norma Millay Ellis, Literary
Executor.

Renascence

All I could see from where I stood
Was three long mountains and a wood;
I turned and looked another way,
And saw three islands in a bay.
So with my eyes I traced the line   5
Of the horizon, thin and fine,
Straight around till I was come
Back to where I'd started from;
And all I saw from where I stood
Was three long mountains and a wood.   10
Over these things I could not see;
These were the things that bounded me;
And I could touch them with my hand,
Almost, I thought, from where I stand.

And all at once things seemed so small   15
My breath came short, and scarce at all.
But, sure, the sky is big, I said;

Miles and miles above my head;
So here upon my back I'll lie
And look my fill into the sky.   20
And so I looked, and, after all,
The sky was not so very tall.
The sky, I said, must somewhere stop,
And—sure enough!—I see the top!
The sky, I thought, is not so grand;   25
I 'most could touch it with my hand!
And, reaching up my hand to try,
I screamed to feel it touch the sky.

I screamed, and—lo!—Infinity[1]
Came down and settled over me;   30
Forced back my scream into my chest,
Bent back my arm upon my breast,
And, pressing of the Undefined
The definition on my mind,[2]
Held up before my eyes a glass   35
Through which my shrinking sight did
    pass
Until it seemed I must behold
Immensity made manifold;
Whispered to me a word whose sound
Deafened the air for worlds around,   40
And brought unmuffled to my ears
The gossiping of friendly spheres,
The creaking of the tented sky,
The ticking of Eternity.

I saw and heard, and knew at last   45
The How and Why of all things, past
And present, and forevermore.
The universe, cleft to the core,
Lay open to my probing sense
That, sick'ning, I would fain pluck thence   50
But could not—nay! But needs must suck
At the great wound, and could not pluck
My lips away till I had drawn
All venom out.—Ah, fearful pawn![3]
For my omniscience paid I toll[4]   55
In infinite remorse of soul.
All sin was of my sinning, all
Atoning mine, and mine the gall
Of all regret. Mine was the weight
Of every brooded wrong, the hate   60
That stood behind each envious thrust,

Mine every greed, mine every lust.
And all the while for every grief,
Each suffering, I craved relief
With individual desire—   65
Craved all in vain! And felt fierce fire
About a thousand people crawl;
Perished with each—then mourned for
    all!
A man was starving in Capri;[5]
He moved his eyes and looked at me;   70
I felt his gaze, I heard his moan,
And knew his hunger as my own.
I saw at sea a great fog bank
Between two ships that struck and sank;
A thousand screams the heavens smote;   75
And every scream tore through my
    throat.
No hurt I did not feel, no death
That was not mine; mine each last breath
That, crying, met an answering cry
From the compassion that was I.   80
All suffering mine, and mine its rod;[6]
Mine, pity like the pity of God.
Ah, awful weight! Infinity
Pressed down upon the finite Me!
My anguished spirit, like a bird,   85
Beating against my lips I heard;
Yet lay the weight so close about
There was no room for it without.
And so beneath the weight lay I
And suffered death, but could not die.   90

---

1. **Infinity,** when capitalized, as here, stands for God, the One, the First Cause.
2. **pressing of the Undefined/The definition on my mind,** revealing to my mind the meaning of that Being who cannot be defined in the usual sense of the word because to define means to set limits (*Latin:* definire, to limit) and limits cannot be set to the Infinite.
3. **fearful pawn,** one of the sixteen chessmen of least value and with greatest limitation of movement on the chessboard. Here: an insignificant person full of fear.
4. **For my omniscience paid I toll,** for my all-knowing I paid a price. I had become one with all; I suffered with all.
5. **Capri** (kə prē´), an Italian island south of Naples.
6. **All suffering mine, and mine its rod.** In the moment of attunement with the Infinite, the poet was at one both with the sufferer and with that (the rod) which caused the suffering.

Deep in the earth I rested now;
Cool is its hand upon the brow
And soft its breast beneath the head
Of one who is so gladly dead.
And all at once, and over all, 95
The pitying rain began to fall;
I lay and heard each pattering hoof
Upon my lowly, thatchèd roof,
And seemed to love the sound far more
Than ever I had done before. 100
For rain it hath a friendly sound
To one who's six feet underground;
And scarce⁷ the friendly voice or face:
A grave is such a quiet place.

The rain, I said, is kind to come 105
And speak to me in my new home.
I would I were alive again
To kiss the fingers of the rain,
To drink into my eyes the shine
Of every slanting silver line, 110
To catch the freshened, fragrant breeze
From drenched and dripping apple trees.
For soon the shower will be done,
And then the broad face of the sun
Will laugh above the rain-soaked earth 115
Until the world with answering mirth
Shakes joyously, and each round drop
Rolls, twinkling, from its grass-blade top.
How can I bear it; buried here,
While overhead the sky grows clear 120
And blue again after the storm?

O, multicolored, multiform
Belovèd beauty over me,
That I shall never, never see
Again! Spring silver, autumn gold, 125
That I shall never more behold!
Sleeping your myriad magics through,
Close sepulchered away from you!
O God, I cried, give me new birth,
And put me back upon the earth! 130
Upset each cloud's gigantic gourd⁸
And let the heavy rain, down poured
In one big torrent, set me free,
Washing my grave away from me!

I ceased; and, through the breathless
 hush 135
That answered me, the far-off rush
Of herald wings came whispering
Like music down the vibrant string
Of my ascending prayer, and—crash!
Before the wild wind's whistling lash 140
The startled storm clouds reared on high
And plunged in terror down the sky,
And the big rain in one black wave
Fell from the sky and struck my grave.
I know not how such things can be 145
I only know there came to me
A fragrance such as never clings
To aught save happy living things;
A sound as of some joyous elf
Singing sweet songs to please himself, 150
And, through and over everything,
A sense of glad awakening.
The grass, a-tiptoe at my ear,
Whispering to me I could hear;
I felt the rain's cool finger tips 155
Brushed tenderly across my lips,
Laid gently on my sealèd sight,
And all at once the heavy night
Fell from my eyes and I could see—
A drenched and dripping apple tree, 160
A last long line of silver rain,
A sky grown clear and blue again.
And as I looked a quickening gust
Of wind blew up to me and thrust
Into my face a miracle 165
Of orchard breath, and with the smell—
I know not how such things can be!—
I breathed my soul back into me.

Ah! Up then from the ground sprang I
And hailed the earth with such a cry 170
As is not heard save from a man
Who has been dead, and lives again.
About the trees my arms I wound;
Like one gone mad I hugged the
 ground;

7. **scarce,** here: the word means "seldom met."
8. **gourd** (gôrd), a plant that bears fruit with a shell
which is often dried and used to make dippers.

TWO APPLES
Peter Thomson
Courtesy, Vincent
FitzGerald and Company

I raised my quivering arms on high; 175
I laughed and laughed into the sky,
Till at my throat a strangling sob
Caught fiercely, and a great heartthrob
Sent instant tears into my eyes;
O God, I cried, no dark disguise 180
Can e'er hereafter hide from me
Thy radiant identity!
Thou canst not move across the grass
But my quick eyes will see Thee pass,
Nor speak, however silently, 185
But my hushed voice will answer
      Thee.
I know the path that tells Thy way
Through the cool eve of every day;

God, I can push the grass apart
And lay my finger on Thy heart! 190

The world stands out on either side
No wider than the heart is wide;
Above the world is stretched the sky—
No higher than the soul is high.
The heart can push the sea and land 195
Farther away on either hand;
The soul can split the sky in two,
And let the face of God shine through.
But East and West will pinch the heart
That cannot keep them pushed apart; 200
And he whose soul is flat—the sky
Will cave in on him by and by.

FOR UNDERSTANDING

The feeling that one needs to be reborn spiritually often has its beginnings in the frustrations and failings of one's personal life, as well as in one's concern over the sufferings and crimes of humanity. And nearly always the rebirth involves some sort of suffering or atonement by which the soul is purged and washed clean. These are the themes explored in Millay's "Renascence."

1. What personal frustrations seem to beset the narrator?

2. What sufferings and crimes of the world trouble her? How do they affect her?

3. What does the narrator suffer before she is reborn?

4. How does her rebirth change her?

FOR INTERPRETATION

Discuss the meaning of the following quotations and show how they relate to one another in telling the story of the narrator's rebirth.

1. And all I saw from where I stood
   Was three long mountains and a wood.
   Over these things I could not see;
   These were the things that bounded me;
   (lines 9–12)

2. I screamed, and—lo!—Infinity
   Came down and settled over me;
   (lines 29–30)

   . . . .

   Until it seemed I must behold
   Immensity made manifold;
   (lines 37–38)

3. All suffering mine, and mine its rod;
   Mine, pity like the pity of God.
   Ah, awful weight! Infinity
   Pressed down upon the finite Me!
   (lines 81–84)

4. Before the wild wind's whistling lash
   The startled storm clouds reared on high
   And plunged in terror down the sky,
   And the big rain in one black wave
   Fell from the sky and struck my grave.
   (lines 140–144)

5. O God, I cried, no dark disguise
   Can e'er hereafter hide from me
   Thy radiant identity!
   (lines 180–182)

   . . . .

   God, I can push the grass apart
   And lay my finger on Thy heart!
   (lines 189–190)

6. The world stands out on either side
   No wider than the heart is wide;
   Above the world is stretched the sky—
   No higher than the soul is high.
   (lines 191–194)

FOR APPRECIATION

Structure

Note the division of the poem into ten stanzas. Try to summarize the thought in each of them in a sentence or two in order to better see the planned framework of the poem. Also, compare the following: lines 1–16 with lines 151–160; lines 105–112 with lines 153–162; lines 1–28 with lines 187–202. Show how these comparisons argue for the idea that the poem was carefully planned.

Symbolism

1. What do the wind and the rain symbolize? Be prepared to argue for or against the notion that they are well-chosen symbols.
2. What does the poet's touching the sky symbolize?
3. What is the symbolic meaning of the "great wound"?

LANGUAGE AND VOCABULARY

To develop large speaking, reading, and writing vocabularies, you must become interested in words: in how words acquire meanings, in how words change, and in how to add meanings to words you already know. The study of synonyms and antonyms helps sharpen your understanding of the distinctions that set words apart. Test your word knowledge by giving a synonym and an antonym for the italicized word or words in each phrase.

1. *stigma* of a fiction *monger*
2. certain *alacrity* in his gait
3. all had *furtive* appearances
4. *fervent* explorations
5. *inured* to my high-handed raids
6. *bogus* refugees
7. filed *sullenly* aboard
8. *languid* with rest
9. *precariously* rooted shrub
10. *salient* characteristics

Archibald MacLeish

1892–1982

When Archibald MacLeish died, just short of his ninetieth birthday, obituary writers often referred to him—unofficially, of course—as America's poet laureate. Robert Frost had been so considered before his death in 1962. MacLeish was born in Glencoe, Illinois, and educated at Yale and at Harvard Law School. He was foremost a poet, then a dramatist, an essayist, a lawyer, and a public official; in the latter capacity he served as Librarian of Congress and as an assistant secretary of state.

Impressed with the writings of Ezra Pound and T. S. Eliot in the 1920s, MacLeish lived for a time in Paris and experimented with the concepts espoused by the Imagists. Although not a member of this group, he wrote "Ars Poetica," which soon became famous because it seemed to be the Imagist manifesto, with its insistence on concrete imagery. Some critics were quick to point out, however, that the poem violated the Imagist dictum, as it leaned heavily on meaning in insisting what a poem "should be."

Although his earlier work was influenced by the Imagists, MacLeish's later poetry moved away from the cataloging of images and toward a simple lyric eloquence with which he treated world social and political concerns. His long narrative poem, *Conquistador* (1932), a story of the Spanish conquest of Mexico, won for him the first of three Pulitzer Prizes. Alert to the threat of fascism and to the actuality of dictatorial brutality in the 1930s, MacLeish attempted to arouse a lethargic American public through radio plays, such as *The Fall of the City* (1937) and *Air Raid* (1938). His humanitarian concerns led him to aid in the foundation of the United Nations Educational, Scientific, and Cultural

PORTRAIT OF ARCHIBALD MACLEISH
First and foremost a poet, MacLeish was also a dramatist, essayist, lawyer, and public official.

Organization (UNESCO). In 1958 he turned to the Book of Job as the basis for his biblical allegory *J. B.* The play won a Pulitzer Prize in Drama and was successfully produced on Broadway. In his declining years MacLeish continued to speak and to write in defense of democracy and express his faith in the promise of America.

Ars Poetica*

A poem should be palpable and mute
As a globed fruit

Dumb
As old medallions to the thumb

Silent as the sleeve-worn stone   5
Of casement ledges where the moss has grown—

A poem should be wordless
As the flight of birds

A poem should be motionless in time
As the moon climbs   10

Leaving, as the moon releases
Twig by twig the night-entangled trees,

Leaving, as the moon behind the winter leaves,
Memory by memory the mind—

A poem should be motionless in time   15
As the moon climbs

A poem should be equal to:
Not true

For all the history of grief
An empty doorway and a maple leaf   20

For love
The leaning grasses and two lights above the sea—

A poem should not mean
But be.

*__Ars Poetica__ (ärs pō e′ ti ka), Latin for the "art of
poetry."

*The artist, who served in World War II, was known
for his use of flat colors and stark geometric shapes.*

LIGHTS IN AN AIRCRAFT PLANT, Ralston Crawford
National Gallery of Art, Washington, D.C.
Gift of Mr. and Mrs. Burton G. Tremaine

Lines for an Interment

Now it is fifteen years you have lain in the meadow:
The boards at your face have gone through: the earth is
Packed down and the sound of the rain is fainter:
The roots of the first grass are dead.
It's a long time to lie in the earth with your honor: 5
The world, Soldier, the world has been moving on.
The girls wouldn't look at you twice in the cloth cap:
Six years old they were when it happened:
It bores them even in books: "Soissons[1] besieged!"
As for the gents they have joined the American Legion: 10
Belts and a brass band and the ladies' auxiliaries:
The Californians march in the OD silk.[2]

1. **Soissons,** a city in northeast France.
2. **OD silk,** olive drab.

We are all acting again like civilized beings:
People mention it at tea . . .The Facts of Life we have learned
are Economic: 15
You were deceived by the detonations of bombs:
You thought of courage and death when you thought of warfare.
Hadn't they taught you the fine words were unfortunate?
Now that we understand we judge without bias:
We feel of course for those who had to die: 20
Women have written us novels of great passion
Proving the useless death of the dead was a tragedy.
Nevertheless it is foolish to chew gall:
The foremost writers on both sides have apologized:
The Germans are back in the Midi[3] with cropped hair: 25
The English are drinking the better beer in Bavaria.[4]
You can rest now in the rain in the Belgian meadow—
Now that it's all explained away and forgotten:
Now that the earth is hard and the wood rots:
Now you are dead . . .   30

3. **Midi,** the south of France, an area famous for its resorts.
4. **Bavaria,** an area in southern Germany, a popular haunt of English tourists.

UNDERSTANDING AND APPRECIATION

"Ars Poetica"

1. List the five adjectives the poet uses in the first four stanzas to describe how a poem should be. How does each relate to speech? How does each relate to sound? According to these five adjectives, what qualities does the poet value in a poem, an image, or speech?

2. The adjective *palpable* means "capable of being touched or felt or imagined." What tangible or palpable images does the poet use to pair with the adjectives in the first four stanzas?

3. Lines 9–10 are seemingly contradictory. How does the poet explain this apparent paradox in line 14?

4. In lines 17–18, how is it possible for a poem to be "Not true"?

5. What images does the poet suggest as representative of the "history of grief" and of "love"?

6. Since the poet insists that a poem is to be composed of a series of images, how can the poem "be" but not "mean"?

"Lines for an Interment"

1. To whom is the poet speaking? What is the tone he establishes in line 5?

2. In line 6, MacLeish says that "the world has been moving on." How does he prove his point?

3. In line 15, the poet says "The Facts of Life we have learned are Economic." Explain how this is in ironic contrast with the next three lines.

4. Recall that Germany fought both England and France as well as the United States in World War I. In lines 25–26, is MacLeish really trying to prove that the world has been moving on in a progressive sense? Explain his reference to the Midi and to Bavaria.

5. In the last line of the poem MacLeish omits the word *that* (which he had used in the two previous lines). Is this a significant omission? Does it help you see something about the direction of events since the war?

e. e. cummings

The most unconventional of the modern American poets, edward estlin cummings was born in Cambridge, Massachusetts, educated at Harvard (his father taught in the Divinity School), and served briefly as a volunteer ambulance driver in France during World War I. As a poet and painter, cummings flouted the conventional, and early in life brought on controversy over his writings, paintings, and his way of living.

Believing that most people are without souls and move about in a stifling world of half-light, empty platitudes, and robotlike conformity, cummings celebrated the iconoclastic individual who lives in constant childlike wonder over the possibilities of joy and romantic love. In his war with accepted typography, cummings refused to capitalize his initials or his last name, used punctuation in his verse only as a stylistic device, and altered parts of speech by turning verbs into nouns and vice versa. His lines of poetry are often set on the page in odd configurations of syllables that provide intriguing puzzles for readers. Dedicated to the natural, instinctive world, he was bitterly opposed to scientists, philosophers, warmongers, and religious zealots because he felt they were trying to alter it. In the eyes of his contemporaries, cummings was a self-styled madcap/misfit who celebrated a life of extreme individuality.

cummings's works include several collections of his poems; two plays; a satirical ballet, *Tom* (1935), based on *Uncle Tom's Cabin;* and his semi-fictional *The Enormous Room* (1922). The latter is an account of the three months he spent in a French detention camp early in World War

SELF-PORTRAIT OF E. E. CUMMINGS
National Portrait Gallery, Smithsonian Institution

I as the result of a misunderstanding with French authorities.

Throughout his writing cummings deals in opposites, in contrasts between order and disorder, between natural, instinctive life and a machine-made world. Critics generally agree that cummings was one of the best writers of modern lyrical verse.

old age sticks

old age sticks
up Keep
Off
signs)&

youth yanks them   5
down(old
age
cries No

Tres)&(pas)
youth laughs   10
(sing
old age

scolds Forbid
den Stop
Must   15
n't Don't

&) youth goes
right on
gr
owing old   20

l(a

l(a
le
af
fa
ll
s)
one
l
iness

i thank You God for most this amazing

i thank You God for most this amazing
day: for the leaping greenly spirits of trees
and a blue true dream of sky; and for everything
which is natural which is infinite which is yes

(i who have died am alive again today,   5
and this is the sun's birthday; this is the birth
day of life and of love and wings; and of the gay
great happening illimitably earth)

how should tasting touching hearing seeing
breathing any—lifted from the no   10
of all nothing—human merely being
doubt unimaginable You?

(now the ears of my ears awake and
now the eyes of my eyes are opened)

UNDERSTANDING AND APPRECIATION

"old age sticks"

1. In this ironic comment on the conservatism of
old age versus the radicalism of youth, who "sticks
up" signs of "Keep Off" and "No Trespassing"?
Who tears down the signs?
2. What words does old age use to scold?
3. What does youth continue to do in the last
stanza? Explain the irony here.

"l(a"

Explain the relationship between the concrete
image inside the parentheses and the abstract
word outside the parentheses.

"i thank You God for most this amazing"

1. What has made the day "amazing" for the poet?
2. Who has been lifted "from the no / of all
nothing"?
3. cummings delighted in the sonnet form. Note,
however, that here he is not constrained to a tight
rhyme scheme. What words are "glancing
rhymes," or sound similarities, in the first stanza?

COMPOSITION

Now try your hand at writing abstract/concrete
poetry, using contrasting ideas and actions as
cummings did. Be certain, in arranging letters,
words, and syllables, that a reader can comprehend your images and central idea.

Langston Hughes 1902–1967

Popularly called "poet laureate of the black race" because he articulated the concept of black pride so capably, Langston Hughes was a man whose many accomplishments won him an international reputation. During a forty-year span, Hughes wrote poetry, novels, short stories, biographies, children's books, translations, and opera librettos. Many of his books have been translated into other languages, and his plays have been performed around the world. At the time of his death, he had the distinction of being the only American black man of letters able to support himself by his writing alone.

Hughes was born in Joplin, Missouri, received his public school education in Kansas and Ohio, and had a year at Columbia University before going to sea on a freighter putting in at the Canary Islands, the Azores, and West Africa. After living briefly in Paris, he returned to the United States and, while a busboy at a Washington hotel, was "discovered" by Vachel Lindsay, who included some of Hughes's poems in one of his public readings. By then associated with the Harlem Renaissance writers, Hughes published his first book of poems, *The Weary Blues,* in 1926. After resuming his schooling, he graduated from Lincoln University in Pennsylvania in 1929 and published *Not Without Laughter,* his first novel, in 1930. In the years following, his writings and honors multiplied and he was elected to the American Academy of Arts and Letters in 1961. Poetry, however, continued to be his primary interest. Among his many books of poetry are *Fine Clothes to the Jew* (1927), *Dear Lovely Death* (1931), *Shakespeare in Harlem* (1941), *Selected Poems* (1959), and *Ask Your Mama: Twelve Moods for Jazz* (1961). He also coauthored with Arna

PORTRAIT OF LANGSTON HUGHES, Winold Reiss
National Portrait Gallery, Smithsonian Institution

Bontemps *The Poetry of the Negro* (1950) and edited *New Negro Poets: U.S.A.* (1964). Some of Hughes's best-known writing was prose. In newspaper columns for the *New York Post* and *Chicago Defender,* he created a comic character, Jesse B. Semple ("Simple" for short), a resident of Harlem whose fictional adventures and "cracker-barrel" philosophy amused a host of readers between 1950 and 1965.

Theme for English B

The instructor said,

> *Go home and write*
> *a page tonight.*
> *And let that page come out of you—*
> *Then, it will be true.*   5

I wonder if it's that simple?
I am twenty-two, colored, born in
    Winston-Salem.
I went to school there, then Durham, then here
to this college on the hill above Harlem.
I am the only colored student in my class.   10
The steps from the hill lead down into Harlem,
through a park, then I cross St. Nicholas,
Eighth Avenue, Seventh, and I come to the Y,
the Harlem Branch Y, where I take the elevator
up to my room, sit down, and write this page: 15

It's not easy to know what is true for you or me
at twenty-two, my age. But I guess I'm what
I feel and see and hear, Harlem, I hear you:
hear you, hear me—we two—you, me,
    talk on this page.
(I hear New York, too.) Me—who?   20
Well, I like to eat, sleep, drink, and be in love.
I like to work, read, learn, and understand life.
I like a pipe for a Christmas present,
or records—Bessie, bop, or Bach.*
I guess being colored doesn't make me *not* like   25
the same things other folks like who are
    other races.
So will my page be colored that I write?

---

*__Bessie, bop, or Bach.__ __Bessie Smith__ (1898–1937) was
one of the most gifted blues singers of the 1920s and
early 1930s. Her first recording, "Down Hearted Blues"
(1923), was an enormous success. __Bop__ is a form of jazz.
__Johann Sebastian Bach__ (1685–1750) is famous for his
church music and his work in counterpoint and fugue.

Being me, it will not be white.
But it will be
a part of you, instructor.   30
You are white—
yet a part of me, as I am a part of you.

That's American.
Sometimes perhaps you don't want to be
        a part of me.
Nor do I often want to be a part of you.   35
But we are, that's true!
As I learn from you,
I guess you learn from me—
although you're older—and white—
and somewhat more free.   40

This is my page for English B.

UNDERSTANDING AND APPRECIATION

1. What are the instructor's directions? What information does the student give about himself in the two stanzas following the instructor's directions?
2. In an autobiographical account, Hughes wrote that he was always in love with Harlem. In lines 18–20, what is his use of *apostrophe* to show his feeling of closeness to this "city within a city"? What relationship does the writer see between the instructor and himself?
3. Critics agree that much of Hughes's poetry has the spontaneous feel of improvisation and is marked by such ease of expression and naturalness that the lines almost seem not to have been "composed" at all. Discuss whether you feel this to be true for "Theme for English B," noting the presence or absence of difficult vocabulary and imagery.

COMPOSITION

Take the assignment given the student in "Theme for English B" and write a page that comes "out of you." You may begin your composition by telling about yourself as Hughes did. Note that Hughes included significant information such as the fact that he was "the only colored student" in his class, how he felt about Harlem, and how he felt about being an American. Write only a page but be sure to tell something of what you "feel and see and hear."

Countee Cullen

Countee Cullen, a prominent figure in the Harlem Renaissance, was educated at New York University and Harvard. He modeled his poetry on the sonnets and quatrains of the nineteenth-century English romantic poets and on the verse forms of Edwin Arlington Robinson. The themes of Cullen's poems—the psychological impact of racial prejudice and the black American's search for an African heritage —were, however, new to American poetry.

Cullen published verse in several magazines and his longer works include *The Medea and Other Poems* (1935); *The Lost Zoo* (1940), a children's book; *One Way to Heaven* (1932), a satire on elite black society in Harlem; and *St. Louis Woman,* a musical play written in collaboration with Arna Bontemps. *On These I Stand,* a collection of the poems by which he wished to be remembered, was published posthumously in 1947.

PORTRAIT OF COUNTEE CULLEN

From the Dark Tower

We shall not always plant while others reap
The golden increment of bursting fruit,
Not always countenance, abject and mute,
That lesser men should hold their brothers cheap;
Not everlastingly while others sleep   5
Shall we beguile their limbs with mellow flute,
Not always bend to some more subtle brute;
We were not made eternally to weep.

The night whose sable breast relieves the stark,
White stars is no less lovely being dark,   10
And there are buds that cannot bloom at all
In light, but crumple, piteous, and fall;
So in the dark we hide the heart that bleeds,
And wait, and tend our agonizing seeds.

Any Human to Another

The ills I sorrow at
Not me alone
Like an arrow,
Pierce to the marrow,
Through the fat   5
And past the bone.

Your grief and mine
Must intertwine
Like sea and river,
Be fused and mingle,   10
Diverse yet single,
Forever and forever.

Let no man be so proud
And confident,
To think he is allowed   15
A little tent
Pitched in a meadow
Of sun and shadow
All his little own.

Joy may be shy, unique,   20
Friendly to a few,
Sorrow never scorned to speak
To any who
Were false or true.

Your every grief   25
Like a blade
Shining and unsheathed
Must strike me down.
Of bitter aloes* wreathed,
My sorrow must be laid   30
On your head like a crown.

---

*__aloes__ (al′ ōz),   a bitter drug made from the juice of the
leaves of certain aloe plants.

From ON THESE I STAND by Countee Cullen: "Any Human to Another."
Copyright, 1935, by Harper & Row, Publishers, Inc. Renewed, © 1963, by
Ida M. Cullen. Reprinted by permission of Harper & Row, Publishers, Inc.

YOUNG MAN IN A VEST, William H. Johnson
National Museum of American Art, Smithsonian Institution
Washington, D.C.

UNDERSTANDING AND APPRECIATION

1. What is the metaphorical significance of the
title: "From the Dark Tower"?
2. How does the image in the last two lines of
"From the Dark Tower" reinforce and complete
the hope implied in the first two lines?
3. In "Any Human to Another," what images does
Cullen use to suggest grief?
4. The English poet and cleric John Donne (1572–
1631) wrote: "No man is an island, entire of itself;
every man is a piece of the continent, a part of the
main; if a clod be washed away by the sea, Europe
is the less, as well as if a promontory were . . . any
man's death diminishes me, because I am involved
in mankind. . . . " Relate this concept of Donne's to
that in "Any Human to Another."
5. In ancient Greece and Rome those who were
honored were crowned with wreaths of inter-
twined flowers or leaves. Explain the metaphor the
poet uses in the last three lines.

Karl Shapiro   1913–

Karl Shapiro was born and reared in Baltimore, attended public schools there, and studied at both the University of Virginia and Johns Hopkins University. He published his first book of verse, *Poems,* in 1935, and during the time he served in the South Pacific in World War II, he published three more volumes of verse: *Person, Place and Thing* (1942), in which the poem "Auto Wreck" appears; *The Place of Love* (1942); and *V-Letter and Other Poems* (1944). The latter was awarded the Pulitzer Prize.

Shapiro served briefly as poetry consultant to the Library of Congress, taught English at several universities, was editor of two literary magazines, and has since continued to teach and write. His later works include several volumes of poetry, a novel, and books of critical essays. In the mid-1940s Shapiro aroused considerable controversy when he published the blank verse *Essay on Rime* in which he took a strong stand against poetic tradition by insisting on the primacy of intuition and emotion over poetic analysis, and by reasserting the importance of Whitman over Eliot and other modern poets.

PORTRAIT OF KARL SHAPIRO, Jill Krementz

Auto Wreck

Its quick soft silver bell beating, beating,
And down the dark one ruby flare
Pulsing out red light like an artery,
The ambulance at top speed floating down
Past beacons and illuminated clocks   5
Wings in a heavy curve, dips down,
And brakes speed, entering the crowd.
The doors leap open, emptying light;
Stretchers are laid out, the mangled lifted
And stowed into the little hospital.   10
Then the bell, breaking the hush, tolls once,

And the ambulance with its terrible cargo
Rocking, slightly rocking, moves away,
As the doors, an afterthought, are closed.

We are deranged,[1] walking among the cops   15
Who sweep glass and are large and composed.
One is still making notes under the light.
One with a bucket douches ponds of blood
Into the street and gutter.
One hangs lanterns on the wrecks that cling,   20
Empty husks of locusts, to iron poles.

Our throats were tight as tourniquets,
Our feet were bound with splints, but now
Like convalescents intimate and gauche,[2]
We speak through sickly smiles and warn   25
With the stubborn saw of common sense,
The grim joke and the banal resolution.
The traffic moves around with care,
But we remain, touching a wound
That opens to our richest horror.   30

Already old, the question Who shall die?
Becomes unspoken Who is innocent?
For death in war is done by hands;
Suicide has cause and stillbirth, logic.
But this invites the occult mind,   35
Cancels our physics with a sneer,
And spatters all we knew of denouement[3]
Across the expedient and wicked stones.

1. **deranged,** emotionally upset.
2. **gauche** (gōsh), clumsy, awkward.
3. **denouement** (dā′ nü man′), usually, the solution or
the unraveling of the plot in a story or play.

UNDERSTANDING AND APPRECIATION

1. The images crowding each other in the first stanza suggest the intensity of the poem. What is "quick soft silver . . . beating, beating"? Identify the assonance and alliteration in the first line. What is "pulsing out red like an artery" in the third line of the first stanza?

2. The word *toll* is usually used to mean the sound (or stroke) of a bell that is rung for the dead. What does this suggest about the "mangled" that are placed on stretchers?

3. There is no emotional outcry over the tragedy by the speaker or those in the crowd. How are the police described?

4. What metaphor does Shapiro use for the wrecked vehicles?

5. In the third stanza, explain the reference to tourniquets, splints, and convalescents.

6. What "old" question is asked in the final stanza?

Margaret Walker   1915–

Anguished over the prejudice against black people she found in both the South and North, Margaret Abigail Walker grew up wanting to write the songs of her people. The daughter of a Methodist minister, she spent her girlhood in Birmingham, Alabama, and received graduate degrees from both Northwestern and Iowa State universities. She has worked as a social worker, newspaper reporter, magazine editor, and college English teacher in North Carolina and West Virginia. Her most recent teaching position was at Jackson State College in Jackson, Mississippi.

For My People, Walker's first book of poetry, was published in 1942 as a result of her winning the Yale University Younger Poets competition; it continues to be recognized as an outstanding contribution to American literature. It is made up of three divisions: a grouping of direct poems in which she speaks for her people, a grouping of folk ballads in which she uses black dialect, and a grouping of sonnets. Among her other writings is *Jubilee* (1966), a long re-creation of the life and times of her great-grandmother, a slave. The book is noteworthy as the first Civil War novel by a black writer. Her second volume of poetry, *Prophets for a New Day,* was published in 1970.

For My People

For my people everywhere singing their slave songs repeatedly:
    their dirges and their ditties[1] and their blues and jub-
    ilees, praying their prayers nightly to an unknown god,
    bending their knees humble to an unseen power;

For my people lending their strength to the years, to the gone   5
    years and the now years and the maybe years, washing
    ironing cooking scrubbing sewing mending hoeing plowing
    digging planting pruning patching dragging along never
    gaining never reaping never knowing and never
        understanding;

For my playmates in the clay and dust and sand of Alabama   10
    backyards playing baptizing and preaching and doctor
    and jail and soldier and school and mama and cooking
    and playhouse and concert and store and hair and Miss
    Choomby and company;

1. **dirges . . . ditties,** funeral hymns . . . short simple songs.

"For My People" from FOR MY PEOPLE by Margaret Walker, published by Yale University Press, 1942.

For the cramped bewildered years we went to school to learn   **15**
    to know the reasons why and the answers to and the
    people who and the places where and the days when,
    in memory of the bitter hours when we discovered we
    were black and poor and small and different and nobody
    cared and nobody wondered and nobody understood;   **20**

For the boys and girls who grew in spite of these things to be
    man and woman, to laugh and dance and sing and play and
    drink their wine and religion and success, to marry
    their playmates and bear children and then die of consump-
    tion and anemia[2] and lynching;   **25**

For my people thronging 47th Street in Chicago and Lenox
    Avenue in New York and Rampart Street in New Orleans,
    lost disinherited dispossessed and happy people
    filling the cabarets[3] and taverns and other people's
    pockets needing bread and shoes and milk and land   **30**
    and money and something—something all our own;

For my people walking blindly spreading joy, losing time
    being lazy, sleeping when hungry, shouting when
    burdened, drinking when hopeless, tied and shackled
    and tangled among ourselves by the unseen creatures   **35**
    who tower over us omnisciently and laugh;

For my people blundering and groping and floundering in
    the dark of churches and schools and clubs and
    societies, associations and councils and committees
    and conventions, distressed and disturbed and de-   **40**
    ceived and devoured by money-hungry glory-craving
    leeches, preyed on by facile force of state and fad
    and novelty, by false prophet and holy believer;

For my people standing staring trying to fashion a better
    way from confusion, from hypocrisy and misunder-   **45**
    standing, trying to fashion a world that will hold
    all the people, all the faces, all the adams and eves
    and their countless generations;

2. **anemia** (a nē′ mē ə), condition in the blood characterized by a reduction of red blood cells.
3. **cabarets** (kab′ ə rāz′), restaurants with entertainment.

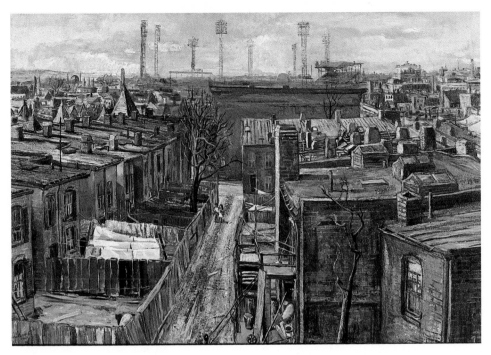

THE COUPLE, John Farrar, Barnett-Aden Collection, Anacostia Neighborhood Museum, Washington, D. C.

Let a new earth rise. Let another world be born. Let a bloody
   peace be written in the sky. Let a second generation   **50**
   full of courage issue forth; let a people loving freedom come to growth. Let a beauty full of healing and
   a strength of final clenching be the pulsing in our
   spirits and our blood. Let the martial songs be
   written, let the dirges disappear. Let a race of men   **55**
   now rise and take control.

UNDERSTANDING AND APPRECIATION

Form and Phrasing

In this powerful poem, the reader is caught up
and carried along in the rhythm of word forms,
use of parallel structure, and alliterative phrasing
as the poet builds toward her concluding verse
paragraph.

1. In the second paragraph, what does the poet say
her people have been doing over the "gone / years
and the now years and the maybe years"? Why do
you think Walker uses no commas or inner punctuation to set apart her words in series?

2. As revealed in the fourth paragraph, what did
her people go to school to learn? What did they
discover?

3. What do the people need, as revealed in the
sixth paragraph? Who are "the unseen creatures /
who tower over us omnisciently and laugh" in the
seventh?

4. In her concluding paragraph, how does the
author imply that the "new earth" would come
about? Is there a better solution?

MODERN DRAMA
Eugene O'Neill 1888–1953

At the turn of the century, as the famous romantic actor James O'Neill skillfully played the sentimental, melodramatic role of the Count of Monte Christo, he typified the best of American theater of the time. For several decades previously, European drama had been turning away from nineteenth-century melodrama and farce toward realism and expressionism. The best of these plays came primarily from the Scandinavian playwrights, Henrik Ibsen (1828–1906) and August Strindberg (1849–1912). Ibsen's realism attempted to show ordinary life with all its problems; Strindberg's expressionism dealt with psychology, the mind and its emotions.

Breaking loose from the set conventions that had held American theater in their grip was a coterie of adventurous young playwrights who began writing in the early decades of the twentieth century. But the Paul Bunyan of them all was James O'Neill's son, Eugene O'Neill. In his many plays, the dramatist pioneered the development of realistic, naturalistic, and expressionistic drama in the United States.

Eugene O'Neill was introduced to the theater through the stage door—he toured with his parents, managed the theatrical company of his father, and even did some acting—all before he had any idea of becoming a playwright. He was not an eager student and, after suspension from Princeton University, spent much of his time sailing as a merchant seaman on tramp steamers, beachcombing in Buenos Aires, gold-prospecting in Honduras, and frequenting waterfront bars in New York City. If his health had not failed, he might never have tried playwriting. When he entered a tuberculosis sanitarium in 1912 he was ill and despondent; when he left six months later he had found his vocation. By this time, work as a newspaper reporter had already aroused his interest in writing and after he turned his efforts to drama, he drove himself in ceaseless study and

PORTRAIT OF EUGENE O'NEILL, Soss Melik
National Portrait Gallery, Smithsonian Institution

experimentation to bring new artistry and originality to the American theater.

After attending a playwright's workshop at Harvard in 1914, he allied himself with the Provincetown (Massachusetts) Players, who produced ten of his short plays within three years. And though audiences may have been shocked at the frank, brutal language his plays contained, they recognized the vitality O'Neill was able to bring to his characters. Because the Provincetown Players were in revolt against what O'Neill called "the worn-out traditions, the commercial theater, the tawdry artificialities of the stage," they offered the young playwright the freedom to work out his innovative ideas as he wished.

Broadway beckoned in 1920. Although O'Neill won the Pulitzer Prize (the first of three) for *Beyond the Horizon* (1920), his first full-length play, it is a static, conventional tragedy in comparison with *The Emperor Jones* (1920) and *The Hairy Ape* (1921), two experimental plays that left no doubt about O'Neill's power to move an audience. His two central characters, the tragic hero Brutus Jones, giant black "emperor" of a West Indian island, and York, the stupid and profane stoker known to his shipmates as "the hairy ape," set New York talking about the daring young playwright. O'Neill obviously had found his subject, psychological revelation, and he was determined to show the world that the stage could handle it as brilliantly as the novel.

Between 1924 and 1931, O'Neill produced four major works that established his reputation internationally and made him the first American to win the Nobel Prize in Drama (1936). Two of these plays might be given particular mention because of their innovative staging and technical invention: *Desire Under the Elms* (1924) and *Strange Interlude* (1928). For the former, a stage set was designed that let the audience view action simultaneously in the kitchen, parlor, and upstairs bedrooms at the same time they saw the melancholy exterior of the Cabot farmhouse. For his nine-act *Strange Interlude* (really three plays in one), O'Neill introduced the use of stream-of-consciousness technique to the stage by having each actor's dialogue interspersed with that actor's thoughts, spoken aloud as asides for only the audience to hear while action was frozen on the stage. Through this technique, O'Neill sought to show how people disguise their true feelings with meaningless words.

A brilliant domestic comedy, *Ah, Wilderness* (1933), marked O'Neill's only deviation from a seeming compulsion to write tragedy. This is understandable in view of his childhood—spent in an environment filled with alcoholism and drug addiction. In fact, it is two tragedies that most critics say are O'Neill's greatest work: *The Ice Man Cometh* (1946) and *Long Day's Journey into Night* (1956).

As we look back on O'Neill's career, we realize that in almost every play he wrote he was trying, with "deep pity and understanding," to probe human nature, to show his audience the causes for neuroses and frustrations and tragedy. His last plays are such a far cry, in scope and setting, from his early one-act sea plays that we sometimes wonder whether they were written by the same man, though they surely were. O'Neill's early plays are slight and sometimes sentimental; but every audience that listened to their flat prose rhythms and their obsession with the ominous, omnipresent sea knew, without being told, that they were in the presence of a man with strong, true theatrical instincts. Once he had left his beachcombing days behind, the stage became his whole world. Into his plays he put his deep knowledge of man's nature, and he wrote with as sure a mastery of stagecraft as Nathaniel Hawthorne had of fiction and Emily Dickinson of the poetic mode. The time and the setting of his plays are of little import. Their themes of illusions, frustrations, dreams, and death are universal.

ILE
(A Play in One Act)

CHARACTERS

BEN   (the cabin boy)

THE STEWARD

CAPTAIN KEENEY

SLOCUM   (second mate[1])

MRS. KEENEY

JOE   (a harpooner)

Members of the crew of the steam whaler *Atlantic Queen*

SCENE

CAPTAIN KEENEY'S *cabin on board the steam whaling ship* Atlantic Queen—*a small, square compartment about eight feet high with a skylight in the center looking out on the poop deck. On the left (the stern of the ship) a long bench with rough cushions is built in against the wall. In front of the bench, a table. Over the bench, several curtained portholes.*

In the rear, left, a door leading to the CAP-TAIN'S sleeping quarters. To the right of the door a small organ, looking as if it were brand-new, is placed against the wall.

On the right, to the rear, a marble-topped sideboard. On the sideboard, a woman's sewing basket. Farther forward, a doorway leading to the companionway, and past the officers' quarters to the main deck.

In the center of the room, a stove. From the middle of the ceiling a hanging lamp is sus-pended. The walls of the cabin are painted white.

There is no rolling of the ship, and the light which comes through the skylight is sickly and faint, indicating one of those gray days of calm when ocean and sky are alike dead. The silence is unbroken except for the measured tread of someone walking up and down on the poop deck[2] overhead.

It is nearing two bells—one o'clock—in the afternoon of a day in the year 1895.

At the rise of the curtain there is a moment of intense silence. Then the STEWARD *enters and commences to clear the table of the few dishes which still remain on it after the* CAPTAIN'S *dinner. He is an old, grizzled man dressed in dungaree pants, a sweater, and a woolen cap with earflaps. His manner is sullen and angry. He stops stacking up the plates and casts a quick glance upward at the skylight; then tiptoes over to the closed door in rear and listens with his ear pressed to the crack. What he hears makes his face darken and he mutters a furious curse. There is a noise from the doorway on the right and he darts back to the table.*

BEN *enters. He is an overgrown, gawky boy with a long, pinched face. He is dressed in sweater, fur cap, etc. His teeth are chattering with the cold and he hurries to the stove, where he stands for a moment shivering, blow-ing on his hands, slapping them against his sides, on the verge of crying.*

1. **second mate,**   the officer third in command of the ship. (The ship's captain and the first mate are his superiors.)

2. **poop deck,**   the aftermost deck of a ship.

THE STEWARD (*in relieved tones—seeing who it is*). Oh, 'tis you, is it? What're ye shiverin' 'bout? Stay by the stove where ye belong and ye'll find no need of chatterin'.

BEN. It's c-c-cold. (*Trying to control his chattering teeth—derisively.*) Who d'ye think it were —the Old Man?

THE STEWARD (*makes a threatening move—*BEN *shrinks away*). None o' your lip, young un, or I'll learn ye. (*More kindly.*) Where was it ye've been all o' the time—the fo'c's'tle?[3]

BEN. Yes.

THE STEWARD. Let the Captain see ye up for'ard monkeyshinin' with the hands and ye'll get a hidin' ye'll not forget in a hurry.

BEN. Aw, he don't see nothin'. (*A trace of awe in his tones—he glances upward.*) He jest walks up and down like he didn't notice nobody— and stares at the ice to the no'th'ard.

THE STEWARD (*the same tone of awe creeping into his voice*). He's always starin' at the ice. (*In a sudden rage, shaking his fist at the skylight.*) Ice, ice, ice! Damn the ice! Holdin' us in for nigh on a year—nothin' to see but ice— stuck in it like a fly in molasses!

BEN (*apprehensively*). Ssshh! He'll hear ye.

THE STEWARD (*raging*). Aye, damn him, and damn the Arctic seas, and damn this stinkin' whalin' ship of his, and damn me for a fool to ever ship on it! (*Subsiding as if realizing the uselessness of this outburst— shaking his head—slowly, with deep conviction.*) He's a hard man—as hard a man as ever sailed the seas.

BEN (*solemnly*). Aye.

THE STEWARD. The two years we all signed up for are done this day. Two years o' this dog's life, and no luck in the fishin', and the hands half starved with the food runnin' low, rotten as it is; and not a sign of him turnin' back for home! (*Bitterly.*) Home! I begin to doubt if ever I'll set foot on land again. (*Excitedly.*) What is it he thinks he's goin' to do? Keep us all up here after our time is worked out till the last man of us is starved to death or frozen? We've grub enough hardly to last out the voyage back if we started now. What are the men goin' to do 'bout it? Did ye hear any talk in the fo'c's'tle?

BEN (*going over to him—in a half whisper*). They said if he don't put back south for home today they're goin' to mutiny.

THE STEWARD (*with grim satisfaction*). Mutiny? Aye, 'tis the only thing they can do; and serve him right after the manner he's treated them—'s if they weren't no better nor dogs.

BEN. The ice is all broke up to s'uth'ard. They's clear water s'far 's you can see. He ain't got no excuse for not turnin' back for home, the men says.

THE STEWARD (*bitterly*). He won't look no-wheres but n'th'ard where they's only the ice to see. He don't want to see no clear water. All he thinks on is gettin' the ile—'s if it was our fault he ain't had good luck with the whales. (*Shaking his head.*) I think the man's mighty nigh losin' his senses.

BEN (*awed*). D'you really think he's crazy?

THE STEWARD. Aye, it's the punishment o' God on him. Did ye ever hear of a man who wasn't crazy do the things he does? (*Pointing to the door in the rear.*) Who but a man that's mad would take his woman—and as sweet a woman as ever was—on a stinkin' whalin' ship to the Arctic seas to be locked in by the rotten ice for nigh on a year, and maybe lose her senses forever—for it's sure she'll never be the same again.

BEN (*sadly*). She useter be awful nice to me before—(*His eyes grow wide and frightened.*) —she got—like she is.

THE STEWARD. Aye, she was good to all of us. 'Twould have been hell on board without her; for he's a hard man—a hard, hard man—a driver if there ever was one. (*With a grim laugh.*) I hope he's satisfied now— drivin' her on till she's near lost her mind. And who could blame her? 'Tis a God's

---

3. **the f'c's'tle** (fōk′ sal), the forecastle, or forward part of a ship, where the sailors' quarters are housed.

wonder we're not a ship full of crazed people—with the ice all the time, and the quiet so thick you're afraid to hear your own voice.

BEN (*with a frightened glance toward the door on right*). She don't never speak to me no more—jest looks at me 's if she didn't know me.

THE STEWARD. She don't know no one—but him. She talks to him—when she does talk—right enough.

BEN. She does nothin' all day long now but sit and sew—and then she cries to herself without makin' no noise. I've seen her.

THE STEWARD. Aye, I could hear her through the door awhile back.

BEN (*tiptoes over to the door and listens*). She's cryin' now.

THE STEWARD (*furiously—shaking his fist*). Blast him for the devil he is!

[*There is the noise of someone coming slowly down the companionway stairs. The* STEWARD *hurries to his stacked-up dishes. He is so nervous from fright that he knocks off the top one, which falls and breaks on the floor. He stands aghast, trembling with dread.* BEN *is violently rubbing off the organ with a piece of cloth which he has snatched from his pocket.* CAPTAIN KEENEY *appears in the doorway on right and comes into the cabin, removing his fur cap as he does so. He is a man of about forty, around five-ten in height but looking much shorter on account of the enormous proportions of his shoulders and chest. His face is massive and deeply lined, with gray-blue eyes of a bleak hardness, and a tightly clenched, thin-lipped mouth. His thick hair is long and gray. He is dressed in a heavy blue jacket and blue pants stuffed into his sea-boots.*

He is followed into the cabin by the SECOND MATE, *a rangy six-footer with a lean weather-beaten face. The* MATE *is dressed about the same as the* CAPTAIN. *He is a man of thirty or so.*]

KEENEY (*comes toward the* STEWARD *with a stern look on his face. The* STEWARD *is visibly frightened and the stack of dishes rattles in his trembling hands.* KEENEY *draws back his fist and the* STEWARD *shrinks away. The fist is gradually lowered and* KEENEY *speaks slowly*). 'Twould be like hittin' a worm. It is nigh on two bells, Mr. Steward, and this truck not cleared yet.

THE STEWARD (*stammering*). Y-y-yes, sir.

KEENEY. Instead of doin' your rightful work ye've been below here gossipin' old woman's talk with that boy. (*To* BEN, *fiercely.*) Get out o' this, you! Clean up the chart room. (BEN *darts past the* MATE *to the open doorway.*) Pick up that dish, Mr. Steward!

THE STEWARD (*doing it with difficulty*). Yes, sir.

KEENEY. The next dish you break, Mr. Steward, you take a bath in the Bering Sea at the end of a rope.

THE STEWARD (*tremblingly*). Yes, sir.

[*He hurries out. The* SECOND MATE *walks slowly over to the* CAPTAIN.]

MATE. I warn't 'specially anxious the man at the wheel should catch what I wanted to say to you, sir. That's why I asked you to come below.

KEENEY (*impatiently*). Speak your say, Mr. Slocum.

MATE (*unconsciously lowering his voice*). I'm afeared there'll be trouble with the hands by the look o' things. They'll likely turn ugly, every blessed one o' them, if you don't put back. The two years they signed up for is up today.

KEENEY. And d'you think you're tellin' me somethin' new, Mr. Slocum? I've felt it in the air this long time past. D'you think I've not seen their ugly looks and the grudgin' way they worked?

[*The door in rear is opened and* MRS. KEENEY *stands in the doorway. She is a slight, sweet-faced little woman, primly dressed in black. Her eyes are red from weeping and her face drawn and pale. She takes in the cabin*

THE ICEBERGS, Frederic Edwin Church
Dallas Museum of Fine Arts, Texas

One of America's foremost nineteenth-century landscape artists, Church excelled at the realistic depiction of dramatic natural scenes.

with a frightened glance and stands as if fixed to the spot by some nameless dread, clasping and unclasping her hands nervously. The two men turn and look at her.]

KEENEY *(with rough tenderness).* Well, Annie?

MRS. KEENEY *(as if awakening from a dream).* David, I—(*She is silent. The* MATE *starts for the doorway.*)

KEENEY *(turning to him—sharply).* Wait!

MATE. Yes, sir.

KEENEY. D'you want anything, Annie?

MRS. KEENEY *(after a pause, during which she seems to be endeavoring to collect her thoughts).* I thought maybe—I'd go up on deck, David, to get a breath of fresh air. (*She stands humbly awaiting his permission. He and the* MATE *exchange a significant glance.*)

KEENEY. It's too cold, Annie. You'd best stay below today. There's nothin' to look at on deck—but ice.

MRS. KEENEY *(monotonously).* I know—ice, ice, ice! But there's nothing to see down here but these walls. (*She makes a gesture of loathing.*)

KEENEY. You can play the organ, Annie.

MRS. KEENEY *(dully).* I hate the organ. It puts me in mind of home.

KEENEY *(a touch of resentment in his voice).* I got it jest for you.

MRS. KEENEY *(dully).* I know. (*She turns away from them and walks slowly to the bench on left. She lifts up one of the curtains and looks through a porthole; then utters an exclamation of joy.*) Ah, water! Clear water! As far as I can see! How good it looks after all these months of ice! (*She turns round to them, her face transfigured with joy.*) Ah, now I must go up on deck and look at it, David!

KEENEY *(frowning).* Best not today, Annie. Best wait for a day when the sun shines.

MRS. KEENEY (*desperately*). But the sun never shines in this terrible place.

KEENEY (*a tone of command in his voice*). Best not today, Annie.

MRS. KEENEY (*crumbling before this command—abjectly*). Very well, David. (*She stands there staring straight before her as if in a daze. The two men look at her uneasily.*)

KEENEY (*sharply*). Annie!

MRS. KEENEY (*dully*). Yes, David.

KEENEY. Me and Mr. Slocum has business to talk about—ship's business.

MRS. KEENEY. Very well, David. (*She goes slowly out, rear, and leaves the door three-quarters shut behind her.*)

KEENEY. Best not have her on deck if they's goin' to be any trouble.

MATE. Yes, sir.

KEENEY. And trouble they's goin' to be. I feel it in my bones. (*Takes a revolver from his coat pocket and examines it.*) Got your'n?

MATE. Yes, sir.

KEENEY. Not that we'll have to use 'em—not if I know their breed of dog—jest to frighten 'em up a bit. (*Grimly.*) I ain't never been forced to use one yit; and trouble I've had by land and by sea s'long as I kin remember, and will have till my dyin' day, I reckon.

MATE (*hesitatingly*). Then you ain't goin'—to turn back?

KEENEY. Turn back? Mr. Slocum, did you ever hear o' me pointin' s'uth for home with only a measly four hundred barrel of ile in the hold?

MATE (*hastily*). No, sir—but the grub's gittin' low.

KEENEY. They's enough to last a long time yit, if they're careful with it; and they's plenty o' water.

MATE. They say it's not fit to eat—what's left; and the two years they signed on fur is up today. They might make trouble for you in the courts when we git home.

KEENEY. Let them make what law trouble they kin! I've got to git the ile! (*Glancing sharply at the* MATE.) You ain't turnin' no sea-lawyer, be you, Mr. Slocum?

MATE (*flushing*). Not by a sight, sir.

KEENEY. What do the fools want to go home fur now? Their share o' the four hundred barrel wouldn't keep 'em in chewin' ter-bacco.

MATE (*slowly*). They want to git back to their folks an' things, I s'pose.

KEENEY (*looking at him searchingly*). 'N you want to turn back, too. (*The* MATE *looks down confusedly before his sharp gaze.*) Don't lie, Mr. Slocum. It's writ down plain in your eyes. (*With grim sarcasm.*) I hope, Mr. Slocum, you ain't goin' to jine the men agin me.

MATE (*indignantly*). That ain't fair, sir, to say sich things.

KEENEY (*with satisfaction*). I warn't much afeard o' that, Tom. You been with me nigh on ten year and I've learned ye whalin'. No man kin say I ain't a good master, if I be a hard one.

MATE. I warn't thinkin' of myself, sir—'bout turnin' home, I mean. (*Desperately.*) But Mrs. Keeney, sir—seems like she ain't jest satisfied up here, ailin' like—what with the cold an' bad luck an' the ice an' all.

KEENEY (*his face clouding—rebukingly but not severely*). That's my business, Mr. Slocum. I'll thank you to steer a clear course o' that. (*A pause.*) The ice'll break up soon to no'th'ard. I could see it startin' today. And when it goes and we git some sun Annie'll perk up. (*Another pause—then he bursts forth.*) It ain't the money what's keepin' me up in the northern seas, Tom. But I can't go back to Homeport with a measly four hundred barrel of ile. I'd die fust. I ain't never come back home in all my days without a full ship. Ain't that truth?

MATE. Yes, sir; but this voyage you been icebound, an'—

KEENEY (*scornfully*). And d'you s'pose any of 'em would believe that—any o' them skippers I've beaten voyage after voyage? Can't you hear 'em laughin' and sneerin'—

Tibbots 'n' Harris 'n' Simms and the rest—and all o' Homeport makin' fun o' me? "Dave Keeney what boasts he's the best whalin' skipper out o' Homeport comin' back with a measly four hundred barrel of ile?" (*The thought of this drives him into a frenzy, and he smashes his fist down on the marble top of the sideboard.*) I got to git the ile, I tell you. How could I figger on this ice? It's never been so bad before in the thirty year I been acomin' here. And now it's breakin' up. In a couple o' days it'll be all gone. And they's whale here, plenty of 'em. I know they is and I ain't never gone wrong yit. I got to git the ile! And I ain't agoin' home till I do git it!

[*There is the sound of subdued sobbing from the door in rear. The two men stand silent for a moment, listening. Then* KEENEY *goes over to the door and looks in. He hesitates for a moment as if he were going to enter—then closes the door softly.* JOE, *the harpooner, an enormous six-footer with a battered, ugly face, enters from right and stands waiting for the* CAPTAIN *to notice him.*]

KEENEY (*turning and seeing him*). Don't stand there like a gawk, Harpooner. Speak up!

JOE (*confusedly*). We want—the men, sir—they wants to send a depitation aft to have a word with you.

KEENEY (*furiously*). Tell 'em to go to—(*Checks himself and continues grimly.*) Tell 'em to come. I'll see 'em.

JOE. Aye, aye, sir. (*He goes out.*)

KEENEY (*with a grim smile*). Here it comes, the trouble you spoke of, Mr. Slocum, and we'll make short shift of it. It's better to crush such things at the start than let them make headway.

MATE (*worriedly*). Shall I wake up the First and Fourth,[4] sir? We might need their help.

KEENEY. No, let them sleep. I'm well able to handle this alone, Mr. Slocum.

[*There is the shuffling of footsteps from outside*

and five of the crew crowd into the cabin, led by JOE. *All are dressed alike—sweaters, sea-boots, etc. They glance uneasily at the* CAPTAIN, *twirling their fur caps in their hands.*]

KEENEY (*after a pause*). Well? Who's to speak fur ye?

JOE (*stepping forward with an air of bravado*). I be.

KEENEY (*eyeing him up and down coldly*). So you be. Then speak your say and be quick about it.

JOE (*trying not to wilt before the* CAPTAIN'S *glance and avoiding his eyes*). The time we signed up for is done today.

KEENEY (*icily*). You're tellin' me nothin' I don't know.

JOE. You ain't p'intin' fur home yit, far 's we kin see.

KEENEY. No, and I ain't goin' to till this ship is full of ile.

JOE. You can't go no further no'th with the ice afore ye.

KEENEY. The ice is breaking up.

JOE (*after a slight pause during which the others mumble angrily to one another*). The grub we're gittin' now is rotten.

KEENEY. It's good enough fur ye. Better men than ye are have eaten worse.

[*There is a chorus of angry exclamations.*]

JOE (*encouraged by this support*). We ain't agoin' to work no more 'less you puts back for home.

KEENEY (*fiercely*). You ain't, ain't you?

JOE. No; and the law courts'll say we was right.

KEENEY. We're at sea now and I'm the law on this ship! (*Edging up toward the harpooner.*) And every mother's son of you what don't obey orders goes in irons.

[*There are more angry exclamations from the crew.* MRS. KEENEY *appears in the doorway*

---

4. **the First and Fourth,** the first and fourth mates.

in the rear and looks on with startled eyes. None of the men notice her.]

JOE *(with bravado).* Then we're agoin' to mutiny and take the old hooker home ourselves. Ain't we, boys?

[As he turns his head to look at the others, KEENEY'S *fist shoots out to the side of his jaw.* JOE *goes down in a heap and lies there.* MRS. KEENEY *gives a shriek and hides her face in her hands. The men pull out their sheath knives and start a rush, but stop when they find themselves confronted by the revolvers of* KEENEY *and the* MATE.*]*

KEENEY *(his eyes and voice snapping).* Hold still! *(The men stand huddled together in a sullen silence.* KEENEY'S *voice is full of mockery).* You've found out it ain't safe to mutiny on this ship, ain't you? And now git for'ard where ye belong, and—*(He gives* JOE'S *body a contemptuous kick.)* Drag him with you. And remember, the first man of ye I see shirkin' I'll shoot dead as sure as there's a sea under us, and you can tell the rest the same. Git for'ard now! Quick! *(The men leave in cowed silence, carrying* JOE *with them.* KEENEY *turns to the* MATE *with a short laugh and puts his revolver back in his pocket.)* Best get up on deck, Mr. Slocum, and see to it they don't try none of their skulkin' tricks. We'll have to keep an eye peeled from now on. I know 'em.

MATE. Yes, sir.

[He goes out, right. KEENEY *hears his wife's hysterical weeping and turns around in surprise—then walks slowly to her side.]*

KEENEY *(putting an arm around her shoulder— with gruff tenderness).* There, there, Annie. Don't be afeard. It's all past and gone.

MRS. KEENEY *(shrinking away from him).* Oh, I can't bear it—Oh, I can't bear it any longer!

KEENEY *(gently).* Can't bear what, Annie?

MRS. KEENEY *(hysterically).* All this horrible brutality, and these brutes of men, and this terrible ship, and this prison cell of a room, and the ice all around, and the silence. *(After this outburst she calms down and wipes her eyes with her handkerchief.)*

KEENEY *(after a pause during which he looks down at her with a puzzled frown).* Remember, I warn't hankerin' to have you come on this voyage, Annie.

MRS. KEENEY. I wanted to be with you, David, don't you see? I didn't want to wait back there in the house all alone as I've been doing these last six years since we were married—waiting, and watching, and fearing—with nothing to keep my mind occupied—not able to go back teaching school on account of being Dave Keeney's wife. I used to dream of sailing on the great, wide, glorious ocean. I wanted to be by your side in the danger and vigorous life of it all. I wanted to see you the hero they make you out to be in Homeport. And instead—*(her voice grows tremulous)*—all I find is ice and cold—and brutality! *(Her voice breaks.)*

KEENEY. I warned you what it'd be, Annie. "Whalin' ain't no ladies' tea party," I says to you, and "You better stay to home where you've got all your woman's comforts." *(Shaking his head.)* But you was so set on it.

MRS. KEENEY *(wearily).* Oh, I know it isn't your fault, David. You see, I didn't believe you. I guess I was dreaming about the old Vikings in the story books and I thought you were one of them.

KEENEY *(protestingly).* I done my best to make it as cozy and comfortable as could be. *(*MRS. KEENEY *looks around her in wild scorn.)* I even sent to the city for that organ for ye, thinkin' it might be soothin' to ye to be playin' it times when they was calms and things was dull-like.

MRS. KEENEY *(wearily).* Yes, you were very kind, David. I know that. *(She goes to left and lifts the curtains from the porthole and looks out—then suddenly bursts forth.)* I won't stand it—I can't stand it—pent up by these walls like a prisoner. *(She runs over to him and* *throws her arms around him, weeping. He puts his arm protectingly over her shoulders.)* Take me away from here, David! If I don't get away from here, out of this terrible ship, I'll go mad! Take me home, David! I can't think any more. I feel as if the cold and the silence were crushing down on my brain. I'm afraid. Take me home!

KEENEY *(holds her at arm's length and looks at her face anxiously).* Best go to bed, Annie. You ain't yourself. You got fever. Your eyes look so strange-like. I ain't never seen you look this way before.

MRS. KEENEY *(laughing hysterically).* It's the ice and the cold and the silence—they'd make anyone look strange.

KEENEY *(soothingly).* In a month or two, with good luck, three at the most, I'll have her filled with ile and then we'll give her everything she'll stand and p'int for home.

MRS. KEENEY. But we can't wait for that—I can't wait. I want to get home. And the men won't wait. They want to get home. It's cruel, it's brutal for you to keep them. You must sail back. You've got no excuse. There's clear water to the south now. If you've a heart at all, you've got to turn back.

KEENEY *(harshly).* I can't, Annie.

MRS. KEENEY. Why can't you?

KEENEY. A woman couldn't rightly understand my reason.

MRS. KEENEY *(wildly).* Because it's a stupid, stubborn reason. Oh, I heard you talking with the second mate. You're afraid the other captains will sneer at you because you didn't come back with a full ship. You want to live up to your silly reputation even if you do have to beat and starve men and drive me mad to do it.

KEENEY *(his jaw set stubbornly).* It ain't that, Annie. Them skippers would never dare sneer to my face. It ain't so much what anyone'd say—but—*(he hesitates, struggling to express his meaning)*—you see—I've always done it—since my first voyage as skipper. I always come back—with a full ship—and

—it don't seem right not to—somehow. I been always first whalin' skipper out o' Homeport, and—don't you see my meanin', Annie? *(He glances at her. She is not looking at him, but staring dully in front of her, not hearing a word he is saying.)* Annie! *(She comes to herself with a start.)* Best turn in, Annie, there's a good woman. You ain't well.

MRS. KEENEY *(resisting his attempts to guide her to the door in rear).* David! Won't you please turn back?

KEENEY *(gently).* I can't, Annie—not yet awhile. You don't see my meanin'. I got to git the ile.

MRS. KEENEY. It'd be different if you needed the money, but you don't. You've got more than plenty.

KEENEY *(impatiently).* It ain't the money I'm thinkin' of. D'you think I'm mean as that?

MRS. KEENEY *(dully).* No—I don't know—I can't understand—*(Intensely.)* Oh, I want to be home in the old house once more and see my own kitchen again, and hear a woman's voice talking to me and be able to talk to her. Two years! It seems so long ago—as if I'd been dead and could never go back.

KEENEY *(worried by her strange tone and the faraway look in her eyes).* Best go to bed, Annie. You ain't well.

MRS. KEENEY *(not appearing to hear him).* I used to be lonely when you were away. I used to think Homeport was a stupid, monotonous place. Then I used to go down to the beach, especially when it was windy and the breakers were rolling in, and I'd dream of the fine, free life you must be leading. *(She gives a laugh which is half a sob.)* I used to love the sea then. *(She pauses; then continues with slow intensity.)* But now—I don't ever want to see the sea again.

KEENEY *(thinking to humor her).* 'Tis no fit place for a woman, that's sure. I was a fool to bring ye.

MRS. KEENEY *(after a pause—passing her hand over her eyes with a gesture of pathetic weari-*

ness). How long would it take us to reach home—if we started now?

KEENEY *(frowning).* 'Bout two months, I reckon, Annie, with fair luck.

MRS. KEENEY *(counts on her fingers—then murmurs with a rapt smile).* That would be August, the latter part of August, wouldn't it? It was on the twenty-fifth of August we were married, David, wasn't it?

KEENEY *(trying to conceal the fact that her memories had moved him—gruffly).* Don't *you* remember?

MRS. KEENEY *(vaguely—again passes her hand over her eyes).* My memory is leaving me—up here in the ice. It was so long ago. *(A pause—then she smiles dreamily.)* It's June now. The lilacs will be all in bloom in the front yard—and the climbing roses on the trellis to the side of the house—they're budding. *(She suddenly covers her face with her hands and commences to sob.)*

KEENEY *(disturbed).* Go in and rest, Annie. You're all worn out cryin' over what can't be helped.

MRS. KEENEY *(suddenly throwing her arms around his neck and clinging to him).* You love me, don't you, David?

KEENEY *(in amazed embarrassment at this outburst).* Love you? Why d'you ask me such a question, Annie?

MRS. KEENEY *(shaking him fiercely).* But you do, don't you, David? Tell me!

KEENEY. I'm your husband, Annie, and you're my wife. Could there be aught but love between us after all these years?

MRS. KEENEY *(shaking him again—still more fiercely).* Then you do love me. Say it!

KEENEY *(simply).* I do, Annie.

MRS. KEENEY *(gives a sigh of relief—her hands drop to her sides.* KEENEY *regards her anxiously. She passes her hand across her eyes and murmurs half to herself).* I sometimes think if we could only have had a child—(KEENEY *turns away from her, deeply moved. She grabs his arm and turns him around to face her—intensely.)* And

I've always been a good wife to you, haven't I, David?

KEENEY *(his voice betraying his emotion).* No man has ever had a better, Annie.

MRS. KEENEY. And I've never asked for much from you, have I, David? Have I?

KEENEY. You know you could have all I got the power to give ye, Annie.

MRS. KEENEY *(wildly).* Then do this, this once, for my sake, for God's sake—take me home! It's killing me, this life—the brutality and cold and horror of it. I'm going mad. I can feel the threat in the air. I can hear the silence threatening me—day after gray day and every day the same. I can't bear it. *(Sobbing.)* I'll go mad, I know I will. Take me home, David, if you love me as you say. I'm afraid. For the love of God, take me home!

[She throws her arms around him, weeping against his shoulder. His face betrays the tremendous struggle going on within him. He holds her out at arm's length, his expression softening. For a moment his shoulder sags, he becomes old, his iron spirit weakens as he looks at her tear-stained face.]

KEENEY *(dragging out the words with an effort).* I'll do it, Annie—for your sake—if you say it's needful for ye.

MRS. KEENEY *(with wild joy—kissing him).* God bless you for that, David!

[He turns away from her silently and walks toward the companionway. Just at that moment there is a clatter of footsteps on the stairs and the SECOND MATE *enters the cabin.]*

MATE *(excitedly).* The ice is breakin' up to the no'th'ard, sir. There's a clear passage through the floe, and clear water beyond, the lookout says.

[KEENEY straightens himself like a man coming out of a trance. MRS. KEENEY looks at the MATE with terrified eyes.]

KEENEY (*dazedly—trying to collect his thoughts*). A clear passage? To no'th'ard?

MATE. Yes, sir.

KEENEY (*his voice suddenly grim with determination*). Then get her ready and we'll drive her through.

MATE. Aye, aye, sir.

MRS. KEENEY (*appealingly*). David!

KEENEY (*not heeding her*). Will the men turn to willin' or must we drag 'em out?

MATE. They'll turn to willin' enough. You put the fear o' God into 'em, sir. They're meek as lambs.

KEENEY. Then drive 'em—both watches. (*With grim determination.*) They's whale t'other side o' this floe and we're agoin' to git 'em.

MATE. Aye, aye, sir.

[*He goes out hurriedly. A moment later there is the sound of scuffling feet from the deck outside and the* MATE'S *voice shouting orders.*]

KEENEY (*speaking aloud to himself—derisively*). And I was agoin' home like a yaller dog!

MRS. KEENEY (*imploringly*). David!

KEENEY (*sternly*). Woman, you ain't adoin' right when you meddle in men's business and weaken 'em. You can't know my feelin's. I got to prove a man to be a good husband for ye to take pride in. I got to git the ile, I tell ye.

MRS. KEENEY (*supplicatingly*). David. Aren't you going home?

KEENEY (*ignoring this question—commandingly*). You ain't well. Go and lay down a mite. (*He starts for the door.*) I got to git on deck.

[*He goes out. She cries after him in anguish, "David!" A pause. She passes her hand across her eyes—then commences to laugh hysterically and goes to the organ. She sits down and starts to play wildly an old hymn.* KEENEY *reenters from the doorway to the deck and stands looking at her angrily. He comes over and grabs her roughly by the shoulder.*]

KEENEY. Woman, what foolish mockin' is this? (*She laughs wildly and he starts back from her in alarm.*) Annie! What is it? (*She doesn't answer him.* KEENEY'S *voice trembles.*) Don't you know me, Annie?

[*He puts both hands on her shoulders and turns her around so that he can look into her eyes. She stares up at him with a stupid expression, a vague smile on her lips. He stumbles away from her, and she commences softly to play the organ again.*]

KEENEY (*swallowing hard—in a hoarse whisper, as if he had difficulty in speaking*). You said— you was agoin' mad—God!

[*A long wail is heard from the deck above, "Ah, bl-o-o-o-ow!"[5] A moment later the* MATE'S *face appears through the skylight. He cannot see* MRS. KEENEY.]

MATE (*in great excitement*). Whales, sir—a whole school of 'em—off the starb'd quarter 'bout five miles away—big ones!

KEENEY (*galvanized into action*). Are you lowerin' the boats?

MATE. Yes, sir.

KEENEY (*with grim decision*). I'm acomin' with ye.

MATE. Aye, aye, sir. (*Jubilantly*.) You'll git the ile now right enough, sir.

[*His head is withdrawn and he can be heard shouting orders.*]

KEENEY (*turning to his wife*). Annie! Did you hear him? I'll git the ile. (*She doesn't answer or seem to know he is there. He gives a hard laugh, which is almost a groan.*) I know you're foolin' me, Annie. You ain't out of your mind—(*anxiously*)—be you? I'll git the ile now right enough—jest a little while longer, Annie—then we'll turn home'ard. I can't turn back now, you see that, don't you? I've

5. **Ah, bl-o-o-o-ow!** the cry of the lookout when he sights the spray blown by a whale.

got to git the ile. (*In sudden terror.*) Answer me! You ain't mad, be you?

[*She keeps on playing the organ, but makes no reply. The* MATE'S *face appears again through the skylight.*]

MATE. All ready, sir.

[KEENEY *turns his back on his wife and strides to the doorway, where he stands for a moment and looks back at her in anguish, fighting to control his feelings.*]

MATE. Comin', sir?

KEENEY (*his face suddenly grown hard with determination*). Aye.

[*He turns abruptly and goes out.* MRS. KEENEY *does not appear to notice his departure. Her whole attention seems centered in the organ. She sits with half-closed eyes, her body swaying a little from side to side to the rhythm of the hymm. Her fingers move faster and faster and she is playing wildly and discordantly as the curtain falls.*]

FOR UNDERSTANDING

1. Why is the day upon which the play begins of great importance to the crew of the whaler? What are they planning to do?
2. What evidence does the steward cite to support his contention that the captain is crazy?
3. How does seeing Keeney subdue the mutineers affect his wife's behavior? What does she beg him to do and why?
4. What makes Keeney decide not to turn back home?

FOR INTERPRETATION

In nearly all the plays he wrote, O'Neill tried with "deep pity and understanding" to explore human nature and show his audience the neuroses and frustrations that could end in tragedy. All his works show the compassion with which he treated his characters.

As set forth in the speech beginning, "Woman, you ain't adoin' right . . . " (p. 711), explain why

Keeney feels trapped. Do you feel sympathy for him in his dilemma? How is Annie Keeney also "trapped"? Discuss.

FOR APPRECIATION

Staging

1. One of O'Neill's trademarks was his sure instinct for staging that produced just the atmosphere or effect he desired. In this play it was important that he convey the dread monotony of Annie Keeney's existence on the ice-bound ship. Discuss details of the stage set or scene that contribute to this monotony. How has the captain's behavior over the long months of the ship's imprisonment contributed to the monotonous atmosphere?
2. Whether a play is being read or performed, meaningful stage directions are essential to present the action as the playwright has intended it. Check the stage direction that precedes Captain Keeney's assent to his wife's wish. What does this tell either actor or reader about the effect that turning back would have had on Captain Keeney's character?
3. The organ, which obviously doesn't belong on the rough whaler any more than Annie Keeney, is interpreted by many to represent a symbol of the home. How, then, would reader or audience interpret the wild, discordant music as the play closes?

COMPOSITION

Select any two of the six characters listed in the cast and write a page of dialogue in which you have them exchange thoughts related to some problem on their ill-starred voyage—the endless ice, the dwindling food supply, plans for mutiny, worries about loved ones at home.

To do this well, you will need to envision the characters you choose as whole individuals and imagine what their lives might be like. Consider what is meaningful to them and what they would be likely to talk about. For example, what would Annie Keeney be thinking if she were talking to the steward? What would Ben, the cabin boy, say to Joe, a harpooner? Be sure to include stage directions (enclosed in parentheses) to help your reader interpret your dialogue.

A TWENTIETH-CENTURY WRITER LOOKS BACK

In "A Christmas Memory," Truman Capote looks back on his childhood in the 1930s. As a small boy, he and his mother went to live with cousins in Alabama. One of his elderly relatives was Sook Falk, a timid, childlike woman. She was given charge of Truman, and soon became a kindred spirit to the shy, imaginative boy. The time was the Great Depression, a period of severe economic hardship, anxiety, and constant "making do." But in this fictionalized account the family's straitened circumstances are eclipsed by the warmth and richness of the friendship Capote describes.

Truman Capote   1924–1984

Truman Streckfus Persons spent most of his childhood in New Orleans and Monroeville, Alabama. It was his mother's second marriage that gave him the name Capote and brought him to New York, where he continued his schooling. After dropping out of school at seventeen, he worked briefly as a protégé of a fortuneteller and then for the *New Yorker* magazine, beginning as an errand boy.

Intent upon a writing career, Capote, who had won first prize in a short-story contest when he was eight, began publishing other stories in magazines in 1945. In 1948 his *Other Voices, Other Rooms,* a novel of childhood and Southern decadence, won acclaim for its poetic use of language and authenticity of dialogue. The collections, *Tree of Night* (1949) and *Local Color* (1950), further advanced his reputation as a stylist of remarkable ability. In 1951 his novel *The Grass Harp* revealed his empathy for children and eccentrics. In addition to travel sketches he also wrote *Breakfast at Tiffany's* (1958).

In midlife Capote developed an interest in

PORTRAIT OF TRUMAN CAPOTE
Capote's literary output has ranged from works of poetic fiction to works of hard-hitting nonfiction.

journalism, in contrast to the highly imaginative nature of much of his fiction, and secured reportorial assignments for the *New Yorker* that included covering the mass murder of a farm family in Kansas. From this came *In Cold Blood* (1966), a book-length work detailing actual events but using many of the techniques of the novel. Although it resulted in mixed critical furor, it made the best-seller list and was also made into a film. As a whole, Capote's efforts at dramatic writing brought only limited success. However, a number of his television adaptations, among them "A Christmas Memory" and "The Thanksgiving Visitor," are considered classics.

A CHRISTMAS MEMORY

Imagine a morning in late November. A coming of winter morning more than twenty years ago. Consider the kitchen of a spreading old house in a country town. A great black stove is its main feature; but there is also a big round table and a fireplace with two rocking chairs placed in front of it. Just today the fireplace commenced its seasonal roar.

A woman with shorn white hair is standing at the kitchen window. She is wearing tennis shoes and a shapeless gray sweater over a summery calico dress. She is small and sprightly, like a bantam hen; but, due to a long youthful illness, her shoulders are pitifully hunched. Her face is remarkable—not unlike Lincoln's, craggy like that, and tinted by sun and wind; but it is delicate too, finely boned, and her eyes are sherry-colored and timid. "Oh my," she exclaims, her breath smoking the windowpane, "it's fruitcake weather!"

The person to whom she is speaking is myself. I am seven; she is sixty-something. We are cousins, very distant ones, and we have lived together—well, as long as I can remember. Other people inhabit the house, relatives; and though they have power over us, and frequently make us cry, we are not, on the whole, too much aware of them. We are each other's best friend. She calls me Buddy, in memory of a boy who was formerly her best friend. The other Buddy died in the 1880's, when she was still a child. She is still a child.

"I knew it before I got out of bed," she says, turning away from the window with a purposeful excitement in her eyes. "The courthouse bell sounded so cold and clear. And there were no birds singing; they've gone to warmer country, yes indeed. Oh, Buddy, stop stuffing biscuit and fetch our buggy. Help me find my hat. We've thirty cakes to bake."

It's always the same: a morning arrives in November, and my friend, as though officially inaugurating the Christmas time of year that exhilarates her imagination and fuels the blaze of her heart, announces: "It's fruitcake weather! Fetch our buggy. Help me find my hat."

The hat is found, a straw cartwheel corsaged with velvet roses out-of-doors has faded: it once belonged to a more fashionable relative. Together, we guide our buggy, a dilapidated baby carriage, out to the garden and into a grove of pecan trees. The buggy is mine; that is, it was bought for me when I was

Few American painters have been as well known and well loved as Grandma Moses, who took up painting at the age of seventy-seven.

OUT FOR THE CHRISTMAS TREES
Grandma Moses
Grandma Moses Properties

born. It is made of wicker, rather unraveled, and the wheels wobble like a drunkard's legs. But it is a faithful object; springtimes, we take it to the woods and fill it with flowers, herbs, wild fern for our porch pots; in the summer, we pile it with picnic paraphernalia and sugar-cane fishing poles and roll it down to the edge of a creek; it has its winter uses, too: as a truck for hauling firewood from the yard to the kitchen, as a warm bed for Queenie, our tough little orange and white rat terrier who has survived distemper and two rattle-snake bites. Queenie is trotting beside it now.

Three hours later we are back in the kitchen hulling a heaping buggyload of wind-fall pecans. Our backs hurt from gathering

them: how hard they were to find (the main crop having been shaken off the trees and sold by the orchard's owners, who are not us) among the concealing leaves, the frosted, deceiving grass. Caarackle! A cheery crunch, scraps of miniature thunder sound as the shells collapse and the golden mound of sweet oily ivory meat mounts in the milk-glass bowl. Queenie begs to taste, and now and again my friend sneaks her a mite, though insisting we deprive ourselves. "We mustn't, Buddy. If we start, we won't stop. And there's scarcely enough as there is. For thirty cakes." The kitchen is growing dark. Dusk turns the window into a mirror: our reflections mingle with the rising moon as we work by the fireside in the firelight. At last, when the moon is quite high, we toss the final hull into the fire and, with joined sighs, watch it catch flame. The buggy is empty, the bowl is brimful.

We eat our supper (cold biscuits, bacon, blackberry jam) and discuss tomorrow. Tomorrow the kind of work I like best begins: buying. Cherries and citron, ginger and vanilla and canned Hawaiian pineapple, rinds and raisins and walnuts and whiskey and oh, so much flour, butter, so many eggs, spices, flavorings: why, we'll need a pony to pull the buggy home.

But before these purchases can be made, there is the question of money. Neither of us has any. Except for skinflint sums persons in the house occasionally provide (a dime is considered very big money); or what we earn ourselves from various activities: holding rummage sales, selling buckets of hand-picked blackberries, jars of homemade jam and apple jelly and peach preserves, rounding up flowers for funerals and weddings. Once we won seventy-ninth prize, five dollars, in a national football contest. Not that we know a fool thing about football. It's just that we enter any contest we hear about: at the moment our hopes are centered on the fifty-thousand-dollar Grand Prize being offered to name a new brand of coffee (we suggested "A.M."; and, after some hesitation, for my friend thought it perhaps sacrilegious, the slogan "A.M.! Amen!"). To tell the truth, our only *really* profitable enterprise was the Fun and Freak Museum we conducted in a back-yard woodshed two summers ago. The Fun was a stereopticon[1] with slide views of Washington and New York lent us by a relative who had been to those places (she was furious when she discovered why we'd borrowed it); the Freak was a three-legged biddy chicken hatched by one of our own hens. Everybody hereabouts wanted to see that biddy: we charged grown-ups a nickel, kids two cents. And took in a good twenty dollars before the museum shut down due to the decease of the main attraction.

But one way and another we do each year accumulate Christmas savings, a Fruitcake Fund. These moneys we keep hidden in an ancient bead purse under a loose board under the floor under a chamber pot under my friend's bed. The purse is seldom removed from this safe location except to make a deposit, or, as happens every Saturday, a withdrawal; for on Saturdays I am allowed ten cents to go to the picture show. My friend has never been to a picture show, nor does she intend to: "I'd rather hear you tell the story, Buddy. That way I can imagine it more. Besides, a person my age shouldn't squander their eyes. When the Lord comes, let me see him clear." In addition to never having seen a movie, she has never: eaten in a restaurant, traveled more than five miles from home, received or sent a telegram, read anything except funny papers and the Bible, worn cosmetics, cursed, wished someone harm, told a lie on purpose, let a hungry dog go hungry. Here are a few things she has done, does do: killed with a hoe the biggest rattlesnake ever seen in this county (sixteen rattles), dip snuff (secretly), tame humming-birds (just try it) till they balance on her finger, tell ghost stories (we both believe in ghosts) so tingling they chill you in July, talk to herself, take walks in the rain, grow the prettiest japonicas in town, know the recipe for every sort of old-time Indian cure, including a magical wart-remover.

Now, with supper finished, we retire to the room in a faraway part of the house where my friend sleeps in a scrap-quilt-covered iron bed painted rose pink, her favorite color. Silently, wallowing in the pleasures of conspiracy, we take the bead purse from its secret place and spill its contents on the scrap quilt. Dollar bills, tightly rolled and green as May buds. Somber fifty-cent pieces, heavy enough to weight a dead man's eyes.

---

1. **stereopticon** (ster' ē op' tə kən), compound slide projector that can project pictures in quick succession so that one fades into the other.

Lovely dimes, the liveliest coin, the one that really jingles. Nickels and quarters, worn smooth as creek pebbles. But mostly a hateful heap of bitter-odored pennies. Last summer others in the house contracted to pay us a penny for every twenty-five flies we killed. Oh, the carnage[2] of August: the flies that flew to heaven! Yet it was not work in which we took pride. And, as we sit counting pennies, it is as though we were back tabulating dead flies. Neither of us has a head for figures; we count slowly, lose track, start again. According to her calculations, we have $12.73. According to mine, exactly $13. "I do hope you're wrong, Buddy. We can't mess around with thirteen. The cakes will fall. Or put somebody in the cemetery. Why, I wouldn't dream of getting out of bed on the thirteenth." This is true: she always spends thirteenths in bed. So, to be on the safe side, we subtract a penny and toss it out the window.

Of the ingredients that go into our fruitcakes, whiskey is the most expensive, as well as the hardest to obtain: State laws forbid its sale. But everybody knows you can buy a bottle from Mr. Haha Jones. And the next day, having completed our more prosaic shopping, we set out for Mr. Haha's business address, a "sinful" (to quote public opinion) fish-fry and dancing café down by the river. We've been there before, and on the same errand; but in previous years our dealings have been with Haha's wife, an iodine-dark Indian woman with brassy peroxided hair and a dead-tired disposition. Actually, we've never laid eyes on her husband, though we've heard that he's an Indian too. A giant with razor scars across his cheeks. They call him Haha because he's so gloomy, a man who never laughs. As we approach his café (a large log cabin festooned inside and out with chains of garish-gay naked light bulbs and standing by the river's muddy edge under the shade of river trees where moss drifts through the branches like gray mist) our steps slow down. Even Queenie stops prancing and sticks close

by. People have been murdered in Haha's café. Cut to pieces. Hit on the head. There's a case coming up in court next month. Naturally these goings-on happen at night when the colored lights cast crazy patterns and the victrola wails. In the daytime Haha's is shabby and deserted. I knock at the door, Queenie barks, my friend calls: "Mrs. Haha, ma'am? Anyone to home?"

Footsteps. The door opens. Our hearts overturn. It's Mr. Haha Jones himself! And he *is* a giant; he *does* have scars; he *doesn't* smile. No, he glowers at us through Satan-tilted eyes and demands to know: "What you want with Haha?"

For a moment we are too paralyzed to tell. Presently my friend half-finds her voice, a whispery voice at best: "If you please, Mr. Haha, we'd like a quart of your finest whiskey."

His eyes tilt more. Would you believe it? Haha is smiling! Laughing, too. "Which one of you is a drinkin' man?"

"It's for making fruitcakes, Mr. Haha. Cooking."

This sobers him. He frowns. "That's no way to waste good whiskey." Nevertheless, he retreats into the shadowed café and seconds later appears carrying a bottle of daisy yellow unlabeled liquor. He demonstrates its sparkle in the sunlight and says: "Two dollars."

We pay him with nickels and dimes and pennies. Suddenly, jangling the coins in his hand like a fistful of dice, his face softens. "Tell you what," he proposes, pouring the money back into our bead purse, "just send me one of them fruitcakes instead."

"Well," my friend remarks on our way home, "there's a lovely man. We'll put an extra cup of raisins in *his* cake."

The black stove, stoked with coal and firewood, glows like a lighted pumpkin. Eggbeaters whirl, spoons spin round in bowls of butter and sugar, vanilla sweetens the air,

2. **carnage,** extensive and bloody slaughter.

ginger spices it; melting, nose-tingling odors saturate the kitchen, suffuse the house, drift out to the world on puffs of chimney smoke. In four days our work is done. Thirty-one cakes, dampened with whiskey, bask on window sills and shelves.

Who are they for?

Friends. Not necessarily neighbor friends: indeed, the larger share are intended for persons we've met maybe once, perhaps not at all. People who've struck our fancy. Like President Roosevelt. Like the Reverend and Mrs. J. C. Lucey, Baptist missionaries to Borneo who lectured here last winter. Or the little knife grinder who comes through town twice a year. Or Abner Packer, the driver of the six o'clock bus from Mobile, who exchanges waves with us every day as he passes in a dust-cloud whoosh. Or the young Wistons, a California couple whose car one afternoon broke down outside the house and who spent a pleasant hour chatting with us on the porch (young Mr. Wiston snapped our picture, the only one we've ever had taken). Is it because my friend is shy with everyone *except* strangers that these strangers, and merest acquaintances, seem to us our truest friends? I think yes. Also, the scrapbooks we keep of thank-you's on White House stationery, time-to-time communications from California and Borneo, the knife grinder's penny post cards, make us feel connected to eventful worlds beyond the kitchen with its view of a sky that stops.

Now a nude December fig branch grates against the window. The kitchen is empty, the cakes are gone; yesterday we carted the last of them to the post office, where the cost of stamps turned our purse inside out. We're broke. That rather depresses me, but my friend insists on celebrating—with two inches of whiskey left in Haha's bottle. Queenie has a spoonful in a bowl of coffee (she likes her coffee chicory-flavored and strong). The rest we divide between a pair of jelly glasses. We're both quite awed at the prospect of drinking straight whiskey; the taste of it brings screwed-up expressions and sour shudders. But by and by we begin to sing, the two of us singing different songs simultaneously. I don't know the words to mine, just: *Come on along, come on along, to the dark-town strutters' ball.* But I can dance: that's what I mean to be, a tap dancer in the movies. My dancing shadow rollicks on the walls; our voices rock the chinaware; we giggle: as if unseen hands were tickling us. Queenie rolls on her back, her paws plow the air, something like a grin stretches her black lips. Inside myself, I feel warm and sparky as those crumbling logs, carefree as the wind in the chimney. My friend waltzes round the stove, the hem of her poor calico skirt pinched between her fingers as though it were a party dress: *Show me the way to go home,* she sings, her tennis shoes squeaking on the floor. *Show me the way to go home.*

Enter: two relatives. Very angry. Potent with eyes that scold, tongues that scald. Listen to what they have to say, the words tumbling together into a wrathful tune: "A child of seven! whiskey on his breath! are you out of your mind? feeding a child of seven! must be loony! road to ruination! remember Cousin Kate? Uncle Charlie? Uncle Charlie's brother-in-law? shame! scandal! humiliation! kneel, pray, beg the Lord!"

Queenie sneaks under the stove. My friend gazes at her shoes, her chin quivers, she lifts her skirt and blows her nose and runs to her room. Long after the town has gone to sleep and the house is silent except for the chimings of clocks and the sputter of fading fires, she is weeping into a pillow already as wet as a widow's handkerchief.

"Don't cry," I say, sitting at the bottom of her bed and shivering despite my flannel nightgown that smells of last winter's cough syrup, "don't cry," I beg, teasing her toes, tickling her feet, "you're too old for that."

"It's because," she hiccups, "I *am* too old. Old and funny."

"Not funny. Fun. More fun than anybody. Listen. If you don't stop crying you'll be

"Now a nude December fig branch grates against the window. The kitchen is empty, the cakes are gone. . . ."

so tired tomorrow we can't go cut a tree."

She straightens up. Queenie jumps on the bed (where Queenie is not allowed) to lick her cheeks. "I know where we'll find real pretty trees, Buddy. And holly, too. With berries big as your eyes. It's way off in the woods. Farther than we've ever been. Papa used to bring us Christmas trees from there: carry them on his shoulder. That's fifty years ago. Well, now: I can't wait for morning."

Morning. Frozen rime lusters the grass; the sun, round as an orange and orange as hot-weather moons, balances on the horizon, burnishes the silvered winter woods. A wild turkey calls. A renegade hog grunts in the undergrowth. Soon, by the edge of knee-deep, rapid-running water, we have to abandon the buggy. Queenie wades the stream first, paddles across barking complaints at the swiftness of the current, the pneumonia-making coldness of it. We follow, holding our shoes and equipment (a hatchet, a burlap sack) above our heads. A mile more: of chastising thorns, burs and briers that catch at our clothes; of rusty pine needles brilliant with gaudy fungus and molted feathers. Here, there, a flash, a flutter, an ecstasy of shrillings remind us that not all the birds have flown south. Always, the path unwinds through lemony sun pools and pitch vine tunnels. Another creek to cross: a disturbed armada of speckled trout froths the water round us, and frogs the size of plates practice belly flops; beaver workmen are building a dam. On the farther shore, Queenie shakes herself and trembles. My friend shivers, too: not with cold but enthusiasm. One of her hat's ragged roses sheds a petal as she lifts her head and inhales the pine-heavy air. "We're almost there; can you smell it, Buddy?" she says, as though we were approaching an ocean.

And, indeed, it is a kind of ocean. Scented acres of holiday trees, prickly-leafed holly. Red berries shiny as Chinese bells: black crows swoop upon them screaming. Having stuffed our burlap sacks with enough greenery and crimson to garland a dozen windows, we set about choosing a tree. "It should be," muses my friend, "twice as tall as a boy. So a boy can't steal the star." The one we pick is twice as tall as me. A brave handsome brute that survives thirty hatchet strokes before it keels with a creaking rending cry. Lugging it like a kill, we commence the long trek out. Every few yards we abandon the struggle, sit down and pant. But we have the strength of triumphant huntsmen; that and the tree's virile, icy perfume revive us, goad us on. Many compliments accompany our sunset return along the red clay road to town; but my friend is sly and noncommittal when passers-by praise the treasure perched in our buggy: what a fine tree and where did it come from? "Yonderways," she murmurs vaguely. Once a car stops and the rich mill owner's lazy wife leans out and whines: "Giveya two-bits cash for that ol tree." Ordinarily my friend is afraid of saying no; but on this occasion she promptly shakes her head: "We wouldn't take a dollar." The mill owner's wife persists. "A dollar, my foot! Fifty cents. That's my last offer. Goodness, woman, you can get another one." In answer, my friend gently reflects: "I doubt it. There's never two of anything."

Home: Queenie slumps by the fire and sleeps till tomorrow, snoring loud as a human.

A trunk in the attic contains: a shoebox of ermine tails (off the opera cape of a curious lady who once rented a room in the house), coils of frazzled tinsel gone gold with age, one silver star, a brief rope of dilapidated, undoubtedly dangerous candy-like light bulbs. Excellent decorations, as far as they go, which isn't far enough: my friend wants our tree to blaze "like a Baptist window," droop with weighty snows of ornament. But we can't afford the made-in-Japan splendors at the five-and-dime. So we do what we've always done: sit for days at the kitchen table with scissors and crayons and stacks of colored paper. I make sketches and my friend cuts them out: lots of cats, fish too (because they're easy to draw), some apples, some watermelons, a few winged angels devised from saved-up sheets of Hershey-bar tin foil. We use safety pins to attach these creations to the tree; as a final touch, we sprinkle the branches with shredded cotton (picked in August for this purpose). My friend, surveying the effect, clasps her hands together. "Now honest, Buddy. Doesn't it look good enough to eat?" Queenie tries to eat an angel.

After weaving and ribboning holly wreaths for all the front windows, our next project is the fashioning of family gifts. Tie-dye scarves for the ladies, for the men a home-brewed lemon and licorice and aspirin syrup to be taken "at the first Symptoms of a Cold and after Hunting." But when it comes time for making each other's gift, my friend and I separate to work secretly. I would like to buy her a pearl-handled knife, a radio, a whole pound of chocolate-covered cherries (we tasted some once, and she always swears: "I could live on them, Buddy, Lord yes I could—and that's not taking His name in vain"). Instead, I am building her a kite. She would like to give me a bicycle (she's said so on several million occasions: "If only I could, Buddy. It's bad enough in life to do without something *you* want; but confound it, what gets my goat is not being able to give somebody something you want *them* to have. Only one of these days I will, Buddy. Locate you a bike. Don't ask how. Steal it, maybe"). Instead, I'm fairly certain that she is building me a kite—the same as last year, and the year before: the year before that we exchanged slingshots. All of which is fine by me. For we are champion kite-fliers who study the wind like sailors; my friend, more accomplished than I, can get a kite aloft when there isn't enough breeze to carry clouds.

Christmas Eve afternoon we scrape together a nickel and go to the butcher's to buy Queenie's traditional gift, a good gnawable beef bone. The bone, wrapped in funny paper, is placed high in the tree near the silver star. Queenie knows it's there. She squats at the foot of the tree staring up in a trance of greed: when bedtime arrives she refuses to budge. Her excitement is equaled by my own. I kick the covers and turn my pillow as though it were a scorching summer's night. Somewhere a rooster crows: falsely, for the sun is still on the other side of the world.

"Buddy, are you awake?" It is my friend, calling from her room, which is next to mine; and an instant later she is sitting on my bed holding a candle. "Well, I can't sleep a hoot," she declares. "My mind's jumping like a jack rabbit. Buddy, do you think Mrs. Roosevelt will serve our cake at dinner?" We huddle in the bed, and she squeezes my hand I-love-you. "Seems like your hand used to be so much smaller. I guess I hate to see you grow up. When you're grown up, will we still be friends?" I say always. "But I feel so bad, Buddy. I wanted so bad to give you a bike. I tried to sell my cameo Papa gave me. Buddy —"she hesitates, as though embarrassed—"I made you another kite." Then I confess that I made her one, too; and we laugh. The candle burns too short to hold. Out it goes, exposing

the starlight, the stars spinning at the window like a visible caroling that slowly, slowly daybreak silences. Possibly we doze; but the beginnings of dawn splash us like cold water: we're up, wide-eyed and wandering while we wait for others to waken. Quite deliberately my friend drops a kettle on the kitchen floor. I tap-dance in front of closed doors. One by one the household emerges, looking as though they'd like to kill us both; but its Christmas, so they can't. First, a gorgeous breakfast: just everything you can imagine— from flapjacks and fried squirrel to hominy grits and honey-in-the-comb. Which puts everyone in a good humor except my friend and I. Frankly, we're so impatient to get at the presents we can't eat a mouthful.

Well, I'm disappointed. Who wouldn't be? With socks, a Sunday school shirt, some handkerchiefs, a hand-me-down sweater and a year's subscription to a religious magazine for children. *The Little Shepherd*. It makes me boil. It really does.

My friend has a better haul. A sack of Satsumas,[3] that's her best present. She is proudest, however, of a white wool shawl knitted by her married sister. But she *says* her favorite gift is the kite I built her. And it *is* very beautiful; though not as beautiful as the one she made me, which is blue and scattered with gold and green Good Conduct stars; moreover, my name is painted on it, "Buddy."

"Buddy, the wind is blowing."

The wind is blowing, and nothing will do till we've run to a pasture below the house where Queenie has scooted to bury her bone (and where, a winter hence, Queenie will be buried, too). There, plunging through the healthy waist-high grass, we unreel our kites, feel them twitching at the string like sky fish as they swim into the wind. Satisfied, sun-warmed, we sprawl in the grass and peel Satsumas and watch our kites cavort. Soon I forget the socks and hand-me-down sweater.

---

3. **Satsumas** (sat sü′ məs), plums of a variety that originated in Satsuma, Japan.

I'm as happy as if we'd already won the fifty-thousand-dollar Grand Prize in that coffee-naming contest.

"My, how foolish I am!" my friend cries, suddenly alert, like a woman remembering too late she has biscuits in the oven. "You know what I've always thought?" she asks in a tone of discovery, and not smiling at me but a point beyond. "I've always thought a body would have to be sick and dying before they saw the Lord. And I imagined that when He came it would be like looking at the Baptist window: pretty as colored glass with the sun pouring through, such a shine you don't know it's getting dark. And it's been a comfort: to think of that shine taking away all the spooky feeling. But I'll wager it never happens. I'll wager at the very end a body realizes the Lord has already shown Himself. That things as they are"—her hand circles in a gesture that gathers clouds and kites and grass and Queenie pawing earth over her bone—"just what they've always seen, was seeing Him. As for me, I could leave the world with today in my eyes."

This is our last Christmas together.

Life separates us. Those who Know Best decide that I belong in a military school. And so follows a miserable succession of bugle-blowing prisons, grim reveille-ridden summer camps. I have a new home too. But it doesn't count. Home is where my friend is, and there I never go.

And there she remains, puttering around the kitchen. Alone with Queenie. Then alone. ("Buddy dear," she writes in her wild hard-to-read script, "yesterday Jim Macy's horse kicked Queenie bad. Be thankful she didn't feel much. I wrapped her in a Fine Linen sheet and rode her in the buggy down to Simpson's pasture where she can be with all her Bones . . ."). For a few Novembers she continues to bake her fruitcakes single-handed; not as many, but some: and, of course, she always sends me "the best of the batch." Also, in every letter she encloses a dime wadded in toilet paper: "See a picture show and write me the story." But gradually in her letters she tends to confuse me with her other friend, the Buddy who died in the 1880's; more and more thirteenths are not the only days she stays in bed: a morning arrives in November, a leafless birdless coming of winter morning, when she cannot rouse herself to exclaim: "Oh my, it's fruitcake weather!"

And when that happens, I know it. A message saying so merely confirms a piece of news some secret vein had already received, severing from me an irreplaceable part of myself, letting it loose like a kite on a broken string. That is why, walking across a school campus on this particular December morning, I keep searching the sky. As if I expected to see, rather like hearts, a lost pair of kites hurrying toward heaven.

FOR UNDERSTANDING

1. Although "A Christmas Memory" takes the reader twenty years back into the past, how does the author make the account seem as though it were taking place in the present?
2. What are the three main activities that Buddy and his friend engage in prior to Christmas?
3. Why do they mail the fruitcakes to people they hardly know?
4. What gifts would Buddy and his friend like to give each other? What is the gift each makes for the other?
5. After they have opened their gifts, what do they do on Christmas morning? What does Buddy's friend say that shows her happiness at this time?

FOR INTERPRETATION

1. In this reminiscence, the author draws a vivid and complete picture of his "best friend" without even giving her name. She is a timid spinster in her sixties. He is a boy of seven. In paragraph three, what is the most significant line that explains why the two get along so well together?

2. Psychologists agree that our attitudes toward life are developed in our early years. What do the other relatives in the household, whom we never actually meet, represent to Buddy? What do you think might be their lasting effect upon his life?

3. What do you interpret to be the meaning of the "lost pair of kites hurrying toward heaven" in the story's ending?

FOR APPRECIATION

Imaginative Language

"A Christmas Memory" abounds in descriptive passages filled with imaginative language. A prominent characteristic of Capote's writing style is his skill in appealing to all the senses with imaginative or figurative language. Among the literary techniques and devices he uses are *simile* (comparison using *like* or *as*) and *metaphor* (implied comparison); *personification* (giving human qualities to an animal, object, or idea); *onomatopoeia* (words that imitate sounds); and *alliteration* (repeating a sound in a word series to create a rhythmic image).

1. In paragraph two, what simile appears in Capote's description of his friend that characterizes her movements?

2. On page 715, in the paragraph beginning "Three hours later . . ." what example do you find of onomatopoeia? What alliteration do you find in the sentence immediately following?

3. The paragraph beginning "Now, with supper finished . . ." (p.716) contains much figurative language.

   a. What similes describe the dollar bills and the nickels and quarters?

   b. How is personification used in describing the fifty-cent pieces?

   c. What alliteration is found in the author's description of the pennies?

4. The description of the two friends' expedition to the far woods to get their Christmas tree is filled with sensory imagery. Reread the two paragraphs beginning "Morning. Frozen rime lusters the grass . . ." (p. 719) and note the imagery that appeals to the physical feelings of the reader. What is the line that personifies the Christmas tree as it is being cut?

LANGUAGE AND VOCABULARY

One reason Capote's descriptions are so alive is his use of imaginative and colorful verbs. On a separate sheet of paper, supply a more ordinary or everyday verb for each of those in italics in the following quotations:

1. The hat is found, a straw cartwheel *corsaged* with velvet roses. . . .

2. Besides, a person my age shouldn't *squander* their eyes.

3. He *glowers* at us through Satan-tilted eyes.

4. My dancing shadow *rollicks* on the walls. . . .

5. Frozen rime *lusters* the grass. . . .

6. *Lugging* it like a kill, we commence the long trek out.

7. And there she remains, *puttering* around the kitchen.

COMPOSITION

Choose either of the following writing exercises:

1. Write about the usual procedure for the trimming of *your* Christmas tree, patterning your description after Capote's paragraph beginning: "A trunk in the attic contains: . . ." Tell where the trimmings are stored, who trims the tree, what trimmings you use, whether you make or buy your decorations, how your tree usually looks when you put the finishing touches on it. Use as much imaginative language as possible.

2. Describe a special family tradition or ritual. Use concrete details and imaginative language.

COMPOSITION WORKSHOP

THE BIBLIOGRAPHY

The goal of a research paper on a literary topic is to increase the reader's knowledge of a work of literature, related works of literature, an author, or a historical period. The first step toward achieving this goal is to examine what others who have studied the topic have said about it. After presenting their observations to the reader, the writer of a research paper is free to offer his or her own insights and conclusions on the topic.

Because the research paper includes a report of others' findings and observations, it is necessary to document the sources used. The sources are identified in the bibliography at the end of the paper and in footnotes at the bottom of pages throughout it.

The documentation of a research paper actually takes place while information is being collected for it. The process begins with the bibliography cards the writer prepares while he or she is locating promising sources. The first thing the writer must do is judge the usefulness of each source. Sometimes a quick survey of a book or article whose title sounds promising reveals that it does not actually cover the topic the writer is interested in. Sometimes the survey shows that the book or article provides information already collected from another source.

In evaluating sources, keep in mind that some will be more authoritative and reliable than others. The bibliographies you will come across when searching for possible sources will always include the standard works in a field. If you see a work included in three or four different bibliographies, you can assume that it is a standard and reliable work on your topic. The date of publication will also give you some idea of the usefulness of a particular source. A book published in the late 1890s or early 1900s will generally be of limited value if your topic is one still actively investigated.

After locating sources that seem promising, the next step is to evaluate each one carefully, looking for material that has some bearing on your topic. It is rarely necessary to read every source from beginning to end. In gathering information for a typical research paper, you will probably rely on six to ten sources. Of these, you might read one or two from cover to cover because they supply much valuable information. In the other sources only a chapter or even a few pages may need to be read. Experienced writers examine tables of contents and indexes and often rely on quick-reading techniques in order to locate information that is more usable in those sources and which need not be read completely. Keep in mind that your examination of a source may lead you to conclude that it is of no value to you. Should this occur, the bibliography card for the source should be eliminated.

TAKING NOTES

The information collected from usable sources can be kept in a regular notebook or on separate sheets of paper. But experienced researchers usually prefer 3 x 5- or 4 x 6-inch note cards, because they are easy to use and store. A major advantage of these cards is that they can easily be reorganized when it comes time to outline and write the paper. The source's author and the title should appear below the note that is made on each card. The numbers identifying the page or pages from which the note was taken should also be included, because they will be needed when the time comes to prepare footnotes. Other necessary information (place of publication, publisher, and date) is on the source's bibliography card.

Three kinds of notes are usually taken for a research paper. The first summarizes material found in a source. This summary may be of the basic background material or of a lengthy argument that a writer makes. Since the summary is written by the researcher, no quotation marks are necessary. A footnote identifying the source of the summary will, however, be needed, so the pages summarized must be indicated. On the next page is an example of a summary note. The note summarizes a chapter from a biography of the American novelist F. Scott Fitzgerald. Note that the card has a heading that tells the writer at a glance what part of the topic the note relates to.

The second kind of note researchers take is the kind that paraphrases the language of the source. In a paraphrase, the writer uses his or her own

Summary

SAMPLE
NOTE CARD

```
Family Background

On his mother's side, Fitzgerald was the grandson of a

successful businessman who had come to St. Paul, Minnesota,

from Ireland in 1857.  On his father's side, Fitzgerald was

descended from a prominent Maryland family related to

Francis Scott Key.  When Fitzgerald's father failed to pros-

per in St. Paul, he tried his luck in Buffalo for a few years,

then moved the family back to St. Paul when Scott was twelve.

Turnbull, Andrew, Scott Fitzgerald pp. 3-17
```

Direct Quotation

SAMPLE
NOTE CARD

```
Fitzgerald's Generosity

"Wherever they went, Fitzgerald insisted on being host,

and James Rennie (an actor friend) was appalled by the

tips which were sometimes as large as the bill itself.

Realizing it would be fruitless to argue, he adopted

the strategy of calling Fitzgerald's attention to

something behind him and pocketing the overtip while

his back was turned."

Turnbull, Andrew, Scott Fitzgerald, p. 163
```

words but follows the sense of the original passage very closely. A paraphrase is often used to substitute simpler language for a source's more difficult language. When key words and phrases from the original source are included in a paraphrased note, they must be set off by quotation marks.

The final kind of note is a direct quotation from the source. Writers collect direct quotations of very important material only. Direct quotations are normally no longer than a single paragraph. Since direct quotations are another writer's exact words, they must always be enclosed in quotation marks. Note the sample direct quotation note card shown above.

Carefully taken notes make the final draft of a research paper much easier to assemble. Take time to record the results of your research carefully and accurately.

ASSIGNMENT 1

Review and evaluate the possible sources for your research paper. Read the most pertinent sources carefully, and identify the passages in other sources that merit careful study. Reject sources that provide little or no information on your topic or that duplicate better sources. Eliminate bibliography cards for rejected sources.

ASSIGNMENT 2

Take notes on the sources you will use for your research paper. Follow the form outlined here. If you are uncertain whether or not you will use a particular piece of information, take notes on it anyway. Unnecessary information can always be eliminated later.

THREE FLAGS (detail), Jasper Johns
Whitney Museum of American Art, New York City
Anniversary gift of Mr. and Mrs. Charles Gilman,
Mr. and Mrs. L. Lauder, Mr. Alfred A. Taubman

Contemporary Literature

1945–

The Second World War brought "unthinkable" horrors: the liquidation of six million Jews in the Nazi holocaust, the bombing of Pearl Harbor, the destruction of major European cities, and the unleashing of the atomic bomb on Hiroshima and Nagasaki. The profound impact of these events was intensified by the new anxieties created by the cold war that followed. Shaken by "man's inhumanity to man" and by the world's new potential for atomic self-destruction, writers began questioning human nature itself. How civilized was a world in which such horrors could take place? What was the true nature of the individual? Could self-knowledge be achieved, and if so, could such knowledge produce a more civilized world?

The Horrors of World War II

THE CONTEMPORARY AMERICAN NOVEL

Important as the war was, only a few enduring "war novels" were written in its aftermath. *The Naked and the Dead* (1948) by Norman Mailer (see page 760), *Slaughterhouse-Five* (1969) by Kurt Vonnegut, and several books by John Hersey are among those still being read. But one can cite far more examples of postwar novels dealing with questions of the self and issues related to self-knowledge.

One of the great early books on the theme of self-knowledge was Robert Penn Warren's *All the King's Men* (1946). Although politics plays a major role in the story and much of the action centers on the rise and fall of Willie Stark, a Louisiana politician, the deeper themes of the novel are carried by its narrator, Jack Burden, who discovers how painful it is to achieve self-knowledge. Burden says, in fact, that only if self-knowledge has been paid for in blood can one be sure one has gained it. J. D. Salinger's *A Catcher in the Rye* (1951) deals less with the attainment of self-knowledge than with the attempt to preserve the integrity of the self in a world full of "phoniness" and insensitive people.

The Theme of Self-Knowledge

The above novels are realistic, but as we move deeper into the contemporary period we find more and more writers turning away from realism and making extensive use of symbolism, fantasy, myth, surrealism, and ironic or antic comedy.

One of the earliest novelists in this tradition was Ralph Ellison, whose *Invisible Man* was published in 1952. Though the nameless hero

Alexander Calder's innovative mobiles—hanging sculptures of delicately balanced shapes turning in the air—brought him worldwide fame in the decades after World War II.

BIG RED, Alexander Calder
Whitney Museum of American Art, New York City
Gift of the Friends of the Whitney Musuem of American Art

(who winds up in a coal cellar) is black, he can be said to represent a much broader slice of twentieth-century humanity. At the end of the novel he says, "Who knows but that, on the lower frequencies, I speak for you?"

Bernard Malamud

If all people are black (and white), then perhaps it is also true that "all men are Jews," as Bernard Malamud (see page 746) has said. The statement seems to mean—at least in the novel *The Assistant* (1957)—that all people suffer. Or perhaps we should say that we are all victims, as is the hero of *The Fixer* (1966), who, ironically, is condemned to death for being a Jew, even though he rejects Jewish religious beliefs.

Saul Bellow

Saul Bellow (see page 752), who won the Nobel Prize in 1976, specializes in creating comic heroes who also are victims—of the modern world, of others, even of themselves. His most famous victim-heroes are Augie March of *The Adventures of Augie March* (1953) and Henderson of *Henderson the Rain King* (1959). Augie's adventures consist chiefly in his escapes from the influence of others who try to dominate him, until he comes finally to accept himself. Henderson is on a quest for a self to accept. He ultimately decides not to be a "being person" but to

In the 1950s, Frankenthaler and other American artists began experimenting with a variety of new techniques and ideas. Together, they were called the abstract expressionist movement.

ARDEN, Helen Frankenthaler
Whitney Museum of American Art, New York City

accept himself as a "becoming person," even though, to use his own language, such persons are "very unlucky, always in a tizzy."

With the novels of John Barth we seem to reach an impasse insofar as the theme of self-knowledge is concerned. In books like *The End of the Road* (1958) and *The Sot-Weed Factor* (1960), the self is seen as nothing more than a series of roles or masks. And as the "Founder's Scroll" reads in *Giles Goat-Boy* (1966), "Self-knowledge is always bad news."

John Barth

Once we enter the seventies and eighties, it becomes extremely difficult to predict which novelists will survive and which will fall by the wayside in years to come. The best one can do is point up some names and titles that have caught the attention of a significant number of discriminating readers and critics.

John Updike (see page 778) is a prolific writer who has produced such recent novels as *Rabbit Redux* (1971), *The Coup* (1978), and *Rabbit Is Rich* (1981), which won a Pulitzer Prize in 1982. Another prolific novelist is Anne Tyler (see page 787), who has published a novel almost every other year since she first broke into print. Her most recent titles are *Earthly Possessions* (1977), *Morgan's Passing* (1980), and *Dinner at the*

John Updike

Diebenkorn was one of many artists in the post-war decades whose work reflected a brooding sense of personal isolation and alienation.

WOMAN IN A WINDOW
Richard Diebenkorn
Albright-Knox Art Gallery, Buffalo, New York
Gift of Seymour H. Knox

Joyce Carol Oates

Homesick Restaurant (1982). Still another highly productive novelist is Joyce Carol Oates (see page 784). The winner of a National Book Award in 1970 for *Them,* Oates's most recent novels are *A Bloodsmoor Romance* (1982) and *Mysteries of Winterthurn* (1984).

Among less productive but no less influential or ambitious authors of novels are William Styron, Alex Haley, Joan Didion, Alice Walker, John Irving, Eudora Welty, Thomas Pynchon, and Donald Barthelme.

William Styron

William Styron, who won a Pulitzer Prize in 1968 for *The Confessions of Nat Turner,* most recently published *Sophie's Choice* (1980), a novel dealing with a survivor of the holocaust. A long-time best seller, it was also made into a successful movie. Alex Haley's *Roots* (1975) also

A recent development in American art has been the emergence of photo realism, in which objects are depicted with an odd and startling clarity.

LEONARDO'S LADY, Audrey Flack
Collection, The Museum of Modern Art, New York City,
National Endowment for the Arts and an Anonymous Donor

achieved great popular success and was made into a multi-part television series. Joan Didion is an important essayist and recently published a book on El Salvador. Her novels include *Play It As It Lays* (1970) and *A Book of Common Prayer* (1976).

Alice Walker became the first black American to win a Pulitzer Prize for Fiction with *The Color Purple* (1982), a novel in the form of a series of letters written by a young Southern black woman to God. John Irving is best known for his recent *The Hotel New Hampshire* (1981) and for *The World According to Garp* (1978). Eudora Welty (see page 740), a regional short story writer, is also a novelist of distinction and won a Pulitzer Prize in 1973 for *The Optimist's Daughter*.

Alice Walker

Eudora Welty

Thomas Pynchon published two novels in the sixties—*V.* (1963) and *The Crying of Lot 49* (1966). *Gravity's Rainbow* (1973) further increased his stature, especially among those who enjoy a highly intellectual sort of novel. Like Welty, Donald Barthelme (see page 773) is best known as a short-story writer. He has published two novels, however—*Snow White* (1965) and *The Dead Father* (1975)—and promises more.

Post-modernism

Critics who have sought a label for work that is distinctive to our time have come up with such terms as "postmodernism" or "contemporary modernism" to distinguish the work of such writers as John Barth, Donald Barthelme, Thomas Pynchon, and Kurt Vonnegut from such literary predecessors as Faulkner, Hemingway, and other "modernists." While the term "postmodernist" has not yet been adequately defined, there is a growing consensus among critics that the best writing of our time has a distinctive quality of its own.

THE SHORT STORY

All of the writers named above also write short stories. Anne Tyler, for example, typically turns her energies toward short fiction between novels. John Updike and Joyce Carol Oates are masters of the short story, and both have many collections of stories in book form. Donald Barthelme is primarily a writer of short fiction, as is his brother Frederick, who is gradually making a reputation of his own.

Flannery O'Connor

Not mentioned in our discussion of the American novel because she wrote only two is one of the greatest short story writers of modern times, Flannery O'Connor (see page 764). Her stories are written with a cool passion and a depth of moral conviction that is matchless. Some other topflight short story writers in America today are Anne Beattie, Kay Boyle, Elizabeth Hardwick, Isaac Bashevis Singer, and Jean Stafford.

Although we could name many more contemporary short story writers as well, there is little doubt that this form of literature has suffered a decline in recent years. Not as many major magazines publish short stories as used to in the past, and those that do, publish fewer stories than they once did. Perhaps one reason for this development is that many people are turning to movies and television for the kind of entertainment they used to get from short fiction. If so, it seems a shame, for neither television nor the film is a substitute for reading.

CONTEMPORARY DRAMA

Williams, Miller, Albee

Tennessee Williams and Arthur Miller won Pulitzer Prizes back to back in 1948 and 1949 for *A Streetcar Named Desire* and *Death of a Salesman*, respectively, and these two dramatists continued to be the major talents on the American stage for many years. Competing with them for the limelight in the sixties and seventies was Edward Albee, who won the New York Drama Critics' Circle Award for the 1962–1963 season with *Who's Afraid of Virginia Woolf?* and who later earned two Pulitzer Prizes —in 1967 for *A Delicate Balance* and in 1975 for *Seascape*.

At a time when other sculptors were creating abstract works, Segal began producing his "realistic" plaster sculptures, cast from actual people and presented with props from everyday life.

CINEMA, George Segal
Albright-Knox Art Gallery, Buffalo, New York
Gift of Seymour H. Knox

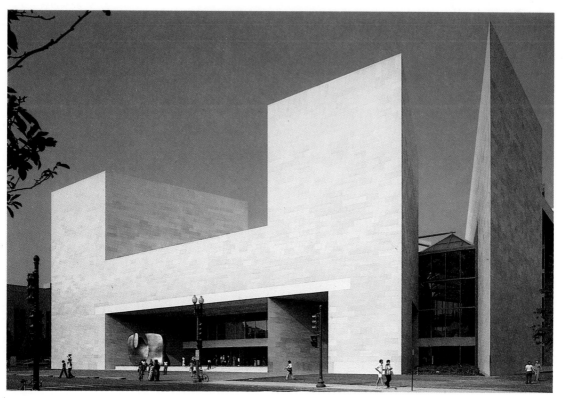

The East Building, National Gallery of Art, Washington, D.C., designed by architect I. M. Pei. Pei's massive, streamlined buildings embody many elements of the so-called International style, which has dominated American architecture since the 1920s.

Apart from these three exceptional writers, the seventies and early eighties have seen a number of strong individual efforts, such as Jason Miller's *That Championship Season* (1972), Miguel Piñero's *Short Eyes* (1973), Beth Henley's *Crimes of the Heart* (1980), and Charles Fuller's *A Soldier's Play* (1981). But none of these authors has as yet produced a significant body of high quality drama on the level of Albee, Williams, or Arthur Miller.

Shepard, Mamet

Two dramatists who have received considerable recognition from critics and serious theatergoers and who have written a relatively large number of plays are Sam Shepard and David Mamet. Neither has yet had any great success on Broadway, but even Eugene O'Neill began in a small way, and possibly one or both playwrights will still achieve popular success in the future. Sam Shepard's *Buried Child* won the Pulitzer Prize for Drama in 1979, and Mamet's *American Buffalo*, which had a long run off-Broadway and won the New York Drama Critics' Circle Award for the 1976–1977 season, opened on Broadway in 1983.

Probably America's most influential architect in the years since World War II has been Philip Johnson, who designed this "glass house" in New Canaan, Connecticut, in 1949. Johnson promoted the International style, not only because of its reliance on modern materials like concrete, steel, and glass, but also because of its emphasis on buildings as "machines for living."

POETRY

Robert Frost

The most dominant figure in American poetry in the fifties and early sixties was Robert Frost, a remarkable poet in that much of his work appealed to both the critic and the common man and woman. When President John F. Kennedy asked Frost to read a poem at his inauguration, it was a high point for the art of poetry, and the United States had come as close as it had been in many decades to having a nationally recognized major poet.

Robert Lowell

After Frost, America's most distinguished poet in the minds of many poets and critics was Robert Lowell (see page 800). Lowell, however, never achieved the popularity of his fellow New Englander; moreover, he was basically an antiestablishment figure. Although he served briefly (1947–1948) as Poetry Consultant to the Library of Congress in Washington, D.C., Lowell typified the schism of American society created by the war in Vietnam. Lowell himself marched on the Pentagon in protest against that war, and his decline of President Johnson's invitation to participate in a Festival of the Arts appeared on the front page of the *New York Times*. Since Lowell's death in September 1977, we have had no one dominant poet of the stature of Lowell and Frost.

This is not to say that there are not many excellent poets writing in America today. Indeed, there may be more than ever. There is Robert Penn Warren (see page 794), for example, who has twice won the Pulitzer Prize for Poetry. James Dickey (see page 806) is a vigorous and prolific poet, who has written on as broad a spectrum of subjects as any serious poet we have had. There is Richard Wilbur (see page 804), who writes accomplished formalistic poetry at a time when most poets have forgotten what rhyme sounds like. The metaphysical poetry of Elizabeth Bishop (see page 796) continues to challenge readers with its penetrating wit, while that of Gwendolyn Brooks (see page 798)—the first black woman to win the Pulitzer Prize—moves and sustains us with its concern for the individual and the community.

Many Poets, Many Styles
The past thirty years have been a time of rich creativity for scores of American poets, whose backgrounds, subjects, techniques, and passions vary widely. From the harsh, staccato rhythms of Sylvia Plath (see page 812) to the deceptively simple revelations of Anne Sexton (see page 808); from the gentle lyrics of Linda Pastan (see page 814) and Audre Lorde (see page 815) to the vivid, sometimes painful descriptions of Jesús Papoleto Meléndez (see page 817), C. K. Williams (see page 816), and Gary Soto (see page 819)—contemporary poetry offers an embarrassment of riches to choose from. Whatever the state of the other arts, American poetry has never been so alive and vigorous.

CONTEMPORARY NONFICTION

Nonfiction Subjects
A glance at the nonfiction best-seller list in any given week will reveal the American public's wide range of interests. The subjects range from health and beauty to history and biography, from politics and pop psychology to sports and humor, from money and business to travel and leisure. The titles on the list change frequently, reflecting current trends and issues. But however interesting and helpful they may be, most of these books will soon be forgotten; only a rare few among them will be read a decade hence.

Novelistic Elements
Prominent among the books that tend to endure beyond their brief appearance on the best-seller list are biographies and social or political histories. Focusing on the controversial people and events of our time, such books recount stories as gripping as any fiction—with the added "kick" of being true. In fact, some of the most interesting experiments in nonfiction over the past twenty years actually read more like fiction than nonfiction. Probably the best known of these works is Truman Capote's *In Cold Blood* (1966), a dramatic mixture of fact and imaginative reconstruction that almost single-handedly launched a new genre: the "nonfiction novel." In fact, one of the hallmarks of much contemporary nonfiction is its increasing reliance on novelistic elements. Among these are a more vivid and subjective narrative style, a greater concentration on revealing incidents, and a deeper and more specula-

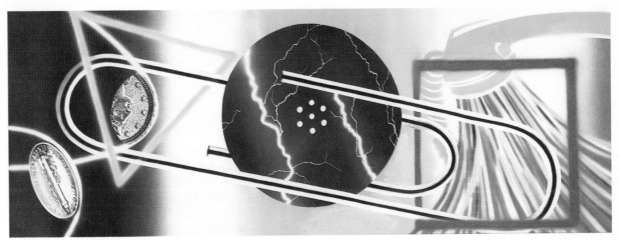

One of the so-called pop artists of the 1960s, Rosenquist drew on his experience as a billboard painter in the Times Square area of New York City for his huge-scale closeups of everyday items.

HELLO HELLO HELLO
James Rosenquist
The Brooklyn Museum, Brooklyn, New York

tive exploration of personality. These are among the elements that distinguish today's literary nonfiction (personal essays, memoirs, and social commentaries) from documentary nonfiction (news articles and more traditionally objective biographies).

It takes a writer of considerable skill, of course, to tell a true story in a way that combines popular appeal with enduring human and literary value. Three contemporary writers who have achieved this feat in the field of autobiography are James Baldwin, with *Notes of a Native Son* (1955), Maxine Hong Kingston, with *The Woman Warrior* (1976), and Maya Angelou (see page 820), with her compelling four-part autobiography (1971–1983). Among the many American writers who have achieved distinction as political and social commentators in recent years are Norman Mailer, Joan Didion, and Tom Wolfe.

Autobiography

Just as histories, biographies, and autobiographies feed our hunger to explore other lives, travel books answer our longing to know about faraway places. More than simply describing the look and feel of other environments, they provide insights into the possibilities of human nature. Different ways of life are very largely the product of people's interaction with their surroundings; places help nations and individuals become what they are.

Travel Writing

Two contemporary American writers who have looked deeply into their own country and thus helped us see more deeply into ourselves are N. Scott Momaday (see page 825) and William Least Heat Moon (see page 828). It is fitting that a book of American literature should conclude with a fresh look at the land whose existence made that literature possible, and whose spirit and potential have inspired so many fine writers over the past three centuries.

A Fresh Look

Contemporary Literature

THEODORE ROOSEVELT 1901–1909

WILLIAM H. TAFT 1909–1913

WOODROW WILSON 1913–1921

WARREN G. HARDING 1921–1923

CALVIN COOLIDGE 1923–1929

HERBERT HOOVER 1929–1933

FRANKLIN D. ROOSEVELT 1933–1945

Stock market crash begins
Great Depression, 1929

U.S. in World
War I, 1917–1918

U.S. women get
the vote, 1920

U.S. in World
War II, 1941–1945

1910   **1920**   **1930**   **1940**

1905	ROBERT PENN WARREN
1907	JESSAMYN WEST
1909	EUDORA WELTY
1911	ELIZABETH BISHOP
1914	BERNARD MALAMUD
1915	SAUL BELLOW
1917	ROBERT LOWELL GWENDOLYN BROOKS
1921	RICHARD WILBUR
1923	NORMAN MAILER JAMES DICKEY
1924	TRUMAN CAPOTE
1925	FLANNERY O'CONNOR
1928	ANNE SEXTON
1931	
1932	SYLVIA PLATH
1934	
1936	
1938	
1939	
1941	

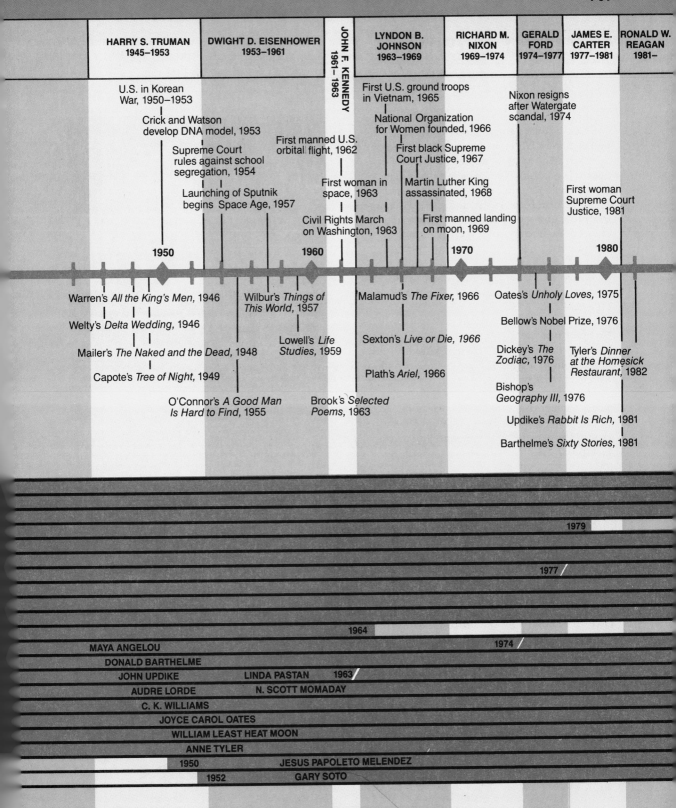

| HARRY S. TRUMAN 1945–1953 | DWIGHT D. EISENHOWER 1953–1961 | JOHN F. KENNEDY 1961–1963 | LYNDON B. JOHNSON 1963–1969 | RICHARD M. NIXON 1969–1974 | GERALD FORD 1974–1977 | JAMES E. CARTER 1977–1981 | RONALD W. REAGAN 1981– |

U.S. in Korean War, 1950–1953

Crick and Watson develop DNA model, 1953

Supreme Court rules against school segregation, 1954

Launching of Sputnik begins Space Age, 1957

First manned U.S. orbital flight, 1962

First woman in space, 1963

Civil Rights March on Washington, 1963

First U.S. ground troops in Vietnam, 1965

National Organization for Women founded, 1966

First black Supreme Court Justice, 1967

Martin Luther King assassinated, 1968

First manned landing on moon, 1969

Nixon resigns after Watergate scandal, 1974

First woman Supreme Court Justice, 1981

1950   **1960**   **1970**   **1980**

Warren's *All the King's Men*, 1946

Welty's *Delta Wedding*, 1946

Mailer's *The Naked and the Dead*, 1948

Capote's *Tree of Night*, 1949

O'Connor's *A Good Man Is Hard to Find*, 1955

Wilbur's *Things of This World*, 1957

Lowell's *Life Studies*, 1959

Brook's *Selected Poems*, 1963

Malamud's *The Fixer*, 1966

Sexton's *Live or Die, 1966*

Plath's *Ariel*, 1966

Oates's *Unholy Loves*, 1975

Bellow's Nobel Prize, 1976

Dickey's *The Zodiac*, 1976

Bishop's *Geography III*, 1976

Tyler's *Dinner at the Homesick Restaurant*, 1982

Updike's *Rabbit Is Rich*, 1981

Barthelme's *Sixty Stories*, 1981

1979

1977

1964

1974

MAYA ANGELOU

DONALD BARTHELME

JOHN UPDIKE   **LINDA PASTAN**   1963

AUDRE LORDE   **N. SCOTT MOMADAY**

C. K. WILLIAMS

JOYCE CAROL OATES

WILLIAM LEAST HEAT MOON

ANNE TYLER

1950   **JESUS PAPOLETO MELENDEZ**

1952   **GARY SOTO**

Eudora Welty

1909–

Eudora Welty was born in Jackson, Mississippi, and has lived all her life there, in a house built by her family. Though she has traveled a good deal and does not confine her stories to the South, her work has a distinctively Southern flavor. Her first published stories appeared in the middle and late 1930s, and she early caught the attention of such important writers and critics as Katherine Anne Porter, Cleanth Brooks, and Robert Penn Warren. By 1980, when her *Collected Stories* appeared, she had published four story collections and five novels. One of the latter, *The Optimist's Daughter,* won the Pulitzer Prize in 1973.

Of her writing Welty has said that she tries "to enter into the mind, heart, and skin of a human being who is not myself. Whether this happens to be a man or a woman, old or young, with skin black or white, the primary challenge lies in making the jump itself. It is the act of a writer's imagination that I set most high." You be the judge of how successfully she enters the skin of the ancient black woman, Phoenix Jackson, in the following story.

PORTRAIT OF EUDORA WELTY

A WORN PATH

It was December—a bright frozen day in the early morning. Far out in the country there was an old Negro woman with her head tied in a red rag, coming along a path through the pinewoods. Her name was Phoenix Jackson. She was very old and small and she walked slowly in the dark pine shadows, moving a lit-

tle from side to side in her steps, with the balanced heaviness and lightness of a pendulum in a grandfather clock. She carried a thin, small cane made from an umbrella, and with this she kept tapping the frozen earth in front of her. This made a grave and persistent noise in the still air, that seemed meditative like the chirping of a solitary little bird.

She wore a dark striped dress reaching down to her shoe tops, and an equally long apron of bleached sugar sacks, with a full pocket: all neat and tidy, but every time she took a step she might have fallen over her shoelaces, which dragged from her unlaced shoes. She looked straight ahead. Her eyes were blue with age. Her skin had a pattern all its own of numberless branching wrinkles and as though a whole little tree stood in the middle of her forehead, but a golden color ran underneath, and the two knobs of her cheeks were illumined by a yellow burning under the dark. Under the red rag her hair came down on her neck in the frailest of ringlets, still black, and with an odor like copper.

Now and then there was a quivering in the thicket. Old Phoenix said, "Out of my way, all you foxes, owls, beetles, jack rabbits, coons and wild animals! . . . Keep out from under these feet, little bobwhites. . . . Keep the big wild hogs out of my path. Don't let none of those come running my direction. I got a long way." Under her small black-freckled hand her cane, limber as a buggy whip, would switch at the brush as if to rouse up any hiding things.

On she went. The woods were deep and still. The sun made the pine needles almost too bright to look at, up where the wind rocked. The cones dropped as light as feathers. Down in the hollow was the mourning dove—it was not too late for him.

The path ran up a hill. "Seem like there is chains about my feet, time I get this far," she said, in the voice of argument old people keep to use with themselves. "Something always take a hold of me on this hill—pleads I should stay."

After she got to the top she turned and gave a full, severe look behind her where she had come. "Up through pines," she said at length. "Now down through oaks."

Her eyes opened their widest, and she started down gently. But before she got to the bottom of the hill a bush caught her dress.

Her fingers were busy and intent, but her skirts were full and long, so that before she could pull them free in one place they were caught in another. It was not possible to allow the dress to tear. "I in the thorny bush," she said. "Thorns, you doing your appointed work. Never want to let folks pass, no sir. Old eyes thought you was a pretty little *green* bush."

Finally, trembling all over, she stood free, and after a moment dared to stoop for her cane.

"Sun so high!" she cried, leaning back and looking, while the thick tears went over her eyes. "The time getting all gone here."

At the foot of this hill was a place where a log was laid across the creek.

"Now comes the trial," said Phoenix.

Putting her right foot out, she mounted the log and shut her eyes. Lifting her skirt, leveling her cane fiercely before her, like a festival figure in some parade, she began to march across. Then she opened her eyes and she was safe on the other side.

"I wasn't as old as I thought," she said.

But she sat down to rest. She spread her skirts on the bank around her and folded her hands over her knees. Up above her was a tree in a pearly cloud of mistletoe. She did not dare to close her eyes, and when a little boy brought her a plate with a slice of marble-cake on it she spoke to him. "That would be acceptable," she said. But when she went to take it there was just her own hand in the air.

So she left that tree, and had to go through a barbed-wire fence. There she had to creep and crawl, spreading her knees and stretching her fingers like a baby trying to climb the steps. But she talked loudly to herself: she could not let her dress be torn now, so late in the day, and she could not pay for having her arm or her leg sawed off if she got caught fast where she was.

At last she was safe through the fence and risen up out in the clearing. Big dead trees, like black men with one arm, were standing in the purple stalks of the withered cotton field. There sat a buzzard.

"Who you watching?"

In the furrow she made her way along.

"Glad this not the season for bulls," she

said, looking sideways, "and the good Lord made his snakes to curl up and sleep in the winter. A pleasure I don't see no two-headed snake coming around that tree, where it come once. It took a while to get by him, back in the summer."

She passed through the old cotton and went into a field of dead corn. It whispered and shook and was taller than her head. "Through the maze now," she said, for there was no path.

Then there was something tall, black, and skinny there, moving before her.

At first she took it for a man. It could have been a man dancing in the field. But she stood still and listened, and it did not make a sound. It was as silent as a ghost.

"Ghost," she said sharply, "who be you the ghost of? For I have heard of nary death close by."

But there was no answer—only the ragged dancing in the wind.

She shut her eyes, reached out her hand, and touched a sleeve. She found a coat and inside that an emptiness, cold as ice.

"You scarecrow," she said. Her face lighted. "I ought to be shut up for good," she said with laughter. "My senses is gone. I too old. I the oldest people I ever know. Dance, old scarecrow," she said, "while I dancing with you."

She kicked her foot over the furrow, and with mouth drawn down, shook her head once or twice in a little strutting way. Some husks blew down and whirled in streamers about her skirts.

Then she went on, parting her way from side to side with the cane, through the whispering field. At last she came to the end, to a wagon track where the silver grass blew between the red ruts. The quail were walking around like pullets, seeming all dainty and unseen.

"Walk pretty," she said. "This the easy place. This the easy going."

She followed the track, swaying through the quiet bare fields, through the little strings of trees silver in their dead leaves, past cabins silver from weather, with the doors and windows boarded shut, all like old women under a spell sitting there. "I walking in their sleep," she said, nodding her head vigorously.

In a ravine she went where a spring was silently flowing through a hollow log. Old Phoenix bent and drank. "Sweet-gum makes the water sweet," she said, and drank more. "Nobody know who made this well, for it was here when I was born."

The track crossed a swampy part where the moss hung as white as lace from every limb. "Sleep on, alligators, and blow your bubbles." Then the track went into the road.

Deep, deep the road went down between the high green-colored banks. Overhead the live-oaks met, and it was as dark as a cave.

A black dog with a lolling tongue came up out of the weeds by the ditch. She was meditating, and not ready, and when he came at her she only hit him a little with her cane. Over she went in the ditch, like a little puff of milkweed.

Down there, her senses drifted away. A dream visited her, and she reached her hand up, but nothing reached down and gave her a pull. So she lay there and presently went to talking. "Old woman," she said to herself, "that black dog come up out of the weeds to stall you off, and now there he sitting on his fine tail, smiling at you."

A white man finally came along and found her—a hunter, a young man, with his dog on a chain.

"Well, Granny!" he laughed. "What are you doing there?"

"Lying on my back like a June-bug waiting to be turned over, mister," she said, reaching up her hand.

He lifted her up, gave her a swing in the air, and set her down. "Anything broken, Granny?"

"No sir, them old dead weeds is springy enough," said Phoenix, when she had got her breath. "I thank you for your trouble."

"Where do you live, Granny?" he asked, while the two dogs were growling at each other.

"Away back yonder, sir, behind the ridge. You can't even see it from here."

"On your way home?"

"No sir, I going to town."

"Why, that's too far! That's as far as I walk when I come out myself, and I get something for my trouble." He patted the stuffed bag he carried, and there hung down a little closed claw. It was one of the bob-whites, with its beak hooked bitterly to show it was dead. "Now you go on home, Granny!"

"I bound to go to town, mister," said Phoenix. "The time come around."

He gave another laugh, filling the whole landscape. "I know you old colored people! Wouldn't miss going to town to see Santa Claus!"

But something held old Phoenix very still. The deep lines in her face went into a fierce and different radiation. Without warning, she had seen with her own eyes a flashing nickel fall out of the man's pocket onto the ground.

"How old are you, Granny?" he was saying.

"There is no telling, mister," she said, "no telling."

Then she gave a little cry and clapped her hands and said, "Git on away from here, dog! Look! Look at that dog!" She laughed as if in admiration. "He ain't scared of nobody. He a big black dog." She whispered, "Sic him!"

"Watch me get rid of that cur," said the man. "Sic him, Pete! Sic him!"

Phoenix heard the dogs fighting, and heard the man running and throwing sticks. She even heard a gunshot. But she was slowly bending forward by that time, further and further forward, the lids stretched down over her eyes, as if she were doing this in her sleep. Her chin was lowered almost to her knees. The yellow palm of her hand came out from the fold of her apron. Her fingers slid down and along the ground under the piece of money with the grace and care they would have in lifting an egg from under a setting hen. Then she slowly straightened up, she stood erect, and the nickel was in her apron pocket. A bird flew by. Her lips moved. "God watching me the whole time. I come to stealing."

The man came back, and his own dog panted about them. "Well, I scared him off that time," he said, and then he laughed and lifted his gun and pointed it at Phoenix.

She stood straight and faced him.

"Doesn't the gun scare you?" he said, still pointing it.

"No, sir, I seen plenty go off closer by, in my day, and for less than what I done," she said, holding utterly still.

He smiled, and shouldered the gun. "Well, Granny," he said, "you must be a hundred years old, and scared of nothing. I'd give you a dime if I had any money with me. But you take my advice and stay home, and nothing will happen to you."

"I bound to go on my way, mister," said Phoenix. She inclined her head in the red rag. Then they went in different directions, but she could hear the gun shooting again and again over the hill.

She walked on. The shadows hung from the oak trees to the road like curtains. Then she smelled wood-smoke, and smelled the river, and she saw a steeple and the cabins on their steep steps. Dozens of little black children whirled around her. There ahead was Natchez shining. Bells were ringing. She walked on.

In the paved city it was Christmas time. There were red and green electric lights strung and crisscrossed everywhere, and all turned on in the daytime. Old Phoenix would have been lost if she had not distrusted her eyesight and depended on her feet to know where to take her.

She paused quietly on the sidewalk where people were passing by. A lady came along in the crowd, carrying an armful of red-, green-, and silver-wrapped presents; she gave off perfume like the red roses in hot summer, and Phoenix stopped her.

"Please, missy, will you lace up my shoe?" She held up her foot.

"What do you want, Grandma?"

"See my shoe," said Phoenix. "Do all right for out in the country, but wouldn't look right to go in a big building."

"Stand still then, Grandma," said the lady. She put her packages down on the sidewalk beside her and laced and tied both shoes tightly.

"Can't lace 'em with a cane," said Phoenix. "Thank you, missy. I doesn't mind asking a nice lady to tie up my shoe, when I gets out on the street."

Moving slowly and from side to side, she went into the big building, and into a tower of steps, where she walked up and around and around until her feet knew to stop.

She entered a door, and there she saw nailed up on the wall the document that had been stamped with the gold seal and framed in the gold frame, which matched the dream that was hung up in her head.

"Here I be," she said. There was a fixed and ceremonial stiffness over her body.

"A charity case, I suppose," said an attendant who sat at the desk before her.

But Phoenix only looked above her head. There was sweat on her face, the wrinkles in her skin shone like a bright net.

"Speak up, Grandma," the woman said. "What's your name? We must have your history, you know. Have you been here before? What seems to be the trouble with you?"

Old Phoenix only gave a twitch to her face as if a fly were bothering her.

"Are you deaf?" cried the attendant.

But then the nurse came in.

"Oh, that's just old Aunt Phoenix," she said. "She doesn't come for herself—she has a little grandson. She makes these trips just as regular as clockwork. She lives away back off the Old Natchez Trace." She bent down. "Well, Aunt Phoenix, why don't you just take a seat? We won't keep you standing after your long trip." She pointed.

The old woman sat down, bolt upright in the chair.

"Now, how is the boy?" asked the nurse.

Old Phoenix did not speak.

"I said, how is the boy?"

But Phoenix only waited and stared straight ahead, her face very solemn and withdrawn into rigidity.

"Is his throat any better?" asked the nurse. "Aunt Phoenix, don't you hear me? Is your grandson's throat any better since the last time you came for the medicine?"

With her hands on her knees, the old woman waited, silent, erect and motionless, just as if she were in armor.

"You mustn't take up our time this way, Aunt Phoenix," the nurse said. "Tell us quickly about your grandson, and get it over. He isn't dead, is he?"

At last there came a flicker and then a flame of comprehension across her face, and she spoke.

"My grandson. It was my memory had left me. There I sat and forgot why I made my long trip."

"Forgot?" The nurse frowned. "After you came so far?"

Then Phoenix was like an old woman begging a dignified forgiveness for waking up frightened in the night. "I never did go to school, I was too old at the Surrender," she said in a soft voice. "I'm an old woman without an education. It was my memory fail me. My little grandson, he is just the same, and I forgot it in the coming."

"Throat never heals, does it?" said the nurse, speaking in a loud, sure voice to old Phoenix. By now she had a card with something written on it, a little list. "Yes. Swallowed lye. When was it—January—two, three years ago—"

Phoenix spoke unasked now. "No, missy, he not dead, he just the same. Every little while his throat begin to close up again, and he not able to swallow. He not get his breath. He not able to help himself. So the time come around, and I go on another trip for the soothing medicine."

"All right. The doctor said as long as you came to get it, you could have it," said the nurse. "But it's an obstinate case."

"My little grandson, he sit up there in the

house all wrapped up, waiting by himself," Phoenix went on. "We is the only two left in the world. He suffer and it don't seem to put him back at all. He got a sweet look. He going to last. He wear a little patch quilt and peep out holding his mouth open like a little bird. I remembers so plain now. I not going to forget him again, no, the whole enduring time. I could tell him from all the others in creation."

"All right." The nurse was trying to hush her now. She brought her a bottle of medicine. "Charity," she said, making a check mark in a book.

Old Phoenix held the bottle close to her eyes, and then carefully put it into her pocket.

"I thank you," she said.

"It's Christmas time, Grandma," said the attendant. "Could I give you a few pennies out of my purse?"

"Five pennies is a nickel," said Phoenix stiffly.

"Here's a nickel," said the attendant.

Phoenix rose carefully and held out her hand. She received the nickel and then fished the other nickel out of her pocket and laid it beside the new one. She stared at her palm closely, with her head on one side.

Then she gave a tap with her cane on the floor.

"This is what come to me to do," she said. "I going to the store and buy my child a little windmill they sells, made out of paper. He going to find it hard to believe there such a thing in the world. I'll march myself back where he waiting, holding it straight up in this hand."

She lifted her free hand, gave a little nod, turned around, and walked out of the doctor's office. Then her slow step began on the stairs, going down.

FOR UNDERSTANDING

1. At what time of year does the story take place? Is there any particular significance to that time?

2. Toward what city is Phoenix headed?

3. What is the main purpose of her journey?

4. How does Phoenix acquire the ten cents she has at the end of the story?

5. What does she intend to do with the money?

FOR INTERPRETATION

Below are some quoted sections of I Corinthians 13 in the Bible. What connections can you establish between the biblical quotations and the story?

Charity suffereth long, and is kind; charity envieth not; charity vaunteth not itself, is not puffed up,

Doth not behave itself unseemly, seeketh not her own, is not easily provoked, thinketh no evil;

Rejoiceth not in iniquity, but rejoiceth in the truth;

Beareth all things, believeth all things, hopeth all things, endureth all things.

Charity never faileth. . . .

And now abideth faith, hope, charity, these three; but the greatest of these is charity.

FOR APPRECIATION

Symbolism

Fiction writers generally choose the names of their characters with care. When a character is given an unusual name, the name is especially likely to have symbolic significance. In Egyptian mythology a *phoenix* was a bird that consumed itself by fire every 500 years and rose renewed from its own ashes. The phoenix, then, is a potential symbol of renewal or self-regeneration.

In what way or ways is Phoenix Jackson like the mythical bird?

Theme

Since Phoenix Jackson is such a key character in this story, Welty could easily have entitled it "Phoenix," "Phoenix Jackson's Journey," or something similar. Yet she chose the title "A Worn Path."

1. Why do you suppose she chose this title?

2. What does it tell you about the theme?

3. State the theme of the story in a sentence or two.

Bernard Malamud   1914–

When Bernard Malamud was young his parents owned a grocery store in Brooklyn. They worked long hours, and when he was not working at the store himself, he spent his time wandering through Brooklyn neighborhoods, much as the hero of the following story does. Later, he settled down in a furnished room and for almost ten years wrote about his experiences during the day while teaching at night. Malamud continued to teach even after becoming established as a major writer. For nearly a generation he has been a college teacher, first at Oregon State University and then at Bennington College in Vermont.

Malamud's first published novel was *The Natural,* in 1952. He won the National Book Award with his first collection of short stories, *The Magic Barrel,* in 1959. In 1967 he won both a National Book Award and a Pulitzer Prize for his novel *The Fixer.* His novel *Dubin's Lives* (1979) is a book about a prize-winning biographer. His most recent novel is *God's Grace* (1982).

PORTRAIT OF BERNARD MALAMUD

A SUMMER'S READING

George Stoyonovich was a neighborhood boy who had quit high school on an impulse when he was sixteen, run out of patience, and though he was ashamed every time he went looking for a job, when people asked him if he had finished and he had to say no, he never went back to school. This summer was a hard time for jobs and he had none. Having so much time on his hands, George thought of going to summer school, but the kids in his classes would be too young. He also considered registering in a night high school, only he didn't like the idea of the teachers always telling him what to do. He felt they had not respected him. The result was he stayed off the streets and in his room most of the day. He was close to twenty and had needs with the neighborhood girls, but no money to spend, and he couldn't get more than an occasional few cents because his father was poor, and his sister Sophie, who resembled George, a tall bony girl of twenty-three, earned very little and what she had she kept for herself. Their mother was dead, and Sophie had to take care of the house.

Very early in the morning George's father got up to go to work in a fish market. Sophie left about eight for her long ride in the subway to a cafeteria in the Bronx. George had his coffee by himself, then hung around in the house. When the house, a five-room railroad flat above a butcher store, got on his nerves he cleaned it up—mopped the floors with a wet mop and put things away. But most of the time he sat in his room. In the afternoons he listened to the ball game. Otherwise he had a couple of old copies of the *World Almanac* he had bought long ago, and he liked to read in them and also the magazines and newspapers that Sophie brought home, that had been left on the tables in the cafeteria. They were mostly picture magazines about movie stars and sports figures, also usually the *News* and *Mirror*. Sophie herself read whatever fell into her hands, although she sometimes read good books.

She once asked George what he did in his room all day and he said he read a lot too.

"Of what besides what I bring home? Do you ever read any worthwhile books?"

"Some," George answered, although he really didn't. He had tried to read a book or two that Sophie had in the house but found he was in no mood for them. Lately he couldn't stand made-up stories, they got on his nerves. He wished he had some hobby to work at—as a kid he was good in carpentry, but where could he work at it? Sometimes during the day he went for walks, but mostly he did his walking after the hot sun had gone down and it was cooler in the streets.

In the evening after supper George left the house and wandered in the neighborhood. During the sultry days some of the storekeepers and their wives sat in chairs on the thick, broken sidewalks in front of their shops, fanning themselves, and George walked past them and the guys hanging out on the candy store corner. A couple of them

he had known his whole life, but nobody recognized each other. He had no place special to go, but generally, saving it till the last, he left the neighborhood and walked for blocks till he came to a darkly lit little park with benches and trees and an iron railing, giving it a feeling of privacy. He sat on a bench here, watching the leafy trees and the flowers blooming on the inside of the railing, thinking of a better life for himself. He thought of the jobs he had had since he had quit school —delivery boy, stock clerk, runner, lately working in a factory—and he was dissatisfied with all of them. He felt he would someday like to have a good job and live in a private house with a porch, on a street with trees. He wanted to have some dough in his pocket to buy things with, and a girl to go with, so as not to be so lonely, especially on Saturday nights. He wanted people to like and respect him. He thought about these things often but mostly when he was alone at night. Around midnight he got up and drifted back to his hot and stony neighborhood.

One time while on his walk George met Mr. Cattanzara coming home very late from work. He wondered if he was drunk but then could tell he wasn't. Mr. Cattanzara, a stocky, baldheaded man who worked in a change booth on an IRT station, lived on the next block after George's, above a shoe repair store. Nights, during the hot weather, he sat on his stoop in an undershirt, reading the *New York Times* in the light of the shoemaker's window. He read it from the first page to the last, then went up to sleep. And all the time he was reading the paper, his wife, a fat woman with a white face, leaned out of the window, gazing into the street, her thick white arms folded under her loose breast, on the window ledge.

Once in a while Mr. Cattanzara came home drunk, but it was a quiet drunk. He never made any trouble, only walked stiffly up the street and slowly climbed the stairs into the hall. Though drunk, he looked the same as always, except for his tight walk, the quietness, and that his eyes were wet. George liked Mr. Cattanzara because he remembered him giving him nickels to buy lemon ice with when he was a squirt. Mr. Cattanzara was a different type than those in the neighborhood. He asked different questions than the others when he met you, and he seemed to know what went on in all the newspapers. He read them, as his fat sick wife watched from the window.

"What are you doing with yourself this summer, George?" Mr. Cattanzara asked. "I see you walkin' around at nights."

George felt embarrassed. "I like to walk."

"What are you doin' in the day now?"

"Nothing much just right now. I'm waiting for a job." Since it shamed him to admit he wasn't working, George said, "I'm staying home—but I'm reading a lot to pick up my education."

Mr. Cattanzara looked interested. He mopped his hot face with a red handkerchief.

"What are you readin'?"

George hesitated, then said, "I got a list of books in the library once, and now I'm gonna read them this summer." He felt strange and a little unhappy saying this, but he wanted Mr. Cattanzara to respect him.

"How many books are there on it?"

"I never counted them. Maybe around a hundred."

Mr. Cattanzara whistled through his teeth.

"I figure if I did that," George went on earnestly, "it would help me in my education. I don't mean the kind they give you in high school. I want to know different things than they learn there, if you know what I mean."

The change maker nodded. "Still and all, one hundred books is a pretty big load for one summer."

"It might take longer."

"After you're finished with some, maybe you and I can shoot the breeze about them?" said Mr. Cattanzara.

"When I'm finished," George answered.

Mr. Cattanzara went home and George continued on his walk. After that, though he had the urge to, George did nothing different from usual. He still took his walks at night, ending up in the little park. But one evening the shoemaker on the next block stopped George to say he was a good boy, and George figured that Mr. Cattanzara had told him all about the books he was reading. From the shoemaker it must have gone down the street, because George saw a couple of people smiling kindly at him, though nobody spoke to him personally. He felt a little better around the neighborhood and liked it more, though not so much he would want to live in it forever. He had never exactly disliked the people in it, yet he had never liked them very much either. It was the fault of the neighborhood. To his surprise, George found out that his father and Sophie knew about his reading too. His father was too shy to say anything about it—he was never much of a talker in his whole life—but Sophie was softer to George, and she showed him in other ways she was proud of him.

As the summer went on George felt in a good mood about things. He cleaned the house every day, as a favor to Sophie, and he enjoyed the ball games more. Sophie gave him a buck a week allowance, and though it still wasn't enough and he had to use it carefully, it was a helluva lot better than just having two bits now and then. What he bought with the money—cigarettes mostly, an occasional beer or movie ticket—he got a big kick out of. Life wasn't so bad if you knew how to appreciate it. Occasionally he bought a paperback book from the news-stand, but he never got around to reading it, though he was glad to have a couple of books in his room. But he read thoroughly Sophie's magazines and newspapers. And at night was the most enjoyable time, because when he passed the storekeepers sitting outside their stores, he could tell they regarded him highly. He walked erect, and though he did not say much to them, or they to him, he could feel approval on all sides. A couple of nights he felt so good that he skipped the park at the end of the evening. He just wandered in the neighbor-

One of America's best-loved twentieth-century painters is Edward
Hopper, whose blunt, haunting scenes skillfully capture the
loneliness and transience of many American lives in the 1930s.

APPROACHING A CITY
Edward Hopper
The Phillips Collection, Washington, D.C.

hood, where people had known him from the
time he was a kid playing punchball whenever there was a game of it going; he wandered
there, then came home and got undressed for
bed, feeling fine.

For a few weeks he had talked only once
with Mr. Cattanzara, and though the change
maker had said nothing more about the
books, asked no questions, his silence made
George a little uneasy. For a while George
didn't pass in front of Mr. Cattanzara's house
anymore, until one night, forgetting himself,
he approached it from a different direction
than he usually did when he did. It was already past midnight. The street, except for
one or two people, was deserted, and George
was surprised when he saw Mr. Cattanzara

still reading his newspaper by the light of the
street lamp overhead. His impulse was to stop
at the stoop and talk to him. He wasn't sure
what he wanted to say, though he felt the
words would come when he began to talk; but
the more he thought about it, the more the
idea scared him, and he decided he'd better
not. He even considered beating it home by
another street, but he was too near Mr.
Cattanzara, and the change maker might see
him as he ran, and get annoyed. So George
unobtrusively crossed the street, trying to
make it seem as if he had to look in a store
window on the other side, which he did, and
then went on, uncomfortable at what he was
doing. He feared Mr. Cattanzara would
glance up from his paper and call him a dirty

rat for walking on the other side of the street, but all he did was sit there, sweating through his undershirt, his bald head shining in the dim light as he read his *Times,* and upstairs his fat wife leaned out of the window, seeming to read the paper along with him. George thought she would spy him and yell out to Mr. Cattanzara, but she never moved her eyes off her husband.

George made up his mind to stay away from the change maker until he had got some of his softback books read, but when he started them and saw they were mostly story books, he lost his interest and didn't bother to finish them. He lost his interest in reading other things too. Sophie's magazines and newspapers went unread. She saw them piling up on a chair in his room and asked why he was no longer looking at them, and George told her it was because of all the other reading he had to do. Sophie said she had guessed that was it. So for most of the day, George had the radio on, turning to music when he was sick of the human voice. He kept the house fairly neat, and Sophie said nothing on the days when he neglected it. She was still kind and gave him his extra buck, though things weren't so good for him as they had been before.

But they were good enough, considering. Also his night walks invariably picked him up, no matter how bad the day was. Then one night George saw Mr. Cattanzara coming down the street toward him. George was about to turn and run but he recognized from Mr. Cattanzara's walk that he was drunk, and if so, probably he would not even bother to notice him. So George kept on walking straight ahead until he came abreast of Mr. Cattanzara and though he felt wound up enough to pop into the sky, he was not surprised when Mr. Cattanzara passed him without a word, walking slowly, his face and body stiff. George drew a breath in relief at his narrow escape, when he heard his name called, and there stood Mr. Cattanzara at his elbow, smelling like the inside of a beer barrel. His eyes were sad as he gazed at George, and George felt so intensely uncomfortable

he was tempted to shove the drunk aside and continue on his walk.

But he couldn't act that way to him, and, besides, Mr. Cattanzara took a nickel out of his pants pocket and handed it to him.

"Go buy yourself a lemon ice, Georgie."

"It's not that time anymore, Mr. Cattanzara," George said, "I am a big guy now."

"No, you ain't," said Mr. Cattanzara, to which George made no reply he could think of.

"How are all your books comin' along now?" Mr. Cattanzara asked. Though he tried to stand steady, he swayed a little.

"Fine, I guess," said George, feeling the red crawling up his face.

"You ain't sure?" The change maker smiled slyly, a way George had never seen him smile.

"Sure I'm sure. They're fine."

Though his head swayed in little arcs, Mr. Cattanzara's eyes were steady. He had small blue eyes which could hurt if you looked at them too long.

"George," he said, "name me one book on that list that you read this summer, and I will drink to your health."

"I don't want anybody drinking to me."

"Name me one so I can ask you a question on it. Who can tell, if it's a good book maybe I might wanna read it myself."

George knew he looked passable on the outside, but inside he was crumbling apart.

Unable to reply, he shut his eyes, but when—years later—he opened them, he saw that Mr. Cattanzara had, out of pity, gone away, but in his ears, he still heard the words he had said when he left: "George, don't do what I did."

The next night he was afraid to leave his room, and though Sophie argued with him he wouldn't open the door.

"What are you doing in there?" she asked.

"Nothing."

"Aren't you reading?"

"No."

She was silent a minute, then asked, "Where do you keep the books you read? I never see any in your room outside of a few cheap trashy ones."

He wouldn't tell her.

"In that case you're not worth a buck of my hard-earned money. Why should I break my back for you? Go on out, you bum, and get a job."

He stayed in his room for almost a week, except to sneak into the kitchen when nobody was home. Sophie railed at him, then begged him to come out, and his old father wept, but George wouldn't budge, though the weather was terrible and his small room stifling. He found it very hard to breathe, each breath was like drawing a flame into his lungs.

One night, unable to stand the heat anymore, he burst into the street at one A.M., a shadow of himself. He hoped to sneak to the park without being seen, but there were people all over the block, wilted and listless, waiting for a breeze. George lowered his eyes and walked, in disgrace, away from them, but before long he discovered they were still friendly to him. He figured Mr. Cattanzara hadn't told on him. Maybe when he woke up out of his drunk the next morning, he had forgotten all about meeting George. George felt his confidence slowly come back to him.

That same night a man on a street corner asked him if it was true that he had finished reading so many books, and George admitted he had. The man said it was a wonderful thing for a boy his age to read so much.

"Yeah," George said, but he felt relieved. He hoped nobody would mention the books anymore, and when, after a couple of days, he accidentally met Mr. Cattanzara again, *he* didn't, though George had the idea he was the one who had started the rumor that he had finished all the books.

One evening in the fall, George ran out of his house to the library, where he hadn't been in years. There were books all over the place, wherever he looked, and though he was struggling to control an inward trembling, he easily counted off a hundred, then sat down at a table to read.

FOR UNDERSTANDING

1. How old is George at the time of the story?
2. Why doesn't he want to go to summer school?
3. Why does he not try evening high school?
4. What makes Mr. Cattanzara different from George's other neighbors?
5. Why does George lie to Mr. Cattanzara about his plan to read good books?
6. What is the significance of Mr. Cattanzara's giving George a nickel near the end of the story?

FOR INTERPRETATION

Examine the following assumptions and discuss them in light of this selection:
1. The chief factor standing in the way of George's self-realization is his unwholesome environment.
2. The chief factor causing George to move toward self-realization is his need for love and respect.
3. If George had managed to get a job, his conscience would have stopped bothering him.
4. In order to succeed in life people need to have models of success to stimulate them.
5. To develop oneself fully, one must have an education.

FOR APPRECIATION

Conflict

What are the forces that move George in a positive direction and what are those that influence him negatively? What forces *within* George might be listed on the one side and on the other? Do the inner or the outer forces seem to be the more powerful? Does the conflict seem to be evenly or unevenly balanced?

Climax

A turning point and minor climax occur when George tells Mr. Cattanzara that he is reading good books. After this, George's fortunes definitely improve in the sense that his neighbors and family gain greater respect for him. At the same time, however, the reader is well aware that this moment is not the true climax of the story. How does the reader know this? When does the true climax occur?

Saul Bellow   1915–

Saul Bellow has been acknowledged to be one of America's greatest writers since the mid-fifties, and judging from his intense and chillingly vivid most recent novel, *The Dean's December* (1982), his creative powers have not waned.

Born in Lachine, Quebec, Bellow was raised in Chicago—the setting for a good deal of his fiction—and educated at the University of Chicago and Northwestern. He has written nine novels to date, as well as several works of nonfiction, stories, and plays. He has won three National Book Awards and a Pulitzer Prize. In 1976 Saul Bellow received the Nobel Prize in Literature "for the human understanding and subtle analysis of contemporary culture that are combined in his work." You will see this combination in the story you are about to read. Bellow has taught at a number of universities in the United States and is currently a member of the Committee on Social Thought at the University of Chicago.

PORTRAIT OF SAUL BELLOW

A FATHER-TO-BE

The strangest notions had a way of forcing themselves into Rogin's mind. Just thirty-one and passable-looking, with short black hair, small eyes, but a high, open forehead, he was a research chemist, and his mind was generally serious and dependable. But on a snowy Sunday evening while this stocky man, buttoned to the chin in a Burberry coat and walking in his preposterous gait—feet turned outward—was going toward the subway, he fell into a peculiar state.

He was on his way to have supper with his fiancée. She had phoned him a short while ago and said, "You'd better pick up a few things on the way."

"What do we need?"

"Some roast beef, for one thing. I bought a quarter of a pound coming home from my aunt's."

"Why a quarter of a pound, Joan?" said Rogin, deeply annoyed. "That's just about enough for one good sandwich."

"So you have to stop at a delicatessen. I had no more money."

He was about to ask, "What happened to

the thirty dollars I gave you on Wednesday?" but he knew that would not be right.

"I had to give Phyllis money for the cleaning woman," said Joan.

Phyllis, Joan's cousin, was a young divorcee, extremely wealthy. The two women shared an apartment.

"Roast beef," he said, "and what else?"

"Some shampoo, sweetheart. We've used up all the shampoo. And hurry, darling, I've missed you all day."

"And I've missed you," said Rogin, but to tell the truth he had been worrying most of the time. He had a younger brother whom he was putting through college. And his mother, whose annuity wasn't quite enough in these days of inflation and high taxes, needed money too. Joan had debts he was helping her to pay, for she wasn't working. She was looking for something suitable to do. Beautiful, well educated, aristocratic in her attitude, she couldn't clerk in a dime store; she couldn't model clothes (Rogin thought this made girls vain and stiff, and he didn't want her to); she couldn't be a waitress or a cashier. What could she be? Well, something would turn up and meantime Rogin hesitated to complain. He paid her bills—the dentist, the department store, the osteopath, the doctor, the psychiatrist. At Christmas, Rogin almost went mad. Joan bought him a velvet smoking jacket with frog fasteners, a beautiful pipe, and a pouch. She bought Phyllis a garnet brooch, an Italian silk umbrella, and a gold cigarette holder. For other friends, she bought Dutch pewter and Swedish glassware. Before she was through, she had spent five hundred dollars of Rogin's money. He loved her too much to show his suffering. He believed she had a far better nature than his. She didn't worry about money. She had a marvelous character, always cheerful, and she really didn't need a psychiatrist at all. She went to one because Phyllis did and it made her curious. She tried too much to keep up with her cousin, whose father had made millions in the rug business.

While the woman in the drugstore was wrapping the shampoo bottle, a clear idea suddenly arose in Rogin's thoughts: Money surrounds you in life as the earth does in death. Superimposition is the universal law. Who is free? No one is free. Who has no burdens? Everyone is under pressure. The very rocks, the waters of the earth, beasts, men, children—everyone has some weight to carry. This idea was extremely clear to him at first. Soon it became rather vague, but it had a great effect nevertheless, as if someone had given him a valuable gift. (Not like the velvet smoking jacket he couldn't bring himself to wear, or the pipe it choked him to smoke.) The notion that all were under pressure and affliction, instead of saddening him, had the opposite influence. It put him in a wonderful mood. It was extraordinary how happy he became and, in addition, clear-sighted. His eyes all at once were opened to what was around him. He saw with delight how the druggist and the woman who wrapped the shampoo bottle were smiling and flirting, how the lines of worry in her face went over into lines of cheer and the druggist's receding gums did not hinder his kidding and friendliness. And in the delicatessen, also, it was amazing how much Rogin noted and what happiness it gave him simply to be there.

Delicatessens on Sunday night, when all other stores are shut, will overcharge you ferociously, and Rogin would normally have been on guard, but he was not tonight, or scarcely so. Smells of pickle, sausage, mustard, and smoked fish overjoyed him. He pitied the people who would buy the chicken salad and chopped herring; they could do it only because their sight was too dim to see what they were getting—the fat flakes of pepper on the chicken, the soppy herring, mostly vinegar-soaked stale bread. Who would buy them? Late risers, people living alone, waking up in the darkness of the afternoon, finding their refrigerator empty, or people whose gaze was turned inward. The roast beef looked not bad, and Rogin ordered a pound.

While the storekeeper was slicing the meat, he yelled at a Puerto Rican kid who was reaching for a bag of chocolate cookies, "Hey, you want to pull me down the whole display on yourself? You, *chico,* wait a half a minute." This storekeeper, though he looked like one of Pancho Villa's bandits, the kind that smeared their enemies with syrup and staked them down on anthills, a man with toadlike eyes and stout hands made to clasp pistols hung around his belly, was not so bad. He was a New York man, thought Rogin—who was from Albany himself—a New York man toughened by every abuse of the city, trained to suspect everyone. But in his own realm, on the board behind the counter, there was justice. Even clemency.

The Puerto Rican kid wore a complete cowboy outfit—a green hat with white braid, guns, chaps, spurs, boots, and gauntlets—but he couldn't speak any English. Rogin unhooked the cellophane bag of hard circular cookies and gave it to him. The boy tore the cellophane with his teeth and began to chew one of those dry chocolate disks. Rogin recognized his state—the energetic dream of childhood. Once, he, too, had found these dry biscuits delicious. It would have bored him now to eat one.

What else would Joan like? Rogin thought fondly. Some strawberries? "Give me some frozen strawberries. No, raspberries, she likes those better. And heavy cream. And some rolls, cream cheese, and some of those rubber-looking gherkins."

"What rubber?"

"Those, deep green, with eyes. Some ice cream might be in order, too."

He tried to think of a compliment, a good comparison, an endearment, for Joan when she'd open the door. What about her complexion? There was really nothing to compare her sweet, small, daring, shapely, timid, defiant, loving face to. How difficult she was, and how beautiful.

As Rogin went down into the stony, odorous, metallic, captive air of the subway, he was diverted by an unsual confession made by a man to his friend. These were two very tall men, shapeless in their winter clothes, as if their coats concealed suits of chain mail.

"So, how long have you known me?" said one.

"Twelve years."

"Well, I have an admission to make," he said. "I've decided that I might as well. For years I've been a heavy drinker. You didn't know. Practically an alcoholic."

But his friend was not surprised, and he answered immediately, "Yes, I did know."

"You knew? Impossible! How could you?"

Why, thought Rogin, as if it could be a secret! Look at that long, austere, alcohol-washed face, that drink-ruined nose, the skin by his ears like turkey wattles, and those whisky-saddened eyes.

"Well, I did know, though."

"You couldn't have. I can't believe it." He was upset, and his friend didn't seem to want to soothe him. "But it's all right now," he said. "I've been going to a doctor and taking pills, a new revolutionary Danish discovery. It's a miracle. I'm beginning to believe they can cure you of anything and everything. You can't beat the Danes in science. They do everything. They turned a man into a woman."

"That isn't how they stop you from drinking, is it?"

"No. I hope not. This is only like aspirin. It's superaspirin. They called it the aspirin of the future. But if you use it, you have to stop drinking."

Rogin's illuminated mind asked of itself while the human tides of the subway swayed back and forth, and cars linked and transparent like fish bladders raced under the streets: How come he thought nobody would know what everybody couldn't help knowing? And, as a chemist, he asked himself what kind of compound this new Danish drug might be, and started thinking about various inventions of his own, synthetic albumen, a cigarette that lit itself, a cheaper motor fuel. Ye gods, but he needed money! As never before. What was to be done? His mother was growing more and more difficult. On Friday night, she had neglected to cut up his meat for him, and he was hurt. She had sat at the table motionless, with her long-suffering face, severe, and let him cut his own meat, a thing she almost never did. She had always spoiled him and made his brother envy him. But what she expected now! Oh, Lord, how he had to pay, and it had never even occurred to him formerly that these things might have a price.

Seated, one of the passengers, Rogin recovered his calm, happy, even clairvoyant state of mind. To think of money was to think as the world wanted you to think; then you'd never be your own master. When people said they wouldn't do something for love or money, they meant that love and money were opposite passions and one the enemy of the other. He went on to reflect how little people knew about this, how they slept through life, how small a light the light of consciousness was. Rogin's clean, snub-nosed face shone while his heart was torn with joy at these deeper thoughts of our ignorance. You might take this drunkard as an example, who for long years thought his closest friends never suspected he drank. Rogin looked up and down the aisle for this remarkable knightly symbol, but he was gone.

However, there was no lack of things to see. There was a small girl with a new white muff; into the muff a doll's head was sewn, and the child was happy and affectionately vain of it, while her old man, stout and grim, with a huge scowling nose, kept picking her up and resetting her in the seat, as if he were trying to change her into something else. Then another child, led by her mother, boarded the car, and this other child carried the very same doll-faced muff, and this greatly annoyed both parents. The woman, who looked like a difficult, contentious woman, took her daughter away. It seemed to Rogin that each child was in love with its own muff and didn't even see the other, but it was one of his foibles to think he understood the hearts of little children.

A foreign family next engaged his attention. They looked like Central Americans to him. On one side the mother, quite old, dark-faced, white-haired, and worn out; on the other a son with the whitened, porous hands of a dishwasher. But what was the dwarf who sat between them—a son or a daughter? The hair was long and wavy and the cheeks smooth, but the shirt and tie were masculine. The overcoat was feminine, but the shoes— the shoes were a puzzle. A pair of brown ox- fords with an outer seam like a man's, but Baby Louis heels like a woman's—a plain toe like a man's, but a strap across the instep like a woman's. No stockings. That didn't help much. The dwarf's fingers were beringed, but without a wedding band. There were small grim dents in the cheeks. The eyes were puffy and concealed, but Rogin did not doubt that they could reveal strange things if they chose and that this was a creature of remark- able understanding. He had for many years owned de la Mare's *Memoirs of a Midget*. Now he took a resolve; he would read it. As soon as he had decided, he was free from his consum- ing curiosity as to the dwarf's sex and was able to look at the person who sat beside him.

Thoughts very often grow fertile in the subway, because of the motion, the great company, the subtlety of the rider's state as he rattles under streets and rivers, under the foundations of great buildings, and Rogin's mind had already been strangely stimulated. Clasping the bag of groceries from which there rose odors of bread and pickle spice, he was following a train of reflections, first about the chemistry of sex determination, the X and Y chromosomes, hereditary linkages, the uterus, afterward about his brother as a tax exemption. He recalled two dreams of the night before. In one, an undertaker had of- fered to cut his hair, and he had refused. In another, he had been carrying a woman on his head. Sad dreams, both! Very sad! Which was the woman—Joan or Mother? And the undertaker—his lawyer? He gave a deep sigh, and by force of habit began to put together his synthetic albumen that was to revolutionize the entire egg industry.

Meanwhile, he had not interrupted his examination of the passengers and had fallen into a study of the man next to him. This was a man whom he had never in his life seen before but with whom he now suddenly felt linked through all existence. He was middle-aged, sturdy, with clear skin and blue eyes. His hands were clean, well formed, but Rogin did not approve of them. The coat he wore was a fairly expensive blue check such as Rogin would never have chosen for himself. He would not have worn blue suède shoes, either, or such a faultless hat, a cumbersome felt animal of a hat encircled by a high, fat ribbon. There are all kinds of dandies, not all of them are of the flaunting kind; some are dandies of respectability, and Rogin's fellow passenger was one of these. His straight-nosed profile was handsome, yet he had betrayed his gift, for he was flat-looking. But in his flat way he seemed to warn people that he wanted no difficulties with them, he wanted nothing to do with them. Wearing such blue suède shoes, he could not afford to have people treading on his feet, and he seemed to draw about himself a circle of privilege, notifying all others to mind their own business and let him read his paper. He was holding a *Tribune*, and perhaps it would be overstatement to say that he was reading. He was holding it.

His clear skin and blue eyes, his straight and purely Roman nose—even the way he sat —all strongly suggested one person to Rogin: Joan. He tried to escape the comparison, but it couldn't be helped. This man not only looked like Joan's father, whom Rogin detested; he looked like Joan herself. Forty years hence, a son of hers, provided she had one, might be like this. A son of hers? Of such a son, he himself, Rogin, would be the father. Lacking in dominant traits as compared with

Joan, his heritage would not appear. Probably the children would resemble her. Yes, think forty years ahead, and a man like this, who sat by him knee to knee in the hurtling car among their fellow creatures, unconscious participants in a sort of great carnival of transit—such a man would carry forward what had been Rogin.

This was why he felt bound to him through all existence. What were forty years reckoned against eternity! Forty years were gone, and he was gazing at his own son. Here he was. Rogin was frightened and moved. "My son! My son!" he said to himself, and the pity of it almost made him burst into tears. The holy and frightful work of the masters of life and death brought this about. We were their instruments. We worked toward ends we thought were our own. But no! The whole thing was so unjust. To suffer, to labor, to toil and force your way through the spikes of life, to crawl through its darkest caverns, to push through the worst, to struggle under the weight of economy, to make money—only to become the father of a fourth-rate man of the world like this, so flat-looking with his ordinary, clean, rosy, uninteresting, self-satisfied, fundamentally bourgeois face. What a curse to have a dull son! A son like this, who could never understand his father. They had absolutely nothing, but nothing, in common, he and this neat, chubby, blue-eyed man. He was so pleased, thought Rogin, with all he owned and all he did and all he was that he could hardly unfasten his lip. Look at that lip, sticking up at the tip like a little thorn or egg tooth. He wouldn't give anyone the time of day. Would this perhaps be general forty years from now? Would personalities be chillier as the world aged and grew colder? The inhumanity of the next generation incensed Rogin. Father and son had no sign to make to each other. Terrible! Inhuman! What a vision of existence it gave him. Man's personal aims were nothing, illusion. The life force occupied each of us in turn in its progress toward its own fulfillment, trampling on our individual humanity, using us for its own ends like mere dinosaurs or bees, exploiting love heartlessly, making us engage in the social process, labor, struggle for money, and submit to the law of pressure, the universal law of layers, superimposition!

What the blazes am I getting into? Rogin thought. To be the father of a throwback to *her* father. The image of this white-haired, gross, peevish, old man with his ugly selfish blue eyes revolted Rogin. This was how his grandson would look. Joan, with whom Rogin was now more and more displeased, could not help that. For her, it was inevitable. But did it have to be inevitable for him? Well, then, Rogin, you fool, don't be a damned instrument. Get out of the way!

But it was too late for this, because he had already experienced the sensation of sitting next to his own son, his son and Joan's. He kept staring at him, waiting for him to say something, but the presumptive son remained coldly silent though he must have been aware of Rogin's scrutiny. They even got out at the same stop—Sheridan Square. When they stepped to the platform, the man, without even looking at Rogin, went away in a different direction in his detestable blue-checked coat, with his rosy, nasty face.

The whole thing upset Rogin very badly. When he approached Joan's door and heard Phyllis's little dog Henri barking even before he could knock, his face was very tense. I won't be used, he declared to himself. I have my own right to exist. Joan had better watch out. She had a light way of by-passing grave questions he had given earnest thought to. She always assumed no really disturbing thing would happen. He could not afford the luxury of such a carefree, debonair attitude himself, because he had to work hard and earn money so that disturbing things would *not* happen. Well, at the moment this situation could not be helped, and he really did not mind the money if he could feel that she was not necessarily the mother of such a son as his subway son or entirely the daughter of that awful, obscene father of hers. After all, Rogin was not himself so much like either of his parents, and quite different from his brother.

Joan came to the door, wearing one of Phyllis's expensive housecoats. It suited her very well. At first sight of her happy face, Rogin was brushed by the shadow of resemblance; the touch of it was extremely light, almost figmentary, but it made his flesh tremble.

She began to kiss him, saying, "Oh, my baby. You're covered with snow. Why didn't you wear your hat? It's all over its little head" —her favorite third-person endearment.

"Well, let me put down this bag of stuff. Let me take off my coat," grumbled Rogin, and escaped from her embrace. Why couldn't she wait making up to him? "It's so hot in here. My face is burning. Why do you keep the place at this temperature? And that damned dog keeps barking. If you didn't keep it cooped up, it wouldn't be so spoiled and noisy. Why doesn't anybody ever walk him?"

"Oh, it's not really so hot here! You've just come in from the cold. Don't you think this housecoat fits me better than Phyllis? Especially across the hips. She thinks so, too. She may sell it to me."

"I hope not," Rogin almost exclaimed.

She brought a towel to dry the melting snow from his short black hair. The flurry of rubbing excited Henri intolerably, and Joan locked him up in the bedroom, where he jumped persistently against the door with a rhythmic sound of claws on the wood.

Joan said, "Did you bring the shampoo?"

"Here it is."

"Then I'll wash your hair before dinner. Come."

"I don't want it washed."

"Oh, come on," she said, laughing.

Her lack of consciousness of guilt amazed him. He did not see how it could be. And the carpeted, furnished, lamplit, curtained room seemed to stand against his vision. So that he felt accusing and angry, his spirit sore and bitter, but it did not seem fitting to say why. Indeed, he began to worry lest the reason for it all slip away from him.

They took off his coat and his shirt in the bathroom, and she filled the sink. Rogin was full of his troubled emotions; now that his chest was bare he could feel them even more and he said to himself, I'll have a thing or two to tell her pretty soon. I'm not letting them get away with it. "Do you think," he was going to tell her, "that I alone was made to carry the burden of the whole world on me? Do you think I was born to be taken advantage of and sacrificed? Do you think I'm just a natural resource, like a coal mine, or oil well, or fishery, or the like? Remember, that I'm a man is no reason why I should be loaded down. I have a soul in me no bigger or stronger than yours.

"Take away the externals, like the muscles, deeper voice, and so forth, and what remains? A pair of spirits, practically alike. So why shouldn't there also be equality? I can't always be the strong one."

"Sit here," said Joan, bringing up a kitchen stool to the sink. "Your hair's gotten all matted."

He sat with his breast against the cool enamel, his chin on the edge of the basin, the green, hot, radiant water reflecting the glass and the tile, and the sweet, cool, fragrant juice of the shampoo poured on his head. She began to wash him.

"You have the healthiest-looking scalp," she said. "It's all pink."

He answered, "Well, it should be white. There must be something wrong with me."

"But there's absolutely nothing wrong with you," she said, and pressed against him from behind, surrounding him, pouring the water gently over him until it seemed to him that the water came from within him, it was the warm fluid of his own secret loving spirit overflowing into the sink, green and foaming, and the words he had rehearsed he forgot, and his anger at his son-to-be disappeared al-

together, and he sighed, and said to her from the water-filled hollow of the sink, "You always have such wonderful ideas, Joan. You know? You have a kind of instinct, a regular gift."

FOR UNDERSTANDING

1. What is Rogin's profession?
2. What does Rogin say people mean when they say they would not do a thing "for love or money"?
3. What important change in behavior at the dinner table has Rogin noticed in his mother?
4. What are Joan's Christmas presents to Rogin? What is his reaction to the presents?
5. What people does the man sitting on the subway next to Rogin resemble?

FOR INTERPRETATION

Be prepared to answer orally or in writing one or more of the following, according to the directions of your teacher.
1. Why is Rogin so preoccupied with making money?
2. What does "superimposition is the universal law" mean?
3. Why does the realization that everyone is under pressure and affliction make Rogin feel wonderful?
4. Rogin is quite concerned about Joan's spending money, yet he himself spends lavishly at the delicatessen. Explain why.
5. Early in the story there is a passing reference to scientists changing a man into a woman. How many later references to sex determination can you find? What is the function of these?
6. We see Joan largely through Rogin's eyes. What sort of a person is she, in reality? Be sure you can justify your opinions.

FOR APPRECIATION

Characterization

The English novelist and critic E. M. Forster

made a useful distinction between what he called "flat" and "round" characters. A flat character is one-sided and can be summed up rather simply. Joan's cousin Phyllis might be an example from this story. A round character, in contrast, is a character who is complex and developed fully. Rogin is clearly an example. We get to know him almost as well as we may know some of our own friends.

Which items in the list below characterize Rogin? Be sure you can support your opinion by references to the story.

1. He is still a child.

2. He sleeps through life.

3. He is oppressed by the need to play the male role.

4. He is fundamentally bourgeois.

5. He badly needs security, wants to belong.

6. He is the victim of social forces beyond his control.

Theme

In a story that focuses as strongly on character as this story does, what can we say about theme? Is Bellow interested solely in drawing a portrait? If not, what is the point or meaning of this particular story?

COMPOSITION

Compare Phoenix Jackson of "A Worn Path" with Rogin of "A Father-to-Be" with respect to the "flat/round" distinction mentioned above under "Characterization" (p. 758). Which of the two characters is "flatter"? Is it appropriate or inappropriate that that character be "flat"? Why?

Note: "Flat" and "round" applied to characters in fiction are *descriptive* terms. They are not evaluative. A flat character is not necessarily "bad," nor is a round character necessarily "good."

Norman Mailer

1923–

When at the age of twenty-five Norman Mailer published *The Naked and the Dead,* a realistic and naturalistic novel about jungle warfare in the South Pacific during World War II, he became an instant celebrity. He has been in the limelight for literary or other reasons ever since. Mailer was mainly a novelist in his early career, publishing *Barbary Shore* in 1951 and *The Deer Park* four years later. And he certainly has continued to be a novelist as his recent novel, *Ancient Evenings* (1983), testifies.

But novel-writing alone has not satisfied Norman Mailer. He has produced films, and he has run for mayor of New York (1969). During the Vietnamese war he joined in a national march on Washington and was arrested for his participation in a march on the Pentagon. He published a book about these experiences—*The Armies of the Night* (1968)—which won a National Book Award and a Pulitzer Prize. Other nonfiction includes such items as *Of a Fire on the Moon* (1970), dealing with spaceflight; *Marilyn* (1973), a biography of the actress Marilyn Monroe; and a penetrating study of capital punishment, *The Executioner's Song* (1979).

PORTRAIT OF NORMAN MAILER

THE NOTEBOOK

The writer was having a fight with his young lady. They were walking toward her home, and as the argument continued, they walked with their bodies farther and farther apart.

The young lady was obviously providing the energy for the quarrel. Her voice would rise a little bit, her head and shoulders would move toward him as though to add weight to her words, and then she would turn away in disgust, her heels tapping the pavement in an even, precise rhythm which was quite furious.

The writer was suffering with some dignity. He placed one leg in front of the other, he looked straight ahead, his face was sad, he would smile sadly from time to time and nod his head to every word she uttered.

"I'm sick and tired of you," the young lady exclaimed. "I'm sick and tired of you being so superior. What do you have to be superior about?"

"Nothing," the writer said in so quiet a voice, so gentle a tone that his answer might as well have been, "I have my saintliness to be superior about."

"Do you ever give me anything?" the young lady asked, and provided the response herself. "You don't even give me the time of day. You're the coldest man I've ever known."

"Oh, that's not true," the writer suggested softly.

"Isn't it? Everybody thinks you're so nice and friendly, everybody except anybody who knows you at all. Anybody who knows you, knows better."

The writer was actually not unmoved. He liked this young lady very much, and he did not want to see her unhappy. If with another part of his mind he was noticing the way she constructed her sentences, the last word of one phrase seeming to provide the impetus for the next, he was nonetheless paying attention to everything she said.

"Are you being completely fair?" he asked.

"I've finally come to understand you," she said angrily. "You don't want to be in love. You just want to say things you're supposed to say and watch the things you're supposed to feel."

"I love you. I know you don't believe me," the writer said.

"You're a mummy. You're nothing but a . . . an Egyptian mummy."

The writer was thinking that when the young lady became angry, her imagery was at best somewhat uninspired. "All right, I'm a mummy," he said softly.

They waited for a traffic light to change.

He stood at the curb, smiling sadly, and the sadness on his face was so complete, so patient and so perfect, that the young lady with a little cry darted out into the street and trotted across on her high heels. The writer was obliged to run a step or two to catch up with her.

"Your attitude is different now," she continued. "You don't care about me. Maybe you used to, but you don't care any more. When you look at me, you're not really looking at all. I don't exist for you."

"You know you do."

"You wish you were somewhere else right now. You don't like me when I'm nasty. You think I'm vulgar. Very well, then, I'm vulgar. I'm too vulgar for your refined senses. Isn't that a pity? Do you think the world begins and ends with you?"

"No."

"No, what?" she cried.

"Why are you angry? Is it because you feel I didn't pay enough attention to you tonight? I'm sorry if I didn't. I didn't realize I didn't. I do love you."

"Oh, you love me; oh, you certainly do," the young lady said in a voice so heavy with sarcasm that she was almost weeping. "Perhaps I'd like to think so, but I know better." Her figure leaned toward his as they walked. "There's one thing I will tell you," she went on bitterly. "You hurt people more than the cruelest person in the world could. And why? I'll tell you why. It's because you never feel anything and you make believe that you do." She could see he was not listening, and she asked in exasperation, "What are you thinking about now?"

"Nothing. I'm listening to you, and I wish you weren't so upset."

Actually the writer had become quite uneasy. He had just thought of an idea to put into his notebook, and it made him anxious to think that if he did not remove his notebook from his vest pocket and jot down the thought, he was likely to forget it. He tried repeating the idea to himself several times to

fix it in his memory, but this procedure was never certain.

"I'm upset," the young lady said. "Of course, I'm upset. Only a mummy isn't upset, only a mummy can always be reasonable and polite because they don't feel anything." If they had not been walking so quickly she would have stamped her foot. "What are you thinking about?"

"It's not important," he said. He was thinking that if he removed the notebook from his pocket, and held it in the palm of his hand, he might be able to scribble in it while they walked. Perhaps she would not notice.

It turned out to be too difficult. He was obliged to come to a halt beneath a street light. His pencil worked rapidly in nervous elliptic script while he felt beside him the pressure of her presence. *Emotional situation deepened by notebook*, he wrote. *Young writer, girl friend. Writer accused of being observer, not participant in life by girl. Gets idea he must put in notebook. Does so, and brings the quarrel to a head. Girl breaks relationship over this.*

"You have an idea now," the young lady murmured.

"Mmm," he answered.

"That notebook. I knew you'd pull out that notebook." She began to cry. "Why, you're nothing but a notebook," she shrieked, and ran away from him down the street, her high heels mocking her misery in their bright tattoo upon the sidewalk.

"No, wait," he called after her. "Wait, I'll explain."

It occurred to the writer that if he were to

do such a vignette, the nuances could be altered. Perhaps the point of the piece should be that the young man takes out his notebook because he senses that this would be the best way to destroy what was left of the relationship. It was a nice idea.

Abruptly, it also occurred to him that maybe this was what he had done. Had he wished to end his own relationship with his own young lady? He considered this, priding himself on the fact that he would conceal no motive from himself, no matter how unpleasant.

Somehow, this did not seem to be true. He did like the young lady, he liked her very much, and he did not wish the relationship to end yet. With some surprise, he realized that she was almost a block away. Therefore, he began to run after her. "No, wait," he called out. "I'll explain it to you, I promise I will." And as he ran the notebook jiggled warmly against his side, a puppy of a playmate, always faithful, always affectionate.

FOR UNDERSTANDING

1. Name at least two of the young lady's criticisms of the writer.
2. In a general way, how does the writer react toward the young lady?
3. What action of the writer produces the climax?

FOR INTERPRETATION

Answer one or more of the following, according to the direction of your teacher.
1. What does the young lady imply by calling the writer an Egyptian mummy?
2. Why do you suppose that Norman Mailer chose the title that he did?

3. In the second sentence of the last paragraph, what are the implications of the word "yet"?
4. Analyze as fully as you can the meaning of the phrase, "a puppy of a playmate," which is used to describe the notebook at the end of the story.
5. In the quarrel between the writer and the young lady, whose side do you take? Why do you choose the side that you do?

FOR APPRECIATION

Distance

Writers may stand at varying distances from the characters and situations they write about. In "A Worn Path," for example, the narrator is very close to the character of Phoenix Jackson and in full sympathy with her. We could say that, in that story, the "distance" between narrator and character is very slight.

There is a greater distance between narrator and main character in "A Summer's Reading" and a still greater distance in "A Father-to-Be." In the latter story, we have a sense of the narrator looking down on the character of Rogin to some degree. There is at least some sense of *ironic detachment;* that is, there is a discrepancy between the values of the narrator and those of the character.

This matter of distance can be very important to our understanding of the meaning and the values being conveyed in the story. If, for example, we did not feel the considerable distance between the narrator and the character of Rogin in "A Father-to-Be," we might think that what happens at the end is perfectly acceptable to the narrator; but it is *not* acceptable.

How distant is the narrator of "The Notebook" from his characters? In answering this question, consider the fact that the main characters are called "the writer" and "the young lady." Finally, try to determine where the narrator stands regarding the quarrel. Whose side is he on?

Flannery O'Connor

1925–1964

No serious discussion of the twentieth-century American short story can ignore Flannery O'Connor's work. In that genre she was simply as good a writer as we have had. Born and raised in Savannah, Georgia, she moved to a farmhouse in Milledgeville, Georgia, at the age of thirteen, when her father died. She attended a local college for women, then studied at the University of Iowa, where she earned an M.A. in creative writing. After graduation, she lived briefly in New York and Connecticut. Then, at about the same time that her first novel, *Wise Blood* (1952), was published, she learned that she was suffering from lupus, the same chronic illness that had killed her father.

O'Connor went back to Georgia to live with her mother in Milledgeville. Over the next few years there, despite her illness, she wrote the great majority of her painstakingly crafted short stories and a second novel, *The Violent Bear It Away* (1960). Her first volume of stories, *A Good Man Is Hard to Find,* was published in 1955. A second collection, *Everything That Rises Must Converge,* was published in 1964, a few weeks before her death from lupus.

Like the story you are about to read, almost all of O'Connor's fiction is set in the rural South,

PORTRAIT OF FLANNERY O'CONNOR

in Georgia or Tennessee. Moral values are at the core of all her writing. Though her work is often humorous and ironic, O'Connor was one of the most serious and deeply religious writers of our time.

THE LIFE YOU SAVE MAY BE YOUR OWN

The old woman and her daughter were sitting on their porch when Mr. Shiftlet came up their road for the first time. The old woman slid to the edge of her chair and leaned forward, shading her eyes from the piercing sunset with her hand. The daughter could not see far in front of her and continued to play with her fingers. Although the old woman lived in this desolate spot with only her daughter and she had never seen Mr.

Shiftlet before, she could tell, even from a distance, that he was a tramp and no one to be afraid of. His left coat sleeve was folded up to show there was only half an arm in it and his gaunt figure listed slightly to the side as if the breeze were pushing him. He had on a black town suit and a brown felt hat that was turned up in the front and down in the back and he carried a tin tool box by a handle. He came on, at an amble, up her road, his face turned toward the sun which appeared to be balancing itself on the peak of a small mountain.

The old woman didn't change her position until he was almost into her yard; then she rose with one hand fisted on her hip. The daughter, a large girl in a short blue organdy dress, saw him all at once and jumped up and began to stamp and point and make excited speechless sounds.

Mr. Shiftlet stopped just inside the yard and set his box on the ground and tipped his hat at her as if she were not in the least afflicted, then he turned toward the old woman and swung the hat all the way off. He had long black slick hair that hung flat from a part in the middle to beyond the tips of his ears on either side. His face descended in forehead for more than half its length and ended suddenly with his features just balanced over a jutting steeltrap jaw. He seemed to be a young man but he had a look of composed dissatisfaction as if he understood life thoroughly.

"Good evening," the old woman said. She was about the size of a cedar fence post and she had a man's gray hat pulled down low over her head.

The tramp stood looking at her and didn't answer. He turned his back and faced the sunset. He swung both his whole and his short arm up slowly so that they indicated an expanse of sky and his figure formed a crooked cross. The old woman watched him with her arms folded across her chest as if she were the owner of the sun, and the daughter watched, her head thrust forward and her fat helpless hands hanging at the wrists. She had long pink-gold hair and eyes as blue as a peacock's neck.

He held the pose for almost fifty seconds and then he picked up his box and came on to the porch and dropped down on the bottom step. "Lady," he said in a firm nasal voice, "I'd give a fortune to live where I could see me a sun do that every evening."

"Does it every evening," the old woman said and sat back down. The daughter sat down too and watched him with a cautious sly look as if he were a bird that had come up very close. He leaned to one side, rooting in his pants pocket, and in a second he brought out a package of chewing gum and offered her a piece. She took it and unpeeled it and began to chew without taking her eyes off him. He offered the old woman a piece but she only raised her upper lip to indicate she had no teeth.

Mr. Shiftlet's pale sharp glance had already passed over everything in the yard—the pump near the corner of the house and the big fig tree that three or four chickens were preparing to roost in—and had moved to a shed where he saw the square rusted back of an automobile. "You ladies drive?" he asked.

"That car ain't run in fifteen year," the old woman said. "The day my husband died, it quit running."

"Nothing is like it used to be, lady," he said. "The world is almost rotten."

"That's right," the old woman said. "You from around here?"

"Name Tom T. Shiftlet," he murmured, looking at the tires.

"I'm pleased to meet you," the old woman said. "Name Lucynell Crater and daughter Lucynell Crater. What you doing around here, Mr. Shiftlet?"

He judged the car to be about a 1928 or '29 Ford. "Lady," he said, and turned and gave her his full attention, "lemme tell you something. There's one of these doctors in Atlanta that's taken a knife and cut the human heart—the human heart," he repeated, leaning forward "out of a man's chest and held it in his hand," and he held his hand out, palm up, as if it were slightly weighted with the human heart, "and studied it like it was a day-old chicken, and lady," he said, allowing a long significant pause in which his head slid forward and his clay-colored eyes brightened, "he don't know no more about it than you or me."

"That's right," the old woman said.

"Why, if he was to take that knife and cut into every corner of it, he still wouldn't know no more than you or me. What you want to bet?"

"Nothing," the old woman said wisely. "Where you come from, Mr. Shiftlet?"

He didn't answer. He reached into his pocket and brought out a sack of tobacco and a package of cigarette papers and rolled himself a cigarette, expertly with one hand, and attached it in a hanging position to his upper lip. Then he took a box of wooden matches from his pocket and struck one on his shoe. He held the burning match as if he were studying the mystery of flame while it traveled dangerously toward his skin. The daughter began to make loud noises and to point to his hand and shake her finger at him, but when the flame was just before touching him, he leaned down with his hand cupped over it as if he were going to set fire to his nose and lit the cigarette.

He flipped away the dead match and blew a stream of gray into the evening. A sly look came over his face. "Lady," he said, "nowadays, people'll do anything anyways. I can tell you my name is Tom T. Shiftlet and I come from Tarwater, Tennessee, but you never have seen me before: how you know I ain't lying? How you know my name ain't Aaron Sparks, lady, and I come from Singleberry, Georgia, or how you know it's not George Speeds and I come from Lucy, Alabama, or how you know I ain't Thompson Bright from Toolafalls, Mississippi?"

"I don't know nothing about you," the old woman muttered, irked.

"Lady," he said, "people don't care how they lie. Maybe the best I can tell you is, I'm a man; but listen, lady," he said and paused and made his tone more ominous still, "what is a man?"

The old woman began to gum a seed. "What you carry in that tin box, Mr. Shiftlet?" she asked.

"Tools," he said, put back. "I'm a carpenter."

"Well, if you come out here to work, I'll be able to feed you and give you a place to sleep but I can't pay. I'll tell you that before you begin," she said.

There was no answer at once and no particular expression on his face. He leaned back against the two-by-four that helped support the porch roof. "Lady," he said slowly, "there's some men that some things mean more to them than money." The old woman rocked without comment and the daughter watched the trigger that moved up and down in his neck. He told the old woman then that all most people were interested in was money, but he asked what a man was made for. He asked her if a man was made for money, or what. He asked her what she thought she was made for but she didn't answer, she only sat rocking and wondered if a one-armed man could put a new roof on her garden house. He asked a lot of questions that she didn't answer. He told her that he was twenty-eight years old and had lived a varied life. He had been a gospel singer, a foreman on the railroad, an assistant in an undertaking parlor, and he come over the radio for three months with Uncle Roy and his Red Creek Wranglers. He said he had fought and bled in the Arm Service of his country and visited every foreign land and that everywhere he had seen people that didn't care if they did a thing one way or another. He said he hadn't been raised thataway.

A fat yellow moon appeared in the branches of the fig tree as if it were going to roost there with the chickens. He said that a man had to escape to the country to see the world whole and that he wished he lived in a desolate place like this where he could see the sun go down every evening like God made it to do.

"Are you married or are you single?" the old woman asked.

There was a long silence. "Lady," he asked finally, "where would you find you an innocent woman today? I wouldn't have any of this trash I could just pick up."

The daughter was leaning very far down, hanging her head almost between her knees watching him through a triangular door she had made in her overturned hair; and she suddenly fell in a heap on the floor and began to whimper. Mr. Shiftlet straightened her out and helped her get back in the chair.

"Is she your baby girl?" he asked.

"My only," the old woman said, "and she's the sweetest girl in the world. I would give her up for nothing on earth. She's smart too. She can sweep the floor, cook, wash, feed the chickens, and hoe. I wouldn't give her up for a casket of jewels."

"No," he said kindly, "don't ever let any man take her away from you."

"Any man come after her," the old woman said, "'ll have to stay around the place."

Mr. Shiftlet's eye in the darkness was focused on a part of the automobile bumper that glittered in the distance. "Lady," he said, jerking his short arm up as if he could point with it to her house and yard and pump, "there ain't a broken thing on this plantation that I couldn't fix for you, one-arm jackleg or not. I'm a man," he said with a sullen dignity, "even if I ain't a whole one. I got," he said, tapping his knuckles on the floor to emphasize the immensity of what he was going to say, "a moral intelligence!" and his face pierced out of the darkness into a shaft of doorlight and he stared at her as if he were astonished himself at this impossible truth.

The old woman was not impressed with the phrase. "I told you you could hang around and work for food," she said, "if you don't mind sleeping in that car yonder."

"Why listen, lady," he said with a grin of delight, "the monks of old slept in their coffins!"

"They wasn't as advanced as we are," the old woman said.

The next morning he began on the roof of the garden house while Lucynell, the daughter, sat on a rock and watched him work. He had not been around a week before the change he had made in the place was apparent. He had patched the front and back steps, built a new hog pen, restored a fence, and taught Lucynell, who was completely deaf and had never said a word in her life, to say the word "bird." The big rosy-faced girl followed him everywhere, saying "Burrttddt ddbirrrttdt," and clapping her hands. The old woman watched from a distance, secretly pleased. She was ravenous for a son-in-law.

Mr. Shiftlet slept on the hard narrow back seat of the car with his feet out the side window. He had his razor and a can of water on a crate that served him as a bedside table and he put up a piece of mirror against the back glass and kept his coat neatly on a hanger that he hung over one of the windows.

In the evenings he sat on the steps and talked while the old woman and Lucynell rocked violently in their chairs on either side of him. The old woman's three mountains were black against the dark blue sky and were visited off and on by various planets and by the moon after it had left the chickens. Mr. Shiftlet pointed out that the reason he had improved this plantation was because he had taken a personal interest in it. He said he was even going to make the automobile run.

He had raised the hood and studied the mechanism and he said he could tell that the car had been built in the days when cars were really built. You take now, he said, one man puts in one bolt and another man puts in another bolt and another man puts in another bolt so that it's a man for a bolt. That's why you have to pay so much for a car: you're paying all those men. Now if you didn't have to pay but one man, you could get you a cheaper car and one that had had a personal interest taken in it, and it would be a better car. The old woman agreed with him that this was so.

Mr. Shiftlet said that the trouble with the world was that nobody cared, or stopped and took any trouble. He said he never would have been able to teach Lucynell to say a word if he hadn't cared and stopped long enough.

"Teach her to say something else," the old woman said.

"What you want her to say next?" Mr. Shiftlet asked.

The old woman's smile was broad and toothless and suggestive. "Teach her to say 'sugarpie,'" she said.

Mr. Shiftlet already knew what was on her mind.

The next day he began to tinker with the automobile and that evening he told her that if she would buy a fan belt, he would be able to make the car run.

The old woman said she would give him the money. "You see that girl yonder?" she asked, pointing to Lucynell who was sitting on the floor a foot away, watching him, her eyes blue even in the dark. "If it was ever a man wanted to take her away, I would say, 'No man on earth is going to take that sweet girl of mine away from me!' but if he was to say, 'Lady, I don't want to take her away, I want her right here,' I would say, 'Mister, I don't blame you none. I wouldn't pass up a chance to live in a permanent place and get the sweetest girl in the world myself. You ain't no fool,' I would say."

"How old is she?" Mr. Shiftlet asked casually.

"Fifteen, sixteen," the old woman said. The girl was nearly thirty but because of her innocence it was impossible to guess.

"It would be a good idea to paint it too," Mr. Shiftlet remarked. "You don't want it to rust out."

"We'll see about that later," the old woman said.

The next day he walked into town and returned with the parts he needed and a can of gasoline. Late in the afternoon, terrible noises issued from the shed and the old woman rushed out of the house, thinking Lucynell was somewhere having a fit. Lucynell was sitting on a chicken crate, stamping her feet and screaming, "Burrddttt! bddurrd-dtttt!" but her fuss was drowned out by the car. With a volley of blasts it emerged from the shed, moving in a fierce and stately way. Mr. Shiftlet was in the driver's seat, sitting very erect. He had an expression of serious modesty on his face as if he had just raised the dead.

That night, rocking on the porch, the old woman began her business at once. "You want you an innocent woman, don't you?" she asked sympathetically. "You don't want none of this trash."

"No'm, I don't," Mr. Shiftlet said.

"One that can't talk," she continued, "can't sass you back or use foul language. That's the kind for you to have. Right there," and she pointed to Lucynell sitting cross-legged in her chair, holding both feet in her hands.

"That's right," he admitted. "She wouldn't give me any trouble."

"Saturday," the old woman said, "you and her and me can drive into town and get married."

Mr. Shiftlet eased his position on the steps.

"I can't get married right now," he said. "Everything you want to do takes money and I ain't got any."

"What you need with money?" she asked.

"It takes money," he said. "Some people'll do anything anyhow these days, but the way I think, I wouldn't marry no woman that I couldn't take on a trip like she was somebody. I mean take her to a hotel and treat her. I wouldn't marry the Duchesser Windsor," he said firmly, "unless I could take her to a hotel and giver something good to eat.

"I was raised thataway and there ain't a thing I can do about it. My old mother taught me how to do."

"Lucynell don't even know what a hotel

Boldly expressionistic, Arthur Dove's paintings often depicted the sun or the moon in a simplified, dramatic fashion. He was one of the very first American abstract painters.

HIGH NOON, Arthur G. Dove
Wichita Art Museum, Wichita, Kansas
Roland P. Murdock Collection

is," the old woman muttered. "Listen here, Mr. Shiftlet," she said, sliding forward in her chair, "you'd be getting a permanent house and a deep well and the most innocent girl in the world. You don't need no money. Lemme tell you something: there ain't any place in the world for a poor disabled friendless drifting man."

The ugly words settled in Mr. Shiftlet's head like a group of buzzards in the top of a tree. He didn't answer at once. He rolled himself a cigarette and lit it and then he said in an even voice, "Lady, a man is divided into two parts, body and spirit."

The old woman clamped her gums together.

"A body and a spirit," he repeated. "The body, lady, is like a house: it don't go anywhere; but the spirit, lady, is like a automobile: always on the move, always——"

"Listen, Mr. Shiftlet," she said, "my well never goes dry and my house is always warm in the winter and there's no mortgage on a thing about this place. You can go to the courthouse and see for yourself. And yonder under that shed is a fine automobile." She laid the bait carefully. "You can have it painted by Saturday. I'll pay for the paint."

In the darkness, Mr. Shiftlet's smile stretched like a weary snake waking up by a fire. After a second he recalled himself and said, "I'm only saying a man's spirit means more to him than anything else. I would have to take my wife off for the weekend without no regards at all for cost. I got to follow where my spirit says to go."

"I'll give you fifteen dollars for a weekend trip," the old woman said in a crabbed voice. "That's the best I can do."

"That wouldn't hardly pay for more than the gas and the hotel," he said. "It wouldn't feed her."

"Seventeen-fifty," the old woman said. "That's all I got so it isn't any use you trying to milk me. You can take a lunch."

Mr. Shiftlet was deeply hurt by the word "milk." He didn't doubt that she had more money sewed up in her mattress but he had already told her he was not interested in her money. "I'll make that do," he said and rose and walked off without treating with her further.

On Saturday the three of them drove into town in the car that the paint had barely dried on and Mr. Shiftlet and Lucynell were married in the Ordinary's office while the old woman witnessed. As they came out of the courthouse, Mr. Shiftlet began twisting his neck in his collar. He looked morose and bitter as if he had been insulted while someone held him. "That didn't satisfy me none," he said. "That was just something a woman in an office did, nothing but paper work and blood tests. What do they know about my blood? If they was to take my heart and cut it out," he said, "they wouldn't know a thing about me. It didn't satisfy me at all."

"It satisfied the law," the old woman said sharply.

"The law," Mr. Shiftlet said and spit. "It's the law that don't satisfy me."

He had painted the car dark green with a yellow band around it just under the windows. The three of them climbed in the front seat and the old woman said, "Don't Lucynell look pretty? Looks like a baby doll." Lucynell was dressed up in a white dress that her mother had uprooted from a trunk and there was a Panama hat on her head with a bunch

of red wooden cherries on the brim. Every now and then her placid expression was changed by a sly isolated little thought like a shoot of green in the desert. "You got a prize!" the old woman said.

Mr. Shiftlet didn't even look at her.

They drove back to the house to let the old woman off and pick up the lunch. When they were ready to leave, she stood staring in the window of the car, with her fingers clenched around the glass. Tears began to seep sideways out of her eyes and run along the dirty creases in her face. "I ain't ever been parted with her for two days before," she said.

Mr. Shiftlet started the motor.

"And I wouldn't let no man have her but you because I seen you would do right. Goodby, Sugarbaby," she said, clutching at the sleeve of the white dress. Lucynell looked straight at her and didn't seem to see her there at all. Mr. Shiftlet eased the car forward so that she had to move her hands.

The early afternoon was clear and open and surrounded by pale blue sky. Although the car would go only thirty miles an hour, Mr. Shiftlet imagined a terrific climb and dip and swerve that went entirely to his head so that he forgot his morning bitterness. He had always wanted an automobile but he had never been able to afford one before. He drove very fast because he wanted to make Mobile by nightfall.

Occasionally he stopped his thoughts long enough to look at Lucynell in the seat beside him. She had eaten the lunch as soon as they were out of the yard and now she was pulling the cherries off the hat one by one and throwing them out the window. He became depressed in spite of the car. He had driven about a hundred miles when he decided that she must be hungry again and at the next small town they came to, he stopped in front of an aluminum-painted eating place called The Hot Spot and took her in and ordered her a plate of ham and grits. The ride had made her sleepy and as soon as she got up on the stool, she rested her head on the counter and shut her eyes. There was no one in The Hot Spot but Mr. Shiftlet and the boy behind the counter, a pale youth with a greasy rag hung over his shoulder. Before he could dish up the food, she was snoring gently.

"Give it to her when she wakes up," Mr. Shiftlet said. "I'll pay for it now."

The boy bent over her and stared at the long pink-gold hair and the half-shut sleeping eyes. Then he looked up and stared at Mr. Shiftlet. "She looks like an angel of Gawd," he murmured.

"Hitchhiker," Mr. Shiftlet explained. "I can't wait. I got to make Tuscaloosa."

The boy bent over again and very carefully touched his finger to a strand of the golden hair and Mr. Shiftlet left.

He was more depressed than ever as he drove on by himself. The late afternoon had grown hot and sultry and the country had flattened out. Deep in the sky a storm was preparing very slowly and without thunder as if it meant to drain every drop of air from the earth before it broke. There were times when Mr. Shiftlet preferred not to be alone. He felt too that a man with a car had a responsibility to others and he kept his eye out for a hitchhiker. Occasionally he saw a sign that warned: "Drive carefully. The life you save may be your own."

The narrow road dropped off on either side into dry fields and here and there a shack or a filling station stood in a clearing. The sun began to set directly in front of the automobile. It was a reddening ball that through his windshield was slightly flat on the bottom and top. He saw a boy in overalls and a gray hat standing on the edge of the road and he slowed the car down and stopped in front of him. The boy didn't have his hand raised to thumb the ride, he was only standing there, but he had a small cardboard suitcase and his hat was set on his head in a way to indicate that he had left somewhere for good. "Son," Mr. Shiftlet said, "I see you want a ride."

The boy didn't say he did or he didn't but he opened the door of the car and got in, and Mr. Shiftlet started driving again. The child held the suitcase on his lap and folded his arms on top of it. He turned his head and looked out the window away from Mr. Shiftlet. Mr. Shiftlet felt oppressed. "Son," he said after a minute, "I got the best old mother in the world so I reckon you only got the second best."

The boy gave him a quick dark glance and then turned his face back out the window.

"It's nothing so sweet," Mr. Shiftlet continued, "as a boy's mother. She taught him his first prayers at her knee, she give him love when no other would, she told him what was right and what wasn't, and she seen that he done the right thing. Son," he said, "I never rued a day in my life like the one I rued when I left that old mother of mine."

The boy shifted in his seat but he didn't look at Mr. Shiftlet. He unfolded his arms and put one hand on the door handle.

"My mother was a angel of Gawd," Mr. Shiftlet said in a very strained voice. "He took her from heaven and giver to me and I left her." His eyes were instantly clouded over with a mist of tears. The car was barely moving.

The boy turned angrily in the seat. "You go to the devil!" he cried. "My old woman is a flea bag and yours is a stinking pole cat!" and with that he flung the door open and jumped out with his suitcase into the ditch.

Mr. Shiftlet was so shocked that for about a hundred feet he drove along slowly with the door still open. A cloud, the exact color of the boy's hat and shaped like a turnip, had descended over the sun, and another, worse looking, crouched behind the car. Mr. Shiftlet felt that the rottenness of the world was about to engulf him. He raised his arm and let it fall again to his breast. "Oh Lord!" he prayed. "Break forth and wash the slime from this earth!"

The turnip continued slowly to descend.

After a few minutes there was a guffawing peal of thunder from behind and fantastic raindrops, like tin-can tops, crashed over the rear of Mr. Shiftlet's car. Very quickly he stepped on the gas and with his stump sticking out the window he raced the galloping shower into Mobile.

FOR UNDERSTANDING

1. How old is the daughter? How old does her mother say she is?
2. How much does Lucynell's mother offer Mr. Shiftlet for her daughter?
3. What is the name of the restaurant where Mr. Shiftlet takes Lucynell?
4. How does the boy in the restaurant refer to Lucynell? What other person is referred to by the same phrase?
5. What prayer does Mr. Shiftlet pray to God and how is he answered?

FOR INTERPRETATION

Near the end of the story, as Mr. Shiftlet is driving away from the restaurant, we read: "Occasionally he saw a sign that warned: 'Drive carefully. The life you save may be your own.'" This is the title of the story. It is also a slogan commonly used on American highways. Think about that slogan for a minute or two. It is urging you as a driver to drive carefully so that you will not kill yourself. In other words, it is appealing to essentially selfish motives. You are not to drive carefully to save the lives of innocent animals or children, or of your own family, or of old people. You are to drive carefully because the life you save may be *your own*.

Only half conscious of what we see around us anyway, most of us probably think the slogan is a clever one—never examining its deeper implications. But Flannery O'Connor was one of those upon whom nothing is lost. She saw the enormous irony of the slogan and built a story around it.

Try to explain how the following statements from the story relate to the discussion above:

1. The world is almost rotten.
2. Nowadays, people'll do anything anyways.
3. People don't care how they lie.
4. There's some men that some things mean more to than money.
5. I wouldn't give her up for a casket of jewels.
6. Mr. Shiftlet said that the trouble with the world was that nobody cared, or stopped and took any trouble.
7. I was raised thataway and there ain't a thing I can do about it. My old mother taught me how to do.

FOR APPRECIATION

Characterization and Symbolism

Sometimes the details a writer uses to characterize a figure in a story make it clear that the figure is to be taken symbolically. What details in the portrait of the young Lucynell, for example, make it clear that she is symbolically an angel?

Some details in Mr. Shiftlet's portrait suggest that he may be intended as a Christ symbol. His figure forms a cross, for example, in an early part of the story. Later he acts as if he had "just raised the dead" when he resurrects the old car, and we may be reminded of Christ raising Lazarus from the dead. Can you relate the following details to the life of Christ:

1. Shiftlet's gaunt figure lists slightly to the side.
2. Shiftlet is wounded.
3. Shiftlet is a carpenter.

Of course Shiftlet is not wholly a Christ symbol —his figure forms a *crooked* cross and it is a machine, not a person, that he raises from the "dead." If he were really a Christ figure, he would surely not desert an angel of God.

That Shiftlet is a Christ symbol may seem impossible, but it is an "impossible truth," just as the fact that he has a moral intelligence is described in the story as an impossible truth. For he *does* have a moral intelligence; in fact, he often says morally intelligent things—"Nowadays, people'll do anything anyways," for example—but he does not live by his words. There is a split in Shiftlet between his speech and his action. Perhaps it is akin to the split within the many people who *call* themselves Christian and *profess* a concern for others while living as if the only life they cared to save were their own.

Donald Barthelme   1931–

Donald Barthelme was born in Philadelphia, Pennsylvania, but grew up in Texas and studied at the University of Houston. He has written two novels, *Snow White* and *The Dead Father,* and a book for children, *The Slightly Irregular Fire Engine.* In 1983 a play of his was produced in New York, off Broadway. Barthelme is best known, however, for the sketches that he regularly contributes to *The New Yorker* (and occasionally other magazines), which he has collected and published under such titles as *Come Back, Dr. Caligari; City Life;* and *Sadness.* A collection of his best work, *Sixty Stories,* was published in 1981. Donald Barthelme's books have been translated into more than a dozen languages, and he is one of America's most widely influential authors.

PORTRAIT OF DONALD BARTHELME

HEROES

—These guys, you know, if they don't know what's the story how can they . . .

—Exactly.

—So I inform myself. *U.S. News & World Report. Business Week. Scientific American.* I make it a point to steep myself in information.

—Yes.

—Otherwise your decisions have little meaning.

—Right.

—I mean they have *meaning,* because no decisions are meaningless in and of themselves, but they don't have *informed* meaning.

—Every citizen has a right.

—To what?

—To act. According to his lights.

—That's right.

—But his lights are not going to be that great. If he doesn't take the trouble. To find out what's the story.

—Take a candidate for something.

—Absolutely.

—There are all these candidates.

—More all the time. Hundreds.

—Now how does the ordinary man—

—The man in the street—

—*Really know.* Anything. About these birds.

—The media.

—Right. The media. That's how we know.

—Façades.

—One of these birds, maybe he calls you on the telephone.

—Right.

—You're flattered out of your skull, right?

—Right.

—You say, Oh my God, I'm talking to a *senator* or something.

—You're covered with awe.

—Or whoever it is. He's got your name on a little card, right? He's holding the card in his hand.

—Right.

—Say your name is George. He says, Well, George, very good to talk to you, what do you think about the economy? Or whatever it is.

—What do you say?

—You say, Well, Senator, it looks to me like it's a little shaky, the economy.

—You've informed yourself about the economy.

—Wait a minute, wait a minute, that's not the point. I mean it's *part* of the point but it's not the *whole* point.

—Right.

—So you tell him your opinion, it's a little shaky. And he agrees with you and everybody hangs up feeling good.

—Absolutely.

—But this is the point. Does he *act* on your opinion?

—No.

—Does he even remember your opinion?

—He reaches for the next card.

—He's got an awful lot of cards there.

—Maybe two hundred or three hundred.

—And this is just one session on the phone.

—He must get tired of it.

—Bored out of his skull. But that's not the point. The point is, the whole thing is meaningless. You don't know one thing more about him than before.

—Well, sometimes you can tell something. From the voice.

—Or say you meet him in person.

—The candidate. He comes to where you work.

—He's out there in the parking lot slapping skin.

—He shakes your hand.

—Then he shakes the next guy's hand. What do you know after he's shook your hand?

—Zero. Zip.

—Let me give you a third situation.

—What?

—You're standing on the sidewalk and he passes in his motorcade. Waving and smiling. What do you learn? That he's got a suntan.

—What is the reality? What is the man behind the mask? You don't learn.

—Therefore we rely on the media. We are *forced* to rely on the media. The print media and the electronic media.

—Thank God we got the media.

—That's what we have. Those are our tools. To inform ourselves.

—Correct. One hundred percent.

—*But.* And this is the point. There are distortions in the media.

—They're only human, right?

—The media are not a clear glass through which we can see a thing clearly.

—We see it darkly.

—I'm not saying these are intentional. The ripples in the clear glass. But we have to take them into consideration.

—We are prone to error.

—Now, you take a press conference.

—The candidate. Or the President.

—*Sometimes they ask them the questions that they want to be asked.*

—Pre-prepared questions.

—I'm not saying all of them. I'm not even saying most of them. But it happens.

—I figured.

—Or he doesn't pick the one to answer that he knows is going to shoot him a toughie.

—He picks the guy behind him.

—I mean he's been in this business a long time. He knows that one guy is going to ask

*A kaleidoscope of multiple images taken from various
media, this composite picture projects a powerful
impression of modern American urban life.*

ESTATE, Robert Rauschenberg
Philadelphia Museum of Art, Philadelphia, Pennsylvania
Given by the Friends of the Philadelphia Museum of Art

him about the economy and one guy is going to ask him about nuclear holocaust and one guy is going to ask him about China. So he can predict—

—What type of question a particular guy is going to pop on him.

—That's right. Of course some of these babies, they're as smart as he is. In their own particular areas of expertise.

—They can throw him a curve.

—He's got egg on his face.

—Or maybe he just decides to tough it out and *answer* the question.

—But what we get, what the public gets—

—The tip of the iceberg.

—There's a lot more under the surface that we don't get.

—The whole iceberg.

—We're like blind men feeling the iceberg.

—So you have to have *many, many* sources. To get a picture.

—Both print and electronic.

—When we see a press conference on the tube, *it's not even the whole press conference.*

—It's the highlights.

—Just the highlights. Most of the time.

—Maybe there was something that you wanted to know that got cut out.

—Five will get you ten there's something touching your vital personal interests that got cut out.

—Absolutely.

—They don't do it on purpose. They're human beings.

—I know that. And without them we would have nothing.

—But sometimes bias creeps in.

—Very subtle bias that colors their objectivity.

—Maybe they're not even aware of it but it creeps in. The back door.

—Like you're looking at the newspaper and they have pictures of all the candidates. They're all out campaigning, different places. And maybe they run one guy's picture twice as big as another guy's picture.

—Why do they do that?

—Maybe it's more humanly interesting, the first guy's picture. But it's still bias.

—Maybe they ought to measure them, the pictures.

—Maybe they *like* the guy. Maybe they just like him as a human being. He's more likable. That creeps in.

—One-on-one, the guy's more likable.

—But to be fair you should print the guy's picture you don't like as big as this guy's.

—Or maybe the guy they don't like, they give him more scrutiny. His personal life. His campaign contributions.

—Or maybe you want a job if he gets elected. It's human.

—That's a low thought. That's a *terrible* thought.

—Well, be realistic.

—I don't think that happens. There aren't that many jobs that they would want.

—In the *government* there aren't that many jobs?

—That were better than their present jobs. I mean which would you rather be, some government flunky or a powerful figure in the media?

—The latter. Any day in the week.

—I mean what if you're the *Wall Street Journal,* for instance? A powerful voice. A Cassandra crying in the wilderness. They're scared of what you might reveal or might not reveal. You can hold your head up. You bow to no man, not even presidents or kings—

—You have to stand up if he comes into the room, that's the rule.

—Well, standing up is not bowing.

—The thing is to study their faces, these guys, these guys that are running, on the tube. *With the sound turned off.* So you can see.

—You can read their souls.

—You can't read their souls, you can get an idea, a glimpse. The human face is a dark pool with dark things swimming in it, under the surface. You look for a long time, using your whole experience of life. To discern what's with this guy.

—I mean he's trying to look good, the poor sucker, busting his chops to look good in every nook and cranny of America.

—What do we really know about him? What do we know?

—He wants the job.

—Enormous forces have pressured him into wanting the job. Destiny. Some people are bigger than you or I. A bigger destiny. It's tearing him apart, not to have the job, he sees some other guy's got the job and he says to himself, My destiny is as big as that guy's destiny—If I can just get these jackasses to elect me.

—The rank and file. Us.

—If I can just get them to rally to my banner, the dummies.

—You think he thinks that?

—What's he going to think? It's tearing him apart, not to be elected.

—We're mere pawns. Clowns. Garbage.

—No. Without us, they can't realize their destinies. Can't even begin. No way.

—We make the judgments. Shrewd, informed judgments. Because we have informed ourselves.

—Taking into account the manifold distractions of a busy fruitful life.

—If it is fruitful.

—It's mostly going to be fruitful. If the individual makes the effort, knows what's the story—

—How did they know before they had the media?

—Vast crowds would assemble, from every hearth in the land. You had to be able to make a speech, just a dilly of a speech. "You shall not crucify mankind upon a cross of gold"—William Jennings Bryan. You had to be larger than life.

—The hearer of the speech knew—

—They were noble figures.

—They had to have a voice like an organ.

—The vast crowd swept by a fervor, as if by a wind.

—They were heroes and the individual loved them.

—Maybe misled. History sorts it out.

—Giant figures with voices like a whole church choir, plus the organ—

—A strange light coming from behind them, maybe it was only the sun. . . .

FOR UNDERSTANDING

1. What does the character mean by saying "Façades" in response to, "The media. That's how we know"?

2. What are the three voter-meets-candidate situations envisioned by the characters? Are these, in fact, the most likely ways a voter gets to meet a candidate for a high political office?

FOR INTERPRETATION

1. What is the card that the senate candidate is holding in his hand when he telephones the voter?

2. To get at the truth of what a political candidate is like, what does the one character recommend doing to the television set? How is this ironic?

3. Referring to pre-media candidates, one character says, "They were heroes and the individual loved them." Why is "individual" ironic here?

4. What is the "strange light" coming from behind pre-media political candidates?

5. Why is the story called "Heroes"?

FOR APPRECIATION

Point of View

In this story we have what might be called an "effaced" (erased) narrator point of view. That is, no one tells the story. The characters speak directly to each other.

1. What is the advantage of this technique, so far as reader involvement is concerned?

2. How does the reader know where the author stands when the latter uses an effaced narrator? (Hint: Consider the effect of the choice of the italicized word in the following speech from near the end of the story: "You had to be able to make a speech, just a *dilly* of a speech.")

John Updike   1932–

Originally, John Updike, who was born and raised in the small town of Shillington, Pennsylvania, near Reading, wanted to be a poet or a painter. He has continued to write poetry all his life, but after the appearance of his first novel, *The Poorhouse Fair,* in 1959, he has been known mainly as a novelist and short story writer. Updike joined the staff of *The New Yorker* magazine after graduation from college and has been working there ever since, doing book reviews as well as publishing his stories and poems. He has been an unusually prolific writer: for nearly a generation he has published a book of poems, a collection of stories, or a novel every year. He won a National Book Award in 1963 for his novel *The Centaur.* Among his most successful novels are *Rabbit Run* (1960), *Rabbit Redux* (1971), and *Rabbit Is Rich* (1981).

PORTRAIT OF JOHN UPDIKE

THE ALLIGATORS

Joan Edison came to their half of the fifth grade from Maryland in March. She had a thin face with something of a grownup's tired expression and long black eyelashes like a doll's. Everybody hated her. That month Miss Fritz was reading to them during homeroom about a girl, Emmy, who was badly spoiled and always telling her parents lies about her twin sister Annie; nobody could believe, it was too amazing, how exactly when they were despising Emmy most Joan should come into the school with her show-off clothes and her hair left hanging down the back of her fuzzy sweater instead of being cut or braided and

her having the crust to actually argue with teachers. "Well I'm sorry," she told Miss Fritz, not even rising from her seat, "but I *don't* see what the point is of homework. In Baltimore we never had any, and the *little* kids there knew what's in these books."

Charlie, who in a way enjoyed homework, was ready to join in the angry moan of the others. Little hurt lines had leaped up between Miss Fritz's eyebrows and he felt sorry for her, remembering how when that September John Eberly had half on purpose spilled purple Sho-Card paint on the newly sandpapered floor she had hidden her face in her arms on the desk and cried. She was afraid of the school board. "You're not in Baltimore now, Joan," Miss Fritz said. "You are in Olinger, Pennsylvania."

The children, Charlie among them, laughed, and Joan, blushing a soft brown color and raising her voice excitedly against the current of hatred, got in deeper by trying to explain, "Like there, instead of just *reading* about plants in a book we'd one day all bring in a flower we'd *picked* and cut it open and look at it in a *microscope.*" Because of her saying this, shadows, of broad leaves and wild slashed foreign flowers, darkened and complicated the idea they had of her.

Miss Fritz puckered her orange lips into fine wrinkles, then smiled. "In the upper levels you will be allowed to do that in this school. All things come in time, Joan, to patient little girls." When Joan started to argue *this,* Miss Fritz lifted one finger and said with the extra weight adults always have, held back in reserve, "No. No more, young lady, or you'll be in *serious* trouble with me." It gave the class courage to see that Miss Fritz didn't like her either.

After that, Joan couldn't open her mouth in class without there being a great groan. Outdoors on the macadam playground, at recess or fire drill or waiting in the morning for the buzzer, hardly anybody talked to her except to say "Stuck-up" or "Emmy." Boys were always yanking open the bow at the back of her fancy dresses and flipping little spitballs into the curls of her hanging hair. Once John Eberly even cut a section of her hair off with a yellow plastic scissors stolen from art class. This was the one time Charlie saw Joan cry actual tears. He was as bad as the others: worse, because what the others did because they felt like it, he did out of a plan, to make himself more popular. In the first and second grade he had been liked pretty well, but somewhere since then he had been dropped. There was a gang, boys and girls both, that met Saturdays—you heard them talk about it on Mondays—in Stuart Morrison's garage, and took hikes and played touch football together, and in winter sledded on Hill Street, and in spring bicycled all over Olinger and did together what else, he couldn't imagine.

Charlie had known the chief members since before kindergarten. But after school there seemed nothing for him to do but go home promptly and do his homework and fiddle with his Central American stamps and go to horror movies alone, and on weekends nothing but beat monotonously at marbles or Monopoly or chess Darryl Johns or Marvin Auerbach, who he wouldn't have bothered at all with if they hadn't lived right in the neighborhood, they being at least a year younger and not bright for their age, either. Charlie thought the gang might notice him and take him in if he backed up their policies without being asked.

In Science, which 5A had in Miss Brobst's room across the hall, he sat one seat ahead of Joan and annoyed her all he could, in spite of a feeling that, both being disliked, they had something to share. One fact he discovered was, she wasn't that bright. Her marks on quizzes were always lower than his. He told her, "Cutting up all those flowers didn't do you much good. Or maybe in Baltimore they taught you everything so long ago you've forgotten it in your old age."

Charlie drew; on his tablet where she could easily see over his shoulder he once in a while drew a picture titled "Joan the Dope": the profile of a girl with a lean nose and sad mincemouth, the lashes of her lowered eye as black as the pencil could make them and the hair falling, in ridiculous hooks, row after row, down through the sea-blue cross-lines clear off the bottom edge of the tablet.

March turned into spring. One of the signals was, on the high school grounds, before the cinder track was weeded and when the softball field was still four inches of mud, Happy Lasker came with the elaborate airplane model he had wasted the winter making. It had the American star on the wingtips and a pilot painted inside the cockpit and a miniature motor that burned real gas. The buzzing, off and on all Saturday morning, collected smaller kids from Second Street down to Lynoak. Then it was always the same: Happy shoved the plane into the air, where it climbed and made a razzing noise a minute, then nose-dived and crashed and usually burned in the grass or mud. Happy's father was rich.

In the weeks since she had come, Joan's clothes had slowly grown simpler, to go with the other girls', and one day she came to school with most of her hair cut off, and the rest brushed flat around her head and brought into a little tail behind. The laughter at her was more than she had ever heard. "Ooh. Baldypaldy!" some idiot girl had exclaimed when Joan came into the cloakroom, and the stupid words went sliding around class all morning. "Baldy-paldy from Baltimore. Why is old Baldy-paldy red in the face?" John Eberly kept making the motion of a scissors with his fingers and its juicy ticking sound with his tongue. Miss Fritz rapped her knuckles on the window sill until she was rubbing the ache with the other hand, and finally she sent two boys to Mr. Lengel's office, delighting Charlie an enormous secret amount.

His own reaction to the haircut had been quiet, to want to draw her, changed. He had kept the other drawings folded in his desk, and one of his instincts was toward complete sets of things, Bat Man comics and A's and Costa Rican stamps. Halfway across the room from him, Joan held very still, afraid, it seemed, to move even a hand, her face a shamed pink. The haircut had brought out her forehead and exposed her neck and made her chin pointier and her eyes larger. Charlie felt thankful once again for having been born a boy, and having no sharp shocks, like losing your curls to make growing painful. How much girls suffer had been one of the first thoughts he had ever had. His caricature of her was wonderful, the work of a genius. He showed it to Stuart Morrison behind him; it was too good for him to appreciate, his dull egg eyes just flickered over it. Charlie traced it onto another piece of tablet paper, making her head completely bald. This draw-

ing Stuart grabbed and it was passed clear around the room.

That night he had the dream. He must have dreamed it while lying there asleep in the morning light, for it was fresh in his head when he woke. They had been in a jungle. Joan, dressed in a torn sarong, was swimming in a clear river among alligators. Somehow, as if from a tree, he was looking down, and there was a calmness in the way the slim girl and the green alligators moved, in and out, perfectly visible under the window-skin of the water. Joan's face sometimes showed the horror she was undergoing and sometimes looked numb. Her hair trailed behind and fanned when her face came toward the surface. He shouted silently with grief. Then he had rescued her; without a sense of having dipped his arms in water, he was carrying her in two arms, himself in a bathing suit, and his feet firmly fixed to the knobby back of an alligator which skimmed upstream, through the shadows of high trees and white flowers and hanging vines, like a surfboard in a movie short. They seemed to be heading toward a wooden bridge arching over the stream. He wondered how he would duck it, and the river and the jungle gave way to his bed and his room, but through the change persisted, like a pedalled note on a piano, the sweetness and pride he had felt in saving and carrying the girl.

He loved Joan Edison. The morning was rainy, and under the umbrella his mother made him take this new knowledge, repeated again and again to himself, gathered like a bell of smoke. Love had no taste, but sharpened his sense of smell so that his oilcloth coat, his rubber boots, the red-tipped bushes hanging over the low walls holding back lawns all along Grand Street, even the dirt and moss in the cracks of the pavement each gave off clear odors. He would have laughed, if a wooden weight had not been placed high in his chest, near where his throat joined. He could not imagine himself laughing soon. It

Stark in its simplicity, Noland's painting conveys the kind of cheerful cruelty children sometimes inflict on one another.

seemed he had reached one of those situations his Sunday school teacher, poor Miss West with her little mustache, had been trying to prepare him for. He prayed, *Give me Joan.* With the wet weather a solemn flatness had fallen over everything; an orange bus turning at the Bend and four birds on a telephone wire seemed to have the same importance. Yet he felt firmer and lighter and felt things as edges he must whip around and channels he must rush down. If he carried her off, did rescue her from the others' cruelty, he would have defied the gang and made a new one, his own. Just Joan and he at first, then others escaping from meanness and dumbness, until his gang was stronger and Stuart Morrison's garage was empty every Saturday. Charlie would be a king, with his own touch football game. Everyone would come and plead with him for mercy.

His first step was to tell all those in the cloakroom he loved Joan Edison now. They cared less than he had expected, considering how she was hated. He had more or less expected to have to fight with his fists. Hardly anybody gathered to hear the dream he had pictured himself telling everybody. Anyway that morning it would go around the class that he said he loved her, and though this was what he wanted, to in a way open a space between him and Joan, it felt funny nevertheless, and he stuttered when Miss Fritz had him go to the blackboard to explain something.

At lunch, he deliberately hid in the variety store until he saw her walk by. The homely girl with her he knew turned off at the next street. He waited a minute and then came out and began running to overtake Joan in the block between the street where the other girl turned down and the street where he turned up. It had stopped raining, and his rolled-up umbrella felt like a commando's bayonet. Coming up behind her, he said, "Bang. Bang."

She turned, and under her gaze, knowing she knew he loved her, his face heated and he stared down. "Why, Charlie," her voice said with her Maryland slowness, "what are you doing on this side of the street?" Carl the town cop stood in front of the elementary school to get them on the side of Grand Street where they belonged. Now Charlie would have to cross the avenue again, by himself, at the dangerous five-spoked intersection.

"Nothing," he said, and used up the one sentence he had prepared ahead: "I like your hair the new way."

"Thank you," she said, and stopped. In Baltimore she must have had manner lessons. Her eyes looked at his, and his vision jumped back from the rims of her lower lids as if from a brink. Yet in the space she occupied there was a great fullness that lent him height, as if

he were standing by a window giving on the first morning after a snow.

"But then I didn't mind it the old way either."

"Yes?"

A peculiar reply. Another peculiar thing was the tan beneath her skin; he had noticed before, though not so closely, how when she colored it came up a gentle dull brown more than red. Also she wore something perfumed.

He asked, "How do you like Olinger?"

"Oh, I think it's nice."

"Nice? I guess. I guess maybe. Nice Olinger. I wouldn't know because I've never been anywhere else."

She luckily took this as a joke and laughed. Rather than risk saying something unfunny, he began to balance the umbrella by its point on one finger and, when this went well, walked backwards, shifting the balanced umbrella, its hook black against the patchy blue sky, from one palm to the other, back and forth. At the corner where they parted he got carried away and in imitating a suave gent leaning on a cane bent the handle hopelessly. Her amazement was worth twice the price of his mother's probable crossness.

He planned to walk her again, and further, after school. All through lunch he kept calculating. His father and he would repaint his bike. At the next haircut he would have his hair parted on the other side to get away from his cowlick. He would change himself totally; everyone would wonder what had happened to him. He would learn to swim, and take her to the dam.

In the afternoon the momentum of the dream wore off somewhat. Now that he kept his eyes always on her, he noticed, with a qualm of his stomach, that in passing in the afternoon from Miss Brobst's to Miss Fritz's room, Joan was not alone, but chattered with others. In class, too, she whispered. So it was with more shame—such shame that he didn't believe he could ever face even his parents again—than surprise that from behind the dark pane of the variety store he saw her walk by in the company of the gang, she and Stuart Morrison throwing back their teeth and screaming and he imitating something and poor moronic John Eberly tagging behind like a thick tail. Charlie watched them walk out of sight behind a tall hedge; relief was as yet a tiny fraction of his reversed world. It came to him that what he had taken for cruelty had been love, that far from hating her everybody had loved her from the beginning, and that even the stupidest knew it weeks before he did. That she was the queen of the class and might as well not exist, for all the good he would get out of it.

FOR UNDERSTANDING

1. What is the name of the town where the story takes place? Briefly characterize it.
2. What does Charlie do mostly after school during the week? What does Charlie do mostly on weekends?
3. What is the first thing Charlie does after deciding he loves Joan? Why does he do it?
4. What does Charlie imagine will happen after he and Joan get together?
5. Roughly how old are the main characters in this story?

FOR INTERPRETATION

1. Why does the narrator say that Charlie is even worse than the other students (paragraph five)?
2. What is the first hint the reader gets that Joan may be becoming a member of the group?
3. Interpret Charlie's dream, and explain why the story is called "The Alligators."

4. Why does Charlie feel the need at one point in the story to "change himself totally"?
5. What are some of the elements that Charlie pictures in this "total change"? Explain the irony here.
6. Why does Charlie feel *shame* when he sees Joan walking with gang members? Why will this shame make it difficult for him to "ever face his parents again"?

FOR APPRECIATION

Point of View

In third-person point of view, the narrator uses such pronouns as *she, her, he, him, it, they, them*—the third-person pronouns. In discussing third-person point of view, we often distinguish between "limited" and "omniscient" viewpoints. In a *limited viewpoint,* the author restricts the *persona,* or narrative voice, by focusing on the thoughts and experiences of only one character, or by entering into the consciousness of only one character. The *omniscient,* or all-knowing, point of view is at the other end of the scale. An omniscient narrator or persona may describe and comment on all the characters and actions and may enter the mind of more than one character.

1. How would you describe the point of view of this story? Is it limited? omniscient? neither of these? both? Explain.
2. At the beginning of the story, the statement is made about Joan that "Everybody hated her." Near the end of the story we read: ". . . everybody had loved her from the beginning. . . ." How do you explain this contradiction?

Theme

"The Alligators" is a story about a certain growth in self-awareness.

1. Try to describe the theme in your own words.
2. Why is the point of view particularly appropriate for the expression of this theme?

Joyce Carol Oates 1938–

Born in Lockport, New York, Joyce Carol Oates has become one of the most productive writers of our time. An acknowledged master of the short story, she has published numerous collections of her stories. She has also written some excellent literary criticism, and recently she published the text of *Three Plays*, which were produced off Broadway in the seventies. With her novel *Them* she won the National Book Award in 1970. Her novel *Bellefleur* (1980) was a best-seller. Her two most recent novels are *A Bloodsmoor Romance* (1982) and *Mysteries of Winterthurn* (1984).

PORTRAIT OF JOYCE CAROL OATES

JOURNEY

You begin your journey on so high an elevation that your destination is already in sight—a city that you have visited many times and that, moreover, is indicated on a traveler's map you have carefully folded up to take along with you. You are a lover of maps, and you have already committed this map to memory, but you bring it with you just the same.

The highway down from the mountains is broad and handsome, constructed after many years of ingenious blasting and leveling and paving. Engineers from all over the country aided in the construction of this famous highway. Its cost is so excessive that

many rumors have circulated about it—you take no interest in such things, sensing that you will never learn the true cost anyway, and that this will make no difference to your journey.

After several hours on this excellent highway, where the sun shines ceaselessly and where there is a moderate amount of traffic, cars like your own at a safe distance from you, as if to assure you that there are other people in the world, you become sleepy from the monotony and wonder if perhaps there is another, less perfect road parallel to this. You discover on the map a smaller road, not exactly parallel to the highway and not as direct, but one that leads to the same city.

You turn onto this road, which winds among foothills and forests and goes through several small villages. You sense by the attitude of the villagers that traffic on this road is infrequent but nothing to draw special attention. At some curves the road shrinks, but you are fortunate enough to meet no oncoming traffic.

The road leads deep into a forest, always descending in small cramped turns. Your turning from left to right and from right to left, in a slow hypnotic passage, makes it impossible for you to look out at the forest. You discover that for some time you have not been able to see the city you are headed for, though you know it is still somewhere ahead of you.

By mid-afternoon you are tired of this road, though it has served you well, and you come upon a smaller, unpaved road that evidently leads to your city, though in a convoluted way. After only a moment's pause you turn onto this road, and immediately your automobile registers the change—the chassis bounces, something begins to vibrate, something begins to rattle. This noise is disturbing, but after a while you forget about it in your interest in the beautiful countryside. Here the trees are enormous. There are no villages or houses. For a while the dirt road runs alongside a small river, dangerously close to the river's steep bank, and you begin to feel apprehension. It is necessary for you to drive very slowly. At times your speedometer registers less than five miles an hour. You will not get to the city before dark.

The road narrows until it is hardly more than a lane. Grass has begun to grow in its center. As the river twists and turns, so does the road twist and turn, curving around hills that consist of enormous boulders, bare of all trees and plants, covered only in patches by a dull, brown lichen that is unfamiliar to you. Along one stretch rocks of varying sizes have fallen down onto the road, so that you are forced to drive around them with great caution.

Navigating these blind turns, you tap your horn to give warning in case someone

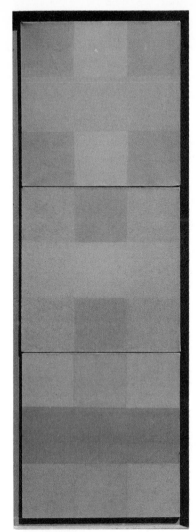

TRIPTYCH BLUE
Ad Reinhardt
Dayton Art Institute, Dayton, Ohio

should be approaching. But it is all unnecessary, since you come upon no other travelers.

Late in the afternoon, your foot numb from its constant pressure on the accelerator, your body jolted by the constant bumps and vibrations of the car, you decide to make the rest of your journey on foot, since you must be close to your destination by now.

A faint path leads through a tumble of rocks and bushes and trees, and you follow it enthusiastically. You descend a hill, slipping a little, so that a small rockslide is released; but you are able to keep your balance. At the back of your head is the precise location of your parked car, and behind that the curving dirt road, and behind that the other road, and then the magnificent highway itself: you understand that it would be no difficult feat to make your way back to any of these roads, should you decide that going by foot is unwise. But the path, though overgrown, is through a lovely forest, and then through a meadow in which yellow flowers are blooming, and you feel no inclination to turn back.

By evening you are still in the wilderness and you wonder if perhaps you have made a mistake. You are exhausted, your body aches, your eyes are seared by the need to stare so intently at everything around you. Now that the sun has nearly set, it is getting cold; evenings here in the mountains are always chilly.

You find yourself standing at the edge of a forest, staring ahead into the dark. Is that a field ahead, or a forest of small trees? Your path has long since given way to wild grass. Clouds obscure the moon, which should give you some light by which to make your way, and you wonder if you dare continue without this light.

Suddenly you remember the map you left back in the car, but you remember it as a blank sheet of paper.

You resist telling yourself you are lost. In fact, though you are exhausted and it is almost night, you are not lost. You have begun to shiver, but it is only with cold, not with fear. You are really satisfied with yourself. You are not lost. Though you can remember your map only as a blank sheet of paper, which can tell you nothing, you are not really lost.

If you had the day to begin again, on that highway which was so wide and clear, you would not have varied your journey in any way: in this is your triumph.

UNDERSTANDING AND INTERPRETATION

In a story as short as this, you can be fairly certain that each detail counts for something. Explain the significance of as many of the following details as you can.

1. You are a lover of maps.

2. On the big highway cars "like your own" travel "at a safe distance" from you.

3. The second road leads deep into a forest, but you cannot look at it.

4. On the third road there are no villages or houses.

5. You remember the map as a blank sheet of paper.

FOR APPRECIATION

Structure

Short as it is, this story is very highly structured, especially with respect to several progressions that flow through it. For example, the "you" in the story goes from a first-rate highway to a curving paved road, to an unpaved dirt road, to a faint path, to no path at all. Another progression is a movement from the familiar to the unfamiliar. Still another begins with "sleepy from the monotony." What are the other steps in this progression? How does it end? What other progressions, if any, can you trace?

Symbolism

How can you decide whether or not this story should be interpreted symbolically? For one thing, you might observe that "you" has no name and no background. Notice that the mountain and the city are also nameless; in fact, there isn't a single proper name in the whole story. In short, it is not the things and person that are important but what they stand for.

1. What, in your opinion, does the journey of "you" symbolize?

2. How does your tracing of the progressions in the story help you to see its symbolic import?

Anne Tyler

1941–

Though born in Minneapolis, Minnesota, Anne Tyler spent her high school years in Raleigh, North Carolina. She went to college at Duke University and later at Columbia University. She was a Russian language major in college but also wrote stories and in fact finished her first novel while she was still in her early twenties. Since then, she has written eight others, including *Celestial Navigation, Earthly Possessions*, and her most recent, *Dinner at the Homesick Restaurant*, which was nominated for a National Book Award. Tyler has said that she writes because she wants to live other lives—"I've never quite believed that one chance is all I get."

PORTRAIT OF ANNE TYLER

AVERAGE WAVES IN UNPROTECTED WATERS

As soon as it got light, Bet woke him and dressed him, and then she walked him over to the table and tried to make him eat a little cereal. He wouldn't, though. He could tell something was up. She pressed the edge of the spoon against his lips till she heard it click on his teeth, but he just looked off at a corner of the ceiling—a knobby child with great glassy eyes and her own fair hair. Like any other nine-year-old, he wore a striped shirt and jeans, but the shirt was too neat and the jeans too blue, unpatched and unfaded, and would stay that way till he outgrew them. And his face was elderly—pinched, strained, tired —though it should have looked as unused as his jeans. He hardly ever changed his expression.

She left him in his chair and went to make the beds. Then she raised the yellowed shade, rinsed a few spoons in the bathroom sink, picked up some bits of magazines he'd torn the night before. This was a rented room in an ancient, crumbling house, and nothing you could do to it would lighten its cluttered look. There was always that feeling of too many lives layered over other lives, like the layers of brownish wallpaper her child had peeled away in the corner by his bed.

She slipped her feet into flat-heeled loafers and absently patted the front of her dress, a worn beige knit she usually saved for Sundays. Maybe she should take it in a little; it hung from her shoulders like a sack. She felt too slight and frail, too wispy for all she had to do today. But she reached for her coat anyhow, and put it on and tied a blue kerchief under her chin. Then she went over to the table and slowly spun, modelling the coat. "See, Arnold?" she said. "We're going out."

Arnold went on looking at the ceiling, but his gaze turned wild and she knew he'd heard.

She fetched his jacket from the closet—brown corduroy, with a hood. It had set her back half a week's salary. But Arnold didn't like it; he always wanted his old one, a little red duffel coat he'd long ago outgrown. When she came toward him, he started moaning and rocking and shaking his head. She had to struggle to stuff his arms in the sleeves. Small though he was, he was strong, wiry; he was getting to be too much for her. He shook free of her hands and ran over to his bed. The jacket was on, though. It wasn't buttoned, the collar was askew, but never mind; that just made him look more real. She always felt bad at how he stood inside his clothes, separate from them, passive, unaware of all the buttons and snaps she'd fastened as carefully as she would a doll's.

She gave a last look around the room, checked to make sure the hot plate was off, and then picked up her purse and Arnold's suitcase. "Come along, Arnold," she said.

He came, dragging out every step. He looked at the suitcase suspiciously, but only because it was new. It didn't have any meaning for him. "See?" she said. "It's yours. It's Arnold's. It's going on the train with us."

But her voice was all wrong. He would pick it up, for sure. She paused in the middle of locking the door and glanced over at him fearfully. Anything could set him off nowadays. He hadn't noticed, though. He was too busy staring around the hallway, goggling at a freckled, walnut-framed mirror as if he'd never seen it before. She touched his shoulder. "Come, Arnold," she said.

They went down the stairs slowly, both of them clinging to the sticky mahogany railing. The suitcase banged against her shins. In the entrance hall, old Mrs. Puckett stood waiting outside her door—a huge, soft lady in a black crêpe dress and orthopedic shoes. She was holding a plastic bag of peanut-butter cookies, Arnold's favorites. There were tears in her eyes. "Here, Arnold," she said, quavering. Maybe she felt to blame that he was going. But she'd done the best she could: baby-sat him all these years and only given up when he'd grown too strong and wild to manage. Bet wished Arnold would give the old lady some sign—hug her, make his little crowing noise, just take the cookies, even. But he was too excited. He raced on out the front door, and it was Bet who had to take them. "Well, thank you, Mrs. Puckett," she said. "I know he'll enjoy them later."

"Oh, no . . ." said Mrs. Puckett, and she flapped her large hands and gave up, sobbing.

They were lucky and caught a bus first thing. Arnold sat by the window. He must have thought he was going to work with her; when they passed the red-and-gold Kresge's sign, he jabbered and tried to stand up. "No, honey," she said, and took hold of his arm. He settled down then and let his hand stay curled in hers awhile. He had very small, cool fingers, and nails as smooth as thumbtack heads.

At the train station, she bought the tickets and then a pack of Wrigley's spearmint gum. Arnold stood gaping at the vaulted ceiling, with his head flopped back and his arms hanging limp at his sides. People stared at him. She would have liked to push their faces in. "Over here, honey," she said, and she

THE RED BRIDGE
J. Alden Weir
The Metropolitan Museum of Art
New York City

nudged him toward the gate, straightening his collar as they walked.

He hadn't been on a train before and acted a little nervous, bouncing up and down in his seat and flipping the lid of his ashtray and craning forward to see the man ahead of them. When the train started moving, he crowed and pulled at her sleeve. "That's right, Arnold. Train. We're taking a trip," Bet said. She unwrapped a stick of chewing gum and gave it to him. He loved gum. If she didn't watch him closely, he sometimes swallowed it—which worried her a little because she'd heard it clogged your kidneys; but at least it would keep him busy. She looked down at the top of his head. Through the blond prickles of his hair, cut short for practical reasons, she could see his skull bones moving as he chewed. He was so thin-skinned, almost transparent; sometimes she imagined she could see the blood travelling in his veins.

When the train reached a steady speed, he grew calmer, and after a while he nodded over against her and let his hands sag on his knees. She watched his eyelashes slowly drooping—two colorless, fringed crescents, heavier and heavier, every now and then flying up as he tried to fight off sleep. He had never slept well, not ever, not even as a baby. Even before they'd noticed anything wrong, they'd wondered at his jittery, jerky catnaps, his tiny hands clutching tight and springing open, his strange single wail sailing out while he went right on sleeping. Avery said it gave him the chills. And after the doctor talked to them Avery wouldn't have anything to do with Arnold anymore—just walked in wide circles around the crib, looking stunned and sick. A few weeks later, he left. She wasn't surprised. She even knew how he felt, more or less. Halfway, he blamed her; halfway, he blamed himself. You can't believe a thing like this will just fall on you out of nowhere.

She'd had moments herself of picturing some kind of evil gene in her husband's ordinary, stocky body—a dark little egg like a black jelly bean, she imagined it. All his fault. But other times she was sure the gene was hers. It seemed so natural; she never could do anything as well as most people. And then other times she blamed their marriage. They'd married too young, against her parents' wishes. All she'd wanted was to get away from home. Now she couldn't remember why. What was wrong with home? She thought of her parents' humped green trailer, perched on cinder blocks near a forest of masts in Salt Spray, Maryland. At this distance (parents dead, trailer rusted to bits, even Salt Spray changed past recognition), it seemed to her that her old life had been beautifully free and spacious. She closed her eyes and saw wide gray skies. Everything had been ruled by the sea. Her father (who'd run a fishing boat for tourists) couldn't arrange his day till he'd heard the marine forecast— the wind, the tides, the smallcraft warnings, the height of average waves in unprotected waters. He loved to fish, offshore and on, and he swam every chance he could get. He'd tried to teach her to bodysurf, but it hadn't worked out. There was something about the breakers: she just gritted her teeth and stood staunch and let them slam into her. As if standing staunch were a virtue, really. She couldn't explain it. Her father thought she was scared, but it wasn't that at all.

She'd married Avery against their wishes and been sorry ever since—sorry to move so far from home, sorrier when her parents died within a year of each other, sorriest of all when the marriage turned grim and cranky.

But she never would have thought of leaving him. It was Avery who left; she would have stayed forever. In fact, she did stay on in their apartment for months after he'd gone, though the rent was far too high. It wasn't that she expected him back. She just took some comfort from enduring.

Arnold's head snapped up. He looked around him and made a gurgling sound. His chewing gum fell onto the front of his jacket. "Here, honey," she told him. She put the gum in her ashtray. "Look out the window. See the cows?"

He wouldn't look. He began bouncing in his seat, rubbing his hands together rapidly.

"Arnold? Want a cookie?"

If only she'd brought a picture book. She'd meant to and then forgot. She wondered if the train people sold magazines. If she let him get too bored, he'd go into one of his tantrums, and then she wouldn't be able to handle him. The doctor had given her pills just in case, but she was always afraid that while he was screaming he would choke on them. She looked around the car. "Arnold," she said, "see the . . . see the hat with feathers on? Isn't it pretty? See the red suitcase? See the, um . . ."

The car door opened with a rush of clattering wheels and the conductor burst in, singing "Girl of my dreams, I love you." He lurched down the aisle, plucking pink tickets from the back of each seat. Just across from Bet and Arnold, he stopped. He was looking down at a tiny black lady in a purple coat, with a fox fur piece biting its own tail around her neck. "You!" he said.

The lady stared straight ahead.

"You, I saw you. You're the one in the washroom."

A little muscle twitched in her cheek.

"You got on this train in Beulah, didn't you. Snuck in the washroom. Darted back like you thought you could put something over on me. I saw that bit of purple! Where's your ticket gone to?"

She started fumbling in a blue cloth

purse. The fumbling went on and on. The conductor shifted his weight.

"Why!" she said finally. "I must've left it back in my other seat."

"What other seat?"

"Oh, the one back . . ." She waved a spidery hand.

The conductor sighed. "Lady," he said, "you owe me money."

"I do no such thing!" she said. "Viper! Monger! Hitler!" Her voice screeched up all at once; she sounded like a parrot. Bet winced and felt herself flushing, as if *she* were the one. But then at her shoulder she heard a sudden, rusty clang, and she turned and saw that Arnold was laughing. He had his mouth wide open and his tongue curled, the way he did when he watched "Sesame Street." Even after the scene had worn itself out, and the lady had paid and the conductor had moved on, Arnold went on chortling and la-la-ing, and Bet looked gratefully at the little black lady, who was settling her fur piece fussily and muttering under her breath.

From the Parkinsville Railroad Station, which they seemed to be tearing down or else remodelling—she couldn't tell which—they took a taxicab to Parkins State Hospital. "Oh, I been out there many and many a time," said the driver. "Went out there just the other——"

But she couldn't stop herself; she had to tell him before she forgot. "Listen," she said, "I want you to wait for me right in the driveway. I don't want you to go on away."

"Well, fine," he said.

"Can you do that? I want you to be sitting right by the porch or the steps or whatever, right where I come out of, ready to take me back to the station. Don't just go off and——"

"I *got* you, I got you," he said.

She sank back. She hoped he understood.

Arnold wanted a peanut-butter cookie. He was reaching and whimpering. She didn't know what to do. She wanted to give him anything he asked for, anything; but he'd get it all over his face and arrive not looking his best. She couldn't stand it if they thought he was just ordinary and unattractive. She wanted them to see how small and neat he was, how somebody cherished him. But it would be awful if he went into one of his rages. She broke off a little piece of cookie from the bag. "Here," she told him. "Don't mess, now."

He flung himself back in the corner and ate it, keeping one hand flattened across his mouth while he chewed.

The hospital looked like someone's great, pillared mansion, with square brick buildings all around it. "Here we are," the driver said.

"Thank you," she said. "Now you wait here, please. Just wait till I get——"

"*Lady*," he said. "I'll wait."

She opened the door and nudged Arnold out ahead of her. Lugging the suitcase, she started toward the steps. "Come on, Arnold," she said.

He hung back.

"Arnold?"

Maybe he wouldn't allow it, and they would go on home and never think of this again.

But he came, finally, climbing the steps in his little hobbled way. His face was clean, but there were a few cookie crumbs on his jacket. She set down the suitcase to brush them off. Then she buttoned all his buttons and smoothed his shirt collar over his jacket collar before she pushed open the door.

In the admitting office, a lady behind a wooden counter showed her what papers to sign. Secretaries were clacketing typewriters all around. Bet thought Arnold might like that, but instead he got lost in the lights—chilly, hanging ice-cube tray lights with a little flicker to them. He gazed upward, looking astonished. Finally a flat-fronted nurse came in and touched his elbow. "Come along, Arnold. Come, Mommy. We'll show you where Arnold is staying," she said.

They walked back across the entrance hall, then up wide marble steps with hollows worn in them. Arnold clung to the bannister.

There was a smell Bet hated, pine-oil disinfectant, but Arnold didn't seem to notice. You never knew; sometimes smells could just put him in a state.

The nurse unlocked a double door that had chicken-wired windows. They walked through a corridor, passing several fat, ugly women in shapeless gray dresses and ankle socks. "Ha!" one of the women said, and fell giggling into the arms of a friend. The nurse said, *Here* we are." She led them into an enormous hallway lined with little white cots. Nobody else was in it; there wasn't a sign that children lived here except for a tiny cardboard clown picture hanging on one vacant wall. "This one is your bed, Arnold," said the nurse. Bet laid the suitcase on it. It was made up so neatly, the sheets might have been painted on. A steely-gray blanket was folded across the foot. She looked over at Arnold, but he was pivoting back and forth to hear how his new sneakers squeaked on the linoleum.

"Usually," said the nurse, "we like to give new residents six months before the family visits. That way they settle in quicker, don't you see." She turned away and adjusted the clown picture, though as far as Bet could tell it was fine the way it was. Over her shoulder, the nurse said, "You can tell him goodbye now, if you like."

"Oh," Bet said. "All right." She set her hands on Arnold's shoulders. Then she laid her face against his hair, which felt warm and fuzzy. "Honey," she said. But he went on pivoting. She straightened and told the nurse, "I brought his special blanket."

"Oh, fine," said the nurse, turning toward her again. "We'll see that he gets it."

"He always likes to sleep with it; he has ever since he was little."

"All right."

"Don't wash it. He hates if you wash it."

"Yes. Say goodbye to Mommy now, Arnold."

"A lot of times he'll surprise you. I mean there's a whole lot to him. He's not just—"

"We'll take very good care of him, Mrs. Blevins, don't worry."

"Well," she said. "'Bye, Arnold."

She left the ward with the nurse and went down the corridor. As the nurse was unlocking the doors for her, she heard a single, terrible scream, but the nurse only patted her shoulder and pushed her gently on through.

In the taxi, Bet said, "Now, I've just got fifteen minutes to get to the station. I wonder if you could hurry?"

"Sure thing," the driver said.

She folded her hands and looked straight ahead. Tears seemed to be coming down her face in sheets.

Once she'd reached the station, she went to the ticket window. "Am I in time for the twelve-thirty-two?" she asked.

"Easily," said the man. "It's twenty minutes late."

"What?"

"Got held up in Norton somehow."

"But you can't!" she said. The man looked startled. She must be a sight, all swollen-eyed and wet-cheeked. "Look," she said, in a lower voice. "I figured this on purpose. I chose the one train from Beulah that would let me catch another one back without waiting. I do not want to sit and wait in this station."

"Twenty *minutes*, lady. That's all it is."

"What am I going to do?" she asked him.

He turned back to his ledgers.

She went over to a bench and sat down. Ladders and scaffolding towered above her, and only ten or twelve passengers were dotted through the rest of the station. The place looked bombed out—nothing but a shell. "Twenty minutes!" she said aloud. "What am I going to do?"

Through the double glass doors at the far end of the station, a procession of gray-suited men arrived with briefcases. More men came behind them, dressed in work clothes, carrying folding chairs, black trunklike boxes with silver hinges, microphones, a wooden lectern, and an armload of bunting. They set the lectern down in the center of the floor, not six feet from Bet. They draped the bunting across it—an arc of red, white, and blue. Wires were connected, floodlights were lit. A microphone screeched. One of the workmen said, "Try her, Mayor." He held the microphone out to a fat man in a suit, who cleared his throat and said, "Ladies and gentlemen, on the occasion of the expansion of this fine old railway station——"

"Sure do get an echo here," the workman said. "Keep on going."

The Mayor cleared his throat again. "If I may," he said, "I'd like to take about twenty minutes of your time, friends."

He straightened his tie. Bet blew her nose, and then she wiped her eyes and smiled. They had come just for her sake, you might think. They were putting on a sort of private play. From now on, all the world was going to be like that—just something on a stage, for her to sit back and watch.

FOR UNDERSTANDING

It is a familiar saying that our best laid plans often go wrong. What happens to Bet at the end of this story is a good example.
1. Why does Bet want the cab driver to wait at the hospital?
2. What does she discover at the ticket window?
3. What is ironic about the fact that the mayor intends to give a twenty-minute speech?
4. Interpret the last line of the story: "From now on, all the world was going to be like that—just something on a stage, for her to sit back and watch."

FOR INTERPRETATION

Be prepared to discuss your opinions of the statements that follow and the extent to which the story does or does not bear them out.

1. If we truly love someone, we do what is best for her or him, regardless of our own feelings or desires.
2. Rational solutions to problems are not necessarily the best solutions.
3. Standing staunch is a virtue.
4. When we have something distasteful to do, it's best to do it without leaving ourselves any time to think.
5. No one can fully prepare for what life may bring.
6. People who see things through are always more admirable than those who run away.

FOR APPRECIATION

Symbolism
One of the most important tasks of a good short story writer is to make everything hang together. Sometimes, it is a symbol that helps to crystallize a story in a writer's mind. Tyler probably knew early on that she wanted to write about Bet and Arnold, but what probably pulled everything into perspective for her was the symbol that ultimately became the title of the story.
1. What does the title mean to you?
2. Do you agree or disagree that it serves to crystallize the story, and why?

Structure: Foreshadowing and Flashback
Foreshadowing and *flashback* are aspects of structure that are more commonly seen in longer, rather than shorter, works of literature, but there are instances of both in this short story. *Foreshadowing* is simply the hinting at something that will occur later in the story.

A *flashback* is a device by which the author presents scenes or incidents that occurred prior to the opening of the story. Notice that in this story Tyler uses as a flashback a recollection of Bet's, in order to sketch in some details about her past life.
1. How many examples of foreshadowing can you find in "Average Waves"? What purposes do these examples serve?
2. Locate the flashback mentioned above and note how smoothly the author moves into and out of it.
3. How essential is this flashback to the design and meaning of the story?

Robert Penn Warren   1905–

Robert Penn Warren, who was born in Guthrie, Kentucky, has long been one of the outstanding literary figures of the twentieth century. While still an undergraduate, he became associated with a group of writers known as the Fugitives at Vanderbilt University, and he went on to distinguish himself as an author of nonfiction, fiction, literary criticism, and poetry while teaching at Louisiana State University, at the University of Minnesota, and at Yale University.

With his colleague, Cleanth Brooks, Warren coauthored two of the most influential textbooks of all time—*Understanding Poetry* (1938) and *Understanding Fiction* (1943). In 1947 he won the Pulitzer Prize for Fiction with his novel, *All the King's Men,* a book about politics and the quest for self-knowledge. Robert Penn Warren has twice won the Pulitzer Prize for Poetry, with *Promises* in 1958 and again in 1979 with *Now and Then.*

PORTRAIT OF ROBERT PENN WARREN
Conrad Albrizio
National Portrait Gallery, Smithsonian Institution, Washington D.C.
Gift of Robert Penn Warren

First Dawn Light

By lines fainter gray than the faintest geometry
Of chalk on a wall like a blackboard, first light
Defines the window edges. Last dream, last owl-cry
Now past, now is the true emptiness of night.

For not yet first bird-stir, first bird-note, only   5
Your breath as you wonder what daylight will bring—and you try
To recall what the last dream was, and think how lonely
In sun-blaze you have seen the buzzard hang black in the sky.

For day has its loneliness, too, you think, even as
First bird-stir does come, first twitter, faithless and fearful   10
That new night, in the deep leaves, may lurk. So silence has
Returned. Then, sudden, the glory, heart-full and ear-full,

THE ARTIST'S STUDIO IN AN AFTERNOON FOG, Winslow Homer
Memorial Art Gallery of the University of Rochester, New York, P.T. Miller Fund

For triggered now is the mysterious mechanism
Of the forest's joy, and yours, by temperature or beam,
And until a sludge-thumb smears the sunset's prism,   15
You must wait to resume, in night's black hood, the reality of dream.

UNDERSTANDING AND INTERPRETATION

1. When does "the true emptiness of night" come?
2. Why is the first twitter of the birds "faithless and fearful"?
3. What triggers the forest's and people's joy in the early morning?
4. What does the speaker mean by "the reality of dream"?
5. How is the ending of the poem ironic?

FOR APPRECIATION

1. Describe the rhyme scheme of the poem.
2. Demonstrate that the basic rhythm of the poem is iambic hexameter.
3. How does the last line diverge from this pattern?
4. When two accents appear in succession, we sometimes refer to it as a *spondee*. Locate several instances of this in "First Dawn Light."

Elizabeth Bishop   1911–1979

Elizabeth Bishop once compared her life and behavior to that of a sandpiper—"just running along the edges of different countries and continents, looking for something." Born in Worcester, Massachusetts, in 1911, Bishop traveled widely, beginning shortly after her graduation from college. From 1951 to 1966, she lived in Brazil and served as coeditor of a volume of *Contemporary Brazilian Poetry*. Her first book of poems—*North and South*—was published in 1946. With her second volume, *A Cold Spring,* she received the Pulitzer Prize in 1956. Her *Complete Poems* appeared in 1969 and won the National Book Award. A second volume of *Complete Poems* appeared in 1983.

The poem on the next page is based on the *villanelle* form. In this form the first and third lines of the first three-line stanza alternate as the last lines of the succeeding four three-line stanzas. Then they must be used again as the last two lines of the final four-line stanza.

PORTRAIT OF ELIZABETH BISHOP

Casabianca

Love's the boy stood on the burning deck
trying to recite "The boy stood on
the burning deck." Love's the son
    stood stammering elocution
    while the poor ship in flames went down.   5

Love's the obstinate boy, the ship,
even the swimming sailors, who
would like a schoolroom platform, too,
    or an excuse to stay
    on deck. And love's the burning boy.   10

One Art

The art of losing isn't hard to master;
so many things seem filled with the intent
to be lost that their loss is no disaster.

Lose something every day. Accept the fluster
of lost door keys, the hour badly spent.   5
The art of losing isn't hard to master.

Then practice losing farther, losing faster:
places, and names, and where it was you meant
to travel. None of these will bring disaster.

I lost my mother's watch. And look! my last, or   10
next-to-last, of three loved houses went.
The art of losing isn't hard to master.

I lost two cities, lovely ones. And, vaster,
some realms I owned, two rivers, a continent.
I miss them, but it wasn't a disaster.   15

—Even losing you (the joking voice, a gesture
I love) I shan't have lied. It's evident
the art of losing's not too hard to master
though it may look like (*Write* it!) like disaster.

UNDERSTANDING AND INTERPRETATION

"Casabianca"

1. What are the different people or things that love is said to be?
2. Why do the swimming sailors envy the boy?

"One Art"

1. In what sense is losing an art?
2. Where does the poem shift from offering instruction to a more personal tone?
3. To whom is *"Write* it!" addressed?
4. How does the speaker feel about losing the "you" referred to in the final stanza?

FOR APPRECIATION

"One Art"

1. A villanelle is a difficult poem to write because the first and third line of the first stanza must be reused so often. (Specifically, each must be reused three times.) Normally, these lines are repeated word for word. What sort of variety in this normal use does Bishop practice with her third line?
2. The first line of the poem is more precisely repeated in its subsequent appearances, but in one place the repetition is not exact. Find it and describe the difference. Can you relate that difference to the meaning of the poem as a whole?

Gwendolyn Brooks   1917–

In 1950 Gwendolyn Brooks became the first black woman to win a Pulitzer Prize. She received it for her second volume of poetry, *Annie Allen* (1949). Her first book of poems, *A Street in Bronzeville*, had appeared in 1945. She published a novel, *Maud Martha*, in 1953, followed by more poetry—*The Bean Eaters* (1960) and *In the Mecca* (1968). These five volumes were brought together under one cover in 1971 in a book entitled *The World of Gwendolyn Brooks*. Brooks has lived nearly all her life on the South Side of Chicago, the area about which she writes. In 1968 she was named Poet Laureate of Illinois. An autobiography, *Report from Part One*, appeared in 1972.

PORTRAIT OF GWENDOLYN BROOKS

Looking

You have no word for soldiers to enjoy
The feel of, as an apple, and to chew
With masculine satisfaction. Not "good-by!"
"Come back!" or "careful!" Look, and let
   him go.
"Good-by!" is brutal, and "come back!"
   the raw   **5**
Insistence of an idle desperation
Since could he favor he would favor now.
He will be "careful!" if he has permission.
Looking is better. At the dissolution
Grab greatly with the eye, crush in a steel **10**
Of study—Even that is vain. Expression,
The touch or look or word, will little avail.
The brawniest will not beat back the storm
Nor the heaviest haul your little boy from
   harm.

UNDERSTANDING AND INTERPRETATION

1. Whom is the speaker addressing?
2. Explain the title.
3. What does the speaker mean by "if he has permission"?
4. What does "expression" (line 11) mean? Why is expression of little avail?

FOR APPRECIATION

Modern poets often shape traditional verse forms to their own ends. "Looking" is a *sonnet*, a fourteen-line poem with five stresses to a line (usually iambic). This particular sonnet is most similar to a form often called the "Spenserian" (after the English poet Edmund Spenser). In such a sonnet the *quatrains*—four-line units—are connected by interlacing the rhymes: *abab bcbc cdcd ee*. This kind of sonnet usually deals with a single idea or emotion, and its final couplet is frequently used as a sort of summary of or conclusion for what has gone before.

Discuss "Looking" as a variation of the Spenserian sonnet form.

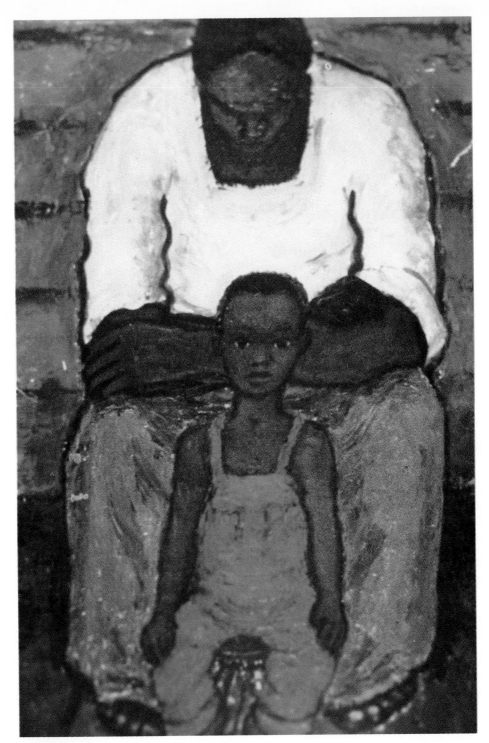

THE MATRIARCH
Ellis Wilson
The Barnett-Aden Collection, Anacostia Neighborhood Museum, Washington, D.C.

Robert Lowell   1917–1977

Robert Lowell was born into a distinguished Boston family. One of his ancestors was the first woman to step off the *Mayflower*, and he was related to two well-known American poets: James Russell Lowell and Amy Lowell. But Robert Lowell soon rebelled against his family, Harvard University, Boston tradition, even America. In the middle of his college education he left Harvard for Kenyon College in order to study with John Crowe Ransom. During the same period, he left the traditional Protestantism of his family and became a Roman Catholic. His adopted religion strongly influenced his first two volumes of poetry, *Land of Unlikeness* (1944) and *Lord Weary's Castle* (1946). The latter volume was highly praised by famous literary figures and it also brought Lowell—who was barely thirty years old—a Pulitzer Prize and an appointment as consultant in poetry at the Library of Congress.

In the fifties, Lowell studied the work of the famous psychoanalyst Sigmund Freud and in three successive books, *Life Studies* (1959), *For the Union Dead* (1964), and *Near the Ocean* (1967), closely examined his own personality and experience. His self-analytical approach gave rise to a school of "confessional poetry," which eventually numbered among its practitioners some of the greatest poets of the era. In exploring himself, Lowell was in many ways exploring twentieth-century humankind, for although he was not an "average person," his problems—mental illness, marital difficulties,

PORTRAIT OF ROBERT LOWELL

opposition to war—were typical of our time. His work has been described as "a mirror to his culture, supplying society with elements for advance." And the same critic has said of Lowell that "His power as a poet derives from his understanding that . . . he can be a man of letters only insofar as he can remain a man among men."

Robert Lowell is often considered the most influential of all contemporary American poets. He knew virtually all the major poets of his time and taught such famous poets as Anne Sexton and Sylvia Plath, among many others. It may be well therefore to look closely at one of his poems as a way of discovering how to read contemporary poetry. We have chosen for this purpose a late poem of Lowell's, one dealing with Henry David Thoreau, an American writer of the previous century, whom you have already met in this book (see page 190).

Thoreau 2*

He thought New England was corrupted by
too much communion with her saints,
our fears consoled and iced, no hope confirmed.
If the high sun wandered and warmed a winter day
and surprised the plodding circuit of our lives,   5
we winced and called it fickleness and fools-thaw—
"However bad your life, meet it, live it,
it's not as bad as you are." For Thoreau,
life in us was like water in a river:
"It may rise higher this year than all others."   10
Adrift there, dragging forty feet of line,
he felt a dull, uncertain, blundering purpose
jerking, slow to make up its mind, and knew
the light that blinds our eyes is not the sun.

* The "2" after "Thoreau" merely indicates that this is
the second of two poems addressed to Thoreau.

"Thoreau 2" from HISTORY by Robert Lowell. Copyright © 1967, 1968, 1969, 1970, 1973 by Robert Lowell. Reprinted by permission of Farrar, Straus & Giroux, Inc.

READING CONTEMPORARY POETRY

The poem probably seems difficult to you on first reading. That is not surprising. One should not expect a good poem to be immediately clear on first reading, nor should readers expect contemporary poetry to be traditional in form or structure.

Why should a contemporary poem be so unlike traditional poetry? Someone once asked the poet-critic Mark Van Doren a question about this. Specifically, Van Doren was asked, "Why don't poets write love poems like Robert Burns?" (Burns is a Scottish poet of the eighteenth century; he wrote "My Luve is Like a Red, Red Rose" and "Flow Gently, Sweet Afton," among many other poems.) Van Doren answered simply, "Because Burns did it so well."

A similar question might be asked and a similar answer given about artists in virtually every other field as well: "Why don't painters paint like Edward Hopper any more?" The answer would be that Hopper had already done it so well. Actually, if all poets wrote like Burns and if all artists painted like Hopper, this would be a very dull world indeed.

In any case, artists of all kinds want to be original; they want to express themselves. They do not want to copy what someone else has done. So we may begin to approach a contemporary poem by expecting the unfamiliar, and we *look at what is there.*

Organization

Looking at "Thoreau 2," the first thing we might notice is that the poem is fourteen lines long. It also has five iambic beats in most lines. But here the similarity to the traditional sonnet ends. We do not find a traditional rhyme scheme, nor do we find either of the two most familiar arrangements: an eight-line unit *(octave)*, followed by a six-line unit *(sestet),* which characterizes the Italian, or Petrarchan, sonnet; or the three *quatrains* (four-line units), followed by a *couplet* (two-line unit), which is characteristic of the Shakespearian or English sonnet.

What do we find? Look closely at the poem, and ask yourself what are its four basic divisions.

If you use the end-stopped lines as a clue, you will find that the first unit ends at line three. Line six is another natural break, even though it is not marked by a period. It is at this point that Lowell lets Thoreau speak for himself. Line ten—where Thoreau stops speaking—is end-stopped and marks the third division. And of course the last stop is the end of the poem. The basic division, then, is 3–3–4–4. In view of what we normally expect in a sonnet, this is most unusual.

It is unusual, that is, until we see that were we to make a two-part division, we would get 6–8, which would be the traditional octave and sestet turned upside down. In Lowell's poem the first six lines (sestet) offer a statement (in lines one to three) followed by an illustration (in lines four to six). The next eight lines (octave) consist of Thoreau's statements (lines seven to ten) and Lowell's conclusion (lines eleven to fourteen). Our contemporary poet has turned the traditional Italian sonnet form on end.

Rhyme

Let's turn next to rhyme. Normally, we say we have end rhyme when there is a correspondence of sound in the vowels and succeeding consonants of the accented syllables at the end of a line in two or more lines of verse. A perfect rhyme for Lowell's "saints," for example, would be "paints" or "taints." The rhyme scheme of an Italian sonnet is *abba abba cde cde, or cdc cdc, or cde dce.* Using "rhyme" in its traditional sense, it is clear that none of these fits this poem. In fact, there appears to be no rhyme scheme at all.

But what is the purpose of rhyme, we might ask. Basically, rhyme affords sensuous pleasure to the ear and also serves to unify the poem. In the case of "Thoreau 2," there may not be rhyme in the conventional sense, but there is a great deal of assonance, which performs the same functions. Consider the end of lines two and four, for instance:

> w**i**th h**e**r s**ai**nts
> w**i**n t**e**r d**ay**

Not only is the vowel sound in "saints" identical to that in "day," they are preceded by two other identical vowels. In addition to that, the consonants *w*, *r*, *n*, and *t* are also found in both lines.

In short, these two lines are far more closely connected by similarity of end sounds than are most traditional rhyming lines. Note that the function of this similarity in sound is to bind the first and second three-line units to each other. The vowel identity between "by" and "lives" binds the same two units together by connecting the first line of the poem to the fifth.

1. What other sound links can you find in the poem?

2. Look for all the long "i" sounds in the poem. Do you agree that the interweaving of this sound ties the whole poem together as a unit?

UNDERSTANDING AND INTERPRETATION

1. Roughly translate into your own words the meaning of the first three lines of "Thoreau 2."

2. How do the next three lines serve as an illustration of what the first three are saying?

3. What is the significance of the quotation from Thoreau in line ten?

4. If the light that blinds our eyes is not the sun, what might it be?

Nesting

Discovering, discovering trees are green at night,
braking headlights-down, ransacking the roadside
for someone strolling, fleeing to her wide goal;
passing blanks, the white Unitarian Church,
dark barn on my bulwark, two scowling unlit shacks,   5
the town pool just drained, the white lighthouse unplugged,
watching the beerfroth on the muddy breakers,
dwarfed by the STATE OF MAINE, white iceberg at drydock.
The question, my questioners? It's not for them—
crouched in the gelid drip of the pine in our garden,   10
invisible even when found, till we toss a white raincoat
over your sky-black, blood-trim quilted stormcoat—
you saying *I would prefer not*, like Bartleby:
small deer tremble and steely in wet nest!

UNDERSTANDING AND INTERPRETATION

1. "Nesting" is about a father searching for a daughter, who he thinks has run away from home. Where does he find her?
2. Name the "blanks" he passes in his search.
3. In line nine, who might "them" be? (Hint: They are the same people to whom the speaker says, "The question, my questioners?")
4. Why is the poem called "Nesting"?

FOR APPRECIATION

1. What is the basic division of Robert Lowell's poem "Nesting"?
2. What is the relationship in meaning between the two major parts?
3. In line 13, Lowell quotes, in italics, a line from Herman Melville's famous short story, "Bartleby the Scrivener" (see p. 255). What does Lowell's use of the line here tell you?

Richard Wilbur   1921–

Born in New York City, Richard Wilbur was educated at Amherst College and Harvard University and went on to teach at Harvard, Wellesley College, Wesleyan University, and Smith College. The winner of many awards, including the National Book Award and the Pulitzer Prize (for *Things of This World*, a collection of poems), Wilbur is one of the few distinguished modern poets who has continued to adhere to traditional verse forms. In addition to his own poetry, Wilbur has translated poems from several languages, notably French and Russian. Several of his translations of French plays have been produced in New York.

PORTRAIT OF RICHARD WILBUR

Juggler

A ball will bounce, but less and less. It's not
A light-hearted thing, resents its own resilience.
Falling is what it loves, and the earth falls
So in our hearts from brilliance,
Settles and is forgot.   5
It takes a skyblue juggler with five red balls

To shake our gravity up. Whee, in the air
The balls roll round, wheel on his wheeling hands,
Learning the ways of lightness, alter to spheres
Grazing his finger ends,   10
Cling to their courses there,
Swinging a small heaven about his ears.

But a heaven is easier made of nothing at all
Than the earth regained, and still and sole within

The spin of worlds, with a gesture sure and noble   15
He reels that heaven in,
Landing it ball by ball,
And trades it all for a broom, a plate, a table.

Oh, on his toe the table is turning, the broom's
Balancing up on his nose, and the plate whirls   20
On the tip of the broom! Damn, what a show, we cry:
The boys stamp, and the girls
Shriek, and the drum booms
And all comes down, and he bows and says goodbye.

If the juggler is tired now, if the broom stands   25
In the dust again, if the table starts to drop
Through the daily dark again, and though the plate
Lies flat on the table top,
For him we batter our hands
Who has won for once over the world's weight.   30

UNDERSTANDING AND INTERPRETATION

1. What comparison between a ball and the earth is being made in the first five lines?
2. What does the speaker mean by "to shake our gravity up"?
3. Describe the two shows the juggler puts on.
4. Specifically how does the audience react to the juggler?
5. What is the "point" of the poem, as revealed in the last line?

FOR APPRECIATION

This poem tells a little story, paints a vivid picture, and contains some deeper meanings about life. The poem also has a very strict technical form.
1. How many lines are there in each stanza?
2. What is the metrical pattern of each stanza (i.e., how many beats to the line)?
3. What is the rhyme scheme of each stanza?
4. Are the metrical and rhyme schemes consistent throughout the poem?

James Dickey 1923–

Born in Atlanta, Georgia, James Dickey is currently Poet-in-Residence at the University of South Carolina in Columbia, where he lives. He was a fighter pilot in two wars and a star football player in high school and college. Dickey continues to combine poetry writing and academic interests with an active, athletic life. He is a great outdoorsman and a lover of nature—interests one can find reflected in his novel *Deliverance* (1970), which was made into a motion picture. A volume of his poems, *Buckdancer's Choice*, won the National Book Award in 1966. His most recent book of poems is *Puella* (1982).

PORTRAIT OF JAMES DICKEY

The Rain Guitar

—England, 1962—

The water-grass under had never waved
But one way. It showed me that flow is forever
Sealed from rain in a weir. For some reason having
To do with Winchester, I was sitting on my guitar case
Watching nothing but eelgrass trying to go downstream with all the right motions 5
But one. I had on a sweater, and my threads were opening
Like mouths with rain. It mattered to me not at all
That a bridge was stumping
With a man, or that he came near and cast a fish
thread into the weir. I had no line and no feeling. 10
I had nothing to do with fish
But my eyes on the grass they hid in, waving with the one move of trying
To be somewhere else. With what I had, what could I do?
I got out my guitar, that somebody told me was supposed to improve
With moisture—or was it when it dried out?—and hit the lowest 15
And loudest chord. The drops that were falling just then

Hammered like Georgia railroad track
With E. The man went into a kind of fishing
Turn. Play it, he said through his pipe. There
I went, fast as I could with cold fingers. The strings shook   20
With drops. A buck dance settled on the weir. Where was the city
Cathedral in all this? Out of sight, but somewhere around.
Play a little more
Of that, he said, and cast. Music-wood shone,
Getting worse or better faster than it liked: 25
Improvement or disintegration
Supposed to take years, fell on it
By the gallon. It darkened and rang
Like chimes. My sweater collapsed, and the rain reached
My underwear. I picked, the guitar showered, and he cast to the mountain   30
Music. His wood leg tapped
On the cobbles. Memories of many men
Hung, rain-faced, improving, sealed-off
In the weir. I found myself playing Australian
Versions of British marching songs. Mouths opened all over me; I sang,   35
His legs beat and marched
Like companions. I was Air Force,
I said. So was I; I picked
This up in Burma, he said, tapping his gone leg
With his fly rod, as Burma and the South   40
west Pacific and North Georgia reeled,
Rapped, cast, chimed, darkened and drew down
Cathedral water, and improved.

UNDERSTANDING AND INTERPRETATION

1. Explain the significance of each of the following places in the poem: Winchester, Georgia, the South Pacific, Burma.
2. In what branch of the armed services did the speaker serve?
3. How does the last word of the poem resolve one of its key tensions?
4. What is the basic theme of the poem?

FOR APPRECIATION

There is no end rhyme and no regularity of meter or line length in this poem. However, James Dickey has taken great pains to control the sound, as you will become aware when you answer the following questions.

1. Scan the following and try to describe how the sound and the arrangement of words suggest the meaning:

It mattered to me not at all
That a bridge was stumping
With a man

2. Study carefully the sound pattern in the last two lines of "The Rain Guitar." What consonant sound is repeated nine times in the two lines? What vowel sound is repeated often? Look carefully for any other vowel and consonant repetitions. What did you find?

Anne Sexton   1928–1974

Anne Sexton lived most of her life in or near Newton, Massachusetts, where she was born. She was almost thirty before she first started to write—during a recovery from a nervous breakdown. She was a poet of the "confessional" school; many of her early poems dealt with the depression, despair, and suffering of her years of emotional illness. She won the Pulitzer Prize for Poetry in 1967 for *Live or Die*. *The Complete Poems* was published posthumously in 1981. Anne Sexton was a superlative reader of her own work, a "presence" one could not easily forget.

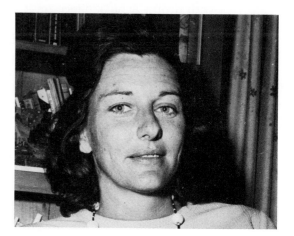

PORTRAIT OF ANNE SEXTON

A Little Uncomplicated Hymn
for Joy

Is what I wanted to write.
There *was* such a song!
A song for your kneebones,
a song for your ribs,
those delicate trees that bury your heart;   5
a song for your bookshelf
where twenty hand-blown ducks sit in a Venetian row;
a song for your dress-up high heels,
your fire-red skate board,
your twenty grubby fingers,   10
the pink knitting that you start
and never quite finish;
your poster-paint pictures,
all angels making a face,
a song for your laughter   15
that keeps wiggling a spoon in my sleep.

Even a song for your night
as during last summer's heat wave
where your fever stuck at 104 for two weeks,
where you slept, head on the window sill,   20
lips as dry as old erasers, your thirst
shimmering and heavy as I spooned water in,
your eyes shut on the thumping June bugs,
the lips moving, mumbling,
sending letters to the stars.   25
Dreaming, dreaming,
your body a boat,
rocked by your life and my death.
Your fists wound like a ball,
little fetus, little snail,   30
carrying a rage, a leftover rage
I cannot undo.

Even a song for your flight
Where you fell from the neighbor's tree hut,
where you thought you were walking onto solid blue air,   35
you thought, *why not?*
and then, you simply left the boards behind
and stepped out into the dust.

O little Icarus,
you chewed on a cloud, you bit the sun   40
and came tumbling down, head first,
not into the sea, but hard
on the hard packed gravel.
You fell on your eye. You fell on your chin.
What a shiner! What a faint you had   45
and then crawled home,
a knocked-out humpty dumpty
in my arms.

O humpty-dumpty girl,
I named you Joy,   50
That's someone's song all by itself.
In the naming of you I named
all things you are . . .
except the ditch
where I left you once,   55
like an old root that wouldn't take hold,
that ditch where I left you
while I sailed off in madness
over the buildings and under my umbrella,

sailed off for three years   60
so that the first candle
and the second candle
and the third candle
burned down alone on your birthday cake.
That ditch I want so much to forget   65
and that you try each day to forget.

Even here in your school portrait
where you repeat third grade,
caught in the need not to grow—
that little prison—   70
even here you keep up the barrier
with a smile that dies afraid
as it hides your crooked front tooth.
Joy, I call you
and yet your eyes just here   75
with their shades half-drawn over the gunsights,
over your gigantic knowledge,
over the little blue fish who dart back and forth,
over different streets, the strange rooms,
other people's chairs, other people's food,   80
ask, "Why was I shut in the cellar?"

And I've got words,
words that dog my heels,
words for sale you might say,
and multiplication cards and cursive writing   85
that you ignore to teach my fingers
the *cat's cradle* and the *witch's broom*.
Yes! I have instructions before dinner
and hugs after dinner and still those eyes—
away, away,   90
asking for hymns . . .
without guilt.

And I can only say
a little uncomplicated hymn
is what I wanted to write   95
and yet I find only your name.
There *was* such a song,
but it's bruised.
It's not mine.

You will jump to it someday   100
as you will jump out of the pitch of this house.

It will be a holiday, a parade, a fiesta!
Then you'll fly.
You'll really fly.
After that you'll, quite simply, quite calmly   105
make your own stones, your own floor plan,
your own sound.

I wanted to write such a poem
with such musics, such guitars going;
I tried at the teeth of sound   110
to draw up such legions of noise;
I tried at the breakwater
to catch the star off each ship;
and at the closing of hands
I looked for their houses   115
and silences.
I found just one.

　　you were mine
　　and I lent you out.

I look for uncomplicated hymns   120
but love has none.

UNDERSTANDING AND INTERPRETATION

1. Interpret the line: "There *was* such a song!"
2. Approximately how old was Joy when her mother left her?
3. Why is humpty-dumpty a good image for Joy?
4. Interpret the couplet:

　　you were mine
　　and I lent you out.

5. The speaker concludes the poem by saying that love has no uncomplicated hymns. What does she mean by this, and why do you agree or disagree with her?

FOR APPRECIATION

1. What details/similarities can you find near the beginning and near the end of the poem that help to tie it together?
2. Study the final line or two of each section of the poem. What common thread can you find in them?
3. Sexton has been called a "confessional" poet because of her tendency to speak in personal terms about intimate details from her own life. What sort of standards do you think might be appropriate for judging the value of this kind of poetry? Is this a good confessional poem? Discuss.

Sylvia Plath   1932–1963

Born and raised in Massachusetts, Sylvia Plath had a very distinguished academic career at Smith College and began publishing stories and poems at an early age. Nevertheless, she suffered a severe mental breakdown while in college—an experience she wrote about in her well-known novel, *The Bell Jar*, which was published in England in January 1963, about a month before she committed suicide.

Although she published only one volume of poems (*The Colossus*, 1960) in her lifetime, she wrote poetry feverishly during her last years, and three books of poems have appeared since her death—*Ariel, Crossing the Water,* and *Winter Trees.* In 1981 her husband, the English poet Ted Hughes, edited *The Collected Poems.*

PORTRAIT OF SYLVIA PLATH

Mirror

I am silver and exact. I have no preconceptions.
Whatever I see I swallow immediately
Just as it is, unmisted by love or dislike.
I am not cruel, only truthful—
The eye of a little god, four-cornered.   5
Most of the time I meditate on the opposite wall.
It is pink, with speckles. I have looked at it so long
I think it is a part of my heart. But it flickers.
Faces and darkness separate us over and over.
Now I am a lake. A woman bends over me,   10
Searching my reaches for what she really is.
Then she turns to those liars, the candles or the moon.
I see her back, and reflect it faithfully.
She rewards me with tears and an agitation of hands.
I am important to her. She comes and goes.   15
Each morning it is her face that replaces the darkness.
In me she has drowned a young girl, and in me an old woman
Rises toward her day after day, like a terrible fish.

THE CONVERSATION, Hobson Pittman
North Carolina Museum of Art, Raleigh, Gift of the Artist

UNDERSTANDING AND INTERPRETATION

1. Why does the speaker describe itself as "exact"?
2. What does "four-cornered" refer to?
3. How does the speaker become a lake?
4. In what sense are the candles and the moon "liars" from the speaker's point of view?
5. Interpret the last two lines.

FOR APPRECIATION

The Persona

In many poems and short stories, the *I* (whether expressed or implied) refers to the author, and the thoughts, feelings, and memories being revealed are clearly the author's own. For example, in "A Little Uncomplicated Hymn for Joy," and in "The Rain Guitar," Anne Sexton and James Dickey are speaking in their own voices and from very personal points of view. Nevertheless, it is best, at first reading, to assume that the voice speaking to us in a poem or short story is *not* the voice of the author. In many poems and stories, the *I* is a voice created by the author to narrate the particular poem or story. We call this created voice the author's *persona*. Keep this in mind: the voice used by the author is not necessarily his or her own; it may be a voice adopted by the author for the purposes of the poem. As you study a poem, look for evidence to indicate whether the speaker is the author or a persona created by the author.

1. Notice that "Mirror" is a first-person poem. How can you be sure that the *I* speaking is not Sylvia Plath, the person?
2. Why might Plath choose to adopt the persona she does in this poem?

Linda Pastan   1932–

Linda Pastan was born and raised in New York City and graduated from Radcliffe College in 1954. She did graduate work at Simmons College and Brandeis University. Her first book of poems, A Perfect Circle of Sun, *was published in 1971. Since that time, she has been quite prolific and her poems have been appearing regularly in the best magazines in the country. A collection of her verse,* PM/AM, New and Selected Poems, *was published in 1982.*

I Am Learning to Abandon the World

I am learning to abandon the world
before it can abandon me.
Already I have given up the moon
and snow, closing my shades
against the claims of white.   5
And the world has taken
my father, my friends.
I have given up melodic lines of hills,
moving to a flat, tuneless landscape.
And every night I give my body up   10
limb by limb, working upwards
across bone, towards the heart.
But morning comes with small
reprieves of coffee and birdsong.
A tree outside the window   15
which was simply shadow moments ago
takes back its branches twig
by leafy twig.
And as I take my body back
the sun lays its warm muzzle on my lap   20
as if to make amends.

UNDERSTANDING AND INTERPRETATION

1. What might have caused the speaker to want to abandon the world in the first place?
2. What specific examples of abandoning the world does the speaker give?

3. Why is the sun an especially good symbol for the return of life?
4. What does the speaker mean when she writes that the tree "takes back its branches"?
5. What implicit comparison is made in the next-to-last line?

Audre Lorde   1934–

*Born and raised in New York City, Audre Lorde also went to college there,
graduating with a B.A. from Hunter College of the City University of New York in
1959 and from Columbia University with a Masters in Library Science in 1961. She
worked as a librarian in the sixties, but turned more and more to publishing poetry,
issuing a volume every other year on the average from 1968 on. From a Land
Where Other People Live, a book of poems, was nominated for a National Book
Award in 1974. A collection of Lorde's best poems—Chosen Poems: Old and
New—was published in 1982.*

Memorial I

If you come as softly
as wind within the trees
you may hear what I hear
see what sorrow sees.

If you come as lightly   5
as the threading dew
I shall take you gladly
nor ask more of you.

You may sit beside me
silent as a breath   10
and only those who stay dead
shall remember death.

If you come I will be silent
nor speak harsh words to you—
I will not ask you why, now,   15
nor how, nor what you knew.

But we shall sit here softly
beneath two different years
and the rich earth between us
shall drink our tears.   20

"Memorial I" is reprinted from COAL by Audre Lorde, by permission of
W. W. Norton & Company, Inc. Copyright © 1968, 1970, 1976 by Audre
Lorde.

UNDERSTANDING AND INTERPRETATION

1. In this poem a living speaker is addressing a
person who has died. How does the speaker want
the dead person to come to her?
2. If the person comes this way, what will the
speaker do?
3. What will the two of them do together?
4. What does the speaker mean by "only those who
stay dead/shall remember death"?
5. How do you interpret "beneath two different
years"?

FOR APPRECIATION

One of the main reasons this poem is so effective is
the richness of its sound patterns and the control
the poet has over them.
1. The rhyme scheme of the stanzas is basically
abcb. What additional similarities in rhyme can you
find by comparing the second and the fourth
quatrains? the first and the fifth?
2. One of the softer consonants in English is "s,"
which may be sounded as *s*, *z*, or *sh*. How many of
these can you find in this quiet poem?
3. Listen for assonance within lines. How many
examples can you find?

C. K. Williams   1936–

C. K. Williams was born in Newark, New Jersey, and educated at Bucknell University and the University of Pennsylvania. He received a Guggenheim Fellowship in 1974 and has been a contributing editor of American Poetry Review. *He has also translated works of classical Greek authors. Among his books are* A Day for Anne Frank, Lies, I Am the Bitter Name, *and* With Ignorance. *His most recent book of poems* Tar, *was nominated for the National Book Award in 1983.*

Ten Below

It is bad enough crying for children
suffering neglect and starvation in
    our world
without having on a day like this
to see an old cart-horse covered
    with foam,
quivering so hard that when he stops   5
the sheels* still rock slowly in place
like gears in an engine.
A man will do that, shiver where
    he stands,
frozen with false starts
before decisions, just staring,   10
but with a man you can take his arm,
talk him out of it, lead him away.

What do you do when both hands
and your voice are simply goads?
When the eyes you solace see space,   15
the wall behind you, the wisp of grass
pushing up through the curb at
    your feet?
I have thought that all the animals
we kill and maim, if they wanted to

could stare us down, wither us   20
and turn us into smoke with their
    glances—
they forbear because they pity us,
like angels, and love of something else
is why they suffer us and submit.

But this is Pine Street, Philadelphia,
    1965.   25
You don't believe
in anything divine being here.
There is an old plug with a worn
    blanket
thrown over its haunches. There is
    a wagon
full of junk—pipes and rotted
    sinks,   30
the grates from furnaces—and there
is a child walking beside the horse
with sugar, and the mammoth head
    lowering,
delicately nibbling from those vulnerable
fingers. You can't cut your heart out.   35
Sometimes, just what is, is enough.

By permission of C. K. Williams.

* **sheels,** parts of a harness.

UNDERSTANDING AND INTERPRETATION

1. In the opening stanza, Williams mentions children, the horse, and "a man." What connection or connections do you find in the stanza among these?

2. What is the "something else" in line 23?
3. In the first line of the last stanza, the speaker mentions three specific things. Why does he choose to be so specific here?
4. What is the meaning of the last line of the poem? Is it a good final line? Why or why not?

Jesús Papoleto Meléndez   1950–

*Of Puerto Rican ancestry, Jesús Papoleto Meléndez was born in El Barrio in New York City in 1950. He published a book of poems—*Street Poetry and Other Poems*—when he was only twenty-one years old. The poem that appears below was printed in a collection,* Nuyorican Poetry (1975), *edited by two other Nuyorican (Puerto Rican/New York) poets, Miguel Algarín and Miguel Piñero. Meléndez has also written plays.*

Bruja*

a plastic Bruja
fell
from a 4th floor windowsill
against the cold concrete
of sidewalks   5
that describe this metal city.
it did not break.
but it will not grow
this plastic flower that is store-bought
impersonating Spirits   10
that are real.
no it will not grow.
it is not real in that way
in that respect.

now had it been a Brúja from Puerto Rico   15
broken-away from the join of its family
beneath trees & rocks
in jungles
of birds that sing
& animals   20
that crawl within the dirt

*A tropical/jungle plant that grows in Puerto Rico. It is very thick and heavy. A single leaf of this plant can be taken anywhere, resoiled, and a new plant will grow from it. Each leaf is seeded. *Bruja* also means "witch."

and eat the fruits that grow from trees/
had that Bruja that fell
come from where the Sun sinks close enough
to touch the trees   25
& be blessed as a Natural God
(unlike airplanes)
had that Bruja that fell against the concrete
been one of those
the same that grow   30
on Doña Juana's windowsill
the ones that she brought back
from her last trip to the Island
the one about her father's death   there
her plants grow   35
in all colors of the Sun & Moon
& in all seasons of this Earth & stretch
to enter onto the walls
that make her home/
had that fallen Bruja been one of those   40
it would have dug its hole
in through that concrete that is man-made
& found itself a home
deep
where the Earth is warm again   45
& soon
it would have grown between the cracks
the Sun makes when it's hot
& it would have joined the flowers
of colors that are different   50
& that have come to meet
on this battlefield of concrete
& then
that same Bruja that once felt
the cold of steel & asphalt   55
it would have raised its hand
to throw its brick
too.

FOR UNDERSTANDING

1. What does the speaker mean by "the Island"?
2. In what kind of physical environment is the speaker living at present?
3. Who is growing a Bruja plant? Where and when did she get it?

FOR INTERPRETATION

1. What is meant by "this battlefield of concrete"?
2. Under the headings of Natural and Man-Made, make two lists of images from the poem. Where would the speaker feel more comfortable? Why?
3. Interpret the last three lines of the poem.

Gary Soto   1952–

Raised in Fresno, California, Gary Soto has worked on farms in the San Joaquin Valley, though later he became a teacher at the University of California, Berkeley. His first book of poems, The Elements of San Joaquin, *was published when he was only in his mid-twenties. Soto is now a highly regarded young poet whose work appears in numerous magazines. He also publishes books of his poetry regularly, his most recent collection being* Where Sparrows Work Hard *(1981).*

Salt

For Juan Rodriguez

I

There was nothing to eat, father. We
Were sent out, a sack in our hands,
A pebble in each pocket. Conejo,* mother said,
Frog or catfish. The road was long
But never long enough. We walked toward   5
The lake that was little more than a mirror.
The day was clear, and what the wind turned over
We took in our hands and imagined it to be bread.
We broke this wish in halves, and ate.

II

Some way from home, I threw my stone,   10
Juan set his sack on fire and it
Was licked clean with flame. We ran
Toward some cows, fenced and mooing.
I wrung their ears, as I might the wash,
But nothing was squeezed into our hands.   15
They were licking saltrock and rock.
Juan shooed them away. He chipped
A piece off and we sucked until our tongues
Were stropped raw and bleeding,
And what was lost, the salt gave back.   20

"Salt" by Gary Soto first appeared in POETRY, June, 1978. Copyright © 1978 by The Modern Poetry Association. Reprinted by permission of the Editor of Poetry.

* **conejo,** Spanish, "rabbit."

UNDERSTANDING AND INTERPRETATION

1. Why did the children have a sack and pebbles?
2. What did they do with these things and why?
3. How do you interpret the last line? That is, what one thing or state would have been lost yet given back by the salt?

4. The speaker paints a sad portrait—a father gone, a mother with no food to put on the table, two children expected to find food in an arid land with no food to yield. How would you respond to someone who said that such a picture is too sad to contemplate, that poets should not write about such things?

Maya Angelou   1928–

When her parents' marriage broke up, Maya Angelou was sent to live with her paternal grandmother, Ann Henderson, in Stamps, Arkansas. She lived there until 1940, when she rejoined her mother in San Francisco. Angelou grew up a many-talented woman—an actress, a singer, a songwriter and composer, a playwright and a screenwriter, a newspaper columnist, a poet, and a college lecturer at such schools as the University of Kansas and Yale University. In the 1970s she published three parts of her autobiography—*I Know Why the Caged Bird Sings* (1970), *Gather Together in My Name* (1974), and *Singin' and Swingin' and Gettin' Merry Like Christmas* (1976). In 1981 she added a fourth volume to this series: *The Heart of a Woman.*

PORTRAIT OF MAYA ANGELOU

from I KNOW WHY THE CAGED BIRD SINGS

My First Life Line

For nearly a year, I sopped around the house, the Store, the school and the church, like an old biscuit, dirty and inedible. Then I met, or rather got to know, the lady who threw me my first life line.

Mrs. Bertha Flowers was the aristocrat of Black Stamps. She had the grace of control to appear warm in the coldest weather, and on the Arkansas summer days it seemed she had a private breeze which swirled around, cooling her. She was thin without the taut look of wiry people, and her printed voile dresses and flowered hats were as right for her as denim overalls for a farmer. She was our side's answer to the richest white woman in town.

Her skin was a rich black that would have peeled like a plum if snagged, but then no one would have thought of getting close enough to Mrs. Flowers to ruffle her dress, let alone snag her skin. She didn't encourage familiarity. She wore gloves too.

I don't think I ever saw Mrs. Flowers

laugh, but she smiled often. A slow widening of her thin black lips to show even, small white teeth, then the slow effortless closing. When she chose to smile on me, I always wanted to thank her. The action was so graceful and inclusively benign.

She was one of the few gentlewomen I have ever known, and has remained throughout my life the measure of what a human being can be.

Momma had a strange relationship with her. Most often when she passed on the road in front of the Store, she spoke to Momma in that soft yet carrying voice, "Good day, Mrs. Henderson." Momma responded with "How you, Sister Flowers?"

Mrs. Flowers didn't belong to our church, nor was she Momma's familiar. Why on earth did she insist on calling her Sister Flowers? Shame made me want to hide my face. Mrs. Flowers deserved better than to be called Sister. Then, Momma left out the verb. Why not ask, "How *are* you, *Mrs.* Flowers?" With the unbalanced passion of the young, I hated her for showing her ignorance to Mrs. Flowers. It didn't occur to me for many years that they were as alike as sisters, separated only by formal education.

Although I was upset, neither of the women was in the least shaken by what I thought an unceremonious greeting. Mrs. Flowers would continue her easy gait up the hill to her little bungalow, and Momma kept on shelling peas or doing whatever had brought her to the front porch.

Occasionally, though, Mrs. Flowers would drift off the road and down to the Store and Momma would say to me, "Sister, you go on and play." As I left I would hear the beginning of an intimate conversation. Momma persistently using the wrong verb, or none at all.

"Brother and Sister Wilcox is sho'ly the meanest—" "Is," Momma? "Is"? Oh, please, not "is," Momma, for two or more. But they talked, and from the side of the building where I waited for the ground to open up

and swallow me, I heard the soft-voiced Mrs. Flowers and the textured voice of my grandmother merging and melting. They were interrupted from time to time by giggles that must have come from Mrs. Flowers (Momma never giggled in her life). Then she was gone.

She appealed to me because she was like people I had never met personally. Like women in English novels who walked the moors (whatever they were) with their loyal dogs racing at a respectful distance. Like the women who sat in front of roaring fireplaces, drinking tea incessantly from silver trays full of scones and crumpets. Women who walked over the "heath" and read morocco-bound books and had two last names divided by a hyphen. It would be safe to say that she made me proud to be Negro, just by being herself.

She acted just as refined as whitefolks in the movies and books and she was more beautiful, for none of them could have come near that warm color without looking gray by comparison.

It was fortunate that I never saw her in the company of powhitefolks. For since they tend to think of their whiteness as an evenizer, I'm certain that I would have had to hear her spoken to commonly as Bertha, and my image of her would have been shattered like the unmendable Humpty-Dumpty.

One summer afternoon, sweet-milk fresh in my memory, she stopped at the Store to buy provisions. Another Negro woman of her health and age would have been expected to carry the paper sacks home in one hand, but Momma said, "Sister Flowers, I'll send Bailey up to your house with these things."

She smiled that slow dragging smile, "Thank you, Mrs. Henderson. I'd prefer Marguerite, though." My name was beautiful when she said it. "I've been meaning to talk to her, anyway." They gave each other age-group looks.

Momma said, "Well, that's all right then. Sister, go and change your dress. You going to Sister Flowers'."

The chifforobe was a maze. What on

earth did one put on to go to Mrs. Flowers' house? I knew I shouldn't put on a Sunday dress. It might be sacrilegious. Certainly not a house dress, since I was already wearing a fresh one. I chose a school dress, naturally. It was formal without suggesting that going to Mrs. Flowers' house was equivalent to attending church.

I trusted myself back into the Store.

"Now, don't you look nice." I had chosen the right thing, for once.

"Mrs. Henderson, you make most of the children's clothes, don't you?"

"Yes, ma'am. Sure do. Store-bought clothes ain't hardly worth the thread it take to stitch them."

"I'll say you do a lovely job, though, so neat. That dress looks professional."

Momma was enjoying the seldom-received compliments. Since everyone we knew (except Mrs. Flowers, of course) could sew competently, praise was rarely handed out for the commonly practiced craft.

"I try, with the help of the Lord, Sister Flowers, to finish the inside just like I does the outside. Come here, Sister."

I had buttoned up the collar and tied the belt, apronlike, in back. Momma told me to turn around. With one hand she pulled the strings and the belt fell free at both sides of my waist. Then her large hands were at my neck, opening the button loops. I was terrified. What was happening?

"Take it off, Sister." She had her hands on the hem of the dress.

"I don't need to see the inside, Mrs. Henderson, I can tell . . ." But the dress was over my head and my arms were stuck in the sleeves. Momma said, "That'll do. See here, Sister Flowers, I French-seams around the armholes." Through the cloth film, I saw the shadow approach. "That makes it last longer. Children these days would bust out of sheet-metal clothes. They so rough."

"That is a very good job, Mrs. Henderson. You should be proud. You can put your dress back on, Marguerite."

"No ma'am. Pride is a sin. And 'cording to the Good Book, it goeth before a fall."

"That's right. So the Bible says. It's a good thing to keep in mind."

I wouldn't look at either of them. Momma hadn't thought that taking off my dress in front of Mrs. Flowers would kill me stone dead. If I had refused, she would have thought I was trying to be "womanish" and might have remembered St. Louis. Mrs. Flowers had known that I would be embarrassed and that was even worse. I picked up the groceries and went out to wait in the hot sunshine. It would be fitting if I got a sunstroke and died before they came outside. Just dropped dead on the slanting porch.

There was a little path beside the rocky road, and Mrs. Flowers walked in front swinging her arms and picking her way over the stones.

She said, without turning her head, to me, "I hear you're doing very good school work, Marguerite, but that it's all written. The teachers report that they have trouble getting you to talk in class." We passed the triangular farm on our left and the path widened to allow us to walk together. I hung back in the separate unasked and unanswerable questions.

"Come and walk along with me, Marguerite." I couldn't have refused even if I wanted to. She pronounced my name so nicely. Or more correctly, she spoke each word with such clarity that I was certain a foreigner who didn't understand English could have understood her.

"Now no one is going to make you talk—possibly no one can. But bear in mind, language is man's way of communicating with his fellow man and it is language alone which separates him from the lower animals." That was a totally new idea to me, and I would need time to think about it.

"Your grandmother says you read a lot. Every chance you get. That's good, but not good enough. Words mean more than what is set down on paper. It takes the human voice to infuse them with the shades of deeper meaning."

I memorized the part about the human voice infusing words. It seemed so valid and poetic.

She said she was going to give me some books and that I not only must read them, I must read them aloud. She suggested that I try to make a sentence sound in as many different ways as possible.

"I'll accept no excuse if you return a book to me that has been badly handled." My imagination boggled at the punishment I would deserve if in fact I did abuse a book of Mrs. Flowers'. Death would be too kind and brief.

The odors in the house surprised me. Somehow I had never connected Mrs. Flowers with food or eating or any other common experience of common people. There must have been an outhouse, too, but my mind never recorded it.

The sweet scent of vanilla had met us as she opened the door.

"I made tea cookies this morning. You see, I had planned to invite you for cookies and lemonade so we could have this little chat. The lemonade is in the icebox."

It followed that Mrs. Flowers would have ice on an ordinary day, when most families in our town bought ice late on Saturdays only a few times during the summer to be used in the wooden ice-cream freezers.

She took the bags from me and disappeared through the kitchen door. I looked around the room that I had never in my wildest fantasies imagined I would see. Browned photographs leered or threatened from the walls and the white, freshly done curtains pushed against themselves and against the wind. I wanted to gobble up the room entire and take it to Bailey, who would help me analyze and enjoy it.

"Have a seat, Marguerite. Over there by the table." She carried a platter covered with a tea towel. Although she warned that she hadn't tried her hand at baking sweets for some time, I was certain that like everything else about her the cookies would be perfect.

They were flat round wafers, slightly browned on the edges and butter-yellow in the center. With the cold lemonade they were sufficient for childhood's lifelong diet. Remembering my manners, I took nice little lady-like bites off the edges. She said she had made them expressly for me and that she had a few in the kitchen that I could take home to my brother. So I jammed one whole cake in my mouth and the rough crumbs scratched the insides of my jaws, and if I hadn't had to swallow, it would have been a dream come true.

As I ate she began the first of what we later called "my lessons in living." She said that I must always be intolerant of ignorance but understanding of illiteracy. That some people, unable to go to school, were more educated and even more intelligent than college professors. She encouraged me to listen carefully to what country people called mother wit. That in those homely sayings was couched the collective wisdom of generations.

When I finished the cookies she brushed off the table and brought a thick, small book from the bookcase. I had read *A Tale of Two Cities* and found it up to my standards as a romantic novel. She opened the first page and I heard poetry for the first time in my life.

"It was the best of times and the worst of times . . ."[1] Her voice slid in and curved down through and over the words. She was nearly singing. I wanted to look at the pages. Were they the same that I had read? Or were there notes, music, lined on the pages, as in a hymn book? Her sounds began cascading gently. I knew from listening to a thousand preachers that she was nearing the end of her reading, and I hadn't really heard, heard to understand, a single word.

"How do you like that?"

---

1. These are the opening words of Charles Dickens's *A Tale of Two Cities.*

It occurred to me that she expected a response. The sweet vanilla flavor was still on my tongue and her reading was a wonder in my ears. I had to speak.

I said, "Yes, ma'am." It was the least I could do, but it was the most also.

"There's one more thing. Take this book of poems and memorize one for me. Next time you pay me a visit, I want you to recite."

I have tried often to search behind the sophistication of years for the enchantment I so easily found in those gifts. The essence escapes but its aura remains. To be allowed, no, invited, into the private lives of strangers, and to share their joys and fears, was a chance to exchange the Southern bitter wormwood for a cup of mead with Beowulf or a hot cup of tea and milk with Oliver Twist. When I said aloud, "It is a far, far better thing that I do, than I have ever done . . ."[2] tears of love filled my eyes at my selflessness.

On that first day, I ran down the hill and into the road (few cars ever came along it) and had the good sense to stop running before I reached the Store.

I was liked, and what a difference it made. I was respected not as Mrs. Henderson's grandchild or Bailey's sister but for just being Marguerite Johnson.

Childhood's logic never asks to be proved (all conclusions are absolute). I didn't question why Mrs. Flowers had singled me out for attention, nor did it occur to me that Momma

2. The famous last words of Sidney Carton, a major character in Dickens's *A Tale of Two Cities.*

might have asked her to give me a little talking to. All I cared about was that she had made tea cookies for *me* and read to *me* from her favorite book. It was enough to prove that she liked me. . . .

FOR UNDERSTANDING

1. What contrast is there between the manner of address that Mrs. Henderson (Momma) and Mrs. Flowers use toward each other?

2. What "corrections" in her Momma's speech would Maya like to have made?

3. What was the only significant difference between the two older women?

4. From what book does Mrs. Flowers read to Maya?

5. What is the basic purpose of Mrs. Flowers reading to Maya?

6. What does Mrs. Flowers make Maya promise to do the next time the latter comes for a visit?

FOR INTERPRETATION

1. In what sense did Mrs. Flowers throw Maya her "first life line"?

2. What are some of the qualities that make Mrs. Flowers a "gentlewoman"?

3. Why does Maya say, "It would be fitting if I got sunstroke and died before they came outside"?

4. What is the very first "lesson in living" that Mrs. Flowers teaches Maya? Why is it an especially appropriate lesson?

5. Do you think the meeting between Mrs. Flowers and Maya was arranged by Mrs. Henderson (Momma)? Why would she want to arrange such a meeting?

N. Scott Momaday 1934–

N. Scott Momaday was born in Lawton, Oklahoma, and is a full-blooded American Indian. Both of his parents were teachers and Momaday himself holds a Ph.D. degree from Stanford University, where he is a professor of English and comparative literature.

Dr. Momaday's first book, *House Made of Dawn* (1968), won the Pulitzer Prize for Fiction. *The Way to Rainy Mountain,* published in the following year, deals with his own Kiowa Indian tribe, and helped to make him a nationally known writer. Momaday also writes poetry. The following essay, which appeared in *Life* magazine, will show that his prose is also highly poetic.

PORTRAIT OF N. SCOTT MOMADAY

A VISION BEYOND TIME AND PLACE

When my father was a boy, an old man used to come to [my grandfather] Mammedaty's house and pay his respects. He was a lean old man in braids and was impressive in his age and bearing. His name was Cheney, and he was an arrowmaker. Every morning, my father tells me, Cheney would paint his wrinkled face, go out, and pray aloud to the rising sun. In my mind I can see that man as if he were there now. I like to watch him as he makes his prayer. I know where he stands and where his voice goes on the rolling grasses and where the sun comes up on the land. There, at dawn, you can feel the silence. It is cold and clear and deep like water. It takes hold of you and will not let you go. (From *The Way to Rainy Mountain.* The University of New Mexico Press.)

I often think of old man Cheney, and of his daily devotion to the sun. He died before I was born, and I never knew where he came from or what of good and bad entered into his life. But I think I know who he was, essentially, and what his view of the world meant to him and to me. He was a man who saw very deeply into the distance, I believe, one whose vision extended far beyond the physical boundaries of his time and place. He perceived the wonder and meaning of Creation itself. In his mind's eye he could integrate all the realities and illusions of the earth and sky; they became for him profoundly intelligible and whole.

Once, in the first light, I stood where Cheney had stood, next to the house which my grandfather Mammedaty had built on a rise of land near Rainy Mountain Creek, and watched the sun come out of the black horizon of the world. It was an irresistible and awesome emergence, as waters gather to the flood, of weather and of light. I could not have been more sensitive to the cold, nor than to the heat which came upon it. And I could not have *foreseen* the break of day. The shadows on the rolling plains became large and luminous in a moment, impalpable, then faceted, dark and distinct again as they were run through with splinters of light. And the sun itself, when it appeared, was pale and immense, original in the deepest sense of the word. It is no wonder, I thought, that an old man should pray to it. It is no wonder . . . and yet, of course, wonder is the principal part of such a vision. Cheney's prayer was an affirmation of his wonder and regard, a testament to the realization of a quest for vision.

This native vision, this gift of seeing truly, with wonder and delight, into the natural world, is informed by a certain attitude of reverence and self-respect. It is a matter of extrasensory as well as sensory perception, I believe. In addition to the eye, it involves the intelligence, the instinct, and the imagination. It is the perception not only of objects and forms but also of essences and ideals, as in this Chippewa song:

> *as my eyes*
> *search*
> *the prairie*
> *I feel the summer*
> *in the spring*

Even as the singer sees into the immediate landscape, he perceives a now and future dimension that is altogether remote, yet nonetheless real and inherent within it, a quality of evanescence and evolution, a state at once of being and of becoming. He beholds what is there; nothing of the scene is lost upon him. In the integrity of his vision he is wholly in possession of himself and of the world around him; he is quintessentially alive.

Most Indian people are able to see in these terms. Their view of the world is peculiarly native and distinct, and it determines who and what they are to a great extent. It is indeed the basis upon which they identify themselves as individuals and as a race. There is something of genetic significance in such a thing, perhaps, an element of being which resides in the blood and which is, after all, the very nucleus of the self. When old man Cheney looked into the sunrise, he saw as far into himself, I suspect, as he saw into the distance. He knew certainly of his existence and of his place in the scheme of things.

In contrast, most of us in this society are afflicted with a kind of cultural nearsightedness. Our eyes, it may be, have been trained too long upon the superficial, and *artificial,* aspects of our environment; we do not see beyond the buildings and billboards that seem at times to be the monuments of our civilization, and consequently we fail to see into the nature and meaning of our own humanity. Now, more than ever, we might do well to enter upon a vision quest of our own, that is, a quest after vision itself. And in this the Indian stands to lead by his example. For with respect to such things as a sense of heritage, of a vital continuity in terms of origin and of destiny, a profound investment of the mind and

A different type of "seeing" from the kind Momaday describes is involved in this painting by Larry Poons. One of the so-called op artists of the 1960s, Poons's work was characterized by startling optical effects that made his canvases seem to shimmer.

TRISTAN DA CUGNA, Larry Poons
National Gallery of Art, Washington, D.C.
Gift of Mr. and Mrs. Burton Tremaine

spirit in the oral traditions of literature, philosophy, and religion—those things, in short, which constitute his vision of the world—the Indian is perhaps the most culturally secure of all Americans.

As I see him, that old man, he walks very slowly to the place where he will make his prayer, and it is always the same place, a small mound where the grass is sparse and the hard red earth shows through. He limps a little, with age, but when he plants his feet he is tall and straight and hard. The bones are fine and prominent in his face and hands. And his face is painted. There are red and yellow bars under his eyes, neither bright nor sharply defined on the dark, furrowed skin, but soft and organic, the colors of sandstone and of pollen. His long braids are wrapped with blood-red cloth. His eyes are deep and open to the wide world. At sunrise, precisely, they catch fire and close, having seen. The low light descends upon him. And when he lifts his voice, it enters upon the silence and carries there, like the call of a bird.

FOR UNDERSTANDING

1. According to Momaday, what did old man Cheney do daily?
2. What attitudes does Momaday say are necessary to "see truly"?
3. According to Momaday, what kind of a quest do Americans need to go on?
4. What things constitute the Indian's vision of the world?

FOR INTERPRETATION

1. What does it mean to see far beyond the physical boundaries of time and place?
2. Why do you suppose Momaday capitalizes the word "creation"?
3. What doe he mean by saying that wonder is the principal part of a vision beyond time and place?
4. Why is the ending of the essay particularly appropriate?

William Least Heat Moon 1939–

William Least Heat Moon—whose non-Indian name is William Trogdon—was born in Kansas City, Kansas, in 1939. He is of mixed blood, being part Sioux Indian. His father called himself Heat Moon—the moon of the seventh month, according to the Siouan peoples—and his older brother thus took the name Little Heat Moon. He, coming last, was named Least Heat.

When he lost his job teaching English in college in Missouri (because of declining enrollment), he decided to take what little money he had and make a tour around the United States in a small truck, avoiding as many main roads and large towns as possible, visiting instead the small towns that dotted the small highways. He then published *Blue Highways: A Journey into America,* which has been highly praised by such writers as N. Scott Momaday and Robert Penn Warren.

PORTRAIT OF WILLIAM LEAST HEAT MOON

from **BLUE HIGHWAYS**

Starting Out

The vernal equinox came on gray and quiet, a curiously still morning not winter and not spring, as if the cycle paused. Because things go their own way, my daybreak departure turned to a morning departure, then to an afternoon departure. Finally, I climbed into the van, rolled down the window, looked a last time at the rented apartment. From a dead elm sparrow hawks used each year came a high *whee* as the nestlings squealed for more grub. I started the engine. When I returned a

season from now—if I did return—those squabs would be gone from the nest.

Accompanied only by a small, gray spider crawling the dashboard (kill a spider and it will rain), I drove into the street, around the corner, through the intersection, over the bridge, onto the highway. I was heading toward those little towns that get on the map—if they get on at all—only because some cartographer has a blank space to fill: Remote, Oregon; Simplicity, Virginia; New Freedom, Pennsylvania; New Hope, Tennessee; Why, Arizona; Whynot, Mississippi. Igo, California (just down the road from Ono), here I come. . . .

The first highway: Interstate 70 eastbound out of Columbia, Missouri. The road here follows, more or less, the Booneslick Trail, the initial leg of the Oregon Trail; it also parallels both the southern latitude of the last great glacier in central Missouri as well as the northern boundary of the Osage Nation. The Cherokee[1] and I had skirmished its length in Missouri and Illinois for ten years, and memory made for hard driving that first day of spring. But it was the fastest route east out of the homeland. When memory is too much, turn to the eye. So I watched particularities.

Item: a green and grainy and corrupted ice over the ponds.

Item: blackbirds, passing like storm-borne leaves, sweeping just above the treetops, moving as if invisibly tethered to one will.

Item: barn roofs painted VISIT ROCK CITY—SEE SEVEN STATES. Seven at one fell swoop. People loved it.

Item: uprooted fencerows of Osage orange (so-called hedge apples although they are in the mulberry family). The Osage made bows and war clubs from the limbs; the trunks, with a natural fungicide, carried the first telegraph lines; and roots furnished dye to make doughboy uniforms olive drab. Now the Osage orange were going so bigger tractors could work longer rows.

At High Hill, two boys were flying gaudy butterfly kites that pulled hard against their leashes. No strings, no flight. A town of surprising flatness on a single main street of turn-of-the-century buildings paralleling the interstate, High Hill sat golden in a piece of sunlight that broke through. No one moved along the street, and things held so still and old, the town looked like a museum diorama.

Eighty miles out, rain started popping the windshield, and the road became blobby headlights and green interstate signs for this exit, that exit. LAST EXIT TO ELSEWHERE. I crossed the Missouri River not far upstream from where Lewis and Clark on another wet spring afternoon set out for Mr. Jefferson's *"terra incognita."* Then, to the southeast under a glowing skullcap of fouled sky, lay St. Louis.

I crossed the Mississippi as it carried its forty hourly tons of topsoil to the Louisiana delta.

The tumult of St. Louis behind, the Illinois superwide quiet but for the rain, I turned south onto state 4, a shortcut to I-64. After that, the 42,500 miles of straight and wide could lead to hell for all I cared; I was going to stay on the three million miles of bent and narrow rural American two-lane, the roads to Podunk and Toonerville. Into the sticks, the boondocks, the burgs, backwaters, jerkwaters, the wide-spots-in-the-road, the don't-blink-or-you'll-miss-it towns. Into those places where you say, "My god! What if you lived here!" The Middle of Nowhere.

The early darkness came on. My headlamps cut only a forty-foot trail through the rain, and the dashboard lights cast a spectral glowing. Sheet lightning behind the horizon of trees made the sky look like a great faded orange cloth being blown about; then darkness soaked up the light, and, for a moment, I was blinder than before.

In the approaching car beams, raindrops spattering the road became little beacons. I bent over the wheel to steer along the divider stripes. A frog, long-leggedy and green, belly-flopped across the road to the side where the puddles would be better. The land, still cold and wintery, was alive with creatures that trusted in the coming of spring.

On through Lebanon, a brick-street village where Charles Dickens spent a night in the Mermaid Inn; on down the Illinois roads—roads that leave you ill and annoyed, the joke went—all the way dodging chuckholes that *Time* magazine said Americans would spend 626 million dollars in extra fuel swerving around. Then onto I-64, a new interstate that cuts across southern Illinois and Indiana without going through a single town. If a world lay out there, it was far from me. On and on. Behind, only a red wash of taillights.

---

1. **The Cherokee.** Moon called his wife "The Cherokee" because she was part Cherokee Indian.

At Grayville, Illinois, on the Wabash River, I pulled up for the night on North Street and parked in front of the old picture show. The marquee said TRAVELOGUE TODAY, or it would have if the O's had been there. I should have gone to a cafe and struck up a conversation; instead I stumbled to the bunk in the back of my rig, undressed, zipped into the sleeping bag, and watched things go dark. I fought desolation and wrestled memories of the Indian wars.

First night on the road. I've read that fawns have no scent so that predators cannot track them down. For me, I heard the past snuffling about somewhere close.

Paying Attention

Not out of any plan, but just because it lay in front of me, I headed for the Bluegrass region. I took an old road, a "pike," the Kentuckians say, since their first highways were toll roads with entrances barred by revolving poles called "turn pikes." I followed the old pike, today route 421, not out of any plan either, but because it looked pleasant—a road of white fences around Thoroughbred farms. Many of the fence planks now, however, were creosoted and likely to remain the color of charred stumps until someone invents a machine to paint them.

Along the Leestown Road, near an old whitewashed springhouse made useless by a water-district pipeline, I stopped to eat lunch. Downstream from the spring where butter once got cooled, under peeling sycamores, the clear rill washed around clumps of new watercress. I pulled makings for a sandwich from my haversack: Muenster cheese, a collop of hard salami, sourdough bread, horseradish. I cut a sprig of watercress and laid it on, then ate slowly, letting the gurgle in the water and the guttural trilling of red-winged blackbirds do the talking. A noisy, whizzing gnat that couldn't decide whether to eat on my sandwich or ear joined me.

Had I gone looking for some particular place rather than any place, I'd never have found this spring under the sycamores. Since leaving home, I felt for the first time at rest. Sitting full in the moment, I practiced on the god-awful difficulty of just paying attention. It's a contention of Heat Moon's—believing as he does any traveler who misses the journey misses about all he's going to get—that a man becomes his attentions. His observations and curiosity, they make and remake him.

Etymology: *curious,* related to *cure,* once meant "carefully observant." Maybe a tonic of curiosity would counter my numbing sense that life inevitably creeps toward the absurd. *Absurd,* by the way, derives from a Latin word meaning "deaf, dulled." Maybe the road could provide a therapy through observation of the ordinary and obvious, a means whereby the outer eye opens an inner one. STOP, LOOK, LISTEN, the old railroad crossing signs warned. Whitman calls it "the profound lesson of reception."

New ways of seeing can disclose new things: the radio telescope revealed quasars and pulsars, and the scanning electron microscope showed the whiskers of the dust mite. But turn the question around: Do new *things* make for new ways of seeing?

A Place Never Dreamed Of

There's something about the desert that doesn't like man, something that mocks his nesting instinct and makes his constructions look feeble and temporary. Yet it's just that inhospitableness that endears the arid rockiness, the places pointy and poisonous, to men looking for its dicipline.

Up along blue road 9 in the Little Hatchet Mountains—just desert hills here— I stopped for a walk in the scrub. Every so often I paused to listen. Like a vacuum. Pascal should have tried these silences.[2] I yelled

---

2. **Pascal should have tried these silences.** The reference is to Blaise Pascal, a French philosopher, author of *Pensées* (Thoughts). One of Pascal's "thoughts" is "The eternal silence of these infinite spaces frightens me."

GRAND CANYON, Thomas Moran
Thomas Gilcrease Institute of American History and Art, Tulsa, Oklahoma

my name, and the desert took the shout as if covetous of any issue from life.

Walking back to the highway, I saw a coil of sand loosen and bend itself into a grainy S and warp across the slope. I stood dead still. A sidewinder so matched to the grit only its undulating shadow gave it away. And that's something else about the desert: deception. It can make heat look like water, living plants seem dead, mountains miles away appear close, and turn scaly tubes of venom into ropes of warm sand. So open, so concealed.

For the fourth time that day, I crossed the Continental Divide, which, at this point, was merely a crumpling of hills. The highway held so true that the mountains ahead seemed to come to me. Along the road were small glaring and dusty towns: Playas, a gath-

ering of trailers and a one-room massage parlor ($3.00 for thirty-five minutes the sign said); and Animas, with a schoolyard of Indian children, their blue-black heads gleaming like gun barrels in the sun. Then the road turned and went directly for an immense wall of mountain that looked impossible to drive through and improbable to drive around. It was the Chiricahuas, named for the Apache tribe that held this land even before the conquistadors arrived.

I crossed into Arizona and followed a numberless, broken road. A small wooden sign with an arrow pointing west:

PORTAL
PARADISE

In the desert flatness, the road began twisting

for no apparent reason, tacking toward the Chiricahuas. It had to be a dead end—there could be no opening in that sheer stone obtrusion, that invasion of mountain looked as if it had stridden out of the Sierra Madres, had seen the New Mexican desert, and stopped cold in its Precambrian tracks.

The pavement made yet another right-angle turn, and a deep rift in the vertical face of the Chiricahuas opened, hidden until the last moment. How could this place be? The desert always seems to hold something aside. The constriction of canyon was just wide enough for the road and a stream bank to bank with alligator juniper, pine, sycamore, and white oak. Trees covered the water and roadway and cut the afternoon heat. Where the canopy opened, I could see canyon walls of yellow and orange pinnacles and turrets, fluted and twisted, everything rising hundreds of feet. More deception: in the midst of a flat, hot scarcity, a cool and wet forest between rock formations that might have come from the mind of Antonio Gaudi. I couldn't have been more surprised had the last turn brought me into Jersey City. And that was the delight—I'd never heard of the Chiricahuas. I expected nothing.

Portal consisted of a few rock buildings and not a human anywhere. Three miles up the canyon I forded Cave Creek and pulled in under some big juniper and sycamore. Ghost Dancing[3] sat so my bunk was at the edge of the stream; I wanted to hear water that night and wash away the highway wearies. I took an apple and went to the creek. The place drowsed. I was sitting in the northeast corner of the great Sonoran Desert, while at my feet a pair of water bugs swam in slow tandem as if shadows of each other. Evergreens resinated in the air, and bleached clouds moved high over three rhyolite monoliths cut from the spewings of an ancient volcano to which the Chiricahuas are a tombstone. Before any men, wind had come and inscribed the rock, and water had incised it, but who now could read those writs?

I was in one of the strangest pieces of topography I'd ever seen, a place, until now, completely beyond my imaginings. What is it in man that for a long while lies unknown and unseen only one day to emerge and push him into a new land of the eye, a new region of the mind, a place he has never dreamed of? Maybe it's like the force in spores lying quietly under asphalt until the day they push a soft, bulbous mushroom head right through the pavement. There's nothing you can do to stop it.

Reaching Farther Out

I followed the road, the road followed the Klickitat, and the river followed the rocky valley down to the Columbia. At The Dalles another dam—this one wedged between high walls of basalt. Before the rapids here disappeared, Indians caught salmon for a couple of thousand years by spearing them in midair as the fish exploded leaps up the falls; Klickitats smoked the salmon over coals, pulverized the dried flesh, and either packed it in wicker baskets lined with fishskins for use during the winter or they tied the cooked salmon in bundles for trading to other tribes. The fish kept for months and some even ended up with Indians living east of the Rockies.

The cascades provided such a rich fishing site that Lewis and Clark called The Dalles "the great mart of all this country." Natives found a new source of income in the falls when white traders came with boats to be portaged. One fur trader complained, as did many early travelers, that the Indians were friendly but "habitual thieves"; yet he paid fifty braves only a quid of tobacco each to carry his heavy boats a mile upriver.

East of the dam, the land looked as

---

3. **Ghost Dancing.** This is the name Moon gave to his 1975 half-ton Ford Econoline van. The phrase refers to ceremonial dances of the Plains Indians, dances meant to bring dead warriors back to life.

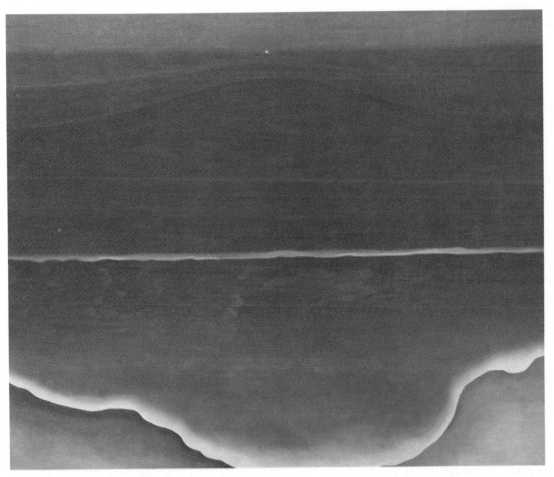

The paintings of Georgia O'Keeffe explore the natural shapes and rhythms of the American Southwest, a part of the country that has inspired many of her finest landscapes and abstractions.

WAVE NIGHT, Georgia O'Keeffe
Addison Gallery of American Art
Phillips Academy, Andover, Massachusetts

though someone had drawn a north-south line forbidding green life: west, patches of forest; east, a desert of hills growing only shrubs and dry grasses. The wet coastal country was gone. A little before sunset, in the last long stretch of light, I saw on a great rounded hill hundreds of feet above the river a strange huddle of upright rocks. It looked like Stonehenge. When I got closer, I saw that it was Stonehenge—in perfect repair. I turned off the highway and went down to the bottom-land peach groves, where a track up the hill

led to the stones. They stood a hundred yards south of several collapsed buildings.

In truth, the circle of menhirs was a ferro-concretehenge, but it was as arresting on its hill as the real Stonehenge on Salisbury Plain. From it, I could see the river Lewis and Clark had opened the Northwest with and awakened a new consciousness of nationhood; I could look across to a far riverside section of the Oregon Trail now buried under I-80. The setting sun cast an unearthly light on the sixteen-foot megaliths and turned the enormous pyramid of Mount Hood, fifty miles away, to a black triangle. I felt again the curious fusion of time—past with present—that occurred at the Nevada petroglyphs.

A flaking wooden sign said a highway engineer and rail magnate, Sam Hill, whose grave was just down the slope, had built the replica in the twenties as a memorial to doughboys "sacrificed to the heathen god of war." Over several smooth declivities in the concrete slabs appeared almost imperceptible notations from other travelers: A.J. WILSON NYC. HELLO STUPID. KT 1936. BOB AND JANEY WAS HERE. The monument had become a register, and the scribbles gave a historical authenticity that masked its bogus one. The twentieth century had made the stones an equivalent to the petroglyphs. . . .

The hills went dark, the volcano vanished against the black sky, blue ice stars shone as thick as mottles on a trout. A few lights from Biggs, Oregon, several miles across the river, gleamed off the slick water.

The loneliness again. Now I had only the idea of the journey to keep me going. Black Elk[4] says it is in the dark world among the many changing shadows that men get lost. Instead of insight, maybe all a man gets is strength to wander for a while. Maybe the only gift is a chance to inquire, to know nothing for certain. An inheritance of wonder and nothing more.

Stars shone with a clarity beyond anything I could remember. I was looking into—actually seeing—the past. By looking up into the darkness, I was looking into time. The old light from Betelgeuse, five hundred twenty light-years away, showed the star that existed when Christopher Columbus was a boy, and the Betelgeuse he saw was the one that burned when Northmen were crossing the Atlantic. For the Betelgeuse of this time, someone else will have to do the looking. The past is for the present, the present for the future.

Astronomers say that when telescopes of greater range can be built, ones that can look down the distant curves of the universe billions of light-years away, they might show existence at the time of creation. And if astrophysicists and countless American Indians are correct in believing that a human being is composed of exploded bits of heavenly matter, billions of galactic atoms, then astronomers may behold us all in the stellar winds; they may observe us when we were something else and very much farther away. In a time when men counted only seven planets, Whitman recognized it:

> Afar down I see the huge first Nothing, I knew I was even there,
> I waited unseen and always, and slept through the lethargic mist,
> And took my time.

There came a dry rustle in the desert bush—a skunk, rabbit, coyote, I didn't know what, but it pulled me back to Sam Hill's Stonehenge, now just an orbit of shadows. The people who built the British Stonehenge used it as a time machine whereby starlight—the light of the past—could show them a future of equinoxes, solstices, eclipses. Across America I had been looking for something similar. An old urge in man. It seemed the journey had led here.

What was this piece of ground I stood on? Fifty miles away rose the ancient volcano like those that puffed out the first atmosphere, and under me lay the volcanic basalt ridge the old river had cut through. For thousands of years, chinook and chum and bluebacks swam upriver to regenerate, and Indians followed after the salmon; and then new people came down the river after everything. South lay the Oregon Trail under four lanes of concrete marked off by the yellow running lights of the transports; south, too, were glinting rails of the Union Pacific. North a ghost town crumbling, and around me a circle of stones for the dead of the first war called a "world war."

---

4. **Black Elk.** Moon brought with him a book, Neihardt's *Black Elk Speaks.* Black Elk was an Indian.

Astronomer Edwin Hubble observed a galaxy moving away from Earth at nine hundred million miles an hour and concluded that the universe is dispersing itself to emptiness. Perhaps so, but the things I saw on the mountain—and more that I didn't—all had come together briefly while I stood as witness. Now atomic physicists, those who watch the dance of the universe, were saying that in the pursuit of matter one ends up not so much with things as with interconnections—interconnections that give the particularities not merely definition but (even more) their moment, their meaning. Whitman: "A vast similitude interlocks all."

Who can say how a man comes to see? I appeared surrounded by tombstones: the volcano dead, the basalt solidified, the fast river of cataracts drowned, the Indians and explorers and settlers and thirteen doughboys and Sam Hill too (his tombstone said "Amid nature's great unrest, he sought rest"), all in their graves. That's how a man sees the continuum: by the tracks it leaves.

All of those things—rock and men and river—resisted change, resisted the coming as they did the going. Hood warmed and rose slowly, breaking over the plain, and cooled slowly over the plain it buried. The nature of things is resistance to change, while the nature of process is resistance to stasis, yet things and process are one, and the line from inorganic to organic and back again is uninterrupted and unbroken.

The Ghost Dancers[5] showed both man's natural opposition to change he doesn't understand and his natural failure in such opposition. But it is man's potential to try to see how all things come from the old intense light and how they pause in the darkness of matter only long enough to change back into energy, to see that changelessness would be meaninglessness, to know that the only way the universe can show and prove itself is through change. His job is to do what nothing else he knows of can do: to look about and draw upon time.

A man lives in things and things are moving. He stands apart in such a temporary way it is hardly worth speaking of. If that perception dims egocentrism, that illusion of what man is, then it also enlarges his self, that multiple yet whole part which he has been, will be, is. Ego, craving distinction, belongs to the narrowness of now; but self, looking for union, belongs to the past and future, to the continuum, to the outside. Of all the visions of the Grandfathers the greatest is this: *To seek the high concord, a man looks not deeper within—he reaches farther out.*

5. **The Ghost Dancers.** Here, the reference is to the Indian dancers, not to Moon's truck.

FOR UNDERSTANDING

1. When did Moon start on his journey?
2. What kinds of places did he intend to visit?
3. Specifically where did he spend his first night?
4. What are the Chiricahuas?
5. Describe the town of Portal.
6. What are the "circle of menhirs" that Moon finds in Oregon? To what does he compare them?

FOR INTERPRETATION

1. What is an advantage of looking for any place rather than a particular place?
2. Interpret: "A man becomes his attentions."
3. In your opinion do "new *things* make for new ways of seeing"? Explain.
4. Why does Moon mention that the fur trader paid a quid of tobacco to each Indian who carried his heavy boats?
5. Interpret: "The past is for the present, the present for the future."
6. What does Moon mean by saying that we see the continuum by the tracks it leaves?
7. What distinction does Moon make between the Ego and the self?

COMPOSITION WORKSHOP

A WORKING OUTLINE

Once all the raw material for a research paper has been collected and documented on bibliography cards, the gathered material must be examined and sorted through. A preliminary plan or working outline must then be drawn up. Once the working outline has been developed, the actual writing of the paper can begin.

For every research paper on a literary topic, a very rough plan actually comes into being once the writer identifies the topic. If the writer has chosen to write about a particular literary work or works, for example, he or she says in effect: "I have read this work of literature and believe I understand it fairly well. I will find out what others who have read the work have said about it. Then I will present my own conclusions, which may or may not match the conclusions others have come to." If the writer has chosen to investigate some aspect of an author's life, he or she says in effect: "I have read many works by this author and note that certain points of view and concerns arise again and again. I will find out what others who have studied the author's works and life have said about the connection between them. Then I will come to my own conclusions about how the author's life influenced the works." Other types of topics are, of course, common. But at the moment any topic is selected, a rough plan similar to these is usually adopted.

The assembly of the actual working outline begins with a review of all of the gathered information. A considerable amount of time may have gone by since the research began, and information collected earlier may prove less useful than material collected more recently. Or information gathered earlier may turn out to be unrelated to the topic as it has developed. No topic is changeless, and ideas usually change and become more exact as the gathering of information proceeds. The writer must eliminate information that turns out to be inferior or unrelated, even though valuable time may have been spent collecting it.

Once useless information has been eliminated, the writer can begin to structure a working outline. The first entry in the outline will be the introduction to the paper. However, while the introduction is always the first item in the outline, it should always be the last part of the paper to be written, because before the body of the paper is complete, the writer cannot possibly know what its exact contents will be. The remaining items in the outline will, of course, depend upon the topic. But in order to see how a typical outline might be put together, let us examine a possible topic for a research paper.

Let us assume that you have read Stephen Crane's short novel, *The Red Badge of Courage*. In the novel, Henry Fleming, a young teenage boy who joins the Union Army during the American Civil War, learns that war is not the heroic and glorious enterprise he thought it was. As you read the novel, you saw that the boy ran from his first battle. But eventually he becomes a fighting machine, the kind of fearless soldier all military officers dream of commanding. In the novel's most dramatic scene, he single-handedly turns his fellow soldiers into fierce warriors. His heroism wins the respect and admiration of all.

Your reading of this great American novel has convinced you that part of its message has to do with how a young boy finds out what it means to be a hero. Although originally frightened, he manages to find the inner resources to overcome his fear and become a true hero. But your reading of the book also suggests that perhaps the author's main message has to do with the nature of such heroism. Through his description and commentary, the author might be saying that the more heroic men act in war, the more mechanical and inhuman they become. You note, for example, that Crane uses words generally associated with animals when he describes the army as a unit. You note also that his language is beautifully descriptive. But when the soldiers themselves talk, they find it difficult to express themselves and are very inarticulate. And you notice that when Henry becomes a true hero, he loses control of his reason and becomes something between an animal and a machine.

As you gather information for your paper, you notice that the authors of many of the sources you consult comment upon Henry's growth as a soldier and a person. Many also comment on the horror of war that Crane graphically presents in the novel. But what you believe Crane is saying about the nature of the war hero is not often referred to. So you decide to make that view of the book's message your major conclusion. You will review standard interpretations and then present the conclusion your own reading and research has lead you to. Your working outline for your paper on Stephen Crane's novel might therefore look like this:

    I. Introduction
   II. Summary of Plot
  III. Henry Fleming's Growth
  IV. Crane's View of War
   V. The Nature of the War Hero
  VI. Conclusion

FOOTNOTES

As in any other piece of practical writing, the research writer follows the preliminary outline in writing the paper. The writer uses the direct quotations, paraphrases, and summaries collected from other sources during the research and develops paragraphs that make up each section of the paper. Because the research paper is a documented piece of writing, the writer must include footnotes that tell a reader where a quotation or idea came from.

Footnotes are numbered consecutively throughout a paper. The number of the footnote is placed outside whatever punctuation goes with the sentence or paragraph:

As Thomas Beer pointed out, veterans were convinced that Crane had seen action as a soldier.[7]

The footnotes themselves are usually positioned at the bottom of the page on which the material to be footnoted appears. They may, however, be presented on separate sheets of paper after the body of the research paper and before the bibliography. When footnotes are given at the bottom of a page, they are often separated from the text by a solid line.

A source is fully identified in a footnote when it is first referred to. If the writer has carefully collected material from sources, all the information needed to write the footnotes is already available on the note cards. Here is the standard footnote form for a first reference to both a book and an article:

[1]John Crowe Ransom, *The New Criticism* (New York: New Directions, 1941) 138.

[4]John Crowe Ransom, "The Poet as Woman," *Southern Review* 2 (1937): 803.

If your paper gives the author's full name, it is omitted from the footnote. The footnote then begins with the title of the source being referred to.

After a source has been referred to for the first time, later footnotes may be kept very brief. If only one source by a particular author has been referred to, the source need contain only the author's last name followed by the page reference:

[9]Ransom 141.

If more than one work by the same author has been referred to earlier, a later reference should also include the title to avoid confusion:

[10]Ransom, *The New Criticism* 163.

THE FINAL DRAFT

The final draft of a research paper should always include the paper's title centered on a title page, followed by the writer's name. On the page following the title page, an outline is often provided. This is a final outline, not the working outline. It is prepared after the paper has been written. In addition to noting the paper's parts, it often begins with a thesis statement which tells the reader what the writer hopes to accomplish in the paper.

A research paper should always be typed if possible. The text should be double-spaced and the footnotes and bibliography should be single-spaced. If the paper must be written in longhand, it should be prepared very carefully. A neat appearance tells the reader that the writer has done a lot of hard work with great care.

ASSIGNMENT 1

Carefully examine all the information that you have gathered for your research paper. Eliminate all information that turns out to be unusable. Then develop a preliminary working outline.

ASSIGNMENT 2

Follow the preliminary outline you developed and write the first draft of your paper. Study the first draft carefully over a period of time and make whatever changes are necessary. Then prepare a final draft of your paper. Be sure to use the proper form for the footnotes and bibliography.

HANDBOOK OF LITERARY TERMS

Allegory: A literary technique in which characters, events, and details of setting have a literal and symbolic meaning. Writers use allegory to suggest various beliefs about philosophical and moral issues. Nathaniel Hawthorne's "Dr. Heidegger's Experiment" (p. 222) is a well-known American allegory. (See **Parable, Symbolism.**)

Alliteration: The repetition of the same beginning consonant sounds in closely associated words or accented syllables. Here is an example from Edna St. Vincent Millay's "Renascence" (p. 678): "The soul can split the sky in two." Alliteration is used to create melody, to call attention to key words, and to reinforce rhythmic patterns. (See **Assonance, Consonance, Rhythm.**)

Allusion: A brief reference to historical events or characters or to another literary work with which the author presumes the reader is familiar. Assuming that the reader does understand the reference, an allusion can help establish characterization and tone and add depth to a work. For example, Oliver Wendell Holmes makes an allusion to Greek mythology in this line from his poem "Old Ironsides" (p. 292): "The harpies of the shore shall pluck / The eagle of the sea!" The allusion to the harpies, grotesque mythological monsters, effectively contrasts the ship's former glory to the possibility of its ending up in a scrap heap.
See page 42.

Almanac: An annual table or book of tables containing a calendar of days, weeks, and months and often including astronomical data, weather predictions, and other miscellaneous information. Among the earliest American almanacs were Benjamin Franklin's *Poor Richard's* almanacs (p. 98).
See page 98.

Analogy: A comparison of two things that are essentially unalike but that can be shown to have some similarities. Analogy can be used in effective ways to explain, describe, or convince. Claude McKay draws an analogy in his sonnet "America" (p. 676) when he writes of the enormous effect America exerts on his life: "Her vigor flows like tides into my blood, / . . . Her bigness sweeps my being like a flood." (See **Metaphor, Simile.**)

Anapest (anapestic foot): A foot of poetry consisting of two unaccented syllables followed by one accented syllable (˘ ˘ ′). Use of the anapest gives a feeling of swiftness to a line and emphasizes the last word. (See **Foot.**)

Anecdote: A short, entertaining story. It differs from a short story in that an anecdote does not have a complex plot or elaborate characterization. An anecdote does, however, have a definite beginning, middle, and end. The final section often emphasizes the lesson or moral of the story. The outlandish "Canterbury tale" related in *The History of the Dividing Line"* (p. 49) is an example of an amusing anecdote. (See **Fable.**)

Aphorism: A short statement expressing a general truth or some practical wisdom. Ralph Waldo Emerson is well known for his aphoristic style, that is, his ability to incorporate aphorisms, or memorable statements, in his writing. "A foolish consistency is the hobgoblin of little minds" is a famous aphorism from his essay "Self-Reliance" (p. 187). Benjamin Franklin's *Poor Richard's* almanacs (p. 98) also contain many well-known aphorisms.
See page 99.

Apostrophe: A figure of speech in which a thing is addressed directly, as though it were a listening person. Thus, in "Theme for English B" (p. 691) Langston Hughes addresses Harlem, saying "Harlem, I hear you. . . ." An apostrophe may be addressed to a person (in which case there would be no personification) if the person is not living or conceived to be literally listening. (See **Personification.**)

Aside: In a play, a speech given by an actor that the other actors on stage are not supposed to hear. The Stage Manager in Thornton Wilder's play *Our Town* (p. 469) comments on the action in a series of extended asides.

Assonance: The repetition of similar vowel sounds. Assonance differs from rhyme in that rhyme uses the same vowel and final consonant sounds *(pain, main)*, while assonance uses different consonants with the same vowel sound *(pain, maim)*. Note the examples of assonance in these two lines from "Memorial I" (p. 815) by Audre Lorde:

> I will not ask you why, now,
> nor how, nor what you knew.

(See **Alliteration, Consonance.**)

Atmosphere: The overall mood or emotional aura of a literary work. Atmosphere is created by the handling of such elements as setting, character, and theme. It is often described by the same adjectives we would use to describe the weather: *gloomy, cheerful, threatening, tranquil,* and the like. (See **Setting, Tone.**)

Autobiography: The story of a person's life written by that person. Benjamin Franklin's *Autobiography* (p. 93), Frederick Douglass's *My Bondage and My Freedom* (p. 300), and Maya Angelou's *I Know Why the Caged Bird Sings* (p. 820) are all autobiographical selections. (See **Biography, Nonfiction.**)

Biography: An account of a person's life written by another individual. In some biographies, the writer uses only facts and documented materials. Other biographies are made more interesting by conversations and scenes imagined by the author. All such works based on an individual's life are categorized as nonfiction. (See **Autobiography, Nonfiction.**)

See also page 161.

Blank verse: Poetry written in unrhymed iambic pentameter, that is, lines of ten syllables with the even-numbered syllables accented and the odd-numbered syllables unaccented. Blank verse is well suited to epic and dramatic poetry because its rhythm closely resembles that of normal English speech. See, for example, Robert Frost's "Birches" (p. 646): "Whĕn Í sĕe bírchĕs bénd tŏ léft ănd ríght." The accents may not always be quite as regular as this, but there will always be five per line. (See **Iambic pentameter.**)

See also page 656.

Character: A person or an animal presented in a literary work. A *dynamic* character is one whose personality or attitude changes over the course of the work. The turning point in a dynamic character's growth often coincides with the climax of the plot. Because George Stoyonovich gains new knowledge of himself during "A Summer's Reading" (p. 746), he is a dynamic character. A *static* character is one whose personality and attitude do not change over the course of a literary work. In a literary work, a character who is drawn in three dimensions is called a *rounded* character. Such a character shows enough different qualities and personality traits to seem believable. The opposite of a rounded character is a *stock* or *flat* character, or *stereotype*. Such a character is either so predictable or one-sided that he or she is not believable. The protagonist or hero of a literary work must be a rounded character. A stock or flat character in the role of hero would be unsubstantial and unconvincing.

See page 758.

Characterization: The means used by a writer to show what his or her characters are like. These means may include (1) direct description, (2) presentation of the character in action, (3) presentation of the thoughts of the character, (4) comparison of one character with another, and (5) reactions to or discussions of the character by other characters.

See pages 230, 772.

Chronological: A pattern of organization in writing in which events are presented in the order in which they happen. A story such as "The Sculptor's Funeral" (p. 529) by Willa Cather uses this kind of organization. (See **Flashback, Time sequence.**)

Classicism: A movement or body of doctrine in art, literature, and music reflecting the qualities of early Greek and Roman culture. Classicism emphasizes such ideas and attitudes as formal elegance, simplicity, order, and proportion. Classicism is often contrasted with romanticism, which is concerned with emotions, passions, personal themes, and freedom of expression. Thomas Jefferson's Declaration of Independence (p. 112) is regarded as a model of classical prose. (See **Romanticism.**)

Climax (or **turning point**): The turning point of the action in a literary work, when the conflict must be resolved. The climax is the point of highest interest and emotional involvement for the reader. (See **Dénouement, Plot.**)

See also page 221.

Comedy: A work of literature that (1) ends happily and (2) aims primarily to amuse. (See **Tragedy.**)

Conceit: A poetic metaphor, or comparison, that expresses a striking parallel between two seemingly dissimilar things. For example, in his poem "Huswifery" (p. 36), Edward Taylor compares the making of

cloth to the gaining of salvation or grace from God. The use of conceit implies intellectual ingenuity on the part of the writer. Emily Dickinson, T. S. Eliot, and John Crowe Ransom are especially noted for their use of the conceit.

See also page 37.

Conflict: A struggle between opposing forces in a literary work. An *external* struggle may be between characters or between a character and a set of circumstances or a force of nature. An *internal* struggle takes place within a character whose instincts, emotions, or values are in conflict. Conflict provides the drama, interest, and suspense that make a reader want to know how the issue will be resolved. Although many stories have more than one conflict, there is usually one central or primary one. In "The Sculptor's Funeral" (p. 529), there is a basic conflict between "ruffianism and civilization." (See **Plot.**)

See also pages 221, 352, 403, 539.

Connotation: The emotional associations a word evokes. The dictionary definition of the word *snake* is "a reptile having a long, tapering cylindrical body." When the word is applied to a person, it has the connotations of evil and treachery. (See **Denotation.**)

Consonance: The repetition of similar consonant sounds with different vowels. For example, the words *till, tall; ball, bull;* and *compact, deduct* demonstrate consonance. Consonance at the end of two or more lines of poetry is called *half rhyme* or *slant rhyme* because the final consonants in the stressed syllables are the same, but the vowels preceding them sound different. (See **Alliteration, Assonance.**)

Couplet: A pair of rhyming lines in a poem. An iambic couplet is a couplet written in iambic feet. Here are two iambic couplets from John Greenleaf Whittier's *Snow-Bound* (p. 288):

> The sun that brief December day
> Rose cheerless over hills of gray,
> And, darkly circled, gave at noon
> A sadder light than waning moon.

Dactyl (dactylic foot): A foot of poetry consisting of one accented and two unaccented syllables (´ ˘ ˘). This foot evokes a stately, measured feeling, although it is usually not used exclusively throughout an entire poem. (See **Foot.**)

Denotation: The specific or literal meaning of a word without its emotional coloration or association. For example, the denotation of *gorilla* is "a large anthropoid ape having a stocky body and coarse, dark hair." If the word, however, suggests to the listener or reader a brutish or thuglike person, the word has acquired connotations.

Denote: To reveal or indicate.

Dénouement (or **falling action**): The concluding section in a literary work that follows the climax. The dénouement explains the outcome of the conflict and shows its effects on the characters. This section ties up the loose ends of a story, novel, or play. (See **Climax, Resolution.**)

Description: One of the four forms of discourse (persuasion, exposition, narration, description). It has as its purpose the picturing of persons, places, or things. In a literary work, description creates the environment in which the action takes place by giving details of time, place, character, and situation. (See **Discourse.**)

See page 52.

Determinism: In literature, a theory embracing the idea that what a person thinks, does, and says is a result of heredity and environment over which she or he has little or no control. American novelists Frank Norris, Theodore Dreiser, and Jack London often portray individuals shaped by biological, social, and economic forces beyond the individuals' control and comprehension. (See **Naturalism, Realism.**)

Dialect: The characteristic speech of a region or social group, distinguished from standard English by its pronunciation, sentence structure, and vocabulary. In the United States, there are three main geographical divisions of dialects: northern, midland, and southern. For *The Adventures of Huckleberry Finn* (p. 456), in particular, Mark Twain was accorded worldwide acclaim for his skill in recording dialects.

See page 455.

Dialogue: Conversation between two or more people in a play, novel, short story, poem, letter, or essay. The use of dialogue is prevalent in modern literature as a way of revealing character, building suspense and conflict, and carrying the action forward. In drama, of course, dialogue alone carries the work to its climax.

Diction: A writer's choice of words. Writers choose words and develop a style that is appropriate to the material they are writing. For example, the simple language of Amy Lowell's poem "Peace" (p. 643) reflects the simplicity of the incident in the poem. The diction of Thomas Paine's famous essay series *The Crisis* (p. 105) reflects the eloquent style of his time and his desire to persuade the American people to his point of view. (See **Style.**)

Discourse: Discourse is verbal expression or composition, either written or spoken. Its four chief forms, or modes, are *description, exposition, narration,* and *persuasion* or *argumentation.*

Description *describes*—with the purpose of picturing a scene or an individual. It is usually subordinated to other forms of composition, such as narration.

Exposition *explains*—with the purpose of giving information. The playing directions included in a card game or background information preceding a story, play, or ceremony are examples of exposition.

Narration *narrates*—with the purpose of telling a story or recounting an event or series of events in a certain sequence.

Persuasion *persuades*—with the purpose of bringing a reader or listener to a particular opinion or action. Also termed *argumentation*, it attempts to convince rather than to explain.

See page 56.

Drama (or **play**): A composition in prose or poetry written for performance by actors on a stage. Except for stage directions, a drama consists entirely of dialogue that must reveal character, build suspense and conflict, and carry the action forward to a climax and resolution. (See **Tragedy.**)

See also page 700.

Dramatic irony: See **Irony**.

Dramatic poem: A narrative poem in which one or more characters speak and each speaker always addresses a specific listener. Robert Frost's "The Death of the Hired Man" (p. 651) is one of the best-known dramatic poems in American literature.

Effect: The overall impression the writer strives to create in a literary selection. Edgar Allan Poe wrote that he always began a writing by considering the effect he wished to make on his readers. In his "The Fall of the House of Usher" (p. 233), for example, he produces the effect of terror by very carefully blending the details of setting, characterization, and action. (See **Mood.**)

See also pages 233, 246.

Elegy: A mournful, melancholy poem lamenting the passing of life and beauty or meditating on the nature of death. Walt Whitman's "When Lilacs Last in the Dooryard Bloom'd" (p. 318) is an elegy that mourns the death of Abraham Lincoln.

End-rhyme: The rhyme that occurs at the ends of lines of poetry. The pattern formed by the end-rhymes is the *rhyme scheme*. In Edna St. Vincent Millay's poem "Renascence" (p. 678) note the end-rhyme in the first two lines:

> All I could see from where I stood
> Was three long mountains and a
> wood.

(See **Rhyme scheme.**)

End-stopped line: A line of poetry in which a grammatical pause (such as the end of a phrase or clause) coincides with the end of the line. Each of the twelve lines is end-stopped in Bradstreet's "To My Dear and Loving Husband," (p. 30) which begins:

> If ever two were one, then surely we.
> If ever man were loved by wife, then
> thee;
> If ever wife was happy in a man,
> Compare with me ye women if you
> can.

(See **Run-on line**.)

Epic: A long narrative poem describing the great feats of a superhuman hero. The themes of epic poetry are often abstract and universal rather than subjective and personal, as in lyric poetry. The protagonist of the epic embodies the cultural ideals of a society, such as courage, honesty, strength, and justice. One of the most famous epics in American literature is Henry Wadsworth Longfellow's *Hiawatha*.

Epigram: A short, pointed, or witty saying. Many of Benjamin Franklin's sayings in his *Poor Richard's* almanacs (p. 98) have an epigrammatic quality.

Epigraph: A quotation or motto set at the beginning of a literary work or a division of it to suggest its theme. T. S. Eliot uses an epigraph to introduce "The Hollow Men" (p. 671).

Epithet: A descriptive phrase that is often substituted for the person's real name or title. In *The Crisis,* Number I (p. 105), Thomas Paine uses the epithets "the summer solider" and "the sunshine patriot" to characterize those who fail to serve their country in time of crisis.

Essay: A short literary composition on a single subject, usually reflecting on life or presenting the writer's view of some subject. There are two general divisions of essays, informal and formal. An *informal* essay generally has a personal flavor, uses humor, and has an easy, rambling style. It often reveals a great deal about the personality of the writer. A *formal* essay is sober, dignified, and logically organized; it is usually longer than an informal essay. Serious magazine articles and scientific reports are examples of formal essays. A well-known formal essay is the Declaration of Independence (p. 112), in which Thomas Jefferson enumerates the reasons why the American colonies should separate themselves from England. Ralph Waldo Emerson's "Self-Reliance" (p. 187) is another example of the formal essay. One type of formal essay is the *critical* essay, which deals with a particular work of art, a particular artist, or some issue concerning the arts. An example of the critical essay is Edgar Allan Poe's "A Theory of the Short Story" (p. 232).
See pages 56, 353.

Exaggeration: See **Hyperbole**.

Exposition: One of the four forms of discourse, exposition is explanatory information given in a piece of writing about characters, setting, time, and prior happenings so that the reader can understand the action that follows. The exposition provides the answers to the questions who, where, when, and why. The author may present the characters, setting, and basic situation in a block at the beginning of a piece of writing or, as in Thornton Wilder's *Our Town* (p. 469), a character (the Stage Manager) may provide exposition throughout the work. Lines of dialogue or descriptive sentences may present exposition less obviously. Even the names of the characters may provide exposition indirectly by giving indications of personality traits. In general, exposition is any writing that explains something. (See **Discourse**.)

Expressionism: A movement in literature and art emphasizing emotional content, subjective reactions of characters, and symbolic or abstract representations of reality. The expressionistic plays of August Strindberg, the Swedish dramatist, have had an important influence on modern American drama, especially on the work of Eugene O'Neill (p. 700).

Fable: A brief story that illustrates a lesson or moral. The characters are often animals that speak and act like people. James Thurber (p. 557) wrote many fables that are wisely critical of human behavior. (See **Anecdote, Fantasy.**)

Falling action: See **Dénouement, Plot**.

Fantasy: A piece of writing that consciously breaks free from reality. A fantasy may take place in a nonexistent or unreal world, as in a fable or fairy tale. Fantasy may also describe physical or scientific principles contrary to present experience. Sometimes fantasy is used purely to delight the reader. At other times it is used by the writer to make a satiric comment about the real world.

Feminine rhyme: A rhyme in which the last two syllables of two or more lines rhyme. The first syllable is accented, while the second is unaccented: *glancing, dancing.* The effect is one of delicacy, lightness, and sometimes restlessness. The rhythm feels hanging and incomplete. Feminine rhyme is also called weak rhyme. (See **Rhyme.**)

Fiction: A piece of writing created by the writer's imagination. Although fiction may spring from actual personal experience, it involves characters, scenes, and actions that the author imagines to advance the theme. Fiction is most often written in prose, such as short stories, novels, and dramas. Narrative poems such as Frost's "The Death of the Hired Man" (p. 651) can also be a form of fiction. According to the nineteenth-century American writer Henry James, the chief function of fiction is to entertain. Fiction may also give insights into other cultures or point up moral and psychological insights, as in Hawthorne's "Dr. Heidegger's Experiment" (p. 222). Fiction is one of the most telling ways for an individual to communicate a vision of the world.

Figurative language: Language that uses figures of speech, such as hyperbole, simile, metaphor, personification, symbol, or other forms of imagery. Figurative language is used to gain impact, freshness of expression, or pictorial effect. In "From the Dark Tower" (p. 693), Countee Cullen effectively uses figurative language both to catch the reader's attention and to express his own deep feelings about racial pride and prejudice. (See **Hyperbole, Metaphor, Personification, Simile, Symbol.**)

Flashback: A device or technique used by an author to present information about what has happened prior to the opening of a short story, novel, play, or narrative poem. It is often more dramatic or interest catching to "flash back" to the past to pick up necessary information than to present it in what might become a tedious chronological account. A device particularly useful in films, flashback may be thought of as a scene that interrupts a chronological narrative to supply information about the past. Flashback appears in literature in a variety of forms, including dream sequence, narratives by characters, and recollections such as those of Molly Morgan in John Steinbeck's book *The Pastures of Heaven* (p. 605). (See **Time sequence.**)

See also pages 615, 793.

Folk tale: A fictional piece of writing characterized by exaggerated characters and events, simple language or dialect, elemental emotions, and a story that has been passed down through generations. "The Celebrated Jumping Frog of Calaveras County." (p. 445) has elements of a folk tale. (See **Tall tale.**)

Foot: A single unit of accented and unaccented syllables that, when repeated, form the pattern we call rhythm. The most common English feet are the following:

iambic (˘´): Thĕ ráil/roăd tráck
trachaic (´˘): Márў/hád ă/líttlĕ/lámb
anapestic (˘˘´): Lĭke ă chíld
dactylic (´˘˘): Thís ĭs thĕ/fórĕst prĭ/
    mévăl
spondaic (´´): Gráy dáwn
pyrrhic (˘˘): Ănd ă

Lines are measured and named by the number of feet they contain. A line with one foot is called a *monometer*; two feet, *dimeter*; three feet, *trimeter*; four feet, *tetrameter*; five feet, *pentameter*; six feet, *hexameter*. (See **Anapest, Dactyl, Iamb, Pyrrhic, Rhythm, Spondee, Trochee.**)

See also page 148.

Foreshadowing: The hint or suggestion of a coming event used to create suspense and heighten the reader's interest. Foreshadowing is a technique the author can use to vary the time sequence of a plot. Stephen Vincent Benét uses foreshadowing in the opening paragraph of "Trials at Salem" (p. 70) to create suspense. (See **Plot, Suspense, Time sequence.**)

> See also pages 77, 793.

Form: See **Structure**.

Free verse: Poetry that has an irregular rhythmic beat instead of the usual metrical patterns. In conventional poetry, the metrical unit is the foot or the line; in free verse, the units are sometimes paragraphs or long stanzas. See, for example, Whitman's "One's-Self I Sing" (p. 316).

> See pages 314, 328, 662.

Gothic: In literature, a style characterized by gloomy settings, violent or grotesque action, and a mood of decay, degeneration, and decadence. These gothic elements are found in Edgar Allan Poe's "The Fall of the House of Usher" (p. 233).

Haiku: A seventeen-syllable poem that is purposely short enough to be spoken in one breath. The subject is one scene or observation. The imagist poets were influenced by Oriental verse forms, particularly by the haiku.

Half-rhyme: See **Consonance**.

Harlem Renaissance: A flowering of literature, especially poetry, by black writers during the 1920s and 1930s in the Harlem district of New York City.

> See page 632.

Hero: See **Protagonist**.

Humor: The literary expression of amusing or ridiculous incidents. Humor depends in part on the fact that a situation, statement, or personality trait is unexpected. Humor also depends on the reader's emotional distance from a situation. A third aspect of humor is its connection with wish fulfillment and fantasy. Humor involves the ability to see the comical and ludicrous aspects of a situation and to present them in an amusing way.

> See page 562.

Hyperbole: A figure of speech that uses obvious and intentional exaggeration for special effect. Hyperbole is often used by writers such as Mark Twain and James Thurber for humorous effect. (See **Figurative language.**)

> See also page 118.

Iamb (iambic foot): A foot of poetry consisting of one unaccented syllable followed by one accented syllable (˘´). (See **Foot.**)

Iambic pentameter: A line of poetry consisting of five iambic feet in which an unaccented syllable is followed by an accented syllable (˘´). Because the iambic pattern is the most natural in English, it occurs often in poetry, including blank verse. Iambic pentameter is the prescribed rhythm of the sonnet form. See, for example, Claude McKay's sonnet "America" (p. 676). (See **Blank verse.**)

Identification: The sense of recognition aroused in a reader by a sympathetic character. The reader may identify with a character who seems to have personality traits, feelings, or problems that are similar to the reader's own. The character may also have been in situations that the reader would like to experience.

Imagery: Words and phrases that appeal to the reader's senses and imagination. Imagery is created by using figures of speech, such as similes and metaphors, or vivid words to produce a mental picture. Note the picture evoked in the poem "Ars Poetica" (p. 684) when MacLeish says that a poem should be (among other things):

"Dumb / As old medallions to the thumb. . . ."

Imagism: The theory and practice of a group of early twentieth-century poets in Great Britain and the United States who believed that poetry should employ the language of common speech; have complete freedom in subject matter; create new rhythms; and present clear, precise, and concentrated images. Amy Lowell's "Night Clouds" and "Peace" (p. 643) are imagist poems. (See **Objectivism.**)

See also page 630.

Impressionism: A literary practice that does not stress reality but rather the impressions of the author (or one of the characters). Impressionism may also be defined as an artistic theory that claims that the dominant purpose of literature is to explain effects upon intellect, feelings, and conscience rather than to provide detailed descriptions of objective settings and events. Impressionism is a personal style of writing in which the author develops characters and paints scenes as they appear to him or her at a given moment rather than as they are (or may be) in actuality. (See **Expressionism, Imagism, Stream of consciousness, Surrealism, Symbolism.**)

Intention: The effect or the meaning that the writer wishes the work to have. We typically discover intention, however, not from direct statements by the writer but rather from inferences we make from the work itself. (See **Theme.**)

See pages 42, 77.

Internal rhyme: Rhyme that occurs within a line of poetry. The rhyme is usually with the end-line word, as in this line from Sidney Lanier's "Song of the Chattahoochee" (p. 377): "And the lordly *main* from beyond the *plain*."

Irony: The contrast between appearance and reality. This incongruity may be between what a speaker says and what the words actually mean (*verbal irony*). Note that verbal irony is conscious if a character deliberately conceals the truth. It is unconscious if the character does not understand the full meaning of his or her statements. The incongruity may also be between what a character expects and what actually happens (*situational irony*) Situational irony is demonstrated in "A Mystery of Heroism" (p. 416) when the water is spilled at the end of the story. Sometimes irony arises because of the contrast between what a character knows and what the reader realizes (*dramatic irony*). Irony, like humor, may surprise the reader with the unexpected. However, the ironic surprise comes from the contrast between the truth and what merely appears to be true. As a literary technique, irony can range from the light and amusing to the more grimly serious.

See pages 423, 465, 763.

Journal: A daily personal record of occurrences, observations, and experiences. Sarah Kemble Knight's (p. 43) journal of 1704 provides the modern reader with a detailed picture of provincial New England at the beginning of the eighteenth century. (See **Autobiography.**)

See also pages 29, 48.

Legend: A tradition or story handed down from earlier times and popularly accepted as true. "It Was the Wind that Gave Them Life" (p. 58) is an account of Creation based on ancient Navaho legend.

See page 57

Local color: See **Regionalism.**

Lyric poetry: Poetry that explores a person's intimate emotions and sensations. A lyric poem has as its focus a single subject or mood. It creates a single, intense impression for the reader through its use of vivid language. Its sound pattern may come close to sounding like music. Sara Teasdale's "The Solitary" (p. 666) and "The Look" (p. 667) are fine examples of lyric poetry.

See page 675.

Masculine rhyme: A rhyme of the final accented syllable in two or more lines: *joy, toy.* Masculine rhyme has a forceful, vigorous effect. Masculine rhyme is also called *strong rhyme.* (See **Feminine rhyme, Rhyme.**)

Measure: See **Meter.**

Metaphor: An implied comparison between two unlike things. In "A Little Uncomplicated Hymn" (p. 808), poet Anne Sexton creates a metaphor when she calls her child's ribs "those delicate trees." Metaphor is closely allied to *simile,* which is a stated comparison—generally introduced by *like* or *as*—between two things. If Sexton had written "Your ribs are like trees," she would have written a simile. Both metaphor and simile are figures of speech. (See **Analogy, Simile.**)

Metaphysics: Investigation of and speculation about objects, ideas, and realms beyond what can be known from direct observation and experience. *Metaphysical poetry* is a term applied to writing that is highly intellectual and philosophical, that makes extensive use of ingenious conceits, and that usually combines intense emotion with mental ingenuity. Among leading American poets of this school are Edward Taylor (p. 33) and T. S. Eliot (p. 670).

Meter: A rhythmic pattern determined by the number and kind of feet in a line of poetry. Meter is also called *measure.* (See **Foot, Rhythm, Scansion.**)

See also page 148.

Moment of illumination: The moment in a story at which its full meaning becomes clear. At such moments, all the parts of the story fit into place, and the reader sees the unity of the whole.

See page 222.

Monologue: In a play, a lengthy speech by one character; in a prose piece, an extended record of a single character's thoughts. This literary technique gives the reader an intimate sense of the character. (See **Soliloquy.**)

Mood: The tone that prevails in a literary work. The mood that Edgar Allan Poe establishes in "The Fall of the House of Usher" (p. 233) is one of decay and horror. (See **Atmosphere, Tone.**)

Myth: See **Legend.**

Narration: One of the four chief forms of discourse, narration is writing or speaking that tells a story that may be as long as a novel or as short as a fable. A poem that tells a story is also an example of narration. (See **Discourse.**)

Narrative poetry: Poetry that tells a story. The epic and the ballad are types of narrative poems. Robert Frost's "The Death of the Hired Man" (p. 651) and Edgar Allan Poe's "The Raven" are two of the best-known narrative poems in American literature.

Narrator: The person in a literary work who is telling the story. The narrator may be a character in the work or the author of the piece. (See **Point of view.**)

Naturalism: In literature, an attempt to achieve fidelity to nature by rejecting idealized portrayals of life. Naturalistic writers hold that human existence is shaped by heredity and environment, over which one has no control and can exercise little, if any, choice. Naturalistic literature, emphasizing the animal nature of human beings, portrays characters engrossed in a brutal struggle for survival. The most highly regarded American naturalistic writers are Stephen Crane, Frank Norris, and Theodore Dreiser. (See **Determinism, Realism, Romanticism.**)

See also page 363.

Nonfiction: A factual report dealing with events and people that exist or existed in real life. *Documentary nonfiction* includes biographies and news articles in which the writer presents objective facts about the subject. *Literary nonfiction* includes autobiographies, memoirs, and personal essays in which the writer is more subjective in making judgments and interpreting facts. N. Scott Momaday's *A Vision Beyond Time and Place* (p. 825) is an example of literary nonfiction.

Novel: A fictional prose piece. Broadly, a novel is written to entertain, to present an issue, or to give a historical background. Like the short story, the novel is developed through characterization, plot, and setting. The basic difference between a short story and a novel is length. Since a novel is much longer, it has greater scope. It can therefore deal with more characters who can change and develop over time. A novel can also include subplots in addition to the main conflict, which can be more complex than in a short story. Finally, a novelist can vary the settings and give them more details than a short story writer can. (See **Characterization, Plot, Setting.**)

See also pages 505, 520, 727.

Objectivism: A term first used by William Carlos Williams to refer to poetry in which objects are perceived, selected, and presented for their value simply as objects, rather than for their capability to serve as symbols of emotions or concepts. A good example of objectivism is Williams's poem "The Red Wheelbarrow" (p. 664). Note how the first two lines ("so much depends / upon") alert the reader at the outset to the poet's insistence on *perceiving* the objects in the poem as they simply are, rather than as symbols of some idea in the poet's mind. (See **Imagism.**)

Octave: An eight-line unit of poetry, such as the first eight lines of an Italian sonnet. In such a sonnet, these lines present a problem or issue that is either resolved or reacted to in the following six lines, or sestet. (See **Sonnet.**)

Ode: A lyric poem with a dignified theme that is phrased in a formal, elevated style. Odes are often written for a special occasion.

See page 312.

Onomatopoeia: The use of words whose sounds suggest their meaning, such as *moo, buzz,* and *snap.* In these opening lines from Edgar Allan Poe's "The Bells" (p. 248), the word *tinkle* is onomatopoeic:

> Hear the sledges with the bells
> Silver bells!
> What a world of merriment their melody foretells!
> How they tinkle, tinkle, tinkle,
> In the icy air of night!

See page 251.

Oral literature: Literature that is not written down but passed on by word of mouth. Indian songs and Negro spirituals are oral literature, as are many traditional ballads.

See pages 10, 57.

Oratory (or **rhetoric**): The art of public speaking. Effective public speaking makes use of repetition, rhythm, irony, alliteration, vivid imagery, and allusions. Public speakers try to reach their audiences with short, clear, and concise sentences. For examples of oratory, see Patrick Henry's "Liberty or Death" speech (p. 101) and Abraham Lincoln's "Gettysburg Address" (p. 304).

Parable: A brief, simple story about common everyday affairs that is designed to teach the reader something. A parable illustrates a profound moral or religious truth. Hawthorne gave the subtitle "A Parable" to his story "The Minister's Black Veil" (p. 213). (See **Allegory, Fable.**)

Parody: A humorous imitation of a character, a literary work, or a manner of speaking. The imitation is often amusing because of the exaggeration of the original.

Pathos: In literature, an ability or power to call forth feelings of pity, compassion, and sadness. In "The People Will Live On" (p. 659), Sandburg uses pathos to invoke the reader's sympathy for the general plight of humanity.

Personification: A figure of speech in which animals, ideas, or inanimate objects are given human qualities. A personification is a kind of metaphor. Carl Sandburg personifies Chicago in his poem by the same name (p. 658) by speaking to the city as though it possessed human attributes. (See **Metaphor.**)

See page 118.

Persuasion: One of the four forms of discourse, persuasion (also known as argumentation) is writing or speaking that tries to move a listener or reader toward a particular belief or action. Newspaper editorials and television commercials are examples of written and spoken persuasion. Jonathan Edwards's sermon "Sinners in the Hands of an Angry God" (p. 54) is an example of a persuasive essay. (See **Discourse.**)

See also pages 56, 100, 115.

Plot: The arrangement of incidents in a piece of literature. In a well-constructed plot, each incident develops logically from a previous event. The three major elements of plot are exposition, conflict, and climax. Some writers consider characterization more important than plot, which they feel is only a mechanical way to display characters. For the reader, plot is the element that gives structure and unity to the narrative. (See **Climax, Conflict, Dénouement, Exposition.**)

See also page 221.

Poetry: The term describing the many rhythmic forms people use to express profound and imaginative views of their world and their relationship with it. Poetry is generally characterized by its vivid language and emotional power. Richard Lederer, chairman of the English Department of St. Paul's School, Concord, New Hampshire, captures the essence of poetry in these words: "Poetry is the heartbeat of life. Poems are life transmuted into diamonds, compact, and indestructible. The first literature of every country is its poetry. It is the oldest language we have, the most primitive, the most elemental, and the most natural expression of ourselves as human beings" (*The New Yorker,* May 16, 1983). It is generally agreed that there are three elements common to most poetry: a specific content, a more or less definite form, and a particular effect.

See pages 143, 441, 629, 645, 656, 675, 801.

Point of view: The observation point from which the author tells the story. The two basic points of view are first person, "I," and third person, "he, she, it." A first-person point of view tends to involve the reader more and to encourage identification and sympathy with the characters. If the first-person narrator is the main character in the story, the author is using a *first-person participant* point of view. If the first-person narrator is not the main character, the point of view is *first-person observer*, as in Melville's "Bartleby" (p. 255). A story told in the third person that concentrates on the thoughts of one character uses a *third-person limited* point of view. Eudora Welty's "A Worn Path" (p. 740) is an example. The author may also use a *third-person omniscient* point of view to let the reader know the thoughts of several characters. This technique is used in Porter's "The Jilting of Granny Weatherall" (p. 549). Analysis of a playwright's point of view is more complex, since it is usually behind the scenes. In a drama, the individual characters reveal their point of view in their speeches. (See **Narrator.**)

    See also pages 29, 555, 777, 813.

Propaganda: See **Persuasion**.

Prose: A literary piece that is not written in a rhythmic pattern. Unlike poetry, prose cannot be broken down into units of metrical feet. The reasons an author has for writing a piece of prose determine the way it is organized and worded. A novel written for entertainment is quite different from a scientific report on the life cycle of the medfly, but both are prose.

Protagonist (or **hero**): In a literary work, the main character in whom the reader has the greatest interest. The protagonist must be a *rounded character*, that is, one who shows enough different qualities and personality traits to seem human and believable. The enemy of a protagonist is an *antagonist*. (See **Character.**)

Pun: A humorous play on words in which a word or phrase has two or more meanings. In Flannery O'Connor's "The Life You Save May Be Your Own" (p. 764), Mr. Shiflet makes a pun when he says he had been in the "Arm Service." Obviously, he means the Armed Service. As Mr. Shiflet has lost half of one arm, the author is making a pun on *arm* and *armed*.

Pyrrhic (**pyrrhic foot**): A foot of poetry consisting of two unaccented syllables (ˇ ˇ). Like the spondee, it is often substituted for a few syllables in a poem of mainly iambic feet to give a quick, light feeling. (See **Foot, Meter.**)

Quatrain: A four-line unit of a poem with a particular rhyme scheme. Quatrains usually follow an *abab*, *abba*, or *abcb* rhyme scheme. The subject of a quatrain is usually a variation on the basic theme of the poem. Emily Dickinson's "This Is My Letter to the World" (p. 433) is a poem composed of two quatrains. (See **Rhyme scheme.**)

Realism: In literature, a theory of writing in which the familiar, ordinary aspects of life are depicted in a matter-of-fact, straightforward manner designed to reflect life as it actually is. In its careful descriptions of everday life, realism often deals with the lives of the so-called middle or lower classes. (See **Naturalism, Romanticism.**)

    See also pages 358, 362.

Refrain: A group of words, usually a phrase or a sentence, repeated at intervals in a poem and generally at the end of a stanza. Perhaps the most famous refrain in American literature is the line repeated at the end of several stanzas of Edgar Allan Poe's "The Raven":

    Quoth the Raven, "Nevermore."

Regionalism: In literature, an emphasis on the accurate portrayal of life in a particular geographical region. The term may be used interchangeably with *local-color* writing, but sometimes the latter term has a narrower and less favorable connotation, as though the local colorist were interested in the region mainly for its oddities. Mary E. Wilkins Freeman and Willa Cather are American regionalists.

    See pages 360, 376, 385.

Resolution: The outcome of a conflict in a literary work. The resolution of a story, play, or novel becomes clear when the work reaches its climax. (See **Climax, Dénouement.**)

Revelation: See **Moment of illumination.**

Rhetoric: See **Oratory.**

Rhyme: In poetry, the repetition and variation of similar sounds to create a pattern. The rhyme may emphasize or vary the poem's basic rhythm; it is also the device used to set off particular lines as separate units, or stanzas. The two types of rhyme are masculine and feminine. *Masculine rhymes* are those that rhyme the final accented syllable in two or more lines. *Feminine rhymes* are those that rhyme the last two syllables of two or more lines; the first syllable is accented and the second is unaccented. (See **End-rhyme, Internal rhyme, Rhyme scheme.**)

      See also page 802.

Rhyme scheme: The pattern of end-rhymes in a poem. To determine the rhyme scheme used, designate the word at the end of the first line as *a*. Every other end word that rhymes with this word is also *a*. The next different end word is designated *b*, and so forth. For example, a rhyme scheme *abab* is a quatrain in which every other line rhymes. (See **End-rhyme.**)

Rhythm: The repetition of regular patterns of accented and unaccented syllables. Rhythm is described in terms of the type and number of metrical feet that appear most frequently in the poem as a whole. A *foot*, the basic unit of measurement, is the single combination of accented and unaccented syllables that, when repeated, form the pattern called rhythm. Rhythm is seldom constant throughout a poem, but varies to suit the mood. Changes in rhythm are produced by substituting different metrical

feet and by changing the pattern of rhymes at the ends of the lines. Use of alliteration, assonance, and consonance also produces variety. Ideally, the rhythm of a poem complements its ideas and feelings and reinforces its mood. To determine the rhythm of a poem, read it aloud (See **Alliteration, Assonance, Consonance, Foot.**)

Romanticism: The term *romanticism* cannot be precisely applied to a specific state of mind, point of view, or literary technique. It may be called a literary attitude in which imagination is considered more important than formal rules, reason, and a sense of fact. In effect, romanticism places emphasis on the individual as opposed to social convention and tradition; on mystery and the supernatural as opposed to common sense; on the infinite as opposed to the finite; on the imaginative and emotional as opposed to the rational. Romanticism appeals to the heart rather than to the head. (See **Classicism, Realism, Transcendentalism.**)

     See also pages 165, 358.

Run-on line: A line of poetry having a thought that carries over to the next line without a pause. In the following lines from John Crowe Ransom's "Parting, Without a Sequel" (p. 674), there are two run-on lines:
> Then all the blood
> Forsook the face. She was too pale
> for tears,
> Observing the ruin of her younger
> years.

(See **End-stopped line.**)

Sarcasm: See **Irony.**

Satire: A literary technique in which the author ridicules certain kinds of behavior in order to change them. Satire can run from gentle scoffing to scathing mockery. While readers may sympathize with a humorous or ironic character, they do not usually find character traits that are the object of satire likable or sympathetic. In the excerpt from *The Adventures of Huckleberry Finn* (p. 456), Mark Twain satirizes Huck's taste in poetry and the furnishing of the Grangerford home described by Huck.

Scansion: The division of a line of poetry into metrical feet by indicating accented and unaccented syllables. In scansion, the diacritical mark (˘) indicates an unaccented syllable. The mark (′) indicates a stressed syllable. A vertical line (/) is used to separate metrical feet. Scansion enables the reader to determine the meter of a poem and to see how a poet establishes rhythmical effects. (See **Foot, Meter.**)

See also page 149.

Sestet: A unit of six lines of verse. In an Italian sonnet, these six lines of verse resolve or react to the issue raised in the preceding octave (eight lines of verse). A sestet usually has a rhyme scheme of *cdedce* or *cdccdc* and may or may not be set off as a stanza. (See **Sonnet.**)

Setting: The time and place in which events occur in a literary work. The setting contributes to the atmosphere and theme of a work. Plot and setting are usually related elements that are dependent on each other. The fiendish setting of Washington Irving's "The Devil and Tom Walker" (p. 125) is certainly consistent with the mood of the narrative. (See **Atmosphere, Exposition, Plot, Theme.**)

See also pages 133, 221, 229, 246.

Short story: A relatively brief fictional narrative in prose. There have always been stories in one form or another, springing from an inborn creative need to tell and to hear stories. Ancient Egyptians, the Hebrews in Palestine, the Greeks and the Romans, and so on to this day, all told stories. In America, the short story flowered with such speed and brilliance that it is sometimes called an American art form. Edgar Allan Poe tried to define the genre, but modern writers have since gone beyond the bounds of his definition. It is safe to say, though, that the short story, like the novel, is developed through characterization, plot, and setting. The basic difference between a novel and a short story is length. A short story may be only 500 words long (the short-short story), or it may run from 12,000 to 15,000 words (the novelette). Unlike a novel, a short story has the scope to present only a limited number of major characters. In addition, a short story generally focuses on one principal conflict that is immediately established. Finally, a short story is unlike the novel in that there is usually a single setting.

See pages 221, 232, 524, 732.

Simile: A figure of speech in which a comparison is made between two unlike things using the words *like* or *as*. Similes are an important literary device because they enable writers to convey what is unfamiliar in terms of something familiar. Thus what is unknown takes on the qualities of what is known. For example, in Robert Frost's "Birches" (p. 646), the ice-bent trees are said to look "Like girls on hands and knees that throw their hair / Before them over their heads to dry in the sun." (See **Analogy, Metaphor.**)

Situational irony: See **Irony**.

Slant rhyme: See **Consonance**.

Soliloquy: A speech, usually in a play, delivered by a character who is alone or who thinks she or he is alone. A soliloquy reveals to the audience what the character is thinking or gives information that is important for understanding the action of the play.

Song: A lyric poem that can be set to music. Song lyrics are usually short, simple, and emotional. The three Chippewa love songs (p. 63) express hope, exultation, and sadness.

See pages 61, 296.

Sonnet: A rigidly structured poem of fourteen lines in a single stanza written in iambic pentameter and using one of two set rhyme schemes. There are two major forms of the sonnet, the Shakespearean and the Petrarchan, or Italian. The *Shakespearean* sonnet consists of three quatrains (a four-line unit) and ends with a rhymed couplet (a two-line unit) that usually comments on the first twelve lines. The rhyme scheme is *abab cdcd efef gg.* See, for example, Claude McKay's "America" (p. 676). The *Italian* sonnet is divided into an octave (an eight-line unit) with the rhyme scheme *abba abba* and a sestet (a six-line unit) with a rhyme scheme that is usually *cdccdc* or *cdedce.* The octave presents the subject—a doubt, a reflection, or a problem—and the sestet resolves or reacts to the octave. "From the Dark Tower" (p. 693) by Countee Cullen is a variation of the Italian sonnet form; the last six lines rhyme *ccddee.* (See **Rhyme scheme.**)

See also pages 798, 802.

Spondee (spondaic foot): A foot of poetry consisting of two accented syllables. (″). The spondee is often used for a few syllables as a substitute for the iambic foot. Since most multisyllabic words in English have accented and unaccented syllables, English poetry generally uses two monosyllabic words to form a spondee. *Fóotbáll* is one of the few examples in English of a one-word spondee. The slow, heavy spondaic rhythm adds a feeling of force and importance to the poetic line. (See **Foot, Meter.**)

Stanza: A subdivision of a poem consisting of two or more lines that use a common pattern of rhythm, rhyme, and length. Stanzas are easily recognized because of their fixed patterns of rhymes and number of lines. Stanzas are generally set off by extra space above and below their first and last lines. Stanzas often reflect the thought divisions of a poem, each stanza developing a differ-

ent aspect of the theme. Because different stanzas may deal with separate thoughts, the stanza may be compared to a paragraph in prose. (See **Couplet, Octave, Quatrain, Sestet.**)

Stereotype: See **Character.**

Stream of consciousness: A technique used by writers to show the thoughts, feelings, associations, reflections, and memories that flow in random fashion through a character's mind. It is one of the most revealing means of psychological characterization, since it brings the reader and the character close together without the intrusion of others. Katherine Anne Porter demonstrates this device for in-depth characterization in "The Jilting of Granny Weatherall" (p. 549).

See page 555.

Stress (or **accent**): The emphasis given to a syllable in a poetic foot. Repetition of combined accented and unaccented syllables results in the pattern we call *rhythm.* (See **Foot, Rhythm.**)

See also page 148.

Strong rhyme: See **Masculine rhyme.**

Structure (or **form** or **organization**): The planned framework of a piece of literature. In a poem, structure refers to stanza divisions, verse form, and rhythm patterns; it also includes the arrangement of images and ideas in the poem that produces one dominant impression. In drama, structure is the logical division of the play into acts and scenes. In a short story or novel, plot is considered the basic framework. In a formal essay, structure is the outline for presenting the information.

See pages 103, 547, 637, 793.

Style: The distinctive, individual quality that distinguishes the work of one writer from another. The style of writing includes the author's choice of words, use of figurative language, and grammatical structure. Style also reflects the personality of the writer as well as the historical period in which the author writes. Style is an important element in poetry for conveying meaning since there is little room for an elaborate exposition.

See pages 21, 42, 97, 115, 189, 199, 455, 599.

Subplot: A minor conflict, as distinguished from the principal, central conflict in a literary work. (See **Conflict.**)

Surrealism: A style in literature and painting that stresses the subconscious or the nonrational aspects of human existence. In "The Fall of the House of Usher" (p. 233), Poe makes use of surrealism in his description of the decayed mansion and its deranged occupants. (See **Expressionism, Romanticism.**)

Suspense: The technique of keeping the reader uncertain, anxious, or apprehensive about what is going to happen in the story, especially to a character with whom the reader is sympathetic. Suspense is a valuable tool in gaining and holding the reader's interest. If the ending is uncertain, suspense lies in trying to outguess the author, as in "A Horseman in the Sky" (p. 397). If the ending is inevitable, the suspense lies in the reader's apprehension about when and where it will occur, as in "Bernice Bobs Her Hair" (p. 567). (See **Foreshadowing, Plot.**)

Symbol: An object, a character, or an event that stands for something else. Its meaning goes beyond its literal significance. A *conventional* symbol is an object, a character, or an event that is generally acknowledged as representing something else. For example, the image of Uncle Sam is a conventional

symbol of the United States, and a picture of an airplane on a map symbolizes an airport. Conventional symbols are found all around us—on traffic signs, for example, and as trademarks and insignias. A *contextual* symbol is one that grows out of the particular context of a literary work. For example, in the last six lines of "Birches" (p. 646), Frost makes the birch tree an appropriate symbol of a human's dilemma: the desire both to escape the earth and to return to it.

Symbolism: The practice of representing objects or ideas by symbols or of giving things a symbolic character and meaning. Symbolism is also applied to a nineteenth-century movement in the literature and art of France that was a revolt against realism. Symbolists of this era tried to suggest various aspects of life through the use of symbols and images.

See pages 673, 745, 772.

Sympathy and detachment (or **distance**): The "distance" between character and author or character and reader. If we feel close to a character, we are sympathetic; we identify with him or her. If we stand apart from a character, we speak of ourselves as "detached"; we tend to be observers of her or him.

See page 763.

Tall tale: A simple, humorous narrative using realistic details and common speech to relate extravagant happenings. The main character of a tall tale is often a superhuman figure. (See **Folk tale.**)

See also page 454.

Tension: An unsettled state induced in the reader at or near the beginning of a literary work. Generally, a work of literature moves from tension to relaxation, from relative instability to relative stability. (See **Conflict.**)

Theme: The central, underlying meaning or main idea of a literary work. The theme is conveyed through the characters, images, and action. Usually the theme is not stated directly. However, after reading a selection, the reader can usually determine the theme by completing the following sentence: "In this selection, the writer is trying to show. . . ." In poetry, the theme is often implied in the title, in certain key words, and in the figurative language used.

Time sequence: The framework in which an author unfolds the plot of a literary work. Events may develop chronologically, in the order in which they happen. See, for example, the development of the plot in "Testimony of Trees" (p. 617). Techniques that vary the chronological time sequence include *flashback*, shown in the selection from *The Pastures of Heaven* (p. 605), and *foreshadowing*, used in "Average Waves in Unprotected Waters" (p. 787). (See **Flashback, Foreshadowing.**)

Tone: The writer's attitude toward the subject. In prose, tone may be revealed by the author's word choice, arrangement of ideas and events, and use of literary techniques, such as humor, irony, and satire. In poetry, tone is conveyed by rhythm, rhyme, choice of words, images, length of lines, and even punctuation and the arrangement of the words on the page. Tone may also refer to the writer's attitude toward the reader. (See **Atmosphere, Mood.**)

See also page 209.

Tragedy: A literary work with a serious theme carried to a catastrophic conclusion. Traditionally, tragedy traces the career of a noble person whose character is flawed by some defect (jealousy, excessive ambition, pride, and the like) and whose actions cause him or her to break some moral precept or divine law, with ensuing downfall and de-

struction. Though defeated, the tragic hero usually gains a measure of wisdom or self-awareness. (See **Comedy, Conflict.**)

Transcendentalism: A form of philosophical romanticism that places reliance on human intuition and conscience. Transcendentalism holds that human inner consciousness is divine, that the whole of God's moral law is revealed in nature, and that ultimate truth can be discovered by people's inmost feelings and a morality guided by conscience. (See **Romanticism.**)

See also pages 165, 168.

Trochee (trochaic foot): A foot of poetry consisting of an accented syllable followed by an unaccented syllable (´˘). The trochee is often used for emphasis, variety, or feeling in a poem using mostly iambic feet. The rhythm of the trochee is best suited to light poems and songs and hence is often found in nursery rhymes such as "Márў hád ă líttlĕ lámb." (See **Foot, Rhythm.**)

Turning point: See **Climax.**

Understatement: The saying of less than what one truly means or the representation of something as less than it is in fact. Understatement is a form of irony; it is the opposite of exaggeration, or overstating one's meaning.

Verse: A single line of poetry.

Villanelle: A short poem of fixed form written in five three-line stanzas and a concluding four-line stanza. Only two rhymes are employed in the entire length (nineteen lines) of a villanelle. Elizabeth Bishop's "One Art" (p. 797) is a villanelle that varies slightly from traditional form. (See **Rhyme scheme.**)

Weak rhyme: See **Feminine rhyme.**

GLOSSARY

This Glossary contains those relatively common yet difficult words used in the selections contained in this book. Many of the words occur two or more times in the book. The definitions are in accord with how the words are used in the selections.

Technical, archaic, obscure, and foreign words are footnoted with the selections as they occur.

The pronunciation symbols used in both the Glossary and the footnotes follow the system used in the *Thorndike/Barnhardt Advanced Dictionary* (1979). For words having more than one pronunciation, the first pronunciation is the one used here, and regional pronunciations may therefore vary from some pronunciations provided in this Glossary.

Syllable division and stress marks for primary and secondary accent marks used in the pronunciations also follow the system used in the *Advanced Dictionary*, including putting stress marks after the syllables stressed.

The following abbreviations are used to indicate parts of speech:

n. noun	*adj.* adjective
v. verb	*adv.* adverb

abuse (ə byüs′) *n.* rough or cruel treatment.
accelerate (ak sel′ə rāt) *v.* speed up; hasten.
accomplished (ə kom′plisht) *adj.* expert; skilled.
accoutrements (ə kü′trə mənts) *n.* equipment.
accumulate (ə kyü′myə lāt) *v.* collect little by little.
accustomed (ə kus′təmd) *adj.* usual; habitual.
acquiesce (ak′wē es′) *v.* agree to; consent.
acquisition (ak′wə zish′ən) *n.* something one gets by continued effort.
admirably (ad′mər ə blē) *adv.* most satisfactorily.
admission (ad mish′ən) *n.* confession; an admitting that something is true.
admonishing (ad mon′ish ing) *adj.* gently scolding; warning.
admonition (ad′mə nish′ən) *n.* earnest advice; a warning.
advent (ad′vent) *n.* a coming; an arrival.
adversary (ad′vər ser′ē) *n.* an opponent.
adversity (ad vėr′sə tē) *n.* great misfortune.
affable (af′ə bəl) *adj.* courteous and pleasant.
affectations (af′ek tā′shənz) *n.* mannerisms or behavior assumed to impress others; pretenses.
afflicted (ə flikt′əd) *adj.* suffering severely.

affliction (ə flik′shən) *n.* condition of continued distress; misfortune; misery.
aggravates (ag′rə vāts) *v.* annoys; irritates.
aggravating (ag′rə vāt′ing) *v.* annoying; irritating.
aghast (ə gast′) *adj.* horrified; dumbfounded.
agitation (aj′ə tā′shən) *n.* a violent moving or shaking.
agony (ag′ə nē) *n.* great emotional distress.
ague (ā′gyü) *n.* any fit of shaking or shivering. Also, a fever marked by shivering.
alacrity (ə lak′rə tē) *n.* quickness; liveliness.
allegiance (ə lē′jəns) *n.* the loyalty citizens owe their country.
alleviation (ə lē′vē ā′shən) *n.* a lessening; a making easier to bear.
allotted (ə lot′əd) *v.* assigned.
ambiguity (am′bə gyü′ə tē) *n.* lack of clarity; vagueness; uncertainty.
amble (am′bəl) *n.* an easy, slow pace in walking.
ambush (am′bush) *n.* a secret or concealed place where soldiers or others lie in wait to make a surprise attack.
amends (ə mendz′) *n.* something done to make up for a wrong or an injury done.
ample (am′pəl) *adj.* abundant; more than enough.
anguish (ang′gwish) *n.* great despair; extreme mental pain or suffering.
anguished (ang′gwisht) *adj.* tormented; filled with extreme mental pain; distressed.
animation (an′ə mā′shən) *n.* liveliness of manner.
annexed (ə nekst′) *v.* added to.
annuity (ə nü′ə tē) *n.* an investment that provides a fixed yearly income during one's lifetime.
anticipate (an tis′ə pāt) *v.* expect; look forward to.
appalled (ə pôld′) *v.* shocked; filled with horror.
apprehending (ap′ri hend′ing) *n.* arresting.
apprehension (ap′ri hen′shən) *n.* expectation of misfortune; fear; dread of impending danger.
appropriate (ə prō′prē it) *adj.* especially right or proper for the occasion; suitable.
arbitrary (är′bə trer′ē) *adj.* based on one's wishes or will, not on law or rules; using or abusing unlimited power; tyrannical.
arduous (är′jü əs) *adj.* hard to do; difficult.
aristocratic (ə ris′tə krat′ik) *adj.* stylish or grand in tastes, opinions, and manners; snobbish.
arrayed (ə rād′) *v.* dressed in fine clothes.
arrogance (ar′ə gəns) *n.* excessive pride.
arrogantly (ar′ə gənt lē) *adv.* in an overbearing, rude manner.

articulate (är tik′yə lit) *adj.* distinctly marked off.

artifice (är′tə fis) *n.* a clever device.

artificial (är′tə fish′əl) *adj.* not natural; man-made.

ascertainable (as′ər tān′ə bəl) *adj.* able to be determined; making sure of.

ascribed (ə skrībd′) *v.* thought of as caused by or coming from.

askance (ə skans′) *adv.* with disapproval and distrust.

assailed (ə sāld′) *v.* attacked with hostile words, arguments, etc.

assessors (ə ses′ərz) *n.* persons who estimate the value of property or income for taxation.

associated (ə sō′shē āt əd) *v.* connected with.

assurance (ə shur′əns) *n.* certainty; confidence.

assured (ə shurd′) *adj.* certain; confident.

asunder (ə sun′dər) *adv.* into pieces.

attainted (ə tānt′əd) *adj.* utterly disgraced.

auspicious (ô spish′əs) *adj.* favorable; with signs that point to a successful outcome.

austere (ô stir′) *adj.* stern; harsh.

authenticity (ô′then tis′ə tē) *n.* genuineness; condition of being real and true.

avarice (av′ər is) *n.* too great a desire for money or property; greed for wealth.

aversion (ə vėr′zhən) *n.* a strong or fixed dislike.

badgered (baj′ərd) *adj.* tormented by nagging.

banal (bə nal′) *adj.* commonplace; trite.

barbarous (bär′bər əs) *adj.* not civilized; savage.

barrier (bar′ē ər) *n.* something that separates or keeps apart.

beldames (bel′dəmz) *n.* old women.

beleaguered (bi lē′gərd) *adj.* being surrounded by armed forces in order to cause surrender.

bellicose (bel′ə kōs) *adj.* quarrelsome and angry.

benign (bi nīn′) *adj.* kindly in feeling; gracious.

bereft (bi reft′) *adj.* left desolate and alone.

beseech (bi sēch′) *v.* ask earnestly; beg.

bestow (bi stō′) *v.* give as a gift.

boisterous (boi′stər əs) *adj.* noisy and loud.

bondage (bon′dij) *n.* lack of freedom; slavery.

bounteous (boun′tē əs) *adj.* plentiful; abundant.

buccaneering (buk′ə nir ing) *n.* using unlawful means.

budge (buj) *v.* move slightly.

cached (kasht) *v.* hid; put in a safe place.

calamity (kə lam′ə tē) *n.* a great misfortune, such as a flood or fire, or a personal loss.

canvassing (kan′vəs ing) *v.* examining to discover how a group will vote. Also, seeking votes.

capacity (kə pas′ə tē) *n.* ability to learn or do.

capitulate (kə pich′ə lāt) *v.* surrender, usually on certain terms or conditions; give in.

cargo (kär′gō) *n.* load of goods carried by a ship or an aircraft; freight.

caricature (kar′ə kə chúr) *n.* a drawing that exaggerates the peculiarities or defects of a person.

carnage (kär′nij) *n.* slaughter of many people.

caulk (kôk) *v.* fill up to prevent leaking; make watertight.

caution (kô′shən) *n.* great care; regard for safety.

cautious (kô′shəs) *adj.* very careful.

cavalcade (kav′əl kād) *n.* a procession of people on horseback.

celestial (sə les′chəl) *adj.* heavenly; very good or beautiful.

celibacy (sel′ə bə sē) *n.* unmarried state.

censure (sen′shər) *n.* expression of disapproval.

censurer (sen′shər ər) *n.* critic; one who disapproves of the actions of others.

ceremonial (ser′ə mō′nē əl) *adj.* very formal.

chastise (cha stīz′) *v.* punish; reprove or scold.

chastising (cha stīz′ing) *adj.* punishing.

circumstantial (sėr′kəm stan′shəl) *adj.* based or depending on appearance rather than on fact.

citations (sī tā′shənz) *n.* honorable mentions for bravery in war.

civilized (siv′ə līzd) *adj.* refined; showing culture and good manners.

clarity (klar′ə tē) *n.* clearness.

clemency (klem′ən sē) *n.* mercy or leniency.

collapse (kə laps′) *v.* fall in; cave in; break down. *n.* a falling or caving in; a breakdown; failure.

combatants (kəm bat′nts) *n.* persons who are fighting each other.

comely (kum′lē) *adj.* pleasing; pleasant to look at.

commemorate (kə mem′ə rāt) v. honor the memory of a person or an event.

commendably (kə men′də blē) adv. in a praiseworthy manner.

commotion (kə mō′shən) n. bustle or stir.

compassion (kəm pash′ən) n. feeling for another's sorrow or hardship leading to help; sympathy.

compel (kəm pel′) v. force someone to do something against his or her will.

competently (kom′pə tənt lē) adv. capably.

complacently (kəm plā′snt lē) adv. in a self-satisfied manner.

compliance (kəm plī′əns) n. doing as another asks; acting in agreement with a request; consenting to do as another asks or suggests.

compulsory (kəm pul′sər ē) adj. required.

conceited (kən sē′tid) adj. having too high an opinion of oneself or one's ability; vain.

conciliatory (kən sil′ē ə tôr′ē) adj. soothing or calming.

condemned (kən demd′) adj. and v. doomed; sentenced.

confiscation (kon′fə skā′shən) n. a seizing or taking and keeping for the public treasury.

conformity (kən fôr′mə tē) n. action in agreement with a generally accepted set of standards.

confounded (kon′foun′did) adj. confused.

conjecture (kən jek′chər) n. a guess; supposition. v. guess; suppose to be true.

conqueror (kong′kər ər) n. a victor; a person who gets something by fighting or by winning a war.

conscious (kon′shəs) adj. being aware.

consecrate (kon′sə krāt) v. make holy or sacred; honor.

consequence (kon′sə kwens) n. importance; a result; an effect.

consistency (kən sis′tən sē) n. a keeping to the same principles, course of action, etc.

consolation (kon′sə lā′shən) n. comfort; an easing of grief, worry, etc.

conspicuous (kən spik′yü əs) adj. outstanding.

conspiracy (kən spir′ə sē) n. a plot; a secret plan.

constituents (kən stich′ü ənts) n. the voters in a district.

contemplated (kon′təm plāt əd) v. looked at and studied thoughtfully.

contemplates (kon′təm plāts) v. thinks about for a long time; studies carefully.

contemporaries (kən tem′pə rer′ēz) n. persons of the same age.

contempt (kən tempt′) n. scorn; disgust combined with strong disapproval; disdain.

contemptuous (kən temp′chü əs) adj. scornful.

contending (kən tend′ing) v. struggling; fighting.

contention (kən ten′shən) n. statement maintained as true; belief.

contentious (kən ten′shəs) adj. fond of arguing.

continuity (kon′tə nü′ə tē) n. an unbroken series; a connected whole.

continuum (kən tin′yü əm) n. thing that remains the same; chain of connected events, etc.

contracted (kən trakt′əd) v. agreed; promised.

contradict (kon′trə dikt′) v. deny; say the opposite of what was said earlier; disagree with.

contradiction (kon′trə dik′shən) n. a statement opposite to one already made.

contrive (kən trīv′) v. plan with skill; design.

contriving (kən trīv′ing) v. planning or managing with skill.

converging (kən vėrj′ing) v. meeting at a given point; coming together.

conveyance (kən vā′əns) n. a vehicle for carrying people.

convictions (kən vik′shənz) n. firm beliefs.

convoluted (kon′və lüt əd) adj. coiled; twisting and turning.

cope (kōp) v. deal with successfully.

corpulent (kôr′pyə lənt) adj. stout; fat.

corridors (kôr′ə dərz) n. long hallways or passageways.

corrupted (kə rupt′əd) v. made worse or wicked.

cosmopolitan (koz′mə pol′ə tən) adj. worldly; feeling at home in all parts of the world.

countenance (koun′tə nəns) n. the face; expression of the face; one's features.

counterfeit (koun′tər fit) v. pretend; sham.

courteous (kėr′tē əs) adj. polite; civil; thoughtful.

credible (kred′ə bəl) adj. believable; reliable.

credulous (krej′ə ləs) adj. too ready to believe.

crisis (krī′sis) n. a state of danger. Also, a deciding event.

crystalline (kris′tl ən) adj. clear and transparent like glass.

cumbersome (kum′bər səm) adj. hard to manage; clumsy; unwieldy.

curtly (kėrt′lē) adv. rudely, briefly; abruptly.

cynicism (sin′ə siz′əm) n. disbelief; a doubting the sincerity and goodness of others. Also, a sneer or sarcastic remark.

debonair (deb′ə ner′) adj. pleasant and courteous.

debris (də brē′) n. ruins; wreckage; rubbish.

debtor (det′ər) n. person who owes something to another.

deception (di sep'shən) *n.* something that is false or misleading; pretense.

decorum (di kôr'əm) *n.* proper behavior; good taste in manners, conduct, speech, etc.

decrepit (di krep'it) *adj.* broken down or weakened by old age; old and feeble.

dedicated (ded'ə kāt əd) *v.* given wholly to a specific purpose.

deference (def'ər əns) *n.* great respect.

deferential (def'ə ren'shəl) *adj.* respectful.

defiant (di fī'ənt) *adj.* openly resisting; refusing to recognize or obey authority.

defiantly (di fī'ənt lē) *adv.* challengingly.

deficiency (di fish'ən sē) *n.* lack of something that is needed or required.

dejectedly (di jek'tid lē) *adv.* sadly.

deliberate (di lib'ər it) *adj.* done on purpose; carefully thought out beforehand; intentional.

deliberation (di lib'ə rā'shən) *n.* discussion of reasons for and against something; debate; careful thought.

delicate (del'ə kit) *adj.* very fine; frail.

delirium (di lir'ē əm) *n.* wild enthusiasm. Also, temporary disorder of the mind aroused by fever, drunkenness, etc.

delusion (di lü'zhən) *n.* a deception; a false and often harmful belief about something.

delusive (di lü'siv) *adj.* misleading; deceptive.

demeanor (di mē'nər) *n.* the way a person looks or acts; behavior; manner.

deposed (di pōzd') *v.* declared under oath; testified.

depravity (di prav'ə tē) *n.* wickedness; corruption.

deprecating (dep'rə kāt ing) *adj.* expressing strong disapproval of.

derisively (di rī'siv lē) *adv.* mockingly; scornfully.

designate (dez'ig nāt) *v.* indicate definitely.

desolate (des'ə lit) *adj.* forlorn; wretched; dismal.

desolation (des'ə lā'shən) *n.* ruin; despair.

desperate (des'pər it) *adj.* hopeless; ready to run any risk; not caring what happens because all hope is gone.

desperation (des'pə rā'shən) *n.* despair; hopelessness.

despondent (di spon'dənt) *adj.* downcast; discouraged; dejected.

despotism (des'pə tiz'əm) *n.* tyranny.

destination (des'tə nā'shən) *n.* place to which a person or thing is going or is being sent.

destined (des'tənd) *v.* intended; set apart for a particular purpose or use.

destiny (des'tə nē) *n.* fate; one's lot or fortune.

Pronunciation Key

hat, āge, fär; let, ēqual, tėrm;
it, īce; hot, ōpen, ôrder;
oil, out; cup, pút, rüle;
ch, child; ng, long; sh, she;
th, thin; ŦH, then; zh, measure;
ə represents *a* in about, *e* in taken,
i in pencil, *o* in lemon, *u* in circus.

---

destitute (des'tə tüt) *adj.* in great need; having nothing; without.

detached (di tacht') *adj.* aloof; reserved.

devastation (dev'əs tā'shən) *n.* complete ruin.

devote (di vōt') *v.* give full attention to.

diabolical (dī'ə bol'ə kəl) *adj.* having to do with the devil; wicked; fiendish.

digits (dij'its) *n.* fingers.

dilapidated (də lap'ə dā'tid) *adj.* fallen into ruin or disrepair; shabby; tumbledown.

dilemma (də lem'ə) *n.* difficult choice; a fix; predicament.

diligence (dil'ə jəns) *n.* constant and earnest effort to accomplish what is undertaken; hard work.

diligent (dil'ə jənt) *adj.* hard-working.

dimensions (də men'shənz) *n.* size; extent.

dingy (din'jē) *adj.* dirty-looking; grimy; lacking brightness or freshness.

dirges (dėrj'əs) *n.* funeral songs or tunes; mournful music.

disarms (dis ärms') *v.* makes one forget one's anger and feel friendly.

disaster (də zas'tər) *n.* a great misfortune; an event that causes much suffering or loss.

discern (də zėrn') *v.* understand; see clearly.

discernible (də zėr'nə bəl) *adj.* capable of being seen clearly.

discerning (də zėr'ning) *adj.* keen in seeing and understanding; wise.

disconcerted (dis'kən sėrt'əd) *v.* disturbed so suddenly or badly as to cause a person to lose control of a situation.

discreetly (dis krēt'lē) *adv.* with caution.

discriminating (dis krim'ə nā'ting) *adj.* using careful judgment; making careful, sometimes slight distinctions; being judgmental.

dishevelled (də shev'əld) *adj.* mussed; untidy.

disinherited (dis'in her'it əd) *adj.* having all one's rights and privileges taken away.

disintegration (dis in'tə grā'shən) *n.* a breaking up; a falling apart.

dismal (diz'məl) *adj.* dark and gloomy; dreary.

dismay (dis mā′) *n.* fear; alarm.

dispersed (dis pėrst′) *v.* scattered.

disposition (dis′pə zish′ən) *n.* a person's character or usual way of thinking and acting.

dispossessed (dis′pə zest′) *adj.* being deprived of one's home and belongings.

disputes (dis pyüts′) *n.* quarrels; arguments.

dissipation (dis′ə pā′shən) *n.* lack of self-control; excesses.

dissolution (dis′ə lü′shən) *n.* a breaking up or an ending of an association of any kind.

distinction (dis tingk′shən) *n.* a difference from others.

distortions (dis tôr′shənz) *n.* exaggerations that twist the truth; misrepresentations.

distracted (dis trakt′əd) *adj.* upset and confused.

distraction (dis trak′shən) *n.* something that draws away the mind, attention, etc.

distraught (dis trôt′) *adj.* very distressed; frantic.

diverse (də vėrs′) *adj.* different; varied.

diversion (də vėr′zhən) *n.* distraction.

docile (dos′əl) *adj.* obedient; easily managed.

dominion (də min′yən) *n.* rule or government; control.

drenched (drencht) *adj.* soaked; thoroughly wet.

drivel (driv′əl) *n.* silly talk; nonsense.

drowsed (drouzd) *v.* dozed; slept lightly.

drudgery (druj′ər ē) *n.* work that is hard, tiresome, or disagreeable.

dwindled (dwin′dld) *v.* gradually became smaller.

earnestly (ėr′nist lē) *adv.* seriously; intently.

eccentric (ek sen′trik) *adj.* odd; peculiar; out of the ordinary. *n.* person who behaves in an unusual manner.

effect (ə fekt′) *n.* a result; something that happens directly and immediately.

effrontery (ə frun′tər ē) *n.* impudence; boldness.

egotism (ē′gə tiz′əm) *n.* habit of thinking, talking, or writing too much about oneself.

elaborate (i lab′ər it) *adj.* overdone and complicated; worked out with great care and exactness.

elapsed (i lapst′) *v.* passed; slipped by.

eloquence (el′ə kwəns) *n.* using language so as to stir the feelings; fluent speech.

elusive (i lü′siv) *adj.* hard to describe or understand; baffling.

emaciated (i mā′shē āt əd) *adj.* unnaturally thin and wasted; thin and bony.

embattled (em bat′ld) *adj.* armed for war; prepared to fight or defend oneself.

emblem (em′bləm) *n.* an object, often a flag or badge, that stands for an invisible quality, idea, etc.; a sign that represents an idea.

eminent (em′ə nənt) *adj.* famous; outstanding; distinguished.

endeavor (en dev′ər) *n.* an earnest attempt.

endeavors (en dev′ərz) *v.* tries hard.

engrossed (en grōst′) *v.* wholly occupied; had all one's attention taken by.

enigmatic (en′ig mat′ik) *adj.* like a puzzle or a riddle; puzzling; baffling.

enormous (i nôr′məs) *adj.* huge; vast.

enterprising (en′tər prī′zing) *adj.* daring; likely to start projects and have new ideas.

enticing (en tīs′ing) *v.* tempting; luring.

entreaty (en trē′tē) *n.* an earnest request.

enumerations (i nü′mə rā′shənz) *n.* lists or counts.

enunciation (i nun′sē ā′shən) *n.* clear speaking; distinct pronunciation.

epileptic (ep′ə lep′tik) *adj.* characterized by violent jerking movements.

equable (ek′wə bəl) *adj.* changing little; uniform; even; pleasant.

equanimity (ē′kwə nim′ə tē) *n.* steadiness; evenness of mind or temper; composure.

equilibrium (ē′kwə lib′rē əm) *n.* state of balance.

equity (ek′wə tē) *n.* fairness; justice.

equivalent (i kwiv′ə lənt) *n.* something equal in value to something else.

equivocal (i kwiv′ə kəl) *adj.* being intentionally confusing; having two or more meanings.

eradicate (i rad′ə kāt) *v.* get rid of entirely.

essential (ə sen′shəl) *adj.* very important; necessary.

eternal (i tėr′nl) *adj.* lasting throughout time; always and forever the same; constant.

eternity (i tėr′nə tē) *n.* time without beginning or ending; all time; endlessness. Also, the endless period after death.

ethereal (i thir′ē əl) *adj.* heavenly. Also, light; airy.

evinces (i vins′əz) *v.* shows clearly; proves.

exasperated (eg zas′pə rāt′d) *adj.* extremely annoyed; angry.

exasperating (eg zas′pə rāt′ing) *adj.* annoying.

exasperation (eg zas′pə rā′shən) *n.* extreme annoyance; irritation; anger.

excruciating (ek skrü′shē ā′ting) *adj.* causing great suffering; very painful.

exemptions (eg zemp′shənz) *n.* freedom from a duty, obligation, rule, etc., imposed on others.

exhilarated (eg zil′ə rāt′əd) *adj.* being in high spirits; excited and happy.

exhilaration (eg zil'ə rā'shən) *n.* great joy and excitement.

existence (eg zis'təns) *n.* life.

expatriated (ek spā'trē āt əd) *adj.* banished; exiled; being forced to leave a place.

expediency (ek spē' dē ən sē) *n.* desirability or fitness of something; usefulness.

expletives (ek'splə tivz) *n.* swear words; curses.

explicit (ek splis'it) *adj.* outspoken; definite.

extenuate (ek sten'yü āt) *v.* excuse in part; make the seriousness of something seem less.

extort (ek stôrt') *v.* obtain by threats, force, fraud.

extremity (ek strem'ə tē) *n.* the end; the last part or point.

exuberant (eg zü'bər ənt) *adj.* overflowing with good cheer; joyous.

façades (fə sädz') *n.* outward appearances.

facetiously (fə sē'shəs lē) *adv.* jokingly; in fun.

facilitate (fə sil'ə tāt) *v.* help bring about; assist.

falter (fôl'tər) *v.* waver; hesitate; draw back.

familiars (fə mil'yərz) *n.* spirits or demons supposed to serve particular persons.

famished (fam'isht) *adj.* starved; very hungry.

fantastic (fan tas'tik) *adj.* fanciful; absurd; very odd or queer; wild and strange.

feigned (fānd) *adj.* pretended; false.

felicity (fə lis'ə tē) *n.* great happiness; bliss.

felonious (fə lō'nē əs) *adj.* criminal; villainous.

ferociously (fə rō'shəs lē) *adv.* fiercely; cruelly.

ferocity (fə ros'ə tē) *n.* savage cruelty; fierceness.

festooned (fə stünd') *v.* decorated with garlands.

fetch (fech) *v.* go and get; bring.

feud (fyüd) *n.* a long and deadly quarrel between families, tribes, etc.

fickleness (fik'əl nəs) *n.* changeableness.

fiend (fēnd) *n.* an evil spirit; devil; demon.

fissure (fish'ər) *n.* a long, narrow opening; a crack.

floundering (floun'dər ing) *v.* plunging about; struggling without making much progress.

fluctuating (fluk'chü āt ing) *v.* changing continually; varying from time to time.

foibles (foi'bəlz) *n.* weaknesses; little faults or failings.

forego (fôr gō') *v.* give up; do without.

forlorn (fôr lôrn') *adj.* left alone and neglected.

formidable (fôr'mə də bəl) *adj.* hard to overcome; to be dreaded; powerful; mighty.

fortitude (fôr'tə tüd) *n.* courage in facing pain, danger, trouble, etc.; firmness of spirit.

fragile (fraj'əl) *adj.* easily broken, damaged, or destroyed; delicate; frail.

Pronunciation Key

hat, āge, fär; let, ēqual, tėrm;
it, īce; hot, ōpen, ôrder;
oil, out; cup, pùt, rüle;
ch, child; ng, long; sh, she;
th, thin; ᴛʜ, then; zh, measure;
ə represents *a* in about, *e* in taken,
i in pencil, *o* in lemon, *u* in circus.

---

frenzy (fren'zē) *n.* frantic condition.

futility (fyü til'ə tē) *n.* uselessness; ineffectiveness.

gait (gāt) *n.* a person's manner of walking.

galaxy (gal'ek sē) *n.* a system or band of stars across the sky.

genetic (jə net'ik) *adj.* having to do with the principles of heredity.

ghastly (gast'lē) *adj.* horrible; shocking.

grandeur (gran'jər) *n.* magnificence or splendor of appearance, style of living, etc. *n.* magnificence.

grappled (grap'ld) *v.* struggled by seizing one another; fought closely.

grudge (gruj) *v.* give or let have unwillingly.

guile (gīl) *n.* deception; slyness; cunning.

habitation (hab'ə tā'shən) *n.* place to live in.

haggard (hag'ərd) *adj.* looking worn from pain, worry, etc.; careworn; gaunt.

haggle (hag'əl) *v.* bargain about the terms of something; quarrel.

haranguing (hə rang'ing) *v.* using noisy, violent speech; speaking loudly and strongly.

harassed (har'əst) *adj.* troubled and annoyed.

harbor (här'bər) *v.* give shelter to; protect.

hazard (haz'ərd) *n.* risk; danger; peril.

heinous (hā'nəs) *adj.* very wicked; hateful.

hideous (hid'ē əs) *adj.* very ugly; frightful.

holocaust (hol'ə kôst) *n.* great or wholesale destruction.

hostility (ho stil'ə tē) *n.* unfriendliness; enmity.

hypnotic (hip not'ik) *adj.* causing sleep or a sleeplike state.

hypocrisy (hi pok'rə sē) *n.* an outward show of goodness; a pretending to be what one is not.

hypocritical (hip'ə krit'ə kəl) *adj.* false; deceitful; insincere.

hypothesis (hī poth'ə sis) *n.* a theory; an explanation; a reasonable guess.

hysteria (hi ster'ē ə) *n.* unrestrained excitement or emotion.

ignominiously (ig′ nə min′ē əs lē) *adv.* contemptuously; humiliatingly.

illiteracy (i lit′ər ə sē) *n.* lack of education and of cultural knowledge. Also, inability to read and write.

illiterate (i lit′ər it) *adj.* unable to read or write; showing a lack of education.

illusion (i lü′zhən) *n.* a false impression; something that deceives the eye; a dream.

imaginative (i maj′ə nə tiv) *adj.* being able to form ideas of things in the mind; inventive; fanciful.

imbecility (im′bə sil′ə tē) *n.* great stupidity.

immensity (i men′sə tē) *n.* a very great size or extent; vastness.

immobile (i mō′bəl) *adj.* motionless; not moving.

immortal (i môr′tl) *adj.* everlasting; deathless; divine. Also, remembered or famous forever.

impecunious (im′pi kyü′nē əs) *adj.* having little or no money; poor.

impel (im pel′) *v.* drive or force; cause.

imperative (im per′ə tiv) *adj.* not to be avoided; essential.

imperceptible (im′pər sep′tə bəl) *adj.* very slight.

imperious (im pir′ē əs) *adj.* haughty or arrogant; overbearing; domineering.

impersonating (im pėr′sə nāt ing) *v.* pretending to be someone else.

impertinence (im pėrt′n əns) *n.* rudeness; impudence.

impertinent (im pėrt′n ənt) *adj.* rudely bold.

imperturbably (im′pər tėr′bə blē) *adv.* calmly; in an unexcited, undisturbed manner.

impervious (im pėr′vē əs) *adj.* waterproof. Also, not open to argument, suggestions, etc.

impetuous (im pech′ü əs) *adj.* hasty; headlong.

impetus (im′pə təs) *n.* a driving force; cause of action; energy.

impious (im′pē əs) *adj.* ungodly; very wicked.

importunate (im pôr′chə nit) *adj.* annoyingly persistent; asking repeatedly.

importunities (im′pôr tü′nə tēz) *n.* repeated demands.

imposing (im pō′zing) *adj.* impressive because of size, appearance, dignity, etc.

impregnable (im preg′nə bəl) *adj.* cannot be overcome; impossible to conquer.

impressionable (im presh′ə nə bəl) *adj.* easily influenced.

impressive (im pres′iv) *adj.* striking; imposing.

impropriety (im′prə prī′ə tē) *n.* lack of correct conduct; a wrong act.

impulse (im′puls) *n.* a sudden inclination or tendency to act; something done in haste.

impute (im pyüt′) *v.* blame; attribute.

inaccessible (in′ək ses′ə bəl) *adj.* out of reach.

inane (in ān′) *adj.* silly; senseless; stupid.

inarticulate (in′är tik′yə lit) *adj.* indistinct and hard to understand.

inaudible (in ô′də bl) *n.* so softly as not to be heard.

incantations (in′kan tā′shənz) *n.* sets of words spoken as a magic charm or to cast a magic spell.

incapacitated (in′kə pas′ə tāt əd) *adj.* disabled; being incapable of doing anything.

incensed (in senst′) *adj.* very angry; enraged.

incentives (in sen′tivz) *n.* whatever urges a person on; causes of action or effort; motives.

incessant (in ses′nt) *adj.* never stopping.

incidents (in′sə dənts) *n.* separate happenings or events of little importance.

inclination (in′klə nā′shən) *n.* preference or liking for; a tendency.

inclined (in klīnd′) *v.* leaned or bowed.

incoherence (in′kō hir′əns) *n.* disconnected thought or speech.

incomparable (in kom′pər ə bəl) *adj.* unequalled; matchless.

inconceivable (in′kən sē′və bəl) *adj.* impossible to imagine.

incorrigible (in kôr′ə jə bəl) *adj.* unmanageable; too firmly fixed in bad ways, etc., to be reformed.

incredible (in kred′ə bəl) *adj.* hard to believe.

indecorous (in dek′ər əs) *adj.* improper.

indicted (in dīt′əd) *adj.* being charged with or accused of a crime.

indictment (in dīt′mənt) *n.* a formal, usually written accusation.

indispensable (in′dis pen′sə bəl) *adj.* absolutely necessary; essential.

indisputable (in′dis pyü′tə bəl) *adj.* undoubted; certain; unquestionable; undeniable.

ineffable (in ef′ə bəl) *adj.* too great to be described in words.

inestimable (in es′tə mə bəl) *adj.* priceless.

inevitable (in ev′ə tə bəl) *adj.* sure to happen; certain to come; not to be avoided.

inexorably (in ek′sər ə blē) *adv.* relentlessly.

inexplicable (in′ik splik′ə bəl) *adj.* cannot be explained; mysterious.

inexplicably (in′ik splik′ə blē) *adv.* mysteriously; in a manner not easily explained.

infallible (in fal′ə bəl) *adj.* absolutely reliable.

infamous (in′fə məs) *adj.* in public disgrace; shamefully bad.

infidel (in′fə dəl) *adj.* unbelieving; irreligious. *n.* an unbeliever.

inflexibly (in fleks′ə blē) *adv.* stubbornly; steadfastly.

infuse (in fyüz′) *v.* pour ideas or knowledge into the mind; instill.

ingenious (in jē′nyəs) *adj.* skillful; inventive.

iniquity (in ik′wə tē) *n.* evil; sin; wickedness.

initial (i nish′əl) *adj.* occurring at the beginning; first; earliest.

innate (i nāt′) *adj.* inborn; natural.

innumerable (i nü′mər ə bəl) *adj.* too many to count; countless.

inquisitive (in kwiz′ə tiv) *adj.* curious; prying into other people's affairs.

inscrutable (in skrü′tə bəl) *adj.* hard to understand or explain.

insensible (in sen′sə bəl) *adj.* unfeeling.

insidious (in sid′ē əs) *adj.* crafty; tricky; sly.

insignificance (in′sig nif′ə kəns) *n.* unimportance; uselessness; smallness.

insistence (in sis′təns) *n.* a firm demand; an urging.

insolent (in′sə lənt) *adj.* insulting.

instinct (in′stingkt) *n.* the inborn tendency to act in a certain way.

insufferable (in suf′ər ə bəl) *adj.* unbearable.

integrate (in′tə grāt) *v.* bring together (parts) into a whole.

integrity (in teg′rə tē) *n.* uprightness; soundness of character.

intelligible (in tel′ə jə bəl) *adj.* understandable.

intensified (in ten′sə fīd) *adj.* strengthened.

interminable (in tèr′mə nə bəl) *adj.* endless; very long and tiring.

intermission (in′tər mish′ən) *n.* a pause; a time between periods of activity.

intervene (in′tər vēn′) *v.* interfere; act as a go-between to explain something.

intimate (in′tə mit) *adj.* personal; private.

intimated (in′tə māt əd) *v.* suggested indirectly.

intolerable (in tol′ər ə bəl) *adj.* unbearable; not to be endured.

intolerance (in tol′ər əns) *n.* denial of the right of others to differ; unwillingness to put up with people whose ways, ideas, etc., differ from one's own.

intricate (in′trə kit) *adj.* complicated; having many twists and turns.

---

intuitively (in tü′ə tiv lē) *adv.* without relying on reason; instinctively.

invisible (in viz′ə bəl) *adj.* not capable of being seen; unseen.

irked (èrkt) *adj.* disgusted or annoyed; irritated.

irreparable (i rep′ər ə bəl) *adj.* cannot be repaired, put right, or made good.

irresistible (ir′i zis′tə bəl) *adj.* overwhelming; too great to be withstood.

irresponsible (ir′i spon′sə bəl) *adj.* without a sense of duty; untrustworthy; unreliable.

irreversible (ir′i vèr′sə bəl) *adj.* unable to be changed; unalterable.

irritation (ir′ə tā′shən) *n.* annoyance; vexation.

jubilantly (jü′bə lənt lē) *adv.* triumphantly; joyfully.

judiciously (jü dish′əs lē) *adv.* wisely; sensibly.

knavery (nā′vər ē) *n.* dishonesty; trickery.

lanced (lanst) *adj.* being cut open with a sharp knife.

legacy (leg′ə sē) *n.* a gift left to a person by the will of someone who has died.

lethargic (lə thär′jik) *adj.* dull; slow; sluggish.

levy (lev′ē) *v.* wage; carry on.

listlessly (list′lis lē) *adv.* wearily; indifferently.

loathsome (lōтн′səm) *adj.* disgusting; hateful.

loiter (loi′tər) *v.* hang about; linger aimlessly.

lugubriousness (lü gü′brē əs nəs) *n.* extreme sadness; gloominess; sorrow.

luminous (lü′mə nəs) *adj.* full of light; shining.

lustrous (lus′trəs) *adj.* bright; shining.

magnanimity (mag′nə nim′ə tē) *n.* nobility of soul or mind.

magnificence (mag nif′ə səns) *n.* grand beauty; richness of material, color, etc.; splendor.

magnitude (mag′nə tüd) *n.* great importance, effect, or consequence.

malady (mal′ə dē) *n.* any bodily disorder or disease, especially one that is chronic.

malefic (mə lef′ik) *adj.* extremely harmful; evil.

malevolence (mə lev′ə ləns) *n.* ill will; spite.

malicious (mə lish′əs) *adj.* spiteful.

manifold (man′ə fōld) *adj.* many and various.

marital (mar′ə təl) *adj.* of or having to do with marriage.

martial (mär′shəl) *adj.* warlike; suitable for war; of or having to do with the army or navy.

maturity (mə chûr′ə tē) *n.* full development; an adult; a grown-up.

maudlin (môd′lən) *adj.* tearful and silly.

media (mē′dē ə) *n.* the various forms of communication, such as newspapers, television, and radio, that reach large numbers of people.

meditate (med′ə tāt) *v.* think quietly about.

meditative (med′ə tā′tiv) *adj.* thoughtful; fond of engaging in deep, serious thought.

meditatively (med′ə tā′tiv lē) *adv.* thoughtfully; reflectively.

medley (med′lē) *n.* a mixture; a jumble.

melancholy (mel′ən kol′ē) *n.* sadness; gloominess. *adj.* sad; gloomy; depressing.

memento (mə men′tō) *n.* something serving as a reminder of what is past or gone; souvenir.

memorable (mem′ər ə bəl) *adj.* worth remembering; noteworthy.

menace (men′is) *n.* a threat; a danger.

mentor (men′tər) *n.* a wise and trusted advisor.

mercenaries (mėr′sə ner′ēz) *n.* soldiers serving for pay in a foreign army.

miscellaneous (mis′ə lā′nē əs) *adj.* of mixed and varied character or composition.

miserable (miz′ər ə bəl) *adj.* very unhappy or unfortunate; distressed.

misrepresentations (mis′rep′ri zen tā′shənz) *n.* wrong ideas.

mitigate (mit′ə gāt) *v.* soften; ease; make easier to bear.

mocked (mokt) *v.* made fun of; laughed at.

mode (mōd) *n.* the way in which one lives; one's style of living.

mollified (mol′ə fīd) *adj.* calmed; pacified.

momentum (mō men′təm) *n.* force that moves something along.

monotonous (mə not′n əs) *adj.* without change; wearying because of its sameness; boring.

monotony (mə nōt′n ē) *n.* wearisome sameness; dullness; boredom.

monstrous (mon′strəs) *adj.* huge; enormous. Also, shocking; horrible; dreadful.

mood (müd) *n.* state of mind or feeling.

morose (mə rōs′) *adj.* gloomy; sullen; ill-humored.

mortgaged (môr′gijd) *v.* and *adj.* pledged as security for money loaned.

multiplicity (mul′tə plis′ə tē) *n.* a great variety; a great many.

musing (myü′zing) *adj.* thoughtful. *v.* looking thoughtfully at something; thinking; pondering.

mutinous (myüt′n əs) *adj.* rebellious.

mutiny (myüt′n ē) *v.* rebel; refuse to obey orders.

mutual (myü′chü əl) *adj.* felt or done in the same way by two persons, for or toward each other.

myriad (mir′ē əd) *adj.* countless; innumerable.

neglected (ni glekt′əd) *v.* left undone or uncared for; didn't attend to.

nocturnal (nok tėr′nl) *adj.* relating to the night.

nonchalance (non′shə ləns) *n.* cool unconcern; indifference.

nonconformity (non′kən fôr′mə tē) *n.* failure or refusal to follow established standards of business, conduct, etc.; not acting according to rules.

nuances (nü äns′əs) *n.* shades of expression, meaning, feeling, etc.

nullifying (nul′ə fī ing) *v.* canceling; wiping out.

obdurate (ob′dər it) *adj.* stubborn or unyielding.

objectivity (ob′jek tiv′ə tē) *n.* condition of being impersonal; considering facts only.

obligation (ob′lə gā′shən) *n.* duty because of kindness received; responsibility.

obliterate (ə blit′ə rāt′) *v.* blot out; destroy.

obliterated (ə blit′ə rāt′əd) *v.* wiped out; erased.

oblivion (ə bliv′ē ən) *n.* condition of being entirely forgotten.

obloquy (ob′lə kwē) *n.* public reproach or condemnation; blame. Also, disgrace; shame.

obscurity (əb skyür′ə tē) *n.* lack of clearness or understanding; vagueness; doubt.

obsequious (əb sē′kwē əs) *adj.* flattering; fawning.

obstinate (ob′stə nit) *adj.* not giving in; stubborn; unyielding in doing things one's own way.

obtrusion (əb trü′zhən) *n.* something that stands out or sticks up.

obviously (ob′vē əs lē) *adv.* unmistakeably; plainly; undoubtedly.

occult (ə kult′) *adj.* mysterious; ghostly.

odious (ō′dē əs) *adj.* very displeasing; hateful.

officiating (ə fish′ē āt ing) *v.* performing the duties of any office or position; serving or acting in some official capacity.

ominous (om′ə nəs) *adj.* threatening; foretelling misfortune; unfavorable.

omnipotent (om nip′ə tənt) *adj.* having all power or great power or influence; almighty.

oppressively (ə pres′iv lē) *adv.* threateningly.

ostentation (os′ten tā′shən) *n.* showing off; a rich display intended to impress others.

overwhelmed (ō′vər hwelmd′) *v.* crushed; overcame completely.

pallid (pal′id) *adj.* lacking normal color; pale.

pallor (pal′ər) *n.* lack of color due to fear, illness, etc.; paleness.

palsied (pôl′zēd) *adj.* shaking; trembling.

paradoxical (par′ə dok′sə kəl) *adj.* being full of contradictions.

parallels (par′ə lels) *v.* runs in the same direction as and along the side of.

paralyzed (par′ə līzd) *adj.* being powerless or helplessly inactive.

pariah (pə rī′ə) *n.* an outcast; any person generally despised.

parsimony (pär′sə mō′nē) *n.* stinginess; extreme economy.

participant (pär tis′ə pənt) *n.* a person who takes part in or shares in.

patent (pat′nt) *n.* an official document giving rights and privileges.

pathological (path′ə loj′ə kəl) *adj.* exaggerated to the point that mental disorder seems likely.

pavilions (pə vil′yənz) *n.* buildings forming a hospital.

pawns (pôns) *n.* persons used by someone to gain some advantage.

pedantic (pi dan′tik) *adj.* scholarly in a dull and narrow way.

peered (pird) *v.* looked closely in order to see clearly.

penitentially (pen′ə ten′chəl ē) *adv.* regretfully.

pensioned (pen′shənd) *adj.* living on a fixed sum of money paid for past service.

pensive (pen′siv) *adj.* thoughtful in a serious or sad way.

pensively (pen′siv lē) *adv.* dreamily; thoughtfully.

perception (pər sep′shən) *n.* understanding.

perfidy (pėr′fə dē) *n.* base treachery; disloyalty.

perilous (per′ə ləs) *adj.* dangerous; risky.

perish (per′ish) *v.* be destroyed; die.

perpetual (pər pech′ü əl) *adj.* unending; eternal.

perplexed (pər plekst′) *adj.* bewildered; puzzled.

perplexity (pər plek′sə tē) *n.* bewilderment.

Pronunciation Key

hat, āge, fär; let, ēqual, tėrm;
it, īce; hot, ōpen, ôrder;
oil, out; cup, pùt, rüle;
ch, child; ng, long; sh, she;
th, thin; ŦH, then; zh, measure;
ə represents *a* in about, *e* in taken,
i in pencil, *o* in lemon, *u* in circus.

---

persecution (pėr′sə kyü′shən) *n.* persistent harm; systematic punishment or oppression.

perseverance (pėr′sə vir′əns) *n.* a sticking to a purpose or an aim; great steadfastness.

persistent (pər sis′tənt) *adj.* continuing; enduring.

pertinacity (pėrt′n as′ə tē) *n.* great determination; holding firmly to a purpose, action, or opinion.

pertinently (pėrt′n ənt lē) *adv.* to the point.

perusal (pə rü′zəl) *n.* reading or studying.

pervaded (pər vād′əd) *v.* spread throughout.

perverseness (pər vėrs′nəs) *n.* willfulness; obstinately opposing what is wanted, reasonable, or required.

petitioned (pə tish′ənd) *v.* made a formal, written request for (something).

phantasm (fan′taz′əm) *n.* something seen only in the imagination; a ghost.

phenomenon (fə nom′ə non) *n.* a rare event; a marvel.

picturesque (pik′chə resk′) *adj.* quaint or interesting enough to be used as the subject of a picture.

pierce (pirs) *v.* go through; make a hole in.

pilgrimage (pil′grə mij) *n.* a long journey.

piteous (pit′ē əs) *adj.* causing great sorrow.

pivoting (piv′ət ing) *v.* turning or rotating.

placid (plas′id) *adj.* calm; unruffled.

plague (plāg) *v.* vex; annoy; bother; tease.

plaintive (plān′tiv) *adj.* mournful; sad.

plausibility (plô′zə bil′ə tē) *n.* appearance of being true or reasonable.

plight (plīt) *n.* condition or situation, usually bad.

pompous (pom′pəs) *adj.* self-important.

ponderous (pon′dər əs) *adj.* very heavy; massive.

portaged (pôr′tijd) *v.* carried overland from one river, lake, etc., to another.

portend (pôr tend′) *v.* to indicate beforehand; predict.

portent (pôr′tent) *n.* a warning of coming evil; an omen of ill fortune.

portentous (pôr ten′təs) *adj.* threatening; ominous.

posterity (po ster′ə tē) *n.* descendents; offspring; future generations.

potential (pə ten′shəl) *n.* a possibility; what one is capable of doing or becoming.

precarious (pri ker′ē əs) *adj.* not safe or secure.

precariously (pri ker′ē əs lē) *adv.* uncertainly; dangerously; unsafely.

precept (prē′sept) *n.* rule of action or behavior.

precious (presh′əs) *adj.* much loved; greatly prized.

precipice (pres′ə pis) *n.* a cliff or steep mountainside.

precipitate (pri sip′ə tit) *adj.* very hurried; sudden; hasty; rash.

precipitated (pri sip′ə tāt əd) *v.* brought about suddenly; caused to happen.

precise (pri sīs′) *adj.* very definite or correct.

precocious (pri kō′shəs) *adj.* being too knowledgeable for one's age.

preconceptions (prē′kən sep′shənz) *n.* ideas or opinions formed beforehand.

predisposing (prē′dis pōz′ing) *adj.* having a tendency to; being susceptible.

prejudice (prej′ə dis) *n.* opinion formed without taking time and care to judge fairly; bias.

preliminaries (pri lim′ə ner′ēz) *n.* introductory remarks or actions.

prelude (prel′yüd) *n.* anything serving as an introduction.

premises (prem′is əz) *n.* a building (or buildings) and its grounds.

preposterous (pri pos′tər əs) *adj.* absurd.

prescience (prē′shē əns) *n.* knowledge of what is going to happen; foresight.

presentiment (pri zen′tə mənt) *n.* a feeling that something, often something evil, will happen.

prestige (pre stēzh′) *n.* good reputation based on one's abilities, etc.; reputation or distinction.

preternatural (prē′tər nach′ər əl) *adj.* supernatural; abnormal.

prevail (pri vāl′) *v.* win out; succeed; overcome.

prevalent (prev′ə lənt) *adj.* common; usual.

primitive (prim′ə tiv) *adj.* very simple; rough.

principles (prin′sə pəlz) *n.* basic truths; rules of conduct; beliefs.

privilege (priv′ə lij) *n.* a special right, advantage, or favor.

probing (prōb′ing) *adj.* searching into.

procession (prə sesh′ən) *n.* a body of people moving forward; persons marching or riding.

proclamation (prok′lə mā′shən) *n.* a public announcement.

profitable (prof′ə tə bəl) *adj.* useful; beneficial. Also, yielding a financial gain.

profoundly (prə found′lē) *adv.* very deeply.

prone (prōn) *adj.* having a tendency toward something; liable.

propaganda (prop′ə gan′də) *n.* the spreading of opinions and beliefs, usually following a plan. Also, opinions and beliefs spread in this way.

prophecy (prof′ə sē) *n.* a telling what will happen.

propitious (prə pish′əs) *adj.* favorable; friendly.

proprieties (prə prī′ə tēz) *n.* usual standards for proper behavior.

propriety (prə prī′ə tē) *n.* correct behavior.

prosaic (prō zā′ik) *adj.* ordinary; unexciting.

prosecute (pros′ə kyüt) *v.* carry out; pursue.

prosperous (pros′pər əs) *adj.* successful; doing well.

prostrate (pros′trāt) *adj.* lying flat or at full length.

protracted (prō trakt′əd) *adj.* prolonged; extended; drawn out.

proverbially (prə vėr′bē ə lē) *adj.* well-known.

provisions (prə vizh′ənz) *n.* supply of food and drink, etc.

provocation (prov′ə kā′shən) *n.* act of stirring up or making angry.

provoking (prə vō′king) *v.* irritating.

prowess (prou′is) *n.* unusual skill or ability.

prudence (prüd′ns) *n.* caution; foresight.

prudent (prüd′nt) *adj.* sensible; wise.

pursue (pər sü′) *v.* follow; chase; hunt.

pursuit (pər süt′) *n.* a chase or hunt. Also, one's business or occupation.

quagmire (kwag′mīr′) *n.* soft, muddy ground.

quarry (kwôr′ē) *n.* animal chased in a hunt; anything hunted or eagerly pursued.

quartered (kwôr′tərd) *v.* lodged; stayed.

quavered (kwā′vərd) *v.* said in trembling tones.

queasy (kwē′zē) *adj.* easily upset.

quelled (kweld) *v.* put down by force; crushed.

querulous (kwer′ə ləs) *adj.* complaining; fretful.

quest (kwest) *n.* a search or hunt.

quivered (kwiv′ərd) *v.* trembled; shook.

railed (rāld) *v.* scolded; complained bitterly.

rambler (ram′blər) *n.* a person who wanders about; a walker.

rampant (ram′pənt) *adj.* unchecked; angry and excited; violent.

rancor (rang′kər) *n.* spite; bitterness; ill will.

ransack (ran′sak) *v.* search everywhere for.

ravine (rə vēn′) *n.* a long, deep, narrow gorge.

realm (relm) *n.* kingdom; an area in which someone rules.

rebellious (ri bel′yəs) *adj.* defiant; disobedient.

receded (ri sēd′əd) *v.* moved back; withdrew.

recompense (rek′əm pens) *n.* payment or reward.

reconciled (rek′ən sīld) *adj.* being no longer opposed to; being in agreement with.

reconciliation (rek′ən sil′ē ā′shən) *n.* bringing together again in friendship; settlement of disagreements or difference.

rectitude (rek′tə tüd) *n.* upright conduct; honesty.

reimbursing (rē′im bėrs′ing) *v.* paying back.

relinquish (ri ling′kwish) *v.* give up; let go.

reluctance (ri luk′təns) *n.* unwillingness.

remnant (rem′nənt) *n.* piece left over; fragment.

remonstrances (ri mon′strəns əs) *n.* protests.

remonstrated (ri mon′strāt əd) *v.* protested; objected to; reasoned in complaint or protest.

remorse (ri môrs′) *n.* painful regret for having
done wrong.

remunerative (ri myü′nə rā′tiv) *adj.* profitable.

rendezvous (rän′də vü) *n.* a meeting place.

repentance (ri pen′təns) *n.* sorrow for having
done wrong; regret.

repine (ri pīn′) *v.* be discontented; complain.

reprieves (ri prēvz′) *n.* reliefs or delays.

repulsed (ri pulst′) *v.* thrust back; driven back.

reputable (rep′yə tə bəl) *adj.* well thought of.

reputation (rep′yə tā′shən) *n.* what people think
and say the character of a person is; one's good
name.

requisite (rek′wə zit) *adj.* necessary; required by
the circumstances.

resentment (ri zent′mənt) *n.* the feeling that one
has been injured or insulted; indignation.

reserved (ri zėrvd′) *adj.* disposed to keep to oneself; self-contained.

resignation (rez′ig nā′shən) *n.* patient acceptance.

resilience (ri zil′ē əns) *n.* power of springing back;
buoyancy; cheerfulness.

resolute (rez′ə lüt) *adj.* determined; firm.

resolutely (rez′ə lüt′lē) *adv.* determinedly.

resolution (rez′ə lü′shən) *n.* determination; power
of holding firmly to a thing decided upon.

resolve (ri zolv′) *n.* determination.

respective (ri spek′tiv) *adj.* individual; particular;
belonging to each.

retribution (ret′rə byü′shən) *n.* a deserved punishment; return for evil done.

revelation (rev′ə lā′shən) *n.* anything made
known; a discovery.

revered (ri vird′) *v.* honored greatly; respected.

Pronunciation Key

hat, āge, fär; let, ēqual, tėrm;
it, īce; hot, ōpen, ôrder;
oil, out; cup, pùt, rüle;
ch, child; ng, long; sh, she;
th, thin; ᴛʜ, then; zh, measure;
ə represents *a* in about, *e* in taken,
i in pencil, *o* in lemon, *u* in circus.

---

reverence (rev′ər əns) *n.* a feeling of deep respect.

revile (ri vīl′) *v.* call bad names; abuse with words.

ridiculous (ri dik′yə ləs) *adj.* silly; absurd.

robust (rō bust′) *adj.* strong and healthy; sturdy.

rummaging (rum′ij ing) *v.* searching in a disorder-
ly way.

sacrament (sak′rə mənt) *n.* a religious ceremony; a
rite.

sacrilegious (sak′rə lij′əs) *adj.* being disrespectful
of anyone or anything deserving respect.

sagacious (sə gā′shəs) *adj.* wise; shrewd.

sallow (sal′ō) *adj.* having a yellowish or brownish–
yellow color.

sanctity (sangk′tə tē) *n.* holiness; sacredness.

sarcasm (sär′kaz′əm) *n.* hurtful mockery; taunt-
ing; harsh, bitter irony.

sarcastic (sär kas′tik) *adj.* mocking; sneering.

saturated (sach′ə rā′tid) *adj.* soaked thoroughly.

sauntering (sôn′tər ing) *v.* strolling lazily along.

scandal (skan′dl) *n.* shameful action.

scandalous (skan′dl əs) *adj.* disgraceful; shameful.

scowled (skould) *v.* looked angry; frowned.

scrutinizing (skrüt′n īz ing) *adj.* examining closely; inspecting carefully.

scrutiny (skrüt′n ē) *n.* close examination.

self-reliance (self′ri lī′əns) *n.* trust in one's own
acts, abilities, etc.

sententiously (sen ten′shəs lē) *adv.* briefly, but
filled with meaning.

sentimentality (sen′tə men tal′ə tē) *n.* tendency to
be influenced by one's emotions.

serenely (sə rēn′lē) *adv.* calmly; peacefully.

shackled (shak′əld) *v.* restrained; hampered.

sheer (shir) *adj.* absolute; unmixed.

significant (sig nif′ə kənt) *adj.* full of meaning;
having or expressing a hidden meaning.

silhouette (sil′ü et′) *n.* in outline; a dark image
outlined against a lighter background.

simplicity (sim plis′ə tē) *n.* lack of pretense.

simulated (sim'yə lāt əd) v. pretended; shammed.

simultaneously (sī'məl tā'nē əs lē) adv. at the same time; together; as one.

singular (sing'gyə lər) adj. extraordinary; unusual; strange; odd. Also, being the only one of its kind.

sloughs (slouz) n. soft, deep, muddy places.

snare (sner) n. pitfall; trap.

sojourner (sō'jėrn'ər) n. a visitor; a traveler.

solace (sol'is) v. comfort; cheer up.

solemn (sol'əm) adj. serious; grave. Also, sacred.

solicitous (sə lis'ə təs) adj. anxious; concerned.

solicitude (sə lis'ə tüd) n. anxious care; concern.

solitude (sol'ə tüd) n. isolation; being alone.

sophistication (sə fis'tə kā'shən) n. worldly experience or ideas.

sorcery (sôr'sər ē) n. magic; witchcraft.

sordidness (sôr'did nəs) n. meanness; ugliness.

spasm (spaz'əm) n. a sudden, brief spell of unusual energy or activity.

spectacle (spek'tə kəl) n. a public show or display.

spectral (spek'trəl) adj. ghostly; mysterious.

speculation (spek'yə lā'shən) n. buying or selling.

speculative (spek'yə lā'tiv) adj. uncertain; risky; based on theory rather than on fact.

squalid (skwol'id) adj. very dirty; filthy; disgusting.

squander (skwon'dər) v. waste foolishly.

squeamish (skwē'mish) adj. being too particular or too conscientious; too scrupulous.

stagnant (stag'nənt) adj. foul from standing still.

stealthily (stel'thə lē) adv. secretly; slyly.

steep (stēp) v. involve deeply in something.

strategically (strə tē'jik lē) adv. as having importance based on careful military planning.

subdued (səb düd') v. conquered; overcame.

subjugation (sub'jə gā'shən) n. conquest; defeat.

sublime (sə blīm') n. something that is lofty, noble, exalted, etc. adj. noble; grand; glorious.

submission (səb mish'ən) n. a surrender; a yielding to the power or authority of another.

submit (səb mit') v. give in; yield.

substantial (səb stan'shəl) adj. strong; firm; solid.

subtle (sut'l) adj. faint; mysterious; so fine and delicate as to be almost unnoticeable.

subtleties (sut'l tēz) n. qualities that are clever or skillful but difficult to detect.

succession (sək sesh'ən) n. a coming one after another.

succinctly (sək singkt'lē) adv. briefly and clearly.

succor (suk'ər) n. assistance; help; aid; relief.

suffice (sə fīs') v. be enough; be sufficient.

suffuse (sə fyüz') v. spread over or throughout.

sullen (sul'ən) adj. silent because of bad humor or anger; showing bad humor or anger.

sundry (sun'drē) adj. different; various; several.

superb (sù pėrb') adj. very fine; first-rate.

supercilious (sü'pər sil'ē əs) adj. haughty, proud, and contemptuous.

superficial (sü'pər fish'əl) adj. shallow; not real or genuine.

superfluous (sù pėr'flü əs) adj. needless; unnecessary; unwanted.

superstition (sü'pər stish'ən) n. a belief in omens and magic.

superstitious (sü'pər stish'əs) adj. believing in omens and magic. Also, being afraid of the unknown or mysterious.

supinely (sü pīn'lē) adv. flat on one's back.

supplication (sup'lə kā'shən) n. a humble prayer.

surly (sėr'lē) adj. bad-tempered and unfriendly.

surmised (sər mīzd') v. supposed; guessed.

surveyed (sər vād') v. measured the land (for position, boundaries, etc.).

swarthy (swôr'ᴛHē) adj. having a dark skin.

swathed (swāᴛHd) v. wrapped closely or tightly.

swerve (swėrv) v. turn aside suddenly.

symbol (sim'bəl) n. something that stands for or represents an idea, quality, condition, etc.

symptom (simp'təm) n. a sign indicating the kind of illness.

synthetic (sin thet'ik) adj. made artificially by chemical reaction.

tacit (tas'it) adj. implied or understood without being openly expressed.

tantalized (tan'tl īzd) v. teased or tormented.

tantrums (tan'trəmz) n. fits of bad temper.

tedious (tē'dē əs) adj. wearisome; tiresome.

tempered (tem'pərd) adj. softened; moderated.

temperamentally (tem'pər ə men'tlē) adv. by nature or disposition.

tempo (tem'pō) n. the time or rate of movement.

temporal (tem'pər əl) adj. concerned with earthly affairs; worldly.

tenacious (ti nā'shəs) adj. sticky; holding fast.

tentatively (ten'tə tiv lē) adv. with hesitation.

termagant (tėr'mə gənt) n. a violent, quarreling, scolding woman.

testimony (tes'tə mō'nē) n. whatever is used as evidence or proof.

testy (tes'tē) adj. easily irritated; impatient.

timorously (tim'ər əs lē) adv. fearfully; timidly.

tolerance (tol'ər əns) n. a putting up with people whose opinions or ways differ from one's own.

topography (tə pog′rə fē) *n.* the features of a landscape including hills, valleys, streams, etc.

torrent (tôr′ənt) *n.* a rushing stream of water.

tradition (trə dish′ən) *n.* old-time customs and beliefs, etc.

tranquil (trang′kwəl) *adj.* calm; peaceful; quiet.

transfigured (trans fig′yərd) *adj.* changed in appearance.

transient (tran′shənt) *adj.* passing soon; not lasting; fleeting; short-lived; temporary.

travail (trə vāl′) *n.* toil; labor; hard work.

tread (tred) *n.* the act or sound made by someone walking.

tremendous (tri men′dəs) *adj.* very great; huge. Also, dreadful; alarming; awful.

tremulous (trem′yə ləs) *adj.* trembling; quivering.

trepidation (trep′ə dā′shən) *n.* nervous dread.

trespass (tres′pəs) *v.* go on another's property without permission.

trivial (triv′ē əl) *adj.* not important; small.

tumult (tü′mult) *n.* noise and uproar.

tyranny (tir′ə nē) *n.* cruel and unjust use of power.

unalienable (un ā′lyə nə bəl) *adj.* that cannot be given or taken away or transferred to another.

unappalled (un′ə pôld′) *adj.* not dismayed; not filled with horror.

unceremonious (un′ser ə mō′nē əs) *adj.* not as courteous as would be expected; informal.

uncomplicated (un kom′plə kā′tid) *adj.* simple.

unconscionable (un kon′shə nə bəl) *adj.* unreasonable; unfair.

unfaltering (un fôl′tər ing) *adj.* unhesitating; unwavering.

unique (yü nēk′) *adj.* having no like or equal; rare.

unlamented (un′lə ment′əd) *adj.* unmourned.

unobtrusively (un′əb trü′siv lē) *adv.* inconspicuously.

unremitting (un′ri mit′ing) *adj.* never stopping.

unscrupulous (un skrü′pyə ləs) *adj.* not careful about right and wrong; having no conscience.

unwarrantable (un wôr′ən tə bəl) *adj.* not justifiable or defensible; improper.

urgency (ėr′jən sē) *n.* the need to act at once.

usurer (yü′zhər ər) *n.* person who lends money at an extremely high rate.

usurpations (yü′zər pā′shənz) *n.* seizing and holding of the place or power of another.

utterly (ut′ər lē) *adv.* completely; totally.

vacate (vā′kāt) *v.* leave empty or unoccupied.

vagaries (və gėr′ēz) *n.* whims; odd fancies.

vagrant (vā′grənt) *n.* a tramp; someone without a settled home.

vague (vāg) *adj.* not clear in meaning.

valiant (val′yənt) *adj.* brave; courageous.

valid (val′id) *adj.* sound or true; correct.

valise (və lēs′) *n.* a small traveling bag or suitcase.

valor (val′ər) *n.* bravery; courage.

vanity (van′ə tē) *n.* self-pride; conceit.

vanquished (vang′kwisht) *adj.* defeated.

variance (ver′ē əns) *n.* difference; disagreement.

venerable (ven′ər ə bəl) *adj.* worthy of respect.

venomous (ven′ə məs) *adj.* spiteful; malicious.

veracious (və rā′shəs) *adj.* truthful; reliable. Also, true.

veranda (və ran′də) *n.* a large porch along one or more sides of a house.

verbose (vər bōs′) *adj.* using too many words.

vestige (ves′tij) *n.* trace; the faintest mark.

vexation (vek sā′shən) *n.* annoyance.

vigilance (vij′ə ləns) *n.* watchfulness; caution.

vigilant (vij′ə lənt) *adj.* keeping steadily on the alert; wide-awake.

vivacious (vī vā′shəs) *adj.* lively; bright; sprightly.

vociferation (vō sif′ə rā′shən) *n.* loud, noisy shouting.

volubly (vol′yə blē) *adv.* in a loud, talkative way.

voodoo (vü′dü) *n.* a religion that originated in Africa whose mysterious rites and practices include sorcery, magic, and conjuring.

vulnerable (vul′nər ə bəl) *adj.* sensitive to criticism; defenseless; open to attack.

wan (won) *adj.* lacking normal color; pale.

warily (wer′ə lē) *adv.* carefully; cautiously.

weir (wir) *n.* a barrier or dam across a river.

wheedle (hwē′dl) *v.* persuade by flattery; coax.

whim (hwim) *n.* a sudden fancy or notion.

whimper (hwim′pər) *n.* a low, mournful cry.

winced (winst) *v.* drew back sharply; flinched.

woeful (wo′fəl) *adj.* sad; sorrowful; wretched.

wretchedness (rech′id nəs) *n.* misery; distress.

FINE ART INDEX

FINE ART SOURCES

PHOTO CREDITS

SKILLS INDEX

GENERAL INDEX

In this index, titles of literary works are shown in italics. Numbers in boldface refer to pages on which the biographical notes of authors appear. Names of authors represented in this textbook and other references appear in regular type.